# DICTIONARY OF
# BEHAVIORAL SCIENCE

# DICTIONARY OF BEHAVIORAL SCIENCE

Compiled and Edited by

## BENJAMIN B. WOLMAN

### In Collaboration With

Gerhard Adler
Kurt A. Adler
George W. Albee
Anne Anastasi
Petr K. Anokhin
Silvano Arieti
Benjamin Balinsky
Nancy Bayley
Leopold Bellak
Lauretta Bender
Arnold Bernstein
Manfred Bleuler
Medard Boss
Francis J. Braceland
Jerome S. Bruner
Charlotte Buhler
Leonard Carmichael
George M. Carstairs
Raymond B. Cattell
Isidor Chein
Lee J. Cronbach
Florence L. Denmark
Gordon F. Derner
Morton Deutsch
John Dollard
John C. Eccles
David Elkind
Albert Ellis
John E. Exner
H. J. Eysenck

Charles B. Ferster
Anna Freud
Erich Fromm
G. Allen German
Eleanor J. Gibson
Gustave M. Gilbert
Edward Glover
Joy P. Guilford
Harry F. Harlow
Donald O. Hebb
Edna Heidbreder
Harry Helson
Mary Henle
Ernest R. Hilgard
Robert R. Holt
Lewis A. Hurst
Lothar B. Kalinowsky
Abram Kardiner
Otto Klineberg
David Krech
Wolfgang Kretschmer
Lawrence S. Kubie
Stanley Lesse
Konrad Lorenz
Juan J. Lopez-Ibor
Arthur R. Luria
Margaret S. Mahler
Jules H. Masserman
David C. McClelland
Margaret Mead

Neal E. Miller
Henryk Misiak
Jacob L. Moreno
O. Hobart Mowrer
Gardner Murphy
Lois B. Murphy
Theodore M. Newcomb
Joseph M. Notterman
Carl Pfaffmann
Jean Piaget
Karl H. Pribram
Harold M. Proshansky
John D. Rainer
Carl R. Rogers
Nathaniel Ross
William N. Schoenfeld
Robert R. Sears
Hanna Segal
Virginia S. Sexton
B. F. Skinner
M. Brewster Smith
Hans H. Strupp
John J. Sullivan
Leona E. Tyler
David Wechsler
Michael M. Wertheimer
E. D. Wittkower
Joseph Wolpe
Paul T. Young
Joseph Zubin

 VAN NOSTRAND REINHOLD COMPANY

New York   Cincinnati   Toronto   London   Melbourne

Van Nostrand Reinhold Company Regional Offices:
New York  Cincinnati  Chicago  Millbrae  Dallas

Van Nostrand Reinhold Company International Offices:
London  Toronto  Melbourne

Manufactured in the United States of America

Published by Van Nostrand Reinhold Company
450 West 33rd Street, New York, N.Y. 10001

Published simultaneously in Canada by Van Nostrand Reinhold Ltd.

15 14 13 12 11 10 9 8 7 6 5 4 3 2

**Library of Congress Cataloging in Publication Data**

Wolman, Benjamin B.
  Dictionary of behavioral science.

  1. Psychology—Dictionaries.       I.       Title.
[DNLM: 1. Behavioral       sciences—Dictionary.
2. Psychology—Dictionary. BF 31 W865d 1973]
BF31.W64        150'.3        73-748
ISBN 0-442-29566-9

# PREFACE

There are hundreds of thousands of professionals and millions of college and university students who read psychological, psychiatric, and related literature and millions of interested laymen who are unable to avail themselves of useful information because of the barriers of technical terms. There are, indeed, a few dictionaries on the market covering partial areas, but at the present time, there is not even one comprehensive and authoritative dictionary that covers the entire field. The need for such a dictionary has been apparent and the authors of the present *Dictionary of Behavioral Science* intend to fill the gap.

Our Dictionary covers all areas of psychology such as experimental and developmental psychology, personality, learning, perception, motivation, and intelligence. It also includes all aspects of applied psychology, such as diagnosis and treatment of mental disorders, and social, industrial and educational psychology. The Dictionary covers the disciplines of psychiatry, biochemistry, psychopharmacology and clinical practice. The Dictionary includes terms related to neurology, neurosurgery, genetics, endocrinology, and presents the concepts and techniques of the orthodox and non-Freudian psychoanalysis. The motto of the Dictionary is *Concision and Precision.*

The planning of the Dictionary was done according to the specific disciplines, but it is printed in alphabetic order. Compiling and editing of this Dictionary resembled the writing and editing of close to 20,000 short papers. It certainly required the joint efforts of a large team of prominent psychologists, psychiatrists, and other scholars, and the help of a selected group of editorial assistants and secretarial staff. I am deeply indebted to all of them.

I must thank especially Drs. G. F. Derner, E. Glover, R. R. Holt, and H. Proshansky for their wise comments. Mr. Mike Hamilton gets the credit for initiating this project and Mr. Barry R. Nathan and Mrs. Alberta W. Gordon have earned my profound gratitude for their most cordial help.

B. B. Wolman

v

# ACKNOWLEDGMENTS

I would like to express my profound gratitude to the following people who helped in many ways in the preparation of this DICTIONARY.

*Editorial Assistants*

Melvin Crosby

Patricia Edstrom

Cecille Freilich

Susan Knapp

Barbara Leavy

Ella Lenoff

Michael Moskowitz

Sally Moskowitz

Anne Mulvey

Irwin Schatz

Leonard Temme

*Secretarial Staff*

Robin Haber

Kathy Mankes

Naomi Mankes

Margaret Wiener

We are deeply indebted to the following Publishers who permitted us to adapt their copyrighted material.

(1) Appleton-Century Crofts

Adapted material from "Schedules of Reinforcement," C. B. Ferster and B. F. Skinner, copyright 1957 by Appleton-Century-Crofts, Inc. Reprinted by permission of Appleton-Century-Crofts, Educational Div., Meredith Corp.

(2) Harcourt Brace Jovanovich, Inc.

Adapted material from "Introduction to Psychology," Fifth Edition, Ernest R. Hilgard, *et al.,* copyright 1953, 1957, 1962, 1967, 1971, by Harcourt Brace Jovanovich, Inc. Reprinted with their permission.

Adapted material from "Personality and Motivation Structure and Measurement", Raymond B. Cattell, copyright 1957 by Harcourt Brace Jovanovich, Inc. Reprinted with their permission.

(3) Houghton Mifflin Co.

Adapted material from "Abilities: Their Structure, Growth and Action," Raymond B. Cattell, copyright 1971 by Houghton Mifflin Co. Reprinted with their permission.

(4)Penguin Books Ltd.

Adapted material from "The Scientific Basis of Personality," Raymond B. Cattell, copyright 1965 by Penguin Books Ltd. Reprinted with their permission.

(5)American Psychiatric Association

Adapted material from "Diagnostic and Statistical Manual of Mental Disorders (DSM-II)," copyright 1968 by American Psychiatric Association. Reprinted with their permission.

(6)American Psychological Association

Adapted material from "Ethical Standards of Psychologists," copyright 1963 by the American Psychological Association, Inc.

# EXPLANATORY REMARKS

The guiding ideas of this Dictionary are usefulness, simplicity, and flexibility. We have tried to keep matters as simple as possible and to avoid whatever could hinder easy access and readability. There was no reason to mark the pages with phonics, phonetics, etc. We have assumed that people who read psychology in English do not need to be instructed in spelling.

We have avoided as much as possible superfluous indicators such as q.v., see, synonym, opposite, for we do not believe that someone looking for a specific fact, e.g., a definition of operant conditioning, must be bothered with a host of signs indicating related terms. If he looks for them, he will find them easily; if he does not seek them, there is no need to inform him that the terms he did not seek have been defined elsewhere in the Dictionary. Thus, the word "see" was used sparingly and only when it was absolutely necessary.

The logic of a dictionary required giving priority to nouns. For instance, "phlegmatic type" was defined under "type, phlegmatic." It was necessary, however, to cross reference many terms, and the "phlegmatic type" was listed as "see *type, phlegmatic.*" The same principle was applied to several key terms such as complex, conditioning, reinforcement, scale, syndrome, test and type. Abbreviations have been avoided for they are usually more handicap than help. Adjectives were defined only when necessary; e.g., "narcotic" was defined as a noun. When a term was spelled in more than one way, in most cases, both types of spelling followed one another, divided by a semicolon; e.g., aboulia; abulia.

No entries were signed; the name in front of an entry does not give the author of the entry, but rather indicates the author of the concept, idea, or technique.

The term "mental disorder" was used interchangeably with "behavior disorder."

Finally, the reader will find two appendices of special interest. These are the American Psychiatric Association's Classification of Mental Disorders and the American Psychological Association's statement of Ethical Standards of Psychologists. We believe that these appendices greatly enhance the Dictionary's usefulness and scope.

B.B.W.

# DICTIONARY OF
# BEHAVIORAL SCIENCE

# A

**A** See *angstrom.*

**a%** A traditional Rorschach scoring calculation, representing the proportion of animal content responses in a protocol. Since it is easy to see animal forms in the inkblots, it is expected that they will represent from one-third to one-half of all the responses in most records. Unusually high numbers of animal responses are generally associated with constriction and/or stereotypy while unusually low numbers are associated with the records of the more seriously disturbed subjects.

**A scale** See *scale A.*

**AA** See *achievement age.*

**AAT** See *test, auditory apperception.*

**A/S ratio** (D. O. Hebb) Association-sensation ratio.

**Abadie's sign** (J.M.C. Abadie) The absence of pain when pressure is put on the Achilles tendon.

**abalienated; abalienation** Obsolete terms meaning mental illness or insanity.

**abalienatus** Total destruction of the senses; loss of mental faculties. This term is no longer in use.

**abasement** Degradation of oneself; excessive complying, surrendering, accepting punishment.

**abasement need** See *need, abasement.*

**abasia** The inability to walk due to lack of motor coordination, usually the result of a psychological disturbance rather than an organic cause. This condition often accompanies hysteria. Types of abasia: 1) Astasia-abasia involves the inability to stand or to walk as a result of mental conflict. 2) Ataxic abasia is awkward locomotion. 3) Choreic abasia—the inability to walk because of muscle spasms in the lower limbs. 4) Paralytic abasia—the inability to stand or walk due to organic paralysis. 5) Paroxysmal trepidant abasia—a form of astasia-abasia in which the legs become spastic when walking is attempted. 6) Trembling abasia—the inability to walk because of continuous trembling in the legs.

**abative scoring standardization** (R. B. Cattell) The third possibility in standardization, after *normative* (across people) and *ipsative* (across the same response to different stimuli). Like the ipsative score, it is standardized within one person, but with regard to the same response to the same stimulus *made across a population of occasions.* (Hence, P-technique gives abative standardization.)

**ABBA** Counterbalanced order of presentation of independent variables in a psychological experiment. The one independent variable, condition A is followed by the second independent variable condition B, this followed first by condition B then A.

**abclution** (R. B. Cattell) One of the personality dimensions characterized by rejection of acculturation and refusal to conform to cultural patterns.

**abderite** A stupid person.

**abdominal reflex** See *reflex, abdominal.*

**abducens nucleus** A mass of nerve cells located in the fourth ventricle from which the abducent nerve originates.

**abducent nerve** See *nerve, abducent.*

**aberrant energy expression** The abnormal and unorganized methods of releasing energy that are found as symptoms in the psychoses and neuroses.

**aberration** 1. A deviation from the normal or typical. 2. In an optical system, the passage of light by any pathway other than the most efficient; particularly, passage of light in such a way that rays emanating from the same point fail to converge on the same focus.

**aberration, mental** Deviation from normal mental functioning.

**abetalipoproteinemia** See *syndrome, Bassen-Kornzweig.*

**abience** Avoidance. Abient behavior moves the organism away from exposure to a stimulus.

**ability**  The power to perform an act, either physical or mental, whether innate or acquired by education and practice. *Ability,* as distinguished from aptitude, implies that an act can be performed now. *Aptitude* implies that the individual can develop by training the ability to perform a certain act. *Capability* is the maximum effectiveness a person can attain under optimal conditions of training.

**ability grouping**  Dividing pupils into relatively homogeneous groups with regard to ability, either in a specific subject or in general ability.

**ability test**  See *test, ability.*

**abiotrophy**  An early loss of function or vitality of cells or tissues.

**ablation**  Removal of all or part of an organ, often with the purpose of studying its function.

**ablution**  1. The act of washing the body. 2. A form of hydrotherapy given for insomnia that usually brings quiet, restful sleep. This treatment involves vigorously rubbing with water and then drying each part of the body.

**ablutomania**  A preoccupation with thoughts about washing that frequently accompanies an obsessive-compulsive neurosis.

**Abney's Law**  The principle that the luminance of a given monochromatic light is proportional to the luminosity, $V$, of the light and the radiance, $E$. In mathematical form the law is expressed as follows:

$$B=K\zeta \ V\lambda \ E\lambda \ d\lambda$$

where:

$B$ = luminance
$V\lambda$ = relative luminosity at wave length
$E\lambda$ = energy distribution of light according to a specified physical measure
$K$ = a constant allowing for differences in the magnitude of $B$ and $E$.

**abnormal**  1. Diverging from the normal, not conforming with the general rule. The term usually connotes pathology or deviation from what is considered psychologically adjustive. 2. In a statistical distribution, descriptive of scores which are outside the normal or expected range of scores, departing from the mean interval of the distribution.

**abnormal impulse to work**  See *ergasiomania.*

**abnormal polychromate**  An individual who is able to distinguish most color except for one or two which he fails to perceive or confuses.

**abnormal psychology**  See *psychology, abnormal.*

**abnormality**  Deviation from the norm. The various definitions of abnormality depend on the kind of norm one has in mind: 1. (Statistics) Deviant from the mode, mean, or any other statistical norm. Also unusual, rare, coincidental, improbable. 2. (biology and medicine) Sickness, disease, defect, malformation, malfunction, invalidism and any other somatic or physiologic pathology. 3. (psychology) Disturbed, disorganized, maladjustive behavior; irrational, disturbed, uncontrollable and disbalanced mental processes and/or disintegrated personality structure.

**aboiement**  The uncontrollable and involuntary production of abnormal or unusual sounds. For example, some severely regressive schizophrenic patients make many animalistic noises.

**abomination**  A term that has been used to convey loathing for food. Presently it is used only to express a general loathing and extreme disgust.

**aboral**  The region of the body opposite to the mouth. The term is used in animal psychology.

**abortive decision**  Rushed, premature, ineffectual decision.

**aboulia; abulia**  Inability, usually pathological, to make decisions; loss of will power, inability to carry out decisions.

**above and below**  (A. Adler) The unconscious belief that maleness is superior to femaleness; the conception of man as above and female as below. According to Adler, femininity is a position of inferiority; masculinity is to be strived for as a goal of superiority.

**Abraham, Karl (1877-1925)**  One of the earliest disciples of S. Freud and the first German psychoanalyst. Developed a theory of etiology of mental disorders linked to Freud's psychosexual stages and wrote extensively about characterology and manic-depressive psychosis.

**abreaction**  (psychoanalysis) Lessening the anxiety associated with an experience that originally involved the repression of emotions, by reliving the experience in feeling, thought or action. The freeing of psychic energy by converting repressed ideas or experiences into consciousness. In the early stages of psychoanalysis, abreaction was part of the cathartic method.

**abreaction, motor**  (psychoanalysis) Living through an unconscious emotion or experience by muscular or motor expression.

**abscissa**  1. The horizontal line used as a base line in a two-dimensional graph of Cartesian coordinates. Used to plot measures of the independent variable—synonym: $X$ axis, horizontal axis. 2. The distance of a point $P$ along a line parallel to the $X$ axis as measured from the $Y$ axis (or vertical axis)—synonym: $x$ value, $x$ distance.

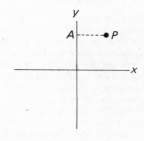

$XX$ is the axis of abscissa.
$AP$ is the abscissa of $P$.

**absence** The short period of time when there is a temporary loss of consciousness during attacks of hysteria and epileptic seizures. During this loss of consciousness there is either suspended or merely automatic activity. Also there is amnesia for the events that occur during such periods.

**absentmindedness** The tendency to be largely unaware of surrounding conditions due to absorption in one's own thoughts.

**Absicht** (from German *ab-sehen*). *Absicht* refers to an intention, aim, goal, or purpose. The usage arises when conceiving of humans as cognitively purposive or as controlled presently by anticipated future states or conditions. The term was important in ethics, for a traditional distinction is made between intention, action, and results. Ethical responsibility, particularly in the Graz school at the beginning of the 20th century, was viewed as residing in the intention. Intention has frequently been confused with intentionality, which as a primarily perceptual or cognitive term does not imply purposive behavior. The root notion is the Aristotelian conception of four types of causality: material, efficient, formal, and final. In human actions *Absicht* refers to a final causality.

**absolute** 1. Independent of comparison with other objects of judgments; not relative. 2. Not subject to change with time or circumstances.

**absolute accommodation** See *accommodation, absolute.*

**absolute error** See *error, absolute.*

**absolute impression** See *impression, absolute.*

**absolute judgment** See *judgment, absolute.*

**absolute-judgment method** See *method, absolute-judgment.*

**absolute limen (RL)** See *threshold, absolute.*

**absolute luminosity** See *luminosity, absolute.*

**absolute measurement** See *measurement, absolute.*

**absolute pitch** See *pitch, absolute.*

**absolute refractory period** See *period, absolute refractory.*

**absolute scale** See *scale, absolute.*

**absolute sensitivity** See *sensitivity, absolute.*

**absolute threshold** See *threshold, absolute.*

**absolute value** See *value, absolute.*

**absolute zero** See *zero, absolute.*

**absorption** 1. Focusing attention on one object, thereby excluding other objects. 2. Excluding reality because the focus of one's attention is on autistic thoughts.

**abstinence syndrome** See *syndrome, abstinence.*

**abstract** (noun) 1. A summary. 2. That which contains within itself all the essential qualities of a larger thing. (adjective) 1. Referring to a quality or aspect that is considered apart from other qualities or from

the object itself. 2. That which is applicable in general rather than in concrete or particular situations. (verb) 1. To separate a part from the whole, to consider a single quality or aspect of an object apart from other aspects and from the object itself. 2. To briefly and uncritically summarize the content of a piece of writing.

**abstract intelligence** See *intelligence, abstract.*

**abstract symbolism** See *symbolism, abstract.*

**abstract thinking** See *thinking, abstract.*

**abstracting-sensation** (C. G. Jung) The isolation of a content or meaning, characterized by sensation, from other irrelevant elements.

**abstracting-thinking** (C. G. Jung) Bringing out a content or meaning that is distinguished from other elements by its logical and intellectual qualities.

**abstraction** 1. Separation and isolation of a particular aspect from a concrete whole; the development of a concept by drawing from a class of objects or events. 2. The concept arrived at by the isolation of a meaning or characteristic from the specific totality considered. 3. Inattention to surrounding situations due to an absorption with one's own thoughts.

**absurdities test** See *test, absurdities.*

**absurdity** Something self-contradictory or meaningless.

**abulia** See *aboulia.*

**abulic** An individual or act characterized by abulia, loss of will power.

**abundancy motive** Desire to experience enjoyment, to obtain gratification, to seek novelty, to discover and understand, to attempt to achieve and create. This motive includes the goals of satisfaction and stimulation. It may often involve the search for tension increase rather than tension reduction.

**AC/A** (psychophysics) The ratio of accommodative convergence to accommodation; it is a description of the near response of an individual which is constant for that individual.

**academic** 1. Relating to formal education, particularly involving the study of books. 2. Pertaining to the theoretical rather than practical issues. In psychology, referring to those experimental programs and schools of thought whose goals are theoretical as opposed to practical application.

**acalculia** A form of aphasia that involves the loss of ability to carry out even simple arithmetic operations.

**acanthesthesia** A variety of paresthesia in which the individual experiences the sensations of pin pricks.

**acarophobia** 1. A morbid fear of mites. 2. Extended to include a wide variety of small animals and objects.

**acatalepsia** Abnormal inability to understand or to reason; impairment of reasoning function.

**acatalepsy** An obsolete term that was used as synonymous with dementia.

**acatamathesia 1.** Inability to understand perceived objects or situations. **2.** Impaired ability to comprehend the meaning of spoken language.

**acataphasia** The inability to arrange words in the correct phrasing and sentence structure of common speech. Also called syntactical aphasia.

**acathexia** Partial or complete inability to retain secretions and excretions of the organism.

**acathexis** (psychoanalysis) The absence of a cathexis. Particular ideas or thoughts that hold no feelings or emotions for an individual are said to be acathected.

**acathisia** The inability to sit down because the thought of such an act or the act itself produces intense anxiety in the individual.

**acathisia paraesthetica** Presently called paresthetic acathisia; another name for acathisia—the inability to sit down due to emotional factors.

**acathisia psychasthenica** Presently called psychasthenic acathisia; the inability to sit down because the thought of such an act or the act itself produces intense anxiety in the individual.

**acathisia spastica** Presently called spastic acathisia; the inability to sit down because the thought or act of sitting results in hysterical convulsive seizures.

**acceleration 1.** A quickening or speeding up. **2.** An increase in the rate of change. Constant acceleration—an increase that is the same in each successive time unit. Positive acceleration—an increase that increases with each successive time unit. Negative acceleration—an increase that is less with each successive time unit.

**acceleration, developmental** Uneven growth; precocious growth of some or all functions.

**acceptance 1.** A positive attitude toward an idea or judgment. **2.** A relationship or attitude that involves the recognition of an individual's worth without condoning or condemning the person's behavior or verbalizations and without implying emotional attachment.

**acceptance in social relations** (B. B. Wolman) Social relations are viewed in the two dimensions of "power" and "acceptance," power being measured in terms of the ability or inability to satisfy needs and acceptance in terms of willingness or unwillingness to do so. Individuals who are willing to satisfy the needs of others are perceived as friendly, those who act against the needs of others are perceived as hostile.

**acceptor of action results (AAR)** An apparatus of the functional system which corresponds to decision making. The apparatus of AAR consists of several functional structures. One of them concerns the ascending tonic influences of the hypothalamus and reticular formation. These influences sustain AAR as a rather heterogeneous apparatus in a long-lasting stable state until the program of action is formed

and the result that was programmed is attained. Another mechanism of the AAR can be called the "Mechanism of collation." Due to the afferent synthesis the afferent features of a probable result are mobilized from memory, as predicted. By means of return afferentation at the acceptor of action results, a collation of features of the real result is combined with the features of what has been predicted by the AAR.

**accessory** Additional help, contributory, assisting. Used to refer to those parts of a sense organ that aid in the organ's more effective functioning.

**accessory catalepsy** See *catalepsy, accessory*.

**accident** Unusual, unpredictable event, usually harmful.

**accident, cerebrovascular** Apoplexy; stroke. A serious and sudden damage caused to the cerebrum by hemorrhage or thrombosis or embolism, associated with partial or complete paralysis, brain damage and psychotic state.

**accident, intentional** An accident occurring because of an unconscious motive.

**accident prone person** A person who acts out and discharges a forbidden and unconscious impulse through accidents.

**accident proneness 1.** Tendency to experience harm or damage. **2.** Unconscious wish to be harmed.

**accident, purposeful** An accident that satisfied some need of the individual. Also called intentional accident. See *accident, intentional*.

**accidental chaining** See *chaining, accidental*.

**accidental errors** See *errors, accidental*.

**accidental reinforcement** See *reinforcement, accidental*.

**accidental stimuli** See *stimuli, accidental*.

**accommodation 1.** The adjustment and adaptation of an organ, a part of an organ, or an organism to existing situations. **2.** The changes in the lens and ciliary muscle of the eye for focusing at different distances. **3.** (J. Piaget) The modification of an existing schema by which a person perceives or thinks as a result of new experiences.

**accommodation, absolute** The adjustment or change in the shape of the lens in response to different distances as considered for each eye separately.

**accommodation, binocular** Simultaneous accommodation of both eyes.

**accomplishment quotient** Also called achievement quotient; the ratio of achievement age, the actual performance in school or on a standardized test and the performance level expected, indicated by the chronological age or estimated by the mental age.

**acculturation 1.** The processes by which children learn the characteristic behavior patterns of their social group. **2.** The processes through which an individual learns the behavior patterns of a particular group, thus enabling the person to get along within that group. 3. The acquisition of the cultural elements of one people by individuals of another group or culture.

**accuracy** 1. Pertaining to exactness, freedom from error. 2. Relating to the degree of correspondence between that which is said or measured and a fact, thing or event. 3. Ratio between number of test items correctly answered and the number of test items attempted.

**accuracy compulsion** (Rorschach) A tendency of the subject to be overly concerned with the form of the inkblots and dissatisfied with his own associations or responses.

**accuracy score**  See *score, accuracy.*

**accuracy test**  See *test, accuracy.*

**ACE Test**  See *test, ACE.*

**acedia**  Listlessness, carelessness, melancholia, and apathy. (This term is rarely used.)

**acenesthesia**  Absence or lack of the feeling or perception of one's own body.

**acerophobia**  Also acerbophobia; an intense fear of sourness.

**acetylcholine**  A compound released at the endings of parasympathetic postganglionic and all preganglionic nerve endings. This base is believed to be responsible for the passage of impulses across synapses thus activating muscles. It also lowers blood pressure and increases peristalsis.

**acetylcholine, metabolism of**  Acetylcholine, produced from acetylation of choline by the enzyme choline acetylase is present in the brain almost entirely in bound form. On nerve stimulation, it is released in its "free" form and is rapidly inactivated by the enzyme cholinesterase through hydrolysis to acetate and choline.

**Ach, Narziss Kaspar (1871-1946)**  Member of Oswald Külpe's "Würzburg school" of imageless thought in Germany, later professor of psychology at Berlin, Königsberg, and Göttingen. His 1904 work on the determining tendency in thought (such as being ready to add or to multiply two digits before they are presented) was a landmark in the psychology of set.

**achievement**  1. Accomplishment, success in bringing about a desired end. 2. That which is successfully attained. 3. The degree or level of success in some specified area or in general. The level of proficiency attained in scholastic or academic work.

**achievement age**  Achievement described in terms of age; the level of attainment that is considered normal for a particular age; the chronological age that is equivalent to a specific level of performance.

**achievement battery**  A group of tests that measure the degree of attainment of skills and knowledge in several areas.

**achievement drive**  See *drive, achievement.*

**achievement motive**  (D. C. McClelland) Technically in psychology a concern to improve, to do things better than one has done them before; measured by counting the frequency with which people think spontaneously in terms of improvement in imaginative stories; related to certain action characteristics like taking moderate risks and preferring concrete feedback on quality of performance which in turn facilitate entrepreneurship and rapid economic growth. Not related to fame or school achievement, or to one's own opinion of how concerned he is to get ahead.

**achievement need**  See *need, achievement.*

**achievement quotient**  Less commonly called accomplishment quotient; the ratio of actual performance level to the expected level of performance.

**achievement test**  See *test, achievement.*

**Achilles jerk**  The reflex movement of the ankle when the Achilles tendon is tapped lightly.

**achluophobia**  An intense fear of darkness.

**achromatic**  1. Lacking in chroma; that is, possessing no hue or saturation but only the dimension of brilliance. Such stimuli are considered "colorless colors," running from black through gray to white. 2. Referring to a lens that has been corrected for chromatic aberration.

**achromatic color response**  A type of Rorschach response in which the black, white, and/or grey features of the inkblots are specifically used to represent color, as for example, "a *black* bat." The scoring symbol 'C' is generally used to denote such responses.

**achromatism**  Complete color blindness.

**achromatopsia**  Inability to discriminate between all hues; all stimuli are perceived as achromatic-gray; total color blindness; also called achromatism.

**acidosis, diabetic**  Occurs in diabetes mellitus and is due to a loss of base in the urine along with the accumulation of ketone acids in the tissues and blood. May result in coma.

**acmaesthesia**  Also acmesthesia; perceiving sharp points by touch but lacking the sensation of pain usually associated with such perceptions.

**acme**  1. The highest point. 2. The highest point of pleasure occurring during sexual intercourse. 3. (medicine) The critical stage or crisis point of a disease.

**acolasia**  An old term for unrestrained self-indulgence or lust.

**aconuresis**  Also enuresis; the uncontrolled or involuntary passage of urine.

**acoria**  1. An insatiable desire for food because the individual never feels full after eating. 2. A form of hunger as a result of the absence of feeling satiated after a meal.

**acoumeter**  Also acumeter; an instrument used to determine auditory acuity or sensitivity of hearing.

Hearing loss is measured in terms of decibels at the various frequencies within the normal range of sensitivity. More commonly called audiometer.

**acousma** A simple auditory hallucination such as hissing or buzzing. A condition on the borderline between illusion and true hallucinosis.

**acoustic spectrum** The range of sound waves within the range of human hearing from about 16–20,000 hertz.

**acoustico-mnestic aphasia** See *aphasia, acoustico-mnestic.*

**acousticophobia** A morbid fear of sounds.

**acoustics** 1. The science of sound, specifically the physics of sound. 2. Those characteristics of a room that affect the distinctness with which sounds can be heard within that enclosure.

**acquired** 1. Obtained. 2. (psychology) Behavior or response that is gained primarily through practice, experience and learning. 3. (biology) Development that is due to environmental influences.

**acquired amentia** See *amentia, acquired.*

**acquired drive** See *drive, acquired.*

**aquired fear** Fear resulting from conditioning.

**acquisition** 1. That which is gained or added by the organism, such as ideas, information or new ways of responding. 2. Increase in the response strength after the behavior has been rewarded.

**acquisition cumulative curve** See *curve, acquisition cumulative.*

**acquisition curve** See *acquisition cumulative curve.*

**acquisitiveness** A strong tendency or desire to possess, and sometimes to hoard certain objects.

**acrai** An Arabian term, no longer used in the United States, that is synonymous with nymphomania and satyriasis.

**acrasia, acrasy** Absence of self-control; intemperance.

**acratia** Impotence; inefficiency; loss of power.

**acroaesthesia** Also acroesthesia; exaggerated sensitivity in the extremities, especially to pain.

**acroanesthesia** Loss of feeling or sensitivity in the extremities.

**acrocinesia** Also acrocinesis; excessive motion or movement as sometimes observed in certain cases of hysteria.

**acrocyanosis** Blueness of the extremities as a result of a vasomotor disturbance. If this condition is chronic and progressive, there is hypertrophy of the soft tissues of the hands and feet. One of the symptoms which accompany severe schizophrenia.

**acrocyanotic** Pertaining to the condition characterized by bluish discoloration of the extremities.

**acrohypothermic** Relating to abnormal coldness of the extremities.

**acromania** An obsolete term that was used to refer to a chronic, incurable and violent form of behavior disorders.

**acromegaly** A condition involving the overgrowth of bones and connective tissue caused by hypersecretion of the anterior pituitary gland during adulthood. The characteristics are enlarged head, hands, feet and some internal organs.

**acromicria** Term used in constitutional medicine, especially by E. Kretschmer and N. Pende, for a condition characterized by the underdevelopment of the extremities and the skull as compared to visceral development. Acromicria congenital is an expression introduced by C. E. Benda for mongolism. See *Down syndrome.*

**acroparesthesia** 1. A sense of numbness, sometimes recurring, in the extremities. 2. A neurosis, chiefly seen in middle-age women, involving tingling or crawling sensations and coldness in the hands.

**acrophobia** An intense fear of being in high places.

**act** "Act" is a basic or primitive term in Act psychology, but in Association or Gestalt psychology is a derived term. The "act issue" is whether to conceive relations or acts as primitive terms of a theory of mind. If mental acts are basic, then relations between elements of experience are formed by mental acts. If relations are embedded in the nature of experience (Stumpf, Wm. James), then both mental acts and Laws of Association, which function to relate elements in experience, are not necessary.

If relations are formed by the integrative action of the nervous system (Koehler), then both mental acts and Laws of Association are not necessary. The act issue starts with two notions: that experience comes in mosaic-like elements and the unity of consciousness is a psychologically real phenomena which must be explained. For Aristotle the common sensibles related the elements of experience; for the British empiricists after Locke, Laws of Association performed that function; for Gestalt psychologists the integrative activity of the nervous system related elements of experience; but for act psychologists the unity of experience is achieved by means of cognitive functions of mind.

**act–habit** Repetitive activities on the part of a child that represent habituation and personality-rooted character traits. This term points out the importance of different cultural aspects of the environment in influencing the development of certain aspects of a child's personality.

**act psychology** Within the domain of mental phenomena act psychology can be distinguished on ontological grounds from other psychological constructions as follows: (1) what exists are contents and their relations (Wundt), (2) what exists are contents, relations, and mental acts or functions (Külpe), and (3) what exists are primarily mental acts within which contents have a secondary existence (Brentano).

Some forms of act psychology, following Aristotle's and Aquinas' philosophical realism, also assert the existence of objects external to the individual. For the Brentano school only real objects are capable of being presented in the sensorium. This position leads to controversies about the existence of objects like mermaids, golden mountains, etc. A realist position was defended by B. Russell, who made a distinction between knowledge by acquaintance and knowledge by description. A mermaid is known not by acquaintance but by description.

Closely related to the tradition of act psychology is J. P. Guilford's Structure-of-Intellect model. In this model knowledge is categorized by contents (figural, symbolic, semantic, behavioral) and form (units, classes, relations, systems, transformations, implications) and mental operations, or acts, into cognition, memory, divergent production, convergent production, and evaluation.

Act psychology can be distinguished from two other views: Association Psychology and Gestalt Psychology. Association Psychology relations arise as a result of the operation of laws of association; in Gestalt Psychology they arise as a result of an integrative activity of the nervous system; in Act Psychology they occur by a mental act.

**act, pure stimulus; r**   (C. L. Hull) An act which, although it does not serve to move the organism closer to a goal, initiates the proprioceptive stimuli that tend to elicit the appropriate operant response.

**ACTH**   See *adrenocorticotropic hormone.*

**acting out**   (psychoanalysis) The reproduction of forgotten attitudes, memories or conflicts by action rather than words without conscious awareness or recognition on the part of the individual. Carrying into action behavior patterns that are appropriate to an older situation but are brought out by the symbolic similarity of the present situation. During psychoanalytic treatment the patient behaves toward the therapist in ways that are reproductions of past attitudes toward parental authority. This is called "acting out in the transference." Acting out can occur outside of the analytic situation but related to it. In these instances, the patient projects his feelings toward the therapist onto people in his everyday environment. Externalization of conflicts through acting out can, with some persons, occur without being related to treatment, as in character disorders. The term acting out, is often applied indiscriminantly to any aggressive or anti-social activity. Such behaviors have an unclear relationship to acting out and, therefore, the term lacks precision except within the context of an analytic situation.

**actinic rays**   Short wave-length light rays, violet and ultra-violet, which produce chemical change.

**action currents**   The changes in the electrical potential of nerves or muscles that occur during physiological activity.

**action, deferred**   (psychoanalysis) When an experience becomes significant and meaningful not at the time the experience took place; that is, when the original experience is revived by some subsequent occurrence.

**action interpretation**   (S. R. Slavson) The nonverbal reaction of a therapist to the statements or acts of a patient. A technique used almost exclusively in activity group psychotherapy.

**action potential**   The entire sequence of changes in the electrical potential associated with impulses in nerves and muscles. Often used as synonymous for action current.

**action, psychomotor**   A behavioral response or action that is the direct result of an idea or perception.

**action psychotherapy**   See *psychotherapy.*

**action research**   Scientific programs or studies designed to yield results that are practical rather than theoretical.

**action, symbolic**   Unconscious and automatic actions that are considered accidental by the individual doing them. These acts may be simple or complex; but either type conceals a definite meaning. Symbolic actions may manifest themselves in such unconscious mannerisms as jingling coins or playing with a moustache.

**action system**   1. All the glands, nerves and muscles involved in the production of a particular response. 2. All the physiological and psychological structures participating in accomplishing a specific behavioral result.

**activation**   A desynchronization of the electrical recordings made from the brain (EEG) when the organism becomes alert.

**activation theory of the emotions**   The assumption that defines emotion as one end of a continuum of activation. The continuum ranges from sleep (no activity) to violent emotion (maximum activity).

**active**   1. Dynamic, functioning, working. 2. Possessing the qualities of movement or change. 3. Alert, showing spontaneity or initiative. 4. Causing action.

**active analysis**   (psychoanalysis) A technique in which the analyst takes a more dominating role in the treatment process. The analyst would offer advice, give interpretations, and give suggestions for the direction of free association. Wilhelm Stekel and Sandor Ferenczi advocated various types of active psychoanalysis.

**active fantasying**   A psychotherapeutic procedure involving the analysis of the patient's spontaneous imagery. Through the analysis of fantasied images, the analyst can uncover the unconscious roots of the patient's conflicts and help the patient bring them into conscious awareness.

**active imagination**   See *imagination, active.*

**active-passive**   1. A polarity believed to be important in governing mental life and most commonly applied to opposing aims of instinctual drives. Activity is evident when a person seeks objects to gratify his needs. Passivity is manifested when a person wishes to have someone gratify his instinctual needs, with him being the receiver of gratification. 2. The child moves from passivity to activity as he learns to perform for himself functions previously performed for him by adults. 3. A specialized psychoanalytic usage referring to the structural concepts of id, ego, and superego, which are considered to be, at various times, either active or passive in relation to one another.

**active therapy**  See *psychotherapy, active.*

**activities, graded**  Occupations and handicrafts that have been classified according to their difficulty; that is, the amount of mental and physical effort needed to complete them. This system is used in occupational therapy to make possible a simultaneous increase in difficulty and in the patient's capacity to perform.

**activity catharsis**  A catharsis in which the repressed feelings and thoughts are conveyed through action rather than verbally. This situation occurs often in activity group psychotherapy.

**activity, group**  An activity in which several individuals participate. In occupational therapy, the main value of such a group is its socializing effect upon the members.

**activity, group immobilizing**  (S. R. Slavson) A form of group psychotherapy in which activities are limited to one specific interest or task for the purpose of binding libidinal energy.

**activity group therapy**  See *psychotherapy, activity group.*

**activity, libido-binding**  (S. R. Slavson) Activities that tie an individual to a particular interest or occupation.

**activity, socializing**  Referring to therapy groups, any activity that results in the interaction of an individual with other members of the group.

**activity wheel**  A drum in which the subject, usually a rat, may run turning the drum. The measure of the activity is the number of revolutions of the drum.

**actual neurosis**  See *neurosis, actual.*

**acuity**  The accurateness or sharpness of perception.

**acuity grating**  A square with alternate black and white lines printed very close together, used to measure visual acuity by determining the minimum separability that is needed so that the objects will be perceived as two distinct things.

**acute**  1. Sharp or pointed at the end. 2. Sensitive to fine discriminations in both perception and thinking. 3. Severe or sharp pains. 4. Of rapid onset and lasting a short time. 5. An angle of less than 90 degrees or containing one or more angles of less than 90 degrees. 6. (psychopathology) Acute disorder or disease with a sudden onset and usually short duration.

**acute affective reflex**  See *reflex, acute affective.*

**acute brain disorder**  A complex of symptoms resulting from temporary impairment of the functions of brain tissue such as the disordered behavior occasionally induced by drugs.

**acute delirium**  A condition of mental confusion and excitement characterized by convulsions and sometimes death.

**acute hallucinosis**  A condition in which the individual experiences hallucinations for not longer than a few weeks. Hallucinosis is typically toxic in origin, particularly associated with acute alcoholism.

**acute mania**  See *mania, acute.*

**acute preparation**  An animal that must be destroyed for humane reasons following an experiment involving unusual surgical techniques.

**acute shock psychosis**  See *psychosis, acute shock.*

**adaptation**  1. (physiology) The change or adjustment of a sense organ to the incoming stimulation. Sensory adaptation—a) decreased sensitivity to stimuli due to prolonged stimulation, also called negative adaptation; b) continued effective sensory responsiveness under changing stimulation. 2. (biology) Structural or behavioral changes of an organism or part of an organism that fits it more perfectly for the environmental conditions under which it must live; changes that have survival value. 3. More generally, any beneficial modification that is necessary to meet environmental demands. Social adaptation—accepting and meeting societal and interpersonal demands. 4. Elimination of irrelevant behavior as learning progresses. 5. (A. Adler) A process of upward adjustment and compensation for man's innate deficiencies. 6. (E. Fromm) Modifications in drives, attitudes and emotions in adjusting to the environment. Although man can adjust himself to most circumstances, there are some limits to the malleability of human nature. 7. (H. Hartmann) A critical concept in Hartmann's theory of the ego. The newborn child has an innate perceptual and protective apparatus which, after the id-ego separation, becomes the conflict-free ego sphere. This apparatus performs the tasks of mastering the reality, called by Hartmann adaption.

**adaptation, brightness**  A decrease in the brilliance of a stimulus which is caused by an increase in the general illumination of the surrounding visual field.

**adaptation, color**  See *color adaptation.*

**adaptation level**  (H. Helson) 1. A hypothesized momentary state of the organism at which stimuli are neutral or indifferent on any attribute. The stimuli above this point have specific characteristics and those below have complementary qualities. For example, in the transition from pleasant stimuli to unpleasant stimuli there is a stimulus or group of stimuli that is neutral. This transitional zone represents the stimuli to which the organism is adapted so far as the particular quality, magnitude or attribute is concerned. 2. Also known as AL, the adaptation level can be operationally defined as the value of that stimulus which elicits a neutral response when a subject judges a set of stimuli in terms of qualitative or numerical rating scales. 3. The theory of adaptation level attempts to evaluate the factors that influence this neutral zone in terms of focal, background and residual stimuli. The AL is seldom, if ever, at the center or at the arithmetic mean of the series. The phenomenon is called decentering. As a result of decentered AL the usual tendency is to overestimate small values of stimuli and to underestimate large values of stimuli although the contrary is sometimes found. These and other puzzles in classical psychophysics are easily explained if it is assumed that the prevailing AL is the effective norm in psychophysical judgments. Harry Helson and his co-workers have proposed quantitative theories embodying AL as a parameter to deal with difficulties in such classical formulations as the Weber-Fechner law and phenomena associated with changed states of adaptation in color vision. It is generally accepted that AL is a weighted geometric mean of focal, background (or contextual), and residual stimuli. While AL denotes the value of stimulus that elicits a neutral or indifferent response, to predict or fit the responses to each of the members of a class of stimuli being judged, it is necessary to know the proper type of S-R function or curve for the data in question.

The adaptation level theory has been utilized in studies of psychophysical judgment, sensory and perceptual processes, language and communication, and in aesthetic, social and personality studies, to mention a few of its numerous applications.

**adaptation, photopic**  See *adaptation, brightness.*

**adaptation syndrome**  See *syndrome, adaptation.*

**adaptation time**  The duration of time from the onset of a stimulus to the moment when the consequent changes in the sense organ being stimulated cease.

**adaptational psychodynamics**  See *psychodynamics, adaptational.*

**adaptative**  Relating to that which aids in adjustment or improvement; appropriate.

**adaptive act**  (H. A. Carr) Adaptation to the environment is of central importance. In the adaptive process motives act upon the organism; there is always a sensory situation and a response to the stimulus. Response is the activity that leads to a change in the entire situation in the direction of satisfaction of the motive. Once the motive is satisfied, the organism does not react to it any longer. The object by which the motive is satisfied is called an incentive. A motive represents a genuine need; the satisfaction of a motive is necessary for the survival and the well-being of the organism. When the adaptive act is completed the action of the motivating stimulus is terminated and the goal of the response accomplished.

**adaptive behavior**  Any behavior that aids the organism in meeting the demands of its environment; adjustive or appropriate responses.

**adaptometer**  Any instrument used to measure the degree of sensory adaptation, but specifically applied to a device that measures dark adaptation.

**addiction**  1. Compulsive craving for something. 2. Overdependence on the intake of certain substances such as alcohol and drugs, or performing of certain acts such as smoking, etc. 3. Inability to overcome a habit or behavioral pattern.

**Addison's disease**  A progressive condition of anemia accompanied by digestive disturbances, weakness, and some pigmentation of the skin, which is caused by ineffective functioning of the adrenal cortex.

**additional response**  Used in Rorschach testing to note instances in which the subject reports a percept during the inquiry phase of the test which he did not report during the free association period.

**additional scores**  See *scores, additional.*

**additive scale**  See *scale, additive.*

**additive W**  A type of response to the Rorschach inkblot test that involves the report of details which the subject eventually combines to form a whole response. See *Rorschach inkblots.*

**ademonia**  A term used in the past for severe mental anxiety or distress; sometimes used as synonymous with melancholy.

**ademosyne**  A term that was used as synonymous with nostalgia.

**adenoid type**  A hypertrophied pharyngeal tonsil or adenoid that is believed to be a sign of a serious constitutional problem. The extreme cases of this type are frequently associated with cretinism and deaf-mutism.

**adephagia**  Also addephagia; a term used in the past indicating an abnormal and insatiable appetite; synonymous with bulimia.

**adequate stimulus**  See *stimulus, adequate.*

**adermonervia**  An obsolete term for anesthesia.

**ADH**  Antidiuretic hormone. See *vasopressin.*

**adhesion**  1. (physics) The molecular attraction between body surfaces that are in contact with one another. 2. (medicine) The abnormal connection betwen organs or parts of organs due to inflammatory growth of new tissues. 3. The connection or sticking together of substances, events, or ideas.

**adiadochokinesis**  Also adiadokokinesis or adiadokokinesia; adiadokocinesis or adiadokocinesia. 1. Inability to perform movements that involve rapid alteration. 2. Continuous movement.

**adience**  (adient behavior) Behavior that moves the organism toward a specific stimulus or exposes the organism to more of the stimulus through action that maintains the stimulus.

**adiposogenital dystrophia**  Also called Froehlich's syndrome. Retarded development of the gonads and increased sugar tolerance, usually occurring in individuals during the pre- or post adolescent period. This condition is the result of an impairment of the pituitary gland or the hypothalamus.

**adj schedule**  See *reinforcement, schedule of: adjusting.*

**adjunctive psychotherapy**  See *therapy, adjunctive.*

**adjusting (adj) schedule**  See *reinforcement, schedule of: adjusting.*

**adjustment**  1. An harmonious relationship with the environment involving the ability to satisfy most of one's needs and meet most of the demands, both physical and social, that are put upon one. 2. The variations and changes in behavior that are necessary to satisfy needs and meet demands so that one can establish a harmonious relationship with the environment.

**adjustment inventory**  See *inventory, adjustment.*

**adjustment mechanism**  A fairly permanent, habitual form of behavior that is adjustive.

**adjustment method**  A psychophysical method in which the subject adjusts a stimulus object in relation to a constant or standard stimulus. The mean of the series of adjustments is taken to be the most representative score. A measure of variability, such as the standard deviation, is also calculated as indicative of the subject's variability.

**adjustment of observations; measurements  1.** Statistical correction of observed data to allow for atypical or disturbed conditions. **2.** The use of the principle of least squares to obtain the best value to represent a series of measurements. See *least squares method.*

**adjustment, optimum**  Survival under the best possible conditions which is the goal of psychotherapy.

**adjustment path analysis**  (R. B. Cattell) A standard framework for analyzing a person's attempts at adjustment in terms of basic alternative paths which can be followed.

**adjustment procedure**  (psychophysics) A means of arriving at the threshold of error by taking the average of the deviations when a subject adjusts a stimulus object until it appears equal to a criterion object.

**adjustment process analysis  (APA) chart**  An abstraction and reduction to a system of the sequences of response possible to the organism in its goal-seeking behavior. An attempt at comprehensive schematization of successive paths and choice-points (Dynamic Crossroads) in the adjustment of the organism, including possibilities for frustration, conflict, and personality learning.

**Adler, Alfred (1870-1937)**  Viennese psychiatrist, an early associate of Sigmund Freud and one-time president of the Vienna Psychoanalytic Society. He broke with Freud in 1911, rejecting Freud's instinct (libido) theory and stressing instead an ego-psychology, and a social personality theory and social psychiatry, calling it "individual psychology". He saw man as aiming towards his own, self-created goals, rather than as the victim of his inherited drives; he viewed man's problem in his insecurity, which is apt to mislead him to emphasize his self-interest only, instead of uniting it with the interests of the community of men of which he ought to feel a part; he believed that neuroses and psychoses are generated by an insufficient development of social feelings towards others. His greatest influence has been in Child Guidance, and his theories sparked Child Guidance movements in Europe and the U. S. A. He lived in New York City from 1926, lecturing and practicing psychiatry, and was professor at the Long Island College of Medicine 1932-37. Among his many books are: *Theory and Practice of Individual Psychology, Social Interest, A Challenge to Mankind, Problems of Neuroses, What Life Should Mean to You, Understanding Human Nature, The Education of Children, The Problem Child* and many others. His theories and techniques are taught and practiced in many Adlerian Institutes and Adlerian Clinics in the U. S. A. and abroad, by societies bearing his name.

**ad lib body-weight**  The weight approached or reached by a mature organism under continuous access to food.

**ad lib feeding**  Providing continuous access to food.

**adolescence  1.** (biology) This approach considers early adolescence as beginning with the onset of the pubescent growth spurt until about a year after puberty. The pubescent growth spurt is marked by a spurt in physical growth, changes in body proportions and the maturation of primary and secondary sex characteristics. Puberty is the climax of pubescence and is characterized by signs of sexual maturity such as the menarche in girls and the presence of live spermatozoa in the male urine. Late adolescence is considered to last until physical growth is relatively complete at which time early adulthood begins. These biological changes vary according to individual, age-stage, and sex. **2.** (chronology) Early adolescence is designated as the age period of 13 through 16 and late adolescence as 17 through 21. Sometimes the age periods established for girls and boys are different, 12 through 21 and 13 through 22 respectively. Either designation is misleading for neither biological nor psychological maturity proceeds at the same rate in all individuals. In addition, all aspects of biological or psychological maturity do not develop at the same rate in the same individual. **3.** (sociology) Considered to be largely a creation of the Western world, social adolescence involves outgrowing the social status of a child but not yet being accorded the privileges of the adult. **4.** (cross-cultural) Adolescence is viewed according to the way of life of the youth through the years and in different parts of the world. By such a comparison certain constants can be identified as characteristic of adolescence regardless of culture. **5.** (theoretical) Adolescence may be defined according to a particular theory. For example, the phenomenologist places emphasis on the adolescent's perception of himself and his environment. In contrast, the psychoanalytic approach, based on Freudian theory, considers early life stages as highly significant and each stage as important for the subsequent stages. **6.** (developmental) Adolescence is considered in relation to other developmental stages and in terms of the psychological dynamics involved. Looking at the role that adolescence plays in total development and in helping the individual establish identity is an example of such an approach.

**adolescent crisis  1.** The emotional changes that occur during adolescence. The adolescent ego is confronted with new challenges: achieving independence, casting off old emotional ties and developing new ones. Both physiological and psychological events, during this time, present problems for the adolescent to deal with before reaching maturity.

**2.** Radical shift of moods typical of adolescent period.

**adrenal cortex** The outermost portion of the adrenal glands where cortin is produced.

**adrenal glands** See *glands, adrenal.*

**adrenal medulla** The part of the adrenal gland which secretes the hormones adrenalin and noradrenaline.

**adrenalin** Also called epinephrine; a hormone secreted by the adrenal medulla. Its general effects are to mobilize the body's resources to cope with an emergency or stressful situation. Specifically, adrenalin stimulates the production of sugar from the liver, increases heart rate, facilitates muscle contraction and inhibits digestion.

**adrenalism** A condition resulting from impairment in the functioning of the adrenal glands. Also called suprarenalism.

**adrenergic** **1.** Pertaining to the type of chemical activity characteristic of adrenalin (epinephrine); adrenalin-like action. **2.** Characterizing the action of certain nerve fibers of the sympathetic nervous system that produce sympathin which is an adrenalin-like substance.

**adrenergic-response state** (R. B. Cattell) A personality dimension showing characteristics generally indicative of high levels of adrenalin secretion, such as high blood sugar, rapid pulse and high blood pressure.

**adrenin** Also adrenine; trade names for adrenalin (epinephrine).

**adrenochrome** An oxidized derivative of adrenaline which has psychotomimetic properties and is believed to be present in an excessive amount in schizophrenic people.

**adrenocortical hormones** See *hormones, adrenocortical.*

**adrenocortical insufficiency** See *Addison's disease.*

**adrenocorticotropic hormone** See *hormone, adrenocorticotropic.*

**adult analysis** **1.** (psychoanalysis) Refers to the psychoanalysis of adult patients. **2.** May refer to non-Freudian approaches to analysis used with adults.

**adult-child interaction test** See *test, adult-child interaction.*

**adult maladjustment, simple** A category including individuals who appear maladjusted although there is no evidence of psychosis or psychopathic personality. Their difficulties and lack of adaptive capacities are seen in relation to specific areas such as marriage or occupations.

**adultomorph** (L. S. Kubie) Refers to psychoanalysts who interpret infant's fantasies in adult terms.

**advantage, law of** See *law of advantage.*

**adventitious deafness** See *deafness, adventitious.*

**adventurousness** **1.** Characterized by risks and hazards, thereby being adventurous. **2.** Possessing courage.

**advisor system** A program established by the United States Service Unit in which groups of platoon leaders were trained in practical psychology. The purpose was to sustain the morale of the soldiers and prevent mental breakdowns. Training included being made aware of the importance of: (1) having an interest in and helping to solve the soldiers' problems; (2) explaining details to new members of the unit; and (3) the proper assignment of tasks. Platoon leaders were carefully selected, for emotional stability was an important factor. They were then trained to create good will within their unit without any loss of fighting efficiency. This program successfully reduced psychoneurotic reactions as well as absences without leave.

**adynamia** Loss of strength; weakness; debility. Also called asthenia.

**aedoeomania** An obsolete term for nymphomania.

**aerial perspective** See *perspective, aerial.*

**aero-acrophobia** Intense fear of being in places that are both open and high; such as in an airplane.

**aëroasthenia** See *aëroneurosis.*

**aëroneurosis** A type of psychoneurosis found in aviators. This condition is characterized by restlessness, anxiety and varying physical manifestations.

**aerophagia** Automatic swallowing or gulping of air, a common symptom of neuroses particularly of hysterical patients.

**aerophobia** A morbid fear of fresh air or drafts.

**aerumna** A term that is no longer used to refer to depression that accompanies a physical disease.

**aeschromythesis** The foul or obscene language of the maniacal or delirious person. This term is no longer used.

**aesthesiometer** Also esthesiometer; an instrument used to measure tactile sensitivity. It is a compass-like device that determines the threshold or minimum spatial separation on the skin at which two points are perceived as two separate points.

**aesthete** Also esthete; an individual who emphasizes the importance of the beautiful as part of experience; one who is very sensitive to beauty.

**aesthetic type; esthetic type** See *type, esthetic.*

**aesthetics** Also esthetics; the study of the constituents of beauty. If such study is experimental it is considered a branch of psychology. However, if such study is rational and a priori it is considered a branch of philosophy.

**affect** **1.** A class name given to feelings, emotions, or dispositions as a mode of mental functioning. **2.** The name given to specific emotions or feelings. **3.** (K. Pribram) A state generated when motivated action becomes unfeasible.

**affect block**  The inability to love due to a fear of love and a fear of emotional ties. As a result of the blocking of affect, this condition involves the incapability for strong emotions and the avoidance of loving by using doubts and uncertainties.

**affect, conversion of**  (S. Freud) Wish-impulses arise during the period of infantile sexuality. At a later time when these impulses are fulfilled, the resulting emotional state is pain rather than the previously felt pleasure. This change or conversion of affect is the essence of repression. These impulses are repressed; and, subsequently, they are symbolically represented in some physical manifestation. The physical symptom is held to be the way that an internal conflict is externally expressed.

**affect, detached**  (S. Freud) An emotional component that has been separated from the idea with which it was originally associated because the idea was unbearable to the ego. Instead the affect becomes attached to other, more acceptable, ideas, which grow to be obsessions.

**affect-energy**  When a stimulus is applied to a whole human organism excitement is produced. The energy resulting from this excitement is called affect-energy or affective energy.

**affect, fading of**  (S. Freud) The dimming of the emotional, as well as ideational, components of impressions as they become more and more remote in the past. Freud conceives of these changes as being the work of the preconscious.

**affect-fantasy**  See *affect-phantasy*.

**affect, flattening of**  In pathological states, a general impoverishment of emotional reactivity which is characterized by incongruous or inappropriate affective behavior or a total lack of response to emotionally tinged stimuli.

**affect, hunger**  (D. Levy) The human being's craving or desire for emotions. This term was originally described with regard to the emotional hunger for maternal love, protection and care that arises when a child is deprived of such parental affection. A more descriptive and precise term would be affection hunger.

**affect, inappropriate**  The display of emotions which are incompatible with the demands of a particular situation.

**affect, inversion of**  (psychoanalysis) A manifestation of ambivalence in the form of a sudden change in emotion from love to hate or vice versa.

**affect, organ localization of**  An emotion may be felt in any body organ. An effect is usually localized in those organs that are reached directly by the autonomic nervous system, such as the stomach, heart and lungs.

**affect-phantasy; affect fantasy**  (C. G. Jung) A fantasy, imagined event or object, that has a strong emotional component attached to it.

**affect, somatic factor**  In addition to the subjective emotional state through which an affect expresses itself, there are physiological or somatic accompaniments of emotional states. A few examples of these physiological changes are nausea, palpitations and sweating.

**affect-tonus**  A basic and normal state of affect; that is, the affect is at an even level due to continuous and stable stimulation. This situation is analogous to muscle tonus. Changes in this normal level represent emotional reactions.

**affect, transformation of in dreams**  (psychoanalysis) The representation of an emotion in a dream by the opposite emotion. A feeling, usually a repressed one, is transformed into its exact opposite and incorporated into a dream. This is one of many processes by which true meaning is obscured in dreams.

**affectability**  An individual's ability to express feelings or emotions.

**affectation**  To assume or exhibit unnatural feelings; an artifical manner in behavior or speech meant to impress the listeners or the onlookers. This manner may be often seen in hysteria or in the manic phase of manic-depressive psychosis.

**affectio hypochondriaca**  An obsolete term for hypochondriasis.

**affection**  1. A general term for feelings and emotions. 2. Caring or loving; tender attachment.

**affection, masked**  (W. Stekel) The display of tender behavior by an individual who is actually feeling hostility and hatred. In addition to referring to an unconscious defense reaction, this term may also refer to a conscious deception.

**affective**  Pertaining to affect or feeling.

**affective arousal theory**  (D. C. McClelland) An attempt to account for the arousal of positive and negative affect in terms of the degree of discrepancy between adaptation level (or expectation) and what actually happens to the organism. If what happens coincides exactly with expectation, no affect is aroused; if it deviates slightly from expectation, positive affect is aroused; if it deviates markedly from expectation, negative affect is aroused. Used to explain how motives become directed toward increasingly sophisticated and complex goals. As cognitive expectations become more complex, moderate deviations from them needed to give positive affect—i.e., new goals—also become more complex. Used also to explain why aesthetic taste moves from simple to more complex forms with growing experience.

**affective disorders**  More recently called affective psychoses. A group of psychoses that are characterized by derangements of emotional expression or mood. The exaggeration of emotional expression is accompanied by signs of intellectual disturbance. Also characteristic of an affective disorder is the rapidity with which symptoms change. In these conditions, all emotional distortions range between the two poles of manic elation and deep depression; the affective psychoses tend to occupy the extremes.

The transition from emotional excitement to depression can occur in various ways. The onset of either an extreme depression or elation does not seem to be related to a specific precipitating life experience and therefore, is distinguished from psychotic depressive reaction and depressive neurosis.

*The Diagnostic and Statistical Manual of Mental Disorders* of the American Psychiatric Association, 1968 (Second Edition, DSM-II) categorizes the major affective disorders (affective psychoses) as follows:

I.   Involutional melancholia
II.  Manic-depressive illnesses (manic-depressive psychoses)
     1. Manic-depressive illness, manic type (manic-depressive psychosis, manic type)
     2. Manic-depressive illness, depressed type (manic-depressive psychosis, depressed type)
     3. Manic-depressive illness, circular type (manic-depressive psychosis, circular type)
        a. manic-depressive illness, circular type, manic
        b. manic-depressive illness, circular type, depressed
III. Other major affective disorder (affective psychosis, other)
IV.  Unspecified major affective disorder

**affective energy**  See *affect-energy.*

**affective epilepsy**  See *epilepsy, affective.*

**affective eudemonia**  Escape from an unbearable reality by fleeing into mental illness. This term puts emphasis on secondary gains which are important in the following examples of affective eudemonia: faxen-psychosis, the Ganser syndrome and certain cases of hypochondriasis.

**affective experience**  See *experience, affective.*

**affective processes in ament**  (A. F. Tredgold) Emotions are weaker in both duration and intensity in a mentally deficient individual than they are in normal people. The acquisition of sentiments consisting of the association of an emotion and an abstract idea are even more markedly defective.

**affective psychosis**  See *psychosis, affective.*

**affective ratio**  See *ratio, affective.*

**affective reaction type**  See *type, affective reaction.*

**affective reintegration**  The reorganization of affects or emotions into harmony following their previous disintegration during the affective psychoses.

**affective rhythm**  (psychobiology) An expression used to mean the routine that utilizes the individual's emotional mood.

**affective state**  A condition involving the experience of emotions.

**affective syndrome**  Another term for affective psychosis which is the category of disorders in which the main symptoms are inappropriate or exaggerated emotional reactions.

**affective tone**  1. The generalized mood or feeling of an experience. 2. (E. B. Titchener) The pleasantness or unpleasantness with regard to a specific stimulus. 3. The subjective correlate of acceptance-rejection behavior.

**affective transformation**  1. (psychoanalysis) The representation in consciousness of a repressed emotion usually by its opposite. 2. The law of affective transformation says that emotionally emphasized values continue to strive to increase their area of dominance. This process is often noticed in schizophrenia and may be observed in other behavior disorders as well.

**affectivity**  1. The tendency to react emotionally. 2. A generalized emotional experience, one that is not identifiable as a specific emotion or with a particular stimulus. 3. The amount of emotion or feeling evident at a specific time.

**affectomotor**  Displaying both muscular activity and emotional excitement. This combination of symptoms is common to many behavior disorders, but affectomotor is usually used to refer specifically to the manic phase of manic-depressive psychosis.

**affectomotoric**  Characterized by intense mental tension and muscular activity.

**affecto-thymia**  (R. B. Cattell) The positive pole of the A personality factor, re-named from Cyclothymia vs. Schizothymia because, though it supports in factorial experiment, the dimension of Bleuler and Kretschmer; it may represent easy versus inhibited emotional response.

**affectus animi**  An expression that was used in the past as a general term for any psychiatric disorder.

**afferent**  Carrying toward; concerned with the transmission of neural impulses toward the central nervous system.

**afferent apraxia**  See *apraxia, afferent.*

**afferent interaction**  See *interaction, afferent.*

**afferent motor aphasia**  See *aphasia, afferent motor.*

**afferent paresis**  See *paresis, afferent.*

**afferent stimulus interaction**  1. (C. L. Hull) A postulate which holds that all afferent neural impulses active in the nervous system at any given time interact and in the process of interacting, modify one another. The behavioral effects of these impulses are more than the mere summation of the effects of each taken separately. 2. This principle is an attempt to provide a behaviorist explanation for patterns of stimuli and other configurational problems dealt with by the Gestalt psychologists. See *Gestalt psychology.*

**afferent synthesis**  The initial stage in the formation of the functional system. It is indispensable for every functional system and precedes "decision making" for the system. As a rule, "decision making" occurs only after the stage of afferent synthesis comes to the end. The afferent synthesis comprises the four most main components: dominating motivation at a given moment, situational afferentation, stimulus afferentation, and continuous extraction of the former experience from memory. All these processes are processed on separate neurons at the very beginning, and only after this processing there takes place integration of many decision making neurons, the processing of four heterogeneous excitations on the neuron synaptic organization is realized in uninterrupted dynamic processes, facilitating mobilization of the indispensable interneuronal connections. Such dynamic processes include ascending activation of the reticular formation, hypothalamus facilitating effect, increase of discrimination, cortico-subcortical reverberation, centrifugal facilitation of excitability of the receptors, etc. All these dynamic processes facilitate the choice of the most adequate aim for the given motivation and a given situation. The existence and interrelations of all the dynamic processes mentioned on separate neurons have been experimentally demonstrated.

**affiliation** 1. Connection or association. 2. (H. A. Murray) An individual's need to draw near and enjoyably cooperate with another, to form friendships and remain loyal, to please and win affection of important others. Also called affiliative need.

**affiliation need**  See *need, affiliation.*

**affiliative behavior**  Behavior designed to establish friendly and satisfying interpersonal relationships.

**affiliative motive**  See *motive, affiliative.*

**affiliative need**  See *affiliation.*

**affinal** 1. From the same origin. 2. Related through marriage.

**affinity** 1. Attraction and relationship. 2. (biology) The relationship between certain groups due to their mutual resemblance which is indicative of a similar origin.

**affusion** 1. To pour water upon the body. 2. A form of hydrotherapy during which the patient stands or sits in a bathtub with a sheet around his body while water is poured on him. Then the patient is towel rubbed until a reaction is observed. The purpose is to reduce fever and calm nervous systems.

**after care**  Treatment and rehabilitation services provided by the community for patients discharged from hospitals.

**afterdischarge**  The continuing discharge of neural impulses after the stimulus has been removed.

**aftereffect** 1. An aftersensation. 2. A sensory experience that continues after the stimulating condition ends. 3. (learning) The strengthening of the connection between a stimulus and a response because the consequence of the act are satisfying. See *afterimage.*

**aftereffect, figural**  The distortion or displacement of visual objects that are placed in a region which had previously been occupied for some time by other visual objects, such as dots, lines, or figures.

**afterexpulsion**  Secondary repression.

**afterimage**  The persistence of sensory excitation in

a given sensory system, following the removal of the adequate stimulus. The most readily observed afterimages occur in vision. There are both positive and negative visual afterimages. A positive afterimage occurs when the observer sees a patch of color similar in both brightness and hue to the original. In negative afterimage, every color appears as the complementary in hue to the original and is opposite in brightness. Also called aftersensation. See *Purkinje afterimage.*

**afterimage, memory**  An afterimage consisting of the revival of an experience immediately after it has occurred.

**afterimage, positive**  Experience of a visual stimulus after it has been removed. The brightness and hue of the afterimage are almost the same as the actual stimulus.

**aftersensation**  The continuation of a sensory experience after the removal of its stimulus. In vision, a positive aftersensation is one in which the image is brighter than the surrounding field and a negative aftersensation is one in which the image is less bright than the surrounding field. Also called afterimage. See *Purkinje afterimage.*

**agamma globulinemia**  Disease caused by sex-linked recessive gene resulting in absence of gamma globulin which is necessary for antibody formation. Not clinically detectable at birth and not damaging unless offending organisms or toxins are present. The body is unable to synthesize antibodies to fight the invasion and survival is made unlikely.

**agastroneuria**  A condition of the stomach characterized by lowered nervous tone. Sometimes called neurasthenia of the stomach.

**AGCT**  See *Army General Classification Test.*

**age** 1. The period of time from birth to any given time in life; the time an organism has lived; chronological age. 2. One of the stages or periods in life; as, middle age. 3. A lifetime; the entire time of a being's existence. 4. The time in life when a particular capacity or qualification arises; as, school age. 5. A particular period in the history of man; as, stone age. 6. (psychology) An individual's development, either mental or anatomical, etc., that is measured by the number of years expected for like development in an average child. Distinguished from chronological age and always with a qualifying expression; as, mental age, anatomical age. Called age equivalents.

**age critique**  (French) Menopause or period of time during which menstruation ceases.

**age equivalent**  The level of an individual's development, regarding any trait or characteristic, that is expressed as equal to the chronological age at which the particular level is normally or on the average attained. Therefore, the mental development characteristic of age eight is designated as mental age eight.

**age-equivalent scale**  See *scale, age-equivalent.*

**age-equivalent score**  See *score age.*

**age-grade scaling**  See *scaling, age-grade.*

**age norm** 1. The average score attained by a large group of children on a standardized test; a representative performance of children at a given age level. 2. The chronological age at which a given score is usually achieved.

**age ratio** The chronological age of a child at one testing divided by the child's chronological age at a later testing. This ratio is a crude measure of a test's predictive power. The test's predictive power depends on the age at which the test is given and the length of time between tests. The younger the age of the child, the poorer the predictive power of the test. The longer the interval between tests, the poorer the prediction from one test to the next. Therefore, prediction will probably be better from ages 5 to 6 (ratio 5/6) than from ages 3 to 4 (ratio 3/4).

**age scale** See *scale, age*.

**age score** See *score, age*.

**agenesis; agenesia** Also called aplasia. The failure, either total or partial, of tissues to develop.

**agenetic** Characterized by the absence or imperfect development of one or more parts of the body.

**agent, catalytic** 1. (chemistry) A substance that changes the velocity of a chemical reaction without being altered itself. 2. (psychology) The patient who initiates catharsis in other members of the psychotherapy group.

**agent provocateur** Varying kinds of influence that act as precipitating or exciting causes of events, diseases or disorders.

**ager naturae** (Latin) The field of nature; the uterus.

**agerasia** An old age that shows youthful appearance, health and vigor.

**ageusia** Also ageusis and ageustia. An impairment or deficiency in the sense of taste. The cause of such a disorder may be either physiological or emotional. There are three types of ageusia which are distinguished on the basis of the location of the defect causing the disturbance in the gustatory apparatus. If the cause is a cortical lesion, the disorder is called central ageusia. If the lesion is located in the nerve between its origin and distribution, the disorder is called conduction ageusia. However, if the defect is in the nerve endings, peripheral ageusia is the name given to it. This condition is common in psychiatric patients, particularly in the depressions. It has also been observed to occur in schizophrenia and hysteria.

**agglutinations, image** See *image agglutinations*.

**aggregate** 1. A mass of distinct units; a group of objects, thoughts, persons, etc. that are brought together but remain separate entities. 2. (mathematics) A sum of a number of quantities.

**aggregation theory** (W. C. Halstead) A theory of intelligence in neurological terms. It postulates that intelligence is a function of the coordinated effort of various sensory and motor areas located throughout the cerebral cortex.

**aggression** 1. Attack or hostile action that may take any form from physical assault at one extreme to gentle verbal criticism at the other extreme. This type of behavior may be directed at any thing or person, including the self. 2. (S. Freud) Aggression is one of the primary instincts. One's natural aggressiveness against the self may be directed against the outer world. Thanatos is, primarily, an instinct of death and all of us carry a certain amount of self-destructiveness within ourselves. It seems that people have to destroy things and other people in order not to destroy themselves. In order to protect oneself from the tendency toward self-destruction, one must find external channels for aggressiveness. 3. (A. Adler) In Adler's theory, aggressiveness is the most general human striving and is a necessity of life. Self-assertion is the underlying principle of aggression. The aggressive drive is the drive to overcome one's feeling of interiority. 4. (J. Dollard & N. E. Miller) According to the frustration-aggression theory interference with goal directed behavior is frustration, and frustration leads to either a substitute response or to aggression, which is also a kind of substitute. If aggression if blocked, it may be directed against a substitute or turned inward to become self-aggression. 5. (H. A. Murray) An individual's need to forcefully overcome opposition, to fight, to punish another, to injure or kill another and to revenge an injury.

**aggression, animal experiments of** Several brain centers have been found to be important in the control of aggressive behavior. Afferent stimulation of the hypothalamus in a decortical cat produces quasi rage. Focal lesions of the hypothalamic ventromedial nucleus results in an exaggeration of aggressive tendencies. The medial hypothalamus appears to be inhibitory for this behavior while the lateral area is excitatory. Stimulation of the amygdala in intact animals also induces rage responses while ablation of this area produces docility in a variety of animals. In monkeys, amygdala lesions are followed by changes in position in the hierarchy of dominance-submission. The function of the amygdala seems to be the control of the excitability of lower central mechanisms for aggressive behavior.

**aggression, antisocial** Unjustifiable aggression from a socially evaluative standpoint; e.g., instrumental, retaliatory, spontaneous.

**aggression need** See *need, aggression*.

**aggression, prosocial** Allegedly justified aggression, e.g., in children, tattling, belligerent rule-stating; in adults, punitive discipline of children and criminals, expressions of moral indignation and outrage, violence in a "good cause" (as in lynching, book or witch-burning, destruction of property/persons conceived to differ in values from one's own, revolution).

**aggressive behavior** The acts of behavioral responses of an organism that display the quality of aggression.

**aggressive instinct** See *Thanatos*.

**aggressiveness** 1. The tendency to display hostility by performing acts of aggression. 2. The tendency to overcome opposition of being self-assertive pushing forward one's own interests. 3. Showing enterprising or energetic behavior. 4. The tendency to be dominating in a social situation.

**agitated depression**  See *depression, agitated.*

**agitation**  1. Restlessness. 2. Excitement. 3. Set in motion. 4. Hurrying.

**agitolalia**  Also agitophasia. Excessively rapid speech due to emotional excitement or stress. Speech is cluttered with sounds that are slurred, omitted, or distorted.

**agitophasia**  Also called agitolalia. The cluttered speech that results from extremely rapid speaking while under excitement and stress. Cluttering involves the omission, slurring or distortion of sounds.

**agnosia**  1. A complete or partial inability to recognize and attach meaning to the impressions of a sense organ. 2. The loss of the memory of familiar objects. An individual with agnosia is unable to correctly perceive and identify familiar objects. This condition can involve any sensory system and is often the result of cortical damage. In visual agnosia, for example, the individual is able to perceive whatever is within his visual field but is unable to recognize what he is seeing.

**agnosia, apperceptive visual**  (H. Lissauer) A form of visual agnosia which is characterized by a disturbance of the visual synthesis of individual cues.

**agnosia, associate visual**  (H. Lissauer) A form of visual agnosia characterized by an inability to recognize the meaning of objects when perceiving their outline.

**agnosia, left-right**  See *apractagnosia.*

**agnosia, speech**  A disturbance of phonemic hearing resulting from damage to the posterosuperior portion of the left temporal lobe characterized by the lack of ability to distinguish sounds and words and repeat them, to produce words spontaneously, difficulty in naming objects and in writing and in general, an impairment of the analysis and synthesis of speech sounds.

**agnosia, tactile**  1. Agnosia due to lesions in the postcentral cortical areas which are characterized by difficulties in the tactile recognition of objects, especially the analysis and synthesis of tactile and kinesthetic stimuli. There are two forms: Wernicke's agnosia and asymbolia. 2. See *agnosia, Wernicke's.* 3. See *asymbolia.*

**agnosia, visual**  Agnosia due to lesions in the secondary visual cortex characterized by an inability to recognize objects or the meanings of objects. There are two forms: apperceptive visual agnosia and associate visual agnosia.

**agnosia, Wernicke's**  (S. Wernicke) A form of tactile agnosia in which the identification of objects through touch is impaired usually associated with lesions closer to the secondary areas of the cortical nucleus of the cutaneous-kinesthetic analyzer.

**agoraphobia**  An intense fear of open spaces.

**agrammaphasia**  Also called agrammatism. A type of aphasia in which the individual forms sentences without regard for grammatical rules.

**agrammatism; agrammatologia, agrammata; agrammataphasia**  A type of aphasia; the inability to communicate that involves the absence of grammatical rules in the formation of words into sentences. Such a loss of the ability to speak coherently may be the result of brain injury or it may accompany a severe mental disturbance such as schizophrenia.

**agraphia**  A type of aphasia; the inability to communicate, characterized by the loss of the power to write any or all of the following: individual letters, syllables, words or phrases. This impairment in the ability to write is usually due to a cerebral lesion but occasionally may be the result of emotional factors. Acquired agraphia is the name given to the condition that results from brain injury or disease which causes a loss of the individual's previous ability to write. Congenital agraphia refers to the situation in which the individual has unusual difficulty learning to write, difficulty that is not consistent with his other intellectual accomplishments.

**agraphia, visual**  Disturbances in writing due to lesions of the occipitoparietal areas characterized by inability to differentiate by writing letters, numerals, or words.

**agreement coefficient**  See *coefficient, agreement.*

**agriothymia**  A term used in the past to mean maniacal or insane ferociousness.

**agriothymia ambitiosa**  A morbid desire to conquer and/or destroy nations.

**agriothymia hydrophobica**  Also called hydrophobic agriothymia; an irresistible impulse to bite.

**agriothymia religiosa**  A morbid desire to destroy other religions and the people advocating them.

**agromania**  An extremely intense impulse to live in open country or in isolation.

**agrypnia**  A term to describe the inability to sleep, specifically a chronic condition of sleeplessness. Such a condition is also called insomnia. Sleeplessness that is associated with mental excitement is called agrypnia excitata. Agrypnia pertaesa is the inability to sleep due to a physical disorder. The sleeplessness brought on because of old age is referred to as agrypnia senilis.

**agrypnocoma**  Also called coma-vigil. A deep sleep from which the person can be easily awakened; sleepless coma. A condition involving variations of coma and wakefulness that can be observed particularly in patients with an organic brain disease.

**agrypnotic**  Relating to, producing or displaying insomnia.

**agyiophobia**  A morbid fear of streets; fear of crossing streets.

**aha or ah-ah experience**  Also called ah-hah experience. The name given to the moment of insight or the realization of a solution in a problem solving situation. The time when all the perceived parts of an experience fit into a meaningful pattern.

**ahedonia**   Inability to experience pleasure.

**ahistorical**   A theoretical approach to the study of behavior that emphasizes present conditions, both within and without the organism, as a means of understanding the present behavior of that organism. The use of any item from the past history of the organism is minimal when present behavior is the object of study.

**ahypnia; ahypnosia**   Terms applied to extremely severe cases of insomnia; inability to sleep. See *agrypnia*.

**aichmophobia**   A morbid fear of pointed objects.

**aidoiomania**   Another term for erotomania; a morbid inclination to love.

**aids**   The development of systems of cognitive ability to cope, through the discovery of some particular response formula which is successful and generates many associated performances.

**ailment, functional**   A mild, temporary symptom resulting from disturbed physiological functioning such as the somatic expression of emotional conflicts.

**ailurophobia**   Also called galeophobia and gatophobia. Morbid fear of cats.

**aim-inhibition**   See *drive, aim-inhibited*.

**aim of instinct**   The aim of an instinct is to return the organism to the relative state of balance that existed before the instinct was aroused. The term homeostatic equilibrium has been used by W. B. Cannon to refer to this state. The aim of an instinct is the disappearance of an unpleasurable state while the object of an instinct is the means through which the aim can be achieved. The psychoanalyst's constancy principle represents a view similar to Cannon's.

**aim-transference**   The shift of objectives from one life situation to another in which the goal is more likely to be achieved. For example, if the goal is success, aim-transference may involve the switch from activities in sports to activities in music.

**aiming test**   See *test, aiming*.

**air-swallowing**   See *aerophagia*.

**akataphasia**   See *acataphasia*.

**akinesia algera**   (P.J. Moebius) A form of hysteria characterized by a general painfulness accompanying any type of movement. Moebius associated this symptom only with conditions of psychogenic origin.

**akinesis; akinesia**   The absence or impairment of voluntary movement. Frequently observed in psychiatric patients, akinesis is usually of functional arigin.

**akinesthesia**   The absence or impairment of the kinesthetic sense which includes the muscles, tendons and joints. This condition involves the inability to perceive movement of one's own body.

**akinetic**   Relating to or characterized by lack of mobility.

**akinetic apraxia**   See *apraxia, akinetic*.

**akoasm; acoasm**   A simple, auditory hallucination of sounds such as crackling or buzzing. See *acousma*.

**AL**   See *adaptation level*.

**alalia**   Speechlessness; the complete absence of the ability to talk as a result of functional causes.

**alarm reaction**   The release of metabolites in the affected tissues as a response to stress. See *adaptation syndrome*.

**albedo**   The reflecting power of a surface or object described in terms of the ratio of the light reflected by the object to the light falling upon that surface. This ratio is completely independent of the degree of illumination. The ratio of reflectance is the same whether the illumination is weak or intense.

**albedo perception**   A form of brightness constancy in which the discrimination or perception of surfaces is made only with regard to their albedo (ratio of reflectance), while disregarding the variations in degree of illumination.

**Albee, George W. (1921- )**   American psychologist, concerned with manpower and the sociology of professions. His survey of the nation's needs and resources for professionals for intervention and prevention, and his long-time advocacy of the position that disturbed behavior does not reflect illness but a damaging and inhumane environment, has affected mental health planning. His research interests in psychopathology have focused on intellectual development of seriously disturbed adults. He served as President of the Division of Clinical Psychology (1966-67) and as President of the American Psychological Association (1969-70).

**albinism**   A congenital deficiency in pigmentation of the skin, hair, and eyes. In extreme cases the skin is a milky color, the hair is very light, and the eyes have deep red pupils and pink or blue irises. This condition also involves color blindness.

**alcheringa**   According to the mythology of the Arunta tribe of Australia, alcheringa is the "dream time" or period in which the subhuman ancestors of their race lived.

**alcoholic**   A person addicted to alcoholic beverages.

**alcoholic dementia**   See *dementia, alcoholic*.

**alcoholic hallucinosis**   See *hallucinosis, alcoholic*.

**alcoholic psychoses**   See *psychoses, alcoholic*.

**alcoholic psychosis, paranoid type**   See *psychosis, alcoholic, paranoid type*.

**Alcoholics Anonymous**   Also called A.A. An organization formed in 1935 by former alcoholics aiming at helping alcoholics in overcoming their addiction to alcohol.

**alcoholism**   1. Addiction to alcoholic beverages. 2. Alcoholic poisoning.

**alcoholomania** An urge for drinking alcoholic beverages.

**alcoholophilia** A liking for alcoholic beverages.

**aldosterone** A steroid isolated from substances of the adrenal cortex and from human urine which causes sodium retention and potassium loss.

**alector** A term that was used to refer to any individual who was unable to sleep.

**alertness** Being quick to understand and to act; rapid perception; watchfulness.

**Alexanderism** An uncontrollable desire to conquer and/or destroy nations; also called agriothymia ambitiosa.

**alexia** Also called word blindness and visual aphasia. A form of aphasia in which there is an absence of the ability to grasp meaning from or to read the written or printed language. This condition is the result of organic brain damage and does not involve any impairment in vision or intelligence. The loss of a previous ability to read is called acquired alexia. If the condition involves an inability to learn to read that is not consistent with the individual's mental age and other intellectual achievements, it is referred to as congenital alexia.

**alexia, visual** Disturbances in reading due to lesions of the occipitoparietal areas and characterized by inability to recognize individual letters, numerals, or words.

**algebraic value** The numerical value that includes the plus or minus sign that preceeds the number.

**algedonic** Pertaining to that dimension of experience or emotion characterized by pleasantness-unpleasantness.

**algesia; algesis** Sensitivity to pain; the ability to feel pain; sometimes referring to a capacity to experience pain that is above the average.

**algesimeter; algesiometer** An instrument with a sharp, pricking stimulus used to measure sensitivity to pain by pressing the calibrated needle against the skin.

**algesthesia; algesthesis 1.** Sensitivity to pain. **2.** General hypersensitivity (hyperesthesia).

**algolagnia** (Schrenck-Notzing) Sadomasochism; experiencing perverse sexual arousal or sexual pleasure as a result of either receiving or inflicting pain. Active algolagnia- sadism; passive- masochism.

**algolagnist** An individual who achieves sexual excitement by either experiencing or inflicting pain.

**algometer** An instrument used to measure sensitivity to pain by employing the pressure of a blunt stimulus against the skin.

**algophilia** Masochism. Experiencing pleasure as a result of receiving pain.

**algophobia** An intense fear of pain.

**algopsychalia** A symptom expressed as pain in the mind that is distinguished, by the patient, from organically caused pain. This symptom is character-istic of some hypochondriacal, depressed and schizophrenic patients. For example, the hypochondriac complains of severe head pains resulting from the pressure of unbearable anxiety.

**alienatio mentis** Literally, alienation of the mind; in general, it denotes insanity.

**alienation 1.** Estrangement; breaking down of a close relationship. **2.** (social psychology) Disruption of feeling of belonging to a larger group such as, for instance, the deepening of the generation gap or increasing of a gulf separating social groups from one another.

**alienist** A physician, usually a psychiatrist, who is considered by the courts to be an expert on mental disorders. Such an individual is accepted as an expert witness regarding the mental responsibility of persons involved in legal actions.

**alimentary behavior, brain mechanism in** The limbic and hypothalamic areas of the brain have been found to be important in the control of alimentary behavior. Stimulation of the lateral hypothalamus causes eating behavior while lesions in this area results in aphasia. The ventromedial hypothalamic areas are important in satiety. Stimulation of this area ends feeding while lesions result in hyperphagia. The hypothalamic areas which control drinking behavior are adjacent to those which control eating. While eating depends on adrenergic excitation, drinking is caused by chalinergic excitation. Empirical studies have used a variety of methods to control feeding and drinking behavior resulting in a multiple-factor theory of regulation of feeding and drinking which seems to be generally accepted. Experiments focusing on the EEG activity during alimentary behavior suggest that satiety may express an internal inhibition which, after consummation is achieved, plays a important role in bringing innate behavior to an end.

**alimentary canal** The body organs from the mouth to the anus, including the esophagus, stomach, and small and large intestine. This system is involved in the passage, digestion, and absorption of food, as well as the elimination of waste products.

**alimentary orgasm** (S. Rado) The period of satisfaction that occurs after hunger is satiated. In psychoanalysis, the gastro-intestinal tract is considered to be important with regard to emotional investment and action.

**allachaesthesia; allesthesia** Also spelled allachesthesia; allaesthesia. Experiencing a tactile sensation at a place other than the point actually stimulated.

**allegoric interpretation** See *interpretation, allegoric.*

**allegorization** (A. Neisser) The formation of new words or phrases; a process frequently observed in schizophrenic patients.

**allele; allelomorph** Alleles (allelomorphs) are alternative forms of a gene found in the corresponding loci on homologous chromosomes. Only two alleles can be present in any one individual, one derived from each parent that have segregated at meiosis. Multiple alleles is the term to designate the situation where more than two alleles exist for a given locus in the population. Each allele carries contrasting Mendelian characteristics and goes to different mature germ cells.

**allelic; allelomorphic**   Referring to, pertaining to or having the characteristics of an allele or allelomorph. For example, blue eyes and brown eyes are allelomorphic characteristics.

**allergic potential scale**   See *scale, allergic potential.*

**allergy**   (C. von Pirquet) An acquired, altered reaction capacity of the tissues to specific substances that are harmless to most people. This involves an antigen-antibody mechanism that is characteristic of many disease processes and causes physical disturbances that may range from mild irritation to shock. The antigens (allergens) may be either proteins, lipids, haptens, or carbohydrates; however, the antibodies are not always demonstrable. There are four general classifications of allergic diseases: (a) Serum sickness, (b) Contact dermatitis, (c) Atopic diseases are those that depend upon an inherited reaction capacity, such as hay fever, asthma and drug sensitivities, (d) Anaphylaxis refers to those responses that are induced by previous sensitization.

**allergy, cerebral**   Bizarre and unusual cerebral disturbances occurring as symptoms in allergic individuals.

**allergy, extrinsic**   An allergic reaction resulting from an allergen that originates outside the body.

**allergy, intrinsic**   An allergic reaction caused by an allergen that originates within the body.

**alliaceous**   (Zwaardemaker) One of the classes of smell sensations, of which garlic is a typical example.

**allied reflexes**   See *reflexes, allied.*

**allocentric**   Referring to those senses that are oriented objectively such as seeing and hearing.

**allocheiria; allochiria**   A condition involving the experiencing of a tactile sensation at a corresponding point on the side of the body opposite to the side that had actually been stimulated.

**alloerotic**   Pertaining to sexual excitement that is directed to or induced by others; referring to the extension of libido outward, upon other individuals; opposite to the self-directed, autoerotic sexuality.

**alloerotism; alloeroticism**   Directing sexual or erotic tendencies toward others and away from the self.

**allolalia**   Unusual or abnormal speech.

**allophasis**   An obsolete term meaning incoherent speech.

**alloplastic**   (psychoanalysis) Referring to directing libido away from the self toward other persons and objects.

**alloplasty**   (psychoanalysis) The process through which the adaptation of libido to the environment occurs; directing libido energies away from the self toward other individuals and objects.

**allopsyche**   Another person's mind or psyche.

**allopsychic**   Denoting mental or psychic processes in the world outside the individual himself.

**allopsychosis**   Referring to psychological processes that are directed outside the self. For example, allopsychic delusions involve the projection of the individual's own impulses and feelings into others.

**all-or-none response**   A reaction, involving individual neurons and muscle fibers, that is either of maximum strength or not at all. Such a response shows no gradation regardless of the intensity of the stimulus, as long as it is above threshold strength.

**allotriogeusia; allotriogeustia**   1. An abnormal appetite. 2. An unusual or perverted sense of taste.

**allotriophagy**   An intense desire or need to eat unusual foodstuffs.

**allotropic**   1. Relating to or exhibiting allotropy. 2. (psychiatry) A personality that is concerned with others; how they feel, what they think.

**allotropy**   1. The occurrence of an element in two or more separate forms with different physical properties. 2. A strange or unusual form. 3. An attraction between unlike structures or cells. 4. The term Adolf Meyer used for allopsyche.

**Allport, Gordon W. (1897-1967)**   American psychologist, personality theorist, and researcher. Received his Ph.D. in psychology (1922) from Harvard where he served as professor of psychology from 1930 until his death. Known principally for his innovative contribution to the psychology of personality. Allport's theory emphasizes unique individuality, human maturity, and conscious forces. Among his many works are *Personality: A Psychological Interpretation* (1937), *Becoming* (1955), *Pattern and Growth in Personality* (1961). In the area of social psychology he also contributed *The Psychology of Rumor* (with L. Postman, 1947), *The Individual and His Religion* (1950) and *The Nature of Prejudice* (1954).

**Allport A–S Reaction Study**   (G. W. Allport and F. H. Allport) An example of a unidimensional approach to the measurement of personality. The Allport A–S Reaction Study is a test designed to measure the incidence in the personality of two traits, ascendance and submission. It is theorized that one trait would be prominent and the other subordinate. The method is to present verbally certain life situations and require the subject to select from the standardized choices the type of behavior most characteristic of his own adjustment to such situations. There are two forms available, one for men and another for women. The score is an algebraic summation of the number of situations in which the person felt that he would be dominant. Such a score is assumed to be representative of some general tendency on the part of the subject. An example of a typical situation is as follows:

a.   At a reception or tea do you seek to meet the important person present?

Frequently
Occasionally
Never

b.  Do you feel reluctant to meet him?

Yes, usually
Sometimes
No

**Allport – Vernon – Lindzey Study of Values**  (G. W. Allport, P. E. Vernon, and G. Lindzey) Revision of Allport – Vernon Study of Values. A questionnaire designed to yield measures of six attitudes believed to be the most revealing aspects of personality. The scoring shows the individual's emphasis on social, theoretical, economic (interest in acquisition of material things), aesthetic, political (interest in interpersonal power relations), and religious values. This instrument is appropriate for use with late adolescent or college age subjects. Each individual is given a total of 180 points which is distributed among the six values; therefore, the scores for each value is the relative strength of that value within the person. The resulting scores are significantly related to various educational and occupational groupings, as well as to academic achievement. This technique requires responses to 15 four-alternative items and 30 two-alternative items. An example of a four-alternative item is the following:

1.  Do you think that a good government should aim chiefly at:

a. more aid for the poor, sick and old
b. the development of manufacturing and trade
c. introducing more ethical principles into its policies and diplomacy
d. establishing a position of prestige and respect among nations.

The subject indicates his order of preference by writing 1, 2, 3, or 4 before each alternative. A two-alternative item is illustrated as follows:
2.  The main objects of scientific research should be the discovery of pure truth rather than its practical applications.

(a) Yes   (b) No

Agreement with (a) and disagreement with (b) is shown by writing 3 under (a) and 0 under (b). A slight preference for (a) over (b) is indicated by writing 2 under (a) and 1 under (b). The opposite is done if the agreement or slight preference is for (b).

**alogia**  1. Senseless or stupid behavior. 2. Inability to speak because of defects in the central nervous system such as a brain lesion; expressive aphasia. 3. The type of mutism, due to lack of ideas, that may be observed in an idiot or imbecile.

**alogous**  A term used in the past to mean irrational or unreasonable.

**Alper's disease**  Severe mental retardation combined with seizure state, caused by destruction of cerebral neurons, while the myelinated structures remain unaffected. The disease is nonlipid and it is most often caused by cerebral anoxia. It is also called progressive infantile cerebral poliodystrophy.

**Alpha, Beta, Gamma hypotheses**  (K. Dunlap) Three hypotheses concerning the relationship of frequency of repetition to the rate of learning. Alpha states that frequency of repetition promotes learning. Beta indicates that frequency of repetition has no effect on the rate of learning. Gamma proposes that frequency of repetition hinders learning. See *hypothesis*.

**alpha error**  See *error, alpha*.

**Alpha Examination; Alpha Test**  A group general intelligence test consisting of eight subtests given to military personnel during World War I. See *test, Army Alpha*.

**alpha movement**  See *movement, alpha*.

**alpha press**  See *press, alpha*.

**alpha response**  A response, in a conditioning situation, that is not considered to be true learning but rather is believed to be the result of sensitization.

**alpha rhythm**  Also called Berger rhythm, Berger wave, and alpha wave. The most common brain waves of the adult cortex. During rest the oscillations are regular and smooth, occurring at a rate of 8-12 per second with an amplitude of 5-15 microvolts.

**Alpha Tests**  See *test, Army Alpha*.

**alphabet content**  (H. Rorschach) The scoring system used when letters of the alphabet are given as responses to the inkblots.

**alt schedule**  See *reinforcement, schedule of: alternate*.

**alter**  To change, vary or modify. In psychology: An individual's concept of another person as distinct and separate from himself.

**alter ego; alteregoism**  A very intimate friend that is considered by the individual as a second or other self. Alteregoism is a close feeling about another person in the same situation as oneself.

**alternate form**  See *form, alternate*.

**alternate responses test**  See *test, alternate responses*.

**alternating personalities**  The appearance, independently, of more than one organization of the mental, social, and moral qualities of an individual as manifested in the person's relations with his social environment.

**alternating vision**  The process of using first one eye and then the other eye for seeing. In most situations, one eye has dominance over the other and suppresses its incoming sensory information.

**alternation of neurosis**  An older expression referring to the temporary or permanent cure of a behavioral disorder by the occurrence of an acute physical ailment.

**alternation problem, double** See *problem, double alternation.*

**alternative (alt) schedule** See *reinforcement, schedule of: alternative (alt).*

**alternative hypothesis** See *hypothesis, alternative.*

**alternative reinforcement** See *reinforcement, alternative.*

**altitude** A dimension of intelligence described as the level of difficulty of the problems that an individual can solve. Other dimensions are extent of intelligence, the variety of problems that can be solved, and speed of intelligence, the time required to solve certain problems.

**altitude test** See *test, altitude.*

**altophobia** Morbid fear of heights.

**altrigenderism** The natural, nonsexual and non-amorous activities that occur between individuals of opposite sexes. Heteroerotism refers to amorous, though not overtly sexual interests. Heterosexuality is the term used when the sexual element becomes involved; heterogenitality is the expression used when referring specifically to sexual intercourse.

**altruism** (A. Comte) Consideration, concern and affection for other people as opposed to self-love or egoism.

**altruistic** Relating to or characterized by altruism; that is, by constructive consideration and interest in others.

**alucinatio** A term that literally means wandering of mind, but is used to refer to an hallucination.

**alusia** An obsolete term for insanity. The literal meaning is to wander in mind.

**alveolar** Relating to an alveolus: 1) A cavity, pit, depression or cell. 2) A cell of air located in the lungs. 3) The bony socket of a tooth.

**alysm** The restlessness that is displayed by persons who are ill.

**alysmus** The mental anguish, anxiety and depression that accompanies an illness.

**alysosis** Also called otiumosis. Boredom; may be observed in simple schizophrenia.

**Alzheimer's disease** (A. Alzheimer) A rare presenile psychosis that is associated with cerebral sclerosis. There is a rapid deterioration of the brain causing progressive mental disorder accompanied by speech difficulties. The individual is hyperactive and restless, displaying both defective memory and disorientation. Although all the symptoms of senile psychosis may be manifested, this disease may occur at a comparatively early age, such as in the forties.

**amacrine cells** Also called inner horizontal cells or association cells. Amacrine cells are retinal cells that connect the bipolar or second order neurons. Although they appear to be without axons, the bodies

of these cells are located in one of the lower rows of the inner nuclear layer. The importance of amacrine cells is believed to be their involvement in summation effects.

**amathophobia** A morbid fear of dust.

**amaurosis** The partial or total loss of sight, from any cause, without changes in the structure of the eye. The temporary blindness that may result from sudden acceleration is called amaurosis fugax. Amaurosis partialis fugax is the partial blindness that may accompany headaches or vertigo. The condition characterized by total blindness existing at birth is called congenital amaurosis. Introducing various poisons and toxic products into the body may result in a type of blindness known as toxic amaurosis. Another type of toxic amaurosis is uremic amaurosis. See *Tay-Sachs disease.*

**amaurotic family idiocy** See *Tay-Sachs disease.*

**amaxophobia** An intense or morbid fear of being in, or riding upon, any vehicle.

**ambidextrality** Referring to or characterized by the use of both sides of the body.

**ambidextrous** 1. Having no preferred side in performing motor functions. The ability to perform motor acts equally well with the right side of the body as with the left side. 2. Equal skill or ability with both the right and left hand.

**ambiequal** (Rorschach inkblots) A personality dimension described as a well-balanced amount of both introtensive and extrotensive tendencies. The person does not appear as either excessively dependent upon others or particularly egocentric.

**ambiguity, intolerance of** A psychological state manifested in a rigid individual and characterized by the tendency to overlook differences and to simplify the environment.

**ambiguity tolerance** The ability and willingness to handle situations in which there are conflicting or alternate outcomes or interpretations, without undue difficulty.

**ambiguous** 1. Unclear; vague; having several meanings. 2. Referring to statements, objects, or situations that have two meanings or give rise to two intepretations.

**ambiguous figure** Any one of a large group of figures which are subject to continuous change in perspective or interpretation when regarded steadily for a period of time. The Necker cube is the most common example.

**ambitendency** The co-existence of opposing actions, each existing independently of the other.

**ambitent** A Rorschach postulate, referring to those instances where the sum of human movement responses is essentially equal to the weighted sum of color responses. When the ratio (Erlebnistypus) manifests such features, the person is considered naturally prone to derive basic gratifications either from within himself or from interaction with his environment.

**ambivalence 1.** The co-existence of opposing emotions, attitudes or traits in the same individual. **2.** The rapid alternation of emotional attitudes towards another. **3.** Being able to attend to or view two or more aspects of an issue or to view a person in terms of more than one dimension or value. **4.** (K. Lewin) The state of being pushed towards or pulled between two opposite goals.

**ambiversion** (C. G. Jung) A personality type balancing between introversion and extroversion, these two traits being present in about equal amounts.

**ambivert** (C. G. Jung) An individual having ambiversions as the prominent personality trait.

**amblyopia** Poor vision having no known connection with any organic defect or problem in the refracting mechanism of the eye. It has been associated with color blindness, albinism, and tobacco, alcohol and other toxic states.

**amblyoscope** An instrument used to determine the point at which two separately presented visual stimuli fuse.

**ambrosiac** A class of odors of which musk is an example.

**ambulatory automatism** See *automatism, ambulatory.*

**ambulatory psychotherapy** See *psychotherapy, ambulatory.*

**ambulatory schizophrenia** See *schizophrenia, ambulatory.*

**amelectic** A state of indifference; apathy.

**ameleia** Indifference, morbid apathy.

**amenomania 1.** A mild form of mania the symptoms of which are gaiety, a fondness for clothes, etc. **2.** Morbidly elevated affective state. **3.** (B. Rush) A term applied to the manic phase of manic depressive psychosis. **4.** A delirium marked by joyousness.

**amenorrhea** An absence of menstruation resulting from emotional conflict situations where a suppression of menstruation in young women is a defense against sexuality and where heterosexual fantasies substitute for the unacceptable aspects of femininity.

**amentia** Obsolete term for mental deficiency.

**American Psychiatric Association, classification of mental disorders** See *classification of mental disorders.*

**Ames demonstrations** Situations devised by Adelbert Ames, Jr. allowing distortions of depth perception by the use of one cue at a time to eliminate conflicting cues.

**ametropia** Errors of refraction due to a defect in the refractive apparatus of the eye. Usually affecting the visual acuity and accomodation of the eye.

**amimia** Language disorder in which the person is unable to communicate with the help of gestures or signs.

**amine** Any compound formed by placing one or more of the hydrogens of ammonia by one or more organic radicals such as $R \cdot NH_2, R \cdot NH \cdot R'$ and $R \cdot N \cdot (R') \ R''$, where $R, \ R'$, and $R''$, may or may not represent the same radical.

**amino acid** Organic compound resulting from the hydrolysis of protein and having the basic formula of $NH_2 \text{–} R \text{–} COOH$ where $R$ = aliphatic radical. These compounds are used by the body of an organism to resynthesize its proteins.

**aminoaciduria** A disorder of amino acid metabolism causing elevated concentrations of one or more amino acids and the presence of excess amino acid in the urine.

**aminoacidurias, no-threshold** Disease in which enzymatic deficiencies are present but in which no increase in plasma concentration of the amino acids occur. See *homocystinuria.*

**aminoacidurias, overflow** A type of aminoacidurias in which amino acid appears in the urine as a result of increased plasma concentration of one or more amino acids, due to an enzymatic deficiency. See *phenylketonuria; maple syrup urine disease; histidinemia; tyrosinosis.*

**aminoacidurias, renal** A group of aminoacidurias which are the result of faulty mechanism of reabsorption of amino acids in the renal tubules. See *Hartnup disease; Joseph's syndrome; methionine malabsorption.*

**amitosis** Cell division with no splitting of the chromosomes.

**amitryptiline** An antidepressant drug of the tricyclic compound group used in the treatment of depressions.

**amnemonic** Relating to an impairment in or loss of memory.

**amnesia 1.** A deficiency in or lack of memory, either partial or total. **2.** An inability to recall past experiences.

**amnesia, anterograde** Loss of memory for those experiences and events following the physical or psychical trauma.

**amnesia, autohypnotic** (C. G. Jung) Descriptive term for repression.

**amnesia, catathymic** Memory loss delimited and confined to a certain recollection or experience.

**amnesia, circumscribed** Memory loss in which the beginning, or the termination of the memory loss is fairly easily defined.

**amnesia, continuous** See *amnesia, anterograde.*

**amnesia, episodic** Forgetting of particular important incidents only.

**amnesia, epochal** Loss of all memory of a certain past period or epoch of one's life usually precipitated by a sudden shock or trauma; the forgotten period varies from a few days to several years.

amnesia, infantile  Loss of memory for the years from birth to about five years to age necessitated by the unacceptable nature of memories concerning the rise of the sexual life and the limits imposed upon the infant's power.

amnesia, post-hypnotic  Loss of memory for what occurred during hypnosis.

amnesia, retrograde  Loss of memory for those events and experiences preceding the cause of the amnesia.

amnestic aphasia  See aphasia, amnestic.

amnestic apraxia  See apraxia, amnestic.

amniocentesis  Recovery of embryonic cells from the amniotic fluid for genetic prognosis assessment purposes.

amobarbital  The generic name of a five-ethyl-five-isoamylbarbituric acid whose trade name is amytal.

amobarbital sodium  The generic name of the sodium derivative of amobarbital which is a central nervous system depressant producing sedation or hypnosis depending on the dose given.

amphetamines  A racemic drug, $C_6H_5CH_2CH(NH_2)CH_3$ used in medicine and psychiatry as a stimulant in depression and a diet pill in obesity.

amphierotism  (S. Ferenczi) Condition in which the individual is able to conceive of himself as a male or a female both together.

amphigenesis  Ability of a primarily homosexual individual to have normal sexual relations with a member of the opposite sex.

amphigenous inversion  See inversion, amphigenous.

amphimixis  1. Contribution by both parents to the heredity of the offspring. 2. (S. Ferenczi) Refers to the union of anal and genital eroticism.

amplitude  1. Size or amount of the movement from point zero during any one cycle of a variable. 2. Size of a sound or light wave from point zero, related to the psychological dimensions of loudness and brilliance respectively.

ampulla  That enlarged area of the semicircular canals where they connect with the vestibule of the inner ear, containing the hair cells serving as the end organs of the sense of equilibrium.

amputee, castration anxiety  See castration anxiety, amputee.

amuck; amok  A state of murderous frenzy. Amuck patients attack murderously whoever is in their way until they themselves collapse. Hypothetically related to psychomotor epilepsy. The term amuck is borrowed from Malayan amog.

amusia  Impairment or loss of ability, most likely due to brain damage, to comprehend or reproduce musical tones.

amychophobia  Morbid fear of being clawed or scratched, of lacerations.

amygdaloid nucleus; amygdala  Almond-shaped mass of grey matter in the cerebrum located approximately under the anterior tip of the temperal lobe. Thought to be one of the interconnected emotional and motivational centers of the old brain.

amyostasia  Muscle tremor.

amytal interview  See interview, amytal.

amytal; sodium amytal  Trade name for a barbiturate used widely as a sedative and hypnotic. Known popularly, and incorrectly, as "truth serum" since it effects lowering of inhibitions but does not allow confession against the individual's will.

anabolism  Synthetic metabolism involving the restoration and building up of tissues.

anaclisis  1. Condition of emotional dependence on others. 2. (psychoanalysis) A condition in which another instinct conditions the satisfaction of the sex drive.

anaclitic depression  See depression, anaclitic.

anaclitic object choice  Choice of a loved object based on the unconscious wish to receive passive gratification.

anacusia; anacusis  Complete and total deafness.

anaesthesia  See anesthesia.

anaesthetic  See anesthetic.

anaglyph  Stereoscopic picture printed in two complimentary colors that are slightly offset which, when viewed through lenses of the same colors, gives the illusion of depth.

anaglyptoscope; anaglyphoscope  Instrument used to demonstrate the importance of shadow and light in perception by reversing the lighting of an object.

anagogic  1. Referring to the spiritual interpretation of words and the Scriptures. 2. Allegoric Scripture interpretation looking for hidden meaning for future life. 3. Of or pertaining to ideals, to the significance, spiritual or ideal, of behavior or the content of the psyche. 4. (C. G. Jung) The ideal, moral or spiritual striving of the unconscious. 5. Dream interpretation which emphasizes the philosophical meaning of the dream.

anagogic interpretation  See interpretation, anagogic.

anagogic symbolism  See symbolism, anagogic.

anagogy, anagoge  1. Interpretation or application of needs that is spiritual in nature, as with the Scriptures. 2. Scripture interpretation, allegorical in nature, seeking obscured meanings concerning future life.

anal birth  Dreams and fantasies whose anal erotic content is expressed in a symbolic wish to be reborn through the anus.

anal character  See character, anal.

anal eroticism  The experience of sexual arousal or excitement through the stimulation of the anus or by activities associated with the anus such as defecation.

**anal-expulsive stage** (K. Abraham) Subdivision of the anal stage in which erotic pleasure is experienced by the passing of the feces. There is little interest in or caring for the external object (parent) and the passing of the feces often has sadistic overtones.

**anal personality** See *character, anal.*

**anal-retentive stage** (K. Abraham) Subdivision of the anal stage in which the child experiences pleasure from holding on to his feces, which may become his love object. Considered to be the source of tenderness.

**anal sadism** See *sadism, anal.*

**anal-sadistic love** Object relationship characterized by a high degree of aggressive as well as love impulses, typically seen in the anal stage.

**anal-sadistic stage** See *anal stage.*

**anal stage** (S. Freud) The second stage of psychosexual development occurring in the second year of life during which the child derives sexual pleasure from the stimulation of the anal zone by the elimination and retention of feces. This stage is characterized by an ambivalence concerning masculine and feminine impulses manifested as active desires to manipulate and to master, and passive wishes to be dependent and taken care of.

**analgesia, analgia** Insensitivity to pain.

**analgesia, congenital** Insensitivity to pain which exists from birth.

**analgesic, analgetic** 1. Pertaining to analgesia. 2. A drug which relieves pain.

**anality** 1. The component of libido which is localized at the anal zone. 2. Instinctual conflict observed during the anal stage of development. 3. Anal eroticism reflecting a fixation of the anal stage.

**analogies test** See *test, analogies.*

**analogy period** (Rorschach) A type of directive inquiry recommended in the Klopfer approach to the Rorschach. In the formal inquiry all questioning concerning responses must be non-directive, and for this reason, some information provided by the subject may lack clarity. The analogy period permits the examiner to ask direct questions after the formal inquiry has been completed.

**analysand** One being psychoanalyzed.

**analysis** 1. Process of reducing or separating out the constituent parts of a complicated phenomenon. 2. Method of understanding a phenomenon in which the conditions under which it occurs are varied. 3. See *psychoanalysis.*

**analysis, character** See *character analysis.*

**analysis, content** (sociology) A method of transcribing qualitative material into quantitative form by counting. The process consists of determining how to break up the data, how to categorize the units, and of forming an appropriate scoring guide which independent judges can use reliably.

**analysis, direct** (J. Rosen) A psychotherapeutic technique of treating psychotics based on modifed psychoanalytic theoretical formulations in which the therapist enters the patient's delusional system and literally interprets his primary process verbalizations. The psychotic symptoms are believed to reflect unconscious processes directly without the erection of defenses or resistances. The therapist utilizes the patients' delusional system, offers support and provides corrective experiences.

**analysis, ego** Interpretation of ego defenses in psychoanalytic treatment leading to an understanding of the reason for the defense against the impulse.

**analysis, graphic** (statistics) The use of graphs to discover significant relationships among variables.

**analysis, group** The investigation of social pathology in a group.

**analysis, intent** Measurement of social interaction by categorizing verbal statements in terms of their intent or purpose, such as seeking support or comfort.

**analysis, item** 1. The process of determining the difficulty, discriminability, internal consistency, and reliability of a test item. 2. The determination of item validity.

**analysis, latent structure** (P. F. Lazarsfeld) A technique for scaling answers to an attitude questionnaire based on the assumption that inconsistent replies can be explained in terms of a deeper, underlying class or classes of attitudes.

**analysis, link** See *link analysis.*

**analysis of covariance** (statistics) The method used to determine whether differences in variance of two or more related dependent variables exposed to two or more experimental conditions are significantly different from what would be expected by chance while controlling the intercorrelation of the various variables.

**analysis of variance** (statistics) A method used to determine whether the differences in the variance in the dependent variable under different experimental conditions could have occurred by chance only.

**analysis, orthodox** See *psychoanalysis.*

**analysis, pattern** 1. A technique for the search of clusters of items which belong together according to a particular criterion. 2. A technique for finding a group of items which are superior in predicting the criterion to each single item along.

**analysis, propaganda** An assessment of propaganda by the study of its techniques, agencies, materials and contents.

**analysis, scalar** See *scalar analysis.*

**analysis, scatter** An analysis of the amount or qualitative pattern of scatter for the purpose of finding significant relationships among the various subtest scores on a test.

**analysis, self**  The attempt to understand one's own motivations, actions, and feelings without the aid of professional guidance. Freud originally suggested all psychoanalysts undergo self-analysis to avoid potential counter-transference problems but later changed this view in favor of a training analysis.

**analysis, syndromal**  (D. Horn) A simplified type of factor analysis in which rated variables are inter-correlated and combined distributions are performed for highly intercorrelated groups of variables.

**analysis, training**  Personal psychoanalysis of the future psychoanalyst for the purpose of training.

**analysis, transactional**  See *psychoanalysis, transactional.*

**analyst**  See *psychoanalyst.*

**analytic group psychotherapy**  See *psychotherapy, analytic group.*

**analytic process**  See *process, analytic.*

**analytic psychotherapy**  See *psychotherapy, psycho-analytic.*

**analytic therapy**  See *psychotherapy, analytical.*

**analytical psychology**  See *psychology, analytical.*

**analytical scale**  See *scale, analytical.*

**analyzer**  (I. P. Pavlov) The first part of a reflex arc which begins in the natural peripheral end of the centripedal nerve and ends in the receptor cells of the central organ.

**anamnesis**  1. Recollection or recalling. 2. Events prior to the onset of a disorder in a personal, medical or family history which are remembered by the affected individual and sometimes considered pertinent to the disorder.

**anancasm**  Stereotyped, repetitive behavior which produces anxiety if not performed.

**anancastia; anankastia**  An obsessive, compulsive or phobic condition in which the individual feels he is being forced to act, think, or feel against his own will.

**anandia**  See *aphonia.*

**anandria**  The absence of male characteristics or of masculinity.

**anaphase**  (biology) The third stage of mitosis in which the halves of the chromosomes migrate to opposite poles of the spindle.

**anaphia**  Loss of the tactile sense, or some deficiency in it.

**anaphrodisia**  The absence of sexual feeling.

**anaphrodisiac**  That which causes or pertains to a lack of sexual or erotic feeling.

**anaphylaxis**  Extreme susceptibility, particularly an allergic condition in which there is hypersensitivity to proteins taken into the body.

**anarthria**  A partial or total inability to speak articulately.

**anasarca hystericum**  1. A temporary swelling, usually of the abdominal area, in a hysterical person. 2. Phantom tumor.

**Anastasi, Anne (1908- )**  American psychologist. Chairman Psychology Department Fordham University. Principal research concerns test construction and evaluation, factor analysis, nature and origin of psychological traits, and role of cultural and experimental factors in the development of individual and group differences. Author of *Differential Psychology* (1958), *Psychological Testing* (1968), *Fields of Applied Psychology* (1964). President of the American Psychological Association, 1971-72.

**anathymiasis**  1. (philosophy) Obsolete Greek term for soul. 2. An obsolete term for hysterical flatus.

**anatomical age**  A measure of skeletal development based on the rato of the ossification of wrist bones to the area of the "carpal quadrilateral."

**anatomy response (An or At)**  (Rorschach) A scoring code for internal bodily details which can be seen only through the use of X-ray or by dissection.

**anchorages**  1. Perceptual anchoring. 2. The standards or reference points against which judgments are made.

**androgen**  A sex hormone present in both sexes but in greater quantity in males which influences the structural and behavioral characteristics associated with maleness.

**androgenic**  That which causes maleness or contributes to maleness.

**androgyneity**  (anthropology) Belief that the individual has bipolar sexual potential until he is transformed into a particular sex by tribal ritual.

**androgynoid**  A male with hermaphroditic features who often appears to be female.

**androgynous, androgynal, androgynoid, androgynic**  The presence of both male and female characteristics in one individual.

**androgyny**  Condition of being androgynous.

**andromania**  Erotic craving for men in a female; nymphomania.

**andromenecism**  See *hermaphroditism.*

**androphobia**  Morbid fear of men.

**androphomania**  Obsolete term for mental disorder characterized by homicidal tendencies.

**anecdotal evidence**  Casual, unsystematic observations which is rarely sufficient evidence for generalizations but can be used to make hypotheses regarding further investigations.

**anecdotal method**  (G. J. Romanes) A method of presenting data using popular accounts based on observation. This method was introduced in 1882 in the book, *Animal Intelligence* which presented data on animal behavior from scientific and popular accounts.

**anechoic** Echo free, especially in reference to a room or enclosed area.

**anemia** An abnormal reduction of the amount of oxygen transported by the blood due to a decrease in the number of erythrocytes per cubic millimeter, in the hemoglobin concentration and in the volume of red cells and characterized by pallor and weakness.

**anemia, cerebral** Impairment of the cerebral blood circulation which can be produced artificially by the injection of mescaline, adrenaline and other toxic elements. These injections can produce symptoms similar to those of catatonic schizophrenia.

**anemia, sickle-cell** A genetically determined metabolic defect, generally found in dark-skinned peoples, especially of African origin, which is characterized by the displacement of a part of the normal hemoglobin by a slightly different and ineffective variety, resulting in a lowered oxygen carrying capacity by the blood. An individual may carry the gene but exhibit no clinical signs of malfunction unless he moves to a high altitude whereupon the disease becomes manifest.

**anemotropism** A response of orientation of the body as a unit to jar currents.

**anencephaly** Absence of the cerebrum and cerebellum and of the flat skull bones.

**aneneia** Deaf-mutism.

**anenthanasia** Painful death.

**anergasia** (A. Meyer) Loss of functional activity due to structural brain disorder.

**anergastic** Pertaining to or the condition of anergasia.

**anergia, anergy** Absence of energy; weakness; passivity.

**anerotic pulse** Weak pressure wave preceding the main pulse beat.

**anerotism** Sexual negativism; avoidance of sexual relations.

**anesthesia; anaesthesia** Impairment or loss of sensitivity to internal and/or external stimulation from functional causes, drugs or neural damage.

**anesthesia, hysterical** A psychogenic disorder in which sensory feeling is absent in a part or parts of the body.

**anethopathy** (B. Karpman) Personality disorder characterized by a lack of moral inhibitions and unethical behavior and also including narcissistic sexual behavior and general egocentricity. Individuals afflicted with anethopathy do not respond to therapy.

**aneuploid** A chromosome number which is not an exact multiple of the haploid number.

**Angell, James (1869-1949)** American psychologist and educator. Graduated U. of Michigan (1890) and Harvard (1892). Studied at University of Berlin and at Halle. President of Yale University (1921-1937). Before switching to administration Angell won distinction for promoting the Functionalist viewpoint in contrast to Wundtian and Titchenerian structural psychology which he believed could not cope with the expanding problems of the then new psychology. Opposing the stand that the chief purpose of psychology is analysis of immediate experience into its elements and their qualities by introspection, functionalism employed introspection and objective methods in studying consciousness. The latter is regarded as a psychophysiological process having adaptive value in adjusting the organism to its environment. Author of *Psychology* (1904) and *Chapters from Modern Psychology* (1912).

**anger** An intense emotional reaction elicited by threat, interference, verbal attack, overt aggression or frustration and characterized by acute reactions of the autonomic nervous system and by overt or covert attack responses.

**angiogram** Procedure enabling the study of blood distribution in the brain by the injection of a dye with a different x-ray density from blood or brain tissue into blood vessels in or near the brain.

**angstrom** (A) Unit of length measure especially of light wave length, $10^{-10}$ meter; $\frac{1}{100,000}$ micron = 0.001 mm. or 0.1 A.

**angular perspective** See *perspective, angular.*

**anhedonia** Lack of reaction to pleasure producing stimuli; inability to experience pleasurable sensations.

**anima** (C. G. Jung) The archetype that is the feminine component of a male's personality, resulting from the accumulated racial experiences of men with women.

**animal magnetism** See *magnetism, animal.*

**animal phobia** See *phobia, animal.*

**animal psychology** See *psychology, comparative.*

**animism** 1. Ascribing life to inanimate nature. 2. (J. Piaget) This phenomenon has been observed in children who ascribe friendly or hostile intention to inanimate objects.

**animistic reasoning** Illogical reasoning based on natural coincidences, such as, for instance, the belief that putting up storm windows will cause a heat wave.

**animus** (C. G. Jung) The archetype that is the masculine component of all women's personalities resulting from the accumulated racial experiences of women with men.

**annoyer** (E. L. Thorndike) Any factor that obstructs stamping in of a response thus preventing learning.

**Anokhin, Petr K. (1898- )** Soviet neurophysiologist, had been working for many years over the functional system theory which he formulated in 1935. This theory made possible creating a new approach towards study of behavioral acts, and to reveal detailed neurophysiological mechanisms of the conditioned reflex of the behavioral act and the psychic activity. The functional system theory permitted 1) formulation of a new theory in evolution of functions, 2) creation of a neurophysiological basis to study psychophysiological peculiarities of behavior and 3) the general theory of functional systems also helped in deciphering of cybernetic, medical, pedagogical and many other regularities where a researcher deals with biological systems. See *functional system; afferent synthesis; acceptor of action results; systemogenesis; biocybernetics; general systems theory.*

**anomalies of sex chromosomes** See *chromosomes, sex, anomalies of.*

**anomaly** See *abnormal.*

**anomaly, autosomal** Defect of number or form of a chromosome other than the sex chromosome.

**anomia** The difficulty of recalling names; a type of aphasia.

**anopia** Blindness.

**anorexia nervosa** (W. Gull) Severe loss of appetite.

**anoxemia** Oxygen deficiency in the circulatory system.

**Anschauung** (German) 1. Observation. 2. Vantage point. 3. Point of view.

**antagonists** 1. Drugs that neutralize the effect of each other. 2. Muscles that act in an opposite direction to one another, such as extensors and flexors. 3. Two colors that produce together an achromatic color.

**antedating response** See *response, antedating.*

**anterior pituitary gland** See *gland, anterior pituitary.*

**anterior-posterior gradient** See *gradient, anterior-posterior.*

**anthropocentrism** 1. The assumption that the man is the center of the universe. 2. Relating the laws of nature to the laws governing the human mind. The philosophical systems of Kant and Hegel are examples of such an approach.

**anthropoid** Resembling human beings; e.g., chimpanzees are anthropoid apes.

**anthropology** The science of the human race. Physical anthropology studies human organisms in their evolution and adjustment to the changing physical environment. Cultural anthropology studies the customs, manners, morals and social structure of prehistorical, primitive and contemporary men.

**anthropometry** Measurement of physical characteristics of the human body.

**anthropomorph** 1. Man. 2. Of the human species or having a human form.

**anthropomorphic** Having a human form or human characteristics.

**anthropomorphism** Attributing human characteristics or abilities to gods, animals, or objects.

**anthroponomy** (W. Hunter) The science of human behavior; psychology.

**anthropos** (C. G. Jung) The archetype of primal man.

**anthrotype** (biology and medicine) Biological type of human organisms; human phenotype.

**anticathexis** (S. Freud) The energy invested by the ego in keeping repressed material in the unconscious; cathexis used for the blocking of unconscious material.

**anticipation method** See *method, prompting.*

**anticipatory error** See *error, anticipatory.*

**anticipatory response** See *error, anticipatory.*

**antidromic conduction** See *conduction, antidromic.*

**antigen** A substance that stimulates and/or activates the production of antibodies.

**Antigone complex** See *complex, Antigone.*

**antisocial behavior** Behavior which violates explicit or implicit rules of property and personal rights or explicit or implicit rules meant to maintain group cohesiveness and interpersonal trust.

**antisocial reaction** (Psychopathic personality) A "character disorder" in which the individual displays immature behavior in the form of persistent, socially incapacitating tendency to seek immediate gratification. There is also a marked inability to discern the consequences of his behavior and to learn from his experiences.

**anvil** Incus.

**anxiety** 1. (S. Freud) The ego's reaction to external threats is called fear. When the ego is exposed to threats from within, that is, coming from the id or the superego, its reaction to such a threat is called anxiety.

The term anxiety has several connotations. Originally Freud believed that anxiety was the result of blocking of sexual impulses. The combination of unsatisfied libido and undischarged excitation was supposed to be the cause of anxiety neuroses, and the thwarted libido was believed to be transformed into a state of anxiety.

Three years after having presented the structural theory in 1923, Freud introduced a new theory of anxiety. The new theory did not discard the old one but reduced the scope of its meaning to particular cases. According to this new theory (1926) anxiety originates from the infant's inability to master the overflow of excitations. A neonate is usually exposed to more stimulation than he can possibly master. Excessive stimulation may become traumatic, and hence create the painful feeling of primary anxiety.

O. Rank (1929) assumed that the birth-trauma is the prototype of all anxiety states. Separation from mother is another severe anxiety-producing factor. Castration fears, guilt feelings, fear of abandonment, and rejection are the most frequently experienced anxiety-producing situations. The feeling of helplessness is one of the most frequent symptoms of neurotic disturbance; it is especially typical of traumatic neuroses. Also the inability to control one's own excitation (whether aggressive or sexual) may create a state of anxiety.

Freud's early theory of anxiety became incorporated in the new and more broadly conceived theory. Since the satisfaction of instinctual demands may create a dangerous situation the ego must control the instinctual impulses. A strong ego accomplishes this task easily, but a weak ego has to invest more energies in an anticathectic effort to ward off the unconscious impulses.

Anxiety is "a specific state of unpleasure accompanied by motor discharge along definite pathways," Freud wrote in 1926. Ultimately, the three types of anxiety-producing situations in childhood can be put together and reduced to one fundamental cause, namely, loss of the love object. Thus, being left alone, being in the dark, and finding a strange person in place of the mother are the main anxiety-producing situations which reflect the feeling of loss of the loved person. In other words, anxiety is a reaction to the absence of, or separation from, the love object. This feeling of loss is experienced in the birth-trauma, in weaning, and later on in castration fear. In all these situations, loss of support causes increased tension, and an economic disturbance demanding some discharge of energy.

The infant longs for the sight of the mother because he knows from experience that she gratifies all his needs without delay. The situation which the infant appraises as "danger" and against which he desires reassurance is therefore one of not being gratified, of an increase of tension arising from non-gratification of his needs—a situation against which he is powerless (Freud, 1926). A strong ego can cope with danger, but a weak ego reacts with anxiety. When the ego is threatened by external reality it develops reality-anxiety. When the superego attacks the ego, feelings of guilt and inferiority, called moral anxiety, ensue. When the id's pressures threaten to break through the ego controls, neurotic anxiety develops.

Reality-anxiety is a reaction of the ego to a danger from without. Anxiety-preparedness may develop in one of the two following manners: either an old danger-signaling experience called "anxiety development" is re-experienced, or a past danger having a paralyzing effect on the individual, is re-experienced. Neurotic anxiety manifests itself in three ways. The first is anxiety-neurosis, typically felt as an overall apprehension and a sense of oncoming doom. Anxiety neurosis is usually caused by the existence of undischarged excitation when blocking libido energy is transformed into an anxiety state. Neurotic anxiety is manifested also in hysteria and in other neuroses. Certain ideas attached to libido become repressed and distorted, as a result of which the energy, whether libidinal or destructive turns into a state of anxiety.

**2.** (H. S. Sullivan) Anxiety results whenever the biological needs of an individual cannot be satisfied in a socially acceptable way. The individual develops a feeling of insecurity and uneasiness. It is always connected with an increased muscle tension. Muscles ready for a socially unacceptable action become inhibited since their activity is likely to invite disapproval. Anxiety is a socially produced muscular tension which interferes with other tensions or normal mental functioning. The relief of this socially created tension brings the pleasant feeling of self-esteem and self-respect, the antithesis of anxiety.

**3.** (K. Horney) See *anxiety, basic.*

**4.** (B. F. Skinner) Anxiety is the result of conditioning. It is the response to a neutral stimulus which has been associated with an aversive stimulus. It is not an inner state but a group of emotional tendencies which are elicited by a specific situation.

**anxiety attack, equivalent of** See *anxiety equivalent.*

**anxiety, basic** (K. Horney) Each individual has two fundamental needs: safety and satisfaction. The gratification of the satisfaction needs without feelings of safety and acceptance produces basic anxiety, a basic feeling which leads to the development of a neurosis. Neurotics fear the world and view it as an unsafe and hostile place, and defend themselves against basic anxiety in four ways: by seeking affection of any form, by being submissive, by gaining power, or by emotional withdrawal.

**anxiety, castration** Anxiety experienced as a defense against castration anxiety, with regression to the anal area as the primary instinctual zone.

**anxiety equivalent** (psychoanalysis) Intense physiological response or bodily disturbance such as rapid heart beat or loss of breath which replaces conscious anxiety or fear.

**anxiety fixation** See *fixation, anxiety.*

**anxiety hysteria** See *hysteria, anxiety.*

**anxiety, objective** Anxiety for which there is an identifiable and intelligible cause or precipitant.

**anxiety, real** Anxiety caused by an actual external danger.

**anxiety, socialized** (A. Davis) The anticipated fear of punishment for a socially unacceptable behavior.

**anxiety tolerance** The ability to function despite anxiety.

**anxiety, urethral** Anxiety associated with urination.

**apandria** Having an aversion to males.

**apareunia** The inability to have sexual intercourse.

**apastia** Abstaining from eating food; a symptom of psychiatric disorder.

**apathy** 1. Absence or deficiency of emotion, excitement, or interest; indifference. 2. Lack of interest in things which others find interesting or stimulating.

**apeirophobia** Fear of boundlessness or infinity.

**aperiodic reinforcement** See *reinforcement, aperiodic.*

aperture, color   See *color aperture.*

aphakia   Loss of the crystalline lens of the eye due to injury or defect.

aphanisis   (E. Jones) Extinction of sexuality.

aphasia   Loss of or impaired ability to speak, write, or to understand the meaning of words, due to brain damage.

aphasia, acoustico-mnestic   Aphasia resulting from lesions of central portions of the left temporal area or of deep portions of the temporal cortex characterized by difficulties in remembering word lists, comprehension and reproduction of long sentences, comprehension of words, and in the ability to name objects.

aphasia, afferent motor   Aphasia resulting from lesions of inferior portions of the post-central area characterized by a disturbance of fine oral movements associated with a loss of precise kinesthetic feedback.

aphasia, amnestic   Disruption of language usage, involving a memory loss for specific words.

aphasia, auditory   Inability to comprehend the spoken word. A form of sensory aphasia.

aphasia, conduction   A form of aphasia characterized by impairment of the ability to differentiate and repeat speech sounds accurately rather than difficulties in spontaneous articulation and associated with lesions in the post-central cortical areas.

aphasia, developmental   Retardation in the child's learning of language which is often out of phase with mental age, and other developmental levels, and trends. Associated with general sensory, perceptual and intellectual inefficiency, perseveration, emotional inability, and often hyperactivity.

aphasia, efferent motor   Aphasia resulting from lesions of the lower part of the left premotor area and characterized by difficulties in the transition from one sound to another, in the smooth articulation of the speech sequences both in repetition and spontaneous speech.

aphasia, expressive   Language disorder characterized by the inability to speak or write appropriately and sometimes accompanied by the inability to perform related gestures.

aphasia, global   Complete loss of all motor and sensory uses of oral and written speech.

aphasia, jargon   Fluent but inappropriate use of words.

aphasia, motor   Inability to speak words.

aphasia, nominal   Inability to speak the intended or correct word.

aphasia, semantic   Impairment or loss of the ability to comprehend the meaning of words.

aphasia, sensory   Inability to comprehend the spoken or written word, with the damage in the dominant hemisphere.

aphasia, syntactic   Impairment or loss of the ability to employ correct grammatical constructions.

aphasia, visual   Impairment or loss of ability to comprehend the written word.

aphemia   Obsolete term for the inability to speak due to a functional or an organic disorder.

aphephobia   Morbid fear of being touched.

aphonia; aphony   Speech loss caused by defects of the larynx or emotional disorder.

aphonia, hysterical   Sudden loss of voice due to emotional problems.

aphoria   (P. Janet) A state of general weakness and lack of energy which does not disappear with regular exercise or physical training and is considered to be a symptom of neurosis.

aphrasia   The inability to understand or articulate correctly phrases or groups of connected words even though single words may be comprehended and spoken correctly.

aphrenia   Loss or impairment of the functioning of the conscious mind.

aphrodisia   Sexual excitement.

aphrodisiac   That which stimulates sexual excitement or is associated with it.

aphtongia   Type of motor aphasia characterized by the inability to control muscle spasms of the tongue.

apiphobia   Abnormal fear of bees.

aplasia; aplasy   See *agenesis.*

aplestia   Extreme greed.

apocleisis   1. Lack of desire for food. 2. Aversion to food.

apopathetic behavior   Behavior clearly influenced by the presence of others but not directed toward them.

apoplectic type   See *type, apoplectic.*

apoplexy   Sudden loss of motor control and consciousness due to a blocked blood vessel or cerebral hemorrhage.

a posteriori   1. Arriving at the cause of an event by inductive reasoning; i.e., deriving general principles from observation and generalization of specific, observed facts. 2. Of reasoning that starts from observed facts; designating what can be known only after actual occurrence of an event.

Apostle of the idiots   Name given to Edouard Seguin (1812-1880) because of his extensive involvement with the care and welfare of the mentally retarded.

apparatus, lie detector   See *lie detector.*

apparatus, mental   (S. Freud) The three mechanisms of personality, the id, the ego and the superego, or the dynamics of the mind upon which the psychoanalytic model of personality structure is based.

apparatus, psychic   See *apparatus, mental.*

**apparent movement** See *movement, apparent.*

**apperception** 1. Clear perception and awareness of something which occurs in the last portion of attentive perception. 2. Process of recognizing relationships between a particular object and the already existing knowledge of similar or related things in such a way that a particular object is more clearly understood. 3. (J. F. Herbart) Theory that learning and understanding occurs through finding relationships between new facts and one's previously existing experience and knowledge.

**apperceptive visual agnosia** See *agnosia, apperceptive visual.*

**appersonation; appersonification** Delusion in which an individual takes on the characteristics and situation of another person, usually an important figure.

**appetite** 1. A motivation, desire, or impulse which stems from internal physiological conditions, though external conditions may serve as influences. Appetites include hunger, thirst, sexual drive, need for air and for rest. 2. The sensory and affective mental processes which are influenced by such physiological conditions mentioned above. 3. (W. McDougall) The building up of instinct energy. 4. (E. C. Tolman) A state of excitation leading to consummatory responses which bring physiological queiscence. There are six appetites, namely food, sex, excretion, specific contact, rest and sensory-motor.

**appilledema** Choking of the optic nerve at the optic foramen caused by abnormal intracranial or intranentricular tension which is usually due to a brain tumor.

**applied psychology** See *psychology, applied.*

**apprehension** 1. Direct, immediate act or process of becoming aware of something, whether objects or facts. 2. Anxiety stemming from fear of some future event.

**apprehension, implicit** Awareness of the sum of items comprising and affecting a total sense experience without discrimination of the particular items themselves.

**approach-approach conflict** See *conflict, approach-approach.*

**approach-avoidance conflict** See *conflict, approach-avoidance.*

**approach gradient** See *gradient, approach.*

**approach learning** See *learning, approach.*

**approach type** (Rorschach) Description or classification of a response according to how the individual approaches the inkblot which might be in terms of the whole or of details, according to shading or to color or through concern with some combination of aspects.

**approximation conditioning** See *conditioning, approximation.*

**appurtenance** (Gestalt) The mutual influence between parts of a field.

**apractagnosia** Agnosia resulting from lesions of the parieto-occipital areas of the cortex characterized by an inability to analyze the spatial relationships represented in pictures, disturbances of movement and action and of memory for spatial schemata.

**apraxia** Impairment or loss of ability to perform purposeful movement, caused by lesions in the motor area of the cortex but with no sensory impairment or paralysis.

**apraxia, afferent** Apraxia resulting from lesions of the post-central cortex characterized by disturbances of the voluntary control of complex movements associated with defective kinesthetic feedback from the motor acts.

**apraxia, akinetic** A condition involving the loss of ability to move spontaneously.

**apraxia, amnestic** Impairment or loss of the ability to remember or act upon a command.

**apraxia, dynamic** Apraxia resulting from lesions of the premotor cortex and characterized by the loss of the continuity of movement.

**apraxia, efferent** See *apraxia, dynamic.*

**apraxia, ideational** Impairment or loss of the ability to conceive a plan for a whole behavioral movement or sequence. Individual acts may be properly carried out but there is a dislocation of the correct overall sequence.

**apraxia, motor** Disorder in which uncomplicated movements become clumsy. Movement of individual fingers is often impaired or lost.

**apraxia, sensory** 1. Inability to distinguish among objects or to identify objects by touching them. 2. Disorder in which the individual is unsure of how to use familiar objects.

**a priori** 1. Arriving at the effect of an event by deductive reasoning; i.e., arriving at the consequence of a specific event on the basis of definitions or general principles which are assumed to be true. 2. Designating that which can be known through reason alone, without necessity of experience of an actual event. Usually with the connotation of assumption on inadequate grounds of proof.

**aptitude** Capacity or potential ability to perform an as yet unlearned task, skill, or act.

**aptitude, mechanical** The inborn ability to deal with and manipulate mechanical objects and machines.

**aptitude, scholastic** The likelihood of achieving a given degree of success in academic pursuits, based on data such as high school record, personal characteristics and achievement tests and estimated in quantitative terms.

**aptitude test** See *test, aptitude.*

**AQ** (Sometimes A.Q.) The ratio between the actual level of scholastic performance and the level which is expected. Actual performance is measured by achievement age or educational age; expected performance is measured either by chronological age or by mental age. The relation between school achievement and chronological age is phrased as acceleration or retardation. The relation between school achievement and mental age is phrased as overachievement or underachievement. These ratios tend to be unreliable.

**aquaphobia** Morbid fear of water and drowning.

**aqueduct of Sylvius** See *cerebral aqueduct.*

**Aquinas, St. Thomas (1225-1274)** Christian theologian in the Middle Ages who discussed social and political questions concerning property, economics, and the political community within a theological framework. He incorporated Aristotelianism with a Christian outlook and emphasized the importance of reason and nature in the universe.

**arachnophobia** Fear of spiders.

**arbitrary origin** See *origin, arbitrary.*

**arbitrary response** (Rorschach) A response which is not related to any of the particular characteristics of the inkblot upon which it is based.

**archetype** (C. G. Jung) The structural component of the collective unconscious which is inherited. It is a deep unconscious representation of an experience that has been common to a human race for countless generations. The archetypes form the core of autonomous partial systems, independent of the consciousness. If one becomes stirred up, the archetype takes "possession" of the individual and causes neurosis. The archetypes are called primordial images, dominants, imagos, mythological images and behavior patterns. The anima, animus and the shadow are the main archetypes.

**area sampling** See *sampling, area.*

**Ares** 1. The god of war in Greek mythology. 2. (B. B. Wolman) The destructive drive, introduced instead of S. Freud's *Thanatos,* the god of death. It reflects the fight for survival. When there is a threat to life, the general drive for life (lust for life) is channeled into Ares which is more primitive and more powerful than Eros.

**aretic behavior** Destructive, hostile, aggressive behavior.

**aretic syndrome in childhood schizophrenia** (B. B. Wolman) Childhood schizophrenia in which the child displays unusual aggressiveness and unprovoked cruelty. Corresponds to paranoid schizophrenia in adults.

**argininosuccinic aciduria** Metabolic disorder possibly transmitted by a recessive gene, with a deficiency in argininosuccinase causing an excess of argininosuccinic acid. Main clinical features are gradual mental retardation, thinness of hair, convulsions, and systolic murmur.

**Argyll-Robertson pupil** A pupil which contracts in the appropriate way in accomodation and convergence but which does not contract adequately in response to light. This is a symptom of neurological damage usually caused by syphilis.

**Arieti, Silvano (1914- )** American psychiatrist born in Italy. Author of *Interpretation of Schizophrenia* (1955), and *The Intrapychic Self* (1967). Editor-in-Chief of the *American Handbook of Psychiatry,* and editor of the *Journal of the American Academy of Psychoanalysis,* and of the *World Biennial of Psychiatry and Psychotherapy.* Pioneer work in the office treatment of schizophrenic patients. Research in the psychodynamics and thought disorders of schizophrenia; in the creative process; in cognition and volition in normality and mental illness.

**Aristotle (384-322 B.C.)** Greek philosopher. He believed that the universe is comprised of matter (hyle) and form (morphe). The soul is the form, the body is the matter. The soul functions on three levels, the vegetative, sensory and rational. Aristotle introduced the idea of association based on contiguity, similarity, and contrast.

**Aristotle's illusion** See *illusion, Aristotle's.*

**arithmetical average** See *mean.*

**Army Alpha Test** See *test, Army Alpha.*

**Army Beta Test** See *test, Army Beta.*

**Army General Classification Test** See *test, Army General Classification.*

**arousal** An increase in the complexity (amount of information, uncertainty) of neural organization manifest by desynchronization of electrical recordings made from the brain (activation).

**arousal threshold** See *threshold, arousal.*

**arrhythmia** An absence of rhythm of the heart due to functional or organic causes.

**arsenic poisoning** See *poisoning, arsenic.*

**art therapy** See *therapy, art.*

**arteriosclerosis** Proliferative and degenerative changes in arteries causing thickening of the walls, loss of elasticity, and sometimes calcium deposits, with a resulting decrease in the flow of blood.

**arteriosclerosis, cerebral** Arteriosclerosis affecting the vessels of the brain and usually occurring in old age. Symptoms vary, but usually include headache, dizziness, noises in the ears, irritability, loss of power of concentration, memory defect, vague dyesthesias and some hypertension.

**arthritic diathesis** See *diathesis, arthritic.*

**arthritis, rheumatoid** A chronic arthritis of organic or psychogenic etiology affecting multiple joints. Psychogenic causes consist of inhibited hostile, aggressive wishes which cannot be expressed.

**Arthur Point Scale of Performance Tests** See *scale, Arthur Point Of Performance Tests.*

**artificial selection** See *selection, artificial.*

**artificialism** (J. Piaget) The tendency of children to attribute the occurrence of natural phenomena such as rain or sunshine to artificial causes or to the intentions of a person.

**as if** (H. Vaihinger) According to Vaihinger's idealistic positivism, human life is guided by goals and ideals which are not necessarily true, but people act upon them "as if" they were true.

**ascendance-submission** A bi-polar continuum in which the ascendance extreme represents tendency to dominate and the submission extreme the tendency to be dominated in social relations. The Allport A–S Reaction Study is used to measure this dimension.

**asemia** Loss of ability to understand or to utilize communication symbols of any sort including words, signs, and gestures.

**Ashby's Law of Requisite Variety** A mathematical statement about information processing which describes the procedure of choosing correct alternatives and rejecting incorrect ones.

**asonia** Inability to distinguish among pitch differences.

**aspiration level** (K. Lewin and K. Dembo) The expected level of future performance. In Lewin's theory the level of aspiration is presented in realistic or unrealistic psychological fields and the degree of reality of a goal influences the individual's estimate of his achievements.

**assertive responses** Aggressive behavior which a person learns to use in anxiety-provoking situations where he feels intimidated and taken advantage of, as a means to reduce the anxiety which is incompatible with the assertive response.

**assertive training** A behavior therapy technique by which anxiety habits of response to interpersonal situations are overcome by encouraging the patient to express other spontaneously felt emotions in the actual situation. For example, he is encouraged to express his habitually inhibited anger when someone takes unfair advantage of him, e.g. pushing ahead of him in line. Apparently, because such expression potentiates the anger or other relevant emotion there is inhibition of anxiety, leading to weakening of the anxiety habit.

**assets-liabilities technique** A counseling technique which requires the client to list his personality assets and liabilities and to work on eliminating the liabilities.

**assimilation** 1. (physiology) The transformation of food into the substances used and stored in the body. 2. A learning process whereby new material is modified and made part of the existing knowledge. 3. (E. Hering) The production of retinal materials when the blue, red, or green cones are stimulated. 4. (J. F. Herbart) The understanding of new material in terms of what is already known. 5. (C. G. Jung) The lateration of an object or situation to fit the needs of the self. 6. The perception of a new situation in a way which makes it appear identical to a familiar situation. 7. (E. L. Thorndike) The animal's reaction to a new situation as if it was a familiar one because of their similarities. 8. (speech) The adjustment of letter sounds to appear like neighboring letter sounds in the mouth position and/or sound itself. 9. The acceptance of a negative fact about oneself into one's experience.

**assimilation law** See *law of assimilation.*

**associate visual agnosia** See *agnosia, associate visual.*

**association** 1. A functional connection between psychological phenomena established through experience or learning whereby the occurrence of one tends to evoke the other. 2. A bond between ideas. 3. The second part of an associational sequence. 4. The strength of the postulated bond between associated members.

**association by contiguity** The law that upon the occurrence of two events close in time, the subsequent occurrence of one event will evoke the other.

**association coefficient** See *coefficient, association.*

**association, constrained** In an association test, a response which is specified in terms of its relationship to the stimulus.

**association cortex** See *cortex, association.*

**association fiber** A neuron which connects different centers in one hemisphere of the brain.

**association, free** See *free association.*

**association, mediate** An ideational association between two terms which is made by indirect linkage through intervening terms.

**association method** See *method, association.*

**association, neutral** 1. The process of joining independent neurons to produce a result. 2. Postulated neural pathways between various structures of the body.

**association of ideas** (history) The process of joining or connecting ideas to form new compound ideas.

**association psychology** See *associationism.*

**association-reaction time** The time between a given stimulus and a response in the form of an association to the stimulus, especially in a word association test.

**association-sensation ratio** (D. O. Hebb) The ratio of the association cortex to the sensation cortex which is considered an index of general learning ability: the larger the ratio the greater the learning potential. Also called A/S ratio.

**association test** See *test, association.*

**association time** 1. See *association-reaction time.* 2. The association-reaction time minus the simple reaction time, an obsolete method of measuring association-reaction time.

**associationism** The theory that the mind consists of irreducible simple elements which are combined by association to produce learning. Aristotle introduced this principle stating four laws of association: the laws of similarity, contiguity in time, difference, and contiguity in space. Rudiments of this theory which became prominant at the beginning of the seventeenth century and continued to develop through the nineteenth century were established by

J. Locke (1632-1704) and D. Hume (1711-1776) who emphasized the importance of sensory perceptions and associations. D. Hartley (1705-1757) clarified this theoretical position in his work stating the principles of contiguity and repetition as necessary for association to occur. J. Mill (1773-1836) elaborated the theory further emphasizing temporal contiguity. Later British associationists such as A. Bain and J. S. Mill introduced other laws such as similarity, difference, intensity, and inseparability. In the nineteenth century, this position was developed by E. L. Thorndike who stressed connections based on contiguity of stimulus and response and I. P. Pavlov who viewed associationism as identical with conditioning.

**associative inhibition**   See *inhibition, associative.*

**associative memory**   See *memory, associative.*

**associative process**   Process in the organism that is a part of an original unlearned or previously learned process.

**associative shifting**   (E. L. Thorndike) The principle that stimuli presented in a similar situation as stimuli which evoked specific responses can evoke the same responses.

**associative strength**   The strength of an associative connection as evinced by the frequency with which the stimulus evokes the particular response.

**associative thinking**   See *thinking, associative.*

**assonance**   A similarity of vowel sounds as in teeth, beach.

**assumed mean**   See *mean, assumed.*

**astasia**   Motor incoordination and unsteadiness in maintaining a standing position.

**astasia-abasia**   See *abasia.*

**astereognosis**   See *agnosia, tactile.*

**asthenia**   Physical weakness or lack of strength and vitality.

**asthenia, mental**   Inability to concentrate on an idea or thought for any length of time; mental weakness or fatigueability.

**asthenia, neurocirculatory**   See *neurocirculatory asthenia.*

**asthenic**   **1.** Depressed or inhibited feeling. **2.** Linear-framed, long-limbed slender body-type. **3.** (E. Kretschmer) Body type associated with schizothymic temperament.

**asthenic habitus**   Body-type characterized by slender linear frame and long limbs.

**asthenic reaction**   A psychoneurotic reaction characterized by chronic aches, pains, physical, and mental fatigue. It usually occurs in young adults and is believed to result from sustained emotional stress which the individual cannot cope with.

**asthenic type**   See *type, asthenic.*

**asthenophobia**   Morbid fear of weakness.

**asthenopia**   Weakness of vision due to fatigue of the ocular muscles or the eye in general.

**asthma**   Symptom complex resulting in an impairment of breathing, especially respiration, and wheezing, caused by an increase of responsiveness to various stimuli of the trachea, major bronchi, manifested by extreme narrowing of airways to various reasons. It is believed that there may be an inherited vulnerability and that emotional factors are also contributory.

**asthma, bronchial**   See *asthma.*

**astigmatism**   Defective vision due to an abnormal curvature of one or more refractive surfaces of the eye such as the cornea, or the lens, which prevents light rays which enter the eye from focusing at a point on the retina. Instead, the light rays spread out in various directions depending upon the type of curvature.

**astrology**   A pseudoscience which concerns itself with the influence of the movements of stars and planets on human events.

**asylum, insane**   An obsolete term for a mental institution.

**asymbolia**   A form of tactile agnosia in which the visual evaluation of tactile cues is impaired usually associated with lesions in posterior cortical areas and involving zones of overlap of the cortical parts of the cutaneous-kinesthetic and visual analyzers.

**asymmetrical distribution**   See *distribution, asymmetrical.*

**asymptote**   A straight line which a curve constantly approaches, but never reaches, or a theoretical limit which a curve approaches.

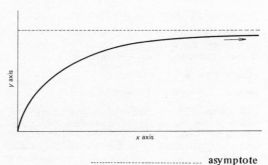

asymptote

**asymptotic curve**   See *curve, asymptotic.*

**asyndesis**   Speech disorder characterized by the juxtaposition of elements without appropriate connections.

**asynergia**   Faulty coordination of groups of muscles that are normally well coordinated.

**asynergic speech**   Asynergia of the vocal apparatus usually due to cerebellar disease; speech becomes irregular, jerky, and explosive.

**ataractic drugs**  Tranquilizers.

**ataraxy**  Complacency; calm, unperturbed mood.

**atavism**  Reappearance of ancestral characteristics after their absence in several generations.

**ataxia**  Incoordination of voluntary muscular action.

**ataxia, intrapsychic**  An emotional state observed in schizophrenics in which the individual appears to separate his own feelings from other mental phenomena.

**ataxia, locomotor**  See *Tabes dorsalis.*

**ataxia, mental**  Lack of correspondence between ideas and affects.

**ataxiagraph**  A device for recording degree of ataxia.

**ataxic abasia**  See *abasia.*

**ataxic paraplegia**  Slow progressive degeneration of the posterior and lateral columns of the spinal chord causing weakness, spasticity, and incoordination of the legs.

**ataxic speech**  See *asynergic speech.*

**ataxic writing**  Uncoordinated writing due to brain damage or lack of skill.

**ataximeter**  1. A device for measuring involuntary sway of an individual standing erect with his eyes closed. 2. Any device for measuring involuntary movement.

**ataxiophobia**  Morbid fear of disorder.

**ataxophemia**  Incoherent speech.

**ATDP**  See *scale, Attitude Toward Disabled Persons.*

**ateliosis**  Dwarfism caused by pituitary disorders without physical malformation.

**atephobia**  Morbid fear of being ruined.

**athetosis**  Condition of slow recurrent apparently purposeless movement primarily of the toes and fingers which results from a brain lesion.

**athletic type**  See *type, athletic.*

**athymia**  (Hippocrates) Melancholy.

**atmosphere effect**  1. The production of a response which is due to habits of responding which are associated with particular words, portions or patterns of the stimulus. 2. Errors in thinking which result from an impression implicit in the statement of premises of the problem.

**atom, social**  (J. L. Moreno) The psychological relations of an individual to the smallest social structure which is the patterns of relationship of the individual to other individuals toward whom he feels attraction or repulsion.

**atomistic psychology**  See *psychology, atomistic.*

**atonicity; atony; atonia**  1. (physiological) Lack or reduction of normal tone or tension in the musculature. 2. (phonetics) Reduction of stress or tone.

**atrophy, optic**  Degeneration of the optic nerve fibers which is classified either primary or secondary depending on the cause.

**atropin**  Drug which relaxes smooth muscles and is used primarily to relax the pupil, the bladder, and the intestines.

**atropine poisoning**  See *poisoning, atropine.*

**attensity**  (F. B. Titchener) The characteristic of attracting attention of a sensation or sense datum.

**attention**  1. Selection and perception of a certain stimulus or of a range of stimuli comprising a part of a complex stimulus situation. 2. Adjustment of the sense organs and/or the central nervous system to allow for maximal stimulation. 3. (E. B. Titchener) State of sensory clearness and vividness; state of consciousness in which one mental content stands out clearly from the rest.

**attention fluctuation**  Intermittent changes in the clarity of perception of an object under conditions of constant and unchanging stimulation.

**attention-getting mechanism**  Behavior designed to gain attention, usually otherwise maladaptive.

**attention reflex**  See *reflex, attention.*

**attention-seeking**  Behavior that secures an orientation of others toward oneself.

**attention-seeking, negative**  (R. R. Sears) Socially unacceptable forms of a.–s., usually considered as mixed with aggression; e.g., in children, temper tantrums, interrupting, disobedience; in adults, quarrelsome behavior, derogation of others, uncooperativeness, demanding aid, as in acute drunkenness, pretended suicide or proposed violence.

**attention-seeking, positive**  (R. R. Sears) Socially acceptable forms of a.–s.; e.g., in children, asking help, talking, performing adult role behavior, asking questions, seeking reassurance, calling attention to successful performances; in adults, persistent talking, mild exhibitionism, pseudo-modesty, self-deprecation, gregariousness.

**attention span**  1. The amount of material or number of separate objects which can be noticed during one brief exposure. 2. The duration of time a person can concentrate on one event or thing.

**attenuation**  1. A reduction in the degree, amount, or worth of anything; to make slim. 2. (statistics) A reduction of a correlation coefficient due to unreliable measurements.

**attitude**  A learned predisposition to react consistently in a given manner (either positively or negatively) to certain persons, objects or concepts. Attitudes have cognitive, affective and behavioral components.

**attitude, masculine, in female neurotics**  See *masculine attitude in female neurotics.*

**attitude scale**  See *scale, attitude.*

**attitude, social**  1. An attitude directed to interindividual or intergroup relations. **2.** An opinion shared by many people.

**Attitude Toward Disabled Persons Scale** See *scale, Attitude Toward Disabled Persons.*

**attonity** Condition of stupor characterized by total or almost total immobility which sometimes occurs in catatonic schizophrenia and depression.

**attribute 1.** A characteristic or fundamental property that is predicted of a subject. **2.** (structural psychology) The most fundamental characteristics of sensation; quality and sensation are the most universally accepted. **3.** An independent dimension of sensation as indicated by discrimination tests.

**Aubert diaphragm** A device for controlling and measuring the amount of light passing through an aperture.

**Aubert-Förster phenomenon** The principle that it is easier to recognize small objects when near as compared to larger more distant objects even though the latter subtend the same visual angle as the former.

**Aubert phenomenon** An optical illusion in which a vertical line inclines to one side as the head is tilted to the opposite side when no other object is present in the visual field.

**audile** An individual for whom auditory rather than visual images are predominant or unusually distinct.

**audio-frequency** Sound waves which are within the range of human hearing, approximately 16-20,000 hertz.

**audiogenic** Caused or produced by sound.

**audiogenic seizure** See *seizure, audiogenic.*

**audiogram** A graphic record of an individual's auditory sensitivity across several frequencies in relation to established norms as measured by an audiometer.

**audiogravic illusion** See *illusion, audiogravic.*

**audiogyral illusion** See *illusion, audiogravic.*

**audiometer** An instrument for measuring the acuity and the range of an individual's hearing.

**audiometric curve** See *audiogram.*

**audio-oscillator** An electronic instrument capable of emitting pure tones of desired frequency and intensity.

**audito-oculogyric reflex** See *reflex, audito-oculogyric.*

**auditory** Pertaining to hearing.

**auditory acuity** Sensitivity of hearing measured in terms of intensity of sound waves; usually equivalent to auditory threshold.

**auditory aphasia** See *aphasia, auditory.*

**auditory apperception test** See *test, auditory apperception.*

**auditory aura** See *aura, auditory.*

**auditory cortex** See *cortex, auditory.*

**auditory flicker** See *flicker, auditory.*

**auditory labyrinth** The portion of the labyrinth of the ear having to do with hearing.

**auditory or acoustic nerve** See *nerve, auditory or acoustic.*

**auditory ossicles** The small bones in the middle ear which conduct sound from the eardrum to the cochlea.

**auditory projection area** The area in the posterior portion of the superior temporal convolution where the auditory nerve terminates and where auditory perception is mediated.

**auditory spectrum** See *acoustic spectrum.*

**auditory threshold** See *threshold, auditory.*

**aulaphobia** Fear of any contact with a wind instrument, especially a flute, which has been sometimes considered a phallic symbol.

**aura 1.** General term for a symptom which precedes the onset of physical or mental disorder and warns of its coming. **2.** (parapsychology) Supposed emanations given off a person's body which are seen or picked up by others who are sensitive.

**aura, auditory** Form of epileptic seizure characterized by sudden occurrence of buzzing sounds sometimes but not always preceding the onset of a grand mal seizure.

**aura cursoria** Aimless running around usually occurring just before an epileptic seizure and associated with its onset.

**aura, epileptic** Psychic, motor or sensory disturbance which precedes an epileptic seizure, serving as a warning signal.

**aura, visual** Form of epileptic seizure characterized by the sudden vision of light flashes sometimes but not usually preceding the onset of a grand mal seizure.

**aural** Related to the ear.

**auricle** The ear flap or external part of the ear.

**auroraphobia** Fear of the northern lights.

**autarchic fiction** See *fiction, autarchic.*

**authoritarian character** See *authoritarian personality.*

**authoritarian cultural lag** (G. M. Gilbert) The persistence of authoritarian attitudes, identifications, and behavioral frames of reference long after a social revolution or upheaval has overthrown traditional authoritarian government. This is thought to make both individuals and their social institutions susceptible to authoritarianism in the guise of self-government and to lead to the establishment of dictatorship as a transitional form of social organization.

**authoritarian group** (K. Lewin) An experimental group in social psychology where all decisions are made by the leader.

**authoritarian personality** Referring to individuals who are characterized by a dependence upon clearly delineated hierarchies of authority.

**authyphobatesis** Obsolete term for spontaneous somnambulism.

**autia** (R. B. Cattell) The high-score of a personality dimension characterized by non-conforming, impractical, "Bohemian," dissociative behavior, with intensive subjective, autistic, inner intellectual life. Involves maladjustment to, and rejection by, social milieu. Appears as first-order questionnaire factor M+ and associated first-order objective test factor U.I. 34+.

**autism** 1. An extreme case of egocentrism, narcissism and inability to relate to other people. 2. Perceiving the outer world in terms of one's own personality, needs, thoughts and ideas, with little if any regard for the reality. 3. Tendency for withdrawal from real life and indulging in daydreaming and bizarre fantasies.

**autism, early infantile** 1. (A. Kanner) A cluster of severe symptoms occurring in infancy. The symptoms include withdrawal, language disturbance and often mutism, fear of change and insistence on sameness, inability to relate to people, repetitive rhythmical movements, apathy and emotional detachment. In some cases the early infantile autism develops into schizophrenia. 2. (M. S. Mahler) Early infantile autism is a type of early childhood schizophrenia, in which the instinctual forces of libido and aggression exist in an unneutralized form. The mother is not perceived by the infant as a separate entity but remains undistinguished from inanimate objects. 3. (B. Rimland) Early infantile autism is basically a cognitive dysfunction. It is the inability to relate new stimulus to previous experiences related to organic impairment, specifically reticular dysfunction. This dysfunction is probably caused by anoxia. 4. (B. B. Wolman) The early infantile autism is a name of a cluster of symptoms which 1) could be caused by organic causes or 2) by psychogenic factors. The latter is a syndrome typical of early childhood schizophrenia called vectoriasis praecocissima. The schizophrenic syndrome of autism is a regression of the infantile ego into the id.

**autism, normal** (M. S. Mahler) The first weeks of extrauterine life are regarded as the normal autistic phase. The instinctual responses to stimuli of a neonate and infant are on a reflex and thalamic level; his ego apparatuses are unintegrated and his defense mechanisms consist of overflow and discharge of somatic reactions. The libido position is predominantly visceral. In the autistic phase the young infant may be likened to a closed monadic system. Mahler conceptualized the state of the sensorium in terms of *normal autism,* for in the first weeks of life, the infant seems to be in a state of primitive negative hallucinatory disorientation, in which need satisfaction belongs to his own omnipotent autistic orbit.

**autistic child** A child who displays autistic symptoms such as repetitive rocking and head banging, apathy, fear of change, insistence on preservation of sameness, lack of interest in people, severe speech disorders with frequent mutism and extreme aloneness. Autistic symptoms start in early infancy and are linked either with organic causes or viewed as a syndrome schizophrenia in childhood. See *autism, early infantile.*

**autistic schizophrenia** See *schizophrenia, autistic.*

**autistic syndrome in childhood schizophrenia** 1. See *autism.* 2. (B. B. Wolman) Corresponds in childhood schizophrenia to simple deterioration and hebephrenia in adults.

**autistic thinking** See *thinking, autistic.*

**autobiography** 1. A biography written by the subject himself recounting memoirs of his life. 2. A document used for psychological, sociological and historicobiographical research which while having the disadvantages of bias due to the author's reasons for writing, his state of mind and age at the time of writing have the advantage of completeness and of being related to a particular area of interest.

**autocentric** Self-centered.

**autochthonus** 1. Found in the area or part of the body in which it originates. 2. Pertaining to ideas that seem to arise independently of an individual's own train of thought.

**autochthonous gestalt** A perceptual unity which arises due to factors that are innate to the perceiving organism rather than to the stimulus.

**autochthonous variable** See *variable, autochthonous.*

**auto-echopraxia** A form of stereotypy in which an individual continually repeats a previously experienced action.

**auto-fellatio** The self-gratifying act of placing one's penis in one's own mouth.

**autofetishism** Sexual feelings towards one's own material possession.

**autoflagellation** Whipping oneself.

**autogenic, autogeny** Self-generated or self-originated.

**autogenic reinforcement** See *reinforcement, autogenic.*

**autognosis** Self-knowledge.

**auto-hypnosis** Self-induced hypnosis.

**autoimmune disease hypothesis** (P.R.J. Burch) Statistically developed explanation for schizophrenia, manic-depressive psychosis, and involutional psychosis using genetic factors.

**autoimmune response** The manufacture of antibodies noxious to the organism's own tissues.

**autokinesis** Movement originated by stimuli arising within the organism.

**autokinetic effect** The illusory erratic and unpredictable movement of a luminous object, fixed in time and space, in an inarticulated surrounding such as darkness.

**autokinetic phenomenon** See *phenomenon, autokinetic.*

**automata theory** The mathematical study of the behavior of robots.

**automated psychodiagnosis** See *psychodiagnosis, automated.*

**automatic action** An act performed without self-awareness.

**automatic writing** 1. Writing while paying attention almost solely to the content rather than to the hand movements or resulting handwriting. 2. Writing of meaningful material unconsciously.

**automatism, ambulatory** Automatic activity which is rhythmic in form.

**automatism, ambulatory comitial** (D. H. Tuke) Automatic acts which are often observed in epileptics.

**automatograph** An instrument for recording automatic movements.

**automaton** 1. A mechanical figure designed to act in a self-motivated or human fashion; a robot. 2. A man who behaves in a machine-like way.

**automaton conformity** (E. Fromm) The posture adopted by a person in order to resolve his fears of freedom and the concomitant isolation by following society's prescription.

**automorphic perception** See *perception, automorphic.*

**automysophobia** Fear of being filthy or smelling bad.

**autonomasia** A type of amnesic aphasia characterized by inability to remember names or nouns.

**autonomic affective apparatus** See *apparatus, autonomic affective.*

**autonomic balance** A wholesome interaction between the divisions of the autonomic nervous system.

**autonomic epilepsy** See *epilepsy, autonomic.*

**autonomic nervous system** See *nervous system, autonomic.*

**autonomy; autonomy drive** (A. Angyal) The tendency to attempt to master or be effective in the environment, to impose one's wishes and designs on it.

**autonomy, functional** (G. W. Allport) The tendency for modes of behavior, once acquired, to become eventually independent of the drives or motives by which they were originally instigated.

**autonomy need** See *need, autonomy.*

**autonomy, primary** (H. Hartmann) In contradistinction to S. Freud, Hartmann postulated that the ego is endowed with an innate apparatus of a conflict-free sphere which includes the functions of motility, perception and thought. The fact that from its inception, the ego is equipped with such an apparatus was called by Hartmann primary autonomy.

**autonomy, secondary** (H. Hartmann) The acquired ability of the ego to resist regression. The stable patterns of the ego, its independence from the id-based impulses, the ability to retain developmental acquisitions are secondary autonomous.

**autopathy** A disease, handicap or disorder that has an afferent cause.

**autophobia** Morbid fear of oneself.

**autophonia, autophony** A condition characteristic of some middle-ear and auditory tube diseases in which the Eustachian tube remains open causing the voice to echo peculiarly.

**autophonomania** Obsolete term for a suicidal mental illness.

**autoplastic** Change, adaptation or alteration of the self.

**auto-sadism** (psychoanalysis) Sadistic tendencies defensively turned toward the self because of the anxiety and guilt associated with aggression directed towards others.

**autoscope** An instrument, device or technique used in the magnification of small, involuntary muscle movements.

**autoscopy** The seeing of one's self as a double, usually in the form of the face and bust which imitates the expressions and movements of the original. The copy is usually misty, hazy and partially transparent.

**autosomal anomaly** See *anomaly, autosomal.*

**autosome** Any chromosome other than the sex chromosomes. Man has 22 pairs and drosophila melanogaster 3 pairs.

**autosuggestion** Communication from oneself to oneself in the attempt to influence or improve health or behavior.

**auxiliary ego** 1. The person who consciously accepts another person's communications, needs, and purposes, in order to aid the other and increase his strength. 2. (J. L. Moreno) In psychodrama, a secondary actor who adopts and enacts supporting roles from the viewpoint of the other.

**auxocyte** A spermatocyte, oocyte or sporocyte during early growth.

**availability principle** The ease and readiness with which a response is elicited is dependent upon how ready for functioning that response is.

**aventyl** Common name for nortriptylene, an antidepressant drug.

**average deviation** See *deviation, average.*

**average variation** See *mean deviation.*

**aversion therapy** See *therapy, aversion.*

**aversive conditioning** See *conditioning, aversive.*

**aversive stimulus** See *stimulus, aversive.*

aviator's neurasthenia  See *neurasthenia, aviator's.*

avoidance-avoidance conflict  See *conflict, avoidance-avoidance.*

avoidance behavior  See *behavior, avoidance.*

avoidance-avoidance conflict  See *conflict, avoidance-avoidance.*

avoidance, free operant  (M. Sidman) Procedure of aversive stimulation used in studying avoidance conditioning. The experimental animal is placed in a usual metal operant conditioning chamber containing an operandum appropriate to the organism. By means of programmed electronic equipment a series of intense but brief shocks are delivered to the subject through the floor of the chamber. The shocks are programmed by two recycling timers. When the subject does not respond to the interval between the shocks, the shock-shock interval or SS interval is specified by the first timer. If the animal responds, the shock can be postponed for the amount of time programmed on the second timer, the response-shock interval, or RS interval. Each shock starts the SS interval anew while each response terminates the SS interval and starts the RS interval. Thus by responding, the animal can reset the RS interval and postpone shock for as long as he responds.

There are no extroceptive stimuli indicating that a shock is impending. Since the duration of the shock is a fraction of a second, the animal does not terminate a shock, but postpones it every time it responds. Thus specification of the SS and RS intervals completely specify the free operant avoidance situation.

avoidance gradient  See *gradient, avoidance.*

avoidance learning  See *learning, avoidance.*

avoidance schedule, Sidman  See *avoidance, free operant.*

awareness  Being conscious of something; the state of perceiving and taking account of some event, occasion, experience or object.

axial gradient  A graded difference that becomes progressively smaller between two aspects, states or conditions located along an axis of an organism.

axiology  A branch of philosophy which deals with the study of values, such as those of religion, ethics and aesthetics.

axiom  1. A truth which is self-evident. 2. A proposition which is commonly accepted as true. 3. A proposition offered as true for the purposes of observing and studying the consequences which follow from it.

axis  One of two or more straight lines meeting at a point called the origin. The horizontal axis is typically identified as the X axis, the vertical as the Y axis, and a third axis at right angles to the first two permits location of all points in three-dimensional space.

axis, vertical  See *Y axis.*

axon  The long and thin efferent part of the neuron. The nerve impulse, produced on the membrane of the axon, travels along the length of the axon.

axon reflex  See *reflex, axon.*

# B

**B** **1.** The total of an organism's body, excepting the nervous system. **2.** A symbol for luminance. **3.** A symbol for any number or variable. **4.** (C. L. Hull) The mean of the amount of responses in a response or alteration cycle.

**babbling** Meaningless vocal sounds uttered by infants prior to their ability to talk.

**Babinski reflex** (J. Babinski) The upward extension versus flexion of toes when the sole of the foot is gently stroked. This reflex is common in infancy but gradually gives way to flexion or contraction of the toes, called the plantar reflex. When this condition occurs beyond infancy it is a sign of neurological disorder—specifically lesion in, or depression of the pyramidal tract.

**baby talk** Early speech characterized by inaccurate pronounciation of various consonants. This form of speech is gradually outgrown unless it is reinforced by the child's environment or the result of some kind of more serious speech disorder.

**bacilli, fear of** See *bacillophobia.*

**bacillophobia** Morbid or pathological fear of bacilli or germs. The fear can extend to include all micro-organisms.

**back disorders, psychogenic** Backaches of emotional origin.

**back wards** Wards in mental hospitals which house severely disturbed patients.

**backward association** A verbal learning term referring to a connection between a particular item in a series and a preceeding item. See *association.*

**backward conditioning** See *conditioning, backward.*

**bad-me** See *personified self.*

**bad object, good object** (Melanie Klein) In the first year of life, at the paranoid-schizoid position, the infant introjects the breasts, and experiences a part of the introjected breasts as a good object and a part as a bad object, reflecting the death instinct. The bad objects are repressed.

**Baillarger, Jules Gabriel Francois (1538-1616)** A French physician considered to have been the first epidemiologist. He provided the first clear description of whooping cough and in a later paper apparently originated the term rheumatism.

**Bain, Alexander (1818-1903)** Scottish professor of philosophy at the University of Aberdeen. He wrote the first systematic textbook of psychology in English (its two volumes appeared in 1855 and 1859), published the first book on mind and body in 1872, and founded the first psychological journal, *Mind,* in 1876.

**balance** **1.** The state in which opposing forces are in an equal relationship. **2.** The state of upright posture characterized by the harmonious adjustment of the muscles against gravity. **3.** (K. Heider) A cognitive system which results when there is consistency in the relationship between either objects, persons, or an object and a person, and an individual's evaluation of them.

**balance of minus judgements** (experimental psychology) When the comparison stimulus is objectively equal to the standard stimulus, the amount of the difference between the percent of plus and minus judgements.

**Baldwin, James Mark (1861-1934)** American philosopher and theorist. Studied at Princeton and at Leipzig (under Wundt). Was professor of philosophy at the University of Toronto (1889-1893), of psychology at Princeton (1893-1903), of philosophy and psychology at Johns Hopkins (1903-1908). The next five years were spent in an advisory capacity at the National University of Mexico. For five years after that he was professor at L'École des Hautes Études Sociales in Paris. He founded laboratories at Toronto (1889); at Princeton (1903); championed work of Hall and Cattell by endorsing evolution, functional approach to psychology, and psychology of individual differences. Specialist in child and social psychology. Co-founder with Cattell of *Psychological Review* (1894) and *Psychological Index* and *Psychological Monographs* and *Psychological Bulletin* (1904). Also published a two-volume

*Dictionary of Philosophy and Psychology* (1901-1902). Wrote *Handbook of Psychology* (1889-1891), *Mental Development in the Child and the Race* (1895), *Social and Ethical Interpretations in Mental Development* (1897) and *History of Psychology* (1913).

**ball and field test**   See *test, ball and field.*

**band chart**   A chart which indicates, usually through the use of different colors, the number, amount or percentage of items, classes, or groups which make up a given total.

**bandwagon effect**   (social psychology)   A social group phenomenon characterized by increasingly large numbers of people associating themselves with the dominant opinion.

**Bar Diagram**   See *Diagram, Bar.*

**baragnosis**   A loss of the perception of weight.

**Barany Test**   See *test, Barany.*

**barbiturate**   Any one of a class of drugs that act as central nervous system depressants.

**baresthesis; baraesthesia**   The sense of pressure.

**barium poisoning**   See *poisoning, barium.*

**barognosis**   The perception of weight; the ability to estimate weight.

**barophobia**   An extreme fear of gravity.

**baroreceptors**   Nerve structures (receptors) which are stimulated by changes of pressure within the organ in which they are located.

**Barr body**   The sex chromatin as seen in somatic cells of the female; named after the discoverer of sexual dimorphism in somatic cells, Dr. Murray Barr. It is best studied by the buccal smear or oral mucosa technique. The number of Barr bodies in a cell is one less than the number of X chromosomes.

**barylalia**   Thick, indistinct speech characteristically seen in patients with organic brain disease and common in the advanced stages of general paresis.

**baryphonia; baryphony**   A form of dysphasia characterized by a thick, heavy voice quality.

**basal age**   The lowest age level at which all items are passed in tests standardized in terms of mental age units.

**basal ganglia**   A group of structures of gray matter deep within the cerebrum which forms part of the neural system that aids in the control of motor responses.

**basal metabolic rate**   Represents the minimum energy expenditure required for the maintenance of vital functions.

**basal metabolism**   The amount of energy expended, measured in calories, per unit of time while at rest; measured after fourteen to eighteen hours of rest. The basal metabolic rate is the minimum energy expenditure necessary for the maintenance of vital functions.

**base line**   The abscissa, or horizontal axis, of a graph.

**base rate problem**   The occurrence of spontaneous remission in patients with or without treatment.

**Basedow's disease**   See *goiter, exophthalmic.*

**basic anxiety**   See *anxiety, basic.*

**basic data relation matrix (BDRM)**   A basically five dimensional (but possibly ten) score matrix containing all the particulars (coordinates) necessary to define a psychological event: a person, focal stimula, a response, an ambient stimulus (background condition), and an observer. Sometimes called "the data box" from which all correlational and analysis of variance procedures must begin. Its value is in pointing comprehensively to all possible relational analyses.

**basic paranoid attitude**   (Melanie Klein) The first stage of the oral phase in which the infant has no experience of the whole person, experiences no ambivalence, and has split his object into an ideal and persecutory one. The prevalent anxiety is of a persecutory nature—a fear that the persecutors may invade and destroy the self and the ideal object.

**basic personality**   (A. Kardiner) The constellation of personality traits which are present in all members of a given culture or society due to common child raising practices.

**basilar membrane**   The delicate membrane in the cochlea which supports the organ of Corti, the organ which converts movements of the basilar membrane into nervous impulses.

**basophobia; basiphobia**   An extreme fear of standing erect or walking.

**Bassen-Kornzweig syndrome**   See *syndrome, Bassen-Kornzweig.*

**bath, brand**   See *cold bath.*

**bathophobia**   A pathological fear of depths.

**bathyesthesis; bathyesthesia**   Deep sensitivity.

**batrachophobia**   An extreme fear of frogs.

**battery of tests**   See *tests, battery of.*

**battle fatigue**   State of physical and emotional exhaustion caused by stress situation in active combat or other hardships of war. It acts as a precipitating factor in causing a variety of behavior disorders. Battle fatigue was called shell shock in World War I.

**Bayes' theorem**   (statistics) An algebraic statement that the probability of an event's having been the consequence of another event is dependent upon the number of mutually exclusive events which may have given rise to that event.

**Bayle's disease**   An obsolete name for general paresis first described in 1822 by the French physician Antoine Bayle.

**Bayley, Nancy (1899-    )**   Developmental psychologist, at University of California (later also

National Institute of Mental Health). Studied psychological and physical growth of sixty healthy children from birth to 36 years. Made analyses of intelligence and of factors influencing IQ and rates of mental growth. Demonstrated low correlations between mental scores obtained before and after one year of age. Found sex differences in determiners of mental abilities, showing boys more permanently affected by early emotional aspects of parent-child interactions, proving that genetic factors play a greater role in girl's abilities. Devised a method of predicting children's adult height from x-rays of bone maturity.

**Bayley scales of infant development** See *scales, Bayley, of infant development.*

**BDRM** See *basic data relation matrix.*

**Beard, George Miller (1840-1883)** An American psychiatrist who introduced the term neurasthenia.

**Beck system** An approach to the Rorschach test developed by Samuel J. Beck following the basic guidelines set forth by Hermann Rorschach and Emil Oberholzer. It is generally considered one of the most conservative approaches to the test, empirically based and following the behavioristic traditions.

**bedlam** State of frenzy, tumult, wild excitement. Bedlam was the name of the Priory of St. Mary of Bethlehem, a mental hospital in London. Bedlam became the common name for any mental hospital and eventually came to its present meaning.

**before-after design** An experimental method or procedure in which all groups, control and experimental, receive pre- and post- tests.

**behavior** 1. The totality of intra- and extraorganismic actions and interactions of an organism with its physical and social environment. Psychology deals with three types of phenomena: 1) Observable behavior, such as nervous tics, stuttering, excessive perspiration, bed-wetting, compulsive acts, impotence, violence, suicidal attempts, etc. 2) Introspectively observable phenomena, i.e., behavior that is not easily observed from without, such as toothache, headache, worry, hunger, and fear. 3) Unconscious processes, i.e., those mental processes which are not accessible even to the experiencing individual himself.
2. Any single activity, movement or response or group of activities, movements or responses of an organism; an activity, movement or response which alters the position of the organism or any part of the organism, in space. 3. (behaviorism) The dependent variable in the science of behavior.
There is considerable disagreement in psychology as to what actually constitutes behavior, although there is a general agreement in that behavior is seen as the activity of an organism. The problem arises in the delimiting of those activities which are considered behaviors. For the behaviorists, an activity, to qualify as a behavior, must be directly observable and measurable. For other psychologists, activities that qualify as behaviors include ideas, thoughts, dreams, images as well as overt muscular and neuro-physiological activities. There is also disagreement in distinguishing activities that are considered behaviors from those activities studied by physiology; i.e., the distinction between talking, perceiving, walking, on the one hand, and breathing, digestion, secreting bile on the other hand.

**behavior, avoidance** Behavior that postpones an aversive event thereby escaping from the conditioned aversive stimuli. The conditioned aversive stimulus is all the stimuli before the aversive stimulus presented minus the stimuli associated with the avoidance response. Thus avoidance behavior is a form of escape behavior.

**behavior contrast** (B. F. Skinner) The observation that in discrimination experiments the latencies of responses to stimuli that occasion reinforcement are longer than the latencies of responses to stimuli that do not occasion reinforcement, when such responses do occur.

**behavior criterion** A standard behavior with which other behaviors are compared.

**behavior determinant** (E. C. Tolman) Any variable which has a causal relation to a behavior.

**behavior disorders** A general term describing disorganized, disturbed, and deranged behavioral patterns. This term is used interchangeably with mental disorders, abnormal behavior, abnormal psychology, and psychopathology.

**behavior dynamics** 1. The study of causes and effects in behavior. 2. Motivation.

**behavior, extrinsic** Behavior which does not have a specific response mechanism; such behavior can be performed in various ways using different kinds of mechanisms.

**behavior field** The sum total at any given time of all events, conditions, and stimuli that impinge upon and influence the behavior of the organism.

**behavior genetics** The field of study dealing with the genetic basis of mechanisms underlying specific behavior patterns.

**behavior homology** A generalization stating the principle of a continuity of behavior patterns from species to species, a specific class of behaviors in lower forms corresponding in function and pattern to that same class of behaviors in man.

**behavior, intrinsic** Behavior which is carried out through a specific mechanism or organ as, for example, eye-blinking.

**behavior, maternal** The behavior involving the care of the young.

**behavior method** An approach which is derived from behaviorism in that the methods and goals, but not some of the negations and philosophical postulates, are accepted. Behavior of organisms is systematically studied as an observable response to carefully defined stimuli. Introspection is not used and mental contents and processes are not dealt with. However, intervening variables that are not directly observable, such as hunger of the organism, are accepted as explanatory constructs if tied down to stimulus and response conditions and if defined in strictly operational terms.

**behavior, molar** 1. A large unified unit of behavior. 2. A large unit of behavior which is not equal to the sum of its parts. 3. (E. C. Tolman) Behavior which is modifiable by learning. The unit of purposive behavior. 4. Behavior which is explained or defined in terms of psychological rather than physiological constructs.

**behavior, molecular** 1. Behavior described in terms of small units. 2. Behavior described in terms of neuromuscular or glandular activities.

**behavior object** An object which usually elicits a socially standardized type of behavior, such as a chair or fork.

**behavior observation** (generic) The recording and measurement of behavior by use of a human observer; may be in naturalistic or controlled settings, with pre- or post-observational categorization with or without supplementary instrumentation. See *time-sampling; behavior unit observation*.

**behavior, overt** Behavior which is easily observable; behavior or response which is visibly accountable or tangible.

**behavior pattern** See *archetype*.

**behavior rating** 1. The observation and recording of the occurrence of specific behaviors or classes of behaviors. 2. The assignment of a rank, score or mark to a specific observed behavior or class of behaviors.

**behavior repertoire** All behaviors which are possible for an organism.

**behavior sampling** The observation and recording of all the behaviors an organism engages in during prescribed segments of time so as to yield a representative sample of the totality of the organism's behavior.

**behavior segment** The smallest descriptive unit of a response to a stimulus.

**behavior shaping** Teaching of new and desired responses by using conditioning techniques of reinforcing any response that approximates the desired one until the correct behavior is learned.

**behavior space** 1. (E. C. Tolman) The space that contains objects perceived by the organism at any one time. The organism perceives the objects as being in a place at a distance and direction from the organism. 2. (K. Lewin) The complex and total set of conditions and relations determining the behavior of the individual, at any given time. The set consists of memories from the past, present influences, contemplations of the future, the perceived objects and the relation between them, the perception of the self in the situation, and a system of values, attitudes and beliefs concerning objects and relationships in the set.

**behavior, species specific** 1. Behavioral patterns shown by most members of the same species when in similar or the same situation. 2. Complex, stereotyped behavior appearing in most members of a species with no evidence of prior opportunity to learn it, thus assumed to be innate.

**behavior, spontaneous** Behavior that occurs ostensibly in the absence of any stimulus that could be shown to occasion, elicit or release the behavior.

**behavior stream** The continuous behavior output of an organism from which behavior theory abstracts such data terms as "response"; the term is paralleled by continuous energy input functions from which behavior theory abstracts such independent variable terms as "stimulus."

**behavior therapy** 1. The class of methods of changing unadaptive habits that is based on experimentally established paradigms. It is applicable to all unadaptive habits that have their origin in learning. The two major branches are classical conditioning, largely involving reciprocal inhibition and mainly applied to neuroses, and operant conditioning applied to unadaptive motor habits, notably those habits of schizophrenics that have been acquired by learning. 2. (B. F. Skinner) Shaping of behavior through manipulation of reinforcement to obtain the desired behavior. The theory is that hypothetical emotional factors and mental states are useless data in the study of psychopathology. The overt behavior is critical which is determined by external forces. Psychopathology is believed to result from underlearning or from learning of inappropriate behaviors which are reshaped by externally given reinforcement. 3. (J. Wolpe) Treatment of neurosis using learning theory techniques. Neurosis is believed to originate when a drive-motivated behavior is arbitrarily punished resulting in feelings of anxiety in similar situations. Therapy consists of reciprocal inhibition involving experimental extinction or counter-conditioning techniques. The patient is asked to perform the anxiety arousing behavior in fantasy or fact in a rewarding atmosphere resulting in the elimination of inhibitions associated with the behavior. Two major methods of behavior therapy are classical conditioning and instrumental conditioning. There are four forms of the latter method: reward training, avoidance learning, omission training, and punishment training.

**behavior therapy, verbal conditioning** The use of operant conditioning techniques in order to guide and increase the verbalized statements of the patient who can find out that his speech will not be disapproved of or punished.

**behavior unit observation (BUO)** Acts defined by pre-established categories are recorded as they occur, without reference to duration or time intervals; measure is either frequency of occurrences during a standard time period of observation, or frequency per unit of time when observations differ in duration.

**behavior, verbal** Behavior which employs words in any form-printed, written, oral, etc.

**behavioral equation** An equation, as follows, expressing the magnitude of a behavioral response act, $a_{jh}$, as a function of the subject's ability, $A$; temperament, $T$; and dynamic, $D$, trait endowments, of behavioral indices, $b_j$'s, peculiar to the focal stimulus and response, $j$, and of modulating influences, $s_h$, peculiar to the ambient situation, $h$.

$$a_{ijh} = \Sigma b_{ja} A_i + \Sigma b_{jt} T_i + \Sigma b_{jd} s_{hd} D_i$$

($i$ being a particular individual). This is the simplest linear and additive form for factor analysis, but can be generalized.

**behavioral genetics** See *behavior genetics.*

**behavioral information** See *information, behavioral.*

**behavioral oscillation** ($sO_R$) See *oscillation, behavioral, or $sO_R$.*

**behavioral situation indices** The values, which are factor loadings, usually written $b$ or $s$ in the behavioral specification equation, which show how much a given source trait is involved in that specific situation and response.

**behaviorism** A theoretical "school of psychology," created by John B. Watson, for which overt behavior was defined as the subject-matter of psychology; designed to broaden systematic psychological study to encompass the lower animals, children, and the mentally abnormal. An atomistic theory for which reflexes and the conditioned reflex were the basic units.

**Behn-Rorschach Test** See *test, Behn-Rorschach.*

**Bekhterev, Vladimir Mikhailovich (1857-1927)** A Russian neuroanatomist, neurophysiologist, psychologist, neuropathologist and psychiatrist. In 1878 he graduated from the Medico-Surgical academy and was assigned to the Chair of Psychiatry under I. P. Merzheyevskii. In 1884-1886 he worked abroad at the laboratories of Kronecker, Gudder, Westphal, Meinert, Wundt, and Flechsig. From 1893-1913 Bekhterev was the Head of the Chair of Psychiatry and Neuropathology of the Academv of Military Sciences in Petersburg. In that period he wrote *Transmitting Pathways of the Spinal Cord and the Brain, Bases of Theory on the Brain Functions* (7 volumes), *Objective Psychology* (3 volumes), *Psyche and Life, Suggestion and its Role in Social Life, General Bases of Diagnosis of the Nervous System Diseases.* He formulated the conception of "combined-motor reflexes" which was an application of the conditioned reflex theory to man. He discovered and described the following new nervous pathways and nervous centers bearing his name: a) a group of cells in the external region of Corpus Posterior; b) vestibular nucleus ("Bekhterev nucleus"); c) Formatio Reticularis; d) four bunches in Brachia Conjunctiva; e) stria medularis was determined to serve for unction of different cerebellum parts; f) external stria inside the brain cortex named after Bekhterev. During his last years, his activity concerned the foundation of the science of reflexology.

**belief-value matrix** (E. C. Tolman) The set of categorizations and classifications (judgments and values) which the individual brings to his interactions with the environment.

**Bell Adjustment Inventory** See *inventory, Bell Adjustment.*

**Bell-Magendie Law** See *law, Bell-Magendie.*

**bell-shaped curve** See *curve, bell-shaped.*

**Bellak, Leopold (1916-    )** American psychiatrist, psychoanalyst, and psychologist. Attempted to bridge these three fields conceptually and experimentally. Created Children's Apperception Test (CAT), formulated multifactorial theory of schizophrenia, and was instrumental in creating Schizophrenia Research Center at National Institute of Mental Health. Organized the first 24-hour walk-in clinic (Trouble Shooting Clinic) and general hospital as community mental health center at Elmhurst General Hospital, New York City. Co-authored with L. Loeb, *The Schizophrenic Syndrome;* described his experimental studies in psychoanalysis in *Broad Scope of Psychoanalysis;* wrote *Emergency Psychotherapy and Brief Psychotherapy* (with L. Small), and *The TAT and CAT in Clinical Use,* and other works.

**Bell's mania** See *mania, Bell's.*

**belonephobia** An extreme fear of needles.

**belongingness, principle of** (E. L. Thorndike) A bond between two items is more readily formed if the properties of one item are closely related to the properties of the other item.

**benadryl** The trade name for diphenhydramine, an anti-histamine compound used orally, topically and parenterally for allergies and for hyperactive children with behavior disorders.

**Bender, Lauretta (1897-    )** American child psychiatrist. Married to Paul Schilder (Austrian psychiatrist and psychoanalyst) until his death, 1941. Author of Visual Motor Gestalt Test (Bender Gestalt Test). Worked in New York City and State psychiatric hospitals for children from 1930. Special contributions made to childhood schizophrenia, brain damaged children, deprivation syndrome in children, learning disabilities, art of children, and physiological and drug-therapies.

**beneceptor** A receptor for stimuli which tend to promote the well-being of the organism.

**Bennett Differential Aptitude Test** See *test, Bennett Differential Aptitude.*

**Bennett Test of Mechanical Comprehension** See *test, Bennett, of Mechanical Comprehension.*

**benzedrine** A trade name for amphetamine.

**benzodiazepine compounds** Include librium and valium. It appears they act by a suppression of excitation in the reticular activating system; they promote muscular relaxation and block convulsive drug or electrically elicited activity. Sedative action seems to be between barbiturates and phenothiazines.

**Berger rhythm** See *alpha rhythm.*

**Bergson, Henri (1859-1941)** French philosopher, professor, whose writings contained much material relevant for psychology; opposed materialistic and positivistic philosophy and atomistic psychology; stressed the dynamic unity of mind and the ego as the unifying substratum of everchanging psychological states; favored intuitive rather than rationalistic approach to reality; received Nobel prize in 1927.

**Beritashvili (Beritoff), Ivan (1885- )** Soviet neurophysiologist. Worked under N.E. Vvedensky (1909-1914). In 1916-1919, Docent of Physiology at Odessa University. Since 1919, professor of the State University in Tbilisi; since 1935, Head of Sechenov Institute of Physiology. He established: 1) role of the spinal nervous elements such as intermediate, motor and gelatinous Rolando's substance in phasic coordinating motion of the extremities (1909-1914); 2) a rhythmic nature of the reciprocal inhibition of skeleton muscles (1912-1914); 3) a nervous mechanism of establishing of the jugular and labyrinth tonic reflexes (1914-1915); 4) formation of bilateral connections—progressive (direct) and return (feedback) under conditioning (1916-1922); 5) formation of conditioned reflexes under a reverse order of the combination, i.e., unconditioned first, then conditioned (1927); 6) appearance of the general inhibition together with inhibition of a definite complex of the brain neurons under each behavioral act (1927-1935); 7) individually acquired feeding or defensive behavior after a one-time perception of the food location or a damaging agent and its regulation by reproduction of an image of the food location or the enemy (1932–1935); 8) regularities of the image-driven psychoneural activity of neocortex (1935, 1947, 1969); 9) an automatized involuntary character of the conditioned reflex, based on structural development of the synaptic apparatus (1961–1969); 10) a neuropsychic mechanism of orientation of animal and man in space (1959); 11) role of cortical and subcortical brain regions in the image-driven psychoneural activity (1961, 1969); 12) image-driven and emotional memory, its characteristic and origination (1968).

**Berkeley growth study** A study aimed at changes in intellectual ability with increasing age. Found that there is little stability in intelligence test scores obtained in testing in infancy and those 5 or 6 years later.

**Bernard, Claude (1813-1878)** French experimental physiologist, credited with coining of the term endocrinology.

**Bernheim, Hippolyte-Marie (1840-1919)** French psychiatrist who investigated hypnotism and suggestibility. Bernheim maintained that all people are suggestible. Bernheim was critical of Charcot's views and techniques.

**Bernoulli trials** (statistics) A series of trials in which there are two and only two possible outcomes for each trial and the outcome of one trial in no way influences the outcome of any other trial.

**Bernreuter Personal Adjustment Inventory** See *Bernreuter Personality Inventory.*

**Bernreuter Personality Inventory (R. G. Bernreuter)** A questionnaire introduced in 1931 which measures six traits: neurotic tendency, self-sufficiency, introversion-extroversion, dominance-submission, confidence and sociability, the last two of which were added by J. C. Flanagan following factor analysis. This inventory is intended for use with children in grades 9 to 16 and with adults. The items are answered yes or no and each is scored in terms of its differentiating ability for a specific trait. Its value lies in initial diagnosis of persons at the extremes of the scale.

**best answer test** See *test, best answer.*

**best reason test** See *test, best answer.*

**bestiality** 1. Any human behavior which is revolting and disgusting. 2. Sexual intercourse with animals.

**beta coefficient** In multiple correlation, the amount that each variable must be multiplied in order to yield the highest correlation.

**beta error** See *error, beta.*

**beta movement** See *movement, beta.*

**beta press** See *press, beta.*

**beta response** An eyelid response which is delayed somewhat after the presentation of the conditioned stimulus.

**beta rhythm; beta waves** A pattern of brain waves observed on an electroencephalograph in which the waves are faster and of less amplitude than alpha rhythm.

**beta test** See *test, Army Beta.*

**beta weight; β-weight** (statistics) In a multiple correlation, the amount by which each variable is multiplied so that each variable or predictor will produce the highest possible multiple correlation with the dependent variable.

**betz cells** Large pyramid shaped cells located in layer V of the motor cortex.

**Bezold-Brücke phenomenon** With an increase in illumination, there is a shift in hue with colors tinged with red and green moving toward the yellow and blue side of the spectrum.

**bias** 1. A tendency towards favoring a certain position or conclusion. 2. A tendency to make errors in a certain direction. 3. A factor in an experimental procedure which systematically introduces error or systematically distorts a set of data. 4. An adjustable set point that regulates a servomechanism. Example: the adjustable setting on a thermostat.

**bibliokleptomania** A pathological tendency to steal books.

**bibliotherapy** Reading used as a therapeutic technique.

**Bichat, Law of** See *law of Bichat.*

**Bidwell's Ghost** See *Purkinje afterimage.*

**bifactor method** (statistics) A factor analytic procedure involving the extraction of a general factor and then the extraction of group factors, or factors of more limited scope.

**bifactoral theory of conditioning** See *conditioning, bifactoral theory of.*

**bilateral** 1. Having two sides. 2. Pertaining to both the right and left sides.

**bilateral transfer** The transference of a skill learned on one side of the body to the other side of the body.

**bilirubin** A chemical substance, the principal pigment of bile. Normally found in feces and, in cases of jaundice, in urine. See *bilirubin encephalopathy.*

**bilirubin encephalopathy** See *Kernicterus.*

**bimodal** (statistics) A descriptive term for a distribution which has two points at which the frequencies are significantly greater than at points on either side of those two points.

**bimodal distribution** See *distribution, bimodal.*

**binary (number) system** A system of numbers consisting of 1 and 0 used in electronic computers.

**binaural** A term pertaining to the functioning of the two ears together, as in normal hearing.

**binaural beat** See *binaural shift.*

**binaural ratio** The ratio of the sound intensities at the two ears.

**binaural shift** The periodic shift in localization or perceived intensity of the sound which occurs when two tones of slightly different frequency are perceived separately by each ear. The fluctuation rate corresponds to the frequency difference.

**bind hypothesis, double** See *hypothesis, double bind.*

**Binet, Alfred (1857-1911)** French psychologist. Director, laboratory of physiological psychology, Sorbonne, Paris; with Theodore Simon constructed first well-known individual scale of intelligence which determined mental age; builder of French psychology and objective scientific psychology, insisting on experimental basis for psychological data; experimented extensively and intensively on functions and phenomena, particularly on thinking; rejected associationism; founded and edited first French psychological journal, *L'Année Psychologique* (1895); author of *L'Étude Expérimentale de l'Intelligence* (1903).

**Binet—Simon Scale** See *test, Binet—Simon.*

**Binet—Simon Test** See *test, Binet—Simon.*

**binocular accommodation** See *accommodation, binocular.*

**binocular flicker** See *flicker, binocular.*

**binocular parallax** See *parallax, binocular.*

**binocular perception** See *perception, binocular.*

**binocular vision** Sight with both eyes fixated on the same object in space.

**binomial expansion** The result of raising to any power an algebraic expression containing two terms.

**Binswanger, Otto (1852-1929)** A German neurologist and psychiatrist.

**biochemical research** Research dealing with the effects of biochemical events on the behavior of organisms and of the reciprocal effect of behavior on biochemical events. Sensory and motor actions can be altered by the injection of chemical agents to particular areas of the brain. Behavior such as learning and memory has been found to affect biochemical systems at the molecular level.

**biocybernetics** A biological branch of application and elaboration of the cybernetic regularities. Mechanisms of self-organization in the living system with the "feed-back" as the decisive factor in the living system. A wide development of biocybernetics took place with the study of the neurocybernetic regularities, such as transmission of information, feed-back, reliability of neurocybernetic patterns, etc. The neurocybernetic approach to study of a neuron and of the brain enabled the building of a great number of models of a neuron and of the whole machine-electronic combinations, as for example, "perceptron" by McCulloch-Pitts. One must, however, notice that "neurocybernetics" is a somewhat artificial limitation of the biocybernetic regularities, since the brain becomes a biosystem if it continuously receives information from the external and internal stimuli through peripheral afferent pathways. At the same time, the brain performs its integrative functions through the activity of the peripheral motor and secretory apparatuses. The biocybernetic regularities are related to the deeper and more narrowly elaborated regularities of the functional system, which is the real working centro-peripheral organization. Biocybernetics also used distinguished properties of living organisms (fine sensibility, speed of movement, principles of organization, etc.) for a constructive improvement of technical and electronic machines.

**bioelectrical potential** The electric charge or potential shown by living tissues, such as neurons and the brain, at any given time.

**biogenesis** The origin and evolution of living things.

**biogenetic law** (E. Haeckel) Ontogenesis, that is the development of the individual, is an abbreviated replica of phylogenesis, that is the development of the species. Also called the law of recapitulation.

**biographical method** See *method, biographical.*

**biological theories of personality** See *personality, theory of: biological.*

*Biographical Sketch of an Infant* By C. Darwin, a diary of the early development of a child.

**biometry**   1. The application of statistical methods to the study of living organisms, their structures and functions. 2. The calculation of the probable human life span.

**bionomics**   See *ecology*.

**biopsychology**   The field of psychology approached from a biological point of view, stressing the organism's adaptiveness to environmental demands and pressures through nervous system, endocrine gland, receptor functioning, etc.

**biosocial theory**   (G. Murphy) Biosocial theory posits the full continuous reciprocity of organism and environment. It emphasizes the fact that observation of personality is possible only when the organism is interacting with a social (or both physical and social) environment. Description of a personality as a self-contained unit (as often occurs in "personality research"), forgetting the situational-ecological context of all personal responses tends to be unrealistic. When considered in terms of the *time dimension*, the organism is continuously both giving and receiving social stimulation, and it is not the life history of the organism as such, but the history of its interactions with other personalities, that constitutes the best present direction for full-fledged personality study.

**biosphere**   1. The total area of the earth and the air surrounding it which contains and supports living organisms. 2. The earth as an environment for living organisms.

**biostatistics**   The collection and analysis of data concerned with the lives of human beings, especially births and deaths.

**biotype**   1. (biology) A group of organisms which share a common hereditary background, although the individuals of the group may vary considerably. 2. (E. Jaensch) One of two kinds of people characterized by an eidetic imagery thought to be physiologically based; the B type is associated with a tendency towards exophthalmic goiter; the T type is associated with a tendency towards tetany.

**biotypology**   The categorization of man into various types (biotypes) dependent upon psychological, physiological and anatomical considerations.

**bipolar**   1. Having two poles or branches at extreme ends. 2. Referring to variables, tests or scales which are meaningful at extreme and opposite ends.

**bipolar factor**   See *factor, bipolar*.

**bipolar neuron**   See *neuron, bipolar*.

**birth order**   The relative order of age in the children of a family.

**birth trauma**   1. (psychoanalysis) The anxiety, thought to be the prototype of all later anxiety, experienced by the infant upon being born and being flooded with stimuli. 2. A physical injury received at and during birth.

**biserial correlation**   See *correlation, biserial*.

**bisexuality**   1. The possession of the anatomical or psychological characteristics of both sexes. 2. The condition of being equally attracted to members of both sexes.

**bite**   (operant conditioning) A deviation from a smooth curve on a cumulative record. It indicates a brief period of slow responding followed by a compensatory high rate which reestablishes the over-all rate.

**bivariate correlation**   See *correlation, simple*.

**bivariate experiment**   A form of design in which only two variables are measured at once, one of them commonly being manipulated and called the independent variable (sometimes called the univariate method). This may be called the classical, traditional experimental design in contrast with the multivariate experiment.

**black box**   A term for a formal model used in an attempt to develop hypothetical constructs to be used in explaining the behavior of organisms. Analogies are drawn between the organism and a black box, i.e., constructs are developed which will account for the output of the system given the input into the system.

**blackout threshold**   The point or level at which an organism loses consciousness, especially in conditions of oxygen deprivation.

**Blacky pictures test**   See *test, Blacky pictures*.

**blank experiment; blank trial**   See *experiment, blank*.

**blanket group**   A classification term referring to those items which do not fit in any of the prescribed categories.

**blast-injection technique**   A means of inducing convulsions in an animal by the prolonged exposure to air blasts or blasts of high frequency sound.

**blastomere**   A cell formed by the division of the fertilized ovum.

**blastula**   The stage of embryonic development formed by the cleavage of the ovum and characterized by a spherical mass of functionally identical cells with a central cavity.

**blend response**   A Rorschach response in which more than one feature of the blot, such as movement, color, form, or shading, contributes to the formulation of the percept. Generally considered to represent a complex affective-thought operation, each of the determinants is scored and given full weight in interpretation. See *additional scores* (for contrasting approach.)

**blepherospasm**   An involuntary spasm or blinking of the eyelids.

**Bleuler, Eugen (1857-1939)**   Swiss physician and psychiatrist. Introduced the word "schizophrenia" and the modern conception of this psychosis, stressed early in the 20th century the need of occupational, social and psychological treatment of schizophrenics and fought against the idea that schizophrenics cannot be successfully treated. The first academic clinician who recognized the significance of Freud's psychoanalysis and helped much in its development. Introduced many psychological and psychopathological conceptions: ambivalence, ambitendence, autism, autistic thinking, etc. Introduced ambulatory assistance to psychiatric patients. Pioneer in the fight against alcoholism and in developing treatment for alcoholics. Stressed the significance of mnemism in psychiatry.

**Bleuler, Manfred (1903-    )** Swiss psychiatrist. Investigated the psychological sequelae of endocrine diseases and introduced the term "endocrine psycho-syndrome". Applied the Rorschach test for sociocultural research. Continued his father's (see Bleuler, Eugen) work on schizophrenia and discovered that the condition of schizophrenia begins to improve from the 5th year on, after the onset of psychosis. Found that children of schizophrenics are healthy and a few are psychopathic. Introduced the principle of active community ("tätige Gemeinschaft") in treatment of mental disorders.

**blind diagnosis** See *diagnosis, blind.*

**blind-matching technique** A validation procedure in which an observer, given one description of a person or event, is required to select another example of that person or event from an independent description of events.

**blind spot** An area of the retina insensitive to light due to the juncture of the optic nerve and the eyeball at that point.

**blindness, hysterical** Blindness occurring although the organ is functional and intact.

**blinking reflex** See *reflex, blinking.*

**block design test** See *test, block design.*

**block sampling** See *sampling, block.*

**blood groups** Five blood types, A, B, O, M and N which are due to the action of single genes. Groups A, B, and O which exhibit linkage are used as markers in experiments designed to map chromosomal pairs. M and N do not manifest linkage.

**blood pressure** The force exerted by the blood against the walls of the arteries. Systolic pressure is the maximum pressure; diastolic pressure is the minimum pressure. There are many physiological and psychological correlates with blood pressure change.

**Blos, Peter (1904-    )** Clinical psychologist and child psychoanalyst. Main contribution in the field of psychoanalytic theory of adolescence. Subdivision of adolescence into five phases, metapsychologically defined and exemplified by clinical material. Similarities and differences established in the developmental lines of male and female adolescence. Adolescent changes in psychic structure are formulated as the Second Individuation Process of Adolescence, Late Adolescent Consolidation and Character Formation. The typical structural differentiations are cued by somatic, genetic and cultural influences. Adolescence is conceived as the terminal stage of childhood, rather than, exclusively, as a recapitulation of prelatency psychosexual development. The oedipus complex reaches its definitive resolution with the closure of adolescence. The transformation of the negative oedipus complex leads to the formation of the adult ego ideal. Special clinical studies in Cryptorchism, Female Delinquency and Acting Out (family myth).

**body build** The individual's body structure taken from the point of view of the pattern of relationships among the members and features of the body-trunk length, girth, limb length, height.

**body-build index** (H. J. Eysenck) An index of constitutional types which groups individuals according to the value obtained from multiplying one hundred times their height divided by six times their transverse chest diameter: mesomorphs fall within one standard deviation of the mean; leptomorphs are those one standard deviation or more above the mean, and eurymorphs are those one standard deviation or more below the mean.

**body image** See *image, body.*

**body-language** The expression of thoughts, emotions, etc. through movement of the body.

**body type** See *type, body.*

**body-weight (in control of level of deprivation)** An accompanying effect of a food deprivation schedule is loss of body-weight which is used as a check on the schedule. Body-weight is usually measured prior to a session and is maintained by feeding the animal up to a prescribed weight following a session.

**Bogardus Social Distance Scale** See *scale, Bogardus Social Distance.*

**Bogen cage** A performance test requiring the solution of a maze problem in three dimensions.

**bone-conduction test** See *test, bone-conduction.*

**Boolean algebra** (G. Boole) An algebra of sets consisting of a system for forming and manipulating sets according to specific postulates.

**borderline intelligence** See *intelligence, borderline.*

**borderline schizophrenia** See *schizophrenia, latent.*

**Boring, Edwin G. (1886-1968)** Long-time head of Harvard's psychology department. Theoretical work on sensory processes, especially audition. Leading professional historian of experimental psychology, who gave particular attention to the competing influences of Zeitgeist and of persons on the development of science. First editor of *Contemporary Psychology.*

**bound energy** (psychoanalysis) Libido under the control of ego processes which is available for dealing with reality and not expended on fantasy and repression.

**Bourneville's disease** See *tuberous sclerosis.*

**Braceland, Francis J. (1900-    )** American psychiatrist, clinician, educator, editor. Psychiatrist-in-chief, the Institute of Living, 1951-65, Senior Consultant, 1965—; Editor, *American Journal of Psychiatry,* 1965—; Chief, psychiatry, Mayo Clinic,

1946-51; Dean, Loyola U. Med. School, 1941-42. Editor and author of four volumes and over 200 psychiatric papers on various aspects of clinical psychiatry and psychiatric education. Chief, Psychiatry, U.S. Navy, WWII, Rear Admiral (Ret.) 1962; President, American Psychiatric Association, 1956-57; President, American Board of Psychiatry and Neurology, 1950-52; Vice President, World Psychiatric Association, 1961-66.

**brachycephaly, brachycephalism** Having a short or broad head with a cephalic index of 81.0 to 85.4.

**brachydactyly** Having abnormally short fingers or toes.

**brachylineal** See *brachymorphy.*

**brachymorphy** Having an abnormally short stature.

**brachyskelic** Having abnormally short legs.

**brachytypical** See *brachymorphy.*

**bradycardia** Slowness of the heart due to functional or organic causes.

**bradyglossia** Slowness of speech resulting from difficulties in the movement of the tongue.

**bradykinesis, bradykinesia** Slowness of movement due to functional or organic causes.

**bradylalia** Slowness of speech of psychological or organic causes.

**bradylexia** Slowness of reading of psychological or organic origin.

**bradylogia** Slowness of speech of psychological or organic causes usually resulting from slowness of thinking.

**bradyorthia** Slowness of speech resulting from organic damage of the speech mechanism.

**bradyphasia** Slowness of thought.

**bradyphrenia** Sluggish mentality of psychological or organic causes.

**bradypragia** Slow action usually referring to physical activity of the body.

**bradypragic** Referring to bradypragia.

**bradyscope** An instrument which presents visual pictures or objects at slow rate of speed.

**bradytrophism** Slow metabolism of nutrition or nutritive movement characteristic of certain diseases.

**braidism** An obsolete term for hypnotism.

**Braille** A system of writing and printing which enables the blind to read, utilizing different combinations of raised points for letters and signs.

**brain** The portion of the central nervous system, composed of nerve tissue, enclosed within the skull, including the cerebrum, midbrain, cerebellum, pons and medulla oblongata.

**brain center** 1. Any area which is the end-point of afferent neurons, or the starting-point of efferent neurons, or an intermediary between the two.

2. Any group of neurons in the brain which are hypothesized to perform a specific function.

**brain damage, effect on IQ test performance** Damage to the right hemisphere results in a lower after birth. Injury to different areas of the brain may result in focalized handicaps but may also result in general intellectual and/or motor impairment.

**brain damage, effect on IQ test performance** Damage to the right hemisphere results in a lower performance level and intact verbal performance while damage to the left hemisphere causes difficulties in the verbal sphere.

**brain disorders** Disorders that are caused by or associated with impairment of functioning of brain tissues and that generally manifest symptoms such as: impairment of orientation; memory impairment; impairment of intellectual functions including calculation, knowledge, learning, comprehension; impairment of judgment; shallowness and lability of affect.

**brain field theory** See *isomorphism.*

**brain lesion, occipitoparietal** 1. See *agnosia, visual.* 2. See *apractagnosia.* 3. See *alexia.* 4. See *agraphia.* 5. See *acalculia.* 6. See *aphasia, semantic.* 7. See *agraphia, visual.* 8. See *alexia, visual.*

**brain lesion, of frontal lobes** Lesions of the frontal lobes result in the impairment of abstract or complex gnostic and intellectual functions, loss of purposeful behavior, of complex forms of behavior, and perseveration. The size, location and extent of the damage to the frontal lobes determines the type of impairment which will occur.

**brain lesion, of occipital lobe** Lesions in the occipital area result in the inability to remember sequential elements of an act. The past is not forgotten.

**brain lesion, of parietal lobe** 1. See *apraxia, afferent.* 2. See *agnosia, tactile.* 3. See *aphasia, afferent motor.*

**brain lesion, of premotor cortex** 1. See *aphasia, efferent motor.* 2. See *apraxia, dynamic.*

**brain localization** The proposition that various behaviors and mental functions are associated with specific and localized areas of the brain.

**brain potential** The level of electrical activity or electric potential in the brain.

**brain stem** That portion of the brain which remains after the cerebrum and cerebellum are removed.

**brain waves** The spontaneous and rhythmic electrical discharges of the living brain, particularly of the cerebral cortex.

**brat syndrome** See *syndrome, brat.*

**breakdown, nervous** A popular term for a sudden neurotic or psychotic disturbance that incapacitates the individual, often to the point of requiring hospitalization.

**breakthrough** 1. Any significant advance, progress or development in research or theoretical knowledge. 2. (psychotherapy) A rather sudden movement towards a goal or manifestation of new and constructive work and attitudes after a period of resistance and little progress.

**Bremerman's limit**  A law which designates the absolute limit to the amount of information processing at a particular time by the following statement: $1.5 \times 10^{47}$ bits per second by one gram of matter.

**Brentano, Franz Clemens (1838-1917)**  German philosopher and psychologist. Studied in Berlin under the Aristotelian scholar, Trendelenburg, and received his Ph.D. degree *in absentia* from Tübingen in 1862 for a thesis on Aristotle's different conceptions of Being. In 1864 he was ordained a priest in the Dominican Order. During the winter of 1866 he was habilitated at Würzburg, and was appointed extraordinarius professor in 1872. Brentano became embroiled in the ecclesiastical controversy over the dogma of the infallibility of the Pope and was allowed to resign from the Dominican Order. At the same time, in 1873, he resigned from Würzburg. In 1874 he was appointed professor at Vienna. He married in 1880 and as a result resigned his post at Vienna; however, he continued to teach as *Privatdozent*. In 1895 he left Vienna for travel and study in Italy. After the outbreak of World War I he went to Zürich where he later died.

Brentano revived an Aristotelian-type psychology. His ontological position is one that recognized mental acts, sensory phenomena, and objects in the external world. In the perception of an object there is simultaneously an awareness of the object and an awareness of the perceiving. There are three types of mental acts which are perceived: (1) Vorstellungen (presentations), (2) Urteile (judging), and (3) Gemütsbewegungen (emotions like love and hate). All thought has a direction and a reference or intention. The content or object of thought has a secondary existence within a mental act, which has primary existence.

Brentano had distinguished students to whom fell the opportunity of recreating European psychology and philosophy after the decline of Hegelianism, and to a lesser extent Kantianism. Among these were Freud, K. Stumpf, F. Hillebrand, K. Twardowski, A. V. Meinong, C. V. Ehrenfels, E. Husserl, A. Marty.

**brevilineal**  A term used by Manouvrier to describe the constitution or body type characterized by a body with lines that are shorter and broader than the average figure.

**brief-stimulus therapy (BST)**  A form of mild electro-shock therapy.

**Briggs Law**  (L. V. Briggs) A statute of Massachusetts which required the psychiatric examination of people indicated for a capital offense and also those people indicated for a crime whose past history include more than one offense for any crime or a conviction on a felony charge. The report would be made available to the court, the probation officer, the district attorney and the defense attorney.

**brightness**  1. The intensity of all visual sense data. 2. The attribute of a film color allowing it to be placed in a series which ranges from dim to brighter

than white under similar viewing conditions. 3. An obsolete term for saturation. 4. A term for a high degree of intelligence understood in relation to those others in the life group of the individual.

**brightness adaptation**  See *adaptation, brightness.*

**brightness constancy**  See *constancy, brightness.*

**brightness contrast**  See *contrast, brightness.*

**brightness threshold**  See *threshold, brightness.*

**bril**  A unit of brightness which has 100 bril equal to 1 millilambert. Smaller and lesser brightnesses are arrived at by the halving method.

**bril scale**  See *scale, bril.*

**Broca, Paul (1824-1880)**  French physician and surgeon. Authority on aphasia and pioneer in science of modern craniology. First to use clinical method successfully for demonstrating localization of functions in the cerebral cortex. Localized articulate speech in the brain (1861).

**Broca's area**  The brain center, located in the inferior frontal gyrus in the left cerebral hemisphere of right-handed individuals, which is highly critical in speech functioning, primarily in articulated or spoken speech. Named after Dr. P. Broca who discovered it.

**broken home**  A home with one parent absent due to divorce, separation, desertion, death, etc.

**bromate poisoning**  See *poisoning, bromate.*

**bromidrosiphobia**  A pathological fear of the offensive odors of the body.

**bronchial asthma**  See *asthma.*

**brontophobia**  The fear of thunder.

**Brookland's experiment**  Demonstrated that adequate stimulation of mentally deficient children resulted in positive changes in social and emotional maturity, affective relationships, and social participation and in a significant increase in intelligence ratings.

**Brosin, Henry W. (1904-    )**  American psychiatrist and psychoanalyst. Worked on toxic-organic reactions including head injuries, malarial therapy, insulin therapy, artifically induced fever therapy; Rorschach method over a wide variety of disorders including the schizophrenias and psychosomatic disorders; psychoanalysis and psychotherapy in psychosomatic disorders and psychoses; since 1955 studied human communication systems including microanalysis of linguistic, kinesic (body motion) and visceral systems in different cultural settings (with G. Bateson, R. Birdwhistell, Charles Hockett, N. A. McQuoun, Frieda Fromm-Reichmann and William Condon).

**Brown–Sequard syndrome**  A paralysis of one side of the body with sensory anesthesia on the opposite side which follows the sectioning of the lateral half of the spinal cord.

**Bruner, Jerome S. (1915-    )**  American psychologist. His work has evolved from an early interest in opinion formation and other social phenomena to concern with perception, thought, learning and language. In the mid-50's he focused on cognitive processes in children and with that, parallel work in the nature of the educational process. Since the late 60's, his subjects have grown younger and experimental apparatus more technical in order to study perception, attending, learning, memory, early language acquisition and problem solving in infants during the first two years of life.

**Brunswik, Egon (1903-1955)** Hungarian systematic psychologist and historian of psychology who, after founding the first psychological laboratory in Turkey, came permanently to the University of California at Berkeley in 1935. Founder of the school of probabilistic functionalism, he made significant contributions to the psychology of perception and to research methodology in psychology.

**Brunswik ratio** A measure of the perceptual constancy prevailing under different experiments, relating the subject's responses to the stimulus variable under various environmental conditions. In an experiment of the constancy of visual brightness the ratio is: (R−S) / (A−S) with S the per cent of reflectance for the stimulus match, A the albedo, or percent of reflectance, for the object to be matched, and R the per cent of reflectance of the object the subject chooses as matching.

**bruxism** The grinding of the teeth during sleep.

**Bryngelson-Glaspey test** See *test, Bryngelson-Glaspey.*

**BSR** Basal Metabolic rate.

**BST** See *brief- stimulus therapy.*

**buccal intercourse** See *intercourse, buccal.*

**Buerger's disease** See *thromboangitis obliterans.*

**buffoonery psychosis** A type of catatonic excitement characterized by disconnected, caricatured grimaces and gestures, and either silence or illogicalities. Believed to be a contrived flight into mental illness in order to escape from reality since patients tend to remain well-oriented.

**bug, cocaine** A sensory disorder occurring in heavy users of cocaine and manifested as itching, biting, sticking and crawling sensations which are attributed by the user to the presence of insects.

**bugger** Colloquialism for homosexual or more specifically for a sodomite.

**Bühler, Charlotte (1893- )** Austrian, then American psychologist. Studied adolescents' problems using diaries. Developed methods for observing infants, experimenting with first social responses of infants. Demonstrated in further behavioral studies of infants, adaptivity and curiosity. Outlined childhood and adolescent development. Used biographies to outline life cycle phases and theory of human development through the life span. Wrote critical studies of psychoanalytic reality principle and of homeostasis theory. Developed the theory of four basic tendencies of life. Introduced values in psychotherapy. Was founding sponsor of Association for Humanistic Psychology and wrote (with Melanie Allen) a book introducing Humanistic Psychology.

**Bühler, Karl (1879-1963)** German physician and psychologist. After some work at Berlin went to Würzburg, as assistant to Oswald Külpe. Made the then final important contribution to the Würzburg School of imageless thought in 1907-1908. Was professor of psychology at Bonn (1909-1913) and then at Munich (1913). After military service during World War I he became professor at the University of Vienna. There, during the years before Nazi annexation of Austria, he gained international recognition for his contributions to the psychology of thought processes, of language, of perception, of Gestalt theory, of the mental development of the child. From 1939 to his death he resided in the U.S. in a kind of academic isolation.

**bulb** A term used for medulla oblongata.

**bulimia** Insatiable hunger related to both increased appetite as well as increased intake of food, often observed in psychotics. Also known as *hyperphagia.*

**bulimy** Bulimia.

**Bunsen-Roscoe law** The principle that visual threshold for light is a function of stimulus intensity multiplied by stimulus duration.

**Buss-Durkee Inventory** A scale which measures hostility developed in 1957 by A. H. Buss and A. Durkee. This inventory consists of a questionnaire made up of seventy-five true-false items which reflect two major factors in aggression: emotional hostility characterized by resentment, suspiciousness, and negativism and overt aggression characterized by verbal and indirect hosility and irritability.

# C

C  See *color response.*

C factor  Factor of cleverness or quickness in thinking uncovered in some factor analyses of intelligence tests.

C group  The control group.

C reaction  A response to stimulation in the human embryo, in which the body bends into a C shape.

CA  See *chronological age.*

cacergasia  Mental deficiency.

cachexia, hypophysical  (M. Simmonds) A state of pathology due to deterioration or traumatic destruction of the anterior lobe of the pituitary gland. The main symptoms are loss of weight, low metabolic rate, general weakness, states of disorientation and loss of memory.

cachexis, cachexia  An advanced state of deterioration and weakness, most often caused by tuberculosis, syphilis, and carcinoma.

cachinnation  Unrestrained laughter that appears to be inappropriate and/or without an evident cause. It is quite often manifest as a symptom of hebephrenic schizophrenia.

cacodaemonomania; cacodemonia; cacodemonomania  A delusional state in which the individual believes himself to be possessed of or by a demon, an evil spirit, or a devil. It is sometimes observed as a symptom of hebephrenic schizophrenia.

cacogenic  A term used to identify the most severely defective individual, physically and/or mentally.

cacogeusia  The perception of bad taste; often reported by individuals with idiopathic epilepsy.

cacopathia  A hippocratic term used to identify a severe emotional illness.

cacosomnia  Insomnia; interrupted sleep; sleeplessness.

cadiva insania  Epilepsy.

caduca passio  Epilepsy; also called "The falling sickness."

caducus morbus  Epilepsy.

Cain complex  See *complex, Cain.*

cainophobia  A fear of new, novel, or unfamiliar objects, surroundings, or people.

caintophobia  See *cainophobia.*

California Achievements Tests  See *tests, California Achievement.*

California first-year mental scale  See *scale, California first year.*

California growth study  Continuation of the Berkeley growth study.

California Infant Scale for Motor Development  See *scale, California Infant, for Motor Development.*

California Personality Inventory  (H. G. Gough) A set of seventeen scales introduced in 1957 for use with normal populations, ages 14 to adult in guidance. The scales assess the presence of traits such as responsibility, socialization and dominance.

California Test of Personality  See *test, California, of Personality.*

California tests of mental maturity  See *tests, California, of mental maturity.*

Calkins, Mary Whiton (1863-1930)  American philosopher and psychologist. Completed work for doctorate at Harvard under James and Münsterberg, but denied degree because Harvard would not award degrees to women. Established the psychology laboratory at Wellesley, the first in a woman's college. Pioneer in dream psychology and one of the original contributors to the systematic psychology of the self. Elected the first woman president of the American Psychological Association. (1905)

callipedia  The wish to bear a beautiful child.

callomania  Delusions of beauty.

**callosum or corpus callosum** Commissural, myelinated nerve fibre that connects the two cerebral hemispheres.

**calorimeter** An instrument for the measurement of heat.

**camisole** A canvas shirt with extra long sleeves that is sometimes used to restrain violent mental patients.

**campimeter** A map of the visual field. See *perimeter*.

**camptocormia** A rare form of hysteria observed most often in soldiers. It is characterized by acute forward flexion of the spine. The patient has extreme difficulty in walking and often suffers tremors. Also known as bent back.

**canalization** 1. (neurology) Formation of neural connections which facilitate the flow of the neural current. 2. (G. Murphy) Establishing of preferences in patterns of behavior.

**cancer, emotional factors in** Emotional factors do not seem to cause malignant growths directly; however, reactions to these diseases are often pathological. Loss of an organ is sometimes responded to as loss of a loved object or as a punishment for a sinful act. Patients with leukemia contracted the disease subsequent to a mourning reaction which consisted of an identification with the lost object followed by a choice of another person as a vicarious object. These patients tended to have mothers for whom they were vicarious objects.

**canchasmus** Inappropriate giggling or laughter that is sometimes observed in patients suffering from hysteria, and frequently in hebephrenic schizophrenia.

**canina appetentia** See *bulimia.*

**cannabis** A narcotic and antispasmotic found in the flowering tops of the more potent Indian and the less potent American cannabis sativa plant which in large doses produced intoxication and mental exaltation. Also known as bang, bhang, gunjah, charas, churrus, hashish, and marihuana.

**cannabis indica** An intoxicant and narcotic that is obtained from Indian hemp.

**cannibalism** A psychotic impulse to eat human flesh.

**Cannon, Walter B. (1871-1945)** American physiological psychologist of motivation and emotion who held that emotion produces bodily changes that prepare the organism for fight or flight. In a pioneer experiment, he demonstrated (by measuring changes in the volume of balloons inflated inside human stomachs) that hunger pangs and stomach contractions are correlated.

**capacitance** The amount of electricity that a condenser or other electronic component can hold.

**capacity** An individual's maximum mental aptitude and/or physical capability.

**capgras syndrome** See *syndrome, capgras.*

**captation** An obsolete term used to identify the initial stage of hypnotism.

**captivation** A light, prehypnotic state.

**carbon dioxide therapy** (L. J. Meduna) The inhalation, through an anesthesia mask, of a mixture of 30 percent carbon dioxide and 70 percent oxygen. The usual procedure consists of a minimum of 20 treatments, 3 times a week.

**carbon monoxide poisoning** See *poisoning, carbon monoxide.*

**carbon tetrachloride poisoning** See *poisoning, carbon tetrachloride.*

**cardiac psychoneurosis** A psychoneurotic fear of coronary disease with no apparent physiological pathology.

**cardiac psychosis** The fearful and confused emotional state that often follows a coronary attack.

**cardiazol** The trade-mark for pentamethylenetetrazol. See *metrazol.*

**cardiograph** An instrument which measures and graphically describes the amplitude and rate of the heart beat.

**cardio-renal disease** Disease of the heart and kidneys.

**cardiotachometer** An instrument that records the total number of heartbeats over extended periods of time.

**cardiovascular** Pertaining to the blood vessels and the heart.

**cardiovascular neurosis** See *neurosis, cardiovascular.*

**carebaria** Unpleasant sensations of heaviness and/or pressure in the head.

**Carmichael, Leonard (1898-   )** American psychologist, physiologist and student of animal behavior. Extensive experimental research on the development of sensory processes and behavior in mammals before birth. With H. H. Jasper devised new apparatus and took the first human electroencephalograms in America. Student of visual fatigue and the electrophysiology of eye movements in reading and other visual tasks. During World War II, Director of office of over 400 workers who made an analytic punch card record of the special skills of all Americans with scientific and specialized skills needed in the war effort. Former President, Tufts University. Former Secretary (administrative head), Smithsonian Institution. Now Vice-President for Research and Exploration, National Geographic Society.

**carnosinemia** A rare aminoaciduria associated with mental retardation.

**carotid sinus syndrome** See *syndrome, carotid sinus.*

**carphology** Aimless picking at bedclothes or pajamas, etc. in patients with fever.

**Carstairs, George M. (1916-   )** Scottish psychiatrist and anthropologist. Has carried out research in culture and personality in North India, research in social psychiatry in Britain, research in transcultural psychiatry in South India.

case history   The complete medical, psychological, and social history of a patient. Psychological test data, personal documents, and transcripts of psychotherapy sessions are all part of a case history.

case study method   An exploratory study of single cases which aims at discovering and forming hypothetical concepts. It deals with complex relationships and tries to discern the relevant variables out of a host of multivariate personality structures and relationships. Most of psychiatric discoveries starting with E. Kraepelin and S. Freud, have been made through detailed case studies of individual patients. Also the discoveries of W. Stern, V. Bekhterev, C. and K. Bühler, and J. Piaget are the result of careful observations conducted on individual cases.

casework, psychiatric   The work with patients conducted by a psychiatric social worker. It may take place within the walls of a mental hospital or at the patient's home. It may be comprised of a few interviews or it may extend to a full fledged prolonged psychotherapy, conducted cojointly with a psychiatrist or a clinical psychologist or independently as the sole treatment.

castrate, castration   The removal of the testes in the male or the ovaries in the female.

castration anxiety   (S. Freud) A fear of genital injury or loss. It is an important part of the *Oedipus Complex* and a source of childhood anxiety. In adults it often manifests itself in the form of a displaced fear of harm to other bodily organs.

castration anxiety, amputee   The amputation often represents symbolic castration. The phenomenon in lower-extremity amputees of the sensation during urination of the stump, rather that the phallus as the source of the stream, supports the psychoanalytic view of castration anxiety.

castration complex   See *complex, castration.*

castrophrenia   A delusion that occurs sometimes in schizophrenic patients, that their enemies are depriving them of and/or controlling their thoughts.

CAT   See *test, Children Apperception.*

catabolism   The process of breaking down complex organic substances into simpler forms. The reverse process of anabolism.

catabythismomania   Impulse to commit suicide by drowning.

catabythismus   Suicide by drowning.

cataclonia   See *cataclonus.*

cataclonic   Relating to cataclonus.

cataclonus   Rhythmic convulsive movements of functional origin.

catagelophobia   Fear of ridicule.

catalentia   An obsolete term for epilepsy.

catalepsia cerea   An obsolete term for catalepsy.

catalepsy   1. A trancelike state in which muscles are held rigid for a long period. 2. A conditon in which a person's limbs will remain in any position in which they are placed. Characteristic of catatonic schizophrenics and of some forms of hysteria. Synonymous with cerea flexibilitas, flexibilitas cerea, and waxy flexibility.

catalepsy, accessory   The conditon called catalepsy involves the waxy flexibility of the muscular system that allows the limbs to be placed in any position, where they will remain indefinitely. Accessory catalepsy is a rarely used term that refers to the catalepsy associated with hysteria, mania, epilepsy, tetanus, and other disorders.

catalepsy, artificial   Catalepsy occurring during hypnosis.

catalepsy, epidemic   Catalepsy affecting many people as a result of imitation.

catalepsy, rigid   See *catalepsy.*

cataleptiform   Resembling catalepsy.

cataleptize   Developing a cataleptic state.

cataleptoid   Resembling catalepsy.

catalexia   A reading disorder characterized by a tendency to reread words and phrases; a form of *dyslexia.*

catalysator; catalyzator   1. A catalyzer. 2. An external agent or stimulus that serves to loosen inhibitions.

catalytic agent   1. A chemical element or substance which increases the speed of a chemical reaction. 2. A member of a psychotherapeutic group who activates emotional discharges in other members.

catalyzing action of hypnosis   The accelerating influence of hypnosis in psychoanalytically oriented psychotherapy such as hypnoanalysis.

catamite   A rare term for a boy who submits to pederasty.

catamnesis   1. The history of a patient following the onset of an illness, mental disturbance, or behavior disorder. 2. The period following the initial examination, or following discharge from treatment.

cataphasia   A disorder in the ability to use language, caused by brain lesions, and characterized by frequent and uncontrollable repetition of the same words or phrases without reference to their meaning.

cataphora   Coma interrupted by intervals of partial consciousness.

cataplectic attack   1. A sudden loss of muscle tone, usually provoked by intense emotion. 2. Part of a syndrome called idiopathic narcolepsy characterized by a sudden urge to sleep and cataleptic attacks.

cataplexy   1. In some animals muscular rigidity caused by an overwhelming sudden emotion such as fear or shock. 2. In humans, sudden loss of muscle tone provoked by intense emotion, often associated with narcolepsy. 3. Hypnotic sleep.

**cataptosis** (C. Galen) An apoplectic or epileptic seizure.

**catastrophe theory** (S. Ferenczi) A theory which maintains that many neurotics view coitus as an activity which may be injurious to their genitals.

**catastrophic behavior** (K. Goldstein) Psychological adaptation to the organically determined disorders of language known as aphasia. This adaptation involved a tendency toward fanatical orderliness, disinterest and aversion as defensive measures to avoid "catastrophic embarrassment."

**catastrophic reaction** A breakdown resulting from an individual's inability to cope with his environment, which may in reality be threatening or dangerous. The individual feels anxious, helpless, and buffeted by his circumstances.

**catathymia** The existence in the unconscious of a complex which produces a pronounced effect in the consciousness.

**catathymic amnesia** Amnesia limited to circumscribed events or periods of a person's life.

**catathymic crisis** A violent nonrepeated act resulting from intolerable tension.

**catatonia** 1. (K. L. Kahlbaum) First described in 1874 and thought to be a brain disease leading to disturbances in motility. 2. In 1896 Kraepelin included it as one of three types of dementia praecox or schizophrenia. See *schizophrenia, catatonic.*

**catatonia, depressive** See *catatonic stupor.*

**catatonia manic** See *catatonic excitement.*

**catatonia mitis** A mild form of catatonia.

**catatonia protracta** A severe form of catatonia.

**catatoniac** An obsolete term for someone suffering from catatonia; synonymous with catatonic schizophrenic.

**catatonic excitement** Excessive motor activity and excitement sometimes seen in catatonic schizophrenia.

**catatonic schizophrenia** See *schizophrenia, catatonic.*

**catatonic stupor** The most prominent symptom of catatonic schizophrenia involving waxy flexibility, extreme negativism, sterotyped behavior and inaccessibility to external stimuli.

**catatonoid attitude** 1. Behavior resembling catatonic behavior. 2. Stereotyped behavior and emotional shallowness typical of latent schizophrenics.

**catch trial** (psychophysics) A trial in which no stimulus or stimulus difference is presented to the subject and a response is a "false alarm", responding to something that is not there. This is an attempt to control the subject's guessing or anticipating a stimulus and for the nervous system producing its own stimuli.

**catecholamine** A group of chemical substances manufactured by the adrenal medulla and secreted during physiological stress.

**categorical** 1. Pertaining to a classification or categorization based on qualitative rather than quantitative distinctions. 2. Unqualified; absolute.

**categorical imperative** 1. An unqualified demand or command. 2. Kant's principle: "Act only on that maxim whereby you can at the same time will that it should become a universal law."

**categorical judgment, law of** See *law of categorical judgment.*

**category** 1. A group having a set of common attributes or qualities. 2. In statistics, a grouping based on qualitative rather than quantitative differences.

**catelectrotonus** Increased excitability of a nerve or muscle near the cathode, as an electric current is passing through the tissue.

**catharsis** 1. The purging of emotions. 2. (Aristotle) The purging or purification of emotions through artistic expression. 3. (psychoanalysis) The expression and discharge of repressed emotions and ideas.

**catharsis, community** The purging of a community's feeling of guilt.

**cathartic** 1. Relating to or using catharsis. 2. A medicine used to produce evacuation of the bowels.

**cathect; cathectize** To charge an object or idea with affect or psychic energy.

**cathectic** Relating to investment of psychic energy.

**cathectical method** Instruction by the Socratic method of skillful questioning.

**cathexis** (psychoanalysis) The investment of an object or idea with psychic energy.

**cathexis, fantasy** The investment of psychic energy in wishes, or fantasies, or to their original source in the unconscious.

**cathexis, hypervectorial** (B. B. Wolman) The overinvestment of psychic energy in one's parents or parental substitutes characteristic of schizophrenics.

**cathexis, interindividual** (B. B. Wolman) The balance of emotional energy of libido or destrudo cathected (invested) in interraction between two or more individuals.

**cathexis, intraindividual** (B. B. Wolman) The balance of emotional energy of libido or destrudo cathected (invested) in various parts of one's personality and parts and organs of one's body.

**cathexis, object** The investment of cathexis in some object outside oneself.

**cathexis, self** The investment of psychic energy in oneself.

**cathode** The negative electrode of an electric circuit.

**catochus** 1. An obsolete term for catalepsy. 2. A phase of ecstasy or trance in which the person is conscious but cannot move or speak.

**catoptrics** Branch of optics dealing with the properties and phenomena of reflected light.

**Cattell Infant Scale** (P. Cattell) A scale of infant intelligence and development from 2 to 30 months, an attempt to extend the Stanford-Binet downward. From 22 months upward the test items include some items from the Stanford-Binet.

**Cattell, Raymond B. (1905-    )** American psychologist. Applied factor-analytic developments and new behavioral test devices to the systematic taxonomy of unitary traits and states. Batteries of known validity provided for 30 indexed traits and 9 states, including anxiety, stress, arousal, etc., as distinct dimensions.
  Discovered most valid objective measures for motivation in men and animals, leading to the dynamic calculus of interest summation, conflict, resolution and integration. Applied this − as tri-vector description − to development of structured learning theory.
  Propounded psychometric and mathematical models − confactor rotation, ipsatization, the profile coefficient, taxonome, P − & dR − techniques, the personality sphere, fluid and crystallized intelligence, and formulae in social psychology for group syntality and leadership interactions.

**caudal** Pertaining to the tail or tail-end of an animal.

**caudate nucleus** Mass of grey matter forming part of the striate body in the subcortical region of the cerebral cortex; next to the thalamus.

**caumesthesia** The experience of heat even when the temperature is not high.

**causal chain** A series of events that are linked causally.

**causal explanation in psychology** 1. Explanation of behavior as the necessary result of antecedent factors. 2. S. Freud accepted a most rigorous determinism that says, "no causes without effects, no effects without cause." 3. K. Guthrie discarded the problem of causation and presented learning in a *post quod* (after which) rather than a *propter quod* (because of which) continuity. 4. C. G. Jung has accepted both Freud's determinism and Adler's purposivism. He held the Kantian position that both principles are methods of cognition rather than laws of nature. 5. K. Lewin viewed behavior and environment as simultaneous facts; the past only effects behavior to the extent that it remains in the present. 6. B. F. Skinner confined his system to description rather than explanation. According to Skinner, a "cause" becomes a "change in an independent variable" and an "effect" a "change in a dependent variable." 7. Some psychologists such as A. Adler, W. McDougall, K. Goldstein, and C. Tolman substituted the notion of causation in psychology by purposivistic theories.

**causal nexus** The causal interconnection between two events or successive phases of a one event.

**causal texture** (E. C. Tolman & E. Brunswik) The property of the environment of being made up of mutually dependent events. The degree of dependence is expressed in terms of probability and not in terms of causal certainty.

**causalgia** Burning pain not caused by heat, sometimes present in nerve injury, particularly injury of the sensory nerves of palms and soles.

**causality** An explanation of phenomena (effects) as the result of antecedent phenomena (causes). See *causal explanation in psychology*.

**causation** See *causality*.

**causation, historical** Explaining present behavior in terms of antecedent causes.

**causation, principle of multiple** The theory that many causes interact to produce an effect.

**causation, systematic** Explaining present behavior in terms of present causes.

**cause and effect test** See *test, cause and effect*.

**CAVD test** See *test, CAVD*.

**CEEB** College Entrance Examination Board.

**ceiling** 1. The maximum score attainable on a test. 2. In statistics, the maximum possible score possible on a test minus an allowance for chance error.

**cell** 1. The structural unit of living organisms. 2. In statistics a compartment formed by the intersection of a row and a column in a table.

**cell-assembly or assembly** (D. O. Hebb) A number of neurons acting temporarily as a system with self-maintained activity; hypothetically, its activity is a representative or ideational process, the unit of perception and thought. It is proposed that a primary assembly is organized as a result of a repeated stimulation such as the sight of a line of a certain slope or a particular hue, a touch at a particular point on the skin, a vowel sound, and so forth. Superordinate assemblies theoretically are organized by the activity of a number of primary assemblies. The assembly may be excited as the direct result of sensory stimulation, or by its associative connections with other assemblies.

**cell, body** Any cell other than a germ cell.

**cell body** The central part of the cell containing the nucleus.

**cell division** See *mitosis*.

**cell, padded** A room with padded walls and floors, used to confine acutely disturbed patients who are potentially destructive to themselves or others.

**cell, Purkinje** A large cell with many dendrites which is located in the middle layer of the cerebullar cortex.

**cellular** Pertaining to cells.

**celom** See *coelom*.

**cenesthesia** 1. The general feeling of the body. 2. The belief that certain bodily sensations are registered in the unconscious without the person being consciously aware of them.

**cenesthesic**  Relating to cenesthesia.

**cenesthopathic**  Relating to general feeling of physical illness.

**cenesthopathy**  The general feeling of physical illness not related to any particular part of the body.

**cenophobia**  See *kenophobia.*

**cenotrope; coenotrope**  An acquired pattern of behavior exhibited by all members of a particular biological group in a common environment and assumed to be the result of both heredity and environment.

**censor, endopsychic**  (psychoanalysis)  The agent within the preconscious responsible for the process of censorship.

**censorship**  (psychoanalysis)  The processes involved in the defensive activity directed against admitting to consciousness disturbing external stimuli or unacceptable impulse-derivatives from the unconscious.

**censorship, dream**  (psychoanalysis)  In dreams, the process which keeps unacceptable wishes or thoughts from breaking through.

**center correlation**  See *correlation center.*

**center, psychical**  An obsolete concept referring to the idea that mind and intelligence were localized in centers within the brain.

**centile**  1. Synonymous with percentile; a score representing the percentage of the distribution which falls below it. 2. One of 100 groups or divisions within a ranked distribution, each representing one percent of the distribution; or the rank order of any of those divisions.

**centile rank**  The number of rank order of a centile; see *centile 2.*

**central conflict**  (K. Horney). The conflict between the real self and the idealized self.

**central constant**  (T. Burrow)  Essentially homeostatic primary principle governing man's total action pattern; relates man as a species to his environment.

**central fissure**  See *central sulcus.*

**central force**  (C. G. Jung)  Refers to the primal libido and means undifferentiated energy or life force.

**central inhibition**  Inhibition of neural impulses by central nervous system processes.

**central limit theorem**  (statistics)  The principle that states that the sampling distribution of the means of random samples will be approximately normal in form regardless of the form of the distribution in the population if the sample size is large enough and if the population variance is finite. The more the population distribution differs from a normal distribution, the larger the sample size must be in order for this principle to be true.

**central lobe**  See *Reil, island of.*

**Central Motive State**  1. (C. T. Morgan)  Drive; motivating force, based on four phenomena: (1) persistence of motivation even when the initial condition does not exist any longer, (2) preparation of the organism for consummatory responses, (3) increased level of activity, (4) the consummatory responses. 2. Hypothetical processes in the central nervous system, not caused by present external stimulation.

**central nervous system**  The brain and the spinal cord.

**central processes**  Processes occurring in the central nervous system.

**central scotoma**  See *scotoma, central.*

**central sulcus**  Groove located in the middle of the lateral surface of the cerebral hemisphere, separating the frontal from the parietal lobe.

**central tendency**  1. (statistics)  The general tendency for scaled ratings to gravitate toward the center of the scale. 2. (biology)  The tendency of inherited biological traits to revert toward the norm.

**central tendency measures**  Statistical measures which attempt to provide a single value representative of a distribution. The most commonly used measures are the mean, median, and mode.

**central vision**  Vision which takes place in the region of the fovea; the area of clearest vision.

**centralism; centralist psychology**  A position which maintains that behavior is a function of the central nervous system. The brain is viewed as the mediator and integrating center between the stimulus and the response.

**centrifugal**  Moving from the center towards the periphery. Sometimes used to describe nerve impulses or fibers.

**centrifugal nerve or neuron**  A sensory or afferent nerve or neuron.

**centripetal**  Moving from the periphery towards the center. Sometimes used to describe nerve impulses or fibers.

**centroid method**  (L. L. Thustone)  A factor analytic method of extracting factors from a correlational matrix in which one axis passes through the center of gravity of the system and the others are orthogonal and thus uncorrelated. By rotating the axis to oblique positions, correlations among factors are revealed.

**cephalad**  Toward the head.

**cephalagia, cephalalgia**  Headache.

**cephalagra**  Headache.

**cephalic**  Pertaining to the head.

**cephalic index**  See *index, cephalic.*

**cephalization**  Concentration of important organs toward the head of the organism.

**cephalocaudal**  Long axis of body, from head to tail.

**cephalocaudal development** The principle that development, especially the embryological, progresses from head to tail.

**cephalogenesis** In embryological development, the stage associated with the development of the primordia of the head.

**ceraunophobia** See *keraunophobia*.

**cerchnus** Obsolete term for hoarseness.

**cerea flexibilitas** See *catalepsy*.

**cerebellar cortex** The gray, outer covering of the cerebellum.

**cerebellar fit** (H. Jackson) Tonic fit associated with tumors of the vermis and characterized by sudden loss of consciousness and falling, dilated and immobile pupils, and rigid extension of the body.

**cerebellar gait** Unsteady gait in which there is a disassociation of movement between the body and legs. The body either lags behind or is thrust forward, resulting in a "drunken" walk.

**cerebellar peduncle** See *peduncle, cerebellar*.

**cerebellar speech** See *asynergic speech*.

**cerebellum** Structure of the brain lying below the cerebrum and above the pons and medulla. Primarily concerned with the regulation of motor coordination.

**cerebral anemia** See *anemia, cerebral*.

**cerebral anemia, acute** Temporary reduced flow of blood to the brain caused by cardiac weakness, or intense fear or anxiety. Symptoms include dulled senses, noises in the ears and spots before the eyes. The skin becomes pale, cold and covered with perspiration.

**cerebral anemia, chronic** Chronic reduced flow of blood to the brain caused by such conditions as pernicious anemia, leukemia or repeated loss of blood. Symptoms include noises in the ears, headache, dizziness, poor memory and insomnia. There may be delusions and hallucinations.

**cerebral anemia, local** Temporary reduced flow of blood to a part of the brain due to a transient spasm or pressure from a tumor causing the closure of an artery. Symptoms reflect function of area involved.

**cerebral aqueduct** A slender elongated cavity in the midbrain connecting the third and fourth ventricles.

**cerebral arteriosclerosis** See *arteriosclerosis, cerebral*.

**cerebral blindness** An inability to see due to lesion or damage in the visual area of the cerebrum.

**cerebral cortex** Mantle of cells covering the cerebrum consisting mainly of cell bodies giving it a grey color. Phylogenetically, the more advanced part of the brain structure.

**cerebral dominance** 1. The principle that the cerebrum is the highest control center in the nervous system. 2. The fact that one brain hemisphere is dominant over the other in the control of body movement, especially handedness.

**cerebral embolism** See *embolism, cerebral*.

**cerebral hemispheres** The two symmetrical halves of the cerebrum which are separated by a deep fissure while connected by a broad band of fibers known as the corpus callosum.

**cerebral integration** The theory that the cerebrum is the integrating center of the organism, serving to integrate and unify all parts of the body and all behavior of the organism.

**cerebral lipidoses** See *lipidoses, cerebral*.

**cerebral lipidosis, infantile** See *Tay-Sachs disease*.

**cerebral palsy** 1. Paralysis due to brain lesion. 2. Infantile spastic diplegia.

**cerebral peduncle** See *peduncle, cerebral*.

**cerebral syphilis** See *syphilis, meningovascular*.

**cerebration** Cerebral physiological activity.

**cerebrospinal** Pertaining to the brain and the spinal cord.

**cerebrospinal fluid** Lymphlike fluid within the cerebral ventricles and between the arachnoid membrane and pia matter of the brain and spinal cord.

**cerebrospinal system** All the nerves in the body except those associated with the autonomic nervous system.

**cerebrotonic type** See *type, cerebrotonic*.

**cerebrum** 1. In vertebrates the largest portion of the brain occupying the entire upper part of the cranium and consisting of the right and left hemispheres. 2. The forebrain and the midbrain.

**ceremonial** A ritualized sequence of behaviors having symbolic and emotional significance beyond the act itself.

**ceremonial, compulsive** Ritualistic repetitive behavior characteristic of the obsessive—compulsive neurotic.

**ceremonial, defensive** An elaborate sequence of behavior devised unconsciously as a defense against anxiety and compulsively executed whenever anxiety threatens.

**certification of psychologists** A statement by an official body that a person has met the required standards and therefore may represent himself as a psychologist.

**cervical** Pertaining to constricted portion or neck.

**CGS system** The generally accepted system of scientific measurement using centimeters, grams and seconds.

**Chaddock reflex** 1. Extension of the big toe on stimulation of the external malleolus, seen in pyramidal tract lesions. 2. Flexion of the wrist and fanning of the fingers caused by irritation of the ulna in hemiplegia.

**chaeraphrosyne** An obsolete term for a state of cheerfulness.

**chaeromania, chairomania** See *cheromania*.

**chain reflex of behavior** A set sequence of behaviors in which the completion of one response is the cue (stimulus) for the next.

**chain schedule** See *reinforcement, schedule of: chained*.

**chained reinforcement** A schedule of reinforcement in which responding to a particular stimulus in one schedule is reinforced by a different stimulus usually under a new schedule, the new schedule being the one in which primary reinforcement takes place.

**chained responses** See *responses, chained*.

**chained (chain) schedule** See *reinforcement, schedule of: chained*.

**chaining, accidental** A process in which a response which frequently precedes a reinforced response shares in the effect of the reinforcement in such a way that the whole sequence becomes a stable part of the organism's behavior. A form of superstitious behavior.

**chance** 1. The probability of an event occurring without any cause. 2. An event is conceived of as being caused by any number of individually unknown factors which combine to give a stable quantititative value. 3. The extent to which an event within a system is caused by factors not in that system.

**chance difference** A difference between two measures which cannot be attributed to a constant error or bias, nor to a true difference but is rather due to random influences.

**chance error** See *error, chance*.

**chance halves correlation** See *correlation, split half*.

**chance variation** Change in the inherited characteristics of an organism due to unknown causes.

**change agent** A term which grew out of the National Training Laboratory experiences with T-groups (T for training) and sensitivity training and which refers to the professional (usually a psychologist) who serves as a leader of the group. The leader conducts group sessions in such a way as to bring about changes in attitudes and behavior of the members of the group that can be brought back to their organizations and have an impact on them.

**change of life** Menopause.

**changing, compulsive** The compulsive need of an individual to continuously change either himself or his environment.

**chaped disk** See *papilledema*.

**character** 1. A consistent and enduring aspect of an individual's personality. 2. The integration of individual traits into a unified whole; personality.

**character, anal** A person with permanent and consistent patterns of overt and covert behavior reflecting issues that were important during the period of learning to control bowel movements. There is a fixation at the anal level due to the child's being unable to reconcile the wish for anal pleasure and the demands of society. The conflict might be resolved by the child's finding pleasure either in anal expulsion which results in such traits as extreme generosity, conceit, suspicion and ambition or in anal retention, resulting in such traits as obstinancy and defiance, parsimony and/or avarice, orderliness and compulsive behavior.

**character analysis** 1. Treatment of a character disorder with psychoanalysis. 2. (W. Reich) Psychoanalytic technique with primary emphasis on the interpretation of the patient's character expressed through his total behavior pattern, and character resistances as revealed in the analytic situation rather than on unconscious material. Unconscious material is interpreted only upon the successful interpretation of the patient's character resistances, an approach which enabled the psychoanalytic treatment of patients who had before been unamenable to psychoanalytic treatment.

**character armor** (W. Reich) An individual's pattern of defenses which are largely ego-syntonic and allow that individual to maintain a certain role in interpersonal relationships; a personality structure as a generalized defense against anxiety.

**character, compliant** (K. Horney) A person who is only submissive and self-effacing and who tends to move toward people.

**character defense** A defense against anxiety which is blended into the personality.

**character disorders** A group of disorders characterized by life-long patterns of deeply ingrained maladaptive behavior.

**character, exploitative** (E. Fromm) An individual who attempts to fulfill his wishes by exploiting others either by force or cunning.

**character formation** The processes leading to character formation; personality development.

**character, genital** (psychoanalysis) The adult stage of psychosexual development characterized by the fusion of pregenital impulses of the oral and anal nature and the primacy of genital eroticism in interpersonal relationships.

**character, hysterical** An individual having a character disorder characterized by excitability, emotional instability, overreaction, dramatization, self-centeredness, and overdependence on others.

**character, membership** 1. (Gestalt) The quality of an element in a whole which is a function of its being a part of the totality. 2. (Gestalt) The concept that the whole is influenced by a change in its elements and that the elements are affected by alterations of the whole.

**character neurosis** 1. Neurotic symptoms which have become accepted by the ego and blended into the personality. 2. (B. B. Wolman) The second level in neurotic deterioration according to the sociogenic classification of mental disorders. Character neurotics seem to have incorporated their neurotic symptoms in their personality structure; the character neuroses are divided into the hyperinstrumental type which corresponds to the sociopathic or psychopathic personality; the dysmutual type, the cyclothymic and passive-aggressive personality; and the hypervectorial type, tne schizoid and compulsive personality.

**character, oral** An individual with permanent and consistent patterns of functioning which reflect fixation on the oral stage as a result of abundant or more frequently, insufficient oral satisfaction. In the former case, the individual develops optimistic but overdependent attitudes; in the latter, depressive and aggressive tendencies may develop. In both cases, narcissistic supplies are demanded from without. The individuals are self-centered and characterized as selfish or "takers." They may be compulsive eaters, drinkers, smokers or talkers.

**character, paranoid** An individual characterized by hypersensitivity, rigidity, unwarranted suspicion, jealousy, envy, feelings of self-importance, and a tendency to blame others and ascribe or project evil motives to them.

**character, receptive** (E. Fromm) Personality type characterized by passivity in social relations, a strong need for support from others, and a dependence on things given to him.

**character structure** The integration of character traits into a unified character or personality.

**character traits** 1. Those aspects of an individual's behavior which are consistent, persistent and stable. 2. (G. W. Allport) Personality trait.

**character, urethral** (psychoanalysis) An individual with permanent and consistent patterns of overt and covert behavior reflecting issues that were most important during the period of learning to control urination. The urethral personality types have usually been punished for enuresis by being put to shame. The bed-wetter would like to hide his deed and to avoid shame; hence the "burning ambition" not to be shamed again and a feeling of envy toward anyone who has not been humiliated. He, however, usually lacks persistence.

**characteristic, acquired** 1. A change in the structure of an organism as a result of the influence of the environment or because of the organism's own activities. 2. A behavioral modification that is learned. See *Lamarck's theory.*

**characterology** A rarely used term for the branch of psychology dealing with character and personality.

**Charcot, Jean Martin (1825-1893)** French neurologist; professor of pathological anatomy, Paris (1860). Appointed to Salpêtriére (1862) where he established a neurological clinic which gained world-wide renown and attracted many students, among them Freud and Janet. Known for his study of hysteria and use of hypnotism.

**Charpentier's bands** Alternating black and white bands seen when a black disk with a white sector is slowly rotated. More rapid rotation causes pastel hues (Fechner's colors) to be seen.

**Charpentier's law** A law of visual perception which states that the product of the area of the image on the fovea and the intensity of light is constant for threshold stimuli.

**chart** A systematic arrangement of data in graphic form.

**chasmus, hystericus** Persistent yawning.

**Checklist, Frostig Sensory-Motor and Movement Skills** A list of various behaviors categorized within seven broad areas of sensory-motor and movement skills including coordination, agility, strength, flexibility, speed, balance and endurance, which was developed primarily as an aid for classroom teachers, school psychologists, and other professional school personnel in the observation and evaluation of selected aspects of the child's motor development. The instrument is not standardized and does not include developmental norms.

**cheimophobia** Fear of cold.

**Chein, Isidor (1912-    )** American psychologist. Contributed to systematic philosophicopsychological theory through analyses of such concepts as attitude, behavior, consciousness and its negations, ego, freedom, heredity, intelligence, mind, morale, motivation, personality, power, prediction, psychological structures, self, typology. Also contributed to the development of the concepts, methodology, and substantive research in the field of *action research,* particularly in the areas of delinquency, drug abuse, intergroup relations, and psychological implications of minority-group membership.

**cheiromancy** See *chiromancy.*

**chemical sense** A sense which is affected only by chemical substances.

**chemoreceptors** Nerve structures which are stimulated by various chemical agents which are produced in or enter into the organism.

**chemotaxis** An involuntary movement of an organism involving change of position toward or away from chemical substances.

**chemotherapy** The employment of chemical substances to effect therapeutic ends, i.e. to cure pathology.

**chemotropism** An involuntary movement of an organism or cells involving change of orientation or growth toward or away from chemical substances.

**cheromania** An obsolete term for the manic phase of manic depressive psychosis.

**cherophobia** Fear of or aversion to gaiety or happiness.

**chess-board illusion** An optical illusion in which a circular black and white check pattern appears to have depth, and the checks seem progressively larger toward the circumference.

**Cheyne-Stokes psychosis** A psychosis characterized by anxiety, restlessness, and Cheyne-Stokes respiration.

**Cheyne-Stokes respiration** Breathing which shows a rapidly diminishing rate followed by a rapidly increasing rate found in premature babies and disorders such as cerebral arteriosclerosis, senility and heart disease.

**Chi** The Greek letter X sometimes used in statistical formulas.

**chiaroscuro response** Any Rorschach response which is determined by the distribution of light and shading in the inkblot. Most approaches to the Rorschach recommend subdividing chiaroscuro responses into three categories depending on whether the light-dark component suggest dimensionality, texture or shading. See *texture; shading; vista responses.*

**chiasma** The place where the optic nerves from each eye unite and then separate.

**chiasms** (R. B. Cattell) Choice points in dynamic adjustment, sometimes called 'dynamic crossroads,' where emotional expression is changed.

**child-centered** 1. Refers to a school or institution in which the primary goal is fulfillment of the child's present needs rather than preparation for adulthood. 2. Refers to families where the child's needs are dominant.

**child development** The study of the child from the developmental point of view.

**child guidance** Methods used in the treatment of behavioral and educational problems in children usually in schools and clinics; generally prophylactic.

**child guidance movement** A movement to establish mental health facilities for children, whose inception was in 1909 with the founding of the Juvenile Psychopathic Institute in Chicago. This center offered performance and intelligence tests in addition to physical examinations while the early clinics were established to treat delinquents; they gradually broadened their treatment orientation to include other behavioral problems. In this milieu, the clinic team emerged consisting of the psychiatrist, clinical psychologist and the psychiatric social worker.

**child-parent fixation** (psychoanalysis) A child's emotional attachment of love, hate, or both toward one of his parents which is so firm as to interfere with his forming other relationships.

**child, problem** A child whose behavior deviates so widely from acceptable social norms that special methods are required for dealing with him.

**child psychiatry** The branch of psychiatry dealing with children.

**child psychology** The branch of psychology dealing with children.

**childhood schizophrenia** See *schizophrenia, childhood.*

**Children's Apperception Test (CAT)** See *test, Children's Apperception.*

**chiromancy** Palmistry.

**chiromania** An obsolete term and concept for the relationship between masturbation and psychiatric disturbance; a morbid impulse to masturbate.

**Chi-Square** $(x^2)$ A formula which determines whether an obtained distribution differs significantly from the expected distribution to such an extent that it would be attributable to the operation of non-chance factors. The formula is:

$$x^2 = \Sigma \frac{(f_o\text{-}f_e)^2}{f_e}$$

Where $x^2$ refers to Chi-Square, $f_o$ is the observed frequency, $f_e$ is the expected frequency, and $\Sigma$ means to take the sum of the values represented by the Chi-Square formula.

**Chi-Square test of goodness of fit** A comparison of an observed distribution with the expected or theoretical distribution of a given population to determine whether or not the two are in reasonable agreement.

**chlorpromazine** A tranquilizing drug. Its commercial name is thorazine.

**choc** An uncoordinated response elicited by a surprise sudden stimulus.

**choc fortuit** (A. Binet) An accidental mental shock usually of sexual nature.

**choice point** The point in a maze or other discrimination apparatus from which it is possible to proceed in more than one direction or make more than one response.

**choice reaction** A type of reaction experiment in which the subject must respond differently in different situations.

**choice reaction time** See *reaction time, choice.*

**choleric type** See *type, choleric.*

**cholinergic** Pertaining to the chemical activity characteristic of acetylcholine or to nerve fibers which release acetylcholine to activate effectors.

**cholinesterase** An enzyme found in blood and in various other tissues which breaks down acetylcholine. By preventing the buildup of acetylcholine at nerve endings it plays an important role in the transmission of nervous impulses.

**cholinesterase, modification by behavior** The alteration of the activity of cholinesterase by environmental stimulation.

**chorda tympani** A branch of the seventh or facial nerve carrying nerve impulses from the taste receptors.

**chorea** A neurological disorder characterized by irregular involuntary movements or spasms of the muscles of the extremities and the face.

**chorea abasia** See *abasia.*

**chorea, epidemic** See *choreomania.*

**chorea, Huntington's** (G. Huntington) Chronic progressive hereditary chorea characterized by loss of coordination, disturbance of speech and mental deterioration.

**chorea rotatoria** Chorea characterized by rotation or oscillation of the head, trunk, or limbs.

**chorea saltatoria** Chorea characterized by involuntary jumping.

**chorea, Syndenham's** The syndrome of chorea following an infection.

**chorea, Syndenham's acute** An actue toxic disorder of the central nervous system secondary to certain infections causing chorea; Saint Vitus' Dance.

**choreiform** Resembling chorea.

**choreoathetosis** Combination of chorea and athetosis. Irregular and involuntary movements of facial and limbic muscles (chorea).

**choreoid** Resembling chorea.

**choreomania** Dancing mania; epidemic of convulsive dancing which occurred in Europe in the fourteenth century, in the wake of the Black Death.

**choroid** 1. Membranous. 2. Choroid coat.

**choroid coat** Vascular layer of the eye that is continuous with the iris and lies between the sclera and the retina.

**choroiditis** Inflammation of the choroid coat.

**chrematophobia** Morbid fear of money.

**chroma** In the Munsell color system the dimension that corresponds most closely to saturation.

**chroma-brightness or brilliance coefficient** The ratio of hue to brightness (brilliance), which varies from a minumum in the yellow to a maximum in the violet.

**chromaesthesia** See *chromesthesia.*

**chromatic** 1. Pertaining to hue. 2. Pertaining to chroma. 3. Pertaining to the chromatic scale.

**chromatic aberration** Error in optical system resulting from unequal refraction of different parts of the spectrum causing indistinct images surrounded by a halo of colors.

**chromatic color** A color possessing hue and saturation.

**chromatic contrast; color contrast** Increased differences in hue between two colors presented simultaneously or in close succession.

**chromatic dimming** Decrease in saturation when light intensity is suddenly decreased after a period of fixation, due to successive contrast.

**chromatic flicker** See *flicker, chromatic.*

**chromatic scale** See *scale, chromatic.*

**chromatic valence** The power of a color stimulus to produce hue in a mixture.

**chromaticity** The quality of a color stimulus determined by its dominant wavelength and its purity.

**chromaticness** The psychological correlate of chromaticity determined by a color stimulus' hue and saturation.

**chromatics** 1. The science of color. 2. The chromatic scale.

**chromatid** A chromosome at prophase and metaphase can be seen to consist of two strands held together by the centromere. Each strand is a chromatid.

**chromatin** The easily stainable protoplasmic substance in the nuclei of cells.

**chromatin negative** Lacking sex chromatin or a Barr body. Normal males are chromatin negative.

**chromatin positive** Possessing sex chromatin or a Barr body, which represents a single X chromosome which is inactive in the metabolism of the cell. Normal females are chromatin positive.

**chromatism** See *photism.*

**chromatophobia** See *chromophobia.*

**chromatopseudopsia** Color blindness.

**chromatopsia** Seeing objects as abnormally colored under unusual conditions such as snow blindness.

**chromatotropism** An orienting response (tropism) toward certain hues or colors.

**chromesthesia; chromaesthesia** A form of synesthesia involving the seeing of colors upon hearing certain words, letters or sounds.

**chromidrosis** A rare condition in which perspiration is colored.

**chromophobia** 1. Fear of colors. 2. Excessive dislike of certain colors.

**chromosomal aberration, chromosomal defect** Non-fatal changes in the structure and number of chromosomes.

**chromosome** Chromosomes are the chromatin strands in the nuclei of somatic and sex cells along which the genes are arranged in linear order. They are composed of DNA on a framework of protein and are the carriers of genetic information. They are visible in a dividing cell as deeply staining rod-shaped or J-shaped structures.

**chromosomes, sex, anomalies of** Sex chromosomes in which there are different constitutions other than the normal XY in the male and the XX in the female. See *Klinefelter's Syndrome; Turner's Syndrome; Triplo-X Syndrome.*

**chronaxia; chronoxic; chronaxy** The excitability of tissues measured in units of time needed for the passage of electric current of voltage twice as intense as the threshold of voltage.

**chronic constipation, psychogenic** See *constipation, chronic, psychogenic.*

**chronic diarrhea** See *diarrhea, chronic.*

**chronic electrode** An electrode for according or stimulating central nervous system tissues implanted through a small hole made in the skull and fixed on the skull permanent.

**chronic mania**  See *mania, chronic.*

**chronological age**  The cumulative age of the individual from birth; calendar age.

**chronological complex**  See *complex, chronological.*

**chronological system**  See *complex, chronological.*

**chronophobia**  Fear of time.

**chronoscope**  An instrument used for the measurement of short intervals of time.

**cibophobia**  Morbid fear of food.

**cineplasty**  A restorative operation performed on a disabled hand which utilizes the remaining muscles in the amputated stump to attach them with ivory pegs through a yoke to an artificial hand.

**cingulectomy**  A form of psychosurgery; surgical removal of the cingulate gyrus.

**circadian rhythms**  Cyclic biological changes that occur within an organism.

**circular conditioned response**  See *circular reflex.*

**circular psychosis**  See *psychosis, manic-depressive.*

**circular reaction**  A behavioral pattern in which the reaction to a stimulus evokes repetition.

**circular reflex**  Special case of response chaining in which the response produces stimuli which themselves increase or prolong that reponse.

**circumstantial (or indirect) validity**  Obtaining the validity of a test X against a criterion Y by evaluating the similarity of X's correlations with variables A, B, C, D, etc., to those of Y with the same variables.

**cistron**  The smallest unit of genetic material that must remain intact to direct the synthesis of a specific polypeptide.

**citrullinemia**  A rare aminoaciduria associated with mental retardation.

**civesticism**  Dressing in inappropriate garments, e.g., an adult who dresses as if he were a little child.

**clairaudience**  Hypothesized ability to hear without using one's ears or any known sensory mediation.

**clairvoyance**  1. A hypothetical ability to see without using the eyes or any sensory mediation. 2. Any sort of perception or knowledge of past, present, or future without known sensory mediation.

**clang association**  Association of words based on their sound.

**Claparède, Edouard (1873-1940)**  Swiss psychologist; functionalist. Established the *International Association of Applied Psychology* and organized its first international congress (1920); founded (with cousin, Théodore Flournoy) *Archives de Psychologie* (1901); studied psychological phenomena in terms of their usefulness in meeting individual's needs and interests; promoted animal psychology and child psychology; advocated improvement of teacher training; established the Rousseau Institute, famed for research in child psychology and development of progressive methods of teaching.

**class interval**  See *interval, class.*

**class, social**  A group of people who have similar level of income, or education, or vocation or inherited status. For instance a society can be divided (on the basis of economic criterion) into high, middle, and low income level classes; on the basis of inherited status in aristocratic class and commoners.

**class theory**  A theory that describes objects or concepts on the basis of their belonging to a certain class.

**classes, informational**  (J. P. Guilford) Conceptions underlying sets of items of information grouped by virtue of their common properties.

**classical conditioning**  See *conditioning, Pavlovian.*

**Classification of Mental Disorders**  Based on the Diagnostic and Statistical Manual of Mental Disorders of the American Psychiatric Association DSM-II, 1968. List of Mental Disorders with Their Code Numbers.

**I. Mental Retardation**
Mental retardation (310-315)
310 Borderline mental retardation
311 Mild mental retardation
312 Moderate mental retardation
313 Severe mental retardation
314 Profound mental retardation
315 Unspecified mental retardation
   .0 Following infection or intoxication
   .1 Following trauma or physical agent
   .2 With disorders of metabolism, growth or nutrition
   .3 Associated with gross brain disease (postnatal)
   .4 Associated with diseases and conditions due to (unknown) prenatal influence
   .5 With chromosomal abnormality
   .6 Associated with prematurity
   .7 Following major psychiatric disorder
   .8 With psycho-social (environmental) deprivation
   .9 With other (and unspecified) condition

**II. Organic Brain Syndromes**
(Disorders Caused by or Associated with Impairment of Brain Tissue Function) In the categories under IIA and IIB the associated physical condition should be specified when known.

**II—A. Psychoses Associated with Organic Brain Syndromes (290-294)**
290 Senile and pre-senile dementia
   .0 Senile dementia
   .1 Pre-senile dementia
291 Alcoholic psychosis
   .0 Delirium tremens
   .1 Korsakov's psychosis (alcoholic)
   .2 Other alcoholic hallucinosis
   .3 Alcohol paranoid state ((Alcoholic paranoia))

.4 Acute alcohol intoxication
.5 Alcoholic deterioration
.6 Pathological intoxication
.9 Other (and unspecified) alcoholic psychosis
292 Psychosis associated with intracranial infection
.0 Psychosis with general paralysis
.1 Psychosis with other syphilis of central nervous system
.2 Psychosis with epidemic encephalitis
.3 Psychosis with other and unspecified encephalitis
.9 Psychosis with other (and unspecified) intracranial infection
293 Psychosis associated with other cerebral condition
.0 Psychosis with cerebral arteriosclerosis
.1 Psychosis with other cerebrovascular disturbance
.2 Psychosis with epilepsy
.3 Psychosis with intracranial neoplasm
.4 Psychosis with degenerative disease of the central nervous system
.5 Psychosis with brain trauma
.9 Psychosis with other (and unspecified) cerebral condition
294 Psychosis associated with other physical condition
.0 Psychosis with endocrine disorder
.1 Psychosis with metabolic or nutritional disorder
.2 Psychosis with systemic infection
.3 Psychosis with drug or poison intoxication (other than alcohol)
.4 Psychosis with childbirth
.8 Psychosis with other and undiagnosed physical condition
(.9 Psychosis with unspecified physical condition)

## II–B. Non-Psychotic Organic Brain Syndromes (309)

309 Non-psychotic organic brain syndromes ((Mental disorders not specified as psychotic associated with physical conditions))
.0 Non-psychotic OBS with intracranial infection
(.1 Non-psychotic OBS with drug, poison, or systemic intoxication)
.13 Non-psychotic OBS with alcohol (simple drunkenness)
.14 Non-psychotic OBS with other drug, poison, or systemic intoxication
.2 Non-psychotic OBS with brain trauma
.3 Non-psychotic OBS with circulatory disturbance
.4 Non-psychotic OBS with epilepsy
.5 Non-psychotic OBS with disturbance of metabolism, growth or nutrition
.6 Non-psychotic OBS with senile or pre-senile brain disease
.7 Non-psychotic OBS with intracranial neoplasm
.8 Non-psychotic OBS with degenerative disease of central nervous system
.9 Non-psychotic OBS with other (and unspecified) physical condition
(.91 Acute brain syndrome, not otherwise specified)
(.92 Chronic brain syndrome, not otherwise specified)

## III. Psychoses not Attributed to Physical Conditions Listed Previously (295-298)

295. Schizophrenia
.0 Schizophrenia, simple type
.1 Schizophrenia, hebephrenic type
.2 Schizophrenia, catatonic type
.23 Schizophrenia, catatonic type, excited
.24 Schizophrenia, catatonic type, withdrawn
.3 Schizophrenia, paranoid type
.4 Acute schizophrenic episode
.5 Schizophrenia, latent type
.6 Schizophrenia, residual type
.7 Schizophrenia, schizo-affective type
.73 Schizophrenia, schizo-affective type, excited
.74 Schizophrenia, schizo-affective type, depressed
.8 Schizophrenia, childhood type
.90 Schizophrenia, chronic and undifferentiated type
.99 Schizophrenia, other (and unspecified) types
296 Major affective disorders ((Affective psychoses))
.0 Involutional melancholia
.1 Manic-depressive illness, manic type ((Manic-depressive psychosis, manic type))
.2 Manic-depressive illness, circular type ((Manic-depressive psychosis, circular type))
.33 Manic-depressive illness, circular type, manic
.34 Manic-depressive illness, circular type, depressed
.8 Other major affective disorder ((Affective psychoses, other))
(.9 Unspecified major affective disorder)
(Affective disorder not otherwise specified)
(Manic-depressive illness not otherwise

297 Paranoid states
.0 Paranoia
.1 Involutional paranoid state ((Involutional paraphrenia))
.9 Other paranoid state
298 Other psychoses
.0 Psychotic depressive reaction ((Reactive depressive psychosis))
(.1 Reactive excitation)
(.2 Reactive confusion)
(Acute or subacute confusional state)
(.3 Acute paranoid reaction)
(.9 Reactive psychosis, unspecified)
(299 Unspecified psychosis)
(Dementia, insanity or psychosis not otherwise specified)

## IV. Neuroses (300)

300 Neuroses
.0 Anxiety neurosis
.1 Hysterical neurosis
.13 Hysterical neurosis, conversion type
.14 Hysterical neurosis, dissociative type
.2 Phobic neurosis
.3 Obsessive compulsive neurosis
.4 Depressive neurosis
.5 Neurasthenic neurosis ((Neurasthenia))
.6 Depersonalization neurosis ((Depersonalization syndrome))
.7 Hypochondriacal neurosis

.8 Other neurosis
(.9 Unspecified neurosis)

## V. Personality Disorders and Certain Other Non-Psychotic Mental Disorders (301-304)

301 Personality disorders
.0 Paranoid personality
.1 Cyclothymic personality ((Affective personality))
.2 Schizoid personality
.3 Explosive personality
.4 Obsessive compulsive personality ((Anankastic personality))
.5 Hysterical personality
.6 Asthenic personality
.7 Antisocial personality
.81 Passive-aggressive personality
.82 Inadequate personality
.89 Other personality disorders of specified types
(.9 Unspecified personality disorder)
302 Sexual deviations
.0 Homosexuality
.1 Fetishism
.2 Pedophilia
.3 Transvestitism
.4 Exhibitionism
.5 Voyeurism
.6 Sadism
.7 Masochism
.8 Other sexual deviation
(.9 Unspecified sexual deviation)
303 Alcoholism
.0 Episodic excessive drinking
.1 Habitual excessive drinking
.2 Alcohol addiction
.9 Other (and unspecified) alcoholism
304 Drug dependence
.0 Drug dependence, opium, opium alkaloids and their derivatives
.1 Drug dependence, synthetic analgesics with morphine-like effects
.2 Drug dependence, barbiturates
.3 Drug dependence, other hypnotics and sedatives or "tranquilizers"
.4 Drug dependence, cocaine
.5 Drug dependence, cannabis sativa (hashish, marihuana)
.6 Drug dependence, other psycho-stimulants
.7 Drug dependence, hallucinogens
.8 Other drug dependence
(.9 Unspecified drug dependence)

## VI. Psychophysiologic Disorders (305)

305 Psychophysiologic disorders ((Physical disorders of presumably psychogenic origin))
.0 Psychophysiologic skin disorder
.1 Psychophysiologic musculoskeletal disorder
.2 Psychophysiologic respiratory disorder
.3 Psychophysiologic cardiovascular disorder
.4 Psychophysiologic hemic and lymphatic disorder
.5 Psychophysiologic gastro-intestinal disorder
.6 Psychophysiologic genito-urinary disorder
.7 Psychophysiologic endocrine disorder
.8 Psychophysiologic disorder of organ of special sense
.9 Psychophysiologic disorder of other type

## VII. Special Symptoms (306)

306 Special symptoms not elsewhere classified
.0 Speech disturbance
.1 Specific learning disturbance
.2 Tic
.3 Other psychomotor disorder
.4 Disorders of sleep
.5 Feeding disturbance
.6 Enuresis
.7 Encopresis
.8 Cephalalgia
.9 Other special symptoms

## VIII. Transient Situational Disturbances (307)

307 Transient situational disturbances
.0 Adjustment reaction of infancy
.1 Adjustment reaction of childhood
.2 Adjustment reaction of adolescence
.3 Adjustment reaction of adult life
.4 Adjustment reaction of late life

## IX. Behavior Disorders of Childhood and Adolescence (308)

308 Behavior disorders of childhood and adolescence ((Behavior disorders of childhood))
.0 Hyperkinetic reaction of childhood (or adolescence)
.1 Withdrawing reaction of childhood (or adolescence)
.2 Overanxious reaction of childhood (or adolescence)
.3 Runaway reaction of childhood (or adolescence)
.4 Unsocialized aggressive reaction of childhood (or adolescence)
.5 Group delinquent reaction of childhood (or adolescence)
.9 Other reaction of childhood (or adolescence)

## X. Conditions Without Manifest Psychiatric Disorder and Non-Specific Conditions (316-318)

316 Social maladjustments without manifest psychiatric disorder
.0 Marital maladjustment
.1 Social maladjustment
.2 Occupational maladjustment
.3 Dyssocial behavior
.9 Other social maladjustment
317 Non-specific conditions
318 No mental disorder

## XI. Non—Diagnostic Terms for Administrative Use (319)

319 Non-diagnostic terms for adminstrative use
.0 Diagnosis deferred
.1 Boarder
.2 Experiment only
.9 Other

**claustrophilia**  A morbid desire to be confined in a small space.

**claustrophobia**  A morbid fear of being confined in a small space.

**clavus**  Severe headache.

**cleft palate**  Congenital effect which results in a fissure of the palate. Its immediate cause is the failure of complete development, by eight to ten weeks, of one or more of the five embryonic processes of the fetus' face. Some children have hearing problems and often have speech problems, and there is, though infrequently, a mild degree of mental impairment and socioemotional deficits.

**clerical test** See *test, clerical.*

**client** (non-directive psychotherapy) A person who receives counseling or non-directive psychotherapy.

**client-centered psychotherapy** See *psychotherapy, client centered.*

**climacophobia** Morbid fear of stairs.

**climacteric psychosis** See *psychosis, involutional.*

**climacterium** 1. A critical period in life. 2. Menopause.

**clinic** An outpatient establishment for the diagnosis and treatment of illness. A mental health clinic deals with mental disorders. Most often mental hospitals operate clinics, but some clinics are operated by groups of psychiatrists, clinical psychologists, and psychiatric social workers.

**clinical method** A variety of research and diagnostic techniques such as interviews, life histories, testing, projective techniques, and case observation.

**clinical psychology** See *psychology, clinical.*

**clinical psychology, legal status** See *certification of psychologists.*

**clinical practice** Treatment of physical diseases and mental (behavioral) disorders.

**clinician** An individual qualified to practice treatment of physical diseases and mental behavior disorders.

**clitoromania** Nymphomania.

**clock** (operant conditioning) A stimulus, some dimension of which changes systematically with time.

**clone** A group of organisms of a common, non-sexual origin, such as, e.g. splitting in protozoa.

**clonic** Relating to clonus.

**clonus** Movement characterized by involuntary alternating rapid muscle contraction and relaxation.

**closure** (Gestalt psychology) The theory of electric circuit has been used by gestalt psychology in their study of brain mechanism. The brain activity follows the principle of equilibrium, and when there is a gap in the current, tensions on both sides of the gap and the electric current closes the gap. Hence the principle of closure which applies to the perception. When a figure is drawn with incomplete lines, the perceive completes it (closes) in his mind and perceives it as complete.

**clouding of consciousness** An impairment of perception and orientation associated with brain disorders.

**cluster analysis** (statistics) A technique for determining the presence of clusters by inspection of a matrix, or correlation table.

**cluster correlation** See *correlation, cluster.*

**Clytemnestra complex** See *complex, Clytemnestra.*

**CNS** Central nervous system.

**coacting group** (social psychology) A group of people cooperating with one another with little if any interaction with one another.

**coaxing-hypnosis** See *mother hypnosis.*

**cocaine** An anaesthetic which is also a mild stimulant.

**cocaine bug** See *bug, cocaine.*

**cochlea** A part of the inner ear which includes the hearing organ.

**cochlear-palpebrol reflex** Tightening or closing of eyelids in response to an auditory stimulus.

**code capacity** (information theory) The maximum of information that can be sent through a code channel.

**code of ethics, ethical code for psychologists** A set of standards for psychologists compiled from real problem situations which psychologists deemed to be of ethical importance. This code, developed by the American Psychological Association, differs from earlier codes which were based on existing codes of other professions in deriving its content from empirical situations relevant to psychologists.

**code test** See *test, code.*

**codeine** A depressant derived from morphine.

**coding** 1. (statistics) The process of transforming a set of scores into a more convenient set. 2. The transformation of messages into signals in an information theory.

**coding key** A list of the classes of data and their respective symbols assigned to each.

**codon** A triplet of three bases in a DNA or RNA which codes for a specific amino acid.

**coefficient** 1. (mathematics) A value by which other values are multiplied. 2. (statistics) A value stating the degree to which a characteristic occurs in specific instances.

**coefficient, agreement** Also called coefficient of agreement. 1. A measure to determine the degree of agreement between a specific item and the rest of the scale. The formula used is as follows:

$$CAg = \frac{a_1 + a_2 + a_3 \ldots + a_n}{N}$$

$CAg$ is the coefficient of agreement, $a_1$ is the total number of responses for subject one that agree with his responses to the item in question, $a_2$ is the same calculation for the second subject and so on, and $N$ is the total number of responses. 2. A measure to determine the amount of agreement among rankings or ratings. The formula that is used is as follows:

$$CA = 100 \left[ \frac{\frac{1 - \Sigma T - \Sigma B}{N}}{2(H - L)} \right]$$

*CA* is the coefficient of agreement, *T* is the top 50% of the rankings, *B* is the bottom 50% of the rankings, *H − L* is the range between the highest and the lowest rank, and *N* is the number of cases.

**coefficient, alienation**  The measure of the degree of absence of a relationship or correlation between two variables. The coefficient is found by using the following formula:

$$k = \sqrt{1 - r^2}$$

where *k* is the alienation coefficient and *r* is the product moment correlation for the two variables in question. See *product moment correlation coefficient*.

**coefficient, association**  A measure of the correlation between dichotomous variables such as male-female.

**coefficient, consistency**  See *coefficient of internal consistency*.

**coefficient, contingency (C)**  A measure of the association of two different sets of data which determines the degree to which the variables are independent of each other and to what extent this can be attributed to chance. The mean square contingency coefficient, the most commonly used measure, is given by the formula; $C = \sqrt{\frac{X^2}{N + X^2}}$

Where *N* = the number of cases and $X^2$ is the symbol for Chi square.

**coefficient, correlation**  See *correlation coefficient*.

**coefficient, dispersion**  An index of variability; it is the ratio of any measure of dispersion over the mean and multiplied by 100. It allows for comparison between scores with unequal means.

**coefficient, j**  (E. S. Primoff) An estimate of the predictive value of each of the subtests of a battery.

**coefficient, multiple determination ($R^2$)**  The degree to which the correlation of two variables in a multiple correlation can be accounted for by the influence of other variables.

**coefficient, nondetermination**  The amount of variance in the dependent variable which is not accounted for by the independent variable.

**coefficient of equivalence, Kuder-Richardson**  Any of several formulas which are variations on the chance-halves correlation, used for the estimation of correlation between comparable forms of a test on the basis of one administration. Also called K-R formulas.

**coefficient of intelligence**  See *intelligence, coefficient of*.

**coefficient of internal consistency**  See *internal consistency, coefficient of*.

**coefficient, path choice**  (R. B. Cattell) Factor analytic technique which measures one person on one set of variables on different occasions.

**coefficient, reliability**  Any measure of reliability which involves the use of correlation coefficients.

**coefficient stability ($r_{st}$)**  The correlation between two applications of a test with a sufficiently large interval between them to reduce the differential effects of practice.

**coefficient, variability**  See *coefficient, variation*.

**coefficient, variation**  (statistics) A measure of relative variability in a frequency distribution given by the formula: $V = \frac{100 \; \sigma}{M}$ where V stands for variability, $\sigma$ is the standard deviation, *M* is the mean of the distribution.

**coelom (celom)**  The embryonic body cavity formed in the lateral mesoderm during the tridermic stage of embryological development.

**coenotype**  See *cenotype*.

**cognition**  1. A general term for any process which allows an organism to know and be aware. It includes perceiving, reasoning, conceiving, judging. 2. A postulated stimulus-stimulus association or perceptual organization thought to account for expectancies of an organism.

**cognition, operation of**  (J. P. Guilford) Immediate discovery, awareness, rediscovery, or recognition of particular items of information; understanding or comprehension.

**cognitive**  Of or related to thoughts and ideas.

**cognitive-awareness level**  (G. A. Kelly) The extent to which a construct used in diagnosis and psychotherapy is useful, effective and noncontradictory.

**cognitive consistency**  The notion that a person's cognitions (beliefs, perceived behaviors, etc.) will tend to be logically and psychologically consistent with one another. If inconsistencies are present, the individual attempts to reduce them by changing his cognitions, behavior, or both so that they are consistent with each other.

**cognitive dissonance**  (L. Festinger) A motivational state which exists when an individual's cognitive elements (attitudes, perceived behaviors, etc.) are inconsistent with each other. The tension produced by this state may be reduced by adding consonant elements; changing one of the dissonant elements so that it is no longer inconsistent with the other, or by reducing the importance of the dissonant elements.

**cognitive-dynamic investment strain**  (R. B. Cattell) A concept referring to the difficulty in having to remember and attend to a large number of minutiae, in order to achieve and maintain goal satisfaction.

**cognitive map**  (E. C. Tolman) A perceptual representation of the maze which an organism develops based on environmental cues and the organism's expectancies, which teaches him the location of the goal.

**cognitive reaction time**  See *reaction time, cognitive*.

**cognitive schema  1.** A perceptual pattern of past experience believed to be imprinted in the organism's structure to which past and future experience are referred for interpretation. **2.** (E. C. Tolman) Cognitive map.

**cognitive sign principle**  The postulate that learning consists of the awareness of the relationship of stimuli to responses or goals rather than the learning of a series of responses.

**cognitive structure**  (K. Lewin) The individual's organization of the world into a unified system of beliefs, concepts, attitudes, and expectations.

**cognitive style**  The mode in which a person organizes and classifies his perceptions of the environment in order to impose order upon a confusing series of events.

**cognitive theory of learning**  A theory of learning which postulates the existence of intervening central processes in learning which are cognitive in nature and which states that learning involves new ways of perceiving rather than of incorporating new responses into the behavior repertoire.

**cognizance need**  See *need, cognizance*.

**cohesion**  The attraction that a group holds for its members and which dictates the capacity of the group to resist dissolution. In order for a group to remain attractive to a member, the resultant force operating on that individual must be greater than zero.

**cohesion, law of  1.** The principle in learning that behaviors which are contiguous in time tend to unify into more complex, higher-order actions. **2.** The principle that parts of a gestalt tend to acquire coherence.

**coitus interruptus**  Sexual intercourse voluntarily interrupted by the male.

**cold spot**  Skin or membrane area sensitive to low temperature.

**colitis**  Inflammation of the colon of organic or psychogenic origin.

**colitis, mucous**  Chronic infection of the mucous membrane of the colon which is often seen in patients who have intense demanding personalities and suffer from constipation or diarrhea.

**colitis, spastic**  Colitis associated with spasms of the colon of physical or psychogenic causes. The psychogenic conflict centers around intense oral aggressive and receptive needs.

**colitis, ulcerative**  An inflammation of the colon characterized by ulceration of the mucosa.

**collecting mania**  See *mania, collecting*.

**collective behavior**  See *mind, collective*.

**collective mind**  See *mind, collective*.

**collective psychology**  See *psychology, social*.

**collective unconscious**  See *unconscious, collective*.

**colliculus**  A prominance in the nervous system. specifically one of the four prominances of the corpora quadrigemine in the brain stem.

**colligation**  A combination of units in which the units remain separate from each other rather than losing their identity in the totality.

**colligation coefficient**  (statistics) An approximation of the relationship between two dichotomous variables. It is a function of the square roots of the products of the frequencies in opposite cells in a four fold table.

**colliquation**  A complete breakdown of cells and tissues.

**color adaptation  1.** The decrease of hue and saturation of a color when it is fixated upon for a prolonged period of time. **2.** Raising an individual's absolute threshold of sensitivity to hue.

**color antagonism**  The mixture of colors which results in achromatic gray.

**color aperture**  Color classified as film colors which are seen as spaces in neutral screens.

**color blindness**  Total or partial inability to perceive colors. Total color blindness results in the perception of colors as shades of gray. The most common form of partial color blindness is the inability to differentiate reds and greens.

**color, complementary**  A color, which when mixed with a particular other color produces gray.

**color contrast**  See *contrast, color*.

**color conversion**  (H. Helson) The changes in lightness and/or chromaticity in color due to any change in viewing conditions such as through simultaneous or successive contrast, changes in spectral energy of source of light, adaptation of the eyes, etc. Usually color conversion is restricted to changes occurring according to the principle of color conversion.

**color deficiency**  See *color blindness*.

**color, induced**  A change in the appearance of a color due to the introduction of another color into the immediate area.

**color memory**  See *memory, color*.

**color mixture**  The operation of combining two or more colors to produce an effect of fusion. The techniques used to accomplish this effect include rapid rotation of colors on a color mixer, simultaneous projection of colored lights on a screen and the mixture of pigments.

**color naming**  A Rorschach answer in which the subject merely identifies areas of the inkblots as to their color. The symbol Cn is typically used to denote such an answer although the criteria for its use differs among various Rorschach systems. Klopfer and Rapaport both include Cn scoring whenever such a response occurs while Hertz and Piotrowski score Cn only when it is clear that the subject has given no thought to a meaningful interpretation of the blot. It is generally regarded as a constricted or disorganized type response.

**color, primary** 1. In a loose sense, any of those colors which, in any system, are of special importance for color classification. 2. One of those colors that cannot be broken down into other component colors: red, green, yellow, and blue. 3. One of those pigments that can be mixed to yield, in reduced color saturation, all the hues: white, black, red, yellow, and blue.

**color purity** The extent to which a color is fully saturated.

**color pyramid** A graphic representation of the relationships of achromatic and chromatic colors to each other in the form of a double pyramid. The base of the pyramid is a triangle, square or circle, depending on which colors are considered to be primary. If the base is a triangle, the primaries are red, green, and blue. If it is a square, yellow is added as the fourth color. The assumption underlying the color base is that there is no basic color. The colors of intermediate hues are placed along the borders of the figures. The center of the geometric figures is gray. The radii extending from this point refer to degrees of saturation. The farther from the center a color is, the more saturated it becomes. The vertical axis of the pyramid represents the dimension of brightness with black at the bottom and white at the top. As one moves from the periphery to the center, the colors become less saturated but of equal brightness. Colors of different tints and shades are found on the sides of the figures from the poles to the periphery of the base.

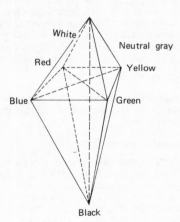

color response (Rorschach) A class of Rorschach responses which includes use of the chromatic features of the blots. It is generally considered to represent affectivity and is weighted in relation to the use of form. Thus, form dominated color responses in

which the form component is secondary or non-existent are considered as lability. Some approaches to the Rorschach, particularly Hertz, Klopfer, and Piotrowski also include special scorings and interpretations for color responses which appear to be "forced" by the subject, or where color is used in an arbitrary manner.

**color shock** An unusual, or startle reaction of Rorschach subjects to the chromatic features of the inkblots. It is manifest in delayed reaction times, sequence alteration, impairment of response quality, and general reduction in response frequency. Most Rorschach authorities have speculated that it is a valid index of neurotic features.

**color sorting test**  See *test, Holmgren.*

**color surface**  The plane surface obtained by cutting through a color pyramid at right angles to the vertical axis of brightness. The surface contains all the possible hues and saturations at that particular level of brightness.

**color temperature**  The temperature of a black body or complete radiator at which it yields a color matching that of a given sample of radiant energy. It is measured on the absolute or Kelvin scale.

**color triangle**  The plane figure forming the base of the color pyramid which shows the relationships between the colors, brightness and saturation.

**color vision, theories of**  1. Theories which attempt to explain how light energy is transformed into visual sensations of different colors. There are three main theories: the Young–Helmholtz, the Hering, and the Ladd-Franklin theory. 2. See *color vision, theory of: Young-Helmholtz theory.* 3. See *color vision, theory of: Hering theory.* 4. See *color vision, theory of: Ladd-Franklin theory.*

**color vision, theory of: Hering theory**  (E. Hering) The perception of color is mediated by three processes in the retina, a black-white, a red-green, and a blue-yellow process. Each member of a pair is differentially stimulated by anabolic building up excitation which produces sensations of black, green and blue and catabolic tearing down stimulation which produces sensations of white, red, and yellow. Mixture of colors is due to the simultaneous stimulation of two halves of non-paired processes. Color blindness results from the absence of one or more of the chromatic processes.

**color vision, theory of: Ladd-Franklin theory** (Ladd-Franklin C.) An evolutionary theory stating that monochromism, total color blindness was the primitive form of perception followed by the evolution of yellow and blue receptors which were succeeded by the development of red and green receptors. The different forms of color blindness result from regressive loss of the use of specific receptors.

**color vision, theory of: Young-Helmholtz theory** (T. Young and H. von Helmholtz) The perception of color is explained by the presence of three types of cones in the retina, red, green and blue. While each cone responds to any wave length, the maximal response occurs to the wave lengths it is most sensitive to. Mixture of colors results from the simultaneous stimulation of two different cones. White results from the simultaneous stimulation of all three cones. Color blindness is due to the partial or total absence of cones.

**color wheel** An apparatus which mixes colors by rapid rotation of a variably colored disk to produce a fusion of the colors.

**color zones** Regions of the retina which respond differentially when stimulated by different colors. Normally, all of the colors can be perceived in the foveal region of the retina. In the middle zone, blues, yellows, and achromatic colors. In the periphery of the retina, all colors are seen as achromatic. The zones are not rigidly separated from each other.

**colorimeter** An instrument used to measure colors by comparing them to a known color mixture.

**Columbia Mental Maturity Scale** See *scale, Columbia Mental Maturity.*

**column** 1. (statistics) A vertical row of values in a statistical table. 2. A bundle of neurons of similar structure and function which extends longitudinally for some distance. It is found in the central nervous system.

**coma** A state of unconsciousness during which most behaviors and reflexes are suspended.

**coma, insulin** Coma induced by a large dose of insulin either accidently or regulated for the purpose of shock therapy.

**coma-vigil** See *agrypnocoma.*

**combat fatigue** See *fatigue, combat.*

**combat neurosis** See *fatigue, combat.*

**combination** (mathematics) A set or group consisting of any number of object items in such a way that no two sets have exactly the same items although an item may occur in more than one set. The ordering of the items is unimportant.

**combination, law of** 1. The principle that two or more stimuli which are presented simultaneously or in close temporal proximity may combine to elicit a response. 2. The principle that two responses which are made simultaneously or in close proximity will occur together upon presentation of the stimulus eliciting either response.

**combination tone** A third tone produced when two tones of similar timbre are sounded simultaneously. There are two kinds of combination tones: summation and difference tones.

**comention** (R. B. Cattell) A personality trait characterized by adherance to cultural prescriptions, obedience to authority and suppression of personal desires.

**cometophobia** Morbid fear of comets.

**commensurable** (mathematics) Referring to two or more variables which can be quantitatively assessed by the same unit of measurement.

**commissural fibers** See *fibers, commissural.*

**common factor** See *factor, group.*

**common factor variance** See *communality.*

**common fate, law of** (Gestalt) The principle that perceived elements which change or move in the same way tend to be apprehended as belonging together.

**common trait** A set of personality characteristics (dimension, trait) which has the same form or pattern of expression for all people and on which, therefore, all people can be given a meaningful numerical value.

**communality** That fraction of the total variance of a test which is due to factors common to all tests subjected to experiment.

**communication** 1. The transmission of energy change from one place to another as in the nervous system or transmission of sound waves. 2. The transmission or reception of signals or messages by organisms. 3. The transmitted message. 4. (Communication theory) The process whereby one system influences another system through regulation of the transmitted signals. 5. (K. Lewin) The influence of one personal region on another whereby a change in one results in a corresponding change in the other region. 6. The message of a patient to his therapist in psychotherapy.

**communication, consummatory** (communication theory) Communication of the sender which expresses his feelings and ideas and which does not require an answer from the receiver.

**communication, mass** The dissemination of information through the mass media.

**communication, mass media of** The instruments of communication which disseminate information to large numbers of people at once such as newspapers, television and radio.

**communication theory** The branch of science which is concerned with communication whether it is physical, mechanical, psychological or social. Models for human communication are developed to parallel machine models.

**communications unit** (communication theory) A unit consisting of a sender, a channel and a receiver. The sender encodes messages to be transmitted via the channel to the receiver which decodes the signals. Parallels are made between machine systems and the human organism.

**community** 1. A group of organisms living in close proximity and having some type of social organization. 2. A group of persons, not in close contact who share a common interest or purpose.

**community catharsis** See *catharsis, community.*

**community-of-content theory** The principle that different complex situations have certain stimuli in common which account for the consistency of responses from situation to situation.

**comparable form**  See *form, comparable.*

**comparative judgment**  See *judgment, comparative.*

**comparative judgment, law of**  See *judgment, comparative, law of.*

**comparative mava method**  A comparison of the estimates of the genetic and environmental variance components across a series of racio-cultural groups (made by the Multiple Abstract Variance Analysis Method) permitting inferences to be made about the environmental influences and genetic structures responsible for the observed variances. Thus, a correlation of variance on an environment feature with the environmental trait variance component permits an estimate of the regression of specific environmental characters upon the environmentally produced part of the trait as such.

**comparative psychology**  See *psychology, comparative.*

**comparison stimulus (Co)**  (psychophysics) Variable stimulus the subject adjusts until, for him, it and the standard stimulus are indistinguishable during a psychophysical experiment.

**compensating error**  See *error, compensating.*

**compensation**  The mechanism of covering up aspects of oneself which are unacceptable and substituting more desired traits in an exaggerated form.

**compensation autonomic**  (E. J. Kempf) A reflexive action to counteract stimuli which produce a fear state in a person. For example, a feeling of social incompetency which causes fear, and reflexly initiates an action to counteract this feeling.

**compensatory rate**  See *rate, compensatory.*

**competence motive**  The individual's active attempt to contact and master his environment as an end in itself as apart from the practical benefits of this activity.

**complacency, principle of**  (R. B. Raup) The tendency of organisms to maintain a physiological state of equilibruim and to return to this state when it is disturbed by external forces.

**complementary color**  See *color, complementary.*

**complementary probabilities**  See *probabilities, complementary.*

**complete learning method; complete mastery method**  Method for measuring the rate of learning by the number of trials taken to learn items to a given criterion.

**completion test**  See *test, completion.*

**complex**  1. A group of related or associated factors. 2. (psychoanalysis) A group of associated ideas and impulses having an emotional meaning which are partly or totally regressed because they are in conflict with the ego and/or the superego.

**complex, Antigone**  (B. B. Wolman) An extreme case of non-sexual love and sacrifice of one's own life for the sake of a beloved person; borrowed from the Greek myth of Antigone, the daughter of Oedipus, who buried the dead body of her brother despite the threat of death penalty. Antigone was punished by death.

**complex, Cain**  A complex characterized by rivalry, competition and destructive feelings toward a brother.

**complex, castration**  (S. Freud) The castration complex is the result of childhood fears of punishment for forbidden sexual desires towards the parent of the opposite sex. In the male it is manifested in a fear of losing his genitals. In the female, it is manifested in the fantasy that the penis has been removed from her as a punishment.

**complex, chronological**  (M. Paine) A systematized complex organized around the experiences of certain epochs of the life of an individual rather than the subject matter in the epoch.

**complex, Clytemnestra**  The occurrence of the wife killing her husband.

**complex, Diana**  Repressed desire of a female to be a male.

**complex, Electra**  (psychoanalysis) Love a girl has for her father with accompanying hostility for her mother; attributed to jealousy of the mother for possession of the father, and to blaming the mother for not giving her a penis or for taking it away from her; feminine version of the Oedipus complex.

**complex, Eshum**  Infrequently used term for castration complex.

**complex, grandfather**  The desire to be the parent of one's own parents.

**complex, Griselda**  Refers to the father's desire to keep the daughter to himself. The father's reluctance to part with his daughter is based on his own unresolved Oedipal conflict in which his yearning was for the mother.

**complex indicator**  (C. G. Jung) In an association test, any behavior caused by a repressed complex such as blushing or responding slowly.

**complex, inferiority**  1. (A. Adler) An abnormal unconscious exaggeration of feelings of insignificance and insecurity resulting in defensive and compensatory behavioral manifestations. 2. (psychoanalysis) Repressed feelings of insignificance arising from the inability to reconcile Oedipal wishes with the reality of childhood inadequacy.

**complex, Jocasta**  (R. de Saussure) An excessive and perverted love of a mother for her son.

**complex, K**  A generalized cortical response evoked by an auditory stimulus occurring during sleep.

**complex, Medea**  The death wishes of a mother toward her children as a means for revenge against her husband.

**complex, mood**  (M. Prince) A systematized complex of dispositions, natural inclinations, desires, and modes of behavior which are suppressed or inhibited for one reason or another.

complex, Oedipus  (S. Freud) Erotic involvement of a male child with his mother accompanied by hostile feelings toward the father. In females, called the Electra complex, it is involvement with the father and resentment toward the mother. Negative Oedipus complex is one erotic involvement with the parent of the same sex and resentment toward the opposite sex. The idea of Oedipus complex was borrowed by Freud from the Greek myth about Oedipus who killed his father and married his mother.

complex, Orestes  (psychoanalysis) The repressed or unconscious desire of a son to kill his mother.

complex, Phaedra  A sexual love of a mother for her son.

complex reaction  See *reaction, complex.*

complex, subject  (M. Prince) A systematic complex or complex of associated experiences organized around subjects or departments of human experience.

complex, systematized  (M. Prince) Image systems of complexes or associated experiences which become organized and fairly distinctly differentiated in the course of the development of every one's personality. Many of these systems may be organized around a predominant emotion, tendency or feeling.

complication experiment  See *prior entry law.*

component instinct  See *instinct, component.*

compos mentis  Of a sound mind; not mentally deficient.

composite image  See *image, composite.*

composite norm  See *norm, composite.*

composite score  See *score, composite.*

compound  A totality formed of independent parts.

compound eye  See *eye, compound.*

compound reaction  See *reaction, compound.*

comprehension test  See *test, comprehension.*

comprehensive solution  See *solution, comprehensive.*

compression  1. The use of one symbol to represent more than one thing at a time. 2. Condensation.

compromise formation  (psychoanalysis) An action or behavior which represents both the work of repressed impulses and of the repressive defensive mechanism of the ego. It is allowed to occur because the repressed impulse becomes disguised in order to escape the censorship of the ego.

compulsion  1. The state in which the person feels forced to behave against his own conscious wishes and judgment. 2. The force which compels a person to action against his own will or forcing a person to act in this way.

compulsion neurosis  See *neurosis, obsessive compulsive.*

compulsive behavior  Irrational and irresistible impulse to perform some act repeatedly.

compulsive personality  See *personality, compulsive.*

computer  An instrument capable of solving problems by applying specific processes to given data and supplying the results of these operations.

computer synthesis scoring  (R. B. Cattell) In a questionnaire containing several factor scales, the usual method scores each only on its own set of items. Computer synthesis allocates available contributions from all scales to any one scale. It increases velocity but vitiates estimates of correlations among the true factors.

Comte, Auguste (1798-1857)  French sociologist who began the positivist movement. He rejected the validity of introspection; all science is social, he held, and deals not with the inferential or speculative but only with the directly observable.

conarium  (R. Descartes) The point of union between the mind and the body in Cartesian philosophy.

conation  The aspect of personality characterized by a conscious willing, strong and purposive action.

conc schedule  See *reinforcement, schedule of: concurrent.*

concentration  1. Exclusive restricted attention to one object or area of study. 2. (I. P. Pavlov) The law of excitation and inhibition which describes the centralization of nerve processes within restricted cortical areas.

concept, congruence of images  See *congruence-of-images concept.*

concept-formation tests  See *tests, concept formation.*

concept-switching task  A task which requires the subject to categorize objects according to one concept, then to find another concept according to which the objects can be classified.

concept validity  See *construct validity.*

conceptual learning  See *learning, conceptual.*

conceptual model  See *model, conceptual.*

conceptual nervous system  See *nervous system, conceptual.*

conceptual thinking and brain processes  See *thinking, conceptual and brain processes.*

concomitant variations  (J. S. Mill) A principle of inductive reasoning which states that when two phenomena vary together, they are either causally related as a cause and effect or have a cause in common.

concordance coefficient (*W*)  (statistics) A statistical estimate of the degree to which judges agree with each other in ranking. The formula is:

$$(W) = \frac{12\Sigma(\Sigma R)^2}{nk^2\,(n^2-1)} - \frac{3^n+1}{n-1},$$

where $\Sigma R$ stands for the sum of the $k$ ranks assigned to each subject by the different judges, and n is the number of subjects.

**concordant** A term used in twin studies to indicate that both members of a twin pair exhibit the trait or disease in question. Concordance rates indicate the percentage of twin pairs in a study that are concordant. Higher concordance rates in monozygotic than dizygotic twin pairs give a preliminary indication of a genetic factor, which can be further explored by studying monozygotic twins reared apart. The twin studies of Franz J. Kallmann in schizophrenia, manic-depressive psychosis and other psychiatric conditions as well as tuberculosis and deafness exemplify this method and extend it by introducing further categories of blood relatives, resulting in a twin-family method.

**concrete intelligence** See *intelligence, concrete.*

**concrete thinking** See *thinking, concrete.*

**concurrent operant** See *operant, concurrent.*

**concurrent (conc) schedule** See *reinforcement, schedule of: concurrent.*

**concurrent validity** See *validity, concurrent.*

**concussion** Shock resulting from a blow or jarring of a part of the body. When blow is to the head, it may be accompanied by unconsciousness, and temporary paralysis.

**condensation** (psychoanalysis) The fusion of any group of unconscious elements into one more acceptable element in order to pass the censorship of the ego.

**Condillac, Étienne Bonnot de (1715-1780)** Influential French empiricist philosopher, who introduced Locke's philosophy to France. Against the doctrine of innate ideas, he developed the philosophy of sensationism: all mental life can be derived from sensory experience. Thus if a statue were endowed with a single sense, it would develop all the mental processes of man.

**condition** 1. The antecedent necessary for an event to occur. 2. The state of a person, situation, or object. 3. To establish a conditioned response. 4. To cause learning in an organism.

**conditional factor** A personality of ability factor found in variables presented under special conditions restricting the range of influences, e.g., without variance in motivation. Opposed to *naturalistic factors.*

**conditional probability** See *probability, conditional.*

**conditional reflex** See *reflex, conditioned.*

**conditionalism** (C. G. Jung) The view that an effect is explicable by its cause and that knowing the cause, one can predict the effect.

**conditioned avoidance** See *conditioning, avoidance.*

**conditioned fear** See *fear, conditioned.*

**conditioned reactive inhibition** See *inhibition, conditioned reactive.*

**conditioned reflex** See *reflex, conditioned.*

**conditioned reinforcement** See *reinforcement, conditioned.*

**conditioned reinforcer** See *reinforcer, conditioned.*

**conditioned response** See *reflex, conditioned.*

**conditioned stimulus** See *stimulus, conditioned.*

**conditioned suppression** See *suppression, conditioned.*

**conditioning, approximation** 1. Conditioning of a complex or rare response through successively rewarding first gross approximations and then closer approximations of the desired response until the desired response is attained and conditioned. 2. Shaping of behavior.

**conditioning, aversive** Form of counter conditioning through the use of punishment; occasionally used in the treatment of homosexuality, stuttering, or alcoholism.

**conditioning, avoidance** An extroceptive stimulus is presented to the experimental subject and after a period of time an unconditioned aversive stimulus is presented. The two stimuli usually overlap in time and terminate together. If the appropriate response is emitted before the onset of the aversive stimulus, it does not occur and the extroceptive stimulus is terminated. The presentation of the neutral extroceptive stimulus before the unconditioned aversive stimulus in a respondent, or Pavlovian conditioning procedure, the onset of the CS followed by the onset of the US. Thus the extroceptive stimulus becomes the CS and the aversive stimulus is the US.

At the same time that this classical conditioning occurs, operant conditioning occurs, since the operant response is reinforced by the termination of the conditioned aversive stimulus and possibly by the nonoccurence of the unconditioned aversive stimulus. In this procedure the conditioned extroceptive stimulus has several properties: (A) It elicits respondent behavior appropriate to the unconditioned aversive stimulus, (B) It is also a conditioned aversive stimulus removal of which is reinforcing. In this sense, avoidance conditioning becomes a special case of escape behavior, (C) It is a discriminative stimulus, it acquires stimulus control of responding.

However, another conditioned avoidance procedure has been developed, the free operant avoidance, in which there is no extroceptive unconditioned stimulus. The aversive stimulus, a very short, intense electric shock, is presented to the organism at regular intervals, say, every ten seconds. This is the shock-shock interval, S-S interval. Each response postpones the occurrence of the shock for a period of time, say twenty seconds. This is the response-shock interval, R-S.

Free operant avoidance behavior is maintained without a conditioned extroceptive stimulus. The stimuli controlling this behavior is still in dispute; thus, the nature of avoidance behavior itself is still unsettled.

**conditioning, backward** (Pavlovian conditioning) One of the common experimental temporal relationships, arranged between the unconditioned stimulus (US) and the conditioned stimulus (CS). Conditioning normally occurs when the onset of the CS is before the onset of the US. In backward conditioning the CS is presented after the onset of the US. If backward conditioning occurs at all, it is not very effective since it has never been conclusively demonstrated.

**conditioning, bifactoral theory of** The proposition that attitudes determine the probability of incidence of conditioning, and properties of the stimulus determine response magnitude.

**conditioning, classical** See *conditioning, Pavlovian.*

**conditioning, cross 1.** Conditioning to any situational stimulus which occurs at the same time as the unconditioned stimulus in the original conditioning procedure. **2.** The conditioning of postural and tonic responses to commonly occurring stimuli.

**conditioning, differential** Establishment and maintenance of a conditioned response to one of two stimuli by reinforcing the response to the one and not reinforcing the response to the other.

**conditioning, higher-order** A type of Pavlovian conditioning in which the original conditioned stimulus is used as the unconditioned stimulus in a new conditioning procedure.

**conditioning, instrumental** Conditioning procedures in which the animal's behavior is instrumental in the obtaining of reward or the avoidance of or escape from punishment. The appropriate response must be performed prior to reinforcement in order to obtain it.

**conditioning, operant** (B. F. Skinner) A form of conditioning in which reinforcement is contingent upon the occurrence of the response. Instrumental and operant conditioning are distinguished primarily, methodologically. Operant conditioning involves the repeated emission of the same response, the operant, while for instrumental behaviors the reinforcement contingent response occurs only once per trial. Consequently the primary measure of operant conditioning tends to be the rate of responding.

Operant conditioning experiments usually involve a small number of subjects observed over a long period of time; thus providing a stable "baseline" or "steady state" with which to compare the experimental effects. With animal subjects the experimental apparatus is usually a sound proof, light resistant box. In its usual form the box contains only the operandum, that upon which the subject responds, sources for light and sound stimuli and a mechanism to deliver reinforcement, usually either food or water. Thus unwanted external influences are minimized and critical variables can be precisely controlled by the experimenter.

In operant conditioning the response conditioned is the operant which is any of a class of behaviors that are equally effective in achieving reinforcement. Thus an operant is defined by the situation in which it occurs. In the experimental situation the operandum defines the operant. When rats are used as subjects, the operandum in the experimental cham-

ber is a bar depressor which delivers reinforcement. In this situation the only behavior that is reinforced is the bar press. It makes no difference how the subject performs the operant, with its paw, nose, or tail; when the bar is pressed, the operant has been performed and the animal is eligible for reinforcement.

Since the dependent variable in operant conditioning is the response rate or the number of events in a given period of time, it becomes meaningful to talk about the amount of responding; twice as many responses mean twice as much behavior. A relationship which is less clear than some other measure is used, e.g. half the latency or half the amplitude. Thus response rate as a measure gives at least a simplicity, if not clarity, to the analysis and interpretation of data. Operant conditioning often leads to a behavior analysis in which explanation of behavior is reduced to description, and causation of behavior reduced to explication of functional relations. Thus the full description of an event is taken to include a description of its functional relationship with antecedent events. Attempts to account for behavior in terms of physiology or biology play little part in operant conditioning.

**conditioning, Pavlovian** (I. P. Pavlov) Often called classical conditioning, respondent conditioning, type 1, and type S conditioning. It is the procedure of presenting two stimuli in one of several temporal arrangements. One stimulus, the unconditioned stimulus, is sufficient to evoke an unconditioned response. By presenting the neutral stimulus followed by the unconditioned stimulus to the experimental subject for a number of times, the neutral stimulus evokes a response similar to the original unconditioned response, and the neutral stimulus becomes a conditioned stimulus capable of evoking a conditioned response. Furthermore, the conditioned response the neutral stimulus evokes through conditioning is a conditioned response, somewhat different and distinguishable from the unconditioned response.

Pavlov developed his theory of conditioning with a physiological orientation explaining the observed facts of conditioning by postulating events in the nervous system of the organism. His basic unit of analysis was the reflex-arc which he divided into three parts; analyzer, connection and effector. The analyzer begins at the peripheral sense receptor and carries the stimulation to the cortical receptor centers. Each analyzer has a special central territory in the cortex which represents a projection in the brain. The sensory stimulation is conducted along the analyzer pathway to its receptor center. The connection is between the receptor and effector. Modifications in the stimulus conditions lead to new connections which in turn lead to new behavioral patterns. Conditioning is the process of creating new connections. The effector is the motor response, or working part of the reflex. Pavlov eventually concluded that reflexes could be formed in the motor regions, therefore the motor region had receptor functions as well.

Three laws govern the excitatory or inhibitory passage of neural energy from one center to another, the process of forming connections: 1) Irradiation, the stimulation in a certain group of nervous cells irradiates over large parts of the cerebrum and the excitation started in a certain cortical point spreads in a wave to surrounding areas. 2) Concentration, the wave of irradiated excitation goes back to the starting point. 3) Induction, once an area is stimulated and irradiates, neighboring areas develop inhibition and force concentration of the stimulated area. This is positive induction. Once an area is inhibited, neighboring areas develop stimulation which force concentration of the inhibition. This is negative induction. Irradiation, concentration, and induction apply to inhibition as well as excitation.

Several types of classical conditioning experimental designs have commonly been distinguished. When the conditioned stimulus (CS) is presented to the subject a fraction of a second to a few seconds prior to the presentation of the unconditioned stimulus (US), the conditioned response (CR) occurs shortly after the CS. The delayed conditioned response occurs when the CS is presented continually for as much as a minute before the US is presented. When there is a pause between the termination of the CS and the presentation of the US it is called trace conditioning, so called because Pavlov concluded that there remained in the organism some trace of the CS after it is discontinued.

Other types of experiments include (a) higher order conditioning where one CS serves as the US for another, second, CS. (b) When conditioning has occurred and the CS will elicit the CR, generalization is said to occur when a wide range of stimuli will elicit the CR. (c) When the subject is trained to respond to one CS and not respond to other stimuli, discrimination is said to have occurred. Repetition of the CS without concomitant repetition of the US, leads invariably to a decline and the eventual extinction of the CR. Without the US reinforcement, extinction always occurs. Among the several types of internal inhibitions that Pavlov distinguished the first type was called extinction; repeated presentation of the CS without the US leads to the suspension of the CR. Another type of internal inhibition was retardation; in trace conditioning the CR does not occur upon the presentation of the CS but occurs after a pause shortly before the US is presented. Differentiated inhibition occurs in discrimination studies where one CS is followed by the US but another CS is not followed by the US. Eventually, only a CR to the former will be established while responses to the latter will be inhibited. Conditioned inhibition is when an indifferent stimulus is added to a well established CS, resulting in the nonoccurrence of the CR. Disinhibition occurs when an external stimulus acts upon the inhibited CS, removing the inhibition resulting in the occurrence of the CR.

**conditioning, pseudo** The elicitation of a response to a previously neutral stimulus when that stimulus is presented following a series of conditioned stimuli.

**conduct** Behavior.

**conduction** 1. The transmission of a neural impulse from one neuron to another. 2. The transmission of sound waves through the ear.

**conduction, antidromic** The passage of a neural im-

pulse from the axons to dendrites, in reversed direction.

**conduction aphasia** See *aphasia, conduction.*

**conduction deafness** See *deafness, conduction.*

**conduction, neural** The transmission of an impulse along nerve fibers and from neuron to neuron.

**conduction unit** 1. The unit whose function is the transmission of impulses from one part of the nervous system to another. 2. (E. L. Thorndike) The hypothesized system of neural connections underlying a particular action which occurs under specific conditions.

**conductivity** 1. The ability of a substance to transmit energy. 2. The ability of a neuron to transmit nerve impulses which is dependent on the size and metabolic state of the neuron.

**cones** Receptor cells in the retina which function to transform the energy of light rays into nervous impulses which produce daylight and color vision.

**confabulated response** (Rorschach) Originally defined by H. Rorschach as a response in which the subject interprets an area of the blot and then assigns the same interpretation to a larger area, or to the entire blot, with general disregard for the appropriateness of concept as related to the larger area. Most contemporary Rorschach systems incorporate this concept and use a scoring of DW or its variations. In the Rapaport approach to the Rorschach, the concept has been extended considerably to account for the broader category of "pathological" verbalizations.

**confabulation** 1. The falsification of memory due to partial amnesia. 2. (Rorschach) Arbitrary elaboration of responses to inkblots without objective support.

**confactor rotation (formerly parallel proportional profiles)** (R. B. Cattell) A method of sorting the rotation problem in psychological factor analysis which gives independence of the need for simple structure methods. It requires two experimental groups and seeks a functional proportionality of factor leadings on the same variables, thus treating factors as influences.

**confession stage** (C. G. Jung) The first stage of analytical psychotherapy in which the patient tells of all that is troubling him.

**confidence interval** The limits outside of which an event is not expected to occur by chance or the distance in sigma units between the fiducial limits.

**confidence, level of** See *limits, fiducial.*

**confidence limits** See *limits, fiducial.*

**configural scoring** See *scoring, configural.*

**configuration** See *gestalt.*

**configuration principle** Refers to the basic interpretive approach used in Rorschach testing, wherein the variety of scores, frequencies, percentages, and ratios are considered inter-dependent and interpretable only as related to each other. This principle generally *prohibits* the formulation of interpretive statements based on single scores or features such as the number of animal responses, or the number of color responses or a simple combination of score frequencies as is found in a psychogram.

**confirmation** (E. C. Tolman) The realization of an expectancy which has the value of a reward.

**confirming reaction** See *reaction, confirming.*

**conflict** Simultaneous instigation of two or more incompatible responses; *types* have been differentiated on the basis of whether the conflicting responses are approach or avoidance: I, approach-approach, II, approach-avoidance, III, avoidance-avoidance, IV, double approach-avoidance, conflict, internalized Type II.
  The instigation is internal (e.g., aggressive or sexual feelings or drive vs. aggression or sex anxiety), thus leading to an approach-avoidance conflict with reference to manipulanda relevant to the drive.

**conflict, actual** (psychoanalysis) A present situation involving a struggle between conscious and unconscious desires, that is, opposite impulses. An actual conflict is believed to be the transformation of a root conflict which is the early source of the struggle. A root conflict remains unresolved in the unconscious, repressed since early infancy.

**conflict, approach-approach** Conflict which occurs when an individual is attracted by and wishes to move toward two positive, attractive goals which are completely or partially incompatible.

**conflict, approach-avoidance** Situation in which both positive and negative stimuli or both approach and avoidance stimuli are inherent in the same goal or in approximately the same place, whether psychologically, geographically or in the same life space. The organism cannot approach one and avoid the other simultaneously which presents conflict.

**conflict, avoidance-avoidance** Situation in which an organism faced with two negative goals or situations must move toward one of them in order to avoid the other. In such a situation, the avoidance gradient of the one being approached increases while that of the other decreases and vice versa, causing the organism to move back and forth if both situations are equally negative and resulting in great stress.

**conflict-free ego sphere** (H. Hartmann) The part of the ego which Hartmann called primary autonomy and which includes perception, motility and memory.

**conflict index, C** A statistic which gives an exact value for the total amount of energy which an organism (or other dynamic system) has bound up in internal conflict.

**conflict, positive-positive** See *conflict, approach-approach.*

**confluence** 1. The flowing together of elements which have been separate such as motives, responses or perceptual elements. 2. (A. Adler) The fusion of several motives into one.

**confluent learning** (R. B. Cattell) Personality learning in which responses are discovered giving simultaneous expression to tensions previously in conflict.

**confusion scales** See *scales, confusion.*

**congenital** Present at birth; not necessarily genetic.

**congenital analgesia** See *analgesia, congenital.*

**congenital aphasia** See *aphasia, developmental.*

**congruence** 1. Agreeable coexistence. 2. (C. Rogers) The integration of experiences into the self, executed on a conscious level.

**congruence-of-images concept** The idea that behavior in a family is partly an effort to develop and maintain shared and congruent images of the various family members; e.g., the image the father has of himself agrees with the daughter's image of the father.

**congruent points** Points on the two retinas which are involved in the perception of a point in an external stimulus.

**congruity** (Osgood, C. E. and Tannenbaum, P. H.) A cognitive state which exists when two objects which have the same evaluative meaning for an individual are positively related in a statement, or when objects which are negatively related have evaluative meaning of the same intensity but of opposite signs.

**conj schedule** See *reinforcement, schedule of: conjunctive.*

**conjoint family therapy** See *psychotherapy, family.*

**conjugate movements** Coordinated movements of the two eyes.

**conjugate schedule** See *reinforcement, schedule of: conjugate.*

**conjunctiva** The mucuous membrane of the inner eyelid and outer eyeball.

**conjunctival reflex** The closing of the eyelid when the cornea is stimulated.

**conjunctive motivation** See *motivation, conjunctive.*

**conjunctive reinforcement** See *reinforcement; schedule of: conjunctive (conj).*

**conjunctive (conj) schedule** See *reinforcement, schedule of: conjunctive (conj).*

**conjunctivity** (H. A. Murray) The coordination and organization of motives, and purposes with actions.

**connection** 1. A link between two phenomena. 2. The link between the receptors and effectors.

**connectionism** 1. The doctrine that the basis of all behavior and learning are connections of stimulus and response which are strengthened to produce stability. 2. (E. L. Thorndike) The theory that the functional bonds between stimulus and response are inherited or acquired neural connections.

**connector** 1. A nerve fiber which joins a receptor and effector. 2. A neuron which connects two neurons.

**consanguinity** Relationship by descent from a common ancestor. Raised consanguinity rates are found in the parentage of persons with recessive diseases.

**conscience 1.** The individual's set of moral values which was thought to be innate by theologians but is now believed to be learned. **2.** (psychoanalysis) See *superego*.

**conscious or consciousness 1.** Referring to the process of being aware or knowing. **2.** Characterizing a person who is aware. **3.** Pertaining to the ability to react to stimulation in the environment. **4.** Pertaining to that which is observable by introspection. **5.** (psychoanalysis) The upper part of the topographic structure where rational processes can take place.

**consciousness, stream of** See *stream of consciousness*.

**consensual eye reflex** See *reflex, consensual eye*.

**consensual validation** (H. S. Sullivan) Validating one's perception against the perception of other individuals, starts at the syntaxic mode or stage of development.

**consentience** (M. Jahoda) The agreement or acceptance of a certain attitude when corroborating evidence is introduced.

**consistency** The agreement of a test with itself. It requires three coefficients (Cattell's conceptualization): 1) The *reliability* (dependability) of a test-retest agreement (over time), 2) The *homogeneity* coefficient defining agreement of parts (over sections), and 3) the *transferability* coefficient expressing degree of agreement of validity over groups (over populations).

**consistency coefficient** See *coefficient of internal consistency*.

**consistency index** See *index, consistency*.

**consistency, internal** An index of the extent to which different parts of a test measure the same function. The degree of internal consistency can be estimated by noting the correlation of the two halves, or by correlating each score with the total score.

**consolidation theory** The theory that when learning ceases, the neurophysiological activities underlying learning continue to function. This hypothesis is used to explain phenomena such as retroactive inhibition.

**conspect reliability coefficient** (R. B. Cattell) The degree of agreement of two psychologists scoring the same recorded or observed responses.

**constancy** The stability of perceptions under varying external conditions.

**constancy, brightness** The fact that an object retains its normal or standard intensity independent of the surrounding stimuli.

**constancy, color** The fact that colors tend to remain the same despite changes in illumination or other conditions.

**constancy hypothesis** The principle that there is a rigid one to one correspondence between the proximal stimulus and the sensory response so that given a particular stimulus, the same response will occur independent of other conditions. This theory is presented as the antithesis of Gestalt theory which stresses relativism in stimulus-response relationships.

**constancy of internal environment** (W. B. Cannon) The postulated tendency for the internal state of the organism to remain relatively constant.

**constancy of the IQ** The tendency of the IQ measure to remain relatively constant from year to year when the individual's score is assessed with the same or similar test.

**constancy principle** (S. Freud) Organic nature tends to return to the initial non-organic phase.

**constancy, size** The stable perception of the size of objects under different viewing conditions.

**constant 1.** A mathematical value that remains unchanged under all conditions. **2.** An experimental condition that is not allowed to vary.

**constant error** See *error, constant*.

**constant method** See *method, constant stimulus*.

**constant stimulus method** See *method, constant stimulus*.

**constellatory construct** See *construct, constellatory*.

**constipation, chronic, psychogenic** Constipation of long duration due to psychological conflicts about giving and retaining.

**constitution 1.** The total hereditary and acquired characteristics which determine an individual. **2.** The nature of a thing.

**constitution, epileptic psychopathic** Complex of negative personality traits and progressive mental and intellectual deficiencies which are manifested by some epileptics and is thought to be related in some way to epilepsy.

**constitution, hyperpituitary** A constitutional type characterized by dysplastic features, massive body parts, and a restless, reasoning mentality. It is associated with pituitary hyperfunction at the end of the normal growth period.

**constitution, hypoadrenal** The constitutional type characterized by deficiency in adrenal activity.

**constitution, hypopancreatic** Condition resulting from progressive intolerance for carbohydrates. A transitory phase to diabetes.

**constitution, hypoparathyroid** The constitutional type characterized by inadequate secretion of the parathyroid glands.

**constitution, hypopituitary** (N. Pende) Constitutional type associated with inadequate secretion of the pituitary gland. Characteristically they exhibit immature secondary sexual features, asthenia, low blood pressure, polyuria, increased carbohydrate tolerance, slow pulse and apathy.

constitutional anomaly  Anatomical and physiological disequilibrium between two or more systems of the body.

constitutional factors  See *factors, constitutional.*

constitutional inadequacy  See *inadequacy, constitutional.*

constitutional medicine  See *medicine, constitutional.*

constitutional psychopath  See *psychopath, constitutional.*

constitutional theory of personality  1. (E. Kretschmer) Personality theory based on the relation between body-type and mental disorder, especially schizophrenic and manic-depressive psychoses. Theory assumes a continuum between abnormal and normal personality types though typology is based primarily on investigation of psychotics. Four body types (see *asthenic, athletic, pyknic* and *dysplastic*) are related to two basic temperaments (see *schizothyme* and *cyclothyme*). These temperaments occur in normal and abnormal variations. Cyclothymic temperament and manic-depressive psychoses are associated with pyknic body-type while schizothymic temperament and schizophrenia are associated with asthenic and athletic body-types. 2. (W. H. Sheldon) Personality theory based on the relationship between body-type and temperament. Body type is classified in terms of three components: ectomorphy, endomorphy and mesomorphy. A person's somatotype is a combination of the three components, each of which is measured along a 7-point scale yielding many possible combinations or somatotypes. Personality is measured in terms of the intercorrelations of sixty traits related to introversion-extroversion and to temperament. The intercorrelation of these traits yields three clusters which constitute the primary components of temperament: cerebrotonia, viscerotonia and somatotonia. The three basic body types are correlated with the three temperamental components: ectomorphy with cerebrotonia, endomorphy with viscerotonia, and mesomorphy with somatotonia. Neither body type nor temperament is completely inherent; early nutritional variables and childhood experiences may influence physique and personality, respectively. Constitutional type provides a substructure of capacities and limitations.

constitutional type  1. A group of enduring physiological, anatomical and psychological qualities which are thought to be a basis for categorizing people. 2. The behavioral traits believed to occur in certain body types. 3. (Hippocrates) A group of characteristics which are believed to be associated with particular diseases. The habitus apoplecticus type was believed to occur in thickset, rounded people. The habitus phthisicus was thought to occur in slender, angular individuals. 4. (Galen) A constellation of traits based on the type of fluid which is basic in the body. The four types include the sanguine, melancholic, choleric and phlegmatic. 5. (E. Kretschmer) See *constitutional theory of personality.* 6. (W. H. Sheldon) See *constitutional theory of personality.*

constrained association  See *association, constrained.*

constraint  The compelling of someone to do or not to do something.

construct  A formally proposed concept representing relationships between empirically verifiable events and based on observed facts. The term was suggested for use instead of concept by K. Pearson.

construct, constellatory  (G. A. Kelly) A construct whose elements also belong to other constructs. The construct boy, for example, may also mean aggressive which is another construct.

construct, core  (G. A. Kelly) A construct which partially determines how a person adjusts himself to the environment.

construct, empirical  A construct determined as a result of experimentation.

construct, hypothetical  Concepts introduced within the framework of a theory with the aim of explaining behavioral data. The logical constructs fill a gap in observation and experimentation, going beyond observable data. They are heuristic in theory formation for they bridge together empirical data and open new vistas for future research. Reinforcement, intelligence, adjustment, learning, superego, oedipus complex, equilibration, etc., are examples of logical, constructs used in various fields of psychological theory.

construct, logical  See *construct, hypothetical.*

construct, pre-emptive  (G. A. Kelly) A construct which cannot be classified in any other way except as the given construct. Right and wrong exemplify such constructs.

construct, preverbal  (G. A. Kelly) A construct having no word symbol which may or may not have developed before the person began to talk.

construct, regnant  (G. A. Kelly) A construct consisting of elements whose function is to be a part of subordinate constructs.

construct validity (or concept validity)  The extent to which a test or operation measures a defined concept or construct, as determined by a correlation coefficient. Since it is mostly factor concepts that can be given measurable form, the term as used in this book refers to a test or test battery's correlation with (loading on) a factor, where the factor is an operationally defined representation of a concept.

construction need  See *need, construction.*

consultant psychologist  See *psychologist, consultant.*

consulting psychologist  See *psychologist, consulting.*

consummatory communication  See *communication, consummatory.*

consummatory response  See *response, consummatory.*

consummatory stimulus  See *stimulus, consummatory.*

contagion  The spread of behavior or feelings to

other people through suggestion, imitation or sympathy.

**contagion, mass** The rapid spread of behaviors among groups of unrelated people who are not necessarily in the same area.

**contaminated response** A Rorschach response in which an unrealistic mixture of content occurs within a single response. The merging of two or more entirely incompatible concepts makes for an obvious bizarreness indicative of serious disturbance in thought.

**contamination 1.** (experimental) A spurious relationship between two variables produced by the independent and dependent variables to influence each other. If an experimenter, for example, has knowledge about one variable, it may influence his findings on the other variable. **2.** (Rorschach) The fusion of two responses which are objectively separate from each other.

**contemporaneous-explanation principle** (K. Lewin) The principle that only present events can influence present behavior.

**content analysis** See *analysis, content.*

**content, dream, latent** (psychoanalysis) The unconscious wishes and impulses whose meaning is hidden from the dreamer due to the transformation of this content into the manifest content by the dream work.

**content, dream, manifest** (psychoanalysis) The dream content as the dreamer perceives and remembers it.

**content, informational** (J. P. Guilford) A parameter of the structure of intellect; it is the substantive aspect of information, by which it is classified in broad categories—figural, symbolic, semantic and behavioral.

**content, law of** See *law of content.*

**content psychology** See *psychology, content.*

**content response** See *response, content.*

**content scores** One of the major components of Rorschach scoring or coding in which standard abbreviations are used to denote the class of content used in a response such as A for animal, H for human, Bl for blood, etc.

**content validity** See *validity, content.*

**context, theory of meaning** See *meaning, context theory of.*

**contiguity** The propinquity of objects or events in space or in time.

**contiguity, law of 1.** (Aristotle) The principle that learning is based on the occurrence of stimulus and response close in time or space. Then when one element occurs, the other follows. **2.** (E. R. Guthrie) The principle that learning depends upon the proximity in time or space of stimulus and response alone. **3.** (C. L. Hull) The hypothesis that learning is based on the proximity of stimulus and response in time or space which is possible due to the gradual decay of the neural excitation underlying the variables. It is believed however that reward is a necessary adjunct to contiguity.

**contiguous conditioning** (E. R. Guthrie) The principle that learning is the result of an association of stimuli and response movements by contiguity. Conditioning occurs after only one trial. Forgetting and extinction result from the inhibition of old connections by new incompatible ones, not from the lack of reinforcement.

**continence 1.** Self-restraint or complete abstinence from sexual activity. **2.** The retention of feces and urine.

**contingency** (statistics) The extent to which the values of one variable depend on the values of another variable.

**contingency coefficient** (*C*) (statistics) A measure of the relationship between two variables. The coefficient is a measure of the degree to which the variables are non-independent of each other more often than would be expected by chance. The formula is: $C = \sqrt{\dfrac{X^2}{n + X^2}}$ where $n$ is the number of paired values in the two variables, and $X^2$ refers to Chi square.

**contingency method** (statistics) A method of measuring the degree to which two variables occur together: the function between actual cell frequencies and the expected cell frequencies in a two-way table.

**contingency table** A two-way table showing the frequencies of two variables which are entered in the vertical and horizontal rows of the table.

**continuity** The quality of uninterrupted movement from one element to another which may be temporal, spatial or logical.

**continuity-non-continuity (in learning theory)** (D. Krech) Terms for alternative assumptions concerning the effects of rewarded and punished responses during discrimination learning. Continuity assumes that the correct response is cumulatively strengthened or weakened with every rewarded or punished choice. Non-continuity assumes that typically the animal first responds on the basis of irrelevant discriminanda prior to making choices based on the correct cues and that only then do rewarded or punished choices affect the acquisition of the correct discrimination. See *hypothesis; discriminandum.*

**continuity of germ plasm theory** The theory that reproductive germ cells are derived from other reproductive germ cells, not from somatic cells so that any environmental influences on the body cells do not affect hereditary transmission.

**continuity, social** The transmission of cultural forms from generation to generation by institutions such as the family, school and church.

**continuity theory of learning** See *learning, continuity theory of.*

**continuous avoidance** See *avoidance, free operant.*

**continuous epilepsy** See *epilepsy, continuous.*

**continuous reinforcement (CRF) schedule** See *reinforcement, schedule of: continuous.*

**continuous scale** See *scale, continuous.*

**continuum** A curve, graph or variable which has no steps between any two points.

**contour** The boundary of a figure.

**contraception** The prevention of fertilization of the ovum by the sperm by artificial means.

**contractility** A fundamental property of a living tissue of shrinking upon stimulation.

**contracture** The failure of a muscle to return to its resting position after contraction.

**contralateral** Referring to the opposite side of the body.

**contrast** The intensification of the difference between two given stimuli produced by the contiguous presentation of these stimuli temporally or spatially.

**contrast, brightness** The intensification of the perceived difference in brillance of two objects which results when two visual stimuli are presented either simultaneously or in close succession.

**contrast, color** The effect which one color has on another when perceived simultaneously or successively. It involves enhancement of complementary colors by each other and the perception of the complement of a neutral surface when the stimulus color is fixated upon.

**contrast, successive** See *contrast, color.*

**contrasuggestibility** The tendency for an individual to take on an opposite attitude to that which was suggested to him.

**contrectation** The touching of and fondling of another person, usually associated with genital excitation.

**control experiment** See *experiment, control.*

**control, experimental** The control and arrangement of all extraneous variables, i.e., all variables other than the independent variable, in order that any change in the dependent variable can be considered a function of the independent variable.

**control group** See *group, control.*

**control, social** The stipulation of rules of conduct by social institutions.

**control, stimulus** See *stimulus control.*

**controlled sampling** See *sampling, controlled.*

**controlled variable** See *variable, controlled.*

**conventions, social** The implicit rules and regulations of social conduct which are tacitly agreed upon by the members of the group.

**convergence** 1. The tendency to move toward one point. 2. The tendency of the eye to move inward toward the source of light so that the image will fall on corresponding parts of the foveas. 3. The inheritance of traits from both father and mother. 4. The principle that a trait is a product of both hereditary and environmental factors. 5. The meeting of two or more nerve impulses from different sensory pathways. 6. (M. Jahoda) The acceptance of an attitude or behavior contrary to one's own because it reflects other valid considerations.

**convergence theory** The theory that psychological phenomena result from the interaction of hereditary or acquired specific traits with specific environmental conditions.

**convergent production, operation of** (J. P. Guilford) Generation of items of information from given items, where the needed information is fully determined by the given information; a search for logical imperatives.

**conversion** 1. A fundamental diametric change of belief or attitude as of religious beliefs. 2. (psychoanalysis) The transformation of psychological conflicts into physical symptoms. 3. (logic) A change of a proposition caused by interchanging the subject and the predicate which results in a distortion in logic. 4. (psychometrics) The translation of scores from one scale to another.

**conversion hysteria** See *hysteria, conversion.*

**conversion seizure** See *seizure, conversion.*

**conviction** Belief without a doubt.

**convolution** A fold on the surface of the cortex of the cerebrum.

**convulsion** Involuntary generalized muscular contraction. May be tonic (without relaxation) or clonic (alternating contraction and relaxation).

**convulsion, clonic** See *convulsion.*

**convulsion, static** A special form of the motor aura of epilepsy which may include forward, backward or related movements.

**convulsion, tonic** Persisting contraction of a muscle.

**convulsive therapy** See *shock therapy.*

**cooperative factor** A factor having the loading pattern on salient variables very similar to that of another independent factor with which its correlation may be negligible.

**coordinate** 1. (mathematics) A point or line of reference which is used to locate a point in space. 2. Equal in rank. 3. To arrange items according to a specific schema.

**coordinated epilepsy** See *epilepsy, coordinated.*

**coordination** 1. The harmonious functioning of parts, especially of muscles in the performance of an action. 2. The similar relationship of two items of a class to a higher or inclusive class.

**coping behavior** (A. Maslow) A behavioral pattern which facilitates adjustment to the environment for the purpose of attaining some goal.

coping style Means by which the person comes to terms with stresses and makes use of opportunities and also the unique organization suggested by the various means employed by the person in adaptive efforts.

coprolaba The uncontrolled use of obscene words.

coprophagia or coprophagy The eating of excrement.

coprophilia An extreme interest in, preoccupation with, or attraction to feces.

coprophobia Morbid fear of excrement.

core construct See construct, core.

corium The outer part of the dermis, the layer underlying the epidermis.

cornea The transparent outer part of the sclerotic layer of the eye.

corneal lens See lens, corneal.

corneal reflection The reflection of light from the surface of the cornea which is used as a technique for studying and photographing eye movements.

Cornell method (L. Guttman) A technique for determining whether an attitude is scalable by ascertaining whether the attitude in question is unidimensional.

Cornell Selective Index (A. Weider, B. Mittelmann, D. Wechsler and H. G. Wolff) A personality inventory introduced in 1944 designed to screen out psychologically unstable men from the armed forces. It consists of ninety-two questions some of which are starred for immediate attention of the tester.

Cornell Word Form Test See test, Cornell Word Form.

corollary 1. A principle which is deduced as a result of proving another proposition. 2. A natural result.

corpora quadrigemina The four masses of nerve tissue at the posterior of the midbrain, one pair of which is the superior collinculli, the center for usual reflexes and the second pair of which is the inferior collinculli, the center of auditory reflexes.

corpus callosum See callosum.

corpus striatum See striate body, or striatum.

corpuscle 1. A small rounded particle. 2. A specialized encapsulated sensory nerve organ. 3. A cell which floats in the blood or lymph.

corpuscle, Krause's An encapsulated neuronal ending, found primarily in the conjunctiva of the eye, the skin of the nipples, and the genitals, and believed to be one type of receptor for cold. Also called Krause ending and Krause's end bulb.

corpuscle, Meissner An encapsulated end organ found primarily in the hairless surface of the soles of the feet and the palms of the hands which functions as a receptor for touch sensations.

correct rejection (signal detection theory) One of four possible outcomes in a single trial of a signal detection experiment. Noise is presented without a signal and the subject correctly detects the absence of a signal. The other outcomes are a hit, a false alarm and a miss.

correction 1. (statistics) The use of specific techniques to minimize chance errors. 2. The use of lenses for the eye to improve impaired vision.

correctional psychology See psychology, correctional.

correlate (noun) 1. A variable which is in some way related to another variable; a correlation exists. 2. A principle that is logically related to another principle or conclusion. (verb) 1. To put a variable, principle or conclusion in relation to something else. 2. To calculate the coefficient of correlation.

correlation 1. Any relationship between two variables. 2. (logic) Any relationship relating two variables such that a change in one of the variables results or is associated with, a change in the other. 3. (statistics) A concomitant variation; the degree to which two variables vary together.

correlation, biserial ($r_{bis}$) A correlation in which one of the variables has only two parts or divisions and the other variable has many classes. For example the correlation of age into two classes, old and young.

correlation, bivariate See correlation, simple.

correlation center A neurological center where two or more afferent neurons unite to influence an efferent system.

correlation, chance halves See correlation, split half.

correlation, cluster A group of variables that are more correlated to each other than to any other group. Any correlation statistically derived from the cluster would be significantly positive.

correlation coefficient (r) (statistics) A numerical index that indicates the degree of relationship of two variables. The Pearson product moment correlation coefficient is the most widely used. The formula is:

$$r = \sqrt{\frac{\Sigma(\check{Y}-\overline{Y})^2}{\Sigma(Y_i-\overline{Y})^2}}$$

where $\check{Y}$ is the predicted value of $Y$, $\overline{Y}$ refers to the mean of the $Y$ values, $Yi$ is one of the variables under consideration and $\Sigma$ means to mathematically sum the values represented by the expressions $(\check{Y}-\overline{Y})^2$ and $(Y_i-\overline{Y})^2$. The values of the correlation coefficient can range from $-1.00$ to $+1.00$ where positive values indicate that a low standing in one variable is associated with a low standing in the other. Negative values indicate an inverse relationship; high standing in one variable is associated with low standing in another.

correlation, curvilinear A correlation whose regression is not linear. It is represented by a curved, rather than a straight line.

correlation graph See scatter diagram.

**correlation hierarchy** A correlation table in which the values are arranged such that the magnitude of correlation either progressively increases or decreases from one corner to the other three. These correlations are seen to originate from common factors.

**correlation, index of** A measure of the relationship of two variables.

**correlation, inverse** A correlation between two variables in which increasing values of one variable are related to decreasing values of the other. Also called negative correlation.

**correlation, linear** A correlation in which the line of regression is in the form of a straight line indicating that for any change in one variable, a proportional change in the other will occur. The degree of correlation is measured by the coefficient of correlation.

**correlation, matrix** A table which includes the correlation coefficients of every variable with every other variable in a particular set. Each test's correlation with itself is usually included.

**correlation, multiple (R)** A coefficient showing the relationship between a number of independent variables and one dependent variable. The multiple correlation is most commonly used when a given relationship is due to multiple causation. The formula is:

$$R_{1.23} = \sqrt{\frac{r_{12}^2 - 2r_{12}r_{13}r_{23}r_{13}^2}{1 - r_{23}^2}}$$

where $R_{1.23}$ is the multiple correlation between the dependent variable 1, and variables 2 and 3, and $r$ refers to the correlation between two variables which are specified by the subscripts.

**correlation, negative** See *correlation, inverse*.

**correlation, partial** The net correlation between two variables when the influence of other variables on their relationship has been eliminated. The formula is:

$$r_{12.3} = \frac{r_{12} - r_{13}r_{23}}{\sqrt{1 - r_{13}^2}\ \sqrt{1 - r_{23}^2}}$$

where $r$ is the correlation between the variables specified in the subscripts.

**correlation, Pearsonian** See *correlation, product moment*.

**correlation, point-biserial** Product moment correlation of a dichotomous variable and a continuous variable.

**correlation, polychoric** A correlation between two variables which are both continuous and normally distributed. The correlations are plotted in a table containing more than four cells.

**correlation, positive** Correlation between variables in which great strength or quantity in one is associated with great strength or quantity in the other. The highest positive correlation is 1.

**correlation, primary** The relationship between two variables which cannot be ascribed to the influence of a third factor.

**correlation, product moment** The most common form of computing correlation, based on product-moments:

$$r = \Sigma xy / N_{\sigma x \sigma y}$$

which assumes rectilinear regression lines.

**correlation, Q** See *P technique*.

**correlation ratio ($\eta^2$)** An index of the degree to which a regression line is nonlinear. The formula most commonly used is:

$$\eta^2 yx = \frac{\Sigma n_j (M_{Yj} - M_Y)^2}{\sum_j \sum_i (Y_{ij} - M_Y)^2}$$

where $\eta^2 yx$ is the correlation ratio for the relation of Y to X, $n_j$ is the number of sample observations in the treatment group $j$, $M_{Yj}$ is the mean for the $j$ observations in group Y, $M_Y$ is the mean error of the total observations in the population Y, $Y_{ij}$ is the value of the $i$th individual in the $j$th category in the Y population, and $\Sigma$ means to mathematically sum all the values represented by the expressions $(M_{Yj} - M_Y)^2$ and $(Y_{ij} - M_Y)^2$.

**correlation, secondary** The correlation between two variables which is due to the existence of a third variable.

**correlation, self** Correlation between random halves of a test, two administrations of the same test or between a test and an equivalent form.

**correlation, simple** The magnitude of the relationship of two variables.

**correlation, Spearman foot rule (R)** (C. Spearman) A coefficient of correlation which is based on gains in rank from the first variable to the second. The formula is:

$$R = 1 - \frac{\sigma \times \Sigma g}{N^2 - 1}$$

where $g$ is the gain by any individual from rank 1 to rank 2, $\Sigma$ means to add all the values represented by the symbol $g$, and $N$ refers to the number of cases involved in the ranking.

**correlation, split half** A method of estimating test reliability by determining the correlation between two comparable halves of a test and applying the Spearman-Brawn formula to compensate for attenuation causing by splitting the test.

**correlation, spurious** A correlation relationship which is caused by a factor or factors external to the variables involved.

**correlation table** A table showing the quantitative relationship between two variables. One variable is entered in the horizontal rows and the other in the vertical.

**correlation, tetrachoric ($r_t$)** A correlation of two variables that are both continuous and normally distributed, and expressed in terms of only two classes: male-female correlated with dullness-brightness would be an example.

correlation, total  The most commonly used form of correlation in which each variable is represented by a series of individual events or scores. This is the correlation of two variables in their original form.

correlation, zero  A correlation showing no relationship, or a correlation having a correlation coefficient of zero.

correspondence  (statistics) A relationship of two variables such that every individual score of one variable is paired with a score of the other.

correspondence theory  (philosophy of science) Also called correspondence rules. A formula translating data and concepts in one field of research in reductionism, when the data and concepts (theoretical reductionism) or the research methods (methodological reductionism) of one science have to be presented as derivations of corresponding data and concepts or research methods of another science.

corresponding points  See identical points.

corterita, U. I. 22  (R. B. Cattell) The factor of cortical alertness and arousal in objective tests, such as reaction time, flicker fusion speed, etc.

cortex  1. The outer layer of an organ. 2. The cerebral cortex when used without qualification.

cortex, "association"  Those parts of the brain which are not directly connected with sensory or motor functions. They are thought to be the areas in which sensations are associated or integrated with motor functions.

cortex, auditory  The area of the cortex which registers auditory stimulation.

cortex, frontal  The outer layer of the frontal lobes.

cortex, parietal, structure and function of  The cutaneous-kinesthetic analyzer which provides the kinesthetic basis of motor activity. It is important for discrimination based upon deep pressure sensitivity. This area follows the principle of functional representation whereby the greater the functional significance of the organ, the greater its area of representation in this central area. In man, the inferior parietal cortex has cutaneous-kinesthetic zones which overlap with the visual analyzers.

cortex, sensory  The part of the cerebral cortex which receives neural impulses from the sensory organs via afferent tracts; the sensory projection areas.

corti  Refers to the structures of the inner ear such as the organ of Corti, the arches and the rods of Corti.

cortical center  1. Areas in the cortex which consist of the incoming sensory fibers. 2. Areas of the cortex which consist of efferent motor fibers.

cortical epilepsy  See epilepsy, Jacksonian.

cortical gray  The median gray color perceived by the dark-adapted eye under conditions of total darkness.

cortical satiation theory  (W. Köhler and H. Wallach) The representation of a stimulus in the brain involves electrical charges and currents which may, if prolonged due to neural defect or overexposure to the stimulus, so fatigue the cortical area that the flow of neural processes is impaired or stopped.

corticalization  An increased control of processes by the cerebral cortex characteristic of organisms who are highly placed in the phylogenetic scale.

corticord substances  Hormones secreted by the adrenal cortex which seem to regulate inflammatory reactions to infection.

corticosteroid toxicity  See toxicity, corticosteroid.

corticotrophic hormone  See hormone, corticotrophic.

cortin  A substance made up of several hormones which is secreted by the adrenal cortex and is important in the regulation of the gonads and the control of salt intake.

cortisone  One of the hormones produced in the adrenal cortex or synthetically which is used mainly in adrenal insufficiency.

co-twin control, method of  An experimental method to ascertain the effects of environmental influence by keeping heredity constant in which one twin is subjected to an experimental manipulation while the other twin is not. The twins are subsequently compared to assess the differences due to learning or environmental effects.

counseling  A form of therapeutic aid offered to individuals to help them understand and resolve their adjustment problems. A variety of diverse techniques are used including the giving of advice, mutual discussion, and administration and interpretation of tests.

counseling, directive  A form of counseling in which the counselor controls and stipulates the condition of the interaction.

counseling, director  Counseling in which the counselor directs the topics and actively suggests courses of action.

counseling interview  See interview counseling.

counseling psychology  See psychology, counseling.

counseling, vocational  Counseling concerning employment and vocational adjustment.

counselor  A professionally trained individual who practices counseling.

counter  (operant conditioning) Stimulus, some dimension of which changes systematically with the number of responses emitted.

counteraction need  See need, counteraction.

counterconditioning  The formation of an alternative response to a stimulus through the establishment of another often incompatible response.

counterego  (W. Stekel) The unconscious part of the psyche which is antagonistic to the ego.

**countertransference** (psychoanalysis) Unconscious feelings evoked in the psychoanalyst by the patient which may adversely affect the necessary objective attitude to the patient and interfere with the treatment.

**courts, juvenile** Courts of justice which deal with people below the legal age of adulthood. The philosophy of these courts is that the child requires rehabilitation, not punishment. Laws concerning juvenile offenses are vague allowing the judge the opportunity to provide the juvenile offender with the best alternative for obtaining help for his problems.

**couvade** The custom prevalent among primitive people of the father taking to bed when his child is born in order to recuperate from the pangs of childbirth.

**covariance** A tendency where a change in one variable is accompanied by a change in another. Covariance is given by the formula:
$$\frac{\Sigma XY}{N}$$
where $X$ and $Y$ are the deviations from the mean, of the two variables in the series, $N$ is the number of cases, and $\Sigma$ means to take the sum of the values represented by $XY$.

**covariation chart** (R. B. Cattell) A correlation chart having three dimensions, people (or organisms), tests (or behavioral preformances), and occasions (on which people and tests interact). The covariation chart shows exhaustively the possibilities of all behavior correlation.

**cover memory** See *memory, screen.*

**covert response** See *response, implicit.*

**covert sensitization** (J. Cautela) A method for overcoming unadaptive appetitive behavior, e.g. overeating or homosexuality, through the verbal evocation of unpleasant responses such as nauseation or disgust. The behavior to be extinguished and the aversive response are evoked simultaneously by verbal cues.

**Coxsackie encephalitis** See *encephalities, Coxsackie.*

**CPI** See *California Personality Inventory.*

**cramp** Painful contraction of a muscle or muscle group which is sustained for a period of time.

**cranial capacity** The cubic content of the cranium.

**cranial division** The upper region of the parasympathetic division of the autonomic nervous system.

**cranial index** See *index, cranial.*

**cranial nerves** See *nerves, cranial.*

**cranial reflex** See *reflex, cranial.*

**craniography** The graphing or photographing of the skull.

**craniology** (F. J. Gall) The belief that mental abilities are localized in different areas of the brain and that the presence of these faculties are determined by the contours of the skull.

**craniometry** The measurement of the skull.

**craniosacral division** The portion of the autonomic nervous system originating in the medulla and lower spinal cord which controls vegetative functions in the body.

**cranium** The skull, especially the part containing the brain.

**creative resultants, principle of** (W. Wundt) The principle that the totality of mental processes equals more than the mere summation of the individual elements.

**cremnophobia** Morbid fear of precipices.

**Crespi effect** A disproportionate increase in learning or the strength of a response in comparison with the reward given to this behavior.

**cretinism** Congenital hypothyroidism. Usually no physical signs at birth except for slow physical and mental development. The skin becomes gradually dry and coarse; vocal expression is hoarse; the genitalia remain infantile. Most cretins are of short physical stature and profoundly retarded.

**crf schedule** See *reinforcement, schedule of: continuous.*

**cri du chat syndrome** Severe mental defect caused by a portion missing from chromosome 5 and associated with oligophrenia, somatic hypotrophia, microcephaly and not uncommonly, congenital heart disease.

**crime** A major transgression of the law which is punishable.

**criminal psychology** See *psychology, criminal.*

**criminal responsibility** A term specified by law to delimit conditions under which the person is held responsible for his actions and can be punished for them.

**criminology** The scientific study of crime and criminals and of the social and psychological factors associated with them.

**crisis theory** See *theory, crisis.*

**crisis therapy** See *therapy, crisis.*

**crispation** Mild contraction of muscles, convulsive or spasmodic.

**criterion analysis** 1. A method of factor analysis using the criterion variable in the test matrix. 2. (H. J. Eysenck) A procedure of factor rotation using two homogeneous groups which are differentiated by the factor which accounts for the greatest amount of variance in the factor matrix.

**criterion rotation** A form of factor rotation in which the difference existing between a control and an experimental or criterion group is made to be the expression of a single factor.

**criterion score** See *score, criterion.*

**criterion variable** See *variable, criterion.*

**critical flicker-fusion frequency** The rate at which a flickering stimulus ceases to be perceived as such and is seen as a continuous fused stimulus.

critical incident technique See *technique, critical incident.*

critical period A point in development at which the individual is optimally ready to learn a particular response pattern. This concept is much like that of maturational readiness.

critical point 1. A point which has been designated as the dividing point which separates ranked scores into distinct groups with reference to some criterion. 2. (S. R. Slavson) Specific time or stage in therapy during which the individual realizes his problems clearly and decides upon a definite course of action to deal with them in a constructive way.

critical ratio (C. R.) The ratio of the difference between two statistics to the standard error of that difference. It is a measure of how probable it is that the obtained statistic is affected by chance. The most commonly used *CR* involves the difference between two means. The formula for uncorrelated means is $C.R. = \dfrac{M_1 - M_2}{\sqrt{\sigma^2_{M_1} + \sigma^2_{M_2}}}$

where $M$ = mean, and $\sigma$ = the standard error of the mean. The difference is not regarded as being significant unless the $CR$ is at least 3.

critical score The score which divides a group of scores or values into distinct groups with reference to some criterion.

Cro-magnon man An upper Paleolithic man manifesting a high level of physical and mental development characteristic of modern man represented by skulls found in Western Europe.

Cronbach, Lee J. (1916- ) American psychologist. Developed (with Meehl) theory of construct validation in psychology; developed (with Gleser) interpretation of tests as aid to decision making; formulated (with Snow) strategy for research on aptitude-treatment interaction; elaborated (with Gleser and others) theory of error and generalization in psychometrics; chaired first committee to develop standards for psychological tests; prepared major textbooks on psychological testing and educational psychology.

cross-adaptation The change in an individual's sensitivity to one stimulus as a function of his adaptation to another stimulus regardless of whether or not both stimuli are in the same modality.

cross-conditioning See *conditioning, cross.*

cross-correspondence (parapsychology) A message arising in automatic writing of one medium which can be understood only by another medium.

cross-cultural approach The study of the effects of social practices and environmental influences upon behavior through the investigation and comparison of several cultures.

cross-modal integration The ability to coordinate information acquired by more than one sense, for instance, tactile and visual, or auditory and visual. Reading is based on the ability to coordinate or integrate the visual sensation of a written or printed word with the sound of the same word spoken. Deficiency or failure of cross-modal integration is believed to be one of the causes of dyslexia (the disability to read).

cross-modality matching (S. S. Stevens) A psychophysical experiment in which the subjects are presented with several standard stimuli, for example, five weights, and the response is to adjust the value of a second continuum, such as loudness, so that the second continuum matches the psychological value of each of the standard stimuli.

cross-parental identification See *identification, cross-parental.*

cross-sectional method See *method, cross-sectional.*

cross-validation A method of determining the validity of a technique or research procedure by administering it to a second group to see if the results coincide with the findings obtained from the administration of this procedure to the original group with whom it has been found to be valid.

crossing over See *crossover.*

crossover Exchange of genetic material between members of a chromosome pair. The chiasmata seen at diplotene are the physical evidence of crossing over.

crucial experiment See *experiment, crucial.*

crude mode See *mode, crude.*

crude score See *score, crude.*

cry, epileptic Strange, abrasive sounds made by an epileptic just prior to the arresting of respiration in a grand mal; thought to be caused by the sudden release of air through the glottis which contracts as the tonic spasm begins.

cry, initial See *cry, epileptic.*

cryptogenic epilepsy See *epilepsy, cryptogenic.*

crystal gazing See *gazing, crystal.*

crystalline lens See *lens.*

crystallized general ability (R. B. Cattell) A general factor, largely in a type of abilities learned at school, representing the effect of past application of fluid intelligence, and amount and intensity of schooling, it appears in such tests as vocabulary and numerical ability measures.

crystallophobia Morbid fear of glass.

crystasthesia A form of perception which is not explainable in terms of known receptors such as clairvoyance or mental telepathy.

crytococcus meningitis See *meningitis, crytococcus.*

crytomnesia The appearance of ostensibly novel experiences, memories, or thoughts, which originate in forgotten or repressed experiences.

cue 1. A signal which elicits behavior based on previous experience. 2. A signal in the perceptual field which the organism uses to make a discrimination.

cue, incidental  See *stimulus, incidental.*

cue reduction  The phenomenon whereby one aspect of a stimulus can elicit a response which was previously evoked by the whole response.

cue reversal  The interchanging of a cue which signaled reward with the cue which signaled nonreward in an experimental situation.

Cullen, William (1710-1790)  Scottish physician who introduced a broad classification of diseases, inclusive of mental illnesses. He coined the term neurosis for diseases which had no local pathology nor caused fever. He divided all neuroses into comata (strokes), adynamias (diseases of the autonomic nerves), spasms (convulsions), and vesanias (mental deficiencies and insanities).

cultural adaptability  The ability of migratory groups to accept the culture of the country they migrated to. Also called acculturation.

cultural anthropology  A branch of anthropology which studies the manners, morals, and social relations of various societies, tribes, and ethnic groups.

cultural deprivation  Substandard living conditions and/or discrimination which prevent certain individuals from participation in the cultural achievements of their society. Cultural deprivation is often quoted among the causes of mental retardation.

cultural determinism  The belief that the culture determines personality structure.

cultural disorganization  A breakdown of traditional cultural bonds and of the importance of values due to transition within a society or the transition of an individual from one society to another.

cultural lag  Residues of cultural values from bygone days, not related to the present day culture.

cultural norm  A set of cultural values generally accepted in a given society.

cultural parallelism  (cultural anthropology) The appearance of similar cultures in two places or two epochs without any connections or influence between the two cultures.

cultural pressure  A dimension found by factoring variables defining modern nations and loading cultural productivity, e.g., Nobel prizes, urbanization, indices of frustration and sublimation, frequency of war, etc.

cultural relativism  The belief that mental health and mental disorder do not have a universal meaning but depend on cultural norms of each particular society. Accordingly people believed to be mentally disturbed could be believed to be normal in another society.

culture  1. The way a certain society lives. 2. The totality of manners, customs, values, of a given society, inclusive of its socioeconomic system, political structure, science, religion, education, art and entertainment. 3. The intellectual aspects of life, such as science, art and religion.

culture area  Geographical boundaries of a culture.

culture epoch theory  A theory that all societies pass through the same periods in their history. A. Comte's theory of the theological, metaphysical and positive stages, and Hegel's thesis, antithesis and synthesis theory are representative examples.

culture-free test  A psychological test that can be administered to individuals in any culture. Test results are not affected by cultural factors.

culture trait  1. Personality trait common to all people belonging to a certain culture. 2. A material or symbolic element of a given culture.

cumulative  1. Constituting that which has been successively put together or summed as each new quantity is added. 2. (statistics) Referring to a method of representing a distribution in which the sum of all elements is taken from the beginning to a certain point by adding each figure successively to the next until all the cases in the distribution have been represented.

cumulative curve  A graphic representation of the sums of the frequencies of a series of scores. Each point on the curve represents the summed total of the number of cases at and below that point (or at and above).

cumulative deficits phenomenon  (M. Deutsch) With persistent influence from a disadvantaged environment there is, over time, an increasingly larger negative effect on the behavior in question.

cumulative distribution  A type of frequency distribution where each plot represents the summed total of the number of cases falling at or below that point (or at or above that point).

cumulative frequency  A graphical or numerical accumulation of cases in which each new case is added to the preceding total.

cumulative frequency curve  See *cumulative curve.*

cumulative record  A continuous summative record to which new data are added to the preceding total.

cumulative scale  See *scale, Guttman.*

cumulative tests  See *tests, cumulative.*

cuneus  A wedge-shaped area on the middle surface of the occipital lobe of the cerebrum.

cunnilingus  Oral stimulation of the female genitals.

cunnus  The external genitals of the female.

Curtis completion form  Projective test used with children 11 and over in which sentences are completed. Scoring method is partially objective, yielding a cumulative point score.

curve, acquisition cumulative  The graphic representation of the rate of response in operant conditioning in which the slope of the cumulative curve reflects the response rate.

curve, asymptotic  A curve which constantly approaches a straight line but never reaches it.

curve, bell-shaped  The graph of a normal distribution.

**curve, distribution** Also called frequency curve, or probability curve, represents graphically the frequency of occurrence.

**curve, fitting** Finding the curve best representing particular empirical data.

**curve, J** (F. H. Allport) A graphic representation of the frequency with which individuals comply with a rule or standard lying within the range of their capacity. The curve approximates the shape of the capital letter J.

**curve, Jordan** (topology) A closed curve of any shape which does not intersect itself, usually used to define regions of life space.

**curve, learning** See *learning, curve*.

**curve, logarithmic** A curve in which each point along one coordinate is the logarithm of the value of the other coordinate. The equation is $y = \log x$. Also called logistic curve.

**curve, mental growth** A graphic representation of mental development as a function of chronological age in which mental age is plotted on the vertical axis and chronological age is on the horizontal axis.

**curve, normal distribution** (K. B. Gauss) A bell-shaped curve which is a graphic description of a theoretical function having as its domain all of the real numbers. It is continuous for all values of a variable $x$ between $-\infty$ and $+\infty$; therefore the graph never touches the horizontal axis. The tails of the curve show decreasing probability densities as the values of $x$ become extreme in any direction. The distribution is absolutely symmetric and unimodal. The mean, median and mode all have the same value of $x$. The height of the curve, denoted by $y$ refers to the probability density for each value of $x$. The entire area cut off beneath the curve by any interval is a probability. The mathematical rule for a normal density function is

$$f(x) = \frac{1}{\sqrt{2\pi\sigma^2}} e - \frac{x - \mu}{2\sigma^2}$$

where $\pi$ and $e$ are mathematical constants, $x$ is the value of the variable, $\mu$ is the mean and $\sigma^2$ is the variance.

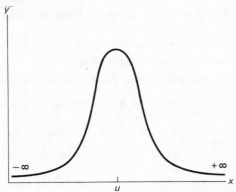

**curve of rest** A graphic description of the gradual change of the psychogalvanic skin response under conditions of no stimulation.

**curve, percentile** (statistics) An ogival-shaped cumulative frequency curve which indicates the cumulative frequencies as percentages of the total number of cases.

**curve, performance** Curve which measures and graphically illustrates performance of a particular behavior as a function of some other variable such as learning, incentive, or time. Such curves are often referred to as learning curves, though what is actually measured is performance.

**curve, retention** (H. E. Ebbinghaus) A graphic representation of the amount of learned material which is remembered over a period of time consisting of a measure of remembering on the vertical axis and a measure of the time elapsed since learning on the horizontal axis.

**curve, S** Referring to a curve that is shaped like an S.

**curvilinear correlation** See *correlation, curvilinear*.

**curvilinear regression** See *regression, curvilinear*.

**curvilinear relationship** A relationship between two variables which is graphically represented by a curved rather than a straight line.

**custodial care** Hospitalization without treatment. For a long time mental hospitals were (some still are) institutions that practiced custodial care.

**cut-off whole** A special classification for scoring Rorschach responses which involve the subject's use of two thirds or more of the blot and the deliberate exclusion of the remainder of the blot to make for a better response. This category, generally scored with the symbol W, was devised by Klopfer and has been adopted in most approaches to the Rorschach although strongly argued against in the Beck approach.

**cutaneous sense** See *sense, cutaneous*.

**cybernetics** (N. Wiener) A science of communication, information and of feedback and control mechanisms which uses servomechanisms.

**cycle disorder** Any behavior disorder with distinct reversal of moods. See *manic-depressive psychosis; dysmutualism*.

**cycle, manic-depressive** The change of mood from depression to elation and reverse, typical of manic-depressive patients.

**cyclophoria** A rotated deviation of the eye due to a muscular imbalance.

**cycloplegia** See *mydriasis*.

**cyclothyme** 1. One who exhibits alternating changes of mood from elation and hyperactivity, to depression and sadness. 2. (E. Kretschmer) Person who has a *cyclothymic* temperament, one of two basic temperaments.

**cyclothymia** Uneven pattern of mood changes from elation and hyperactivity to depression and sadness.

**cyclothymic** (E. Kretschmer) One of two basic temperament classification associated most frequently with the pyknic body-type and characterized by shifts in mood. The extreme cases of cyclothymics develop manic-depressive psychosis.

**cyclothymic personality** Also called affective personality with periods of depression, worry, low energy, pessimism and alternating periods of elation, ambition, enthusiasm and optimism.

**cyclothymic type** See *type, cyclothymic*.

**cynonthropy** A delusion that oneself is a dog.

**cynorexia** See *hyperphagia*.

**cypridophobia** An extreme fear of contracting venereal disease.

**cystathioninuria** A rare aminoaciduria associated with mental retardation.

**cytogenetics** Area of biology concerned with the study of heredity from the viewpoints of cytology and genetics.

**cytology** Area of biology dealing with the study of cells, their formation, structure and functions.

**cytomegalic inclusion body disease** A viral disease; when occurring in pregnant women may affect the fetus and cause congenital mental deficiency. Inclusion bodies can be discovered in urine and the cerebral fluid.

# D

**D** 1. Symbol for drive. 2. (statistics) The symbol for the measure of the scattering of values around a mean or median which includes the middle four-fifths of the cases or the cases between the tenth and the ninetieth percentiles of a frequency distribution. 3. (statistics) The difference between two scores of the same person. 4. (statistics) The symbol for the measure of similarity between set of numbers given by the formula

$$D_{12}{}^2 = \sum_{j-1}^{k} (x_{j1} - x_{j2})^2$$

where $j$ = the number of $k$ variables; the numbers 1 and 2 refer to the two sets of scores and $x_{j1}$ and $x_{j2}$ are the scores of the two sets on variable $j$. 5. (H. Rorschach) A response to parts of an inkblot card in the Rorschach test, which are conspicuous in size. It is believed to indicate interest in the obvious, practical and concrete. 6. (C. Hull) The symbol for the strength of the primary drive which motivates an animal to action after the acquisition of the specific habit involved in the action. It is computed by the formula:

$$D = \frac{D' \times D}{D'}.$$

7. (K. Spence) The symbol for the logarithmic difference between the stimulus used to train an animal and the one used to test him.

**d** 1. (statistics) Symbol for deviation. 2. (statistics) The deviation of a class from the mean of a population. 3. (statistics) The discrepancy between the rank a person receives on two tests. 4. (Rorschach) A score for a response to small visual details of an inkblot card. 5. Diopter. 6. Drive. 7. The number of just noticeable differences found between two stimulus groups.

**d'** 1. (C. Hull) Symbol for $\overset{\circ}{D} - D$. 2. (signal detection theory) An index of the subject's sensitivity in a signal detection sensory experiment. It is the difference between the mean of the distribution of the noise alone from the mean of the distribution of the noise and signal together divided by the standard deviation. The difference between the two distributions are given in terms of standard scores, like $Z$ scores:

$$d' = \frac{M_{SN} - M_N}{\sigma_N}.$$

**D'** (C. L. Hull) The symbol of primary drive components not operative in the formation of a habit.

**$\overset{\circ}{D}$** (C. L. Hull) The symbol of primary drive components not operative in the formation of a habit.

**$\bar{D}$** (C. L. Hull) Symbol equal to the formula

$$100 \, \frac{D + D}{D' + Md}.$$

**d reaction test** See *test, d reaction.*

**d reaction time** See *time, d reaction.*

**dacrygelosis** An obsolete term which indicates alternate spells of crying and laughter.

**dactylology** 1. One-hand alphabet in which symbols are expressed with the fingers. 2. Manual communication of the type generally used by deaf-mutes.

**daemon; daimon** 1. In ancient Greek mythology: a guiding spirit. 2. In medieval terms: an evil spirit that enters a person's body and controls his mind and forces him to act in a bizarre and often antisocial manner.

**daemonic; daimonic** 1. An obsessive thought or feeling that dominates a person's behavior. 2. (R. May) A powerful, uncontrollable drive; a blind push toward self-assertion mainly in rage and sex.

**daemonic character** (S. Freud) A self-destructive drive in masochistic individuals; an expression of the death instinct. The individuals with this self-destructive drive tend to repeat the same actions despite the damage caused to themselves, as if possessed by a daemon.

**daemonophobia** A morbid fear of being attacked by daemons.

**dainties, craving for** An uncontrollable desire for delicacies or some special food. See *opsomania.*

**Daltonism** Red-green color blindness after the English scientist John Dalton (1766-1844), himself color-blind, who gave the first description of this condition.

**damping** The checking or restraining of the amplitude of a vibration either due to sudden or progressive external pressure or internal friction.

**damping constant** The role of decrease of the amplitude presented by a mathematical formula

$$\frac{\sigma}{T}$$

where δ stands for the amplitude, and $T$ stands for the period of time.

**dance therapy** See *psychotherapy, dance.*

**dancing madness** Frenzied dancing such as occurred in Germany during the 14th century. This type of convulsive dance seemed to spread among the masses like an epidemic. It accompanied the outbreak of the Bubonic plague or "Black Death." (1334-1351). See *choreomania* or *choromania; epidemic chorea.*

**dancing mania** 1. An abnormal impulse to dance. 2. A form of psycho-motor over-activity which may take place in conjunction with religious experiences. See *dinomania.*

**dancing mouse** A breed of mouse with a characteristic walking pattern often used in psychological experimentation.

**DAP** See *test, Draw-A-Person.*

**dark adaptation** The process by which the eye becomes sensitive to visual stimuli illuminated by weak light. The process is dependent on the resynthesis of visual purple, rhodopsin, by the rod elements of the retina. See *scotopic adaptation.*

**Darwin, Charles Robert (1802-1882)** Born in Shrewsbery, England and educated at the universities of Edinburgh and Cambridge. In *"The expression of emotions in man and animals"* and *"The descent of man and selection in relation to sex"* he made outstanding contributions to psychology by showing the possibility of not only the evolution of the organic structure but also of the mental functions. Darwin's theory of evolution has become a cornerstone in comparative psychology. Lloyd Morgan, Sechenov, Pavlov, Freud and the functionalists have been inspired by Darwin's theories.

**darwinism** The theory of evolution proposed by Charles Darwin, that through the process of natural selection all organisms have evolved from earlier and primitive organisms. This results in a view of phylogenetic continuity from the primitive to the sophisticated species of organisms.

**DAT** See *test, differential aptitude.*

**data** Plural of datum. Group of factual items collected by observation or experimentation upon which inferences and conclusions are based.

**data processing** A mathematical analysis and description of data.

**datum** Singular of data. An item of information.

**day blindness** An abnormality of the eye in which the central fovea of the retina does not accommodate to high intensities of light stimulation. In such cases, bright light is uncomfortable and vision is better in dim light.

**day dream** See *dream, day.*

**day-dreamer** One who indulges in waking reveries.

**day hospital** See *hospital, day.*

**day residues** Remembrances of experiences of the previous day which, in part, determine the manifest content of a dream.

**daylight vision** See *photopic vision.*

**daymare** An acute state of anxiety of distress induced by fantasies during the waking state.

**Dd** (H. Rorschach) Response to small unusual details in an inkblot card which are perceptually well articulated and which reflect an interest in the fine aspects of situations.

**dd** (H. Rorschach) Response to tiny unusual details in an inkblot card.

**Dds** (H. Rorschach) A response to small unusual details having a small white space which is meaningful in determining the response.

**DDT poisoning** See *poisoning, DDT.*

**DdW** (H. Rorschach) A response to a whole inkblot card determined by a small unusual detail which suggests the given percept.

**de** 1. (H. Rorschach) Response to tiny unusual edge details in an inkblot card which is believed to indicate anxiety and evasion on the part of the subject. 2. See *threshold, difference.*

**deaf mute** One who can neither hear nor speak.

**deafness** Inability to hear sounds. Total deafness is an inability to detect all auditory stimuli. Selective deafness is the loss of sensitivity to a specific range of auditory stimuli. Adventitious deafness is due to injury to the ear, whereas congenital deafness is due to a defect in development. Cortical deafness is due to a malfunction in some area of the cerebral cortex; and nerve deafness results from a malfunction in the pathway from the inner ear to the auditory cortex.

**deafness, conduction** Deafness due to impairment of the conduction structures, the outer ear, eardrum or the middle ear so that sound waves are obtained on their way to the inner ear.

**deafness, hysterical** A form of deafness despite the apparent lack of physiological defect. Hysterical deafness is one of several psychoneurotic conversion reactions, in which the anxiety resulting from an unconscious conflict is converted to some debilitating organic symptom. The specific symptom that develops usually has some compensatory value for the individual.

**de-anal** Transfer of instinctual impulses from the anal region to some other mode of expression.

**de-anality** Referred to instinctual impulses when they find expression in ways unrelated to the anal region.

**de-analize** When instinctual impulses have been transferred from the anal region to some other mode of expression they are said to have been de-analized.

**death** Cessation of bodily and mental functions vital to the organism.

**death feigning** The immobility of some animals in the presence of a threat.

**death instinct** See *Thanatos*.

**death phantasy** Imagining oneself as being dead, and at the same time being aware of what is going on. Typical for manic-depressive patients who often imagine themselves lying in a coffin and watching the reaction of their families and relatives.

**death rate** The ratio of the number of individuals who died at a stated time and place to the total number of individuals at that time and place.

**debilitas animi** An archaic term for mental retardation.

**debilitas erethisica** An archaic term for pathological irritability.

**debility** A physical weakness and lack of vigor.

**decadence** The deterioration of an individual or society resulting from social rather than biological or physical factors.

**deceit, studies of** (H. Hartshorne and M.A. May) Studies of character reported in 1930 in which three areas of moral behavior were assessed: the subject's moral knowledge, his moral attitudes and opinions, and his actual moral behavior. Children, grades five to eight, were tested. Questionnaires and inventories examined moral knowledge and opinions and objective tests ascertained actual behavior. It is believed that these tests of honesty measure deceitfulness, dishonesty, and unfairness. The studies have been criticized because deceit does not seem to be a general measure but specific in particular situations.

**decile** Referring to a division which contains one tenth of the cases in a given distribution of ranked scores.

**decontextualization** (R. R. Sears) A defensive process in which external stimuli (e.g., persons, places, objects) associated with a previous anxiety-evoking experience are avoided or ignored.

**defective, high-grade** A classification of intellectual endowment ranging from IQ 50-69 referring to a person of subnormal intelligence who can adapt to concrete situations with a minimum of supervision.

**defense, isolation** (Rorschach) Isolated comments about the inkblots, rather than responses to them, thought to indicate an effort to avoid those aspects of the blots which may evoke feelings of conflict or anxiety.

**defense mechanism** The term "defense mechanism" was introduced by Freud in 1894. In 1936 Anna Freud described defense mechanisms in detail. Defense mechanisms are methods used by the ego in fighting off the instinctual outbursts of the id and the attacks of the superego. A strong ego does not typically use defense mechanisms, but when it is unable to cope with id and superego pressures, it may resort to the use of these mechanisms. Therefore, all defense mechanisms, except sublimation, indicate an inner conflict and a state of anxiety.

**defense, perceptual** Selective perception of stimuli by which anxiety-provoking stimuli are kept from awareness. Experimentally it has been shown that taboo or offensive words, presented rapidly within a series of neutral words, are either not seen or misperceived, by the subject.

**defensive strategies** (G. M. Gilbert) In contrast to defense mechanisms, defensive strategies involve long-range and overt behavior patterns, especially social role assumptions and interpersonal relations, which serve the purpose of ego enhancement and defense. Examples are: manipulative or opportunistic affiliation, reactive or compensatory aggression.

**deference need** See *need, deference*.

**deficiency, mental** Subnormal intellectual development. Adaptation to the social environment and emotional adjustment as well as the development of learning ability are used in assessing mental-deficiency. IQ scores in intelligence tests more than two standard deviations below the mean are generally considered to be in the mentally deficient range but overall social or behavioral adjustment is the primary consideration in the determination of mental deficiency. IQ scores two to three standard deviations below the mean are in the range of mild mental deficiency; scores three to four standard deviations below the mean are in the moderate range; scores four to five standard deviations below the mean are in the severe range; and scores more than five standard deviations below the mean are in the profound range.

**deflection strain** The strain occasioned by the organism's acceptance of goals or paths-to-goals that are substitutes, in the sense of not being innately preferred; for example, escaping a fire by first moving towards it. Similar to the concept of sublimation, but broader in that it includes acceptance of substitute paths as well as substitute goals.

**deletion** A form of chromosomal aberration in which a portion of chromosome is lost, for example, of the short arm of chromosome 5 in the Cri du chat syndrome.

**delinquency** An infraction of the moral or legal code; if by an individual under 16 or 18 years of age, depending on state law, it is referred to as juvenile delinquency.

**delinquency area** A neighborhood in which the incidence of delinquency is disproportionally high.

**delinquency, juvenile** Relatively minor violation of legal or moral codes by a child or an adolescent which brings him to the attention of a court.

**delinquent** One who offends by negligence, neglect, or violation of a duty or responsibility, or by a minor infraction of a law.

**deliramentum** An archaic term for delirium.

**deliratio senum** An archaic term for senile psychosis.

**deliration** An archaic term for delirium.

**délire** A French term used sometimes to mean delirium, mania, or paranoia.

**délire à quatre** A shared, systematized set of delusions, often of persecution, originating first in one person but then spreading to three others.

**délire d'emblée** (E. Bleuler) A delusion that is complete and stabilized at its outset.

**délire d'énormité** (E. Bleuler) The delusion that the amount of urine to be passed will cause a flood. Consequently such patients may refrain from urinating for long periods of time.

**délire de négation** An archaic term for withdrawal symptoms.

**délire de négation généralise** An archaic term referring to a complete withdrawal from the world, in which the patient has come to believe that the world no longer exists.

**délire du toucher** A compulsion to touch things.

**délire tremblant** Delirium tremens.

**delirium** A non specific term for mental confusion. Often accompanied by delusions and hallucinations. It may be a result of organic brain damage, drugs, fevers, and shock.

**delirium abstinence** A delirious state caused by the discontinuation of the habitual use of one of several drugs or alcohol.

**delirium, acute** (E. Bleuler) A delirium thought to be caused by an infection or schizophrenic processes resulting in convulsions and often, death.

**delirium, alcoholicum** Delirium tremens.

**delirium ebriosorum** Delirium tremens.

**delirium grandiosum** Megalomania.

**delirium metamorphosis** An archaic term for the delusion that the individual's body has turned into a body of a beast.

**delirium, oneiric** An archaic term referring to a delirium accompanied by hallucinations of which the individual has no memory.

**delirium sine materia** An archaic term for a delirium with no apparent physiological cause.

**delirium tremefaciens** Delirium tremens.

**delirium tremens** An acute delirium precipitated usually by alcoholic poisoning but also occurring as a result of brain inflammation and senile psychosis. It is characterized by intense tremors, anxiety, hallucinations, and delusions.

**delirium verborum** A delirious state characterized by great verbiage.

**delirium vesanicum** A non-specific archaic term for a delirium that includes hallucinations, delusions, incoherence, illusions, etc.

**delta movement** See *movement, delta.*

**delusion** 1. A perception contrary to reality despite evidence and common sense. 2. An irrational and obstinate belief in an idea. 3. A system of irrational beliefs that the individual actively defends.

**delusion, asthenic** (P. Janet) Delusions accompanied by psychasthenic activity; the critical powers cease to function and all emotions, thoughts, and acts are expressed.

**delusion, autopsychic** (K. Wernicke) One of a classification of delusions suggested by K. Wernicke. When the individual's personality is the subject of the delusion, it is an autopsychic delusion. When the outside world is the subject of the delusion, it is an allopsychic delusion. When the individual's body is the subject of the delusion, it is a somatopsychic delusion.

**delusion, catathymic** (E. Bleuler) A delusion caused by the affective content of a complex in the unconscious.

**delusion, expansive** The same as delusion of grandeur.

**delusion, explanatory** (E. Bleuler) Refers to the evidence that an individual gives in offering proof of the truth of his delusions. The evidence itself is delusionary.

**delusion, healthy** (C. B. Farrar) The opinion that whether an idea is acceptable or is branded as a delusion depends on its source.

**delusion of grandeur** The exaggerated belief of the individual that he is a great man. He may believe himself to be God, Napoleon, a prince, or a general.

**delusion of interpretation** An interpretation of a delusion given by the individual himself.

**delusion of observation** The same as delusion of reference.

**delusion of persecution** An irrational belief that the individual is a victim of a conspiracy to kill him or to injure him or cause him to fail. It is most common in paranoid individuals where even seemingly innocuous events are taken as proof of the conspiracy.

**delusion of reference** The false belief of the individual that behaviors of others have malign and derogatory reference to the individual when in fact they have no reference to the individual at all.

**delusion, psychasthenic** See *delusion, asthenic.*

**delusion, residual** (C. Neisser) Refers to delusions that are formed in an acute state and maintained in a chronic state.

**delusional system** A system of false beliefs which is resistant to other points of view.

**demand** Any aspect of an organism's internal or external environment that results in a drive.

**demand character** (Gestalt) A stimulus arouses and

directs the appropriate behavior of an organism. The music demands to be listened to or the chocolate cake to be tasted.

**dementia** Non-specific but lasting deterioration of emotion or intellectual powers.

**dementia agitata** (R. Krafft-Ebing) An agitated state of individuals suffering from dementia praecox.

**dementia, alcoholic** The first state of deterioration in Korsakov's alcoholic psychosis.

**dementia apoplectica** The dementia due to cerebral hemorrhage or softening of brain tissues possibly due to cerebral arteriosclerosis.

**dementia arteriosclerotic** Dementia due to cerebral arteriosclerosis. The same as dementia apoplectica.

**dementia atrophic** Presenile psychosis.

**dementia depressive** (E. Kraepelin) See *schizophrenia, catatonic type*.

**dementia, endogenous** (E. Kraepelin) Dementias are endogenous if they: a) arise from internal causes, and, as far as can be seen, are not occasioned by external causes; b) result in more or less general enfeeblement. This distinction is now no longer maintained.

**dementia, epileptic** Deterioration in an epileptic individual, the cause of which apparently is variable from individual to individual.

**dementia infantilis** A degenerative disease of the neurons in the cerebral lobes occurring at about three years of age which leads to a rapid loss of speech and some impairment of motor functions.

**dementia, paralytic** See *paresis*.

**dementia, paralytica** Archaic term for paresis.

**dementia paranoides** (E. Kraepelin) Archaic term for schizophrenia, paranoid type.

**dementia post-traumatic** Impairment of intellectual functioning subsequent to a head injury.

**dementia praecocissima** (S. de Santis) Any of the schizophrenic symptoms appearing in children under five years of age.

**dementia praecox** Schizophrenia.

**dementia praecox, agitated** (E. Kraepelin) A subclass of schizophrenia or dementia praecox distinguished from other forms of schizophrenia by extreme agitation. This term was never widely accepted in the U.S.A.

**dementia praesenilis** Gradual loss of mental powers, intellectual or emotional, seen usually in elderly individuals; however, if observed in younger individuals called dementia praesenilis.

**dementia, primary** Simple schizophrenia.

**dementia psychoasthenic** (P. Janet) From an archaic nosology in which much behavior of schizophrenics is thought to be due to psychological exhaustion arising from uncontrolled thoughts, emotions, illusions, and delusions.

**dementia sejunctiva** Rare term for schizophrenia.

**dementia semantica** A verbal reaction void of feelings.

**dementia, senile** The impairment of intellectual functioning in elderly individuals. It occurs with senile brain disease.

**dementia simplex** Archaic term for simple schizophrenia.

**dementia, traumatic** Intellectual or emotional deterioration caused by injury.

**dementive schizophrenia** (B. B. Wolman) The final stage of deterioration in schizophrenia. The ego and superego no longer interfere with the action of the id, and personality structure breaks down.

**demissio animi** Archaic word for melancholia.

**demi-vierge** (M. Prevost) Refers to a woman that physically is a virgin but psychologically is not a virgin.

**democratic group** 1. Group based on democratic principles. 2. (K. Lewin) An experimental group in sociopsychological research, in which the group members are free to choose whomever they wish to work with, and the leader refrains from imposing his will upon the members of the groups.

**demography** The statistical study of human populations including birth and death rates, income, geographic distribution, mental measurements, etc.

**demon** See *daemon*.

**demonia** Morbid fear of demons.

**demoniac** Archaic term for a mentally disturbed person.

**demonolatry** Worship of a demon or devil.

**demonology** Study of folklore, mythology, and theology dealing with demons and evil spirits.

**demonomania** Obsession with demons.

**demono-melancholia** Same as demonomania.

**demophobia** Morbid fear of crowds.

**demoralization, personal** (R. Park) When an individual reorganizes some values and habits without a concomitant reorganization of his life.

**demorphinization** Termination of the use of morphine.

**demyelination** Loss of myelin.

**denarcism** When the individual is no longer attached to himself; when the psychic energy has been directed to objects external to the individual.

**denatured alcohol poisoning** See *poisoning, ethyl alcohol*.

**dendrite** The part of a nerve cell that receives an impulse from other nerves and carries the impulse toward the nerve body.

**dendron** Same as *dendrite*.

dendrophilia  Love of trees.

dendropsychosis  A strong interest in trees, not necessarily pathological.

denervation  Prevention of the functioning of nerves in part of the body by removing or sectioning them.

denial  Sometimes the weak ego rejects not the past but the present; the defense mechanism called denial is involved in such a rejection. When its actual current life becomes too painful to accept or too difficult to cope with, the infantile ego withdraws from reality, breaking away from the truth, and refusing to acknowledge the existence of painful facts. Memory and perceptions prevent an unlimited escape from reality; but in some pathological cases the hard-pressed ego gives up reality-testing and simply denies facts. Some persons go so far as to deny the loss of beloved ones by acting as if the latter were still around.

denotation  Signifying or designating objects or concepts by some sign, gesture, symbol or word. Distinguished from connotation in which significant aspects are implied rather than denoted.

density  1. A quality characteristic of some types of stimuli; some psychologists maintain that an elementary characteristic of a tone is density, distinct from pitch, volume or timbre with its own absolute and differential thresholds. 2. In statistical theory the probability of instances of a range of events in a continuous probability distribution.

dental age  Dental development measured by the number of permanent teeth a child has to the average number of permanent teeth for his age group.

dentate nucleus  A complex of gray nerve cells, shaped like teeth, located in the cerebellum. There is some evidence that it is involved with the experience of emotion.

Denver system  Classification of chromosomes in a descending order of magnitude, with number one the largest and twenty-two the smallest of the autosomal chromosomes.

de-oral  Removal of oral impulses from the oral zones.

de-orality  The expression of psychic energy normally expressed through the oral region being expressed through some other region.

dependence  1. A relationship between two phenomona in which the occurrence or maintenance of one phenomonon is a necessary condition for the occurrance or maintenance of the other. 2. A reliance on other individuals for the formation and maintenance of opinions and ideas.

dependence need  See need, dependence.

dependence, oral  (psychoanalysis) Wish to be taken care by the mother or a mother substitute.

dependency  1. An action system for which another person's nurturant, helping, caretaking and affectionate activities are the rewarding environmental events; supplicative behavior that elicits such responses from others. 2. (psychoanalysis) An emotional relationship, as above, established in the oral stage of infancy.

dependency motive  Motivation based on a need to be cared for or to gain support through affiliation.

dependent  1. An individual whose social, economic or intellectual wellbeing is maintained by some other individual. 2. A factor contingent upon another factor.

dependent variable  See variable, dependent.

depersonalization  A feeling in an individual that he is no longer himself. His personality, his body, external events, the whole world may no longer appear real.

depolarization  In the normal resting stage of a neuron an electrical equilibrium is established across the neural cell membrane such that the inside of the cell is negatively charged to usually about -70 to -80 millivolts. This is a result of a high concentration of negatively charged ions inside the cell and positively charged ions outside the cell. The membrane normally prevents the positive ions from entering the cell thereby maintaining the equilibrium. When the neuron is fired, the cell membrane permits the positive ions to enter the cell and the depolarization across the membrane takes place. This is the mechanism of neural transmission.

depraved appetite  Archaic term for pica, a craving for unnatural foods.

depression  Feelings of helplessness, hopelessness, inadequacy, and sadness. These may be symptomatic of several disorders; however, these feelings occur also in normal individuals.

depression, adolescent  Mild depression often accompanied with hypochondria and anxiety, usually seen in young men and women.

depression, agitated  A syndrome of abnormal behavior characterized by overactivity, restlessness and tension so that the patient can remain still for only short periods fo time. The agitated-depressed patient is extremely anxious and apprehensive, expecting impending doom. He tends to talk about his fears and despair, and often expresses self-hatred. He shows his depression and suffering as he paces back and forth, wringing his hands, moaning and crying. He is prone to acting out in a hostile manner against others as well as against himself.

depression, ambivalent  (E. Minkowski) Depression in which ambivalence is an outstanding symptom.

depression, anaclitic  (R. Spitz) Syndrome observable in infants having lost their primary care takers and/or object choices in which aggressive and sexual drives, due to the absence of the preferred and accustomed object, are turned inward.

depression, constitutional  Depression thought to have been related to body type or physical constitution of the individual. However, there has been no proof of this.

depression, cyclical  Another term for manic-depres-

*sive, depressed type.* A recurring mood disorder characterized by a severely depressed state and by mental and motor retardation; uneasiness, apprehension, perplexity, and agitation may also be present.

**depression, involutional** Another term for *involutional melancholia*; a mood disorder occurring in older age characterized by worry, anxiety, agitation and insomnia, often with guilt feelings.

**depression, listless** (J. MacCaudy) The individual responds to depressive ideas with effortless resignation.

**depression, reactive** A transient depression attributed to some experience; the individual usually has no history of repeated depressions.

**depression, retarded** A depression in which normal activities are impaired.

**depression, stuporous** A severe depression in which normal activities are omitted.

**depressive anxiety** The anxiety that may accompany a depression.

**depressive neurosis** An excessive depression due to an internal conflict or identifiable event.

**depressive reaction** A transient depression due to some event; the individual usually does not have a history of recurrent depressions.

**depressor nerve** An afferent nerve which depresses motor activity when stimulated, usually a nerve that lowers arterial blood pressure by vasodilation and lowering heart rate.

**deprivation** Dispossession or removal of a needed or desired object. Food and/or water deprivation is often used for a specified duration in animal experiments to create within the organism some definable level of drive; e.g. hungry 22 hours.

**deprivation amentia** (A. Tredgold) Obsolete term for mental deficiency due to the lack or insufficiency of some necessary factors. These factors may be physiological or social.

**deprivation, sensory** A level of stimulation that has been reduced or altered so that it no longer conforms to the individual's normal range or kind of stimulation. Two kinds of deprivations are absolute, reduction and reduced patterning. The former is an attempt to eliminate all stimulus inputs. The latter indicates a situation in which stimulus-input levels are maintained near normal but the patterns inherent in the input are modified or destroyed. Sensory isolation indicates a situation in which the social dimensions, interpersonal communication is limited or absent.

**deprivation, sleep, effects of** The chronic prevention of sleep causes psychotic behavior, a decrease in performance on psychological tests, and in EEG alpha activity. It was found that by the fourth day of wakefulness, the metabolism of carbohydrates increases providing the body with an emergency energy supply needed to master the stress of non-sleep. However, by the seventh day, these emergency provisions begin to fail, producing a decrease in arousal.

This decreased arousal has been suggested as the cause of the psychotic disturbance because of the partial or total blocking of sensory input associated with this level of arousal.

**deprivation syndrome** See *syndrome, deprivation.*

**deprivation, thought** A disturbance in which thoughts are interrupted either by the cessation of thoughts for various periods of time or a thought is obstructed and followed by another, unrelated thought.

**depth** In sensory psychology the perceived distance from the subject of visual or auditory stimuli.

**depth interview** An interview conducted in a permissive atmosphere with freedom for the individual to express himself without fear of disapproval, admonition, dispute, or advice, aimed at offering a comprehensive picture of the subject's feelings, beliefs, and motivations.

**depth perception** 1. Perception of distance between the stimulus and the subject. 2. Perception of three dimensionality or solidity of a stimulus.

**depth psychology** See *psychology, depth.*

**derailment** (E. Kraepelin) Archaic term used to indicate abnormal functioning or disorganization of psychological processes.

**derailment of volition** (E. Kraepelin) Archaic term for the disruption of volition.

**Dercum, Francis Xavier (1856-1931)** American neurologist.

**Dercum's disease (adiposis dolorosa)** Rare disease usually appearing about middle life characterized by obesity, sharp pain in the areas of abnormal fat deposits, and mental deterioration including loss of memory, decreased intelligence and emotional disturbance. Generalized epileptiform convulsions are not infrequent.

**derealization** The feeling that familiar surroundings or people are unreal or have become strange.

**dereism** Autistic thinking which ignores reality.

**dereistic** Unrealistic, fantastic.

**derivative** (psychoanalysis) Some activities by which the id may be expressed. They are usually disguised thereby permitting expression of unconscious wishes without anxiety.

**derivative insight** Insight arrived at without interpretation by the therapist.

**derived emotion** (W. McDougall) Emotions associated with a prospective outcome of an event, such as disappointment, hope, relief, etc.

**derived need** A need which has developed from a basic physiological need of the organism through association and generalization. The concept has fallen into disuse.

**derived primary attention** Habitual passive attention.

derived property (Gestalt psychology) The parts of a perceived object derived from the whole.

derived scale A scale of values obtained by some mathematical transformation of the original scores. This is usually done to facilitate analysis, standardize scores, or meet certain mathematical prerequisites which then permit further mathematical analysis.

derived score A score that is obtained by some mathematical manipulation of the raw data. It may summarize raw data, e.g. a mean data, or transform scores to a derived scale, e.g. z scores.

derma The sensitive layer of the skin below the epidermis.

dermal sensitivity, sense The cutaneous sensations associated with skin receptors.

dermatitis Inflammation of the skin of physical or psychological origin.

dermatography, dermatographa Skin writing; slight scratches or strokes on the skin causing welts.

dermatophobia Fear of the skin.

dermatosiophobia Fear of skin disease.

dermis The sensitive layer of skin, between the epidermis and the subcutaneous tissue.

dermography; dermographism Same as dermatography.

Derner, Gordon F. (1915-    ) American psychologist. Developed the first university based professional school in applied psychology at Adelphi University, Garden City, New York, a program which prepares students at the doctoral level and postdoctoral level for practice in consultation, psychodiagnostics, psychotherapy, psychoanalysis and clinical research; published first book in the United States on the psychology of the tubercular; published papers on diagnostic testing, psychotherapy, clinical supervision, clinical problems and professional problems; leader in establishing psychology as a legally recognized profession; early worker in group process; research and practice in control of smoking; active in cross-cultural and international psychology.

desanimania Archaic term for mental deficiency and/or without psychosis.

Descartes, René (1596-1650) Great early French Renaissance philosopher. Distinguished between mind (unextended substance) and body (extended substance), and held that the two interact. Only man possesses mind or soul; animals—and man's body—are strictly machines or automata. Invented analytical geometry and the graphic system now known as Cartesian coordinates.

descriptive average An estimated mean based on incomplete data.

descriptive principle A generalized description and catagorization of classes of events.

descriptive statistics See statistics, descriptive.

desensitization 1. Weakening of a response with repeated presentations of the stimulus. 2. See systematic desensitization.

deserpine A sedative; one of rauwolfia alcaloids.

desurgency (R. B. Cattell) Agitated, depressed behavior.

desexualization Removing sexual energy from an apparently sexual object; sexual detachment.

design, experimental Plan of an experiment structured to answer specific experimental questions. Design usually specifies: 1) Choice of subjects, species, age, sex, etc. 2) Apparatus used for stimulus presentation and response recording. 3) Experimental procedure. 4) Type of analysis of results.

design, factorial Experimental design incorporating one or more levels of two or more independent variables.

design, panel Study in which one sample of people is interviewed recurrently over a long period of time to investigate the processes of response change, usually in reference to the same variable.

designatory scale A numerical scale in which events or event classes are assigned numbers for identification purposes only; the number assigned is arbitrary and is not correlated in any way with any property of the event or class.

desoxyn Metamphetamine, a stimulant.

despeciation 1. Change in the characteristics of the species. 2. Formerly, the appearance in one individual of several extreme deviations in physical characteristics as a sign of biological inferiority.

Despert Fables (L. J. Despert) An English translation of the Düss Fables, a projective technique designed to determine emotional conflict areas in children. It consists of ten short fables, each of which presents a problem for the child to solve.

destination (communication theory) Recipient of message.

destiny, neurosis of Surrender to an allegedly predestined fate.

destruction method The surgical removal or destruction of a part of the nervous system so as to determine the functions of that part.

destructiveness Expression of aggressive impulses by destroying or defacing objects.

destrudo (B. B. Wolman) The emotional energy of Ares, a primitive, archaic, destructive energy which is normally fused with libido. When libido fails in a state of regression, the destructive energy takes over.

detached affect (psychoanalysis) An affect separated from its generating idea and attached to another idea because the original idea was too threatening, thus the original idea and its affect are maintained independently of each other.

detachment (K. Horney) A neurotic need for self-sufficiency and independence. The individual lacks both feelings for others and social involvement.

**detail response** (Rorschach) A response which involves the use of less than the entire blot. A variety of area descriptions have evolved in different approaches to the Rorschach. Most have sub-divided this category into large or frequently responded to areas, and small or infrequently responded to areas. Some approaches, such as Klopfer, have special score designations which differentiate frequently responded to areas into rare, tiny, edged, or internal categories.

**detection theory** See *signal detection theory.*

**detentio** Archaic term for immobility observed in catalepsy.

**deterioration** Progressive loss of a psychological function.

**deterioration, alcoholic** All psychotic, chronic brain syndromes caused by alcoholism, which are not included in Korsakov's psychosis.

**deterioration, emotional** Progressive lack of appropriate emotional behavior.

**deterioration, epileptic** Progressive intellectual and mental deterioration which occurs gradually in a small percentage of epileptics; the cause of this deterioration and its relation to epilepsy is not known.

**deterioration index** A measure by the Wechsler-Bellevue tests of the loss of mental functions with age. Four of the functions tested that show loss with age are called the "Don't hold functions"; these are: digit span, digit symbol, block design, and similarities. Four functions, called the "hold functions" do not show an appreciable decline with age; these are vocabulary, information, object assembly, and picture completion. The deterioration index:

$$= \frac{\text{Hold} - \text{Don't hold}}{\text{Hold}}.$$

**deterioration, senile** Progressive loss of mental functions associated with old age.

**determinant** An antecedent condition that in some way causes an event. Behavior determinants may be physiological, structural, environmental, and/or organismic.

**determinant, Rorschach** The characteristic of the stimulus pattern used to structure the individual's perception.

**determinant score** One of the major components in Rorschach scoring or coding which refers to the perceived feature or features of the blot, such as form, movement, color, or shading, that precipitate the response of the subject.

**determinate reflex** Response at the site of stimulation.

**determination, coefficient of** Proportional reduction in the variance of the dependent variable as a linear function of the independent variable. This coefficient represents the strength of a linear relationship between variables.

**determining quality** (S. Freud) The characteristics of the traumatic scene that determine the specific neurotic symptoms.

**determining tendency** (N. Ach) The presentation of the aim influences the reaction of the experimental subjects to the stimulus. The subjects' performance is determined not only by what they see but also by what they are requested to see.

**determinism** The doctrine that all phenomena, including behavior, are effects of preceding causes. Thus, with knowledge of the relevent antecedent conditions, the subsequent events can be predicted.

**determinism, biological** The view that constitutional and biological factors determine the psychological and behavioral characteristics of the individual.

**determinism, biosocial** The view that psychological and behavioral characteristics are the result of the interaction of biological and social influences upon the organism.

**detour behavior** Action that leads to a desired end when direct action is obstructed.

**detour problem** A design in problem solving tests in which the goal can only be reached by an indirect route.

**detraction** Lessening the amount of attention without shifting the point of focus.

**detumescence** Subsiding of swelling of the genital organs, after erection.

**deuteranomaly** In color vision, a condition in which an individual mixes unusually large amounts of green to red so as to match a yellow standard, indicating poor sensitivity to green color.

**deutero-learning** 1. Learning about the process of learning, learning the skills that make learning more efficient, learning about how to go about learning. 2. Learning to learn, learning set.

**deuteronopia** Green color blindness.

**deuteropathy** A secondary symptom.

**deutero-phallic** (E. Jones) Second stage of the phallic phase. When the child starts to suspect that not everybody has the same type genital organ but that there are two types of people, male and female.

**deutoplasm** Lifeless parts of the cytoplasm, especially food reserves such as the egg yolk.

**Deutsch, Morton (1920- )** American psychologist. Developed and experimentally tested a theory of cooperation and competition. Has shown that attitudes, perception, task orientation, and communication are profoundly influenced by type of social relationship. One of the first to study experimentally such topics as trust and suspicion, interpersonal bargaining, and conflict resolution. Has demonstrated that conflict becomes more destructive as factors making for a competitive relationship become more dominant.

**development** Refers to increasing complexity and/or organization of processes and/or structure.

**development, genital-physical** A conceptualization of sexual life based on psychosexual and emotional maturity rather than orgastic, anatomical and mechanical desires.

**development, mental** The progressive appearance, change and organization of mental processes and functions which occur from birth until death and which are due to maturation and/or learning.

**development, prenatal** The growth of structures and functions in the fetus while in the uterus. The growth occurring before birth.

**developmental age** An index of maturation determined by a psychometric method and expressed in years.

**developmental aphasia** See *aphasia, developmental.*

**developmental levels** Arbitrary division of the course of life into age ranges. These are: (a) infancy, from birth to 1 year, including the neonate, from birth to one month; (b) childhood, from 1 to 12 years, including early childhood from 1 to 6 years, mid-childhood, from 6 to 10 years, and late childhood, from 10 to 12 years; (c) adolescence, from 12 to 21 years, including early adolescence, from 12 to 14 years, mid-adolescence, from 14 to 16 years, late adolescence, from 16 to 21 years; (d) maturity, from 21 to 65; (e) old age, from 65 on.

**developmental norm** The level of development representative and characteristic of children at a specified age.

**developmental psychology** Concerned with the emotional, attitudinal, social and intellectual processes through which the individual goes during the life-span from conception to death. However, the principle orientation is toward the two decades from birth to about twenty years of age, i.e., the time when changes (both physical and mental) are rapid, and during which behavioral patterns are formed and become relatively stable. "Growth," "development," and "maturation" are often used synonymously to refer to change over time, primarily of immature organisms. See *growth; development; maturation.*

**developmental quotient** A psychometrically derived developmental age divided by the individual's chronological age.

**developmental scale** See *scale, developmental.*

**developmental sequence** In the course of the development of an organism there is a sequence of the appearance and development of structures in the organism. This sequence is, within limits, constant for all organisms of the same, or related species. It is usually assumed that this sequence is within limits, constant for all organisms of the same, or related species. It is usually assumed that this sequence is under genetic control.

**developmental stage** A period in the life of an individual during which specific traits or behaviors become characteristic. For example, during the Freudian oral stage, behaviors appropriate to that stage manifest themselves.

**developmental tasks** Achievements and skills obtained by the developing individual and regarded by a society or culture as appropriate and necessary to his level of development for the acceptable functioning of the individual in that society or culture.

**developmental test of visual-motor integration** See *test, developmental, of visual-motor integration.*

**developmental units** Units of an equal interval scale used to measure development. The IQ was intended to be an equal interval scale in which a change of one unit at age 10 and a change of one unit at age 11 were thought to be changes of equal amounts of development. Generally, however, these scales cannot demonstrate equal intervals.

**developmental zero** Hypothetical point at which life starts; generally agreed to be the moment of fertilization of the egg by the sperm.

**deviate** An individual who differs markedly from the social standard usually in terms of attitudes, moral standards and overt behavior.

**deviation** 1. A departure from the norm. 2. (statistics) The amount by which a score differs from some measure of the distribution of scores.

**deviation, average** The arithmetic mean of the absolute values of deviations of scores from some reference measure of the distribution of scores. The reference measure is usually a measure of central tendency. Absolute value means the numerical value alone regardless of sign, plus or minus; i.e., all minus signs are changed to plus signs before finding the arithmetic mean of the deviations.

**deviation IQ** A measure of intelligence with a test in which the scores are standardized with an average score of 100 and a standard deviation specific to the test used. One such test is the Stanford-Binet with a standard deviation of approximately 16. It is contended that the deviation IQ and the conventional IQ, the quotient between mental age and chronological age, have the same meaning.

**deviation, median** The midpoint of all of the deviations from a measure of central tendency.

**deviation score** See *score, deviation.*

**devolution** Retrograde development, degeneration or the undoing of evolution; involution.

**dexterity** Skill and ease in using the hands.

**dexterity test** See *test, dexterity.*

**dextrad** Toward the right side.

**dextral** Of the right side.

**dextrality** Favoring the use of the right hand over the left.

**dextroamphetamine** Form of amphetamine, commonly known as dexedrine; a stimulant.

**dextrophobia** Fear of objects on the right.

**dextrosinistral** An originally left-handed person trained to use the right hand.

**diabetes** A disease characterized by an excessive discharge of urine and by inordinate thirst.

**diabetes insipidus** Disease in which vast quantities of water are consumed and later eliminated as very diluted urine. Caused by damage to the region of the hypothalamus producing vasopressin.

**diabetes mellitus** An inherited disease characterized by a deficiency in insulin causing an excess of sugar in the blood (hyperglycemia).

**diabetic acidosis** See *acidosis, diabetic.*

**diad** 1. A social group of two individuals. 2. A unit of classification of social interactions. 3. Musical term for the simultaneous occurrence of two tones; a chord of two tones.

**diagnosis** 1. Identification of disease handicaps and disorders on the basis of observed symptoms. 2. Classification of individuals on the basis of observed characteristics and usually abnormalities.

**diagnosis, blind** A psychological evaluation based solely on test material without an interview or further clinical information about the patient.

**diagnosis, differential** Distinguishing between two similar diseases or disorders on the basis of their compared characteristics.

**diagnosis, negative** Identification of a disease or a disorder by elimination; identification of what the disturbance is not.

**diagnosis, social** Mostly used by psychiatric social workers to indicate environmental conditions of a client.

**diagnostic interview** See *interview, diagnostic.*

**diagnostic test** See *test, diagnostic.*

**diagnostic word test** See *test, diagnostic word.*

**diagram, bar** A visual representation of quantities consisting of a series of contiguous rectangles, of width proportional to the size of the class interval it represents, and in height proportional to the quantity in the various intervals.

**dialectic** A branch of logic that arrives at truth through deductive reasoning and counterposition of opposites.

**Diana complex** See *complex, Diana.*

**diaphragm** 1. A muscular partition especially the one that separates the thorax from the abdomen and is the chief muscle of respiration. 2. An aperture between a light source and a surface which controls the amount of light falling on the surface. 3. A contraceptive device.

**diarrhea, chronic** Diarrhea of long duration due to physical or psychogenic causes.

**diarrhea, nervous** Gastrointestinal malfunction characterized by frequent and fluid stools due to disturbances of the autonomic nervous system.

**diary method** Daily record of all events relevant to an object of investigation.

**diaschisis** Temporary cerebral shock; a sudden damage to a part of the brain causes shock to all connected parts. This results in a temporary cessation of function in the related parts.

**diastole** Period of the cardiac cycle during which the heart dilates and the ventricles fill with blood.

**diastolic blood pressure** The blood pressure obtained when the heart cavities are filled with blood.

**diathermy** The application of an oscillating electric current of high frequency for therapeutic purposes.

**diathesis** Inherited predisposition to a particular disease.

**diathesis, arthritic** A constitutional condition occurring in adults which includes the exudative and hypersecretory diathesis and arthritism, thought to occur in a megalosplanchnic hypervegetative constitution.

**diathesis, explosive** (A. Meyer) A subdivision of the traumatic neuroses manifesting intense irritability especially under the influence of alcohol which may lead to unmotivated acts of violence.

**diathesis, exudative** A constitutional condition occurring in children characterized by an irritable skin and chafing, eczema and high susceptibility to external irritants of the skin and mucuous membranes.

**diathesis, neuropathic** Neurasthenia.

**diathesis, traumatophilic** A predisposition to accidents.

**diatonic scale** See *scale, diatonic.*

**diazepam** See *valium.*

**dichoglottic** Of two separate areas of the tongue.

**dichorhinic** Of the simultaneous and usually independent stimulation of both nostrils.

**dichotic** Of separate and usually independent stimulation of both ears.

**dichotonomously distributed data** Data which are divided into two mutually exclusive categories on the basis of the presence or absence of a certain trait.

**dichromatism** Of a type of color blindness in which only two of the primary colors are seen.

**dicrotic notch** The notch in a pulse tracing of a peripheral artery.

**didactic analysis** See *psychoanalysis, didactic.*

**didactic group psychotherapy** See *psychotherapy, didactic group.*

**diencephalon** Part of the forebrain between the prosencephalon and mesencephalon, it includes the thalamus, epithalamus, and hypothalamus.

**difference cannon** (J. S. Mill) Any difference in otherwise identical effects are a result of differences in their antecedents.

**difference threshold (limen)** See *threshold, difference.*

**difference tone** A combination tone, sometimes heard when two tones of similar timbre are sounded together. Its frequency is often the difference between the two tones sounded.

**differential aptitude test** See *test, differential aptitude.*

**differential conditioning** See *conditioning, differential.*

**differential diagnosis** See *diagnosis, differential.*

**differential extinction** See *extinction, differential.*

**differential growth** See *growth, differential.*

**differential inhibition** See *inhibition, differential.*

**differential R-technique** (R. B. Cattell) The basic values are differences between scores on each of a set of variables measured at two occasions. These differences between scores are correlated and factor analyzed. One of the two main methods of determining dimensions of personality change-through-time (state factors). The other method is P-Technique.

**differential reinforcement** See *reinforcement, differential.*

**differential reinforcement of inter response times** See *reinforcement, schedule of: differential reinforcement of low rates of responding (drl); reinforcement, schedule of: differential reinforcement of high rates of responding (drh).*

**differential response** See *response, differential.*

**differential scoring** See *scoring, differential.*

**differential sensibility** See *sensibility, differential.*

**differential threshold** See *threshold, difference.*

**differential tone** See *difference, tone.*

**differentiation** 1. Process of becoming something different than it previously was. 2. (biology) Increase in complexity and organization of tissues during development. 3. (conditioning) Experimental procedure in which responses of a subject are changed from one type or class of responses to another class of desired responses by a process of selectively reinforcing successive approximations to the desired response. As the procedure continues for responses to be reinforced, they must approximate the desired response. 4. (mathematics) In calculus, the process of obtaining a differential coefficient. 5. An increase in the number of individual heterogenous aspects of an originally homogenous field.

**differentiation of the life space** (K. Lewin) A process of development increasing the regions of influence of an individual's life space, thus enlarging and diversifying the field of his activities and social interaction.

**difficulty scale** See *scale, difficulty.*

**difficulty value** See *value, difficulty.*

**diffraction** Bending of a portion of light as it passes the edge of an obstacle as when it passes through an aperture. This phenomenon is common to all wave forms.

**diffraction grating** An apparatus which produces the constituent wave length of an electromagnetic wave, often used to obtain monochromatic light from white light. It consists of a highly polished surface upon which are fine parallel slits. The wave length is of the same order of magnitude as the slit length.

**diffusion** 1. The spread of culture from one social group to another. 2. The scatter of light because of irregularities in the medium. 3. The spread of stimulation through cutaneous tissues.

**diffusion circle** An area of skin surface affected by pressure stimulation within the area.

**digital computer** A computer which can perform mathematical and logical operations with information, numbers, etc., represented in digital form.

**dilantin** Common name for diphenylhydantoin, an anticonvulsant drug used in the treatment of behavior disorders in children and adults and also migraine, neuromuscular disorders and a variety of cardiac abnormalities. It appears to act by decreasing the spread and amplification of the response to a stimulus, exerting a stabilizing effect.

**Dilthey, William** (1833-1911) German philosopher. Announced his cultural science psychology in the 1880's, but principal effects of its impact were not felt until early twentieth century. Emphasized critical study of man in society; regarded man as a unit, as an expression of human character, and led to a psychology of personality. Dilthey charged that laboratory psychology was inadequate to understand man; maintained that cultural science psychology *understands,* natural science psychology *explains;* believed that if human mind was to be understood by the psychologist, psychology had to be brought closer to history, art, literature and ethics; regarded psychology as fundamental to all cultural sciences; rejected natural science psychology; stressed understanding and holism.

**dimorphic** Characterized by two forms.

**diphenylhydantoin** See *dilantin.*

**diploid** The chromosome number of a gamete which contains both members of each chromosome pair. In man, the diploid number is 46, and in drosophila melanogaster it is 8.

**diplopia** Double vision; binocularly seeing two images when only one visual stimulus is presented usually as a result of trouble with motor coordination between the eyes or failure to focus properly.

**dippoldism** Flagellation of children.

**dipsomania** Mental disorder associated with alcoholism which occurs periodically following excessive drinking. It lasts several days, and is characterized by various patterns of responses depending upon the individual.

**direct analysis**   See *analysis, direct.*

**direct inquiry**   (H. Rorschach) Procedure used to supplement the regular inquiry, wherein the subject is provided information concerning the various determinants of responses and asked directly to specify which of those determinants were influential in his formulation of each response. The procedure, similar to Klopfer's Analogy Period, is designed to avoid the problems created by the non-directive questions of the regular inquiry.

**direct measurement**   See *measurement, direct.*

**direct psychoanalysis**   See *psychoanalysis, direct.*

**direct reflex**   See *reflex, direct.*

**direct scaling**   See *scaling, direct.*

**direct therapy**   See *psychotherapy, direct.*

**directed thinking**   Goal directed thought.

**directions test**   See *test, directions.*

**directive counseling**   See *counseling, directive.*

**directive fiction**   See *fiction, directive.*

**directive group therapy**   See *psychotherapy, directive group.*

**directive (or determining) tendency**   See *determining tendency.*

**directive therapy**   See *psychotherapy, directive.*

**dirhinic stimulation**   Simultaneous stimulation of both nostrils by the same odor.

**disability**   Loss or impairment of a bodily organ or a function.

**disaesthesia**   Cutaneous and subcutaneous sensation of discomfort.

**disappearing differences method**   (psychophysics) A modified method of limits in which an appreciable difference between two stimuli is gradually decreased until they appear identical.

**discharge of affect**   (S. Freud) An active reaction to an emotional experience involving the whole range of voluntary and involuntary reflexes by which one's emotions are usually worked off.

**discharge rate**   In institutional statistics, the ratio of the number of patients discharged in a given period of time over either the total number of patients in the original group or the number of patients admitted during the same time period.

**discomfort-relief quotient (DRQ)**   Verbal expression of the ratio of feelings indicating satisfaction over feelings indicating dissatisfaction along some specified dimension, i.e., self or environment.

**discontinuity theory of learning**   The hypothesis that for discrimination learning to occur the organism must attend to the cue of the stimulus upon which the discrimination is dependent. This view is related to insight learning but differs from it insofar as discontinuity theory accepts the possibility of gradual improvement in the task after the discrimination is established.

**discontinuous variable**   A variable the values of which are not on a continuum but has discrete, sharp, and abrupt changes from one magnitude to the next magnitude.

**discordant**   A term used in twin studies to indicate that one member of twin pair exhibits a trait or disease and the other does not. The discordance percentage in monozygotic twins in a systematic study provides a measure of the contribution of non-genetic factors operating from within or outside the organism.

**discrepancy**   Disagreement between fact and theory or between two facts.

**discrete distribution**   See *distribution, discrete.*

**discrete measure**   Measures taken for a quantity that changes discontinuously or discretely.

**discrete variable**   Same as *discontinuous variable.*

**discriminal dispersion**   Frequency distribution of responses in a discrimination situation. The greatest number of responses is to the discriminative stimulus; the more different the stimulus is from the discriminative stimulus the fewer the responses made to it.

**discriminal process**   The process of discrimination between stimuli.

**discriminandum (a, pl.)**   (E. C. Tolman) A term referring to the relatively enduring sensory character of objects as modulated by the sense organ capacities of the given organism, and which permit that organism to make sensory differentiations. Thus discriminanda are differentiated from physical stimuli since discriminanda are defined by physical *and* behavioral-supporting attributes. See *physical stimulus.*

**discriminated operant**   (B. F. Skinner) An operant occasioned by a stimulus as a consequence of previous training.

**discriminating fineness**   (psychometrics) An index of the smallest difference in values of a variable detectable by a test.

**discriminating power**   (psychometrics) A composite of several measures of the ability of a test to differentiate between testees on the relevant dimensions. It includes (a) probability of the test, the probability of correct discrimination among testees by the test (b) discriminating fineness, the smallest amounts of differences detectable by the test (c) discriminating range, the range of scores within which the test is a useful tool.

**discriminating probability of the test**   (psychometrics) An index of the probability of correctly discriminating between testees or the relevant dimensions on the basis of the test. It is the proportion of correct to incorrect discriminations by the test.

discriminating range (psychometrics) The range of scores within which a test or index has reliable discriminating power and outside of which the scores may unduly be influenced by chance factors.

discrimination (R. Merton) Restrictive or hostile acts directed against some group.

discrimination, errorless (H. S. Terrace) Procedure used in operant conditioning to establish responding to the $S^D$ and with an absence of responding to the $S^\Delta$; Thus it is a procedure to establish without errors a discrimination between the $S^D$ and $S^\Delta$. Two ways of doing this are: 1) establishing normally with errors, a discrimination between the $S^D$ and $S^\Delta$, then superimposing new stimuli over the established discriminative stimuli, so each stimulus is a complex of the established discriminative stimulus and the new stimulus. Next, by slowly fading out the old discriminative stimuli, the new stimulus come to be the discriminative stimulus. Thus new $S^D$ and $S^\Delta$ have been established with no responses or errors, to the $S^\Delta$. 2) Presenting the $S^\Delta$ for periods of time, too short for the subject to respond, and at weak stimulus intensities and gradually increasing the duration and intensity of the $S^\Delta$; the discrimination between the $S^D$ and the $S^\Delta$ can be established without errors.

discrimination, index of (psychometrics) An index of the sensitivity of a test or test item to differences in testees on the relevant dimensions measured by the test.

discrimination reaction time See reaction time, discrimination.

discrimination, sensory The process or ability to recognize quantitative or qualitative differences between stimuli.

discriminative approach and avoidance responses A technique used by behavioral therapists to teach patients to discriminate between anxiety arousing and non-anxiety arousing situations.

discriminative learning A learning situation in which the subject learns that responses to one stimulus is reinforced while responses to other stimuli are either not reinforced or punished.

discriminative stimulus A stimulus that occasions the appropriate response as a consequence of conditioning.

discussion leader Individual who promotes free discussion and interchange of ideas in a meeting of usually small groups.

disease A lack of a state of ease; usually an abnormal condition of body or mind, synonymous with disorder, pathology, illness.

disease, Beard's (G. M. Beard) Archaic term for neurasthenia.

disease, Bell's (L. V. Bell) Archaic term for a form of manic type of manic-depressive psychosis.

disease, flight into It is generally recognized that gains and compensations as a result of disease or disorder can be motivating factors to become or remain ill.

disease, Friedmann's (M. Friedmann) Narcolepsy.

disease, Janet's (P. Janet) Psychasthenia.

disease, Little's (W. J. Little) Diplegia.

disease (or disorder), mental Psychopathy.

disequilibrium, mental (P. Dubois) Mental imbalance.

disgust A feeling, attitude or emotion of repulsion, aversion, withdrawal, loathing and possibly nausea.

disinhibition 1. (I. P. Pavlov) A temporary increase in the strength of the conditioned response upon introduction of an irrelevant stimulus. 2. The lessening of cortical control of impulsive or vegetative functions due to drugs or alcohol.

disintegration Disruption of the organization of a unified system; it may refer to disintegration of psychic and behavioral processes.

dismemberment, fear of A fear most often seen in involutional psychosis and in schizophrenia, that the individual is going to lose part of his body.

disorder, functional A pathological state of an organism with no organic basis.

disorder, impulse A category of psychopathic behavior characterized by symptoms or a character structure of impulsive action. The neuroses include kleptomania, pyromania, addiction, sexual perversions and catathymic crises caused by inner tension and unconscious conflict needs which cannot be controlled.

disorder, mental Any gross or disabling disruption of mental or behavioral processes of adjustment whether psychological, social, organic, or functional in origin, regardless of being relatively temporary or chronic. Also called behavior disorder.

disorder of volition See parabulia.

disorder, organic A pathological state of an organism resulting from physical or structural damage.

disorders, classification of mental See classification of mental disorders.

disorders, respiratory 1. Disturbances involving the respiratory apparatus. 2. See asthma, bronchial.

disorganized behavior Behavior, parts of which are not integrated and are often aimed at disparate ends, while the total behavior contradicts itself and leads nowhere.

disorientation Loss of the ability to comprehend spatial, temporal and social relations.

disparagement, mania for (P. Janet) Fear and jealousy of another's success and a desire for one's own triumph not really by success but by belittling the achievements of others.

disparagement syndrome See syndrome, disparagement.

disparate retinal points Areas of both retinas of one individual which in normal binocular stimulation give rise to the perception of different positions in space.

**disparation** The double visual image of an object when the fixation point is either in front of or behind the object.

**dispareunia** See *dyspareunia*.

**disparity, retinal** Differences between the projections on both retinas of one individual when looking at a visual stimulus. This occurs since both retinas are located at different views of the same stimulus complex. These differences in the retinal image are important cues for the perception of depth.

**dispersion** The extent to which scores vary among themselves or deviate from some reference point. Dispersion is measured by the average deviation, interquartile range, or most commonly, the standard deviation.

**dispersion circle** Usually a colored circular visual sensation when light rays from a point source are not focused on a single retinal point, but are dispersed over an area. This is achieved usually by a lens system.

**dispersion coefficient** See *coefficient, dispersion*.

**displaced aggression** An expression of hostility to an individual or object rather than to the source of the hostility.

**displacement** 1. A substitution of one response system for another when the former behavior is prevented in some way. 2. A distortion of eidetic image resulting in a rearrangement of recalled parts. 3. (Rorschach) Focusing attention on insignificant details of the stimulus complex so as to avoid more revealing responses. 4. (psychoanalysis) A defense mechanism; displacement is a shift of emotion, meaning, or fantasy from the person or object toward which it was originally directed, to another person or object. It involves a discharge of aroused emotions toward neutral or less dangerous objects.

**displacement in dreams** In the manifest dream a single element may stand for a whole conglomeration of unconscious, latent dream thoughts. In the waking state instinctual energies are bound and cathected in definite objects. In dreams these mental energy loads shift easily from one object to another. In some dreams significant issues are barely mentioned or represented by symbols while unimportant unconscious elements may be represented in a very clear manner. This phenomenon, displacement, occurs in dreamwork, transforming the psychical intensity, latent thoughts and wishes into sensory experience. The more obscure the dream is, the more displacement there is in the dream.

**disposition** 1. The arrangement of parts or elements of a system such that the action of the system is in part a consequence of its internal structure. 2. A hypothetical organization of psychological and physiological elements such that an individual's behavior in different situations will have similar characteristics. 3. A relatively stable and constant attitude. 4. (W. McDougall) All the innate tendencies and propensities of an individual.

**disposition rigidity** See *perseveration*.

**disposition system** See *complex, mood*.

**dissected-sentence test** See *test, disarranged sentence*.

**disseminated sclerosis** Multiple sclerosis.

**dissimilation** 1. Catabolism. 2. (C. G. Jung) Adjustment of the individual to external forces and consequent estrangement of the individual from himself.

**dissimulation** Feigning or concealing one's real emotions.

**dissociation** A process of preventing motivational systems, complex psychological processes and activities from entering consciousness because of intolerable anxiety. These processes function independently of the rest of the personality.

**dissociative reactions** Neurotic reactions to extreme stress, characterized by the repression of entire episodes in life as in amnesia, fugues, and multiple personalities.

**dissonance** (music) Any combination of tones sounded simultaneously, the effect of which is conventionally heard as being in unrest and tense, and needing at least one other simultaneous group of tones following it for resolution and completion. Dissonance is a matter of degree and contemporary music theory redefining it.

**dissonance, cognitive** See *cognitive dissonance*.

**dissonance reduction** (L. Festinger) The principle that when a tension producing dissonant situation occurs, an individual seeks new information or behaves in a way to reduce the dissonance.

**distal** 1. Far from some reference point. 2. (anatomy) Away from the center of the body or point of attachment to the body.

**distal stimulus** See *stimulus, distal*.

**distal variable** See *variable, distal*.

**distance receptor** Receptors capable of responding to stimuli that are separated from the body by some distance. Among these are visual, auditory, thermal, and olfactory receptors.

**distance vision** See *vision, distance*.

**distoceptor** A distance receptor.

**distortion, parataxic** (H. S. Sullivan) An aspect of interpersonal relations of perceiving and relating to a person as if he was a person with whom one has related to in the past, independent of his objective characteristics.

**distortion, perceptual** An absence of correspondence between the common perception of a stimulus and a perception by an individual.

**distribution, asymmetrical** A statistical distribution in which there is a lack of similarity between the two halves as divided by the mean or median.

**distribution, bimodal** A distribution that has two points at which the frequency is considerably greater than on either side of the points. The points need not be of the same frequency.

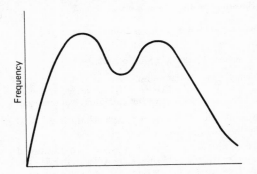

A bimodal distribution

**distribution, binomial** See *normal frequency distribution.*

**distribution, cumulative frequency** See *cumulative frequency distribution.*

**distribution curve** Curve of a frequency distribution; on the horizontal axis the items or values are plotted, and on the vertical axis the frequency of their occurrence is plotted.

**distribution, discrete** A frequency distribution consisting of distinct, separate steps.

**distribution-free** (statistics) Pertaining to nonparametric methods which make no assumptions about the form of distribution of scores in the sampling universe.

**distribution, Poisson** (statistics) A binomial distribution in which the probability of a given event is extremely small.

**distribution, ranked** A distribution of scores or values arranged in order of increasing of decreasing magnitude. A particular rank is indicated by a number specifying its position.

**distribution, rectilinear** A distribution of scores in which each category has approximately the same frequency of cases as opposed to a normal distribution which is characterized by the largest number of cases falling near to the mean.

**distribution, self** (Gestalt psychology) The involuntary change in dynamic relations of a sensory field which results in a higher organization of that field.

**distribution, truncated** (statistics) A distribution having no extreme points due to a failure to obtain extreme cases or an intentional removal of them. It may be unilateral or bilateral.

**disuse principle** The theory that the tendency to make a learned response to a stimulus decreases with disuse over time.

**diuresis** Increased production and secretion of urine.

**divagation** Rambling and incoherent speech.

**divergence** 1. Turning out of both eyes when the distance from the subject to the binocularly fixated point increases. 2. A permanent turning out of one eye respective to the other; wall-eyed.

**divergent production, operation of** (J.P. Guilford) Generation of items of information from given items, where the emphasis is upon a variety of output from the same source; a search for logical alternatives.

**Dix, Dorothea Lynde (1802-1887)** Left home at ten years of age and at fourteen began teaching school at Worchester. Because of tuberculosis she resigned her regular duties and began to give Sunday instruction to women prisoners. This was her first view of prison life, which led her to investigate conditions at poorhouses, insane asylums, and jails. She believed that the living conditions of the insane were due to an antiquated, ignorant, and callous system which needed reform. She was instrumental in the formation of more than thirty institutions for the insane and for having millions of dollars appropriated for improved care in public institutions. In England she was instrumental in having a royal commission investigate insane asylums in Scotland. In Rome she was a moving force in the foundation of a new hospital.

**dizygote twins** Twins which grew from two separate eggs; fraternal twins.

**DL** See *difference threshold.*

**d-lysergic acid dietymide** See *lysergic acid diethylamide.*

**DNA (deoxyribonucleic acid)** The nucleic acid of the chromosomes, in which genetic information is coded.

**doctrine of interest** See *interest, doctrine of.*

**doctrine of temperament, Galen's** (Galen) The belief that personality characteristics result from the different combinations of the four basic elements: earth, air, fire and water, in the physical composition of the person. Sanguine, choleric, phlegmatic and melancholy dispositions were thought to result from different amounts of these elements.

**dolichocephaly** Having a long, narrow head with a cephalic index of less than 75.

**dolichomorph** Tall thin bodily shape.

**doll play, permissive** Examiner is permissive of commonly forbidden thematic content (e.g., aggression), avoids interpretation, and limits interaction to reflection of child's performance.

**doll play, projective** (R.R. Sears) A procedure in which a child is presented with dolls and a doll house or other environmental materials, with encouragement to manipulate them either thematically (e.g., "show what the family does here") or organizationally (e.g., "make a scene").

**Dollard, John (1900-  )** American psychologist. Made a pioneering behavioral study of the caste system in South. Best work done with Neal E. Miller, relating reinforcement learning theory to psychoanalysis and culture theory. Imitation is learned; neurosis is learned. Personality is learned and it varies according to the laws of learning and the specific social conditions under which it is acquired. See *reinforcement learning theory; neurosis; psychotherapy.*

**domal sampling**  A form of area sampling in which a sample of houses are designated and a specific member of each household is interviewed.

**domatophobia**  Fear of being in a house.

**dominance  1.** A drive or desire for ascendancy, being more important or prominant in a relationship. A tendency to control others. **2.** When two or more responses are occasioned by a stimulus, one of them is more likely than the other. **3.** Preferential use of one side of the body over the other; handedness.

**dominance, genetic**  (genetics) The phenotype of one gene of an allele pair is expressed while the phenotype of the other recessive allele, does not appear in the characteristics of the organism.

**dominance, hemisphere**  One hemisphere of the brain controls movement of the body more than the other hemisphere, resulting in handedness.

**dominance, lateral  1.** The tendency for dominance of one side of the brain over the other in most functions. **2.** Preferential use of one hand or side of the body.

**dominance need**  See *need, dominance.*

**dominance, ocular**  The preferred use or greater use of one eye rather than the other which is one form of lateral dominance.

**dominance-submission**  See *ascendance-submission.*

**dominant wave length**  Wave length of a color which when mixed with the appropriate amount of white yields a color that matches a given color.

**dominant**  (genetics) A gene is dominant if it is expressed when heterozygous.

**dominant gene**  See *gene, dominant.*

**dominator-modulator theory**  In color vision the hypothesis that there is a dominant receptor for brightness perception; color discriminations are a function of another receptor, the modulator, which modulates the response of the dominant receptor.

**Donder's law**  See *law, Donder's.*

**Doolittle method**  (statistics) An efficient and systematic method of finding the unknowns in a set of normal equations. This method is often used in solving multiple correlation problems.

**Doppler effect**  If the distance between a sound or light source and an observer changes, the sound pitch or light color appears to change. Thus, for example, the whistle of a train when moving toward an observer appears higher then when it is moving away. When a light source is moving toward an observer it appears more blue than when moving away, then appears more red.

**Dora case**  First of five extensive case histories reported by S. Freud. This one was written in 1901 and published as *Fragment of an Analysis of a Case of Hysteria* in 1905. Freud used the Dora case as a base to further his dream analysis and to account for the repressed part of mental life.

**dorsal**  At or on the back.

**dorso-ventral**  (anatomical) Extending from the dorsal to the ventral axes of the body, from the front to the back.

**DOT**  Dictionary of Occupational Titles.

**dotting test**  See *test, dotting.*

**double alternation problem**  See *problem, double alternation.*

**double aspect theory**  A metaphysical theory, based on Spinoza's philosophy, stating that mental and physical processes represent two aspects of the same occurrences.

**double bind hypothesis**  See *hypothesis, double bind.*

**double blind method**  A research design in which neither the investigator nor the subject knows the nature of the experimental conditions. For example, in drug research neither the investigator nor the participating patients know who is getting the real drug and who is getting the placebo.

**double-entry table  1.** Any statistical table in which values are entered both in the rows and in the columns. **2.** A scatter diagram.

**double orientation**  See *orientation, double.*

**double representation**  The perception of two hues or brightnesses of an object when that object is illuminated by a light of a different color.

**double sampling**  See *sampling, double.*

**double vibration**  See *vibration.*

**double vision**  See *diplopia.*

**doubles, illusion of**  See *illusion of doubles.*

**Downey's Will-Temperament Test**  See *test, Downey's Will-Temperament.*

**Down's syndrome**  See *mongolism.*

**DR or ΔR**  Symbol for change in response.

**drainage hypothesis**  (W. McDougall) A theory of neural inhibition and facilitation which suggests that when two neural groups, anatomically close, are aroused, the neural impulse is drawn from the usual pathway of the weaker neural group and increases the impulse of the more active group.

**drama therapy**  See *psychodrama.*

**dramamine**  An antihistamine drug used to control motion sickness.

**Draw-A-Person Quality Scale**  See *scale, Draw-A-Person Quality.*

**Draw-A-Person Test**  See *test, Draw-A-Person.*

**dream-day; daydream** A fantasy while awake. The individual lets his mind wander aimlessly through gratifying images. The daydream is said to be motivated by unconscious and unfulfilled wishes.

**dream determinant** (psychoanalysis) The principle factor in determining the content and characteristic quality of a dream.

**dream ego** (C. G. Jung) The part of the ego that is dreaming.

**dream interpretation** The process of understanding the unconscious meanings of a dream. There are several levels of meaning. Aside from the symbolism that is individual and characteristic only of the individual and interpretable through dream analysis, it is held that some dream symbols are universal, the meanings of which are shared by all human beings.

**dream, manifest content** (psychoanalysis) The dream as it is remembered; the images, events, people, etc.; "the story line" of the dream.

**dream, perennial** A dream that, after having been dreamt in childhood, appears again in later years.

**dream, reconstruction** (D. B. Levin) A dream in which the sequence of dream elements seems to naturally incorporate a stimulus that wakes the sleeper. For example, the bell of an alarm clock waking the dreamer is included into the dream.

**dream, secondary elaboration of** The differences between the descriptions of a dream and the actual content of the dream. This process continues in the waking state so that a later description of the dream differs from an earlier one.

**dream work** (psychoanalysis) Transformation of an unconscious demand by a substitute wish-fulfillment in dreams. The transformation of the hidden, latent dream content into what the dreamer experiences (manifest dream) is called dream work. The dream work protects the sleep and prevents waking up.

**dreams** 1. Sensations, images, thoughts and emotions experienced in sleep. 2. (S. Freud) Dreams are guardians of sleep and protect the sleeper from being disturbed by unconscious conflicts and annoying external stimuli. Dreams are a compromise between the inner and outer disturbance of sleep and the desire to sleep. The sleeping person "dreams away," as it were, the disturbing factors. The content of the dreams reflects repressed demands for instinctual gratification. The mental functions of the dreams are unconscious with irrational primary processes and "all the absurdities, delusions and illusions" of a psychosis. A dream is a compromise; the unconscious, forbidden impulses appear in the dream in a disguised manner. This disguising is called dream-work, the unconscious wish is called latent dream, the story of the dream is called the manifest dream content. 3. (A. Adler) Dreams serve a problem-solving function offering cryptic solutions to difficulties the dreamer faces. 4. (H.S. Sullivan) Dream satisfies in a symbolic way the needs which could not be discharged in wakeful states thus reducing tension. 5. (W. Dement and C. Fisher) Dreams are sort of "safety valves" reducing the danger of emo-

tional disturbance. Deprivation could produce psychosis. 6. (R. Hernandez-Peon) Dreams are related to disinhibition of cortical and limbic neurons associated with the motivational and muscular systems. The neurons associated with memory functions determine the manifest dream content, the limbic neurons determine the latent dream content. 7. (M. Jouvet and J. Jouvet) The causal-positive area in the thromboencephalic part of the brain is the dream-center.

**dreams, physiology of** The period of dreaming differs from non-dreaming sleep states and periods of wakefulness. These periods are characterized by a low-voltage EEG pattern concomitant with rapid eye movements. The physiological arousal consists of changes in respiration, pulse rate, basal skin resistance, blood pressure and muscular activity. This state recurs periodically from ninety to one hundred twenty minutes which may be due to an internal physiological mechanism involving primitive cerebral structures and perhaps neurohumoral transmitters. If dreaming is prevented, a rebound occurs during the following night in which the subject regains the deficit. Prolonged suppression of dreaming results in serious personality disturbance.

**Dreikurs, Rudolf (1897-1972)** Viennese-born, American psychiatrist and educator. Developed Alfred Adler's system of "Individual Psychology" into techniques for understanding purposes of disturbing behavior in children, and for stimulating cooperative behavior without punishment or reward. Key assumption: the child strives to find a place amongst others. When discouraged from socially useful striving he pursues one or more of the socially useless "Four Goals:" 1) attention, 2) power, 3) revenge, 4) display of inadequacy. Founded Alfred Adler Institutes of Chicago and Tel Aviv. Inspired international movement of Family Education Centers, parent study groups. Opposed "transference" theories by instituting multiple psychotherapy to stress educational task of therapist.

**drh schedule** See *reinforcement, schedule of: differential reinforcement of high rates.*

**drive** 1. An impelling force, push, or pressure. 2. An inner urge that stimulates or prevents action. 3. (W. B. Cannon) A special localized sensation determined by organ stimulation, e.g. the hunger drive is hunger-sensation, pangs caused by the contraction of the stomach. 4. (S. Freud) Drive (Trieb) is an innate force, synonymous to instinct, that facilitates or prevents the discharge of energy; see *instinct.* 5. (C. L. Hull) A general energizer whose reduction is reinforcing. If the reinforcement takes place without learning, the drive is primary; if the reinforcement takes place after prior learning, it is a secondary drive. Thus the primary drives are the unlearned sources of energy in the organism. 6. (N. E. Miller and J. Dollard) Drive is a stimulus that impels the organism to make responses to cues in the stimulus situation. These responses become conditioned if they have been rewarded; thus reward is drive reducing. Primary drives, such as hunger and thirst, are based on physiological processes. Secondary or acquired drives are based on the primary drives.

**7.** (C. T. Morgan) See *Central Motivating State.*
**8.** (B. F. Skinner) Skinner uses the term drive as "a verbal device," a convenient way of referring to the effects of deprivation and satiation. **9.** (W. Stern) Drive is an innate disposition towards the implementation of one's own goals. There are four types of drives, namely: (1) self-preservation, (2) self-development, such as self-adornment, (3) social drives, and (4) human drives such as intellectual and idealistic strivings. **10.** (P. Teitelbaum) Drive is activation of unlearned behavior, in contradistinction from motive, which implies activation of learned behavior. **11.** (C. J. Warden) A behavioral tendency activated by an arousal stemming from deprivation and/or incentive. **12.** (R. S. Woodworth) Woodworth introduced the term drive in 1918 as a factor motivating human behavior. **13.** (P. T. Young) The energy of behavior; the sum of energy released in behavior.

**drive, achievement** The tendency to work with determination toward a specific end that is considered important by the individual.

**drive, acquired** **1.** A need or motive that has been learned through one's life experience as opposed to being an innate drive. **2.** A drive specific to a particular species that comes to be satisfied by learned techniques. See *motivation.*

**drive, aim-inhibited** (S. Freud) Instinctual drives that are modified or held in suspension, under the influence of the ego and superego, allowing gratification different from the original aim. For example, libidinal drives which are powerfully cathected in a love object may become aim-inhibited and result in satisfaction derived from relation to the object without actual sexual gratification.

**drive arousal** Any of a combination of stimulus conditions that activate a specified drive. The conditions can be either external or internal to the organism.

**drive discrimination** (E. C. Tolman) A form of learning dependent on the type of deprivation which an organism has undergone which activates specific drives in the organism.

**drive displacement** After one drive has been aroused but gratification of that drive is prevented, the behavior may change and be appropriate for some other unaroused but gratifiable drive.

**drive for self-aggrandizement** Drive to maintain feeling of personal adequacy expressed primarily in competitive situations.

**drive, homonomy** (A. Angyal) The trend of the individual to adjust himself to the environment, merging his individuality in a union with a social group, or the world order.

**drive, maternal** The tendency of the female organism to care for her young which has both hereditary and learned components.

**drive, primary** Any drive which is universal in a given species, for which there is a physiological basis, and which is independent of learning.

**drive reduction** The lessening of drive behavior (the activity called a drive) and related conditions with the organism usually accomplished through satisfaction of the needs associated with the drive by satiation or through removal of drive arsenal.

**drive-reduction theory** See *theory, drive-reduction.*

**drive, sensory** An intense desire or need for a specific sensory experience.

**drive state** (P. Teitelbaum) The internal state, such as hunger, which influences the excitability of the nervous system and controls its feeding reflexes.

**drive stimulus; $S_D$** (C. L. Hull) An afferent nerve activity arising in those organs in a drive state which, when reduced by some behavior, results in the reinforcement of that behavior.

**drl schedule** See *reinforcement, schedule of: differential reinforcement of low rates.*

**DRQ** See *discomfort-relief quotient.*

**drug addiction** A state of periodic or chronic intoxication detrimental to the individual and to society, produced by the repeated consumption of a drug (natural or synthetic). Its characteristics include: an overpowering desire or need (compulsion) to continue taking the drug and to obtain it by any means, a tendency to increase the dose, a psychic (psychological) and sometimes a physical dependence upon the effect of the drug.

**drumstick** A small protrusion from the nucleus of a polymorphonuclear leucocyte, found in three to five per cent of these cells in females but not in males.

**dual file system** A system in industrial personnel work of summarizing all information in two files: (a) individual endowment profiles, and (b) job profiles.

**dual instinct theory** **1.** (S. Freud) The postulation of two inborn instincts, Eros and Thanatos, as the two forces of life. **2.** See *death instinct.* **3.** See *life instinct.*

**dual personality** See *personality, dual.*

**dualism** **1.** An hypothesis that there are two fundamentally different entities or substances in the world, mind and matter. **2.** (psychology) The proposition that there is a distinction of some kind between the processes of the mind and the processes of the body and there is no way of reducing one to the other.

**duct glands** See *glands, exocrine.*

**ductless glands** See *glands, endocrine.*

**dull normal** A category of intelligence usually delimited by the I.Q. score range from 80 to 90.

**duodenal ulcer** See *ulcer, peptic.*

**duplicity theory** See *theory, duplicity.*

**dura mater** The thick, tough external membrane which covers the brain and spinal cord.

**durance** (H. A. Murray) The temporal unit of life activity which includes all proceedings occurring simultaneously.

**duraplasty**  Treatment of defects in the dura mater.

**Durham rule**  A 1954 law stating that an accused person is not held responsible for an act which is the product of mental defect or disorder.

**Düss Fables**  See *Despert Fables.*

**DV**  Dependent variable.

**dwarfism**  A condition of extreme underdevelopment of the body resulting in small stature.

**dwarfism, panhypopituitary**  A dwarfism which is characterized by the metabolic defects resulting from hypopituitarism.

**dwarfism, renal**  A dwarfism which results from various kinds of chronic renal disease in children, such as congenital kidney malformation, chronic nephritis, renal tubular acidosis.

**dyad**  (R. R. Sears) Two organisms conceived as a single unit because of an interdependence between some aspects of their action or motivational systems; a pair, neither of whose members can achieve full reinforcement, or gratification, without collaboration of the other; e.g., mother and child when attached, a loving husband and wife, twins when reared together, habitual enemies or rivals; a pair whose unique cathexes to one another prevent the replacement of either by a new member without significant emotional disturbance to the remaining original one. See *environmental event.*

**dyadic theory**  (R. R. Sears) A personality or motivational theory that makes explicit the motivational interdependence of the members of two-person (dyadic) units; the dyadic quality of the relationship may be treated either as 1) a phenomenon to be explained developmentally, or as 2) the basic unit whose actions constitute the subject matter of the theory.

**dynaception**  The process, related to sensory perception, in which the organism perceives and responds to his own need state.

**dynamic apraxia**  See *apraxia, dynamic.*

**dynamic crossroads**  Choice-points in the adjustment of the organism, permitting sequences of alternative responses in goal-seeking behavior. These choice-points plus the paths leading to and from them, compose the Adjustment Process Analysis Chart.

**dynamic-effect law**  (R. B. Cattell) The proposition which holds that the habitualization of specific attentions and new behaviors is proportionate to their facilitation of goal attainment.

**dynamic equilibrium**  A characteristic of a system in which the pattern of distribution of energy remains stable despite changes in the total amount of energy. A change in the amount of energy at any one point in the system results in a restructuring of the energy distribution towards the end of maintaining the original distribution pattern.

**dynamic lattice**  (R. B. Cattell) A diagrammatic representation of the relation between an individual's goals and the relatively fixed habits which serve his dynamic purposes (attitudes, interests) in achieving these goals.

**dynamic psychology**  See *psychology, dynamic.*

**dynamic-situations principle**  (V. W. Voecks) The proposition that the stimulus configuration is never set as there are constant alterations of stimuli due to environmental and organismic changes, both of which affect which stimulus elements are received and how they are received.

**dynamic structure factors**  Source traits found among attitude-strength measures of very varied content and representing both ergs and engrams. Distinguished from motivation component factors.

**dynamic subsidiation**  The sequence of subsidiary goals which leads to a final goal.

**dynamic theory**  (W. Köhler) The proposition which holds that brain activity is determined by continual energy changes rather than by fixed relations among anatomic brain structures.

**dynamism**  1. A persistent mode of behaving in a way which brings drive satisfaction; mechanism. 2. (H.S. Sullivan) The smallest unit in the study of an individual's functional activity, that is the relatively enduring pattern of behavior which continuously characterizes the individual in his interpersonal relations. Dynamisms may be either patterns arising from recurring physiological tensions manifested as integrative, disjunctive, or isolative tendencies, patterns arising from particular zones of interaction, or both.

**dynamogenesis; dynamogen**  1. The fact that changes in response are correlated with changes in sensory activity. 2. The fact that motor responses are initiated as a result of sensory stimulation.

**dynamogenesis, principle of**  The proposition that response changes are proportional to the changes in sensory activity.

**dysacousia**  A condition characterized by extreme discomfort caused by ordinary noise.

**dysarthria**  The impairment of speech articulation caused by central nervous system disease.

**dysbulia**  A difficulty in thinking characterized by an inability to concentrate, attend or maintain a train of thought.

**dyseneia**  Defective speech articulation resulting from any kind of deafness.

**dysergasia**  (A. Meyer) A term designating those syndromes usually associated with disordered brain physiology and characterized by hallucination, disorientation, and fears.

**dysesthesia**  An inappropriate, excessive or diminished sensitivity to pain.

**dysgenesis**  1. Faulty development and infertility. 2. The condition in hybrids characterized by infertility with others of the hybrid stock and fertility with the members of either parent's stock.

**dysgenic** 1. A term describing those influences which are detrimental to heredity. 2. Biologically deficient.

**dysgraphia** The inability to express thoughts through writing or written symbols, caused by a brain lesion.

**dyskinesia; dyskinesis** A distortion of or inability to control involuntary movement characterized by involuntary muscular activity such as tics, spasms, or myoclonus.

**dyslalia** Defective speech.

**dyslexia** A reading disorder characterized by the inability to understand what one reads either silently or aloud.

**dyslogia** 1. An impairment of the ability to express ideas through speech caused by mental deficiency. 2. An impairment of speech due to mental deficiency.

**dysmenorrhea** Painful menstruation without apparent organic cause. The psychogenic factor is usually ambivalence concerning the female role.

**dysmnesia** An impairment of memory.

**dysmutual neurosis** See *neurosis, dysmutual.*

**dysmutualism** (B. B. Wolman) A type of mental disorder based on a form of social interaction characterized by an inconsistency of feelings and beliefs and extreme cyclic mood changes, including hysteria (on neurotic level) and manic-depressive psychosis.

**dyspareunia** 1. A deficient capacity for the enjoyment of sexual pleasure. 2. Painful sexual intercourse.

**dysphagia** An inability to swallow due to hysterical spasms of the throat muscles.

**dysphemia** A defective articulation of speech due to functional causes.

**dysphonia** Impairment of voice.

**dysphoria** A generalized feeling of anxiety and restlessness accompanied by depression.

**dysphrasia** A difficulty in speaking or writing which results from mental impairment.

**dysplasis or displasia** 1. Abnormal growth or development. 2. In terms of somatotype, the quantitative amount of a specific component or somatotype whether endomorphic, mesomorphic or ectomorphic, in different regions of the body. Also known as d-component.

**dysplastic type** See *type, dysplastic.*

**dyspnoea; dyspnea** A difficulty in breathing.

**dyspraxia** An impairment in the coordination of movement; an inability to carry out skilled movements.

**dysthmia** Despondent mood or disposition.

**dystrophia** See *dystrophy, pseudohypertrophic muscular.*

**dystrophy, pseudohypertrophic muscular** A familial disease characterized by progressive atrophy of the muscles following early hypertrophy, weakness, inability to rise and move naturally. It occurs in childhood.

# E

**e 1.** Abbreviation for error. **2.** (mathematics) Mathematical constant which is the base of natural logarithms having the value of 2.718281.

**E 1.** Abbreviation for experimenter, often italicized. **2.** Abbreviation for environment.

$_sE_R$  See *excitatory potential.*

$_sE_R$  (C. L. Hull) Generalized reaction potential. The reaction potential of any amount of learning, is $_sE_R = D \times V_1 \times K \times _sH_R$ where $D$ stands for drive operating during the learning process, multiplied by $V_1$ which is the dynamism of the signaling stimulus trace, multiplied by $K$ which is the incentive reinforcement and by $_sH_R$, the habit strength.

$_s\bar{E}_R$  See *momentary effective reaction potential.*

**E scale**  See *scale, E.*

**ear**  Auditory sensory organ consisting of the outer ear, the middle ear, and the inner ear or labyrinth.

**ear drum**  The tympanic membrane which stretches across the inner part of the external auditory canal and conducts vibrations when sound waves reach it.

**ear, inner**  See *labyrinth.*

**ear pulling 1.** Considered to be masturbatory equivalent in psychoanalytic theory. **2.** Viewed as substitute for thumb sucking by Kanner.

**Earle, Pliny (1809-1892)** American psychiatrist who held one of the first professorships of psychological medicine; author of *Curability of Insanity* (1877).

**early recollections** (A. Adler) The earliest childhood recollections offer the clue toward the understanding of a patient, for they represent the patient's attitude toward himself and life. Analysis of the early memories is of utmost importance in individual psychology psychotherapy.

**Ebbinghaus, Hermann (1850-1909)** German psychologist noted for his work in the field of memory and learning. He used experimentally the nonsense syllable. He developed the completion test which has been used in personality and intelligence tests. Serving as his own subject, Ebbinghaus investigated the memory process and association processes through studying the acquisition and retention of lists of words. Ebbinghaus established numerical indices of memory performance. He invented a method of measuring retention called "savings" in which he compared the number of trials to learn a list of nonsense syllables initially to the number of trials required for relearning, and elaborated the curve of retention. Ebbinghaus wrote several books, including *On Memory* (1885).

**Ebbinghaus' curve of retention**  A forgetting curve obtained by Ebbinghaus who measured the retention of nonsense material. The curve demonstrates a rapid drop in retention of material immediately after learning followed by a more gradual decline later on.

**Ebbinghaus illusion**  See *illusion, Ebbinghaus.*

**ebriecation**  (Paracelsus) Term for mental illness associated with alcoholism.

**ebriecation celeste**  (Paracelsus) Deranged exhibition of religious excitement and enthusiasm.

**E/C intervening variable**  The factor that indicates the empirical difference of results between the experimental and the control conditions.

**eccentric**  Deviating noticeably from normality in a manner considered to be odd or unusual without being a distinct sign of mental disorder, though sometimes, it is an early sign of such a disorder.

**eccentric paranoia 1.** Paranoia characterized by acute emotional excitement with frequent hallucinations, abnormal motor activity, and intense involvement with deranged social schemes. **2.** Condition formerly called "religious mania" when involving religious ideas.

**eccentric projection 1.** Location of sensation at the point in space of the stimulating body rather than at the point of sensation in the stimulated organism. Visual and auditory senses are usually projected in this way, while olfactory sensations are generally localized, tactual sensations are located at the point of sensation in the stimulated body. 2. A perceptual theory based upon these phenomena.

**Eccles, John Carew (1903-    )** Neurophysiologist, specially interested in (1) Synaptic transmission in the central nervous system (Nobel award, 1963), (2) The central mechanisms concerned in the control of movement with special reference to the cerebellum, (3) The brain-mind problem. Published books on these three interests are (1) *Physiology of Nerve Cells* (1947); *Physiology of Synapses* (1964); (2) *The Cerebellum as a Neuronal Machine* (1967); *Facing Reality: Philosophical Adventures by a Brain Scientist* (1970).

**ecdemomania**  Unhealthy impulse to roam or travel.

**écho des pensées**  Hallucinations of thoughts reproduced as verbal images; thoughts are heard repeated in speech, including the announcement of future actions.

**echo-phenomena**  A general term indicating repetitive behavior including echopraxia and echolalia.

**echo principle**  Supposition that one animal will imitate another animal if they have been involved simultaneously in the same behavior.

**echo-sign**  Epileptic speech disorder characterized by the repetition of a single word in a phrase.

**echo-speech**  See *echolalia.*

**echokinesis**  See *echopraxia.*

**echolalia**  1. Reiteration by imitation of the words or phrases of another person, characteristic of the catatonic schizophrenia. 2. Infantile speech patterns based on repeating sounds and words.

**echolocation**  Also called facial vision. It is the ability to assess the location of objects from their reflected echoes; it is an unconscious process analogous to radar which detects radio signals above the surface and sonar which discovers sounds under water. Human echolocation was first described by D. Diderot and J. de R. D'Alembert, French philosophers in the eighteenth century. Diderot maintained that blind men judge proximity of fire by the degree of heat and can distinguish an open street by motions of air. Modern researchers (K. M. Dallenbach, D. R. Griffin, W. N. Kellogg) rejected the notion of facial vision but related the perception of blind people to their ability to locate auditory and tactile cues. Some animals display a high degree of echolocation. Dolphins follow fish and catch them following reflected echoes; rats emit sounds and avoid obstacles by perceiving the echoes of their sounds; and bats do not collide with the wires stretched in their caves.

**echomatism**  See *echopraxia.*

**echomimia**  See *echopraxia.*

**echopathy**  Repetition by imitation of the words or actions of another person, characteristic of catatonic schizophrenia.

**echophrasia**  See *echolalia.*

**echopraxia**  Repetition through imitation of the actions or movements of another, as in "mirror-imaging," symptomatic of the catatonic schizophrenic.

**eclactisma**  Movements of the lower portion of the body in a grand mal seizure of epilepsy.

**eclampsia**  1. Epileptic convulsion.  2. Recurrent convulsion occurring during late pregnancy and associated with kidney disorder.

**eclecticism**  Organization of compatible facts and positions from diverse sources and incompatible theories into a consistent system.

**eclimia**  1. Large appetite and increased eating due to insatiable hunger. 2. Bulimia.

**eclipse, mental**  (P. Janet) A belief that one's ideas are stolen from him, characteristic of schizophrenics.

**ecmnesia**  Anterograde amnesia; a rare kind of amnesia.

**ecnoia**  An extreme and prolonged fear reaction.

**ecogenic component in an age curve**  (R. B. Cattell) The part of an age curve of a trait which is freed of influence due to peculiar historical epoch trend (the epogenic component). Ecogenic and epogenic components are to be separated by comparison of curves based on cross-sectional sampling with those from cursive longitudinal sampling.

**ecological validity**  See *validity, ecological.*

**ecology**  The study of organisms in relation to their physical environment and geographical surroundings.

**ecology, human**  The study of human organisms in relation to the physical and social environment which constitutes their life space.

**ecology, psychological**  The interaction of environmental variables and personal susceptibility in the development of a disorder.

**ecomania**  Pathological attitude and behavior syndrome toward members of one's family.

**econetics**  (R. B. Cattell) The subdivision of psychology concerned with relating the psychological meaning of a stimulus situation to the physical, biological, sociological, economic, etc., parameters. Psychophysics is, thus, a limited branch of econetics.

**economic**  Psychoanalytic term for the production, distribution and consumption of psychic energy with the greatest gain for the least effort.

**economic efficiency index**  An index expressing the efficiency of a test installation for industrial purposes by dividing the standard general validity by the cost (in expenditure on the time of various professional and clerical psychometric workers).

**economic type**  See *type, economic.*

**economical**  Minimum possible expenditure of energy resources or materials.

**economics**  1. Study of the production, distribution and exchange of material resources. 2. Theory that a person uses the least possible energy to attain a goal.

**Economo's disease** (K. von Economo) Lethargic encephalitis.

**economy** 1. Principle of arranging any system with minimum possible waste. 2. Tendency of an organism to avoid unnecessary expenditure of energy.

**economy, principle of** Rule in scientific investigation that the simplest of possible explanations be preferred; principle of parsimony.

**ecophobia** Fear of one's own house.

**ecosomatogenic disorders** (B. B. Wolman) Mental disorders of organic origin acquired through interaction with the physical environment. Brain injuries, toxic and infectious mental disorders belong to this category.

**écouteur** Person who experiences excessive pleasure by listening to sexual accounts.

**ecphoria** Recurrence of a memory trace or engram.

**ecphorize** To revive a memory trace or engram.

**ecphory** Reoccurrence of a memory trace or engram.

**ecphronia** Old term for neurotic mania and melancholy.

**ecplexis** (C. Galen) Stupor.

**ecstasy** 1. Overwhelming rapture or joy. 2. Religious trance.

**ecstatic trance** 1. Religious trance. 2. Trance-like state of overwhelming rapture or joy.

**ECT** Electroshock therapy. See *electric convulsive therapy.*

**ectoderm** Outer embryonic layer which gives rise to the epidermis, nails, hair, and other specializations of the outer membrane.

**ectodermal** Pertaining to the ectoderm or outermost embryonic layer which gives rise to the epidermis and its derivatives.

**ectodermogenic neurosyphilis** Syphilitic infection of the nervous system involving the cerebrospinal axis.

**ectomorphic type** See *type, ectomorphic.*

**ectopia pupillae** Abnormality of position of the pupil.

**ectoplasm** 1. Outer layer of a cell or unicellular organism. 2. In occultism and psychic research, a semisolid substance said to emanate from the body of a medium.

**ectype** Physical or mental constitution that varies markedly from the average.

**eczema** An inflammation of the skin characterized by itching, scaling and exudation of serous substances due to physical or psychogenic origin. Psychological causes involve feelings of insecurity, fears of rejection, and an inconsistent overprotective relationship with the mother.

**edema, angioneurotic** See *angioneurotic edema.*

**edge details** 1. A response to a Rorschach inkblot based on the contour of the edge. 2. A scoring category for the Rorschach test based on responses determined by the contour of the inkblot.

**edging** A unique kind of Rorschach test behavior in which the subject "edges" the cards, that is looking at the card with the surface held in a straight line with the line of vision.

**edipism** Injury to the eyes by oneself.

**Edipus complex** See *complex, Oedipus.*

**educability** Potentiality for learning, usually in reference to formal or school learning with I.Q. 50 or M.A. 6 as minimal necessary potential.

**education** 1. Progressive changes of a person affecting knowledge, attitudes, and behavior as a result of formal instruction and study. 2. Development of a person resulting from experience rather than from maturation. 3. Method of analysis through which a general principle emerges. 4. (C. Spearman) Process of relational thinking whereby knowledge of relations and the discovery of correlates leads to discovery of third and fourth neogenetic principles. 5. (H. S. Sullivan) Central processes located between the receptor functions and the effector functions.

**education stage** (C. G. Jung) The third stage of analytical psychotherapy in which the patient adapts to social pressure, demands and needs.

**educational acceleration** Progressing through an educational system more rapidly than normal either by skipping a grade or through special curricula.

**educational age** Performance in academic subjects measured in terms of the average chronological age performing at that level through the use of standardized achievement tests.

**educational guidance** Assisting students to pursue a suitable program of studies in relation to their interests, abilities, future plans, and environmental factors.

**educational measurement** 1. Appraising the abilities of a student through the use of a variety of tests. 2. Test construction and validation for use in schools. 3. Evaluating educational methods.

**educational psychology** See *psychology, educational.*

**educational quotient** Ratio of educational age to chronological age multiplied by 100 which is interpreted as an index of educational achievement.

$$E.Q. = \frac{E.A.}{C.A.} \times 100$$

**Edwards Personal Preference Schedule** (A. L. Edwards) A personality inventory introduced in 1953 which assesses fifteen of the manifest needs defined by H. A. Murray. Attempt was made to reduce variance of scores from social desirability by pairing items deemed equal in social desirability and requiring the subject to make a forced choice preference between these items. The subject's response is believed to reflect his needs rather than his conception of the more desirable characteristic.

**EEG** See *electroencephalogram.*

**E-F scale** Thirty item sub-scale of the Minnesota Multiphasic Inventory of Personality designed to measure ethnocentric and authoritarian attitudes.

**effect** 1. Event that invariably follows a specific other phenomenon as in a causal relationship; a result. 2. Major law of Thorndike's theory of learning stating that annoyance weakens and satisfaction strengthens a stimulus-response connection.

**effect, halo** The tendency to be influenced by a particular trait or overall impression of a person when rating another trait of that person.

**effect, law of** See *law of effect.*

**effect, spread of** The principle that the effect of rewards and punishments of a response spreads to other aspects of the situation.

**effectance motive** General motive encompassing all specific motives.

**effective-habit strength** $(_S\bar{H}_R)$ (C. L. Hull) Functional habit strength; sum of the reaction evocation potentialities set up by a reinforcement process, or by multiple reinforcement processes $(_{SS}H_R)$.

**effective-reaction potential** $(_S\bar{E}_R)$ (C. L. Hull) Reaction potential less inhibitory potential.

**effective stimulus** Stimulus which elicits a response.

**effector** Nerve ending in a muscle or a gland which responds to impulses.

**effeminacy** Physical or psychological feminine characteristics in a man.

**effeminate** Word describing a man who displays marked feminine traits in appearance or in personality.

**effemination** 1. State of being or becoming feminine in physical and psychological characteristics. 2. Homosexuality in which the sexual feelings and the psychological make-up of a man resemble those considered typically feminine.

**efferent** Nerve fibers which conduct impulses from the central nervous system to muscles and glands.

**efferent apraxia** See *apraxia, dynamic.*

**efferent motor aphasia** See *aphasia, efferent motor.*

**efficiency** 1. Ratio of energy expended to work done in a mechanism. 2. Minimum time or energy expended for maximum accomplishment. 3. (Signal detection theory) The square of the ratio of the empirically obtained detectability index for the human observer divided by the index for the ideal observer, the theoretically maximum performance,

$$\eta = \frac{(d' \text{ observed})^2}{d' \text{ ideal}}$$

**efficiency, predictive** See *predictive efficiency.*

**efficient cause** Total of the antecedent conditions of a given event or effect.

**effluvium** 1. Emanations from spiritual bodies in psychical research. 2. Body odor.

**effort** 1. Work done voluntarily or without extrinsic coercion. 2. Increased activity in the face of obstacles. 3. Subjective experience of fatigue or strain accompanying strenuous physical or mental activity.

**effort experience** Kinesthetic experience originating in the muscles involved in activity or effort.

**effort syndrome** 1. Physical symptoms, including shortness of breath, heart palpitation and fatigue out of proportion to the amount of exertion expended; associated with anxiety neurosis. 2. Neurocirculatory asthenia.

**egersis** Extreme wakefulness.

**ego** 1. The self, or the "I" which the individual experiences as himself. 2. (psychoanalysis) Part of a person's mental apparatus which develops gradually under the influence of environmental forces or the id to protect the organism against threats from within and without. The unconscious material of the id becomes transformed into the preconscious ego, in which the primary mental processes give ground to the emerging secondary processes. The main task of the ego is self-preservation of the organism. It performs this task in relation to the external world and to the internal world and in relation to the id by applying the so-called "reality-principle." The ego carries out the intentions of the id but only under conditions that promise a successful fulfillment. The ego brings together, unifies and organizes the mental processes, eliminates contradictions and develops into a coherent and well-functioning unit, practices "reality testing" that is, checks and controls the correctness of perceptions, and steers the entire mental system, avoiding unnecessary risks. The ego adjusts to the environment through control of overt behavior and the regulation of motor functions. When the organism is exposed to external danger, the ego reacts with fear. When the inner pressure stemming from the unconscious threatens the ego, the feeling of anxiety serves as a danger signal.

**ego-alien** (psychoanalysis) Not in harmony with the ego or total self in terms of drives, intellect, emotions, or overt behavior. In this term ego connotes what would currently be called the total self rather than the psychoanalytic concept of ego.

**ego-alter theory** 1. (H. Witkin) Theory that social interaction and social organization results from and is controlled by the individual's perception of himself in relation to the other or others. 2. Theory that the development of social institutions is based on self-interest and the instinct of self-preservation.

**ego analysis** (psychoanalysis) Analysis of the strengths and weaknesses of the ego in order to make constructive use of these forces.

**ego anxiety** (psychoanalysis) 1. Anxiety arising

from threat to the ego caused by the conflicting demands of the id, the ego, and the superego. **2.** Precipitate of ego defenses.

**ego automatisms** (psychoanalysis) Ego functions which are pre-conscious rather than conscious, such as driving a car or speaking a second language. Pathological ego automatisms resemble normal ego automatisms but are not appropriate to the situation, as in echolalia.

**ego, auxiliary**   See *auxiliary ego*.

**ego block**  Anything which interferes with the functioning and growth of the ego.

**ego, body**  Mentally experienced representations of the bodily self.

**ego boundaries** (P. Federn) Hypothetical boundaries existing between the person and the outer world of reality and between the person and his inner unconscious world. In a well functioning individual, the boundaries are cathected and flexible so that the ego is able to admit certain aspects of the unconscious selectively and to test reality demands adequately. In maladjustment, one or both of the boundaries are either too rigid or too weak to exercise their functions properly.

**ego cathexis** (psychoanalysis) Channeling instinctual demands and impulses in a rational, well-adjusted manner by using avenues of gratification in which the demands of the id, the ego, the superego, and of the external world are brought to a rational harmony. Impulses that jeopardize the inner harmony become either "successfully repressed" or sublimated, that is, channeled into new and more acceptable channels.

**ego complex**  (C. Jung) Psychic energy in the human mind centered around the ego or self.

**ego defense** (psychoanalysis) Protection of the ego from unacceptable impulses of the id through the use of unconscious defense mechanisms.

**ego-deficiency symptoms**  (B. B. Wolman) Psychotic symptoms including loss of contact with reality, paranoid delusions, hallucinations, depersonalization and motor and speech disturbances which occur as a result of the collapse of the ego.

**ego development  1.** (S. Freud) The gradual differentiation and evolution of part of the id into the ego. The neonate's mental apparatus, the id, resembles a body floating in water. Under the influence of environmental forces that act on the surface of the id, this surface changes and develops into a sort of protective shell, called the ego. Part of the unconscious material of the id becomes transformed into the preconscious ego, in which the primary mental processes give ground to the emerging secondary processes. This development of ego allows the individual to protect himself from internal and external threats and to differentiate himself from the external world. **2.** (H. Hartmann) Development through maturation and learning of the primary and the secondary autonomous apparati of the ego which constitute the foundation for the ego's relation to external reality. The primary autonomous apparati include the inborn capacities of perception, motility, and thought; the secondary autonomous apparati develops as a result of defense against instinctual drive and leads toward a more structured and independent pattern of behavior.

**ego, duplication of**  Delusion that the individual is more than one person or has multiple identities.

**ego-dystonia**  Mental state of experiencing ideas or impulses which are unacceptable to the ego or self.

**ego-eroticism**  (S. Freud) **1.** The investment of libido in one's own person; the direction of libido to oneself as opposed to external objects. **2.** The egoistic drives or energies that are at the disposal of erotic force and that serve pleasure and enhance the vital functions of the individual.

**ego failure** (psychoanalysis) Failure of the ego to keep balance among impulses coming from the id, demands of the superego, and external reality.

**ego function**  (psychoanalysis) Activities of the ego as opposed to the id or the superego.

**ego-ideal**  (S. Freud)**1.** In earlier works, synonymous with what was later called the superego; representing the biologically and cultural-historically evolved conscience which sets behavioral norms for the individual. **2.** In later works, the ego-ideal represents that part of the superego which carries the child's admiration for idealized parental figures. Identification by introjection results in the individual striving toward perfection by attempting to live up to the expectations or standards of the idealized parental figures, the ego-ideal.

**ego-ideal, narcissistic**  Perfect self-image the child constructs of himself without reference to an ego-ideal based on identification with the parental figures.

**ego identity**  (psychoanalysis) A person's experience of himself as persisting essentially unchanged on as a continuous entity through time as a result of the function of the ego which synthesizes one's ideals, behavior and societal role.

**ego instincts**  (psychoanalysis) Instincts directed toward self-preservation.

**ego-integrative**  Organization of personality into a whole through harmonizing of impulses and desires.

**ego-involvement**  Personal indentification with, or commitment to, a situation or a task.

**ego-libido**  (S. Freud) Libido invested in one's own person; libido directed toward one's self and toward self-preservation, as opposed to external objects.

**ego, loss of boundaries of  1.** Inability of an individual to separate his own self from another, or from the surrounding world. **2.** Breakdown of subject/object distinction.

**ego, mental**  Mentally experienced representation of self or ego.

**ego morphism  1.** (L. Ackerson) Perceiving and interpreting the behavior of others and things in general the way one wants them to be. 2. Using one's personal motivational system as a general standard of reference against which the motives and actions of others are judged.

**ego-neurosis** (psychoanalysis) Disorder occurring when the weak or poorly organized ego is unable to cope with inner and outer pressures; a quantitative disharmony between the id, ego, and superego, and between the total personality and the outer world.

**ego nuclei** (M. Klein) Original components of the ego.

**ego-object polarity** Maintenance of a clear distinction between oneself and all that is other or not self.

**ego perception** (P. Schilder) The ego as a censor.

**ego protective symptoms** (B. B. Wolman) Neurotic symptoms including defense mechanisms indicative of the struggle of the ego to retain the control over unconscious impulses.

**ego resistance** (psychoanalysis) The action or defense mechanism of the ego that prevents the unconscious from becoming conscious.

**ego retrenchment** (psychoanlaysis) The lessening or the disappearance of the need for a particular function of the ego to occur through the use of defense mechanisms.

**ego strength** A source trait showing itself in good emotional stability and capacity to cope with emotional difficulties.

**ego structure** Persisting pattern of personality characteristics that influence ego processes.

**ego subject** (psychoanalysis) The ego as the object of its own libido or instincts as in narcissism and autoerotic gratifications.

**ego-suffering** (psychoanalysis) The direction of aggressive forces stored in the superego against the ego creating guilt feelings such as depression when the superego disapproves of the ego.

**ego syntonic** (psychoanalysis) Ideas, behavior or impulses which are acceptable to the ego or self.

**egocentric** 1. Interested in oneself and one's personal needs and concerns. 2. Behavior directed by personal needs and self-interest.

**egohood** Selfhood; individuality.

**egoism** 1. Action or behavior directed by one's personal needs and interests, disregarding the needs of others. 2. Social philosophy or ethical system based on self-interest as the primary motivation of behavior.

**egoist** One who is motivated primarily by self-interest.

**egoistic** 1. Concerned with one's own interests to the neglect of others. 2. Motivated by self-interest.

**egoity** Selfhood; egohood.

**egoize** To take excessive interest in one's self.

**egology** (S. Rado) Study of the ego or the "I".

**egomania** Extreme preoccupation with self.

**egopathy** Hostile feelings or actions arising from excessive feelings of self-importance and the subsequent desire to put others down.

**egotheism** Deification of the self.

**egotism** See *egoism*.

**egotist** 1. See *egoist*. 2. Conceited person; one who overevaluates himself.

**egotistical** Conceited; thinking very highly of oneself.

**egotize** 1. To take excessive interest in oneself or to act conceited. 2. To display egotism.

**egotropic** (A. Meyer) Egocentric or egocentricity.

**egotropy** (A. Meyer) Narcissism or egocentricity.

**egregorsis** Extreme wakefulness.

**egrimony** Obsolete term for sorrow or sadness.

**eidetic** Mental images of things previously seen characterized by clean or vivid visualization.

**eidetic imagery** Especially clear and detailed visual image of things previously seen, sometimes even months after the actual viewing of them.

**eidetic type** (E. R. Jaensch) Constitutional type based on different kinds of eidetic imagery experienced by people and associated with personality variables arising from differences in perceptual and cognitive functioning.

**Eigenwelt** (Existentialist) Man's relationship with himself.

**Einstellung** (German) Attitude or mental set which predisposes one to behave or respond in a certain way to particular situations.

**eisotrophobia** Fear of mirrors.

**ejaculatio deficiens** Inadequate ejaculation.

**ejaculatio praecox** Premature ejaculation; emission of semen during preparation for sexual intercourse before or immediately upon insertion.

**ejaculation** Expulsion of semen at orgasm.

**ejaculation retardata** Delayed or retarded ejaculation during sexual intercourse.

**EKG** see *electrocardiogram*.

**elaboration** Combining and expanding of ideas and motives characteristic of higher mental processes.

**elation** 1. Extreme joyful excitement. 2. Abnormal or exaggerated gaiety. 3. (W. McDougall) Emotional component of self-display.

**elavil** Common name for amitriptylene, an antidepressant drug.

**Elberfeld horses** Group of horses trained in Elberfeld, Germany around 1900 who appeared to be solving complicated mathematical problems though they were actually trained to tap their feet each time the trainer nodded his head.

**elbow jerk** 1. Sharp reflex of the forearm occasioned by striking the tendon just above the elbow when the arm is partly flexed at the elbow. 2. Triceps reflex.

**elective anorexia** Absence of appetite and restriction of the amount of food eaten through having an extremely negative reaction to the consumption of food.

**Electra complex** See *complex, Electra.*

**electric convulsive (electroshock) therapy** Introduced in 1938 by Cerletti and Bini in Rome, Italy. It is a modification of the original convulsive therapy with pharmacological means (metrazol) by von Meduna. Convulsive therapy is primarily based on an old observation that the symptoms of mental patients may disappear after spontaneous convulsions. The same could be achieved with artificially induced convulsions. Since 1952 the early complications of convulsive treatment are eliminated by means of chemical relaxation of all muscles. This is accomplished by injection of succinyl choline given after induction of barbiturate anesthesia. The treatment itself is given with a short bilateral electrical stimulus. It is painless, and the patient has complete amnesia for the entire procedure. After several treatments some memory disturbance exists but always disappears after a while as thorough psychological testing has proven. Unilateral stimulation over the non-dominant hemisphere avoids memory impairment but is therapeutically less effective. Indications are schizophrenia, and particularly depressions.

**electric organ** Specialized muscular tissue in some primitive fish which can generate potential and store charges and which transmits electric shock through the nervous system upon excitation.

**electrical brain stimulation (ESB)** It has been found that electrical stimulation of the brain by means of implanted electrodes can have both reinforcing and punishing effects on behavior, i.e. the organism will work to be electrically stimulated or will work to avoid electrical stimulation. What effects stimulation will have is a function of the intensity of stimulation and the locus of stimulation.

**electroaesthesiometer** A type of aesthesiometer which measures two-point or spatial thresholds by using an electromagnet to bring the stimulus point into contact with the skin.

**electrocardiogram (EKG)** Graphic record of the electrical activity accompanying the heartbeat made by an electrocardiograph and used as a diagnostic tool.

**electroconvulsive therapy** See *electric convulsive therapy.*

**electrode** Two-poled device used to transmit electric current to tissue; the positive pole is the anode; the negative pole is the cathode.

**electrodermal response (EDR)** See *galvanic skin response.*

**electrodiagnosis** 1. Use of electrical instruments to diagnose conditions of the body. 2. The application of electric current to muscles and nerves for diagnostic purposes.

**electromyogram (EMG)** Graphic record of electrical activity or currents in a muscle. Also called *electromyograph.*

**electronarcosis** A shock treatment which produces a sleep-like coma after an initial convulsive phase.

**electrophobia** Extreme fear of electricity.

**electroretinogram (ERG)** Graphic record of electrical activity in the retina of the eye.

**electroshock therapy** See *electric convulsive therapy.*

**electrotaxis** Response of organisms or cells, either attraction or repulsion, to electrical stimulation.

**electrotherapy** Application of electricity in the treatment of physical or mental disorder.

**electrotonus** The changed electrical and physical condition of a nerve or muscle due to the application of electric current.

**element** 1. A part or constituent of the whole, especially one that cannot be reduced to a simpler unit. 2. (W. Wundt, B. Titchener) The simplest units of consciousness. 3. (G. A. Kelly) One of the events or units of information that are abstracted from a specific construct by a particular person. 4. (information theory) Points in a sample space or a single unit or events in a collection of units or elements.

**elementarism** 1. Belief that a complex whole is reducible to and understandable in terms of its constituent parts which are considered to be independent units. 2. Any approach to psychology which analyzes behavior and mental processes in terms of mental elements. 3. When used derogatorily: preoccupation with simple parts at the expense of the whole.

**eleutheromania** Fanatical interest in freedom.

**Elgin check list** List of behavior patterns more often associated with the psychotic population than with the normal population.

**elimination** The expelling of feces and urine from the body.

**elision** The omission of syllables or sounds in speech.

**Elizur's test for organicity** See *test, Elizur's, for organicity.*

**ellipsis** 1. Omission of whole words in speech or writing with the result that the listener or reader must complete the thought himself. 2. (psychoanalysis) Omission of highly significant words or ideas which might be recovered through free association.

**ellis harmonical** Specialized reed instrument similar to the harmonium used to experimentally study and demonstrate exact intervals and pitches.

**Ellis, Henry Havelock (1859-1939)** British psychologist noted for his study of the psychology of sex.

elucidation stage  (C.. G. Jung) The second stage of analytical psychotherapy in which interpretations of unconscious contents, especially transference material, are made.

emancipation  1. Independence of thought, feeling and behavior due to freedom from control by others, particularly from the control of parents. 2. (psychoanalysis) Resolution of the Oedipal complex and subsequent liberation from parental figures and authority.

emasculation  Castration, either physical or psychological.

embarassment dream  Dream in which the individual sees himself in a painful or shameful situation from which he cannot escape and which is thought to be related to painful childhood experiences.

embedded figure  1. Outline of person or object merged with background in such a way that it is difficult to perceive. 2. Hidden figure.

embolalia  Meaningless words or phrases interspersed in spoken language.

embolism  Obstruction or stoppage of a blood vessel by a blood clot or an air bubble.

embolism, cerebral  Occlusion of a cerebral blood vessel by an embolus, the result appearing like a cerebral hemorrhage.

embolophasia  See embolophrasia.

embolophrasia  Repeated repetition of an unnecessary phrase in spoken language.

embryo  Organism in its early stage of prenatal development; in the human species it is the first six to eight weeks after conception.

embryology  The study of prenatal development of organisms.

embryonic  Related to the embryo or the early stage of an organism's development.

emeotamania  Desire to vomit, often associated with hysteria.

emergency situations  Critical situations where the organism automatically prepares for sudden, sustained action such as fight or flight through the occurrence of automatic facilitating physiological reactions which are under the control of the sympathetic nervous system.

emergency theory of the emotions  1. (W. B. Cannon) Theory that the emotions and accompanying physiological changes controlled by the sympathetic portion of the autonomic nervous system prepare the organism for emergencies; visceral changes such as increased heart rate, rise in blood pressure and dilation of the pupils which are associated with certain emotions also prepare the organism for flight or fight when necessary. 2. (H. Selye) Theory that an organism's adaptation to emergencies or stress is comprised of three phases governed by the autonomic nervous system: the alarm phase in which the organism mobilizes its defenses; the resistance phase in which the body exerts its resources in order to meet continued stress successfully; and the exhaustion stage when the organism has used its protective resources and is no longer able to resist stress.

emergent  1. Phenomenon which cannot be predicted from its parts or reduced to its antecedent events or properties. 2. (Gestalt) The whole as being qualitatively different from its constituent parts and, as such, influencing them.

emergent evolution  Theory that new and unpredicatable phenomena result from the combination or interaction of pre-existing factors or elements.

emetophobia  Extreme fear of vomiting often associated with hysteria.

EMG  See electromyogram.

emission  1. Discharge of semen. 2. Elicitation of a response not associated with an identifiable stimulus.

emission, nocturnal  Discharge of semen in sleep.

emit  Occurrence of a response not associated with any particular or identifiable stimulus.

Emmert's law  See law, Emmert's.

emmetropia, emmetropis  Normal vision due to perfectly functioning refractory system of the eye, which focuses rays directly on the retina without the necessity of accommodation.

emote  To exhibit emotion.

emotion  1. A complex reaction consisting of a physiological change from the homeostatic state, subjectively experienced as feeling and manifested in bodily changes which are preparatory to overt actions. 2. (psychoanalysis) A derivative of instinctual drive representing the tension experienced by the individual making it necessary for him to discharge and eliminate the need. 3. (James-Lange theory) The perception of the physiological reaction to a stimulus. 4. (B. F. Skinner) A hypothetical state that is the predisposition to act in a certain manner that is the function of circumstances in the individual's history. 5. (Cannon-Bard theory) The result of impulses sent to the cortex by the hypothalamus which is stimulated to do so by the receptors of outside stimulation. Impulses to the viscera are sent simultaneously by the hypothalmus, resulting in the energy state accompanying emotion. 6. (K. Pribram) A process of disequilibration (affects, passions) and re-equilibration (coping) that depends on internal control as opposed to that which deploys planned action on the environment (motivation).

emotional  1. Characterized by or associated with emotion or the physiological changes which accompany emotion. 2. Tending toward emotional behavior or responses rather than cognitive behavior or responses.

emotional bias  Prejudice based on emotional causes.

emotional blockage  Inability to remember or to think coherently due to strong emotions usually associated with fear.

emotional centre  Obsolete term for the portion of

the brain thought to control emotional functioning. Thalamic region seems to be related to the function of emotions.

**emotional control** Attempt by an individual to direct his own emotions or the emotions of another.

**emotional disorder** Mental disorder or condition in which emotional reactions are chronically inappropriate or disproportionate given the reality situation.

**emotional expression** Behavioral, visceral, muscular and glandular changes that occur while emoting.

**emotional immaturity** 1. Tendency toward emotional behavior characteristic of children or younger persons. 2. Failure to exhibit emotional behavior considered appropriate to one's age level. 3. Vague term for poor adjustment of any sort.

**emotional instability** Tendency toward rapidly changing and unpredictable emotional behavior.

**emotional maturity** Condition characterized by emotional development, and by exhibition of emotional behavior appropriate to adults rather than to children.

**emotional pattern** 1. The behavioral, physiological and peripheral responses, and the set of relationships, such as intensity and timing, among them usually associated with a particular emotion and supposed to be characteristic of it. 2. The pattern of emotional behavior characteristic of a given individual under various conditions.

**emotional release** 1. Outpouring of emotions which had been suppressed or pent up. 2. Catharsis of emotion.

**emotional stability** Characteristic of having good emotional control and consistency or of not reacting excessively to emotional situations.

**emotional state** Physiological, behavioral, and conscious condition of an organism during emotional or affective experiences and characteristic of emotions.

**emotional surrender** The fusion of patients with another person in a therapeutic setting resulting in loss of their individuality.

**emotionalism, respiratory** See *nervous pseudoasthma.*

**emotionality** 1. Indicates the degree to which a person reacts emotionally. 2. Characteristic of persons who tend to react strongly or excessively to emotional situations.

**emotionality, home setting of** Family situation or home environment characterized by an atmosphere based on emotional influences and factors rather than a rational foundation.

**emotions, abnormal instability of** 1. General term for pathological manifestations of affect or emotions. 2. Thymopathy.

**emotive** Stimuli or situations which evoke an emotional or affective response.

**empathema** Obsolete term for uncontrollable passion.

**empathema atonicum** (M. Good) Melancholy.

**empathema entonicum** (M. Good) Obsolete term for what is currently called the manic phase of manic-depressive psychosis.

**empathema inane** (M. Good) Psychomotor aggression.

**empathetic** 1. Characterized by empathy. 2. Intellectual rather than emotional identification.

**empathize** To experience empathy.

**empathy** 1. Ability to perceive the mood and feelings of another person. 2. Understanding of the feelings, sufferings, or situation of another person without these feelings being communicated by words.

**emphrensy** Obsolete term for enfrenzy.

**empirical** 1. Based on facts and experience, systematic observation and experiment rather than theory on general philosophical principle. 2. Valuing facts and devaluing speculation or rational theory.

**empirical construct** Hypothetical construct based on observed facts.

**empirical equation** Equation based on a set of observations rather than on rational deduction according to the criteria of closeness to fit and parsimony, not theoretical meaning or value.

**empirical law** 1. Principle based on empirical data or experimental findings which states the ongoing relationship between two or more sets of variables. 2. Law based on the inductive rather than the deductive process.

**empirical test** Testing of a hypothesis through the use of facts or experimentation.

**empirical validity** Validity of a test according to how well it actually measures what it was designed to measure, which is determined by correlating the test with another, independent measure.

**empiricism** 1. Philosophical theory that all knowledge originates in experience. 2. Observation in psychology, and sciences in general, which is based on empirical observations and objective facts obtained through natural observation and experimentation as the only valid method and data for scientific investigation. Operational definitions and methods are central and theory-building and hypothetical constructs are generally avoided.

**employment psychology** 1. Area of psychology which deals with selecting the most suitable and most likely to succeed of the applicants for a given occupation through the use of various testing methods. 2. Personnel selection.

**empresiomania** Pathological desire to set things on fire, more commonly called pyromania.

**emprosthotonos** Bending of the body forward.

**empty organism** Term used by opponents of the stimulus-response approach to psychology to criticize the lack of consideration of organismic factors and of hypothetical constructs in such an orientation.

**empty set**   See *null set*.

**empyreumatic**   Category of odors characterized by a tarry or smoky aroma.

**emulation**   Conscious attempt to equal the performance of another with the connotation of imitating that other.

**enantiodromia**   (C.G. Jung) Interplay of opposites through which everything is changed into its opposite eventually.

**enantiopathic**   Leading to the arousal of an opposing passion.

**enantiopathy**   Opposing passion.

**encatalepsis**   (Hippocrates) Obsolete term for catalepsy.

**encephalasthenia**   Extreme mental fatigue.

**encephalitis**   Acute inflammation of the brain or its covering which sometimes results in neurological and personality changes which persist after the inflammation.

**encephalitis, coxsackie**   Mild form of encephalitis, with headaches, lethargy, vomiting, fever and pain of the back of the neck. It is fatal in 80 per cent of the cases in neonates.

**encephalitis, ECHO**   Encephalitis caused by one of the types of ECHO virus, usually types 4, 6, and 9.

**encephalitis, epidemic**   See *encephalitis, lethargic*.

**encephalitis, equine**   Type of encephalitis characterized by headache, nausea, fever, increasing lethargy and vertigo with occasional loss of consciousness and seizures; residual symptoms include intellectual and emotional aberrations, seizures, mental retardation, and visual and language difficulties.

**encephalitis, herpes simplex**   Type of encephalitis with upper respiratory infection, fever and convulsions, from which the person does not awaken. There is often extensive damage to the brain.

**encephalitis, Japanese**   Form of encephalitis with rapid rise of temperature, headaches, confusion and, commonly, transient paralysis of the limbs. Although usually leaving no sequelae, persistent difficulties include paralysis, headaches and, especially in children, intellectual retardation and personality changes.

**encephalitis, lethargic**   1. Sleeping sickness. 2. Inflammation of the brain often resulting in severe personality changes.

**encephalitis, mumps**   A type of encephalitis caused by mumps, although the patients, while suffering from encephalitis, may show no signs of mumps. Symptoms include lethargy, varying degrees of delirium, stupor and coma, and neurological difficulties during the latter half of the first week of the illness. Brainstem symptoms include facial paresis and deafness, with progressive medullary involvement leading to death. The patient may suffer severe peripheral and sphincter weakness and will manifest symptoms of both upper and lower motor neuron difficulty.

Residuals are rare but hearing loss, persistent facial weakness, and personality changes have been reported.

**encephalitis periaxialis diffusa**   See *Schilder's disease*.

**encephalitis, rabies**   Transmitted to humans by the bite of a rabid animal; its symptoms include pain, chills and fever, nausea and vomiting, malaise, headache, vertigo and often mental confusion, irritability and hydrophobia, and most often death.

**encephalitis, rubeola**   A form of encephalitis associated with rubeola, an exanthematous disease characterized by rash and fever. The patient develops encephalitis four to seven days after the appearance of the rash although the severity of the rubeola has no bearing on the likelihood of development of encephalitis. The encephalitis is associated with a rise in temperature, headache, vomiting, ataxia, lethargy frequently progressing to a comatose state, and occasionally seizures. The most common residuals are ataxia and personality changes.

**encephalitis, St. Louis**   A form of encephalitis which usually strikes abruptly with temperature elevation, headache and symptoms and signs of meningeal inflammation. Some difficulties with judgment, emotions and personality may remain for several months or, occasionally, permanently.

**encephalitis, varicella**   A type of encephalitis which occasionally follow a varicella infection, characterized by lethargy, irritability, ataxia, seizures, fever, and paralysis. Residual difficulties include paresis, ataxia, blindness, retardation, speech difficulties, and personality changes.

**encephalization**   1. The brain takes on progressively more control of the functioning of the nervous system and of the activities of the body; ascending the phylogenetic scale, in the evolution of a species, and in the development of the individual. 2. Formation of brain through an evolutionary process.

**encephalocele**   Congenital hernia of the brain which protrudes through an opening of the skull.

**encephalomalacia**   Softening of the brain due to an inadequate supply of blood and resulting in partial or complete deterioration.

**encephalomyelitis**   Inflammation of the central nervous system.

**encephalon**   The brain.

**encephalopathia literatorum**   Obsolete term for mental malfunction allegedly resulting from intense studies.

**encephalopathia puerperalis**   See *puerperal psychosis*.

**encephalopathy**   A general name for various brain diseases.

**encephalopathy, congenital**   Brain disease contracted in utero. It may be caused by the mother's infectious diseases such as syphilis, rubella (also called German measles), influenza, parasitic organisms, etc., blood toxins (toxemia), and intoxications with lead, carbon monoxide, arsenic, etc. The various forms of congenital encephalopathy are associated with mental retardation.

**encephalopsychosis** Mental disorder due to cerebral lesions or a definitely localized disease of the brain.

**encephalopyosis** Brain abscess.

**encephalosis** General term for degeneration of the brain through disease.

**encoding** 1. Transformation of messages into signals which can be transmitted by a communications channel. 2. Transformation of information by an individual into behavior which can function as a signal in a communications system.

**encopresis** Involuntary defecation not caused by illness or any organic malfunction and associated with poor toilet training or emotional problems when it occurs in children.

**enculturation** The process of adjusting to and accepting a culture.

**end** 1. The outcome or result desired from purposive behavior. 2. A goal or purpose.

**end brush** The termination of an axon which is finely branched.

**end button; end foot** Thickening or enlargement of nerve fibers of the end brush which are in contact with the dendrites of other cells at the synapse and are thought to be involved in the firing of cells.

**end plate** Specialized ending of a motor nerve fiber which makes contact with the muscle cell and transmits nerve impulses from the axon to the muscle fiber.

**end pleasure** (psychoanalysis) Intense pleasure associated with release from tension, especially that which occurs with orgasm.

**end spurt** Increase in energy and performance just before completing or learning an activity or work.

**endocathection** 1. (H. A. Murray) The investment of psychic energy in inner thought or emotion for its own sake. 2. Preoccupation with one's own thoughts or inner activities and the withdrawal from external and practical pursuits.

**endocrine gland** Ductless gland of internal secretion, such as the thyroid, whose products go directly into the bloodstream by osmosis.

**endocrine glands** See *glands, endocrine.*

**endocrine psychosyndrome** (M. Bleuler) The majority of endocrine diseases do not provoke a psychosis but they are, however, accompanied by marked personality changes. These personality changes which are described by the term "endocrine psychosyndrome" include 1) increased impulsiveness and excitability in acute cases and decreased in chronic cases; 2) dysfunction of biological rhythms—patients are either inactive and apathetic or tense and hyperactive; 3) mood fluctuations, irritability, anxiety, aggressivity and euphoric states; and 4) disturbances in biological drives—alternations in the urge to be protected against heat and cold, to rest and relax versus being active, to behave sexually or aggressively toward mother or nurse. These morbid alternations may be lasting but more often they occur suddenly and disappear in the same abrupt fashion. These personality changes are similar to those seen in patients with localized cerebral diseases, particularly those of the brain stem and frontal lobes.

**endocrinology** Study of endocrine glands and internal secretions.

**endocrinopathic** Related to or associated with endocrinopathy.

**endocrinopathy** General term for any disorder caused by disease of the endocrine glands.

**endocrinotherapy** The use of preparation made from the secretion from the endocrine glands, such as the pituitary or the thyroid, as therapeutic treatment.

**endoderm** Inner embryonic layer which gives rise to the visceral organs and the digestive tract.

**endogamy** Restriction of marriage to one's own social group, kinship, one's caste or any other specific group to which the individual belongs through custom or tradition.

**endogenous** 1. Arisen from within a given system or structure, as from within the mind of the body or a given biological group. 2. Forms of mental deficiency that are hereditary or determined by genes.

**endolymph** The fluid in the semicircular canal and the labyrinth-like membrane of the internal ear.

**endomorphic type** See *type, endomorphic.*

**endoplasm** Inner cytoplasm of a cell.

**endopsychic** 1. That which is inside the mind; intrapsychic. 2. Referring to unconscious processes.

**endopsychic censor** See *censor, endopsychic.*

**endothelium** 1. The epithelium which lines blood vessels, lymph vessels, and the heart. 2. Simple epithelium which lines closed cavities in the body and which develops from the mesoderm.

**endowment** Natural, innate physical and mental potential; most often used with the connotation of superior potential.

**enelicomorphism** Attributing adult characteristics, behaviors, or abilities to the child; describing a child's characteristics, behaviors or abilities in adult terms.

**enemophobia** Fear of wind.

**energy** (physics) The capacity for doing work.

**energy, kinetic** Energy of a body in motion which is due to the motion.

**energy, psychic** 1. Capacity to do mental or psychic work. 2. Energy invested in or expended through psychological activities or processes or mental pursuits.

**enervate** 1. To lessen energy; to weaken. 2. To surgically remove nerves.

**enfrenzy** To drive crazy, upset or madden.

**engineering psychology** 1. Study of the relationships between man and machines. 2. Adjusting the design of machines to the needs and capacities of man. 3. Study of the effect of machines on man's behavior.

**engram** Intervening variable hypothesized to account for retention and thought to be a permanent change in the state of living tissue as the result of excitation such as that which occurs with learning.

**enomania** See *oinomania*.

**enosimania** An individual's obsessive conviction that he has committed an unforgivable sin.

**entatic** Stimulating; provoking sexual desire or sexual intercourse.

**entelechy** 1. Realization of a potentiality. 2. The completion or perfection of an act. 3. Nonmechanical or immaterial agent considered responsible for material or life processes.

**enteroceptor** See *interoceptor*.

**enterocolitis** Intestinal inflammation associated with nervous disorder.

**enteroperipheral** (H. Spencer) Obsolete term for experience which originates inside the body.

**enteroptosis** Sagging or prolapse of the intestines associated with a particular body type in constitutional medicine.

**entheomania** Extreme fear of evil spirits or demons.

**entity** 1. Relatively autonomous being or object. 2. Discrete part of reality which exists with some degree of independence and maintains itself.

**entoderm** See *endoderm*.

**entomology** Study of insects.

**entomophobia** Morbid fear of insects.

**entoptic** 1. Within the eye. 2. Visual responses which are generated by chemical conditions or mechanical processes inside the eye itself rather than by external stimuli.

**entropy** 1. That part of the energy in a thermodynamic system which is not available for work. 2. (psychoanalysis) The extent to which psychic energy cathected or invested in an object cannot be transferred. 3. (information theory) Specification of the number of possible outcomes a given event might have, increasing as the number of possible outcomes increases while the amount of information contained in any one outcome decreases with an increase in total possible outcomes.

**entropy, social** Principle that energy is consumed in social change leaving less available for further progress and eventually resulting in a static society.

**entry** (statistics) Number, value or symbol which is recorded in a particular position of a statistical calculation.

**enucleation** Removal of a whole organ or tumor without cutting into it, as in the removal of an eyeball.

**enumeration** Counting or identifying each member of a group one by one, often for purposes of classification or induction.

**enuresis** 1. Involuntary passage of urine. 2. Bedwetting.

**environment** Sum total of external conditions, including social and physical factors, which have the potential to influence an organism. See *environmental psychology*.

**environment, internal** The total internal processes occurring within the body, tending toward maintaining homeostasis and considered to act as an influence on any of the organism's activities.

**environmental event** The actions or action-products of one member of a dyad that are essential for allowing the other member to complete his search for gratification or reinforcement; e.g., a mother's responsive smile to her supplicative infant, a wife's retributive criticism of a guilty husband.

**environmental factors** All external conditions which may affect the individual.

**environmental-mold trait** (R.B. Cattell) Personality trait developed by the influence of persistent characteristics of the environment.

**environmental psychology** Environmental psychology is a relatively new field of scientific inquiry which is concerned with the interrelationships between man's physical environment—particularly the built environment—and human behavior and experience. It crystallized as a field in psychology with the publication of *Environmental Psychology: Man and his Physical Setting* by H. M. Proshansky, W. H. Ittelson, and L. G. Rivlin. What distinguishes this field from others concerned with man's environment in relation to human behavior and experience, is its focus on the natural, on-going physical settings that define and guide human interaction. It is problem oriented, interdisciplinary in its conceptual and theoretical orientations, and eclectic in its methodological approaches. The "urban setting" is a primary focus in the interest of many environmental psychologists, studying such issues as "crowding," "safety," "privacy," "territoriality," "place identity," "cognitive mapping," and others in the settings of the home, the school, the office, the neighborhood, the hospital, and the recreational area. What must be noted is that its interdisciplinary emphasis is rooted in its need to have a close working relationship not only with environmental sociologists and anthropologists, but with designers, architects, planners, and other practitioners responsible for designing man's built environment.

**envy** Emotion stimulated by the desire to possess what someone else has.

**enzygotic twins** See *twins, identical.*

enzyme   Organic substance which functions as a catalyst in plants and animals accelerating chemical transformations.

enzyme blocks   Substances or circumstances which prevent enzymes from performing their function.

eonism   See *transvestitism.*

eosinophilic diathesis   (constitutional medicine) Eosinophilic condition resulting from arthritic diathesis.

eosinophils   A type of blood cell which is reduced during physiological stress.

eosophobia   Fear of sunrise, daybreak.

epencephalon   (physiology) The hindbrain or cerebellum rubrick, located below the cerebrum and above the pons and the medulla.

ependyma   Membraneous lining of the central canal of the spinal cord and of the ventricles of the brain.

ephemeral mania   See *mania transitoria.*

ephialtes   Obsolete term for nightmare.

ephialtes vigilantium   Nightmare-like experience while awake.

epicritic   Related to highly developed cutaneous sensitivity capable of delicate discrimination.

epicritic sensibility   (H. Head) Cutaneous sensitivity to light pressure and mild degree of temperature with finely localized responsiveness and highly developed discrimination.

epidemic catalepsy   See *catalepsy, epidemic.*

epidemic encephalitis   See *encephalitis, lethargic.*

epidemic hysteria   See *hysteria, epidemic.*

epidemiologist   A person who studies the incidence, distribution, and control of disease in a population.

epidermis   The outermost layer of the skin composed of epithelial tissue protective in function.

epigastric   Related to or part of the epigastrium which is the surface of the upper and middle portions of the stomach region.

epigastric reflex   Feeling of weakness or sinking in the stomach area frequently associated with anxiety or fear.

epigenesis   1. Hypothesis that new phenomena not present in the original fertilized egg emerge over the course of embryonic development through the interaction of pre-existing elements with pre-natal environmental influences. 2. Appearance of new phenomena not present at previous stages in an organism's development.

epiglottis   Elastic-like membraneous structure which covers the glottis, protecting it during swallowing.

epilempsis   (Hippocrates) Obsolete term for epilepsy.

epilentia   Obsolete term for epilepsy.

epilepsia corticalis continua   See *epilepsy, continuous.*

epilepsia cursiva   Obsolete term for aimless running as a symptom of epilepsy.

epilepsia dromica   Epileptic behavior resembling chorea.

epilepsia gravior   Obsolete term for grand mal seizure.

epilepsia mitior   Obsolete term for petit mal epileptic seizure.

epilepsia partialis continua   Rarely occurring variety of continuous epilepsy specifically characterized by the limitation of jerking movements to one part of the body, usually a peripheral part, and by the resemblance of the movements to irregular muscle contractions.

epilepsia trochaica   See *epilepsia cursiva.*

epilepsia vertiginosa   1. Obsolete term for petit mal epileptic seizure. 2. Disorientation or dizziness which sometimes precedes or takes the place of a grand mal epileptic seizure.

epilepsy   A group of brain disorders associated with changes in the electrical activity of the brain due to brain injury or infectious childhood diseases or endocrine disorders, or one of several other causes. Epilepsy is often characterized by some form of convulsion, though behavioral symptoms vary greatly involving recurrent mental, motor or sensory dysfunction with or without convulsive seizures or loss of consciousness.
 The seizures may be either focal or generalized; the main forms are classified as *grand mal* or major, *petit mal* and *psychomotor.* The "grand mal" seizure is often preceded by an "aura" of psychic, motor or sensory disturbances which serves as a warning followed by complete loss of consciousness and falling to the ground; a tonic phase follows in which the individual stiffens and respiration stops; a clonic phase characterized by jerking movements of the whole body follows the tonic phase, completing the seizure. The "petit mal" seizure refers to recurrent mild seizures of short duration usually consisting of loss of awareness and a sense of disorientation. The "psychomotor" category includes short attacks of extreme motor activity, sometimes violent, of which the individual has no recollection. Some psychomotor epileptics are capable of committing serious crimes of violence without being aware of their own behavior.

epilepsy, affective   (H. Bratz) A form of epilepsy involving exaggerated emotionality usually followed by a seizure. Also called reactive epilepsies by K. Bonhoeffer and epileptic swindle by E. Kraepelin.

epilepsy, akinetic   Form of petit mal epileptic seizure characterized by sudden loss of muscle control, nodding of the head and falling.

epilepsy, autonomic   Form of epileptic seizure confined to the autonomic nervous system and characterized by sweating, changes of temperature, tearing of the eyes, and other symptoms resulting from either sympathetic or parasympathetic discharges.

**epilepsy, continuous** Form of epileptic seizure characterized by continuous myoclonic attacks of one part or side of the body without loss of consciousness.

**epilepsy, coordinated** Form of epileptic seizure characterized by movements which appear coordinated, voluntary and purposeful, although they may be repeated and without direction.

**epilepsy, cryptogenic** Epilepsy for which no cause has been identified.

**epilepsy, essential** See *ideopathic epilepsy.*

**epilepsy, inhibitory** Rare variety of petit mal epileptic seizure characterized by short-term loss of movement in part of the body without tonic and clonic phases and sometimes accompanied by loss of consciousness.

**epilepsy, Jacksonian** (J. H. Jackson) Form of grand mal seizure caused by disease of the cortex in which increasingly severe clonic movements spread from one point outward to include either one or both sides of the body, the more generalized seizures followed by unconsciousness.

**epilepsy, myoclonic** Severe variety of petit mal epileptic seizure characterized by symmetrical jerking of various muscles; the myoclonic EEG pattern is a typical petit mal pattern combined with occasional multiple spike-and-wave complexes.

**epilepsy, nocturnal** Epileptic seizures which occur while sleeping.

**epilepsy, psychic** Any form of epileptic equivalent state associated with or precipitated by a mental or emotional incident; behavioral manifestations include excitement, depression, dream-like states, etc.

**epilepsy, psychopathology of** See *personality, epileptic.*

**epilepsy, reactive** Epileptic seizure which appears to be a reaction to some particular pain or injury, or to a specific pathological focal point.

**epilepsy, regional** See *epilepsy, myoclonic.*

**epilepsy, residual** (E. Kraepelin) Rarely used term for recurrent epileptiform attacks without noticeable changes in personality or strange behavior.

**epilepsy, sensory** Variety of petit mal epilepsy in which the individual experiences sensation disturbances such as loss of sensation on part or all of one side of the body.

**epilepsy, sleep** Obsolete term for narcolepsy.

**epilepsy, tetanoid** (J. Prichard) Epileptic seizure consisting of tonic phase only, not clonic.

**epilepsy, tonic** Epileptic seizure in which only tonic spasms are exhibited, not clonic.

**epileptic aura** See *aura, epileptic.*

**epileptic clouded states** Psychotic behavior exhibited by epileptics before or after a convulsive attack; some epileptics experience hallucinations or fears or become confused, excited or ecstatic. See *aura.*

**epileptic deterioration** See *deterioration, epileptic.*

**epileptic equivalent** See *equivalent, epileptic.*

**epileptic psychopathic constitution** See *constitution, epileptic psychopathic.*

**epilepticism** Obsolete term for status epilepticus.

**epileptiform seizure** See *seizure, epileptiform.*

**epileptoid personality; epileptoidism** A person who exhibits the personality traits associated with the epileptic personality syndrome which includes selfishness, aggressiveness, stubborn uncooperativeness and religious fanatacism; this personality pattern is not found in the majority of epileptics nor exclusively in them.

**epileptology** The study of epilepsy.

**epileptosis** (E. E. Southard) General term for the different forms of psychosis manifested by epileptics.

**epiloia** Tuberous sclerosis.

**epinephrine** See *adrenalin.*

**epinephrine poisoning** See *poisoning, epinephrine.*

**epinosic gain** See *epinosis.*

**epinosic resistance** See *resistance, epinosis.*

**epinosis** (psychoanalysis) Also called secondary gain. An advantage or gain such as achieving social approval, and sympathy derived from neurosis; may lead to resistance in psychoanalysis aimed at perpetuating the epinosic gain.

**epiphenomenalism** The theory that neural processes produce mental activities and consciousness and that mental activities, therefore, can have no determining influence on mental or physical events.

**epiphenomenon** 1. An event which occurs simultaneously with another event but has no causal relationship with it. 2. (pathology) A symptom not related directly to the etiology of the disorder or disease.

**epiphora** Excessive tears due to oversecretion or to obstruction of their flow.

**epiphysis (cerebri)** The pineal gland.

**episcotiser** Instrument for studying short exposure intervals composed of a rotating disc with adjustable open and closed sections which are interposed between an observe and visual stimulus.

**episodic amnesia** See *amnesia, episodic.*

**epistasis** A genetic process in which one combination of non-allelic genes or one hereditary factor has dominance over other such combinations.

**epistatic** Referring to a combination of non-allelic genes or to hereditary factors exercising dominance over such combinations.

epistemology The philosophical investigation of knowledge including its origin, nature, method and limits.

epistemophilia Love of knowledge and for the investigation into things.

epithalamus Brain tissue lying above the thalamus composed of the habenula, the pineal body and the posterior commissure.

epithelium Layer of thin cellular tissue which forms the epidermis, and covers the inner surfaces of the bodily organs or viscera and the hollow linings of the digestive, respiratory and genitourinary systems.

epochal amnesia See amnesia, epochal.

epogenic component in a trait age curve (R. B. Cattell) The departure of an age trend from that most typical for humans, by reason of the special qualities of an epoch. Thus, the population intelligence plots from 1910-1970 are skewed from the ecogenic normal by an unusually rapid increase of education.

epsilon movement See movement, epsilon.

equal and unequal cases method (psychophysics) A variation of the constant stimulus method in which paired stimuli are judged as either equal or unequal.

equal appearing intervals 1. (psychophysics) Intervals determined by the equal sense differences method of measurement; a technique in which an individual finds the midpoint between two different sense stimuli and the two resulting distances are considered equal. 2. (L. Thurstone) Application of the equal sense differences method to any type of scaling judgments by dividing the total number of items of questions into categories composed of equal intervals.

equal interval scale Scale with arbitrarily determined zero point and equal intervals.

equal sense-differences method (psychophysics) A method of measurement in which an individual finds the midpoint between two different sense stimuli, and the two resulting distances are believed to be equal.

equality, law of (Gestalt) Principle that parts of a figure or a field are perceived as being a group or a whole to the extent to which the parts are similar or equal.

equalization of excitation (K. Goldstein) The tendency for excitation to spread out evenly over a functional system thus gradually decreasing the excitation at the stimulus point and increasing in other parts of the system.

equally noticeable 1. (psychophysics) Just noticeable difference. 2. (psychophysics) Differences between stimuli that are believed to be psychologically equivalent differences since they are perceived the same number of times.

equated scores Scores from two different tests of the same variable weighted in such a way as to have a common basis for comparison.

equation method (psychophysics) A procedure in which the subject is asked to adjust a stimulus object to a fixed standard or criterion object. The subject may be asked to equate the two or to relate the stimulus object in some other prescribed way to the criterion.

equation specification An equation for estimating a person's test score knowing his strength in one trait and the loading of that factor on the test. It is a form of the multiple regression equation.

equation, system A mathematical statement of the dynamic aspects of a system based upon the given input and output.

equation, tetrad difference (C. Spearman) An early method of factor analysis used to determine whether the one-factor theory common to all variables of a set is correct. This method originally referred to the nature of intelligence. The equation states that the correlations among various combinations of four factors are due to one factor if the tetrad difference is equal to zero. For example, given four factors, $A$, $B$, $C$, $D$, if one assumes that $G$ is the only factor present in all of the tests, accounting for the variance common to more than one of them, than any tetrad difference should equal to zero such as

$$r_{AB}\, r_{CD} - r_{AC}\, r_{BD} = 0$$

or any other combination of variables. If another factor is found to contribute to the variance of one pair of variables but not to another, then the tetrad difference will no longer be zero, i.e.,

$$r_{AB}\, r_{CD} - r_{AC}\, r_{BD} \neq 0$$

equilibration 1. Adjusting a measuring instrument by equating it with a standard. 2. (J. Piaget) The operation together of the two processes of assimilation and accomodation in the cognitive growth of the child. The child assimilates new information resulting in a modification of (accommodation) existing cognitive structures.

equilibrium 1. A stable or balanced condition within a system as in homeostasis. 2. Maintenance of balance and upright posture in the human body.

equine encephalitis See encephalitis, equine.

equipotent method (R. B. Cattell) A statistical device for comparing source trait factor scores across different cultural, age, etc., groups by adjusting the factor estimation weights peculiar to each group to produce equal multiple correlations of variables with factor scores in the groups compared.

equipotentiality 1. Uniform potential and manifestation of equal potential or power of any sort. 2. The potential for any portion of the embryonic tissue to produce or to develop into any of the parts of the mature organism. 3. Hypothesis that one sensory cue may be substituted for another. 4. Cerebral equipotentiality.

equivalence Relationship between two variables, stimuli, terms or responses such that one may be substituted for another within a specified situation without altering the situation.

equivalence belief (E. C. Tolman) A hypothesized state of an organism based on the organism's behavioral response which indicates the organism is acting toward a subgoal as it would toward the goal as if the subgoal were the goal; equivalence belief parallels secondary reinforcement in other theories.

**equivalence coefficient** The correlation coefficient of two supposedly equivalent forms of the same test given to the same subjects at about the same time; this coefficient indicates the degree of agreement or reliability between the two forms, a high equivalence correlation indicating high reliability and a low coefficient indicating low reliability.

**equivalence, response** The occurrence of the same or similar responses to the same or similar stimuli.

**equivalence, stimulus** The evocation of the same or very similar responses by different stimuli.

**equivalence test** A test which determines which aspects of a stimulus can be varied without changing an organism's previously trained response to that stimulus. Those variations of the original stimulus which continue to elicit the same response are considered equivalent.

**equivalent, anxiety** See *anxiety, equivalent.*

**equivalent, epileptic** Epileptic attacks which are neither grand mal nor petit mal but which take their place, as for example, psychomotor attacks and fugue states.

**equivalent form** See *form, equivalent.*

**equivalent groups** See *groups, equivalent.*

**equivalent of anxiety attack** See *anxiety, equivalent.*

**equivalent, onanistic** (S. Fercenzi) Any act which serves as a substitute for manual masturbation.

**equivalents method** (psychophysics) A method of measurement in which the subject must adjust a stimulus until it seems equal to a criterion object.

**erectio deficiens** Inadequate erection or lack of genital erection.

**erection** The swelling and hardening of erectile tissue such as the penis, clitoris or nipples through the accumulation of blood.

**eremiophobia** Morbid fear of isolated places or of seclusion.

**eremophilia** Abnormal and unhealthy desire to be alone.

**eremophobia** Morbid fear of being by oneself.

**erethism** Abnormally great degree of excitability, sensitivity or irritability in any or all parts of the body.

**erethismic** Pertaining to an abnormally great degree of psychical or physical stimulation.

**erethismus ebriosorum** Rarely used term meaning delirium tremens.

**erethistic** See *eristhismic.*

**erethitic** Associated with exaggerated excitement or excitability.

**erethizophrenia** Extreme cortical excitability.

**ereuthophobia** See *erythrophobia.*

**Erfassungstypus** (H. Rorschach) A subject's mode of approach to the test which is interpretively studied in terms of the sequence of location choices which occurs within each card and to the entire test, together with the ratio of types of location choices through the entire test, such as proportion of Whole responses to usual Detail responses to unusual Detail responses, etc. These data are generally considered as indicative of the style used by the subject in solving his problems.

**erg** (R. B. Cattell) A drive that has been demonstrated by the factor analysis of dynamic variables to be a unitary entity. A factor found in dynamic measures, operationally defining a specific drive or instinct, as clinically and biologically recognized, for example, sex, self-assertion, fear, etc. To be distinguished from drive in general or Ergic Tension.

**ERG** See *electroretinogram.*

**ergasia** (A. Meyer) General term for all of the psychobiological functions or activities within the person taken as a whole.

**ergasiatry** (A. Meyer) Psychiatry.

**ergasic** Related to ergasia; ergastic.

**ergasiology** (A. Meyer) Psychology.

**ergasiomania** An intense need to work and keep busy. This term is infrequently used today. Such a condition is seen in the manic state of manic-depressive psychosis.

**ergasiophobia** General fear of acting or of moving generated by the belief that one's actions will either cause harm to another or to oneself and often associated with the fear of castration and the Oedipal complex.

**ergasthenia** A somewhat outdated term for a frequently encountered condition of fatigue or debility due to overwork or excessive mental and/or physical functioning, particularly noticeable in the manic phase of extreme cases of manic-depressive psychosis.

**ergastic** Related to ergasia; ergasic.

**ergic-tension equation** The equation: $E = S[C + H + (P - aG)] - bG$ expressing the derivation of the ergic-tension level from the influences involved.

**ergodialeipsis** Activity which stops before being completed which is thought to be a form of blocking usually associated with schizophrenia.

**ergograph** Instrument which records the amount of movement of a particular group of muscles of a single part of the body during continuous activity usually in connection with fatigue experimentation.

**ergonomics** The scientific study of the relationships between men and machines, particularly the psychological, biological and cultural with the purpose of adapting machines and jobs to meet the needs of men and of choosing suitable persons for particular jobs or machines.

ergot *Claviceps purpurea*, a fungus which contains alcaloids used for treatment of migraine headaches.

ergot poisoning   See *poisoning, ergot.*

Erlebnistypus (H. Rorschach) A key concept in Rorschach testing representing the ratio of human movement to weighted color responses. Sometimes referred to as experience balance, or experience type; a precise translation from the German has been, at best, difficult in terms of capturing the full sense of Rorschach's meaning. The interpretive meaning goes beyond experience, to a description of "how" a person lives in terms of tendencies and experiences. Depending on the nature of the ratio, a person might be described as extratensive, introversive, ambitent, coarcted, or dilated, any of which relates to styles of living and experiencing.

erogenous or erotogenic zones Areas of the body which give rise to sexual, erotic or libidinal feelings when stimulated.

Eros (S. Freud) Originally Freud postulated two forces present at birth whose aim is individual and species survival, that is, self-preservation and sexual instincts. Later, Freud combined the drive for life under the name Eros which encompasses love directed toward oneself and/or others. The instinctual drive has a source, object and aim.

erotic 1. Sexual sensations, stimuli or feelings which arise from the erogenous zones. 2. Emotions or feelings associated with sexual sensations. 3. Love.

erotic fever   See *fever, erotic.*

erotic organ   See *organ, erotic.*

eroticism or erotism 1. Sexual excitement. 2. A greater than average interest in sexual matters; the tendency to experience sexual arousal more often or more intensely than the average individual; the preoccupation with sexual concerns in areas such as literature, art or history. 3. Sexual arousal through stimulation of non-genital parts of the body such as the mouth or anus.

eroticism, anal   See *anal eroticism.*

eroticism, lip   Erotic satisfaction derived from stimulation of the lips.

eroticism, oral 1. Experiencing of pleasure from oral stimulation and activities such as biting, sucking, chewing and stimulation of the lips and inner mouth. 2. (psychoanalysis) Characteristic of the oral stage of pregenital libidinal development.

erotodromomania Pathological desire to travel, to escape from some upsetting sexual experience.

erotogenesis 1. Originating from sex. 2. The origination of sexual, erotic, or libidinal impulses of behavior.

erotographomania Pathological desire to write love letters in which the love is usually expressed in a vague or sublimated manner, often through religious symbolism.

erotomania Unrestrained and morbid desire for genital relations with members of the opposite sex which is believed to stem from unconscious homosexual impulses.

error 1. A mistake; deviation from what is accurate or true. 2. A belief in something that is not true. 3. (statistics) Deviation from a true score. 4. (experimental) Any change in the dependent variable which is not attributable to the independent variable, whether chance or constant error. 5. (behaviorism) Any inappropriate response which delays the occurrence of the correct response, or any deviation from the experimental conditions or from the requirements of the experimenter.

error, absolute The obtained measurement value or observed score minus the true value. The mean of the measurements is usually considered to be the true value. The sign of this deviation score is disregarded.

error, alpha (statistics) The probability that an obtained result has occurred by chance. This is the risk of mistakenly rejecting the null hypothesis which is kept at a minimal level. The two conventionally accepted levels are .05 and .01.

error, anticipatory An error committed by making a response before the correct time in serial learning experiments.

error, beta (statistics) The probability or risk of accepting the null hypothesis.

error-choice technique   See *forced choice technique.*

error, compensating An error, whether positive or negative which cancels out one or more errors so that the average of the errors tends toward zero.

error, constant An experimental deviation from the correct value of a measure which is consistent in one direction. For example, subjects may consistently underestimate the length of a line.

error, estimation One half of the distance or difference between an upper or a lower threshold.

error, experimental Incorrect value in measurement or measurements due to poor experimental procedure of any sort which includes inadequacy of method, sampling and design, uncontrolled practice effects, and failure to adequately control experimental conditions.

error, instrumental A constant error caused by a precision instrument's deviation from the standard and corrected for by a constant factor.

error of estimate 1. (statistics) The error which occurs from estimating the value of one variable from the value of another variable when using a regression equation. 2. (psychometrics) The anticipated margin of error of an individual's predicted test score on a criterion variable due to the imperfect validity of a test 3. (psychophysics) The point of subjective equality less the standard criterion in comparative judgments.

error of expectation (psychophysics) In the method of limits it is the tendency for the subject to change his responses before a stimulus change because he feels that a stimulus change should have occurred.

**error of habituation** (psychophysics) In the method of limits it is the tendency for the subject to give the same response within a given series even though the stimulus has changed.

**error of measurement** 1. (psychometrics) Departure of an individual test score from its true value due to variations in conditions from one test to another. 2. Departure of an individual test score from its true value which is due to the unreliability of the testing instrument and/or of the tester or experimenter combined.

**error of refraction** The inability to focus visual images upon the retina due either to abnormalities in the optical characteristics of the cornea, lens, aqueous humor or vitreous humor, or to irregular shaping of the eyeball.

**error stimulus** (E. B. Titchener) An error committed in introspective reports of responding to a stimulus as perceived in terms of previous experience rather than responding to stimulus qualities which characterized the object.

**error, systematic** An error resulting from the manner of gathering or interpreting data which indicates bias.

**error variance** That portion of the total variance which is due to uncontrollable factors such as sampling errors or errors of measurement.

**errorless discrimination** See *discrimination, errorless.*

**errors, chance** Mistakes in measurement that are the result of unknown causes and, therefore, cannot be either controlled or predicted. The mean of a series of measurements is taken to be the true value and an accidental error is the departure from this mean. Accidental errors are considered to be due to random or chance factors.

**erythema endemicum** Pellagra.

**erythredema** Also called acrodynia. Occurs in infants, rarely in older children. Main symptoms: anorexia, perspiration, hypertension and moods shifting from apathy to explosive irritability. Linked to mercury poisoning.

**erythrism** The growth of red hair in certain areas of the body, usually the beard or pubic hair, while not in others which is considered a characteristic of certain body types in some older constitutional theories.

**erythroblastosis fetalis** A hemolytic disease of the newborn caused by the development of antibodies in the blood against the Rh - positive factors in the fetal blood. The increased amounts of bilirubin cause jaundice and often kernicterus.

**erythrogenic** Stimulus or radiant energy from which the sensation of red originates.

**erythrophobia** Fear of the color red which is usually associated with a fear of blood.

**erythropsia** Retinal condition in which everything appears tinted with red usually due to overexposure to strong white light.

**escape behavior** Behavior which removes an organism from a pain-producing situation.

**escape training** (experimental) Learning situation in which an organism is exposed to a noxious stimulus from which he may escape by eliciting a particular response.

**Eshmun complex** See *complex, Eshmun.*

**esophagus** The tube which connects the pharynx or mouth to the stomach; the gullet.

**esophoria** An inward deviation of the eye from the correct position necessary for binocular vision resulting from a muscular imbalance.

**esoteric** 1. Understood by, or made for only a special few. 2. Meant for only a special few who have been educated in certain teachings or doctrines. 3. Private or protected from public view.

**esotropia** Optical condition in which one eye deviates inward while the other focuses directly on the object.

**ESP** See *extrasensory perception.*

**esprit de corps** Common feeling shared by member of a group with the connotation of enthusiasm and loyalty.

**Esquirol, Jean Etienne Dominique (1772-1840)** French psychiatrist.

**essay examination** See *examination, essay.*

**essential hypertension** See *hypertension, essential.*

**establishment** (H. Murray) A division of personality along functional lines. Modified versions of Freud's id, ego and superego are the establishments.

**Estes Statistical Model of Learning** (W. K. Estes) Mathematical interpretation of Guthrie's non-continuity S-R learning theory based on the assumption that association occurs through contiguity. Estes' statistical model predicts response probability from a strictly contiguous association viewpoint without utilizing the concepts of reinforcement or extinction.

**esthesia** Sensitivity; capacity for sensation or feeling.

**esthesiogenesis** Producing of a sensory zone reaction.

**esthesiometer** See *aesthesiometer.*

**esthete** See *aesthete.*

**esthetics** See *aesthetics.*

**estimate, unbiased** An estimate based on an adequate and representative sample.

**estimates** 1. Values arrived at by rough rather than exact calculation or by global rather than specific inspection of the data from which the value is obtained. 2. (statistics) To infer a population measure from a sample measure.

**estimation error, or difference** See *error, estimation.*

**estimation, magnitude** (psychophysics) Direct scaling procedure in which a stimulus on a sensory continuum is selected by the experimenter and a number designating its subjective magnitude is assigned to it. The subject is then presented in turn with comparison stimuli and is instructed to assign to each comparison stimulus a number which looks as proportional to its subjective magnitude as compared to the standard. The judgments are in terms of subjective magnitudes consequently the resultant scale is directly obtained.

**estimation method** (psychophysics) The subject estimates the stimuli that are presented.

**estimation, ratio** (psychophysics) Direct scaling procedure in which the subject indicates when the sensory magnitudes of two stimuli stand in a specified ratio to each other. One stimulus is the standard and remains fixed throughout the series; the other stimulus is variable and is adjusted by the subject. The subject's task is to adjust the variable stimulus so that the stimulus magnitude provides a subjective ratio of the variable to the standard that is equal to the ratio specified by the experimenter. For example, the variable stimulus may be adjusted to appear one third as bright as the standard.

**estrogen** Any of the female hormones that stimulates the female to estrus, regulates the estrus cycle and influences the development of secondary sex characteristics.

**estromania** See *nymphomania.*

**estrus or estric cycle** The periodical state of sexual receptivity in female animals accompanied by physiological changes in the reproductive organs.

**Eta coefficient** (X) See *correlation ratio.*

**ethics** The study of moral values and moral behavior.

**ethinamate** Trademark valmid; a depressant.

**ethnic** 1. Groups of biologically related people. 2. Any division or group of people who are related on the basis of common customs or traits.

**ethnocentrism** 1. The tendency to consider one's group, usually national or ethnic, superior to other groups using one's own group or groups as the frame of reference against which other groups are judged. 2. A personality syndrome characterized by perception of social reality as composed of in-groups with which one identifies and out-groups toward which one is hostile; stereotyping people positively or negatively depending on their in-group or out-group membership; authoritarian and power-oriented social relations.

**ethnography** See *ethnology.*

**ethnology** The study of ethnic groups: their origins, customs, culture and pursuits in relation to their geography and to other ethnic groups.

**ethnopsychology** The comparative psychology of peoples and races, particularly nonliterate groups.

**ethology** 1. The science of ethics including the comparative study of ethical systems and the investigation of ethical systems in light of scientific principles. 2. The empirical investigation of character. 3. (sociology) The study of customs, mores and folk ways. 4. (psychology and biology) The comparative study of behavior, particularly lower forms of animal life in relation to their natural habitat.

**ethos** 1. The characteristic outlook or predominant disposition of a racial group or culture. 2. The underlying feeling or spirit associated with a particular outlook on life.

**ethyl alcohol poisoning** See *poisoning, ethyl alcohol.*

**ethylene dichloride poisoning** See *poisoning, ethylene dichloride.*

**ethylene glycol poisoning** See *poisoning, ethylene glycol.*

**etiology** The study of the origins and causes of disease.

**ETS** Educational Testing Service.

**euergasia** (A. Meyer) Normal or healthy mental functions.

**eugenics** The application of scientific genetics to the problem of improving the biological and psychological qualities of mankind. Positive eugenics attacks this task by methods favoring the early and productive unions of persons with superior genetic characteristics. More practicable is the implementation of a voluntary, minimal eugenics, operating through genetic counselling at heredity clinics, aiming at the elimination or reduction of the risks of the procreation of children with severe genetic physical or mental handicaps. Although eugenic ideas are found in Plato and were practised in the Oneida community in Vermont (1841), scientifically informed eugenics only came into its own through the writings of Sir Francis Galton at the turn of the century.

**eumorph, eumorphic** Person whose body type and build is average or normal.

**eunuch** A castrated male.

**eunuchoidism** Condition characterized by lack of fully developed sexual organs and the development of female secondary sex characteristics similar to those of a eunuch but due to disease.

**eupareunia** Sexual intercourse during which orgasm is achieved.

**euphoria** Attitude or mood of complete well-being and optimism.

**euphoric** That which is characterized by euphoria.

**eupraxia** Normal performance of coordinated movements.

**eurhythmia** Smooth congruent relations between different systems of the body.

**eurotophobia** Fear of the female genital organs.

**eurymorph** (H. J. Eysenck) A person whose body-build index is one or more standard deviations below the mean.

**euryplastic** Body type characterized by thick necks, short limbs and rounded body contour.

**eustachian tube** Small valved passageway which connects the middle ear with the mouth and functions to maintain an equilibrium of atmospheric pressure between the middle and the outer ear.

**eusthenic** (E. Kretschmer) Subdivision of the asthenic body type which borders on the athletic type.

**eutelegenesis** Artificial insemination.

**euthanasia** Mercy killing; the act of putting to death as painlessly as possible a person suffering from an incurable or painful disease.

**euthenics** The science concerned with improving the environment and living conditions in order to improve man.

**euthymia** A happy and tranquil mood or disposition.

**evaluation** 1. Determination of the relative value or importance of a score or phenomenon by appraisal or comparison with a standard. 2. (education) Global appraisal or measurement of educational progress or achievement.

**evaluation, operation of** (J. P. Guilford) Inspection or comparison of items of information with respect to given specifications in accordance with logical criteria, such as identity or consistency.

**event** 1. Occurrence or phenomenon which has a definite beginning and end. 2. Occurrence or series of occurrences which are related to an individual's needs in some way and thus form a unity. 3. (H. A. Murray) That part of a projective test which is related to a press or need.

**evil eye** A superstitious belief that certain people have the power to cause evil or to harm others by looking at them.

**evil, St. John's** Obsolete term for epilepsy.

**evivation** 1. Emasculation. 2. Delusion of a male that he has become a woman accompanied by stereotypically feminine feelings and desires.

**evolutility** (biological) Capacity of an organism to change through growth and physical development through nutrition.

**evolution** 1. Process of change through growth and orderly development. 2. Theory that present organisms have developed from pre-existing ones through genetic adaptations to the environment.

**evolution, Darwin's theory of** See *darwinism.*

**evolutionism, evolutism** Characterized by or related to evolution.

**exacerbation** To irritate or exaggerate the violent or bitter symptoms of a disease, of a person's feelings, or of behavior.

**exaltation** 1. Mood of great elation or positive excitement. 2. Abnormal increase in the amount of functioning of an organ.

**examination anxiety** 1. Nervous tension experi-

enced prior to a test due to uncertainty regarding one's performance or ability. 2. (psychoanalysis) Pretest anxiety is exaggerated due to associations, often unconscious, between the test situation and childhood experiences where the individual was punished for doing wrong.

**examination, comprehensive** An examination, which is designed to assess a person's integration and comprehension of a broad field or a range of areas which have been studied for a long period of time.

**examination, essay** Examination in which one must write about one particular topic at some length.

**examination, mental** Test which is administered to assess an individual's mental level or the extent of a person's pathology.

**examination, neurological** The patient is examined to assess the presence and degree of damage to the nervous system. The content of a neurological examination is not homogenous and consistent, probably varying considerably among neurologists. An examination generally includes assessments of the intactness of reflex arcs, the strength of muscles, the quality of voluntary and involuntary movements, visual-motor behavior, quality of language, presence or absence of hyperkinesis. The electroencephalogram, angiogram and air encephalogram are used. Great weight is placed upon the patient's life history, especially the pattern of symptoms.

**examination, psychiatric** Examination of a mental patient aiming at diagnostic evaluation and planning of treatment. It may include several interviews and administration of psychological tests. The main components of the psychiatric examination are history-taking and diagnostic interviewing. In some cases, a neurological and/or any other medical examination may be necessary.

**examination, psychiatric social** Psychodiagnostic evaluation which takes into consideration the influence of sociocultural variables, such as socioeconomic status and family relations.

**examination, psychological** General term for a test which either measures or evaluates abilities, general or specific, or personality traits.

**examination, psychometric** A series of various psychological tests which are administered to an individual in order to test one or several of the factors in his mental ability, such as intelligence, special abilities and disabilities, manual skill, vocational aptitudes, interests, and personality characteristics.

**exanthropia** Obsolete term for disliking society.

**excema, infantile** A psychosomatic disturbance of the skin which occurs in infants.

**exceptional** Differing greatly from others within a given group in one or more characteristics frequently in reference to individual ability differences in children.

**excitability** 1. (physiological) Of a living tissue having the capacity to reach stimulation. 2. Characterized by an easily aroused or excessive emotional reaction. 3. Highly reactive.

**excitant** A stimulus; an object which has the capacity to elicit a response or activity from an organ.

**excitation** 1. The process of causing physiological change in a receptor by stimulation. 2. (I. P. Pavlov) A hypothetical nervous process of the conduction of energy from one center to another in the cortex. 3. The process of causing activity in a nerve or muscle of nerve action. 4. The hypothetical nervous system correlated to the strength of response evoked by a stimulus.

**excitation, deflection of** (S. Freud) The redirection of a response to a stimulus, from the psychical to the somatic sphere.

**excitation gradient** See *generalization gradient*.

**excitation, somatic sexual** (S. Freud) Ongoing visceral excitation caused by pressure on the nerve endings of the seminal vesicles.

**excitatory agent** A stimulus.

**excitatory drive mechanisms** Hormonal or neural mechanisms which cause drive-related behavior.

**excitatory field** Region of the brain near the termination of a neuron at the time it is activated by a specific sensory process.

**excitatory irradiation** See *irradiation, excitatory*.

**excitatory post synaptic potential (EPSP)** A type of synaptic event which causes a rapid depolarization of the neuron. These events convey the neural impulse across a synapse.

**excitatory potential** $_SE_R$ (C. L. Hull) The potentiality of reaction evocation on the hypothesized strength of a response tendency which is arrived at through combining the effects of habit strength and drive: $_SE_R = D \times _SH_R$.

**excitatory tendency** The capacity of a stimulus to elicit a response, usually in terms of quantitative ability.

**excitement** An emotional state characterized by impulsive behavior, activity and a feeling of anticipation.

**excrement, abnormal attraction to** See *coprophilia*.

**executive area** Cortical area which controls other cortical areas through a function of higher integration.

**exercise** 1. Repetition of an act in order to learn it or increase skill. 2. Physical activity to maintain health, improve muscles or for recreational purposes.

**exercise, law of** See *law of exercise*.

**exhaustion** 1. State of depleted metabolism or reduced catabolic rate resulting in fatigue and lowered responsiveness to stimulation. 2. Extreme metabolic depletion which constitutes the final phase of the adaptation syndrome. 3. Hypothetical state of an

action after responding characterized by a higher response threshold and reduced rate and strength of response which is hypothesized to be the result of the loss of energy which occurs with responding and is frequently not replaced.

**exhibition need** See *need, exhibition*.

**exhibitionism** A sexual impulse to exhibit one's genitals which may be displaced to other areas of the body.

**exhilirant** That which causes elation.

**existence, absence of the feeling of physical** See *acenesthesia*.

**existential analysis** (existentialism) A type of psychotherapy designed to help the individual to react spontaneously to life situations and to develop a sense of freedom and responsibility for his own actions.

**existential crisis** A crisis concerning the problem of finding meaning in life.

**existential psychology** See *psychology, existential*.

**existential psychotherapy** See *psychotherapy, existential*.

**existentialism** 1. (philosophy) The name for a group of philosophical systems developed by Sören Kierkegaard, Martin Heidegger, Jean-Paul Sartre and others. There is considerable diversity in their views; Kierkegaard stressed the paradoxality of the concept of being and the idea of individual device. Heidegger bridged existentialism and phenomenology, pointed to the inadequacy of scientific analysis, and developed an existentialist system of being. Sartre maintained that existence is absurd and there is no adequate explanation why things are the way they are. The idea of absurdity and futility of human life was developed by Albert Camus. 2. (psychology) K. Jaspers originated a psychiatric system based on existentialist philosophy. Distinguished between the empirical and the "true" self. Only in situations of extreme despair, called boundary situations, an individual can become aware of his true self. 3. (L. Binswanger) Combined some psychoanalytic ideas with Heidegger's version of existentialism. Neurosis must be explained not in terms of its etiology but its meaning to the patients. 4. (P. Tillich) Combined psychoanalytic ideas with existentialism and protestant philosophy. He maintained that self-affirmation leads to the discovery of being itself. 5. (R. D. Laing) Utilized existentialist concepts in interpreting schizophrenia as "divided self" between what one really is and where one is an object of other people's influences and is unable to live his own life.

**exocathection** (H. A. Murray) Preoccupation with external rather than internal events and involvement in the world of public affairs rather than private pursuits.

**exocrine glands** See *glands, exocrine*.

**exogamy** The restriction of marriage to a person outside one's own group as, for example, the practice of not marrying blood relatives.

**exogenous, exogenetic, exogenic** That which originates outside.

**exolinguistics** (information theory) The study of the relationships between the sender of a message, the receiver and the message itself.

**exophoria** An outward deviation of the eye due to a muscular imbalance.

**exophthalmic goiter** See *goiter, exophthalmic.*

**exopsychic** Mental activity which has effects outside the individual on the physical or social environment.

**exosomatic method or technique** Method which utilizes the resistance of the skin to external electric current in the measurement of psychogalvanic response.

**exoteric** The public or external aspect of a situation or of an interpretation of an idea or thought.

**expansive** Open, unrestricted feeling and expression in physical or verbal behavior.

**expansive delusion** Delusions of grandeur often accompanied by euphoric states including feelings of power, wealth, self-importance and well-being.

**expansiveness** 1. Personality trait characterized by extroverted behavior including friendliness, loquacity and hyper-reactivity. 2. (K. Horney) Neuroticism characterized by egotism, narcissism and perfectionism resulting from the belief of the individual that he has achieved his ideal self.

**expectancy** 1. (statistics) The probability of a thing occurring based on mathematical calculation. 2. An attitude of waiting for or anticipating something accompanied by attention and muscular tension. 3. An intervening variable or learned set which is inferred from behavior whereby a response to a certain cue or stimulus is assumed to lead to another particular situation on the basis of past experience or expectancy.

**expectancy theory** (E. C. Tolman) Cognitive learning consists of the acquisition of expectancies and of the resultant tendency to react to certain objects as signs of certain other objects previously associated with them in the environment.

**expectation** 1. State of anticipation of something often associated with tension or emotion. 2. (statistics) The probability of the occurrence of an event based on mathematical calculation. 3. The true or universal mean.

**experience** 1. The living through and personal encountering of an event. 2. Skill or understanding which is the result of living through something, or of practice, or of participation in something. 3. (E. B. Titchener) The whole of mental phenomena or of consciousness at any particular moment.

**experience, accidental** (psychoanalysis) Refers to experiences that are of external origin rather than inherent in the individual. Two types of accidental experiences are distinguished according to when they occur in the life or mental growth of the individual.

An accidental experience is called dispositional if it happens in the early years of development when it greatly influences the molding of character traits. If an accidental experience occurs later in life, it is called definitive and will have little or no influence on mental development. However, a definitive accident may be important in its affect upon the course of one's career.

**experience, actual** A summary score devised in the Beck approach to the Rorschach which is derived by adding the number of human movement responses to the weighted total of color responses. It is hypothesized to represent the total emotional resources, which, when related to intellect, yields an index of the psychological growth potential. It is also interpreted as the organized emotion operating in the life style of the individaul.

**experience, affective** An event in the life of an individual that involves feelings or emotions.

**experience balance** See *Erlebnistypus.*

**experience type** See *Erlebnistypus.*

**experiment** Controlled arrangement and manipulation of conditions in order to systematically observe particular phenomena with the intention of defining the influences and relationships which affect these phenomena. The variables or conditions in an experiment are the experimental variable which is systematically varied or manipulated by the experimenter; the dependent variable which is the phenomenon to be observed and is assumed to be affected by the manipulation of the experimental variable; all extraneous conditions are held constant as far as possible in that they do not confound results.

**experiment, blank** A kind of experimental control which calls for the occasional introduction of irregular conditions designed to prevent the subject from becoming automatic in his responses or from guessing what is coming. The results of these conditions are not included in the data analysis.

**experiment, complication** See *prior entry law.*

**experiment, control** A repetition of an experiment performed because the initial one was inadequately controlled or not controlled.

**experiment, crucial** An experiment which is critical to the acceptance or rejection of an hypothesis or a theory.

**experiment of nature** The investigation of the reaction of the individual organism to real environmental situations.

**experimental control** See *control, experimental.*

**experimental design** See *design, experimental.*

**experimental error** See *error, experimental.*

**experimental group** See *group, experimental.*

**experimental method** Scientific method and technique of testing hypotheses and gaining information through controlled experimentation.

**experimental neurosis** See *neurosis, experimental.*

**experimental psychology** See *psychology, experimental.*

**experimental series** 1. Trials or observations which are part of the experiment proper, as opposed to pretest, post-test or practice trials. 2. Those trials or observations which were made by the experimental group and those procedures which were applied to them as opposed to the control groups.

**experimental variable** See *variable, experimental.*

**experimenter** 1. One who designs or conducts an experiment. 2. Abbreviation "E."

**experimentum crucis** See *experiment, crucial.*

**explanation** 1. Simplification and classification of a concept or an idea. 2. Accounting for an event or for the nature of an object by delineating those conditions which gave rise to it. 3. Finding the underlying causes.

**explicit** 1. That which is stated directly or is clearly present in the data. 2. Overt.

**explicit behavior** Overt, outward, observable behavior, such as bodily movement.

**exploitation** Taking advantage of another person or group for one's own personal needs without consideration of the needs of that person or group.

**exploitative character** See *character, exploitative.*

**exploratory behavior** Movement or locomotion engaged in most frequently by children, animals and lower organisms when initially orienting themselves to new situations. These movements bring various aspects or pieces of the environment into view of the exploring organism.

**explosive diathesis** See *diathesis, explosive.*

**exponent** (mathematics) A symbol written as a superscript to another symbol or expression which indicates the power to which that symbol or expression is to be raised.

**exposition attitude** (H. A. Murray) The tendency to explain things, to judge, to define relationships, or to demonstrate.

**expression** 1. Anything an organism does which is considered to be indicative of the nature of the organism itself. 2. Verbal, facial or physical responses which are indicative of the emotional state of the individual. 3. (mathematics) A numerical or algebraic statement or symbol.

**expression method** The measurement of emotion or feeling through the investigation of the accompanying physical changes.

**expressive** 1. Responding of an organism. 2. Verbal, physical or facial gestures which indicate an emotion. 3. A portion of an event or situation which particularly indicates the nature of the total event or situation.

**expressive aphasia** See *aphasia, expressive.*

**expressive function** Anything an organism does

which is considered to be indicative of the nature of that organism.

**expressive movements** Distinctive bodily movements such as particular facial expressions or postures which can be used to differentiate one person from another. These are sometimes helpful to personality assessment.

**expressive therapy** See *therapy, expressive.*

**expressivity** The extent to which the genetic complement for a trait or disease, having achieved penetrance, expresses itself. In schizophrenia variable degrees of expressivity are illustrated by the spectrum from seclusive personality, slowly deteriorating schizophrenia of late onset, to rapidly deteriorating schizophrenia of early onset.

**ext schedule** See *reinforcement, schedule of: extinction.*

**extended F+%** A ratio used in the Rapaport approach to the Rorschach which is expressed as the number of "good" pure form responses in proportion to the total number of pure form responses, as related to the number of "good" form-dominated responses in proportion to the total number of form-dominated responses. The ratio is generally interpreted in terms of ego functioning.

**extension** 1. (physics) The occupying of space by physical objects. 2. The supporting and straightening function of a limb. 3. (logic) The category of object or events to which a term applies.

**extension thrust** See *reflex, extension thrust.*

**extensity** The psychological parallel of physical extension which is the raw material or sense data upon which a perception is based as opposed to the extension in space of a physical object.

**extensor** Muscle which functions to straighten a limb by contracting.

**exteraceptor** Sense organ which is stimulated by external sources of energy.

**exteriorization** The relation of one's private life or personal affairs to the external world and objective reality.

**external auditory meatus** Canal which connects the middle ear to the external ear.

**external inhibition** See *inhibition, external.*

**external rectus** External eye muscle which functions to move the eyeball outward.

**external senses** Sensory receptor mechanisms which are stimulated completely or primarily by external stimulation.

**external validation** Validation of a measure by correlating it with an appropriate external criterion as, for example, validating an aptitude test by establishing high positive correlation with school grades.

**externalization** 1. The arousal of a drive by external stimulation rather than by internal stimulation through a learning process of secondary reinforcement. **2.** The process of differentiating the individual self from the external environment which occurs in childhood. **3.** The projection of one's own personal feelings or perceptions onto the external environment. **4.** The attribution of particular aspects of experience to an environment perceived as outside one's own experience.

**extinction** **1.** The gradual diminution of the conditioned response resulting from the withholding of the unconditioned stimulus or the instrumental reward. **2.** (I.P. Pavlov) A type of internal inhibition in which the conditioned response is temporarily decreased following the presentation of the conditioned stimulus without the unconditioned stimulus.

**extinction, differential** Extinction of one response while reinforcing the other.

**extinction, latent** Extinction which occurs without responding as a result of non-reinforced exposure to the previously reinforcing situation.

**extinction ratio** The ratio of unreinforced responses to reinforced responses emitted by the organism during the process of periodic instrumental reconditioning. Unreinforced responses do not elicit reward under experimental conditions; the reinforced response is the previously learned and extinguished response.

**extinction (ext) schedule** See *reinforcement, schedule of: extinction.*

**extinction, secondary** The weakening or extinction of conditioned responses. As the result of a particular conditioned response being extinguished, responses similar to the one being extinguished are likely to become extinct.

**extinctive inhibition** See *extinction, (I.P. Pavlov).*

**extirpation** The surgical removal or destruction of an organ.

**extraception** (H. A. Murray) Orientation or attitude characterized by skepticism and impersonal objectivity.

**extrajection** **1.** (psychoanalysis) Defense mechanism consisting of the projection of one's own feelings, characteristics or processes onto another person. **2.** The symbolic representation of a psychic process or feeling as, for example, writing a poem about anger.

**extramural** That which occurs outside the walls of an institution.

**extraneous** **1.** That which originates externally or pertains to an external or irrelevant factor. **2.** Something which is not pertinent to what is being investigated or considered.

**extrapolate** To infer or estimate from the narration of a variable within the known range the value of that variable beyond the given data or to extend its curve beyond the plotted range.

**extrapunitive** **1.** (S. Rosenzweig) Frustration reaction in which the individual directs hostility, anger, or aggression against the person or thing which he perceives as the source of frustration. **2.** Personality type characterized by extrapunitive frustration reactions.

**extrasensory perception or ESP** Awareness or perception of an external event which is not mediated by any of the known senses. ESP includes the phenomena of clairvoyance, precognition and psychokinesis.

**extraspectral hue** Hue or color not present in the spectrum as, for example, purple, which lies between red and violet or blue.

**extratensive** A Rorschach postulate, referring to those instances where the sum of weighted color responses is substantially greater than the sum of human movement responses. When the ratio (Erlebnistypus) manifests such a characteristic, the person is considered to be one who derives his more basic gratifications from interactions with his environment.

**extratensiveness** (Rorschach) Characterized by strong responsiveness to the environment and outward orientation which may be either passive or active. Passive extratensiveness is associated with conformity and dependance in interpersonal relations and acceptance of surrounding situations; active extratensiveness is associated with creativity in interpersonal relations and striving toward external goals.

**extraversion** **1.** Outward-directed personality orientation characterized by sociability, activity and interest in the public environment rather than inner directed attitudes and interests. **2.** (C. G. Jung) Movement of the libido toward the outer world resulting in all attitudes, values, and interests being directed toward the physical and social environment and an object-directed reference point. **3.** (J. H. Eysenck) A personality type based on particular neural structures which cause a rapid development of reactive inhibition, strong inhibition and a slow dissipation of inhibition. The neurotic form is hysterical conversion.

**extraversion, active** (C. G. Jung) Outward direction of libido which is willed by the subject rather than pulled from an external source or object.

**extraversion-introversion** (C. G. Jung) Bipolar personality dimension which in combination with the four features of thinking, feeling, sensation, and intuition, form the basis of personality typology through which people are divided into the following eight types: extraverted thinking, extraverted feeling, extraverted sensation, extraverted intuition, introverted thinking, introverted feeling, introverted sensation, and introverted intuition. The dimension ranges from outer-directedness on the extraverted extreme and inward-directedness on the introverted extreme.

**extraversion, passive** (C. G. Jung) Outward direction of libido which is compelled by the external object rather than subjectively directed.

**extravert** One who has an extraverted personality.

extraverted feeling type (C. G. Jung) Personality type characterized by acting according to the demands and expectations of a situation, feeling for external objects and the ability to establish friendships.

extraverted intuition type (C. G. Jung) Personality type characterized by a perception of the possibilities for manipulation and control of available external objects.

extraverted sensation type (C. G. Jung) Personality type characterized by a realistic, materialistic outlook and an orientation toward the sensory, concrete features of objects.

extraverted thinking type (C. G. Jung) Personality type characterized by dependence on sensory impressions as a basis for logical analysis and reality-construction, acceptance of the sensory world and an interest in facts and their classification.

extravisual  Outside the field of vision.

extrinsic behavior  See *behavior, extrinsic*.

extrinsic constant  (T. Burrow) Secondary principle governing man's relationship to his environment; refers to cortex mediated behavior.

extrinsic eye muscles  Those eye muscles that rotate the eyeball in different directions.

extrinsic motivation  See *motivation, extrinsic*.

extrinsic reward  See *reward, extrinsic*.

extrinsic thalamus  See *thalamus, extrinsic*.

extrophy  Malformation of an organ.

extropia  The turning outward of one eyeball because of muscular imbalance when the other focuses on an object; walleyedness.

extroversion  See *extraversion*.

exudative diathesis  See *diathesis, exudative*.

exvia-invia  (R. B. Cattell) Factorially established broad dimension within the area of behavior popularly referred to as extraversion-introversion. The precise core concept within extraversion-introversion.

eye  Visual sensory receptor consisting of three layers: the scleratic layer including the white of the eye surrounding the corneal lens which focuses light, the choroid coat which functions to absorb light, and the innermost retinal layer containing the rods and the cones with the fovea on the center of clear vision at its rear. The portion of the eyeball within the eye socket is also part of the eye.

eye, compound  A type of eye found in insects which consists of a series of optical systems whose focus is slightly different which results in the perception of a mosaic rather than a single image.

eye dominance  1. Greater use of one eye than of the other in fixating on objects and greater dependence on the impressions of that eye even though the other eye is functional. 2. One eye leads.

eye ground  That which is seen by the viewer when looking at the back of the eyeball through the pupil with an opthalmoscope.

eye-hand coordination  The cooperative functioning of the eyes and the hands when picking up or moving objects.

eye, light-adapted  1. The eye in its normal condition for daylight vision. 2. An eye which has been exposed to light of a high degree of intensity and has thereby become relatively insensitive to light of lower intensities.

eye movements  The rotary movement and positional changes of the eye as a result of the functioning of the extrinsic eye muscles.

eye span  The amount seen and comprehended in a single fixation pause of the eyes which is measured in terms of the number of letters or words comprehended in reading.

eye-voice span  The distance in terms of letters by which the eye leads the voice in oral reading; the distance between what is being said and what is being focused on.

eyedness  See *eye dominance*.

eyelash sign  The spontaneous reflex movement of the eyelid when the eyelash is stimulated.

Eysenck, Hans J. (1916-    ) British psychologist, German born. He developed and experimentally tested descriptive theory of major dimensions of personality; developed and tested causal theories for these dimensions; linked drug action with personality, and demonstrated the importance of genetic factors in personality development. Originated (with P. Broadhurst) large-scale genetic studies of emotionality, conditioning and arousal in rats. Worked out (with D. Furneaux) model of IQ dependent on speed, error-checking and continuance aspects. Proposed and tested two-factor model for structure of social attitudes, relating these to the political party preference. Promoted development of clinical psychology in England, and played part in origin and growth of behavior therapy; founded and edits *The Journal of Behavior Research and Therapy*.

# F

**F** (Rorschach) Form response.

**F-** (Rorschach) Poor form response.

**F+** (Rorschach) Good form response.

**F+%** A traditional Rorschach calculation used in most approaches to the test, except that of Klopfer (See *form level rating*), and expressed as the proportion of "good" form responses in relation to the total number of form responses. Good and poor form have been variously defined in terms of normative frequency and/or examiners, opinion concerning the appropriateness of the area of the blot used for the response given. Low F+% is generally interpreted as "poor" reality testing.

**F factor** (R.B. Cattell) The factor defining the personality dimension of surgency-desurgency; surgency is social, cheerful versus desurgency being dull, depressed; there is also a difference in tests of speed of reaction time, alkalinity of saliva, etc.

**F ratio** (statistics) An index used to determine whether the difference between two statistics is statistically significant. The F ratio is found by dividing the larger variance ($\sigma_1{}^2$) by the smaller ($\sigma_2{}^2$). The formula is:

$$F = \frac{\sigma_1{}^2}{\sigma_2{}^2}$$

This $F$ is looked up in a table of significance.

**F scale (fascism scale)** (T. W. Adorno et al.) Questionnaire designed to assess how readily the subject would accept antidemocratic ideologies.

**F score** A score on the Minnesota Multiphasic Inventory of Personality that indicates whether or not a testee has complied understandingly to the directions.

**F test (F)** A variance test between two samples to determine whether the difference between them could be ascribed to chance.

**Fables test** A mental test which may be used as a projective or intelligence test in which the subject is required to explain the lesson taught by the fable.

**fabrication 1.** An inappropriate response to test items, often of a fantastic nature. **2.** See *confabulation*.

**fabulation** Fabrication.

**fabulized response** (Rorschach) Included in the Rapaport approach to the Rorschach, as a type of deviant verbalization in which the subject's response includes elaborate and unnecessary descriptions of a generally idiographic nature so as to personalize the response. Occurring in significant quantity in a single record they are considered indicative of psychopathology.

**face-to-face group** Two or more people who are in such close proximity that direct interaction is possible.

**face-to-face interview** See *interview, face-to-face*.

**face validity** The extent to which a test seems to measure the variable to be tested because of its similarity to the criterion measure.

**facial angle** An angle, intended to measure cranial development, which is formed by a line drawn from the base of the nostrils to the opening of the ear and from the base of the nostrils to the forehead.

**facial nerve** See *nerve, facial*.

**facial nucleus** A mass of cells in the base of the brain which give rise to the facial nerve.

**facial vision** See *echolocation*.

**facile ament** (A.F. Tredgold) Mentally defective individual who is "characterless, facile," and particularly amenable to suggestion.

**facilitation** Physiological term referring to the excitation of one neuron by another: in meaning, identical with stimulation, except that it is customary to distinguish between excitation originating outside the nervous system (stimulation) and excitation originating within it (facilitation).

**factitious** Man-made, artificial; not natural or spontaneous.

**factor**  An underlying influence responsible for part of the variability of a number of behavioral manifestations. Therefore, an influence in behavior which is relatively independent of other influences and of a unitary nature.

**factor analysis**  1. Statistical procedure aimed at the generation of hypothetical variates that are weighted sums of observed variates. The former, fewer in number than the latter, are usually expected to describe, summarize, or explain the latter. 2. (C. Spearman) A data-reduction procedure whereby a matrix of obtained measurements of $N$ individuals on $n$ experimental variables is replaced by a smaller matrix of factor coefficients or loadings relating every variable to each of $r$ factors, each an underlying variable, assumed to represent an ability or other kind of trait, which is conceived as a vector in $r$-dimensional space. ($N > n > r$). 3. (L.L. Thurstone) The technique used to show the correlation of all tests of mental ability. Thurstone found that all the tests were positively correlated, indicating a common factor among them. The analysis indicated the following seven primary mental abilities: verbal, number, spatial, perceptual, memory, reasoning and word fluency.

**factor analysis, inverted**  See *Q technique.*

**factor analytic studies**  Studies which attempt to delineate the underlying relationships in a series of correlations.

**factor axes**  A set of coordinates which represents the relationships between factors and the relationships of factors to correlations in the matrix. Axes are located by factor rotation and are the solution regarded as best for a particular study.

**factor, bipolar**  A factor which consists of two mutually exclusive, opposite extremes.

**factor coefficient**  See *factor loading.*

**factor, common**  See *factor, group.*

**factor configurations**  The positions and relations of vectors or lines which represent the various tests in the correlation matrix. The relationship between the angles of each vector represents the correlation. A right angle is a zero correlation; the more acute the angle, the higher the correlation.

**factor group**  A factor present in two or more, but not all tests of a set of tests being factor analyzed which accounts for the high intercorrelations of tests within the set and the lower intercorrelations of these tests outside the group.

**factor loading**  The amount of correlation that a given factor contributes to the variability of a test.

**factor matrix**  A table of factor loadings resulting from a factor analysis; the columns represent the factors extracted and the rows represent the tests.

**factor, number (N)**  A factor found in many tests of ability which is revealed by facility in the manipulation of numbers and in working out simple numerical operations.

**factor, O**  Variables which are present in an orga-

nism at any given moment; internal factors which affect an organism's response such as drive or individual differences. Also called O-variables.

**factor, position**  The influence geographical location or spatial arrangement has upon an organism's response to a particular stimulus as, for example, the tendency to turn a certain way in a maze.

**factor, primary**  1. (factor analysis) Any factor which satisfies the requirements of simple structure. 2. Any factor in a group of factors which could be divided without remainder and without overlapping the covariance of a matrix.

**factor reflection**  Changing the algebraic signs of related measures in a correlation matrix in order to maintain unidirectionality of the variables, or the consequence of rotation.

**factor resolution**  Synonymous with factor structure.

**factor rotation**  In factor analysis movement of the axes of a plot of factors by rotation of their origin to psychologically meaningful positions. The points are then accurately plotted in new dimensions.

**factor, second order**  A factor common to other factors.

**factor structure**  Statistical end point of factor analysis, when the interrelations and relative positions of the vectors have been established and a coordinate system imposed upon their spatial distribution.

**factor theories of learning**  1. Contention that there are two aspects of learning (a) a mechanical, motor process and (b) a mental comprehension of the relationship. 2. A theory in conditioning which maintains that attitudes influence the incidence of conditioning and that stimulus properties determine the magnitude of the response. 3. A theory that says that instrumental and classical or Pavlovian conditioning constitute distinct and separable processes. The characteristics of each remain in dispute, but often instrumental conditioning is said to require reinforcement and occur in the central nervous system, while classical conditioning does not require reinforcement and occurs in the autonomic nervous system. There is currently a feeling that the two processes may be inseparable and the distinction may be a matter of degree resulting from the experimental procedure rather than in the organism.

**factor theory**  Explanation and description of personality and intelligence in terms of statistically derived hypothetical factors used on factor analysis of results of written and motor tests.

**factor theory of intelligence**  Theories of structure and function of intelligence based upon factor analysis of performance on primarily paper and pencil tests. C. Spearman hypothesized a single factor of intelligence which he called "general ability" or "g" and interpreted as a purely intellectual element, pure mind. L.L. Thurstone expanded the number of factors to "seven primary abilities": $V$, verbal; $N$, number; $S$, spatial; $M$, memory; $R$, reasoning; $W$, word-fluency; and $P$, perceptual speed. J.P. Guilford developed a factor theory of intelligence in which each factor is specified by three dimensions: content, operation, and product. The contents are divided into figural, symbolic, semantic, and behavioral contents. The operations are divided into cognition memory, divergent production, and evaluation. The products are divided into implications, transformations systems, relations, classes, and units. Thus there are, in this schema, 120 different factors of intelligence of which Guilford maintains 82 have been demonstrated or discovered.

**factor, unique**  (factor analysis) A factor found in only one test or measure of a correlation matrix; its variance is not shared with the other tests being factorized.

**factor weight**   Synonymous with *factor loading*.

**factorial**  1. Combination of elements or factors, in several or all possible ways. 2. (statistics) A number, $N!$, read "$N$ factorial" representing the product of all numbers from 1 to that number, e.g., $5! = 5 \times 4 \times 3 \times 2 \times 1 = 120$.

**factorial design**  See *design, factorial*.

**factorial theory of personality**  See *personality, factorial theory of*.

**factorial validity**  See *validity, factorial*.

**factoring**  Process of finding factors. The procedure of factor analysis.

**factors, constitutional**  Factors referring to neuro-physiological and chemical aspects of the body.

**faculty**  1. A natural or learned ability to perform a certain act. 2. An obsolete term referring to supposed mental "powers" such as reason, memory, will, perception, and imagination.

**faculty psychology**  (W. Wolff) A theory that the mind is made up of separate and independent areas of power, each of which can be strengthened by exercise.

**fad**  A passing enthusiasm zealously pursued by an individual or group which is not directly useful and meets no major needs.

**faeces amicae in os proprium inicere**  (W. Stekel) A form of sexual perversion in which feces are orally incorporated.

**failure**  1. Someone who has not achieved a minimum economic or social status or who has failed to attain goals he has set for himself. 2. Not obtaining the desired or anticipated results in an experiment.

**faintness**  1. Weakness in intensity. 2. A passing state bordering on loss of consciousness with symptomatic dizziness, overall weakness, and sometimes nausea.

**faith**  Unconditional and complete acceptance of a belief or system of beliefs without substantial evidence, usually accompanied by strong emotions.

**faith healing**  A method or practice of treating mental or physical illness through the patient's belief in divine intervention.

**fall chronometer**  An instrument used to measure time intervals by the fall of a weight.

**fallacia**  An illusion or hallucination.

**fallacia optica**  Optical illusion or hallucination.

**fallacy**  1. Deception. 2. A false idea; also the liability to make a mistake. 3. Reasoning that fails to satisfy the conditions of logical proof or violates the laws of valid argument.

**fallectomy**  A sterilization operation in which the fallopian tubes are cut and tied off.

**falling sickness**  A colloquialism for epilepsy; also called caduca passio.

**Falret, Jean-Pierre (1794-1870)**  A French psychiatrist known for his studies in suicidal tendencies. Also suggested the term "mental alienation" instead of mental illness. First in field to consider mania and depression as stages of the same disorder.

**false alarm**  (psychophysics) A response by a subject as if a stimulus had been presented when in fact no stimulus was presented.

**false association**  (W. Stekel) A dreamer's simultaneous identification with several persons who represent the same love object. Such associations are considered only partly valid and evasive since they may lead the analyst to details concerning one of the people with whom the dreamer identifies as his love object, when in reality this association pertains to another person who is a partial substitute for the real love object.

**false negative**  The number of cases incorrectly excluded from a particular group by the application of certain standards of criteria.

**false positive**  The number of cases incorrectly included in a particular group by the application of certain standards or criteria.

**falsehood, unconscious**  A false or untrue statement made by an individual without his having any conscious awareness of its false nature. The individual has simply come to believe things about himself, other people or situations which are untrue.

**falsification of memory**  1. Detailed and seemingly lucid fabrications of gaps in memory associated with Korsakoff's psychosis. 2. Confabulations.

**falsification, retrospective**  Adding false details and meanings to the recall of past experiences. A common practice of paranoid schizophrenics who may recall experiences which occurred prior to the formation of their delusional system from a delusional point of view.

**fames bovina**  Obsolete term for oxlike hunger.

**fames canina**  Obsolete term for doglike hunger.

**fames lupina**  Obsolete term for wolfish hunger.

**familial**  Pertaining to the family, referring to either heredity or heritage.

**familial dysautonomia**  A hereditary dysfunction of the autonomous nervous system, emotional lability and indifference to pain. Occurs in infancy.

**familial tremor**  A hereditary disease which starts in childhood, associated with tremor and hyperactivity.

**familianism** A tendency to maintain strong intra-familial ties which are culturally transmitted, resulting in intense solidarity among family members.

**famille névropathique** (J. Charcot) A group of degenerative diseases for which heredity was seen as the unique originating cause.

**family** 1. A group of persons related by blood or marriage, the specific members of which differ from culture to culture. Always includes a mother and children, nearly always includes the father. 2. Metaphorically, any group bound by close ties. 3. Biologically, a group of related *genera,* a sub-division of an *order* in the classification of organisms. 4. The *human family:* all men, including extinct species. 5. Any collection of closely related items: a family of words, a family of colors.

**family behavior problem** (social work) Denotes anti-social conduct of an individual within the patient group. Such behavior is usually associated with offenses or delinquency such as assault, and stealing.

**family constellation** (A. Adler) The number and characteristics of the members of a family, the patterns of their mutual relationships, and the order of birth. Considered an important factor in the development of the "style of life."

**family life handicap** (social work) A physical or psychological disability which interferes with or limits an individual's capacities for marriage and home-making.

**family romance** (psychoanalysis) Childhood fantasies in which: 1. the child rejects his own parents and fantasizes that he is the offspring of other, more noble parents thereby making his own developmental need to separate from his real parents more acceptable. 2. the child imagines himself saving the life of some great person, who is really a representative of a parent, and thus resolves his debt to his parents for having given him life.

**family, schismatic** (T. Lidz) Family in which there is chronic parental disharmony and in which the children are forced to take one or the other side in the ongoing battle; the parents tend to devalue each other, making appropriate sex role identification difficult for the children.

**family, skewed** (T. Lidz) Family in which one parent is overwhelming and engulfing and the other is appeasing and submissive, resulting in a lopsided parental situation. Such a family is characterized by a desperate need of all members to avoid anxiety and by the experiencing of individuation as total separation and loss.

**family therapy** See *psychotherapy, family.*

**fanaticism** Excessive enthusiasm for a point of view or cause, evidenced by intense emotions and extreme, though often transient, efforts in its behalf.

**fancy** Fantasy; whimsical imagination.

**fancy, tendency to** A tendency to imagine in a whimsical, wishful way which, in extreme cases, can become morbid and detrimental.

**fantasm; phantasm** A vivid, seemingly real image of an absent person or thing, or of what is assumed by the perceiver to be a disembodied spirit.

**fantastic melancholia** (E. Kraepelin) A term indicating a morbid mental state characterized by bizarre delusions and hallucinations such as evil spirits, death, animals' heads, monsters, angels, and floating heads.

**fantasy; phantasy** Imagining a complex object or event which is pleasant and wish-fulfilling in concrete symbols or images, whether or not the object or event exists.

**fantasy cathexis** See *cathexis, fantasy.*

**fantasy formation; phantasy formation** The process of daydreaming.

**fantasy, pregnancy** (psychoanalysis) The concept that the wish for a child in women is closely related to their oedipal wish of a child with the father, their wish for a penis, their desire for the mother's breast and the wish to retain feces, all of which are the same symbols expressed at different levels of development.

**fantasying, active** (psychoanalysis) A psychotherapeutic technique in which the patient is asked to spontaneously relate his imagery, the analysis of which enables the psychoanalyst to uncover the patient's inner conflicts and subsequently bring them into his conscious awareness.

**far point** The most distant point at which the eye can see an object distinctly under relaxed conditions.

**far sight** A condition of vision characterized by an inability to see near objects clearly, often accompanied by clear vision for distant objects. The most common cause is hyperopia, in which the light rays come to a focal point behind the retina.

**farad** Measure of electrical capacity. It has a charge of one coulomb when the difference in potential between the field and its boundaries is one volt. Usually measured in microfarads 1/1,000,000 farads.

**fasciculus** A bundle or cluster of nerve, muscle, or tendon fibers separated by connective tissue.

**fasciculus cuneatus** An important tract of the dorsal part of the spinal cord which mediates jointly with the fasciculus gracilis the proprioception of touch.

**fasciculus gracilis** An important tract in the dorsal part of the spinal cord which mediates jointly with fasciculus cuneatus the proprioception of touch.

**fascination** The partial mastery of what is experienced as an uncontrollable factor in one's environment by identifying with it. For example, an infant may pay rapt attention to a rattle waved before him, but if it is beyond his reach or if he has not yet learned to grasp and hold, his attention becomes greatly intensified, and he loses himself in the sight

**fetishism, beast** The habitual arousal and gratification of sexual impulses by touching furs or animal skins.

**fetishism, coherent** (M. Hirschfeld) A form of fetishism in which possessions of the loved one are brought into immediate contact by the fetishist with his own body, but are not worn as clothing.

**fetishist** 1. One who believes that certain inanimate objects possess magical powers and worships them accordingly. 2. One who habitually gratifies sexual impulses by handling the possessions or nonsexual parts of the body of the loved one.

**fetishistic** 1. Relating to or exhibiting the worships of certain inanimate objects which are believed to possess magical powers. 2. Relating to or exhibiting a pathological condition in which sexual impulses are habitually aroused and gratified by the possessions or nonsexual parts of the body of the loved one.

**fetology** The study of the fetus.

**fetus, foetus** The unborn offspring of an animal which is in its more advanced stage of development, the earlier stage being referred to as the *embryo*. In human beings, from the end of the third month of pregnancy to birth.

**fever, autarchic** The false and unconditional belief of children in their own omnipotence rather than recognition of their degree of dependence on the environment.

**fever, Christmas** A general term referring to the various syndromes of psychosomatic illness which tend to occur around holidays.

**fever, erotic** The "fever" accompanying erotomania, or unrestrained desire for genital relations with members of the opposite sex.

**fever, psychogenetic** Fever induced by hypnotic suggestion.

**FI schedule** See *reinforcement, schedule of: fixed interval*.

**fiber** 1. A filament or threadlike structure which comprises tissue. 2. A nerve fiber or single neuron. 3. An axon or a dendrite.

**fibers, commissural** Neural tract which connects corresponding areas in the two hemispheres of the brain.

**fibril** Filament-like portion of a neuron which extends through its cell body and out to the periphery.

**fibrillation** The component hair-like filaments which comprise a fiber.

**fibromyositis** See *myositis*.

**fiction** 1. A feigned or imagined state of affairs not considered to be real. 2. A paradoxical concept which is taken as if it is true for the sake of argument, such as $\sqrt{-1}$. 3. (A. Adler) A complex set of principles by which one understands and evaluates his experience and which thus determines his life style.

**fiction, directive** A fantasy or idea of superiority which is originally conceived of as unconscious compensation for feelings of inferiority and which is later reacted to as if it were an absolute truth.

**fidgetiness** A state of restlessness or increased motor activity often caused by anxiety.

**fidgets** A vague uneasiness usually accompanied by increased motor activity.

**fiducial interval** See *interval, fiducial*.

**fiducial limits** See *limits, fiducial*.

**field** 1. An area having boundaries which define both the physical place as well as the kind of activity permitted. 2. (physics) The entire space in which a set of forces operate, such as a magnetic field. 3. (psychology) The complex totality of interdependent social, personal, and physical factors within which a psychological event takes place.

**field cognition mode** (E.C. Tolman) A particular organism's disposition or readiness, resulting from the interaction of perception, memory, and thought, to apprehend some specific characteristic of the field in which he behaves. Thus, the contribution of the organism to the stimulus aspect of the stimulus-response sequence is emphasized.

**field expectancies** (E. C. Tolman) A type of learning in which as a result of repeated presentations of a particular environmental situation, an organism acquires a set to be prepared for further stimuli of a field upon apprehension of the first group of stimuli from this field and set for the interconnections between these groups of stimuli.

**field force** (K. Lewin) A manifestation of directed energy (referred to by other psychologists as libido, instinct, or drive) which has a certain magnitude analagous to that of physical force and which must be defined in terms of the whole field in which it takes place.

**field, leaving the** (K. Lewin) An attempted reduction of conflict or frustration consisting of the individual's removal of himself from the situation.

**field of attention** Those stimuli or ideas to which the organism is attending at any given moment.

**field of awareness** See *field of consciousness*.

**field of consciousness** The totality of that which the individual is aware of at any given time.

**field of regard** All of the external world that can be seen by the moving eye with the head stationary, as distinguished from *visual field*.

**field structure** 1. The patterning of relations among the various parts of the *life space*, or psychological field. 2. The reasonably precise and hierarchical arrangement of psychological facts within the life space which lend it stability.

**field theory** (K. Lewin) A systematic, mathematically described theory of psychology and social psychology which emphasizes the interrelatedness of a present concrete event and the totality of influences both within an individual's personality and his environment which determine behavior. To view a situation in its totality, one must view it as a field, i.e., a totality of interdependent facts. The *psychological field,* or *life space,* of an individual is comprised of the interaction between his personality and his environment. Thus, individual behavior at any given time is the function of one's personality and environment. According to this theory, every concrete situation, rather than just recurring events, is regarded as conforming to psychological laws, and a complete scientific and mathematical representation of such a situation would complete the task of psychology.

**fields of psychology** Since its emergence as a separate field of study, psychology has expanded into a great number of areas. The most basic field of psychology is that of experimental psychology. This field is concerned with precise research of basic psychological problems. The processes investigated may be grouped into several clusters. One such cluster is concerned with the manner in which an organism gathers and receives information about its environment. A second cluster of problems concerns the modification of behavior. Here the psychologist deals with development, learning, thinking, and problem solving; in other words, the way in which the organism learns to react to his environment. A third cluster concerns itself with the general problem of the motivation of behavior, including such topics as reinforcement, emotions, and motives. Some psychologists stress the environmental, sociological point of view, whereas others are more interested in physiology. Those who adopt this latter point of view are the physiological psychologists. Their interests are quite similar to those of physiologists, and they have made great strides in determining the functions of the various areas of the brain. Some of their most recent work deals with the relationship between such physiological processes as reward, punishment, and attention to brain function.

Another field is that of comparative psychology. The comparative psychologist's main interest is in the differences of behavior among the species. They often work with lower animals because of the relative ease in studying their behavior.

Social psychology studies the various factors which are associated with the adjustment of the individual to the specific cultural environment in which he lives. Some of the topics which are of concern to the social psychologist are the conducting of public opinion polls, the social conditions which affect the emergence of religious and political leaders, measurement of attitudes and the determination of those factors which lead to attitude change, the effects of group membership upon individual behavior patterns, group problem solving, conformity and prejudice.

Educational psychology is concerned with the factors which affect performance in the school situation. This field is closely related to that of general psychology which studies learning and motivation in general. The educational psychologist must apply what is known in these areas to the specialized area of the school. It has often been necessary for the educational psychologist to develop his own techniques in dealing with these problems. An example

of this is the development of teaching machines which present material in a way which maximizes effective learning.

The application of psychology to the industrial setting has been an important and widespread development, incorporating many different areas of general psychology. The industrial psychologist concerns himself with such problems as recruiting and training programs for employees, studying consumer motivation, maximizing production by increasing employee morale and motivation, designing advertising campaigns and designing more effective and safer equipment based on psychological knowledge.

The widespread use of psychological tests in schools, business, and the military has led to the development of a field of psychology known as psychometrics. The psychometrist is an expert in test construction, administration, and interpretation. He must have a strong working knowledge of statistical methods in order to assure the reliability and validity of the test results. The psychometrist may also be trained in the administration and interpretation of personality tests, as an adjunct to therapy.

Developmental psychology concerns itself with the patterns of development in children as they grow to adulthood. The developmental (or child) psychologists have accumulated such information as the age norms for weight, height, vocabulary development, motor skills, etc. They have also developed methods of child training, so as to assist the child in his task of growing up.

Some of the most pressing present-day social problems involve the abnormalities in the development and functioning of the personality. Personal maladjustment and mental illness are probably our major medical and social problem. The field of personality and abnormal psychology deals with these problems. Clinical psychologists devote themselves to the diagnosis of personality maladjustments. By means of tests and interviews they attempt to arrive at a meaningful classification of psychopathology. Others are interested in the origins of mental disorders. They have attempted to find the causes of maladjustment in early family life, the stressful events of infancy, physiological causes, social conditions, and others. Another group of clinical psychologists has attempted to develop methods of curing mental disorder. Their methods may be based on individual or group treatment, directive or nondirective participation by the therapist, long- or short-term periods of treatment. In spite of the many different forms the treatment may take, the goal is still the same: the removal of the abnormal condition.

Theoretical psychology is really a combination of all the other fields of psychology. Theoretical psychologists formulate broad scientific systems.

**figural aftereffect** (Gestalt psychology) A perceptual phenomena used to illustrate the tendency to maintain stability in figure-ground relationships by showing that the characteristics of one perceptual field may effect the perception of another.

**figural cohesion** (Gestalt psychology) The tendency of all the parts of a figure to perceptually remain together as one figure. For example, once seen as forming a square, a set of four dots tend to continue to be seen as a square, even when they are combined with other elements.

**figural information**　See *information, figural.*

**figural openness** (Gestalt) Situation in which a figure or figural outline does not surround or enclose the area of a configuration.

**figure-ground** The principle that all perception and even awareness is fundamentally patterned into two parts or aspects that mutually influence each other: a) the *figure,* which has good contour, unity, and is perceived as being separate from the ground, and b) the *ground,* which is relatively homogeneous and whose parts are not clearly shaped or patterned.

**figure, helpful** In the fantasy world of a child, a beneficient and understanding male or female fairy-like creature to whom the child feels he can turn to for help.

**filial generations** The successive generations from a single parent or pair of parents which are designated as first filial ($F_1$), second filial ($F_2$) and so on.

**filicide** 1. Killing of one's own child. 2. One who has killed his own child.

**filiform script** Cursive writing, generally small and rapid, in which words trail off into a single line of indistinguishable letters.

**film color** A texture-free, soft color which lacks localization, as contrasted with the color of the surface of an object, and seems to hover before the observer like a film or cloud.

**filter** 1. Device which transmits only a particular variety and homogenous wave lengths. 2. Capacitor or choke circuit or their combination which regulates and smooths out current flow.

**final** 1. Last in a series of terms or trials. 2. Purposive; pertaining to ends or goals.

**finalism** See *teleology.*

**fine grain rate** See *rate, fine grain.*

**fine tremor** Tremor of 10-12 vibrations per second.

**finger agnosia** Inability to recognize one's fingers.

**finger aphasia** Inability to name one's fingers.

**finger painting** Making pictures or designs by applying paints directly to a surface with the fingers and hands. In psychology, it is often used as a projective technique, or means of stimulating free association.

**finger spelling** A mode of communication used among or with the deaf, and the deaf and blind, in which words are spelled out by means of specific finger movements. For a deaf and blind person to receive a message in this way, he cups his hands around the sender's and feels each movement of the sender's fingers.

**finger-thumb opposition** A significant step in child's motor coordination which occurs at about the age of one year, and which is characterized by picking up objects between the thumb and fingers (partial prehension) and, later, the thumb and fore-finger (final prehension), rather than by scooping movements with the palm and fingers.

**fingers, insane** A low grade inflammation of the fingers to which the mentally ill, particularly general paralytics, are liable. It is less common today than in the past which is probably due to improved hygiene in mental institutions.

**Fisher's test** See *test, Fisher's.*

**fission** 1. Any splitting or cleaving. 2. (biology) Asexual reproduction, characteristic of unicellular animals, in which the mature cell splits into two parts, each of which becomes a separate organism.

**fissure** Any of the deep grooves on the surface of the brain. Any of the shallower ones are known as a *sulcus.*

**fissure of Rolando**　See *central sulcus.*

**fissure of Sylvius** A deep fissure located in the temporal cortex, which divides the temporal lobe from the parietal and frontal lobes. Also called the lateral fissure.

**fistula** A tube or opening in some tissue resulting from incomplete closure of a wound, surgery, or abnormal growth.

**fit** 1. (medicine) A sudden attack, or a convulsion. 2. (statistics) The agreement of probable data with actual data. 3. The adjustment of obtained data to conform to a predetermined standard.

**fittest** From Darwin's concept of the "survival of the fittest," referring to those organisms best adapted to their environment and who thus tend, in the "struggle for existence" to survive and propagate their species.

**fixated conflict** The condition in a stable course of behavior, settled upon after conflict, in which some ergic satisfactions are gained at the cost of loss of others, as shown by simultaneous positive and negative loadings.

**fixatio mononoea** An obsolete term for severe depression.

**fixation** 1. A persistent mode of behavior which has outlived its usefulness or has become inappropriate. 2. The strengthening of a memory or a motor habit by repetition. 3. The directing and focusing of one or both eyes on an object or point, so that the image falls on the *fovea.* 4. (psychoanalysis) A strong and relatively enduring emotional attachment, generally psychosexual in nature, to an object of infancy or childhood which persists into later life and, thus, makes the formation of new attachments and new patterns of behavior rather difficult if not impossible.

**fixation, anxiety** (psychoanalysis) The persistence into later life of anxiety which was originally associated with a dangerous situation of an earlier phase of development.

**fixation, cannibalistic** The fixation of the libido at the late oral, or biting, phase, which may lead to cannibalistic fantasies such as biting, eating, swallowing, and, thus, incorporating a hated object.

**fixation, father** An excessively emotional and possessive attachment to one's father, stemming from the period of infantile sexuality but continued long beyond the point at which Oedipal conflicts should normally have been resolved.

**fixation hysteria** See *hysteria, fixation.*

**fixation, libido** The retention of libido at an early phase of psychic growth.

**fixation, mother** An excessively emotional and possessive attachment to one's mother, stemming from the period of infantile sexuality but continued long beyond the point at which Oedipal conflicts should normally have been resolved.

**fixation of affect** The establishment of a strong and relatively enduring emotional attachment, generally psychosexual in nature, to an object of infancy or childhood which persists into later life and, thus, makes the formation of new attachments and new patterns of behavior rather difficult if not impossible.

**fixation pause** One of the brief moments during which the eyeball is not moving which makes visual discrimination possible.

**fixed alternative** Pertaining to a test or questionnaire which requires that the subject choose one answer from several limited alternatives.

**fixed idea** A persistent, firmly held, but often irrational idea which tends to dominate a person's mental life.

**fixed-interval reinforcement** Partial reinforcement schedule in which the subject is rewarded or reinforced consistently on his first response after the lapse of a certain prescribed amount of time after the preceding reinforcement.

**fixed interval (FI) schedule** See *reinforcement, schedule of: fixed interval (FI).*

**fixed ratio reinforcement** Partial reinforcement schedule in which the subject is rewarded or reinforced consistently with $n$th trial.

**fixed ratio (FR) schedule** See *reinforcement, schedule of: fixed ratio (FR).*

**fixedness; functional fixedness** An inability to be flexible in problem solving which is characterized by maintaining a certain set behavior despite its inappropriateness.

**fixity, social** Pertaining to societies or any grouping of people in which each individual's role, status and possibility for social interaction is rigidly defined, as in feudal or caste societies.

**flaccid** Readily yielding to pressure; soft, flabby; without muscular tone.

**flagellant** 1. One who whips himself or submits to whipping by others for religious purposes or sexual excitement. 2. A religious sect in the thirteenth century in Europe which believed in self-punishment and self-torture as an expression of the Lord's commandment for self-imposed suffering.

**flagellantism** Self-punitive and self-torturing behavior.

**flagellate** To scourge or whip.

**flagellation** The act of whipping, especially as a means for arousing religious or sexual emotions.

**flagellator** One who whips himself or others for religious purposes or sexual excitement.

**flagellomania** Sexual pleasure or stimulation from whipping or being whipped.

**Flajane's disease** See *goiter, exophthalmic.*

**flattening of affect** See *affect, flattening of.*

**flavor** A sensory impression from objects, mainly food, in the mouth which results from the combined experience of taste, smell, pressure, and temperature.

**Flesch index** Formulas used to compute the reading difficulty of a passage of English prose.

**fleshy type** (C. B. Davenport) Constitutional body type characterized by short limbs, thick neck, and rounded or fat body contour.

**flexibilitas cerea** See *catalepsy.*

**flexibility** 1. Adaptability; plasticity. 2. The ability to readily change set, modify behavior, and, thus, respond to changing conditions.

**flexibility, waxy** See *catalepsy.*

**flexion** The act of bending at the joint of a limb or part of the body, which is made possible by certain muscles called *flexors.*

**flexor** A muscle which serves to bend or flex a limb or part of the body.

**flicker** A sensation of fluctuating vision induced by a corresponding change in the visual stimulus.

**flicker, auditory** The perception of a periodically interrupted auditory stimulus as discontinuous.

**flicker, binocular** Flicker evoked by alternating stimuli rapidly from one eye to the other.

**flicker, chromatic** Flicker due to rapid periodic changes in hue, saturation, or both.

**flicker, photometry** Measurement and comparison of brightnesses by determining their critical flicker frequencies when reflected individually against a surface with the same illumination.

**flight into health** See *transference cure.*

**flight of colors** Visual afterimage of a succession of colors or white which sometimes occurs as an aftersensation to a bright or intense light stimulus.

**flight of ideas** A rapid and continuous flow of thought or speech which, while not disjointed or bizarre in content, is characterized by jumping from one topic to another, each topic being only superficially related to the previous one or intervening stimuli in the environment.

**floccillation** See *carphology.*

**flogger** See *flagellator.*

**fluctuation** 1. Constant change; moving back and forth as a wave. 2. (biology) Relatively slight changes or variations due to chance factors which are normally distributed about the mean of a species, as distinguished from mutations. 3. (perception) See *attention fluctuations*. 4. (statistics) Changes in the value of a statistical constant when calculated from successive but otherwise similar random samples.

**fluctuations of attention** See *attention fluctuations*.

**fluency** 1. The ability to verbally communicate with ease. 2. (factor analysis) A factor that characterizes the ability to rapidly think of and verbalize words and associations. It loads on items which require the subject to produce as many words as possible in a given period of time, verbalize associations to inkblots, complete stories, etc.

**fluid** 1. (psychology) Pertaining to an unstable, changing situation with few constraints in which an individual may act freely. 2. (field theory) Characterizing a *field* in which there is an easy flow of communication between the various forces or tensions of the field.

**fluid general ability** (R. B. Cattell) That form of general intelligence which is largely innate and which adapts itself to all kinds of material, regardless of previous experience with it.

**fluttering hearts** A perceptual illusion in which colored figures moved forward and back on a differently colored background appear to be moving from side to side.

**focal** Pertaining to a *focus*.

**focal epilepsy** See *Jacksonian epilepsy*.

**focal length** The specified distance from a given lens which is necessary to bring parallel rays of light to a focus.

**focal symbiosis** See *symbiosis, focal*.

**focus** 1. The point at which parallel rays of light are made to converge after passing through a given lens. 2. To adjust an optical system so as to bring parallel rays of light to a convergence point. 3. To center one's attention on a stimulus.

**focus of attention** That part of a complex experience which at a given moment is the clearest and most outstanding.

**foliate papilla** Minute, nipple-like protrusions, shaped like a leaf, which are found along the sides and back of the tongue.

**folie** The French word for *insanity* which, historically, has been used in combination with other qualifying French words to name various mental disorders.

**folie à deux** Simultaneous occurrence of the same mental disorder in two people who are closely associated with each other where one appears to have influenced the other.

**folie à double forme** An obsolete term for manic-depressive psychosis.

**folie à quatre** The simultaneous appearance of psychoses with similar delusional content in four members of the same family.

**folie à trois** The simultaneous appearance of psychoses with similar delusional content in three members of the same family.

**folie ambitieuse** A generic term referring to various forms of insanity in which grandiose ideas are present.

**folie du doute** (J. P. Falret) Form of anxiety neurosis or obsessive compulsive behavior characterized by excessive doubting to the point of madness as, for example, checking repeatedly to see that a door is locked.

**folie morale, acquired** (E. Kraepelin) Patients classified as psychopathic personalities may eventually develop a clearly defined psychotic condition. Kraepelin called this psychotic state an acquired form of folie morale or moral insanity. See *psychopathic personality; psychosis*.

**folium** A fold or convolution in the grey matter of the *cerebellum*.

**folk psychology** 1. The social psychology of non-literate, primitive societies. 2. A detailed study of the legends, beliefs, and customs of a particular race or people, especially primitive.

**folklore** Legends, beliefs, customs, folk-remedies, songs, and other fragments of culture which have survived from earlier, more primitive stages of a given society.

**folkways** Traditional patterns of behavior, including habits and customs, which characterize a given culture or social group and which exercise a strong though unconscious influence on the behavior of each member.

**fontanel** The "soft spot" in the cranium of an infant which is not ossified.

**foot lambert (ftl)** Unit of measure of luminance.

**foot rule correlation** See *correlation, Spearman foot rule*.

**foramen magnum** Opening in the occipital bone which the spinal cord passes through into the brain where it becomes the medulla.

**force** (field theory) A tendency to act in a certain direction; a cause of any activity.

**forced choice technique** (psychometrics) Method of assessing the attitudes of an individual or the social desirability of alternatives by directing the individual to choose between two equally unlikely, and undesirable alternatives as, for example, whether he prefers ugliness or laziness; the pattern of forced responses is then assessed.

**forced color response** A concept in Klopfer's approach to the Rorschach to denote instances in which the response includes the use of color, but not the color of the perceived object in its natural state. Instead, the subject has "forced" the use of color as it exists on the blot, as for example, "pink mountain lions."

**forebrain** The anterior brain portion of the embryo which develops into the diencephalon and the telencephalon from which arise the olfactory lobes, the cerebral hemispheres, the striate body and the thalamus.

**forecasting efficiency index of (E)** The measure of the extent to which one can predict one variable by knowing another variable and the relationship between them. The formula is:

$$E = 100\left[1 - \sqrt{\frac{N-1}{N-2}}\,(1 - r^2)\right]$$

where $N$ is the number of scores in the sample, and $r$ is the correlation coefficient.

**fore-exercise** Period preceding an experiment or test, the purpose of which is to allow the subject to adapt to the situation or to estimate the approximate strength of the response which is to be measured.

**forensic psychiatry** See *psychiatry, forensic.*

**foreperiod** The initial time interval between the ready signal and the introduction of the stimulus in an experiment, especially reaction time experiments.

**forepleasure** (psychoanalysis) **1.** The pleasure, physical and emotional, occurring with increase in tension especially in sexual areas. **2.** The erotic pleasure which comes from stimulation of an erogenous zone prior to intercourse.

**Forer Structured Sentence Completion Test** See *test, Forer Structured Sentence Completion.*

**foreshortening 1.** The shorter appearance of the length of a line when it is viewed lengthwise; the shortening appears proportionately greater as the closer the line parallels the direction in which one is looking. **2.** The perceptual shortening in a painting or drawing according to the principles of perspective.

**form 1.** The outline, shape or pattern of arrangement of elements of an object or figure. **2.** (Gestalt) The nature of a whole in terms of its organized arrangement of parts or its unity.

**form, alternate** (psychometrics) Tests measuring the same thing but with unequal raw scores that have been standardized through the use of an equivalence table yielding scores that are comparable.

**form-color response (FC response)** (Rorschach) Response to a Rorschach inkblot test which is co-determined by form and color with form being the primary contributor. The form determinant appears to reflect the subject's reasoning powers and contact with the demands of reality. The color determinant appears to reflect affectivity and impulsiveness.

**form, comparable** (psychometrics) General term for different sets of test items which are considered to be different forms of the same test due to similarity of content structure, and the possibility of converting the raw scores from the tests to the same derived score scale.

**form determinant** The use of contour, shape or form as the basis for a Rorschach response which is thought to reflect the formal reasoning power and contact with reality demands of the respondent.

**form, equivalent** Tests measuring the same thing which have raw scores with the same statistical meaning on each form.

**form level rating** A method developed by Klopfer to evaluate the appropriateness of form used in the Rorschach more extensively than afforded by other systems. Each response is weighed on a scale ranging from +5.0 to −2.0 depending on the accuracy, specification, and organization of the percept.

**form, number** See *number form.*

**form quality 1.** (Gestalt) Properties of a whole or entity which does not reside in its constituent parts. **2.** Properties which a part possesses when a constituent of a particular unit or entity but not when in isolation or when it belongs to another unit. **3.** Gestalt qualitaten.

**form response** The most common type of Rorschach answer wherein the response is determined by the shape or form of the blot or the portion of the blot used. No other determinant such as color, movement, or shading is involved in the formulation of the percept. Form may also play a determining role in responses involving other features of the blot and when this occurs, scoring is modified accordingly, such as FC for a form-dominated color response, CF for a color dominated color response which also includes form.

**formal discipline 1.** Formal training or education. **2.** Doctrine that certain subjects should be studied for the constructive exercise of the mind or the positive effect such study will have on intellectual ability in general rather than for its own sake.

**formalism** The systemization of a field of knowledge through strict adherence to consistent orderly organization within a relatively rigid framework which directs and limits theorizing.

**formant** Elements which constitute the timbre or quality which makes one vowel sound different from another.

**formative cell** An embryonic cell.

**formboard test** See *test, formboard.*

**fornication** Generally, sexual intercourse involving persons who are not married to each other.

**fornix** A nerve fiber which connects the thalamus with the hippocampus.

**foster placement** The process of arranging for persons not related to a child to care for and support that child by taking the child into their home and family.

**Four Picture Test** See *test, Four Picture.*

**fourfold table** A statistical table composed of two sets of columns and two of rows.

**Fourier's law** (physics) Principle that any complex sound or light wave may be represented in the form of simple sine waves or as comprised of several simple vibratory movements.

**Fournier's Test** (A. F. Fournier) Test in which the individual is asked to stand up quickly, turn sharply and to start and stop walking on command in order to determine whether there is a disorder of muscular coordination or equilibrium in relation to walking.

**fovea centralis** Center of clearest vision which is a small depression in the retina.

**foveal vision** Seeing with the foveal region of the retina.

**FPT** See *test, Four Picture.*

**FR schedule** See *reinforcement schedule of: fixed ratio.*

**fractional antedating goal response** See *response, fractional antedating goal.*

**fractionation** Physiologically, the dropping-out of neurons from a neural system with repeated activity, the result of changed time properties of the system. The opposite of recruitment, when the changed time properties make it possible to "recruit" neurons not originally part of the system.

**Fragesucht** (German) A compulsion to ask questions without being interested in having them answered.

**frame of reference** 1. A system of attitudes and values which provide a standard against which actions, ideas, and results are judged and which to some extent controls or directs action and expression. 2. The background against which a thing is perceived.

**Franck Drawing Completion Test** See *test, Franck Drawing Completion.*

**fraternal twins** See *twins, fraternal.*

**free association** 1. An unrestricted, random flow of words or ideas. 2. (psychoanalysis) Method employed in which the patient says whatever comes into his mind and speaks freely in order to widen the therapist's access to the patient's unconscious mind and to allow the repressed memory of traumatic experiences to come to the surface in order that the trauma may be resolved.

**free association period** The main procedure in Rorschach testing in which the subject is handed the cards, one at a time, and asked to report what he is reminded of by the blot. The specific instructions to the subject are somewhat different than the free association procedure as employed in psycho-analysis, yet some overlap does exist. In Rorschach testing the subject is asked to report what he sees but is also free to elaborate as extensively or as minimally as he prefers.

**free association test** See *test, free association.*

**free nerve endings** The delicately branched endings of afferent neurons in the skin without specific nerve organs which are thought to be associated with sensitivity to temperature and to pain.

**free recall test** See *test, free recall.*

**free will** The philosophical and religious doctrine that attributes the cause of behavior to volition and independent decisions of the person rather than to external determinants.

**freedom, degrees of** See *degrees of freedom.*

**Fregoli's phenomenon** See *illusion of negative doubles.*

**frequency** 1. The number of cycles per second in a periodic vibration. 2. The number of times a specific phenomenon occurs in a given class interval.

**frequency curve or distribution** A curve showing graphically the frequency of various values in each interval of the distribution.

**frequency diagram** The spatial or graphic representation of a frequency distribution.

**frequency graph** A graphic representation of a frequency distribution. The three most common are the histogram, frequency polygon, and the frequency curve.

**frequency histogram** A graphic representation of a frequency distribution consisting of a series of contiguous rectangles, of width proportional to the size of the class interval, and in height proportional to the frequencies in the various intervals.

**frequency, law of** See *law of frequency.*

**frequency, marginal** 1. (statistics) The sum of the frequencies of a column or a row in a double-entry table which are written in the lower right-hand margin of the table. 2. (testing) The frequency of responses falling outside the modal response.

**frequency polygon** The graphic outline of the frequency distribution made by connecting the plot of the midpoints of the class intervals.

**frequency table** The systematical ordering in tabular form of the values of a frequency distribution.

**frequency theory of hearing** See *hearing, theory of: frequency theory.*

**Freud, Anna (1895-    )** Youngest daughter of Sigmund Freud, born in Austria, active member of the International Psychoanalytical Association since 1922. Emigrated to England in 1938; Director of the Hampstead Child-Therapy Course and Clinic from 1947 onward. Many contributions to the developmental theory of psychoanalysis and its application to educational, diagnostic, therapeutic and preventive work.

**Freud, Sigmund (1856-1939)** Viennese psychiatrist, founder of psychoanalysis. Initially conducted research in neurology, then under the influence of Charcot, Liebeault, and Breuer, treated mental disorders with hypnosis. Developed (jointly with Breuer) the cathartic method of treatment, then psychoanalytic technique. These joint studies were reported in Breuer and Freud's *Studies of Hysteria* (1894). Through the observation of his patients and the analysis of his own dreams, Freud discovered the phenomena of the unconscious and developed the technique of dream analysis (described in *The Interpretation of Dreams*, 1901). In 1905 Freud wrote *Three Essays on Sexuality* in which he applied the biogenetic principle to the study of the phylo and ontogenetic psychosexual development. In 1914, Freud discovered the phenomenon of narcissism and thus interpreted human behavior by means of a single innate drive, the force of love, that is support of life. This force, called Eros, had at its disposal the emotional energy of libido which could be sexual or desexualized, directed toward others (cathected) as object-love or toward oneself as narcissistic self-love. In 1920 Freud again revised his theory of instinctual drives by introducing the concept of the death instinct, called Thanatos, and destructive energy. In 1923 Freud elaborated the so-called structural theory, introducing the concept of a three-partite mental apparatus comprised of the id, ego and superego. In 1927 Freud published the *Future of an Illusion*, a psychoanalytic critique of religion; in 1930 he dissected contemporary civilization and in the last year of life wrote a critical essay on *Moses and Monotheism*.

Freud wrote and worked with patients almost until his last days, despite the fact that he suffered from cancer of the mouth and in the years 1923-1939 he underwent 33 surgical operations.

**Freudian slip** (psychoanalysis) A mistake or substitution of words in speaking or in writing. The mistake is contrary to the conscious wish of the individual. The individual expresses his unconscious and repressed wishes through the erroneous action.

**Freudian theory** See *psychoanalysis.*

**Freudianism, Freudism** See *psychoanalysis.*

**frigidity 1.** Coldness; absence of sexual feeling. **2.** Blocking of the normal expression of sexual desire in females.

**Froelich syndrome** An endocrine disturbance affecting the pituitary gland and resulting in a condition with poor skeletal development, metabolic disturbances, obesity and arrested physical and behavioral development.

**Fromm, Erich (1900-     )** Born in Germany, emigrated to United States in 1934. Has developed a revision of Freud's theory, emphasizing (1) the specific conditions of human existence, (2) the influence of social factors on character ("social character"), (3) the use of psychoanalysis for the understanding of social and historical processes and political leaders, (4) the relevance of values. Proposed a synthesis of Marx's and Freud's concepts. See *psychoanalysis; social character; ethics.*

**frontal cortex** See *cortex, frontal.*

**frontal leucotomy** Frontal lobotomy.

**frontal lobe** See *lobe, frontal.*

**frontal lobe, structure and function of** See *lobe, frontal, structure and function of.*

**frontal lobes brain lesion** See *brain lesion, of frontal lobes.*

**frontal lobotomy** See *lobotomy, frontal.*

**Frosch, John (1909-     )** American psychiatrist and psychoanalyst. Editor of *Journal of American Psychoanalytic Association;* Editor of *Annual Survey of Psychoanalysis;* Professor of psychiatry, New York University College of Medicine. Has been a practicing psychoanalyst for 35 years. Has founded and been Editor-in-Chief of the *Journal of the American Psychoanalytic Association,* the official publication of the American Psychoanalytic Association for the past 25 years. Author of some 35 articles. His recent contributions have been in the area of the borderline problems both in the psychopathology, as well as in the treatment modalities. He has emphasized the concept of the psychotic character and described borderline patients who function most of the time as nonpsychotic, although they may have psychotic breaks from time to time. He has also made contributions to the understanding and the treatment of the disorders of impulse control with special emphasis on the impulse ridden character and introduced the concept of reality constancy as the counterpart to object constancy. This is an ego function which permits an individual to attain an appropriate relationship to reality but is severely disturbed in borderline and psychotic patients.

**Frostig Sensory-Motor and Movement Skills Checklist** See *checklist, Frostig Sensory-Motor and Movement Skills.*

**frottage** Sexual perversion in which orgasm occurs as a result of rubbing against a clothed person of the opposite sex in a crowd.

**fructose intolerance** A deficiency of fructose-1-phosphate alcocase which leads to an inhibition of hepatic release of glucose, resulting in hypoglycemia when fructose containing foods are ingested.

**fruity** A type of smell typified by the smell of fruits.

**frustration** Interference with an ongoing action.

**frustration aggression hypothesis** (J. Dollard and N. E. Miller) Theoretical assumption based on psychoanalytic concepts, that frustration leads to aggression, whether implicit or explicit, and that aggression is always a sign of some sort of frustration.

**fugue states 1.** A long-term amnesia state characterized by the individual leaving his home and changing life-style and conduct. The individual has almost total loss of memory though skills are not affected. When the fugue ends, there is complete restoration of pre-fugue memory and a forgetting of the whole fugue period. **2.** Period of absence associated with epilepsy.

**Fullerton-Cattell law** See *law, Fullerton-Cattell.*

**function 1.** (statistics) A quantity that varies with the variation of another quantity. The variation is not necessarily proportional. **2.** The activity of an organism rather than non-activity; an ongoing process. **3.** The purpose or end product of an organ or organism. **4.** That which is dependent on something else, stated non-quantitatively. **5.** A heading or categorical classification for activities. **6.** An activity or structure that is useful. **7.** (C. Jung) Any transitory manifestation of the psyche or libido.

**function fluctuation** The real variation on a source trait from time to time with internal and external conditions (not in the focal stimulus), differentiating the stability coefficient from the consistency coefficient.

**function, power** See *power function.*

**functional autonomy** See *autonomy, functional.*

**functional autonomy principle** (G. W. Allport) The principle that modes of behavior, though acquired, become independent of the original instigating drive.

**functional disorder** See *disorder, functional.*

**functional fixedness** See *fixedness.*

**functional inferiority** See *inferiority, functional.*

**functional psychology** See *functionalism.*

**functional relation** A dependency between variables such that a change in one will bring about a change in one or more of the others.

**functional system** (P. K. Anokhin) A unit of integrative activity of the brain and organism formulated in 1935 by P. Anokhin. Due to the development of the "systems approach" and "general systems theory," the functional system theory is obtaining a particular significance for research in biology, physiology, neurophysiology, psychology and other sciences where systems analysis is essential. The principal features of the functional system are as follows: (1) system organizing factor, which determines the formation of co-operative relationships between the system components toward obtaining a functional-useful result. Such co-operation of the system components can be possible when the system permanently sorts out "degrees of freedom" of every system component (such as, for example, the

synaptic formation on a neuron). Through return afferentation ("feed-back") the result produces a reorganizing effect upon the co-operative relationships between the system components. (2) Some specific key mechanisms (internal architectonics) enable the investigator to construct a continuous passage ("conceptual bridge") from the level of integration to the level of the finest mechanisms of the brain systemic activity, the molecular level included. These key mechanisms of the functional system provide it with uninterrupted self-organization and plastical adaptation toward changing external conditions. The functional system key mechanisms are the following: a) afferent synthesis, b) decision making, c) acceptor of action results, d) program of action, e) result of action, f) return afferentation which contains all parameters of the result, and g) collation of the real results with those that have been predicted before in the Acceptor of Action Results. By its constructive meaning the functional system theory permits study and evaluation of such compound processes of the whole organism which cannot be either investigated or understood without it.

**functional unity** **1.** The cooperative functioning of various parts or processes to produce an integrated whole or perform one action. **2.** Considering different behavioral patterns as stemming from one trait or organ. Such relationships are investigated systematically through factor analysis.

**functionalism** School of psychology founded at the end of the 19th century by James and Dewey. The major proponents include James R. Angell, Harvey A. Carr, and Edward Robinson. Functionalism began as a protest against structuralism, elementarism and a disjointed molecular approach to the subject matter of psychology. Functionalism treated psychological processes as functions within the context of Darwinian theory. The process of adjustment of the organism to the environment is central as is a pur-positivistic interpretation of the process in which stimuli and responses are a chain of deeds and not separate entities. Functionalism dealt with the

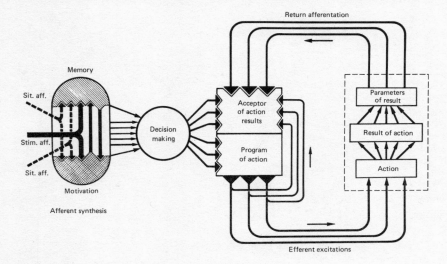

"how" and "why" of psychology rather than the "what." A molecular approach was emphasized in order to understand the totality of the organism and the functions of the mind as mediator between organism and environment. The process of the modification of behavior and of associationism was given importance, resulting in interest in habit formation, learning theory, and the concerns of educational and comparative psychology. Functional psychology also prepared the ground for behaviorism and conditioning as well as for the purposive-hormic theory of McDougall.

**functions maintenance** The physiological activities in an organism which preserve a state of relative inner equilibrium.

**fundamental response processes** Physiological processes assumed to underlie the fundamental colors.

**fundamental tone** The basic or lowest component of a compound tone which identifies the pitch.

**furor, epileptic** State of confusion followed by maniacal attack of violence or rage associated with epileptic equivalent attacks.

# G

**G factor** See *general factor*.

**G force** The force required to go against the force of gravity.

**g score** A key scoring in the Hertz approach to the Rorschach which represents the manner in which a response is organized. See also *organizational activity; z score*.

**gain** An increment or increase in a variable.

**gain, epinosic** Secondary advantages obtained from illness such as the gratification of dependency needs.

**gain, method** See *gain, epinosic*.

**gait, hemiplegic** Gait characterized by stiffly held legs seen in hemiplegic patients.

**gait-stuttering** A halting and hesitant gait analogous to the stammer in speech.

**galactosemia** A congenital metabolic disturbance causing increased galactose in the blood often associated with mental retardation. Gastrointestinal disturbance of varying intensity is characteristic. If severe, death may occur. Cataracts appear between 4 to 8 weeks. Treatment consists of removal of galactose containing substances including milk.

**galeanthropy** The delusion of being a cat.

**galeophobia** Morbid fear of cats.

**gallows humor** See *humor, gallows*.

**Galton bar** (psychophysics) An apparatus for determining the threshold for visual linear distances by the method of just noticeable differences or the method of reproduction. It consists of a meter rod with four sides, one of which facing the experimenter has a millimeter scale. The other sides are painted in grey or black. The rod has riders on it, one at the center and two on opposite sides. One of the markers is placed at a standard distance from the center. The subject is asked to place the second marker at a distance equal to the standard marked off length.

**Galton, Francis (1822-1911)** Versatile British psychologist who, ten years after the publication of *The Origin of Species,* applied Darwinian evolutionary theory to individual differences in human mental capacity in his work, *Hereditary Genius.* Pioneer in mental testing, the eugenics movement, the use of the questionnaire method, and the development of the coefficient of correlation.

**Galton's whistle** (F. Galton) A high-pitched whistle used in the determination of the upper threshold of tonal hearing.

**galvanic** Referring to a steady, direct current such as one from a battery.

**galvanic nystagmus** See *nystagmus, galvanic*.

**galvanic skin response** The changes in the electrical resistance of the skin measured by a galvanometer. It is used as an indicator of emotional arousal and tension.

**galvanometer** A device used to measure the strength of an electric current in amperes and milliamperes.

**galvanotropism or galvanotaxis** An orienting response toward electrical stimulation.

**gambler's fallacy** The failure to recognize the independence of some events that occur in a sequence. A gambler who has lost 10 straight times and feels he has a better chance of winning because of his misfortune is an example of this fallacy.

**game** Play which is organized according to specific rules, usually competitive and with a definite goal.

**game, hallucinatory** Make-believe games created by the child in which he actively invents fantasy objects to amuse himself. These hallucinations differ from real hallucinations which are passively experienced as foreign in that the child realizes the unreality of his fantasy play and can easily revert back to reality when necessary.

**game theory** A mathematical theory which attempts to analyze conflict situations in terms of a game in which each person seeks maximal gain and minimal loss.

**gamete** A mature germ cell (male or female) with haploid chromosome number.

**gametogenesis** The developmental process of the male and female gametes.

**gamma (γ)** (psychophysics) The distance of a stimulus from the threshold.

**gamma movement** See *movement, gamma.*

**gammacism** Speech impairment characteristic of young children in which velars g, k are replaced with dentals such as d and t.

**gamogenesis** Reproduction through fusion of two gametes.

**gamonomania** Excessive desire to marry.

**gamophobia** Fear of marriage.

**gang** A group of persons united together by common interests. It usually refers to children and often has antisocial connotations.

**ganglia** Groups of nerve cells whose cell bodies are located outside of the central nervous system.

**gangliated** Referring to a neuron which passes a ganglion on its course.

**ganglion** A group of nerve cells or cell bodies which are found outside the brain or spinal cord.

**ganglioplexus** A group of cell bodies found in a network of nerve fibers.

**gangliosides** Fat substances of the brain which contain a special fatty acid, neuraminic acid. Often associated with organic disorders caused by abnormal metabolic conditions, such as Tay-Sachs disease.

**Ganser's syndrome** See *syndrome, Ganser's.*

**Ganzfeld** A homogeneous visual field which is uniformly illustrated and which lacks any area or point of unique stimulation.

**gargalesthesia** A tickle sensation.

**gargoylism** See *Hurler's syndrome.*

**gases, psychosis due to** Mental disturbances resulting from the inhalation of poisonous gases such as carbon monoxide which produce a loss of consciousness and prolonged delirium, followed by difficulties in concentration, fatigue, and in some cases by impairment of intellectual functions.

**gastric neurosis** See *neurosis, gastric.*

**gastro-intestinal tract** The region of the stomach and intestines related to digestion.

**gastropaths, false** Individuals who are able to digest allegedly indigestible food but who develop food phobias for other foods due to psychological problems.

**gastro-psychiatry** A psychiatric term referring to a subject's preoccupation with his digestive system.

**gastrula** A stage in the development of an embryo following the blastula stage.

**gastrulation** The development of the didermic gastrula in the embryonic developmental process.

**Gates-MacGinitie Reading Tests** See *tests, Gates-MacGinitie Reading.*

**gating** The blocking of one set of sensations by another occurring usually during attention, when there is selective focusing on one set of sensations while others are held in the background.

**gatophobia** Fear of cats.

**Gaucher's disease** (P. C. E. Gaucher) A rare familial lipidosis occurring in both an acute infantile form and a more chronic adult form. Characterized by enlargement of the spleen, bronzing of the skin, anemia and, in infants, neurological involvement usually leading to death by age two.

**Gaussian or Gauss's curve** See *curve, normal distribution.*

**gaze, fascinating** The intensification of the eyes of the hypnotist on the subject in hypnosis.

**gazing, crystal** A technique used in hypnoanalysis in which a hypnotized subject is instructed to observe a glass ball or a mirror and to produce associations.

**gelasmus** Spasmodic laughter seen in hysterics.

**Gelinean's syndrome** (J. B. Gelinean) See *narcolepsy.*

**gemmation** A type of non-sexual reproduction in which the new organism develops as a bud from the parent.

**gemmule** A small copy of a cell found inside each cell.

**Gemüt or Gemütsbewegung** 1. A general term in German referring to the effective sphere of experience. 2. Mood.

**gender** Denotes sex. It is solely determined by the difference in the physical structure and appearance of the subject, and is used to differentiate male and female.

**gene** The basic unit of heredity. Genes are arranged in a linear fashion along the chromosomes, each gene having a precise position or locus. From the chemical standpoint a gene is a portion of a DNA molecule coded for the synthesis of certain poly-peptide chain.

**gene, dominant** A member of an allele pair which if present determines the phenotype whether either member of the pair is the same or different.

**gene, major** A gene which has a noticeable phenotypic effect.

**gene pair** See *alleles.*

**gene, recessive** The subordinate member of a heterozygous allele pair which does not have an effect on the phenotype and can only exhibit its effect phenotypically in a homozygous state.

**genealogical**  See *genealogy*.

**genealogy**  The study of the descent of a person or family from a progenitor.

**general ability  1.** A term describing the ability to deal with a wide range of problems. **2.** An ability necessary in all intellectual tasks and measured to a degree by cognitive tests. **3.** (C. Spearman) See *general factor*.

**general ability test**  A general intelligence test.

**general adaptation**  See *general adaptation syndrome*.

**general adaptation syndrome**  (H. Selye) Intense physiological changes in various organ systems of the body, especially the endocrine system as a result of stress. The sequence of bodily changes consists of the alarm reaction, resistance, and exhaustion.

**general aptitude**  The potentiality to acquire proficiency in a diversity of skills with a given amount of formal or informal training.

**general aptitude test battery**  A group of subtests developed by the United States Employment Service for use by their counselors. The subtests include a verbal aptitude, numerical aptitude, spatial aptitude, form perception, clerical perception, motor coordination and manual dexterity test.

**general attitude type**  (C. Jung) A categorization of individuals determined by their habitual way of responding to stimuli, whether inward (introversion) or outward (extraversion).

**general consciousness**  Experiences shared by all members of a group.

**general factor  1.** A factor common to all the tests being factor analyzed; also called G factor. **2.** (C. Spearman) The G (general) factor is a common factor which represents a general ability.

**general image**  An image representing anyone of a class of objects for a subject.

**general inhibition**  (R. B. Cattell) A temperament factor in objective tests loading especially reduction of muscular movement under threat, larger G.S.R. response and avoidance of risk behavior. Indexed as U.I. 17 in the universal index series of factors and hypothesized as identical with Pavlov's temperament dimension in animals.

**general intelligence**  A basic intellectual factor which functions in the solution of all intellectual problems.

**general intelligence test**  See *test, intelligence*.

**general juvenile paresis**  See *paresis, general juvenile*.

**general norms**  Average, standard performance under specified conditions which is used as a base for comparison of other's performance under the same conditions.

**general paralysis of the insane**  See *paresis, general*.

**general paresis**  See *paresis, general*.

**general psychology**  See *psychology, general*.

**general semantics**  Science which deals with human reactions to symbols.

**general systems theory**  (L. V. Bertalanffy) The "general systems theory" is a reaction of contemporary science to the overflow of fractional analytic and non-organized researches at the world's numerous laboratories. The "general systems theory" represented by the special annual edition of "General Systems Theory" and by the scientific "Society of General Systems Theory" seeks the most effective theoretical generalizations, which would permit finding a "key" toward the understanding of different classes of phenomena within the system. Failures of the wide application of the "general systems theory" are connected with some of its shortcomings such as: a) it still doesn't have a formulation of the system acceptable for a majority of the investigators; b) it hasn't revealed a system organizing factor, transferring the chaos of a great number of components into an organized multitude, into the system; c) the system is displayed as something homogeneous without operational architectonics which would permit the evaluation of the system functional effect.

**generalization  1.** A statement concerning the classification of a class of objects on the basis of one common denominator. **2.** The subject's realization of a common principle in a class of objects or problems in concept formation and problem solving. **3.** (I. P. Pavlov) Stimuli which were not used in the original conditioning procedure can evoke the conditioned response.

**generalization gradient**  The decrease in the strength of the generalized conditioned response with decreasing similarity of the stimuli used in testing to the original stimulus.

**generalized**  A judgment or principle which, having the qualities common to a class, applies to the members of this class.

**generalized gangliosidosis**  A lipidosis, associated with the involvement of the central nervous system leading to mental retardation as well as liver and kidney failure. Progressive deterioration usually leads to death by age three.

**generalized glycogenesis**  See *Pompe's disease*.

**generalized inhibitory potential**  (C. L. Hull) Conditioned inhibition as a result of stimulus generalization.

**generation  1.** Act of producing offspring. **2.** A group of individuals of the same genealogical rank. **3.** A group of individuals living at the same time. **4.** Statistical concept describing the average duration of life in a group.

**generative**  Having the ability to reproduce.

**generativity**  See *generative*.

**generator potential**  Change in voltage in a receptor cell due to the depolarizing action of a stimulus.

**generic  1.** Pertaining to genus. **2.** General, applying to all instances of a class.

**generic image**  See *image, generic*.

**genesis**  Origin; beginnings; inception.

**genetic**  1. Pertaining to origins, history or development; developmental, as, for example, genetic psychology. 2. The science of genetics, pertaining to genes. 3. Produced or determined by a gene or combination of genes. 4. When combined with nouns denotes "pertaining to generation" or "genesis" as in psychogenetic or psychogenic.

**genetic marker**  A readily recognizable gene which can be used to determine whether another gene is on the same chromosome.

**genetic method**  The understanding of behavior by tracing its hereditary origins and development.

**genetic psychology**  See *psychology, genetic.*

**genetic sequences**  The order in which structures or functions determined by genes appear in development.

**genetic theory or viewpoint**  The point of view that stresses the importance of origins and developmental history in understanding phenomena.

**geneticism**  The doctrine that behavior is inherited.

**genetics**  The scientific study of heredity initiated by the hybridization studies of Gregor Mendel published in 1886.

**genial**  Pertaining to the genetic quality of exhibition of genius.

**geniculate bodies**  Slight enlargements on the lateral surface of the thalamus which function as relay stations for visual and auditory impulses to the appropriate centers in the cortex.

**geniculate neuralgia**  Lesion of the facial nerve at the geniculate ganglion followed by facial paralysis.

**genital**  Pertaining to the organs of reproduction.

**genital character**  See *character, genital.*

**genital eroticism**  Sexual excitement resulting from the stimulation of the genital organs.

**genital love**  1. Love of the genitals during the period of love of an object. 2. (psychoanalysis) Sexually mature love of another person.

**genital primacy**  (psychoanalysis) State of psychosexual development in which the dominant sexual proclivity is coition.

**genital primacy stage**  (psychoanalysis) The final stage of psychosexual development during which the emphasis is on coition and the pleasure is derived from the genital organs.

**genital-psychical development**  Psychosexual development evaluated by the capacity to love on an adult level as opposed to physical prowess.

**genital sensations**  Sexual sensations originating in the genital organs.

**genital stage**  (psychoanalysis) The final stage of psychosexual development in which a person has an affectionate relationship with the sex partner.

**genital zones**  The external genitals and adjacent areas from which genital sensations arise.

**genitality**  Term referring to the genital aspects of sexuality; adult sexuality.

**genitalize**  (psychoanalysis) Regarding objects as symbols of genitals.

**genitals**  The organs of reproduction.

**genius**  1. High intellectual and creative ability 2. A person possessing such ability.

**genome**  All the genes found in a haploid set of chromosomes.

**genophobia**  Fear of sex.

**genosomatogenic disorders**  (B. B. Wolman) Inherited organic mental disorders.

**genotype**  The genetic characters inherent in the alleles present at a particular locus, or the sum total of these characters in the organism under consideration.

**genotypical**  Pertaining to the genotype.

**gens**  A division of an ethnic group whose line of descent runs through the males.

**genus**  A biological classification which consists of closely related species.

**geography, psychological**  The description of a community in terms of its location and psychological influences among members of the group and groups within the community.

**geometric illusion**  A group of illusions determined by distorted lines which cause a misinterpretation of their relationships.

**geometric mean**  The $n$th root of the product of $n$ number of means. For example:

$$\bar{x}_g = \sqrt[n]{\bar{x}_1 \bar{x}_2 \bar{x}_3 \ldots \bar{x}_n}$$

**geometric-optic agnosia**  Lack of sense of direction.

**geophagy**  The eating of dirt.

**geotaxis**  A taxis in which the animal orients to the stimulation of gravity.

**gephyrophobia**  Morbid fear of crossing a bridge or river.

**geriatrics**  A branch of medicine concerned with old age and its ailments.

**geriopsychosis**  A psychosis of old age characterized by the deterioration of the brain tissue and progressive mental deterioration.

**germ**  1. A mass of protoplasm capable of developing into a new organism. 2. A bud.

**germ cell**  A reproductive cell.

**germ plasm**  The tissue making up germ cells which is the main factor in the transmission of hereditary characteristics.

**German,  Gordon  Allen  (1935-     )**  British

psychiatrist. Set up the first academic unit of psychiatry in East and Central Africa at Makerere University, Uganda, in 1966. Has demonstrated that the prevalence of mental disorder amongst Africans is at least as high as in developed countries; in particular that neurotic illness is a common development in unsophisticated Africans. Explored the nature of psychiatric disorder amongst African students; has put forward the hypothesis that the evil consequences of social change rather than social change *per se* are key factors in the etiology of mental illness.

**germinal period**   The early period of embryonic life, approximately two weeks.

**germinal vesicle**   The nucleus of the egg before the development of the polar bodies.

**germinally affected**   Refers to an individual who carries a homozygous recessive gene pair for a morbid trait which is not manifested phenotypically.

**gerontology**   The scientific study of old age.

**gerontophilia**   Love of old people.

**gerophilia**   See *gerontophilia.*

**Gesell, Arnold (1880-1961)**   Child psychologist and pediatrician (Yale). Research on stages of motor development in infancy, popularizing concept of maturation as basis for development; devised method of co-twin control; author of widely read books on characteristics of children at successive age levels from birth to ten years.

**Gesell Development Scales 1.** Scales of development for infants and pre-school children based on normative data of children from the Yale Clinic of Child Development. **2.** See *infant schedule.* **3.** See *pre-school schedule.*

**gestalt**   A configuration or figure whose integration differs from the totality obtained by summing the parts.

**gestalt factor**   Any condition favorable to the perception of a whole or totality.

**Gestalt psychology**   Gestalt psychology, a major revolution in psychology, was founded in Germany around 1910 by Max Wertheimer, Wolfgang Köhler, and Kurt Koffka. It started as a protest against the atomism and the narrowness of the prevailing psychology of the mind, but its criticisms were later applied also to the equally atomistic American behaviorism.

Scientific psychology at the turn of the century modeled itself after the physical sciences as it understood them, seeking to reduce the wealth of experience to elements of the mind. The exact nature and number of elements were under dispute, but sensory elements were generally agreed upon. It was assumed that there is a one-to-one correspondence between local sensory experience and local stimulation. This is the constancy hypothesis, the basis of traditional psychology.

Gestalt psychologists set out by rejecting the constancy hypothesis and other forms of elementarism

in psychology. Rather than starting with a preconception about the nature of scientific analysis, they undertook first of all to make their analysis relevant to its subject matter. This meant a starting point in phenomenology in the sense of a clear and unbiased view of phenomena. Re-examining scientific method, Gestalt psychologists asserted that it need not be atomistic. Field theory in physics provided them with a model entirely different from the interpretation of science by the traditional psychology. They found that in many situations, parts derive their nature and functions from the wholes in which they exist and cannot be understood apart from these wholes. Nor can such dynamic wholes be understood as a summation of independent local constituents. The processes in them are functions of interactions within the total relevant field.

From this point of view, many problems in perception were investigated; the approach was extended to thinking, memory and recall, to values and to problems of motivation, to social psychology and the psychology of art. Through the principle of isomorphism, the hypothesis that there is a structural similarity between the facts of organized experience and the corresponding cortical processes, certain problems of brain physiology were opened up to investigation by Gestalt psychologists. Isomorphism proved to be a powerful heuristic tool and led to the investigation of figural aftereffects, then to the demonstration of cortical currents corresponding to organized perceptions.

**Gestalt therapy**   See *psychotherapy, Gestalt.*

**Gestaltqualität**   The quality of the whole form or configuration as dependent on the combination and patterning of the elements.

**gestation**   The carrying of the embryo in the uterus.

**gestation period**   The period of development of an organism before birth.

**gestational insanity**   A mental disorder which occurs during pregnancy.

**Gestural Interverbal Test**   See *test, Gestural Interverbal.*

**gestural-postural language**   See *language, gestural-postural.*

**gesture**   A movement of a part of the body for the purpose of communication.

**geumophobia**   Morbid fear of taste.

**geusia**   The act of tasting.

**Gheel colony**   A colony in Gheel, Belgium, in existence since the 13th century, which treats psychotic patients in private residences in the community.

**ghost**   A disembodied being who retains some of the bodily characteristics such as visibility.

**gibberish**   Incoherent, incomprehensible language.

**Gibson, Eleanor J. (1910-    )**   American psychologist, best known for research and theory on perceptual learning and development. Applied concepts of conditioning (generalization and differentiation) to verbal learning; made comparative studies of early experience and development of depth perception measured on the "visual cliff" (with Richard Walk); conducts basic research on reading skill and development of economical strategies of perceptual processing.

**giddiness**  Dizziness; having the sensation of whirling about.

**gifted**  1. Possessing a high degree of intellectual ability. 2. Possessing a high degree of a special talent.

**gigantism**  An abnormal increase in stature due to oversupply of the growth hormone by the anterior pituitary gland.

**gigantosomia primordialis**  A rare form of gigantism characterized by well proportioned physique and a normal sex development.

**gigolette**  Descriptive term for a young woman who engages in promiscuous love affairs.

**gigolism**  1. Term describing the action of a professional escort usually to members of the opposite sex. 2. Male prostitution.

**gigolo**  1. Man who serves as a paid escort for women. 2. Man who lives on the earnings of a professional prostitute.

**girdle sensation**  The sensation created by a tightly worn belt appearing as a symptom in particular diseases such as tabis dorsalis.

**given**  1. Potentially specifiable but left undefined. 2. A set of data available at the inception of an investigation.

**gland**  An organ which secretes substances used in the body or excreted. There are two types: endocrine or ductless glands which secrete their substances directly into the blood stream, and exocrine or duct glands whose secretions are discharged through a duct to the outside or other organs of the body.

**gland, anterior pituitary**  A portion of the pituitary gland which responds to physical or emotional stress by secreting the adreno-corticotrophic hormone which stimulates the adrenal cortex to increase its production of hormones.

**gland, parotid**  Large salivary gland located below the external ear under the jaw bone.

**gland, pituitary**  An endocrine gland called the master gland which is located in the central part of the head. It is made of up two parts. The anterior pituitary controls growth and the activity of other endocrine glands. The posterior pituitary controls the water balance.

**glands, adrenal**  A pair of endocrine glands lying over the kidneys. The adrenal medulla is the dark, central portion of the glands that produces epinephrine and norepinephrine (more commonly called adrenalin and noradrenalin). These hormones are important in the body's reaction to stress. The adrenal cortex, the yellowish outer layer of the adrenal glands, releases several hormones called steroids which are involved in the regulation of body metabolism and sexual functions.

**glands, endocrine**  The ductless glands which secrete their substances directly into the bloodstream.

**glands, exocrine**  The duct glands which secrete their substances through a duct to the outside or other organs of the body.

**glands, sudoriferous**  Sweat glands.

**glandular response**  The reaction of the gland when it is stimulated by a substance outside of the gland.

**glans**  The bulblike end of the penis or clitoris.

**glass sensation**  The visual quality produced by a transparent solid.

**glaucoma**  A disease of the eye caused by increased internal pressure from the liquids leading to progressive visual impairment and finally blindness.

**glia**  Specialized supporting tissue within the cerebrospinal axis; neuroglia.

**glial diathesis**  A constitutional condition characterized by an abnormal growth of the primitive or more differentiated glial cells resulting in one of many degenerative scleroses of the corpora striata.

**glioma**  A brain tumor.

**gliosis**  Rapid increase in the production of neuroglia in the brain or spinal cord as a replacement process or due to inflammation.

**global**  Taken as a whole, as an entirety without distinguishing the parts.

**global aphasia**  See *aphasia, global.*

**globus hystericus**  The sensation of having a lump in the throat or of a ball coming from the stomach to strangulate the person.

**glossal**  Pertaining to the tongue.

**glossiness**  A quality of the surface determined by the degree to which it reflects light.

**glossodyma**  A burning sensation of pain in the tongue.

**glossolalia**  Unintelligible speech such as occurs in hypnotic trances, religious ecstasies and sometimes in pathological mental disorders.

**glossopharyngeal nerve**  The ninth cranial nerve which contains nerve fibers which mediate the sensation of taste.

**glossospasm**  A spasm of the tongue consisting of an inward-outward movement, lasting several minutes.

**glossosynthesis**  The formation of nonsense words.

**glottis**  1. The opening between the vocal cords. 2. The opening between the arytenoid of the larynx and the vocal cords found at the upper part of the trachea.

**glove anesthesia**  A functional disorder in the

sensory field in which the person is insensitive to touch in an area corresponding approximately to the part covered by a glove.

**Glover, Edward (1888-1972)** M.D., L.L.D., Hon. Fel. Brit. Psycho. Soc. Originally specialist in diseases of chest. Since 1921, adopted psychoanalytic practice. Wrote extensively on clinical and theoretical aspects of psychoanalysis. Founded Criminological Institute and Clinic for Study and Treatment of Delinquency. Special interests include technique and theory of psychoanalysis, classification of mental disorders, also various social aspects. Author of textbooks of psychoanalytic theory and practice, also on problems of child development and war psychology.

**glucose** Blood sugar.

**gluteal reflex** A reflexive contraction of the glutea caused by the stroking of the buttocks.

**gluttony** Excessive eating.

**glycogen** Stored hydrocarbon which is used by the muscles and tissues in performing work.

**glycogen storage diseases** Group of diseases characterized by abnormal accumulations of glycogen in the body, each disease being characterized by a specific, genetically determined enzymatic deficiency resulting in a defect of carbohydrate metabolism. Disease types I, II, and III result in hypoglycemia and the associated central nervous system manifestations.

**glycosuria** The presence of sugar in the urine resulting from disease or a violent emotional reaction.

**gnostic sensation** Refers to epicritic sensations, the result of delicate sensory discrimination of the cutaneous receptors.

**goal** 1. The end result toward which a living organism is moving. 2. A place which contains a reward, an incentive. 3. A consummatory response.

**goal-directed behavior** Behavior which can be interpreted only in terms of the organism's intention to reach the goal.

**goal gradient** (C. L. Hull) The principle that in closer proximity to the goal, the experimental animal will speed up and make fewer errors in performance.

**goal object** The final result toward which the experimental subject is striving.

**goal orientation** 1. The positioning of the experimental animal or human subject toward the goal. 2. In maze learning, the tendency of the experimental animal to enter alleys in the direction of the goal.

**goal response** 1. A response directed toward the goal. 2. In instrumental conditioning, the response made toward the reward.

**goal set** An anticipation of the goal.

**goal stimulus** A proprioceptive stimulus which arises from goal-directed behavior.

**Goetsch Test** (E. Goetsch) A test for hyperthyroidism.

**goiter, exophthalmic** Disease caused by the overproduction of tyroxin by the thyroid gland. It is characterized by an enlargement of the thyroid gland, tachycardia, nervousness, loss of weight, muscular weakness, disturbances in carbohydrate metabolism and acute thyroid crises.

**golden section** The aesthetic division of a line or an area into two parts $x$ and $y$, so that the ratio of $x$ to $y$ equals the ratio of $y$ to the line or area.

**Goldflam, Samuel (1852-1932)** Polish neurologist who is known for his description of myasthenia gravis.

**Goldstein, Kurt (1878-1956)** German neurologist and Gestalt psychologist who emigrated to the United States in 1935. An organismic personality psychologist whose theory of motivation stressed self-actualization; he found (with Martin Scheerer) that brain injury makes behavior less abstract and more concrete.

**Goldstein-Scheerer Tests** See *tests, Goldstein-Scheerer.*

**Golem** Based on Jewish medieval tradition, a manmade huge monster created from clay by the supernatural power of Rabbi Livay.

**Golgi apparatus** Granule-like structures inside the neuron which are rich in ribonucleic acid and are believed to participate in the synthesis of substances used in maintaining the cell and of transmitter substances which excite or inhibit other cells.

**Golgi-Mazzoni corpuscles** Encapsulated end organs consisting of nerve endings surrounded by a capsule of tissue, similar to the Krause corpuscles, receptors for cold sensations.

**Golgi tendon organ** Kinesthetic end organs which are found in the tendons near the tendon-muscle junctures. By responding to changes in tendon tension, these nerve endings function to provide kinesthetic sensations.

**gonad** The sex gland.

**gonadal, gonadial, gonadic** Pertaining to the gonad.

**gonadocentric** Regarding the genitals as central points.

**gonadotropic hormone** A hormone secreted by the pituitary gland which stimulates the growth and development of the sperm and eggs in the gonads and causes the secretion of androgen and estrogen.

**goneometer** 1. An instrument for measuring angles. 2. An instrument which measures the amount of sway in psychological experiments.

**good and evil test** See *test, good and evil.*

**good continuation** (Gestalt psychology) The principle that a perceived element tends to continue in its direction.

**good Gestalt** A symmetrical, simple configuration.

**good-me** See *personified self.*

**good object** See *object, good.*

**good shape** (Gestalt psychology) The principle that figures, shapes or patterns are perceived in the most stable and uniform manner as possible.

**Goodenough Draw-a-Man Test** See *test, Goodenough Draw-a-Man.*

**goodness of fit** The degree to which any set of empirical observations conforms to a theoretical or standard value.

**Gordon Holmes rebound phenomenon** See *rebound phenomenon of Gordon Holmes.*

**Gordon reflex** (A. Gordon) A great toe reflex evoked in diseases of the pyramidal tract.

**Gottschaldt figures** Simple geometric figures hidden in more complex figures used to test form perception.

**governess psychosis** See *psychosis, governess.*

**Grace Arthur Scale** See *scale, Arthur Point of Performance Tests.*

**gradation methods** Psychophysical techniques measuring change in terms of small equal steps.

**grade 1.** A class consisting of things on the same position on a scale. **2.** In United States schools, a class representing one academic year. **3.** A rating on a test.

**grade equivalent** A score which reflects a person's achievement on a test or battery of tests according to grade norms.

**grade scale** See *scale, grade.*

**grade score** See *score, grade.*

**graded rehearsal** The rehearsal of behaviors which increase in difficulty.

**gradient 1.** Any regular change in a magnitude which slopes from high to low or vice versa. **2.** A change in the motivation to respond which is dependent on a corresponding change in some dimension of stimulation such as time interval or distance.

**gradient, anterior-posterior** The more rapid growth of the head region in comparison with the tail region which results in the cephalocaudal sequence in development.

**gradient, approach** The degree of attractiveness of a positive goal increases as a function of nearness to it or as the goal is approached.

**gradient, avoidance** The attractiveness of a negative goal decreases as it is approached and the tendency to move away from the negative goal increases with closeness to it.

**gradient of effect** The principle that in a series of *S-R* sequences, those sequences which closely follow or precede a reinforced sequence have greater probability of occurrence than those which are remote.

**gradient of reinforcement** The generalization that the closer a response is to the reinforcement, the stronger it becomes.

**gradient of response generalization** The principle that upon learning to emit a particular response to a given stimulus, that stimulus will elicit similar responses from the animal. The greater the similarity in response, the more the stimulus will elicit it.

**gradient of stimulus generalization** The principle that when the animal learns to respond to a given stimulus, he will respond to similar stimuli. This response will not, however, be as strong.

**Graduate Record Examination** A combination of verbal and mathematical tests which are used as measures of aptitude to select candidates for graduate school. Also known as GRE.

**grand mal** A complete epileptic seizure consisting of a sudden loss of consciousness, tonic and clonic spasms, frothing at the mouth and often urine incontinence. Following the convulsions, the person is often confused and falls into a deep sleep. See *epilepsy.*

**grandeur delusions** See *delusions, grandeur.*

**grandfather complex** See *complex, grandfather.*

**grandiose** Referring to delusions of greatness and importance.

**granular layers 1.** The fourth layer of the central cortex consisting of many small multipolar cells with short peripheral processes. **2.** The fifth and seventh layer of the retina.

**graph** The representation of the relationship between two variables by means of lines or geometric figures.

**graph, correlation** See *scatter diagram.*

**graphic** Representation by means of a graph.

**graphic analysis** See *analysis, graphic.*

**graphic individuality** See *individuality, graphic.*

**graphic language** See *language, graphic.*

**graphic method** See *method, graphic.*

**graphic rating scale** See *scale, graphic rating.*

**graphic score** See *score, graphic.*

**graphodyne** A mechanism for recording pressure in handwriting.

**graphology** The study of handwriting for the purpose of deducing the personality characteristics of the writer.

**graphomania** Intense impulse to write.

**graphomaniac** A person exhibiting an inordinate impulse to write.

**graphomotor technique** See *technique, graphomotor.*

**graphophobia** Fear of writing.

**graphorrh(o)ea** Disordered, often meaningless writing observed in pathological states.

**graphospasm** Writer's cramp.

**grasping and groping reflex** See *reflex, grasping and groping.*

**gratification**  Satisfaction of a person's needs or desires.

**gratification, self**  The satisfaction of one's own needs, particularly those having to do with enhancement of self through praise and prestige.

**Graves' disease**  See *goiter, exophthalmic.*

**gray matter**  The part of the brain and spinal cord chiefly made up of nerve cells.

**Gray Oral Reading Test**  See *test, Gray Oral Reading.*

**gray-out**  Partial loss of consciousness due to anemia of the brain or anoxemia.

**GRE**  See *Graduate Record Examination.*

**Great Mother**  See *Magna Mater.*

**Greek love**  Homosexuality among males.

**green**  A visual sensation resulting from the stimulation of the retina with radiation of approximately 510 millimicron wave lengths.

**gregariousness**  1. The proclivity to be in the company of others. 2. The tendency for animals to congregate in herds or flocks. 3. The tendency in humans to live in groups and to desire the company of others.

**grey or gray**  The achromatic color ranging in shade between the extreme limits of black and white.

**grief**  An emotional state resulting from the loss of an important object.

**Grieg's disease**  Mental and physical retardation associated with a deformity of the frontal area of the cranium and characterized by a low forehead, wide bridge of the nose, increased distance between the eyes and divergent strabismus; hypertelorism.

**Griffiths' Scale**  See *scale, Griffiths'.*

**grimace**  A distorted facial expression due to organic or psychological causes.

**Griselda complex**  See *complex, Griselda.*

**gross score**  See *score, gross.*

**ground**  The background in the relationship of figure and ground.

**group**  Two or more individuals, assembled or dispersed, who are united by some common interest, characteristic or attachment and whose actions are interrelated.

**group acceptance**  The reaction of group members to a new or prospective member which establishes the member's role in the group.

**group analysis**  See *analysis, group; group psychoanalysis.*

**group atmosphere**  The feelings and attitudes manifested in a group.

**group behavior**  1. The behavior of a group acting as a whole. 2. The actions of an individual member as influenced by being a member of the group. 3. Ac-

tions characteristic of individuals when in the group but not when outside the group.

**group, blanket**  A group in which criteria for group membership do not exist.

**group boundary**  The regulations which control group activities and group membership.

**group, closed**  A psychotherapy group which does not admit new patients during the course of the treatment.

**group consciousness**  1. An awareness characteristic of the whole group which is more than the sum of the individual consciousness. This concept is synonymous with G. LeBon's group mind and group behavior. 2. An awareness of one individual in a group for another member or for the group as a whole.

**group contagion**  The rapid spread of feelings through the group as a result of an empathic perception of the feelings in others.

**group, control**  A group which is equivalent to the experimental group in every respect except for the independent variable which the experimental group is treated with and the control group is not.

**group decision**  An opinion or judgment arrived at by the group either by consensus or by a majority vote of the members.

**group differences**  Distinguishing disparities between two or more groups with respect to any specific variable.

**group dimension**  A quantitative characteristic by means of which a group can be described.

**group dynamics**  1. The cause and effect relationships which exist in the group. 2. The study of the development of the cause and effect relationships within a group. 3. The techniques for changing the interpersonal relations and attitudes within a group.

**group experiment**  An experiment performed on a large number of interrelated persons.

**group, experimental**  The subjects in an experiment who are exposed to the independent or experimental variable and whose performance is thought to reflect the influence of that condition. This group is matched with the control group in every way except for their exposure to the experimental condition.

**group feeling**  The desire to be with other members of a group.

**group identification**  The process of internalizing the standards and ideals of the group.

**group interval**  A class interval.

**group interview**  The use of the interview technique with several individuals at once.

**group marriage**  A marriage consisting of several men and women.

**group, matched**  (experimental research) One of the groups used in an experiment which are made equivalent in every respect in order to ensure experimental control. Some groups undergo experimental manipulation while others do not. The resulting difference between the initially equal groups is a measure of experimental effect.

**group mean *p* technique** A longitudinal factor analysis carried out, not on an individual, but a group, all members experiencing the same sequence of stimuli.

**group measures** Measures which fall within intervals or classes of scores rather than a group of individual scores.

**group, membership** A group in which the person is an accepted member.

**group mind** (G. LeBon) A term used to explain the behavior of a group which cannot be accounted for by the sum of the traits of the individual members.

**group morale** The prevailing spirit in the group characterized by confidence and a willingness to strive for group goals.

**group norm** See *norm, group.*

**group, open** A psychotherapy group which admits new patients during the course of treatment.

**group processes** The methods used by a group to approach and solve problems and to meet objectives.

**group psychoanalysis** Psychoanalytic technique applied to the group treatment of mental disorders; a particular version of group psychotherapy based on psychoanalytic principles.

**group psychotherapy** See *psychotherapy, group.*

**group psychotherapy, analytic** See *psychotherapy, analytic group.*

**group psychotherapy, didactic** See *psychotherapy, didactic group.*

**group psychotherapy, nondirective** See *psychotherapy, nondirective group.*

**group psychotherapy, psychoanalytic** See *psychotherapy, psychoanalytic group.*

**group rigidity** Resistance to change in a group.

**group, standardization** The group of individuals used for establishing norms for a test which is believed to be representative of the population which will be tested in the future.

**group structure** The relationships of members in a group and the characteristics of the group which determine the interpersonal relations and its relationships with other groups.

**group, structured** (S. R. Slavson) A therapy group in which the selection of members is made according to the criterion of which individuals will effect a most therapeutic change on one another.

**group superego** The aspect of the superego based on identifications with peer groups as opposed to the portion of the superego derived from the introjection of parental values.

**group test** see *test, group.*

**group therapy** See *psychotherapy, directive group.*

**group, therapy** See *psychotherapy, group.*

**group, transitional** A psychotherapy group designed for children in the latency and puberty stage who cannot adjust to the demands of a social club but do not need intensive group psychotherapy.

**grouped distribution** A frequency distribution in which the values of a variable are expressed in ranges.

**grouping** 1. Putting together of objects, animals, humans, or concepts and ideas into one clan or category. 2. Combining scores into classes or categories. 3. (education) Assigning school pupils into classes or grades.

**grouping error** The error introduced when a set of observations is divided into class intervals due to the assumption that the data are uniformly distributed around the midpoint of each interval.

**groups, equivalent** (statistics) Two or more groups which exhibit approximately the same distribution on a particular variable. Mean, standard deviation and range are nearly the same, falling within previously set limits of each other.

**growing pains** 1. Physical pain experienced by the child or adolescent due to the overly rapid development of the bones. 2. Metaphorically, any stress due to development.

**growth** Refers to increments in size or amount.

**growth curve** A graphic representation of the growth rate of an organism over a period of time.

**growth, differential** Growth of one organ or structure proceeds at a different rate than another organ within the same organism.

**growth, mental** The increase with age of any psychological function, specifically of intelligence.

**growth motivation** See *motivation, growth.*

**growth principle** (C. R. Rogers) The principle that in an atmosphere free from coercion and distortion, the creative and actualizing tendencies within an individual will prevail leading to the development of a more adaptive, forward-moving and confident person, with feelings of positive self-regard and worth.

**grumbling mania** See *mania, grumbling.*

**guessed mean** See *mean, assumed.*

**guidance** A type of counseling in which an individual is assisted through the use of interviews and tests, in choosing educational and vocational careers which will offer him maximum satisfaction.

**guidance, child** A term which refers to the preventive measures oriented toward minimizing the possibility of mental disorders in adult life by offering didactic and therapeutic aid to the child and his family members, at a time when the intervention will have a critical prophylactic effect.

**Guilford, Joy Paul (1897-    )** American multivariate experimental psychologist, known for his contributions to psychological measurement and the application of measurement methods and factor analysis to derivation of taxonomies of personality traits, including intellectual abilities. Probably his best contribution was his structure of intellect, a model representing systematically all currently conceivable varieties of intellectual functioning. The model has led to an operational-informational point of view in psychology, which regards the individual as a processor of information in specified codes, according to logical principles.

**Guilford-Zimmerman Temperament Survey** A personality inventory published in 1949, which measures ten traits, products of factorial analyses: general activity, restraint, ascendance, sociability, emotional stability, objectivity, friendliness, thoughtfulness, personal relations, and masculinity. The survey is intended for use with individuals in grades 9 through 16 and with adults.

**guilt** 1. The realization that one has transgressed a moral, social or ethical principle, associated with a lowering of self-esteem and a need to make retribution for the transgression. 2. (psychoanalysis) Feeling which is the result of a conflict between the superego and ego in which the superego, as the internal authority, punishes the ego in the form of feelings of low self-esteem and guilt for allowing the expression or existence of unacceptable impulses. The guilt feeling or moral anxiety in the most extreme form becomes a fear of annihilation, and panic that affection and narcissistic supplies will be withdrawn.

**guilt proneness** A source trait distinct from superego strength but predisposing to guilt-prone, depressive, apprehensive behavior.

**guilt, unconscious sense of** A term referring to the unconscious causes of guilt feelings. A more correct term would be an unconscious need for punishment.

**gumma, intracranial** A form of cerebral syphilis in which a necrotic mass with a tendency to encapsulation and tibrosis may produce intracranial pressure. The associated mental symptoms include an acute organic reaction with delirium, memory loss of recent events and emotional variability. Upon increased intracranial pressure, stupor and a loss of sphincter control occur.

**gust** A unit of taste which equals the subjective strength of a one per cent solution of sucrose.

**gustation** The sense of taste with receptors on the tongue and soft palate.

**gustatism** A syncratic sensation of taste with another sensory modality.

**gustatory center** The center of taste.

**gustatory-lacrimal reflex** Crocodile-tears syndrome.

**Guthrie, Edwin R. (1886-1959)** Behaviorist at the University of Washington. Developed a theory of learning based upon a single law, which he used systematically to account for a broad range of behaviors, including social phenomena, personality and education: whenever a response occurs, it is linked permanently with each stimulus element present at the time the response is made.

**Guttman scale** See *scale, Guttman.*

**guttural** Pertaining to the throat such as sounds originating in the throat.

**gynander, gynandromorph** An organism exhibiting both male and female characteristics due to the development of both types of sex tissue.

**gynandroid, gynandromorphic, gynandrous** Referring to the hermaphroditic combination in an organism in which feminine features predominate.

**gynandry** Feminine pseudohermaphroditism.

**gynecomania** Intense desire for women.

**gynephobia** Fear of women.

**gynomonoecism** The ability of a genetic female to produce spermatozoa in the ovaries.

**gyrectomy** The surgical ablation of any gyrous of the brain. As a treatment for certain forms of mental illness, part of the cortex is excised bilaterally from the frontal lobes of the brain.

**gyrus** A fold or convolution on the surface of the cerebral hemisphere.

**gyrus cinguli or cingulate** Also called gyrus callosus. The central fold of each cerebral hemisphere; it lies above the corpus callosum.

**gyrus fornicatus** See *lobe, limbic.*

**gyrus of Broca** (P. Broca).Motor speech area.

**gyrus, paracentral** A convolution on the middle surface of the cerebral hemispheres which surrounds the upper end of the dentral fissure.

# H

**H** 1. See *mean, harmonic.* 2. (C. L. Hull) Habit strength. Also $_SH_r$ . 3. Rorschach scoring symbol for the perception of human forms.

**H test** See *test, H.*

**Haab's pupil reflex** (O. Haab) The contraction of both pupils when the gaze is directed toward a bright object in a darkened room.

**habenula** 1. The fibers which form the stalk of the pineal body and attach it to the thalamus. 2. A small strip of flesh.

**habit** 1. An acquired act that is practiced regularly and with a minimum of voluntary control. 2. The tendency for a given stimulus to evoke a specific response on occasions subsequent to the original reaction. 3. (J. Dewey) a) Complex and flexible mechanisms of behavior that control the interaction between organism and its environment; b) The mechanisms that "assimilate objective energies, and eventuate in command of environment;" c) Dewey distinguishes between routine habits, those which offer adjustment to a more or less static environment and intelligent habits, which guide the individual to a better adjustment to a changing situation. 4. (C. L. Hull) a) Persistent patterns of behavior that are "set up by virtue of the law of reinforcement;" b) Reinforced conditioned-response patterns. See *habit formation, law of* and *habit strength.*

**habit, accident** The tendency to have accidents as a result of unconscious conflictual needs which are partially satisfied by the consequent injuries.

**habit, act** A characteristic mode of responding resulting from environmental influence.

**habit, complaint** (L. Kanner) A recurrent tendency to hypochondriachal complaints in children as a reaction to emotional or other difficulties.

**habit, deterioration** The loss of socialized behaviors as a result of a regression to less integrated patterns of behavior in mental and organic illnesses.

**habit, family hierarchy** (C. L. Hull) The grouping of alternate routes to a goal in the order of most to least preferred.

**habit formation** The establishment of behavior patterns.

**habit formation, law of** (C. L. Hull) An equation in mathematical learning theory that expresses the relation between habit strength and number of reinforcements. If reinforcements follow each other at evenly distributed intervals, everything else constant, the resulting habit will increase in strength as a positive growth function of the number of trials according to the equation: $_SH_R = 1 - 10^{-aN}$ where $a$ is a constant that specifies the learning rate, $N$ is the total number of reinforcements from $Z$, and $Z$ is the absolute zero of the reaction potential.

**habit hierarchy** 1. (C. L. Hull) The arrangement of responses in terms of their strength which depends on their temporal contiguity with the reinforced response. 2. The hierarchical organization of simpler habits into more complex habit patterns.

**habit, hysterical** A hysterical reaction which develops from a voluntary to an automatic response by means of repetition.

**habit, interference** The weakening of one or both responses which have been established to the same situation.

**habit, motor** A habit defined in terms of the response movements which are involved.

**habit, residual hysterical** Hysteria which continues to exist because of the patient's lack of desire to get well.

**habit, sensory** A learned behavior which consists of the ability to differentiate between stimuli rather than learning to make specific responses.

**habit strength** (C. L. Hull) The strength of the habitual response which is dependent on the number of reinforcements, the amount of reinforcement, the temporal interval between stimulus and the response, and between the response and the reinforcement. Also known as $_SH_R$.

**habit training** The didactic process directed toward the establishment of habitual patterns of behavior in organisms.

**habitat** 1. Natural surroundings and conditions of an animal or vegetable species. 2. (A. Adler) The situations to which a person has been exposed including the social factors that have influenced him.

**habituation** The elimination of a response as a result of a continuous exposure to the stimulus which evoked the response.

**habitus** 1. The general characteristic appearance of the body of an organism. 2. The constitutional predisposition to a disease believed to be associated with a particular body type.

**habitus, affective** The affective organization of a person.

**habitus apoplecticus** See *type, apoplectic.*

**habitus phthisicus** (Hippocrates) A slender constitution thought to be characteristic of tubercular patients.

**habromania** Morbid gaiety.

**haematophobia, hematophobia** See *hemophobia.*

**haemorrhage** The eruption of blood from the vessels.

**hair cells** Cells with hairlike protrusions which function as receptors in the inner ear.

**hair follicle** An epithelial structure in the corium and hypodermis which contains the root of the hair filament.

**hair pulling** A compulsive symptom of pulling the hair from the head which is the expression of unconscious conflicts.

**halfway house** A facility providing professional supervision in a group living arrangement for the patient without a home who is ready to work after having been discharged from a hospital.

**Hall, Granville Stanley (1844-1924)** Early pioneer in and promoter of American psychology, a student of Wundt who founded and served as the first president of the American Psychological Association in 1892, while president of Clark University. He started the *American Journal of Psychology,* edited several other journals, and wrote books on individual differences, developmental psychology and other areas.

**hallucinate** To perceive an external stimulus in any sensory modality which has no basis in reality.

**hallucinatio hypochondriasis** An obsolete term for hypochondriasis.

**hallucination** The perception of an external object in any sensory modality, which arises within the individual himself, without any basis in reality.

**hallucination, auditory** A hallucination associated with sensations of hearing.

**hallucination, diminutive visual** See *hallucination, Lilliputian.*

**hallucination, elementary auditory** The hallucination of amorphous noises such as murmurs, knocks and shooting.

**hallucination, extracampine** A hallucination which is localized outside of the normal range of perception for the organ.

**hallucination, genital** The hallucination of being the victim of obscenity.

**hallucination, gustatory** The hallucination of sensations of taste.

**hallucination, haptic** A hallucination associated with sensations of touch.

**hallucination, hypnagogic** A hallucination occurring between the stage of wakefulness and sleep, usually recognized as an unreal perception.

**hallucination, induced** A hallucination evoked in a person by another person.

**hallucination, Lilliputian** The visual hallucination of objects which appear greatly reduced in size.

**hallucination, macroptic** The visual hallucination of objects which appear greatly increased in size.

**hallucination, memory** A visual image of previously repressed material.

**hallucination, microptic** See *hallucination, Lilliputian.*

**hallucination, motor** See *hallucination, psychomotor.*

**hallucination, negative** The failure to see an object when looking at it.

**hallucination, negative memory** The denial of an event which one has experienced.

**hallucination, olfactory** The hallucination of sensations of smell.

**hallucination, psychic** The hallucination of mental events.

**hallucination, psychomotor** The hallucination that certain parts of a person's body are moving or being moved.

**hallucination, psycho-sensorial** Hallucinations involving both mental events and the sensory organs.

**hallucination, reflex** A hallucination in one sensory area resulting from the stimulation of another sensory organ.

**hallucination, retroactive** See *hallucination, memory.*

**hallucination, slow motion** The hallucination that one is moving very slowly while everything around is accelerated.

**hallucination, space-motor** The sensation that one is moving at an accelerated pace.

**hallucination, teleologic** A hallucination in which the person is directed as to what course he should take.

**hallucination, unilateral** A hallucination involving only one side of the sensory apparatus.

**hallucination, vestibular** False sensory perceptions

resulting from the impairment of the vestibular apparatus which are usually restricted to visual and haptic hallucinations.

**hallucination, visual** A hallucination involving vision.

**hallucinatory game** See *game, hallucinatory.*

**hallucinatory image** A mental image which is mistaken for reality.

**hallucinatory neuralgia** See *neuralgia, hallucinatory.*

**hallucinosis** The state of having recurrent hallucinations.

**hallucinosis, acute** The sudden manifestation of hallucinations as a result of alcohol or drug intoxication or a traumatic event, which ceases within a period of weeks.

**hallucinosis, alcoholic** Hallucinatory states caused by alcohol with the exclusion of delirium tremens, Korsakov's psychosis, and alcoholic deterioration. The hallucinations are usually auditory and threatening to the affected alcoholic.

**hallucinosis, diabetic** Hallucinations occurring in diabetic individuals.

**hallucinosis, uremic** Hallucinations occurring in individuals with kidney disease.

**halo** 1. A ring of light around an object. 2. Honor and glory with which a famous or beloved person is endowed.

**halo effect** See *effect, halo.*

**halving method** See *method, halving.*

**hamartophobia** Fear of sin.

**Hamilton, Gilbert Van Tassel (1877-1943)** American psychiatrist and psychobiologist. Pioneered research on frustration with inter-species comparisons, and developed the first sophisticated theory of objective psychopathology (diagnosis and treatment) based on behavioral principles of learning and frustration rather than mentalistic ones of dissociation and the unconscious. His later research on marriage began the integration of psychoanalytic and learning theories of personality development.

**hammer** See *malleus.*

**Hampstead Baby Profile** An instrument introduced by W. E. Freud in 1967 to assess the development of infants up to about six months of age, based on reports and home observations of the development of infants from the Well-Baby Clinic, a department of the Hampstead Child Therapy Clinic in Hampstead, England.

**Hampstead Index** A system of classification of the data of analytic hours introduced in 1955 by workers from the Hampstead Child Therapy Clinic in Hampstead, England, to provide more readily accessible analytic material for research, teaching and reference purposes. The original categories were evolved from a pilot study of fifty cases which were in daily analysis at the clinic.

**Hampton Court Maze** See *maze, Hampton Court.*

**hand test** See *test, hand.*

**hand-to-mouth reaction** A reaction of bringing all objects within reach of the hand to the mouth, observed in infants until approximately twelve months of age.

**handedness** Preferential use of one hand over the other.

**handicap** A disadvantage which prevents the individual from achieving success of some desired goal.

**handicap, collective life** A term used in social work referring to a person's handicap which interferes with his interpersonal relations.

**handicap, family life** A term used in social work referring to a person's handicap which interferes with his role in marriage.

**handicap, perceptual** A term for neurological dysfunction involving the higher mental functions emphasizing that the perceptual processes are involved in brain damage whether it relates to specific perceptual areas or to the person's perceptual organization in the environment.

**handicraft** Art or craft used as a means of therapeutic treatment.

**handwriting scale** See *scale, handwriting.*

**Hanfman-Kasanin Concept Formation Test** See *test, Hanfman-Kasanin Concept Formation.*

**haphalgesia** The experience of the sensation of pain upon touching an object.

**haphephobia** Fear of being touched.

**haploid** The chromosome number of a normal gamete which contains only one member of each chromosome pair. In man, the haploid number is 23.

**haploidy** The condition of having half the number of chromosomes present in somatic cells.

**haplology** The omission of syllables in words because of rapidity of speech.

**haptephobia** See *haphephobia.*

**haptic** Referring to the cutaneous sensory system.

**haptics** The investigation of the cutaneous sensory system.

**haptometer** An instrument for measuring sensitivity of touch.

**hard colors** Reds and yellows, the colors which separate most easily from the gray field of equal saturation and luminosity.

**hard-of-hearing** Having defective auditory acuity which can be improved by the use of a hearing aid.

**harelip** A cleft of the upper lip caused by a failure in the complete development of the fetus in the first eight to ten weeks after conception.

**Harlow, Harry F. (1905- )** American psychologist,

creator of the learning set phenomenon and the cloth and wire surrogate mothers. Experimentally analyzed the various love or affectional systems giving proper and appropriate emphasis to the age-mate or peer system as contrasted to the other system, particularly the maternal. Published extensive studies on cortical localization of learning, curiosity and manipulation, the induction of depression by various experimental techniques and the experimental alleviation of induced psychopathology.

**harmavoidance need**  See *need, harmavoidance*.

**harmonic 1.** An overtone whose frequency of wave vibration is a multiple of the fundamental tone. **2.** Referring to the combination of simultaneous tones into chords.

**harmonic analysis**  The resolution of a complex wave into its sine and cosine components by the use of Fourier's law or a harmonic analyzer.

**harmonic mean**  See *mean, harmonic*.

**harmony 1.** The combination of parts into a congruous whole. **2.** Good, friendly relations among people. **3.** The combination of tones into chords which are arranged to yield a congruous whole in music.

**harp theory of hearing**  See *hearing, theory of: resonance theory*.

**harpaxophobia**  Fear of robbers.

**harria**  (R. B. Cattell) A factor trait referring to assertive, decisive, realistic behavior.

**Harrower inkblots**  (M. R. Harrower-Erickson and M. E. Steiner) The Rorschach inkblot test adapted for assessing groups. The cards are projected on a screen in front of the subjects who write down what they see. They then locate their responses on diagrams of the blots and add any additional information about their responses which will help the examiner score them. Instructions are given before each step to ensure that all of the information is obtained.

**harshness 1.** A quality of sounds due to an irregular wave form. **2.** A personality characteristic manifested by the lack of sympathetic understanding of others, an unpleasant manner and abrupt speech.

**Hartley, David (1705-1757)**  British physician and philosopher, influenced by Newton, founder of British Associationism; endeavored to integrate philosophy with anatomy, physiology, and physics; based his system of physiological psychology on association. Chief work: *Observations on Man* (1749).

**Hartmann, Heinz (1894-1970)**  Was among the second generation of European psychoanalysts who sought to develop further some aspect of Freudian theory. His *Ego Psychology and the Problem of Adaptation* (1939), regarded as a landmark not only in development of psychoanalysis but in the relationships of the schools, was well received by Anna Freud, and exerted influence in Europe and America. Hartmann revised the concept of the ego, freeing it in part from its dependence on the id.

Further investigation of the problem of the ego appeared justified in view of the fluctuation of Freud's thought on the role of the ego and his own warning not to draw sharp dividing lines between ego, superego, and id, but rather to allow "what we have separated to merge again." Today ego psychology is a central issue in psychoanalytical theory.

**Hartmann, von E. (1842-1906)**  A German philosopher known for his introduction of the unconscious as a critical mental factor, for his opposition of the mechanistic materialism of his time and for his justification of philosophical pessimism which formed a bridge to the more extreme views of pessimism and nihilism of the twentieth century.

**Hartnup disease**  A very rare aminoaciduria associated with mental retardation.

**hashish**  See *cannabis*.

**hate 1.** An enduring character trait consisting of anger, aversion and the desire to hurt the other person. **2.** See *Thanatos*.

**haut mal**  Grand mal epileptic attack; seizure.

**Hawthorne experiment**  A study conducted at the Hawthorne Works of the Western Electric Company which pointed out the existence of implicit, informal group norms which affect the behavior of members in a group as opposed to explicitly stated rules which may not be adhered to by the members.

**Hawthorne studies**  A pioneering series of studies started in 1927 and continuing into the early 1930's done at the Western Electric Company by Elton May, F. J. Roethlisberger, W. J. Dickson, and their associates. The studies showed the importance of the human quality and demonstrated that work efficiency was not just the product of physical or economic conditions. They led to seeing the importance of employee attitudes, a change to the indirect from the direct method of interviewing, the introduction of personal counseling and the awareness of the intricacies of social organization.

**headache, lead-cap**  The sensation that the head is splitting or that one has a heavy weight or constriction around the head.

**headache, migraine**  A headache of organic or psychological etiology characterized by periodic attacks, prodromal disturbances and pain. The physiological mechanisms underlying pain seem to involve the vascular stretching of the cerebral and cranial arteries resulting from vasodilation. Ergot and its derivatives offers relief. Migraines often occur in people who are hostile and envious of intellectually superior people.

**head-banging**  Uncontrolled physical movements characteristic of a young child in a temper tantrum.

**head-knocking**  Hitting the head against the wall or other objects seen in some infants and children.

**head-rolling**  Semicircular movements of the head manifested by some infants before going to sleep.

**health-conscience**  (R. H. Jokl) The transformation

of an unconscious sense of guilt into a conscious repudiation of the illness or symptom and alliance with ego attitudes which are healthy.

**Healy Picture Completion Test**  See *test, Healy Picture Completion.*

**hearing**  The perception of sounds through the auditory sensory apparatus.

**hearing, color**  The syncretic sensation of seeing colors when sounds are heard.

**hearing loss**  The degree of loss of the capacity to hear tones at particular frequencies, expressed in relative terms of the percentage of normal hearing or in absolute terms of decibals of loudness.

**hearing, monaural**  Hearing with one ear.

**hearing theories**  1. Theories which attempt to explain how physical sound vibrations give rise to the neural impulses of hearing. There are five major theories: resonance theories, frequency theories, volley theories, hydraulic theories, and sound-pattern theories. 2. See *hearing, theory of: resonance theory.* 3. See *hearing, theory of: frequency theory.* 4. See *hearing, theory of: volley theory.* 5. See *hearing, theory of: hydraulic theory.* 6. See *hearing, theory of: sound-pattern theory.*

**hearing, theory of: frequency theory**  (E. Rutherford) The theory that the basilar membrane responds as a whole to aural stimuli, then transmits the stimuli to the brain for analysis.

**hearing, theory of: hydraulic theory**  (H. Meyer) The theory that hearing is dependent on the amount of basilar membrane involved in the sensation of different tones.

**hearing, theory of: resonance theory**  (H. von Helmholtz) The theory that pitch is determined by the place on the basilar membrane which is stimulated, the short fibers being sensitive to high pitched sounds, the long fibers to the low-pitched sounds and the fibers in the middle of the membrane being attuned to sounds of medium pitch. Also known as the piano theory, place theory and harp theory.

**hearing, theory of: sound-pattern theory**  The theory that the sense of hearing is dependent on the pattern of vibration on the basilar membrane.

**hearing, theory of: volley theory**  (E. G. Wener and C. W. Bray) The theory that nerve fibers of the basilar membrane respond in groups or volleys, not in unison resulting in more transmission of aural impulses.

**heart neurosis**  See *neurosis, cardiovascular.*

**heart rate**  Rate of ventricular contractions per minute.

**heat**  1. A sensation experienced when the receptors for warm and cold are stimulated simultaneously. 2. See *estrus.*

**heavy metal poisoning**  See *poisoning, lead; poisoning, arsenic; poisoning, mercury; poisoning, thallium; poisoning, barium.*

**Hebb, D.O.**  (1904-  ) Canadian psychologist and author of a neurological theory of thinking. Showed that the development of intelligence and personality in the infant, and normal mental function at maturity, depend on environmental stimulation; "sensory deprivation" results in gross disorders of behavior.

**Hebb's theory of perceptual learning**  (D. O. Hebb) A theory of learning based on the postulation of groups of sensory and motor neurons which work together called cell assemblies. The theory states that perception leads to the formation of interconnections between neural pathways which subsequently act as a unit. Separate assemblies can become coordinated to form a phase sequence which on the perceptual level enables an individual to perceive elements of a whole as a totality. The cell assemblies can undergo changes through fractionation, the loss of synchronization of neurons with the assembly or recruitment, the joining of neurons to the assembly. Learning is believed to result from facilitation established in which one or a group of assemblies facilitates the oncoming of some other units. When something has been learned, one stimulus sets off established phase sequences. In higher organisms, missing elements in a perceived totality do not alter the whole because of the ability to generalize and abstract.

**hebephrenia**  One of the main schizophrenic syndromes. See *schizophrenia, hebephrenic.*

**hebephrenia, engraffed**  (E. Kraepelin) Hebephrenia which is superimposed on an already existing disorder.

**hebephrenic, depressive**  A form of hebephrenia characterized by cycles of depression.

**hebephrenic, manic**  A form of hebephrenia characterized by cycles of mania.

**hebephrenic schizophrenia**  See *schizophrenia, hebephrenic.*

**hebetic**  Referring to puberty, specifically to mental illness during adolescence.

**hebetude**  1. Emotional apathy. 2. Lack of affect or interest exhibited through apathy, dullness, listlessness and indifference to surroundings and usually associated with schizophrenia. 3. Apathy and dullness from any cause.

**hebetudinous**  Characterized by hebetude.

**hebetudo animi**  Imbecility.

**hebetudo mentis**  Imbecility.

**heboid praecox**  See *praecox, heboid.*

**heboidophrenia**  (K. L. Kahlbaum) Obsolete term referring to simple form of schizophrenia.

**Hecker, Ewald**  (1843-1909) German psychiatrist who coined the term hebephrenia.

**hederiform terminations**  Free nerve endings in the skin which serve as sensory end organs for pain.

**hedonia**  Pleasure, enjoyment.

**hedonic**  1. Referring to the feeling of pleasure. 2. Referring to the dimension pleasure-unpleasure.

**hedonism** 1. The psychological principle that the person acts to gain pleasure and avoid pain. 2. The philosophical doctrine which states that pleasure or happiness is the goal of conduct.

**hedonophobia** Fear of pleasure.

**heel-to-knee test** See *test, heel-to-knee.*

**Heidbreder, Edna (1890-   )** American psychologist. Author of *Seven Psychologies* and papers on schools and systems of psychology; co-author (with D. G. Paterson, R. M. Elliott, D. Anderson, H. Toops) of *The Minnesota Mechanical Ability Tests*; constructed scales for measuring introversion–extraversion and inferiority attitudes which were among the first instruments available for the quantitative treatment of traits of personality; identified 'participant' and 'spectator' behavior in an experiment on thinking; conducted a series of experiments on concept-attainment in which that phrase was first defined and used as a technical psychological term.

**Heidegger, Martin (1889-   )** German philosopher significant for existential psychology and psychiatry. Influenced by Edmund Husserl and Sören Kierkegaard. Taught that only man, of all beings, is aware of his existence and that he realizes his existence is not his making or his choice. Discovering his life oriented toward inescapable death, man experiences dread and anguish. He tries to overcome this by conforming to conventional modes of thinking, acting, and speaking. Such camouflages produce a feeling of guilt. Heidegger insisted that only by accepting the inevitability of death and nothingness can man have authentic existence and be truly free. The Swiss psychiatrist, Ludwig Binswanger, elaborated and applied this concept to the field of psychotherapy. Author of *Being and Time* (1927), *What is Metaphysics?* (1929), and a *Postscript* (1947).

**Heidelberg man** The primitive man reconstructed from the jaw dated in the early Middle Pleistocene age which was found in 1907 near Heidelberg, Germany.

**Heinis constant** A measure of the rate of mental growth computed by translating mental age units into values on a scale having theoretically equal mental growth units and dividing the result by chronological age.

**Heinis law of mental growth** The principle that intelligence increases with age according to the following formula:

$$y = 429(1 - e^{\frac{CA}{6.675}})$$

where $y$ = attained intelligence, $e$ = the base of the natural logarithm, and $CA$ = chronological age.

**Hejna test** See *test, Hejna.*

**helicord** 1. Referring to a spiral shape. 2. A warped surface produced by a straight line moving so as to cut or touch a fixed helix.

**helicotrema** The opening which connects the scala vestibuli with the scala tympani in the spinal canal of the cochlea.

**heliocentric theory**  The theory that the sun is the center of the universe.

**heliophobia** Fear of sunlight.

**heliotropism** An orienting movement toward the source of light.

**helix** The curved part of the outer ear.

**Heller's disease** See *dementia infantilis.*

**Hellwag's vowel triangle** A graphic description of the interrelationship of vowel sounds:

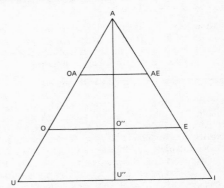

**helmet, neurasthenic** A feeling of pressure over the cranium characteristic of certain cases of neurasthenia.

**Helmholtz, Hermann Ludwig Ferdinand von (1821-1894)** German scholar, physicist, physiologist and psychologist who proposed the principle of conservation of energy, first measured the speed of the neural impulse, and did pioneer work in hearing, vision and perception. Formulated an influential place theory of pitch perception and three-cone theory of color vision. A scientific materialist, he held that perception is a matter of unconscious inference.

**helper, magic** (E. Fromm) A neurotic form of interpersonal relations in which one member endows the other member with omnipotent illusory power in the hope of obtaining security, support, and escape from frightening feelings of isolation.

**helping, mania for** A morbid need to participate in every action in order to gain an advantage for oneself.

**helplessness, psychic** (S. Freud) The experience of the young infant when he is in a dangerous situation in which he cannot gratify his needs which is the prototype for all later experiences of anxiety.

**Helson, Harry (1898-   )** American psychologist, author of the theory of adaptation-level, has worked in psychophysics, sensory processes, perception, color vision, human factors in design of equipment, and other areas. Known also for Helson-Judd effect, reformulation of the Weber-Fechner law and theory of time-order effects (with Michels), and for studies of reversal of classical lightness contrast (von Bezold assimilation). His first major contribution, appearing in journal articles and later in book form, served to introduce Gestalt psychology to English readers. His most recent work, a study of the effects of spectral energy of light sources and chromaticity of backgrounds on pleasantness of object color is the most extensive study in the field of aesthetics of color. See *adaptation-level theory; color conversion; the U-hypothesis; assimiliation and contrast.*

**hemathidrosis** The elimination of blood pigments through the glands of the skin.

**hemeralopia** 1. Day blindness. 2. Night blindness.

**hemeralopsia** See *hemeralopia.*

**hemeraphonia** The loss of the voice during the day characteristic of hysteria.

**hemianaesthesia** A lack of sensitivity in one half of the body.

**hemianalgesia** A lack of pain in one half of the body.

**hemianopia; hemiopia** Unilateral or bilateral blindness in one side of the visual field.

**hemianopsia, heteronymous** Bitemporal loss of vision.

**hemianopsia, homonymous** Loss of vision in the left or right visual field of both eyes.

**hemianthropia** Insanity.

**hemiballism** Violent repeated movements, shaking and twisting of one side of the body resulting from a brain lesion on the opposite side of the body.

**hemichorea** Chorea in which the convulsive movements affect only one side of the body.

**hemichorea, hysterical** Hemichorea caused by hysteria.

**hemichorea, paralytic** Hemichorea occurring with hemiplegia.

**hemichorea, post-hemiplegic** Hemichorea which occurs following an attack of hemiplegia.

**hemichorea, preparalytic** Hemichorea which occurs before an attack of hemiplegia.

**hemichorea, rheumatica** Hemichorea occurring concomitant with rheumatism.

**hemichorea, syphilitic** Hemichorea caused by syphilis.

**hemicrania** 1. Migraine. 2. Pain occurring on one side of the head. 3. Partial anencephalia.

**hemiopia** See *hemianopia.*

**hemiparesis** Paresis of one side of the body.

**hemiplegia** Paralysis of one side of the body.

**hemiplegia cruciata** Paralysis of an upper extremity and a lower extremity of the opposite side.

**hemiplegic gait** See *gait, hemiplegic.*

**hemispheres** The two symmetrical halves into which the cerebrum is divided.

**hemispherical dominance** The tendency of one side of the body to control bodily movements resulting in laterality.

**hemophilus influenzae meningitis** See *meningitis, hemophilus influenzae.*

**hemophobia** Fear of blood.

**hemoptysis, hysterical** The spitting of blood caused by a psychic disorder.

**hemorrhagic arsphenamine encephalitis** See *encephalitis, hemorrhagic arsphenamine.*

**hemothymia** Morbid impulse for blood and murder.

**Henle, Mary (1913-    )** American psychologist. Investigated substitution and other problems of topological psychology. (With MacKinnon) wrote an early laboratory manual in psychodynamics. Edited two volumes of papers on Gestalt psychology. Showed that deductive reasoning does not violate the rules of inference and conducted other studies of cognitive processes. Undertook studies in the history of psychology and systematic analyses of current theories.

**hepatic** Referring to the liver.

**hepatolenticular degeneration** See *Wilson's disease.*

**Herbart, Johann Friedrich (1776-1841)** German philosopher-psychologist, pioneer of quantitative psychology and, according to some, the first educational psychologist. Developed a mathematical theory of how ideas compete for a place in consciousness. His pedagogy was based on the concept of the *apperceptive mass,* the ideas presently in consciousness that determine its receptivity to new ideas.

**Herbartian psychology** (J. F. Herbart) A mechanistic version of the associationist psychology which emphasizes the competitiveness of ideas to reach consciousness. The central thesis of this system is the doctrine of apperception according to which new ideas must be related to a previously acquired mass of ideas, the apperceptive mass, before they can be understood.

**herbivorous** 1. Plant-eating. 2. (T. Bryant) A body type characterized by an athletic build.

**Herculeus morbus** Obsolete term for epilepsy.

**herd instinct** The tendency in certain animals to congregate in flocks or herds.

**hereditarianism** The point of view which emphasizes the importance of heredity in determining behavioral traits.

**hereditary; hereditarial** Referring to the mechanism of transmitting traits from generation to generation and to the characteristics to which one is predisposed resulting from the working of this mechanism.

**hereditary predispostion** An inborn tendency toward a particular disorder whose development depends on environmental influence.

**heredito-constitutional** Aspects of an organism's constitution which reflect the genotype.

**heredity** The process of transmitting characteristics from the progenitor to the offspring which is a function of genes found in chromosomes in the nucleus of each cell. These chromosomes are made of deoxyribonucleic acid (DNA) which contains a code determining particular characteristics of an organism. Hereditary transmission is restricted to the action of the sex cells, the sperm and ova, which fuse to form the new organism.

**heredity, polygenic** Heredity involving many different genes which are expressed in one phenotype.

**hereism** The existence of virtue, goodness and morality in the role of wife and mother named after Hera, the wife of Zeus.

**Hering, Ewald (1834-1918)** Physiologist at Prague who proposed an influential three-cone opponent-process theory of color vision. The cold colors (green, blue and black) result in anabolism, the warm (red, yellow and white) in catabolism of the photo-chemical substance in the retinal cones. Inventor of research apparatus and contributor to the psychology of memory.

**Hering illusion** See *illusion, Hering.*

**Hering's after-image** The positive afterimage perceived following a brief bright stimulus of the same hue and saturation as the original.

**Hering's grays** A set of fifty gray papers ordered from extreme white to extreme black in subjectively equal steps.

**Hering's theory of color vision** See *color vision, theory of: Hering theory.*

**Hering's window** An apparatus used to obtain colored contrast effects. This is a double window with a gray opening and another opening for a colored glass. Any intensities of the lights from the two halves of the window can be controlled by slides to eliminate brightness effects. Objects seen through this apparatus are of the same or complementary color depending on the color of the glass in the opening of the window.

**heritable** Inheritable.

**heritable variation** The variation existing in a species which is transmitted by the genes.

**heritage** 1. Characteristics transmitted biologically from generation to generation. 2. Social customs, traditions and mores transmitted from generation to generation.

**hermaphrodite** A bisexual (or ambisexual) individual. Such an individual has the external genital organs (penis or vagina) of one sex and the inner reproductive structure, and/or the gonads, and/or sex chromatin pattern of the other. In some cases the individual possesses genital organs of both sexes.

**hero-birth, primordial image of** (C. G. Jung) Source of the dream symbol of the individuality of a person on an unconscious level.

**hero-worship** (psychoanalysis) The tendency of people to seek another person to admire and to submit to as a prototype of the father whom they need and long for.

**heroimania** Morbid passion for heroin.

**heroin** A narcotic derivative of morphine which was formerly used as a sedative. Its manufacture or importation into the United States is presently prohibited due to the high danger of addiction and damage to mental and physical health.

**herpes simplex encephalitis** See *encephalitis, herpes simplex.*

**Herpes zoster** A skin eruption characteristic of inflammation of spinal or cranial ganglia of sensory nerves.

**Herring revision** A 1922 revision of the Simon-Binet intelligence test which was used as an alternate in place of the 1916 Stanford scale.

**Hertwig-Magendie phenomenon** (O. Hertwig and F. Magendie) A downward and inward deviation of the eyeball on one side and an upward and outward rotation of the eyeball on the opposite side sometimes charactertistic of a cerebellar lesion.

**hertz (hz)** Cycles per second; a specification of energy in waves, usually used for auditory stimuli.

**hetaera; hetera** Mistress, concubine.

**hetaerism** Referring to a common law marriage.

**heterocentric** Directed toward others, away from oneself.

**heterochrony** 1. A difference in the speed between two processes. 2. A difference in the time of development of an organ from the norm. 3. A difference in the chronaries of functionally related tissue parts.

**heterodox** 1. Referring to opinions and beliefs which differ from those which are generally accepted. 2. Characterizing a person who holds such beliefs.

**heteroerotic** Referring to sexual interest for persons other than oneself.

**heteroerotism** Sexual interest in persons other than oneself, especially of the opposite sex.

**heterogamous** Referring to the differences in the male and female gamete.

**heterogeneity; heterogeny** Referring to differences and dissimilarities of objects in organisms.

**heterogeneous; heterogenous** Characterized by heterogeneity.

**hetero-hypnosis** Hypnosis effected by one person on another.

**heterolalia** See *heterophemy.*

**heteromorphosis** The development of an organ or a part of an organ abnormal to the site after the removal of the original organ.

**heteronomous super-ego** See *super-ego, heteronomous.*

**heteronomy** 1. (A. Angyal) Referring to activities whose source is outside the self. 2. Referring to the direction of one person by another.

heteronymous hemianopsia  See *hemianopsia, heteronymous.*

heterophasia  See *heterophemy.*

heterophemy  The unconscious unintended substitution of words for the desired ones.

heterophilic  Characterized by interest in the opposite sex.

heterophonic  An abnormal change of voice.

heterophoria  Deviation of one eye from the correct position necessary for binocular vision resulting from a muscular imbalance.

heterorexia  Morbid appetite.

heteroscendasticity  Referring to a matrix in which the arrays have significantly different standard deviations.

heterosexual  Referring to attraction for members of the opposite sex.

heterosexual nymphomania  See *nymphomania, heterosexual.*

heterosexuality  1. Attraction for persons of the opposite sex. 2. A developmental level characterized by attraction for the opposite sex or the occurrence of sexual intercourse between members of the opposite sex. 3. The occurrence of sexual intercourse between members of the opposite sex.

heterosis  An increase in growth and a healthier development manifested by first-generation hybrids.

heterosociality  Social relationships with people of the opposite sex.

heterosomal  Referring to the sex chromosome.

heterosome  The chromosome which carries sex determinants.

hetero-suggestibility  The influence of one person over another.

hetero-suggestion  Suggestion which originates in another person.

heterotopia  1. The occurrence of an organ or part of an organ in an unnatural location. 2. The congenital development of gray matter of the spinal cord in the white matter area.

heterotropia  See *strabismus.*

heterozygosis  Having one or more heterozygous pairs of genes resulting from crossbreeding.

heterozygosity  See *heterozygousness.*

heterozygote  An individual who has two different alleles at a given locus on a pair of homologous chromosomes. Adjective: heterozygous.

heterozygotic, heterozygous  Referring to heterozygote.

heterozygousness  Refers to the condition of heterozygosis.

heuristic method  Method which leads to the discovery of new thinking and investigation.

Heymans' law  (C. Heymans) The law relating the threshold value of a stimulus to a simultaneously occurring inhibitory stimulus by the equation: $T_a = T_O + K_a$ where $T_O$ is the threshold of a given stimulus, $T_a$ is the threshold of the stimulus when it is raised by the occurrence of a second stimulus of intensity $x$ and $K_a$ is the coefficient of inhibition which is different in different modalities and with different individuals.

hibernation  1. The state of sleep during the winter characteristic of many animals. 2. A type of therapy using high dosages of chlorpromazine to produce prolonged sleep with a lowered body temperature.

hibernation of ament  The loss of intellectual energy during the winter characteristic of imbecility.

hiccup, hysterical  Hiccough due to mental causes.

hidden-clue test or situation  A test requiring the subject to discover which aspect of the situation will lead to a reward.

hidden figure  See *embedded figure.*

hidden self  The dissociated aspect of the personality.

hierarchy correlation  See *correlation, hierarchy.*

hierarchy of habits  See *habit hierarchy.*

hieroglyphics  A form of writing in which the symbols are pictures designating the word which is represented.

hieromania  Mania for religion.

hieronosus  (Linnaeus) Epilepsy.

hierophobia  Fear of religious things.

high-grade defective  See *defective, high-grade.*

higher centers; higher brain centers  1. Centers of the brain making up the cerebrum. 2. Centers of the brain concerned with complex functions such as learning, memory and intelligence.

higher level skills  (R. H. Seashore) Work technique applicable to a variety of concrete tasks rather than a particular one.

higher mental processes  See *mental processes, higher.*

higher mental processes, organization of  See *mental processes, higher, organization of.*

higher-order conditioning  See *conditioning, higher-order.*

higher response unit  1. A group of stimuli treated as a single stimulus. 2. A complex act formed by integrating simpler acts.

Hilgard, Ernest R(opiequet) (1904-   )  American psychologist and educator, known primarily for his earlier work on conditioned responses and theories of learning and his later work on experimental studies of hypnosis. His general position is a broadly heuristic one, often known in America as functional psychology. The position is represented in his general textbook of psychology and in his occasional writings on education, psychoanalysis, and social problems. See *conditioned responses; functionalism; learning theory; educational psychology;* and *hypnosis.*

**hindbrain** The part of the brain made up of the cerebellum, pons and medulla.

**Hipp chronoscope** (M. Hipp) A clock developed in 1842 and used in reaction-time experiments capable of recording time-intervals of 1/1000 of a second.

**hippanthropy** The belief that one is a horse.

**hippocampus** A large nuclear mass consisting of gray matter lying in the floor of the inferior horn of the lateral ventricle.

**hippus** Independent spasmotic pupillary motion.

**hircine** Pertaining to a cheese-like smell.

**histidinemia** A rare aminoaciduria associated with mental retardation.

**histogram** A graphic representation of a frequency distribution in the form of rectangular bars whose width is equal to the interval of the class and whose height reflects the number of cases in each class.

**histology** The branch of biology which deals with the study of the structure of tissues.

**historical method** (G. W. Allport) The study of individuals by tracing their life events.

**histrionic personality disorder** See *hysterical character.*

**hit** (psychophysics) A correct detection of a stimulus by the subject.

**HIT** See *Holtzman Inkblot Technique.*

**Hitzig's girdle** (E. Hitzig) Insensitivity to pain at the level of the breast which is a sign of tabes dorsalis.

**hoarding orientation** (E. Fromm) A non-productive life style consisting of the proclivity toward keeping one's feelings, thoughts and possessions to oneself as a means of security.

**Hobbes, Thomas (1588-1679)** English philosopher who countered Descartes' doctrine of innate ideas and foreshadowed the thesis of the mind as the tabula rasa in his theory that sense experience forms the content of the mind.

**Hoch, Paul Kerry (1902-1964)** Hungarian born American neuropsychiatrist, specialized in psychosomatic medicine, community psychiatry and hospital adminstration; was a New York State Commissioner of Mental Health.

**hodological space** (K. Lewin) A psychological space which differs from Euclidian space in that direction between regions is important and because the distance between regions is determined by the dynamic qualities of the regions, not by the absolute measure.

**hodology** (K. Lewin) The science of vectors, paths and the direction, distance and force which these locomotions represent reflecting motivations and tensions which guide behavior.

**hodophobia** Fear of traveling.

**Hoffman (or Trommer's) sign** (J. Hoffman) The snapping of the index or ring finger which produces the flexion of the thumb is a sign of hemisplegia of organic origin.

**hog** A slang term for a heroin addict who progressively increases his dose.

**holergasia** (A. Meyer) A psychosis which disrupts the entire personality.

**holergasic, holergastic** Referring to holergasia.

**holism** (K. Goldstein) The principle that an organism is not equal to the sum of its parts and must be studied as a whole. Biological phenomena such as a living organism cannot be evaluated quantitatively but must be described in terms of their qualitative organizations. Increasing knowledge of separate, individual parts does not augment our understanding of the totality except by understanding these parts as expressions of the functioning of the organism as a whole.

**holistic psychology** (A. Maslow) Human beings are fundamentally good and healthy. A full healthy and normal development consists of actualizing oneself and fulfilling one's potentialities. Human needs and motives must be presented in a hierarchical order starting with the most powerful physiological needs such as hunger and thirst, then safety, belongingness, love, esteem, and cognitive and esthetic needs.

**holistic theory of intelligence** The principle that intelligence is a function of the cerebrum as a whole.

**holistic theory of personality** See *holism.*

**Holmes, Gordon, rebound phenomenon** See *rebound phenomenon of Gordon Holmes.*

**Holmgren test** See *test, Holmgren.*

**Holmgren wools** The differently colored skeins of wool used in a test for colorblindness.

**holograph** A document in the handwriting of the author.

**Holt, Robert R. (1917-  )** American psychologist. Developed methods of selecting psychiatric residents, and offered a resolution of the controversy over clinical vs. statistical prediction. Founded and directed (with G.S. Klein) a major center for experimental studies of psychoanalytic propositions (Research Center for Mental Health, NYU); developed a technique for objectively measuring adaptive and maladaptive regression (the primary process and its control) in Rorschach responses, dreams, and other verbal data, and applied it in studies of sensory deprivation, creativity, and LSD effects. Contributed to the clarification and critique of psychoanalytic and personality theories. Methodological and applied studies of personality assessment in clinical and social problems.

**Holtzman Inkblot Technique** (W. H. Holtzman) A projective test developed in 1961 consisting of forty-five inkblots plus two practice blots. The inkblots vary in color, symmetry, form and shading. The subject is asked to give one response to what he sees after which the examiner conducts a brief inquiry. There are two alternate forms allowing for the determination of test-retest rehability and the study of change within an individual. Factor analysis has shown that six variables are tapped: perceptual maturity and integrated ideational activity, perceptual sensitivity, psychopathology of thought, perceptual differentiation, inhibition or inability to perceive; and bodily preoccupation. The last three factors are not stable and differ according to the population tested.

**homeopathic principle**   See *principle, isopathic.*

**homeosis, homoeosis**   The development of an organ in an abnormal site.

**homeostasis**   The maintenance of equilibrium among the bodily processes.

**homeostatic systems**   **1.** Mechanisms which maintain a homeostatic balance. **2.** Physiological process which maintains internal stability in an organism whereby changes in the internal or external environment stimulate other processes to counteract these changes through a feedback mechanism. These mechanisms account for several aspects of innate behavior.

**homichlophobia**   Fear of fog.

**homicidomania**   A mania for killing.

**homilophobia**   **1.** Fear of sermons. **2.** A fear that people in a group will criticize one's appearance.

**homing**   The tendency and ability to return to the original home when removed to a distance characteristic of certain animal species.

**homocystinuria**   Mental deficiency recessively inherited, associated with ocular changes including subluxated lenses. Homocystine is excreted in urine.

**homoerotism, homoeroticism**   Erotic or libidinal feeling directed to a person of the same sex.

**homogametic**   Producing one kind of germ cells. Females have XX chromosomes and are homogametic.

**homogamous**   Evincing qualities of homogamy.

**homogamy**   **1.** Inbreeding in a genetically isolated group resulting in the development of similar traits among the members of the group. **2.** A similiarity in trait or traits among husband and wife.

**homogeneity; homogeny**   **1.** The quality of likeness found in a group of people, data, or objects. **2.** The measure of one single variable by items on a test.

**homogeneity, test for**   See *test of independence.*

**homogeneous reinforcement**   See *reinforcement, homogeneous.*

**homogenitality**   Interest in the genitals of the same sex; homosexuality.

**homology**   Correspondence of structure of organs but not necessarily of their function suggesting common ancestry.

**homonomy drive**   See *drive, homonomy.*

**homonymous hemianopsia**   See *hemianopsia, homonymous.*

**homoscedasticity**   A double-entry table possessing the characteristic of its entries having equal variability.

**homosexual impulses**   Sexual impulses directed toward a person of the same sex.

**homosexuality**   **1.** Sexual intercourse with a member of the same sex. **2.** Sexual feelings for a member of the same sex.

**homosociality**   Social relations with members of the same sex.

**homozygote**   An individual possessing a pair of identical alleles at a given locus on a pair of homologous chromosomes.

**Honi phenomenon**   The absence of the illusion effect of a distorted room in the Ames experiment when the subject is looking at a person whom he knows.

**horizontal-vertical illusion**   See *illusion, horizontal-vertical.*

**horme**   (W. McDougall) The urge to live which is the main purpose of all living organisms.

**hormic psychology**   (W. McDougall) A theory of psychology introduced in 1908 and subsequently modified, based on the three main assumptions that behavior is purposive, that each individual is endowed with certain purposeful behavioral tendencies called instincts and that the entire behavior is determined by these instincts or their derivatives called sentiments or tastes. The basic construct is horme, the purpose to survive, to live, characteristic of all living organisms. To account for the continuity of evolution, a continuity is postulated between inorganic and organic matter suggesting that some trace of mental structure exists in inorganic matter whose activity is also purposive. Instincts, the inherited psychophysical propensities to action, consist of three kinds of functions; cognitive and conative which can be altered by experience, and affective functions which are inherited and cannot be modified by experience. Acquired behavior, however, can be transmitted to the next generation through genes. Seven primary instincts are postulated, each accompanied by an invariable primary emotion: escape associated with fear, combat, and anger, curiosity and wonder, repulsion and disgust, self assertion and elation, self-abasement and subjection and the parental instinct whose primary affect is tender emotion.

**hormic theory**   (W. McDougall) See *hormic psychology.*

**hormone**   A chemical substance produced in one organ and transported by the blood to other cells of the body where it has a physiological regularity effect.

**hormone, adrenocorticotropic**   Secreted by the anterior pituitary gland. This hormone stimulates the adrenal cortex to secrete steroid hormones which in turn regulate the water balance and expenditure of energy.

**hormone, corticotropic**   A hormone secreted by

the anterior pituitary gland which controls the functioning of the adrenal cortex.

**hormones, adrenocortical** Hormones secreted by the adrenal cortex which regulates the water balance and expenditure of energy.

**hormones, sex** Hormones of the male and female which cause the development of secondary sexual characteristics, influence the threshold of arousal, and the emotional manifestations of the sexual drive. Their secretion is affected by the emotional state of the individual.

**Horn-Hellersberg Drawing Completion Test** See *test, Horn-Hellersberg Drawing Completion.*

**Horner's Law** The principle that red-green colorblindness is transmitted from male-to male through the female.

**Horner's syndrome** See *syndrome, Horner's.*

**Horney, Karen (1885-1953)** Psychiatrist and psychoanalyst. Born in Berlin of Norwegian father and Dutch mother. Taught at Berlin Psychoanalytic Institute (1920-1932). Came to U.S. (1932). After 15 years of practice, part of that time in Germany, in Chicago, and in New York, she switched from Freudian orthodoxy, forming her own group, the American Institute of Psychoanalysis. Challenging the biological assumption of Freudian theory, she developed a neo-Freudian approach, stressing social factors in development and functioning of personality. Author of *The Neurotic Personality of Our Time* (1937); *New Ways in Psychoanalysis* (1939); *Our Inner Conflicts* (1945); and *Neurosis and Human Growth* (1950).

**horopter** (optics) The locus of points on which two eyes fixate which are reflected on corresponding points in the two retinas.

**horoscope 1.** A graphic representation of the positions of planets and signs of the zodiac used to predict future events. **2.** The prediction of future events using such a diagram.

**hospital, day** A form of therapeutic facility introduced in the early 1930's which offers a full treatment program to patients who are well enough to remain at home for the night.

**hospitalism** (R. Spitz) A syndrome resulting from institutionalization in infancy with early separation from the mother characterized by a lag in mental and physical development, apathy, immobility, withdrawal reactions in the presence of strangers, frequent infections, cachexia, and sometimes death.

**hostility** The desire to harm another person.

**House-Tree-Person test** See *test, House-Tree-Person.*

**Hovland, Carl Iver (1912-1961)** Social psychologist (Yale). Collaborator with Hull in early studies of verbal learning. Research on communication and persuasion based on learning theory. Influential in organizational affairs in the social sciences nationally.

**Hoyt formula** (C. Hoyt) A formula for the computation of the reliability coefficient using analysis of

variance: $$r = 1 - \frac{V_r}{V_e} = \frac{V_e - V_r}{V_e}$$ where $V_r$ is the variance for the remainder sum of squares and $V_e$ is the variance for examinees.

**H-T-P test** See *test, House-Tree-Person.*

**hue** The perceived dimension of color which corresponds to the wave length of light which stimulates the retina.

**Hull, Clark Leonard (1884-1952)** American behavioristic psychologist. After early research on thinking, aptitude testing and hypnosis, he created a hypothetico-deductive theory of animal and human learning, in the form of a mathematically based "learning theory," which dominated research and theory in these fields for two decades from about 1930. Intellectual leader of the Yale Institute of Human Relations.

**Hull's Mathematico-Deductive Theory of Learning** (C.L. Hull) A theory of learning using mathematical equations, definitions and postulates to explain learning phenomena. The attempt is made to explain observable data in terms of neurophysiological events. Seventeen postulates and seventeen corollaries are presented. It is postulated that biological adaptation facilitates the survival of the organism and when this is not facilitated, the organism is in a state of need. When need is aroused, the organism acts to reduce the need. Behavior is thus goal directed toward the reduction of needs. Any behavior which reduces needs or drives $(S_1)$ is a reinforcer. Conditioning or learning will not occur without need reduction, or reinforcement. Under conditions of reinforcement, specific stimuli evoke specific responses called habits. When the reinforcing need is removed, when habits no longer lead to biological adaptation, they become inhibited, weakened or extinguished. The number of reinforcements strengthens the stimulus-response connection or habit strength $(_SH_R)$. The resulting response or reaction potential $(_SE_R)$ is a function of the Drive $(D)$ or $(S_D)$ and of the reinforcement, or habit strength $(_SH_R)$. In the absence of drive or habit strength, performance will not occur. Two types of inhibitions are postulated, reactive $(I_R)$ and conditioned $(_SI_R)$ inhibition. Reactive inhibition is the reaction of the organism to effort caused by fatigue, pain etc. The increase of this inhibition results in its conditioning producing $(_SI_R)$. In the absence of the goal stimulus or reinforcer, a component of the goal response can occur called the fractional anticipatory goal response $(R_G)$. This serves to explain expectant behavior.

**human engineering** An applied area of psychology and engineering which concerns itself with the design of the physical conditions, machines and other equipment in relation to human capabilities, learning capacities, efficiency and comfort.

**Hume, David (1711-1776)** Influential Scottish philosopher who wrote a major history of England. He argued that the apparent necessary connection between cause and effect may be an illusion produced by repeated contiguity of "cause" and "effect" in time and space.

**Humm-Wadsworth Temperament Scale** See *scale, Humm-Wadsworth Temperament.*

**humor** 1. A positive, pleasant emotional attitude. 2. Any liquid secretion. 3. A comical attitude or expression.

**humor, gallows** Psychiatric term for humorous behavior under conditions of impending death.

**hunger** 1. Desire for food. 2. (experimental) Operational definition of a bodily state in terms of the number of hours of food deprivation. 3. Aching sensations in the stomach region due to muscle contractions. 4. A craving for something one is deprived of.

**Hunt-Minnesota Test for Organic Brain Damage** See *test, Hunt-Minnesota, for Organic Brain Damage.*

**Hunter group** A mucopolysaccharidosis inherited in a sex-linked recessive manner; similar to Hurler's syndrome but affected children are not as severely retarded in motor or intellectual development.

**Huntington's chorea** (G. Huntington) A chronic, progressive hereditary disease which is characterized by irregular movements, disturbance of speech and gradually increasing impairment of intellectual functioning.

**Hurler's syndrome** A mucopolysaccharidosis carried by single recessive genes, characterized by short stature, unusual skeletal deformities, grotesque facial features, deafness, congenital heart disease, mental retardation, and sometimes clouding of the corneas.

**Hurst, Lewis Alfred (1911-    )** South African psychiatrist, whose main contributions have been in the areas of psychiatric genetics, electroencephalographic findings in schizophrenia, manic depressive psychosis, senility and the senile psychoses, and in transcultural psychiatry, notably psychopathology and attitudes to mental health in an urban Bantu group.

**Husserl, Edmund** Philosopher, born 1859, in Prossnitz, Mähren (now Prostejov, Moravia, Czechoslovakia) and died 1938 in Freiburg, Baden-Württemberg. Studied with Stumpf and Brentano and was for a short time an assistant to Weierstrass. Received Ph.D. in 1881. Taught as Privatdozent in Halle 1887-1901, as professor at Göttingen 1901-1916 and at Freiburg from 1916 until his forced retirement by the Nazis. His fundamental goal was a search for the "unshakable foundation of human knowledge." He distinguished sharply between psychology (an empirical science) and logic (an *a priori* science); between science (what is) and ethics (what ought to be); between philosophy viewed as an *a priori* discipline and viewed as historically relative. Paralleling the world of science is the *Lebenswelt,* the study of which is the first task of phenomenology. Husserl distinguished between an empirical and an *a priori* psychology. The former is concerned with the empirical ego and contents of thought of other persons; the latter is concerned with the transcendental ego, intentionality, and mental acts. For Husserl the primary goal is the description of pure intentionality. not objects-as-intended, Brentano's realistic position. Starting from a position near that of Stumpf and Brentano, he developed from a critical realism to a critical idealism. He strongly influenced Scheler, Heidegger, and Merleau-Ponty. Major works of interest to psychologists are: 1) *Die Idee der Phänomenologie: Vorlesungen* (1907) 2) *Cartesian Meditations* (1931) 3) *Die Krisis der Europäschen Wissenschaften und Die Transzendentale Phänomenologie* (1939–not completed at his death)

**hybrid** 1. The progeny of parents who belong to two different species. 2. The offspring of parents, one of whom has and one of whom lacks a particular unit character.

**hydraulic theory of hearing** See *hearing, theory of: hydraulic theory.*

**hydrocephalus** Enlargement of the cranium resulting from an excess of cerebrospinal fluid. Retardation is usually severe or profound.

**hydrocephaly** See *hydrocephalus.*

**hydrochloric acid** A strong acid present in gastric juices in a diluted form. Also called HCL.

**hydrodipsomania** Excessive thirst which occurs periodically.

**hydro-encephalocele** An aberration of brain development in which the brain cavity protruding from the skull connects with the cerebral ventricles.

**hydromyelia** A dilation of the central canal of the spinal cord associated with an increase of fluid in this canal due to tumors of cerebellum or injuries to the spinal chord or characterized by atrophy of the gray matter.

**hydromyelocele** The existence of an excess of fluid in the central canal of the spinal cord.

**hydrophobia** 1. Fear of water. 2. Rabies.

**hydrotherapy** Therapeutic treatment of disease using water administered internally or externally.

**hydroxyprolinemia** A rare aminoaciduria associated with mental retardation.

**hyelophobia** Fear of glass.

**hygiene, mental** The branch of hygiene dealing with the prevention of mental disorder and the preservation and maintenance of optimal modes of living and emotional health.

**hygrophobia** Morbid fear of moisture.

**hylephobia** Fear of forests.

**hypacusia** Partial impairment of hearing.

**hypalgia, hysterical** A decrease in the normal sensitivity of pain in various areas of the body of psychogenic origin. The insensitivity is a defense against repressed unconscious wishes which would cause anxiety if allowed to reach consciousness.

**hyperactive** Overactive.

**hyperacusia, hyperacuses** Supersensitivity of hearing.

**hyperadrenocorticism** A condition involving the overproduction of hormones of the adrenal cortex or the hyperfunctioning of the pituitary gland. It results in Cushing's syndrome.

**hyperalgesia** Excessive sensitivity to pain.

**hyperalgia** See *hyperalgesia.*

**hyperammonemia** A metabolic disorder associated with mental retardation and characterized by episodic vomiting, lethargy, stupor, decline of vision and microcephaly.

**hyperbilirubinemia, neonatal** A condition characterized by an excessive amount of bilirubin in the blood, often resulting in severe neurological involvement and severe psychological problems in the child.

**hypercalcemia** Excessive calcium in the blood causing suppression of CNS activity leading to coma.

**hypercathexis** The overcharge of psychic energy.

**hypercathexis, self** The overinvestment of psychic energy in oneself, seen in narcissistic individuals.

**hyperenesthesia** A feeling of extreme well-being.

**hyperepidosis** An excessive growth of a part of the body.

**hyperergasia** (A.Meyer) The manic, overactive state of manic-depressive psychosis.

**hyperesophoria** An upward and inward deviation of the eye due to a muscular imbalance.

**hyperesthesia** Excessive sensitivity especially to tactile stimuli.

**hyperexophoria** An upward and outward deviation of the eye due to a muscular imbalance.

**hyperfunction** Excessive functioning.

**hypergenitalism** Excessive development of the genital system.

**hyperglycemia** An excess of sugar in the blood commonly caused by diabetes mellitus. If untreated leads to diabetic acidosis and coma.

**hypergnosis, hypergnosia** The projection of inner conflicts onto the environment.

**hyperhistidinemia** A possibly hereditary metabolic disorder associated with mental retardation and characterized by speech defect.

**hyperinstrumental neurosis** See *neurosis, hyperinstrumental.*

**hyperinsulinism** An intermittent or continuous condition causing loss of consciousness caused by excessive production of insulin leading to hypoglycemia.

**hyperkinesis** Excessive movement or motor restlessness.

**hyperkinesthesia** Extreme sensitivity to sensations of the muscles, tendons and joints.

**hyperlogia** Excessive volubility of speech characteristic of excited psychotic states.

**hyperlysinemia** A rare aminoaciduria associated with mental retardation.

**hypermania** An extreme manic state characterized by excessive activity and excitement.

**hypermetropia** A condition of the eye in which incoming parallel light rays focus behind the retina due to an abnormal shortness of the eyeball or to subnormal refraction.

**hypermnesia** Unusual, exaggerated ability to remember.

**hyperopia** See *hypermetropia.*

**hyperorexia** Excessive desire for food.

**hyperosmia** Exaggerated sensitivity to odors.

**hyperphagia** Excessive eating. May be caused by diabetes mellitus or bilateral lesions in the ventromedial hypothalamus.

**hyperphasia** See *hyperlogia.*

**hyperphoria** An upward deviation of the eye due to a muscular imbalance.

**hyperpituitary constitution** See *constitution, hyperpituitary.*

**hyperplasia** Excessive multiplication of cells resulting in an increase in the size of tissues, organs, and bodily parts.

**hyperpnoea** Excessive rate of breathing.

**hyperprolinemia** A rare aminoaciduria associated with mental retardation.

**hyperprosexia** Exaggerated compulsive attention to a particular stimulus.

**hypersarcosinemia** A rare aminoaciduria associated with mental retardation.

**hypersexuality** An excessive need or existence of sexual activity.

**hypersomnia** Excessive sleepiness.

**hypersthenic** Referring to a condition marked by excessive lymphatic functioning and extreme tension and strength.

**hypertelorism** Excessive distance between two parts or organs.

**hypertension, essential** Chronic condition of high blood pressure without any discernible organic cause. The early phase of hypertension can be produced by emotional conflicts, physical work, and renal ischemia.

**hyperthymia** 1. Excessive sensitiveness. 2. Labile, excessive emotionality. 3. State of overactivity. 4. Extreme cruelty or recklessness.

**hyperthyroidism** A condition of excessive thyroid function characterized by an increased metabolic rate, restlessness and excitability and resulting in death if untreated.

**hypertonicity, hypertonia** Excessive state of tension in the muscles.

**hypertrophy** Excessive growth of an organ or tissue due to the multiplication of its cells.

hypervalinemia A rare aminoaciduria associated with mental retardation.

hypervectorial cathexis See *cathexis, hypervectorial.*

hypervectorial childhood neurosis See *neurosis, hypervectorial childhood.*

hypervectorial neurosis See *neurosis, hypervectorial.*

hypervectorial type See *type, hypervectorial.*

hypesthesia; hypaesthesia Impairment of sensitivity to tactile stimulation.

hyphedonia State in which diminution of pleasure sensations occurs in acts which normally give great pleasure.

hypnagogic Inducing sleep; pertaining to the beginning state of sleep.

hypnagogic imagery See *imagery, hypnagogic.*

hypnagogic intoxication See *intoxication, hypnagogic.*

hypnagogic phenomena See *phenomena, hypnagogic.*

hypnagogic reverie See *reverie, hypnagogic.*

hypnagogic visions See *imagery, hypnagogic.*

hypnalgia 1. Pain sensations occurring during sleep. 2. Pain occurring in dreams.

hypnenergia Obsolete term for somnambulism.

hypnic Pertaining to or causing sleep.

hypnoanalysis A form of psychotherapy combining psychoanalytic technique with hypnosis.

hypnobades Obsolete term referring to somnambulist.

hypnobadicus Obsolete term for, relating to, or affected by somnambulism.

hypnobains Obsolete term for somnambulism.

hypnobat Somnambulist; one who walks in his sleep.

hypnobatesis Obsolete term for somnambulism.

hypnobatia Obsolete term for somnambulism.

hypnocarcosis Deep state of sleep induced by hypnosis.

hypnocatharsis Free association while in a hypnotic state.

hypnodia Somnolence.

hypnodrama (J. L. Moreno and J. M. Enneis) A therapuetic technique used when the patient is under hypnosis of dramatizing the patient's conflict with the participation of the therapist or a professional actor in one of the roles.

hypnogenic Producing sleep or hypnosis.

hypnogenic spot See *spot, hypnogenic.*

hypnogenic zone See *spot, hypnogenic.*

hypnograph Instrument measuring physiological functions during sleep.

hypnoid Resembling hypnotic state or sleep.

hypnoidal Mild hypnotic state.

hypnolepsy Narcolepsy.

hypnology The science of hypnotism and sleep.

hypnonergia Obsolete term for somnambulism.

hypnopathy Narcolepsy.

hypnophobia Fear of falling asleep.

hypnophrenosis (C. H. Schutze) Pertaining to various types of sleep disturbance.

hypnopompic Pertaining to the state of awakening.

hypnosigenesis Hypnotic induction.

hypnosigenic Pertaining to hypnotic induction.

hypnosis An artificially induced sleep-like state characterized by increased suggestibility, decreased initiative and will to act on one's own, recollection of events not remembered in the normal state, and often amnesia for that which occurred while hypnotized. The hypnotic state may be superficial or deep depending on the subject's susceptibility. Anesthesia, paralysis and vaso-motor changes can be induced or removed under deep hypnosis. Hypnosis was first brought to psychologists' attention when A. Mesmer demonstrated his "animal magnetism" and "magnetic fluid." Though these concepts were rejected, suggestion and influencing others' minds were recognized as true phenomenon and named hypnotism by J. Braid, a British surgeon. Later, the French physician, A. Liebeault, published a book describing methods of treatment with the use of hypnosis. J. M. Charcot followed with proof that hysterical symptoms could be produced and removed by hypnotic suggestion. Hypnosis has been used in therapeutic treatment of neurotics since the time of S. Freud and J. Breuer.

hypnosis, catalyzing action of The use of hypnosis during various phases of psychotherapy for accelerating the recovery of unconscious material.

hypnosis, induction of The process by which a hypnotist hypnotizes a subject. One of several techniques such as verbal suggestion and/or mechanical or chemical aids may be used depending on the hypnotist's preference and skill, and on the subject's needs and susceptibility. Most techniques have in common the subject's fixation of attention to some small object and the reduction in usual sensory input and motor output through relaxation.

hypnosynthesis (J. H. Conn) A term for hypnotherapy which stresses its function in allowing the patient to view and evaluate his experience objectively and to understand his motives for his behavior.

hypnotherapy Psychotherapeutic treatment by means of hypnosis.

hypnotic 1. Pertaining to hypnosis. 2. A drug that induces sleep.

**hypnotism** The theory and practice of hypnosis.

**hypnotizability** Hypnotic susceptibility.

**hypoacusia** See *hypacusia.*

**hypoadrenal constitution** See *constitution, hypoadrenal.*

**hypoaffective type** See *type, hypoaffective.*

**hypoalgesia** Diminished sensibility to pain.

**hypobulia** Deficiency of will power.

**hypocalcemia** A disorder involving lowered calcium level in the blood. Associated with increased neuromuscular irritability leading to spasms. An idopathic form involves mental retardation.

**hypocathexis** The undercharge of psychic energy.

**hypocathexis, self** The underinvestment of psychic energy in oneself resulting from object hypercathexis.

**hypochondria** Hypochondriasis.

**hypochondriasis** An exaggerated and morbid concern with one's health often focused on a single organ and accompanied by the belief that one is plagued by serious bodily illnesses. It may occur as a specific neurosis or in association with other neurotic disorders.

**hypochondrophthisis** A rarely used term for body atrophy in hypochondriasis.

**hypochoresis** Defecation.

**hypodermic** 1. Referring to the area under the skin. 2. Placed under the skin. 3. An injection given beneath the skin. 4. The syringe used in a hypodermic injection.

**hypoergasia** Depressive stage in manic depressive psychosis.

**hypoevolutism** Inadequate morphological, physiological and psychological development. Term may pertain to either specific or general functions.

**hypofunction** Diminished function or activity.

**hypogenitalism** Various types of deficient genital development.

**hypoglossal nerve** See *nerve, hypoglossal.*

**hypoglossal nucleus** Mass of cell bodies in the lower medulla in which the hypoglossal nerve originates.

**hypoglycemia** Condition caused by low level of glucose in the blood due to excessive utilization of sugar or to interference with the formation of sugar in the blood. In newborns, symptoms may include tremors, cyanosis, seizures, respiratory problems and eye rolling. Later in life, symptoms associated with hypoglycemia are nervousness, profuse sweating and dizziness. There is an approximately 60 percent occurrence of mental retardation in children who develop hypoglycemia in the first year of life.

**hypoglycemia, ketotic** Symptoms of hypoglycemia occur after a short fast; can be precipitated by a high fat and low carbohydrate diet. Seen most frequently in children between 18 months and three years of age.

**hypoglycemic therapy** See *insulin shock therapy.*

**hypognathous** Condition of abnormally small lower jaw.

**hypokinesis** Abnormal reduction of muscle movement.

**hypologia** Abnormal poverty of speech usually of an organic nature.

**hypomagnesemia** A disorder of magnesium metabolism resulting in muscle spasm, tetany and seizures.

**hypomania** Generalized term for a mild form of mania.

**hypomotility** Hypokinesis.

**hyponatremia** A disorder involving low levels of blood sodium. Symptoms may include headache, lethargy, ataxia, hypertension. Seizures frequently occur in affected young children and infants. Death may occur in acute phase. Those surviving may suffer retardation, seizures and spasticity.

**hyponoia** Rare term for hypopsychosis.

**hypopancreatic constitution** See *constitution, hypopancreatic.*

**hypoparathyroid constitution** See *constitution, hypoparathyroid.*

**hypophonia** Incomplete use of voice due to uncoordination of the muscles used in sound production.

**hypophoria** A downward deviation of the eye due to a muscular imbalance.

**hypophrasia** Slowness or lack of speech such as is seen in depression. Bradyphasia.

**hypophrenia** Mental deficiency.

**hypophrenosis** (E. E. Southard) Feeblemindedness.

**hypophysectomy** Surgical removal of the pituitary body.

**hypophysis; hypophysis cerebri** See *gland, pituitary.*

**hypopituitarianism** Inadequate production of the pituitary hormones possibly resulting in impotence, sterility, amenorrhea, hypoglycemia, signs of adrenal cortical failure, hypometabolism and shrinkage of tissue and viscera.

**hypopituitary constitution** See *constitution, hypopituitary.*

**hypoplasia** 1. Underdevelopment of any tissue. 2. Refers to a manikin or a dwarf when relating to the whole organism.

**hypoprosessis** See *hypoprosexia.*

**hypoprosexia** Inadequate attentive ability.

**hypopsychosis** Diminution of mental activity.

**hyposomia** Condition resulting from inadequate amount of sleeping time.

**hypostatic** Referring to those combinations of non-allelic genes or hereditary factors which are mashed by other such combinations, the epistatic, in the genetic process of epistasis.

**hypostenia** Deficient strength; weakness.

**hypotaxia, hypotaxis** See *suggestion, affective.*

**hypotension, orthostatic** Low blood pressure when erect due to organic causes such as diabetes, multiple sclerosis, and adrenal malfunctions or seen as a side effect produced by antihypertensive or tranquilizing drugs.

**hypothalamotomy** Psychosurgical procedure causing partial ablation of the hypothalamic area.

**hypothalamus** Grouping of small nuclei forming part of the diencephalon and generally lying at the junction of the midbrain and thalamus. It is the most important central brain structure involved with autonomic nervous system functions, and together with its connections to the limbic system, is thought to play a major role in emotion and motivation.

**hypothalamus, lateral** The part of the hypothalamus responsible for the control of hunger arousal and food-related activity.

**hypothesis** 1. An assumption; a guess. 2. A tentative statement to be proven or disproven by evidence.

**hypothesis, alternative** 1. (statistics) A statement contrary to the null hypothesis. It is known as $H_A$ or $H_1$. 2. (R. A. Fisher) A statement that the null hypothesis is false. If $H_O = O$, then $H_A \neq O$ where $H_O$ is the null hypothesis, $H_A$ is the alternative hypothesis, = means equal to, and ≠ means not equal to. 3. (J. Neyman and E. S. Pearson) An exact alternate to the null hypothesis which makes the power analysis possible. If $H_O=0$, then $H_A=$ specific number, where $H_O$ is the null hypothesis, $H_A$ is the alternative hypothesis, = means equal to.

**hypothesis, double bind** (G. Bates et al.) The theory that schizophrenia often develops in children who are involved in double bind situations. The child is faced with contradictory messages from his parents. However, the situation is not readily visible as such because the messages are sent on different levels or because of denial. The child cannot escape from the situation or comment on the contradiction, and feels damned regardless of whatever he does.

**hypothesis (in animal learning)** (D. Krech) A term applied to a type of response (whether correct or wrong) displayed by many species during the course of discrimination learning. As originally used by Krech, an hypothesis is a response pattern which can be demonstrated to be (1) systematic (occurring at a frequency beyond chance expectations), (2) purposive (persistence ultimately conditional upon goal attainment), (3) abstractive (guided by attributes common to a set of varying stimuli-configurations), (4) autonomous (reflecting the animal's predilections

and past experiences). See *continuity-non-continuity* (in learning theory).

**hypothesis, mediumistic** (H. G. Baynes) Hypothesis that the schizophrenic person is closer than others to the collective unconscious, is better able to foresee the unconscious trend of events and can therefore recognize early indications of his own disintegration.

**hypothesis, Neyman-Pearson** (statistics) A type of alternative hypothesis which states the exact size of the non-zero effect.

**hypothesis, null** (statistics) An hypothesis stating that an experimental effect does not exist, that the mean of a group is equal to zero, or that there is no difference between means. It is also known as $H_O$.

**hypothetical construct** See *construct, hypothetical.*

**hypothetical process variable** See *variable, hypothetical process.*

**hypothetical state variable** See *variable, hypothetical state.*

**hypothetico-deductive method** (C. L. Hull) A three-step research method applying rigorous deduction from a priori set principles. A system of clear and consistent definitions is introduced, followed by the proposal of a series of highly conceptualized postulates. From these, a series of detailed theorems is rigorously deduced.

**hypothymia** A condition of subnormal intensity of emotions; depression; despondency.

**hypothyroid** Inadequate thyroid secretion.

**hypothyroidism** A condition caused by a deficiency of thyroid hormones, expressed in advanced state as cretinism or myxedema and in mild form as a state having subnormal basal metabolic rates.

**hypothyrosis** Hypothyroidism.

**hypotonia; hypotony** Diminution of normal tension especially introcular pressure.

**hypotonic** 1. Subnormal tension or strength. 2. Pertaining to a solution whose osmotic pressure is less than any other solution taken as standard.

**hypovigility** Subnormal awareness or response to external stimuli, characteristically seen in all categories of schizophrenia.

**hypoxemia** A condition of deficient oxygen in the blood.

**hypoxia** A state in which there is an insufficient amount of oxygen available.

**hypsophobia** Fear of high places.

**hysteria** A mental disorder characterized primarily by dissociation, repression, emotional instability, suggestibility and a variety of psychogenic functional disorders. In the psychoanalytic system, it is classified as a psychoneurosis, two types being distinguished: the conversion type, comprised of mainly somatic symptoms often mimicking organic diseases; and the dissociative type, including alterations in conscious awareness such as amnesia, sleep-walking and split personalities.

Hippocrates coined the term from the Greek word hysteron, meaning uterus. Originally it was applied to a convulsive condition occurring in widows and spinsters presumably due to migration of the uterus. Freud followed by ascribing the cause of his patients functional disorders to frustrated sexual needs. The symptoms are still most commonly thought to arise from repressed conflicts, usually of a sexual nature.

**hysteria, anxiety** (S. Freud) A neurosis characterized by extensive use of the defense mechanism of displacement and often reaction formation and manifesting a variety of symptoms including hypochondriac fears, headaches, restlessness, anxiety states and general irritability.

**hysteria, combat** A functional disorder manifested during combat, the purpose being avoidance of further service in dangerous areas. Termed shell shock during World War I and battle fatigue during World War II.

**hysteria, conversion** A form of psychoneurosis characterized by the transformation of repressed intrapsychic conflicts into overt physical symptoms which have no physiological basis.

**hysteria, epidemic** Hysteria which appears to be attributable to interaction with an hysterical environment.

**hysteria, fixation** Form of hysterical conversion reaction in which a psychological problem manifests itself through a localized physical symptom.

**hysteria, major** A clinical syndrome characterized by several states: the aura, the stage of epileptoid convulsions, the stage of tonic followed by clonic spasms, the stage of dramatic emotional reactions, the stage of delirium. The stages do not necessarily follow the above order. The attack may last up to one half hour.

**hysterical anesthesia** See *anesthesia, hysterical.*

**hysterical aphonia** See *aphonia, hysterical.*

**hysterical blindness** See *blindness, hysterical.*

**hysterical character** See *character, hysterical.*

**hysterical hypalgia** See *hypalgia, hysterical.*

**hysterical neurosis** See *hysteria.*

**hysterical paralysis** See *paralysis, hysterical.*

**hysterical personality** See *character, hysterical.*

**hysteriform** Behavior disorders particularly of a motor nature such as convulsions, of hysteric orgin.

**hysteroid** Resembling hysteria.

**hysterosyntonic** Personality type representing a combination of hysterical and syntonic personalities.

# I

**I fraction** Duration of inspiration divided by the total cycle of inspiration expiration.

**I-persona** (T. Burrow) The personality constellation which synthesizes man's socially symbolic functioning. It is purely partitive and the affective identity exhibited in interrelations.

**$_sI_R$** See *inhibitory potential.*

**iamatology** The science of therapy.

**iatrogenic neurosis; iatrogenic illness** Behavior disorder induced by the physician's diagnosis or attitude.

**iatrogeny** The production of iatrogenic illness.

**iatrotechnique** Treatment method; iatrochemistry is synonymous with chemotherapy.

**ICD** See *International Classification System of Diseases.*

**ichthyophobia** Morbid fear of fish.

**iconolatry** Worship of images.

**iconomania** Morbid worshiping or collecting of images.

**ictal emotions** Suddenly occurring and vanishing emotions, especially depression and anxiety.

**icterus gravis neonatorum** See *kernicterus.*

**ictus** 1. Stress or accentuation of a tone or syllable. 2. Seizure or stroke.

**ictus epilepticus** Obsolete for sudden occurrence of an epileptic seizure.

**id** (S. Freud) The mass of unbound energies, both libidinal and aggressive, which constitute part of the unconscious and influence conscious action by seeking discharge and immediate gratification in accordance with its governing influence, the Pleasure Principle. It is comprised of whatever is innate, inherited or fixed in the constitution and is the link between somatic and mental processes. At birth all mental processes are part of the id. Through gradual contact with environmental demands, part of the unconscious id material becomes bound by pressures subserving these demands and undergoes development into preconscious material from which the ego emerges. The rest remains unconscious and unaltered.

More recent theorists suggest the ego and id are not entirely dichotomously differentiated structures, but rather operate along a continuum, both subserving motivation and discharge, and including ideational activity, with the id operating at the more primitive levels.

**id—ego** (psychoanalysis) The original psychic organization in the newborn out of which the id and ego develop.

**id resistance** See *resistance, id.*

**id sadism** See *sadism, id.*

**idea** 1. Cognitive process such as an image or thought which is not directly sensory in nature. 2. A plan of action or hypothesis.

**ideal** Thought of a personality, type of character, or line of action in emotionally colored terms as representing a goal to be sought after.

**ideal, ego** See *ego-ideal.*

**ideal observer** (signal detection theory) A function that relates an observation to the probability of that observation in a signal detection sensory experiment. The ideal observer is a mathematical expression of the maximum performance possible under the conditions of the experiment.

**ideal type** A perfect or near-perfect representation of all essential characteristics of a given species or category, though no single member embodies them all.

**idealism** A system of philosophical thought which attempts to explain the universe in terms of ideas, rather than in terms of matter or material things.

**idealization** Representation of an object in terms of one's ideals or desires.

**idealized image** (K. Horney) A false and exaggerated estimation of oneself, derived from what one would like to be rather than from what one actually is.

**ideas, flight of** See *flight of ideas.*

**ideas, innate** A philosophical doctrine which claims that all morally correct judgments and scientific principles consist of a priori knowledge of either universal principles governing reality or of objects transcending sensory experience. The knowledge is either present in the individual at birth, or stems from an inborn disposition of the mind to form conceptions under particular circumstances. Plato, ancient Stoics, Spinoza, and Descartes all employed the doctrine of innate ideas in the development of their philosophies.

**ideas of reference** A frequently occurring symptom of paranoid schizophrenia. The schizophrenic ascribes special importance to irrelevant events and believes that they are related to himself.

**ideation** Process of idea or image formation.

**ideational** Pertaining to idea or ideation.

**ideational apraxia** See *apraxia, ideational.*

**ideational fluency** The capacity to produce new ideas.

**ideational learning** See *learning, ideational.*

**idée fixe** See *fixed idea.*

**idée, force** (Fouillée) Postulate that ideas have dynamic influences and can serve as the source of actions.

**identical** Alike, the same; or similar in every respect.

**identical components theory** See *identical-elements theory.*

**identical direction, law of** The principle in binocular vision that objects are localized as if seen by a single, central eye.

**identical-elements theory** (E. L. Thorndike) Proposition that a new task will be learned more easily to the extent that it contains elements like those in already mastered tasks. Called identical components theory by R. S. Woodworth.

**identical points** Pair of points in the two retinae that receive stimuli from a single object at any distance and yield single vision, corresponding points.

**identical series** Type of recognition method used in the experimental study of learning.

**identical twins** See *twins, identical.*

**identical visual direction law** A pair of lines in objective space corresponding in direction in binocular vision, is seen in visual space as a single line. Objects on either line are seen as on a single line.

**identification** 1. The process of recognition. 2. (psychoanalysis) A defense mechanism consisting of the imitation of others in an effort to master too

intense stimuli. Primary identification occurring in normal development during the oral stage is the beginning of the infant's perception of the external world and of his emotional attitudes towards others. It results from the wish to possess the object or the other and is exhibited by taking things into the mouth, thus incorporating whatever is loved and by introjecting others' traits. This is the basis of the superego. Secondary identification is pathological and may occur at later stages. It consists of assuming another's characteristics for purposes of either restoration or mastery. For example, a love-object lost through death, separation or rejection is reestablished through identification with the object. Anxiety caused by a powerful enemy is subdued by the assumption of his powerful traits.

**identification, crossparental** The tendency to identify with the parent of the opposite sex associated with strong attachment to this parent.

**identification test** See *test, identification.*

**identity** 1. The condition of sameness in essential character. 2. The temporally persisting sense of being the same person whereby the individual orients himself to the external world. It is based primarily on coenaesthesia and the continuity of goals and memories. Psychologically, it is called personal identity.

**identity, ego** See *ego identity.*

**identity crisis** 1. Emotional disturbance seen particularly in young people. The individual has difficulty in experiencing or establishing a consistent personality irregardless of changes in time, circumstances, or roles. 2. (E. H. Erikson) Problems of adolescence or adulthood centering around a lack of a sense of personal identity.

**identity hypothesis** See *double aspect theory.*

**ideogenetic** Mental processes employing images of sense impressions rather than ideas that can be verbally expressed.

**ideoglandular** Glandular function evoked by mental impressions.

**ideograph; ideogram** 1. Pictograph; character or figure symbolizing an object or idea. 2. The graphic record obtained from apparatus recording the subject's unconscious movements.

**ideokinetic** See *ideomotor.*

**ideokinetic apraxia** Inability to carry out sequentially correct motor functions, though each single motor response may be intact.

**ideology** 1. A complex system of world, social and/or political philosophy. 2. Theory of the nature of ideas. 3. Psychology before that term was fixed.

**ideometabolic** Metabolic activity resulting from ideas.

**ideomotor** Referring to a motor action which is evoked by an idea.

**ideomotor action** Direct and automatic transfer of ideas into action, such as acts during states of absent-mindedness.

**ideomotor apraxia**  Impairment or loss of the ability to carry out a complex act. The separate behaviors comprising the act may individually be performed properly but the sequence is not correct.

**ideophobia**  Fear of ideas.

**ideophrenia**  (J. Guislain) Delirium characterized by ideational disorders.

**ideoreflex**  Transfer of an idea, suggested either from within or without, into action.

**ideosynchysia**  Obsolete for delirium.

**idioctonia**  Obsolete term for suicide.

**idiocy**  The lowest class of mental deficiency composed of those whose IQ's are below 25. It is usually congenital and accompanied by physical defects.

**idiocy, amaurotic family**  See *Tay-Sach's disease.*

**idiocy, Kalmuk**  Mongolism; Down syndrome.

**idiodynamics**  Point of view that only those environmental aspects that are relevant to a particular individual are attended to.

**idioglossia**  Unintelligible speech.

**idiographic**  Relating to the study of individual cases.

**idiographic science**  (W. Windelband) A science that studies individual and unrepeatable phenomena, such as history. W. Dilthey, G. W. Allport and others maintained that psychology is an idiographic science.

**idiokinesis**  Obsolete term for the origin of a new hereditary character through mutation.

**idiolalia**  Private language invented by those of low mentality.

**idiopathic**  **1.** Primary disease of spontaneous origin, not resulting from an outside agent. **2.** Diseases for which no cause is known.

**idiopathic sterility**  Sterility related to lack of spermatozoa in the semen or faulty ovulation.

**idiophenomena**  Phenomena which are idiographic, due to individual differences.

**idiophonia**  Individual form of dysphonia.

**idiophrenia**  Obsolete term for disorder resulting from organic brain disease.

**idioplasm; idioplasma**  Obsolete for hypothetical structure of the germ plasm.

**idioretinal**  Visual perceptions of light in the absence of external stimulation, caused by physiological changes occurring in the cortex or retina.

**idiosome**  The central apparatus of an auxocyte.

**idiosyncrasy**  A characteristic peculiar to an individual and that can be attributed to any general psychological factor.

**idiosyncratic credit**  The sum of the positive dispositions of group members toward an individual. These credits represent status and allow deviation from group norms, innovation and assertion of influence. The freedom to behave in an idiosyncratic manner increases along with the amount of credit an individual accumulates. Idiosyncratic credit may be acquired as a result of perceived conformity and competence, although other factors such as seniority may enter in.

**idiot**  An individual of the lowest level of mental deficiency, whose IQ is below 25. Idiots are not able to learn to speak, read, write, or avoid the common dangers of living.

**idiot savant**  A mentally retarded person possessing extraordinary ability in one specific area.

**idiotropic**  Introspective.

**idiovariation**  Ongoing process of mutation in the genotypical structure of an organism.

**idol**  **1.** An effigy, natural object or image worshipped as a god. **2.** (F. Bacon) A prejudice usually resulting from mass suggestion or tradition, that interferes with logical thinking.

**idolomania**  Overly passionate worship of idols.

**idolum**  Obsolete for illusion or hallucination.

**I/E ratio**  Rate of inspiration divided by rate of expiration; it may be used as an index of emotionality. It is believed low I/E ratios are indicative of lying.

**I/E scale**  See *scale, I/E.*

**IES test**  See *test, IES.*

**Illinois Test of Psycholinguistic Abilities (ITPA)**  See *test, Illinois, of Psycholinguistic Abilities.*

**illness, advantage by**  See *epinosis.*

**illness as self-punishment**  See *resistance, superego.*

**illumination**  Amount of intensity of light energy that falls on a surface.

**illusio sensus**  Hallucination.

**illusion**  A subjective distortion, occurring in sense perception or memory, of what is objectively present.

**illusion, Aristotle's**  The perception of one object as two, when the object is in contact with the tips of crossed middle fingers.

**illusion, auditory**  A subjective distortion of an auditory stimulus.

**illusion, Ebbinghaus**  The geometrical illusion that a circle surrounded by a ring of smaller circles is of a larger size than the same sized circle surrounded by a ring of circles larger than itself.

**illusion, geometrical**  Class of optical illusions consisting of misperceived direction, size or distance.

**illusion, Hering**  A geometrical optical illusion of straight parallel lines curving inwards when they intersect a series of lines which originate beyond the extremities of the straight lines and intersect above and below them.

**illusion, horizontal-vertical** The illusion that a vertical line drawn at right angles to a horizontal line of the same length is longer.

**illusion, Jastrow** An optical illusion consisting of the upper of two equal-sized ring sectors placed one above the other, appearing smaller.

**illusion, Müller-Lyer** The geometrical illusion that one line is longer than another of equal length when the former has obtuse angles at both ends while the latter has acute angles at both ends.

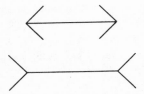

**illusion, oculogyral** The illusory perception of movement of a very dim light in a dark room which occurs following rotation of the body.

**illusion of doubles** Misidentification of known or unknown people in one's environment. It can occur as illusion of either positive or negative doubles. Also called Capgras' syndrome, or illusion of false recognition.

**illusion of false recognition** See *illusion of doubles.*

**illusion of negative doubles** Misidentification of known people in one's environment, as people whose appearances have been altered so they are no longer recognizable. Also called Fregoli's phenomenon.

**illusion of orientation** Misidentification of environmental stimuli due to impaired sensorium. It occurs in typhoid fever, malaria, pneumonia and scarlet fever.

**illusion of positive doubles** Misidentification of people in one's environment as friends or relatives.

**illusion, optical** An illusion of vision usually affecting spatial relations.

**illusion, Ponzo** The geometrical illusion that a horizontal line appearing within the smaller end of a pair of divergent vertical lines is longer than an equal-length line located at a point at which the vertical lines are farther apart.

**illusion, staircase** A reversible figure illusion whereby a staircase can be perceived both as from above or from below with both perspectives alternating.

**illusion, Zoellner** The geometrical illusion that two parallel lines are divergent occurring when one is crossed at sharp angles by many short slanting lines in one direction and the other is crossed by lines going in the opposite direction.

**illusory movement** See *movement, apparent.*

**image** A mental copy arising from memory of a sense experience in the absence of sensory stimulation.

**image agglutinations** (E. Kretschmer) Image groups occurring in dreams that are representative of the day's thoughts and are formed from the conglomeration of discrete images under the influence of affects.

**image, body** 1. Mental representation of one's body derived from internal sensations, emotions, fantasies, posture, experience of and with outside objects and people. 2. Internal, evaluative representation of one's body determined largely by how one thinks it looks to others. Also known as body concept.

**image, generic** A somewhat schematic image representing any one of a class of objects.

**image, idealized** See *idealized image.*

**image, memory** The revival in memory of a past experience, including the recognition that the original percept occurred in the past, in the absence of present sensory stimulation.

**image, percept** See *percept-image.*

**image, primordial** See *archetype.*

**imageless thought** A thought or train of thought lacking sensory content. Within the structuralists school, there was controversy as to whether such thought exists but recent experimental data indicates that it does.

**imagery, composite** A single image composed of parts of several sensory experiences of similar objects.

**imagery, eidetic** See *eidetic imagery.*

**imagery, hypnagogic** Vivid imagery, often of a hallucinatory nature, seen during the pre-sleep stage, and during the time of falling asleep.

**imagery, hypnopompic** Visions occurring during the state after sleep and prior to wakefulness.

**imagination** The constructive reorganization and employment of past perceptual experiences into ideational level images in a present experience. Imagination may be classified according to the function for which it is employed. For example, anticipatory imagination represents movement towards a future goal or the goal itself.

**imagination, active** (C. G. Jung) Technique of analytical psychotherapy used in dream interpretation in which the fantasy of the dream is elaborated through the observation of the fantasy material stimulated by the dream, leading to an understanding of the dream as a whole rather than an understanding of the components of the dream.

**imagination, creative** Self-initiated and self-organized imagination.

**imagination, imitative** Imagination which follows a pattern initiated and organized by another.

**imago** 1. (psychoanalysis) Unconscious, idealized representation of an important figure from childhood, usually a parent, often markedly influencing later life in the form of control of standard. 2. (C. G. Jung) Archetype.

imbalance, muscular  Imbalance in muscles of the opposite function, especially used in reference to the extrinsic muscles of the eyeball causing difficulty in fixating an object with both eyes. Some varieties are heterophoria and strabismus.

imbecile  A mentally deficient individual whose adult IQ is between 25 and 50 and whose mental age is between two and seven years.

imipramine  Drug prescribed in the treatment of depression.

imitation  The performance of an act in the same manner as another seen performing the act.

immanence, theory of life  Closed circle hypothesis of life. Belief that the organism consists of parts or organs which function not only for themselves but also work to keep several other parts in optimal condition. Since each organ is involved in the functioning of others, the life process takes place within a closed circle.

immobility  A state of temporary inability to move, as seen in the death-feigning response or sometimes in hypnosis.

immobility, social  The societal condition in which individuals are not able to change their social class, role, status or occupation.

immobilization-paralysis  See paralysis, immobilization.

immobilizing activity  See activity, immobilizing.

immoral  In violation of social or moral law.

impedance  The property of an electrical circuit which limits the power of the current passing through it.

imperative  Used in reference to actions an individual feels compelled to perform.

imperative, categorical  (E. Kant) An unconditioned demand stemming from an inner law of ethics and morality which is universally binding. The imperative consists of the principle that one's actions are good only if they are valid for all rational beings in the same situation.

imperceptible  A stimulus that is below the threshold of perception.

imperception  Defective perception such as is seen in agnosia.

impersonal projection  See projection, impersonal.

impersonation  The deliberate assumption of another's identity, usually for purposes of obtaining an advantage or privilege.

impetus  (psychoanalysis) The genetically determined force, strength, or energy of an instinctual drive.

implications, informational  (J. P. Guilford) Extrapolations of information in the form of expectancies, predictions, or consequences.

implicit apprehension  See apprehension, implicit.

implicit behavior  See response, implicit.

implicit response  See response, implicit.

impotence  1. The feeling that one is unable to control the course of events. 2. The inability of the male to perform sexual intercourse, related to the lack of erection or inadequate erection or too early ejaculation.

impotence, anal  General constipation or the inability to defecate except under conditions of privacy, resulting from pathological concern with giving offense.

impotence, orgastic  Inability in the male to achieve orgasm or complete sexual satisfaction despite normal erection and ejaculation.

impotentia generandi  Inability of the male to copulate most often due to physiological pathology.

impression  1. The neural effect of sensory stimulation. 2. The psychic effect of stimulation in the form of an unanalyzed sensation.

impression, absolute  A judgment of intensity, weight, brightness, etc. that is made without reference to or direct comparison with a standard.

impression method  See method, impression.

imprinting (ethology)  A learning process; the range of stimuli eliciting the following response in the young of several species becomes narrowed. This is limited to a sensitive period. This period ends in part because the bird flees from strange objects. It is often asserted but questionable that this process is irreversible or that this learning is accomplished without reinforcement.

improvement  The progressive movement towards a given standard or skill in the experimental study of practice. It is exhibited by decrease in time taken to perform the task and increase in accuracy.

improvement over chance  (statistics) A measure of the level of improvement in the dependent variable as compared with the average amount of improvement that would be expected from chance alone.

impuberty; impuberism  The state of not having reached puberty, either chronologically or because of delayed physical or psychological development.

impulse  1. Incitement to action without reflection or deliberation. 2. The wave of active change continuing along a nerve fiber. 3. (psychoanalysis) The psychological presentation of an instinctual drive, in the form of a sudden inclination or desire arising immediately upon confrontation with a certain stimulus.

impulse, component  Impulse arising from a component instinct.

impulse disorder  See disorder, impulse.

impulse fear  A fear that arises from an instinctual or psychological source, as opposed to real fear which is a fear of something real in one's environment.

impulsion  Tendency to immediate action, originating from blind obedience to internal drives.

**impulsive** An act that is the immediate response without deliberation, to the presentation of a stimulus.

**impunitive** 1. (S. Rosenzweig) Frustration reaction in which the individual attempts to justify, rationalize or deny the frustration which has occurred rather than to blame either himself or others for it. 2. Personality type characterized by impunitive frustration reactions.

**inaccessibility** A state, characteristic of autism and schizophrenia, in which the individual is unresponsive to stimulation from others.

**inadequacy** Inability to deal competently with a situation due to lack of skill or mental ability.

**inadequacy, constitutional** Any hereditary physical or mental defect that is largely unmodifiable.

**inadequacy, psychic** (psychoanalysis) The feeling of inability to respond to sexual stimulation in a satisfactory manner.

**inadequate personality** See *personality, inadequate.*

**inadequate stimulus** See *stimulus, inadequate.*

**inappetence** Absence of desire or appetite.

**inappropriate affect** See *affect, inappropriate.*

**inattention** A state in which attention is not focused and wanders unselectively.

**inattention, selective** 1. (H. S. Sullivan) A process used by the self-system to limit and restrict awareness by causing anxiety provoking experiences, threatening to the individual's security and self-esteem, to be ignored, misunderstood, or forgotten. The necessity for restriction of awareness is the result of the limitations of experiences set forth in the socialization process which is transmitted first in one's early childhood at home and is continued through later educational processes. 2. See *defense, perceptual.*

**inborn** Innate; present in the organism at birth.

**inbreeding** Procreation among close relatives which automatically fixes the genes making them homozygous. It is sometimes arranged deliberately in certain species to maintain desirable, hereditary characteristics.

**incendiary mania** Pyromania.

**incentive** 1. Motive for behaving in a certain way. 2. External object which arouses or adds to already existing motivation to maintain a certain goal-directed behavior.

**incest** Sexual relations between opposite-sexed individuals, closely connected by blood kinship, the degree of the kinship being defined by law and social custom.

**incest barrier** (psychoanalysis) The limitation or prohibition placed upon the libido by social law concerning incest, resulting in guilt evoked by thoughts, fantasies or dreams of defying the barrier and in the loosening of libidinal attachment to the family in accordance with the barrier.

**incest taboo** See *taboo, incest.*

**incidence** The frequency with which a condition or event occurs within a given time and population.

**incidental cue** See *stimulus, incidental.*

**incidental learning** See *learning, incidental.*

**incidental memory** See *memory, incidental.*

**incidental stimulus** See *stimulus, incidental.*

**incipient** The beginning or initial phase of a process.

**incipient movement** See *movement, incipient.*

**incoherence** Lack of organization or systematic connection of parts, such as in unintelligible speech marked by disconnectedness.

**incommensurable** Magnitudes or variables requiring different unity scales or standards of measurement or estimation in order to be assessed accurately.

**incompatible** Statements, phenomena, or individuals which are inconsistent or not capable of existing together with the same system.

**incomplete-pictures test** See *test, incomplete pictures.*

**incontinence** Incapacity of self-control of body functions, particularly sexual impulses, urination, and defecation.

**incoordination** Lack of balance or harmony in movements resulting from the inadequate working together of muscles or muscle groups.

**incorporation** 1. Taking into the body and making part of oneself. 2. (psychoanalysis) A form of introjection in which attributes of another are taken into the mind of an individual following the model of oral ingestion and swallowing. It is the primary mechanism in identification.

**increment** The amount or rate of increase or decrease in the progressive change of a magnitude or variable.

**incremental learning theory** See *learning theory, incremental.*

**incubation** 1. A period of no apparent activity in a complex function during which development and change in the function may occur. 2. (G. Wallas) The second of the four stages of creative thought.

**incubus** Nightmare.

**incus** Anvil. The middle bone in the chain of small bones in the middle ear.

**independence-dependence syndrome** See *syndrome, dependence-independence.*

**independence, test of** See *test of independence.*

**independent variable** See *variable, independent.*

**index** A sign or number indicative of change in magnitude, or pointing to a state or fact.

**index, cephalic** Anthropometrical measurement,

given by dividing the maximum breadth of the head by the maximum length and multiplying by 100.

**index consistency (i)** An index measuring the extent to which members of a group give the same responses to identical stimuli within a certain time limit. The formula is:

$$i = \sqrt{\frac{1}{N}\Sigma\cos^\pi - \frac{(BC)^{1/2}}{(AD)^{1/2}(BC)^{1/2}}} \ ,$$

where $A$=the number of responses present both times; $B$ and $C$ = the number of responses present one time and not the other respectively, $D$= the number of responses denied or omitted both times, and $N$= the number of subjects.

**index, cranial** The cephalic index measured on the bare skull.

**index of correlation** See *correlation, index of.*

**index of independence** See *test of independence.*

**index of refraction** See *refraction, index of.*

**index of reliability** See *reliability, index of.*

**index, predictive** See *forecasting efficiency, index of.*

**index, selection** (H. J. Eysenck) A formula used in the determination of the discriminatory usefulness of a test: $D = \dfrac{P}{P+P_m+P_f}$ where $P_m$ equals the proportion of persons who belong in a certain category and whose scores are appropriate to that category; $P$ equals the proportion of individuals who belong in a category but whose scores do not place them there; and $P_f$ equals the proportion of individuals not belonging in the category in which their scores place them.

**indicator, mechanical** A mechanical moving part of an instrument which gives information concerning the state of a phenomenon, usually by bringing a reference point into relation with a scale, such as pointers do on speedometers.

**indifference of medium or indicator** The principle that a personality dimension exists regardless of the form or existence of some particular scale or type of measurement. Thus, the same trait or factor can usually be measured by a number of distinct tests in either Questionnaire Rating, or Objective Test media of observation.

**indifference point** The transition zone between two opposing experiences, such as pleasure and pain, or variables.

**indifferent stimulus** See *stimulus, indifferent.*

**indirect measurement** See *measurement, indirect.*

**indirect method of therapy** See *psychotherapy, client centered.*

**indirect scaling** See *scaling, indirect.*

**indirect vision** See *vision, indirect.*

**indissociation** (J. Piaget) An early stage in the child's development of perception of the physical world in which phenomena are not sharply distinguished from each other or from the self.

**individual differences** See *differences, individual.*

**individual psychology** The name given by Alfred Adler to his personality theory. It is a holistic ego-psychology and a social psychology which assumes that life is movement and must endlessly strive for better adaptation to the environment. This was first called by Adler "The striving for superiority," while any lack of adaptation led to an "inferiority feeling." The age-old conflict as to the primacy of heredity or environment is resolved in this theory by seeing the child as utilizing heredity as well as environment in his endeavor to construct his personality. Within the limits of reality the child has great latitude for doing so. In the course of his striving for better adaptation the child will always set for himself a goal to strive for. Adler stated: "We cannot think, feel, will or act without the perception of a goal." The singlemindedness of this goal striving lead to a unified personality, and the mode of movement of the individual toward his goal was termed by Adler his "style of life." The social character of individual psychology was expressed by Adler as follows: "No psychologist is able to determine the meaning of any expression, if he fails to consider it in its social relation to society." Adler's psychological system was developed in a social science direction. Consciousness itself is considered a social product, and character traits are in Adler's system only the external aspects of the social relationship an individual has to the problems of the outside world. In its stress on ego-psychology and its fight against drive-psychology, the "Individual Psychology" states that instincts would be an inadequate guide for man through the intricacies of our complex world; only goal-directed man can find his way, since all human history is nothing but the activity of man, aiming at his own goals. Adler also contended that civilization, culture, art and science could never have been created by man, if his basic striving had been "back to the womb."

Individual psychology sees neuroses and psychoses as being safeguarding devices, designed (unconsciously) by the individual to defend his self-esteem and his idealized ego against a threatened collapse, when faced with a social problem for which he feels unprepared. His lack of "social interest" forces him from social reality into a world of pretense and illusion. Special innovations in the treatment techniques are the use of "early recollections" and "birth order position" and a relentless stress on the (not conscious) purposiveness of the symptoms.

The optimistic tenor of individual psychology led to the acceptance of its tenets by a great many educators, the child guidance movement and the general public. Societies, individual psychology clinics and Adlerian Institutes carry on the work of "Individual Psychology" in most western countries.

**individual response** See *response, individual.*

**individual test** See *test, individual.*

**individualism** 1. A strong personal attitude or action exhibiting an attitude of independence from group standards. **2.** The theory that the individual is of paramount importance and should take precedence over social or legal action.

**individuality, graphic** The unique characteristics of a person's handwriting which make possible the identification of the writer.

**individualization** The process by which an organism becomes different from all others.

**individuation** **1.** The process by which an organism moves or differentiates from the general class to an individual mode of existence, through the development of particular structures, parts, and functions. **2.** (C. G. Jung) The process by which the various systems within the personality, such as archetypes and complexes, develop to the fullest capacity and become distinct from the original, undifferentiated wholeness in which they originate. Realization of self, the ultimate result, cannot occur unless all systems are completely differentiated and permitted conscious expression. Underdeveloped systems attempt to attract energy from more fully developed ones, causing resistances to growth, irrational behavioral outlets for expression, and consequently neurosis. **3.** (M. S. Mahler) A phase of development, occurring usually between the eighteenth and 36th month, during which the infant manifests progressive independence of the mother through growing ability to satisfy his own desires by increased mobility, dexterity, and tolerance of the mother's absence. The individuation process marks the end of the symbiotic mother-child relationship, during which the infant is completely dependent on the mother.

**indoctrination** **1.** Instruction designed to gain complete and uncritical acceptance rather than critical consideration. **2.** Preliminary training, the purpose of which is to introduce new members to the policies, mores, and practices of a group.

**induced color** See *color, induced.*

**induced movement** See *movement, induced.*

**induced tonus** See *tonus, induced.*

**induction** **1.** The process of deriving the general from the particular. **2.** Arousal in one area resulting from the spread of activity from another part in physiology. **3.** See *induction, positive.* **4.** See *induction, negative.*

**induction coil** An electrical device consisting of two coils, used for physiological stimulation and for the administration of shock in psychological experiments.

**induction, negative** (I. P. Pavlov) The concentration of inhibition due to preceding excitation of neighboring areas.

**induction, positive** (I. P. Pavlov) The concentration of excitation in a stimulated area due to preceding inhibition of neighboring areas.

**induction test** See *test, induction.*

**industrial psychology** The branch of applied psychology concerned with the application of psychological techniques and findings to the solution of problems arising in the industrial or economic field. The first applications were in the use of intelligence and aptitude tests as aids in determining selection and replacement of employees. More recent developments include the involvement of industrial psychologists in training procedures, the counseling of employees, determining effective methods of communication between workers and employers, and in designing the most suitable and effective equipment and working conditions. Industrial psychology is now called industrial and organizational psychology. It is essentially the application of many areas of psychology not only to industry itself but to other organizations where people work. Over the years it has deepened and broadened its scope to include more complex aspects of human behavior in a greater variety of settings. There are three major aspects within the field of industrial and organizational psychology: personnel psychology, industrial-social psychology and human engineering. More recently the term organizational psychology has come to replace the label industrial-social psychology and human factors engineering is replacing human engineering.

**inertia** **1.** The tendency of matter to retain its state of rest or motion as long as it is not acted upon by an external force. **2.** The property in the nervous system of time lag between a stimulus and the onset of its physiological effect.

**infancy** The earliest period of postnatal life, prior to the learning of speech, in which the individual is totally dependent upon parental care.

**Infant Schedule** A Gesell Development Scale used to determine the level of linguistic, motor, and social behavior in infants.

**infant test** See *test, infant.*

**infantile excema** See *excema, infantile.*

**infantile polymorphous perversion** See *perversion, infantile polymorphous.*

**infantile psychosis: treatment design** (M.S. Mahler & M. Furer) Infantile psychosis can be treated only through restoration, as completely as possible, of the mother-child symbiotic dual unity and subsequent facilitation of a separation-individuation process. Mahler & Furer designed a mother-therapist-child tripartite treatment situation in which the first goal was to re-establish a symbiotic-like union with the mother via the therapist as a bridge. This situation facilitated a subsequent separation-individuation process which also enabled the therapist to reconstruct traumata in the psychotic child's past and to observe the emergence of many hitherto absent developmental phenomena. The conflict between the ego and the id produced neurotic-like symptoms which could be dealt with therapeutically.

This therapeutic action research design must be modified for a more general application because of the forbidding cost in manpower. Yet it reaffirms the theory of the symbiosis origin of human emotional development and may eventually facilitate rehabilitation of early and severely disturbed children. The emotional availability of a mothering person in the treatment of the erstwhile psychotic infant is an absolute necessity.

**infantile sadism**  See *sadism, infantile.*

**infantile spastic diplegia**  Bilateral congenital brain defects, or lesions acquired at birth causing the limbs (particularly the lower) to become weak and spastic, Other symptoms may include involuntary movements, ataxia and sometimes mental deficiency.

**infantile symbiotic psychosis**  See *psychosis, symbiotic.*

**infantilism**  Regression or arrested physical or mental development in an older child or adult, characterized by behavior resembling that of the infant.

**infarction, myocardial**  A coronary occlusion produced in the cardiac muscle and related to the existence of hypertension, obesity, diabetes, peptic ulcer, renal disease, and smoking.

**infavoidance need**  See *need, infavoidance.*

**inference**  A judgment or conclusion reached on the basis of former judgments.

**inferiority complex**  See *complex, inferiority.*

**inferiority feelings**  **1.** Feelings of weakness, helplessness and inadequacy. **2.** (A. Adler) Feelings of inferiority, arising from the sense of imperfection and incompletion in a particular sphere of life, which motivates the individual to strive for a higher level of development and as such, are the cause of all improvement in life situation. Each time a new level of achievement is reached, inferiority feelings reappear, continuing to mitigate upward movement. If inferiority feelings become exaggerated by adverse conditions in the home, pathological inferiority complex may develop.

**inferiority, functional**  (A. Adler) One of a subgroup of organ inferiority characterized by work that is quantitatively or qualitatively insufficient to satisfy a standard of required effectiveness.

**inferiority, morphologic**  (A. Adler) One of the subgroups of organ inferiority characterized by a defect in the shape, size, or strength of a particular organ.

**inferiority, organ**  (A. Adler) The belief that the actual or subjectively felt defect in an organ causes feelings of inferiority and attempts at compensation for these feelings.

**infertility**  The inability to produce offspring.

**infinite**  **1.** A quantity greater than any definite quantity. **2.** Not bounded or limited.

**infinitesimal**  **1.** A quantity less than any definite quantity. **2.** Minute.

**informal test**  See *test, informal.*

**information**  **1.** Knowledge of a particular fact or circumstance gained or given through communication, research or instruction. **2.** (behavior theory) That aspect of a stimulus used by the subject in his response. **3.** (information theory) The quantitative property of the set of all possible items that can be communicated under a defined set of circumstances, rather than that item which is actually communicated or its content. If all items of a source of possible items can be predicted, no information will be conveyed by the communication. If all items are as likely to be communicated, maximum information will be conveyed. The bit is the unit of information. **4.** (J. P. Guilford) That which an organism discriminates. Intellectually processed information has some degree of structure, with both substantive (content) and formal (product) aspects.

**information, behavioral**  (J. P. Guilford) Information involved in human interactions where the attitudes, needs, desires, moods, feelings, intentions, perceptions, thoughts, etc. of other people and of ourselves are involved. Conveyed by expressive behavior or "body language" as well as by word symbols.

**information content**  See *content, informational.*

**information, figural**  (J. P. Guilford) Information in concrete form, as perceived or as recalled in the form of images. The term "figural" implies at least minimal structure. Subclasses are along sensory-input lines—visual, auditory, kinesthetic, etc.

**information, semantic**  (J. P. Guilford) Information in the form of meanings to which words commonly, although not always, become attached, hence most notable in verbal thinking and verbal communication, but not identical with words as symbols. Meaningful pictures can also convey semantic information.

**information, symbolic**  (J. P. Guilford) Information in the form of denotative signs, having no significance in and of themselves, such as numbers, letters, and words (as letter structures).

**information test**  See *test, information.*

**information theory**  **1.** The branch of science dealing with the transmission of information as a formal mathematical concept, and originally stemming from probability theory and electrical communications. Modern information theory is based primarily on the work of R. V. L. Hartley who set forth the idea that information could be identified as a stochastic process, one that gives rise to a sequence of symbols to which probability laws apply, and could thus be measured in terms of what could have been communicated under a defined set of circumstances, rather than what actually is communicated.

C. E. Shannon and N. Wiener elaborated the scheme and are largely responsible for the promulgation of information theory in the social sciences, their formulations having been enthusiastically accepted by psychologists such as G. A. Miller and F. C. Frick. Shannon's and Wiener's elaborations consist essentially of the idea that communication is a statistical process which can only be described in probabilistic terms. Maximum information is conveyed when any one item of a source of possible items, is as probable as any other. No information is conveyed when all items of a source of possible items are completely predictable. Based on these premises, a measure of the amount of information associated with a given message was derived by defining a set of conditions the measure had to satisfy. The only measure for any item of a group of items, which satisfies all conditions set forth is the negative logarithm, to the base 2, of the probability of that item. The average information of the group of items, is the average weighted logarithmic measure.

Currently information theory is being applied as a means of psychological experimentation such as language, perception, reaction time, and statistical analyses. **2.** (industrial psychology) The science of the transmission and measurement of information. The basic measure is the "bit." In information theory channel capacity refers to the limit of information that can be handled by any communications channel and, by analogy, human channel capacity refers to the maximum limit of the information that can be received by a human through all sensory modalities. The theory is applicable in human factors engineering, such as determining the perceptual load imposed upon an operator by a sensory-motor task.

**informational classes**  See *classes, informational.*

**informational content**  See *content, informational.*

**informational implications**  See *implications, informational.*

**informational product**  See *product, informational.*

**informational relations**  See *relations, informational.*

**informational systems**  See *systems, informational.*

**informational transformations**  See *transformations, informational.*

**informational units**  See *units, informational.*

**infrahuman  1.** Species, other than man. **2.** Characteristics of a human that resemble those of a lower animal.

**infundibulum**  The stalk by which the pituitary body is attached to the forebrain.

**ingratiation**  A strategy used by a lower status individual to make himself more attractive to a person with higher status and to reduce the power differential between them.

**in-group**  A closely knit group of individuals who feel they belong with each to the exclusion of others.

**inherent**  Existing in, belonging to and permanently forming a part of an individual or object.

**inheritance  1.** Traits transmitted from parent to offspring. **2.** The process by which traits are transmitted from parent to offspring.

**inhibited mania**  See *mania, inhibited.*

**inhibition  1.** The stopping of a process in progress or the prevention of a process from starting when the eliciting stimulus is present. **2.** A mental state which results in a hesitancy or blockage of action. **3.** (psychoanalysis) The prevention of instinctual impulses from reaching consciousness due to the

action of the ego or the superego. **4.** (I. P. Pavlov) A hypothetical cortical process of the diminution or cessation of activity in the cerebrum.

**inhibition, aim**  See *drive, aim-inhibited.*

**inhibition, associative  1.** The weakening of an established bond due to a new association which is made to one of the members of the original association. **2.** The difficulty of establishing a new associative bond because of previously existing associations.

**inhibition, conditioned**  (I. P. Pavlov) The suppression of the conditioned response upon the pairing of the conditioned stimulus with another stimulus without presenting the unconditioned response.

**inhibition, conditioned reactive**  (C. L. Hull) The hypothetical state caused by the conditioning of reactive inhibition to the stimulus that is present when a conditioned response is extinguished, thereby causing the stimulus to have an inhibitory power.

**inhibition, differential**  A hypothesized force within an organism acquired through conditioning causing a decrease in the tendency to respond to one stimulus while a tendency to respond to another, similar, stimulus is left intact.

**inhibition, external**  (I. P. Pavlov) The extinction or cessation of a conditioned response when an extraneous stimulus is presented simultaneously with the conditioned stimulus.

**inhibition, extinctive**  See *extinction, (I. P. Pavlov).*

**inhibition, internal**  (I. P. Pavlov) The principle that an inhibitory process arises in the nervous system to counteract the strength of the conditioned response when the reinforcement is given and causes the diminution of the response when the reward is withheld.

**inhibition of delay**  (I. P. Pavlov) An inhibition which reduces the time interval between the conditioned stimulus and the conditioned response.

**inhibition of inhibition**  See *disinhibition.*

**inhibition of reinforcement**  (C. I. Hovland) The temporary reduction of a conditioned response occurring within reinforcement trials presented in short succession which is reversible following a rest period.

**inhibition, proactive**  The hypothetical process which is used to account for the relatively poorer learning rate of elements later in a series as compared to the learning rate of elements coming earlier in a series.

**inhibition, reactive**  (C. L. Hull) The tendency toward a lessened strength of response due to practice or activity. It is independent of reinforcement and dependent on the time interval since the last response and the number of preceding responses. It is also called $I_R$.

**inhibition, retroactive**  The interference with or impairment of the usual effects of a learning activity when the activity is followed closely by some other activity, especially activity similar to the first.

**inhibition, specific** Inhibition of an ego function such as locomotion or eating, which if performed would cause severe anxiety.

**inhibitory epilepsy** See *epilepsy, inhibited*.

**inhibitory post synaptic potential (IPSP)** A type of synaptic event which has the same form as the excitatory past synaptic potential (EPSP), but which produces a brief hyperpolarization which manifests itself as an inhibition of the neuron when it would normally respond.

**inhibitory potential** (C. L. Hull) $sI_R$; a temporary state of the organism, hypothesized to exist as the result of a response and to reduce the potential of the response's recurrence.

**inhibitory reflex** See *reflex, inhibitory*.

**initial cry** See *cry, epileptic*.

**initial spurt** The relatively high level of performance at the beginning of a series of tasks such as appears frequently in a work curve.

**initiative** The individual's capacity for independent action in starting a series of events, or the action itself.

**injury** Impairment of a structure or function in an organism due to damage from other than natural biological processes.

**ink-blot test** See *test, Rorschach inkblots*.

**innate** Present in the individual at birth.

**innate ideas** See *ideas, innate*.

**inner-directed** (D. Riesman) An individual whose reactions to various environmental pressures are consistent and based on an early-instilled value system.

**inner ear** See *labyrinth*.

**inner-personal region** See *region, inner personal*.

**innervation** 1. The supply of efferent nerves to a muscle or gland. 2. The excitation of a muscle or gland by an efferent nerve.

**innervation ratio** The number of muscle fibers in a motor unit per neuron.

**input** 1. The energy or effort put into a system. 2. (computer technology) The properly coded information fed into the computer. 3. The current or voltage applied to an electronic device or circuit.

**inquiry** The second major procedure in Rorschach testing, following the completion of the free association period (except in the Rapaport system where the inquiry is conducted after the free association to each card). The basic format generally followed is for the examiner to present the cards to the subject a second time, asking non-directive questions so as to understand which portion of the blot was used in the response and which determining features of the blot stimulated the percept. See also *direct inquiry; analogy period; testing-of-limits*.

**insanity** The legal term for severe mental disorder involving irresponsibility and incompetence in the conduction of the individual's affairs.

**insanity, adolescent** 1. (E. Hecker) An obsolete term for hebephrenia. 2. Any psychotic disorder that occurs in adolescence.

**insanity, affective** Another expression for what is now called affective psychosis.

**insanity, legal** Any type or degree of mental disorder which entails legal consequences such as commitment to an institution, appointment of a guardian, or relief of responsibility for crime or contract. Legal insanity involves ignorance of right and wrong, the existence of delusions or the presence of an irresistible impulse.

**insanity, moral** 1. (J. Prichard) Rarely used term describing individuals who manifest uncontrollable violence and extreme lack of concern for the well-being of others without any intellectual impairment. 2. Extreme cases of psychopathic personality.

**insanity, normal** (C. G. Jung) Temporary supplanting of conscious autonomy by the unconscious giving rise to bizarre behavior characteristic of insanity, but occurring in normal individuals usually during periods of great stress.

**insemination** The act of fertilizing or impregnating.

**insensibility** Temporary or permanent absence of a particular quality or mode of sensation.

**insight** 1. Mental discernment or apprehension of the true nature of a problem, object, person, or situation. 2. The faculty involved in grasping the inner character or underlying truth. 3. (psychoanalysis) Awareness of the meaning and unconscious origin of one's behavior, symptoms, and the emotional processes which underlie them, this being a prerequisite to any therapeutic change. 4. (Gestalt) The main factor in learning characterized by grasping of those relationships leading to the solution of a problem, based on perceptual reorganization of previous experience. Once insight occurs it can promptly be repeated and applied to new situations.

**insight therapy** See *therapy, insight*.

**insomnia** Chronic inability to sleep.

**inspection technique** See *technique, inspection*.

**inspiration** 1. The drawing in of air to the lungs. 2. The sudden grasp of the nature of a problem or the occurrence of a creative idea that does not result from previous reasoning or trial and error.

**inspiration-expiration ratio** See *I−E ratio*.

**instability** 1. Excessive or rapidly changing emotions or moods. 2. Lack of steadiness of purpose and self-control.

**instigation** (quantitative) Total combined strength of all instigators to a given response affecting an organism at one time, whether facilitative or inhibitory.

**instigator** A specifiable antecedent to which a given

response is the consequence; *external* instigator is a perceived object or event that initiates or facilitates an action; *internal* instigator may be inferred from external indices of internal changes (e.g., thirst drive equals hours of water deprivation), past experiences (e.g., high achievement motives equals history of parental reward for successful achievement), verbal report (e.g., "I am hungry," or "I am angry.").

**instinct** 1. An innate activity pattern or tendency to action common to a given species. 2. (S. Freud) A constant psychic force with the organism stemming from a certain bodily deficiency or disequilibrium, the aim of which is to remove the excitation and restore equilibrium through its investment in or attachment to an object that will bring satisfaction to the organism. In his final revision of instinct theory, Freud postulated the existence of only two primary instincts, Eros, the aim of which is to bind together, and Thanatos, the aim of which is to destroy connections and reduce living things to an inorganic state. The two instincts may combine into aggressive and sexual instincts of various forms. For example, in sadism, the destructive force is stronger than the aim for intimate union. 3. (W. McDougall) An inherited psychophysical disposition which determines what particular objects the individual will perceive, what he will experience emotionally about them, and how he will react to them behaviorally. McDougall believed the emotional component of instinct is inherited and cannot be modified by experience, as can the sensory and motor components and therefore identification of the distinct primary emotions was the only method of discovering what and how many instincts there are. A list of the primary emotions and thus the primary instincts was compiled and continuously revised. Some of the core instincts include escape, combat, curiosity, repulsion, self-assertion, self-abasement, and parental. 4. (K. Lorenz) Energy which initiates and drives certain behavior patterns and is specific to them. The instinctive activity is characterized by being stereotyped, common to all members of at least one sex of a species, innate, always completed once it is set into motion, and is the goal and terminus of the instinct.

**instinct, aggressive** See *Thanatos.*

**instinct, component** (psychoanalysis) Any of the various pregenital impulses arising from stimulation and tension in specific zones and organs. Each component instinct is disconnected and independent of the others in seeking gratification until puberty when they become fused, and are subordinated to genital primacy, subsequently comprising the elements of forepleasure. Examples are sucking, biting, sadism and masochism, all of which can be pathological if used as the source of end-pleasure.

**instinct, death** See *Thanatos.*

**instinct, destructive** See *Thanatos.*

**instinct, life** See *Eros.*

**instinct, self-preservation** See *Eros.*

**institution, mental** See *mental hospital.*

**institutionalization** 1. The placing of an individual in an institution for corrective or therapeutic purposes. 2. The process by which an individual adapts to the behavior patterns characteristic of the institution in which he lives.

**instruction** The process of imparting knowledge systematically.

**instrument** Any device used in measuring or recording data.

**instrument factor** (R. B. Cattell) A false factor, i.e., not a real personality factor, which sometimes appears when many behaviors are measured by one kind of instrument and which is peculiar to the instrument.

**instrumental** Behavior performed in order to achieve a certain end, as in the subject's response in instrumental conditioning.

**instrumental conditioning** See *conditioning, operant.*

**instrumental error** See *error, instrumental.*

**instrumental learning** See *conditioning, operant.*

**instrumentalism** 1. (J. Dewey) A position attempting the application of scientific methods and critical intelligence to moral and social beliefs through the notion that theory and practice are not opposed and irreconcilable. Using the model of scientific inquiry which, Dewey believed, showed that theory and practice were in fact interdependent, Dewey formulated the view that general ideas are instruments for the reconstruction and reorganization of problem situations. The idea's truth lies in its capacity to reorganize the components of an experience in such a way as to resolve the problem in accordance with the rules of disciplined inquiry. Thus ideas prescribe behavior. 2. (B. B. Wolman) A sociopsychological attitude. Selfishness based on viewing others as instruments to be used for the satisfaction of one's own needs. Originates in the parasitic infant-mother relationship.

**insufficiency, segmental** (A. Adler) Inferiority of a body segment usually observable by a skin disorder of that segment.

**insula** See *Reil, island of.*

**insulin** A hormone secreted by the beta cells of the islets of Langerhans in the pancreas, the purpose of which is to reduce the blood-sugar level. Deficiency in its production results in diabetes for which it is used as a drug.

**insulin coma** See *coma, insulin.*

**insulin shock therapy** Treatment method, introduced by M. Sakel, consisting of the production of hypoglycemic comas and at times, convulsions induced by insulin administration.

**insulin treatment, ambulatory** (P. Polatin and H. Spotnitz) A modified insulin treatment used to relieve extreme anxiety and tension as well as the physical effects of these symptoms, such as appetite and weight loss. Small doses of insulin are administered intramuscularly, inducing hypoglycemia rather than coma. The patient is fully conscious during treatment. This is known also as sub-shock or sub-coma insulin treatment.

**insulinoma** The presence of a tumor in the pancreas which causes it to produce large quantities of insulin irrespective of the body's needs.

**insurance, narcissistic** (S. Rado) The mechanism which inhibits the critical judgment of the ego and thus allows for gratification of forbidden aggressive tendencies resulting in narcissistic satisfaction.

**intake** The initial contact between patient and therapist usually in the form of an evaluative interview upon admission to a clinic or hospital.

**integral** 1. An integer or whole number. 2. The result of mathematical process of integration.

**integrated motivation component** (R. B. Cattell) That component in motivation for a given course of action of which the person is fully aware and which is integrated with his conscious intentions and skills.

**integration** 1. The process or result of the unification of parts into a whole. 2. (psychology) The process by which different parts or characteristics of an individual are combined, organized and worked together at a higher level as a complex whole. 3. (neurology) The combination of discrete neural impulses in a center producing a unified and coordinated activity. 4. (mathematics) The summing of a differential series.

**integration, primary** (psychoanalysis) The conscious recognition of the child, usually before age 5, that his body and mind are distinct from the environment.

**integration, secondary** (psychoanalysis) The process by which psychic components, especially pre-genital sexual components, are unified and socialized into an adult or genital level.

**integration, social** 1. The process of unifying diverse elements of a group or society in such a way that all are guaranteed the same rights and liberties. 2. The process by which an individual adapts to group standards.

**integrative learning** (R. B. Cattell) A type of rewarded learning, important for personality development, in which the organism learns to make a choice or compromise between different goal satisfactions in the interests of a greater satisfaction (of all drives) for the organism as a whole. A learning to control by adjusting goals as distinct from Means—End Learning which is simply the learning of paths to a given goal.

**intellect** 1. The cognitive aspect of the mind including processes of reasoning, relating, judging and conceiving. 2. Mental ability.

**intellect, structure of** (J. P. Guilford) A comprehensive and systematic organization of intellectual abilities, known and hypothesized, in a three-dimensional facet- or matrix-type model, in which the abilities are parallel and are distinguished with respect to kinds of operations, kinds of informational content and kinds of products of information.

**intellectual** 1. Ideas and conceptions having to do with the intellect. 2. Thinking or reasoning of a high quality. 3. A person of high intellect whose interests are mainly in the area of learning and ideas.

**intellectual operations** See *operations, intellectual.*

**intellectualism** The doctrine that reduces all mental processes to only the cognitive aspect of the mind, attempting to explain emotion and volition in terms of the intellect.

**intellectualization** 1. The attempted analysis of a problem in purely intellectual terms. 2. A defense mechanism employing intellectual functions in the attempt to understand or explain a personal problem for the purpose of avoiding the acknowledgement of emotion evoked by the problem.

**intelligence** 1. In its Latin origin, it meant "information," a conception shared today in military circles. Biologically, with the naturalists, in contrast to "instinct" it meant an organism's ability to cope with its environment through learning. In contemporary psychology it is generally defined as a hypothetical construct from which stem an individual's abilities to deal with abstractions, learning, and novel situations. The level of intelligence is measured by standardized intelligence tests, its degree being proportional to the complexity of the test problems. 2. (A. Binet) The ability to judge, comprehend, and reason. Differences in intelligence are identified with differences in developmental levels as represented by the average capacities of individuals of various ages. The measure of an individual's intelligence is his mental age, or the developmental level he achieves, divided by his actual chronological age. 3. (E. L. Thorndike) A composite of a multitude of separate elements of ability broadly categorized within the ability to understand and deal with people (social intelligence), the ability to understand and deal with objects and the appliance of science (concrete intelligence), and the ability to understand and deal with verbal and mathematical symbols (abstract intelligence). Thorndike's is a multi-factor theory of intelligence stating that each mental act involves a number of minute elements operating together. Because many of these operate together and are common to several different mental acts, they can be also classified into separate groups such as verbal meaning, visual perception of relations or comprehension, all of which can then be measured yielding an index of intelligence. 4. (C. Spearman) A general factor ($g$) of mental energy possessed by all individuals in varying degrees which operates in all mental activities in amounts that differ according to the tasks' demands. In addition to $g$, each particular type of mental activity includes its own specific factor ($s$). Spearman's is thus a two-factor theory of intelligence, the $g$-factor being regarded as the essential measure of intelligence and therefore that which must be tapped in testing. An intelligence test conforming to this theory would include items saturated with $g$ so that measurement would cause the testee's level of $g$ to emerge and the effects of $s$ to cancel out. 5. (L.L. Thurstone) A composite of a number of groups of mental operations, each having its own unifying primary factor that is relatively independent of the others. In addition, a second-order general factor is responsible for part of the common ground between some primary factors. Some of the primary factors which have been identified are: the number factor, the ability to do numerical calculations rapidly and accurately; the role memory factor, the ability to memorize quickly; and the verbal factor, involved in verbal comprehension. 6. (D. Wechsler) The individual's global capacity to act purposefully, to think rationally, and to deal effectively with his environment. Intelligence is not, however, the sum of these abilities, because such factors as drive, incentive and motivation influence intelligent behavior, as does the particular way in which the various abilities are combined. In addition, excess of anyone's ability does not necessarily add to behavior's effectiveness as a whole. Despite the fact that intelligence is not the sum of intellectual abilities, it can only be evaluated quantitatively by the measurement of the various aspects of these abilities. If general intelligence is not equated with intellectual ability, there is no contradiction. In Wechsler's system, intelligence is measured by the comparison of an individual's performance with the mean for his chronological age group. This procedure yields an Intelligence Quotient, without the use of the Mental Age concept which is considered erroneous because it presupposes a constancy of relationship between mental and chronological age which is known not to exist.

**intelligence, abstract** The ability to understand and manage abstract concepts, relationships, and symbols.

**intelligence, borderline** The level of intelligence which lies between the normal and subnormal levels. The individual is usually considered legally competent but slightly subnormal in intelligence.

**intelligence, coefficient of** An index of relative intelligence obtained by dividing the testee's score by the norm for his chronological age.

**intelligence, concrete** The ability to deal with situations and problems in a practical and effective way.

**intelligence, marginal** The level of intelligence which is between mental deficiency and normalcy.

**intelligence, mechanical** The inborn capacity to understand mechanical objects and mechanisms.

**intelligence, multimodal theory of** The theory that intelligence is made of a group of abilities or factors rather than one single factor.

**intelligence, nonverbal** Intelligence which is measured by nonverbal or performance tests such as visual-motor coordination.

**intelligence quotient** (W. Stern) An index of rate of development in certain aspects of intelligence during childhood, found by determining what percent a child's mental age is of his chronological age. Among late adolescents and adults, it is an index of relative standing in similar aspects of intelligence, on a standard scale whose mean in the general population is 100 and whose standard deviation is approximately 16. A "verbal IQ" emphasizes abilities important for

general academic aptitude. A "nonverbal IQ" stresses abilities important for mechanical aptitude.

**intelligence scale** A standardized intelligence test.

**intelligence test** See *test, intelligence.*

**intelligibility** Capable of being readily understood.

**intend** In psychological contexts "intend" has different meanings. William James has been quoted using the term in the following clause, "What intelligent consciousness 'means' or intends . . ." This usage is common in introspective psychology in which the meaning of a term is the object to which it refers. The word "hammer" refers semantically (intends) to the thing hammer. The word "hammer" may, however, have other pragmatic meanings. The term "intent" is distinguished from "intend" in that the former is used as a present resolve to perform some future action, whereas the latter is used in the perceptual sense of present consciousness which has a relation to an object or a content.

**intensity** 1. (physics) The magnitude of energy or force per given unit. 2. The unanalyzable quantitative attribute of experience which is roughly correlated with the intensity of the physical energy of the stimulus. 3. The strength of any behavior, emotion, or motivation.

**intent analysis** See *analysis, intent.*

**intentional accident** See *accident, intentional.*

**intentionality** Source of the notion of intentionality is the classical conception in which an individual interacts with an object in such a way that perception of an object is the result of a fusion of *eidola* from the object and a ray emanating from the subject. According to Plato, perception is an interaction of the object with the individual such that wine tastes sour to a sick individual. On the level of thinking, the nature of intentionality is that judgments are "of something" (Plato, *Theaetetus,* 189A).

The term was used by scholastic scholars to distinguish types of mental acts. *First intention* referred to the formation of classes by comparing objects. *Second intention* is what we would call today a second abstractive process from the comparison of classes. As a result of second intentions the primitive terms of logic, such as identity and difference, were constructed.

In the context of mental phenomena, intentionality refers to a relation between an object and a mental act. Within Aristotle's naive realism and substance theory of mind, objects impress their form on the mind, which has the capacity of becoming any form. The form of the object was held to exist in the mind intentionally. This is known as the doctrine of intentional inexistence.

For Brentano intentionality characterized relations between humans and other objects but was not to be found in the physical world. Thus, the distinction between the mental and the physical was the property of intentionality.

Recently G. Bergmann has defined intentionality as "means" in the sentence, "The proposition this is green means this is green." "Means" refers to an intentional relation that is analytic, specific to a world in which there are minds, and which subsists as a logical form.

**inter response time** Time between two successive responses; the response-response interval. IRT's may selectively be reinforced yielding the drl and drh schedules; the former being differential reinforcement of low rates of responding, or large IRT's, the latter being differential reinforcement of high rates of responding, or small IRT's.

**inter schedule** See *reinforcement, schedule of: interpolated.*

**interaction, afferent** (C. L. Hull) The hypothesized mutual influence of the peripheral neural processes involved in perception.

**interaction principle** (C. L. Hull) The principle that all active afferent neural impulses interact at any given moment and partially change as a result of each varying combination.

**interaction process analysis** (F. Bales) A method consisting of four major categories and twelve subcategories by which reactions of members of a group are analyzed for emotional and problem solving responses.

**interactional psychoanalysis** See *psychoanalysis, interactional.*

**interactional psychotherapy** See *psychotherapy, interactional.*

**interactionism** A theory postulating reciprocal causation or interaction between mind and body as the solution to the psycho-physical problem.

**interactionist approach** The Hertz approach to Rorschach interpretation which seeks to integrate Rorschach configurations with socio-educational-situational-life style variables so as to create a broader and potentially objective configurational pattern.

**interactive measurement** See *measurement, interactive.*

**interactive scale units** Units on a psychological scale which are derived from actual physical and social effects of behavior and are thus in units compatible with those of physics. (Opposed to solipsistic measurement, within the individual.)

**interbehavior** (J. R. Kantor) Adjustive interaction between an organism and its environment.

**interbehavioral psychology** See *psychology, interbehavioral.*

**interbrain** Diencephalon.

**intercalation** The automatic, illogical and irrelevant insertion of a sound or word between other words or phrases.

**intercept** The distance from a point of origin to the point at which a line crosses a reference axis.

**intercorrelation** The correlation of each variable with each of the other variables in a group, usually arranged in tabular form.

**intercourse 1.** Interaction in any modality of two or more individuals or groups. **2.** Coitus.

**intercourse, buccal** The application of the mouth to the genitals.

**intercranial stimulation (ICS)** See *electrical brain stimulation.*

**interego** (W. Stekel) Proposed substitute for Freud's term superego to imply the function of the intermediary between crude libidinal impulses and their final conscious aims according to moral principles.

**interest 1.** An enduring attitude consisting of the feeling that a certain object or activity is significant and accompanied by selective attention to that object or activity. **2.** A state of motivation which directs activity toward certain goals. **3.** The element, either acquired or congenital in an individual's make-up, from which an individual would be unable to learn. **4.** (K. Pribram) The resultants of emotional (affective) and motivational (appetitive) processes.

**interest, doctrine of** The belief that learning cannot occur without the student's feeling of interest in the subject or activity and that education should begin with an appeal to the present interests with the aim of continuing to induce broadened and more varied ones.

**interest inventory** See *inventory, interest.*

**interference 1.** Conflict caused by incompatible or competing motives, ideas, precepts, or acts. **2.** The inhibition of a piece of learning or an association by a conflicting memory or thought. **3.** A diminution in the amplitude of sound or light waves taking place when two waves which are out of phase, occur simultaneously.

**interference tube** A complex conducting tube arranged such that sound waves of different lengths periodically cancel those tones to which they are tuned, producing tones of any required degree of purity.

**interindividual cathexis** See *cathexis, interindividual.*

**interjection theory** The theory which attributes the origin of spoken language to automatic or forced exclamatory sounds.

**interlock schedule** See *reinforcement, schedule of: interlocking.*

**interlocking reinforcement** See *reinforcement, interlocking.*

**interlocking (interlock) schedule** See *reinforcement, schedule of: interlocking.*

**intermediate gene** See *gene, intermediate.*

**intermittence tone** See *tone, interruption.*

**intermittent reinforcement** See *reinforcement, intermittent.*

**intermittent schedule** See *reinforcement, intermittent schedule of.*

**intern** An individual who has completed a given course of formal instruction and subsequently practices the profession for which he was trained, under the supervision of experienced professionals.

**internal capsule** A relatively large tract of nerve fibers passing through the corpus striatum.

**internal consistency, coefficient of** An index of the degree to which a consistent score can be obtained from different parts of a test, as exhibited by the degree to which testees score comparably. The degree of internal consistency is usually computed by correlating split-halves of the test items, or by the Hoyt or Kuder-Richardson formulas.

**internal ear** See *labyrinth.*

**internal environment** See *environment, internal.*

**internal inhibition** See *inhibition, internal.*

**internal reinforcement** See *reinforcement, internal.*

**internal secretion** See *secretion, internal.*

**internal validation** See *validation, internal.*

**internalization** (psychoanalysis) The process by which interactions between the individual and the external world are replaced by inner representations of them and their results. The process contributes to super-ego formation and the substitution of outer for inner controls.

**International Classification System of Diseases** The classification system of diseases, developed by the World Health Organization for uniform use throughout the world. The classifications of mental disorders and diseases of the nervous system and sense organs follow:

### MENTAL DISORDERS (290-315)
Psychoses (290-299)
- 290 Senile and presenile dementia
- 291 Alcoholic psychosis
- 292 Psychosis associated with intracranial infection
- 293 Psychosis associated with other cerebral condition
- 294 Psychosis associated with other physical conditions
- 295 Schizophrenia
- 296 Affective psychoses
- 297 Paranoid states
- 298 Other psychoses
- 299 Unspecified psychosis

Neuroses, personality disorders, and other nonpsychotic mental disorders (300-309)
- 300 Neuroses
- 301 Personality disorders
- 302 Sexual deviation
- 303 Alcoholism
- 304 Drug dependence
- 305 Physical disorders of presumably psychogenic origin
- 306 Special symptoms not elsewhere classified
- 307 Transient situational disturbances
- 308 Behavior disorders of childhood
- 309 Mental disorders not specified as psychotic associated with physical conditions

Mental retardation (310-315)
- 310 Borderline mental retardation
- 311 Mild mental retardation
- 312 Moderate mental retardation
- 313 Severe mental retardation
- 314 Profound mental retardation
- 315 Unspecified mental retardation

### DISEASES OF THE NERVOUS SYSTEM AND SENSE ORGANS (320-389)
Inflammatory diseases of central nervous system (320-324)
- 320 Meningitis
- 321 Phlebitis and thrombophlebitis of intracranial venous sinuses
- 322 Intracranial and intraspinal abscess
- 323 Encephalitis, myelitis, and encephalomyelitis
- 324 Late effects of intracranial abscess or pyogenic infection

Hereditary and familial diseases of nervous system (330-333)
- 330 Hereditary neuromuscular disorders
- 331 Hereditary diseases of the striatopallidal system
- 332 Hereditary ataxia
- 333 Other hereditary and familial diseases of nervous system

Other diseases of central nervous system (340-349)
- 340 Multiple sclerosis
- 341 Other demyelinating diseases of central nervous system
- 342 Paralysis agitans
- 343 Cerebral spastic infantile paralysis
- 344 Other cerebral paralysis
- 345 Epilepsy
- 346 Migraine
- 347 Other diseases of brain
- 348 Motor neuron disease
- 349 Other diseases of spinal cord

Diseases of nerves and peripheral ganglia (350-358)
- 350 Facial paralysis
- 351 Trigeminal neuralgia
- 352 Brachial neuritis
- 353 Sciatica
- 354 Polyneuritis and polyradiculitis
- 355 Other and unspecified forms of neuralgia and neuritis
- 356 Other dieases of cranial nerves
- 357 Other diseases of peripheral nerves except autonomic
- 358 Diseases of peripheral autonomic nervous system

Inflammatory diseases of the eye (360-369)
- 360 Conjunctivitis and opthalmia
- 361 Blepharitis
- 362 Hordeolum
- 363 Keratitis
- 364 Iritis
- 365 Choroiditis
- 366 Other inflammation of uveal tract
- 367 Inflammation of optic nerve and retina
- 368 Inflammation of lacrimal glands and ducts
- 369 Other inflammatory diseases of eye

Other disease and conditions of eye (370-379)
- 370 Refractive errors
- 371 Corneal opacity

372 Pterygrium
373 Strabismus
374 Cataract
375 Glaucoma
376 Detachment of retina
377 Other disease of retina and optic nerve
378 Other diseases of eye
379 Blindness
Diseases of the ear and mastoid process (380-389)
380 Otitis externa
381 Otitis media without mention of mastoiditis
382 Otitis media with mastoiditis
383 Mastoiditis without mention of otitis media
384 Other inflammatory disease of ear
385 Meniere's disease
386 Otosclerosis
387 Other disease of ear and mastoid process
388 Deaf mutism
389 Other deafness

**internship, in clinical psychology** One year of supervised training in a clinical facility including diagnosis, therapy, research, seminars, and conferences required to obtain a Ph.D. degree.

**internuncial neurons** See *neurons, internuncial.*

**interoceptive system** The system of receptors located within the body as distinguished from the exteroceptive system, situated near the surface of the body, and the proprioceptive system, situated within the body tissue.

**interoceptor** A sense organ or receptor located inside the body in contrast to one located at the surface or within the body tissue. It receives stimuli related to visceral processes.

**interocular distance** The distance between the central points of the pupils of the two eyes when they are in the normal position for fixation.

**interosystem** (R. Monroe) Any system which functions wholly within the organism and is controlled by the autonomic nervous system, such as the cardiac and respiratory systems.

**interpersonal psychotherapy** See *psychotherapy, interpersonal.*

**interpersonal theory** See *theory, interpersonal.*

**interpolated reinforcement** See *reinforcement, interpolated.*

**interpolated (inter) schedule** See *reinforcement, schedule of: interpolated.*

**interpolation** The calculation, either graphically or by mathematical formula, of a value between two values in a series of measurements.

**interposition** The partial obscuring of one object by another, used as a monocular cue in the perception of distance and depth.

**interpretation 1.** The description, formulation, or reformulation of data, an event, or thought in a more familiar or significant way. **2.** (psychoanalysis) The therapist's formulation or description of the patient's productions, particularly translation of

resistances, defenses, and symbols into terms which are understandable by the patient.

**interpretation, allegoric** The view that assumes a symbolic expression is intentional on the part of the speaker.

**interpretation, anagogic** (C. G. Jung) Interpretation of dreams based on the premise that they not only reflect conflict stemming from infantile wishes, but also the idealistic strivings of the unconscious.

**interpretation of dreams** See *dream interpretation.*

**interpretive therapy** See *therapy, interpretive.*

**interquartile range** (statistics) The distance between the first and third quartiles, encompassing the central fifty percent of the values in the distribution.

**interruption tone** See *tone, interruption.*

**intersensory perception** See *perception, intersensory.*

**intersexuality** The possession of sexual traits of both sexes, especially secondary sex characteristics.

**interstimulation** Behavior which is modified by the presence or perceived presence of others, whether there is intentional communication or not.

**interstitial neurosyphilis** See *syphilis, cerebral.*

**intertone** A tone of intermediate pitch between two tones of nearly equal pitch produced when the two tones are sounded together.

**intertrial interval** See *interval, intertrial.*

**interval, class (i)** (statistics) The number of score units between the upper and lower limits, or the range of values of a class in a frequency distribution.

**interval estimation** (statistics) The estimate of the population parameter in terms of a range of values within which the parameter lies with a certain degree of probability. The length of the confidence interval depends on the variance of the derived sampling distribution.

**interval, fiducial** The distance between certain points or limits beyond which a statistic is not expected to occur except by chance in more than a stated percentage of the samplings.

**interval, intertrial** The interval of time between successive presentations of the stimuli.

**interval, median** The class interval containing the median.

**interval, mode** The class interval which includes the mode.

**interval of uncertainty (IU)** The range between the upper and lower thresholds in judgments of difference.

**interval reinforcement** See *reinforcement, interval.*

**interval scale** See *scale, interval.*

**interval schedule** See *schedule, interval.*

**intervention 1.** Behavior by an organism designed

to alter the environment or its relation to the environment. 2. The therapist's direction of or influence on a client's actions.

**interview** A conversation between a therapist, counselor, or other professional, and a patient, client, or perspective employee, designed to elicit information for the purpose of assessing diagnosis, treatment, qualifications, or aid in research or guidance. According to the purpose of the interview it may be conducted using a directive or non-directive approach. For therapeutic purposes, the non-directive approach is usually preferred.

**interview, amytal** Interview conducted with the patient having been injected with small doses of amytal, inducing a completely relaxed and serene state which facilitates the communication of thoughts and the expression of previously repressed memories, affects and conflicts.

**interview counseling** An interview of an individual with a professional counselor who offers advice and guidance in the appropriate problematical area.

**interview, diagnostic** An interview whose purpose is to establish a diagnosis, treatment and prognosis of a disorder of the one interviewed.

**interview, face-to-face** A type of interview during which the therapist and patient sit opposite each other, characteristic of supportive interviewing and some forms of insight interviewing, such as Sullivanian therapy.

**interview, stress** An interview during which the interviewee is under intentionally induced emotional tension.

**interview, structured** An interview which has a definite predetermined cause.

**interviewer bias** The effect of the interviewer's opinions, values, expectations, and prejudices upon the process and interpretation of an interview.

**intimacy, principle of** (Gestalt psychology) The principle that Gestalts are wholes composed of interdependent parts, none of which may be changed without changing the whole.

**intoxication** A condition of exhilaration, depression, or alternating states between the two, caused by poisoning due to the ingestion of alcohol, drugs, or poison.

**intoxication, hypnagogic** Obsolete term for a hypnopompic state in which process of awakening generates dream images which persist into and may induce action in the awakened state.

**intraception** (H. A. Murray) Orientation or attitude characterized by humanism, feeling and imagination.

**intracranial** Within the cranium or brain.

**intracranial tumor** See *tumor, intracranial.*

**intraindividual cathexis** See *cathexis, intraindividual.*

**intraocular modification** Any change that takes place in the visual stimulus during its passage from the cornea to the ocular nerve, as a result of the general or individual structure of the eye.

**intrapsychic** Arising from or occurring within the psyche, mind, or personality, such as intrapsychic conflicts, the expressions of the existence of two opposing impulses or motivations within the individual.

**intrapunitive** See *intropunitive.*

**intrinsic behavior** See *behavior, intrinsic.*

**intrinsic constant** See *central constant.*

**intrinsic eye muscles** Muscles of the iris and of the ciliary body of the eye.

**intrinsic motivation** See *motivation, intrinsic.*

**intrinsic reward** See *reward, intrinsic.*

**intrinsic thalamus** See *thalamus, intrinsic.*

**introception** Internalization of a social group's standards or motives.

**introjection** The desire to swallow the love object and to identify with it is called introjection. Introjection expresses the primitive and ambivalent attitude that combines love and destruction in a cannibalistic incorporation of the love object, and in identification with the object incorporated. When certain adults are unable to develop more mature object relationships, their weak egos regress to the oral defense mechanism of introjection. Neurotic identification with the love object becomes the only possible object relationship.

**introjection, projection and introjection process** The process of learning and experiencing consisting of introjection, projection, and introjection. The person projects internal states into the environment, then introjects or is receptive to those aspects which will affect him. The introjections circularly determine the following projections. As a result of this process, the world is a meaningful part of the person and exists only as an aspect of that person. It also provides the individual with a system of values which affects his actions, and experiences.

**intropunitive** 1. (S. Rosenzweig) Frustration reaction in which the frustrated individual blames himself for what happened and feels guilty, ashamed, or humiliated because of it. 2. Personality type characterized by intropunitive frustration reactions.

**introspection** Observation and contemplation of one's own mental processes, and experiences; systematic self-observation.

**introspectionism** (W. Wundt) The method of psychology which holds that introspection is the basic method of psychological investigation.

**introspective psychology** See *introspectionism.*

**introversion** 1. Inner-directed personality orientation characterized by interest in personal thoughts and feelings rather than in social concerns or external matters. 2. (C. G. Jung) Dominance of subjective perception and cognition resulting in self-centered orientation and involvement with one's own inner world. **3.** (H. J. Eysenck) A personality type based on particular neural structures which cause a slow development of reactive inhibition, weak inhibition and fast dissipation of inhibition. The neurotic form is characterized by anxiety and depression symptoms.

**introversion, active** (C. G. Jung) Inward direction of libido which is willed by the subject or a voluntary preoccupation with internal subjective reality.

**introversion-extraversion** **1.** (H. J. Eysenck) A factor analyzed bipolar variable basic to the personality. **2.** See *introversion*. **3.** See *extraversion*.

**introversion, passive** (C. G. Jung) Inward direction of libido due to an inability to direct it toward external objects or an inability to relate to external reality.

**introversive** A Rorschach postulate, referring to those instances where the sum of human movement responses is substantially greater than the weighted sum of color responses. When the ratio (Erlebnistypus) manifests such a characteristic, the person is considered prone to derive his more basic gratifications from within himself rather than from interaction with his environment.

**introversiveness** (Rorschach) Characterized by inwardness and a tendency to interpret the world according to personal needs and values usually accompanied by a strong imagination and well-developed cerebral and autonomic processes.

**introvert** One who has an introverted personality or orientation.

**introverted feeling type** (C. G. Jung) Personality type characterized by a dominant subjective orientation such that the individual lives within his own internal world of emotions as a daydreamer or quiet, peaceful person.

**introverted intuition type** (C. G. Jung) Personality type characterized by attention to imagery which influences activity and a tendency to live within himself.

**introverted sensation type** (C. G. Jung) Personality type characterized by attendance to the external world through perceptions dominated by the individual's subjective internal state.

**introverted thinking type** (C. G. Jung) Personality type characterized by thorough organization of ideational patterns until they suit the individual, and some success in social contacts.

**introverted type** See *type, introverted*.

**intuition** Direct and immediate perception, judgment or knowledge, arrived at without prior conscious cogitation or reflective thinking.

**intuitionism** The philosophical theory stressing intuitive knowledge of fundamental truths in ethics, concerning right and wrong, and aesthetics, concerning beauty.

**intuitive type** See *type, intuitive*.

**invalid** **1.** A conclusion, argument, or method which is not logically correct because of violation of the established rules of logic. **2.** A test which does not measure that which it was designed to measure.

**invariance** **1.** The property of remaining constant despite changes in other conditions. **2.** The tendency of an image to retain its original size regardless of changes in the distance of the surface upon which it is projected.

**inventive-response test** An "open-ended" test in which the subject is restricted in response only by the instructions, as opposed to a selective-response test in which given response alternatives restrict the possible responses.

**inventory** A catalog or list used for assessing the presence or absence of certain behaviors, interests, attitudes or other items regarded as relevant for a given purpose.

**inventory, adjustment** A technique used to obtain evidence concerning an individual's adjustment from the individual himself. Also called surveys, schedules or questionnaires. An adjustment inventory contains statements or questions believed to be indicative of good or bad adjustment. The subject is requested to show what is generally or typically true of himself by choosing either "yes-no," "agree-disagree," or "like-dislike," depending on the particular inventory being used. The answers are scored and then compared to norms based on large samples of individuals.

In some cases, such as the SRA (Science Research Associates) Youth Inventory, the subject marks the appropriate answer space only if the statement applies to him. The following are some statements from a few of the areas covered by the SRA Youth Inventory:

| Area | Illustrative Item |
| --- | --- |
| My School | 1. I have difficulty keeping my mind on my studies. |
| Looking Ahead | 35. What shall I do after high school? |
| About Myself | 81. I feel "low" much of the time. |

**Inventory, Bell Adjustment** A personality questionnaire used with subjects fourteen and up, yielding scores on home, health, social and emotional adjustment.

**inventory, interest** A questionnaire used in personality diagnosis, vocational guidance and personnel selection, consisting of items designed to reveal objects and activities preferred by or interesting to the individual.

**Inventory, Minnesota Counseling** (R. F. Berdie and W. L. Layton) An inventory developed from 1953 to 1957 designed for use with secondary school and college applicants in counseling.

**inventory, personality** A questionnaire or checklist which is usually answered by an individual about himself. It generally consists of numerous statements about personal characteristics to which the individual must respond, indicating whether they apply to him or not with "yes," "no" or "doubtful." Norms based on large representative samples are used in interpreting and comparing results.

**inventory test**  See *test, inventory*.

**inverse correlation**  See *correlation, inverse*.

**inverse relationship**  Any relationship in which high values of one variable are associated with low values of the other.

**inverse square law**  See *law, inverse square*.

**inversion**  A choromosomal aberration in which a segment of a chromosome is reversed.

**inversion, amphigenous**  Condition in which the homosexual individual engages in sex relations with those of the opposite sex, in contrast with absolute inversion.

**inversion of affect**  See *affect, inversion of*.

**invert**  An individual who prefers sexual partners of the same sex.

**inverted factor analysis**  See *Q technique*.

**investment**  1. (psychoanalysis) The psychic energy expended upon an object. 2. The potential amount of affect or psychic energy with which an object is charged. Also called cathexis.

**inviolacy motive**  (H. A. Murray) The need to defend onself and prevent self-depreciation.

**involuntary**  An action which occurs without intention or volition.

**involution**  Retrograde change in development accompanied by physiological and psychological deterioration as in senility and sometimes menopause.

**involutional depression**  See *psychotic reaction, involutional*.

**involutional melancholia**  See *psychotic reaction, involutional*.

**involutional psychotic reactions**  See *psychotic reactions, involutional*.

**Iowa Tests of Basic Skills**  See *tests, Iowa, of Basic Skills*.

**I-P-I process**  See *introjection, projection, and introjection process*.

**iproniazid**  A compound $C_3H_{13}N_3O$ which was used as a monoaminooxidase inhibitor antidepressant drug with mental patients until 1961 when it was withdrawn from the market because of the danger of causing an irreversible jaundice.

**ipsation**  Autoerotism.

**ipsative method**  A method of measuring traits using the individual's own behavior as the standard for comparison.

**ipsative scale**  See *scale, ipsative*.

**ipsative scoring**  (R. B. Cattell) Standardization of scores obtained for a given individual. The ipsative scoring accounts for the mean and standard deviation of similar responses given by a certain individual to a variety of stimuli and/or on numerous occasions.

**ipsilateral**  On the same side.

**IQ**  See *intelligence quotient*.

**iris**  The pigmented muscular disc of the eye, located in front of the lens and surrounding the pupil, the contractions of which regulate the amount of light entering the eye.

**irradiation**  1. The spreading of rays of light. 2. An ostensible increase in the size of a small bright stimulus seen on a dark background. 3. The spread of an afferent impulse to adjacent fibers as it approaches and travels through the central nervous system. 4. A spread of excitation in muscle fibers upon increase in the intensity of stimulation. 5. (I. P. Pavlov) The spread of excitation and inhibition through the cerebral cortex. 6. (I. P. Pavlov) The elicitation of the conditioned response by stimuli similar to the conditioned stimulus. 7. The exposure of tissues to radiation.

**irradiation, excitatory**  (I. P. Pavlov) The spreading out of stimulation in the cerebrum.

**irradiation theory**  See *theory, irradiation*.

**irrational type**  See *type, irrational*.

**irreality level**  (K. Lewin) The region of the individual's life space in which actions and thoughts are determined more by needs and desires than by objective recognition of situations. Prejudices and fantasies are of the irreality level.

**irreality-reality dimension**  (K. Lewin) The continuum on which behaviors can be ordered according to the degree they are regulated by either needs and desires, or by the reality demands of the environment.

**irritability**  1. The characteristic property of living matter of being capable of responses to stimulation or excitation. 2. Over-sensitivity to stimulation.

**IRT**  See *inter response time*.

**ischnophonia; ischophonia**  Stammering or stuttering.

**Ishihari test**  See *test, Ishihari*.

**Island of hearing**  See *tonal islands*.

**Island of Reil**  See *Reil, island of*.

**Islands of Langerhans**  See *Langerhans, islands of*.

**isochronism**  1. Correspondence in time or frequency of occurrence between two processes. 2. Having the same chronaxy.

**isocortex**  The most common type cortex of the cerebral hemispheres, composed of six layers of cells originating in the gray matter. Also called neocortex.

**isogenic**  Having identical genotypes as in identical

twins, triplets, etc. A homograft is accepted in these cases.

**isolate** 1. To separate, set apart, or abstract from a class. 2. (psychoanalysis) To separate ideas or memories from their affect. 3. (J. L. Moreno) The individual who scored lowest in a group on the sociogram.

**isolation** (S. Freud) A defense mechanism of the ego. It consists of interposing of a refractory period in which the individual refrains from thinking and acting. It is usually an aftermath of a traumatic or severely unpleasant experience.

**isolation defense** See *defense, isolation.*

**isolation effect** The isolation of an item by use of distinctive type or color in the center of a group in serial learning, resulting in the facilitation of learning.

**isolation, psychic** (C. G. Jung) Withdrawal from social contacts for fear that some unconscious material might be divulged.

**isometric twitch** See *twitch, isometric.*

**isomorphism** 1. (logic) A one-to-one relation between the elements of two distinct sets. 2. (Gestalt) The proposition that there exists a one-to-one correspondence between a stimulus and the excitatory fields in the brain; that is, if there is a perceived difference of size there will be a corresponding difference in the size of the excitatory fields.

**isopathic principle** See *principle, isopathic.*

**isophilia** (H. S. Sullivan) Affectionate behavior with the absence of expressed or sublimated genital lust, towards individuals of one's own sex.

**isophonic contour** A graphic representation of the interdependent relationships between the physical properties of a sound and the corresponding auditory experiences.

**isopodic method** (R. B. Cattell) A method of comparing source trait factor scores across cultural or age groups by producing comparability of a) the scaling of the variables themselves, and b) the factor estimation weights.

**isosensitivity function** See *receiver operating characteristic.*

**isotropic** Items or attributes placed in an ordered series on any nonquantitative basis, as for example, army ranks.

**isovaleric acidema** A rare aminoaciduria associated with mild mental retardation.

**isthmus** 1. The neck or the connecting part of an organ. 2. The part of the brain which connects the spinal cord with the forebrain and the cerebellum.

**item analysis** See *analysis, item.*

**item difficulty** The level of difficulty of a test item. The frequency with which it is passed or failed in a given testee population.

**item scaling** A statistical procedure used for assigning a test item to its place, determined by its level of difficulty.

**item selection** The process by which an item is selected for use on a test on the basis of its validity, reliability, scorability, scalability, and unique contribution.

**item validity** See *validity, item.*

**item weighting** The process by which a test item is assigned the proportion of the total score it will determine.

**items, stop** Starred items in personality inventories which are used to screen individuals who may need psychological help.

**ITPA** See *test, Illinois, of Psycholinguistic Abilities.*

**IU** See *interval of uncertainty.*

**Ivanov-Smolensky technique** See *technique, Ivanov-Smolensky.*

# J

**J** (C. L. Hull) Delay in reinforcement.

**j** The number of standard deviations from the mean.

**j coefficient** See *coefficient, j.*

**J curve** See *curve, J.*

**Jackson, John Hughlings (1834-1911)** A British neurologist who described the seizures due to focal lesions of the cerebral cortex, since called Jacksonian epilepsy. He is also credited with the classic study of aphasia, and with J. A. L. Clarke, the first full description of syringomyelia. His description of paralysis of one-half of the palate, pharynx, and larynx, and flaccid paralysis of the homolateral sternocleidomastoid and part of the trapezius resulted in its being known as Jackson's syndrome.

**Jackson's law** The principle that in deterioration in mental functioning resulting from disease, the order of degeneration is the reverse of the order of development or acquisition.

**jactation or jactitation** Excessive restlessness characterized by irregular and convulsive movements of the body.

**James-Lange theory** Two separate, distinct theories about emotions which are often commonly and incorrectly viewed as one. **1.** C. Lange (1834-1900), a Danish physiologist, studied the circulatory system and concluded that emotions were identical with experiences of vascular change. **2.** W. James (1842-1910) incorporated Lange's idea into his own theory which stated that bodily changes, particularly visceral and muscular changes, immediately followed the perception of an emotion-provoking situation and that one's experience of these physiological changes is the emotion. This theory challenged the popular view that emotions preceded and caused bodily changes.

**James, William (1842-1910)** American psychologist and philosopher, developed pragmatic philosophy and functionalistic psychology. His main work, *Principles of Psychology* (1878), introduced an evolutionary-biological approach to mental life viewed as an important tool in adjustment to life. His theory of emotions assumes that bodily changes follow directly the perception of existing fact, and that our feeling of the same dangers as they occur is the emotions. Thus we feel sorry because we cry, not vice versa. James introduced the concept of "stream of consciousness." Consciousness itself is a product of evolution and has been evolved as all other functions. James stressed pleasure and usefulness as the main motives of behavior.

**Janet, Pierre (1859-1947)** French student of Charcot who had competed with Freud. Studied dissociation and hysteria, and pioneered interest in the unconscious. Fully at home in both medicine and general psychology, he tried to bring the two closer together.

**Jansky-Bielschowsky disease** See *Tay-Sachs disease.*

**Japanese encephalitis** See *encephalitis, Japanese.*

**jargon aphasia** See *aphasia, jargon.*

**Jaspers, Karl (1883-1969)** A Swiss-German existentialist philosopher. Prior to his philosophical work, Jaspers was a practicing psychiatrist. His emphasis, as such, was on the need for detailed descriptions of patient's subjective experiences and on the necessity of empathy with patients' feelings in order for therapy to be successful. *Die Psychologie der Weltanschauungen* ("Psychology of Personal Views on Life") marked his move towards philosophy. As a philosopher, Jaspers' aim was to provide a theory encompassing all problems related to man's existence. Thus he distinguished three modes of being: "being-there," the objective world known through observation and experiment; "being-oneself," man's personal existence dependent upon awareness of self, liberty, and assertion of self by decision and choice; and "being-in-itself," the representative of the world in its transcendence. According to Jaspers, man can participate in all modes at once but can never fully grasp the entire meaning of existence. Communication is central to Jaspers' theory. Man exists only to the extent that he is in communication with others, or to the extent that another existence reflects him. Though he is alone in dealing with inescapable situations such as death, anguish, and struggle, he is not isolated. Freedom, in essence, is man's search for communication with the existence of others.

**Jastrow cylinders** A series of hollow, weighted rubber cylinders used for the determination of thresholds for pressure and kinaesthesis in lifting.

**Jastrow illusion** See *illusion, Jastrow.*

**Java man** Pithecanthropus erectus.

**jealousy, projected** Jealousy derived from an individual's own actual infidelity or from repressed desires for it.

**Jendrassik reinforcement** See *reinforcement, Jendrassik.*

**jnd** See *just noticeable difference.*

**job analysis** A thorough examination and breakdown of the ability and experience requirements, work conditions and opportunities for advancement on a particular job or occupation.

**job placement** The assignment of a person to a job usually on the basis of his aptitude, interest, experience, and personality.

**Jocasta complex** See *complex, Jocasta.*

**joints, disturbances of** 1. Disturbances of joints and the muscular system due to organic or psychogenic causes. 2. See *arthritis, rheumatoid.* 3. See *back disorders, psychogenic.*

**Jones, Ernest (1879-1958)** British psychiatrist and psychoanalyst. One of the earliest disciples of S. Freud; the first British psychoanalyst. Wrote extensively on psychoanalytic technique, dream interpretation, nightmares, etc. Author of the most detailed biography of S. Freud.

**Jordan curve** See *curve, Jordan.*

**Joseph's syndrome** A rare aminoaciduria associated with seizures.

**Jost's law** See *law, Jost's.*

**judgment** 1. The process of discovering an objective or intrinsic relationship between two or more objects, facts, experiences or concepts. 2. That faculty which enables an individual to make judgments. 3. A critical evaluation of a person, object or situation. 4. (psychophysics) A subject's verbal responses to stimuli, concerning its presence or absence and magnitude used for the determination of threshold.

**judgment, absolute** In a series of comparisons, the evaluation of the first of a pair of items prior to the presentation of the second member of the pair.

**judgment, comparative** A report which declares the subject's perception of how two or more stimuli compare on a particular dimension.

**judgment, moral** (J. Piaget) Judgment concerning whether an act is right or wrong. The moral judgment is a function of development.

**Juke family** (R.L. Dugdale) The history of this family was studied in the early part of the century in an attempt to show a family with low intelligence also has generally low social competence.

**Jung, Carl Gustav (1875-1961)** Swiss psychiatrist, founder of "analytical psychology." Discovered "feeling-toned complexes" (1904-09); proposed psychogenic theory of schizophrenia (1907); cooperated with Freud (1907-1913); introduced principle of analysis of analysts (1912); separated from Freud on account of his divergent concepts of libido and of incest. Described psychological typology ("extra- and introversion," 1921). Defined psyche as self-regulating system, aiming at individuation, manifested in compensatory function of dreams, with the symbol as "transformer of energy." Distinguished three layers of psyche: consciousness, the personal unconscious, and the collective unconscious, the latter containing the "archetypes." Explored psychological significance of myth, religion, and alchemy; formulated concept of "synchronicity" as a principle of "acausal connection."

**Jung association test** See *test, Jung association.*

**Jungian typology** See *extraversion-introversion.*

**just noticeable difference** The least difference, usually in a quantitative aspect, between two stimuli, one of which is barely above the threshold. Statistically, the difference is not detected as often as it is.

**just noticeable differences method** See *method, just noticeable differences.*

**juvenile delinquency** See *delinquency, juvenile.*

**juvenile general paresis** See *paresis, general juvenile.*

# K

k  1. (mathematics) The most commonly used symbol for representing a constant. 2. (statistics) The coefficient of alienation, given by the formula

$$\sqrt{1-r^2}$$

where $r$ is the correlation coefficient. 3. (Rorschach) The symbol used to represent a response in which shading was a determinant.

K  (C. L. Hull) Incentive motivation considered as a part of reaction potential.

K'  (C. L. Hull) The physical reward or incentive in motivation.

K complex  See *complex, K*.

K scale  See *scale, K*.

Kahlbaum, Karl Ludwig (1828-1899)  A German psychiatrist who described in 1863 mental deterioration in adolescence and called it *paraphrenia hebetica*. In 1874 he described catatonic stupor and called it *Spannungs Irrsinn* (insanity of tension); he believed that the stupor was caused by a brain disease.

Kahn Test of Symbol Arrangement  See *test, Kahn, of Social Arrangement*.

Kalinowsky, Lothar B. (1899-     )  Born in Berlin, Germany; psychiatrist and neurologist. Interested in somatic treatments in psychiatry since working with malaria treatment in the Viennese Clinic of Wagner-von Jauregg. After work in German neuropsychiatric centers he worked with the Italian psychiatrists Cerletti and Bini at the time of their discovery of electric convulsive treatment. Since 1940 in the United States, continues his work in the field of somatic treatments. Wrote various books, the latest (with H. Hippius) in 1969, *Psychopharmacological Convulsive and other Somatic Treatments in Psychiatry*.

Kallikak family  (H. H. Goddard) A ficticious name given by H. H. Goddard to a family he studied intensively, one branch (496 individuals) of which was noted for its good citizenship and in several cases, distinguished service to the community, while the other branch (480 individuals) showed almost without exception, a record of criminality, degeneracy, insanity, and severe mental retardation.

Kallmann, Franz J. (1897-1965)  Psychiatrist and geneticist, born and trained in Germany, lived and worked in United States from 1936. Developed genetic theory of schizophrenia based on extensive study of families and twins, showing that the risk of schizophrenia in relatives varies directly with the degree of genetic closeness; formulated hypothesis that predisposition is inherited and manifestation depends on constitutional and environmental factors; provided evidence by studies of twins for the role of genetic factors in manic-depressive psychosis, involutional psychosis, homosexuality, and the aging process; demonstrated increasing marriage and fertility rates among hospitalized schizophrenic patients; concerned from an early date with problems of genetic counseling in a psychiatric setting; studied family and mental health problems of persons with early total deafness and established in New York the first psychiatric service for the deaf.

Kanzer, Mark (1908-     )  American psychoanalyst. Main studies have been in the application of psychoanalysis to the understanding of human behavior and the promotion of its potentialities 1) through investigations of the history of psychoanalysis; 2) the evaluation of its methods both in the clinical and behavioral fields; 3) in analytic education, research and administrative organizations; 4) in definition of its terms and concepts.

Kappa effect  (J. Cohen) See *Tau effect*.

Kardiner, Abram (1891-     )  Past Director of Psychoanalytic Clinic and Clinical Professor of Psychiatry at Columbia University. Efforts directed chiefly to a study of human adaptation as seen through traumatic neuroses and cross cultural studies of human development. Books written include: *The Individual and his Society* (1939), *The Traumatic Neuroses of War* (1941), *The Psychological Frontiers of Society* (1945), *The Mark of Oppression* (with L. Ovesey) (1951), *Sex and Morality* (1954), *War Stress and Neurotic Illness* (1947), *They Studied Man* (1958).

**karyotype** The chromosomal set of an individual; often applied to their photo-micrographs arranged according to a standard classification.

**kathisophobia** Fear of sitting down.

**Keeler polygraph** Lie detector.

**Kelley's constant process** (psychophysics) A technique for the treatment of data from the constant stimulus method, consisting of fitting the data to the normal ogive by using the standard deviation instead of h.

**Kelly, George Alexander (1905-1967)** American clinical psychologist; pioneer in clinical psychology; the first to found a psychological clinic for service and training; proposed a personality theory based on the thesis that the important determinant of a person's behavior is his own conception of the world in which he lives and the people he meets; his chief two-volume work, *The Psychology of Personal Constructs* (1955), and his clinical methods had much influence and stimulated research here and abroad; he taught at Ohio State University for 20 years; lectured in Europe, South America, and the Caribbean area.

**keltolagnia** Sexual excitement associated with stealing.

**Kelvin scale** See *scale, Kelvin.*

**kenophobia; cenophobia** Fear of large, empty spaces.

**Kent-Rosanoff test** See *test, Kent-Rosanoff.*

**Kent Series of Emergency Scales** See *scales, Kent Series of Emergency.*

**keraunophobia** Fear of lightning.

**kernicterus** A disease occurring in infancy manifested by jaundice two or three days after birth, which if untreated, produces convulsions, rigidity, coma and death in 75% of the cases. Mental deficiency, epilepsy, chorea or athetosis often result in those who survive. Also called icterus gravis neonatorum. It is caused by blood incompatibility of blood groups Rh, A, B and O of the fetus with the mother's blood.

**kerosene poisoning** See *poisoning, kerosene.*

**ketotic hypoglycemia** See *hypoglycemia, ketotic.*

**key** 1. A central concept upon which others depend or which facilitates understanding of other concepts. 2. A list of symbols or correct answers used in coding or decoding information, or in scoring a test. 3. (operant conditioning) Any object movement which opens or closes an electric circuity thus meeting the criterion of a reinforcement eligible response.

**Kierkegaard, Sören (1813-1855)** Danish philosopher and writer on theology. Objected to Hegelian rationalism and based his philosophy on the absolute dualism of faith and knowledge, and of thought and reality. Considered himself a "religious author," but was not renowned so much for his theological ideas as for his penetrating analysis of man's inner experiences, man's existential problems. Was probably the first to use the term "existence" in the sense existentialists now use it. His main theme is man and his conflicts; man striving for eternity with an infinite God, but frustrated by his own temporality and finitude. Emphasized that religion was a matter for the individual soul. Author of *Either-Or* (1843), *The Concept of Dread* (1844), and *The Sickness Unto Death* (1849). Discovered in the 20th century. Major influence on existential philosophers such as Martin Heidegger.

**kinephantom** A movement illusion seen in shadow movement, in which the shadows of moving objects, such as the spokes of a wheel, are seen as moving in the opposite direction from that of the object.

**kinesthesis** The sense of body movement and movements of particular body parts, such as muscles, tendons and joints. In conjunction with the static sense derived from the semicircular canals of the ear, it yields information concerning the position of the body and limbs in space. Kinesthesis is divided into: muscle sense, sensors within the muscles which are stimulated by muscle contraction; tendon sense, sensors within the tendons; and joint sense, sensors on joint surfaces which are stimulated by joint flexion.

**kinesthetic aphasia** See *aphasia, afferent motor.*

**kinesthetic apraxia** See *apraxia, afferent.*

**kinesthetic feedback** See *feedback, kinesthetic.*

**kinesthetic memory** See *memory, kinesthetic.*

**kinesthetic method** See *method, kinesthetic.*

**kinesthetic response** See *response, kinesthetic.*

**kinetic aphasia** See *aphasia, efferent.*

**kinetic apraxia** See *apraxia, efferent.*

**kinky hair disease** A genetic, sex-linked transmitted metabolic disorder which results in a slight aminoaciduria in the urine and an excess of glutamic acid in the blood. The main clinical features are mental and physical retardation, lack of pigmentation in the hair, epilepsy and microcephaly.

**kinship system** See *system, kinship.*

**Kirchhoff, Theodor (1853-1922)** A German psychiatrist and noted historian of psychiatry.

**Kjersted-Robinson law** The principle that the amount of information learned during a segment of the total learning time is relatively independent of and constant for different lengths of material.

**Klein, Melanie (1882-1960)** Born in Vienna and died in London. Analyzed by Ferenczi and Abraham, she became an original thinker in the field of psychoanalysis and her technical and theoretical work deeply influenced modern psychoanalytic theory. Pioneered the psychoanalysis of children and evolved the play technique which became the basis of most techniques in child psychotherapy. Her theoretical contributions include the description of the early roots of the Oedipus complex and of the superego, and a conceptualization of the early infantile development in terms of the depressive and the paranoid-schizoid positions. The light she threw on the dynamics of early infantile stages is of particular importance for the understanding and psychoanalytical treatment of psychotic states. In 1926, she came to London and exerted a marked influence on the British Psychoanalytic Society.

**Klein's, Melanie, contribution to psychoanalysis** Melanie Klein, the originator of the technique of psychoanalysis of children, evolved a play technique which gave her a means for direct investigation of the mind of a small child, and enabled her to extend and deepen psychoanalytic knowledge. Her early discoveries established the existence of pregenital forms of the Oedipus complex and the superego, and the importance of unconscious fantasy in all aspects of mental functioning. In the latter part of her scientific work she formulated her findings in terms of development of positions. The *paranoid-schizoid* position gets organized in the first months of life. It is characterized by the infant's relation to part objects, primarily the breast. The leading mechanisms of defense are splitting, projective identification and introjection. Both the object and the ego are split into good and bad. The prevalent anxiety is persecutory. Envy is an important pathogenic factor. The *depressive* position is organized when the infant perceives the mother as a whole person. It is characterized by integration, awareness of separateness from the object, and ambivalence. The prevalent anxiety is a loss of the loved object, and guilt. The depressive anxiety and guilt are defended against by manic defenses, but they also give rise to more positive developments linked with reparation. The roots of the Oedipus complex are in the oral phase in the depressive position following the recognition of the mother's separate existence as a person. Jealousy gradually replaces envy. The points of fixation of psychotic illnesses lie in the paranoid-schizoid position and early stages of the depressive position.

**kleptomania** An obsessive impulse to steal often in the absence of economic motive or desire for the particular objects stolen.

**Klineberg, Otto (1899-    )** American social psychologist, born in Quebec, Canada. Research and publications concerning problems of ethnic relations and race differences, international affairs, culture and personality, social and cultural aspects of mental health. Actively engaged in the international development of psychology. Taught for over 30 years at Columbia University, New York; visiting professor, University of Sao Paulo, Brazil; University of Hawaii; University of Paris and Ecole des Hautes Etudes, Paris, 1962-    . Member of Secretariat, Unesco, 1948-49, 1953-55. Former Secretary general and President, International Union of Psychological Science; President and Honorary President, World Federation for Mental Health; Honorary President, European League for Mental Hygiene. One of the first psychologists to question, on the basis of empirical research, the theory of innate psychological differences between racial and ethnic groups. See *race*.

**Klinefelter's syndrome** See *syndrome, Klinefelter's*.

**klinotaxis** A taxis which does not require a receptor itself capable of disciminating the direction of the stimulus source. If the receptor is not equally accessible to stimulation in all directions, the animal can compare intensities by moving the receptors first one way, then another. In these successive comparisons the organism turns until the two sides are equally stimulated.

**Klopfer system** An approach to the Rorschach test developed by Bruno Klopfer, essentially based on a phenomenological approach to understanding behavior and thinking. It has become the most widely used approach to the Rorschach in the United States.

**Klüver-Bucy syndrome** See *syndrome, Klüver-Bucy*.

**knee** A deviation from a smooth curve which is often seen in the early acceleration of interval or ratio segments and which consists of a period of compensatory low response rate following a brief period of rapid responding.

**knee jerk reflex** See *reflex, patellar*.

**knox cube test** See *test, Knox cube*.

**Koenig cylinders** A series of tuned, metal cylinders which emit tones of very high frequency, used in the determination of the upper threshold of pitch.

**Koffka, Kurt (1886-1941)** European-born American psychologist. With Max Wertheimer and Wolfgang Köhler, founder of Gestalt psychology. He was the first to introduce Gestalt psychology to America (1922). Extended this approach to developmental psychology (*Growth of the Mind*); later undertook a systematic overview of the whole field of psychology from the Gestalt point of view (*Principles of Gestalt Psychology*, 1935). Made many experimental and theoretical contributions to perception, including studies of the perception of motion, the constancies, visual organization, and a clarification of the problem of the nature of the stimulus.

**Köhler-Restorff phenomenon** The occurrence of greater frequency of recall in right associates experiments, when the pair is presented in isolation in comparison to presentation as one pair in a series.

**Köhler, Wolfgang (1887-1967)** European-born American psychologist. With Max Wertheimer and Kurt Koffka, founder of Gestalt psychology. Critic of prevailing atomistic theories in psychology, he examined the relations between field theory in physics and the theories and findings of Gestalt psychology, showing similarities between the behavior of physical and of perceptual organizations. This line of thinking later led him to investigation (with Wallach and others) of figural aftereffects and finally to the demonstration (with Held and others) of cortical currents corresponding to organized perceptions. Made many theoretical and empirical contributions to perception. Investigated problem solving in chimpanzees and clarifed concept of insight. (With von Restorff) discovered the isolation effect in memory; contributed to theory of memory and recall; developed nonassociationistic theory of the nature of associations. Analyzed values in terms of requiredness, rejecting purely subjective and relativistic interpretations. His analysis of evolutionary theory showed that the nativism-empiricism dichotomy is insufficient, since it neglects all those factors, either inherited or acquired that organisms share with the rest of nature.

**Kohs Block Design Test**  See *test, Kohs Block Design.*

**Kolb, Lawrence C. (1911-    )** American psychiatrist, educator, author. Contributed to understanding of the body image separating clinically the healthy from the psychopathological responses following trauma, mutilation and disease, and described the features which discriminate body concept and percept as well as delineating preventive and therapeutic approaches to the variant expressions. Also wrote on related pain expressive behavior and its management; superego defects productive of homosexual acting out. Earlier work on the traumatic neuroses induced by environmental stress and physiology of micturition. In recent years has chaired the Columbia University Department of Psychiatry, and directed the New York State Psychiatric Institute. Author of *Urban Challenges to Psychiatry; Mental Deficiency* and 150 other articles.

**Korsakoff psychosis**  See *psychosis, Korsakoff.*

**Korsakov's syndrome or psychosis**  Excessive neural irritation generally caused by alcoholism and severe deficiencies in food intake, characterized by disturbances of memory and loss of orientation.

**Korte's laws**  Laws stating the conditions for optimal apparent movements when two stationary visual stimuli are given in succession. They are: 1) when intensity is held constant, the time interval for optimal phi directly varies with the distance between stimuli; 2) when time is held constant, the distance for optimal phi varies directly with intensity; 3) when distance between stimuli is held constant, intensity for optimal phi varies inversely with the time interval.

**KPR**  See *Kuder Preference Record.*

**K-R formulas**  See *coefficient of equivalence, Kuder-Richardson.*

**Kraepelin, Emil (1856-1926)**  German psychiatrist, a student of Wundt, who, in applying Wundtian methods to the study of abnormal states, was a pioneer in experimental psychopathology. Late in the nineteenth century he formulated a system for classifying the psychoses that has been highly influential ever since. He classified mental disease into two major groups: dementia praecox and manic depressive psychoses. Maintained strict somatic view; helped to initiate abnormal psychology. Author of *Lehrbuch der Psychiatrie* (1933).

**Krafft-Ebing, Richard (1840-1903)**  A German psychiatrist primarily noted for his work in sexology. He was the first to definitely establish the relationship between general paralysis and syphilis before the Wassermann reaction was discovered and in his work *Psychopathia Sexualis* in 1886, he described aberrations of the sexual drive.

**Krause's corpuscle**  See *corpuscle, Krause's.*

**Krech, David (né Krechevsky, I.) (1909-    )**  American experimental psychologist, brain researcher, social psychologist and textbook author. His behavioral research culminated in his "hypothesis" and "non-continuity" theories for animal cognitive learning; after early ablation experiments on animal brains, he initiated the Berkeley research program on brain chemistry and behavior and made the initial observation of chemical and anatomical brain residuals consequent upon psychologically enriched experiences; founded, in 1936, the Society for the Psychological Study of Social Issues; with collaborators wrote three texts: *Theory and Problems of Social Psychology, Individual in Society, Elements of Psychology.*

**Kretschmer, Ernst (1889-1964)**  German neuro-psychiatrist and psychotherapist. Designed the first psychiatric characterology, described the sensitive psychogenesis of delusions and postulated multidimensional diagnosis and therapy. Psychophysiological theory of hysteria (conscious will and hypobulic mechanisms). Understanding of neurosis caused by ambivalence of impulses and insufficience of maturation; connection between adolescence and psychic disorders. Wrote first *Medical Psychology.* Found correlation between schizophrenia and leptosome, athletic, dysplastic body built; between manic-depressive psychoses and pyknic habitus. Constitutional correspondence: leptosome-schizothyme, athletic-barykinetic, pyknic-cyclothyme temperaments. Investigated relationship between character, genius and society.

**Kubie, Lawrence S. (1896-    )**  American psychiatrist and psychoanalyst; taught, practiced and conducted research in psychiatry, clinical neurology, experimental neuropathology, psychoanalysis, and psychosomatic medicine. Kubie examined critically the fundamental concepts of psychoanalytic theory and practice, as well as the biological basis of psychiatry, and tried to reconcile the constitutional factors with psychoanalysis.

**Kuder Preference Record**  A self-report inventory designed to reveal relative interest in ten broadly defined vocational areas, such as scientific, musical, etc. by the administration of items dealing with the interests as well as five sections dealing with personality data, such as family relations, and conflict avoidance.

**Kuder-Richardson coefficients of equivalence**  See *coefficients of equivalence, Kuder-Richardson.*

**Kuf's Disease**  (H. Kufs) A type of amaurotic familial idiocy which occurs in the teens. Also see *Tay-Sachs disease.*

**Kuhlmann-Anderson Test**  See *test, Kuhlmann-Anderson.*

**Kuhlmann-Binet Test**  See *test, Kuhlmann-Binet.*

**Külpe, Oswald**  Philosopher, psychologist. Born August 3, 1862 in Kandava, Latvia; died December 30, 1915 in Munich of influenza. In 1881 he studied history at Leipzig, then followed several years of academic *Wanderjahren* studying at Berlin, Göttingen, and Dorpat. He received his Ph.D. at Leipzig under Wundt in 1887. He was professor at Würzburg in 1894; in 1909 he went to Bonn and in 1912 to Munich.

Külpe is best known in psychology as the founder of the Würzburg School of *Denkpsychologie*. His intellectual development went from early adherence to Wundt's psychology of contents towards Brentano's psychology of acts. His is a middle position between these two extremes in that he recognized the existence of conscious contents (Gedanken), relations between them, and psychic functions like abstracting (Denken). Impalpable acts were a species of *Denken* and included the attribution of meaning, thinking and judging, which were conceived to be other than relations between contents.

Compared with Brentano, who was a distinguished Aristotelian scholar, Külpe was an outstanding Kantian scholar. His general philosophical position was that of Critical Realism.

His students included K. Bühler, O. Selz, and E. Bloch. Wertheimer received his degree at Würzburg at the time of Külpe's leadership, but could not be considered one of the followers of the school.

Külpe published quantitatively little by the scale of academicians of his time, but qualitatively his work was well reasoned and therefore influential. Among his works are: 1893, *Grundiss der Psychologie,* English translation by Titchener; 1895-1929, *Einleitung in die Philosophie,* (many editions); 1907-1912, *I. Kant* (two editions).

**Kundt's rule** The principles that: 1) distances which have been divided by regular gradation lines appear greater than those which are unmarked and 2) that in the attempt to bisect a horizontal line using only one eye, there is a liklihood that the dividing point will be placed too near the nasal side of the eye used.

**kurtosis (Ku)** The relative degree of flatness or peakedness in a frequency curve in the region of the mode.

**kuru** A neurological disorder, occurring mainly in Australia and the South Pacific, the etiology of which is unknown. It results in progressive motor incoordination, mental disturbances especially in affect, and often death within six to nine months after onset.

**Kwashiorkor** A tropical and subtropical children's disease caused by an inappropriate protein diet. Main symptoms include impaired growth, edema, severe apathy and often mental retardation.

**Kwint psychomotor test** See *test, Kwint psychomotor.*

**kymograph** An instrument essentially consisting of a rotating drum covered with paper, used for making graphic records of temporal variations in physiological and psychological processes.

**kymography** A technique used for the measurement of motions in an organ.

**kyphoscoliosis** A lateral curvature of the spine with an anteroposterior hump on the spinal column.

**kyphosis** An angular curvature of the spine which resembles a mild humpbacked condition.

# L

**L** Lumen.

$_sL_R$ (C. L. Hull) The stimulus strength which will just barely evoke a response; reaction threshold.

**L-data** Life-record data, obtained by rating the individual as he reacts in life situations. Quantifiable data not arising from standard key-score tests; hence, subject to disagreement among observers as to the score value to be assigned a given performance. L-Data constitute one of the three Media of Observation, the other two being Q-Data and T-Data.

**L method** (statistics) A short cut method for selecting a small number of items which will predict a criterion as well as or better than one that was computed from the entire pool or population from which the smaller sample was drawn.

**laboratory training** A general term for group approaches in which the goals are some degree of self-understanding, the understanding of the conditions which facilitate or inhibit group functioning, the understanding of interpersonal operations in groups and developing skills for diagnosing individual, group and organizational behavior. The primary use of these groups is in industry where problems arise due to interpersonal or group conflicts. The first organization to offer such assistance to industry was the National Training Laboratories or NTL.

**labyrinth** Part of the auditory apparatus composed of a system of intercommunicating canals and cavities within the cochlea.

**lacuna** A gap in evidence or data occurring in memory or consciousness.

**Ladd-Franklin, Christine (1847-1930)** American psychologist. A versatile scientist who was trained at Johns Hopkins, Göttingen, and Berlin. Probably best known for her theory of color vision, an elaboration of Hering's evolutionary color vision theory. An associate editor of Baldwin's *Dictionary of Philosophy and Psychology* (1901-02) and a frequent contributor to mathematical, philosophical, and psychological publications. She lectured in logic and psychology at Johns Hopkins (1904-1909). In 1910 moved to Columbia where she remained until her death.

**Ladd-Franklin theory** See *color vision, theory of: Ladd-Franklin theory.*

**lagophthalmos, lagophthalmus** A disturbance of the seventh cranial nerve consisting of the failure of the upper eyelid to move downward when the individual attempts to close his eyes.

**Laing, Ronald D. (1927-    )** Scottish psychiatrist and psychoanalyst. Experiences as practicing psychiatrist led to questioning psychiatric assumptions as to what mental illness is. Research in mental hospital, clinic, and home settings, brought to light many observations in social *impasses,* and the behavior that ensues. Work with psychedelics in social situations led to need to envisage chemistry *in vivo,* as part of the social process, conditioned thereby, and conditioning. Subsequently involved in developing theory in the area between social controls, behavior, and experience. Presently associated with experiments with reciprocal influences of disturbed and disturbing environment and disturbed and disturbing modes of experience.

**laissez-faire group** (K. Lewin) Group in social psychology with a passive leader who avoids taking the initiative.

**lallation** 1. Infantile or unintelligible speech. 2. The substitution of the *l* sound for more difficult consonants such as *r.*

**Lamarckian evolution** (J.B.P.A. de Monet de Lamarck) The theory that characteristics acquired during the life of an organism through use, disuse, or adaptation of organs to changes in the environment can be transmitted to the offspring.

**lambda (λ)** Wave length.

**lambda ratio** A primary Rorschach index as formulated in the Beck approach to the test and represented by the proportion of pure form responses to all non-pure responses in the record. It is related to, but computed differently than, the F% used in other approaches to the test. Either lambda or the F% are interpreted as representing affect-free functioning.

**lambert** A unit of luminance equal to the brightness of a perfectly diffusing surface reflecting light at a rate of one lumen per square centimeter, or to $1/\pi$ candles per square centimeter. The millilambert, one thousandth of a lambert, is more commonly used.

**Lambert's law** A law of the relation between physical intensity of light and the angle of incidence with the reflecting surface, stating that the incidence, emission and reflection of light, vary directly as the cosine of the angle of the rays perpendicular to the surface.

**La Mettrie, Julien Offray de (1709-1751)** French physician-philosopher who also worked in Holland and Germany. Holding that thought is only the outcome of the mechanical action of the brain and nervous system, he was an extreme scientific materialist and hedonist. Among his influential writings was *Man, a Machine,* published in 1848.

**Landolt circles** Incomplete circles having gaps of varying sizes used in the determination of visual acuity.

**Lange, Carl George (1834-1900)** A Danish physiologist who almost simultaneously with William James, proposed a theory of emotions stating that emotion is the organism's feeling of the physiological changes which directly follow perception of an object, situation or thought. This has since been known as the James-Lange theory of emotion.

**Langerhans, islands of** Small masses of cells in the pancreas which secrete insulin.

**language centers** Areas in the cerebral cortex which function in different aspects of spoken and written language and in music.

**language, gestural-postural** A form of non-verbal communication by means of gestures and postures.

**language, graphic** Communication by means of recorded symbols.

**language, irrelevant** (L. Kanner) Words, utterances, or phrases within the context of intelligible speech or alone, which are understood and have meaning for only the speaker. Irrelevant language is seen most commonly in schizophrenia and early infantile autism.

**Laplacian curve** The normal frequency curve.

**lapsus calami** A slip of the pen.

**lapsus linguae** A slip of the tongue.

**lapsus memoriae** A slip of the memory.

**larval sadism** See *sadism, larval.*

**larvated epilepsy** See *epileptic equivalent.*

**laryngeal reflex** See *reflex, laryngeal.*

**laryngograph** An arrangement for obtaining a graphic record on a kymograph of movements of the larynx during speech.

**laryngoscope** An instrument composed essentially of a system of mirrors, used in examining the larynx.

**Lasegue sign** A symptom indicative of disease of the sciatic.

**Lashley jumping stand** Apparatus used to train and test animal visual discrimination. The subject, most often a rat, stands on a platform and is faced with two doors, one of which is locked. Each door has a different stimulus pattern. The response is the rat jumping through the unlocked door to the food reinforcement on the other side.

**Lashley, Karl Spencer (1890-1958)** American physiological psychologist who discovered in pioneer ablation experiments on the rat, that memory for learned habits is not precisely localized in the brain; performance decrement is proportional to the *amount* of brain tissue removed, not to its *location.* Formulated the principles of mass action and equipotentiality in brain function.

**latency stage** (S. Freud) The fourth stage of psychosexual development occurring from the age of six to eleven during which the Oedipal incestuous and aggressive wishes have been repressed and the child identifies with the parent of the same sex. During this stage, the child gives up interest in persons of the opposite sex which are prototypes of the parent, and tends to associate with members of his own sex.

**latent dream content** See *content, dream, latent.*

**latent extinction** See *extinction, latent.*

**latent learning** See *learning, latent.*

**latent structure analysis** See *analysis, latent structure.*

**lateral dominance** See *dominance, lateral.*

**lateral fissure** See *fissure of Sylvius.*

**lateral geniculate body** A sensory relay nucleus which is part of the visual system. It is part of the thalamus where the optic tract synapse joins with visual fibers which project to the visual region of the cerebral cortex.

**lateral hypothalamus** See *hypothalamus, lateral.*

**Latin square** An experimental pattern or design which provides as many different trials as there are experimental conditions, every subject being exposed to all conditions in varying serial orders from other subjects.

**law, Bell-Magendie** A statement of the principle that the ventral roots of the spinal nerves are motor in function while the dorsal roots are sensory in function.

**law, Donder's** Principle that the position of the eyes in looking at an object is independent of the movement of the eyes to that position; regardless of previous fixation points, every point on the line corresponds to a definite, invariable angle of the eyes.

**law, Emmert's** Generalization that a projected image, either eidetic image or after-image, tends to increase in size in proportion to the distance to which it is projected onto a ground.

**law, Fullerton-Cattell** A generalization proposed as a substitute for Weber's law which states that the errors of observation and of just noticeable differences are proportional to the square root of the magnitude of the stimuli, though subject to variations which must be accounted for in each case.

**law, inverse square** A law of physics which states that the intensity of energy emanating from a stimulus, decreases proportionately to the square of the distance from the source to the sense receptor. Sound, light, heat, and odor follow this principle.

**law, Jost's** The principle that given two associations of equal strength and unequal age, repetition increases the strength of the older more than the younger, and the older loses strength less rapidly with the passage of time.

**law of advantage** Also called principle of advantage; the principle that when two or more incompatible and inconsistent responses occur to the same situation one has an advantage over the others, being more reliable and occurring more frequently.

**law of assimilation** (E. L. Thorndike) Also called law of analogy; it is a replica of association by similarity. It says that learners tend to reply in a similar way as they replied before to a similar situation.

**law of Bichat** Proposed by Marie Francois Bichat (1771-1802), a French anatomist. There are two main body systems which are in inverse relationship, called the vegetative and the animal, with the former providing for assimilation and augmentation of mass and the latter providing for the transformation of energy.

**law of categorical judgment** (W. S. Torgenson) A theory derivative of the law of comparative judgment which should provide an equal interval category scale. It assumes: 1) the psychological continuum of an individual can be divided into categories 2) a category boundary is not a stable entity but projects a normal distribution on the continuum 3) the subject's responses are predicated on the position of the category boundary; thus, the boundaries between adjacent categories behave like stimuli. The law of categorical judgment may be written: $C_A - R_1 = Z_{A1} \sqrt{\sigma A^2 - \sigma 1^2 - 2r_{A1} \sigma_A \sigma_1}$ which is directly comparable to the law of comparative judgment of Thurstone.

**law of closure** See *closure.*

**law of coercion to cultural-genetic mean** (R. B. Cattell) The tendency of social pressure to force behavior to the existing central norm.

**law of comparative judgment** (L.L. Thurstone) A mathematical model which explicates a theoretical assumption about the effects of the stimulation by two stimuli, $S_1$ and $S_2$

$$R_2 - R_1 = Z_{21} \sqrt{\sigma_2^2 + \sigma_1^2 - 2r_{21}\sigma_1\sigma_2}$$

in which $R_2$ is the mean of the responses to stimulus two; $R_1$ is the mean of the responses to stimulus one; $Z_{21}$, the standard score of the distribution of differences between the two distribution responses to the two different stimuli, $\sigma_2^2$, the standard deviation of the distribution of the responses to stimuli two; $\sigma_1^2$, the standard deviation of responses to stimuli one.

**law of content** 1. The principle that the meaning of verbal material or mental processes is influenced by the situation surrounding them. 2. The hypothesis that the degree of retention depends on the similarity between the learning situation and the retention condition.

**law of effect** (E. L. Thorndike) Learning theory law stating that annoyance weakens and satisfaction strengthens a stimulus-response connection.

**law of exercise** (E.L. Thorndike) Principle that repetition of an act promotes learning and makes subsequent performance of that act easier, other things being equal.

**law of frequency** The principle that the more an act or an association is repeated the more rapid is the acquisition or learning of that act or association, other things being equal.

**law of prepotency of elements** (E. L. Thorndike) The learner tends to select relevant elements in his response to a complex situation.

**law of readiness** (E. L. Thorndike) The proposition which holds that when a conduction unit is ready to conduct, conduction by it is satisfying, as long as nothing is done which alters its action.

**law of recapitulation** See *biogenetic law.*

**law of recency** 1. The principle or generalization that a specific item will tend to remind the individual of a more recent association than one farther in time. 2. The generalization which holds that the more recent the item, event or experience, the better it is remembered.

**law of use** The generalization that an association or a function is facilitated by use or practice.

**law, power** See *Steven's power law.*

**law, Talbot-Plateau** Principle that with a surface illuminated by a light flickering so quickly no interruption is apparent, the brightness is less than the brightness of steady illumination to a degree equal to the ratio between the time during which the light actually reaches the surface and the whole period.

**laws, Mendelian** See *Mendelian laws.*

**lead poisoning** See *poisoning, lead.*

**leadership** 1. The exercise of authority in initiating, directing, or controlling the behavior or attitudes of others, with their consent. 2. Those qualities of personality and training which make the guidance and control of others successful.

**learning, approach** Learning specific behaviors in order to attain particular rewards.

**learning, avoidance**  A type of training in which the organism is allowed to avoid a noxious stimulus if he makes the required response.

**learning, conceptual**  The learning of new concepts or the alteration of old ones.

**learning contingencies**  Variables present in the learning situation.

**learning, continuity theory of**  The principle that in discrimination learning, there is an increment of learning for every reinforced response to the stimulus.

**learning curve**  A graphic representation of the changes at successive units of practice over the course of learning. Units of practice, recorded on the abscissa, are usually in terms of time spent or number of trials required; the progress in performance, recorded on the ordinate, is usually in terms of amount recalled, time required for successful completion of the task, or number of errors. The form of the curve differs according to the measure used for the ordinate.

**learning, ideational**  Learning involving the use of ideational material, either as in learning through the connection of ideas or memorization, in contrast to rote and motor learning.

**learning, incidental**  The occurrence of learning in the absence of formal instruction, intent to learn and ascertainable motive. If indeed there is no motive operating, incidental learning suggests contiguity alone is a sufficient condition for learning.

**learning, instrumental**  See *conditioning, operant.*

**learning, latent**  Learning which is not manifested in performance but which reveals itself in later performances that follow an intervening activity which does not involve the behavior in question nor any reward for behavior. The change in performance is attributed to the addition of a motive in later performances.

**learning, linear-operator model of**  (B. B. Bush and F. Mosteller) Mathematical model of learning which assumes that an organism perceives and responds to some fraction of the total stimulus complex. This fraction of stimulus elements attended to is measured as a kind of sum of the weighted element. This theory incorporates two parameters a) the positive influence of reinforcement and b) the negative punishing influence of the work required in responding. The linear-operator is: $Qp = p \, a(1-p) - bp$ where $Qp$ is the operator $Q$ operating on $p$, the probability that a response will occur during a specified time, $a$ is the parameter associated with reward, $b$ is the parameter associated with work or punishment, $p$ is the probability of the response.

**learning, motor**  Any form of learning which is described in terms of the activities of muscles and glands which it involves.

**learning, perceptual**  Learning of a new perceptual response or learning which consists of modifying an already existing perceptual response.

**learning, programmed**  A learning method consisting of materials which are presented in a predetermined order with provisions enabling the student to check his answers and to proceed at his own pace. The most common method of programmed learning involves the use of teaching machines, although some programs have been prepared in workbook form.

**learning, response**  Learning to make a specific set of responses to reach a goal rather than learning the route or topography of the environment.

**learning, reversal**  Experimental technique in which the correct response, usually one of two possible responses, after some specified amount of training, is changed to the other response.

**learning, serial or serial-order**  Learning of responses in a specific order which is often used in rate learning.

**learning set**  1. A generalized approach to problem situations which includes the assumption by the subject that a specific method can be discovered to solve the problem. The approach itself is a result of learning. 2. An orienting factor which determines which kinds of responses will be made and which kinds omitted in a particular kind of problem situation. The manner of approach to solving the situation has been previously learned, not the particular solution.

**learning, social**  Learning of social standards, values and customs.

**learning, subliminal**  The acquisition of a habit which cannot be remembered because the learning of it was not on a conscious level or because it has not progressed far enough.

**learning theory**  A large body of concepts exploring the process of learning, starting with associationism, through the various theories of conditioning and cognition. At the present time, several theoretical systems and subsystems started by Pavlov, Bekhterev, Hull, and Skinner as well as specialized approaches of the mathematical learning theories, gestalt inspired learning theories and others vie for the so far unattainable position of a generally accepted theory of learning.

**learning theory, incremental**  The average measure of learning as presented in the typical learning curve shows a gradual change over trials. This is so common that it has provided a basis for the inference that learning is a gradual process. It is contended that a stimulus is complex and gradually more and more stimulus elements come to be associated to the reinforced response.

**learning types**  Individual kinds of learners distinguished by the types of imagery they tend to rely on and the methods of learning they employ.

**learning, verbal**  The learning to respond verbally to a verbal stimulus, ranging from learning to associate two nonsense syllables to learning to solve complex problems stated in verbal terms.

**learning, whole method of**  Learning characterized by the successive repetition of the complete material, from the beginning to the end.

least action, law of (Gestalt) The principle that an organism will tend to follow the course of action which requires the least effort or expended energy under prevailing conditions. Course of action and energy expended can be influenced by the particular individual's personality characteristics so that an objectively easy course may be difficult for an individual because of the amount of emotional investment required. Also called principle of least energy expenditure, and least effort principle.

least group size The principle that the optimal size of a class or learning group is the smallest number of individuals which represent all the abilities required for the learning tasks to be undertaken.

least noticeable difference See *just noticeable difference.*

least squares method See *method of least squares.*

leaving the field See *field, leaving the.*

left-right agnosia See *apractagnosia.*

legal insanity See *insanity, legal.*

legal responsibility See *responsibility, legal.*

Leibniz, Gottfried Wilhelm von (1646-1716) German philosopher and mathematician. He developed an elaborate systematic position, published as the *Monadology* in 1714, which contained a strict parallelist analysis of the mind-body problem: mental and bodily events are like synchronous clocks that do not affect each other.

Leigh's encephalomyelopathy A genetic metabolic disorder transmitted by an autosomal recessive resulting in high level pyruvates in the blood. The main clinical features are failure to thrive, lack of movement, hypotonia, spasticity, absent reflexes, optic atrophy, nystagmus, and convulsions.

Leiter International Performance Test See *test, Leiter International Performance.*

lencotomy, frontal Frontal lobotomy.

Lennox syndrome A type of myoclonic epilepsy in older children.

Lennox, William Gordon (1884-1960) An American neurologist noted for his work in epilepsy.

lens A transparent structure in the eye capable of changing its convexity, the function of which is to form an image on the retina of the object being looked at. Also called crystalline lens.

lens, corneal A plastic lens worn on the tears of the cornea which is used to correct impaired vision. Also known as contact lens.

leptokurtosis The relative degree of peakedness about the mode of a frequency curve.

leptomorph (H. J. Eysenck) A person whose body-build index is one or more standard deviations above the mean.

leptosome An individual of slender or asthenic body build.

LES See *local excitatory state or potential.*

lesbianism Homosexuality in women.

lesion A change in tissue due to injury, disease or surgical procedures.

Lesse, Stanley (1922-    ) American psychiatrist and neurologist. Demonstrated the direct relationship between the quantitative degree of anxiety and the development and amelioration of other symptoms and signs, and the predictable relationship between the various components of anxiety to each other. Introduced futurologic research with projections as to how the health sciences will be at the end of the century. Introduced future oriented psychotherapy as a therapeutic technique. Described the multivariant masks of depression, performed the original research studies and presented the initial publications on the use of psychotherapy in combination with tranquilizing drugs and antidepressant drugs. Presented the original descriptions of the psychopathology and psychodynamics of pain of psychogenic origin, particularly a typical facial pain. Described psychotherapy as a placebo phenomenon and interrelated unintended psychotherapeutic effects with placebo effects. Research into the relationship of socioeconomic and sociopolitical phenomena and its relationship to psychotherapeutic techniques.

lethal disease Fatal disease, a disease that ends in death.

lethal equivalent A gene carried in the heterozygous state which if homozygous, would be lethal. Thalassemia minor and major, approximate this situation.

lethargic encephalitis See *encephalitis, lethargic.*

leucotomy Lobotomy.

leucotomy, pre-frontal Pre-frontal lobotomy.

leukodystrophy See *sulfatide lipidosis.*

level 1. An area, region, position or degree in which all things are equal in quality. 2. (psychophysics) The condition of reactivity of a receptor compared with its established average threshold. 3. The position or rank obtained on a test. 4. The plane or standard of intellectual, sensory and motor efficiency.

level, maintenance 1. A state of development at maturity when the organism's growth, weight, and size stabilize and remain at this maximal level. 2. The unvarying ability to perform an act due to overlearning or repeated practice.

leveling effect An effect due to practice or repetition under certain conditions of measurement, which results in a second set of observations to cluster more closely around the mean, the standard deviation and range being less than in the first set of observations.

levitation Rising in the air without material support, usually in reference to dream experience.

Levy inkblots A special series of inkblots which are designed to facilitate movement (*M*) responses.

Lewin, Kurt (1890-1947) German child psychologist; emigrated to America in 1933. Created a field theory of action and emotion modeled on modern physical theory and topology. Known especially for studies of conflict, level of aspiration, substitution, regression, and for development of research and theory on small group dynamics. Applied latter to problems of food utilization and housing congestion in World War II. See *field theory; topological psychology.*

**LGB** See *lateral geniculate body.*

**libertarianism** See *free will.*

**libertine** Sexually unrestrained and promiscuous individual.

**libertinism** Unrestrained sexual activity especially with reference to the male.

**libidinal types** (S. Freud) Freud distinguished three libidinal types, the erotic, obsessional and narcissistic. See *type.*

**libido** (S. Freud) A quantitatively variable force related to sexual excitation. The totality of mental energy at the disposal of Eros, the instinct of love.

**libido object** See *object, libido.*

**lie detector** Apparatus which measures physiological changes in pulse, respiration, blood pressure and psychogalvanic skin response of a person to whom questions are posed which he must answer. The assumption is that the emotional disturbance associated with telling a lie will exhibit itself in the above physiological changes though such physiological changes accompany emotionality of any sort.

**Liebeault, Ambroise-August (1823-1904)** A French physician who was one of the first to employ hypnosis in the treatment of his patients and is one of those responsible for its growth as a method of treatment.

**life-goal** (A. Adler) The goal of attaining superiority to compensate for an individual's real or imagined inferiority. It is present implicitly in all strivings though is seldom consciously acknowledged.

**life history** A detailed description of the environmental and internal events in the development of an individual or group from birth to the present or death.

**life instinct** See *Eros.*

**life lie** (A. Adler) An individual's belief that he will fail in his life plan because of circumstances beyond his control.

**life plan** (A. Adler) The complete pattern of defensive behaviors used by an individual to prevent his assumed superiority from being disproved by reality.

**life space** (K. Lewin) The entire set of phenomena in the environment and in the organism itself which influence present behavior or the possibility of behavior. Emphasis is placed on the interaction between the organism and its environment in an organized, unified field.

**life span** 1. The length of life from birth to death of an individual. 2. The characteristic length of life of a species.

**life style** (A. Adler) The characteristic mode of living of a person, of the way in which he pursues his goals.

**light-adapted eye** See *eye, light-adapted.*

**likelihood criterion ratio** (signal detection theory) The decision rule the subject uses to determine his responses in a psychophysical experiment. It can be estimated in the experiment by the likelihood ratio.

**likelihood ratio** 1. (J. Neyman and E. S. Pearson) A procedure for finding the best statistic test for testing any hypothesis which will give the most powerful test for the hypothesis. It consists of the probability of obtaining the sample result under the null hypothesis relative to the probability of obtaining the sample result under the alternate hypothesis. 2. (signal detection theory) An expression of the likelihood that the observed responses obtained arose from signal plus noise relative to the likelihood that the responses arose from noise alone.

**Likert scale** See *scale, Likert.*

**limbic lobe** See *lobe, limbic.*

**limbic system** A group of functionally related structures including the transitional cortex and subcortical nuclei, about which much controversy exists as to function and definition, but generally thought to be related to the integration of emotional patterns and primary drives.

**limen** See *threshold.*

**limen, absolute (RL)** See *threshold, absolute.*

**limen gauge** (Von Frey) An instrument consisting of two levers, one which is activated by a spring that is controlled by the other lever, used for the application of pressure to the skin at regular intervals.

**limen, sense** See *threshold, absolute.*

**liminal sensitivity** See *sensitivity, liminal.*

**liminal stimulus** See *stimulus, liminal.*

**limit, physiological** See *physiological limit.*

**limited aims psychotherapy** See *psychotherapy, limited aims.*

**limited hold** (operant conditioning) On interval schedules, FI, VI, etc., the organism is eligible for reinforcement after a time from the previous reinforcement. When the organism is eligible, a response is reinforced (reinforcement occurs only after a response). Limited hold is the period during which a response will be reinforced. At the end of the limited hold, a response is not reinforced until the next limited hold occurs.

**limited-term psychotherapy** See *psychotherapy, limited-term.*

**limits and differences method** (E. Kraepelin) A modification of the limits method, consisting of the statistical treatment of judgments obtained by the normal limits method.

**limits, fiducial** The points or limits to the right or left of some measure of central tendency beyond which a statistic is not expected to occur except by chance alone in more than a stated percentage of the samplings.

**limits method** See *method, just noticeable difference.*

**limophoitas** Psychotic episode caused by starvation.

**limophtisis** Physical and mental emaciation caused by starvation.

**Lincoln-Oseretsky Motor Development Scale** See *scale, Lincoln-Oseretsky Motor Development.*

**line of direction** The line of sight from an object to the nodal points of the eyes.

**line of regard** See *regard, line of.*

**linear correlation** See *correlation, linear.*

**linear function** A relationship between two variables which is represented by a straight line whose equation is $y = mx + b$ where $m$ is the slope of the line and $b$ is the point at which the line crosses the $y$ axis.

**linear graph** The representation of the relationship between two variables by means of lines.

**linear-operator model of learning** See *learning, linear-operator model of.*

**linear perspective** See *perspective, linear.*

**linear regression** A regression whose equation develops a line that best fits the mean of the rows or columns in a correlation table, and is approximately straight.

**linear system** A system in which the units of input are summated in a simple straight line method; or in which the response to a complex input is the summation of the individual responses of the input.

**linguistics** The scientific study of the origin, structure, and evolution of language.

**link analysis** The design of systems in which connections between parts are as efficient as possible, the number of links being minimal and their value maximal. For example, the design of an efficient typewriter keyboard.

**link-defect hypothesis** An explanation for the abnormalities of perception, attention, cognition, etc. in mentally defective children. Mental functions are seen as complex processes which are formed in the course of a child's development. If the process of formation is disturbed, if a step or link is missed due to illness, trauma, inborn defect, etc., the disturbance may affect further mental development and lead to a number of secondary symptoms and consequences.

**Link Instrument Trainer** An apparatus used in training airplane pilots, which without leaving the ground, simulates operating conditions for a plane.

**linkage 1.** The tendency for characteristics to be linked together in hereditary transmission, the offspring showing either both traits or neither. **2.** The connection between stimulus and response.

**linophobia** Fear of ropes.

**lip eroticism** See *eroticism, lip.*

**lip key** An instrument used in reaction time experiments for measuring the start of lip movements in speech.

**lip-reading** A method used by the deaf for understanding spoken speech, consisting of observation of the speaker's lip movements.

**lipid histiocytosis, kerasin type** See *Gaucher disease.*

**lipid histiocytosis, phosphatide type** See *Niemann-Pick disease.*

**lipidoses, cerebral** A group of rare diseases characterized by the accumulation of particular complex lipids in the central nervous system and associated with a mental defect which is familial, an enlarged liver and spleen.

**lipidosis** Disorder of lipid metabolism.

**lipids** A group of non-water soluble fats; a major chemical component of the brain.

**Lissajou's figures** Closed figures produced by the reflection of a beam of light from small mirrors attached to the surfaces of two tuning forks which vibrate in perpendicular planes to one another.

**Lissauer's dementia paralytica** See *dementia paralytica, Lissauer's.*

**Listing's law** A law of eye movement stating that when the eye moves from the primary position to another position, the axis around which the eye in the new position moves, is the same as if the eye had turned around a fixed axis at right angles to the initial and final lines of regard.

**literacy test** See *test, literacy.*

**lithic diathesis** A hereditary metabolic dysfunction characterized by renal disorders and a tendency to form urinary calculi.

**Little Hans** (S. Freud) A case of a phobia of a horse in a five year old boy analyzed by S. Freud and Hans' father. A classical illustration of the dynamics of the phobia, in that there is a clear sexual component, for Hans was in a state of intensified sexual excitement with nightly masturbation, with repression (of Hans' death wishes for the father), projection (Hans feared that someone would do to him what he wished to do), and displacement (from the father onto the horse), with concern about the missing penis of the woman, the anatomical difference being seen as a possible consequence of masturbation.

**Little's disease** See *infantile spastic diplegia.*

**Lloyd Morgan's canon** The principle that in the interpretation of behavior, attribution of the behavior in terms of lower rather than higher level of functioning is preferred.

**load** 1. The number of patients or clients a therapist, social worker, or counselor conducts treatment with. 2. (statistics) The multiplication of a set of values by a constant for the purpose of rendering the set comparable to another set. 3. (statistics) A weight or factor loading.

**loading** A value varying between +1 and -1 which is obtained from factor analysis and shows the extent to which increases in the strength of a factor bring about increases in the dependent behavior score.

**lobe** 1. A rounded projection of an organ. 2. One of the main sections of the cerebrum; the frontal, parietal, temporal, occipital, or central lobes.

**lobe, central** See *Reil, island of.*

**lobe, frontal** The part of each central hemisphere in front of the central fissure.

**lobe, frontal, structure and function of** The frontal lobe is characterized by the predominance of associative layers and fiber tract connections to other cortical areas through which it receives processed information from subcortical layers. As a result of these interconnections, these areas influence both afferent and efferent stimulation. It has been found that the frontal lobes are important in regulating complex behavior, the organization and planning of purposeful activities, and the coordination of intention with the action. Lesions of these areas result in the impairment of planned, purposeful behavior.

**lobe, limbic** A convolution on the medial surface of the brain, consisting of the gyrus cinguli, isthmus hippocampi, and the gyrus hippocampi. Also called gyrus fornicatus.

**lobe, occipital** The dorsal portion of the cerebral hemispheres of the brain which contains the centers for vision.

**lobe, parietal** The part of the cerebral cortex between the frontal and occipital lobes and behind the central fissure.

**lobe, temporal** The section of the cerebral hemisphere lying below the lateral fissure and in front of the occipital lobe, that is the cortical area for the reception of auditory stimuli.

**lobectomy** Surgical removal of a lobe or an organ or gland. Commonly refers to the removal of the prefrontal region of the frontal lobes.

**lobectomy, pre-frontal** Surgical removal of the prefrontal region of the frontal lobes of the brain.

**lobotomy** The surgical severing of the nerve fibers of the frontal lobes of the brain which connect with the thalamus and the hypothalamus. This is a form of psychosurgery which is sometimes used in the treatment of mental disorder.

**lobotomy, frontal** See *lobotomy.*

**lobotomy, transorbital** A surgical procedure consisting of partial ablation of the prefrontal area, preferred to the classical prefrontal lobotomy because undesirable side effects such as incontinence and apathy are less likely to occur.

**local excitatory state or potential** The reaction of nervous tissue to stimuli consisting of a localized increase in negativity on the surface of the membrane and in a spike potential if the stimulation is above threshold.

**local rate** See *rate, local.*

**local sign** See *sign, local.*

**localization** 1. The mental reference of a sensory or perceptual process to its source in space. 2. The reference of mental and nervous functions to their particular sources in the various parts of the nervous system.

**location chart** (Rorschach) Reproductions of the inkblots on a single side of the record blank used by the examiner for the purpose of locating and recording the positions of the subject's responses.

**location score** One of the major components in Rorschach scoring or coding which denotes the general area of the blot used in a response, such as the whole blot, a common detail area, or an unusual detail area.

**Locke, John (1632-1704)** Philosopher and politician and early British empiricist. Held that the *idea* is the fundamental unit of mind; all ideas come from sensation or reflection. Formulated the principle of association, and distinguished between *primary* qualities of perception (number, weight, etc.) which correspond to characteristics of the real object and *secondary* qualities (color, sound, etc.), which are "aroused in us" by the powers of the real object.

**locomotion** 1. The movement of an organism from one area to another. 2. (K. Lewin) A change in the valence or value of regions within the individual's life space resulting in a change in the relationship of the individual to his life space.

**locomotor** The organs upon which movement from place to place depends.

**locomotor ataxia** See *tabes dorsalis.*

**locus** 1. A place or spot on the surface of the body or an organ. 2. (mathematics) The sum of all possible positions of a moving element.

**Loeb, Jacques (1859-1924)** German zoologist and physiologist who moved to America in 1891. Developed the tropistic theory of animal behavior. He also proposed that associative memory is the criterion of consciousness.

**logagnosia; logamnesia** Sensory aphasia.

**logarithmic curve** See *curve, logarithmic.*

**logarithmic mean** See *mean, logarithmic.*

**logic, affective** A sequence of judgments which on the surface appear to be logical chains connected by reasoning but in actuality are linked by emotional factors.

**logical construct** See *construct, hypothetical.*

**logical positivism** Also called physicalism; a philosophical school associated with a group of Viennese philosophers (Wiener Kreis, that is, the Vienna Circle) who saw the main task of philosophy in stating scientific data in the language of physical science and development of a system of symbolic logic to be used as the vehicle for scientific research and communication. The logical positivists maintained that a great many philosophical issues must be dismissed as pseudo-problems. C.L. Hull, K. Lewin, B.F. Skinner, S.S. Stevens, and other psychologists have been influenced by the logical positivists.

**logistic curve** See *curve, logarithmic.*

**logospasm** Explosive speech.

**loloneurosis** Stammering.

**lolopathy** Speech disorder.

**lolophegia** Inability to speak caused by paralysis of facial muscles.

**lolophobia** Morbid fear of speaking.

**Lombroso, Cesare (1836-1909)** Italian anthropologist and criminologist who wrote on the connection between genius and insanity. He advocated the view of the innate disposition to criminal behavior associated with degeneration of hereditary cells. He found most criminals have physical signs (stigmata of degeneration) bearing witness to the innate, constitutional disposition to crime.

**long-circuiting** The renunciation of immediate satisfaction in the interests of attaining relatively remote goals. A recently discovered, objective test factor, indexed as U.I. 35, is believed to embody the most important features of this concept.

**long term memory (LTM)** See *memory, long term.*

**longitudinal studies** Studies which focus on the change in a person or group of people over an extended period of time.

**Lopez Ibor, Juan Jose (1907-    )** Spanish psychiatrist, head of Department of Psychiatry and Psychological Medicine at the Madrid University. Former President of the World Psychiatric Association, Honorary Member of the Royal Psychiatric College, London, Member of the Academia Leopoldina Gesellschaft, German Fed. Republic, Honorary Member of the American Psychiatric Association. Developed a new theory of schizophrenic characteristics and new concepts of depressions, partly extended in the concept of depressive equivalents (Maudsley Lecture, 1970). Described anxiety equivalents which include ailments considered to be neurological, such as paresthesic meuralgia, etc. Studied psychological aspects of anxiety; 1st publication "Vital Anxiety" (*Angustia Vital,* 1950), 2nd edition in 1960. Introduced new ideas concerning the dynamic of neuroses, published as "Neuroses as illness of the mind" (*Neurosis como enfermedades del animo,* 1966), and modified the

therapeutic technique. Apart from these clinical and psychological publications, conducted physiopathological studies of anxiety and the use of neuroleptics. Several publications on social psychiatry, psychiatric assistance and its organization, especially in European countries. Also critical studies on the results obtained in the so-called "Therapeutic Communities." Wrote on depressions in young people and their relation to severe cases of drug addiction. Presently studies the subconscious elements of psychotherapeutic directions from Mesmer toward post-Freudian techniques.

**Lorenz, Konrad (1903-    )** Austrian physician, founder of ethology, director of Max Planck Institute for Behavior Physiology. Discovered several aspects of animal behavior, among them the innate behavior coordinaters (Erbkoordinationen), fixed action patterns (F.A.P.) stimulus selection, signal movements in introspecific communication. He found "inner releasing schemata," imprinting, and other phylogenetically determined behavior mechanisms. Lorenz developed new observational and experimental techniques in the study of animal behavior.

**Lowe's syndrome** A genetic metabolic disorder which appears to be sex-linked resulting in aminoaciduria in the urine and acidosis in the blood. The main clinical features are mental retardation, glaucoma, cataracts, rickets and hypotonia.

**LS** See *sensitivity, luminal.*

**LSD** See *lysergic acid diethylamide.*

**lumbar puncture** The withdrawal of a sample of cerebrospinal fluid for diagnostic purposes, by the insertion of a hypodermic needle between the lumbar vertebrae.

**lumen** The strength of light energy or the unit of luminous flux, determined by the amount of light within a solid angle of unit size coming from a uniform point source of one candle-power.

**luminal** Common name for phenobarbital.

**luminance** Light energy transmitted, reflected or emitted from a source; the actual strength of light in the whole of the space involved.

**luminosity** The physical correlate of brightness of light, dependent on and modified by the prevailing physical conditions such as distance, reflectance, and conditions of illumination, and not on the physical intensity of the light itself.

**luminosity, absolute** The relative brightness of a light expressed in absolute terms such as lumens per watt.

**luminosity coefficients** The numbers which any color mixture data must be multiplied by in order that the sum of the three products equals the luminances of the particular desired color sample.

**luminosity curve** The brightness value of the various spectral stimuli through the visible range, plotted as curves with wave length on the abscissa and luminosity on the ordinate.

**luminous flux** The rate of passage of light determined by the experience of the brightness it produces on a surface at right angles to its direction.

**lupus erythematosis** A chronic lupus disease of the skin of unknown origin sometimes affected by emotional factors which is characterized by red, scaly patches of different sizes.

**Luria, A.R. (1902- )** Soviet psychologist and neuropsychologist. His basic works were concerned with the analysis of brain mechanisms of psychological processes, psychological methods of diagnostics of local brain lesion, as well as the basic problems of the development of behavioral process and the role of speech in organization of human behavior. Main publications: *The Nature of Human Conflicts; Higher Cortical Function in Man; Human Brain and Psychological Processes; Restoration of Functions after Brain Trauma; Traumatic Aphasia; The Mind of a Mnemonist; The Man with a Shattered World; The Working Brain.*

**Luria technique** (A. R. Luria) A method for measuring emotional tensions in which the subject simultaneously responds to words in a free association test and presses the fingers of one hand on a sensitive tremor recorder while holding the other hand as still as possible.

**lust for life** 1. (I. P. Pavlov) The main reflex whose goal is self-preservation. It is composed of positive movement reflexes toward conditions favorable for life and negative movement reflexes guarding the organism against injury. 2. (B. B. Wolman) All living organisms carry a certain amount of mental energy, a derivative from the universal biochemical energy. This energy is activated by threats to one's life. The built-in release apparatus, the force that opens the valves or ignites the motor and facilitates the discharge of energy is called a drive or instinctual drive. Since this force activates the energies for survival, it was named "Lust for Life." At a certain level of evolution, a part of this force has been directed into procreative activities, and the Lust for Life can be channelled into a drive for war, called Ares, and the drive for love, called Eros.

**Lustprinzip** (S. Freud) The urge for immediate discharge of energy which brings satisfaction to libidinal or destructive drives. Usually translated as the pleasure principle.

**lux** A unit of illumination, equal to the density of luminance flux on a surface area of one square meter which is at right angles to the rays and at a distance of one meter or foot from a point source of one candle-power.

**lycanthopy** The belief by an individual that he can change himself into a wolf.

**lygophilia** A morbid desire to stay in dark and gloomy places.

**lymph** A body fluid, chiefly derived from the blood but which also may contain food products, that slowly travels through the lymphatic system of ducts and vessels to the large veins near the heart where it is transferred into the blood stream.

**lymphoma** A group of malignant diseases of lymphoid tissue.

**Lyon hypothesis** This hypothesis seeks to explain the puzzle that females homozygous for an $X$-limited mutant gene are no more markedly affected than homozygous males. Some mechanism of dosage compensation is indicated. Dr. Mary Lyon (1962) stated a detailed hypothesis containing the following three points 1) the condensed sex chromosome is genetically inactivated, 2) the inactivated $X$ could be either the paternal or maternal $X$ in the cells of the same individual and, 3) the inactivation occurs early in embryonic life.

**lypothymia** 1. Depression. 2. Involutional psychosis.

**lysergic acid diethylamide (LSD)** One of a group of psychomimetic drugs which produces symptoms similar to those of psychosis such as disturbance in thought processes, severe anxiety, general confusion and delusions.

**lyssophobia** Fear of going insane.

# M

**m** **1.** In general formulas, symbol for a number. **2.** Meter. **3.** (Rorschach) Inanimate movement.

**M** **1.** Symbol for arithmetic mean. **2.** Symbol for illumination. **3.** (C. Hull) Symbol for the maximum learning. **4.** (Rorschach) Movement response. **5.** Associative memory factor symbol.

**MA** See *mental age.*

**Mach, Ernst (1838-1916)** Austrian philosopher, and a physicist, a thinker and an experimentalist. Made many contributions, theoretical and experimental, to the study of vision, hearing, and to time and space perception; tried to make psychology less philosophical, more quantitative and objective; his ideas influenced logical positivism (the "Vienna Circle"), American operationism, and Einstein's earlier work; William James called him "pure intellectual genius."

**Machover Draw-A-Person Test** See *test, Draw-a-Person.*

**MacQuarrie Test for Mechanical Ability** See *test, MacQuarrie for Mechanical Ability.*

**macrocephaly** Increase in size of brain leading to mental retardation, impaired vision and sometimes convulsions.

**macrocosm** The universe or society as a totality.

**macrogenitosomia** A syndrome characterized by premature physical development concomitant with the occurrence of secondary sex characteristics. It is caused by tumors of the pineal gland.

**macropsia** An impairment of vision in which objects appear larger than they really are due to retinal pathology.

**macroscopic** **1.** Large enough to be seen without the aid of special lenses. **2.** Perceived as a whole disregarding the details.

**macrosplanchnic** Referring to a body build in which the trunk is disproportionally large in relation to the extremities.

**macula acoustica** A thickening of the utricle and saccule wall in the inner ear made up of cells of unknown functions.

**macula lutea** A yellowish area about 2 millimeters in diameter in the center of the human retina containing the fovea.

**Maddox rod test** See *test, Maddox rod.*

**magazine** (operant conditioning) Device which makes food, water, etc. available to the organism usually during reinforcement.

**Magendie, François (1783-1855)** French physiologist, pioneer of experimental physiology, author of several medical books. He made important contributions to medicine; demonstrated in 1822 that the dorsal roots of the spinal nerves were sensory in function and the ventral roots motor; the claim of famous British anatomist, Charles Bell, to priority in this discovery (1809) began one of the greatest controversies, never conclusively settled.

**magic** **1.** The act of producing desired effects and control of natural phenomena through various techniques such as prayer or incantation. **2.** The production of illusions by means of sleight of hand.

**magical thinking** See *thinking, magical.*

**magilalia** Hesitancy in speaking.

**Magna Mater** **1.** The symbol of universal motherhood. **2.** (C. G. Jung) The archetypal primordial image of the mother, based on the cult of Cybele, a goddess known to the Romans as the Great Mother of the Gods.

**magnetism, animal** (F. A. Mesmer) The hypothetical force which induces hypnosis by being transferred from the hypnotist to the subject.

**magnitude estimation** See *estimation, magnitude.*

**magnitude scales** See *scales, magnitude.*

**Mahler, Margaret Schoenberger (1897- )** American psychoanalyst and child psychiatrist. M.D. (Jena, Germany), Sc.D. (Med.) Honoris Causa. Faculties New York and Philadelphia Psychoanalytic Institutes. Psychoanalyst-Teacher. Director of Research Masters Children's Center, New York City. Recipient of: Brill Memorial Plaque, 1962, of the New York Psychoanalytic Society; Agnes Purcell McGavin Award of the A.P.A., 1969; The Scroll of the N.Y. Psychoanalytic Institute, 1970 Freud Anniversary Lectureship; The Frieda Fromm-Reichman Award of 1970 of the American Academy of Psychoanalysis; A Festschrift: Separation-Individuation with contributions of 27 psychoanalysts. Author of more than eighty scientific articles, chapters and books, some of them translated into Italian, German, French and Spanish. Pioneering contributions to psychoanalytic developmental psychology, to the natural history of infantile psychosis and to tics and motor neurosis in child- and adulthood as well as the application of the concepts of separation-individuation to reconstruction in the psychoanalytic situation of borderline cases (adult and adolescent).

**maieusiophobia**  Morbid fear of childbirth.

**main score**  (H. Rorschach) The number of responses to inkblots which the subject gives during the test precluding the additional responses which are added as afterthoughts.

**maintenance functions**  See *functions, maintenance.*

**maintenance level**  See *level, maintenance.*

**maintenance schedule**  See *schedule, maintenance.*

**major gene**  See *gene, major.*

**major solution**  See *solution, major.*

**Make-A-Picture-Story Test**  See *test, Make-A-Picture-Story.*

**make-believe**  The pretense that fantasy is a real characteristic of children's play and associated with varying degrees of recognizing the unreality of the situation.

**maladaptation**  The failure of an organism to develop biological characteristics necessary to insure success in interaction with the environment.

**maladjustment**  The failure of an individual to develop behavioral patterns necessary for personal and social success.

**malaise**  A slight feeling of being ill or unwell.

**malformation**  An abnormal development of an organ or part of the body.

**malfunction**  Failure of an organismic process, organ or system to work properly.

**malignant**  Referring to a disease or tumor with a poor prognosis, usually threatening life.

**malingering**  The pretense of illness or disability in order to obtain certain benefits.

**malleation**  A repeated spasmodic motion of the hands involving striking at an object.

**malleus**  Bony transmitter of aural vibrations from the outer ear through the middle ear to the inner ear.

**Malleus Maleficarum**  A book depicting the ideology of the witch-hunting movement written by J. Sprenger and H. Kraemer in 1487 with the approval of the Church, the University of Cologne and the monarch, Maximilian I, king of Rome. The textbook describes the destruction of heretics and the mentally ill, branded as witches, with detailed instructions on the process of identifying and convicting these individuals.

**malpractice**  Behavior of a professional person contrary to the established ethical code due to negligence, ignorance or intent which may result in legal action.

**Malthus' theory; Malthusianism**  (T. R. Malthus) The doctrine concerning population growth which states that the population of a species increases geometrically while the food supply increases arithmetically suggesting the necessity of some form of population control including war, famine, and natural disasters.

**malum minus**  The petit mal type of epilepsy.

**mammalia**  The highest class of vertebrates which includes organisms which bear their young within a uterus, nourish them by milk from the mammary glands after birth and have hair.

**mammalingus**  (E. Jones) The concept of fellatio towards a woman which stresses the woman's act of suckling the man.

**mammillary bodies**  Two small rounded bodies in the posterior hypothalamus.

**man-to-man rating**  See *rating, man-to-man.*

**management, psychology of**  The manipulation and direction of people and their work environment in order to obtain more effective and favorable results.

**mand**  (B. F. Skinner) A speech sequence whose function is to make a demand on the recipient who subsequently grants the request thus rewarding the speaker.

**mandala**  1. An oriental geometric circular symbol representing unity. 2. (C. G. Jung) The symbol expressing the archetype of man's striving for unity. It is representative of the integration of the conflicting elements of conscious and unconscious through the emergence of the self.

**mania**  1. Impulsive, uncontrollable behavior characterized by violent and excessive motor activity and excitement. 2. The overactive phase of manic-depressive psychosis. 3. Uncontrollable urge to do a certain thing.

**mania a potu**  Alcoholically induced state characterized by extreme excitement and sometimes other-directed violence.

**mania, absorbed**  A condition in which the patient has focused his attention upon his own thoughts to the exclusion of reality. This situation has been distinguished from a condition which it resembles called a stupor because in the latter situation this is a lack of attention and mental activity.

**mania, acute**  Manic state which has sudden onset

and terminates rather than persisting over a long period of time.

**mania, akinetic** A disorder characterized by the symptoms of mania as well as lack of movement.

**mania, ambitious** Obsolete term for delusions of grandeur or any mental disorder characterized by grandiose ideas.

**mania, anxious** Variation of manic-depressive psychosis characterized by anxiety and excitement rather than depression.

**mania, Bell's** (L. V. Bell) Acute mania.

**mania, chronic** Mania or manic state which persists over a long period of time or permanently.

**mania, collecting** Uncontrollable urge to collect things, often useless items, and thought to be associated with anal erotic impulses.

**mania concionabunda** Obsolete term for strong uncontrollable urge to give speeches to the public.

**mania, ephemeral** See *mania transitoria*.

**mania errabunda** Obsolete term for uncontrollable desire to wander aimlessly away from home which is often associated with senility.

**mania, grumbling** The state of exaltation and restlessness concomitant with feelings of dissatisfaction, capriciousness and complaining.

**mania, incendiary** Pyromania.

**mania, inhibited** (E. Kraepelin) Variation of the manic state characterized by cheerfulness, inhibited psychomotor activity and flight of ideas.

**mania, metaphysical** Obsolete term for folie du doute.

**mania, mitis** Mild form of mania currently called hypomania.

**mania, muscular** Obsolete term for mania characterized by normally voluntary muscular movements occurring automatically.

**mania, recurrent** General term for mania which occurs periodically.

**mania, puerperal** Obsolete term for mania occurring after childbirth and previously thought to be attributable in a casual way to the puerperium, though today the puerperium is considered just one of several contributing factors.

**mania, recurrent** General term for mania which occurs periodically.

**mania, religious** Acute state of excitement characterized by religious hallucinations and hyperactivity.

**mania senilis** Mania associated with old-age and senility.

**mania sine delirio** Mild form of mania currently called hypomania, a more appropriate term.

**mania, stuporous** Manic phase of mania in which an individual is aloof and often does not talk.

**mania transitoria** Obsolete term for rare variety of spontaneous mad exaltation which is characterized by incoherence, insomnia and total or partial lack of awareness of surroundings.

**mania, wandering** Form of mania in which the individual has uncontrollable urge to leave home and wander about.

**maniac** One who exhibits mania or maniacal behavior.

**maniacal chorea** Chorea accompanied by extreme mental disturbance.

**maniaphobia** Morbid fear of going insane.

**manic behavior** Elated, hyperactive behavior.

**manic-depressive psychosis** See *psychosis, manic-depressive*.

**manic-depressive psychosis, circular type** See *psychosis, manic-depressive, circular type*.

**manic depressive psychosis, depressed type** See *psychosis, manic depressive, depressed type*.

**manic-depressive psychosis, manic type** See *psychosis, manic-depressive, manic type*.

**manifest anxiety scale** See *scale, manifest anxiety*.

**manifest dream content** See *content, dream, manifest*.

**manifest schizophrenia** See *schizophrenia, manifest*.

**manifold** 1. A group of objects which have something in common. 2. A classification which contains two or more subdivisions.

**Manikin Test** See *test, Manikin*.

**manipulanda** (E. C. Tolman) The aspects of an object or situation which allow the animal to manipulate it motorically.

**manipulandum** (operant conditioning) That part of the experimental chamber upon which the organism responds. This term, no longer the preferred term is being replaced by the word operandum.

**manometric block** Obstruction of the free flow of cerebrospinal fluid.

**manoptoscope** An apparatus consisting of a hollow cone through which the subject looks, which measures eye dominance.

**mantle** The part of brain which includes corpus callosum, fornix and the convolutions.

**mantle layer** The middle embryonic layer of the neural plate which develops into the gray matter of the central nervous system.

**manual method** See *method, manual*.

**maple syrup urine disease** A rare aminoaciduria associated with mental retardation. A hereditary metabolic disorder. In infantile form it is associated with hypertonicity, vomiting, seizures and often death.

**MAPS**  See *test, Make-A-Picture Story.*

**marasmus**  1. A wasting or withering of the tissues, usually from improper nutrition. 2. (R. Spitz) A condition in infants in which there is a gradual wasting of the body. The last stage of the grief reaction, in infants older than six months who are separated for a long period from their primary caretaker.

**Marbe's law**  More common responses in word association tests have a shorter latency than the less common responses.

**marginal intelligence**  See *intelligence, marginal.*

**marginal layer**  The outer layer of the walls of the embryonic neural plane which gives rise to the nerve fibers.

**marginal man**  (social psychology) A person who is not assimilated into a group or culture and is uncertain about his group membership.

**marihuana; marijuana**  A drug derived from the hemp plant, cannabis indica, which produces feelings of mental exaltation, loss of inhibitions, intoxication and a distorted sense of time.

**mark**  1. A distinguishing characteristic. 2. A score indicating the value or level of the performance of a subject.

**marker variable or marker**  A variable, usually a test score, previously known to load (correlate with) a factor highly and consistently through different studies. Therefore, (a) a marker which loads highly on a factor helps to identify that factor, and (b) scores on marker tests can be used to estimate scores on the factor (Factor Score).

**market research**  See *research, market.*

**marketing orientation**  (E. Fromm) A non-productive life-style characterized by the perception of oneself as a commodity and of one's self-worth as dependent on one's market value.

**Markov process**  (statistics) A model which represents joint probabilities sequentially and conditional probabilities in order to determine statistically the future values of a random variable.

**masculine protest**  1. (A. Adler) The desire to dominate and be superior. 2. (A. Adler) The desire of the female to be a male.

**Mashburn Complex Coordinator**  An apparatus to measure eye-hand and eye-foot coordination. The subject is asked to line up rows of red and green lights with a stick and rudder bar; the score is the number of matchings in a limited amount of time.

**masked epilepsy**  See *epileptic equivalent.*

**masking**  1. The partial or complete obscuring of sensory stimulus by another. 2. The partial or complete interference of one tone by another.

**Maslow's theory of personality**  (A. H. Maslow) The theory that two basic types of motivation are important: deficiency motivation as oxygen, food and water, and growth motivation, strivings for knowledge and self-actualization. There is a postulated hierarchy of motivation according to which physiological needs must be satisfied first followed by safety needs, love, esteem needs and finally the need for self-actualization.

**masochism**  1. Sexual perversion in which the individual derives sexual pleasure from the infliction of pain upon himself. 2. The deriving of pleasure from being maltreated or from suffering. 3. (psychoanalysis) Aggression turned toward the self because of the anxiety inherent in expressing it outward.

**mass action, principle of**  (K. S. Lashley) The theory that learning depends on the areas of the cortex as a whole based on animal experiments which have shown that the effect of brain tissue removal on learning depends on the quantity of ablated tissue rather than its location.

**mass communication**  See *communication, mass.*

**mass contagion**  See *contagion, mass.*

**mass media of communication**  See *communication, mass media of.*

**mass method**  See *method, mass.*

**mass movement**  See *movement, mass.*

**mass observation**  See *observation, mass.*

**mass polarization**  See *polarization, mass.*

**mass psychology**  See *psychology, mass.*

**mass reflex**  See *reflex, mass.*

**Masserman, Jules H.** (1905-    )  American neurologist, psychiatrist and psychoanalyst. After early work on cerebrospinal fluid and neurophysiology, conducted research demonstrating the following biodynamic principles applicable to animals and man: 1) that behavior is actuated by varying physiologic needs, 2) that it is contingent on the organism's genetic and experiential *concepts* of its milieu, 3) that versatility of adaptation to stress is similarly determined and 4) that when these adaptive ranges are exceeded in circumstances of conflict or uncertainty, somatic dysfunctions and drug addictions stereotyped, regressive or "dereistic" patterns develop analogous to clinical neuroses or psychoses. As President of the International Association of Social Psychiatry (1970-    ), Masserman proposed that all effective therapy must satisfy three ultimate (Ur-) needs of man: 1) physical well-being and creativity, 2) social security and 3) philosophic serenity.

Author of 8 books, editor of 34 others, and contributor of over 250 articles on history, music, biography and philosophy as well as neurology, pharmacology and psychiatry.

**Masson disc**  A white disc upon which black squares are arranged along one radius so that when the disc is rotated, a series of concentric rings of diminishing grayness is seen. The first ring from within which becomes indistinguishable from the background reflects the difference threshold of brightness vision.

**mastery motive**  See *motive, mastery.*

**masturbation** The deriving of sexual satisfaction by manual or mechanical stimulation of the genitals.

**MAT** See *test, Miller Analogies.*

**matched group** See *group, matched.*

**matched sample** See *sample, matched.*

**matching test** See *test, matching.*

**mate** 1. To copulate. 2. To enter into a long-term relationship with a member of the opposite sex.

**materialism** 1. A philosophical point of view that matter is the only reality. 2. A value system which stresses the pursuit and acquisition of material goods and comforts at the expense of intellectual and cultural activities.

**maternal behavior** See *behavior, maternal.*

**maternal drive** See *drive, maternal.*

**maternal overprotection** See *overprotection, maternal.*

**mathematical axis** 1. A straight line around which a plane figure can be rotated to form a solid figure. 2. A pair of intersecting coordinates which are used to determine the position of a point or a series of points forming a surface or curve.

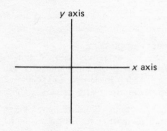

**mathematical model** See *model, mathematical.*

**mathematico-deductive method** See *method, mathmatico-deductive.*

**matriarchy** 1. A society in which lineage and inheritance are determined through the female line. 2. A society ruled by a woman.

**matrix** 1. The context. 2. (mathematics) A table of numbers arranged in rows and columns which undergoes certain mathematic operations.

**matrix correlation** See *correlation, matrix.*

**matrix, product** (factor analysis) The result obtained when factor loadings of variables are multipled together.

**maturation** The process of changing from an immature (small, undifferentiated) to a mature or adult state.

**maturation-degeneration hypothesis** The principle that an organism's functions and abilities develop to a certain optimal stage then decline.

**maturation hypothesis or theory** The theory that some modes of behavior are solely determined by heredity but cannot be manifested until the appropriate organs and neural connections have matured.

**maturity, emotional** See *emotional maturity.*

**maturity rating** See *rating, maturity.*

**MAVA** See *multiple abstract variance analysis.*

**maximal sensation** See *sensation, maximal.*

**maximum likelihood estimators** (statistics-R.A. Fisher) Statistics chosen as estimators of population parameters which will maximize the likelihood of the sample results that are observed to occur.

**Maxwell discs** Slotted color discs which overlap when fitted on a rotating spindle. When rotated at a speed above the critical flicker frequency, a color mixture occurs whose hue and brightness is proportional to the amount of color exposed by the overlapping.

**Maxwell triangle** See *color triangle.*

**Maxwell's demons** (C. Maxwell) A metaphorical way of discussing physical forces and concepts as if they were humanlike with human attributes.

**maze** An apparatus of varying complexity used to study learning and motivation behavior which consists of a series of pathways, some of which are blind alleys, which eventually lead to the end or goal point.

**maze, Hampton Court** A 6 by 8 foot instrument designed to test learning in rats introduced by W. S. Smell, and based on the pattern of Hampton Court, England.

**maze, multiple T** A series of T maze runways with the starting box at the base of the first T and the goal at one end of the last cross bar.

**maze, stylus** A maze which a person traces with a stylus.

**maze, T** A pathway in the shape of a T with the starting box at the base and goal boxes at either ends of the cross piece. For each trial, reinforcement may be available in either or both goal boxes. Often used in animal learning and discrimination studies with the discrimination stimuli at the choice point.

**McArdle's syndrome** See *syndrome, McArdle's.*

**McDougall, William** (1871-1938) British-born psychologist and physician. Professor of psychology, Harvard University (1920-1927), Duke University (1927-1938). Chief exponent of hormic psychology whose basic proposition is that all behavior is purposive or goal-seeking. Opposed concept of psychology as science of consciousness; was first to propose definition of psychology as the study of behavior. Wrote *Physiological Psychology* (1905), *Introduction to Social Psychology* (1908), *The Group Mind* (1920), *Outline of Psychology* (1923), *Outline of Abnormal Psychology* (1926), and *The Energies of Men* (1932).

**MCI** See *inventory, Minnesota Counseling.*

**MCI**   See *mother-child interaction.*

**McNaghten rule**   See *M' Naghten rules.*

**mdn**   See *median.*

**Mead, Margaret (1901-   )** American anthropologist. Developed method of studying childhood in primitive cultures; the study of cultural character; extended its application to the study of modern cultures and the study of cultures at a distance; developed the theory of cultural transformation through across the board cultural change and the application of anthropological methods to culture building.

**mean** $(\bar{x})$ A measure of central tendency which is the arithmetic average of the scores. Obtained by the formula: $\bar{x} = \frac{\Sigma x}{N}$, $x$ refers to the individual scores, $N$ is the number of scores, and $\Sigma$ is to take the sum of the values represented by the expression.

**mean, assumed**   An arbitrary value near the middle of a group distribution which is chosen in a short-cut method of determining the mean. The algebraic sum of the deviations from the assumed mean divided by the number of deviations is subsequently added or subtracted from the assumed mean to arrive at the actual mean of the series.

**mean deviation**   See *deviation, average.*

**mean-error procedure**   See *adjustment method.*

**mean geometric**   See *mean, logarithmic.*

**mean gradation method**   See *equal sense differences method.*

**mean, harmonic**   The reciprocal of the arithmetic mean of the reciprocals of a series of values. The formula for $H$ or $M_H$ is

$$\frac{1}{H} = (\frac{1}{N})\Sigma(\frac{1}{X})$$

where $N$ = number of cases and $X$ = any score.

**mean, logarithmic**   The $n^{\text{th}}$ root of the product of $n$ number of values or means, used in averaging ratios, rates of change, and means which are distinctly different but which have comparable standard deviations. Also called geometric mean. The formula is:

$$M_2 = \sqrt{a \cdot b \cdot c}$$

**mean rate**   See *rate, mean.*

**mean square**   The square root of the average of the squares of all the values in a set.

**mean-square contingency coefficient** (statistics) A statistic which determines whether the entries in a two-way contingency table could have been produced by chance factors. The symbol is $\Phi^2$.

**mean-square error**   See *variance.*

**mean variation**   See *deviation, average.*

**meaning**   1. That which is intended. 2. That which a symbol or symbolic act signifies. 3. The emotional or cognitive import of something for an individual.

**meaning, context theory of** (E. Titchener) The hypothesis that the meaning of an experience consists of the mental images which are associated with this experience. The meaning develops from actual sensory experience which is gradually replaced by mental images which symbolize the experience.

**means-end capacity** (E. C. Tolman) The hypothesized ability of an organism to respond to relationships between means objects and goal objects, specifically to respond to cues which lead to the goal such as distances, directions, and sequence.

**means-end expectancy** (E. C. Tolman) A state of expectation for the goal resulting from the immediate perception of means-end stimuli.

**means-end learning**   A type of rewarded learning in which skills are acquired for the purpose of achieving a single, relatively restricted goal, usually tangible and external; for example, a rat satisfying hunger by running a maze.

**means-end readiness** (E. C. Tolman) A state of innate or acquired readiness to form particular expectancies.

**means-end relations** (E. C. Tolman) The intervening objects and signs between a means and an end goal which are meaningful to an organism due to his previous experience.

**measure**   1. A quantitative result of measurement. 2. A standard used in measurement. 3. A statistic.

**measurement, absolute**   1. A measurement that disregards the plus or minus sign of the value. 2. A measurement that is obtained by units derived from that which is being measured and is, therefore, independent of comparison with other variables.

**measurement, direct**   Measurements taken directly without transformation to another scale of measurement.

**measurement, indirect**   Measurement in which the obtained values must be transformed to another scale or used in an intermediary process to obtain the desired quantification such as in the calculation of rectangular area from values of length and width.

**measurement, interactive** (R. B. Cattell) Measurement reflecting the exchange between an individual and his environment.

**measurement, mental**   1. The use of quantitative methods to measure psychological processes. 2. Psycho-physical methods of measurement.

**measurement methods**   See *methods, measurement.*

**meatus**   The external and internal canals of the temporal bone of the skull. The external passage leading from the outside to the middle ear cavity transmits soundwaves from the outside to the ear. The internal canal which leads from the cavity of the inner ear to the interior of the skull transports the auditory and facial nerves with blood-vessels.

**mechanical aptitude**   See *aptitude, mechanical.*

**mechanical indicator**   See *indicator, mechanical.*

**mechanical intelligence** See *intelligence, mechanical.*

**mechanical stimulation** See *stimulation, mechanical.*

**mechanism** 1. A system which operates like a machine. 2. The manner in which an end is produced. 3. A habitual manner of behaving which accomplishes a desired end. 4. (psychoanalysis) Unconscious determinants of behavior resulting from repressed wishes and impulses.

**mechanistic theory** The doctrine that all aspects of the universe including organisms and their psychological processes can be explained in terms of mechanical laws. Free will, motivation and purpose are denied as important variables in attaining ends.

**mechanoreceptor** Nerve structures (receptors) which are stimulated by movement of or change of pressure within the organ in which they are located.

**mecholyl** A drug which causes a rapid drop of blood pressure.

**Medea complex** See *complex, Medea.*

**median (md)** A measure of central tendency which is the point that divides the distribution into two parts such that an equal number of scores fall above and below the point.

**median deviation** See *deviation, median.*

**median grey** A brightness of gray forming the midpoint of a scale of brightness ranging from pure white to pure black.

**median interval** See *interval, median.*

**mediate** 1. Interposed between two items. 2. To act as an arbitrator between disputants. 3. To be a link between two processes, specifically thought processes. 4. Dependent upon an intervening process.

**mediate association** See *association, mediate.*

**mediated generalization** Similar responses and associated proprioceptive stimuli that becomes attached to different stimuli, consequently retarding the formation of a discrimination. This concept has been used to extend the stimulus-response formulations to symbols using human subjects.

**mediation theory** The doctrine that stimuli do not directly initiate behavior but stimulate intervening processes which activate the instrumental behavior.

**mediator** (communication theory) Functions of receiving and sending message are united. A system between the source and destination of a message.

**medicine** 1. Any substance, material or method used in the treatment of disease. 2. The science of treating diseases. The branches of medicine include: 1) Anatomic medicine, dealing with anatomic changes in diseased organs and their association to symptoms manifested during life; 2) Clinical medicine, the study of disease by direct observation and treatment of the patient; 3) Experimental medicine, based upon experiments on animals and the observation of pathologic changes induced in diseases and

the effect of drugs dispensed; 4) Physical medicine, a consultative, diagnostic, and therapeutic aid coordinating and integrating the use of physical and occupational therapy, and physical rejuvenation on the professional direction of the ailing and injured; 5) Preventive medicine, dealing with any activity which seeks to prevent disease, prolong life, and support physical and mental health and effectualness, especially the science of etiology and epidemiology of disease processes. They deal with those predisposing factors increasing an individual's suseptibility to disease, the initiating and precipitating factors of disease, and those factors which in noninfective or degenerative disease, result in their advance; 6) Psychosomatic medicine, dealing with the interrelationship between the psychic and physical components of illness; 7) Social medicine, an approach to the preservation and promotion of health, and to the prevention, amelioration, and cure of disease, having its foundation in a dynamic sociology and biology, comprised of the study of man and his environment. It is an attempt at the integration of the fields of clinical and social pathology, their workers, and their methods. The data so obtained is consistently guided by the concepts of the normal variability of human beings, and their capacity for adaptability.

**medicine, constitutional** The branch of medicine which concerns itself with the patient's constitution and his vulnerability to disease.

**medium** 1. The instrumentality through which something is accomplished. 2. Anything which fills the space through which a substance such as waves passes. 3. (parapsychology) A person who is believed to be controlled by disembodied spirits during a trance and to be able to receive and to impart messages from deceased people.

**medulla** 1. The inner part of an organ. 2. Abbreviation for medulla oblongata, the bulb at the top of the spinal cord which is the lowest part of the brain and the seat of nerve centers controlling autonomic functions such as respiration, heart rate, and gastrointestinal functions, and contains all of the ascending and descending fiber tracts interconnecting the brain and the spinal cord with many important nerve cell nuclei.

**Meduna, Ladislas J. von (1896-1964)** Hungarian-born American psychiatrist who suggested the use of convulsive agents in the treatment of schizophrenics.

**megalocephalia** See *macrocephaly.*

**megalomania** An exaggerated overestimation of one's own value, importance and abilities.

**Meier Art Judgment Test** See *test, Meier Art Judgment.*

**meiosis** The special type of cell division occurring in the gonads by which the gametes, containing the haploid chromosome number, are produced from diploid cells. This mechanism ensures that the chromosome number does not double with each new generation.

**mel** A unit of a ratio scale for pitch developed by

establishing a tone of 1,000 cycles per second equal to 1000 mels. The steps of the scale are constructed by the method of fractionation whereby the subject adjusts a stimulus tone equal to one-half the standard tone of 1000 mels, then adjusts the next tone and continues in this manner to produce a scale of subjectively equal intervals.

**melancholia, abdominal** (T. S. Clouston) Describes patients suffering from profound depression with intensely believed in delusions concerning the stomach and bowels.

**melancholia, agitated** The expression, melancholia agitata, was employed in the latter half of the nineteenth century to refer to the excited phase of catatonia. The Anglicized term, agitated melancholia, then became associated with manic-depressive psychosis and involutional melancholia. Neither term is much in use today. The condition described by the term agitated melancholia involves a state of severe anxiety, most commonly occurring late in life.

**melancholia; melancholy** 1. An obsolete term for intense depression, loss of interest in external stimuli, and feelings of guilt. 2. (psychoanalysis) The pathological reaction to a loss of an object characterized by intense depression, disinterest in the outside world and guilt feelings resulting from previously repressed intense hostility directed at the internalized object.

**melancholic type** See *type, melancholic.*

**membership character** See *character, membership.*

**membership group** See *group, membership.*

**memory** 1. The characteristic of living organisms involving the reliving of past experience and consisting of four phases: learning, retention, recall, and recognition. 2. The totality of experiences which can be remembered. 3. A specific past experience which is recalled.

**memory afterimage** See *afterimage, memory.*

**memory, associative** The recalling of a past experience by remembering a fact or incident associated with it which evokes the experience.

**memory color** The effect of a color perceived previously on a present experience of the same color.

**memory, curve** See *curve, retention.*

**memory drum** An apparatus for the presentation of material to be learned by the subject at a constant rate of speed. It is used to test verbal recall of serially presented words and of paired associate words.

**Memory-for-Designs Test** See *test, Memory-for-Designs.*

**memory image** See *image, memory.*

**memory, incidental** The occurrence of a memory without intent to remember.

**memory, kinesthetic** Memory that is in terms of ideal representation of movement sensations.

**memory, long term (LTM)** The ability to respond to a stimulus, recite a list, remember an association, and so on, after a long period of time since the material was presented. Its slow rate of decay and great amount of remembered material distinguish it from short term memory.

**memory, operation of** (J. P. Guilford) The commission of information to memory storage, to be distinguished both from the memory store itself and from the process of retrieval of information from storage.

**memory, organic** A change in living tissue which persists and modifies subsequent activity of that tissue and which results from the activity or functioning of the tissue itself.

**memory, physiological** (M. Prince) The storing of somatic experiences without the organism's awareness of it.

**memory, racial** The part of person's mental apparatus which is believed to be inherited from ancestors, and transmitted from generation to generation.

**memory, screen** (psychoanalysis) Fragmentary childhood memories which are similar in structure to manifest dream content in that they have been subjected to the operations of condensation and displacement, and usually serve as a cover for other repressed memories. Also called cover memory.

**memory, short term (STM)** The correct recall or appropriate performance immediately or shortly after the presentation of the material. Its rapid decay and limited amount of material distinguishes it from long term memory.

**memory span** Greatest number of items an individual can correctly reproduce immediately after one presentation. Series of items of a single type.

**memory-span method** Test of memory span by the presentation of several series of items varying in length from what is expected the subject will recall to what is known to be beyond his ability to recall. The number correctly reproduced in fifty percent of the trials is taken as the measure of memory span.

**memory system** An artificially developed device for remembering material usually consisting of the formation of associative connections between the material to be learned and previous knowledge.

**memory trace** The hypothetical neurological change which occurs when material is learned; it is postulated to account for the retention of learned material.

**memory, unconscious** (psychoanalysis) Repressed ideas and affects which influence behavior through their derivatives which enter consciousness.

**menarche** The first menstruation in the human female.

**mendacity** Pathological lying.

**Mendel, Gregor Johann (1822-1884)** Czech priest and biologist, abbot of the Augustinian monastery in Brno, Czechoslovakia; laid foundation for modern genetics; experimented on crosses between varieties of plants, mostly peas; discovered two laws of inheritance (Mendel's laws); his published report of 1866 was ignored for over 30 years; died without recognition for his scientific work.

**Mendelian Law of Independent Assortment** The principle that alleles or homologous chromosomes segregate independently of other alleles in other chromosome pairs.

**Mendelian Law of Segregation** The principle that genes maintain their integrity as they divide and recombine from generation to generation.

**Mendelian laws** Laws of hereditary transmission of characteristics which state that traits are inherited according to the Mendelian ratio which refers to the frequency of dominant to recessive phenotypes in the particular generation. The crossing of pure dominant with pure recessive parents produces a first generation consisting of three dominant phenotypes to one recessive.

**Mendelian ratio** The frequency of the dominant and recessive phenotype in the offspring from a specific type of mating.

**Mendelism** The doctrine of inheritance based on the principles that elements called genes exist which are responsible for the transmission of unit characters, and that the genetic elements are segregated independently of each other in the reproduction process.

**meninges** The three membranes, the dura matter, the arachnoid layer and the pia matter which cover the brain and spinal cord.

**meningitis** Inflammation of the meninges.

**meningitis, cryptococcus** A form of meningitis, frequently associated with leukemia and lymphoma in children, in which signs and symptoms include a positive Kernig's sign, nuchal rigidity, increased intracranial pressure, irritability, somnolence, anorexia, vomiting and fever.

**meningitis, hemophilus influencae** Type of meningitis with symptoms of anorexia, fever and seizures. Sequelae include upper motor neuron disease with resultant spasticity, hemiparesis, deafness, intellectual and motor retardation, seizures, and rarely, brain abcesses.

**meningitis, neonatal** Occurring in .01 percent of full-term infants, its symptoms include vomiting, anorexia, lethargy, twitchings, tremors, increase in startle response, jaundice, bulging fontanelle, and seizures.

**meningitis, pneumococcal** A type of meningitis with symptoms including lethargy, fever and seizures.

**meningitis, staphylococcal** A relatively rare form of bacterial meningitis which usually results from an infection of the skin, ears, or paranasal sinuses. There are multiple intracerebral and meningeal abscesses along with lethargy, fever and seizures leading to death if not properly treated. Sequelae include

spasticity, deafness, seizures, and motor and mental retardation.

**meningitis, streptococcal** A form of bacterial meningitis most commonly found in the first few months of life in which a focus of infection in the skin, ears, and nasopharynx is frequently present. It results in a deposition of a purulent exudate over the convexity of the brain along with lethargy, fever, and seizures. Sequelae include spasticity, deafness, seizures, and motor and mental retardation.

**meningovascular syphilis** See *syphilis, meningovascular.*

**menopause** Also called climacterium; the normal cessation of menstruation which takes place usually in the late forties.

**menotaxis** A taxis in which the animal orients at a constant angle rather than directly toward or away from the stimulus source.

**menstruation** The monthly discharge of blood and uterine material which occurs in the sexually mature female.

**mensuration** The measurement process.

**mental abilities, primary** 1. The hypothetical fundamental and basic units which constitute all distinguishable mental abilities. 2. (L. L. and L. G. Thurstone) Seven unit traits, derived through factor analysis, which are held to account for most variance in ability: verbal comprehension (V); word fluency (W); number (N); space (S); associative memory (M); perceptual speed (P); and reasoning (R) or induction (I).

**mental age** (A. Binet) The degree of intelligence of an individual determined by comparing his ability with the ability of other individuals of the same age. This concept is based on the principle that intellectual ability can be measured and that it increases progressively with age.

**mental apparatus** See *apparatus, mental.*

**mental chemistry** The doctrine that mental elements are fused by association into complex processes which no longer resemble the original elements.

**mental deficiency** See *deficiency, mental.*

**mental development** See *development, mental.*

**mental disease** See *disease, mental.*

**mental disorder** 1. Behavior disorder. 2. Severe maladjustment. 3. Includes mental diseases and all forms of psychopathological behavior.

**mental disorders, classification of** See *classification of mental disorders.*

**mental disorders of old age** See *senility.*

**mental examination** See *examination, mental.*

**mental faculty** See *faculty psychology.*

**mental function** 1. A mental process. 2. A particular type of ability such as intelligence.

**mental growth** See *growth, mental.*

mental growth curve  See *curve, mental growth*.

mental healing  The curing of disorders by suggestion or faith.

mental health  A state of relatively good adjustment, feelings of well-being and actualization of one's potentialities and capacities.

Mental Health Study Act  An act passed by the Congress of the United States of America in 1955 pointing out the human and economic problems of mental illness and stating its support of research aiming at the prevention of mental disorders.

mental hospital  An institution, either privately or state owned, in which in and out rehabilitative care is administered to mentally disturbed persons through various forms of therapy, such as psychotherapy, occupational therapy, and chemotherapy.

mental hygiene  See *hygiene, mental*.

mental illness  A disorder of behavior of organic or non-organic origin which is severe enough to require professional help. This term is used exchangeably with mental and behavior disorder.

mental institution  See *mental hospital*.

mental maturity  1. The attainment of an adult level of mental development. 2. An average adult level of intelligence.

mental measurement  See *measurement, mental*.

mental process  See *process, mental*.

mental processes, higher  Complex functions such as thinking, intelligence, memory, in contrast to sensory or motor functions.

mental processes, higher, organization of  Higher mental processes are described in terms of two principles: the reflex structure of mental activity and the systemic organization of higher mental processes in man which are of social origin. The reflex processes underlying mental activity are complex and dynamically organized involving different cerebral structures. The mental functions are dynamic systems in which different groups of cortical areas participate. These higher mental processes are developed from intercommunication among individuals and are mediated by a second signaling system. At different stages of development, the same mental function involves different cortical areas and dynamic systems.

mental retardation  1. Subnormal intellectual development due to social and environmental factors with no organic component, carrying with it the implication of reversibility. 2. See *deficiency, mental*.

mental scale  See *scale, mental*.

mental set  See *set, mental*.

mental structure  See *structure, mental*.

mental test  See *test, mental*.

mentalism  The doctrine that mental phenomena or mental processes cannot be reduced to physical phenomena.

menticide  The systematic attempt to break down a person's beliefs, standards, and values and to inculcate other views.

meprobamate  A minor tranquilizer, usually prescribed for anxiety, phobic states, insomnia, irritability and hyperactivity.

mercury poisoning  See *poisoning, mercury*.

merergasia  (A. Meyer) A syndrome consisting of a partial disorganization of personality.

merit ranking  Ordering of data, persons, objects, etc. with respect to the magnitude of a particular trait.

merit rating  The evaluation of an individual's performance on a specific job or task.

merit scale  Ranking of data or subjects according to the average of merits which were assigned by the raters.

Merkel corpuscle  A sense receptor, believed to be associated with pressure and touch which is located in the mouth and tongue.

Merkel's laws  (Merkel) A principle which holds that equal above threshold sense differences correlate with equal stimulus differences.

Merleau-Ponty, Maurice (1907-1961)  French existential philosopher. Attempted to integrate phenomenology and psychology. Made perception the foundation of his philosophy because he regarded it as man's primordial contact with the world. Wrote *The Structure of Behavior* (1942) and *Phenomenology of Perception* (1945).

Merrill-Palmer scale  (Merrill, Palmer) A test designed to measure intellectual ability, including verbal and performance materials within a 93 item-series that has been standardized for children ages 24-63 months.

mescaline  A narcotic drug which produces auditory and visual hallucinations. It is derived from the cactus plant. Mescaline, when ingested, is known to alter one's state of consciousness and has been used in therapy to make a patient behave as if he were back in his childhood. The drug can produce an effect which simulates a psychotic state. The intake of mescaline produces hallucination (a feeling that part of the body is missing), the tasting and smelling of peculiar odors, the development of paranoid ideas, the hearing of colors, the seeing of sounds, depressive or euphoric states. Some physiological effects are dilation of the pupils, body tremors, poor coordination, and difficulty in spatial discrimination.

mesencephalon  The midbrain consisting of the corpora quadrigemina, lamina, the cerebral peduncles, the tegmentum and the nerve tracts known as the crura cerebri. It developed from the middle portion of the primitive embryonic brain.

Mesmer, Franz Anton (1734-1815)  Austrian physician; believed in animal magnetism, an invisible power, which some men could utilize to cure diseases; expelled from Vienna for practicing what came to be called mesmerism, moved to Paris, where his method of treatment gained wide popularity; commission of scientists and physicians under presidency of Benjamin Franklin verified mesmeric phenomena but attributed them to causes other than animal magnetism; unable to prove his theory, branded as an impostor, had to leave Paris; died in Switzerland.

**mesmerism** (F. A. Mesmer) Obsolete term for hypnotism.

**mesmerization** Hypnosis.

**mesmerize** To hypnotize.

**mesoblast** See *mesoderm.*

**mesocephalic** The moderate relationship of the head between its length and width. In somatometry, having a cephalic index of 76.0 to 80.9.

**mesoderm** The middle layer in an embryo which develops into bone and muscle. Also called mesoblast.

**mesodermogenic neurosyphilis** See *neurosyphilis, mesodermogenic.*

**mesognathous** A condition in which the upper jaw has a mild degree of anterior projection when compared to the profile of the facial skeleton. In craniometry, having a gnathic index of 98.0 to 102.9.

**mesokurtosis** A frequency curve whose distribution, particularly its peak, is similar to the peak found in a normal curve.

**mesomorphic type** See *type, mesomorphic.*

**mesomorphy** (W. Sheldon) One of the three basic bodily builds which relates to the 3 primary temperments. According to this classification, the physique is marked by a prominence of muscle, bone and connective tissue.

**mesosomatic** (E. J. Eysenck) A subject who falls within one standard deviation of the mean after standard scores for height and chest measurements have been multiplied.

**message** 1. Symbolic communication between individuals. 2. (communications theory) The part of the output of one unit which is fed into the receiver of another unit as input.

**messenger RNA** A type of ribonucleic acid which transfers genetic information from the cell nucleus to the cytoplasm.

**metabolism** The physical and chemical reactions of the organism by which protoplasm is produced and destroyed and which manufacture energy necessary for the organism to perform its vital activities.

**metacholine chloride** A compound used as a measure of gross autonomic activity and to predict differential response to electroshock therapy.

**metachromatic leukodystrophy** See *sulfatide lipidosis.*

**metaerg** (R. B. Cattell) A trait, motivational in nature, which is affected by environmental factors, as opposed to constitutional influences.

**metagnomy** A belief that knowledge can be obtained by superhuman methods from spiritual beings; superhuman knowledge.

**metalanguage** 1. The aspect of language concerned with rules for the correct use of language such as grammar and syntax. 2. Terminology which expresses from dissimilar disciplines in a common manner.

**metallophonia** A metallic quality of the voice.

**metals, psychosis due to** Psychotic symptoms may appear in persons who have had prolonged exposure to metallic poisoning, such as lead or mercury. Because of the effects of these toxins on the neurological structures, patients may not recover, although recovery is not ruled out.

**metamers** Colors with different spectral qualities but which are perceived as identical under specific conditions.

**metamorphopsia** The distortion of visually perceived objects when the retina has been displaced.

**metamorphoses, delirium of** See *lycanthropy.*

**metamorphosis** 1. Radical, striking change. 2. The abrupt, observable change in the post-embryonic development of an organism, such as a tadpole into a frog.

**metamorphosis sexualis paranoica** A rare delusion, seen in paranoid patients who believe that they have been changed into the opposite sex.

**metamphetamine** A drug of the amphetamine group used in the treatment of depression and, in children, in the treatment of hyperactive behavior. However, it is infrequently prescribed because of cardiovascular effects when given in high dosages.

**metaphase** A stage in mitosis when the split chromosomes group together in the equatorial plane of the spindle. The metaphase occurs after the prophase and before the anophase.

**metaphoric language** 1. The use of metaphors. 2. In psychoanalytical theory, a form of thinking which resembles the primary process. The metaphor is a device which expresses a vital emotion and experience which originally occurred in the pregenital stage and of repressed Oedipal wishes. Metaphoric thinking may take place in dreams and in regressed states of neurotics.

**metaphorical combinations** A connection between different spheres of experience made by symbols or images.

**metaphrenia** A condition which is characterized by a compulsion with time and money.

**metaphysical mania** See *mania, metaphysical.*

**metaphysics** The branch of philosophy which concerns itself with the ultimate nature of existence. It includes ontology, the science of being, cosmology, the science of the nature of the universe and more widely epistemology, the theory of knowledge.

**metapsychics** See *parapsychology*.

**metapsychology** (psychoanalysis) The study of mental processes in terms of dynamic, economic, structural, genetic, adaptive and topographic approaches. *Dynamic:* deals with two innate motivational forces (instinctual drives), namely the libidinal Eros and the aggressive Thanatos. *Economic:* dwells upon the use of mental energies. *Structural:* divides the personality structure into id, ego and superego. *Genetic:* analyzes the origin of the mental phenomena and their development. *Adaptive:* deals with the interaction with the environment and the ensuing intrapsychic harmony. *Topographic:* divides the mind into conscious, preconscious and unconscious.

**metatheory** See *metapsychology*.

**metathetic** (S. S. Stevens) A sensory continuum in which just noticeable differences are thought to be subjectively equal. The physiological processes underlying the discrimination for metathetic continua are suggested to be the substitution of one locus of neural activity for another locus of activity. Pitch is one such continuum.

**metempirical** Beyond the empirical method; speculative or intuitive; evading empirical evidence.

**metempsychosis** A belief in the transmigration of the human soul into another corporal being.

**metencephalon** The part of the embryonic brain from which the medulla oblongata develops.

**methadone** A synthetic narcotic drug which is used in the relief of pain and the treatment of heroin addiction.

**methamphetamine hydrochloride** A central stimulant and vasoconstrictor compound soluble in water which is a methyl derivative of amphetamine or a desoxyn derivation of ephedrine.

**methionine** A rare aminoaciduria associated with mental retardation.

**method** A systematic procedure; a chosen path of dealing with facts or hypotheses.

**method, absolute-judgment** A psychophysical method that involves the evaluation of each of a series of stimuli without direct comparison to a standard; the utilization of absolute impressions.

**method, association** The study of association responses to given stimuli in an attempt to determine personality or behavioral traits.

**method, biographical** The systematic utilization and analysis of background information of a person in the investigation of cause-and-effect relationships between events in the person's life and development.

**method, constant** See *method, constant stimulus*.

**method, constant stimulus** (G. T. Fechner) A psychophysiological technique used for determining absolute and difference thresholds by requiring the subject to compare various stimuli with a standard or by stating when he notices a given stimulus. The thresholds are then determined as the value which is perceived in exactly fifty per cent of the cases.

**method, contingency** (statistics) A method of determining the degree to which two variables are dependent on each other. It is obtained by taking a function of the differences between the actual frequencies of the cells of a two-way table and the frequencies that would be estimated if the two variables were independent.

**method, cross-sectional** A method of studying large groups of people by assessing their standing on a particular variable at a given time rather than looking at how they change on this variable over a longer period of time. This method is used to establish standards.

**method, graphic** 1. The use of graphs to present or to analyze data. 2. A technique of recording responses in the form of a graph.

**method, halving** A psychophysical technique of constructing ratio scales of sensory magnitude in which the subject is asked to compare pairs of stimuli so that the intervals between them are perceived as equal.

**method, impression** A method used in the experimental study of feeling, that is dependent on the subject's introspective report of the affective experience produced by various stimuli.

**method, just noticeable difference** (psychophysics) A procedure for determining the smallest difference in a stimulus that can be discriminated by a subject. The technique consists of increasing the difference between two nondiscriminable stimuli, decreasing the difference between two discriminable stimuli, and taking the average of the point at which difference between the former is discerned and the point at which difference between the latter is imperceptible.

**method, kinesthetic** A technique for treating speech and reading defects and disabilities by focusing attention onto the various movement sensations associated with correct and faulty speech and reading.

**method, limits** See *method, just noticeable difference*.

**method, manual** The method of communication among deaf people consisting of sign language and gestures.

**method, mass** A technique for measuring large numbers of persons simultaneously.

**method, mathematico-deductive** (C. L. Hull) The use of mathematical equations to delineate postulates and definitions from which detailed theorems are deduced.

**method, metric** 1. The use of quantitative measurement, especially measurement using the metric system. 2. (psychophysics) Psychophysical methods of measurement.

**method, minimal change** (psychophysics) A technique for determining the differential threshold. The experimenter presents the subject with a series of stimuli which vary slightly in ascending or descending order which the subject is asked to compare with a standard.

**method, moving average** (statistics) A method of evening-out a series of items by substituting for frequencies of a number of groups, the average of the groups.

**method, moving total** (statistics) A method of evening-out a series of items by replacing each item with the sum of the item and a number of neighboring items.

**method, Müller-Urban** (psychophysics) A technique used to analyze data obtained by the method of constant stimuli based on the assumption that the best measure of the absolute or difference threshold value is the median of the best fitting ogive curve for the observed distribution.

**method, multigroup** (R. B. Cattell) A factor analytic procedure of simultaneously extracting the factors from the correlation matrix instead of successively.

**method, multiple-choice** A test or experiment in which the subject or animal is given several choices, only one of which is correct or which leads to a reward. In a discrimination experiment, the correct choice is usually marked by a specific cue which the animal must learn.

**method, obstruction** A technique for measuring the relative strength of various drives or motivations by juxtaposing one against the other in order to see which will determine an animal's behavior. The animal is forced to endure a negative stimulus in order to reach a positive goal; the technique measures to what extent a negative stimulus will be endured in particular conditions.

**method of adjustment** (psychophysics) The subject manipulates a continuously variable comparison stimulus until it appears equal to the standard stimulus. Several measures are usually taken. It is often used to determine the differential threshold or the point of subjective equality (PSE).

**method of least squares** (mathematics) A method for obtaining the best fitting curve for a series of quantitative data by making minimum the sum of the squares of the differences between the points to be fitted and the corresponding points on the fitted line.

**method of limits** (psychophysics) Most commonly used method for determining absolute thresholds. The experimenter presents a series of stimuli, each differing by a small discrete amount from the preceding stimulus. For each stimulus in the series the experimenter records the response of the subject. In this method usually two types of stimulus series are employed: a) an ascending series in which the initial stimulus of the series is presented below the threshold and each succeeding stimulus is increased by a constant small step until the subject reports detection; b) A descending series in which the initial stimulus is above the threshold and each succeeding stimulus is decreased by a constant small step.

**method of residues** See *residues, method of.*

**method of successive-intervals** See *successive-intervals, method of.*

**method of successive-practice** See *successive-practice, method of.*

**method, prompting** The method of measuring retention by the number of prompts needed to reproduce a previously presented series of items until the entire series can be reproduced without prompting.

**method, rank order** A method of ranking items or events according to the order of their rank.

**method, right and wrong cases** See *method, constant stimulus.*

**method, scientific** The techniques and procedures of naturalistic observation and experimentation used by scientists to deal with facts, data and their interpretation according to certain principles and precepts.

**method, scopic** A method of recording quantitative data by means of visual observation as opposed to graphic methods in which they are recorded by instruments.

**method, sense ratio** See *estimation, ratio.*

**method, serial-anticipation** See *method, prompting.*

**method, subtraction** 1. A method used to obtain a value of interest by subtracting the value of one observation from another. 2. (psychophysiology) In reaction time experiments, a method for measuring the amount of time necessary to make a choice, by subtracting from the time of the compound reaction, the amount of time used in the simple reaction.

**method, successive-approximation** See *conditioning, approximation.*

**method, successive reproduction** A method for measuring retention by asking the subject to reproduce learned material at relatively long intervals.

**methodology** A branch of logic and/or philosophy of science which analyzes research procedures.

**methods, measurement** Quantitative methods in psychological experiments. The measurement of psychological constructs by tests, and scales which are treated statistically.

**methyl alcohol poisoning** See *poisoning, methyl alcohol.*

**methylphenidate** A central nervous system stimulant frequently prescribed for the treatment of depression.

**metonymy** Disturbance in the logical use of language; the use of inappropriate, non-idiomatic, autistic forms of speech.

**metrazol** A trade name for pentylenetetrazol which in doses of 0.1 gr (1 ½ gr) is used as a circulatory and respiratory stimulant and in doses of 0.4-0.5 gr (6–7½ gr) is given intravenously and used in shock treatment of mental disorders.

**metric method** See *method, metric.*

**metronome** An apparatus which marks off short periods of time. It is used in timing various activities and was formerly used in obtaining graphical records of time intervals in psychological experiments.

**metronoscope** An apparatus which exposes short pieces of reading material for variable intervals to test or practice reading speed.

**Metropolitan Achievement Tests** See *tests, Metropolitan Achievement.*

**Meyer, Adolf (1866-1950)** American psychiatrist who stressed a holistic and integrative view including counseling, advice, and social service. The patient was viewed as a psychobiological whole. He interpreted behavior in terms of overt reactions and did not concern himself with a postulated set of unconscious mechanisms. The approach was keeping an open mind with the patient in order to understand the patient's cues. He introduced the term "mental hygiene" which developed into a movement for the prevention and cure of mental illness.

**Meynert, Theodore (1833-1892)** Viennese physician who emphasized the neurological and physiological aspect of mental disorder. He theorized that psychosis is due to a variety of changes in the circulatory nervous system and developed a classification of mental illness on a purely anatomical basis involving the working of the central nervous system.

**M-F test 1.** Test for measuring an individual's psychosocial gender role (masculinity or femininity). **2.** A test for such measurement in adults devised by L. M. Terman and Catherine C. Miles.

**Michigan Picture Test** See *Test, Michigan Picture.*

**Michotte, Albert van den Berk (1881-1965)** Belgian phenomenological experimental psychologist at the University of Louvain. During World War II, he and his students undertook extensive experiments on the perception of motion and of causation, demonstrating (contrary to David Hume's philosophical analysis) that impressions of causality depend not upon past experience but upon time, space, and speed relationships in the stimulus pattern.

**microcephaly** A condition characterized by the smallness of the head with associated subnormal mental development, produced by an incomplete development of the brain due to a premature closing of the skull.

**micron** The unit of length equal to one millionth of a meter.

**microphobia** Morbid fear of small objects.

**microphonia** Weak, hardly audible voice.

**micropsia** Disorder of visual perception in which objects are perceived much smaller than they really are.

**microsplanchnic** (A. Viola) A body type characterized by a small trunk and relatively long limbs.

**microtome** An instrument used for cutting thin sections of tissue for microscopic preparations.

**micturition** Discharge of urine; urination.

**midbrain** See *mesencephalon.*

**midparent** The average measure for both parents of any characteristic such as height.

**midpoint** The halfway point in a given interval or range.

**midrange values** The mean of the highest and lowest scores in a distribution which is a crude measure of central tendency.

**midscore** The median.

**Mignon delusion** The delusional fantasy of a child that his parents are not his real parents and that his true parents are distinguished people.

**migraine headache** See *headache, migraine.*

**milestone sequence** (J. Loevinger) A trait which develops in stages independent of age.

**milieu therapy** A therapeutic process which stresses changes in the patient's physical and social environment, with emphasis on the social.

**military psychology** See *psychology, military.*

**Mill, James (1773-1836)** British philosopher-empiricist whose doctrine represented the culmination of the philosophy of associationism. A strict elementist, he held that the mind consists of sensations and ideas; there is only one principle needed to explain mind: association. Any mental whole equals the sum total of its constituent elements.

**Mill, John Stuart (1806-1873)** British empiricist whose influential "mental chemistry" differed sharply from the arch-associationism of his father, James Mill. Compounds of ideas can, he held, have properties not deducible from the properties of the elemental ideas composing them. Also influential was his epistemological position that matter is the permanent possibilities of sensation.

**Mill's canons** (J. S. Mill) Five principles of inductive reasoning: the law of agreement states that given a large number of instances of a phenomenon which have a common factor, that factor causes the phenomenon most probably; the law of difference which holds that differences occurring among otherwise similar phenomena are due to events preceding them; the law of agreement and difference which states that the factor which is present when the phenomenon is present and absent if the event is absent must be a cause of the occurrence; the law of residues which states that the unexplained residue of an event is due to an unexplained remainder in the preceding condition; and the law of concomitant variation which states that the factors which vary together have a common cause.

**Miller Analogies Test** See *test, Miller Analogies.*

**Miller, Neal E. (1909-    )** American psychologist. Developed and experimentally tested theory of conflict and displacement, developed (with John Dollard) learning theory of psychotherapy, showed that fear can motivate, and reduction in it reinforce, learning; credited (with Delgado and Roberts) with first demonstration of instrumental learning motivated by direct electrical stimulation of the brain, one of the early investigators to use a variety of behavioral techniques to study the effects of direct electrical and chemical stimulation of the brain, proved that such stimulation of specific sites in hypothalamus can have a variety of motivational effects similar to those of normal hunger and thirst; proved that a variety of autonomically mediated visceral responses are subject to instrumental learning.

**millilambert** A measuring unit of luminance equal to one thousandth of a second.

**millimicron** A unit of measurement for light waves equal to one thousandth of a micron or one millionth of a millimeter.

**mimesis** 1. Imitation. 2. Meaningful response to species-specific behavior without previous learning.

**mind** 1. The organized totality of mental or psychical processes of an organism. 2. The totality of structures which are postulated to account for the occurrence of behaviors and processes. 3. (structuralism) The sum total of conscious experience. 4. The self or psyche. 5. The intellect. 6. A characteristic manner of thinking, feeling, and behaving such as the American mind.

**mind-body problem** The philosophical and psychological issue concerning the relation of the mind or mental processes to the body, the physical or physiological processes. Several views have been suggested: the theory that the mind and body are separate and should be studied as such is called dualism. The view that the mind and body influence each other is known as interactionism. According to the theory of psychophysical parallelism, the mind and body have parallel effects and change in parallel manner but do not interact. The isomorphic view is that a point-by-point correspondence exists between conscious experience and brain areas. The double language theory states that mental and bodily processes describe the same phenomenon in two different terminologies. Epiphenomenalism holds that mental processes are products of bodily processes and unimportant in themselves. The materialistic view also states that only the body is real while the idealistic viewpoint is that the mind is real and that bodily activity is simply a phenomenon of the mind.

**mind, collective** 1. A consensus. 2. The mental processes or behaviors which characterize the group rather than the individuals.

**miniature system** See *system, miniature.*

**minimal brain dysfunction syndrome** A concept which attempts to explain the etiology of learning disturbances for which there are no severe neurological signs. Developmental dyscrasias, learning disabilities and visual—motor perceptual irregularities are taken as signs of brain dysfunction, reflecting disorganized central nervous system functioning. The concept is applied to children with average, below average and above average intelligence with mild to severe learning and/or behavioral disabilities, manifested by impairment in perception, conceptualization, language, memory, and control of attention, impulse or motor function.

**minimal change method** See *method, minimal change.*

**minimum audible field (MAF)** Auditory threshold measuring technique in which the subject faces the source of sound in a free field room. The sound intensity is measured at the position in which the observer's head was located.

**minimum audible pressure** Auditory threshold measuring technique in which the sound intensity is measured against the eardrum.

**Minnesota Clerical Aptitude Test** See *test, Minnesota Clerical Aptitude.*

**Minnesota Counseling Inventory** See *inventory, Minnesota Counseling.*

**Minnesota Multiphasic Personality Inventory** A paper-and-pencil personality questionnaire with 550 items consisting of items borrowed from older inventories and rephrased diagnostic cues used by clinical workers. The subject answers true, false or cannot say to such items as: "I believe I am being plotted against"; "I drink an unusually large amount of water everyday"; "I wish I could be as happy as others seem to be." The content of the items are diverse, reporting observable behavior, feelings, symptoms of abnormal behavior, and general social attitudes. Scoring yields a profile on the subject with separate scores for scales of: hypochondriasis; depression; hysteria; psychopathic deviation; masculinity-femininity; paranoia; psychasthenia; schizophrenia; hypomania. Also scored are control scales (?,L,F,K) which identify or make allowance for exceptional response styles. ? identifies the frequency of the cannot say response. The L score, or Lie score, indicates the trustworthiness of the subjects answers. The F, or False, score consists of responses given extremely rarely; a high F indicates carelessness, misunderstanding and otherwise invalid answers. The K scale assesses the subject's defensiveness and is used as a weight in correcting the regular scale.

**Minnesota Paper-Form Board** A test of mechanical ability introduced in 1948 which consists of problems requiring the subject to identify the correct geometric figures from five choices when only two or more parts of the figure are shown. The test is believed to measure the ability to visualize and manipulate geometric forms which is related to mechanical ability.

**Minnesota Rate of Manipulation Test** See *test, Minnesota Rate of Manipulation.*

**Minnesota Spatial Relations Test** See *test, Minnesota Spatial Relations.*

**Minnesota Test for Aphasia** See *test, Minnesota, for Aphasia.*

**miolecithal** Referring to eggs which have little or no yolk.

**miosis**  See *myosis.*

**mirror drawing**  Drawing performed while viewing the design and one's hand in the mirror, used in psychological experiments or test of eye-hand coordination.

**mirror reading**  See *reading, mirror.*

**mirror reversal**  1. The reversal of right and left positions of objects when they are perceived in the mirror. 2. A change in the right and left positions of an object.

**mirror writing**  Reverse writing that looks as usual writing when put against a mirror.

**misanthropy**  Aversion, dislike of mankind.

**miscegenation**  Mixing of different races in marriage.

**misogynist**  A person who hates women.

**misogyny**  Hatred of women.

**misologia**  Fear and aversion of speaking.

**misoneism**  Avoidance of change and dislike of new subjects, events and people.

**misopedia**  Hatred of children.

**miss**  (signal detection theory) One of four possible outcomes in a single trial of a signal detection experiment. Both a signal and noise are presented together and the subject incorrectly responds that no signal was presented, only the noise. The other three possible outcomes are a hit, false alarm, and a correct rejection.

**mitis mania**  See *mania, mitis.*

**mitochondria**  Bodies in the cell which oxidize sugars and fats to produce adenosine triphosphate, an energy-rich substance utilized by the cells.

**mitosis**  Cell division which results in the formation of two daughter cells, each having one-half of the chromosomal material from the original cell. This process begins with the division of the fertilized ovum and continues in the somatic cells of the body.

**mix schedule**  See *reinforcement, schedule of: mixed.*

**mixed (mix) schedule**  See *reinforcement, schedule of: mixed.*

**mixed schizophrenic**  See *schizophrenic, mixed.*

**mixoscopia**  An unusual form of voyeurism where orgasm is reached while looking at sexual relations between one's love object and another person.

**mixovariation**  (genetics) Combination of several hereditary factors over several generations.

**MMPI**  See *Minnesota Multiphasic Personality Inventory.*

**M'Naghten Rules**  A legal test of insanity. Often used in the U.S.A. A person accused of a crime must be declared legally insane and thus not guilty by reason of insanity if the court decides that "he was laboring under such a defect of reason, from disease of the mind, as not to know the nature and quality of the act he was doing or . . .did not know he was doing what was wrong."

**mneme**  (R. Semon) The basic principle which is believed to account for memory. The memory trace.

**mnemonics**  Artificial devices used to facilitate recall and memory.

**mnemotaxis**  A taxis in which the animal orients on the basis of a whole configuration of stimulus cues and not to the selective stimulation of special parts of the receptor.

**mnemotechnics**  The art of facilitating memory.

**mobility, social**  Pertaining to societies or any grouping of people in which the role and status of each individual is flexible and changing, thus allowing for free interaction among its members.

**mobilization vs. regression**  (u.i. 23) in the Universal Index  (R. B. Cattell) A source trait visible as a pattern in objective tests and characterized at one pole by ability to mobilize one's skills quickly and at the other by general regression of interest and control.

**modality**  In personality, the division into ability, temperament, and dynamic traits.

**modality, sense**  See *sense.*

**mode ($M_O$)**  1. (statistics) A measure of central tendency which is the most frequently occurring value in a series. 2. The peak (or peaks) in a frequency curve. 3. A characteristic action pattern which satisfies needs.

**mode, crude**  (statistics) The midpoint of the interval containing the greatest number of cases.

**mode interval**  See *interval, mode.*

**mode, parataxic**  (H. S. Sullivan) The second stage in perceiving. The child in parataxic mode perceives the world in a prelogical order viewing himself as the center of the universe.

**mode, prototaxic**  (H. S. Sullivan) The earliest stage in perceiving. The infant's prototaxic mode is a state of unconscious and diffused experiences.

**mode, refined**  (statistics) An estimation of the mode of a population from which a given sample was drawn.

**mode, syntaxic**  (H. S. Sullivan) The third stage in perceiving. The school-age child learns to validate his perceptions against the perceptions of others and arrives through this consensual validation at a correct perception of reality.

**model**  1. A copy of the authentic thing. 2. A criterion or something ideal used for comparison purposes. 3. An actual representation of how a system functions with all of its interrelated parts. 4. A system of principles or hypotheses which is postulated to explain relationships in the data and is usually presented in mathematical terms.

**model, conceptual** A graphic or schematic representation of a concept.

**model, mathematical** The use of mathematical formulas or equations to systematize and order psychological data showing the relationship of some aspects of the data to others.

**model, mathematical learning** Use of mathematics to describe, summarize, and express relationships, predict and suggest further investigation in the field of learning. Feedback models, cybernetics, information-theory, and game theory have been the sources of the most influencial mathematical models of learning.

**model, schematic** A model which manifests the significant relationships between concepts.

**model, stochastic** See *stochastic models of behavior.*

**modeling** A behavior therapy technique designed to modify behavior through perceptual learning and by allowing the individual to imitate.

**modification** 1. Any change in structure, function or behavior. 2. (genetics) Any change in the phenotype due to environmental influences without a corresponding change in the genotypic configuration.

**modifiers (modifying genes)** Genes, usually polygenes, which influence the penetrance and expressivity of specific genetic mechanisms. In the view of Franz J. Kallmann these genes relate to constitution or somatotype which influences the manifestation of both schizophrenic and manic-depressive psychosis.

**modulation theory** (R. B. Cattell) The theory that a stimulus situation can be divided into two parts—a *focal stimulus* and an *ambient stimulus*—the second of which is capable of momentarily changing the individual's level on states and certain traits. The behavioral equation thus acquires modulator (s) terms, in addition to behavioral indices (b) terms, the former changing the state level, the latter expressing the effect of the state upon behavior.

**modulator, visual** (R. Granit) A hypothesized receptor in the retina which yields the sensation of a specific hue.

**Moebius, Paul Julius (1853-1907)** A German psychiatrist and sexologist. He studied famous men and originated the branch of psychiatry called pathography which deals with psychopathology in superior men.

**mogigraphia** Writer's cramp.

**molar behavior** See *behavior, molar.*

**molecular behavior** See *behavior, molecular.*

**molimen** Physiological and psychological distress which causes difficulties in performing even simple tasks.

**molimen, menstrual** Premenstrual tensions which may include psychological and physiological symptoms.

**molimen, virile** Obsolete term for fatigue characteristic of the climacterium in the male.

**moment** 1. A very small interval of time. 2. The measure of a force determined by its effect in causing circular movements in a body. 3. (statistics) The average of the deviations from the mean, after each deviation has been raised to a certain power. The general formula is $\Sigma\ (x^n)/N$ where $x$ is any deviation, $n$ is the power to which $X$ is raised, $N$ is the number of cases in the series, and $\Sigma$ is the summation sign.

**momentary effective reaction potential** $(_S\bar{E}_R)$ (C. L. Hull) Reaction potential modified by the oscillation factor.

**moments of a distribution** (statistics) The expectations of different powers of the random variable. The first moment about the origin of a random variable $x$ is $E(x)=$ mean. The second moment is $E(x^2)$, the third is $E(x^3)$, etc. When the mean is subtracted from $x$ before it is raised to a power, the moment is about the mean. $E(x - E(x))^2$ is the second moment about the mean; $E(x - E(x))^3$ is the third moment about the mean, etc. The higher moments reflect features of the distribution such as the degree of skewness or kurtosis which are important for statisticians in developing theoretical distribution which will fit the observed data.

**monadic theory** A psychological theory which treats each organism as an independent unit; e.g., most cognitive and developmental stage theories (Freud, Werner, Piaget).

**monaural hearing** See *hearing, monaural.*

**mongolism; mongoloidism** A common subgroup of mental deficiency. Retardation is usually moderate. Characterized by broad face, flat nose, slanted eyes, coarse and deeply fissured tongue, and broad and clumsy hands and feet. Also called Down syndrome. Typically, mongoloids have 47 chromosomes, having trisomic chromosome 21.

**monism** A philosophical theory of unity of nature. A belief that mind and matter are one and the same thing.

**monitor** To watch or supervise an individual or machine in order to insure continued normal functioning.

**monoamine oxidase; MAO** An enzyme which can oxidase or inhibit various amino substances.

**monochorionic twins** See *twins, identical.*

**monocular vision** See *vision, monocular.*

**monogamy** Marriage of one woman to one man.

**monohybridity; monohybridism** A state of being heterozygous for one single pair of genes.

**monomania** 1. Obsolete: a mild form of insanity in which the patient's mind concentrates on one topic only. 2. Exaggerated concern with one idea or topic.

**mononoea** See *monomania.*

**monoplegia** Paralysis of one limb or any other one part of the body.

**monosomy** A condition in which one chromosome of a pair is missing, resulting in a single member of that pair instead of the normal diploid number. Thus in Turner's syndrome there is a single X chromosome instead of the normal female double X complement.

**monovular twins** See *twins, identical.*

**monozygote** That which develops from one egg or zygote as, for example, identical twins.

**monozygotic** A term used to describe twins derived from a single fertilized ovum. Synonyms — identical or uniovular twins. Also see *twins, identical.*

**monozygotic twins** See *twins, identical.*

**Monroe Diagnostic Reading Test** See *test, Monroe Diagnostic Reading.*

**mood complex** See *complex, mood.*

**mood system** See *complex, mood.*

**Mooney Problem Checklist** An inventory developed in 1950 for use with persons in high school and college which consists of a record of different types of problems. The individual is asked to consider this list and to choose those problems which are relevant to him. The checklist is used as a screening device for finding people with problems, and as a means to facilitate counseling or psychological interviews.

**moral anxiety** See *anxiety, superego.*

**moral idiot** (E. Bleuler) An individual in whom the ability to sympathize with others is absent while his ability to experience other kinds of emotions is essentially unimpaired.

**moral imbecile** (E. Bleuler) An individual whose ability to sympathize with others is inadequately developed while his ability to experience other kinds of emotions is essentially unimpaired.

**moral insanity** See *insanity, moral.*

**moral judgment** See *judgment, moral.*

**moral oligophrenic** (E. Bleuler) Individual whose ability to sympathize with others is either stunted (moral imbecile) or entirely absent (moral idiot), while his ability to experience other kinds of emotions is essentially unimpaired.

**moral realism** (J. Piaget) The attitude characteristic of small children that morality is inherent in an act as an objective fact and that it is observable to all.

**moral treatment in psychiatry** The forerunner of the modern therapeutic community which emphasized the humane treatment of mentally ill people. The movement dates back to the thirteenth century when psychotic patients were taken care of in the homes of citizens of Gheel in Belgium and was propelled by the liberation of patients from chains by P. Pinel in 1793. B. Rush supported this movement in the United States emphasizing the release of patients from mechanical restraint, the improvement in patient care, kindness, attention to the patient's psychological needs, and a stress on supporting the patient's self-respect.

**morale** An attitude in individuals or in a group characterized by confidence, control, and motivation.

**morality, sphincter** (S. Ferenczi) The rudiments of the superego which originate from the rewards and punishments centering around toilet training.

**Morel, Benedict Augustin (1809-1873)** French psychiatrist who viewed most mental diseases as a result of "hereditary weakness." He believed that mental disease is a product of a hereditary malformation called degeneration, and they are accompanied by a series of symptomatic physical signs called "stigmate of degeneration." He divided all mental diseases into five groups, namely hereditary, toxic, sympathies (brain disease), emotional (hysteria,) and sociopathic psychoses. He coined the term dementia praecox, later called schizophrenia.

**Moreno, J.L. (1890-     )** American psychiatrist of Austrian education. Credited with the development of sociometry and psychodrama. Coined the terms encounter and encounter group, group therapy and group psychotherapy; developed a psychodramatic theory of personality and its application to 1) the treatment of mental disorders, 2) analysis of social and cultural phenomena, and 3) a new theory of society (sociatry).

**mores** Social customs without legal sanction which are believed to be conducive to social welfare and which put a pressure on the members to conform under the threat of societal condemnation.

**Morgan, Conway Lloyd (1852-1936)** Early comparative psychologist who in 1894 formulated a psychological version of the principle of parsimony, later known as Lloyd Morgan's canon: one must not interpret an animal's activity as the outcome of the exercise of a higher psychical faculty, if it can be interpreted as the outcome of the exercise of one which stands lower in the psychical scale.

**Morgan's canon** (L. Morgan) The principle that a behavior should not be interpreted as the result of the functioning of a higher mental process if it can be explained in terms of a lower psychical process.

**moria** An obsessive desire to joke.

**Moro response** The infant's response to stimuli such as a strong blow to the surface on which he is lying, characterized at first by general clutching movements of the extremities and gradually evolving into a discrete rapid body jerk. Also known as the startle response.

**moron** A level of feeblemindedness which is defined as the range of IQ from fifty to seventy. This category includes people who are believed to be capable of supporting themselves by performing simple tasks under supervision.

**morpheme** The smallest linguistic unit which is still meaningful.

**morphine** A colorless, narcotic drug derived from opium which is chiefly used to reduce pain and to induce sleep.

**morphinomania** Morbid desire or craving for morphine.

**morphogenesis** The structural development of parts of an organism.

**morphologic inferiority** See *inferiority, morphologic.*

**morphology** The branch of biology dealing with the study of form and structure of organisms.

**Morquio's syndrome** A type of mucopolysaccharidosis which is transmitted in an autosomal recessive fashion and characterized by normal intelligence, cloudy corneas, and severe bony changes leading to marked curvature of the spine.

**mortido** S. Freud called the mental energy at the disposal of Eros, the life instinct, libido, but did not coin any term for the destructive energy activated by the instinct of death, Thanatos. E. Federn called the destructive energy mortido; B. B. Wolman called it destrudo.

**morula** A stage in the embryological development of an organism before the fertilized egg reaches the thirty-two cell stage and the formation of the blastula.

**mosaic** An individual or tissue with at least two cell lines differing in genotype or karyotype, derived from a single zygote.

**Mosaic Test** See *test, Mosaic.*

**mother-child interaction (MCI)** (generic) Standardized assessment situations in which mother-child interactions are observed and recorded for either monadic or dyadic analysis.

**mother complex** See *Oedipus complex.*

**mother figure** 1. A person who replaces one's real mother and becomes the object of habitual responses originally developed in relation to the real parent. 2. A mature individual with whom a younger, immature person identifies and who comes to exercise such parental functions as advice and encouragement.

**mother hypnosis** (S. Ferenczi) The concept that submission to hypnotic states can be traced to blind obedience to one's parents, in this case transference of maternal fixation; also called "coaxing-hypnosis."

**mother imago** See *imago.*

**mother, schizophrenogenic** (A. Kanner) A woman whose behavior causes her child to become a schizophrenic.

**mother substitute** See *surrogate.*

**mother surrogate** See *mother figure; surrogate.*

**motion study** The study of the movements made in the performance of a task in order to determine the most efficient method of carrying out this task.

**motivation** 1. A process (appetitive as opposed to affective) that effects changes in the environment (acts) consonant with internal representations (plans, programs). 2. (V. G. Dethier) A specific state of endogenous activity in the brain which, under certain internal conditions and sensory input, leads to behavior which results in changes in the interior milieu and reduction of the initial activity.

**motivation component factors** (R. B. Cattell) Components, found in measurement *devices,* which may enter into any dynamic structure factor—principally, factors *a* (conscious id), $\beta$ (realized ego), $\gamma$ (ideal self), and $\delta$ (unconscious, physiological).

**motivation, conjunctive** (H. S. Sullivan) The desire for a lasting satisfaction.

**motivation, deficiency** (A. H. Maslow) Needs for food, oxygen and water which motivate behavior. These needs must be satisfied before other needs, higher in the hierarchy are considered.

**motivation, extrinsic** Motivation which stems from positive or negative reinforcements which are external to the behavior itself rather than inherent in it: studying to get good grades not because the studying is enjoyable.

**motivation, growth** (A. H. Maslow) Strivings toward self-actualization and knowledge which motivate behavior when lower physiological needs are satisfied.

**motivation, intrinsic** Motivation as an incentive which originates within the behavior itself rather than externally as in playing a musical instrument for enjoyment.

**motivational hierarchy** (A. Maslow) A hierarchy of human motives which determine behavior. The physiological needs are postulated to be the most basic. Needs for security and safety are at the next level. Love, affection, and belongingness form the next category followed by needs for esteem, mastery, competence and prestige. The highest level need is the need for self-actualization which does not appear until the lower level needs are satisfied.

**motive** 1. A state within an organism which energizes and directs him toward a particular goal. 2. The reason an individual offers to explain his behavior. 3. An unconscious cause of behavior.

**motive, affiliative** Need or tendency to depend upon or seek out others, for the purpose of forming friendships and other kinds of attachments.

**motive, mastery** The drive to achieve, to be successful.

**motone** (H. A. Murray) A motor-muscular action pattern.

**motoneuron** A neuron which is directly connected to a muscle or gland thus stimulating or inhibiting it.

**motor abreaction** See *abreaction, motor.*

**motor aphasia** See *aphasia, motor.*

**motor apraxia** See *apraxia, motor.*

**motor area** The area of the cortex consisting of the ascending precentral Rolandic convolutions and neighboring areas which when electrically stimulated elicits contraction of certain muscles and the associated bodily movement.

**motor end plate**   See *motor point.*

**motor equivalence**   The principle that a goal can be reached by many different actions requiring different muscular movements.

**motor function**   Any activity resulting from the excitation of muscles and glands by efferent neural fibers.

**motor habit**   See *habit, motor.*

**motor learning**   See *learning, motor.*

**motor nerve**   See *nerve, motor.*

**motor neuron**   See *neuron, motor.*

**motor point**   The point of contact between a motor neuron and a muscle.

**motor primacy theory**   The theory that the mechanisms underlying motor functions develop before those responsible for sensory functions.

**motor reaction type**   See *reaction type, motor.*

**motor root**   A ventral root of the spinal cord involved in motor functions.

**motor sensation**   See *sensation, motor.*

**motor set**   See *set, motor.*

**motor theory of consciousness**   (J. B. Watson) The principle that the subjective perception of consciousness depends on the motor and glandular reactions the subject makes.

**motor unit**   The motor neuron, its axon and the muscular and glandular areas which it supplies.

**motoric region**   (K. Lewin) The expressive part of personality, reflected by the external appearance and responses of the person.

**motorium**   The brain areas which directly control the activity of the voluntary or skeletal muscles.

**mouches volantes**   French word meaning flying flies which is used to refer to minute particles in the vitreous or aqueous humor of the eye which sometimes appear to be in motion in the field of vision. They are usually unnoticeable.

**movement, alpha**   A form of apparent movement where there appears to be change of size in parts of a figure exposed in succession.

**movement, apparent**   Subjective visual perception of movement in the absence of real physical movement. The most common examples are the phi phenomenon, the autokinetic effect, and the aftereffect of seen movement.

**movement, beta**   A form of apparent movement occurring when different sized or positioned objects exposed in succession give the appearance of movement. The time interval between exposures is crucial. Also called optimal movement.

**movement, delta**   A form of apparent movement obtained under certain conditions of stimulus size, intensity of illumination and distance and time between stimuli. When these requirements are met and the second stimulus is brighter than the first, movement of the brighter stimulus to the darker stimulus is reported.

**movement determinant**   See *movement response.*

**movement, epsilon**   The visual perception of movement when a white line against a black background is changed into a black line against a white background, one of various types of apparent movement.

**movement, gamma**   A form of apparent movement characterized by perceived expansion and contraction of a figure which is suddenly shown or withdrawn, or is exposed to sudden change in illuminations.

**movement, illusion**   See *movement, apparent.*

**movement, incipient**   The imperceptible or barely perceptible beginning of a movement that is not overtly carried out such as occurs in the speech organs during internal speech.

**movement, induced**   The illusory movement of the inner object of a pair of stimulus elements arranged such that one is the surround for the other, regardless of which object is set in motion. The perceived direction of movement is rigidly determined by the direction of the objectively moving surround.

**movement, mass**   (sociology) A unified attempt by a large number of individuals to effect a social change by working as a group.

**movement, optimal**   See *movement, beta.*

**movement response**   A Rorschach response in which the subject perceives in the "static" blots some form of action, expression, posture, or life. Rorschach restricted this classification to those responses in which the movement was human or human–like and used the symbol *M* for the scoring. Rorschach's basic position is also followed in the Beck and Rapaport approaches to the test; however, other approaches such as Klopfer, Hertz, and Piotrowski have defined two other classes of movement responses. One involves animal movement which is scored *FM* and the second involves movement perceived in inanimate objects, scoring using the symbol *m*. Human movement responses are generally conceded to be related to the inner life of the subject, especially his organized fantasy world while animal and inanimate movement responses are interpreted as being less sophisticated or controlled energies.

**movement, stroboscopic**   The illusion of movement occurring when fixed, separate stimuli are presented in succession. The most common example is the motion picture where if succession is rapid enough, there is no perceived separation of images but rather perceived smooth motion.

**Movigenic Movement Scale**   See *scale, Movigenic Movement.*

**moving average method**  See *method, moving average*.

**moving total method**  See *method, moving total*.

**Mowrer, O. Hobart (1907-    )**  American psychologist whose work includes three stages: 1) research on visual and vestibular functions with special reference to spatial orientation and reflex habituation; 2) work with laboratory animals involving issues in systematic learning theory, analogues of certain clinical dynamisms, competitive and cooperative problem solving, and signaling behaviors from which human language evolved; and 3) interest in disordered interpersonal relationships and their rectification in small groups and the role of psychopharmacology in this connection.

**mucopolysaccharidosis**  Disorder  of  mucopolysaccharide metabolism.

**mucous colitis**  See *colitis, mucous*.

**Müller, Georg Elias (1850-1934)**  Early German experimental psychologist at the University of Göttingen. Did seminal research in psychophysics, vision, physiological psychology, and memory. He discovered the associative and retroactive inhibitions, the paired associates type of learning, and developed better and more reliable apparatus. He also furthered the studies in color vision, space perception, and attention. He was the head of the Göttingen laboratory, a rival of Wilhelm Wundt's Leipzig laboratory, which under his direction became an influential experimental center, turning out many distinguished students and much important research.

**Müller, Johannes (1801-1858)**  German physiologist and comparative anatomist, professor at Berlin University; experimented on sensation; published monumental *Handbook of Human Physiology* which contained new physiological material; formulated theory of specific nerve energies which profoundly influenced research on sensation; coined the phrase "nemo psychologus nisi physiologus" (no one can be a psychologist unless he is a physiologist).

**Müller—Lyer illusion**  See *illusion, Müller-Lyer*.

**Müller—Schumann Law**  The principle that the association of two items causes difficulties in associating either one with a third item.

**Müller—Urban method**  See *method, Müller—Urban*.

**Müller—Urban weights**  (psychophysics) A technique used for determining the best value of $h$, the measure of precision of the fit of the data under the normal curve. When p=.50, the weight equals the maximal value of 1.00. At the extremes of the distribution, p.=.01 and p=.99, the weights are at a minimum.

**mult schedule**  See *reinforcement, schedule of: multiple*.

**multicellular**  Many-celled.

**multidimensional analysis of deviant behavior**  The analysis of a person in terms of a number of variables chosen for their importance in the establishment and maintenance of social response patterns.

**multigroup method**  See *method, multigroup*.

**multimodal theory of intelligence**  See *intelligence, multimodal theory of*.

**multiple abstract variance analysis (MAVA) design**  A research design for discovering relative proportions of environmental vs. hereditary determination for personality traits (Nature-Nurture Ratio).

**multiple choice method**  See *method, multiple-choice*.

**multiple choice test**  See *test, multiple choice*.

**multiple correlation**  See *correlation, multiple*.

**multiple determination coefficient**  See *coefficient, multiple determination*.

**multiple discrimination technique**  (statistics) A technique in which a subject is assigned a number which places him in more than one category. It is a form of the Fisher's discriminant function technique.

**multiple-factor**  Pertaining to a theory or process which is believed to have more than one factor underlying it.

**multiple-factor inheritance**  The transmission of a trait determined by more than one pair of genes.

**multiple personality**  See *personality, multiple*.

**multiple regression equation**  See *regression equation, multiple*.

**multiple response, principle of**  A complex and varied reaction to a new stimulus.

**multiple response test**  See *test, multiple response*.

**multiple (mult) schedule**  See *reinforcement, schedule of: multiple*.

**multiple sclerosis**  Hardening of the nerve tissues causing emotional disorder, speech defects, tremor, etc.

**multipolar nerve cell**  A cell which has more than one pole.

**multivariate analysis**  (statistics) Any technique designed to assess the existence and size of effect of many variables acting simultaneously.

**multivariate experiment**  An experimental design in which several stimulus conditions are simultaneously varied and/or several responses simultaneously measured, the relations being determined factor analytically or by path coefficients, partial correlations, etc.

**mumps encephalitis**  See *encephalitis, mumps*.

**Murphy, Gardner (1895-    )**  American psychologist. Wrote extensively on history of psychology and social psychology. Conducted research in social and developmental psychology jointly with his wife Lois

B. Murphy. Created the biosocial theory of personality based on the analysis of biological and social factors, conditioning and perception. Developed a field-theoretical approach to social problems and studied, on behalf of UNESCO, social tensions in India.

As Director of Research at the Menninger Foundation directed a major program in personality, stressing developmental factors and perceptual learning, and developed (with E.E. Green) the concept of biofeedback as applied to self-deception. Also contributed to research in parapsychology.

**Murphy, Lois Barclay** (1902-   ) American specialist in child development. Introduced American study of childhood sympathy; coping styles and devices; vulnerability and resilience. With Ruth Horowitz (Hartley) and L.K. Frank introduced the concept of "projective techniques"; integrated projective methods and naturalistic observations in studies of individual children. Directed a multi-disciplinary longitudinal series studying mid-west children. Contributed to integration of child development and psychoanalytic theory. Collaborated with Gardner Murphy on a volume on experimental social psychology, and with others in psychodynamic studies of learning at the college level.

**Murray, H. A.** (1893-   ) American psychologist who developed a system of needs believed to be characteristic of man and presented them in his book *Explorations in Personality.* He was instrumental in beginning an assessment of men in the United States Army during the Second World War. He is best known for his projective technique, the Thematic Apperception Test which is designed to elicit interpersonal conflicts related to the above needs.

**muscle spindle**  See *spindle, muscle.*

**muscle, striate or striped**  A skeletal muscle which is under voluntary control and has a striped appearance.

**muscular mania**  See *mania, muscular.*

**music preference test**  A test of personality through measuring factors of appreciative response to music.

**mutagen**  Any substance or force which increases the mutation rate, e.g. ionizing radiation.

**mutation**  A permanent heritable change in the genetic material. It is usually defined as a change in a single gene and is then often named a point mutation, in contrast to the less common usage to indicate a change in the number or arrangement of chromosomes. Schizophrenia and manic-depressive disorder if caused by single recessive and single dominant mode of inheritance respectively must have originated as point mutations. According to Frazer Roberts, genetic diseases which originate in this way through mutation often run an evolutionary course from dominance to recessiveness.

**mutism**  1. The lack of speech, resulting from congenital deafness, lack of proper development of the speech apparatus. 2. The voluntary or involuntary lack of speech due to emotional conflicts.

**muton**  In molecular genetics, the unit of mutation, possible as small as one nucleotide pair.

**mutualism** (B. B. Wolman) A sociopsychological give and take attitude based on the desire to satisfy the needs of others and have one's own needs satisfied by them. Mature sexual relationship is the prototype of mutualism.

**mydriasis**  Dilation of pupils.

**mydriatics**  Cocaine, atropine, epinephrine and any other substance that causes dilation of the pupils.

**myelination; myelinization**  The formation of myelin or its accumulation in the process of development or regeneration of a nerve.

**myelitis**  Inflammation of the spinal cord or of the bone marrow.

**myeloblastoma**  A malignant tumor caused by overgrowth of myeloid cells.

**Myers-Briggs Type Indicator** (I. B. Myers) A test designed in 1962 on the assumption that individuals differ in their preferences in perception and judgment. It measures the four sets of traits postulated by C. G. Jung: extraversion–introversion, sensing–intuiting, thinking–feeling, and judgment–perception. Each item calls for a choice between two contrasting alternatives, which are both from the same category. The subject's score is based on the number of times he chooses a category. His type is designated by the letters of his predominant mode in each of the categories.

**myocardial infarction**  See *infarction, myocardial.*

**myoclonic epilepsy**  See *epilepsy, myoclonic.*

**myoclonus**  Alternating contraction and relaxation of a muscle which usually does not cause movement.

**myokinetic psychodiagnosis** (E. Mira) A technique based on the symbolic interpretation of movements developed in 1940. The subject is blindfolded and asked to draw ten lines with each hand, to the left, or right toward and away from the subject, with the drawing board in a vertical position, upward or downward; the lines are measured in terms of slope and direction of drift of center of gravity. Based on work with abnormal subjects, the movements are interpreted as distinct personality signs. Drifts away from the body are believed to indicate aggressive attitudes toward others. An inward drift is thought to refer to self-aggression or suicidal trends. An upward drift indicates elation; a downward drift, depression.

**myopathy**  Any disease of the muscle.

**myopia**  Nearsightedness.

**myopsychopathy**  Muscular disease frequently associated with mental disorder or mental deficiency.

**myosis**  Extreme contraction of the pupil of the eye due to drugs or disease.

**myositis**  Inflammation of the muscle tissue due to muscle tension of physical or psychogenic origin.

The psychogenic cause is a chronically suppressed emotional state.

**mysoline** Common name for the anticonvulsant drug, primodine.

**mysophobia** Fear of contamination.

**mysticism** 1. The belief in supernatural, religious and/or spiritual sources of knowledge. 2. The belief in direct contact with God or other spiritual forces.

**mythological image** See *archetype*.

**mythological theme** See *theme, mythological*.

**mythomania** A morbid interest in and liking of myths often accompanied by distortions and fabrications.

**myxedema; myxodema** A disorder due to a decrease or absence of the thyroid hormone characterized by a sallow, thick skin, low metabolism, and physical and mental retardation. It is a constitutional disorder occurring in adults and older children.

# N

**N** **1.** (statistics) The number of observations in the data. **2.** (C. L. Hull) The number of rewards which are given. **3.** Symbol for need in the Thematic Apperception Test.

**näive misperception** That demonstrated factor in misperception which arises from interpreting others' behavior in terms of one's own, as a result of low intelligence or limited experience.

**Nancy School** A school founded by H. Bernheim in 1882 which promulgated the belief that hypnotism is a natural phenomenon induced by suggestion.

**nanism** Dwarfism.

**nanometer ($\eta m$)** N M = $10^{-9}$ meter, formerly called a millimicron; the preferred term is now nanometer.

**narcissism** **1.** Love of the self; egoism. **2.** (psychoanalysis) Erotic gratification derived from love of one's own body, qualities and attributes. **3.** (K. Horney) The loving of the unrealistic attributes of the idealized image of oneself.

**narcissism, primary** (psychoanalysis) The earliest stage of life in which all the energies at the disposal of the love instincts are invested in oneself.

**narcissism, secondary** Narcissism occurring in later life when object love is thwarted and libido is turned back to one's own person.

**narcissistic disorders** **1.** Behavior disorders characterized by excessive narcissism. **2.** (S. Freud) Schizophrenia is a narcissistic disorder because schizophrenics are unable to develop object relations. Schizophrenia represents a regression to narcissism, that is loss of objects, loss of contact with reality and breakdown of the ego. As a result, schizophrenics are unable to develop transference. **3.** (B. B. Wolman) The hyperinstrumental-narcissistic type of disorders characterized by intense self-cathexis of libido and object cathexis of destrudo. More severe cases of this disorder are the sociopathic, i.e., psychopathic personality and psychopathic psychosis.

**narcissistic insurance** See *insurance, narcissistic.*

**narcoanalysis** Treatment of mental disorders with the use of chemically induced sleep. Widely used in the second World War with intravenous injections of sodium amythal or sodium pentothal. Also used for extracting confessions from criminals under the name truth serum. Various forms are called narcosynthesis, narcosuggestion, and narcotherapy.

**narcolepsy** Recurrent and sudden uncontrollable tendency to fall into deep sleep of short duration associated with epilepsy, some tremors and encephalitis.

**narcomania** A morbid desire for relief from physical pain by using narcotics.

**narcosynthesis** The use of the material obtained from a patient under narcotics for a postnarcotic psychotherapy.

**narcotherapy** The use of narcotics in the treatment of mental disorder.

**narcotic** Sleep-inducing drug.

**nardil** A common name for phenelzine.

**nares** The nasal passages.

**National Intelligence Scale** See *scale, National Intelligence.*

**nativism** A theory that maintains that practically all functions of the organism, including the mental ones are inherited.

**natural sciences** Sciences which study nature; e.g. physics, chemistry, biology, geology, etc. W. Windelband counterposed the natural sciences to cultural sciences (humanities). Some philosophers of science maintain that all sciences are natural sciences, for psychology, sociology, history, archeology, etc., study certain fractions of the universe.

**natural selection** (C. Darwin) The survival of the fittest in the struggle for survival. As a result of this struggle, the poorly equipped individuals, unable to adjust to changing conditions, perish, while the superior individuals survive.

**naturalistic observation** Observation conducted in natural surroundings, such as practiced by J. Piaget in developmental psychology and K. Lorenz in ethological studies of animals.

**nature-nurture problem** One of several highly controversial issues in psychiatry and psychology related to the relative importance of heredity (called nature) versus environment (called nurture) in the development of normal and abnormal behavior. The nativists stress the role of heredity, while the empiricists emphasize the effect of sociocultural and socioeconomic factors, family dynamics and rearing practices, etc.

**nature-nurture ratio** A statistic giving the extent to which endowment of a personality trait tends to be fixed genetically rather than determined by environmental experience.

**Neanderthal man** An extinct, prehistorical human race. Its remnants were found in the valley of Neanderthal.

**near-point-of convergence** The limit of seeing a close point as single. If the object is brought closer to the eyes, it looks double.

**Necker cube** An ambiguous figure that is a line drawing of a cube drawn as if it were transparent, with all twelve angles showing. When regarded steadily, there is continuous shift in the angle of interpretation, for example it can be regarded as viewed from above or below.

**necromimesis** Belief that one is dead.

**necrophilia** Desire for sexual relations with a corpse.

**necrophobia** Morbid fear of dead bodies.

**need** 1. The condition of lacking, wanting or requiring something which if present would benefit the organism by facilitating behavior or satisfying a tension. 2. (H.A. Murray) A construct representing a force in the brain which directs and organizes the individual's perception, thinking, and action, so as to change an existing, unsatisfying situation. A need may be evoked by internal processes or environmental forces and is accompanied by particular emotions and modes of behavior designed to change the initiating circumstance and satisfy the organism. From intensive study of a number of subjects, Murray compiled a list of common essential needs. The original list includes needs for: *abasement,* to admit inferiority, blame, error, to accept punishment or criticism and to passively submit to external forces; *achievement,* to independently master objects, others, and ideas, and to increase self-esteem by successful exercise of talent; *affiliation,* to draw near, cooperate and remain loyal to another who is seen as similar to oneself and a friend; *aggression,* to oppose, fight, injure or punish another; *autonomy,* to be independent, unattached, and unrestricted; *counteraction,* to overcome failure and weakness through resumed action and repression of fear; *dependence,* to defend oneself against assault, criticism, and blame and to justify or conceal a failure, error, or humiliation; *deference,* to support, praise,

honor, or admire a superior and to conform to custom; *dominance,* to influence or control others' behavior; *exhibition,* to impress others; *harm-avoidance,* to avoid pain, injury, illness, and death; *infavoidance,* to avoid humiliation; *nurturance,* to support, protect, comfort, heal and gratify the needs of the helpless; *order,* to organize, balance, and arrange objects in the environment; *play,* to seek enjoyment and relaxation without further purpose; *rejection,* to separate oneself from a negatively cathected object; *sentience,* to seek and enjoy sensuous impressions; *sex,* to form and pursue an erotic relationship; *succorance,* to be gratified by an allied object and always have support and protection; *understanding,* to question, answer, speculate, formulate, analyze, and generalize.

**need, cognizance** (H.A. Murray) The need to investigate, explore, observe, be curious, and ask questions.

**need, construction** (H.A.Murray) The need to organize and build things.

**need, felt** A need of which one is consciously aware.

**need, gratification** Reduction of a need through consummatory behavior.

**negative acceleration** A gradual decline of speed; a consecutively smaller increment, e.g. mental growth slows down with age.

**negative attention seeking** See *attention seeking, negative.*

**negative doubles, illusion of** See *illusion of negative doubles.*

**negative feedback** See *feedback, negative.*

**negative induction** See *induction, negative.*

**negative movement reflex** See *reflex, negative movement.*

**negative Oedipus complex** Oedipal involvement with the parent of the same sex.

**negative reinforcement** See *reinforcement, negative.*

**negative response** See *response, negative.*

**negative taxis** See *taxis.*

**negative therapeutic reaction** See *resistance, superego.*

**negative transference** See *transference, negative.*

**negative tropism** See *tropism.*

**negativism, sexual** (M. Hirschfeld) Lack of sexual interests believed to be caused by a deficiency of the sexual glands.

**nembutal** Common name for pentobarbital.

**neocortex** See *isocortex.*

**neololia** A tendency of forming new words, neologisms.

**neomnesis** Selective memory with a particular ability for recollection of recent events.

**neonatal hyperbilirubinemia** See *hyperbilirubine-mia, neonatal.*

**neonatal meningitis** See *meningitis, neonatal.*

**neonate** Newborn.

**neopallium** A large part of the cerebral hemisphere with the exclusion of the rhinencephalon.

**neophobia** Morbid fear of anything new.

**neophrenia** (K.L. Kahlbaum) An obsolete term for childhood psychosis.

**neoplasm** A new growth, tumor.

**neopsychoanalysis** A school of psychoanalysis which repudiates the importance of biology, the instincts, and the role of insight in promoting therapeutic change.

**neostriatum** Parts of the corpus striatum which includes the putamen and caudate nucleus.

**nerve** A bundle of neuron fibers.

**nerve, abducens; abducent** The sixth cranial nerve. It innervates the external rectus muscle of the eye, carrying to this muscle a motor component and carrying from it a sensory component mediating proprioception.

**nerve, auditory or acoustic** The portion of the eighth cranial nerve concerned with hearing.

**nerve block** Disruption of the passage of nerve excitation.

**nerve ending** The termination of a nerve either in a center or periphery but not at a synapse.

**nerve, facial** The seventh cranial nerve which carries efferent impulses to the facial muscles and afferent impulses from the taste buds in the front portion of the tongue.

**nerve, hypoglossal** The twelfth pair of cranial nerves. A motor nerve innervating the muscles of the tongue.

**nerve, motor** An efferent nerve which transmits impulses to muscles and glands.

**nerve, oculomotor** The third cranial nerve containing components which innervate all the extrinisic eye muscles except the superior oblique and the lateral rectus and containing afferent proprioceptive fibers.

**nerve, optic** The second cranial nerve which functions as a connection between the visual centers and the retina.

**nerve, pathetic** See *nerve, trochlear.*

**nerve, pneumogastric** See *nerve, vagus.*

**nerve, sensory** Afferent nerve from a sense receptor to the central nervous system.

**nerve, trochlear** The fourth cranial nerve which carries different impulses to the superior oblique eye muscles.

**nerve, vagus** The tenth cranial nerve which distrib-

utes motor and sensory nerve fibers to many parts of the body, including the lungs, stomach area, external ear, larynx, pharynx and heart.

**nerves, cranial** Twelve pairs of nerves originating or terminating within the cranium.

**nervous pseudo-asthma** Physiological changes in respiration due to emotion as, for example, shortness of breath, constriction of the throat, or panting. Also known as respiratory emotionalism.

**nervous system** The entire apparatus comprised of nerve tissues, including: 1. the cerebrospinal nervous system, which is comprised of the brain, the brain stem, the spinal cord, all cranial and peripheral nerves and ganglions and 2. the autonomic nervous system, comprised of the parasympathetic or craniosacral division, the sympathetic or peripheral and orthosympathetic or thoracicolumbar divisions.

**nervous system, autonomic** A system of ganglia, nerves, and plexuses which innervate the viscera, heart, blood vessels, smooth muscles, and glands. It was once thought to be completely self-regulating, but is now known to be only partially independent. Includes the sympathetic and parasympathetic nervous system.

**nervous system, conceptual** A model which attempts to present the neurological or physiological correlates of behavioral acts. It is a hypothetical model and chiefly of heuristic value.

**nervous system, parasympathetic** A subdivision of the autonomic nervous system which selectively stimulates various visceral organs, stimulation resulting in an effect opposite from the sympathetic nervous system.

**nervous system, sympathetic** A component of the autonomic nervous system which centers about two chains of ganglia running along the sides of the spinal cord and connects with many sympathetic ganglia, facilitating widespread discharge. Stimulation by this system usually results in an effect opposite from the parasympathetic nervous system.

**nervous tissue** Accumulation of nerve cells, i.e. the neurons.

**neural circuit** The path of transmission of an impulse from a receptor via connecting neurons to an effector.

**neural conduction** See *conduction, neural.*

**neural crest** See *cephalogenesis.*

**neural current** The electrical change which occurs along nerve fibers and across the synapse during the transmission of an impulse.

**neural excitation** The activity in a neural fiber induced by stimulation of the neuron.

**neural fold** See *cephalogenesis.*

**neural groove** See *encephalogenesis.*

**neural induction** The effect which one neuron or group of neurons has on another. Positive induction means that neural activity is facilitated. Negative induction refers to the inhibition of neural activity.

**neural noise** Spontaneous neural activity occurring in the nervous system which may give rise to sensations when in fact no stimulus was presented. During threshold determinations neural noise may be responsible for many responses during latch trials. Since neurons are spontaneously active, stimulation does not so much initiate neural activity but modifies existing activity.

**neural plate** See *cephalogenesis.*

**neural reinforcement** See *reinforcement, neural.*

**neural reverberation** (D.O. Hebb) The maintenance and continuation of neural activity after the stimulus which initiated it ceases.

**neural satiation** A state of relative insensitivity to stimulation in the nerve fibers directly following a period of stimulation by a group of closely related stimuli.

**neural set** See *set, neural.*

**neural tube** See *cephalogenesis.*

**neuralgia** Sharp, stabbing, paroxysmal pain of a nerve without structural changes in the nerve.

**neuralgia, hallucinatory** The sensation of local pain with no actual peripheral nerve pain.

**neuraminic acid** An acid obtained from the ganglioside part of brain lipids. Also found in mammary glands of some animals.

**neurasthenia** See *asthenic reaction.*

**neurasthenia, abdominal** A type of neurasthenia in which the dominant symptoms are those which relate to the gastrointestinal tract.

**neurasthenia, aviator's** A neurosis believed to occur among aviators and characterized by anxiety, restlessness, and various physical symptoms.

**neuraxis** The brain and the spinal cord.

**neurin** 1.The protein substance of nerve tissue. 2. (W. McDougall) The energy believed to account for nerve excitation.

**neurinomatosis; neurofibromatosis** A tumorous disease. A growing number of neurofibromas appear in the skin and along peripheral nerves. Often associated with mental retardation. Transmitted by dominant genes.

**neurite** Axon.

**neuritis** Inflammation of peripheral nerves.

**neuroarthritism** A disease of gout and neurological rheumatoid disease.

**neurobiotaxis** The tendency of nerve cells to draw to the source of their nutrition.

**neuroblast** A newly formed nerve cell.

**neurocirculatory asthenia** 1.Anxiety neurosis characterized by shortness of breath, heart palpitations, and a vague feeling of effort and fatigue out of proportion with amount of energy expended. 2. Effort-syndrome.

**neurocyte** Nerve cell; neuron.

**neurodermatitis** A skin disease characterized by localized, circumscribed, symmetrical patches of pruritic dermatitis which is exacerbated by emotional problems.

**neurofibril** A fibril of a nerve cell.

**neurofibroma** A tumor characterized by proliferation of neurofibrils.

**neuroglia** 1.Supporting tissues in nerve cells derived mainly from the ectoderm. 2. Certain cells of the nervous system such as astrocytes and oligodendroglia.

**neurohumor** The chemical substance in the nerve cell which facilitates the conduction of nerve impulses at the synapse.

**neurological examination** See *examination, neurological.*

**neurology** A branch of medicine devoted to the study and treatment of anatomy and physiology of normal and abnormal structure and functions of the nervous system.

**neuromuscular junction** The point where a motor nerve meets the muscle it activates.

**neuron** The complete nerve cell, the basic structural and functional unit of the nervous system. It consists of the axon, dendrites, cell body, and myelin sheath.

**neuron, bipolar** A neuron which is characterized by the extension in opposite directions of the two long processes of the cell—the axon and dendrite. This cell is contrasted with the regular sensory neuron which is characterized by the cell body's being off to one side while the axon seems to be continuous with the dendrite.

**neuron, motor** An efferent neuron which transmits impulses to muscles and glands.

**neurons, internuncial** Neurons which connect sensory and motor neurons within the central nervous system.

**neuropathic diathesis** See *diathesis, neuropathic.*

**neuropathy** Any disease of the nervous system.

**neurophysiology** The branch of physiology which deals with the functions of the nervous system especially the study of the transmission of the nerve impulse.

**neuropil** A network of neurofibrils which are non-myelinated at the synaptic function between two neurons.

**neuropsychiatry** In the nineteenth century, the name of the profession and discipline concerned with the diseases of the nervous system, organic and non-organic. Today, the term is used for a branch of psychiatry distinctly concerned with neurological causes, symptoms and cures of mental disorders.

neuropsychology A branch of psychology which studies the nervous system and its impact on behavior. A great many psychologists in the U.S.S.R. are neuropsychologists.

Neurosis (300) Also called psychoneurosis, a loosely used term applied to a variety of comparatively mild disorders. The following description is taken with abbreviations from the Diagnostic and Statistical Manual of Mental Disorders (DSM II) published by the American Psychiatric Association in 1968. Anxiety is the chief characteristic of the neuroses. It may be felt and expressed directly, or it may be controlled unconsciously and automatically by conversion, displacement and various other psychological mechanisms. Generally, these mechanisms produce symptoms experienced as subjective distress from which the patient desires relief.

The neurosis, as contrasted to the psychoses, manifests neither gross distortion or misinterpretation of external reality, nor gross personality disorganization. A possible exception to this is hysterical neurosis. which some believe may occasionally be accompanied by hallucinations and other symptoms encountered in psychosis. Traditionally, neurotic patients, however severely handicapped by their symptoms, are not classified as psychotic because they are aware that their mental functioning is disturbed.

## 300.0 Anxiety neurosis
This neurosis is characterized by anxious over-concern extending to panic and frequently associated with somatic symptoms. Unlike phobic neurosis, anxiety may occur under any circumstances and is not restricted to specific situations or objects. This disorder must be distinguished from normal apprehension or fear, which occurs in realistically dangerous situations.

## 300.1 Hysterical neurosis
This neurosis is characterized by an involuntary psychogenic loss or disorder of function. Symptoms characteristically begin and end suddenly in emotionally charged situations and are symbolic of the underlying conflicts. Often they can be modified by suggestion alone.

## 300.13 Hysterical neurosis, conversion type
In the conversion type, the special senses or voluntary nervous system are affected, causing such symptoms as blindness, deafness, anosmia, anaesthesias, paraesthesias, paralyses, ataxias, akinesias, and dyskinesias. Often the patient shows an inappropriate lack of concern or belle indifference about these symptoms, which may actually provide secondary gains by winning him sympathy or relieving him of unpleasant responsibilities. This type of hysterical neurosis may be distinguished from psychophysiologic disorders, which are mediated by the autonomic nervous system; from malingering, which is done consciously; and from neurological lesions, which cause anatomically circumscribed symptoms.

## 300.14 Hysterical neurosis, dissociative type

In the dissociative type, alterations may occur in the patient's state of consciousness or in his identity, to produce such symptoms as amnesia, somnambulism, fugue, and multiple personality.

## 300.2 Phobic neurosis
This condition is characterized by intense fear of an object or situation which the patient consciously recognized as not real danger to him. His apprehension may be experienced as faintness, fatigue, palpitations, perspiration, nausea, tremor, and even panic. Phobias are generally attributed to fears displaced to the phobic object or situation from some other object of which the patient is unaware. A wide range of phobias has been described.

## 300.3 Obsessive compulsive neurosis
This disorder is characterized by the persistent intrusion of unwanted thoughts, urges, or actions that the patient is unable to stop. The thoughts may consist of single words or ideas, ruminations, or trains of thought often perceived by the patient as nonsensical. The actions vary from simple movements to complex rituals such as repeated handwashing. Anxiety and distress are often present either if the patient is prevented from completing his compulsive ritual or if he is concerned about being unable to control it himself.

## 300.4 Depressive neurosis
This disorder is manifested by an excessive reaction of depression due to an internal conflict or to an identifiable event such as the loss of a love object or cherished possession.

## 300.5 Neurasthenic neurosis (Neurasthenia)
This condition is characterized by complaints of chronic weakness, easy fatigability, and sometimes exhaustion. Unlike hysterial neurosis the patient's complaints are genuinely distressing to him and there is no evidence of secondary gain.

## 300.6 Depersonalization neurosis (Depersonalization syndrome)
This syndrome is dominated by a feeling of unreality and of estrangement from the self, body, or surroundings. This diagnosis should not be used if the condition is part of some other mental disorder, such as acute situational reaction. A brief experience of depersonalization is not necessarily a symptom of illness.

## 300.7 Hypochondriacal neurosis
This condition is dominated by preoccupation with the body and with fear of presumed diseases of various organs. Though the fears are not of delusional quality as in psychotic depressions, they persist despite reassurance. This condition differs from hysterical neurosis in that there are no actual losses or distortions of function.

## 300.8 Other neuroses
This classification includes specific psychoneurotic disorders not classified elsewhere such as "writer's cramp" and other occupational neuroses.

**neurosis, actual** (psychoanalysis) A neurosis involving a physiological as opposed to psychological basis for symptoms. Originally this concept was associated with Freud's first or toxicologic theory of anxiety. The existence of actual neuroses as clinical entities separate from the psychoneuroses has been questioned by other investigators. See *psychoneurosis; neurosis.*

**neurosis, anxiety** A controversial term. The Diagnostic and Statistical Manual of Mental Disorders (II) describes it as follows: Characterized by anxious over-concern extending to panic and frequently associated with somatic symptoms.

**neurosis, cardiovascular** A neurosis with manifestations of cardiovascular disorder which have no physiological basis.

**neurosis, character** See *character neurosis.*

**neurosis, combat** See *fatigue combat.*

**neurosis, dysmutual** (B.B. Wolman) A neurosis characterized by inconsistency in interpersonal relations and manifested in dissociative and conversion reactions.

**neurosis, experimental** **1.** State of stereotyped, compulsive or inhibited behavior, hyper-emotionality, chaotic and random responding, or inability to respond induced in experimental animals by impossible tasks or difficult discrimination problems particularly when failure to make the correct response results in severe punishment. **2.** (I.P. Pavlov) An induced acute neurotic state in animals produced by requiring very fine discriminations which the animal is unable to perform. Differences in the preneurotic behavior of the animals are related to the type of neurosis which develops.

**neurosis, gastric** A disturbance of digestion due to a psychological conflict involving dependent infantile fixations.

**neurosis, hyperinstrumental** (B.B.Wolman) A neurosis manifesting anxiety and depressive reactions and characterized by intense selfish, narcissistic interest in oneself.

**neurosis, hypervectorial** (B.B.Wolman) A neurosis manifesting obsessive, phobic, or neurasthenic reactions and characterized by excessive object hypercathexis.

**neurosis, transference** (psychoanalysis) An artificial neurosis occurring during psychoanalytic treatment in which the patient re-enacts all of his Oedipal conflicts with the analyst, who represents the important figures in the patient's life.

**neurosis, traumatic** A neurotic disorder precipitated by a trauma such as an incident or emotional upheaval.

**neurosis, vegetative** Neurosis characterized by disturbances of the autonomic nervous system functioning where the outward-directed action is suppressed and the withheld emotional tension induces chronic internal vegetative changes.

**neurosyphilis** Syphilis which affects the nervous system resulting in locomotor ataxia if the spinal cord is affected or general paresis in infections of the brain.

**neurosyphilis, interstitial** See *syphilis, cerebral.*

**neurosyphilis, mesodermogenic** Neurosyphilis involving the meninges, blood vessels and neural membranes which develop from mesodermal embryonic layers.

**neurotic** One who exhibits neurotic behavior.

**neurotic character** See *character neurosis.*

**neurotic depressive reaction** See *depression, reactive.*

**neurotic process factor** (R. B. Cattell) A characterological trait factor whose scores are of crucial importance in influencing the severity and expression of neurosis. Among Neurotic Contributory factors, that subclass which most significantly and meaningfully discriminates between neurotics and normals, hence is believed to be central in the etiology of neurosis.

**neurotic resignation** See *resignation, neurotic.*

**neurotic symptoms** Some symptoms, such as anxiety, apprehension, depressive moods, excessive fatigue, etc. are common to most if not to all neuroses. Some other symptoms, such as compulsions are typical only for a certain type neurosis.

**neurotic trend** See *trend, neurotic.*

**neuroticism** **1.** The condition of being neurotic. **2.** (R. B. Cattell) Neurosis which is characteristic in varying degrees of all people.

**neurovegetative system** The parasympathetic branch of the autonomic nervous system which is the aspect of the nervous system controlling the vegetative processes.

**neurovisceral gangliosidosis** See *generalized gangliosidosis.*

**neutral stimulus** See *stimulus, neutral.*

**neutralization** (H. Hartmann) The transformation of aggressive and sexual energy into energy which is free from the pressure of instinctual needs and is available for use in the development of ego functions.

**neutralizer** (S. Slavson) A term in group psychotherapy for a member who controls and nullifies the aggressive and impulsive behaviors of other members.

**nevus; naevus** Birthmark.

**new look** (D. Krech) A phrase from women's fashions (circa 1948 when longer, fuller skirts replaced short, spare war-time dresses) applied by Krech to the then new approach to perceptual research which emphasized the dependence of perception upon the psychological attributes of the perceiver. This research concern threatened for a time to become a "movement." The incipient "movement" however quietly reverted to what has become a continuing research and theoretical orientation.

**Newcomb, Theodore M. (1903- )** American social psychologist. Demonstrated close relationship in small college community between attitude change and position in status structure; 25 years later, these changes persisted on the part of individuals whose social environments were supportive of changed attitudes. Showed, in different setting, that interpersonal attraction among initial strangers changed over period of months in ways predictable from similarity of relatively unchanging values and attitudes. Extended this formulation, derived from Heider's balance theory, by showing that positive and negative attraction have different effects on interpersonal balance.

**nexus 1.** The connection between two variables. **2.** The causal connection between two items or variables which makes them interdependent.

**Neyman-Pearson hypothesis** See *hypothesis, Neyman-Pearson.*

**nialamide** An antidepressant drug of the monoamine oxidase inhibitor group used in the treatment of depression.

**niamid** Common name for nialamide.

**Niemann-Pick disease** A lipidosis similar to Tay-Sachs disease but not confined to the first year of life.

**Nietzsche, Friedrich (1844-1900)** German philosopher, advocate of extreme individualism. Invented the term "id", representative of unconscious blind forces. Criticized the overvaluation of consciousness, maintaining that it is merely the surface, while "the great basic activity is the unconscious."

**nightmare 1.** A dream depicting fearful events and marked by acute anxiety. According to psychoanalytic theory: 1) a nightmare represents the failure of the dream's function of protecting sleep; 2) in a nightmare a wish one is afraid of comes true. **2.** (E. Jones) Nightmares originate in incestuous impulses symbolized by witches, devils, and vampires.

**nirvana 1.** A state of satisfaction and bliss. **2.** (Buddhism) The state of life which is the prime goal when all desires are eliminated and the self is merged with the cosmos.

**nirvana-principle** (S. Freud) The inherent tendency of drives to eliminate all energy and to bring the life processes to an end, to reduce them to the inorganic state, thus attaining perfect equilibrium.

**Nissl granules** Granular bodies found in the cell body and dendrites of a neuron; chromophil granules.

**no-threshold aminoacidurias** See *aminoacidurias, no-threshold.*

**nocireceptor** A receptor for pain stimuli.

**noctambulism** Sleepwalking or somnambulism.

**nocturnal enuresis** Bedwetting at night, in sleep.

**nocturnal epilepsy** See *epilepsy, nocturnal.*

**noise, neural** See *neural noise.*

**noise, sensory** See *neural noise.*

**nomenclature of mental disorders** The American Psychiatric Association published in 1968 the Diagnostic and Statistical Manual of Mental Disorders (DSM II). See *Classification of mental disorders.*

**nominal aphasia** See *aphasia, nominal.*

**nominal scale** A scale in which numbers are assigned to events or event classes for identification and with no reference to any property of the event or class. Thus the number does not represent any dimension of the event or class, e.g. numbers on the members of a football team.

**nominalism** (philosophy) A theory that maintains that only objects and bodies exist, while concepts, abstractions, and generalizations are merely names of classes or groups of objects or bodies.

**nominating technique** A rating technique in which the rater chooses the person who conforms best or worst to the criterion. J.L. Moreno's sociogram and B.B. Wolman's statogram apply this technique.

**nomograph; nomogram 1.** (mathematics) A graphic presentation of a mathematical function or of any other relationship. **2.** (statistics) A graphic presentation consisting of three parallel lines representing three interrelated variables; the values of two are known and the value of the third is inferred by dividing a straight edge.

**nomology 1.** The science of law. **2.** (A. Kaplan) Referring to cases or experiments whose focus is the testing of hypotheses for the purpose of deriving general laws.

**nomothetic** Referring to methods and procedures used to formulate general laws or statements.

**nomothetic science** (W. Windelband) A science which aims at the discovery of general laws.

**non-additive** A group of elements which cannot be added to one another.

**non-continuity (in learning theory)** See *continuity-non-continuity (in learning theory).*

**nondetermination coefficient** See *coefficient, nondetermination.*

**nondirective group psychotherapy** See *psychotherapy, nondirective group.*

**nondirective psychotherapy** See *psychotherapy, client centered.*

**nondiscriminated avoidance** See *avoidance, free operant.*

**non-disjunction** The failure of two members of a chromosome pair to disjoin during the anaphase of cell division, so that both pass to the same daughter cell. This is the underlying reason of trisomy 21 accounting for one variant of Down's syndrome or mongolism.

**non-linear regression** See *regression, nonlinear.*

**non-permissiveness** (developmental psychology) In child rearing, preventing the occurrence of undesired behaviors by non-punitive means, such as 1) distraction, 2) negative evaluation in advance, 3) expression of counter-values with expectancy that child will adopt them. See *permissiveness.*

**nonsense figure** A figure which has no meaning in terms of resembling real objects or geometric figures.

**nonsense syllables** (H. Ebbinghaus) A group of letters which can be pronounced but which are meaningless as words. They are used in the rote-learning experiments.

**nonverbal intelligence** See *intelligence, nonverbal.*

**nonverbal tests** See *tests, nonverbal.*

**noology** The study of the human mind.

**noradrenaline** Norepinephrine.

**norepinephrine** A substance secreted by the adrenal medulla and formed at sympathetic nerve endings which functions as a neural transmitter and produces bodily reactions characteristic of emotional excitement.

**norm, composite** A norm arrived at by combining two or more scores.

**norm, group** 1. Representation of the performance of a given group. 2. Social norm.

**norm-of-reaction concept** The principle that each genotype has a range of possible phenotypes that can be developed depending on the influence of the environment.

**norm, percentile** (statistics) A norm which is defined in terms of the percentage standing of scores or individuals in the population in question as opposed to the means or averages.

**normal; normality; normalcy** 1. Being and acting according to some accepted standards. 2. Being healthy, wholesome, and free of conflict.

**normal distribution curve or frequency** See *curve, normal distribution.*

**normal insanity** See *insanity, normal.*

**normative science** A science that sets norms and determines what ought to be done, e.g. education is such a science, for it determines the ends and means of upbringing children, teaching and guiding.

**normative scoring** Standardization of scores obtained by a sample or a population. Normative scoring standardization uses the mean and the sigma of scores of a sample or a population.

**nortriptyline** An anti-depressant drug of the tricyclic compound group used in the treatment of depressions.

**nosogenesis; nosogeny** The beginning and development of a disease.

**nosology** The study and classification of diseases; this term applies also to the study of behavior disorders.

**nosophobia** Morbid fear of diseases.

**nostalgia** Homesickness.

**not-me** See *personified self.*

**("not-R")** The residual responding which makes up the behavior stream apart from the experimentally measured response, R.

**Nothnagel, C. W. H. (1841-1905)** Austrian neurologist who is known for his early work on the localization of brain function.

**notogenesis** The stage of embryonic development in which the notochord and the mesoderm develop.

**notomania** Excessive homesickness.

**Notterman, Joseph M. (1923- )** American experimental psychologist. Main studies in field of feedback paradigms of behavior. Principle research in kinesthetic feedback of motor responses, particularly in context of operant conditioning. Has demonstrated that systematic variations in response force, duration, and time integral of force ("effort") occur as a function of reinforcement contingencies, and response-induced feedback. Has also written extensively on perception of changing stimuli as related to feedback control of behavior, and on heart rate conditioning.

**noumenal** Pertaining to perception or knowledge based on pure thought with no reference to time or space.

**nous** (Greek) Reason.

**noxious** Harmful, damaging, hurting.

**nuclear cluster** A correlation cluster which consists of the variables overlapping from several phenomenal clusters.

**nuclear sexing procedures** Screening techniques helpful in the search for anomalies of the sex chromosomes.

**nucleus** 1. The central part of a living cell containing specialized substances, which is distinctly separated from the rest of the cell material or cytoplasm. 2. The central or focal part about which material gathers. 3. A group of cells within the cerebrum of the brain. 4. A cluster.

**null hypothesis** See *hypothesis, null.*

**null set (∅)** A set containing no objects or elements.

**nulliplex inheritance** Inheritance which is determined by two recessive genes, each contributed by one parent.

**Number Completion Test** See *test, Number Completion.*

**number factor** See *factor, number.*

**number form** An imaginary form which represents a number series; each number has a definite position in space.

**numerical value**   A number which is expressed as an absolute number, regardless of the sign.

**nursing, psychiatric**   See *psychiatric nursing.*

**nurturance need**   See *need, nurturance.*

**nurture**   The environmental aspects which influence an organism from the time of conception. This term is used in the nature-nurture controversy which attempts to assess whether heredity or environment is the determining influence in development.

**nutrient**   A substance which can be absorbed into the body and transformed into food for the tissues.

**nyctalopia**   Inability to see in darkness.

**nyctophobia**   Morbid fear of darkness.

**nymphomania**   An excessive heterosexual drive in females.

**nymphomania, heterosexual**   Excessive desire of woman for men.

**nystagmus**   A fluctuating movement of the eyeballs which may be congenital or due to intracranial disease.

**nystagmus, galvanic**   Nystagmus produced by passing an electric current through the labyrinthine area.

# O

O **1.** Abbreviation for observer; plural: Os. **2.** Abbreviation for organism. **3.** (Rorschach) Abbreviation for original response. **4.** Abbreviation for oscillation. **5.** (structuralism) The trained introspectionist who observes.

$_SO_R$ (C. L. Hull) Behavioral oscillation or the oscillatory weakening potential which is associated with $_SE_R$, effective reaction potential.

**O factor** See *factor, O.*

**O-technique** (R. B. Cattell) A factor analysis technique which correlates the relationships among functions by yielding a correlation of classes of occasions and, by inference, their similarity. This technique is used to compare the same person on different occasions, as, for example, on two different tests.

**O variable** See *variable, O.*

**oasthouse urine disease** A rare aminoaciduria associated with mental retardation; malabsorption of methionine.

**object 1.** Anything which is concrete, stable, and visible. **2.** Any aspect of the environment of which an individual is aware or towards which an attitude is directed or to which a response is made which may be material, abstract or social. **3.** An aim, purpose or goal of an individual or group. **4.** A stimulus or that which elicits an instinctive response or reaction. **5.** Anything which exists independent of a perceiver or subject.

**object-assembly test** See *test, object-assembly.*

**object cathexis** See *cathexis, object.*

**object, good** (M. Klein) The introjected object which helps and supports the ego in binding its death instinct by libido.

**object hypercathexis** The overinvestment of psychic energy in objects outside of oneself.

**object libido** (psychoanalysis) Sexual energy or drive which is directed outward toward external objects or persons rather than toward the erogenous zones or the self.

**object loss 1.** (psychoanalysis) The real loss of a loved one due to death, illness, or some other cause. **2.** (psychoanalysis) The experiencing of loss of love by an individual even though such a loss of love or threat of loss has not really happened.

**object love** (psychoanalysis) The direction of sexual energy or libido outward to an external object or person and the investment of libido in an external object.

**object relations** (psychoanalysis) The relationships of an individual including those in which there is either libidinal and/or aggressive instinctual gratifications and those where instinctual gratification is sublimated. These include primitive types of relationships such as symbiotic and transitional object relations and mature forms of object relations.

**object relations technique** A projective technique used with children, consisting of two sets of four pictures of one-person, two-person, three-person, and group relationships. Color is used to intensify the threat element and to encourage emotional involvement.

**objective-analytic (O-A) battery** A group of tests for measuring each of the eighteen main personality dimensions found in Objective Tests. A general purpose test for objective test measurement of personality factors.

**objective anxiety** See *anxiety, objective.*

**objective examination** An examination which has a scoring standard so prescribed and unequivocal as to leave no element of subjectivity or chance to the scorer. The most common types of such tests are completion tests, multiple choice and true-false.

**objective test** A test in which the subject's behavior is measured, for inferring personality, without his being aware in what ways his behavior is likely to affect the interpretation.

**oblique muscles** A pair of eye muscles, the inferior and the superior which rotate the eyeball. The inferior oblique rotates the eyeball downward and outward and the superior oblique rotates the eyeball upward and outward.

**oblique solution** (factor analysis) A set of factors which are correlated since they are not at right angles to each other.

**obliviscence** 1. Forgetfulness. 2. The gradual disappearance of ideas over time.

**obnubilation** Obscuring of consciousness; stupor.

**obscenity** Violation of established norms of what is believed to be proper, modest or in good taste; lewd or pornographic actions or communication. This includes pictures, gestures, writings, and speech often dealing with the subjects of sex or excretory functions. The interpretation of and criteria for what constitutes obscenity varies culturally and is often determined legislatively or in the courts.

**observation** 1. An intentional or explicit examination of a situation in order to ascertain facts or particulars about it. 2. A score or value which represents an observed fact. 3. The communication, usually casual, of what has been observed.

**observation, mass** The technique of ascertaining public opinion through the sampling of opinions of representative people of a group.

**observer** 1. An individual who examines a situation or an object closely in order to report on it or understand it clearly. 2. One who participates in introspective observations. 3. Abbreviation: "O."

**observer, participant** One who observes a social event or happening while participating in it himself simultaneously.

**observer reliability** The degree to which two observers agree on some measure of behavior observation when they observe the same series of events independently; Pearson $r$ is a common expression of agreement when the measure is of frequency of occurrence in a set of 30 or more observations; "percent agreement" is often used when each observation involves 2 or more parameters (e.g., agent, object, intensity, category of action), the formula being 2 × total number of agreements on recorded observations by $A$ and $B$ divided by the total number of recorded observations by $A$ plus same by $B$.

**obsession** An idea or impulse which persistently preoccupies an individual even though the individual prefers to be rid of it. Obsessions are usually associated with anxiety or fear and may be of relatively long or short duration and may constitute a minimal or a major disturbance of or interference with normal functioning and thinking.

**obsessional neurosis** See *neurosis, obsessive-compulsive*.

**obsessive-compulsive behavior** Behavior characterized by repetitive, irrational thoughts called obsessions and actions called compulsions.

**obsessive-compulsive neurosis** See *neurosis, obsessive-compulsive*.

**obstacle sense** The ability to avoid objects in one's

way without seeing them usually developed by blind persons and sometimes by others; this depends largely upon echo-location which is hearing sounds bounce off objects.

**obstipation** Severe constipation usually of functional origin.

**obstruction** The sudden ceasing, blocking or disappearance of thought which is a symptom of mental disturbance.

**obstruction method** See *method, obstruction*.

**obtained score** A raw score which is a score obtained directly from a test and one which has not been converted to standard units or submitted to any statistical treatment.

**Occam's razor** The principle of scientific thinking which states that the most simple adequate explanation of a thing is to be preferred to any more complex explanations.

**occasionalism** (philosophy) A post-Cartesian school which proposes that God intervenes in bodily and psychic processes which may be transformed into each other without any other intervention.

**occipital lobe** See *lobe, occipital*.

**occipital lobe brain lesion** See *brain lesion, of occipital lobe*.

**occipitoparietal brain lesion** See *brain lesion, occipitoparietal*.

**occlusion** 1. The obstruction of a passageway. 2. The exhibition of fewer than the usual number of motor unit responses due to an overlap of neuronal fields.

**occultism** The belief that nature can be controlled through magical procedures. Also the attempt to control nature through such means.

**occupational ability** The measurement of an individual's aptitude for a certain vocation or work by means of a standard test; several different occupational ability tests are usually administered at one time and the results are reported as a profile or pattern.

**occupational analysis** See *job analysis*.

**occupational norm** The average or usual score or pattern of scores for a particular occupational category or profession.

**occupational test** See *test, occupational*.

**occupational therapy** See *therapy, occupational*.

**oceanic feeling** (psychoanalysis) Sensation of unlimited omnipotence, of boundlessness, and of being at one with the universe.

**ochlophobia** Fear of crowds.

**ocular dominance** See *dominance, ocular*.

**ocular pursuit** See *pursuit, ocular*.

**oculocardiac reflex** See *reflex, oculocardiac*.

**oculogyral illusion or movement** See *illusion, oculogyral.*

**oculomotor nerve** See *nerve, oculomotor.*

**odd-even technique** A method of estimating test reliability by determining the correlation between the odd and the even test items and applying the Spearman-Brown formula to compensate for attenuation caused by splitting the test.

**odor prism** (H. Henning) A diagrammatic illustration of the relations between the six basic classes of odors and the mixed colors.

**odorimetry** Olfactometry or the measurement of odors.

**oedipal conflict** (S. Freud) Conflict experienced by the boy during the phallic stage concerning his incestuous wishes for his mother and fear that the father will castrate him.

**Oedipus complex** See *complex, Oedipus.*

**ogive** 1. A curve which has a double bend. 2. (statistics) A mathematical curve which is shaped like the letter S.

**Ohm's law** 1. (acoustics) The ear hears a complex tone as a combination of simpler tones; often the ear can break down a complex tone into its simpler components by a physical separation of the complex acoustic wave. 2. (electricity) The amount of electrical current in a circuit is directly proportional to the electro-motive force and inversely proportional to the circuit resistance.

**oikiomania** Pathological attitude and behavior syndrome toward members of one's own family.

**oikiophobia** See *oikophobia.*

**oikofugic** Relating to the urge to travel or wander about.

**oikophobia** Fear of one's own home or house.

**oikotropic** Homesick.

**oinomania** Excessive desire for liquor caused by excessive drinking; dipsomania.

**old age, mental disorders of** See *senility.*

**olfaction** The sense of smell, the receptors of which are located in the nose and are made up of hair cells in the olfactory epithelium.

**olfactometer** An instrument used in threshold experiments to regulate the intensity and the amount of a smell stimulus.

**olfactory area** The part of the cerebral cortex where the centers for smell are located.

**olfactory brain** The rhinencephalon.

**olfactory bulb, or lobe** One of two oval masses of grey matter located on the bottom of the cranium above the nasal cavity extending outward toward the eyes. These bulbs or lobes mediate smell and are an extension of the cerebrum.

**olfactory cells** Spindle-shaped cells in the nasal cavities, membranes which function as sense receptors for smell stimuli.

**olfactory nerve** The first cranial nerve which connects the olfactory region in the cerebrum with the olfactory cells.

**oligoencephaly** (C. E. Benda) The primary oligophrenia, an idiopathic mental deficiency characterized by asymmetries in the physical development. There are usually noticeable differences between the right and left sides of the body, irregularities in the nervous system, and low resistance to disease.

**oligomenorrhea** Scanty, infrequent menstruation sometimes due to psychological regression to the oral state of development because of fear of the sexual role.

**oligophrenia** Mental deficiency.

**oligophrenic response** A peculiar type of Rorschach response in which discrete parts of figures, particularly human, are reported while the majority of subjects see the entire figure. These types of responses, generally rare, are most commonly associated with severe intellectual retardation or those severe disturbances in which intellectual ties to reality are extensively impaired.

**omission training** A type of training in which a particular undesired response is not rewarded.

**omnibus test** See *test, omnibus.*

**omnipotent infantile sadism** See *sadism, omnipotent infantile.*

**onanism** 1. Coitus interruptus or withdrawal of the penis before ejaculation. 2. Masturbation.

**onanistic equivalent** See *equivalent, onanistic.*

**one-tailed test** See *test, one-tailed.*

**one-trial learning** 1. The total mastery of a skill or of an association on the first trial; the mastery of an increment of learning or association on one trial. 2. (E. R. Guthrie) The acquisition of the complete associative strength of a stimulus pattern on the first pairing of it with a response. 3. (B. F. Skinner) Maximum probability that a particular response will follow a particular stimulus as the outcome of one rewarded pairing.

**one-way screen** A screen or mirror which can be seen through from only one direction. This allows an individual to observe a person or group without the observed knowing they are being watched.

**oneirism** Experiencing of a dreamlike state while awake.

**onomatomania** Obsession by words or names.

**onomatophobia** Fear of hearing a particular name.

**onomatopoiesis** Creating a word which imitates the sound of the action or thing which the word represents. The creation of such words is characteristic of certain forms of schizophrenia.

**ontogenesis; ontogeny** The origin and development of the individual organism.

**ontogenetic; ontogenic** Relating to ontogenesis.

**ontology** The branch of philosophy concerned with the study of the nature of being.

**onychophagia** (A. Kanner) Nailbiting which is thought to be a form of neurotic behavior and a means of releasing inner tension.

**oocyte** The female egg cell before the maturation process is complete.

**oogonia** The first phase in the development of mature female reproductive cells.

**open-cue situation** Learning situation in which the means or materials necessary for solution of the problem or attainment of the goal are available to the subject. The task is to use the means appropriately in order to reach the goal.

**open-ended question** Any question which allows the person answering flexibility of form and substance in his response.

**open group** 1. A group which admits new members. 2. A psychotherapeutic group in which every member follows his own therapeutic course; when some members are discharged (or leave), new members are admitted.

**operandum** (operant conditioning) Any object movement which is classified as a response and as such is reinforced. The word operandum is preferred and is replacing the earlier word, "manipulandum."

**operant** (B. F. Skinner) A unit of behavior defined by its effect on the environment. It is a class of responses all members of which are equally effective in achieving reinforcement under a set of given conditions.

**operant avoidance** See *avoidance, free operant.*

**operant behavior** Behavior which is identified in terms of its effect on the environment.

**operant, concurrent** (operant conditioning) Two or more topologically different responses, at least with respect to locus, capable of being performed at the same time or in rapid succession with little mutual interference. Stimuli and reinforcements are independently programmed for each response.

**operant conditioning** See *conditioning, operant.*

**operant level** (operant conditioning) The rate of occurrence of the operant before conditioning, before it occasions reinforcement.

**operant reserve** See *reflex, reserve.*

**operating characteristic** 1.The probability of accepting the null hypothesis in every possible situation of a test of significance. 2. Quantitative statement of the expected effects of a particular procedure or thing.

**operation of cognition** See *cognition, operation of.*

**operation of convergent production** See *convergent production, operation of.*

**operation of divergent production** See *divergent production, operation of.*

**operation of evaluation** See *evaluation, operation of.*

**operation of memory** See *memory, operation of.*

**operational analysis** (communication theory) The quantitative analysis of output and input in a transmission system; such a system may be composed of organisms or other measurable units.

**operational definition** A definition of a fact or a concept in terms of "operations" such as controlled observation or experimentation performed by the researcher. Intelligence, e.g., is what intelligence tests measure.

**operational-informational psychology** See *psychology, operational-informational.*

**operational term** A term which has been defined by the procedures used to arrive at it.

**operationalism** See *operationism.*

**operationism** (P. W. Bridgman) A radical version of empiricism. According to Bridgman, any scientific concept must be presented in terms of the operations performed by the scientist. Accordingly, the true meaning of a term is to be found by observing what a man does with and not by what he says about it. Although at a later stage (1936), Bridgman assumed that in final analysis "science is only my private science," a great many psychologists embraced operationism as the proper guidepost in psychological research. According to S. S. Stevens "the propositions of science have empirical significance only where their truth can be demonstrated by a set of concrete operation," and "only those propositions which are public and repeatable are admitted to the body of science."

**operations, intellectual** (J. P. Guilford) Major kinds of intellectual activities or processes; things that an organism does in the construction of information and its use. One of the parameters of the structure of intellect, including the categories of cognition, memory, divergent production, convergent production, and evaluation.

**operator** (mathematics) A symbol which indicates an operation is to be performed on another symbol or number.

**operon** Unit or gene action postulated by Jacob and Monod, consisting of an operator gene and a closely linked structural gene(s) whose action it controls.

**ophidiophilia** Morbid attraction for snakes.

**ophidiophobia** Morbid fear of snakes.

**ophthalmia** Inflammation of the outer tissues of the eye, especially of the conjunctiva.

**ophthalmology** Branch of medicine which deals with the structure, the functions, and the diseases of the eye.

**ophthalmometer** Instrument which measures the curvature of the front surface of the eye.

**opiate** 1. Drug which contains opium or a derivative of opium. 2. Anything which relaxes, soothes, or quiets a person.

**opinion poll** A survey of opinions which is gathered by questioning a sample of people on a specific issue or issues.

**opinionaire** Questionnaire used in a study of public opinion.

**opiomania** Addiction to opium or an opium derivative.

**opium** A narcotic drug which comes from a species of poppy and which depresses the higher nervous centers and induces a euphoric condition. Codeine and morphine are the most common derivatives.

**opposites test** See *test, opposites.*

**optic atrophy** See *atrophy, optic.*

**optic chiasma** See *chiasma.*

**optic disc** Retinal area where the optic nerve fibers gather before leaving the retina. This area is extremely insensitive to light and is called the blind spot.

**optic lobes** The upper part of the corpora quadrigemina.

**optic nerve** See *nerve, optic.*

**optic thalamus** See *thalamus.*

**optical axis** The line passing through the curvature center of both the lens and the cornea which is the center of vision.

**optical illusion** See *illusion, optical.*

**optimal movement** See *movement, beta.*

**optical projection** See *projection, optical.*

**optimal stimulation principle** (C. Leuba) Generalization that an organism learns those responses and behaviors which lead to an optimal level of excitation and stimulation.

**optimal tension level** The amount of tension thought to be necessary for mental health.

**optimism** An attitude or personality trait characterized by cheerfulness; a tendency to have faith in the future and the tendency to perceive most situations and things as good.

**optimum adjustment** See *adjustment, optimum.*

**optional-content drawings** A projective technique used with children in which the child is asked to draw whatever he wishes or to complete elaborate already provided stimulus patterns, sometimes being asked to relate a story concerning the drawing. Drawings and stories are both interpretable.

**optogram** A light-reflecting image of an object on the retina.

**optokinetic reaction** Eye movements which are caused by visual stimulation and the apparent movement which sometimes results in the visual field.

**optometry** 1. The measurement of the eye and its functions. 2. The applied art of improving vision by fitting glasses or suggesting visual exercises and training but not through the use of surgery or the prescription of drugs.

**oral-aggressive type** See *type, oral-aggressive.*

**oral character** See *character, oral.*

**oral characteristics** Traits of a person which reveal a fixation at the oral stage characterized by dependence, and passivity.

**oral dependence** (psychoanalysis) The desire to return to the security of the infantile oral stage of development which consisted of the protection of the mother in combination with the intense gratification provided by the mother's breasts and milk.

**oral eroticism or erotism** See *eroticism, oral.*

**oral incorporation** (psychoanalysis) The desire to incorporate the mother or any other love object.

**oral-passive type** See *type, oral–passive.*

**oral personality** See *character, oral.*

**oral sadism** See *sadism, oral.*

**oral stage** (S. Freud) The first psychosexual stage occurring in the first year of life during which the infant's sexual pleasure is derived from the stimulation of the mouth. The infant's first sexual excitations are related to sucking in the feeding process, which becomes the prototype of later sexual satisfaction and the mother, the object involved in the feeding process becomes the prototype of all later love object relations.

**oral test** See *test, oral.*

**orality** See *eroticism, oral.*

**order need** See *need, order.*

**order of a matrix** (statistics) Matrix size stated in terms of the number of its rows and its columns which is written in this form: "in the order of $m$ by $n$ (rows by columns)."

**order of magnitude** Arrangement of values, objects or data in a sequence which goes from the lowest or smallest in magnitude to the highest or largest.

**order of merit** Arrangement of people, data or objects in a sequence determined by their magnitude or importance with respect to a particular characteristic or quality.

**ordinal** Pertaining to or indicating order or succession as in ordinal numbers.

**ordinal position** A specific position in a succession, usually indicated by the ordinal numbers.

**ordinal scale** See *scale, ordinal.*

**ordinate** 1. The vertical axis of a two-dimensional graph. 2. The shortest distance from a point to the horizontal axis of a two dimensional chart measured along a line parallel to the vertical axis.

**Orestes complex** See *complex, Orestes.*

orexis  The conative and affective components of an act or behavior as opposed to the cognitive aspect.

organ  A structure of an organism which is specialized for a particular function or functions.

organ, erotism  The investment of erotic energy in an organ or part of one's body.

organ inferiority  See *inferiority, organ.*

organ of Corti  Numerous hair cells in a bony cavity of the inner ear which move when stimulated by sound or air waves and set off neural impulses which produce auditory sensations.

organ, sense  1. An end organ usually including the endings of afferent neurons and associated cells which are specialized to receive specific types of stimulation. 2. A receptor.

organic variable or O variable  See *variable, organic or O.*

organic view of psychopathology  The belief that mental disturbances are caused by hereditary factors or acquired through physical damage or disease.

organicism  1. Philosophical view that life is the end-product of organization. 2. Principle that all disorders are organic in origin, whether mental or physical. 3. (H. Spencer) Belief that social groups are analogous to individual persons.

organism  Any living being which has the potential to maintain itself and exist independently as a self-contained system with functions such as respiration, digestion, etc. This includes all plants and animals.

organismic  1. Of an organism or pertaining to one. 2. Any psychological viewpoint which rejects a dualistic approach to the organism and utilizes a holistic or functionalist orientation in psychological investigation and experimentation as, for example, organismic psychology and behaviorism. 3. Characteristics of an integrated organism which are the product of integration and interactivity. 4. (J. R. Kantor) Interbehavioral psychology.

organismic psychology  1. Psychological orientation which stresses investigation of the total biological organism as the proper subject matter of psychology. A molar of holistic approach is characteristic as is the rejection of dualism and mind-body distinctions. 2. (J. R. Kantor) School of psychology which states that psychological organisms are simultaneously physical and biological objects which always function as a whole within a definite environment. The subject matter of psychology is the interbehavior of organism with objects, events, and other organisms. The field of interbehavior between organism and environment is the subject matter of psychology.

organization  1. The arrangement of elements or parts in an integrated or cooperative way. 2. The amount of integration or cooperation in a complex whole. 3. (Gestalt) The process through which psychophysical excitations form themselves into an integrated stable field or gestalt.

organizational activity  The composite perceptual-association process which appears in some but not all Rorschach responses. It is most clearly identified where two or more elements of a blot are organized into a relationship with a meaning described to the organized elements. Rorschach implied that all percepts using the entire blot manifest organizational activity. Beck and Hertz (see *z score* and *g score*) have developed a quantitative method for differentiating the organizational activity when it occurs to the whole blot or as it occurs by combining adjacent or distant details of the blots. The organizational activity is interpreted as directly related to intellectual functioning but also involving non-intellectual features.

organon  1. Body of principles and tenets which indicate how knowledge should be acquired, investigated and increased. 2. A scientific method.

organotherapy  Treatment of a body with natural organic substances such as, for example, hormones, with the intention of restoring health to the body by replacing or supplementing a vital substance that was lacking.

orgasm, alimentary  (S. Rado) Experience of well-being and release of tension by an infant at the height of breast-feeding.

orgastic impotence  See *impotence, orgastic.*

orgiastic  1. Like an orgy in nature. 2. Characterized by excitement, frenzy, or emotional intensity.

orgone theory  (W. Reich) A dissident psychoanalytic theory that there is a vital, primal raw-material energy called orgone which permeates the space and accounts for the functions of life.

orientation  1. Awareness of one's position or direction in space and time whether in relation to other persons, situations, physical reality or a goal. 2. The tendency to move toward a source of stimulation or a particular direction, as in tropisms. 3. A pre-disposition or frame of reference which influences reactions to certain stimuli, situations or behaviors. 4. (personnel) The process of initiating an individual to a work situation and of instructing him about rules, regulations and responsibilities as an introduction to a new situation, particularly a new job. 5. The position a thing or organism is in or the position taken by it. 6. General viewpoint which influences choice of scientific method, selection of methodology, etc.

orientation, double  (E. Bleuler) Ability to maintain contact with reality and acceptable daily functioning on same level while exhibiting delusions in certain areas.

orientation, illusion of  See *illusion of orientation.*

orienting response  A reaction of attention to a given stimulus.

origin, arbitrary  (statistics) Any arbitrary chosen zero point against which other values are defined by being measured as deviations.

original response  A special Rorschach scoring category, using the symbol O, to denote responses which occur no more than once in 100 records.

**original score**  See *score, raw.*

**ornithophobia**  Fear of birds.

**orthodox analysis**  See *psychoanalysis.*

**orthogenesis**  (biology) The theory that maintains that nature has an intrinsic tendency to develop in a definite direction determined by the germ plasm.

**orthogenic**  Corrective, improving, making things straight.

**orthognatic or orthognathous skull**  A skull with a profile of 85° to 93°. The forehead and the jaws form an almost vertical line.

**orthogonal solution**  (factor analysis) A solution in which the axes symbolizing factors are at right angles with one another which indicates they are uncorrelated or independent.

**orthopsychiatry**  A cross disciplinary science combining child psychiatry, developmental psychology, pediatrics, and family care, devoted to the discovery, prevention and treatment of mental disorders in childhood and adolescence.

**orthoptics**  System of training techniques which are designed to facilitate cooperative functioning of the two eyes especially in cases of muscular imbalance.

**orthorater**  Brand name of an instrument which tests visual acuity, color vision, steropsis, and phoria.

**orthostatic hypotension**  See *hypotension, orthostatic.*

**orthriogenesis**  (P. Federn) Regaining of its full development by the ego which is said to occur spontaneously at the moment of awakening when the ego has its cathexis restored which had disappeared in sleep.

**oscillation**  1. Swinging back and forth or fairly steady direction reversal. 2. (C. L. Hull) The continual quantitative and qualitative variability of response to the same environmental stimulation which is thought to be a function of the normal probability law. 3. (factor analysis) The amount of general response variability which characterizes a person's responses to the same situation or test on different occasions.

**oscillation behavioral** $_sO_R$  (C. L. Hull) The incessant variability or oscillatory weakening potential of the effective reaction potential $_s\bar{E}_R$; the reaction potential's standard deviation.

**oscillograph**  An instrument which produces a graphic record of the wave form of an electric current.

**oscillometer**  An instrument which records mechanical oscillations or vibratory motion.

**Oseretsky scale**  See *scale, Oseretsky.*

**osmosis**  A penetration of a porous substance, membrane, etc. by fluids.

**osphresiolagnia**  Morbid concern with bodily odors.

**osphresiophobia**  Morbid fear of odors.

**Ostwald colors**  A large series of achromatic and chromatic color samples classified according to an arbitrary letter-number notation system. Each color sample represents a particular pigment mixture of full color content, white content, and black content.

**OT**  See *occupational therapy.*

**Otis Quick-Scoring Mental Ability Test**  See *test, Otis Quick-Scoring Mental Ability.*

**Otis Self-Administering Test of Intelligence**  See *test, Otis Self-Administering, of Intelligence.*

**otitis media**  Inflammation of the middle ear.

**otogenic tone**  See *tone, otogenic.*

**otohemineurasthenia**  Deafness in one ear caused by non-organic factors.

**otoliths**  Small calcium deposits in the endolymph of the inner ear which help maintain equilibrium by activating neuronal endings when the head moves.

**otology**  The science of the ear.

**outer-directed**  (D. Riesman) Individual who is motivated by public opinion rather than by his own convictions and who tends to conform to the desires of other persons, seeking social approval as a primary goal.

**outgroup**  1.(social psychology) Any group to which a designated person does not belong. 2.Any persons who are not members of a particular group being considered. 3. Any individuals, whether members of a group or not, who do not belong to one's own group.

**outpatient treatment**  Ambulatory, non-hospital treatment in private practice or a clinic.

**ovariotomy**  Removal of the ovaries by surgery.

**ovary**  The female reproductive organ which produces the ovum or egg cell and the female sex hormones, the estrogens. It is one of a pair of glandular organs which are connected to the uterus by the fallopian tubes.

**over-all rate**  See *rate, over-all.*

**overachievement**  Performance which exceeds expectations made on the basis of mental aptitude.

**overcompensation**  Using more effort than is necessary to make up for weakness or deficiency.

**overdetermination**  (S. Freud) The assumption that mental processes are caused by more than one factor, that is, they are overdetermined.

**overflow aminoacidurias**  See *aminoacidurias, overflow.*

**overinclusion**  (N. Cameron) Inability to eliminate inappropriate or inefficient responses associated with a particular stimulus from the behavioral repertoire.

**over-learning**  Learning in which practice continues after the desired criterion of learning is reached.

**overprotection, maternal**  Excessive protection and indulgence of the child by the mother which usually results in later passivity, dependence, and inability to tolerate frustration in the overprotected child.

**overreaction** A greater reaction than would be expected to a situation, usually of an emotional nature.

**overt behavior** See *behavior, overt.*

**ovoplasm** The cytoplasm of an unfinished ovum.

**ovum** A female germ cell.

**oxycephaly** Having an elongated or can-shaped head.

**oxyesthesia** Hypersensitivity; hyperesthesia.

**oxygeusia** Unusually acute sense of taste.

**oxyopia** Excellent vision; unusually sharp vision.

**oxyphonia** Unusually shrill voice.

**ozostomia** Bad breath; halitosis.

# P

**P** 1. Person. 2. Perceptual speed. 3. Probability ratio. 4. (H. J. Eysenck) Symbolizes the degree of personality organization. 5. (Rorschach) Popular response scoring code. 6. (physiology) Symbolizes drive state.

**p factor** A factor of behavioral inertia; the tendency to maintain an activity once it has started.

**P-technique** (R. B. Cattell) A factor analytic design which measures a single person on the same set of variables over a number of different occasions. Correlations between the variables are computed over these occasions as entries, then factor analyzed. P-technique and Incremental Factor Analysis are the two main methods for determining dimensions of personality change-over-time (or states).

**padded cell** See *cell, padded.*

**pain** 1. The opposite of pleasure; that which is not pleasant. 2. The sensation which results from too much stimulation of the free nerve endings pain receptors in the skin and where tissue is damaged.

**pain, referred** Pain which is perceived or felt as coming from some other location than that which was stimulated.

**pain sense** See *sense, pain.*

**pain spot** A small area of the skin especially sensitive to pain.

**paired associates** Pairs of words or nonsense syllables used in experiments of learning.

**paired associates method** The method of measuring retention in which items to be learned are presented in pairs. In testing retention the first member of each pair is given and the subject asked to respond with the second.

**paired-choice tests** See *tests, paired-choice.*

**paired-comparison method** A technique used in psychophysics and social psychology in which the subject is asked to compare each stimulus with every other.

**Paired Hands Test of Friendliness** See *test, Paired Hands, of Friendliness.*

**paleologic thinking** (Van Domarus) Paralogic thinking which is characteristic of schizophrenic thinking disorders.

**paleomnesis** Memory of the distant past of one's life.

**paligraphia** Obsessive repetition of letters, words, or phrasing in writing.

**palilalia** Speech disorder consisting of the increasingly rapid repetition of words and phrases.

**palilexia** Abnormal rereading of words and phrases.

**pallesthesia** Sensitivity to vibrations experienced when a vibrating tuning fork is placed over bony surfaces.

**pallium** Old word for the cerebral cortex; neo-pallium refers to newer areas and archi-pallium to older areas of the cortex.

**palmar reflex or response** See *reflex, palmar.*

**palmesthesia** See *pallesthesia.*

**palmistry** Interpreting the personality characteristics, past or future of an individual by reading the lines and other characteristics of the hand.

**palsy, cerebral** See *cerebral palsy.*

**panel design** See *design, panel.*

**panhypopituitary dwarfism** See *dwarfism, panhypopituitary.*

**panic, primodial** Combination of fright and anger reaction with disorganized motor responses characteristic of many schizophrenic children.

**panmixia** Equal, unrestricted mating of different races or different ethnic groups.

**panphobia; panophobia; pantophobia** Fear of everything.

**panpsychism** Belief that only psychological or mentalistic reality exists.

**pansexualism** The view that human behavior and motivation can be fully explained in terms of the sex drive or motive.

**Panum's area** Areas of the two retinas within which one identical stimulus is perceived when two separate stimuli are presented, one in each eye, in which case they fall within the limits of Panum's area and binocular fusion occurs.

**paper and pencil test** See *test, paper and pencil.*

**papilledema** Usually bilateral edema, or accumulation of fluids in the optic nerve often caused by brain tumor.

**parabiosis** Temporary loss of nerve conductivity.

**parabulia** Inability to make decisions.

**paracentral vision** See *vision, paracentral.*

**parachromatopsia** Partial color-blindness.

**paracousia; paracusia; paracusis** 1. Deafness to deep tones which is selective or relative. 2. The supposed ability of partially deaf people to hear better when there is background noise. 3. Any hearing disorder except deafness.

**paracusis imaginaria** Hallucination of audition.

**paradigm** A pattern or model which illustrates all the possible functions or forms.

**paradoxia sexualis** Manifestation of sexual impulses or behavior not characteristic of the chronological age of the individual.

**paradoxical cold** The sensation of coldness when a relatively warm object stimulates a cold receptor or spot on the skin.

**paradoxical warmth** The sensation of warmth when a relatively cold object stimulates a warm receptor or spot on the skin.

**paragenital** Intercourse in which conception is prevented.

**parageusia** 1. A distorted or perverted sense of taste. 2. Taste hallucination.

**paragrammatism** Speech disorder in which there is faulty syntactical or grammatical relationships.

**paragraphia** The omission and incorrect inclusion of words in speech or writing due to cerebral injury or nervous disorder.

**parahypnosis** The kind of sleep occasioned by hypnotism and sleep walking.

**parakinesia** Movement carried out in a grotesque, awkward manner.

**parakinesis** The lifting up of material things by supernatural powers in psychical research.

**paralalia** Speech disorder characterized by the inability to make certain sounds or the emission of incorrect sounds.

**paralalia literalis** The inability to form certain sounds correctly often accompanied by stammering.

**paraleresis** A mild form of delirium.

**paralexia** The incorrect reading of words including the transposition of word order and the inclusion of additional words.

**paralipophobia** Fear of neglecting responsibilities.

**parallax** The apparent movement of objects when the viewpoint is shifted laterally in the field of vision. Things beyond the fixated point move with the shift; things closer to the observer than the fixated point appear to move against the direction of the shift.

**parallax, binocular** Difference in optic angle or viewpoint of the eyes due to their separation laterally.

**parallax threshold** (binocular vision)

$$p = \left(\frac{a}{y-x} - \frac{a}{y}\right) = \frac{ax}{y(y-x)}$$

where $x$ is the distance of two points, $y$ is the further point, distant from the nodal point of both eyes, $a$ is the stereo base (interocular distance) and $p$ is the parallax threshold measured in radians.

**parallel law** (T. Fechner) Psychophysical generalization that when two different intensity stimuli are presented to a sense modality, sensory adaptation and fatigue result in a decrease of the absolute intensity, but the ratio of the difference between the two stimuli remains the same.

**parallel proportional profiles** (R. B. Cattell) Procedure method of factor analysis which utilizes several matrices at once and applies the parsimony principle to the complete set instead of applying it to analysis of each matrix separately.

**parallelism, psychological** Doctrine that assumes the relationship between mental and physical processes to be parallel and concomitant without assuming any causal connection between them.

**paralog** Nonsense word of two syllables.

**paralogia** The suppression of a logically connected idea in speech and the substituting of another one related to it.

**paralogia, metaphoric** Speech disorder characterized by the suppression of a general idea by a more narrow idea which replaces it.

**paralogia, thematic** Abnormal speech characterized by the incessant preoccupation with one subject.

**paralogical thinking** Irrational, fallacious thinking without the person being aware of the logical errors.

**paralogism** Fallacy which is not intentioned or goes unnoticed.

**paralysis** Partial or complete impairment of function in the voluntary musculature.

**paralysis agitans** See *Parkinsonism.*

**paralysis, familial periodic** A paralysis due to an

autosomal mode of inheritance characterized by spontaneous attacks or attacks induced by the injection of salt-retaining adrenocortical steroids which may last from a few hours to several days.

**paralysis, general** See *paresis, general.*

**paralysis, hysterical** Paralysis which is psychogenic in origin rather than organic.

**paralysis, immobilization** The often hysterical persistence of immobilization of a limb or body part after healing, in patients who have been immobilized for some time by casts or splints.

**paralytic abasia** See *abasia.*

**paralytic dementia** See *paresis.*

**parameter** Any device employed in psychoanalytic technique which is not interpretation is called a parameter. Examples are advice, reassurance, suggestion, etc. A parameter should not be used until and unless the analyst is convinced that without it the analysis will not progress. The classic example is that of advising a phobic patient to confront his feared situation, after exhaustive analysis has failed to impel him to go of his own will. In employing a parameter, the analyst must be convinced that nothing else will suffice to move the patient, that it can be given up as quickly as possible, and that the patient attains full insight into the reasons for using it.

**paramimia** Apraxic disorder in which gestures are distorted and do not express feelings.

**paramnesia** 1. Déjà vu or false recognition. 2. Memory distortion or false memory.

**paramutualism** See *dysmutualism.*

**paranoid; paranoea** Psychotic disorder characterized by extensive systemized delusions with little deterioration or general dementia. Most usual are delusions of persecution, of grandeur, or of both.

**paranoid character** See *character, paranoid.*

**paranoid defenses** Feelings that others are hostile to oneself.

**paranoid personality** See *character, paranoid.*

**paranoid reactions** Ascribing one's own feelings, mostly hostile ones, to other people.

**paranoid schizophrenia** See *schizophrenia, paranoid.*

**paranosic gain** See *paranosis.*

**paranosis** Also called primary gain. The alleviation of anxiety resulting from the reduction of instinctual pressure through their partial discharge in the formation and maintenance of neurotic symptoms.

**paraphasia** Habitual inclusion of extremely inappropriate words or phrases in one's speech.

**paraphasia, verbal** Verbal response characterized by the introduction of inappropriate words or phrases and associated with lesions of the auditory speech areas of the cortex.

**paraphia** 1. Distorted or perverted sense of touch. 2. Malfunction of tactile sensibilities.

**paraphilia** Sexual perversion or distortion of sexuality.

**paraphonia** Pathological change in voice quality or any other abnormal voice condition.

**paraphrasia** Misuse or improper construction of words and phrases.

**paraphrenia** An obsolete term for schizophrenia and paranoia.

**paraphrenia hebetica** (K. L. Kahlbaum) An obsolete term for mental deterioration in adolescence.

**paraplegia** Paralysis of the lower limbs which is sometimes affected by emotional problems.

**parapraxis** A generic term for minor errors in behavior such as slips of the tongue, small accidents, forgetting things and mistakes in writing.

**parapsychology** The study of forms of interaction between individual and environment which cannot at present be explained in terms of known physical energies. Attempts to achieve the full description and systematic understanding of alleged telepathy (communication between one organism and another through means other than the known senses); clairvoyance (perception of objective stimuli or events by extra-sensory means); precognition (telepathy or clairvoyance relating to *future* occurrences); and psychokinesis (the control of the movements of physical objects without the use of known physical energies). It attempts to gather, classify, and explain all such events, and to develop experimental control, full replication, and a systematic scientific-philosophical interpretation.

**parasexuality** Perverted or abnormal sexual behavior.

**parasitophobia** Fear of parasites.

**parasomnia** Sleep disturbances or perversions usually associated with nervous system lesions.

**parasympathetic nervous system** See *nervous system, parasympathetic.*

**parataxic** 1. Characterized by emotional maladjustment. 2. Referring to a lack of congruity among various aspects of the personality.

**parataxic distortion** See *distortion, parataxic.*

**parataxic mode** (H. S. Sullivan) A prelogical second mode of experiencing the world characterized by an autistic interpretation of events and people and a subjective, personal system of communication. It is associated with young children and sometimes seen in adults.

**parateresiomania** 1. Extreme impulse to observe or to peep. 2. Scoptophilia.

**parathion poisoning** See *poisoning, parathion.*

**parathymia** Display of an inappropriate reaction or of the opposite mood from what would be expected from the situation. This is an affect disturbance characteristic of schizophrenia.

**parathyroidism** Over-functioning of the parathyroid glands.

**paratype** Environmental influences.

**parceled factor analysis** (R. B. Cattell) A method of economically factoring large matrices by packaging the variables and undoing later.

**parenchyma; parencyme** The actual specific tissue of a gland or an organ as opposed to the connective or supporting tissue.

**parental attitudes** Attitudes which parents exhibit towards their children have a great effect upon the shaping of the child's development from infancy and subsequent personality characteristics and behavior as, for example, attitudes of rejection or lack of a meaningful relationship with the mother appear to be factors connected with psychopathic personality patterns.

**paresis** Partial motor paralysis characteristic of psychosis which results from a syphilitic infection of the brain.

**paresis, afferent** (O. Foerster) A disturbance of movement due to very severe lesions of the postcentral area in which the patient cannot carry out movements because impulses are transmitted simultaneously to agonist and antagonist muscles, although he retains strength in his muscles. In less severe cases, the person may be unable to place his hand in a desired position or to manipulate objects.

**paresis, general** A psychosis due to syphilis of the central nervous system. It is characterized by a variety of mental and neurological symptoms resulting from progressive brain pathology.

**paresis, general juvenile** A psychosis due to inherited syphilis which does not differ appreciably from the adult form, usually observed in children aged 12-14.

**paresthetic acathisia** See *acathisia, paresthetic.*

**parietal brain lesion** See *brain lesion, parietal.*

**parietal cortex, structure and function of** See *cortex, parietal, structure and function of.*

**parietal lobe** See *lobe, parietal.*

**Parkinson, James (1755-1824)** British physician best known for his treatise on a neurological condition currently called parkinsonism or Parkinson's disease which is characterized by the symptoms of rigidity, tremor, akinesia, and loss of movement.

**Parkinsonism; Parkinson's disease** A syndrome which in the idiopathic case is characterized by tremor, rigidity, a masking of the face, and a loss of spontaneous and automatic movement. It predominantly occurs in males over the age of fifty. The onset is usually slow, insidious, and local and gradually spreads to other parts of the body producing an abnormal posture and gait, and distortions in the musculature of the body. The symptoms are exacerbated by emotional stress and abate during sleep.

**parnate** Common name for tranylcypromine, a powerful antidepressant.

**parole** Release from imprisonment or from restraint upon the condition of good behavior, usually used in reference to the discharge of prisoners from penal institutions or correctional facilities with the condition that they report to a parole officer.

**parosmia** Disturbance of the olfactory sense.

**parotid gland** See *gland, parotid.*

**paroxysm** Spasm; convulsion.

**paroxysmal choreoathetosis** Tonic or choreotype movements of limbs, trunk and face. Probably inherited.

**paroxysmal trepidant abasia** See *abasia.*

**Parry's disease** See *goiter, exophthalmic.*

**parsimony law** Scientific principle which states the simplest of alternative explanations of a situation or phenomenon is to be preferred.

**Parson Language Sample** A diagnostic language test derived from Skinnerian learning theory with an emphasis on the delineation of observable vocal and nonvocal responses, thus allowing the definition of the conditions controlling the responses. The seven subtests reflect Skinner's major classes of language behavior: naming response; verbal repetition response; response showing comprehension; gestural exchange; and demand response. The first three subtests assess vocal responses; the next three assess nonvocal responses; and the seventh assesses both vocal and nonvocal responses.

**part method of learning** See *learning, part method of.*

**parthenogenesis** Development of an organism from an unfertilized egg which occurs primarily in some insects, crustacea, and worms.

**parthenophobia** Morbid fear of girls.

**partial correlation** See *correlation, partial.*

**partial regression equation** See *regression equation, multiple.*

**partial reinforcement** See *reinforcement, partial.*

**participant observer** (H. S. Sullivan) The role of the therapist consisting at once of skill and expertise in both observation of the patient's interactions and participation in the interpersonal process of therapy.

**participation, law of** 1. Taking part in an activity or occurrence. 2. (L. Levy-Bruhl) Tendency to perceive similar things as not just similar but the same which is characteristic of primitive thinking and also functions in magic. 3. (J. Piaget) Tendency of children to confuse their wishes with outer events.

**participation, mystical** (L. Levy-Bruhl) Condition in which an individual experiences himself as one with the object of his perception or thought and is unable to distinguish between himself and such an object.

**partile** (statistics) Generic name for one of a set of points which divide a serially ordered distribution into any number of groups or classes, each of which includes an equal number of scores or values. The most common partile division is into 100 equal points each of which is a percentile.

**partition measure** (statistics) Any division which separates one part of a frequency distribution from another as, for example, a partile measure.

**partition scales** See *scales, partition*.

**parturition** The act of childbirth.

**passive-aggressive personality** See *personality, passive-aggressive*.

**passive vocabulary** The amount of words a child understands without being able to use them actively in speaking.

**passivism** Total sexual submission of males.

**pastoral psychiatry** See *psychiatry, pastoral*.

**PAT** See *test, Picture Arrangement*.

**patellar reflex** See *reflex, patellar*.

**paternalism** 1. The principle or practice of dealing with individuals in the way a father relates to his children which implies protection and control. 2. Denial of the right to control their own affairs to adults who occupy a subordinate position.

**path** 1. Conduction line along a nerve network. 2. An alley in a maze. 3. (K. Lewin) That part of the psychological environment along which locomotion occurs. The direction and regions along which locomotion occurs is determined by the strength and fluidity of region boundaries and by dynamic factors.

**path-transformation coefficient** (R. B. Cattell) A statistic which relates experiences on life-adjustment paths to learning and other forms of personality change. It states what such path experience does to the individual, after the path or choice has been made; that is, it states, in the broadest sense, what he learns from it.

**pathergasia** (A. Meyer) Any physical defect or malfunction which interferes with the personal psychological adjustment of the individual.

**pathermia** (R. B. Cattell) One pole of a personality dimension, characterized by emotional immaturity and affectivity, in the sense of reacting to problems with cognitively unfocused feelings rather than with realism and objectivity.

**pathetic nerve** See *nerve, trochlear*.

**pathetism** Hypnotism; mesmerism.

**pathobiology** The study of diseases or disorders which are biological in origin.

**pathocure** Disappearance of a neurotic condition at the same time an organic disease occurs.

**pathogen** Any organism, generally a microorganism, that can infect a host with a disease, i.e. that gives rise to pathology or suffering.

**pathogenesis** 1. The process by which suffering and disease is generated. 2. The history and origins of suffering and disease.

**pathogenic** Having the potential to give rise to suffering or disease.

**pathognomy** 1. Diagnosis of or recognition of the characteristics of a disease. 2. Recognition of the characteristics of feelings and emotions.

**pathological** Abnormal; caused by disease.

**pathology** 1. A condition of the organism that gives rise to suffering. Usually implies an abnormal or disordered condition of the body or its parts. 2. The medical discipline which studies such conditions.

**pathomimesis; pathomimicry** Mimicking or feigning of a disease.

**pathomorphism** Abnormal body build.

**pathopsychology** See *psychopathology*.

**pathos** 1. Great suffering, mental anguish or unhappiness, psychological in origin rather than physiological. 2. That which arouses sympathy or sorrow. 3. The private emotional components of an art work rather than its universal elements. 4. (sociology) The feeling that a revered tradition or idea should not be criticized or discussed.

**patient** A person who receives treatment.

**Paton, Stewart** American psychiatrist and neurologist who wrote the first American psychiatric textbook (1905) and established the first American University mental health clinic at Princeton University (1910).

**patrilineal** Kinship or relationship on the father's side.

**pattern analysis** See *analysis, pattern*.

**pattern discrimination** Responding to a whole pattern rather than to the individual components which comprise it.

**pattern, sensory** Perceptual or sense data which exhibit overall unity or interrelationship such that the total design on the relationships is emphasized rather than the sensory properties taken separately.

**pattern similarity coefficient** (R. B. Cattell) A statistic ($r_p$), ranging from +1.00 to -1.00, which expresses the degree of similarity or dissimilarity between two Profiles of Factor Scores. (Profiles can be for single individuals or for groups of individuals). This statistic takes into account shape, level, and emphasis of the profiles, and, for profile comparison purposes, therefore, it is superior to the usual correlation coefficient, which considers only shape. Also known as Profile Similarity Coefficient.

**pattern, variable** (T. Parsons and E. Shils) Five bipolar dimensions along which any action may be categorized and its meaning defined: 1) specific or diffuse, 2) affective or non-affective, 3) performance quality or quantity, 4) particular or universal, 5) self-oriented or collectively oriented.

**patterning** 1. Imposing a pattern or system of organization upon a group of data. 2. Learning to respond to a whole set of data or stimuli pattern rather than to parts.

**Pavlov, Ivan Petrovich (1849-1936)** Russian physiologist, created an epoch in some fields of physiology, such as digestion and the higher nervous activity. In 1874 he graduated from Petersburg University and in 1879 from the Petersburg Medico-Surgical Academy. After graduation from the Academy he went abroad where he worked at the laboratories of Ludwig and Heidenhain. In 1874-1885 he worked at the Clinic of the Russian clinician-therapeutist S. P. Botkin, as the head of Botkin's experimental physiological laboratory. In 1890 Pavlov was appointed Professor of Pharmacology at the Medico-Surgical Academy and in 1896 Head of the Physiology Department of the Academy. In 1904 Pavlov was awarded the Nobel prize for his work on the physiology of digestion where the surgical method of application of chronical fistula was first employed systematically. In 1905 Pavlov was elected as a member of the Russian Academy of Sciences. I. P. Pavlov discovered a new regularity of the brain activity, the conditioned reflex. This "Doctrine on the higher nervous activity" became a new chapter in the physiology of the brain. During 35 years of research in this field Pavlov and his numerous disciples covered a wide range of fundamental problems in the study of the brain related also to such sciences as medicine, pedagogy, art, etc. Pavlov discovered a new form of inhibition specific for the higher nervous activity which he called "internal inhibition" or "conditional inhibition", different from all other types of specific and unconditioned inhibitions. The conditioned-reflectory regularities have become a general model of the entire behavior, and the study of neurophysiological mechanisms and the theory of the higher nervous activity can be rightfully considered milestones in the history of the science of the brain.

**Pavlovian conditioning** See *conditioning, Pavlovian.*

**pavor nocturnus** (Latin) Night panic. Waking up in the middle of the night panic stricken, agitated, and sometimes hallucinated, then falling back asleep with complete amnesia.

**Payne Sentence Completion Blank** A projective technique for children in the upper grades and high school which requires the child to complete a sentence stem.

**Pcs** (S. Freud) The preconscious. The middle layer in Freud's topographic theory of personality, between the conscious and unconscious layers. The preconscious contains memory traces. It is, as it were, in one's mind but not on his mind at a particular moment.

**PE** See *probable error.*

**Peabody Picture Vocabulary Test** See *test, Peabody Picture Vocabulary.*

**peak top diagram** A diagram constructed by plotting each frequency above the midpoint of its class interval and connecting the points by a line.

**Pearson, Karl (1857-1936)** British biomathematician and statistician who, in addition to undertaking extensive statistical investigations of psychological questions, invented the product-moment coefficient of correlation, $r$, which has been named after him. He devised the system of generalized frequency curves; invented "chi-square" test of good fit and worked out its distribution; derived "Pearson's product moment" formula and two equivalent formulas; elaborated correlation theory on three variables and on other aspects of correlation and of regression.

**Pearsonian correlation** See *correlation, product movement.*

**peccotiphobia** Morbid fear of committing a sin.

**pecking order** 1. Hierarchy of privilege and dominance observed by some animal groups, and particularly studied in chickens. 2. Accepted hierarchy of privilege and dominance established in some small groups by intimidation and aggressiveness.

**pedagogical psychology** See *psychology, educational.*

**pederasty** Anal intercourse with a boy or young man.

**pederosis** (A. Forel) A sexual desire for children commonly found among certain types of psychopathic personalities and also some psychoneurotic patients.

**pediatrics** A branch of medicine devoted to the study, treatment and prevention of childhood diseases.

**pedication** Pederasty.

**pedigree** Genealogy.

**pedigree method** The study of the distribution of traits in families in order to determine hereditary mechanisms. This method is of historical interest.

**pedologia** Soviet name for the study of child development. Child psychologists in the U.S.S.R. in the years 1918-1935 were called pedologists.

**pedomorphism** Attributing childish characteristics, behaviors, or abilities to adults; describing adult characteristics, behavior or abilities in childish terms.

**peduncle** A stalklike bundle of nerve fibers connecting various parts of the brain.

**peduncle, cerebellar** One of three bonds of fibers connecting the cerebellum to the brain stem.

**peduncle, cerebral** One of two large bands of white matter containing descending axons of upper motor neurons connecting the cerebral hemispheres to the pons and forming the main connection with the spinal cord.

**Peking man** (anthropology) A primitive form of man similar to the Neanderthal man the remains of which were found near Peking.

**pellagra** A nutritional deficiency of nicotinic acid characterized by diarrhea and dermatitis of sun-exposed surfaces and in severe cases, disturbances of the central nervous system, such as delirium, acute mania and depression.

**pellet**   1. Small piece of food usually standardized by size, weight, and content which is used in animal experimentation. 2. Small round object which is used in infant development studies for the infant to manipulate.

**penetrance**   The percentage of cases in which genetic complement for a trait or disease is manifested in the developed organism or phenotype. The penetrance of the single genetic mechanism in schizophrenia is calculated as being of the order of 60 to 70% in the twin-family studies of Franz J. Kallmann.

**peniaphobia**   Morbid fear of becoming poor.

**penilingus**   Fellatio.

**penis envy**   (S. Freud) A reaction of little girls at the phallic stage to the discovery of sexual differences. The girls feel they have been deprived of the penis (castrated) and wish to have it back. The resolution of the feminine castration complex and Oedipal wish is associated with the substitution of desiring having a child instead of having a penis.

**penology**   The scientific study of the treatment of criminals which may be punitive or preventive in orientation.

**pentobarbital**   A drug of the barbiturate family used to alleviate acute anxiety and fear.

**pentothal**   Trademark for thiopental, a narcotic.

**peotillomania**   Pulling of one's own penis as a nervous tic and not masturbation.

**peptic ulcer**   See *ulcer, peptic.*

**percentile**   1. (statistics) One of the 99 points which divide a group of scores or ranked distribution into 100 equal parts, each containing 1/100th of the scores or people. Percentiles are ranked from the bottom up from 1 to 99. Thus, the 62nd percentile indicates that 62% of the total group are below that point and 38% fall above it. 2. (statistics) Centile rank or division.

**percentile curve**   See *curve, percentile.*

**percentile norm**   See *norm, percentile.*

**percentile rank**   See *rank, percentile.*

**percentile scale**   See *scale, percentile.*

**percentile score**   See *score, percentile.*

**percept**   1. The object of perception. 2. A single instance of perception. This refers to the perceptual experience but not to the physical objects of perception which are stimuli.

**percept-image**   A concrete fantasy or memory image of hallucinatory clarity, commonly seen in schizophrenic patients.

**perception**   1. The process of obtaining information about the world through the senses. 2. (nativism) The view that perception of the world as it exists is inborn. The adherents of this group were R. Descartes and I. Kant. 3. (empiricism) The view that perception is based on previous experience, on the association of elements. This view is characteristic of British associationists. 4. (E.B. Titchener and W. Wundt) Perception is the result of learning added to raw sensations. The perceptions must be analyzed in order to yield the more basic psychological elements of sensation. 5. (J.J. Gibson) Perception is the result of physical stimuli impinging on sense receptors. The emphasis is on the biological context which is believed to explain true perception. 6. (Gestalt) Perception results from an innate organizing process. The basic unit is a configuration which is a whole that is greater than the sum of its parts and which determines the parts. An isomorphism between the organizing processes in perceived configurations and the chemical-electrical events taking place in the brain is postulated. 7. (A. Ames) The transactional approach states that perception is based on assumptions about the construction of reality. Each individual is believed to develop a restricted set of perceptions through his own unique transactions with the environment to handle the infinite variety of possible retinal images which he receives. Perception becomes a learned act of constructing reality to fit one's assumptions about it.

**perception, allocentric**   (E. G. Schachtel) Perception which is independent of the individual's immediate needs, of the stereotyped interpretation or the symbolic representation of an object.

**perception, automorphic**   The tendency to view or think of others as similar to oneself, strengthened by ignoring differences and accentuating similarities.

**perception, binocular**   Perception of only one visual field through the cooperative acting of both eyes. Binocular vision is the primary way of perceiving three-dimensionality and of seeing things in space in reference to the person seeing.

**perception, extra-sensory**   See *extra-sensory perception.*

**perception, intersensory**   Perception with more than one sense modality.

**perception of time**   (P. Fraisse) The attention to, or apprehension of, change through the integration of a series of stimuli and characterized by the ability to conceive of duration, simultaneity, and succession. The perception of time is generally broken down into various categories: conditioning to time, which includes the temporal orientation of organisms, the periodicity of their behavior in terms of the circadian, or day-night, 24-hour cycle; the perception of the passage of time, duration, the ability to estimate various segments of time (ten seconds, ten minutes, etc.); control over time which is characterized by an active orientation of the self in time, in the present, the past and the future; and the experience of time, which includes the differences between "psychological" time and "clock" time and how the individual views and experiences time—its passage, its role in his life, and what it is.

**perception, sense**   The awareness of the world as based on the stimulation of the sense organs.

**perception, social**   1. Perception of social phenomena which includes persons and groups. 2. Perception of the behaviors of another which reveal his feelings, intentions, and attitudes.

**perception, subliminal** The perception of stimuli below the threshold which are not perceived consciously but can influence behavior.

**perceptual anchoring** A frame of reference against which a perceptual response or judgment is made. This frame of reference in combination with the properties of the object itself influences the response.

**perceptual defense** See *defense, perceptual*.

**perceptual distortion** See *distortion, perceptual*.

**perceptual field** All those elements of the external environment which an organism perceives or experiences as he experiences them. This may include illusory or distorted elements.

**perceptual handicap** See *handicap, perceptual*.

**perceptual learning** See *learning, perceptual*.

**perceptual restructuring** The process of changing an already existing perception which entails changing the pattern of a percept.

**perceptual schema** The cognitive patterns which serve as a frame of reference against which an organism reacts to the environment and external stimuli.

**perceptual segregation** Separation of part of a perceptual field from the total field.

**perceptual set** See *set, perceptual*.

**perceptual speed** One of several hypothetical units which constitute the primary mental abilities. This ability consists of quick, efficient handling of perceptual forms.

**perceptualization** 1. Organization of sensory elements into a meaningful whole. 2. Awareness of a new or different meaning for a percept.

**percipient** 1. The perceiver. 2. (parapsychology) The person who receives the messages in telepathic communication.

**performance** 1. Activity. 2. Behavior in which an organism engages in response to a task or activity which leads to results, especially to a result which modifies the environment in some way.

**performance curve** See *curve, performance*.

**performance test** See *test, performance*.

**periblepsis** Strange staring expressing bewilderment, typical for a delirious state.

**perimacular vision** See *vision, perimacular*.

**perimeter** (vision) Instrument which maps the visual areas of the retina defining the sensitivity of the retinal field by determining what can be seen when different parts of the field are stimulated. It is used to measure the extent of achromatic and chromatic vision and to isolate areas of visual defect. The device consists of a circular band which rotates upon which stimuli are moved outward and inward. The subject fixates his eye at the center of rotation.

**period** 1. (physics) The time interval of a complete cycle of an event which happens regularly as, for example, the time it takes for a sound to occur. 2. (physiology) The length of time the menstrual flow lasts, or the menstrual period.

**period, absolute refractory** Short period of time following the discharge of a neuron, during which the neuron cannot be fired again.

**periodic mania** See *mania, periodic*.

**periodic reinforcement** Reinforcement which occurs intermittently rather than continuously according to a consistent predetermined time schedule.

**peripheral region** (K. Lewin) In differentiated personality structure, the peripheral region represents the acquired and not-fundamental personality traits.

**peripheral vision** Vision which takes place in the outer regions of the retina; the area of rods and color vision.

**peripheralism** A position which maintains that behavior should be viewed as a function of events taking place in the periphery of the organism.

**peristalsis** Progressive wavelike contraction which occurs in the alimentary tract forcing the contents of the tract downward.

**peritoneum** Membrane lining of the inside of the abdominal cavity which surrounds the enclosed viscera.

**permeable** 1. That which can be penetrated, permeated or passed through without being ruptured as with membranes which allow certain liquid to pass through. 2. A boundary which can be penetrated from the outside. 3. (topology) The degree to which activities or regions can be affected by forces from outside the region of the life space. 4. (G. A. Kelly) A construct which has the capacity to accept new elements into its field of applications.

**permissive relation** The relation of one factor to another such that a certain level must be reached on the former before the latter can function on the criterion at all.

**permissiveness** (developmental psychology) Allowing a child to express his feelings and ideas in ways that are cognitively and emotionally appropriate to his age and experience; often used in reference to parental non-punitive treatment of sexual, aggressive, or other behavior which by tradition is subject to socialization pressures.

**permutations** A statistical rule concerning the number of ways that $N$ objects may be arranged in order according to the formula:
$$N! = (1)(2)(3)...(N-1) \ (N) \text{ where } 0! = 1$$

**perphenazine** A drug used as a tranquilizer and in the treatment of nausea.

**perseveration** 1. A tendency for organismic activity to occur without exteroceptive or specifiable stimuli. 2. A tendency to finish whatever was begun or difficulty experienced in changing methods while doing a task. 3. Pathological repeating of a word or phrase.

**perseverative trace**   See *trace, perseverative.*

**persona**   (C. G. Jung) An autonomous partial system or complex representing an individual's conscious attitude toward the outer world in accordance with his own inner archetypal needs. The ego is the core of the persona.

**personal data sheet**   A questionnaire which asks for specific biographical information about the individual usually inquiring about name, age, sex, occupation, interests, etc. It may include some psychological questions but based on habits and factual data rather than personality questions which would necessitate inferences.

**personal document analysis**   (G. W. Allport) In accordance with his idiographic view of psychology, Allport stressed the importance of analysis of personal diaries, letters, inventories, etc. as case study research techniques.

**personal equation**   1. Difference in performance which is due to individual differences. 2. Difference in simple reaction time between two persons. 3. Personal idiosyncrasies which must be considered in analyzing situations if the actual dynamics of situations are to be determined.

**personal identity**   See *identity.*

**personal unconscious**   See *unconscious, personal.*

**personalistic psychology**   See *psychology, personalistic.*

**personality**   The pattern of traits characterizing an individual person, trait here meaning any psychological characteristic of a person, including dispositions to perceive different situations similarly and to react consistently despite changing stimulus conditions, values, abilities, motives, defenses, and aspects of temperament, identity, and personal style. Though the pattern of such characteristics is necessarily unique, personality comprises all of a person's traits, not merely the ones that differentiate him from others. A descriptive, not a causally efficacious concept, personality (and traits) may be interpreted in terms either of observable consistencies in behavior or of inferred dispositions to behave (behavior being construed in the widest sense, to include implicit, only self-observable thoughts, feelings and emotions, impulses, dreams, and percepts, as well as actions and words observable by others). The full pattern or organization of traits becomes manifest only over the entire life span, so that personality is, in Murray's phrase, the study of lives; but the term is commonly used to refer to the observable and inferrable pattern at any one time. Personality is not synonymous with person, a more inclusive term denoting an individual human organism, which consists not only of a personality but that of a physique, an anatomy, a physiology, a social role and status, a being who expresses and transmits a culture—the focus of all the human (e.g., behavioral and medical) sciences.

**personality (a psychometric conception)**   An individual's unique pattern of characteristics, including his positions on a large number of trait variables.

**personality, anal**   See *character, anal.*

**personality, basic**   (A. Kardiner and R. Linton) A theory which maintains that common child raising methods practiced in a given society determine certain basic personality traits such as, e.g. assertion, aggressiveness, cooperation, etc. These traits, called "basic personality" determine the ethnic or national characteristics common to all members of a given social group notwithstanding the differences between the various individuals.

**personality, compulsive**   A personality type characterized by an excessive rigid involvement with standards, morality and conformity and a tendency to be orderly, inhibited and pedantic.

**personality disorder, iatrogenic**   Personality disorder caused by diagnostic or treatment exacerbation.

**personality disorders**   See *character disorders.*

**personality, dual**   1. Dissociation. 2. A form of personality disorder in which the personality is divided, as it were, into two separate, distinct parts, each of which functions with its own fairly independent organization and mental life though there is some degree of unity between them.

**personality dynamics**   The motivations, emotions, and other internal forces which underlie behavior.

**personality, epileptic**   Complex of negative traits and related behavioral manifestations including aggressiveness, selfishness, religious fanaticism, morbid egotism, temper tantrums and stubborn uncooperativeness found in some epileptics. This personality syndrome is not exhibited by the majority of epileptics nor exclusively by epileptics; the relationship between epilepsy and this pattern is unclear.

**personality, factorial theory of**   (R. B. Cattell) Concluding that clinical observation alone is not sufficiently reliable to develop and test theories of personality structure, Cattell began in 1940 what became a thirty-year factor analytic investigation of correlations, over people and over time, in life (L), questionnaire (Q) and behavioral test (T) data. The resulting concepts in traits and states, e.g., surgency, ego strength, regression, superego, anxiety and arousal, cover some *thirty primaries, twelve secondaries,* etc., in a hierarchy. A specific response behavior $a_j$ is estimated according to the model:

$$a_j = b_{j1}\,T_1 + \ldots b_{jp}T_p + b_{j1s}S_1 + \ldots . b_{jsq}S_q +$$

specific terms, where the $T$'s are $p$ broad common traits and the $S$'s are $q$ broad common states. The model, when the $T$'s are known ability, temperament and dynamic traits, has yielded excellent criterion predictions. The $b$ terms (behavioral indices or loadings) describe the environment, thus brought to interaction with the individual personality vector of $T$'s. The *dynamic calculus* is the more specialized development of this theory in the dynamic realm.

**personality, inadequate**   Class of personality disturbances in which the individuals are characterized by inadaptability, social incompatibility and inadequate responses to intellectual, emotional, social, and physical demands without being grossly physically or mentally deficient on examination.

**personality inventory**  See *inventory, personality*.

**personality measurement**  A general term for a variety of psychological techniques which measure various aspects of personality. Personality measurement techniques include paper-pencil tests, projective techniques, interest inventories, attitudes scales, rating and performance techniques, etc.

**personality, multiple**  An extreme form of dissociative reaction to stress in which two or more separate personalities exist. The person may shift from one personality to another which is often very different from the other. Each personality has no memory of the other's thoughts and actions. One of the personalities may function unconsciously and be aware of the conscious personality but it manifests itself early indirectly as in automatic writing.

**personality, oral**  See *character, oral*.

**personality, passive-aggressive**  Behavior syndrome characterized by passivity and aggressiveness with the aggressiveness often expressed passively by obstructionism, stubbornness, pouting, etc. This pattern usually reflects hostility and resentment at the individual's inability to establish a satisfactory relationship with a person or institution upon which he is overdependent.

**personality, prepsychotic**  An individual whose behavior is indicative of an approaching psychosis.

**personality, sociopathic**  Personality disorder characterized by poor social relationships and inability to conform to cultural, ethical, and social norms. This broad category may include antisocial, asocial, or dyssocial attitudes and behavior and often sexual anomalies.

**personality sphere**  (R. B. Cattell) Essentially, the range of measurable human personality.

**personality tests**  See *tests, personality*.

**personality, theories of: biological**  1. Theories of personality which emphasize the biological nature of personality. 2. See *constitutional theory of personality: W. H. Sheldon*. 3. See *holistic theory of personality*. 3. See *Maslow's theory of personality*.

**personality trait**  Any respect in which one person differs from others. It can often be represented by a linear dimension. Otherwise, it is a matter of presence or absence, or membership in categories.

**personality types**  Classification of human beings according to certain distinct personality features and typical behavioral patterns. There are several personality typologies (Eysenck, Freud, Fromm, Hippocrates, Jung, Kretschmer, Sheldon, Wolman, etc.), which describe particular personality types. See *type*.

**personification**  1. Attribution of personal characteristics to inanimate objects, an abstraction, or various phenomena of nature. 2. (H.S. Sullivan) An abstract of what an individual perceives as the pattern of another's interaction with him or his interaction with another, based on feelings, attitudes and conceptions which grow from recurrent interpersonal experiences with need satisfaction and anxiety. Personifications are not accurate representations of the person to whom they refer but images formed to better deal with others. The individual's first personifications are of the good mother, who satisfies needs, and the bad mother, who causes anxiety, neither of which is a true picture of the 'real' mother.

**personified self**  (H.S. Sullivan) The personification referring to one's self, based on the rudimentary personifications of: good-me, the organization of interpersonal experiences in which satisfaction and tenderness have been forthcoming from the mother because she was pleased with the infant's behavior; bad-me, the organization of interpersonal experiences in which anxiety has been evoked by the mother; and not-me, the organization of interpersonal experiences in which horror, dread, and intense-anxiety has been evoked. The personified self is part of the self-system and as such works to protect the individual from anxiety threatening to his security by interfering with objective self-evaluation.

**personnel management**  Supervision of the employees of a firm or institution which entails interviewing job applicants, selection, training and placement of personnel, and dealing with problems which affect employees.

**personnel psychology**  Personnel psychology is perhaps the earliest aspect of industrial and organizational psychology. It revolves around the study of individual differences and the comparative analysis of candidates for a position. Its roots stem from psychometrics, educational psychology, learning theory and applied personality theory. Organizational psychology studies people within organizations to implement effective coordination and control. It is closely related to social psychology and sociology. In human factors engineering, the working environment is manipulated to bring about compatibility with the individual. Human factors engineering is related to the general field of applied psychology, to industrial engineering and to psychophysiology.

**personnel research**  See *research, personnel*.

**personology**  1. The study of personality. 2. The principle that behavior should be studied in terms of its relevance to the personality. 3. (H. A. Murray; R. W. White) Scientific biography; the study of lives.

**perspective, aerial**  A cue to depth perception in which as distance increases color quality becomes less saturated and increasingly blurred while outlines within the image become less sharp.

**perspective, alternating**  Changes in the perception of a stimulus pattern that lead to multiple interpretations as a result of the sense of a third dimension, created by the part of a figure or drawing that appears, alternately, closer and farther away as the figure is fixated. See *ambiguous figures; reversible figures*.

**perspective, angular**  Represents the relationship between lines in the visual field and those formed by the images of the lines projected on the retina.

**perspective, linear** The apparent change in size of objects at different distances from the eye and the principles according to which distance determines the varying sizes of the visual image.

**perturbation** (information theory) A disturbance or excess presented with or superimposed upon the necessary information of a message. Such disturbance tends to obscure the message and thus lessens the probability that the receiver will respond appropriately to the message.

**perversion** A socially disapproved or prohibited form of conduct, particularly in sexual life. Interpretation varies and the term itself is becoming outmoded.

**perversion, infantile polymorphous** (S. Freud) The theory that a child's sexual instinct has no specific direction which results in the child's inclinations which might be considered perverted if performed by an adult.

**pesticide poisoning** See *poisoning, DDT; poisoning, parathion.*

**petrification** The process of being petrified or turned to stone which is sometimes interpreted as being a punishment for unacceptable voyeuristic or scopophilic impulses.

**peyote** An hallucinogenic drug derived from a cactus which causes psychedelic effects such as radical mood changes, delusions and hallucinations.

**PF Study** See *Picture-Frustration Study.*

**Pfaffmann, Carl** (1913-    ) U.S. physiological psychologist, pioneered electrophysiological studies of sense of taste. First to show limited specificity of single afferent taste fibers and introduced the neural pattern concept of taste discrimination. Showed that increased taste preferences not due to increased sensitivity of receptor. With Carr also found no receptor change from gonadal hormones again indicating stability of peripheral receptors. With Pfaff and Scott did find differential processing of olfactory information in preoptic brain area related to mating behavior and olfactory sensory responses in hypothalamus. His correlated studies of physiology and behavior clarified mechanisms underlying the sensory basis of reinforcement and the "Pleasures of Sensation."

**Phaedra complex** See *complex, Phaedra.*

**phagocyte** White blood cell; defends the organism against foreign bodies.

**phagomania** Morbid urge for overeating.

**phagophobia** Morbid fear of food and of gaining weight.

**phallic character** (psychoanalysis) An individual with permanent and consistent patterns of functioning which reflect reaction formation to castration fear experienced during the oedipal stage. Self-assuredness and boastfulness, combined with narcissism, vanity and sensitiveness are the main characteristics. Exhibitionistic and overtly aggressive behavior is a reaction formation to castration fear. In women, penis envy may be elaborated either by the assumption of a masculine role or by vindictive behavior toward males.

**phallic sadism** See *sadism, phallic.*

**phallic stage** (S. Freud) The third stage of psychosexual development occurring from the age of three to seven during which the child derives pleasurable sensations from stimulation of the genital organs. During this stage, each child has the desire to displace the parent of the same sex and to possess the parent of the opposite sex. These wishes are repressed because of castration anxiety for the boy and fear of loss of the mother's love for the girl.

**phallic symbol** (S. Freud) In dreams, knives, sticks, swords, etc. are phallic symbols as they represent the phallus.

**phallus** Penis in a state of erection.

**phaneromania** A morbid, compulsive urge to touch one's own body, e.g. such as one's nose, breasts, lips, etc.

**phantasm** See *fantasm.*

**phantasmagoria** Raising or recalling spirits of the dead.

**phantasmoscopia** Hallucinations of ghosts and spirits.

**phantasy** See *fantasy.*

**phantasy formation** See *fantasy formation.*

**phantom limb** The illusion of sensations in an amputated limb or stump. The prosthesis can even be experienced as a natural limb.

**pharmacogenetics** The sphere of biochemical genetics dealing with drug responses and their genetically controlled variations. Genetically controlled variation in response to certain anti-depressant agents is an example.

**pharmacologic therapy** Chemotherapy; treatment of mental patients with chemical substances, especially stimulants for depressive states and tranquilizers for excited states.

**pharynx** A part of the throat which leads to the larynx and esophagus.

**phase difference** (audition) Differences in the phase sequences of two sound waves as when crest does not correspond with crest and trough does not correspond with trough. Phase difference aids in the localization of sounds.

**phase sequence** (D.O. Hebb) A series of cell-assembly actions, theoretically constituting the stream of thought.

**phasmophobia** Morbid fear of ghosts.

**phenelzine** An antidepressant drug of the monoamine oxidase inhibitor group used in the treatment of depression and psychosis.

**phengophobia** Morbid fear of daylight.

**phenobarbital** A drug of the barbiturate family

used in the alleviation of acute anxiety and fear and also to control seizures.

**phenocopy** A phenotypic trait resulting from a specific genotype is mimicked by the interplay of an environmental effect, e.g., temperature or sunlight which duplicates hereditary traits of the skin.

**phenomena, hypnagogic** Processes occurring during the hypnagogic state.

**phenomenal field** See *field of consciousness.*

**phenomenal regression** See *regression, phenomenal.*

**phenomenal report** A verbal report of what one has experienced in a given experimental situation from a phenomenological viewpoint.

**phenomenal self** See *self, phenomenal.*

**phenomenon, autokinetic** The perception by various individuals of different amounts of apparent movement when exposed to a stationary light for some time.

**phenomenology** 1. The science of the subjective processes by which phenomena are presented. It deals with mental processes and concentrates on the ideal, essential elements of experiences. 2. The investigation of occurrences or phenomena as they happen directly in experience without interpretation.

**phenomotive** (W. Stern) A motive which can be discovered and observed introspectively.

**phenothiazine poisoning** See *poisoning, chlorpromazine.*

**phenylketonuria (PKU)** A genetic metabolic disorder transmitted as an autosomal recessive causing a lack in the enzyme necessary for the oxidation of phenylalanine resulting in an accumulation of phenylpyruvic acid. The clinical picture is of a severely retarded child with blond hair, blue eyes, fair skin, eczema and microcephaly.

**phenylpyruvic oligophrenia** See *phenylketonuria.*

**phenylthiocarbamide** A substance whose taste in people is determined by a single gene pair. The ability to taste is dominant.

**phi coefficient ($r_\phi$)** The measure of association appropriate when two variables are divided into two qualitatively separate classes of observations, working from a four-fold contingency table. The formula is:

$$r_\phi = \frac{bc - ad}{\sqrt{(a+c)\ (b+d)\ (a+b)\ (c+d)}}$$

where the letters refer to the cell and marginal frequencies.

**phi-gamma function ($\phi(\tau)$)** The integration of a normal distribution of psychophysical judgments obtained by the method of constant-stimulus difference stated in terms of h; an index of precisely how closely the data are centered about the mean. The formula is:

$$P = \int_{-\infty}^{\tau} \frac{11}{\sqrt{\pi}}\, e^{-\tau}\, d\gamma,$$

where the $\int_{-\infty}^{\tau}$ is the derivative from negative infinity to gamma, $e$ is the common log base

(2.718281) raised to the negative gamma power ($-\tau$) and d$\tau$ is the change observed in the gamma value.

**phi-gamma hypothesis** The assertion or assumption that the data obtained by the method of constant stimulus difference will fit the phi-gamma function.

**phi phenomenon** (M. Wertheimer) The production of apparent movement by the successive appearance of two stationary stimuli, like the flashing of two lights. It is perceived as the movement of a single stimulus from one point in space to another.

**philomimesia** A compulsion to imitate and/or mimic.

**philosophy of psychology** Philosophical problems in psychology, such as theory formation, conceptualization, causation, reductionism, etc. Most of these problems belong to philosophy of science applied to psychology.

**phlegmatic type** See *type, phlegmatic.*

**phobia** Morbid fear based on displacement of an original fear, e.g., a patient afraid of his aggressive, genocidal impulses may develop agoraphobia, (fear of open places), thus preventing himself from acting out his aggressive impulses.

**phobia, animal** 1. Severe and unreasonable fear of animals, which may come from learning by experience or by being told of danger from imagination concerning the feared animal or identification with someone who fears the animal in question. 2. (psychoanalysis) Extreme fear of an animal involving the repression and projection of unacceptable impulses onto the animal.

**phobia, school** Fear of attending school, most commonly seen in elementary school children usually as a result of anxiety about separation from the mother.

**phobic reactions** Irrational fearful responses.

**phobophobia** A morbid fear of ever experiencing fear.

**phocomelia** A deformity of limbs in which the hands are attached directly to the shoulders with arms missing.

**phonantograph** An instrument which records sound waves graphically.

**phonation** Production of the sounds of speech.

**phone** Element of speech; a single symbol in the system of phonetics.

**phoneidoscope** A device which facilitates the visual observation of sound waves by reflecting light off a film which is made to vibrate.

**phonelescope** An instrument which makes possible the observation, measurement, and photographic recording of sound waves through the use of a recorder which is attached to a vibrating diaphragm.

**phoneme** 1. Similar speech sounds which are considered to be the same sound and may be spelled with the same or with equivalent letters. 2. An hallucination in which speaking or distinct sounds are heard as in hearing "voices".

**phonetics** Study of the production of vocal sounds with emphasis on their relation to language, though including psychological, physiological, and physical relationships and data.

**phonism** A form of synasthesia in which a sensation of sound is produced by a sensation in another sense modality or a thought.

**phonogram** 1. A symbolic illustration of a vocal sound. 2. A diagram which illustrates the vocal organs in the process of producing vocal sounds.

**phonomania** Homicidal impulses.

**phonophobia** Morbid fear of sounds including one's own voice.

**phonoscope or phonoprojectoscope** General term for any instrument which makes sound waves visible.

**phoria** The way the eyes turn or orient themselves to sight an object.

**phorometry** Measurement of the amount of balance or imbalance which exists in the external muscles which turn the eyeballs.

**phosphene** A phosphorescent form of light seen in the dark which is produced by the eyeball being distorted due to the normal process of accommodation and convergence or to pressure externally or to mechanical distortion.

**phot** A unit of illumination the same as that light produced at a surface which is one centimeter distant from a uniform point source of light of one candlepower strength.

**photerythrosity** Increased sensitivity to the red end of the spectrum exhibited by some people.

**photic driving** Stimulation of the brain rhythmically through the application to the eyes of a stroboscopic light to heighten brain waves. Alpha rhythm may be made to correspond with the light.

**photism** 1. Hallucination of light. 2. A form of synesthesia, in which a visual sensation of color or light is produced by a sensation in another sense modality or thought.

**photochromatic interval** Stimulus intensity range over which colored or chromatic stimulus can be perceived as light but cannot yet be seen as color or hue.

**photoma** Visual hallucination; seeing a flash of light without external stimulation.

**photomania** A morbid craving for light.

**photometric measure** Measure of light energy given in photometric terms as opposed to physical terms or sensation terms.

**photometry** The science of the measurement of light.

**photophobia** An extreme dislike of light.

**photopic adaptation** See *adaptation, brightness.*

**photopic vision** See *vision, photopic.*

**photoreceptor** Receptors which are stimulated by light and function in vision such as the retinal rods and cones.

**phototropism** An automatic movement (tropism) toward light (positive) or away from light (negative) caused by chemical or physical factors.

**phrenitis** (Hippocrates) An ancient term for the inflammation of the brain.

**phrenology** An obsolete theory which linked mental faculties to particular parts of the skull and maintained that the shape of the skull is indicative of the predominance of a particular faculty.

**phronemophobia** A morbid fear of reasoning.

**phthisic type** See *type, phthisic.*

**phyloanalysis** (T. Burrow) Method of treating behavior disorders which is based on the assumption that the disorders of individuals and of society are the result of impaired tensional balance which affects the individual's internal and external relationships.

**phylobiology** (T. Burrow) Behavioral science which investigates the phyletic motivation of organisms' reactions as they mediate the individual's rapport with the environment. It assumes biological unity to be a central principle directing motivation.

**phylogenesis; phylogeny** The origin and evolutionary development of a species.

**phylogenetic; phylogenic** Pertaining to the origin and development of a species.

**phylogenetic principle** See *principle, phylogenetic.*

**phylogeny** The evolutionary development of a species.

**phylum** Classification of biological species.

**physical therapy** See *physiotherapy.*

**physicalism** See *logical positivism.*

**physiogenesis** The origin of a normal or abnormal function of the organism.

**physiognomy** 1. Using the external appearance of the face and other external bodily features as a means of mental characteristics or attitudes. 2. Facial expression.

**physiological age** The level of physiological development attained at a certain chronological age.

**physiological limit** The point beyond which there can be no further gain in efficiency due to practice. The limit is not necessarily set by the physiological structure of the organism.

**physiological memory** See *memory, physiological.*

**physiological psychology** See *psychology, physiological.*

**physiological therapy** See *therapy, physiological.*

**physiology** Branch of biological science which investigates the functions of living organisms or of their parts and structures.

**physiopathology** Study of physiological disorders including both organic and functional disturbances.

**physiotherapy** Branch of medicine which deals with physical forms of treatment such as hydrotherapy, massage, and the use of light, heat, cold, etc.

**physique** Overall body structures and organization; general physical appearance.

**physostigmine poisoning** See *poisoning, physostigmine.*

**pia mater** Vascular membrane consisting of a network of blood vessels enclosed in thin tissue covering the surface of the brain and the spinal cord.

**Piaget, Jean (1896-     )** Swiss psychologist, who started his scientific career as a zoologist and later, as a philosopher. His diverse interests led him to do postdoctoral work with the psychiatrist, Bleuler, in Zurich and with Dr. Simon in Paris. It was during an attempt to standardize Burt's reasoning tests upon Parisian children that the zoologist and philosopher was transformed into the child psychologist and epistemologist. After his work in Paris, Piaget was successively Director of Research at the Rousseau Institute in Geneva, Privat Docent at the Faculty of Science of the University of Geneva, Professor of Psychology and of the Philosophy of Science at the University of Neuchatel, Professor of General Psychology at the University of Lausanne, Professor of Sociology and of Experimental Psychology at the University of Geneva. He was named Titular Professor of Genetic Psychology at the Sorbonne in 1952. Piaget is currently co-director of the Institute of Educational Science in Geneva, as well as Professor of Experimental Psychology at the Faculty of Science at the University of Geneva. Piaget devoted his research and theoretical talents to the systematic understanding of the mental evolution of the child, as well as to problems of epistemology. His current bibliography totals to more than 18,000 printed pages. Many of his works have been translated into numerous languages and some of them are now regarded as classics in the field. Piaget has received honorary degrees from universities around the world, including, most recently, the University of Pennsylvania. He is the founder of the Center for the Study of Genetic Epistemology in Geneva, which each year brings together scholars from all over the world to deal with problems of epistemology. Under Piaget's editorship, the Center has published more than twenty volumes of original research on epistemological problems.

**piano theory of hearing** See *hearing, theory of: resonance theory.*

**pica** 1. The eating of non-nutritional substances such as paint, cornstarch or hair. 2. The craving for unusual foods which occurs frequently during pregnancy.

**Pickford Projective Pictures Test** See *test, Pickford Projective Pictures.*

**Pick's disease** (A. Pick) A presenile endogeneous disorder of insidious origin characterized by a progressive state of dementia resulting from circumscribed cerebral atrophy. A disturbance of abstract thinking and aphasia may occur. The onset occurs usually in the range of forty-five to fifty years with a preponderance of women being afflicted.

**pictograph; pictogram** See *ideogram.*

**Picture Arrangement Test** See *test, Picture Arrangement.*

**picture completion test** See *test, picture completion.*

**Picture-Frustration Study** (S. Rosenzweig) A controlled projective technique introduced in 1945 which measures a person's reaction to frustration. It consists of twenty-four cartoon-like drawings, each depicting a situation in which one person is frustrated by another. The comments of the frustrator are written and the subject is asked to provide the response of the frustrated person which is interpreted in terms of direction of the response and type of response. An overall conformity rating can be determined. There is a form for adults, for children and for the study of attitude toward minority groups developed by J. F. P. Brown.

**picture impressions test** See *test, picture impressions.*

**picture interpretation test** See *test, picture interpretation.*

**Picture World Test** See *test, Picture World.*

**Piderit drawings** Large series of very simple outlines of the human face which illustrate various emotional expressions. These are cut up into interchangeable pieces which are used to study how changing the expression on one part of the face affects overall expression and also to see how many potential varieties of emotional facial expression there are.

**Piéron, Henri (1881-1964)** One of the first major experimental psychologists in France, long-time professor at the Collège de France in Paris. Author of books on experimental psychology in 1928 and on mental development and intelligence in 1930, he also edited the major French psychological journal, *L'Année Psychologique.*

**pigmentary retinal lipoid neuronal heredo-degeneration** See *Spielmeyer-Vogt's disease.*

**Pillars of Corti** See *rods of Corti.*

**pilomotor response** See *response, pilomotor.*

**pilot study** A short-range exploratory study which is carried out as preparation for a larger, more involved study in order to test the feasibility of proposed methods or projects and to ascertain to some degree what problems may be encountered and what the outcome may be.

**pineal body or gland; epiphysis cerebri** 1. A small glandular outgrowth of the thalamic region at the top of the third ventricle. 2. According to Descartes, the place where soul and body interact.

**Pinel, Philippe (1745-1826)** French psychiatrist who during the French Revolution removed the chains from the inmates of the Salpetriere hospital and introduced a liberal approach to the inmates whom he perceived as victims of diseases, deserving humane treatment.

**Pinel's system** (P. Pinel) Eighteenth century classification system of mental disorder which divided psychiatric disorders into four categories: melancholias, manias with delirium, manias without delirium, and dementia or mental deterioration. The Pinel system included a systematic description of mental disturbances and of symptoms.

**pinocytosis** Absorption of fluid by cells which is a means of metabolic transport in the central nervous system.

**Pintner-Paterson Scale of Performance Tests** See *tests, Pintner-Paterson Scale of Performance.*

**Piotrowski system** An approach to the Rorschach test developed by Zygmunt Piotrowski. It represented an empirically based approach which differs significantly from methods developed by H. Rorschach and other Rorschach systematizers.

**Piper's law** The threshold for luminance in a consistently stimulated area of the retina is inversely proportional to the square root of the stimulated area.

**pitch, absolute** 1. The pitch of a sound as a function of its vibration rate. 2. Ability to recognize and reproduce notes accurately without comparing any particular note or tone with another.

**Pithecanthropus erectus** An extinct ape considered to be closely related to modern man and classified as the lowest human in the evolutionary scale yet discovered. The species is identified and represented by a skull found in Java.

**pithecoid** Like an ape or monkey.

**pithiatism** 1. The use of persuasion or forced suggestion to treat hysteria and other nervous disorders. 2. Rarely used term for hysteria.

**Pitre's rule** The general course of recovery from aphasia for a multilingual person begins first and is most complete with the most familiar, fluent language and proceeds gradually to less well-known languages.

**pituitarism** Pituitary gland overactivity.

**pituitary-adrenal axis** A system in the body of an organism which responds to situations of stress by secreting a hormone from the pituitary gland which activates the adrenal gland to secrete its substances that are necessary for the organism to fight harm or infection.

**pituitary gland, hypophysis cerebri** See *gland, pituitary.*

**PKU** See *phenylketonuria.*

**place theory of hearing** See *hearing, theory of: resonance theory.*

**placebo** 1. A substance with no medicinal properties which causes a patient to improve because of his belief in its efficacy. 2. (experimental) A substance administered to a control group in an experiment in which the experimental group receives a drug in order to eliminate the effect of the act of administering the drug.

**placebo therapy** See *therapy, placebo.*

**placement** (personnel) Assignment of people to jobs according to abilities, experience, and interests in order that the person be well-suited and satisfied in the job.

**placement test** See *test, placement.*

**placenta** Vascular structure in mammals which attaches the fetus to the uterus and transmits nourishment and respiration from the mother to the fetus.

**placing reaction** When a few weeks old infant is supported under his arms and the dorsal part of the feet touches a table, he lifts his legs and places the feet on the table.

**plan** A neural program for effective action.

**planchette** Instrument used in automatic writing experiments. It consists of a pencil just above or on a smooth surface which records involuntary movements of the hand.

**plantar reflex** See *reflex, plantar.*

**plantigrade** Type of standing or locomotion in which the whole foot touches the ground as in bears and man.

**plasm** 1. Plasma or liquid portion of blood and lymph. 2. Cellular substance.

**plasma** The liquid portion of blood and lymph consisting of a solution containing proteins and similar to interstitial body fluid.

**plasmon** (biology) Hereditary elements in the egg cytoplasm as opposed to the genome characteristics.

**plasticity** 1. Potential for flexible response. 2. Adaptability. 3. Teachability or possessing the capacity for learning.

**plateau** A flat period in a learning curve which indicates an apparent stop of learning which occurs temporarily during the process of learning a complicated task or skill.

**Plato (427-347 B.C.)** Greek philosopher, born in Athens, wrote Phaedo, Republic, Symposium and several other works. Plato believed in immortality of the soul. The soul has three parts, the highest one being the reason; the middle emotion and will; the lowest part is comprised of sensuous desires and appetites. The reason is located in the brain, the emotions in the heart, and the appetites in the liver. The rational part of the soul existed before birth; when the soul enters the human body, it acquires the two irrational parts.

**platycephaly** Flattening of the crown of the skull.

**platykurtosis** The relative degree of flatness of a frequency curve.

**play need** See *need, play.*

**play therapy** With children, the use of dolls and other play material as a measure of securing free expression of feelings and ideas; attributes of the play, including thematic content and organization, are treated as expressions in the therapeutic sense, with the usual interventions: reflection, interpretation, confrontation, etc.

**pleasure-pain principle** See *principle, pleasure-pain.*

**pleasure principle** (S. Freud) The principle which dominates id activity, calling for immediate reduction of tension through the satisfaction and gratification of all instinctual demands and impulses.

**"pleasures of sensation"** The hedonic or affective responses to certain classes of stimuli. Thus moderately sweet solutions are pleasant. Other stimuli may elicit displeasure, e.g. bitter solutions or pain prick. Weak lights and sounds may be pleasant, intense sounds and lights, unpleasant. Such affective aspects of sensation relate to the value or reinforcement value of stimuli as contrasted with the cognitive purely informational properties of sensory experience.

**pleiotropy** If a single gene or gene pair produces multiple effects, it is said to exhibit pleiotropy. Certain neurological syndromes exemplify this.

**pleniloquence** Compulsive, excessive talking.

**pleocytosis** Excessive cells in the cerebrospinal fluid associated with meningeal irritation.

**pleonexia** Morbid greediness.

**plethysmograph** An instrument used to record changes in the volume of a part of a body resulting from fluctuations in blood supply.

**plexus** A network of nerves, blood vessels, veins or lymphatics.

**plot** 1. (statistics) To record scores or make entries on a scatter diagram or frequency table. 2. Scatter diagram.

**pluralism** 1. The condition or situation of being plural. 2. Philosophical doctrine that reality consists of several irreducible, ultimate elements rather than only one.

**plutomania** Extreme greediness or desire for riches.

**PMD** See *dystrophy, pseudohypertrophic muscular.*

**pneumococcal meningitis** See *meningitis, pneumococcal.*

**pneumogastric nerve** See *nerve, vagus.*

**pnigerophobia** Morbid fear of being smothered.

**pnigophobia** Morbid fear of choking.

**Poetzl phenomenon** To dream about parts of a tachistoscopically viewed picture which were not consciously noticed or reported at the time of viewing.

**Poggendorf illusion** A geometrical illusion that the seen sections of a straight diagonal line, the center part of which is concealed behind a pair of vertical or horizontal parallel lines, are not parts of the same line.

**poinephobia** Morbid fear of being punished.

**point-biserial correlation** See *correlation, point-biserial.*

**point, critical** See *critical point.*

**point estimation** (statistics) The use of sample values or statistics to predict population parameters. It is so called because a single value or point in the space of all values is taken as an estimate.

**point for point correspondence** The relationship between two variables so that for every point on one variable, there is a corresponding point on the other variable.

**point hour ratio** Grade-point average which is an index of grades with each course letter grade weighted according to the number of credit hours the course is assigned and given a numerical value according to a sliding scale as follows: $A = 4$, $B = 3$, $C = 2$, and $D = 1$. The over-all average is calculated by multiplying the numerical value by the number of credit hours of the course and dividing the sum of these scores by the total number of credit hours.

**point of regard** See *regard, point of.*

**point of subjective equality (PSE)** (psychophysics) The value of the comparison stimulus energy which is equally likely to be judged as higher or lower than the test stimulus. It is the value of the comparison stimulus that is subjectively equal to the standard stimulus for the given stimulus conditions.

**point-sampling** A succession of behavior observations made for only an instant at regular intervals; measure is the frequency of occasions on which the act was occurring at the instant of recording.

**point scale** See *scale, point.*

**point, score** See *score, raw.*

**"poison-pen" psychotherapy** See *psychotherapy, "poison-pen".*

**poisoning, arsenic** Early signs of acute toxicity are limited; mainly to gastrointestinal symptoms of vomiting and watery, bloody diarrhea. In the terminal stages, seizures and coma are present. Chronic toxicity is characterized by burning sensations, optic neuritis and chronic gastrointestinal upset.

**poisoning, atropine** Symptoms include blurred vision, fever, lethargy, delirium, excitability, confusion, comas, seizures resulting from the disruption of parasympathetic nervous system functioning by the inhibition of the acetylcholine effect. In cases of acute toxicity, permanent central nervous system effects are not common.

**poisoning, barium** Acute toxicity results in muscle spasms, vomiting, weakness, cardiac irregularities and, if untreated, death. Chronic toxicity is rare.

Severe and prolonged seizures may result in chronic cerebral changes.

**poisoning, bromate** Predominant symptoms of poisoning are those of renal and central nervous systems. In acute toxicity the patient vomits violently and experiences colic and diarrhea, with lethargy, coma and seizures following. Difficulties with anuria are very common and may lead to permanent renal failure and death.

**poisoning, carbon monoxide** Inhalation of carbon monoxide results in tissue anoxia, with symptoms ranging from headache to light-headedness to coma and death. Permanent intellectual impairment is a common consequence when the person has been comatose.

**poisoning, carbon tetrachloride** May occur through ingestion or inhalation with primary symptoms of liver, kidney, and central nervous system damage. If chronic may lead to confusion, blurred vision, personality alteration and memory loss.

**poisoning, chlorpromazine** Acute toxicity with this tranquilizing drug of the phenothiazine group. It causes lethargy, usually some degree of hypotension, nausea, occasionally visual difficulties, tremors and disturbance in voluntary motor movement. Residuals are rare, but include hepatic and hematologic difficulties.

**poisoning, DDT** Acute toxicity with the common insecticide results in irritability, excitability, muscular tremors, weakness and eventually major motor seizures. Chronic exposure can result in paresthesias, tremors, and personality changes. There are often permanent residuals if the patient has reached the seizure stage.

**poisoning, epinephrine** Causes stimulation of the sympathetic nervous system and acute toxicity. Leads to central nervous system excitement, irritability, fever, rapid heart activity, dilation of the pupils and frequently, seizures and ensuing coma. Chronic toxicity may lead to personality disorders.

**poisoning, ergot** Causes contraction of the smooth muscles of the gut, uterus and arterioles and results in light-headedness, seizures and coma.

**poisoning, ethyl alcohol** Toxicity leads to central nervous system symptoms including incoordination, slowing of reaction time, blurred vision progressing to gross incoordination, impairment of judgment, stupor, and coma.

**poisoning, ethylene dichloride** Primary involvement is of the central nervous system with lesser involvement of the liver, kidney and heart. Symptoms of poisoning, include stupor, progressing to coma along with vomiting and hypertension.

**poisoning, ethylene glycol** Results in kidney and liver damage and symptoms include stupor, coma and possibly seizures.

**poisoning, heavy metal** See *poisoning, lead; poisoning, arsenic; poisoning, mercury; poisoning, thallium; poisoning, barium.*

**poisoning, kerosene** The patient suffers from pulmonary edema, with central nervous system depression leading possibly to coma and seizures. Chronic exposure may lead to peripheral neuritis and personality changes.

**poisoning, lead** Acute toxicity leads to nausea, vomiting, weakness, and pain in the extremities and abdomen. Chronic lead poisoning leads to peripheral neuritis and involvement of the central nervous system with resultant changes in level of consciousness, convulsions, changes in pulse rate, spasticity and, commonly, mental retardation.

**poisoning, mercury** Acute toxicity leads to gastrointestinal disturbances of vomiting, abdominal colic, and bloody diarrhea and sometimes to prominent central nervous system symptoms. Chronic toxicity leads to fatigue, irritability, muscular weakness, psychotic personality changes and, occasional seizures.

**poisoning, parathion** A type of organo phosphate insecticide with symptoms including nausea, epigastric pain, excessive perspiration, vomiting, diarrhea, respiratory failure and central nervous system involvement manifested in anxiety, confusion, withdrawal, depression and later, coma. Permanent central nervous system residuals including changes in personality, judgment and intellect have been reported.

**poisoning, phenothiazine** See *poisoning, chlorpromazine.*

**poisoning, physostigmine** Acute toxicity with this autonomic group drug leads to abdominal colic, perspiration, tremors, bronchospasm, seizures, coma and death.

**poisoning, salicylate** Usually caused by acetysalicylic acid (aspirin) overdose, early symptoms of toxicity are hyperventilation and vomiting, followed by lethargy, disorientation and coma. Chronic toxicity symptoms include muscle tenderness and spasm, decreased auditory acuity, paresthesias, excitability, delirium, and hallucinations.

**poisoning, thallium** Toxicity results in neurological symptoms including myoclonic jerking and rigidity. Chronic ingestion often results in residual cerebral difficulties including intellectual, motor and personality changes.

**poisoning, toluene** Toluene is a common constituent of airplane glue and is thought to be the offending agent in patients who suffer from toxicity secondary to glue sniffing. Symptoms include light-headedness, euphoria, headache, visual blurring, tremors and, in later stages, coma and seizures. Chronic symptoms include personality changes, irritability and headache.

**poisoning, trichloroethylene** Acute toxicity results in central nervous system depression initially, leading to light-headed sensations, headache, and hyperactivity followed by coma. Chronic toxicity often leads to lethargy and personality change. Liver damage is occasionally a limiting factor in the patient's recovery.

**poisoning, triorthocresyl phosphate** The usual sequelae of ingestion are demyelinization of peripheral nerves and, to some extent, degenerative changes within the spinal cord. Lower motor neuron paralysis, particularly of the distal muscles of the extremities, is common. Acute toxicity leads to weakness of the distal muscles with footdrop, wrist drop, loss of deep tendon reflexes and, in more severe cases, weakness of the ocular, laryngeal, and respiratory muscles.

**Poisson distribution** See *distribution, Poisson.*

**Poisson series** A frequency distribution in which the frequencies are listed by:

$$e^{-m} \quad (1, m, \frac{m^2}{2!}, \frac{m^3}{3!}, \frac{m^4}{4!} \ldots)$$

where $m$ is the mean value of the distribution, and $e^{-m}$ is the common log base (2.718281) raised to the negative mean value of the distribution.

**polar continuum** A continuum or series which ranges from one opposite to another. The opposite are the end points as in the personality scale for submission-dominance.

**polar variable** See *variable, polar.*

**polarization, mass** The focusing of attention of a large number of people upon the same information or communication.

**poliodystrophy** See *Alper's disease.*

**poliomyelitis** A disease, often paralytic, which includes symptoms of malaise, muscle pains, stiffness and motor weariness. Difficulties with this autonomic nervous system lead to symptoms of hypertension, perspiration and, occasionally, vomiting. Death is more common in adults than in children.

**polyandry** Marriage of one woman with more than one man.

**polychloric correlation** See *correlation, polychloric.*

**polychromatic** Multi-colored.

**polydactylism** Possessing more than five fingers or toes.

**polydipsia** Excessive craving for fluids.

**polygamy** Marriage of one man with more than one woman, or one woman with more than one man.

**polygenic** Polygenic inheritance is inheritance by many genes at different loci, with small additive effects. Synonyms: multifactorial or quantitative. This type of mechanism is the major one involved in the genetic transmission of intelligence.

**polygenic heredity** See *heredity, polygenic.*

**polygraph** An apparatus for the simultaneous recording of a number of physiological reactions or activities.

**polygyny** Marriage of one man with more than one woman.

**polyhybridity; polyhybridism** (genetics) Difference in more than three hereditary characteristics in a hybrid or a hybrid possessing several hereditary differences.

**polymorphism** 1. The derivation of several varieties of animal or individual from the same parent. 2. Organism which passes through several stages or forms or possesses several varieties.

**polyneuritic psychosis** See *Korsakov's syndrome.*

**polyneuritis** Condition of inflammation of several peripheral nerves simultaneously which is due to an infection or to poisoning and causes great pain, atrophy of muscles, and paralysis.

**polyopia** Abnormality of the refractive visual mechanism which causes several images of an object to form on the retina.

**polyparesis** See *paresis, general.*

**polypeptidorrhachia** Meningitis caused by polypeptides in the cerebrospinal fluid.

**polyphagia** Excessive craving for food.

**polyploid** Any multiple of the basic haploid chromosome number, other than the diploid number.

**polypnoea** Respiration which is heavy, forced or rapid and may be due to physical or psychical causes.

**Pompe's disease** A genetic metabolic disorder transmitted by autosomal recessive gene resulting in an excess of glycogen in the blood leucocytes and body tissues. The main clinical features are: failure to thrive, cardiomegaly and later cardiac failure, hypotonia, and enlarged tongue.

**ponophobia** Morbid fear of being overworked.

**pons Varolii** Part of the hind brain whose nerve fibers arch across the medulla connecting the cerebrum and the cerebellum.

**Ponzo illusion** See *illusion, Ponzo.*

**pooling procedures** Combining scores from different tests or values obtained through using various measures and treating them as one variable which often entails weighting some of the values in order to compensate for differences in scoring or methods of measures from one procedure to the other.

**popular response** A Rorschach scoring category, using the symbol P, to denote responses which occur very frequently. Authorities differ on the statistical criterion necessary for a response to be classified as popular. Rorschach suggested any response occurring once in three records while others have varied the criterion upward to as much as once in six records. Lists of popular responses vary from system to system with the largest number, 15, provided in the Beck approach.

**population** 1. All of the organisms living in a particular geographical area as opposed to a limited number of the total which is a sample. 2. The total group of cases or people upon which a statement is based rather than the smaller sample which is observed or experimentally tested as representative of the total group.

**porencephaly** Presence of cavities in the substance of the brain due to a developmental abnormality.

**poriomania** Extreme desire to wander aimlessly which is sometimes associated with criminal behavior and/or amnesia during the travelling period.

**pornographomania** Extreme desire to write obscene letters.

**porphyria** Inherited metabolic disorder characterized by pathological amounts of porphyrins in the blood, urine, and other tissues.

**Porter's law** Generalization that increase in the critical flicker-fusion frequency is a function of the log brightness of the stimulus independent of the wavelength.

**Porteus Maze Test** See *test, Porteus Maze.*

**position** 1. The location of a thing in space in relation to other objects or to some reference point. 2. (social psychology) The rank or location of a person within a social structure or hierarchy of influence or power. 3. Taking a stand in relation to a theoretical issue or preference for a particular attitude. 4. (topology) Life space region in which a thing occurs, an event happens, or a fact lies.

**position factor** See *factor, position.*

**position, primary** The position of the eyes when the head is erect and the eyes are fixated on an object that is distant and straight in front in the median and horizontal planes.

**position, secondary** Any position of the eyes other than the primary position, especially rotation from the primary position around either the vertical or horizontal axis.

**positive abnormalities** Personal traits which have a positive and helpful effect on an individual's personal and social functioning.

**positive after-image** See *after-image, positive.*

**positive attention seeking** See *attention seeking, positive.*

**positive correlation** See *correlation, positive.*

**positive doubles, illusion of** See *illusion of positive doubles.*

**positive induction** See *induction, positive.*

**positive movement reflex** See *reflex, positive movement.*

**positive-positive conflict** See *conflict, approach-approach.*

**positive reward** See *reinforcement, positive.*

**positive taxis** See *taxis.*

**positive transference.** See *transference.*

**positive tropism** See *tropism.*

**positivism** Philosophical and scientific viewpoint that knowledge concerns observable phenomena, experience and facts and which regards metaphysical concepts and questions about ultimate reality as unnecessary and unscientific. This approach in psychology underlies behaviorism and involves a reductionistic and empirical orientation.

**post-infectious psychosis** See *psychosis, post-infectious.*

**postpartum psychosis** See *psychosis, postpartum.*

**postpuberal stage** See *stage, postpuberal.*

**postremity principle** (V.W. Vocks) Organisms tend to repeat a certain pattern of behavior performed in a given situation when a similar situation occurs.

**postulate** An underlying principle which is thought or assumed to be true. Scientists set postulates in the belief that these postulates have heuristic value and will be of help in further research.

**postural reflexes** See *reflexes, postural.*

**potamophobia** Morbid fear of rivers.

**potassium metabolism disturbance** Characterized by weakness, paralysis of the flaccid variety and, frequently, electrocardiogram changes.

**potence; potency** 1. Power or authority. 2. Latent power. 3. The ability of the male to perform the sex act. 4. (topology) The relative amount of influence any particular part of the life space has upon behavior.

**potential** 1. Having potency. 2. Latent ability to do something especially in relation to intellectual capability or talent. 3. Amount of electrical charge.

**potlatch** (anthropology) Ritual of some Northwest American Indians in which the giving away or destroying of possessions results in a gaining of prestige.

**power** 1. (mathematics) The product of a number multiplied times itself one or more times. The number of times it is to be multiplied is signified by the superscript. 2. Muscular strength. 3. The degree of magnification of a lens. 4. The control which a person has over other people; social power. 5. The degree to which a person possesses a trait. 6. (B.B. Wolman) A behavioral dimension defined as ability to satisfy needs. The amount of power an individual possesses indicates how well he can protect life and satisfy the needs of his own and of others. Omnipotence is the summit of power, death is the zero point. Power can be used for satisfaction of needs or for the prevention of satisfaction. The direction power is used is called acceptance.

**power factor** 1. A general intellectual factor which indirectly affects all aspects of intelligence and energizes them, reflecting the efficiency level of overall brain functioning. 2. (B.B. Wolman) The ability to satisfy needs of oneself and of others, or both, or to prevent their satisfaction. In interindividual relations power can be used for the protection or the destruction of life and can be presented in a linear scale ranging from a zero point which indicates no power to higher plus numbers indicating more and more power.

**power function** (statistics) An index of whether or not a given hypothesis should be rejected at a given level of risk when other related hypotheses are assumed as true.

**power law**   See *Steven's power law.*

**power politics type**   See *type, power politics.*

**power spectrum**   (audition) Graphic illustration of the mean square amplitude of a sound wave which is used to analyze the intensity of a mixed noise or sound.

**power test**   See *test, power.*

**practice curve**   A curve which represents progress in learning. The number of trials is marked along the horizontal axis, the successes and/or failures are marked along the vertical axis.

**practice effect**   The amount or degree of improvement which results from practice.

**practice limit**   The law of diminishing returns applies to most cases of practice. Where there are no returns (no improvement) the practice has reached its limit.

**practice material**   Material given to a testee before a test which enables some degree of familiarization with the test, and puts the testee at ease.

**practice theory of play**   (K. Groos) The belief that children's play prepares them for future tasks in life. This theory was based mainly on observation of animal life.

**pragmatism**   (C. Peirce and W. James) A philosophical-epistemological theory. According to Peirce, pragmatism is a method of classification of the meaning of linguistic signs thus permitting unambiguous communication of knowledge. According to James, the meaning and truth of ideas depends on their testability in real life. The main task of thought is the achievement of "satisfactory relations with our surroundings."

**Prägnanz, law of**   (Gestalt) The general principle of learning in Gestalt psychology; Prägnanz means the goal directed tendency to restore the balance of the organism. Whenever there is a disequilibrium of forces in a psychological field, a learning process takes place and restores the equilibrium. Since learning is an improvement in Gestalt, the tendency to attain the most complete figure is called Prägnanz.

**praxiology**   1. Psychology viewed as the study of actions, and overt behavior. 2. (B.B. Wolman) Any normative science, such as, e.g. education, social philosophy, ethics, etc., that sets norms and goals for human actions.

**precipitating factor**   The onset of mental i.e. behavior disorders is usually caused by several factors, mainly the predisposing ones acting upon an organism for a long time and the precipitating factors that turn a latent condition into a manifest disease or disorder.

**precision index; $h$**   Indicates how close the measures come to the mean.

$$h = \frac{1}{\delta\sqrt{2}}$$

**precision law**   (Gestalt) Shaping up of perception; assuming precise contours. Precision law is another version of Prägnanz.

**precocity**   A too early, somewhat premature development.

**precognition**   (parapsychology) Knowledge of a future event which could not have been rationally inferred.

**preconditioning**   Presentation of two stimuli consecutively without reinforcement. The conditioning of the experimental subject to the second stimulus is called preconditioning.

**preconditioning, sensory**   (W. J. Brogden) Procedure in which two conditioned stimuli are paired during preconditioning sessions. One conditioned stimulus is then paired with the unconditioned stimulus during the conditioning stage of the experiment after which the other conditioned stimulus, the one not paired with the unconditioned stimulus, is tested for conditioning.

**preconscious**   (S. Freud) The middle stratum or "mental province" in Freud's topographic theory lying between the conscious and the unconscious. It includes what the individual is unaware of at a certain moment but may become conscious of at any time.

**predelay reinforcement**   See *reinforcement, predelay.*

**predementia praecox**   The personality configuration of the pre-schizophrenic characterized by evasion into day-dreams and flight from reality demands.

**predication**   1. Attributing certain characteristics to the subject of a proposition as in associating a predicate with a subject. 2. The psychological processes involved with making an association between concepts or ideas.

**predictability**   See *predictive efficiency.*

**prediction**   A statement concerning future outcome of an event. In a testing situation, the predictive value is related to the validity coefficient.

**predictive efficiency**   A measure of the proportion of correct predictions of a test.

**predictive index**   See *forecasting efficiency, index of.*

**predictive validity**   The degree to which a test measures what it is supposed to measure; it is ascertained by comparing it to an independent interim.

**predisposing factors in mental disorders**   Factors which increase the probability of the development of a mental disorder.

**preference method**   A research technique. The experimental subject is presented with two mutually exclusive stimuli and he has to choose one of them.

**"Preformationist" Concept of Development**   An approach to understanding the development of the child which assumes that the basic developmental pattern exists at birth. According to this concept, the human personality emerges to its full maturity according to a preformed pattern.

**preformism**  The belief that any evolutionary process and individual development is an evolvement of preexisting conditions in respectively, the origins of nature and/or embryonic state.

**prefrontal area**  The anterior part of the frontal lobe of the brain.

**prefrontal leucotomy**  See *lobotomy.*

**prefrontal lobectomy**  See *lobectomy, prefrontal.*

**preganglionic neuron**  A neuron of the autonomic nervous system; its cell body is located in the spinal cord or brain and its axon terminates in an autonomic ganglion.

**pregenital phases of sexuality**  (S. Freud) The oral, anal, and urethral phases of psychosexual development.

**pregnancy fantasy**  See *fantasy, pregnancy.*

**prejudice**  An attitude which predisposes an individual to make either negative or positive judgments about persons, objects, concepts, or groups, prior to objective evaluation. The term is usually applied when negative attitudes are held.

**premenstrual tension**  Premenstrual disturbances of mood.

**premonition**  1. An anxiety ridden anticipation of an adverse event. 2. (parapsychology) A supernatural revelation of future adversities.

**premorbid history**  The history of an individual before his illness or disorder.

**premotor cortex, brain lesions of**  See *brain lesions, of premotor cortex.*

**premsia**  (R. B. Cattell) One pole of a personality dimension, characterized by protected emotional sensitivity, dependence, lack of aggressiveness, and tender-mindedness.

**prenatal development**  See *development, prenatal.*

**preparatory interval**  The time between a ready or warning signal and the presentation of a stimulus.

**preparatory response**  Any response which does not directly bring satisfaction or is not immediately goal-directed but which is related to goal activity.

**prepotence**  (A. A. Ukhtomski) The modification of an action caused by the force of sheer neural strength with no regard for reality, adaptiveness, and with no benefit of cognition and little involvement of affect.

**prepotent response**  The response which is made when stimuli appropriate to two separate responses are present.

**prepsychotic personality**  See *personality, prepsychotic.*

**prepubertal stage**  The transitional period, usually one or two years, between childhood and adolesence which directly precedes puberty.

**prerecognition hypothesis**  An inferred or unverbalized expectation of what is about to occur which is thought to be generated by previous experiences in similar situations.

**Pre-School Schedule**  A Gesell Development Scale used to determine the level of linguistic, motor, and social behavior in pre-school children.

**presenile psychosis**  See *Alzheimer Disease; Pick's Disease.*

**presentation**  1. The exposing of a subject in an experiment to the stimulus object. 2. The materials used as stimuli in an experiment. 3. The qualities and aspects of a thing as known. 4. The object known through the act of perceiving. 5. (J. F. Herbart) The second of the five formal steps in teaching which involves any form of placing subject matter in question before the person so that he might understand. 6. (psychoanalysis) The means through which an instinctual drive is expressed, including the instinct and some vehicle of expression.

**press**  (H. A. Murray) The property of power an environmental object or person holds, having a facilitating or impeding effect on the individual's efforts to achieve a certain goal. Some press, significant in childhood are press-birth of sibling, press-family discord, and press-sex exposure.

**press, alpha**  (H. A. Murray) The properties of environmental objects and people as they exist in reality.

**press, beta**  (H. A. Murray) The properties of environmental objects and people as they are interpreted or perceived by the individual.

**pressure balance**  1. A mechanism used to control the amount and rate of application of pressure to the skin. 2. An instrument employed for testing judgments of lifted weights.

**pressure gradient**  (psychophysiology) The gradual diminution in all directions from the center of pressure when point pressure is applied to the skin.

**pressure, social**  See *social pressure.*

**presthesia**  An abnormal exceptional cutaneous sensation such as tingling, itching, and burning occurring in spinal cord lesions, in peripheral neuritis and as a conversion symptom of psychogenic origin.

**prestige motive**  The desire or push to gain position in the eyes of one's peers or in general.

**preverbal construct**  See *construct, preverbal.*

**Pribram, Karl H.** (1919-  ) American brain scientist and experimental psychologist. Known for pioneering experiments relating cerebral function to behavior. Discovered the effects of limbic forebrain stimulation on visceral-autonomic functions and of limbic resection on the four F's (feeding, fighting, fleeing and sex); the relationship of frontal to limbic cortex and both to context-dependent cognitive processes; the separate roles in visual, auditory, gustatory and somesthesic memory of portions of the primate posterior association cortex; the primarily sensory nature of the functions of motor cortex in controlling behavioral acts (via receptor regulation). Developed and extensively tested an influential cognitive theory of motivation based on computer technology (with George Miller and Eugene Galanter); and a theory of perception based on optical information processing (holography).

**primacy, law of** The proposition that that which is learned first in a series will be remembered better than the others.

**primacy zone** (psychoanalysis) In the psychosexual development of the individual, the erotic zone which is in ascendancy at the moment, i.e. in the phallic stage, the phallic zone is primary.

**primal-horde stage** A hypothetical stage in the development of human society, occurring before the primitive clan stage in which human groups probably consisted of a dominant male, his females, and subordinate males.

**primal sadism** See *sadism, primal.*

**primal scene** (psychoanalysis) A recollection, which may be actual observation, fantasy, or some mixture of the two, from childhood which relates to an early sexual experience, especially concerning sexual intercourse between the parents.

**primary color** See *color, primary.*

**primary correlation** See *correlation, primary.*

**primary data** The data as originally obtained and collected, before sorting, classification, and analysis.

**primary drive** See *drive, primary.*

**primary factor** See *factor, primary.*

**primary gain** See *paranosis.*

**primary group** An intimate face-to-face group, such as the family or a small club, which exerts an enduring influence on the individual.

**primary hue** A color primary.

**primary integration** See *integration, primary.*

**primary mental abilities** See *mental abilities, primary.*

**primary narcissism** See *narcissism, primary.*

**primary position** See *position, primary.*

**primary process** See *process, primary.*

**primary process thinking** See *thinking, primary process.*

**primary quality** A fundamental or basic aspect of an object which is necessary for the object's perceptual existence. Thus the orange color of an orange is not primary while its spatial dimensions are.

**primary reinforcement** See *reinforcement, primary.*

**primary repression** See *repression, primary.*

**primary stimulus generalization** See *stimulus generalization, primary.*

**primate** The highest order of mammals including the lemuridae, a sub-order of monkey-like animals,

and the anthropoidae, a suborder which includes monkeys, apes, and man.

**prime number** A number which can be divided only by itself or by the number one.

**primidone** An anticonvulsant drug closely related to the barbiturates, used in the treatment of epilepsy.

**primipara** A female who has only once borne offspring.

**primordial dwarfism** See *dwarfism, primordial.*

**primordial image** See *archetype.*

**primordial panic** See *panic, primordial.*

**Prince, Morton (1854-1929)** American psychiatrist, who described cases of multiple personality.

**principle** 1. A working hypothesis or a maxim used in guiding conduct. 2. A guideline or canon of scientific investigation. 3. A fundamental law or statement of a unity in nature. 4. The essential ingredient of a substance which produces its characteristic reaction.

**principle, constancy** (S. Freud) The proposition that the mental apparatus attempts to maintain excitation at the lowest or at a constant level. The mind strives towards rest or repose and, when excited, acts so as to remove the excitation and thus return to a quiescent state. Freud's constancy principle corresponds to homeostasis.

**principle, homeopathic** See *principle. isopathic.*

**principle, interaction** See *interaction principle.*

**principle, isopathic** (E. Jones) A term to describe the process in which the cause of something can cure its effect, i.e. guilt caused by hate is relieved with the expression of that hate.

**principle of color conversion** (H. Helson) In any viewing situation there is established a level of adaptation such that objects with reflectances (luminances) above adaptation level are tinged with the hue of the illuminant, objects below adaptation level are tinged with the after-image complementary to the hue of the illuminant, while objects near, or at, adaptation level are either achromatic or are of weak or uncertain chromaticity.

**principle of dynamogenesis** See *dynamogenesis, principle of.*

**principle of inertia** (F. Alexander) The same principle as that of repetition-compulsion, but with stress laid upon the fact that the tendency to automatic action is greater than activity which involves constantly changing and active mental efforts.

**principle of interdependence** The basic format for the Piotrowski interpretation of Rorschach data predicated on the application of logical relationships between Rorschach components. It is similar, but not identical, to the configuration principle following more closely along lines such as would be found in the programming of a computer.

**principle of intimacy**   See *intimacy, principle of.*

**principle of least energy expenditure**   See *least action, law of.*

**principle of reduced cue**   See *reduced cue, principle of.*

**principle, phylogenetic**   The doctrine which holds that the individual tends in the course of his own development to exhibit behaviors that repeat the history of his species; ontogeny (individual development) recapitulates phylogeny (species development).

**principle, pleasure**   See *pleasure principle.*

**principle, pleasure-pain**   (psychoanalysis) Bipolar principle that people attempt to seek pleasure and avoid pain. The stimulation of the organism by inner or external forces causes disbalance of energy or tension. Tension is experienced as unpleasure or pain, and the instinctual forces press for an immediate discharge of energy so as to re-establish the equilibrium that existed previously. The discharge of energy brings relief and is experienced by the individual as pleasure or gratification of the instinctual demands. The perfect pleasure is the perfectly balanced state of the organism.

**prior entry, law of**   The principle that of two perceived stimuli, one attended to and the other not, the stimulus that is attended to will be perceived as having been introduced significantly sooner than the other.

**prism**   A wedge-shaped lens possessing the property to refract or bend light waves passing through it so that the light waves are broken down into their component wave lengths, resulting in the spectrum, or band, of colors.

**prism diopter**   (optics) The strength of a prism measured by 100 times the tangent of the angle through which the light waves are refracted.

**prison neurosis**   See *chronophobia.*

**prison psychosis**   See *psychosis, prison.*

**privation**   A condition of an involuntary lack of the means necessary for the satisfaction of a need.

**privileged communication**   A legal, medical, or psychotherapeutic document or recorded statement which is not accessible to public inspection. The communication between psychiatrists and psychologists and their patients or clients is privileged communication.

**proactive inhibition**   See *inhibition, proactive.*

**probabilism**   The position that it is possible to make predictions of future events through the use of logical operations in a rational and empirical study of past experience. A one-to-one correspondence between cause and effect is not assumed; rather, it is assumed that predictions with validity can be made within the limits of mathematical probability.

**probabilistic functionalism**   A theoretical approach holding that behavior is best understood in terms of its probable success in attaining goals.

**probabilities, complementary**   The sum of the probabilities that an event occurs and does not occur, given by the formula: $p + q = 100$ where $p$ is the probability that an event accurs and $q$ that it does not occur.

**probability**   1. (mathematics) The degree to which it is likely that an event will occur as opposed to alternate events which might occur. The formula most often used is

$$P(A) = \frac{\#(A)}{\#(S)}$$

where *(P)A* refers to the probability of event *A*. *#(A)* is the number of outcomes in event *A* and *#(S)* is the total number of outcomes in the entire population of the experiment. 2. The quality of being probable, or likely of occurring. 3. See *probability theory.*

**probability, conditional**   The relative frequency with which one event occurs as dependent upon the occurrence of another event.

**probability curve**   A normal frequency curve unless otherwise qualified.

**probability function**   The relation that is graphed in a normal frequency curve.

**probability integral**   1. The integral of the probability function. 2. The area falling below the normal frequency curve between two given abscissa points.

**probability learning**   In choice behavior the probability of a response tends to approach the probability of the reinforcement.

**probability matching**   In a choice situation in which the only discriminative stimulus is the reinforcement or lack of reinforcement of the previous trial the probability of a subject's responses come to match the probability of the reinforcement.

**probability of response**   The actual frequency of occurrence of a response in relation to the theoretical maximum frequency of that response under a specified set of stimulus conditions.

**probability ratio**   The ratio obtained by dividing the number of circumstances under which an event could occur by the total number of events that could occur in a certain defined set. It is written: $P/Q$.

**probability sampling**   See *sampling, random.*

**probability table**   A table which gives the frequency with which a given variable will probably occur given certain specified conditions.

**probability theory**   The treatment of probability, the science of measuring or predicting chance, in mathematics based upon the postulates regarding the uniformity of nature, laws of change, equality of opportunity of occurrence of events, and the cancellation of complementary errors with sufficient observations.

**probable error (PE)**   The index of a measure is variability derived in terms of the extent to which the obtained values of the measure deviate from the mean of the measure. The probable error is equal to

0.6745 of the standard error, half of the deviations from the mean falling within ± 1 probable error.

**proband** In genetic family trait studies, the original cases which must be representative of the trait in question that are the starting points of the family study.

**probation** A period of time in which a person is allowed to prove his ability to meet set requirements whether of achievement or of conformity to social regulations.

**probe technique** Common method to measure short term retention. A series of items are presented to the subject, who is tested on only one of them. At the time of the presentation the subject does not know which item will be tested.

**problem behavior** 1. Behavior perplexing to the observer or to the actor. 2. Behavior which creates a problem for the actor or others due to the antisocial or abnormal nature of the behavior.

**problem box** A box which must be opened in order to receive a reward. The opening of the box requires the successful manipulation of the fastenings.

**problem checklist** A self-report form consisting of various situations that often give rise to concern (sex, academic, vocational achievement), the subject being asked to check those items he feels are particularly pressing for him.

**problem child** See *child, problem.*

**problem, double alternation** An experimental situation in which the strategy for maximum success requires the subject to respond twice in one way and then to respond twice in another way. No extroceptive stimulus or cue is used to signal the response alternation.

**problem solving** The process involved in the determination of the correct sequence of alternatives leading to a desired goal.

**proceeding** (H. A. Murray) The physiologist's basic data or unit of observation consisting of interaction of sufficient duration to include the important elements of a particular behavioral sequence.

**process, analytic** In psychoanalysis as a psychotherapeutic method, includes establishing the analytic situation, the growth and interpreting of the transference neurosis and the working through of the end phase. The regression in the treatment resulting in the emergence of unresolved childhood conflicts and in their eventual resolution allows for greater maturity, mastery and insight on the part of the patient.

**process, interpersonal** The quality of psychotherapy characterized by the attitudes, affects, etc. of the patient and psychotherapist towards each other which are not products of the transference or countertransference.

**process, mental** 1. Action of an organism which involves the mind. 2. The phenomena of mental life.

**process, primary** The mental process in the id by which there is immediate and direct satisfaction of libidinal or instinctual wishes. Primary processes are unconscious and include such irrational elements as condensation, distortion, displacement, etc.

**process schizophrenia** See *schizophrenia, process.*

**process, secondary** (psychoanalysis) The activity of the conscious part of the psyche which determines and governs the ego activity that will be used in order to satisfy instinctual impulses.

**process, unconscious** The mental processes which exist at the unconscious level.

**process variable, hypothetical** See *variable hypothetical process.*

**processing error** An error which is introduced into the data in the process of producing, collecting, or analyzing.

**processomania** A term for mania for litigation introduced by Bianchi.

**prochlorperazine** Compasine, a tranquilizer.

**procreation** The biological processes of reproduction of the species.

**prodigy** A person manifesting any outstanding trait, ability, or quality, especially at an early age.

**prodrome** Early warning sign or symptom of an oncoming disease.

**product, informational** (J. P. Guilford) A parameter of the structure of intellect, it is the formal aspect of information, by which it is classified in six categories—units, classes, relations, systems, transformations, and implications.

**product matrix** See *matrix, product.*

**product moment** In correlation technique, the deviations from the means of the variables, or from some other measure as origin, raised to a power, multiplied and summated.

**product moment correlation** (r) See *correlation, product moment.*

**product, scalar** See *scalar product.*

**product scale** An original scale consisting of a series of products or performances that are assigned numbers representing merit against which the performance or product of a subject is judged, his performance being given the number of the standard performance it most closely resembles.

**production methods** (psychophysics) The subject directly manipulates the stimuli so they reflect a specified subjective relation.

**productive character orientation** (E. Fromm) A life style characterized by an interest in people and things and by giving rather than taking.

**profession** An occupation which requires general and specialized education at a high level and which generally has some code of ethics defining the role the profession should play in society.

**professional code** A set of ethical principles

adopted by a professional group to serve as a guide-line for the performance of the respective members.

**proficiency** An ability of a certain degree, usually of a high degree, that is necessary for the performance of a task or the involvement in a vocation.

**profile analysis** A procedure used in assessing an individual's uniqueness and trait organization which consists of establishing patterns of traits in the profile of the individual.

**profile chart** A curve which unites points depicting the individual's scores on various measures, the various scores having been made comparable by a statistical treatment.

**profile test** See *test, profile.*

**progeria** A kind of dwarfism combined with infantile traits and premature senility.

**progesterone** A hormone secreted by the ovaries which prepares the uterus lining for pregnancy.

**prognathous** A term describing a skull which is characterized by the protrusion of the upper jaw beyond the plane of the forehead.

**prognosis** A prediction of the outcome of an activity or process, especially of a disease or mental disorder, including an indication of the duration, severity, and course.

**prognostic test** See *test, prognostic.*

**program** A list of coded instructions for the computer which are necessary to solve a problem.

**programmed learning** See *learning, programmed.*

**programming** A method of preparing a computer to perform certain operations on data fed into the machine by instructing the computer in "language" which it can read and understand.

**progression, law of** (J. Delboeuf) The proposition that successive increments of sensation increase in an arithmetic progression while the corresponding stimulus increments increase in a geometric progression.

**progressive matrices test** See *test, progressive matrices.*

**progressive relaxation** See *relaxation, progressive.*

**project** A planned undertaking or procedure, with a well worked-out field but not necessarily a fully defined goal.

**projection** 1. (anatomy) A protruding part. 2. The transmission of nerve impulses to specific areas of the cerebral cortex from lower centers. 3. The attribution of one's faults to others. 4. (testing) The perception of one's needs and goals in unstructured stimuli. 5. (psychoanalysis) Projection is a defense mechanism diametrically opposed to introjection. It is an externalization of wishes that leads to paranoid distortion of reality. The primitive, archaic ego draws a line between "something to be swallowed," which is pleasurable, and "something to be spit out," which is unpleasurable. What was "inside" was believed to be a part of the ego, and what was spit out becomes an alien body. When the weak ego harbors desires and feelings that invite the superego's harsh disapproval, the ego may ascribe them to the outer world. Forbidden homosexual impulses are a case in point, for most homosexuals "project" their homosexual urges and believe that other people of the same sex desire them. Neurotic and psychotic individuals, who cannot admit their own hostility will frequently ascribe it to others in delusions of persecution.

**projection fibers** Neurons which lead into and away from sensory areas.

**projection, impersonal** Attributing one's unobjectionable, impersonal or neutral actions or qualities to another.

**projection, optical** 1. The formation of an image of an object using an optical instrument such as a slide projector. 2. The objective referent of sensation in the environment. 3. The localization of objects in space which correspond to the image on the retina as determined by the refractive mechanism of the eye.

**projective doll play** See *doll play, projective.*

**projective play** Play in which the child using play materials such as dolls and a doll house, expresses unconscious ideas, attitudes, and feelings that the child would otherwise be unable to express and that are useful in coming to an understanding of the dynamics of the child.

**projective techniques** Methods used to discover an individual's attitudes, motivations, defensive maneuvers and characteristic ways of responding through analysis of their responses to unstructured, ambiguous stimuli.

**prolactin** A pituitary hormone associated with the secretion of milk.

**prolegomena** A lengthy and detailed introduction to a scholarly work or course of study.

**proliferation** A multiplication of cells in a living body, especially through cell division.

**prolonged sleep treatment** See *sleep treatment, prolonged.*

**promiscuity** Non-selectivity in social or sexual intercourse.

**prompting method** See *method, prompting.*

**pronation** Movement into a prone position, especially a movement of the hand orienting the hand downward.

**proof** Facts, evidence or valid generalizations which convincingly support a proposition. Proof may be inductive, reasoning from the particular to the general, or deductive, reasoning from the general to the specific.

**propaganda** Actions or expressed opinions of individuals or groups which are actively organized in an attempt to influence the actions or opinions of other individuals or groups.

**propaganda analysis** See *analysis, propaganda.*

**propensity** **1.** An hypothesized strong and persistent characteristic of a person, from hereditary sources or from habit, which leads or inclines the person to certain goal-seeking behavior. **2.** (W. McDougall) A substitution for instinct to avoid difficulties with the latter term. **3.** (R. B. Cattell) A disposition permitting the individual to acquire certain behaviors more readily than others. The dispositions may be innate or acquired. See *erg; metanerg.*

**proper subset** See *subset, proper.*

**prophecy formula** (statistics) A formula used in the estimation of scores expected on some future measurement.

**prophylaxis** The prevention of disease or disorder through the use of systematic measures.

**proposition** **1.** A formulation of a plan or procedure to be acted upon. **2.** (logic) A verbal or symbolic statement which is offered to be tested for truth.

**propositional speech** Speech which is characterized by the meaning yielded from relationships among the words as opposed to the meaning yielded from the addition of the distinct words.

**proprioception** The sense of body position and movements.

**proprioceptive cues** Cues which are sensitive to body position or movement.

**proprioceptive sensation** See *sensation, proprioceptive.*

**proprioceptor** A receptor which is sensitive to the position and movement of the body and its limbs which include: (1) receptors sensitive to the body's orientation in space, and to body rotation which are located in the vestibule of the inner ear and in the semicircular canals; and (2) receptors which are sensitive to the position and movement of body members, giving rise to kinesthetic sensations, located in the muscles, tendons, and joints.

**proprium** (G. W. Allport) Aspects of the personality which seem peculiarly individual and collectively constitute the individual's uniqueness and sense of individuality.

**prosencephalon** The forebrain.

**Proshansky, Harold M.** (1920- ) American psychologist. Began his research in social perception working with Gardner Murphy and Otto Klineberg. Carried out the first systematic attempt to use an especially designed projective technique to measure a social attitude. Subsequently continued to do research on perception, attitude changes, and ethnic prejudice. Most significant contribution came as a result of his collaboration with W. H. Ittelson and L. Rivlin in their pioneering research in the definition of the field of environmental psychology. Since 1958 has developed with Ittelson and Rivlin a behavioral mapping technique for the study of how individuals use physical space, and continues to carry out research with respect to such physical settings as hospitals, family settings, and others. See *environmental psychology.*

**prosthesis** An artificial device substituting for a missing part of the body such as, e.g., an amputated leg.

**protanopia** Partial color blindness; inability to distinguish between blue-green and red.

**protein** A complex nitrogeneous substance of high molecular weight which is found in different forms in animals and plants and is a characteristic of living matter.

**protensity** The attribute of a mental process characterized by its temporality or movement forward in time.

**protest, masculine** (A. Adler) Submission to inferiority is feminine, rebellion against it is masculine. The rebellion against inferiority, whether experienced by men or women, was called by Adler "masculine protest." The masculine protest is a universal and normal compensatory mechanism.

**prothetic** (S. S. Stevens) A sensory continuum in which just noticeable differences are thought not to be subjectively equal. It is suggested that the physiological processes underlying sensory discrimination for prothetic continua involve the addition of neural excitation to ongoing neural activity. Two prothetic continua are brightness and loudness; apparently it is the Stevens' power law that relates stimulus energy to subjective sensation.

**protocol sentences** (L. J. J. Wittgenstein) A fundamental concept in logical positivism, first introduced by Wittgenstein in 1921. The protocol sentences, also called basic statements, represent simple names of simple objects arranged in a most simple order. R. Carnap assumed that these sentences describe what is given in immediate sensory experience; thus they need no further explanation. They can be expressed in any form of language. O. Neurath maintained that these protocol sentences must be conveyed in an intersubjective language.

**protoneuron** A most primitive nerve unit which hypothetically exists in lower organisms which have no nervous system. Protoneurons transmit impulses indiscriminately, in all possible directions.

**protoplasm** The essential substance of living cells.

**prototaxic; prototaxic mode** (H. S. Sullivan) The first and earliest mode of experience characteristic of an infant which is undifferentiated, global, unorganized. It consists of changing momentary states which are unformulated and incommunicable.

**prototype** **1.** (biology) The earliest, aboriginal type. **2.** The original pattern from which other patterns evolved.

**protozoa** (biology) Most primitive organisms; some of them are unicellar, some multi-nucleic organisms or colonies.

**proverb test** See *test, proverb.*

**proximal variable** See *stimulus, proximal.*

**proximity principle** (Gestalt) Wertheimer distinguished several determinants in the organization of perception, among them proximity, similarity and closure. Proximity of dots to one another determines their perception as a figure.

**proximo-distal trunk** The development of the body proceeds from the center toward its distant parts; e.g. the shoulders develop before the arms, the arms grow before the hands.

**pruritus, psychogenic** An irritating itching of psychogenic origin in which an inhibited sexual excitement is a dynamic factor.

**PSE** See *point of subjective equality.*

**psellism** Speech defect; stammering.

**pseudo conditioning** See *conditioning, pseudo.*

**pseudoamentive syndrome in childhood schizophrenia** (B. B. Wolman) The most severe level of childhood schizophrenia, corresponding roughly to the dementive level of schizophrenia in adults. In the most severe cases, development is stopped before it had a chance to start; motor coordination, metabolism, sleep and waking states, food intake, speech and mental development are affected.

**pseudogeusia** False perception of taste.

**pseudohypertrophic muscular dystrophy** See *dystrophy, pseudohypertrophic muscular.*

**pseudohypoparathyroidism** Failure of venal tubes to respond to parathyroid hormone. Symptoms include hypocalcemia, mental retardation and skeletal deformities.

**pseudologia fantastica** Morbid extensive fabrication aimed at self-aggrandizement, easily renounced when confronted with facts.

**pseudomental deficiencies** Conditions simulating mental deficiency in which there is a deficit in intellectual development and inadequate behavior which are not the result of poor innate intellectual endowment. A combination of factors such as auditory or visual handicaps and emotional disturbances may interfere with intellectual development to the point that the child appears mentally defective.

**pseudonomania** The impulse to falsify.

**pseudoscope** An optical instrument which transposes the visual images so that what is normally seen by the left eye is seen by the right and vice versa and which inverts distance relations so that hollow objects appear solid and solid objects appear hollow.

**psi process** (parapsychology) The intra-individual mental processes, unable to be described in terms of presently accepted natural laws, which are involved in the ability to send or receive telepathic messages.

**psoriasis** A skin disease characterized by chronic inflammation, red patches with white scales which is of organic or psychogenic origin. The psychogenic causes relate to wishes for exhibitionism which are punished.

**psychalgia** Experiencing pain without an organic cause.

**psychasthenia** (P. Janet) Janet divided all neuroses into hysterias and psychasthenias; psychasthenia included anxiety stages, phobias and obsessions.

**psyche** Mind, self, soul; the spiritual as distinct from the bodily nature of persons.

**psychedelic drugs** Drugs which produce a mental state characterized by an 'expanded' sense of consciousness, extreme feelings of despair or euphoria and sometimes concomitant perceptual distortions and hallucinations.

**psychergograph** An apparatus designed for the measurement of fatigue and discrimination, used for submission of a series of new stimuli for the discrimination as soon as a correct response was made to a former stimulus. Also called serial discrimeter.

**psychiatric criminology** A branch of psychiatry devoted to the study, diagnosis, treatment, and prevention of mentally abnormal criminals. Psychiatric criminology is also related to the study of the legal aspects of crime and the judicial and penitentiary systems.

**psychiatric interview** Usually, the initial interview with a patient to be admitted for treatment in a public or private ambulatory or confined setting. The aim of the psychiatric interview is to establish a tentative diagnosis of the disorder.

**psychiatric nosology** A classification of mental disorders.

**psychiatric nursing** A specialty in nursing. A psychiatric nurse is a registered nurse who has received advanced training in clinical psychiatry and holds, usually, an M.A. degree. Most frequently a psychiatric field nurse plays the role of a ward administrator and mother-surrogate to hospitalized patients, and assists the psychiatrists in all aspects of psychiatric treatment.

**psychiatric social examination** See *examination, psychiatric social.*

**psychiatric social work** A social work specialty devoted to mental disorders emphasizing the role of community and family life on the origin of mental disorders and their prevention.

**psychiatric social worker** A social worker who specializes in dealing with mentally disturbed people. Psychiatric social workers work in mental hospitals and clinics, conduct field studies, visit the families of the patients, place patients in institutions and homes and administer intake interviews related to the social background and etiology of mental disorders. A great many psychiatric social workers take an active part in the psychotherapeutic process either jointly with psychiatrists and clinical psychologists or independently.

**psychiatrist** A physician who specializes in the diagnosis and treatment of mental disorders using physical, chemical or psychological methods. Psychiatrists work in mental hospitals, clinics, and private practice, as well as in public mental health and research.

**psychiatry** Psychiatry started as a medical specialty related to the study, diagnosis, treatment and prevention of organic and non-organic mental disorders. Psychiatry today includes a variety of scientific disciplines such as endocrinology, biochemistry, genetics, neuropathology, psychoanalysis, psychopharmacology, psychopathology, sociology, and various theories of normal and abnormal behavior, and it deals with problems related to public mental health, social and community problems and a host of research problems in several aspects of medicine, psychology, and the social sciences.

**psychiatry, child**   A branch of psychiatry devoted to the study, diagnosis, treatment and prevention of mental disorders in children and adolescents.

**psychiatry, community**   A branch of social psychiatry applied to cooperation with communities and prevention of mental disorders. Community psychiatry deals with the establishment of mental health centers, clinics and after-care institutions.

**psychiatry, forensic**   The field of applied psychology or psychiatry which concerns itself with legal, judicial, or correctional procedures. The focus of clinical expertise is typically on such matters as the determination of responsibility or sanity of a defendant in a criminal trial, suitability for guardianship or custody of a child in divorce proceedings, commitment of an incompetent to a state mental hospital, recommendation for parole of an offender, etc.

**psychiatry, hospital**   A branch of psychiatry related to establishing, directing and reforming institutionalized treatment of mental disorders. The main areas of research of hospital psychiatry are the conversion of custodial type hospitals in therapeutic centers and the development of new methods of treatment and staff-patient relationships in mental hospitals.

**psychiatry, pastoral**   1. A branch of psychiatry related to religion. 2. Psychiatric type counseling with mental patients, conducted by clergymen.

**psychiatry, political**   A study of psychopathological phenomena in public life.

**psychiatry, psychoanalytic**   A branch of psychiatry which applies psychoanalytic principles and techniques to the study, diagnosis, treatment and prevention of mental disorders.

**psychiatry, social**   The study of social and cultural factors of mental disorders. Social psychiatric research encompasses ethnology, cultural anthropology, sociology, social psychology, mental hygiene, community psychiatry, hospital psychiatry, language and communication and several other ancillary disciplines. Social psychiatry studies the roles of sex, socioeconomic class, ethnic group, ecology and their impact on the etiology and choice of symptoms in various types of behavior disorders, as well as the epidemiology of mental disorders.

**psychic**   1. Related to psyche, mind. 2. (parapsychology) An individual or an object believed to be involved with supernatural, spiritual powers.

**psychic apparatus**   See *apparatus, mental.*

**psychic determinism**   A belief that the entire overt and covert behavior can be presented as a chain of causes and effects.

**psychic impotence**   1. Pathological temporary inability to perform actions and mental activity ordinarily performed.   2. Impotence resulting from psychological factors.

**psychic inadequacy**   See *inadequacy, psychic.*

**psychic isolation**   See *isolation, psychic.*

**psychic research**   (parapsychology) Study of supranatural phenomena such as occultism, extrasensory perception and telepathy.

**psychical satiation**   See *satiation, psychical.*

**psychoacoustics**   A discipline that links physics and psychology which deals with the physical phenomena of sound as related to audition, as well as with the physiology and psychology of sound receptor processes.

**psychoactive agent**   1. Psychotropic drug.   2. A chemical substance that affects the mind. A mood altering drug; a drug that alters states of consciousness.

**psychoanalysis**   A scientific approach to the study of human functioning, normal and abnormal, originated by Sigmund Freud and expanded in method, form, content, theory, and application by him and his followers.

Psychoanalysis is (1) a particular method of investigating the mind; (2) a systematic body of knowledge arrived at by use of a specific method, accompanied by a gradually evolving body of theory which has expanded, particularly with the development of ego psychology, from an early preoccupation with psychopathology into a general psychology; (3) a specific method of treatment of psychological disorders.

1. The psychoanalytic method of investigation is designed to bring about accessibility to the unconscious process in the patient in a setting which enables him to master, through insight, the forces hitherto totally unknown to him which have seriously impaired his ability to feel and to function satisfactorily in his life situation. By the use of free association, the reclining position, the benevolent but neutral attitude of the analyst, the frustration of infantile wishes in relation to the analyst, and the requirement that the patient will verbalize what he might otherwise carry out in action, regression is brought about in relation to the analyst. This, encouraged by the analyst's interventions to remove resistances (consisting mostly of ego defenses), facilitates the appearance of the transference neurosis, together with the therapeutic alliance. The latter may be described as the effect of a split in the patient's ego, whose healthy part enables him to ally himself with the analyst in an attempt to elicit the unconscious, regressive memories and experiences which come to consciousness in the transference neurosis. Dreams, fantasies, behavior, thought processes, cognitive and affective processes are made comprehensible through interpretation, the basic tool of psychoanalysis.

The process of working-through, a repetition and

elaboration of the relationship between the present and the past, results in the final resolution of the terminal phase of analysis.

2. The psychoanalytic body of knowledge has been refined and reformulated into a general theory called *metapsychology*. The facets of metapsychology are (1) the dynamic, referring to the constantly active interplay of forces within the individual; (2) the economic, referring to the shifts of psychic energy; (3) the genetic, which means the instinctual and ego developmental sequences culminating in the formation of the individual personality; (4) the structural, referring to the characteristics and interactions within and between the id, ego, and superego, and the adaptive. Certain analysts might add the topographical aspect, the unconscious, preconscious, and conscious characteristics of psychic functioning, but others would maintain that these terms can apply to each one of the metapsychological concepts, and therefore cannot be put into a separate category.

3. Psychoanalysis as a therapy has been most effective in its purest form in the treatment of psychoneurotic individuals who are capable of the therapeutic split of the ego and the alliance with the analyst described above, who are sufficiently intelligent to grasp the interpretations presented to them, and whose life situation is not so irreversibly traumatic as to be impervious to change. It is also necessary for individuals in analysis to have a sufficiently intact ego to be able to synthesize their insights so as to formulate and independently carry out their own individual way of life.

The consistent handling of the transference and the analysis of resistances are the main elements of the psychoanalytic technique. The increasing knowledge of ego psychology, especially concerning early developmental phases, has provided new means of strengthening the ego, neutralizing aggression and preparing otherwise inaccessible patients for a closer approach to psychoanalytic treatment proper. Improved methods and extra-analytic devices (parameters) have been applied especially in psychoanalytically-oriented psychotherapy. The aim of all types of psychoanalytic treatment is to enable the patient to develop the capacity to love, to work effectively, and to function in society with a well-defined and satisfying sense of identity.

**psychoanalysis, didactic** Psychoanalysis of an individual in fulfillment of requirements to become a psychoanalyst.

**psychoanalysis, direct** (J. Rosen) A method of psychotherapy, used primarily with schizophrenics, characterized by an attempt to convey to the patient the therapist's ability to fully understand what is going on in the patient's mind. This is accomplished through direct interpretation of the patient's behavior, letting him know in definitive terms how the therapist sees his behavior.

**psychoanalysis, interactional** (B. B. Wolman) A modification of psychoanalytic theory and technique. This theory introduced the concept of interindividual cathexis and the driving force called Lust for Life, divided in two instinctual drives, Eros (love) and Ares (destructiveness). The interactional

psychotherapeutic technique is based on explicit manipulation of transference viewed as interindividual cathexis and on search for identity.

**psychoanalysis, transactional** (E. Berne) A theoretical and treatment approach which emphasizes the levels of interactions and communications within a person and among individuals. The levels in interactions in a person are denoted "adult," "parent," and "child"; therapy consists in analyzing the origin and development of these levels and in determining ways to integrate them within the personality.

**psychoanalyst** A psychiatrist or clinical psychologist who is fully trained in the theory and practice of psychoanalysis and who employs these principles in treatment.

**psychoanalytic group psychotherapy** See *psychotherapy, psychoanalytic group.*

**psychoanalytic psychiatry** See *psychiatry, psychoanalytic.*

**psychoanalytic psychology** See *psychology, psychoanalytic.*

**psychoanalytic psychotherapy** See *psychotherapy, psychoanalytic.*

**psychobiogram** (E. Kretschmer) A means of investigating the personality, the first two parts consisting of data relating to the individual's history and heredity and the other parts consisting of data relating to the individual's temperament, social attitudes, physical findings, intelligence, etc.

**psychobiology** (A. Meyer) An organismic approach to the study and treatment of normal and abnormal behavior which emphasizes the holistic functioning of the individual in his environment.

**psychodiagnosis, automated** The diagnosis of mental disorders using machinery which elicits and records the diagnostic information.

**psychodiagnostics** The use of the individual's behavior and results on psychological tests for the study of the individual's personality.

**psychodometer** A mechanical device utilizing a tuning fork, which is used in the measurement of response time.

**psychodrama** (J. L. Moreno) A projective technique and form of group psychotherapy in which a person is asked to act out meaningful situations in the presence of people who act as auxiliary egos confronting the person on various issues, the therapist, and the audience. Each member of this drama has specific functions designed to help the subject understand himself and to act spontaneously which facilitates self-understanding.

**psychodynamics, adaptational** (S. Rado) A system of psychoanalytic psychotherapy which emphasizes the need to counter the regressive trend in psychoanalytic treatment with a force toward progression. That is, in psychoanalytic treatment, the patient, following a regressive trend, tends to parentify the therapist. In this system, the therapist counters this trend by not allowing himself to be pushed into the role of parent, thus bolstering the patient's self-confidence. There is an emphasis on understanding the patient in terms of motivation and control, the cultural context, and background and life-history.

**psychoepistemology** (J. P. Guilford) Basic kinds of information as distinguished in the structure of intellect in terms of interactions of kinds of content and kinds of products.

**psychogalvanic response; psychogalvanic reflex** See *galvanic skin response.*

**psychogalvanometer** Lie detector.

**psychogenesis.** 1.Having psychological origins; developing from a thought or idea; generated by the mind, as for example, a psychogenic disorder. **2.** Having psychological determinants.

**psychogenic disorder** A functional disorder having no observable organic basis which is probably due to emotional conflict or stress.

**psychogeusia** Perception of taste.

**psychognosis** Diagnosis of mental state.

**psychokinesis; psychokinesia; PK** (parapsychology) The hypothetical ability of an individual to directly influence the movement or condition of an inanimate object or of a physical system without any known physical or sensory mediation.

**psycholagny** Fantasy that causes sexual arousal.

**psycholepsis; psycholepsy** A sudden and intense decrease in one's normal level of mental tension, resulting in depression, which is generally associated with individuals who are emotionally unstable.

**psycholinguistics** The investigation and study of the relationships between the language spoken by an individual or group and the characteristics of the individual or group.

**psychological examination** See *examination, psychological.*

**psychological field** See *life space.*

**psychological scale** See *scale, psychological.*

**psychological space** See *life space.*

**psychological test** See *examination, psychological.*

**psychological warfare** A general concept which refers to the total attempt to lower the ability of the enemy to wage war by weakening his morale, and to raise one's own ability to wage war.

**psychologist** A psychologist, whatever his specific field, has two roles of a professional man and scientist. As a professional psychologist he holds a job and earns a living, and as a scientist he is interested in expanding the knowledge of behavior and in developing theories which will provide interpretation of this knowledge. The number of vocational settings in which the professional psychologist may find himself is quite large. He may find himself at a school,

prison, hospital, clinic, in business, the military, or government.

Traditionally, psychology is an academic subject. Most psychologists teach in a college or university, devoting themselves to teaching and research. Depending on particular circumstances, the proportion of time devoted to both areas varies greatly. Typically, the psychologist teaches three to four courses, and spends the rest of his time carrying on research, either on his own, or with the cooperation and assistance of his colleagues and students. He may also spend some of his time in the administrative problems involved in departmental education. Other psychologists have their primary appointment as members of a hospital or clinic. The duties of the clinical psychologist often are more varied than those of the academic psychologist. Again, depending on individual circumstances, the clinical psychologist may do either research, or therapy, or a combination of both. Very often the clinical psychologist also holds a position as a member of the staff at a college; either one associated with the hospital or clinic at which he works, or at a nearby university. In some cases his primary appointment is in the university, and his secondary post is in a guidance clinic or hospital operated by the school.

An increasing number of psychologists work directly for industry or as a part of the military. In such a position they may involve themselves with the various problems of training, selection, morale, social relations, or the adaptation of equipment to the capacities of the human operator, or any of the other problems involving human factors that industry or the military may encounter. Like his colleagues, the industrial or military psychologist may hold a secondary appointment with a nearby college or university.

**psychologist, consultant** A psychologist who professionally helps organizations with their psychological problems.

**psychologist, consulting** A psychologist who professionally helps individuals with problems of vocational, educational, and maladjustment nature.

**psychologist, school** A psychologist specializing in problems associated with elementary and secondary educational systems, who utilizes psychological concepts and methods in programs or actions which attempt to improve learning conditions for students. Such actions include counseling teachers and students, diagnostic testing in areas of personality and scholastic ability, designing more efficient and psychologically sound classroom situations, and acting as a catalyst for teacher involvement in reforms and innovations.

**psychology** Psychology is the science of human and animal behavior. Behavior is part of the totality of life processes. Life processes include metabolism, growth, decline, digestion, elimination, circulation. These physiological processes and especially those related to the nervous and glandular systems, form the foundation of behavior. Behavior means the action of the organism as a whole. When an organism runs for life, his various organs, such as the heart, lungs, muscles, are involved. The study of the structure and function of the various organs belong to physiology, but the escape from danger is an action of the organism as a whole; it is its behavior. Behavior is thus the subject matter of psychology. Behavior includes several types of action. In the first category belong the overt and observable actions of the organism, such as its reactions to external stimuli and spontaneous acts stemming from within. All organisms respond to the sight or smell of food; all organisms seek food spontaneously; all organisms fight for survival and most engage in sexual and parental activities.

Psychologists try to assess correctly what organisms do. They use observation, experimentation, measurement, and other research methods. Psychologists study first what organisms do and how they do it, but the scientific inquiry does not stop at the what and the how level. Sciences reach beyond the observable data looking for actions that are unobservable in a direct manner but which can be inferred. When a scientist sees smoke, he seeks the causes of the smoke. Astronomers discovered remote planets before they could be seen; the impact of these remote planets led scientists to assume their existence which was later proved with the help of powerful telescopes.

A similar development took place in psychology. When an experimenter applies a mild electric shock to a subject's finger, the subject withdraws the finger immediately. The observable facts are stimulus and response, but a response is not merely the result of a stimulus. Not all human beings respond in the same way to a given stimulus; some people react vehemently, while others may inhibit their response. Some severely disturbed individuals, schizophrenics, may not react at all to a stimulus which would cause pain and tears in others.

But what is pain? Physiologists study nerve centers' reaction to pain but can psychologists confine their study to facial expressions, tears, and screams? All these symptoms are the smoke that implies the existence of fire. Pain may lead to facial grimaces, tears, and screams. External observers can see the observable reactions, but only the person who experiences the pain, as it were, knows the cause of his grimaces and tears. This observation of one's own feelings and thoughts, called introspection, is associated with the name of William Wundt.

The introspective data are less objective and less reliable than data obtained by rigorous observation and experimentation. Yet it is an undeniable fact that one may be in pain even when the wound is not visible and one may experience auditory hallucinations and hear voices when no one is around. Psychologists have thus developed sophisticated research methods for objective study of those introspective, covert parts of human behavior. There is, however, also a third category of behavior, in addition to the observable and introspectionistic data. One may be unaware of one's true feelings and desires and be surprised when these hidden, unknown-to-oneself wishes lead to overt and unpredictable actions. People may be surprised by their own irrational reactions; some people forget or deny their sexual and aggressive impulses that come true in their dreams, slips of the tongue, and occasionally in uncontrollable overt actions.

The entire province of behavior which cannot be observed from without or by introspection is called unconscious or unconsciousness, and is associated with the name of Sigmund Freud.

**psychology, abnormal** Psychopathology; a branch of psychology devoted to the study of abnormal behavior; a study of behavior and personality disorders, including neuroses, psychoses, psychosomatic and organic mental disorders, and mental deficiencies.

**psychology, analytical** The system created by Carl Gustav Jung. It distinguishes three layers of the psyche: *conscious mind, personal unconscious* "comprising all acquisitions of personal life," and *collective unconscious,* not individually acquired but inherent in the specifically human psychic structure and as such the impersonal substratum of the psyche. The collective unconscious contains the *archetypes* as "determinants" or "regulators" of all psychic processes. Archetypes as such are irrepresentable patterns of behavior. Jung has used the analogy of the axial system of crystals, performing the crystalline structure in the mother liquid without material existence of its own. Archetypes manifest themselves in consciousness as *archetypal images* or ideas which are constellated by the encounter with reality, e.g. man and woman *project* on each other the contrasexual images of *anima* resp. *animus;* mother is experienced as the Great Mother, nourishing and devouring, etc.

Jung's *typology* describes two attitude types: *extra-* and *introversion,* and four function types: intellect, intuition, feeling, sensation. Attitude types as well as function types stand in a complementary relationship, e.g. where intellect is the superior (differentiated) function, feeling is inferior. This polarity creates a dynamic tension, aiming at the *union of opposites.*

The psyche is a *self-regulating system* in which conscious and unconscious stand in a compensatory relationship, the latter functioning as the regulator of the former. The unconscious has thus a potentially constructive function; the causal point of view has to be complemented by a *final point of view* which interprets psychological facts as symbolic expressions of psychic development. The *constructive/prospective* aspect of the unconscious expresses itself mainly in *dreams* (for which reason dream analysis plays a predominant role in psychotherapy). They are "the self-portrayal, in symbolical form, of the actual situation in the unconscious." *Symbols* express contents which transcend consciousness; they are the "best possible expression for a complex fact not yet clearly apprehended by consciousness" (this in contradistinction to a semeiotic use of symbols designating a known thing, as in psychoanalysis). Thus they are *transformers of energy.* The psyche aims at constantly progressing assimilation of unconscious contents, leading to the integrated personality (*process of individuation*). The center of the total personality is the *self,* in contradistinction to the *ego* as center of consciousness.

**psychology and other sciences** A considerable part of human behavior depends upon the biochemical changes in nerve cells, metabolic processes, and glandular secretion. Modern study of heredity revealed that what one inherits from his parents is largely the result of chemical processes.

Other sciences closely related to psychology are neuroanatomy and neurophysiology. Neurological studies of the structure and functions of the nervous system form an indispensable prerequisite for the understanding of human behavior. The central and autonomic parts of the nervous system control human behavior and a considerable part of abnormal behavior is caused by deficiences and diseases in the nervous system.

Also history, the science of human past, and the study of contemporary and past cultures and social systems can be of great help in understanding human nature. A psychologist versed in history, anthropology, and sociology is able to develop a broader outlook on human behavior.

The relationship between psychology and the sciences that study the organism and society is a close one. Psychology deals with the interaction between organism and environment. There is a particular area where medical science and psychology are closely interrelated. A special science of psychosomatics studies the impact of psychological factors on the organism. Peptic ulcers, for instance, are a physical disease caused by emotional disturbances.

The knowledge of psychology may prove indispensable for the understanding of social institutions and cultural issues in the past and the present. Psychology holds a key position in behavioral sciences, and is often used as a basic explanation for a variety of social phenomena. Psychology helps to explain the origin and the development of government, law, economic life, education, and mental health and at the present time psychological research is applied to all these areas.

**psychology, applied** 1. The utilization of theories and principles developed through psychology for practical ends. 2. General term for various subdivisions of psychology each of which deals with a specific practical end. These include educational psychology, vocational guidance and counseling, psychology of learning, industrial psychology, human engineering and personnel psychology. Applied psychology also includes psychotechnology which is the body of principles utilized in applied psychology and psychotechnics which deal with the specific procedures and skills of applied psychology.

**psychology, atomistic** Any system of psychology which suggests that psychological phenomena should be broken down into their component elements for investigation which exist independent of the whole and that psychology should be approached by dealing with small, simple bits of behavior or of mental content. Early behaviorism, associationism, and sensationism were atomistic psychologies.

**psychology, clinical** A branch of psychology devoted to the study, diagnosis and treatment of behavior disorders.

**psychology, comparative** A branch of psychology which deals with the comparison of behaviors of organisms of different species.

**psychology, content** F. Brentano distinguished between psychology concerned with the act of perceiving (the act psychology) and the one concerned with what is perceived (the content psychology). According to this distinction, the psychological systems of Wundt, Ebbinghaus, Titchener, et al. were content psychologies.

**psychology, correctional** The application of techniques of clinical and counseling psychology to the rehabilitation of offenders during incarceration. More broadly, the participation of psychologists in the personnel aspects of prison administration and supervision of inmate behavior and welfare.

**psychology, counseling** A branch of psychology related to clinical psychology but different in that the problems it deals with are generally of a less serious nature. Personal, as well as vocational and academic guidance is provided.

**psychology, criminal** The study of the personalities, motives, etiology and pathology of criminals as well as psychological intervention in correctional procedures and rehabilitation.

**psychology, depth** Any psychological theory which studies unconscious phenomena, e.g. psychoanalysis, individual psychology, analytical psychology.

**psychology, differential** Branch of psychology which studies individual and group psychological differences, their kind, cause, amount and consequences.

**psychology, dynamic** 1. Any psychological system which is primarily concerned with cause and effect relationships or which stresses drives and motives. 2. (R. S. Woodworth) An outgrowth of the functionalism of Dewey and James, this psychological theory is primarily concerned with the causation of behavior which is defined in terms of a dynamic factor. The living organism is interjected between the stimulus and the response. The stimulus-response relation is the mechanism of behavior but the driving power behind it is the drive that activates the mechanism. The S-R chain was modified into an S-O-R chain, O standing for the structures and functions of the organism. The concept of general motivation was introduced; the motivating drives can be organic, such as hunger or fatigue, or inorganic, such as self-assertion or curiosity. To the observable stimulus and response factors were added the drives that act as motivating forces within the organism and together with the stimuli represent the totality of factors that cause action.

**psychology, educational** A branch of psychology concerned especially with increasing the efficiency of learning by applying psychological knowledge about learning and motivation to practices and procedures in school.

**psychology, existential** A movement in psychology based on the philosophical principles of existentialism which emphasizes that each individual must exert his freedom of choice in a chaotic world. This orientation opposes the abstractions of both academic psychology and traditional psychoanalysis while emphasizing the importance of individual existence.

**psychology, experimental** 1. The use of systematic, controlled scientific methodology in the investigation of psychological phenomena. 2. The systematic presentation of the methodology and results of an experiment, usually within the context of a laboratory experiment.

**psychology, female** The psychological study of women with special reference to their particular needs, problems and experiences. There are a wide range of approaches to the field of study, ranging from orthodox psychoanalytic concepts, to K. Horney's and C. M. Thompson's, and to more recent and radical ideas which have discarded such concepts as penis envy in an attempt to develop new and nonstereotypical means of studying women.

**psychology, general** A set of psychological data and theories which apply to people in general.

**psychology, genetic** The branch of psychology which studies phenomena in terms of their hereditary origin and development.

**psychology, Gestalt** See *Gestalt psychology.*

**psychology, holistic-dynamic** (A. Maslow) Maslow's theory is based on the innate goodness of human nature. The fundamental human needs are good or neutral rather than evil. A normal development consists primarily of self-actualizing and fulfillment of the inner potentialities. Men are made bad by adverse environmental factors.

**psychology, humanistic** An offshoot of existentialism and phenomenology, the humanistic school was started by A. Maslow and A. Sutich. Humanistic psychology stresses the holistic approach, creativity and self-actualization, intentionalism, free choice and spontaneity.

**psychology, interbehavioral** (J. R. Kantor) The definition of psychology as the study of evolved interaction between the organism and the environment. The unit of study is the event consisting of the interbehavior of the organism with other organisms and objects which are existentially and structurally separate. Configurations constituting events are determined by previous interbehaviors.

**psychology, introspective** See *introspectionism.*

**psychology, mass** The study of the behavior of groups or crowds.

**psychology, military** The branch of psychology which concerns itself with psychological problems in the Armed Forces, such as selection, assignment, training, morale, and motivation of personnel, and the design of military equipment.

**psychology, operational-informational** (J. P. Guilford) An act-content system of psychology based upon the structure of intellect, in which the taxon-

omy of acts includes five basic kinds of operation, and the taxonomy of content is a psychoepistemology.

**psychology, organismic** 1. Several psychological theories stress the role of the organism in its totality and its adjustive functions. 2. (K. Goldstein) Goldstein's organismic theory is best known under the name of holism or holistic theory. 3. (J. R. Kantor) Under the influence of Adolf Meyer's psychobiology, Kantor views all actions of the organism in their totality; physical and mental functions are but two aspects of interbehavior, that is adjustive interaction between the organism and its environment. Kantor rejects the idea that psychological phenomena must be reduced to physiology. 4. (A. Angyal) Angyal introduced the concept of "biosphere" which represents a holistic unity of the organism and its environment, thus coming close to both K. Goldstein and K. Lewin. The biosphere can be divided into organism (subject) and environment (object). The biosphere has three dimensions, namely the vertical, progressive, and transverse. The vertical dimension reflects overt behavior motivated by the deeper layers of personality; the progressive dimension includes goal-directed behavior; and the transverse dimension serves the overall coordination of personality.

**psychology, pedagogical** See *psychology, educational.*

**psychology, personalistic** A psychological school that was started under the influence of Dilthey's "understanding" psychology, Windelband's concept of idiographic sciences, and Brentano's intentionality. Edward Spranger's personalistic theory combined the above mentioned three elements stressing the need to understand the unique and goal-directed patterns of every human being. These particular patterns are "personality types" and Spranger's theory evolves around the understanding of human personality. Wilhelm Stern developed a full-fledged personalistic theory, describing personality as "unitas multiplex", unity in complexity. Stern maintained that personality is comprised of traits which are organized in a particular manner, making each person unique. Gordon W. Allport represented the American school of personalism; he viewed personality traits as determinants of human behavior. A personality trait is a neuropsychic system which controls the perception of stimulus and responses to them. Personality structure is a dynamic organization of these psychological systems which determines the individual's adjustment to his environment.

**psychology, physiological** Branch of psychology which experimentally investigates the physiological bases of behavior including the anatomical structures and physiological processes which are related to psychological events, psychological process, and mental functions. The nervous system, the endocrine system, and neurological processes are central areas of concern.

**psychology, psychoanalytic** A system of psychology which applies the principles of psychoanalysis to the study of personality and behavior.

**psychology, schools of** See *schools of psychology.*

**psychology, social** The branch of psychology concerned with the study of individuals in groups. It deals with the psychological processes and interpersonal interactions in groups and between groups. The emphasis is on individual behavior rather than on the group as a unity.

**psychology, stimulus-response** A branch of psychology which focuses on determining the relationship between stimuli and responses. While central processes which may be involved in this connection may be postulated, the emphasis is usually on the objective features of the overt stimulus and response.

**psychology, structural** A school of psychology that started under the influence of W. Wundt. The subject matter of psychology is experience; the method of psychology is a specific type of observation, introspection, which is the self-observation of the experiencing individual. The mind is viewed as a sum of mental states and processes. The basic units of consciousness are sensations, images and affections. Sensations are the elements of perception, images are the elements of ideas, and affections are the elements of emotions. Each of these units can be further classified according to the attributes of quality, intensity, duration, and clearness except for affections for which clearness has no meaning. Questions concerning these mental processes can be posed by asking "what," "how," and "why." "What" and "how" seek to describe mental phenomena, "what" deals with facts, and "how" with combinations of facts and their interrelationships. In order to answer "why" physiological parallels of psychological phenomena must be investigated. The primary aim of psychology, however, is to analyze the structure of the mind, the morphological aspects rather than to investigate the function of mental processes. This school of thought was dominant in Germany and the United States until the 1920's when Functionalism and Behaviorism were introduced.

**psychology, topological** (K. Lewin) A descriptive psychological system using the terms of the formal relationships of the geometrical system known as topology. Using the theoretical relationships among the various terms, empirically testable hypotheses are generated.

**psychology, understanding** (W. Dilthey) The main object of the natural sciences is to explain (*erklären*), but the task of psychology is to understand (*verstehen*). Psychological research must deal with the human mind as a whole, and understand the totality of life in human inner experience. Psychology is a humanistic science (*Geisteswissenschaf*) in contradistinction to the empirical, natural sciences. According to Dilthey, psychology should be the foundation of all humanistic sciences such as the study of religion, law, economics and political science, for "all cultural systems . . . can be understood only in terms of the mind."

**psychomathematics** The use of certain mathematical formulas to work out variations of human personality and abilities.

**psychometric constant delta** Δ A constant in the method of constant stimuli, the product of $h$ times $I$, $h$ being equal to $\dfrac{1}{\sigma\sqrt{2}}$ and $I$ being equal to a constant of the individual observer.

**psychometric examination** See *examination, psychometric.*

**psychometric function** A mathematical formula which expresses the relation between the quantitative variation in a stimulus and the judgments of a subject who is reporting about the stimulus.

**psychometry** 1. The measurement of individual differences in behavior. 2. (parapsychology) The alleged process of obtaining information concerning a human event by touching an object related to the event.

**psychomotor attack** Form of epileptic seizure characterized by short attacks of extreme motor activity, sometimes violent, of which the individual has no subsequent recollection, and which usually originates in the temporal lobe. Lesions of the posterior inferior surface, the lateral part, or the insula of the frontal lobe can also initiate the seizure.

**psychomotor center** The area of the cerebrum which is involved in the control of movement that is psychically rather than extra-psychically or organically determined.

**psychomotor retardation** The slowing down of psychomotor reactions.

**psychomotor tests** See *tests, psychomotor.*

**psychoneural parallelism** The proposition which holds that there is a corresponding neural activity for every conscious or mental event.

**psychoneurosis** See *neurosis.*

**psychoneurotic schizophrenia** See *schizophrenia, psychoneurotic.*

**psychonomics** 1. A term for psychic laws. 2. (rare) The study of environmental factors in relation to psychological development.

**psychonosology** The classification of mental disorders.

**psychopath, constitutional** An old term for antisocial personality.

**psychopathology** The study of mental, that is, behavior disorders.

**psychopathology of epilepsy** See *personality, epileptic.*

**psychopedics** The branch of psychology dealing with the guidance and psychological treatment of children.

**psychopharmacology** 1. The study of chemical substances that affect the mind. 2. The study of the effects of chemical substances upon mental states.

**psychophysical dualism** See *dualism.*

**psychophysical function**  See *psychometric function*.

**psychophysical method**  The standard methods used in investigating psychophysical problems such as the method of average error, method of equal-appearing intervals, constant methods and method of limits.

**psychophysics  1.** The branch of psychology which investigates the relationships between stimulus magnitudes, the differences between stimuli and the corresponding sensory experiences. **2.** (G. Fechner) The science of the relations between mind and body. **3.** (logical positivism) The utilization of a human as an instrument of observation of a variable, the variable being one that can be arranged along a physical continuum, governed by a set of specified conditions.

**psychophysiological disorders**  Physical disorders, presumably of psychogenic origin, which are characterized by physiological changes accompanying certain emotional states.

**psychophysiology**  See *psychology, physiological*.

**psychoprocess**  Term referring to central controls which determine which stimuli will affect the organism.

**psychoses, alcoholic**  Psychoses caused by poisoning with alcohol.

**psychosexual immaturity**  The inability to respond sexually at an age-appropriate level.

**psychosexual stages**  (S. Freud) Five biologically determined stages of development: the oral, anal, phallic, latency, and genital stages.

**psychosis**  Mental disorder that interferes seriously with the usual functions of life. The following overall description is taken from the Diagnostic and Statistical Manual (DSM) of the American Psychiatric Association published in 1968. A detailed description of the various psychoses is given elsewhere in the Dictionary in alphabetic order.

Psychoses are described in two places in the Manual, here with the organic brain syndromes and later with the functional psychoses. The general discussion of psychosis appears here because organic brain syndromes are listed first in DSM-II.

Patients are described as psychotic when their mental functioning is sufficiently impaired to interfere grossly with their capacity to meet the ordinary demands of life. The impairment may result from a serious distortion in their capacity to recognize reality. Hallucinations and delusions, for example, may distort their perceptions. Alterations of mood may be so profound that the patient's capacity to respond appropriately is grossly impaired. Deficits in perception, language and memory may be so severe that the patient's capacity for mental grasp of his situation is effectively lost.

Some confusion results from the different meanings which have become attached to the word "psychosis". Some non-organic disorders, in the well-developed form in which they were first recognized, typically rendered patients psychotic. For historical reasons these disorders are still classified as psychoses, even though it now generally is recognized that many patients for whom these diagnoses are clinically justified are not in fact psychotic. This is true particularly in the incipient or convalescent stages of the illness.

II-A.  PSYCHOSES ASSOCIATED WITH ORGANIC BRAIN SYNDROMES (290-294)

290 Senile and pre-senile dementia
 .0 Senile dementia
 .1 Pre-senile dementia
291 Alcoholic psychosis
 .0 Delirium tremens
 .1 Korsakov's psychosis (alcoholic)
 .2 Other alcoholic hallucinosis
 .3 Alcohol paranoid state ((Alcoholic paranoia))
 .4 Acute alcoholic intoxication
 .5 Alcoholic deterioration
 .6 Pathological intoxication
 .9 Other (and unspecified) alcoholic psychosis

292 Psychosis associated with intracranial infection
 .0 Psychosis with general paralysis
 .1 Psychosis with other syphilis of central nervous system
 .2 Psychosis with epidemic encephalitis
 .3 Psychosis with other and unspecified encephalitis
 .9 Psychosis with other (and unspecified) intracranial infection

293 Psychosis associated with other cerebral condition
 .0 Psychosis with cerebral arteriosclerosis
 .1 Psychosis with other cerebrovascular disturbance
 .2 Psychosis with epilepsy
 .3 Psychosis with intracranial neoplasm
 .4 Psychosis with degenerative disease of the central nervous system
 .5 Psychosis with brain trauma
 .9 Psychosis with other (and unspecified) cerebral condition

294 Psychosis associated with other physical condition
 .0 Psychosis with endocrine disorder
 .1 Psychosis with metabolic or nutritional disorder
 .2 Psychosis with systemic infection
 .3 Psychosis with drug or poison intoxication (other than alcohol)
 .4 Psychosis with childbirth
 .8 Psychosis with other and undiagnosed physical condition
 (.9 Psychosis with unspecified physical condition)

II-B.  NON-PSYCHOTIC ORGANIC BRAIN SYNDROMES (309)

309 Non-psychotic organic brain syndromes ((Mental disorders not specified as psychotic associated with physical conditions))
 .0 Non-psychotic OBS with intracranial infection

(.1 Non-psychotic OBS with drug, poison, or systemic intoxication)
    .13 Non-psychotic OBS with alcohol (simple drunkenness)
    .14 Non-psychotic OBS with other drug, poison, or systemic intoxication
.2 Non-psychotic OBS with brain trauma
.3 Non-psychotic OBS with circulatory disturbance
.4 Non-psychotic OBS with epilepsy
.5 Non-psychotic OBS with disturbance of metabolism, growth or nutrition
.6 Non-psychotic OBS with senile or pre-senile brain disease
.7 Non-psychotic OBS with intracranial neoplasm
.8 Non-psychotic OBS with degenerative disease of central nervous system
.9 Non-psychotic OBS with other (and unspecified) physical condition
    (.91 Acute brain syndrome, not otherwise specified)
    (.92 Chronic brain syndrome, not otherwise specified)

### III. PSYCHOSES NOT ATTRIBUTED TO PHYSICAL CONDITIONS LISTED PREVIOUSLY (295-298)

295 Schizophrenia
.0 Schizophrenia, simple type
.1 Schizophrenia, hebephrenic type
.2 Schizophrenia, catatonic type
    .23 Schizophrenia, catatonic type, excited
    .24 Schizophrenia, catatonic type, withdrawn
.3 Schizophrenia, paranoid type
.4 Acute schizophrenic episode
.5 Schizophrenia, latent type
.6 Schizophrenia, residual type
.7 Schizophrenia, schizo-affective type
    .73 Schizophrenia, schizo-affective type, excited
    .74 Schizophrenia, schizo-affective type, depressed
.8 Schizophrenia, childhood type
.90 Schizophrenia, chronic undifferentiated type
.99 Schizophrenia, other (and unspecified) types

296 Major affective disorders (affective psychoses)
.0 Involutional melancholia
.1 Manic-depressive illness, manic type ((Manic-depressive psychosis, manic type))
.2 Manic-depressive illness, depressed type ((Manic-depressive psychosis, depressed type))
.3 Manic-depressive illness, circular type ((Manic-depressive psychosis, circular type))
    .33 Manic-depressive illness, circular type, manic
    .34 Manic-depressive illness, circular type, depressed
.8 Other major affective disorder ((Affective psychoses, other))
(.9 Unspecified major affective disorder
    (Affective disorder not otherwise specified)

(Manic-depressive illness not otherwise specified)

297 Paranoid states
.0 Paranoia
.1 Involutional paranoid state ((Involutional paraphrenia))
.9 Other paranoid state

298 Other psychoses
.0 Psychotic depressive reaction ((Reactive depressive psychosis))
(.1 Reactive excitation)
(.2 Reactive confusion)
    (Acute or subacute confusional state)
(.3 Acute paranoid reaction)
(.9 Reactive psychosis, unspecified)

299 Unspecified psychosis)
    (Dementia, insanity or psychosis not otherwise specified)

**psychosis, acute shock** A sudden but short term psychological disturbance common during active warfare. This condition is marked by complete unconsciousness, insensitivity to pain, fluttering eyelids, closed eyes, and flaccid limbs.

**psychosis, affective** The name given to what used to be called an affective disorder. An affective psychosis is characterized by derangements of mood involving the domination of mental activity by either extreme depression or elation.

**psychosis, akinetic** (C. Wernicke) The extreme catatonia that is marked by stupor and almost no movement is referred to as akinetic motor psychosis.

**psychosis, alcoholic** Psychotic state caused by alcohol poisoning. There are five types of alcoholic psychoses, namely alcoholic deterioration, alcoholic hallucinosis, alcoholic paranoia or paranoid state, delirium tremens, and Korsakov's psychosis.

**psychosis, alcoholic, paranoid type** Also called alcoholic paranoia. A paranoid state accompanied by jealousy and delusions of infidelity by the alcoholic spouse or lover.

**psychosis, alternating** A term descriptive of manic-depressive psychosis which involves alternating symptoms of elation and depression.

**psychosis, arteriosclerotic** A severe psychic disturbance associated with arteriosclerosis with symptoms ranging from mild emotional deviations to extreme psychotic responses and disorders of intellect, thought, and orientation.

**psychosis, circular** See *psychosis, manic-depressive*.

**psychosis, climacteric** See *psychosis, involutional*.

**psychosis, governess** Schizophrenia in a very severe form.

**psychosis, iatrogenic** A severe behavior disorder induced by the physician's diagnosis, attitudes and/or behavior and not the result of the specific treatment for the complaint.

**psychosis, Korsakoff** A disorder, generally caused by alcohol, metallic poisons, infections or the encephalopatimes, which is characterized by polyneuritis as the outstanding physical condition and loss of memory for current events as the outstanding mental condition.

**psychosis, manic-depressive** A psychosis characterized by extreme mood swings, remission and recurrence. It is usually observed in patients with no history of affective psychosis and in the absence of an apparent precipitating event.

**psychosis, manic-depressive, circular type** A psychosis characterized by at least one occurrence of both a depressive episode and a manic one.

**psychosis, manic depressive, circular type, depressed** The depressed episode of the manic-depressive psychosis, circular type.

**psychosis, manic-depressive, depressed type** A psychosis consisting of depressed episodes and characterized by a depressed mood, mental and motor retardation, apprehension, and agitation. Hallucinations and delusions which occur are due to the mood disorder.

**psychosis, manic-depressive, manic type** A psychosis consisting of manic episodes which are characterized by extreme elation, flight of ideas, loquacity, accelerated speech and accelerated motor activity.

**psychosis, organic** Severe mental disorder which is due to an empirically identifiable structural change or impairment of the nerve tissues, such as alcoholic psychosis.

**psychosis, post-infectious** A mental disorder which follows an acute disease such as influenza, pneumonia, typhoid fever, and acute rheumatic fever. Its characteristics include mild confusion and suspicion, irritability and depressive reactions.

**psychosis, postpartum** A psychotic episode precipitated by giving birth.

**psychosis, prison** A kind of mental disorder which is precipitated by imprisonment, the form of the disorder depending upon the individual involved.

**psychosis, schizoaffective** A disorder which is manifested by disturbances of thinking, mood, and behavior, especially with pronounced elation or depression. DSM II lists this disorder as one of the types of schizophrenia.

**psychosis, symbiotic** (M. S. Mahler) A form of mental illness occurring in children aged one to four whose origin lies in the symbiotic phase. This syndrome develops when the young child finds it impossible to separate from his mother and fails to progress to the next stage of separation and individuation because of panic inherent in this separation. Psychosis develops when the symbiotic union of mother and child is threatened. The belief is that a constitutional predisposition toward the development of this state must be present in a child who then responds to the mother in ways to elicit from her similar symbiotic needs.

**psychosis, toxic-infectious** A mental disorder which accompanies or follows an infective illness or poisoning by some external poison. It is characterized by delirium, dazed and stuporous condition, epileptiform attacks, hallucination, and incoherence and confusion.

**psychosis, Windigo** A psychosis found in certain Indian tribes, the Ojibwa, Chippewa, Eastern Cree, which is characterized by a morbid craving for human flesh and by the delusion of a transformation into Windigo, a mythological giant feared by the tribes.

**psychosocial** That which is both social and psychological.

**psychosocial stages of development** (G. M. Gilbert) According to biosocial theory, an epigenetic series of psychosocial stages from infancy to mature social adulthood best depicts the development of the integrated human personality. The stages suggested are: 1) (birth to 3rd year) ego emergence and dependency; 2) (3rd to 7-8th year) primary group interaction; 3) (7-8th year to puberty) secondary socialization; 4) (puberty through adolescence) adult role anticipation; 5) (early adulthood) social role assumption.

**psychosomatic** Involving both the mind and the body, psyche and soma.

**psychosomatic disorder** Generally a disorder of the body having psychogenic determinants.

**psychosomatic medicine** A specialty in medicine dealing with the diagnosis and treatment of psychosomatic disorders.

**psychostimulants** Drugs which stimulate the nervous system. See *amphetamines; methylphenidate; tranylcypromine; phenelzine; nialamide.*

**psychosurgery** Introduced by the Portuguese neuropsychiatrist Moniz in 1935; had been preceded by some operations on mental patients performed by the Swiss psychiatrist Burckhardt in 1890. After Moniz, Freeman and Watts in the United States standardized the operation performing cuts in the connections between frontal lobe cortex and thalamus (lobotomy). Today smaller, so-called stereotaxic operations are aimed at circumscribed structures in the brain. Electrocoagulation or radium-like substances are used.

**psychosynthesis** (S. Potter) A movement counter to psychoanalysis which attempts to restore useful inhibitions and to return the id to its rightful place. There is the attempt to keep the id and ego separate with the reality oriented ego in a dominant position.

**psychotechnics** The use of psychological principles, laws and knowledge in the attempt to control or alter behavior.

**psychotechnology** The body of psychological facts, principles, methods and concepts which are used in the application of psychology to practical problems.

**psychotherapist** A person who is trained in and practices psychotherapy.

**psychotherapy** Psychotherapy is a loose term encompassing a variety of treatment techniques of organic and non-organic mental (i.e., behavior) disorders. In a narrower and most commonly used sense psychotherapy means psychological treatment of mental disorders in contradistinction to the physical and chemical treatment methods. Psychotherapy is practiced primarily by psychiatrists and clinical psychologists, but several other professionals, notably the psychiatric social workers, psychiatric nurses, pastoral counselors, general physicians and others practice psychotherapy to some extent.

With the advent of Freud's discoveries, psychotherapy has been viewed as a form of psychological treatment in which a trained person (psychotherapist) establishes a professional relationship with a person (patient, client) suffering from emotional problems for the purpose of alleviating or modifying troublesome symptoms or patterns of behavior. The resulting changes are seen as promoting personality growth and mental health.

Freud attempted to draw a sharp distinction between psychoanalysis (as a method of treatment) and other forms of psychotherapy, which he regarded as closer to suggestion and hypnosis. In contrast, psychoanalysis was characterized as a radical treatment designed to overcome infantile conflicts. Extending over months and years, psychoanalysis focuses on a thorough analysis of (a) the transference and (b) resistances. The therapist's technical maneuvers are restricted to clarifications and interpretations of the patient's free associations, with a minimum of suggestion, advice, and directiveness. These maneuvers are considered to strengthen the patient's ego by undoing repressions and other defenses. "Orthodox psychoanalysis" has given way to numerous modifications, such as "psychoanalytically oriented psychotherapy" or "psychotherapy based on dynamic principles," which make use of Freudian teachings but adapt them in various ways to the needs of the patients and other circumstances. Differences between therapeutic approaches tend to be in degree rather than kind.

All forms of psychotherapy are based on common psychological principles operating in any helping relationship, including comfort, support, guidance, reassurance, guilt-reduction through confession, and hope. The therapist fosters an atmosphere of trust through interest, respect, understanding, and empathy, and he encourages open and direct communication by refraining from criticism and censure. These so-called nonspecific factors generally result in a diminution of fears and anxieties and mobilize the patient's abilities to cope with his problems. Intertwined with the nonspecific factors are more specific techniques designed to produce changes in symptoms (e.g., phobias, obsessive-compulsive acts), and maladaptive patterns of behavior. These techniques include not only interpretations of unconscious fantasies and beliefs but also suggestions, modeling of fearless behavior, setting an example of reasonableness and rationality, promoting the acquisition of self-understanding through insight, and the management of reward and punishment. Through his interaction with the therapist and experimentation outside the therapeutic situation, the patient acquires more adaptive skills in interpersonal relations. Consequently, psychotherapy is not a form of medical treatment for a disease (formerly called "neurosis"), but it represents a more or less systematic attempt to help a patient achieve maturity, autonomy, responsibility, and skill in adult living.

Psychotherapy takes many forms (e.g., group psychotherapy, psychodrama, play therapy), is based on diverse theoretical principles and assumptions, and is being extended to widely divergent patient groups. Psychotherapy is now frequently distinguished from behavior modification, an approach based on learning theories, with focus on the direct modification of symptoms.

**psychotherapy, active analytical** (W. Stekel) A method of dream interpretation, also called active analysis, in which the analyst intervenes directly in a patient's free associations by making revelations and giving advice suggested by the manifest dream content.

**psychotherapy, Adlerian** (A. Adler) The rationale of this psychotherapy is derived from A. Adler's individual psychology. There are no rigid rules in this treatment method, and the individual-psychological treatment is conceived as a relationship in which two people have to cooperate in a common task. Transference phenomena are viewed as the patient's distortions, and the therapist must interpret them as such. The task of the physician or psychologist is to give the patient the experience of contact with a fellow-man, and then to enable him to transfer this awakened social feeling to others.

**psychotherapy, ambulatory** The treatment of persons with psychological and behavior disorders on an out-patient basis.

**psychotherapy, analytic group** (S. R. Slavson) A method of treatment of behavior disorders in which interpretations are offered to patients, activity and verbalization are encouraged and interpreted in the hope of achieving insight. A particular version of group psychoanalysis.

**psychotherapy, analytical** (C. G. Jung) Psychoanalytic treatment similar to Freud's technique in that free association and dream interpretation are used but deviating from it in that libido is viewed as the general energy of life manifesting itself in creativity as well as sexual drive, and the mind is viewed as bipolar in nature, with one side in ascendency. Dream analysis is employed not only as a means of understanding the causative role of past experiences in present problems but also as a means of understanding the current concerns and future hopes of the patient. Four stages of the analysis are distinguished but not seen as consecutive or mutually exclusive and in each there is a different technical approach: the first stage is confession (cathartic method); the second stage is elucidation or interpretation (especially of the transference); the third stage is education (adapting to social demands and pressures); the fourth stage is transformation or individuation where the unique pattern of the patient is discovered and developed. The goal of the analysis is seen as the development of the unique pattern of personality with a re-balancing of the compensatory relationship between the conscious and the unconscious, accomplished by a progressive integration or constructive synthesis of unconscious contents into the conscious. Towards this goal, the analysis is seen as a dialectical process between two people, the analyst being part of the process and approaching each patient individually. The chair, as well as the couch, is used to facilitate the dialectic interpretations of the transference and dreams are often prospective or constructive rather than reductive in that the transference and dreams are seen as communications of unconscious parts of the personality to be integrated into the conscious as well as expressions of regressive and repressed infantile sexual impulses. "Active imagination" is often used in understanding the dream because free associations to the dream reveal meanings of specific contents and not the meaning of the dream itself.

**psychotherapy, assignment** (J. L. Moreno) Psychotherapeutic help given to a patient in a small work or play group after the group has been assessed sociometrically.

**psychotherapy, client-centered** (C. Rogers) Client-centered therapy is a continually developing approach to human growth and change, developed originally by Carl Rogers in the 1940's. Its central hypothesis is that the growth potential of any individual will tend to be released in a relationship in which the helping person is *experiencing* and *communicating* attitudes of realness, caring, and a deeply sensitive non-judgmental understanding. These concepts have been carefully defined theoretically as congruence, unconditional positive regard, and empathy. This kind of a relationship has been shown by empirical research to have constructive effects with troubled persons, normal people (in encounter groups), hospitalized schizophrenics, and students in classrooms.

Client-centered therapy is process oriented, not diagnostically or theoretically oriented. It draws its hypotheses from the raw data of the process of therapy as preserved in recorded and filmed interviews. It has been determined to test all its hypotheses through appropriate research and has probably sponsored more investigations than any other approach.

It is a mode of dealing with persons which has application in every field of human endeavor where healthy psychological growth and improvement in interpersonal relationships constitute goals. It has found use not only in psychotherapy, but in education, in conflict situations (racial and industrial), religious work, social work, encounter groups, and international student groups.

**psychotherapy, dance** Dance techniques to express one's unconscious conflicts used for psychotherapeutic purpose.

**psychotherapy, didactic group** A method of treatment of individuals in a group in which the group experience serves to educate the individual about the processes of psychotherapy, and to help him to clarify his own problems. The pedagogical methods

may include the patient's bringing up problems for general discussion, the therapist lecturing on particular topics, and/or the use of a textbook to suggest topics of discussion which the patients may comment on or associate to.

**psychotherapy, direct** (K. Platonov) A therapeutic method which uses explanation and persuasion to arouse the patient's cortex, and to remove pathological bonds in the cortex by means of conscious and critical analysis of the pathogenic situation by the therapist.

**psychotherapy, directive** A form of psychotherapy in which the therapist plays an active role giving reassurance and advice, asking questions and offering information.

**psychotherapy, directive group** (S. R. Slavson) A type of therapeutic treatment for a group designed to help the group members adjust to their environment which includes activities such as didactic and educational group work, group counseling and guidance, and therapeutic recreation.

**psychotherapy, existential** Therapy based on phenomenological and existential principles. This therapeutic technique emphasizes the direct approach to life and a thorough investigation of the individual's experiences and consciousness in order to reconstruct and unify the individual's existence. The various existential techniques stress the understanding of the individual and giving meaning to his life.

**psychotherapy, family** Psychotherapy in which the processes of the family as a unit as well as the individual family members are treated. The family meets as a group with the psychotherapist and interpretations are made of the interactions among the family members and of individual psychodynamics involved in those interactions.

**psychotherapy, filial** (B. G. Guerney) Play psychotherapy in which parents are trained and used as psychotherapists with their own children.

**psychotherapy, Gestalt** (F. Perls, P. Goodman, R. Hefferline) A form of psychotherapy based on the theory that psychopathology results from the disturbance of figure-ground development. The therapy consists of analyzing the internal experience in order to achieve a "good gestalt" within the person. Dissociated areas of the personality are thus accepted.

**psychotherapy, group** A form of treatment of behavior disorders in which two or more patients and the psychotherapist participate to resolve difficulties and effect therapeutic changes.

**psychotherapy, implosive** A therapy developed by Stampfl based on the technique of extinguishing fear reactions by having the patient imagine the feared stimuli. The therapy is called implosive because the patient is not actually harmed while imagining. A frightening stimulus is apt to produce an inner explosion—an implosion—of panic.

**psychotherapy, interactional** (B. B. Wolman) A psychotherapeutic technique. The rationale is derived from Wolman's modification of psychoanalysis and the assumption that psychotherapy is an inter-actional process. The main features of this technique are the manipulation of transference phenomena and adjustment of the technique to the type of socio-genic disorder, namely the hyperinstrumental, dysmutual, and hypervectorial, and the five levels of regression, namely neurotic, character neurotic, la-tent, manifest, and dementive psychotic.

**psychotherapy, interpersonal** (H. S. Sullivan) A treatment technique which emphasizes the interper-sonal nature of the events occurring in the treatment as well as in the patient's life in an attempt to help the patient become conscious of those parts of him-self he has a stake in keeping out of awareness.

**psychotherapy, limited aims** Psychological treat-ment with goals which are somewhat more restricted than usual, due often to forces or conditions in the patient's life not allowing for longer, more compre-hensive treatment. A goal of this treatment is often the solution of some pressing life problems rather than the in-depth analysis and restructuring of the patient's personality.

**psychotherapy, limited term** Psychotherapy in which the termination date is established at the inception of treatment.

**psychotherapy, nondirective** See *psychotherapy, client-centered.*

**psychotherapy, nondirective group** A form of group psychotherapy utilizing concepts derived from the Rogerian school of client-centered therapy. The basic assumption is that man has inherent potential for goodness, and self-healing. The focus of the group is the problem of most concern to the group or individual. The belief is that in an accepting, secure atmosphere the individual recognizes his needs and learns ways to obtain satisfaction. The role of the leader is that of a catalyst who clarifies and guides but never interprets.

**psychotherapy, "poison-pen"** (J. G. Watkins) The use of the writing of angry letters for cathartic purposes which are discussed with the therapist rath-er than mailed.

**psychotherapy, psychoanalytic** A simplified and shorter method of treatment based on modified prin-ciples of psychoanalysis.

**psychotherapy, psychoanalytic group** 1. A form of group psychotherapy utilizing the concepts of psychoanalysis. 2. (A. Wolf) The application of psychoanalytic concepts as transference, free associa-tion, dreams, and historical development in groups. The group re-creates the original family facilitating the resolution of problems. The members serve as co-therapists and representative of standards for each other, especially through the use of the technique of "going around," in which each member free associ-ates about another member. The group meets once a week with the therapist and once a week without him. 3. (S. H. Foulkes) A meeting of six to eight people with a group analyst once a week where no directions are given. Any communication is consid-ered free association and a reflection of the group interaction. The role of the therapist is that of a conductor who interprets and analyzes and offers minimal private information. 4. (W. R. Bion) The treatment of individuals in a group where the focus is on group behavior. The group is seen as a series of emotional states or basic assumption cultures. Its behavior is analyzed in terms of its movements to or away from the central problem. 5. (H. Thalen) Treatment of individuals in a group where the focus is on group interaction which is seen as a functional process. Emphasis is placed on the emotional and cognitive factors in the group and the relationship of the individuals to the group culture. 6. (B. B. Wol-man) A psychotherapy group must be balanced verti-cally and horizontally, according to Wolman's classi-ficatory system of mental disorders. The vertical balance requires participation of hyperinstrumental, hypervectorial and dysmutual patients, with none of these three clinical types dominating the group. The horizontal balance is based on avoidance of too extreme differences in the level of regression; e.g. a group comprised largely of character neurotics may have neurotic and latent psychotic members, but must not accept manifest or dementive psychotics.

**psychotherapy, rational** (A. Ellis) Rational psycho-therapy or rational-emotive therapy (RET) is a form of cognitive-behavior therapy which emphasizes a philosophic rather than a psychodynamic approach to the prevention and treatment of emotional distur-bances. It utilizes emotive-evocative techniques (such as direct confrontation) and behavior therapy meth-ods (such as activity homework assignments). It es-pecially teaches the individual that his emotional Consequences (C) do not stem mainly from the Activating Events (A) of his past or present life but from his Belief System (B); and it shows him how to clearly distinguish his rational Beliefs (rB's) from his irrational Beliefs (iB's) about himself and the world and how to use the logico-empirico or scientific method of vigorously Disputing (D) his irrational Beliefs until he significantly changes them. RET thereby helps the individual minimize his current self-defeating behavior and his future disturbability by becoming more realistic (that is, desiring rather than demanding) in his general outlook.

**psychotherapy, reconstructive** A form of psycho-therapy which focuses on the reconstruction of childhood and adult experiences which are instru-mental in the patient's problems.

**psychotherapy, relationship** Psychotherapy in which the relationship between the psychotherapist and patient serves as the means and end of the psycho-therapy. The relationship becomes the significant growth experience, with the focus on the patient's experiencing himself within the context of the rela-tionship. Reliance is placed on the dynamic effect of various maneuvers in the relationship or on the sup-portive value that a positive, friendly contact with another human being can have to another troubled, confused, or unhappy person.

**psychotherapy, role-divided** Individual or group psychotherapy in which more than one therapist participates.

**psychotherapy, short contact** Psychotherapy of short duration often used in child-guidance clinics.

**psychotherapy, will** (O. Rank) A form of psychotherapy, based on the theory of the birth trauma. Rank encouraged the patient to assert his will, as in the separation from the womb, to achieve independence.

**psychotic** An individual afflicted with psychosis.

**psychotic depressive reaction** A form of psychosis which is characterized by a depressive mood attributable to some event or experience, with no history of repeated depressions or mood swings.

**psychotic, involutional** See *psychotic reactions, involutional.*

**psychotic reactions, involutional** Psychotic reactions usually seen in menopausal women but also in aging men. It is characterized by intense depression and feelings of worthlessness.

**psychotomimetic** Appearing to mimic a psychosis. As for example, the effects of lysergic acid diethylamide.

**psychotomimetic drugs** Drugs which produce a state similar to that of psychosis.

**ptosis** 1. Falling. 2. Paralytic drooping of the eyelid.

**pubertas praecox** See *macrogenitosomia.*

**puberty** The developmental state or period in which the reproductive organs reach maturity and the individual begins to exhibit secondary sex characteristics. Although there is much variability among individuals, the end of the stage for males is generally given as fourteen and thirteen for females.

**puberty rites** Initiation through precept and ritual into the adult life of a community consisting of indoctrination into tribal lore, ceremonies, etc.

**pubesence; pubescency** The period or process of reaching puberty.

**public opinion** The general state of feeling, opinion, or attitude of a large and major segment of the population on an issue or group of issues.

**pudendum; pudenda** The external genital organ.

**puerilism** The condition of acting like a boy or child; an adult participating in immature behavior.

**puerperal mania** See *mania, puerperal.*

**pulfric phenomenon or effect** When an object is moving in a pendular movement in one plane it will appear to be moving in an ellipse whose plane is perpendicular to the frontal plane when viewed through a filter of medium density.

**punched card technique** The use of cards with holes punched in them at appropriate places to record and process data, usually in a computer system.

**punishment training** A type of training in which a particular response elicits a negative reinforcer.

**pupil** The aperture on the iris of the eye which changes dimension in response to the brightness of light and to control the amount of the light passing through it on the way to the retina.

**pupillary reflex** See *reflex, pupillary.*

**Purdue pegboard** A test measuring gross arm, wrist and finger movements which requires the subject to combine pegs, washers, and collars into various assemblages.

**Purdue perceptual-motor survey** A test for the qualitative assessment of perceptual-motor abilities in the early grades. The survey consists of twenty-two scorable items divided into eleven subtests: walking board, jumping, identification of body parts, imitation of movement, obstacle course, muscular strength tests, angels in the snow, chalkboard, rhythmic writing, ocular control, and visual achievement forms.

**pure C response** The Rorschach response determined only by color, with no form involvement whatsoever. Such responses, sometimes described as crude color responses, are generally interpreted as representing a substantial loss of control with emotion being in near complete command of behavior. It is typically found in records of very seriously disturbed subjects.

**pure line** See *line, pure.*

**pure number** (statistics) A number which is not dependent on the units of measurement of the quantities used in its determination.

**pure stimulus act** See *act, pure stimulus.*

**puritis** 1. Itching resulting from sensory nerve irritation. 2. Functional or psychological itching.

**Purkinje afterimage** The second positive visual aftersensation, appearing most plainly in the hue complementary to that of the primary sensation.

**Purkinje cell** See *cell, Purkinje.*

**Purkinje figures** The shadowy network on the retina which results from the thin network of blood vessels lying between the sensitive cells and the incoming light and which may be seen under certain conditions.

**Purkinje phenomenon** With decreasing illumination, the red or long-wave end of the spectrum decreases in brilliance more rapidly than the blue, or short-wave end.

**Purkinje-Sanson images** The three images of an object an eye is fixated on which can be seen by an observer of the eye. The images are reflected from the surface of the cornea, from the front of the cornea, and from the back of the cornea.

**purposive psychology** The belief that behavior, rather than being simply a complex set of reflexes or mechanistic physiological processes, is characterized by purpose.

**purposivism** An approach to psychology holding

that purposes interact with certain stimulus conditions in yielding behavior.

**pursuit, ocular** The continuous perception of a moving object by successive fixations of the eyes.

**pursuit reaction** Movements meant to maintain the perception of a moving stimulus.

**pursuitmeter** An instrument which measures the subject's ability to manipulate his behavior in accord with changes in a constantly moving stimulus.

**Putnam, James Jackson (1846-1918)** An American psychiatrist who founded the American Psychoanalytic Society in 1910.

**puzzle-box** An enclosure which prevents the experimental animal from attaining the goal box until he has successfully manipulated a mechanism which opens the enclosure.

**pygmalionism** The condition characterized by the falling in love with one's own creation.

**pygmeism** A constitutional anomaly which is characterized by a dwarfed but well-proportioned body when viewed in comparison with others in the specific racial group.

**pyknic type** See *type, pyknic.*

**pylorus** The opening which leads from the stomach into the duodenum.

**pyramidal tract** The nerve fibers which pass through the medullary pyramids and form an efferent path originating in the precentral gyrus of the cerebral cortex, and leading to the motor centers of the brain stem and cord.

**pyrexiophobia** Fear of fever.

**pyrolagnia** Experiencing of sexual arousal and excitement at the sight of fire.

**pyromania** Pathological desire to set things on fire, or empresiomania.

**pyromania, erotic** See *pyrolagnia.*

**pyromaniac** Person who exhibits pyromania.

**pyrophobia** Fear of fire.

**pyrosis** Heartburn.

**Q** 1. See *quartile deviation.* 2. See *questionnaire.*

*Q* 1. A symbol for luminous energy. 2. (Rorschach) A general symbol sometimes used by the examiner to indicate qualification, restriction, or a self-doubting expression on the part of the subject.

**Q-correlation** See *P-technique.*

**Q data (or factors)** Responses and response factors based on questionnaire behavior taken only as behavior.

**Q-sort** (W. Stephenson) A personality inventory introduced in 1953 in which the subject or a judge is asked to sort a series of statements into a pile showing which best applies to the subject.

**Q-technique** 1. A factor analysis from correlating persons instead of tests. The transpose of R-technique. 2. (R. B. Cattell) A factor analysis technique which investigates the relationships among people by correlating the performance of different persons in relation to a population of tasks under constant conditions.

**Q' technique** Finding types as clusters, not factors, from an $r$ (shape method) or $r_p$ matrix of relations among person profiles, preferably scored on factors as elements.

**quadriplegia** A kind of paralysis which affects both the arms and legs.

**quale** Any bit of experience which is investigated as it is without referring to the context, relations, or meaning involved with it.

**qualification grid** A "ready reckoner" device for calculating job adjustment or success scores from personality factor profiles, with an implicit formula.

**quantum hypothesis** See *quantum theory.*

**quantum theory** (G. von Bekesy) The hypothesis that changes in sensation occur in discrete steps and not on a continuum. This implies that sensory discrimination is fundamentally a discontinuous process characterized by finite quantal steps. This is predi-

cated on the all-or-nothing principle in neural activity.

**quartile** 1. One of the three points which divide a serial ranked distribution into four segments, each segment containing one-fourth of the scores. 2. One of the four segments of the subdivided segment.

**quartile deviation** A rough measure of variability which is equal to one-half of the distance separating quartiles one and three.

**quasi measurement** The attachment of a numerical value to a datum even though the rules of measurement proposed by a theorist are not followed.

**quasi need** (K. Lewin) A state of tension which initiates activity directed at a specific goal with its origin not in a biological deficit but in an intention or purpose.

**quaternity** 1. A unit which is composed by the union of four factors. 2. (C. G. Jung) Describes the four dimensional structural concept of personality, the four dimensions being: thinking, feeling, intuiting, and sensing.

**questionnaire; questionary** A set of questions, often elaborate, which is designed so as to investigate a given subject.

**Quincke's tubes** 1. A set of glass tubes which produce sound when blown across the open end and which are used to obtain high pitches in studies of hearing. 2. A kind of interference tube.

**quota control** A technique used in population sampling where the number chosen of a certain element is proportionate to the number of elements in the population as a whole.

**quota sampling** See *sampling, stratified.*

**quotient** The number which is yielded when one number (the dividend) is divided by another number (the divisor).

**quotient, intelligence** See *intelligence quotient.*

# R

**r** See *correlation, product moment.*

*r* (statistics) The symbol for the product-moment correlation coefficient.

**R** 1. A symbol for response; see *response.* 2. A symbol which denotes a general reasoning factor in reference to primary mental ability. 3. (Rorschach) A symbol which stands for the total number of responses given by a subject to the Rorschach test.

*R* 1. (statistics) A symbol of the multiple correlation coefficient. 2. (Statistics) A symbol for footrule correlation, a rarely used statistic.

$R_G$ (C. L. Hull) The symbol representing a goal-attaining, or consummatory, response.

$r_t$ (statistics) The symbol for the tetrachoric correlation coefficient.

**R-correlation** (R. B. Cattell) A factor analysis technique which investigates how closely two functions or tasks are related by correlating them for a large number of subjects.

**R-technique** A design which measures a group of persons on the same set of variables at one occasion then factor analyzes the correlations between these variables to determine personality dimensions descriptive of inter-individual differences at any one time (or traits).

**rabies** See *encephalitis, rabies.*

**rabies encephalitis** See *encephalitis, rabies.*

**race** (physical anthropology) A large subdivision of mankind characterized by a common ancestry and having a number of common characteristics, particularly physical or visible.

**racial memory** See *memory, racial.*

**racial prejudice** The irrational belief in the association of good or bad qualities to any one racial group.

**racial unconscious** See *collective unconscious.*

**racism** A belief which utilizes common ancestry or somatic racial characteristics as the basis for discrimination in the granting of political, social, or economic rights.

**radiance** The measure of radiant energy in terms of the emission rate and the area of the source. It is the analog of luminance, the measure of radiant energy in terms of the light produced.

**radical** 1. A term descriptive of persons, plans, etc. which seek rapid, fundamental and substantive change. 2. (mathematics) The sign for square root, $m$, indicating that the quantity within is to be factored into its roots.

**radix** A term used for nerve fibers located at the point of entry or departure from the central nervous system.

**ramifying linkage method** (R. B. Cattell) A system method for isolating all types or clusters in an $r$ or $r_p$ matrix.

**ramus; ramus communicans** 1. A branch from a nerve or vein. 2. One of the nerve tracts which connects the sympathetic ganglia (the sympathetic nervous system) to the spinal cord (central nervous system) and to visceral and peripheral organs.

**random** Occurring by chance, without voluntary control.

**random activity** Movement that is carried out without foresight or plan or purpose, that is not the result of instinct or habit, that is not directed toward any goal and that is not elicited by any specific cueing stimulus.

**random error** 1. That part of variability which can be attributed to chance. 2. The average deviation of a sample from the mean of a large number of observed values or scores.

**random observation** Any observation which is not part of a systemized series of observations and which has not been planned in advance.

**random sample** A number of cases of any sort drawn from a population in such a way that every item in the population has an equal chance of being chosen as every other.

**random sampling**  See *sampling, random.*

**range** 1. (statistics) A measure of variability that is computed by subtracting the lowest score in a distribution from the highest score. 2. (sociology) Any geographical area occupied by a species, group or individual.

**range effect**  In a pursuit or tracking reaction, the making of too small a movement when the target motion is large and too large a movement when the target motion is small.

**range of audibility or hearing**  The range which stretches between the upper and lower limits of hearable tones, measured in cycles per second. The average range is 20 to 20,000 cycles per second.

**rank** 1. (noun) The position of an item or datum in relation to others which have been arranged according to some specific criterion. 2. (verb) To put items in an order, from lowest to highest (or highest to lowest) according to some criterion.

**rank correlation**  See *rank-difference correlation.*

**rank-difference correlation (p)**  A technique for ference between two sets of values or magnitudes which have been ranked,

$$p = 1 - \frac{\sigma \Sigma d^2}{N(N^2-1)}$$

where $d$ is the difference between ranks, $N$ is the number of cases ranked, and $\Sigma$ means the sum of all the values represented by $d^2$.

**rank order**  The arrangement of a series of values, scores, or individuals in the order of their magnitude (decreasing or increasing). The intervals between the values are not necessarily equal.

**rank-order method**  See *method, rank-order.*

**rank, percentile**  (statistics) The position or magnitude of a value or score in a sequentially-ordered series defined in terms of the percentage of values or scores which fall at or below that position.

**ranked distribution**  See *distribution, ranked.*

**rapport** 1. A comfortable and warm atmosphere between two individuals, especially between a tester and the testee. 2. A special relationship which exists between the hypnotist and his subject, rendering the latter extremely sensitive to stimuli from the former. 3. (parapsychology) The relationship between a medium and the spirit control.

**rare detail; *dr***  (Rorschach) A response on Rorschach utilizing a small and generally unused portion of the blot.

**rat-man**  (S. Freud) A patient of Freud's who had suffered from severe obsessions and fears. Freud used his knowledge of the case, gained through an eleven month analysis, to illustrate the dynamics of the obsessive-compulsive neurosis.

**rate, compensatory**  (operant conditioning) A higher than average response rate following a lower than normal rate, tending to restore the over-all rate to its earlier value. Also possibly a lower than normal rate

following a higher rate with the same effect on over-all rate.

**rate, fine grain**  (operant conditioning) The response rate, number of responses by time, over the shortest unit of time.

**rate, local**  (operant conditioning) Response rate over a short time; it is given by the tangent of the cumulative curve at any point ignoring the fine curve.

**rate, mean**  (operant conditioning) Responses per unit of time calculated for an interval during which local rates have changed.

**rate, over-all**  (operant conditioning) Mean response rate for a long period of time, from minutes to hours. Frequently applied to response rates between reinforcements.

**rate, response**  (operant conditioning) Responses per unit of time usually responses per second.

**rate, running**  (operant conditioning) The sustained constant rate, often the only important rate other than zero which is often observed in some schedules.

**rate score**  The number of test items which are completed in a specified amount of time.

**rate, terminal**  (operant conditioning) The response rate reached at the moment of reinforcement.

**rate test**  See *test, rate.*

**rating** 1. The analysis of qualitative data by scaling. The essential operation consists of making a judgment about an aspect of the data in terms of more, equal, or less. 2. The rank or score given to data.

**rating behavior**  See *behavior, rating.*

**rating, man-to-man**  The comparison of an individual with other individuals who exemplify different degrees of a trait to determine the subject's endowment of this trait.

**rating, maturity**  The determination of the degree of an individual's development along a certain dimension in comparison with the norm of the group to which he belongs.

**rating scale**  An instrument which allows a rater to record the estimated magnitude of a trait or quality for the case in question.

**rating, sociability**  An index of the degree to which a person is sociable and interacts with others.

**ratio** 1. A relationship between two things, whether in number, degree, or quantity. 2. Specifically, a quotient, as in intelligence quotient, which is equal to the product of the mental age divided by the chronological age.

**ratio, affective**  A calculation, used in the Beck approach to the Rorschach, representing the ratio of number of responses given to the last three cards of the test versus the number given to the first seven cards. Since the last three cards are the only ones in the test which are entirely chromatic, the ratio is believed to afford some index of the manner in which the subject responds to the external world. Other approaches to the Rorschach, such as Klopfer, Hertz, and Piotrowski, include emphasis on the number of responses to the last three cards but compute the ratio differently, as a percentage (8-9-10%) by comparing these responses to all of the responses in the protocol.

**ratio correlation**  See *correlation, ratio.*

**ratio estimation**  See *estimation, ratio.*

**ratio, Mendelian**  See *Mendelian ratio.*

**ratio scale**  See *scale, ratio.*

**ratiocination**  The act or process of thinking, reasoning or of drawing a deductive conclusion.

**rational equation**  A mathematical equation which embodies an hypothesis derived from data and based on assumptions regarding the nature of a specific psychological process. They are generated in an attempt to predict psychological phenomena, the general nature of the parameters being dictated by theory and the exact values determined by the available data.

**rational learning**  Meaningful learning which includes an understanding of the material and an understanding of the relationships among the component facts.

**rational number**  Any number which can be expressed as the quotient of two whole numbers or integers.

**rational psychotherapy**  See *psychotherapy, rational.*

**rational type**  See *type, rational.*

**rationale**  The basic or underlying reason for an opinion, hypothesis or action.

**rationalization**  An effort to distort reality in order to protect one's self-esteem. In its attempt to mediate between the id and reality, the weak ego ascribes rationality to the irrational demands of the id. A strong ego can cope with failures and frustrations, but a weak ego would rather distort the truth than admit defeat. Rationalization is used as a cover-up for mistakes, misjudgments, and failures. It tries to justify behavior by reasons that are made to sound rational.

A common type of rationalization is known as "sour grapes," taking its name from the fable about the fox who, upon failing to get the grapes he desired, consoled himself by calling them "sour." People rationalize in the same way; it takes a mature personality with a strong ego to admit that not all desirable grapes are also attainable. A neurotic tends to make himself believe that sweet grapes are sour rather than admit that he failed.

**rauwolfia compounds**  Compounds derived from the rauwolfia plant and used in the treatment of the psychoses. See *reserpine.*

**Ravens Controlled Projection Test**  See *test, Ravens Controlled Projection.*

**raw score**  See *score, raw.*

**Ray, Isaac (1807-1881)**  American psychiatrist. One of the pioneers of the mental hygiene movement and one of the founding fathers of the American Psychiatric Association.

**Rayleigh equation**  A quantitative statement describing the proportion of red and green stimuli necessary for the normal human eye to perceive yellow. The normal mixture is a spectrum red of 670 m$\mu$ and a spectrum green of 535 m$\mu$ to yield a yellow of 589 m$\mu$, while, for color-blind or -weak person, more red or green may be required, depending on the predominant weakness.

**reaction**  A response of an organism to a stimulus.

**reaction, complex**  In a reaction time experiment, the requirement that the subject choose or make a discrimination between two or more stimuli.

**reaction, compound**  In a reaction time experiment, the requirement that the subject discriminate between two stimuli or recognize a stimulus before reacting.

**reaction, confirming**  The hypothetical reaction which occurs in the nervous system of the organism when the goal is achieved.

**reaction formation**  (psychoanalysis)  A defense mechanism which consists of counteracting the unconscious drive derivative with the opposite conscious attitude such as feeling conscious aversion toward a person toward whom the individual feels unconscious attraction. A strong ego is in control of the entire system; it satisfies some of the id cravings, while it postpones or modifies others and flatly rejects and suppresses those demands which it deems unacceptable. A weak ego resorts to the use of defense mechanisms against impulses. One of these defenses is the development of an attitude diametrically opposed to the id desires. For instance, an individual with strong homosexual impulses may crusade against homosexuality. An individual who hates his father and is very unhappy about it may develop a ritual of affection directed toward his father; an individual torn by an impulse to be dirty may develop compulsive cleanliness.

**reaction key**  A switch interrupting a circuit, much like a telegraph key, which is used in measuring reaction time.

**reaction threshold**  See *threshold, response.*

**reaction time**  1. The minimal amount of time between the onset of the stimulus and the beginning of the subject's response. 2. See *reaction time: sensory preparation.* 3. See *reaction time: motor preparation.*

**reaction time, choice**  When a subject has learned various responses to various stimuli, the time measured from the presentation of a certain stimulus to the beginning of the response of the subject that is correct for that stimulus.

**reaction time, cognitive**  The time measured from the presentation of a stimulus to the beginning of the response of the subject when he has recognized the stimulus.

**reaction time, discrimination** The time measured from the presentation of two stimuli to the beginning of the subject's response to the correct stimulus.

**reaction time, motor preparation** The readiness of the subject to make a particular movement as a response in a reaction time experiment.

**reaction time, sensory preparation** The readiness of the subject to receive a particular stimulus in a reaction time experiment.

**reaction type** In reaction time experiments, those people whose responses are governed or dominated by a particular set, either sensory or motor.

**reaction type, motor** In reaction time experiments, those individuals whose behavior is characterized by a set to respond as quickly as possible with attention to the movement.

**reaction type, sensory** In reaction time experiments, those individuals whose behavior is characterized by a set to apprehend the incoming stimuli.

**reactive epilepsy** See *epilepsy, reactive.*

**reactive inhibition, conditioned** See *inhibition, reactive conditioned.*

**reactive schizophrenia** See *schizophrenia, reactive.*

**readiness law** See *law of readiness.*

**reading disability** Problem or disturbance in the reading ability or progress of a child. It can be due to or associated with a number of factors, including lower scores on the Verbal, Performance and Full Scales of the Wechsler Intelligence Scale for Children (WISC); higher Performance Scale scores than Verbal Scale scores on the WISC; slow development of vocabulary; difficulty with auditory-visual integration and with the perception of auditory stimuli; visual-perceptual difficulties; difficulty in copying a visually presented standard pattern; neurological dysfunction; and inadequate resolution of internal and external conflicts.

**reading, mirror** Reading from right to left.

**reading quotient** An index, obtained by dividing the child's reading age, as obtained from a standardized test, by his chronological age, reflecting the child's reading ability in comparison with other children his age.

**reading readiness** Denotes the stage at which the child, due to developmental, experimental and situational factors, is able to profit by certain conditions of reading instruction.

**reading, remedial** Specific techniques designed to correct particular faulty reading habits.

**reading span** The number of words which can be perceived and comprehended by the subject in a single fixation period, that is, the period of time when the eye is not moving in the reading process.

**reagin** An antibody which may precipitate intense allergic responses.

**real** 1. Whatever exists. 2. (J. F. Herbart) The world is comprised of small units or things which he called the "reals." All reals react to external pressure by self-preservation. The human soul is one of those reals and ideas or presentations are the self-preservation reactions of the soul. The totality of these ideas form the consciousness.

**real anxiety** See *anxiety, real.*

**real base factor analysis** (R. B. Cattell) A system whereby factors are not artificially reduced to equal unit variance, but retain their real differences of "size" from experiment to experiment. This permits an integration of psychometric and manipulative experimental approaches not previously possible. With this design there goes also the possibility of referring scores to a true zero.

**realism** Philosophical school which accepts the existence of the universe independently of human cognition. Naive realism assumes that the world is as perceived by the sensory apparatus; critical realism views human perception as imperfect and demands validation of perceptions by improved cognitive tools, measurement and critical analysis.

**realism, moral** (J. Piaget) Children's belief that the right and wrong ideas are objective, rigid and self-evident.

**reality** The aspect of the universe which is not fantasied.

**reality principle** (S. Freud) The guiding principle of the ego in contradistinction to the id's pleasure principle; it is the ability to postpone or renounce immediate gratification in order to avoid unpleasant consequences and/or secure a greater reward in the future.

**reality testing** (S. Freud) An ego function; an appraisal and evaluation of inner and external stimuli of the possibilities of successful satisfaction of instinctual impulses, of the inner resources and of the totality of circumstances followed by an adjustment to the external requirements.

**reality therapy** See *therapy, reality.*

**reasoning** Rational, logical thinking.

**rebound phenomenon of Gordon Holmes** A test for ataxia illustrating the lack of cerebellar control of coordinated movement.

**recall** The repetition of reinstitution in memory of previously learned materials.

**recall method** Method of measuring retention by reproduction of items which were presented to an adopted criterion of learning.

**recall test** See *recall method.*

**recapitulation theory** The premise that the individual organism in the process of growth and development passes through a series of stages representing stages in the evolutionary development of the species. Also called the biogenetic law.

**receiver** (communication theory) The structure or process which translates a signal into a message; in an animal it is the sense organs and their connections to the brain.

**receiver operating characteristic curve** (signal detection theory) Usually referred to as the ROC curve. It is a description of a subject's performance in a signal detection psychophysical experiment. The ROC is the probability of a correct detection by the subject, of a signal when the signal is given, a hit, plotted as a function of the probability of the subject's reporting that a signal was presented when actually there was no signal presented; a false alarm. The ROC is a graphic description of the sensory capacities of the individual subject.

**receiving hospital** An institution which is designed specifically to receive people suspected of mental disorder for diagnosis and early or short treatment. Commitment is not required although if short treatment is not deemed desirable, the patient is normally referred to other institutions for treatment.

**recency, law of** See *law of recency*.

**recenter** To substitute a better figure-ground relation for an inadequate one; to transfer the anchor of a perceptual field to a different part.

**recept** 1. (neurology) The process or change which occurs in the afferent side of a neural transit. 2. A mental image formed from that which is common in a series of percepts.

**receptive character** See *character, receptive*.

**receptor** A specialized part of the body connected to sensory neurons sensitive to different kinds of stimuli. There are four general classes of receptors: photic receptors which respond to light; mechanical receptors which respond to mechanical stimuli; chemical receptors; and thermal receptors sensitive to warm and cold.

**recessive** A gene is recessive when it is expressed only when homozygous.

**recessive gene** See *gene, recessive*.

**recessive trait** See *trait, recessive*.

**recidives in schizophrenia** See *schizophrenia, recidives in*.

**recidivism** The repetition or occurrence of criminal or delinquent behavior or of mental disorder, especially when recurrence leads to a second conviction or commitment.

**reciprocal inhibition** (C. S. Sherrington) A term which indicates that elicitation of a particular spinal reflex is accompanied by the inhibition of another, and vice versa. Its use was expanded by Wolpe to subsume all cases in which the elicitation of one response seems to bring about a decrement in the strength of a simultaneous response. When a learned response is reciprocally inhibited, its habit strength is diminished. This fact has been the basis of numerous methods of weakening unadaptive habits, especially anxiety response habits, and has been a central focus of behavior therapy.

**reciprocal innervation** 1. A system whereby contraction of one of a pair of antagonistic muscles results in the relaxation of the other. 2. In the autonomic nervous system, an arrangement in which stimulation of the same organ by the sympathetic nervous system results in an opposite effect from the parasympathetic.

**reclining position of the patient** The requirement of psychoanalytic treatment that the patient lie on a couch which facilitates the development of transference.

**recognition method** Means of measuring information retention by administering tests on which items that have been presented earlier appear along with new related items, and requesting the subject to choose those which have been previously presented.

**recognition test** See *recognition method*.

**reconditioning** The strengthening or re-establishment after extinction of a conditioned response through the reintroduction of the unconditioned stimulus.

**reconstruction** (psychoanalysis) One of the tasks in psychoanalytic treatment. Recollection of the past in transference permits the resolution of repressed infantile conflicts. S. Freud compared reconstruction to archeological excavation.

**reconstruction method** Method of measuring retention or learning in which the subject is asked to reconstruct items in the order they were originally presented. The degree to which the reconstruction coincides with the original order is taken as the measure of retention. The number of trials or time required to reproduce the arrangement correctly is taken as the measure of learning.

**reconstructive psychotherapy** See *psychotherapy, reconstructive*.

**record, cumulative** (operant conditioning) A graph produced by the cumulative recorder of response rate. On the vertical axis the cumulative number of responses is recorded; on the horizontal axis cumulative time is recorded. Usually events such as reinforcements, stimulus changes, etc. are indicated.

**recorder, cumulative** (operant conditioning) Most common device used to record responses in operant conditioning. It produces a graph of the total number of responses as a function of time. In other words it provides a graph of the response rate. When in operation a motor drives paper at a constant speed. Each response moves a recording pen a constant amount. The result is a graph with time on the abscissa and responses on the ordinate.

**recovery** Regaining health; restoration of a normal physical or mental state.

**recovery, spontaneous** 1. The reappearance of an

extinguished conditioned response following rest. The response is weaker and will be extinguished if not reinforced. 2. The disappearance of symptoms and general improvement of mental patients without treatment.

recovery time  The period of time which follows a response in which the response cannot be repeated or elicited.

recreational therapy  See *therapy, recreational*.

recruitment  See *fractionation*.

rectilinear distribution  See *distribution, rectilinear*.

rectilinear regression  See *regression, linear*.

recurrent mania  See *mania, recurrent*.

red nucleus  A group of neurons located in the front part of the tegmentum in the midbrain, giving rise to the rubrospinal fluid.

redintegration  1. The re-establishment or re-forming of a whole. 2. The principle which is characterized by the recall of other elements in the whole or the whole itself when a few of the elements are present in consciousness. 3. (H. Hollingworth) The principle which holds the psychological consequence of an event as a whole tends to be elicited by the presence of a single element of that event. 4. The principle which holds that a stimulus which is contiguous with a response elicited by another stimulus will in the future tend to elicit that response, i.e., the principle operative in classical conditioning.

reduced cue, principle of  A learning principle which holds that with repetition of a stimulus-response unit a progressively smaller part of the stimulus is required to elicit the response.

reduced eye  A simplified and schematic representation or model of the average, unaccommodated human eye.

reduced score  A score which has been lessened by some constant in order to facilitate computation.

reduction division  (biology) The formation of gametes or sex cells through a process in which half of the normal number of chromosomes go to the daughter cells; meiosis.

reductionism  The belief that a certain science can be presented in terms of another science, either in the methods of research (methodological reductionism) or in its data and theory (theoretical reductionism)

reductionism, methodological  The application of research techniques borrowed from one scientific discipline to research problems of another discipline, e.g. Pavlov borrowed his psychological research techniques from biology; Margaret Mead, in anthropology, borrowed from psychology.

reductionism, theoretical  The belief that the entire subject matter of one science can be presented in terms of another science, e.g. psychology can be presented in neurophysiological terms. In psychology one can distinguish six distinct approaches to

this problem: 1) Radical reductionism (Bekhterev, Hebb, Watson, et al.) which assumes identity in the subject matter described in both sciences. 2) Hoped-for-reductionism (Pavlov, Freud, Hull, et al.) which assumes that some day psychological data will be presented in physico-chemical terms. 3) Logical reductionism (Feigl, Nagel, et al.) assumes that the logical constructs can be presented in the same way in both sciences. 4) Transitionism (B. B. Wolman) assumes an evolutionary mind-body continuum. 5) Rejection of reductionism (K. Lewin, Skinner). 6) Dualism (practically all psychologists prior to the twentieth century) which believes in two separate substances, mind and body.

reductive interpretation  (C. G. Jung) An interpretation in which behavioral products are not seen as symbols but rather as a sign or symptom of the unconscious processes.

redundancy  See *T function*.

reference axes  (factor analysis) The axes of two orthogonal, or independent factors in relation to the location of other factor axes.

reference group  (sociology) A group with which an individual identifies himself. When an individual's behavior at a particular time is determined by the norms of one of the groups he belongs to (e.g. his economic, religious, or occupational group).

reference, ideas of  Morbid viewing of one's own emotions, thoughts, and attitudes projected on others as originating in them.

reference, objective  A quality of pointing to the objective world which is inherent in certain perceptual processes.

reference vector  (factor analysis) The set of coordinates or axes that test vectors are located in reference to, giving grounding lines or planes which allow the geometrical and trigonometrical expression of the mathematical relations found in the correlation matrix. These axes must retain the same origin as the test vectors in rotation but may be rotated around the origin.

referent  The object, abstraction, event, or experience to which the meaning of a word or other symbol points.

referral  Referring a client or patient to another therapist, agency, or institution.

referred pain  See *pain, referred*.

referred sensation  See *sensation, referred*.

refined mode  See *mode, refined*.

reflected color  Color which is perceived as reflected from an object.

reflection  1. See *introspection*. 2. Going over the meaning, value, or significance of experiences, facts, or events. 3. (physics) The reversal or turning back of particles or waves which strike a surface. 4. The image of an object in a mirror. 5. (factor analysis) The alteration of the algebraic signs in some of the columns and the corresponding rows in order to make consistent the interpretation of the factor loadings as related to certain tests.

**reflection angle** (optics) The angle formed by the path of a beam of light and the line perpendicular to the surface at the point from which the beam is reflected.

**reflection of feelings** (C. Rogers) A counseling or psychotherapeutic technique in which the therapist restates or reiterates what the patient has said in an attempt to accentuate the emotional tone rather than the intellectual meaning.

**reflection response** (Rorschach) A response in which one-half of the inkblot is reported as a reflection of the other half.

**reflex** 1. A simple stimulus response connection believed to be unlearned and characteristic of a species. 2. (H. Spencer) The simplest reactions which are unflexible and gross adjustments to the environment. 3. (I. P. Pavlov) Inborn permanent and unchangeable reactions of organisms to stimulation from the external world which take place through the activity of the nervous system. 4. (B. F. Skinner) Any observed correlation of stimulus and response which constitutes the simple unit of behavior. 5. A mechanical act requiring no thought.

**reflex, abdominal** Contraction of the muscles in the abdominal wall in response to the stroking of the skin of the belly.

**reflex, acute affective** (E. Kretschmer) An involuntary emotional reaction to definite and strong stresses that fades away after a period of rest. Originally identified in soldiers during wartime. Two examples are compulsive crying and fine muscular tremblings.

**reflex, alternating response** Two responses or reflexes that follow one another in their occurrence, usually in a series. For example, the alternating flexion and extension in walking movements.

**reflex-arc** (J. Dewey) The neurological unit which in theory consists of the receptor, an intermediate neuron and an effector.

**reflex, attention** A reflexive change in pupil size when attention is fixed upon something suddenly.

**reflex, audito-oculogyric** Movement of the eyes in the direction of a sudden sound.

**reflex, axon** A peripheral reflex which is thought to be mediated by collateral branches of the afferent neurons activating an effector, a muscle or a gland.

**reflex, Bekhterev-Mendel** (V. M. Bekhterev and K. Mendel) A dorsal flexion of the foot with a flexion of the knee and hip on the same side upon release of a foot passively bent in a plantar direction. This reflex is seen in pyramidal tract disease.

**reflex, blinking** The closing of the eyelids caused by the exposure to bright light, by an attention shift or by tearing.

**reflex circle** The tendency for muscle contractions

to stimulate proprioceptive reflex loops, strengthening in turn the muscular contraction.

**reflex circuit** See *reflex-arc.*

**reflex, conditioned** (I. P. Pavlov) A new and temporary connection between stimulus and response which is the main function of the higher parts of the central nervous system. It is formed when an indifferent stimulus is simultaneously presented with a stimulus which elicits an unconditioned reflex. Following repeated presentations, the indifferent stimulus alone will evoke the same reflex.

**reflex, consensual eye** The contraction of the pupil in the shaded eye when the other pupil is stimulated by a bright light.

**reflex, cranial** A reflex controlled by one of the cranial nerves.

**reflex, direct** Reflex in which both the receptor and effector are on the same side of the body.

**reflex, grasping and groping** The reflexive clutching by the fingers or toes of any object that stimulates the palm or sole.

**reflex, inhibitory** The reflexive relaxation of one of a pair of antagonistic muscles following the excitation of the other muscle of the pair.

**reflex, knee jerk** See *reflex, patellar.*

**reflex, laryngeal** Coughing caused by irritation of the larynx.

**reflex, mass** Indiscriminate response of a large group of effectors to a given stimulus.

**reflex, negative movement** (I. P. Pavlov) A form of the general instinct of life consisting of movements which guard the organism against injury.

**reflex, oculocardiac** A decrease of heart rate as a result of pressure upon the eyeballs.

**reflex or response, palmar** Reflexive hand-grasp action of the newborn.

**reflex, patellar** Spontaneous forward extension of the lower leg elicited by a sudden sharp tap against the patellar tendon which is just below the knee cap.

**reflex, plantar** Spontaneous flexing of the toes which is produced by stroking the sole of the foot.

**reflex, positive movement** (I. P. Pavlov) One form of the general instinct of life consisting of movements toward conditions favorable for life.

**reflex, pupillary** The change in the size of the pupil as the muscle of the iris contracts or relaxes, responding to altered light intensity or to a changed fixation point.

**reflex reserve** (B. F. Skinner) Total number of responses made when the response no longer occasions reinforcement, i.e. during extinction. It was a measure of resistance to extinction. The term is no longer used.

**reflex, Schaeffer** (M. Schaeffer) A pathological reflex manifested by dorsal reflexion of the big toe when the Achilles tendon is pinched.

**reflex sensitization principle** The proposition which holds that a response may sometimes be elicited by a previously less effective or neutral stimulus following repeated elicitation of a response by a stimulus.

**reflex, spinal** A reflex which is mediated by the spinal cord and does not require the brain for the connection of afferent and efferent fibers.

**reflex time; reflex latency** The time which is measured from the application of a stimulus and the beginning of a reflex response.

**reflex, unconditioned** (I. P. Pavlov) An innate reflex derived from the reflex of life whose purpose is the preservation of life, which is connected with a definite sensory mechanism or analyzer and a center in the nervous system.

**reflexes, allied** Two or more simultaneous or closely associated reflexes that combine to form a response unit.

**reflexes, postural** The group of reflexes which help to maintain posture and keep the body in relatively stationary position.

**reflexology** 1. A system of laws in the field of learning experiments, in which a simple reflex connection, such as might be due to a neurological reflex arc, is supposed to exist between the stimulus and the response. 2. (V. M. Bekhterev) A theory that explains all behavior in terms of conditioned and unconditioned reflexes or combinations of them.

**refraction** A change or bending in the direction of flow of a wave, especially of a light wave.

**refraction, index of** A number giving the degree to which a light wave is bent in the passage from one transparent medium to another and dependent upon the nature of the two media and the curvature of the bounding surface.

**refractory period** 1. A brief period of time which follows the stimulation of a nerve during which it cannot be restimulated by another stimulus. 2. A brief period of time which follows the initial movement of a movement system or set of similar movements in which a second movement cannot be initiated even if it is not antagonistic to the first.

**refractory period, relative** A period of time following stimulation of a nerve in which the nerve can be restimulated only by the application of a significantly more powerful stimulus.

**regard, field of** Total space visible by rotation of the eye with the head stationary.

**regard, line of** An imaginary straight line from the fixation point to the center of the rotation of the eye.

**regard, point of** Fixation point.

**regeneration** (biology) Restoration of a lost part of the body by growth.

**region, inner personal** (K. Lewin) That part of the personality, topographically represented as a concentric circle within the larger circle representing the perceptual-motor region. The inner personal region is composed primarily of needs (physiological conditions, desires, intentions), some of which are peripherally located and therefore more accessible to the environment than others which are more centrally located.

**regional epilepsy** See *epilepsy, myoclonic.*

**register, vocal** See *vocal register.*

**regnancy** (H. A. Murray) The unit composed of the total physiological processes occurring at a single moment, which constitute dominant configurations in the brain. A single process comprising part of the regnancy is referred to as a regnant process.

**regnant construct** See *construct, regnant.*

**regression** 1. A movement backward. 2. A return to earlier or less mature behaviors or earlier or less mature levels of organization of behavior. 3. (psychoanalysis) One of the defense mechanisms in which the individual, faced with an anxiety arousing instinctual wish or impulse, returns to a stage which has previously been cathected by libido and is thus less anxiety and guilt provoking. There are two forms of regression: that in which there is a return to the original object and that in which there is a return to the level of infantile sexual organization. The return to an earlier level of organization always carries with it characteristics of the later level, possibly allowing the reworking of earlier conflicts by a more mature ego organization. 4. During the generalized weakening of retention, the tendency for memories to be lost in the inverse order of their acquisition. 5. (genetics) In individuals of the species, the tendency to return to the typical form. 6. (conditioning) The reappearance of a previously extinguished conditioned response after punishment. 7. (conditioning) During the extinction of a conditioned response to a stimulus, the reappearance of a previously extinguished conditioned response to that same stimulus. 8. (statistics) The relationship between two paired variables in which the predicted score of the dependent variable is nearer to the sample mean than is the value of the independent variable.

**regression analysis** (statistics) Adapted from the least square multiple regression equation, this procedure is used in predicting the value of a continuous, quantitative variable from a non-quantitative category or rating score.

**regression coefficient (b)** 1. (statistics) the multiplier of the independent term in the linear regression equation. It is represented by the formula:

$$b = r \frac{\sigma_y}{\sigma_x}$$

where $r$ is the correlation coefficient, and $x$ is the variance of a particular set of scores. 2. The constant in a linear regression equation which measures the slope of a regression line.

**regression curve** A smooth curve fitted to the means of a group of variables in a correlation table.

**regression curvilinear** See *regression line, curvilinear.*

**regression equation** An equation taking the form $Y = bX + a$ and employed for computing the deviation from average of one variable from the given value of another by the formula:

$$Y^1 = by.x \ (X-M_x) + M_y \text{ where}$$
$$Y^1 = \text{the predicted score}$$
$$by.x = \text{regression coefficient}$$
$$M_x = \text{mean of } x$$
$$M_y = \text{mean of } y$$
$$X = \text{given x value.}$$

**regression equation, multiple** (statistics) Equation for computing a criterion variable score for an individual from his scores on several other variables. The criterion valuable score is derived from the correlation of each of these variables with the criterion and from their intercorrelations.

**regression equation, partial** See *regression equation, multiple.*

**regression, filial** The tendency of parents who possess characteristics that widely depart from the mean of the species to produce offspring who depart less widely.

**regression in the service of the ego** (E. Kris) A temporary return to an earlier level of functioning to serve reality needs. This regression aids ego functions being controlled, circumscribed and reversible and promotes imaginative creative thinking because the primary processes become available to secondary process functions.

**regression line** 1. A line that shows the relationship between two variables. 2. A line that is the best fit for a relationship according to some theorem. It may be a curve or a straight line.

**regression line, curvilinear** The line that best fits the means in a correlation table. A regular curve, not a straight line.

**regression, linear** The regression that occurs when the line that best fits the means in a correlation table forms a line that is approximately straight.

**regression, non-linear** A regression line that is not a straight line. It includes curvilinear regression lines.

**regression, phenomenal** The size of an object one perceives that lies between what would be expected from the actual physical stimulus size of the object and what would be expected from object constancy. This entails a shift toward true physical size and away from perfect perceptual constancy.

**regression, teleologic** (S. Arieti) Regression for the purpose of avoiding anxiety and re-establishing a psychic equilibrium, a typical occurrence in schizophrenia.

**regressive behavior** Behavior more appropriate to an earlier level of development.

**regressive electroshock therapy** See *therapy, regressive electroshock.*

**regulator gene** According to the operon theory of gene action of Jacob and Monod, a regulator gene synthesizes a repressor substance which inhibits the action of a specific operator gene, thus preventing the synthesis of messenger RNA by that operon.

**rehabilitation** The process of restoring a person to the best possible level of functioning following a physical, mental or emotional disorder. This process involves training him to find employment and helping him to adjust to his status in the interpersonal sphere.

**reification** Dealing with ideas and concepts as if they were concrete objects.

**Reil, island of** A section of the cortex located at the bottom of the Sylvian fissure and covered by cortical folds present only in primates. Also called insula.

**Reilly bodies** Unusual cytoplasmic granules in white blood cells.

**reinforcement** 1. (I. P. Pavlov) Reinforcement takes place when the conditioned stimulus is presented simultaneously or at an effective interval before the unconditioned stimulus. 2. (E. L. Thorndike) Pleasure producing, rewarding stimuli, called "satisfiers," stamp in, that is strengthen the responses. Thorndike's "stamping in" corresponds to reinforcement. 3. (C. L. Hull) Primary reinforcement takes place whenever an effector activity ($R$) is closely associated with a stimulus afferent impulse or trace ($s$) and the conjunction is closely associated with the rapid diminution in the motivational stimulus ($S_D$ or $S_G$), there will result an increment ($\Delta$) to a tendency for that stimulus to evoke the response 4. (B. F. Skinner) Presenting a reinforcing stimulus when a response occurs, or arranging such presentation is operant reinforcement. Presenting a conditioned and an unconditioned stimulus at approximately the same time is respondent reinforcement.

**reinforcement, accidental** The unplanned coincidence of a response and a reinforcing event. For example, in certain programs designed to establish a discrimination, the appearance of the discriminative stimulus may coincide with a response in its absence. Also called incidental or spurious reinforcement.

**reinforcement, alternative** Reinforcement that occurs according to either a fixed-ratio or fixed-interval schedule, depending on which condition is satisfied first. For example, the alternative conditions might be 50 responses or two minutes. In such a situation, if the 50 responses occurred before the two minutes passed, a reinforcement would be given; if not, reinforcement would take place after the two minute time period had elapsed.

**reinforcement, aperiodic** Reinforcement schedule in which reinforcement occurs irregularly and intermittently, not continuously.

**reinforcement, conditioned** A rewarding event or

state of affairs which obtains its effectiveness from a prior learning or conditioning experience.

reinforcement, differential Selective reinforcement of a response to one stimulus with a greater amount of reinforcement than a response to another stimulus. This operation results in discrimination.

reinforcement, homogeneous The simultaneous presentation of two stimuli each of which elicits the same or similar response.

reinforcement, interlocking A kind of intermittent reinforcement consisting of decreasing ratio of required responses per reinforcement.

reinforcement, intermittent See reinforcement, schedule of.

reinforcement, intermittent schedule of See reinforcement, schedule of.

reinforcement, internal A bodily process which increases the probability of the occurrence of a certain response.

reinforcement, interpolated The insertion of one block of one schedule of reinforcements into another for a brief period of time.

reinforcement, Jendrassik A method of increasing a reflex response, usually the patellar reflex, by having the subject interlock his hands and pull and presenting the usual stimulus the moment the subject begins to pull.

reinforcement mechanisms Areas of the brain which are positively or negatively reinforcing. The posterior hypothalamus and midbrain have positive rewarding qualities more effective as rewards than food. Stimulation of the dorsal diencephalic zone is a negative reinforcement which an organism tries to avoid.

reinforcement, negative The use of coercive stimuli for reduction or prevention of probability of reinforcement.

reinforcement, neural The rewarding effect that one response has on a simultaneously occurring response resulting in a stronger response.

reinforcement of affect (S. Freud) The process in which the suppressed ideas and the mechanism of suppression combine their forces producing mutual cooperation.

reinforcement, partial 1. Intermittent reinforcement or reinforcement which does not occur on every trial but only sporadically, resulting in slower learning rate and slower extinction rate than continuous reinforcement. 2. Presentation of only part of a reward or of reinforcing conditions.

reinforcement, positive A reinforcer which when presented as a consequence of a particular response or behavior increases the occurrence of that response.

reinforcement, predelay A modification of the delayed response technique. The experimental arrival is rewarded at a certain place, then prevented for a while from returning to that place. The return of the animal to the same place after a period of delay.

reinforcement, primary 1. A stimulus increasing the probability of a response without necessitating the learning of the value of the reinforcer. 2. The reduction of a primary-drive state through drive-stimulus reduction.

reinforcement, schedule of (operant conditioning) In the operant situation usually not every response is reinforced. In the laboratory and in life, similar behaviors seldom have the same effect upon the environment in two instances; therefore, the effect called reinforcement is seldom the consequence of every response. Most reinforcements are intermittent. A schedule of reinforcement is the prescription or rule for presenting and terminating reinforcing stimuli that are contingent upon behavior.

The schedule specifies in what way the presentation of the reinforcing stimulus is dependent upon the occurrence of the response. A schedule, therefore, may be defined without reference to its effect upon behavior.

Schedules have regular, orderly and profound effects on the organism's behavior. Each schedule produces a characteristic behavior which may be steady, constant, or cyclic with predictable changes. Just by looking at a record of responses it is often possible to tell what schedule was operative without knowing what type of organism was responding.

reinforcement, schedule of: adjusting (ADJ) Intermittent schedule in which the value of the interval or ratio is changed in some systematic way after reinforcement as a function of the immediately preceding performance. The change in performance requirement occurs from reinforcement to reinforcement in the adjusting schedule while in the interlocking schedule the change in requirement occurs within the reinforcement.

reinforcement, schedule of: alternate (ALT) Intermittent reinforcement schedule in which a response is reinforced either by a fixed ratio or fixed interval schedule whichever is satisfied first. Thus, e.g. in ALT FI 5 FR 300, the first response is reinforced either after a period of 5 minutes if 300 responses have not been made, or upon the completion of 300 responses before 5 minutes have past.

reinforcement, schedule of: chained (CHAIN) Intermittent schedule similar to a tandem schedule; however, a stimulus change is correlated to the completion of the first part of the schedule. The second stimulus controls behavior appropriate to the second part of the schedule.

reinforcement, schedule of: concurrent (CONC) (B. F. Skinner) Two or more schedules independently arranged, but operative at the same time. Each independent schedule is programmed on a separate operandum. For example, in a CONC FI 5 FR 300 reinforcements are programmed to be delivered on one operandum after the first response, five minutes after the previous reinforcement has been delivered on that operandum; at the same time reinforcements are programmed to be delivered after 300 responses on the other operandum. The organism has free access to both operandi; however, since it is impossible to respond on both operandi simultaneously, the organism chooses the operandum, thus choosing the schedule. Concurrent schedules are one way of studying choice behavior and establishing preferences with an operant paradigm.

**reinforcement, schedule of: conjugate** (B. F. Skinner) Schedule in which responses initiate or terminate a constant, subthreshold change in stimulation. Thus, for example, if the subject does not respond, the intensity of illumination constantly but gradually decreases until darkness is reached. If the subject responds, the stimulus change can be terminated or reversed; the more he responds, the brighter it gets. The point is, in conjugate schedules, that stimulus intensities are scheduled to change on a continuum and responses either terminate or reverse the direction of this.

**reinforcement, schedule of: conjunctive (CONJ)** (B. F. Skinner) Intermittent reinforcement schedule in which both a ratio and interval must be satisfied for a response to occasion a reinforcement. Thus, for example, in ALT FI 5 FR 300 a response is reinforced 5 minutes after the previous reinforcement and after at least 300 responses have been made.

**reinforcement, schedule of: continuous (CRF)** (B. F. Skinner) A nonintermittent reinforcement schedule in which every emitted response is reinforced.

**reinforcement, schedule of: differential reinforcement of high rates (DRH)** (B. F. Skinner) Reinforcement occurs when the response rate is above some specified value.

**reinforcement, schedule of: differential reinforcement of low rates (DRL)** (B. F. Skinner) Reinforcement schedule in which a response is reinforced only when a specific time has elapsed since the immediately preceding response. Thus reinforcement is contingent upon a low rate of responding.

**reinforcement, schedule of: extinction (EXT)** (B. F. Skinner) A nonintermittent schedule in which every emitted response has the same effect on the environment, i.e. no response is reinforced.

**reinforcement, schedule of: fixed interval (FI)** (operant conditioning) Intermittent reinforcement schedule in which the presentation of the reinforcing stimulus to the organism is contingent upon the first response the organism makes after a fixed period of time since the previous reinforcement. All other responses made before or after the reinforcement have no effect upon the presentation of the reinforcement. This schedule is designated usually in minutes; thus FI 5 means that the first response made five minutes after the previous reinforcement is reinforced.

**reinforcement, schedule of: fixed ratio (FR)** An intermittent reinforcement schedule in which a response is reinforced upon completion of a fixed number of responses counted from the preceding reinforcement. The ratio refers to the ratio of responses to reinforcement. This schedule is indicated

by the addition of the ratio after FR; thus in FR 100 the one-hundredth response after the previous reinforcement is reinforced.

**reinforcement, schedule of: interlocking (INTER)** Intermittent reinforcement schedule in which a response is reinforced upon completion of a number of responses; but this number changes during the interval that follows the previous reinforcement. For example, immediately after reinforcement, 300 responses may be required for another reinforcement; but this may be reduced as a linear function of time, so that after 10 minutes one response will occasion reinforcement. Therefore, if the organism responded rapidly it would have to have emitted nearly the 300 responses. If responding was slower, it would have been reinforced after a smaller number of responses. Of course, many different cases are possible. In an increasing interlocking schedule ratio, requirements increase as some function of time.

**reinforcement, schedule of: intermittent** (B. F. Skinner) One or two classes of reinforcement schedules in which only certain selected occurrences of a response are reinforced. The schedule is the rule followed by the environment; in an experiment, by the apparatus in determining which among the many occurrences of a response will be reinforced. The intermittent schedules include: fixed ratio (FR), fixed interval (FI), variable ratio (VR), variable interval (VI), alternative (ALT), conjunctive (CONJ), interlocking (INTER), tandem (TAND), chained (CHAIN), adjusting (ADJ), multiple (MULT), mixed (MIX), interpolated (INTER), concurrent (CONC). The second class of reinforcement schedules is the non-intermittent schedules.

**reinforcement, schedule of: interpolated (INTER)** (B. F. Skinner) An intermittent schedule in which a small block of reinforcements, contingent on one schedule, may be introduced into a background of another schedule. For example, a block of 10 reinforcements on a FR 50 is inserted into a six hour period of reinforcement on FI 10.

**reinforcement, schedule of: mixed (MIX)** Intermittent schedule similar to a multiple schedule except stimuli are not correlated with the schedules. For example, MIX FI 5 FR 50 indicates a schedule in which reinforcement occurs after either a 5 minute interval or 50 responses. These possibilities occur either randomly or in a determined proportion in a given program.

**reinforcement, schedule of: multiple (MULT)** Intermittent schedule consisting of two or more independent schedules alternating at random and presented successively to the organism. Each schedule correlates with a different discriminative stimulus which is presented as long as the schedule is operative. For example, in MULT FI 5 FR 100 the response key is sometimes red, and sometimes green, the former when reinforcement is occasioned after 100 responses.

**reinforcement, schedule of: non-intermittent** (B. F. Skinner) One of two classes of reinforcement schedules in which every response has the same environmental effect, i.e. each response is equally effective in producing reinforcement. The non-intermittent schedules are continuous reinforcement (CRF) and extinction (EXT). The second class of reinforcement schedules is the intermittent schedules.

**reinforcement, schedule of: second order** The behavior specified by a complete schedule is treated as a unitary response which is itself reinforced according to some schedule of primary reinforcement; thus a way of specifying schedules of schedules. For example, FR 3 (FI 2) indicates a second order schedule in which primary reinforcement is contingent upon completion of three successive FI 2 schedules. This schedule FR 3 (FI 2) in which there are no extroceptive stimulus changes upon completion of the FI schedules is, in the terminology of Ferster and Skinner, a tandem schedule, TAND FI 2 FI 2 FI 2.

**reinforcement; schedule of: tandem (TAND)** Intermittent schedule in which reinforcement is contingent upon the completion of two schedules, the second beginning when the first has been completed. However, there is no change in stimulus correlated with the change in schedule. For example, in TAND FI 10 FR 5, reinforcement occurs after 5 responses, counted only after a response that occurred 10 minutes after the previous reinforcement. In TAND FR 300 FI 5, 300 responses must be made, followed by a 5 minute period whereupon a response occasions the reinforcement.

**reinforcement, schedule of: variable interval (VI)** Intermittent reinforcement schedule in which responses are reinforced after a time interval from the previous reinforcement. This time interval is variable between reinforcements and is usually a random series of intervals having a given mean and lying within an arbitrary range. The average interval of reinforcements, usually in minutes, is indicated by addition of a number to the letters VI, thus VI 5 indicates a variable interval schedule with a mean interval of 5 minutes.

**reinforcement, schedule of: variable ratio (VR)** Intermittent reinforcement schedule in which a response is reinforced upon completion of a number of responses counted from the preceding reinforcement. The specific ratios are from a random series of ratios having a given mean and lying within an arbitrary range. The mean ratio may be noted by a number; for example, VR 100 indicates that on the average, the one-hundredth response is reinforced.

**reinforcement, secondary** A stimulus which derives its reinforcing qualities from previous conditioning experience in which it has been associated with a primary reward.

**reinforcement, serial** Reinforcement of any particular response in serial learning.

**reinforcement, successive differential** See *conditioning, approximation.*

**reinforcement withdrawal** A therapeutic method of withholding reinforcement for responses to reduce the probability of the recurrence of these responses.

**reinforcer, conditioned** A stimulus which has reinforcing properties by virtue of previous learning or conditioning experience.

**reinforcing stimulus** The unconditioned or rewarding stimulus which is presented or naturally experienced following the subject's having performed the correct response.

**reintegration** See *redintegration.*

**Reix limen (RL)** (psychophysics) German phrase for absolute threshold.

**rejection 1.** The act of determining something or somebody as worthless, or tossing something aside as unimportant, or of refusing to place or locate something in a certain class or category. **2.** (psychoanalysis) A mechanism involving the denial of gratification to an instinctual demand while tolerating the existence of the demand in the conscious mind.

**rejection need** See *need, rejection.*

**relapse** A recurrence of symptoms after cure or a period of improvement.

**relation measure** (statistics) A mathematical formulation which describes the change in one variable paralleling the change in another variable.

**relations, informational** (J. P. Guilford) Definitive connections between items of information based on variables or points of contact that apply to them.

**relationship psychotherapy** See *psychotherapy, relationship.*

**relative refractory period** See *refractory period, relative.*

**relativism, cultural** The belief that the concepts of behavior disorders depend on a particular cultural setting, and individuals believed to be mentally disturbed in one culture may appear normal in another.

**relaxation, progressive** (E. Jacobson) A relaxation training technique in which the person, starting with the most easy muscles to control, learns to relax muscle groups, leading eventually to being able to relax his whole body.

**relaxation therapy** See *therapy, relaxation.*

**relearning and saving method** See *saving method.*

**release phenomenon 1.** (neurology) The activity in a lower center of the brain when a higher controlling center is not functioning. **2.** The inhibited motor discharge occurring when a higher brain center is damaged.

**release therapy** See *therapy, release.*

**releaser** (ethology) A stimulus which is highly specific and which elicits species-specific behavior.

**reliability** The degree to which results are consistent on repetition of the experiment.

**reliability coefficient** See *coefficient, reliability.*

**reliability, index of** An estimate of the correlation between the obtained scores on a test and the theoretically true scores on the test.

**reliability sampling** A measure of the reliability of two or more samples derived from the same population.

**reliability, split-half method of** A measure of reliability in which items from one part of a test are correlated with items from another part of the test.

**religious mania** See *mania, religious*.

**religious therapy** See *therapy, religious*.

**religious type** See *type, religious*.

**remedial instruction** Didactic techniques used with children with learning difficulties

**remedial reading** See *reading, remedial*.

**remission** Disappearance of symptoms.

**remote association** In verbal learning, the connection between one item in a list and one removed from it by at least two steps.

**remote association test** See *test, remote association*.

**remote conditioning** See *track conditioned response*.

**renal aminoacidurias** See *aminoacidurias, renal*.

**renal dwarfism** See *dwarfism, renal*.

**renifleur** An individual for whom sexual excitement is associated with certain odors.

**repetition compulsion** 1. (S. Freud) The conservative tendency of instincts to recreate and repeat an earlier state. The repetition of the experience is an active attempt to master the anxiety experienced previously. It functions to bind energy and reduce tension and manifests a tendency of the instincts to return to the inorganic state. 2. An irrational need to repeat a particular behavior.

**repetition, law of** The proposition which holds that a function is facilitated by being used or exercised and is weakened by disuse.

**replication** The breaking down of an experiment into various components, each containing the essential parts to allow for a comparison between the several replicas, enabling the discrimination between the effect of the experimental conditions and those of irregular or variable conditions.

**report method** Method of measuring retention in which the subject is asked to report his observations after witnessing an event or examining a picture or number of objects for a given length of time. The number of correctly reported items is taken as the measure of retention.

**representation** An obsolete term (*Darstellung*) used loosely as an idea, concept, perception, etc.

**representative design** 1. (E. Brunswik) An experimental procedure utilizing the covariation of a group of variables in the study of stimulus-response relationships. 2. A type of experiment in which a representative or stratified sample of subjects is included.

**representative factors** 1. Those activities which are hypothesized to allow the organism to continue or to renew a response despite the withdrawal of the original stimulus. 2. The verbal symbols and imagery serving as mediators of ideational activity.

**representative measure or score** A number—the mean or median, for example—which can stand for all the scores collectively.

**representative sampling** See *sampling, representative*.

**repression** (psychoanalysis) The main defense mechanism. Repression is an unconscious exclusion from the consciousness of objectionable impulses, memories and ideas. The ego, as it were, pushes the objectionable material down into the unconscious and acts as if the objectionable material were nonexistent.

**repression, primary** (psychoanalysis) That process which originally expels the instinctual derivative from the conscious mind.

**repression resistance** See *resistance, repression*.

**repression, secondary** (psychoanalysis) That process which prevents the return to the conscious mind of the expelled instinctual derivative.

**reproduction** 1. The making or creation of a near copy of something. 2. (biology) The creation of a new organism by a parent organism or by parent organisms. 3. (learning) The doing of a task in the manner in which it was first learned.

**reproduction method** 1. See *adjustment procedure*. 2. A means of assessing retention through the reproduction as completely as possible of learned material.

**reproductive facilitation** (learning) An increase in the level of reproduction of some learned material as a result of some activity which occurs between the learning trials and the reproduction trials.

**reproductive function** 1. The sum of the activities, operations or processes involved in the making or creation of a new organism. 2. A specific act, such as sexual intercourse, involved in the creation of a new organism.

**reproductive interference** (learning) A decrease in the reproduction of some learned material as a result of some activity which occurs between the learning trials and the reproduction trials.

**reproductive strength** An expression of the summation of all factors which tend to increase the probability that a specific response will be made.

**research** 1. A detailed and systematic attempt, often prolonged, to discover or confirm through objective investigation the facts pertaining to a specified problem or problems and the laws and principles controlling it. 2. Library, record, document, or other investigation which attempts to uncover or develop new facts concerning some subject, especially towards the end of developing an historical understanding or perspective of the subject.

**research for action** Research aiming at social change.

**research, market** 1. The systematic investigation of buying and selling behavior. 2. The systematic investigation of the expected volume of sales under specific circumstances.

**research, personnel** Investigation of the individual and of groups with reference to work situations and work conditions both physical and social as a means of dealing with personnel needs and problems and of meeting management needs and goals.

**reserpine** A purified alkaloid extract of Rauwolfia which produces a generally depressant effect. It has been used in the treatment of the psychoses, hyper-aggressivity and hyperactivity. The complications—initial considerable sleepiness, increase in heart rate and, in high doses, Parkinsonian symptoms—have led generally to the use of the phenothiazines in the treatment of these conditions.

**residential treatment** See *treatment, residential.*

**residual** 1. That which remains after certain events or processes, especially accidents, illnesses or operations. Residual vision is the vision which remains after being partially blinded. 2. The difference between a computed and observed value. 3. (factor analysis) The variance remaining once the variance of all factors has been extracted.

**residual epilepsy** See *epilepsy, residual.*

**residual matrix** The matrix which remains following the extraction of the variance due to a factor.

**residues, method of** (J. S. Mill) One of the working principles of induction which holds that the unexplained remainder of an antecedent condition or event results in the unexplained remainder of an effect.

**resignation, neurotic** (K. Horney) A solution for inner conflicts, involving the avoidance of and withdrawal from the situations, events and experiences which would tend to bring the conflict into awareness.

**resistance** (psychoanalysis) Resistance is a continuation of repression which interferes, often actively, with the progress of the analysis. The patient resists in various ways, working for or reaching the goal for which he entered analysis. It is an expression of the wish to maintain the repression of the unconscious desires. The analysis of the resistances, along with the analysis of the transference, forms the basic task of psychoanalysis.

**resistance, epinosic** Resistance aimed at the perpetuation of secondary gain. The patient may wish to stay neurotic and gain all the sympathy and consideration that can be wrung from the sick role. It comes from the ego, as if the ego feared to give up its neurotic mechanisms and face a head-on collision with instinctual forces. This form of resistance occurs most frequently at the beginning of treatment, and in the final stage, when the patient is expected to abandon infantile modes of emotional life.

**resistance, id** (psychoanalysis) Resistance dominated by the repetition compulsion. The resistance takes the form of repeating the same process rather than recollecting it. Id resistances cannot be easily lifted because they hinge on the basic rules of unconscious behavior—the constancy and pleasure principles. A prolonged process of working through is required.

**resistance, repression** (psychoanalysis) Resistance in which the patient attempts to maintain the repression of unacceptable instinctual derivatives by forgetting most recent events; by being unable to free associate; by preventing a continuous flow of free associations in that they go in every possible direction; and by accepting the analyst's interpretation and applying it to everyone but himself.

**resistance, superego** Resistance to psychoanalytic treatment stemming from the superego. It originates from a sense of guilt requiring punishment for alleviation and, therefore, opposes any success in treatment. Also called negative therapeutic reaction.

**resistance, transference** Resistance in which the patient attempts to avoid the treatment of the neurosis by acting-out his transference-love or -hate for the analyst. The task of the analyst is to transform the acting-out of these past feelings into a recollection of them.

**resolving power** 1. The ability or capacity of the eye to perceive two distinct objects when the two objects are viewed simultaneously. 2. The ability of the eye to perceive two distinct objects when the two objects are casting images in close proximity on the retina.

**resonance** 1. The vibration of an object resulting from force applied with periodic frequency, especially the vibrations in an object in response to external sound. 2. A deep, rich and vibrant vocal quality.

**resonance theory of hearing** See *hearing, theory of: resonance theory.*

**resonator** An instrument or device which makes use of the principle of resonance in the intensification of a tone.

**respiratory disorders** See *disorders, respiratory.*

**respondent behavior** Behavior which is elicited by a particular stimulus.

**response; *R*** 1. An answer, especially a formal answer, such as to a question on a test or questionnaire. 2. Any process in the body, muscular, glandular, etc., which results from stimulation. 3. A psychic process which results from previous psychic processes, sensory or imaginal. 4. Any overt or covert behavior; the class or the organisms executing processes.

**response amplitude** 1. A quantitative measure of a response, assessed in terms of some predetermined dimension. 2. See *response magnitude.*

**response, antedating** A response which occurs earlier than usual in a sequence of events.

**response, anticipatory** See *error, anticipatory.*

**response circuit** The neuronal chain or loop from the receptors to the effectors.

**response class; R class** A category of behaviors or parts of behaviors of an organism all of which tend to produce the same, or similar, effects on the organism's environment or changes in his relation to the environment.

**response, consummatory** A concluding response in a series of responses which brings the organism to a state of adjustment in a situation which has been partly or totally determined by the preparatory responses.

**response, content** (Rorschach) A scoring category for responses of what the subject sees such as a bat or an ice-cream sundae.

**response, differential** Response to only one of several stimuli; as a consequence of training, responses to the other stimuli do not occur.

**response differentiation** See *conditioning, approximation.*

**response equivalence** See *equivalence, response.*

**response, fractional antedating goal** 1. A component of the goal response which occurs in the absence of its goal reinforcer. It occurs earlier in the series of conditioned component responses than it originally occurred. 2. Symbol: $r_G$.

**response generalization principle** The principle which holds that when an organism is conditioned to a particular stimulus, that stimulus becomes effective in eliciting other responses.

**response hierarchy** A class of behaviors, parts of behaviors, or behavior patterns which are arranged in the order of the probability of their elicitation in a certain stimulus situation.

**response, implicit** Muscular and glandular responses not directly observable without the appropriate instruments.

**responses incompatible** Responses which cannot occur at the same time and place though either may be elicited by the same stimulus.

**response, individual** A response to a word on an association test that is uncommon and does not appear on standard lists, such as the Kent-Rosanoff, of response frequencies.

**response inhibition** (O. H. Mowrer) The inhibition of a response by internal cues in the presence of the eliciting stimulus.

**response, kinesthetic** (Rorschach) A response which projects movement, action, or life onto the inkblots.

**response latency** 1. Time between stimulus onset and the response in experimental procedures with discrete trials or inter-response times in operant conditioning procedures. 2. A measure of response strength.

**response learning** See *learning, response.*

**response magnitude** See *response strength.*

**response, negative** A response which tends to move the organism away from something, which tends to remove the organism from exposure to a stimulus, either by leaving the situation or by behavior designed to remove or cancel the stimulus in question.

**response-oriented theories or systems** All approaches to or systems of psychology whose primary datum or dependent variable is the response. Such systems include functional psychology, behaviorism, stimulus-response psychology, act psychology and reaction psychology.

**response pattern** A qualitative and quantitative grouping of responses into a distinct unit of activity.

**response, pilomotor** Spontaneous reaction of the hair moving or stiffening as occurs in times of fear and shivering or with goose-pimples.

**response probability** 1. Relative frequency of a response over a number of opportunities. 2. A possible measure of response strength.

**response-produced conflict** A conflict caused by the elicitation of a response which has been previously punished.

**response-reinforcement contingency** The relationship between a response and the rewarding stimulus.

**response, selective** A response which has been differentiated and chosen from a number of possible alternative responses.

**response, serial** A response occurring in an ordered sequence of responses.

**response set** 1. In reaction time experiments or similar situation, the concentration on the muscular, or response, phase of the experiment rather than on the sensory, or perceptual phase in which the subject is ready to perceive the stimuli. 2. The readiness to respond in a certain pattern, to perform one type of response over another.

**response-shock interval** (B. F. Skinner) The time which elapses between the last response and the occurrence of a shock as an aversive stimulus in avoidance conditioning.

**response, species specific** See *behavior, species specific.*

**response, stereotyped** 1. A behavior or response that is consistently occasioned by some problem situation, varies little in its topography, and is little altered by its consequences. 2. Successive occurrences of a response which does not vary in its topography.

**response strength** A measure of the magnitude or intensity of a response. It is important to realize that a response is an arbitrarily defined bit of behavior and among the measures of response strength are frequency, latency rate, amplitude, duration. There is no simple relationship among these measures and each can be independently effected by the reinforcement contingencies. Thus it is not justified to say that response strength changed unless the aspect of the response being measured is specified.

response threshold   See *threshold, response.*

response time   See *reaction time.*

response topography   See *topography, response.*

response variable   See *variable, response.*

responses, chained (operant conditioning)   A sequence of responses in which one response produces the necessary stimulus conditions for the next response. The topography of the chained responses may or may not be the same.

responsibility, legal   The accountability for actions and their consequences in those who are assumed to be able to conform to laws, customs, and standards of the society.

rest-cure   A method of treatment not widely used or recognized, which stresses the importance of rest, environmental change, fattening diet, massage and mild exercise.

restructure   1. (E. C. Tolman) To alter the relative position of part-regions without changing their total number. 2. (K. Lewin) The basic change in the relationships of the psychological field, usually through changes internal to the person rather than changes in the environment or external conditions.

retained members method   A type of recall method of measuring retention using a series of items to be learned that exceeds the memory span and giving an insufficient number of presentations for complete learning.

retardate, familial   Diagnostic term referring to a mildly retarded individual with a genealogical history of retardation who exhibits no physiological causes for the retardation.

retardation   1. The slowing down of a process. 2. The slowing down of an individual's mental development. 3. (I. P. Pavlov) A type of internal inhibition in which the conditioned response is delayed due to the presentation of the unconditioned stimulus several minutes after the beginning of the conditioned stimulus.

retention   1. (physiology) The inability or refusal to empty the bladder or rectum. 2. (learning) The fact that a learned behavior will persist after a period of time has passed in which the behavior has not been performed.

retention curve   See *curve, retention.*

reticular activating system   A structure consisting of a network of nerve fibers found at the upper part of the spinal cord whose function is to regulate attention and arousal by activating the cerebral cortex and to screen out sensory stimuli.

reticuloendothelial system   Hypothesized by F. J. Kallman to be Macrophage system (RES), man's defense mechanism against schizophrenia.

reticulum   (biology) A finely interwoven network in a cell or in some delicate tissue system.

retifism   A pathological condition in which one's sexual needs are satisfied by the foot or shoe of the loved one which is responded to as if it were the genitals.

retinal disparity   See *disparity, retinal.*

retinal field   The specific pattern of rods and cones activated by the particular image falling on the retina.

retinal image   The image of external objects formed on the retina by the structures of the eye.

retinal light   An idioretinal sensation of light, occurring in the absence of any type of stimulation and presumably due to the intrinsic neuronal activity of the cortex and retina.

retinal oscillations   The excitation effect of a single momentary stimulus characterized by variations in the state of excitation of the visual neural apparatus and experienced as a succession of dark and bright phases.

retinal rivalry   An irregular alternation of images when the two eyes are focused on different sensory fields that cannot be somehow fused or are not subject to a unitary interpretation.

retinal zones   See *color zones.*

retinene   A retinal pigment which is related to carotene and from which, in the presence of vitamin A and certain proteins, visual purple is formed.

retinitis   Inflammation of the retina.

retinoscope   A mirror with a small aperture at its center through which light passes and through which the observer is able to examine the interior of the eye.

retroactive association   A connection which is made between an item in a list to be learned and any item which precedes it in the list.

retroactive inhibition   See *inhibition, retroactive.*

retrobulbar   1. Situated behind the eyeball. 2. Behind the medulla oblongata.

retrogenesis   The hypothesis which holds that new growth process develops out of undifferentiated tissue rather than out of a fully developed structure.

retrospection   The systematic review and observation of an experience after it has already happened, especially as soon after its occurrence as possible.

return afferentation   (P.K. Anokhin) A pattern of afferent parameters characterizing the useful result received by the functional system. Return afferentation is composed of quite various sensory modalities, which on the whole give an adequate reflection of the result received (visual, tactile, auditory, etc.). It must be distinguished from the proprioceptive afferentation which, though being a "return" from muscles, has a correcting effect upon the action itself. The result of this correction is a pattern of afferent excitations which corresponds to the result received in accordance with the decision made and with the acceptor of action results already formed, where collation of both complexes of afferent features takes place. The difference between the parameters of the return afferentation and of those predicted on the basis of afferent synthesis elicits disintegration that serves as a stimulus to the immediate formation of a new, more adequate program. The idea and formulation of the return afferentation were elaborated on the basis of study of an organism's compensatory adaptation under disturbed functions by P. K. Anokhin. Being a pattern of afferent parameters of the result received, the return afferentation is anticipation of the "feed-back" as the basic regularity of cybernetics.

**return sweep** The movement of the eyes in reading from the end of one line back to the beginning of the next.

**reverberatory circuit** A neuronal system in the brain or autonomic nervous system which is able to maintain activity after the demise of the initiating impulse. It is known to exist in the autonomic nervous system and hypothesized to exist in the central nervous system.

**reverie** A dream-like state in which the subject experiences visions or ideational mental processes.

**reverie, hypnagogic** Reverie occurring in a hypnagogic state.

**reversal** (psychoanalysis) The transformation of one instinctual derivative into its opposite.

**reversal learning** See *learning, reversal.*

**reversible figure** A specific form of ambiguous figure in which there is a ready and rapid reversal of the perspective.

**reversible perspective** See *alternating perspective.*

**reversion** 1. The inheritance and manifestation of a recessive trait that was not manifested in the parent(s). 2. A regression or return to an earlier developmental level. 3. Atavism, or the reappearance of a hereditary characteristic after absence in immediately preceding generations.

**revival** The recall or reproduction of an experience.

**reward** A stimulus, stimulus-object, situation or verbal statement which is presented upon completion of a successful performance of a task and which tends to increase the probability of the behavior involved.

**reward expectancy** (E. C. Tolman) A hypothesized process which is aroused when an organism encounters the circumstances which have been associated with a reward. It is a set or readiness which moves the animal to search for a goal, is built up over a number of trials and is associated with a certain place or pathway.

**reward, extrinsic** A reward which is external to the behavior being rewarded or which is perceived by the subject as not being logically or intrinsically connected to the thing being rewarded.

**reward, intrinsic** A reward which is closely connected to or part of the behavior or task being rewarded and cannot be separated from it.

**reward learning (or operant conditioning)** Learning new paths or responses towards a goal, under the influence of the 'law of effect', i.e. the tendency of rewarded behaviors to be remembered. See *operant conditioning.*

**reward, positive** See *reinforcement, positive.*

**reward, primary** A stimulus object or situation which is satisfying for the organism without the animal's having to learn to like it—food, drink, sex objects.

**reward, secondary** See *reinforcement, secondary.*

**reward training** A type of learning in which a correct response is rewarded.

**Rh blood factor** An agglutinating factor present in the blood named after the rhesus monkey in whom it was first found. When introduced into an organism who lacks it, it causes the production of antibodies. Rh positive in children of Rh negative mothers causes jaundice, paralysis and convulsions at birth and mental deficiency.

**rheobase** The strength of direct electrical current which is just sufficient to excite a nerve or muscle.

**rheotropism; rheotaxis** A tropistic response to water in which the tropism is a turning in line with the direction of the flow of water.

**rheumatoid arthritis** See *arthritis, rheumatoid.*

**rhinencephalon** The area of the brain which includes the olfactory bulb and a portion of the forebrain in the lateral fissure which includes the hippocampus pyriform lobes and fornix. It is chiefly concerned with the reception and integration of olfactory impulses and with the regulation of appropriate motor activities in response to such impulses.

**RHO:** $\rho$ The coefficient of correlation for squared rank differences:

$$\rho = 1 - \frac{6\Sigma D^2}{N(N^2-1)}$$

with $D$ equal to the deviation in ranks and $N$ the number of ranked cases.

**rhodopsin** Visual purple, the pigmented substance which stimulates the rods of the retina. It bleaches in bright white light and recovers in darkness and is thought to be the material involved in the reception of faint visual stimuli.

**ribosomal RNA** A type of ribonucleic acid which lines up amino acids in the ribosomes to form proteins according to a particular sequence.

**ribosomes** Small bodies in the cytoplasm of a cell which synthesize proteins.

**Ribot, Théodule Armand (1839-1916)** French psychologist who, while not undertaking many experiments himself, wrote many books on psychology. He familiarized himself with the new developments in British and German psychology, publishing books on these in French in 1870 and 1879.

**right and wrong cases method** See *method, constant stimulus.*

**right and wrong test**　See *M'Naghten rules.*

**right associates method**　A common procedure in the investigation of learning and retention. Items which are generally verbal are presented in pairs; the first of each pair, generally not in the same order as the first series, is presented briefly and the subject attempts to reproduce the second, yielding the number of retained members or successes.

**righting reflex**　A reflex or reflexive act which serves to return the organism to an upright position when thrown off balance or when placed on its back.

**rigidity**　1. (physiology) A state of strong muscular contraction. 2. The inability to alter one's opinions, attitudes or actions when they are inappropriate.

**risk level**　The percentage of samples which can be expected to fall outside the particular statistical limits, such as the five or ten per cent level. Therefore, at the five percent level, the chances are one out of twenty, that the obtained statistic, with repeated samplings, will be significantly less or greater than one would expect from chance fluctuation.

**ritalin**　Common name for methylphenidate.

**RNA (ribonucleic acid)**　A nucleic acid formed upon a DNA template and taking part in the synthesis of polypeptides. There are three varieties: 1) Messenger RNA—the template upon which polypeptides are synthesized. 2) Transfer RNA (soluble RNA), which collaboratively with ribosomes brings activated amino acids into position along the messenger RNA template. 3) Ribosomal RNA, a component of the ribosomes, which serves as a non-specific site of polypeptide synthesis.

**RNA, effects of behavior on**　Experiments have shown that rotation in rabbits cause the production of RNA in the nerve associated with equilibrium. The process of learning has been found to produce a change in RNA bases.

**RNA, virus**　A type of messenger RNA which codes genetic information for virus protein *in vitro* and codes for more than one distinct protein.

**R-O-C**　See *Receiver Operating Characteristic Curve.*

**rod vision**　Vision in which only the rods function, the cones not being involved.

**rods of Corti**　Tiny columnar cells which line the organ of corti in the inner ear, forming arches.

**rods; retinal rods**　Structures in the retina which are rod shaped and which are thought to be the specific structures for the reception for grey or achromatic visual qualities at the lower intensities.

**Roe, Anne (1904-　)**　American psychologist. Except for several years as a Training Unit Chief in the Veterans Administration, has been chiefly engaged in research. Made earliest clinical studies of living artists and scientists. Developed new classification of occupations based on psychological aspects, and has contributed largely to theoretical development of field of occupational psychology. Other research topics have included intellectual functions in normal, asphasic, and mentally disordered adults; behavior of newborn infants; development of foster children from different backgrounds; behavior and evolution; psychology of creativity; relations between early experiences and career patterns; aspects of use of woman-power.

**Rogers, Carl R. (1902-　)**　American psychologist and educator. Developed the client-centered approach to psychotherapy and the principles and theory which were deduced from his experience in working with individuals in the therapeutic process. Led and sponsored research in the process of psychotherapy, its outcomes, the attitudinal conditions which foster therapeutic growth and personal growth, and the application of these principles in groups as diverse as college students and confirmed schizophrenics. His theory is based on the hypothesis that given the proper psychological climate of attitudinal conditions, the individual has within himself the capacity and the strength to gain insight into and to cope with his problems. He and others have put this hypothesis to work in ways which have helped to revolutionize the concept of the helping relationship in therapy, in educational guidance, in education itself, in encounter groups, in the ministry and in other professions.

**Rolando's fissure**　Central sulcus.

**Rolando's sulcus**　Central sulcus.

**role**　A pattern of behavior that is characteristic or expected of an individual occupying a particular position within a social system.

**role action pattern**　The pattern of special responses that actually distinguishes a person in a particular role.

**role construct repertory test**　See *test, role construct repertory.*

**role-directed psychotherapy**　See *psychotherapy, role-directed.*

**role playing**　1. The taking on or performing of a role. 2. Behaving according to a role which is not ones own. 3. A means of studying a role in all its manifestations and concrete details by enacting the role in a contrived situation, allowing for a better and more objective understanding. 4. (psychotherapy) The adoption of the role of an important other in the person's life so as to come to a better understanding of the other or the adoption of social roles so as to better understand how he conceives of and functions in them.

**role therapy**　See *therapy, role.*

**Romberg sign**　The swaying which is evident in a person with locomotor ataxia when he tries to stand quietly with eyes closed and feet together.

**root conflict**　A central conflict having its roots in infancy and playing a part in the entire development of the personality, especially in the formation of later conflicts and complexes.

**root-mean-square (RMS)**　The square root of the

sum of several values squared, divided by the number of values in the sample. The formula is:

$$RMS = \sqrt{\frac{\Sigma X^2}{N}}$$

**root, sensory**  Any dorsal root of the spinal cord involved in sensory functions.

**root, spinal**  The end part of the spinal nerves which connects with the spinal cord, including the ventral motor roots and dorsal sensory roots.

**rooting reflex**  The head-turning and mouth-opening movements in the infant when his cheek is stroked which is involved in the reflex to turn toward the breast when being nursed.

**Rorschach, Hermann (1884-1922)**  Swiss psychiatrist who in 1911 at the age of 27 began his experiments with inkblots to study reflex hallucinations. Studying as many as 40 inkblots, Rorschach ultimately settled on the 10 which comprise his now famous test. Rorschach's monograph, *Psychodiagnostik,* had been intended as a preliminary report; however, a few months following its publication in 1921, he developed peritonitis after an attack of appendicitis and died in April, 1922, at the age of 37. His work, though incomplete, became a milestone from which much of modern clinical psychology developed. See *test, Rorschach inkblots.*

**Rorschach test**  See *test, Rorschach inkblots.*

**Rosenzweig Picture-Frustration Test**  See *test, Rosenzweig, Picture-Frustration.*

**Rossolimo reflex**  (G. I. Rossolimo) A plantar flexion of the toes which is elicited by tapping the balls of the toes. It is a pathological reflex exhibited when the lower motor neuron is removed from the usual suppressor effect of higher centers, such as in lesions of the pyramidal tract.

**rotary pursuit**  A pursuit reaction test requiring the subject to follow the path of an irregularly moving object with an indicator.

**rotation**  A technical term for the shifting of factor axes and their hyperplanes from the positions initially obtained after Factor Extraction.

**rotation, orthogonal**  (factor analysis) A rotation of the factor axes to the point where they meet at right angles. The correlation of two factors in this configuration is zero.

**rotation perception**  The sensation which occurs when there is an alteration in the rate or direction of the rotation of a person's body, resulting from movement of the fluids in the semicircular canals which excites the receptors. When the rate of rotation is reduced the sensation is that of rotating in the opposite direction.

**rotation system**  A method sometimes used in group therapy in which the therapist works with the individual patient in a sequence in front of the group.

**rote learning**  Memorization in which the task is to commit the various components of the material to memory with little or no understanding, requiring only the ability to later reproduce what has been learned in the exact form in which it was presented.

**Rotter Incomplete Sentence Blank**  A projective technique for college age individuals developed in 1950 by J. B. Rotter and J. E. Rafferty. It is designed to estimate the person's degree and areas of maladjustment for diagnostic purposes.

**rounding off**  Process of eliminating or discarding one or more digits to the right of a particular digit. The last digit is increased by one if the dropped digit directly following it is greater than five. If this digit is less than five, the preceding digit is left unchanged. When this digit is exactly five, the preceding digit if it is odd is increased, while if it is even it is left unchanged.

**RR interval**  See *inter response time.*

**R/S**  See *response-shock interval.*

**RS interval**  See *avoidance, free operant.*

**rubeola encephalitis**  See *encephalitis, rubeola.*

**Rubin, Edgar J. (1886-1951)**  Danish phenomenologist, a student of G. E. Müller at Göttingen, whose 1915 doctoral dissertation, in which he studied the difference between figure and ground in visual perception, greatly influenced later Gestalt psychology. Occupied the chair in psychology at Copenhagen for many years.

**Rubin's figure**  An ambiguous figure which can be perceived either as a goblet or as two profiles facing each other.

**Ruffini corpuscle or cylinder**  A specialized, branched-nerve end organ found in the subcutaneous tissues which is thought to mediate warmth sensations.

**Ruffini papillary ending**  Nerve endings thought to mediate pressure sensation which are located in the papillary layer of the skin.

**run**  1. A single exposure to a task or stimuli or a single performance of a task, i.e., a trial. 2. An execution of an operation which may then be repeated. 3. To repeatedly expose an animal to an experimental situation such as a maze.

**running rate**  See *rate, running.*

**runway**  A straight pathway, usually without interruption, leading from the starting box to the goal box in which some form of reinforcement, usually positive, is available. The runway is usually either covered or elevated.

**Rush, Benjamin (1745-1813)**  Often called the father of American psychiatry. In 1812 he wrote *Diseases of the Mind,* the first textbook on mental diseases by an American. He was a prime force in the push to get American medicine and the public at large to accept the idea that insanity was the result of internal disturbances rather than of mysterious outside forces. Rush believed in the relief a patient might experience upon talking to a doctor but also advocated treating patients more actively, and somewhat inhumanely—using tricks, terrifying the patient, and tranquilizing and gyrating chairs. Although he used seemingly merciless devices, Rush was sincere in his concern for his fellow human beings and managed to help change the American medical profession's approach to the treatment of mental disorder.

# S

**S** 1. A symbol for stimulus. 2. A symbol for sensory intensity, when the response is the stimulus. 3. A symbol for the space factor of the factors comprising primary mental abilities. 4. (psychophysics) A symbol for the standard stimulus.

**(S)** 1. A symbol for a subject in an experiment. 2. (Rorschach) A symbol for a response to white space on the card.

$\sigma^2$ The symbol used to refer to variance.

$\sigma_M$ The symbol used to refer to the standard error of the mean.

$\Sigma$ The symbol for summation. It is placed before a variable all of whose values are algebraically summed. It is read "sum of."

$S^-$ (respondent conditioning) In Pavlovian conditioning discrimination studies, the test stimulus that is presented to the subject but which has never been paired with the US. Thus if the subject discriminates, the $S^-$ should not elicit the conditioned response.

$S^t$ (respondent conditioning) In Pavlovian conditioning discrimination studies, the CS that is consistently paired with the US.

$S^A$ (operant conditioning) In discrimination studies the stimulus in the presence of which a response is never reinforced.

$S^D$ (operant conditioning) The discriminative stimulus in discrimination studies. The stimulus in the presence of which responses are reinforced and responses in the absence are not reinforced.

$S_D$ See *drive stimuli.*

$S_G$ (C. L. Hull) A symbol for fractional goal stimulus, which is a proprioceptive stimulus resulting from a fractional antedating goal response ($r_G$).

$S \leftrightarrow R$ (J. R. Kantor) A symbol denoting stimulus-response interaction or interbehavior.

**S curve** See *curve, S.*

**S factor** A special or specific factor derived in a factor-analysis of tests of ability which is unique for the test in question, representing the kind of ability necessary to do well on the test.

**S population** See *stimulus, population.*

**S variable** See *stimulus variable.*

**saccadic movement** A rapid jump of the eye from one fixation point to another, especially in reading.

**sacral division** An anatomic division of the autonomic nervous system comprising that part in the region of the sacrum.

**sadism** A sexual perversion in which sexual excitement and orgasm are dependent upon the infliction of pain and humiliation of others.

**sadism, anal** (psychoanalysis) The manifestation of destructive and aggressive tendencies in the anal stage of development.

**sadism, id** The most primitive instinctual destructive urges seen in the early years of infancy, related to the desire for omnipotent gratification.

**sadism, infantile** Sadism occurring in early childhood.

**sadism, larval** (M. Hirschfeld) Concealed sadism.

**sadism, omnipotent infantile** See *sadism, id.*

**sadism, oral** Aggressive, primordial urges toward omnipotent mastery and gratification expressed in fantasy through the oral apparatus.

**sadism, phallic** Aggressive urges in the phallic stage of development during which the child interprets the sexual act as a violent, aggressive activity.

**sadism, primal** The part of the death instinct which remains within the person, partially bound with the libido and partially directed at the self.

**sadism, superego** The aggressive, cruel aspects of the conscience part of the superego whose energy is derived from the aggressive, destructive forces of the id. The intensity of this sadism depends on the intensity and strength of the child's own infantile violent and sadistic fantasies which are controlled by the superego.

**sadism, unconscious** Primordial destructive wishes which one is born with which in the infant are directed toward omnipotent power in fantasy and partially exist in the unconscious fantasies of adults.

**sadomasochism** The tendency toward both sadism and masochism. There is the simultaneous existence of submissive and aggressive attitudes in social and sexual relations with others, usually with the presence of a considerable degree of destructiveness.

**safety motive** 1. (K. Horney) A measure by which the neurotic attempts, in indirect ways, to protect himself from the hostility in his environment and, more broadly, to protect himself from any kind of threat. 2. The tendency to seek security.

**sagittal** 1. A term describing the arrow-shaped suture located between the two parietal bones of the skull. 2. A plane which divides the body into halves, passing through the sagittal suture along the long axis of the body.

**sagittal axis** (optics) The line or plane passing outward from the center of the retina, through the center of the lens and pupil, and projecting to the center of the object in view in the field of vision.

**sagittal fissure** The large longitudinal fissure dividing the two cerebral hemispheres.

**Saint Dymphna** Patron of the mentally disturbed, who was murdered in Gheel, Belgium by her psychotic father.

**Saint John's evil** Obsolete name for epilepsy.

**Saint Vitus' dance** See *chorea, Sydenham's acute.*

**Sakel, Manfred (1900-1957)** A German psychiatrist who developed the idea of using insulin to treat psychotics, especially the inducement of insulin shock in schizophrenics.

**salaam spasm** Movements of the head and upper part of the body which are rhythmic and periodic; usually seen in children.

**salicylate poisoning** See *poisoning, salicylate.*

**salient variable similarity index for factors (s)** A formula based on a count of salients, common salients, and common variables in the studies, whereby the P value of a given factor match between studies can be assessed.

**salivary reflex** The reflex characterized by the production and flow of saliva upon perceiving food.

**salpingectomy** A sterilization operation in which the fallopian tubes are cut and tied off.

**saltatory spasm** A clonic spasm causing the patient to leap or jump.

**Saltpetriére school** A school of psychopathology founded by J. Charcot and based on hypnotic phenomena.

**sample** A subgroup of a population which is used as a representative of an entire population and from which conclusions are drawn which are said to be characteristic of the entire population.

**sample bias** Any factor in a sample or in the method of drawing a sample that lessens the representative quality of that sample.

**sample, matched** A sample which is equivalent in all necessary respects to another sample under consideration.

**sample, stratified** A sample which has been divided into separate, non-overlapping categories. The sample is obtained by random selection and the number of cases in each category is proportional to the number in the population.

**sampling** The process by which a subset of persons or observations from a larger set is drawn and studied in order to make inferences about the characteristics of the larger population.

**sampling, area** Survey procedure which takes all of a particular class of respondents within a specified area such as one ten-block square or from within several specifically selected areas which are chosen to be representative of a larger area.

**sampling block** 1. The categorization of respondents or elements to be sampled into groups which are representative of the total population and the selection of a certain number of cases from each category. 2. The selection of respondents from each of certain geographic areas.

**sampling, controlled** Sampling methods in which the influenced factors are regulated and not left to chance.

**sampling, double** Using two different techniques for generating samples at different stages of the investigation. A form of mixed sampling.

**sampling errors** Errors resulting from the fact that the sample is not completely representative of the population. The standard error is obtained by subtracting the mean of the sample from the population mean.

**sampling population** The population from which the sample is going to be drawn.

**sampling, random** (experimental) The procedure of choosing a representative sample from a population whereby everyone in the parent population has an equal chance of being chosen. This procedure is used when the population values of the variables of interest are unknown.

**sampling, representative** The drawing of a sample which adequately reflects the characteristics of the population from which the sample is drawn.

**sampling servo** An instrument used in the measurement at regular intervals of errors in a process, applying corrections proportional to the error.

**sampling stability** A state which is achieved when successive samplings from a population yield consistent results and are regarded as reliable.

**sampling, stratified** (experimental) The procedure of choosing a representative sample from a population by choosing specific individuals who are similar to the people in the population. This procedure is used when the population values of the variables of interest are known.

**sampling theory** The theory which is involved with drawing samples which are representative of a population.

**sampling validity** A measure to determine how well a certain test item measures what the test as a whole is measuring.

**sampling variability** A measure of the extent to which a sample differs from a truly random sample which is estimated from the standard deviation.

**San Filippo syndrome** A mucopolysaccharidosis not involving skeletal abnormalities. Initially, mild retardation followed by rapid deterioration between the second and fourth years.

**sanguine type** See *type, sanguine.*

**Sansom image** See *Purkinje-Sansom image.*

**saphism** Female homosexuality; lesbianism; the name saphism is derived from Sapho, an ancient Greek poetess.

**Sargent Insight Test** See *test, Sargent Insight.*

**SAT** See *test, scholastic aptitude.*

**satiation, psychical** (K. Lewin) The experience that upon repetition of an act, the act gains a negative valence for a person causing him to try to leave the situation. The process of satiation is identified by the criteria of variation, dissolution of perceptual and action unities, inattention and forgetting. The speed of satiation depends on the structure of the task, upon the state of tension of the whole person, upon whether the task is a peripheral or central one, and upon the personality of the person. Satiation shows that repetition of a task does not always result in an improvement in performance.

**satisfaction** 1. The state of pleasure in an organism when it has achieved the goal of the dominant motivating tendencies. 2. The feeling state in a person who has gratified an appetite or motive.

**satisfier** (E.L. Thorndike) A reward or any external situation or circumstance leading to satisfaction.

**saturated test** (factor analysis) A test having a high factor loading—a high correlation with a certain factor.

**saturation** 1. With colors, purity and fullness of hue of the color. 2. (factor analysis) The degree to which a test is correlated or loaded with a certain factor. 3. (chemistry) The degree to which a chemical substance has been dissolved or absorbed by a liquid.

**satyriasis** Excessive sexual drive in males.

**savant, idiot** See *idiot savant.*

**saving method** (H. Ebbinghaus) The method of measuring retention which can be used when a subject has forgotten what he has learned. The difference between the time required for the first and subsequent learnings or the time saved is taken as the measure of retention present at the time of relearning. Also called relearning and saving method.

**scala** A perilymphatic space of the cochlea.

**scala media** The smallest tube of the cochlea which contains the organ of Corti.

**scala tympani** A spiral tube in the cochlea filled with endolymph, extending from the round window to the apex connecting to the scala vestibuli.

**scala vestibuli** A spiral tube in the cochlea, filled with a fluid which receives sound vibrations from the stapes, communicating them to the organ of Corti.

**scalability** 1. The ability to be arranged in a normal progression or to be fitted into a progression. 2. The characteristic of a test or test item that makes it possible to estimate a subject's response to any single item, knowing his test score.

**scalar analysis** The process of determining where an item is situated on a scale.

**scalar product** (statistics) The length of vector A multiplied by the length of vector B, multiplied by the cosine of the angular separation between the two vectors. The scalar product is the cosine of the angle if the two vectors are of unit length.

**scale** 1. Any series of items which is progressively arranged according to value or magnitude into which an item can be placed according to its quantification. 2. A physical device which is representative of a scale (yardstick). 3. A series of test items which have been arranged according to their value or magnitude of difficulty. 4. The rules which are applied when assigning an item to a class. 5. (L. Guttman) An attitude-measuring device which meets the standards for being scaled.

**scale, A** Questionnaire designed to measure degree of intolerance for ambiguity, vagueness and indefiniteness.

**scale, absolute** A scale that begins at an absolute zero point and has equal intervals between all subsequent points on the scale.

**scale, additive** A scale whose units can be summated because the units are equal at all points on the scale.

**scale, age** Also called age-equivalent scale. A scale in which the units of measurements are the differences between successive age equivalents, each difference assumed to be equal to any other.

**scale, age-equivalent** Also called age scale. A scale whose units of measurement are the differences between successive age equivalents, each difference assumed to be equal to any other. For example, a child with a mental age of ten is said to be one year older mentally than a child whose development is that of nine-year-olds. See *age equivalent.*

**scale, allergic potential** Scale developed for the evaluation of a patient's predisposition to allergic reaction, using family history of allergy, eosinophilic count, skin-test reactions and how easily a certain clinical symptom can be diagnosed as related to certain allergens.

**scale, analytical** A test or scale designed and used for a diagnostic purpose.

**scale, Arthur Point of Performance Tests** (G. Arthur) An intelligence test for school children developed in 1933 which consists of eight performance subtests. Six of these subtests are restandardized versions of the Pintner-Paterson Scale, the Knox Cube Test, the Seguin Form Board, the Two-Figure Form Board, the Casuist Form Board, the Manikin, the Feature Profile, the Mare and Foal, and the Healy Picture Completion I. The two additional tests are the Porteus Maze and the Kohs Block Design Test. The scale yields an IQ score which is determined by the number of successes, or the time required on each test, or the degree of accuracy or a combination of these. An alternate form of the scale is available for retesting and for use with pre-school children. This version consists of four of the subtests from Form I plus the Arthur Stencil Design.

**scale, attitude** A measuring device consisting of a set of items, of predetermined scale value, which are to be marked as favorable or unfavorable.

**scale, attitude toward disabled persons** (H. E. Yuker, J. R. Block, and W. J. Campbell) A scale introduced in 1960 to ascertain attitudes toward disability.

**scale, Bayley, of Infant Development** (N. Bayley) Test to assess an infant's developmental progress which reflects the notion that development is an interaction of mental, physical and social factors. Includes a motor scale, mental scale and a behavioral index, although the index is not as carefully standardized.

**scale, Bogardus Social Distance** A rating scheme requiring the subject to indicate the degree of intimacy to which he would be willing to accept a certain person or a representative of a certain social group.

**scale, bril** A scale of visual brightness based upon the fractionation method for scaling subjective magnitude.

**scale, California Infant, for Motor Development** Test battery divided into subtests, seventy-six items used in assessing motor development from birth to three years. Representative items are: sits with support expected at 3.5 months; walks alone two or three steps without support at 13.0 months; walks alone upstairs at 24.3 months; walks upstairs, alternating forward foot at 35.5 months; and, the last item in the test, walks downstairs, alternating forward foot at 50.0 months.

**scale, chromatic** Musical scale with half-tone intervals between the notes.

**scale, Columbia Mental Maturity** (B. Burgomeister, L. H. Blum, I. Lorge) A scale of general ability developed in 1953 for children aged three to twelve. It consists of sets of drawings printed on a card. The child is asked to point to the one which does not belong with the others.

**scale, continuous** A scale in which the function or trait is measured on a continuum.

**scale, developmental** A check list or inventory of behaviors. The behaviors of an individual are checked on the inventory, compared with the norms of the scale and an estimate of the individual's developmental stage is reached.

**scale, diatonic** A stepwise organization of tones which forms the basis of most western music. A diatonic scale can be formed with any tone as a starting point by producing two successively higher tones each separated from each other by whole steps. Between the third and the fourth tone is a half step. Whole steps separate the fourth from the fifth, the fifth from the sixth, and the sixth from the seventh. Between the seventh and the eighth is a half step. Thus, the successive eight tones, the octave, are separated from each other by whole steps except between the third and fourth tones and between the seventh and eighth tones which are separated by half steps. This is the major scale. In the minor scale, of equal importance, the half steps between the sixth, seventh, and eighth tones are varied depending on the specific form desired; but invariably the half step is between the second and third tones.

**scale, difficulty** A test in which the items are arranged in order of difficulty.

**scale, Draw-A-Person Quality** (M. E. Wagner and H. J. P. Schubert) A scale based on the Draw-A-Person Test in which the person's drawing is scored according to an artistic scale of 0 to 8.

**scale, E** Attitude scale which measures tendency toward ethnocentricism.

**scale, grade** A scale, standardized to measure a person's development in terms of grade norms.

**scale, graphic rating** A type of rating scale for describing the strength of a particular characteristic representative of a person. The scale is usually in the form of a line with gradations marking the range of the trait from minimum to maximum.

**scale, Griffiths'** (R. Griffiths) A scale introduced in 1954 to assess the abilities of infants. It determines the level of development of five areas: locomotor, personal-social, hearing and speech, hand and eye development, and performance. The scale yields a general quotient derived by dividing the mental age by the chronological age.

**scale, Guttman** (L. Guttman) A unidimensional attitude scale in which the items are arranged in such a way that a person who agrees with a particular item automatically agrees with the items lower in rank and disagrees with those higher in rank.

**scale, Humm-Wadsworth Temperament** (D. G. Humm and G. W. Wadsworth) A personality inventory introduced in 1935 designed to assess if a person has paranoid, hysteric, manic, depressive, or schizoid tendencies.

**scale, I/E** Introversion/extroversion scale; a scoring key for the Minnesota Multiphasic Personality Inventory, yielding points on the introversion and extroversion dimension.

**scale, interval** A type of scale which does not have an absolute zero point but possesses equal intervals and magnitude.

**scale, ipsative** A scale which employs the characteristic behavior of an individual as the standard of comparison, so that a response is rated in terms of how it compares to the individual's common response.

**scale, K** A scoring scale of the Minnesota Multiphase Personality Inventory used for the detection of malingering.

**scale, Kelvin** A temperature scale using absolute zero or the complete lack of heat, -273° C, as its starting point. Also called absolute scale.

**scale, Likert** A type of attitude scale which requests the subject to indicate the degree of agreement or disagreement, on a three- or five-step scale, with stated attitudes.

**scale, Lincoln-Oseretsky Motor Development** A sensorimotor diagnostic test battery with thirty-six items of high reliability and good discrimination for children between six and fourteen years of age. The test is useful in the assessment of general motor ability rather than in the differential evaluation of psychomotor abilities.

**scale, mental** A scale involving the application of different numerical scores to different levels of mental performance.

**scale, national intelligence** A group test developed for the National Research Council of America consisting of a battery of tests designed to assess intelligence. There are two forms, Form A and Form B.

**scale, nominal** The simplest type of scale which labels objects by letters or numbers for identification or classification. It does not possess equal intervals, magnitude relationships or an absolute zero point.

**scale, ordinal** A type of scale which arranges objects with reference to their magnitude and assigns numbers accordingly—first, second, third, etc. It does not possess equal intervals or an absolute zero point.

**scale, percentile** A scale which indicates the percentile rank of each score or value of the population.

**scale, point** Test items or set of problems each of which is assigned a numerical score. Performance is rated according to total number of points earned.

**scale, psychological** A device used in the measurement and assessment of psychological functioning, such as attitudes, mental ability, degree of psychopathology, etc.

**scale, ratio** A type of scale with magnitude, an absolute zero point, and equal intervals which can be added or divided. All statements of ratio must be based on this scale.

**scale, sixteen D** (N. Bayley) A score defining the level of intelligence derived from a multiple of the standard deviation from the mean score obtained at age sixteen on several standardized tests. This score allows for the comparison of growth levels at different ages determined by tests having disparate age ranges and scoring systems.

**scale, stuttering Iowa** A scale which is composed of thirty-three nine-second samples of phonographically recorded stuttered speech, ranked using the equal-appearing intervals method on the basis of the degree of stuttering which is thought to be manifested in the samples. A stutterer in speech is compared with the samples and then assigned the scale value of the sample which it most closely resembles.

**scale, T** A scale which is based on the standard scores of the distribution obtained from unselected twelve-year-olds for any given test. The distribution is given a mean of fifty. Any score which equals five times the value of the standard deviation either above or below the mean is given the value of zero or one hundred. The scores between zero and one hundred progress in steps equal to .1 standard deviation.

**scale, Taylor Manifest Anxiety** (J. A. Taylor) A verbal measure of anxiety developed in 1956 which consists of a questionnaire made up of items believed to indicate anxiety to which the subject must answer true or false according to whether the statement describes him. This scale has a statistically significant but not very high validity when compared with physiological and other verbal measures of anxiety.

**scale, Thorndike's Handwriting** (E. L. Thorndike) A scale composed of handwriting samples rated in terms of the probability they exhibit against which another sample may be compared and then graded.

**scale, Thurstone Attitude** A scale constructed using the method of equally appearing intervals and consisting of a series of statements assigned a scale value of favorability in respect to a specified attitude object, on the basis of the proved judgments of a hundred or more raters. The score is the mean of the total of the values of those with which the subject indicates he agrees.

**scale, value** 1. The number that is assigned to an item according to a certain scale. 2. The number or name that is assigned to a division or a point on a scale; the reference points.

**scale, Vineland Social Maturity** (E. A. Doll) A survey of a person's maturity and social development introduced in 1936 and designed for use with individuals from infancy to the age of thirty years. The scale determines the levels of development in six categories: self-help, self-direction, locomotion, occupation, communication and socialization, from interviews with someone who knows the person or the subject himself. Items are grouped according to age and scored yielding a social age which is divided by the chronological age to produce a social quotient.

**scale, Wechsler Adult Intelligence** (D. Wechsler) An intelligence test developed and standardized in 1955 on white subjects, ages 16-64. It is a modified version of the Wechsler-Bellevue scale consisting of eleven subtests. The six verbal subtests include Information, Comprehension, Arithmetic, Similarities, Digit Span and Vocabulary. The performance tests are Digit Symbol, Picture Completion, Block Design, Picture Arrangement and Object Assembly. These subtests measure verbal, numerical, social and visual-motor capabilities. The test yields a Verbal, Performance and Full Scale Intelligence Quotient with a mean of 100 and a standard deviation of 15. Also known as the WAIS.

**scale, Wechsler-Bellevue** (D. Wechsler) An intelligence test for adults developed in 1939 and standardized on an American population aged 7-69. It consists of eleven subtests. The six verbal subtests are Information, Comprehension, Digit Span, Arithmetic, Similarities and Vocabulary. The five performance tests include Picture Arrangement, Picture Completion, Block Design, Object Assembly and Digit Symbol. These subjects measure verbal, numerical, social and perceptual-motor abilities. For a more recent version, see *Wechsler Adult Intelligence Scale.*

**scale, Wechsler Intelligence, for Children** (D. Wechsler) An intelligence test for children ages 5 years 0 months to 15 years 11 months developed and standardized in 1949 on a group of white children. The scale consists of twelve subtests, one of which is an alternate performance test. The verbal tests are Information, Comprehension, Arithmetic, Similarities, Vocabulary and Digit Span. The performance tests include Picture Completion, Picture Arrangement, Block Design, Object Assembly, Coding and the alternate test, Mazes. These tests measure verbal, numerical, social and visual-motor adaptability. The test yields a Verbal, Performance and Full Scale Intelligence Quotient with a mean of 100 and a standard deviation of 15. Also known as the WISC.

**scale, Wechsler Preschool and Primary, of Intelligence** (D. Wechsler) An intelligence scale for children ages 4-6½ developed and standardized in 1963. It includes eleven subtests of which one verbal subtest is an alternate. The six verbal subtests are Information, Vocabulary, Arithmetic, Similarities, Comprehension and the alternate test, Sentences. The performance tests include Animal House, Picture Completion, Mazes, Geometric Design and Block Design. These tests assess verbal, numerical, social and visual-motor capabilities. The test yields a Verbal, Performance and Full Scale Intelligence Quotient score with a mean of 100 and a standard deviation of 15. Also known as the WPPSI.

**scales, confusion** Scales produced by indirect scaling procedures are sometimes called confusion scales.

**scales, Fels, of Parental Behavior** (H. Champney) Scales designed to assess the child's home environment as a function of parental behavior and introduced in 1941. Thirty scales comprise this battery appraising dimensions such as child-centeredness, protectiveness, readiness of criticism, restrictiveness of regulations, severity of penalties, discord at home. The ratings are based on information obtained during several home visits including clinical impressions which are analyzed in terms of intra-rater and inter-rater reliability.

**scales, handwriting** (T. S. Lewinson and J. Zubin) A series of twenty-two scales developed in 1942 to evaluate the dynamic aspects of handwriting and describe an individual's movement impulses which are expressed in the handwriting. Each scale, representing one element of handwriting is divided into seven categories: the middle, called the balance, subdivides the scale into the contraction categories which indicate increasing degrees of control and the release categories which indicate increasing degrees of undercontrol. Twenty subjects were tested, both normal and abnormal, to produce the frame of reference for these scales. The findings suggest that the most striking difference between the normal and abnormal performance is in the consistency of handwriting, normals being consistent and abnormals manifesting variability.

**scales, Kent Series of Emergency** A brief general intelligence test consisting of ten orally given questions used in situations requiring a quick estimate of intellectual ability. Also called the Kent EGY test.

**scales, magnitude** Direct ratio scales based on the direct judgment of the ratios.

**scales, partition** Of direct equal interval scales based on the direct judgment of the intervals.

**scaling** The methods of determining which properties of a number scale apply to the dimension of objects, and which transformations of the scale values leave these scale dimensions invariate. Three characteristics of a scale are order, distance, and origin. Depending on whether none, one, two, or three of these are present in a scale, the scale is designated as nominal, ordinal, interval, or ratio. The type of valid mathematical functions possible on a scale is determined by the type of scale and its characteristics.

**scaling, age-grade** Standardizing a test on a population of school children who are at the normal or average age for their grade in school.

**scaling, direct** (S. S. Stevens) Methods of obtaining units of measurement on a scale in which direct quantitative judgments of a particular stimulus dimension are made by the subject. The subject not only judges stimuli A B on a given continuum as he does in an indirect scaling procedure, but he specifies the particular relationship among the subjective experiences, e.g. the subject may adjust stimulus B so that it appears one half the size of stimulus A.

**scaling, indirect** Methods for obtaining scales of sensation in which the subject differentiates stimuli on the basis of order, e.g. which tone is louder, stimulus A or B? If A is judged as louder 50% of the time, it is concluded that stimulus A is louder than stimulus B. If stimulus B is just noticeably higher than stimulus A and stimulus C is just noticeably higher than stimulus B, then the distance on the psychological continuum that separates B and A is assumed to be equal to the distance that separates C and A: one "just noticeable difference", one jnd. Thus jnd's are assumed to be equal, and a scale constructed on this assumption is an indirect scale.

**scaling, test** The procedure of assigning test items to specific positions on a scale after having administered the scale to a trial sample of people.

**scallop** (operant conditioning) A positively accelerated part of a cumulative response record indicating an increase in the response rate. The scallop is the typical steady state performance of a FI.

**scalogram** A cumulative scale, also called Guttman scale.

**scapegoating** 1. Process by which a person, group or object becomes the focus of displaced aggression. 2. (family therapy) Process in which one member of the family is identified as the "bad" or "crazy" member and is regularly put into a position in which other members of the family unconsciously support, as well as outwardly condemn, his unacceptable activities; the problems of the family are blamed upon this member.

**scatology** Morbid interest in excrement.

**scatter** 1. The degree to which a distribution of measurements or scores are closely grouped around the mean or dispersed over a wide range, most commonly measured by the standard deviation. 2. The extent to which items passed or failed by an individual on a test are of widely varying levels of difficulty.

**scatter analysis** See *analysis, scatter.*

**scatter diagram** A correlation diagram or chart that shows the relationship of two variables. The scores for the X variable are plotted along the horizontal axis and the scores for the Y variable are entered along the vertical axis. A point is made at each intersection.

**scatterplot** See *scatter diagram.*

**Schaeffer reflex** (M. Schaeffer) See *reflex, Schaeffer.*

**schedule** 1. A detailed plan for a series of operations. 2. A form used to guide experimental proceedure and gathering of data. 3. A questionnaire.

**schedule, Edwards Personal Preference** An instrument used with college students and adults which is designed, through a forced-choice method, to show the relative importance within the subject of fifteen key needs or motives, including achievement, dominance, debasement, change, nurturance, autonomy.

**schedule, maintenance** The provision of food, water and exercise to maintain an organism at a stable level of growth.

**schedule of reinforcement** See *reinforcement schedule.*

**schedule of reinforcement: adjusting (ADJ)** See *reinforcement, schedule of: adjusting.*

**schedule of reinforcement: alternate ALT** See *reinforcement, schedule of: alternate.*

**schedule of reinforcement: chained (CHAIN)** See *reinforcement, schedule of: chained.*

**schedule of reinforcement: concurrent (CONC)** See *reinforcement, schedule of: concurrent.*

**schedule of reinforcement: conjugate** See *reinforcement, schedule of: conjugate.*

**schedule of reinforcement: conjunctive (CONJ)** See *reinforcement, schedule of: conjunctive.*

**schedule of reinforcement: continuous (CRF)** See *reinforcement, schedule of: continuous.*

**schedule of reinforcement: differential interresponse time reinforcement** See either *reinforcement, schedule of: differential reinforcement of low rates of responding (DRL)* or *reinforcement, schedule of: differential reinforcement of high rates of responding (DRH).*

**schedule of reinforcement: extinction (EXT)** See *reinforcement, schedule of: extinction.*

**schedule of reinforcement: fixed interval (FI)** See *reinforcement, schedule of: fixed interval.*

**schedule of reinforcement: fixed ratio (FR)** See *reinforcement, schedule of: fixed ratio.*

**schedule of reinforcement: interlocking (INTER)** See *reinforcement, schedule of: interlocking.*

**schedule of reinforcement: intermittent** See *reinforcement, schedule of: intermittent.*

**schedule of reinforcement: interpolated (INTER)** See *reinforcement, schedule of: interpolated.*

**schedule of reinforcement: mixed (MIX)** See *reinforcement, schedule of: mixed.*

**schedule of reinforcement: multiple (MULT)** See *reinforcement, schedule of: multiple.*

**schedule of reinforcement: nonintermittent** See *reinforcement, schedule of: nonintermittent.*

**schedule of reinforcement: second order** See *reinforcement, schedule of: second order.*

**schedule of reinforcement: tandem (TAND)** See *reinforcement schedule of: tandem.*

**schedule of reinforcement: variable interval (VI)** See *reinforcement, schedule of: variable interval.*

**schedule of reinforcement: variable ratio (VR)** See *reinforcement, schedule of: variable ratio.*

**schedule, self-demand** A schedule for feeding infants in which the infant is fed when he gives indications of being hungry rather than by a predetermined schedule of feeding time.

**schedule, Sidman Avoidance** See *avoidance, free operant.*

**Scheie's syndrome** A disorder of mucopolysaccharide metabolism which is transmitted as an autosomac recessive trait and is characterized by a coarse appearance, cloudy corneas, limitation of motion at the joints, normal intellect, and cardiac vascular changes.

**schematic model** See *model, schematic.*

**Schilder's disease** One of the group of progressive diffuse sclerosis diseases commonly occurring early in life and characterized by symptoms such as visual failure, mental deterioration and spastic paralysis. Also called encephalitis periaxialis diffusa.

**schismatic family** See *family, schismatic.*

**schizoaffective psychosis** See *psychosis, schizoaffective.*

**schizogenic family** A family unit believed to have caused schizophrenia in one or more of its children.

**schizogenic mothers** See *schizophrenogenic mothers.*

**schizoid** 1. Pertaining to schizophrenia. 2. Schizoid character. 3. Schizophrenic-like behavior.

**schizoid character** An individual with a character disorder characterized by social withdrawal. Such individuals are shy, oversensitive, seclusive and often appear detached and eccentric, and sometimes withdraw into autistic fantasies and daydreams though some reality contact is maintained.

**schizoid personality** see *schizoid character.*

**schizophrenia** A group of psychotic reactions characterized by fundamental disturbances in reality relations and concept formations, and behavioral, affective and intellectual disturbances in varying degrees. There is often progressive deteriorating and regressive behavior. Several varieties classified according to symptomatology are distinguished. Formerly called dementia praecox.

**schizophrenia, ambulatory** 1. Schizophrenic disorder which does not require hospitalization. 2. Relates to schizophrenic patients who are treated on an out-patient basis.

**schizophrenia, aretic** (B.B. Wolman) An aggressive, pugnatious syndrome of childhood schizophrenia.

**schizophrenia, autistic** The autistic phase in childhood schizophrenia.

**schizophrenia, catatonic** A type of schizophrenia characterized by conspicuous motor behavior, exhibiting either marked generalized inhibition, such as stupor, mutism, negativism, waxy flexibility and inaccessibility to external stimuli, or excessive motor activity and excitement.

**schizophrenia, childhood** Diagnostic category for those children exhibiting a schizophrenic state, including such symptoms as withdrawal from people and reality, escape into a fantasy world, disturbance in the ability to make affective contact with the world, autistic thought processes, mutism, excessive inhibition or uninhibition of impulse expression, identification with animals or objects, stereotyped gestures, impassivity or extreme outbursts of rage and anxiety, bizarre posturing, and vasovegetative functioning.

Childhood schizophrenia is seen as a mental catastrophy that took place even before the ego had the opportunity to grow and exert control over the id; there is an arrest in the development of the personality structure. This is in contradistinction to adulthood schizophrenia which is seen as the failure of an impoverished ego; the personality structure is regressed.

**schizophrenia, childhood, sociopsychosomatic theory of** (B. B. Wolman) The classification of childhood schizophrenia based on etiology and personality characteristics which corresponds to particular stages in which the disorder was proposed. The pseudo amentive schizophrenia, formed during the pre-verbal stage, is the most severe form of this illness and corresponds to dementive schizophrenia in adults. The other three types of schizophrenia are the autistic, corresponding to adult hebephrenia; the symbiotic, parallel to adult catatonia; and the aretic, which corresponds to the adult paranoid syndrome.

**schizophrenia, deteriorating stage of** The stage at which the patient is in a regressed affectless stage.

**schizophrenia, hebephrenic** A type of schizophrenia characterized by marked silliness, inappropriate affect, giggling, delusions, hallucinations and regressive behavior.

**schizophrenia, latent** A form of schizophrenia in which the person has not yet broken with reality but may develop a psychosis if exposed to unfavorable circumstances of life. It is characterized by a considerable unevenness in mental functioning with mental functioning breaking down in emotionally loaded areas and threatening situations, strict control of id impulses, coldness shallowness, non-attachment, and difficulty in accepting friendship and love.

**schizophrenia, manifest** A schizophrenic reaction which is observable. A fully developed schizophrenic disorder.

**schizophrenia, mixed** A form of schizophrenia characterized by symptoms usually manifested in two or more of the four categories of schizophrenia: hebephrenic, simple, catatonic and paranoid, so that a classification in one of the above categories cannot be made.

**schizophrenia, paranoid** A type of schizophrenia characterized by autistic thinking, delusions of persecution and/or grandeur, ideas of reference and often hallucinations.

**schizophrenia, postemotive** Schizophrenia, the onset of which is precipitated by a severe physical, social or sexual trauma.

**schizophrenia, process** Several authors distinguish process schizophrenia from reactive schizophrenia.

The process schizophrenia is characterized by a gradual decline of activity, dullness, autism, ideas of reference, thought disturbances, prolonged history of maladjustment, poor physical health, difficulties at home and in school, abnormal family relationships and somatic delusions.

**schizophrenia, psychoneurotic** (P. Hoch and P. Polatin) A syndrome characterized by a pervading anxiety which affects all areas of life and the presence of all symptoms of neurotic illnesses at the same time. The patient may have short psychotic episodes or may become schizophrenic in the future.

**schizophrenia, reactive** Schizophrenia characterized by a radical onset, oscillations between excitement and stuporous depression and by periods of almost normal functioning alternating with states of confusion.

**schizophrenia, recidives in** Recurring and intermittent schizophrenic episodes which occur after a long remissions period, the recurring episodes often duplicating past episodes although there are often new features.

**schizophrenia, simple** A type of schizophrenia characterized chiefly by reduction in external attachments and interests and impoverishment of human relationships, often accompanied by apathy and indifference.

**schizophrenia, sociopsychosomatic theory of** See *sociopsychosomatic theory of schizophrenia.*

**schizophrenia, thanatotic** (K. R. Eissler) Schizophrenic syndrome associated with the wish to die.

**schizophrenic paradox** (B. B. Wolman) Schizophrenic's renunciation of his own life in order to protect those who are supposed to protect him.

**schizophrenic reaction** See *schizophrenia.*

**schizophrenogenic mothers** (A. Kanner) Mothers whose personality and behavior are believed to have caused schizophrenia in their offspring.

**schizothyme** 1. Person who has schizothymic tendencies. 2. (E. Kretschmer) Person characterized by a schizothymic temperament, one of two basic temperaments.

**schizothymia** Schizoid-like behavior or characteristics within the limits of normality.

**schizothymic** 1. Schizoid behavior or characteristics within the limits of normality. 2. (E. Kretschmer) Basic temperament characterized by introversion, sensitivity, moodiness and seriousness, associated with the asthenic and the athletic body types and to a lesser degree with the dysplastic type.

**schizothymic type** See *type, schizothymic.*

**Schoenfeld, William N. (1915- )** American psychologist and university educator. Principal research areas: behavior theory, conditioning, social psychology, psychophysics and perception. Co-author (with F.S. Keller) of first textbook based on reinforcement theory; and, formulator of first systematic organization of reinforcement schedules (as presented in *Stimulus Schedules: the t-t Systems,* with B. K. Cole, et al., co-authors).

**scholastic achievement test** See *test, scholastic achievement.*

**scholastic aptitude test** See *test, scholastic aptitude.*

**school and college ability test** See *test, school and college ability.*

**school phobia** See *phobia, school.*

**school psychologist** See *psychologist, school.*

**schools of psychology** There are several independent theoretical systems in psychology not related to one another. Historically speaking, the earliest two systems were proposed by Plato and Aristotle, and later by Plotinus, St. Augustine and others influenced by Plato, and St. Thomas Aquinas and others inspired by Aristotle. In modern times the faculty psychology competed with associationism.

The nineteenth century witnessed the birth of scientific research in psychology; Wundt and Titchener developed the structural psychology (structuralism) and James Dewey, Angell and others started the functional psychology (functionalism).

The main currents in twentieth century psychological theory can be roughly divided into three major groups or schools, namely the conditioning-behavioristic school which includes the teachings of Pavlov, Watson, Hull, Skinner and others; the psychoanalytic school which encompasses the works of Freud, Adler, Jung, Sullivan and others; the third current which includes several distinct schools, such as personalistic psychology, phenomenology, Gestalt, field theory and others.

**Schopenhauer, Arthur (1788-1860)** German philosopher. Developed a solipsistic theory of cognition viewing the world as man's will and idea. Believed that insanity (madness-Irrsinn) originates in the unconscious.

**Schreber case** (S. Freud) Interpretation of an autobiographical description of a paranoid schizophrenic by the judge David Paul Schreber.

**science** 1. An organized and systematic body of knowledge. 2. The study of phenomena in order to produce precise and valid information hitherto unknown with proof to support its validity.

**scientific method** See *method, scientific.*

**scintillating scotoma** See *scotoma, scintillating.*

**sciosophy** Non-scientific system of thought such as astrology.

**scleroderma** A disease characterized by patches of hardened skin tissue, atrophy of the epidermis and pigmentation. Psychogenic causes may lead to susceptibility to the disorder in patients who are threatened by a loss of security.

**sclerosis, tuberous** See *epiloia.*

**scopic method** See *method, scopic.*

**scopophilia; scoptophilia** Sexual pleasure derived from looking; also called voyerism.

**score** 1. A quantitative value assigned to a datum, usually a test response, attitude, etc. 2. The sum or total of a number of credits or scores obtained by an individual.

**score, accuracy** The proportion or number of test items that the subject answered correctly.

**score, age** Also called age equivalent score. A test score that expresses the individual's performance as the age at which most individuals reach that particular level of performance. See *age equivalent*.

**score, composite** The average of a person's scores when they are expressed in common units. The scores may be weighted.

**score criterion** The dependent variable in an experimental situation.

**score, crude** 1. The raw score which has not been analyzed. 2. The approximate score.

**score, derived** 1. A score derived by the mathematical manipulation of another score or measure. 2. A score that has been converted from one scale into the units of another scale.

**score, deviation** (statistics) An individual score obtained by subtracting from any raw scores. Another value may be substituted for the mean, but it will be indicated.

**score, grade** A score which describes a person's achievement in terms of grade level for which his performance is average.

**score, graphic** A score which is represented by a line or other figural diagram.

**score, gross** The score expressed in the original units of measurement.

**score, original** See *score, raw*.

**score, percentile** A score which indicates the percentage of cases or persons falling below a particular score in a given sample.

**score, point** See *score, raw*.

**score, raw** A score which is presented in the original test units; a value that has not been treated statistically.

**score, sigma** See *score, standard*.

**score, standard** 1. Any score using as its unit the standard deviation of a population which it is using as its criterion. 2. The difference between the obtained score ($x$) and the mean ($M_x$) divided by the standard deviation ($\sigma$). It is known as the $z$ score. The formula is:

$$z = \frac{x - M_x}{\sigma_x}$$

**score, time** The amount of time required to perform a particular task.

**score, transmuted** A score which has been translated into the units of another scale.

**score, z** See *score, standard*.

**scores, additional** Used in the Klopfer approach to the Rorschach to identify responses which have more than one determining feature, i.e. form, color, movement, or shading. Klopfer's system requires that only one determinant be selected as the "main" feature responsible for the response. Where multiple determinants occur, one is selected as "main" and the others are scored as "additional." Klopfer's method of interpretation generally weighs additional scorings differently from main scores.

**scores, ungrouped** Scores which have not been tabulated into classes or groups.

**scoring, configural** A method of determining a subject's criterion score used in pattern analysis. Each individual in a particular answer pattern is assigned the same score for that pattern. This set of scores is the best prediction of the subject's criterion score according to the least squares requirement.

**scoring, differential** Procedure of scoring responses on a battery of tests in different ways so as to get measures of more than one variable.

**scotoma** A blind or partially blind spot in the visual field surrounded by normal or near normal vision.

**scotoma, central** A blind or partially blind spot limited to the area of the retina normally associated with clearest vision (the macular luteu).

**scotoma, mental** Lack of insight; mental blind spot.

**scotoma, scintillating** The usually temporary appearance of bright flashes before the eyes.

**scotopic adaption** Adaption to darkness.

**scotopic vision** Twilight vision.

**screen memory** Recollection of an insignificant item used unconsciously as resistance against recalling an emotionally significant event.

**screening** The selection of individuals or items for inclusion or exclusion in a test group, procedure or other situation.

**scrying** Crystal gazing.

**SD ($\sigma$)** See *standard deviation*.

**seance** A group meeting or sitting, usually in darkness, for the purpose of obtaining and investigating psychic phenomena.

**Sears, Robert R. (1908-    )** Child psychologist whose behavioral research explored the influence of parental child-rearing practices on aggression, dependency, sex-typing, identification and other motivational systems. Devised standardized methods of behavior observation for fantasy expression (doll play) and mother-child interactions. Emphasized dyadic approach to theoretical analysis of personality development. See dyad.

**Sechenov, Ivan Mikhailovich (1829-1905)** Russian physiologist considered to be the "Father of Russian Physiology"; created the school of Russian physiologists. Between 1850 and 1855, Sechenov was a student of the Faculty of Medicine of the Moscow University, where he had a chance to listen to K. F. Rulye, F. I. Inozemtzev, et al. Sechenov was influenced by the revolutionary ideas of a leader of Russian Enlightenment, N. G. Chernishevskiu. Sechenov worked at European laboratories under C. Ludwig, J. Müller, Du Bois-Reymond, Claude Bernard, et al. He was interested in the physiology of the nervous system where he made a remarkable discovery, namely the process of central inhibition. In the book, *Reflexes of the Brain* (1863) Sechenov demonstrated the possibility of scientific materialistic interpretation of man's psychic activity. He also investigated gas exchange and gas contents in blood; he introduced the method of "Toricelli vacuum" for extraction of gases from blood.

**second order factor** A factor which describes the correlations among first-order factors after they have been rotated to simple structure. A dimension of co-variation in the correlations between factors. Second order factors describe more massive, broader organizations of personality.

**second order schedules** See *reinforcement, schedule of: second order.*

**second signal system** (I. P. Pavlov) The ability to signal to oneself, in contrast to the external signal of the conditioned stimulus.

**secondary correlation** See *correlation, secondary.*

**secondary elaboration** (S. Freud) The putting together of non-related elements or thoughts and considering them to be a whole, as in dreams.

**secondary extinction** See *extinction, secondary.*

**secondary gain** See *epinosis.*

**secondary inhibitor** A neutral stimulus which becomes an inhibitor as a result of its association with an inhibitor.

**secondary integration** See *integration, secondary.*

**secondary narcissism** See *narcissism, secondary.*

**secondary position** See *position, secondary.*

**secondary process** See *process, secondary.*

**secondary reinforcement** See *reinforcement, secondary.*

**secondary repression** See *repression, secondary.*

**secondary reward** See *reinforcement, secondary.*

**secondary sex characteristics** See *sex, secondary characteristics.*

**secretion** Production of substance by a bodily organ, e.g. tears; the secretion of the tear glands is exogenous and the thyroxin hormone, secretion of the thyroid gland, is endogenous.

**secretion, internal** The secretion of the endocrine glands.

**security operations** (H. S. Sullivan) Activities employed by the self-system to reduce or relieve tension and maintain self-esteem and a feeling of safety.

**sedative** Any drug which quiets functioning or activity. The barbiturate, a cellular depressant, is commonly used.

**segmental behavior** Behavior controlled by a segment of the spinal cord.

**segmental insufficiency** See *insufficiency, segmental.*

**segregation** 1. (genetics) Breaking up of a pair of gametes permitting new combinations of genes in sexual reproduction 2. (Gestalt) Breaking up of elements in perception and forming a new figure-ground combination. 3. (social psychology) Isolating of individuals or groups from the rest of the population; forming ghettos and/or forming separate dwelling units, schools, and means of locomotion for the segregation of groups in order to isolate them from the non-segregated population.

**seizure, audiogenic** Convulsion caused by prolonged exposure to intense high frequency sound.

**seizure, conversion** A seizure due to psychological causes with no organic or physical basis.

**seizure, epileptiform** 1. A convulsion or attack which resembles an epileptic attack but which is caused by some other disease or injury to the brain. 2. Hysterical behavior which leads to epileptic-like symptoms such as convulsions.

**seizure, gustatory** A form of epilepsy in which the seizure pattern includes the sensation of a peculiar taste.

**selection** 1. (statistics) The choice of an item, individual, or experimental stimulus for inclusion in a group, test, category or experiment. 2. (genetics) The process by which particular genes or gene combinations change from generation to generation as a result of biological advantages favoring change. 3. (industrial psychology) The process of selection attempts to optimize the number of successful employees hired by an organization. It represents the earliest function performed by psychologists employed in industry beginning with the work of Münsterberg, published in 1913.

**selection, artificial** The process by which animals or plants that possess desirable characteristics are chosen for hybridizing or homogeneous breeding.

**selection index** See *index, selection.*

**selection method** See *method, recognition.*

**selection, natural** (C. Darwin) Biological law synonymous to the survival of the fittest. In the process of natural selection, individuals who carry characteristics which do not foster successful adjustment to the environment cannot survive, thus they do not transmit maladjustive traits, and only the traits which help survival are genetically transmitted.

**selection ratio** A statistical technique that gives the functional value of any selection instrument. The selection ratio is defined as the ratio of the number of available jobs to the number of applicants for the jobs.

**selective answer test**  See *test, selective answer.*

**selective inattention**  See *inattention, selective.*

**selective response**  See *response, selective.*

**selective silence**  A brief period occurring in conversation, association tests, or therapy, in which a subject withholds a response, indicating an anxiety-provoking topic has been touched upon.

**self  1.** The ego. **2.** The traits and characteristics making up the individual. **3.** (W. James) That which a person considers part of or representing himself. There are many selves representing an individual, such as the material self, the social self, and the spiritual self. **4.** (C. G. Jung) An archetype which develops during middle age and represents the reconciliation of opposites and the fusion of the conscious and the unconscious. It is the center of the personality providing stability and equilibrium and is thus the goal of life. It does not develop until the other aspects of the personality are developed and individuated. **5.** (C. Rogers) The portion of the personality which consists of perceptions of "I" or "me" and develops out of the organism's interaction with the environment. It strives for consistency, introjects the values of others which may be perceived in a distorted way, and changes as a result of maturation and learning. **6.** (H. S. Sullivan) See *self-system.* **7.** (A. Adler) A subjective system which makes experiences meaningful for the individual and seeks experiences which will fulfill the person's life style. It gives meaning to life creating the goal as well as helping to fulfill it.

**self-acceptance**  A healthy attitude toward one's worth and limitations consisting of an objective recognition of each quality and an acceptance of each as being part of the self.

**self-actualization  1.** (K. Goldstein) Striving toward completeness; fulfillment of one's potentialities. **2.** (A. Maslow) Developing and fulfilling one's innate, positive potentialities.

**self-administering test**  See *test, self-administering.*

**self-analysis**  See *analysis, self.*

**self-cathexis**  See *cathexis, self.*

**self-concept**  The individual's appraisal or evaluation of himself.

**self-consistency  1.** Individuals, items, or theories which do not contradict themselves in any aspect, action or phase. **2.** (B. Lecky) A theory of personality growth which postulates that growth consists of the development of a self-image and progressive harmonizing of subsequent behavior consistent with that image.

**self-correlation**  See *correlation, self.*

**self-demand schedule**  See *schedule, self-demand.*

**self-distribution**  See *distribution, self.*

**self-dynamism**  (H. S. Sullivan) See *self-system.*

**self-effacement**  (K. Horney) One of the major neurotic solutions to conflict consisting of identification with the hated self and consequent idealization of compliancy, dependency, and love.

**self-extinction**  (K. Horney) Neurotic behavior in which the individual has no experience of himself as an entity, attempts to live through others' experiences, and sees himself only as a reflection of others.

**self-feeling**  (W. McDougall) Various simple feelings which form the nucleus of an individual's self-regard. They may be of either a positive nature, derived from praise or achievement, or of negative nature, resulting from criticism or under-achievement.

**self-gratification**  See *gratification, self.*

**self-gratification mores**  (G. Murphy) The mores which set forth the means for obtaining non-utilitarian satisfactions. Also called self-maintenance mores.

**self-hypercathexis**  See *hypercathexis, self.*

**self-hypocathexis**  See *hypocathexis, self.*

**self-image**  (K. Horney) The perfect and ideal self which the individual imagines himself to be after identification with an idealized conception of what he should be.

**self-inventory**  A self-making questionnaire on which the subject marks the traits he believes are his own.

**self-maintainence mores**  See *self-gratification mores.*

**self-marking test**  See *test, self-marking.*

**self, phenomenal  1.** The self as it is experienced directly as the focus in the interaction of person and environment. **2.** The self as it is personally perceived and directly known as in the self-image or self-concept.

**self-preservation instinct**  See *Eros.*

**self-report inventory**  See *self-inventory.*

**self-sentiment**  (R. B. Cattell) A control of impulse, temperamental capacity to integrate, and strong investment of appropriate behavior integrated about the self-concept (or, roughly, self-respect). Aspects of this concept are involved in questionnaire factor $Q_3$ (usually called Self-Sentiment Control), objective test factor UI 36 (usually called Strength of Self-Sentiment Development), and a purely dynamic factor measured by the Motivational Analysis Test. Since these three factors are not identical empirically, they are best thought of as representing somewhat different aspects of the self-sentiment concept, with some common core of similarity.

**self-system**  (H. S. Sullivan) A secondary dynamism, dissociated from the rest of the personality, the organization of which controls awareness. It includes the personified self as well as the processes by which anxiety-provoking experiences and perceptions are kept from awareness. The self-system is purely the product of interpersonal experiences arising from anxiety encountered in the pursuit of need satisfaction and has no particular zones of interaction or physiological apparatus behind it but rather uses all zones and apparatus.

**semantic aphasia**  See *aphasia, semantic.*

**semantic conditioning**  Conditioning of a word to an object which the word represents.

**semantic differential test**  See *test, semantic differential.*

**semantic information**  See *information, semantic.*

**semantic therapy**  An ancillary method in psychotherapy; the explanation of meaning of words is used to help emotional conflicts.

**semantics**  The study of meaning of symbols; interpretation of symbols.

**semiotics**  The study of relationships between verbal and other symbols, and what they represent.

**senile dementia**  See *dementia, senile.*

**senility**  1. A general term including a variety of mental disorders occurring in old age which consist of two broad categories, organic and functional disorders. Organic disorders are characterized by intellectual impairment, poor memory, and labile emotions, due to infection, intoxication, circulatory disturbances or brain disease. The functional disorders include physical reactions of vertigo, fatigue, and headaches and psychological reactions of insomnia, doubt, hypochondriasis, delusions and feelings of physical decline. 2. See *dementia, senile.* 3. See *geriopsychosis.* 4. See *psychotic reactions, involutional.*

**sensation**  Immediate elementary experiences requiring no verbal, symbolic or conceptual elaboration, and related primarily to sense organ activity such as occurring in the eye or ear and in the associated nervous system leading to a particular sensory area in the brain. In so far as the only verifiable statements about sensations become statements about behavior, sensation denotes a construct whose meaning is derivative of responses of the organism to specified stimuli.

Sensation is typically though somewhat vaguely and arbitrarily distinguished from perception in that the latter tends to be more complex and more dependent upon learning, motivational, social and personality factors than the former.

**sensation, affective**  Also called feeling-sensation. An inseparable blending of feeling or affective elements with sensation elements.

**sensation increment**  (psychophysics) An increase in the intensity of the subjective sensory experience.

**sensation level**  The degree of intensity of a sensation such as in audition; the intensity in decibels of a sound.

**sensation, maximal**  The intensity level of the sensation which is not augmented upon increase of the physical stimulus.

**sensation, motor**  Sensation which arises from the receptors in the muscles, joints, and tendons.

**sensation, proprioceptive**  Sensation from inside the body.

**sensation, referred**  The experience of sensation at a point other than that which was stimulated.

**sensation, subjective**  Sensations which do not result from external stimulation but are related to phenomena within the organ such as ringing in the ears.

**sensation threshold**  See *threshold, absolute.*

**sensation type**  See *type, sensation.*

**sensation unit**  1. A small discriminible experience which can occur in any sensory modality. 2. The just-noticeable-difference. 3. (audition) A unit of physical intensity of a stimulus equal to the decibel. It is measured in logarithms and is abbreviated as SU.

**sense**  1. At least five criteria differentiate among primary sense modalities. They have 1) different receptive organs that 2) respond to characteristic stimuli. Each set of receptive organs has 3) its own nerve that goes to 4) a different part of the brain and 5) the resultant sensations are different on the basis of these criteria. Nine and perhaps eleven different senses have been identified: vision, audition, kinesthesis, vestibular, tactile, temperature, pain, taste, and smell. 2. The activity of a sense organ and correlated neural activity. 3. Apparently intuitive judgment in which the relevant stimuli are unidentified or obstructed.

**sense, cutaneous**  The sense of pressure, pain, cold, warmth and touch whose receptors lie beneath the skin or in the mucous membranes.

**sense datum**  That fundamental unit which is experienced upon stimulation of a sense receptor.

**sense distance**  The interval on a scale of sensation which separates two sensations.

**sense experience**  The awareness of the sensation resulting from the stimulation of the sensory receptor.

**sense-feeling**  The dimension of pleasantness and unpleasantness of a sensory experience.

**sense limen**  See *threshold, absolute.*

**sense modality**  See *modality, sense.*

**sense organ**  See *organ, sense.*

**sense, pain**  Sensory modality of free nerve endings receptive to pain which is distributed over the periphery of the body and many internal surfaces.

**sense perception**  See *perception, sense.*

**sense quality**  1. The character of a sensation which distinguishes it from other senses. 2. A sense datum characteristic of a particular modality.

**sense-ratios method**  See *method, sense-ratios.*

**sense, systemic**  The sense whose receptors lie in the internal organs. Also known as interoceptive sense.

**sensed difference** A noticeable difference between two sensations which are presented simultaneously or successively.

**sensibility** The capacity to sense or to be stimulated by sense stimuli.

**sensibility, differential** Ability to discriminate between two stimuli as measured by a differential threshold.

**sensibility, subcutaneous** Sensitivity to stimulation of the receptors lying beneath the skin.

**sensitive zone** A part of the body highly responsive to a particular kind of stimulus, e.g. skin is a tactile sensitive zone.

**sensitivity** 1. The reciprocal of threshold; one over threshold. 2. The responsiveness of an organism to stimulus energy or energy changes.

**sensitivity, absolute** The ability to respond to stimuli of minimal intensity.

**sensitivity, liminal** An individual's sensory acuity as measured by the average stimulus that just barely evokes a response.

**sensitivity training** Training in human relations which is an outgrowth of the thinking of K. Lewin and C. Rogers and began with the meeting of a group in Bethel, Maine in 1947. The focus of the group is personal and interpersonal interactions. The members are taught to observe their interactions with others and the nature of the group process. There are many forms and emphases in the groups. The groups may be composed of strangers or they may be acquainted with each other. They may be workers in an organization, couples, male, female, etc. Some groups meet once a week, some more often, even during an entire weekend. There is at least one leader whose function is to facilitate the understanding of interpersonal relations. Presently, this term usually refers to groups in which personal and interpersonal issues are the primary forces rather than the observation of group processes or organizational behavior.

**sensitization** The process of a receptor becoming more susceptible to a given stimulus.

**sensor** A receptor that responds to energy or energy changes.

**sensori-motor activity** Responses resulting from the reception of sensory stimulation.

**sensorium** 1. Obsolete term for the sensory areas of the brain. 2. The total sensory mechanism.

**sensory** Referring to the total apparatus and experience of sensation including the sense organs, stimuli impinging on the sense receptors, afferent neurons, brain centers' receiving the impulses and the processes involved in the experience of sensation.

**sensory adaptation** 1. The decrease in sensitivity to stimuli due to prolonged stimulation, also called negative adaptation. 2. The continuation of effective sensory responsiveness to changing stimulation.

**sensory aphasia** See *aphasia, sensory*.

**sensory apraxia** See *apraxia, sensory*.

**sensory areas** Areas in the cerebral cortex which receive neural impulses from sense organs.

**sensory basis of reinforcement** Property of many sensory stimuli that reinforce behavior in their own right as a result of their stimulus properties and innate central nervous system connections. Head turning to one side or the other may be rapidly conditioned in the neonate by presentation of a sweet nipple. Patterns of visual or auditory stimuli may reinforce motor responses that turn on such stimuli. Adversive reinforcement is also observed in which organisms avoid and learn instrumental responses to turn off or reduce noxious stimulation.

**sensory circle** Area of the skin in which two points stimulating the skin are perceived as a single point. This was explained as the skin area in which the terminals of a single sensory neuron are distributed.

**sensory clearness** See *attensity*.

**sensory code** The information content of a pattern of neural discharge frequencies about the nature of the stimulus impinging on a sense receptor.

**sensory cortex** See *cortex, sensory*.

**sensory deprivation** See *deprivation, sensory*.

**sensory development, stages of** (E. Schactel) Modes of perceiving, by which the individual objectifies his environment and shapes his experiences, which define an ontogenic hierarchy ranging from the dominance of autocentric modes (olfactory, gustatory, tactile) to the dominance of allocentric modes (auditory and visual).

**sensory discrimination** See *discrimination, sensory*.

**sensory drive** See *drive, sensory*.

**sensory epilepsy** See *epilepsy, sensory*.

**sensory field** The totality of stimuli which impinge on a receptor or organism as a whole at a specific time.

**sensory habit** See *habit, sensory*.

**sensory integration** (H. Birch and M. Bitterman) The postulate that the contiguous stimulation of two afferent areas results in a relationship between them whereby the activation of one will cause the other to be aroused.

**sensory interaction** The reciprocal interdependence of sensory processes occurring simultaneously.

**sensory-motor arc** Path of a neural impulse from the receptor through its afferent fibers to the central nervous system where it synapses with motor, efferent fibers which eventually terminate with response effectors.

**sensory nerve** See *nerve, sensory*.

**sensory noise** See *neural noise*.

**sensory organization** 1. The process by which

sensory processes become meaningfully coordinated. **2.** (Gestalt) The patterning of stimuli in the sensory field which produces a meaningful percept.

**sensory pattern**  See *pattern, sensory.*

**sensory preconditioning**  See *preconditioning, sensory.*

**sensory process**  **1.** The process underlying sensation which originates in the receptor. **2.** The process of becoming aware of sensations.

**sensory projection area**  See *sensory areas.*

**sensory reaction type**  See *reaction type, sensory.*

**sensory receptors**  See *receptor.*

**sensory root**  See *root, sensory.*

**sensory stimulus**  See *stimulus, sensory.*

**sensory system**  The sensory unit consisting of the sensory organs, afferent neurons and the sensory projection areas in the cerebral cortex.

**sensual**  Referring to satisfaction obtained from indulging in activities involving the senses, such as food and sex.

**sensum**  See *sense-datum.*

**sensuous**  Referring to the sense aspect of experience or the ability for the senses to be aroused.

**sentence completion test**  See *test, sentence completion.*

**sentence repetition test**  See *test, sentence repetition.*

**sentience**  **1.** The capacity of the organism to receive stimuli. **2.** Sensation without concomitant associations which is hypothesized as the most primitive form of cognition.

**sentience need**  See *need, sentience.*

**sentiment**  **1.** An attitude. **2.** An emotional disposition. **3.** A soft, gentle feeling. **4.** An expression of a subdued emotion, or of an emotionally colored attitude.

**separation anxiety**  (psychoanalysis) Anxiety caused in a child by actual separation from his mother or by a threat thereof.

**separation-individuation, normal**  (M. S. Mahler) From the fifth month on, the infant begins to differentiate gradually his own self, especially his bodyself boundaries, from the symbiotic dual unit; he starts to disengage himself and to separate his mental representation from that of his mother. Toward the end of the second quarter of the first year, there are unmistakable signs that symbiosis is overlapped by what Mahler calls the "separation-individuation" process. During the process of the child's separation-individuation, the mother's role shifts from that of complement and buffer (as it had been in the autistic and symbiotic phases) to that of support and encouragement for the toddler's strivings toward and gradual attainment of ego, i.e. self-autonomy.

**separation-individuation: subphases of the normal process**  Four steps or subphases of the separation-individuation process were described by Mahler and her co-workers: 1) Differentiation (also called "hatching" from the symbiotic dual unity's common membrane); 2) The Practicing Period; 3) The Rapprochement Subphase (Mahler); 4) The Subphase "On the Way to Emotional Object Constancy."

**sequels**  The pathological aftereffect of an illness.

**sequence**  **1.** (mathematics) A series of consecutive quantities in which each is obtained by performing a specific operation on the preceding quantity. **2.** (H. Rorschach) The order of the different types of responses which the subject makes, such as whole and detail response.

**sequence alternation**  One element of basic Rorschach interpretation in which the sequence of response determinants, such as movement, form, color, or shading, are studied in their consecutive relation to each other. This method of response analysis often reveals those responses which are most idiographic to the individual.

**sequence analysis**  In Rorschach interpretation, the examination of each response in its chronological order in the protocol for basic structure, relevance to the blot area relation to preceding and subsequent responses, and its basic content. It is generally considered the second of three interpretive steps in working with Rorschach data, the first being interpretation from quantitative structural data and the third being a broad qualitative analysis of verbalizations and content.

**sequential analysis**  Discussion of results obtained in research which aims at acceptance, rejection or modification of conclusions arrived at in that research.

**sequential test**  See *test, sequential.*

**serial-anticipation method**  See *method, prompting.*

**serial discrimeter**  See *psychergograph.*

**serial or serial-order learning**  See *learning, serial or serial-order.*

**serial position effect**  The effect of a position of a certain item within a series on the speed of learning process.

**serial reinforcement**  See *reinforcement, serial.*

**seriation**  **1.** Forming of series. **2.** Organizing of data into statistical series.

**series, Poisson**  See *Poisson series.*

**serotonin**  A substance found in the brain, the intestines, and the platelets which induces vasoconstriction and muscular contraction. It has been suggested that this substance is involved in the development of mental disorders. This hypothesis is based on studies which show that certain indoles which antagonize serotonin produce aberrant behavior and that the displacement of serotonin from the brain by certain psychotropic drugs produces abnormal behavior in animal and human subjects. It may be that abnormal levels of serotonin underlie mental disorders.

**serpasil** Common name for reserpine, a purified alkaloid extract of rauwolfia.

**servomechanism** A system or mechanism which controls the rate of operation of another system according to a specified plan such as a thermostat.

**set** 1. (mathematics) A well defined collection of elements. 2. A temporary but often recurring tendency of a person or an organism to respond toward certain environmental stimuli in a predetermined way. 3. The establishment of a fixed behavior pattern; stereotyping.

**set learning** See *learning, set.*

**set, mental** Readiness for a particular kind of action usually due to instructions given previously.

**set, motor** The readiness of an organism to react motorically in a particular way to an expected stimulus which involves the adjustment of the muscles in anticipation of the action.

**set, neural** A readiness of an organism to respond in a specific way which is explained in terms of a state of neural excitation of a response circuit.

**set, perceptual** A predisposition to perceive the environment in a particular way, usually influenced by some sort of pattern.

**set, postural** Tonic muscle contractions which ready the organism to begin a specific action.

**set, stimulus** A readiness to attend to the stimulus rather than on making a response in reaction time experiments.

**sex** 1. Male or female gender. 2. Biological division of animal and human organism on the basis of their reproductive role. The male organism produces spermatozoa and possesses a necessary fertilization organ; the female organism produces ova capable of becoming fertilized by the spermatozoa and possesses the necessary organs for prenatal and postnatal care of the offspring.

**sex chromosomes** Chromosomes responsible for sex determination. In man, XX is female and XY is male.

**sex determination** Genetic mechanism which determines the difference between the two sexes, specifically the sex chromosomes X and Y. Under usual conditions a fertilized egg with two XX chromosomes becomes a female; a fertilized egg with one X and one Y chromosome becomes a male.

**sex differences** Innate or acquired, organic and/or behavioral differences between the two sexes.

**sex hormones** See *hormones, sex.*

**sex-influenced** A trait which is not sex-linked but is expressed to a different degree or with a different frequency in male and female is termed sex-influenced. Involutional psychosis is a good example.

**sex-limited** A trait expressed in one sex only is termed sex-limited.

**sex-linkage** Inheritance by genes on the sex chromosomes. Several neurological syndromes exhibit sex-linked transmission.

**sex need** See *need, sex.*

**sex reversal** 1. Changing of the anatomical sex. 2. Change in fundamental sexual characteristic. In some cases, when the female ovaries or male gonads are destroyed, or when there is an innate pathological discrepancy between the chromosomal and anatomical change, the apparent sexual characteristics and behavior can be changed into opposites.

**sex role** Behavioral patterns expected from an individual by his social group believed to be typical of his sex. Some sex determinant behavioral patterns are biologically determined, such as, e.g. menstruation and pregnancy in females. Certain behavior patterns are culturally influenced, such as, e.g. ascendance-submissiveness, or occupational choices. Sex role is often called psychosexual role.

**sex, secondary characteristics** Characteristics which distinguish between the sexes and are not directly related to sexual and reproductive functions, e.g. pubic hair, voice, stature, etc.

**sex-typed skills** Skills which are designated as either masculine or feminine.

**sex-typed trait** A trait identified as either masculine or feminine.

**sex-typing** The designation in a culture of certain behaviors as feminine or masculine and the training of children to adhere to these roles.

**sexism** A belief that utilizes sex differences as the basis for discrimination in the granting of political, social or economic rights.

**sexoesthetic inversion** The assumption of manners, habits, and garments of the opposite sex.

**sexology** Scientific study of sexual life.

**Sexton, Virginia Staudt (1916-   )** American psychologist. Principal research interests: history of psychology; international developments in psychology; and psychology of women. Published (with H. Misiak) *Catholics in Psychology* (1954); *History of Psychology: an Overview* (1966); and *Historical Perspective in Psychology: Readings* (1971).

**sexual behavior** The totality of normal and abnormal, conscious and unconscious, overt and covert sensations, thoughts, feelings and actions related to sexual organs and other erotogenic zones, including masturbation, heterosexual and homosexual relations, sexual deviations, goals and techniques.

**sexual deviation** 1. Sexual behavior which does not conform with social norms of a certain culture. 2. The Diagnostic and Statistical Manual of the American Psychiatric Association (DSM II, 1968) describes sexual deviation as follows:

|      |                        |
|------|------------------------|
| .0   | Homosexuality          |
| .1   | Fetishism              |
| .2   | Pedophilia             |
| .3   | Transvestitism         |
| .4   | Exhibitionism          |
| .5   | Voyeurism              |
| .6   | Sadism                 |
| .7   | Masochism              |
| .8   | Other sexual deviation |

**sexual exhibitionism**  See *exhibitionism.*

**sexual frigidity**  Sexual inadequacy in females; covers a variety of symptoms, such as lack of sexual desires, total inability of reaching orgasm, inability of reaching vaginal orgasm or orgasm in coitus, complete or partial anesthesia of sexual organs, vaginism, etc.

**sexual negativism**  See *negativism, sexual.*

**sexual perversion**  See *sexual deviation.*

**sexual reflex**  1. Erection. 2. Orgasm.

**sexual reproduction**  The process of creating a new organism through the union of male and female sex cells.

**sexual selection**  Selection of sexual mates which leads to natural selection. The prevalence of certain sex characteristics sought after fosters, through heredity, a prevalence of these characteristics in the forthcoming generations.

**sexual symbolism**  The use of substitute objects to represent sexual organs or actions, such as receptacles for female organs and sharp objects for male organs.

**Sh R**  (Z. Piotrowski) Shading response is a Rorschach inkblot test indicating self-control and inhibition of overt emotional reactions.

**shading response**  A type of Rorschach response in which the chiaroscuro features (light-dark distribution) contribute to the development of a response in a manner other than creating a textural quality or a sense of depth. Shading responses are generally considered indicative of painful affects, mainly anxiety.

**shading shock**  An unusual or startle response of Rorschach subjects to the achromatic or chiaroscuro features of the blots. It may be manifest in delayed reaction time, alteration in approach, reduction of response quality and/or frequency. It is generally interpreted as a response to threat and associated with insecurity, extensive anxiety, or over-emphasis on introspection.

**shadow**  (C. G. Jung) The archetype consisting of man's animal instincts inherited in his evolution from lower life forms. It contains sexual and aggressive impulses which cannot be approved by the conscious ego. When these impulses pierce the consciousness they may be repressed into the personal unconscious and form a part of a complex.

**Shannon's tenth theorem**  See *Ashby's Law of Requisite Variety.*

**shape constancy**  Perceiving an object as having the same shape irrespective of the perceiver's vantage point.

**shaping**  See *conditioning, approximation.*

**Sheldon, William H. (1899-  )**  American psychologist. Developed and experimentally investigated a constitutional theory of personality. Investigated the composition of the human body, the components of temperament, and the relation between physiology and personality; developed 7-point measuring scales for assessing body-type and temperament; applied theoretical findings to the area of delinquency; investigated the relation between physical structure and organic disease. See *constitutional theory of personality.*

**shell shock**  See *battle fatigue.*

**Sherrington, Charles S. (1857-1952)**  Distinguished British neurophysiologist. His 1906 *Integrative Action of the Nervous System* presented the results of many experiments on reflexes, the synapse, and the control of reflex arcs by higher nervous centers, and developed many concepts and principles (such as neural summation, reciprocal inhibition, and facilitation) that served as the foundation of physiological psychology for many decades.

**shifting, law of**  (E.L. Thorndike) The law of associative shifting means that it is easy to have associated the responses which the learner is capable of with situations to which he is sensitive.

**shock therapy**  The treatment of mentally ill persons by passing an electric current through the brain or by the administration of drugs which produces convulsions.

**short term memory (STM)**  See *memory, short term.*

**Siamese twins**  See *twins, Siamese.*

**sickle-cell anemia**  See *anemia, sickle-cell.*

**Sidman avoidance schedule**  See *avoidance, free operant.*

**sigma** ($\sigma$)  1. One thousandth of a second. 2. The symbol of standard deviation.

**sigma score**  See *standard score.*

**sign-gestalt**  (E.C. Tolman) The process of cognitive learning is based on expectations of attainment of certain goals or objects called sign-gestalts.

**sign learning**  (O.H. Mowrer) Learning by contiguity with the participation of autonomic nervous system.

**sign, local**  (H. Lotze) An inherent qualitative factor by means of which one visual or tactual sensation can be distinguished from others in respect to position in space.

**sign-significance relation**  The expectancy of a given phenomenon.

**sign stimulus**  See *stimulus, sign.*

**sign stimulus, super-normal**  See *stimulus, super-normal sign.*

**signal detection theory** (psychophysics) A method of dealing with sensory discrimination without using the threshold concept, since classical psychophysics assumes that there is a real sensory threshold. Signal detection theory provides a method of separating the sensitivity of the subject from his criterion of response. The basic signal detection experiment involves the detection of signals (stimuli) that are weak relative to a background noise against which they are presented. This detection becomes a function of the signal intensity and background noise intensity. On some trials the noise is presented without a signal and on other trials both are presented together. The subject attempts to determine if the signal was present or not. There are four possible results on any trial; the signal may or may not be presented and in each case the response may or may not be correct.

A response is a function of the stimulus input, the sensations, and the decision rule used by the subject. The specific decision rule in the specific situation depends on the value or relative loss of the types of errors and the relative worth of the types of correct responses; this defines the optimum strategy. The subject's sensitivity is depicted as a graph of the probability of a yes response to the signal and noise together—a correct determination; as a function of the probability of a yes response to the noise alone—a false alarm. Any deviation from this obtained function, called d', on the receiver operating characteristic (ROC) curve is indicative of a change in the subject's sensitivity. Thus the ROC curve serves as a baseline or characteristic performance level with which to compare other individuals or changes in the sensitivity of the same individual as a function of some independent variable.

**significance** (statistics) A statement that the probability of obtaining the observed effect by chance only is small and designated by the alpha error.

**significant difference** A difference between two statistics, computed from two separate samples. This difference is of a magnitude such that the probability that the samples were drawn from the same universe is less than some predetermined level.

**similarity paradox** See *Skaggs-Robinson hypothesis.*

**simple interview** An interview with an individual who forms part of a sample of a population.

**simple schizophrenia** See *schizophrenia, simple.*

**simple structure** A criterion for rotation of factors, which is attained when the number of zero or near-zero loadings (Hyperplane Count) is maximized for each factor.

**single variable, rule of** The rule of experimentation which states that only one factor at any given time should be treated as an independent variable. When two equivalent groups differ, the difference can be attributed to only one factor.

**sitomania** Morbid craving for food; bulimia.

**sitophobia** Fear of food.

**situation, analytic** Setting of the psychoanalytic process, characterized by a one-to-one relationship between analyst and patient, the patient being required to recline so he cannot see the analyst and to relate without censoring all thoughts and feelings as they occur.

**situation test** See *test, situation.*

**situationism** (K. Lewin) Dealing with psychological phenomena in a given situation at a given time. Viewing behavior in a context of interaction between the organism and its environment as it occurs at a certain moment, as a momentary situation.

**sixteen D scale** See *scale, sixteen D.*

**size constancy** See *constancy, size.*

**size-weight illusion** See *illusion, size-weight.*

**SK** See *skewness.*

**Skaggs-Robinson hypothesis** (E. B. Skaggs and E.S. Robinson) The learning of identical materials, the learning of one enchancing the retention of the other; as the materials become more dissimilar, one interferes with the retention of the other, and when the material is completely dissimilar, retention increases again, although it never attains the level obtained at the point of maximal similarity of material.

**skew-deviation** See *Hertwig-Magendie phenomenon.*

**skewed family** See *family, skewed.*

**skewed regression** See *regression, non-linear.*

**skewness (SK)** The extent to which a frequency curve is twisted, so that it extends farther to one side of the central tendency than to the other. It is positively skewed if it leans to the right and negatively skewed if it leans to the left.

**skiascope** An instrument used for measuring the refractive condition of the eye.

**skill** An acquired aptitude.

**Skinner, B.F.** (1904- ) American psychologist, working in the experimental analysis of operant behavior. Developed laboratory methods and extended principles to verbal behavior, psychotherapy, education, and the design of cultures. See *operant behavior.*

**Skinner box** A typical research apparatus is a device known as the Skinner box, named for its inventor B. F. Skinner. The dimensions of the box are about 12 inches cubed. There is a small lever projecting out of one wall of the apparatus. When the experimental animal (usually a rat) depresses the lever, a piece of food is released into the compartment for the animal to consume. The animal is rewarded for pressing the lever, and thus continues to press it as long as it is hungry. The pattern of the animal's behavior can be varied by varying the procedure. For example, if the animal receives food once for every ten pressings, he will press the bar very rapidly. On the other hand, if it receives food only on the first response after a one minute period has lapsed, his behavior will be quite different. As a rule, the animal does very little for the first part of the minute, but toward the end of the time limit it presses the bar rapidly.

**Skinner's operant conditioning** See *conditioning, operant.*

**Slater, Eliot T. O. (1904-   )** British psychiatrist. Principally engaged in work on the genetics of mental disorders. Studied parents and children of manic-depressives, proposing hypothesis of major dominant gene. Conducted the first British major study of twins of psychotic patients. Twin studies, and later follow-up studies, of "hysteria" led to the conclusion that this was a pseudo-syndrome without genetical basis. Studies of schizophrenia-like psychoses in epileptics (with A.W. Beard and E. Glithero) suggested a discrete syndrome of organic but not genetic causation. Twin studies (with J. Shields) in the neuroses suggested an important genetical contribution to anxiety states, but a negligible one to the reactive depressions.

**sleep  1.** A state of bodily rest combined with inhibition of voluntary activities, decrease in metabolism, and complete or partial suspension of consciousness. **2.** (I. P. Pavlov) Sleep is the most general internal inhibition which creates a balance between the processes of destruction and restoration. **3.** (S. Freud) A temporary regression into a position resembling intrauterine life. **4.** (H. Pieron) During the waking state a fatigue product, called hypnotism, is accumulated in the blood and cerebrospinal fluid. The abundance of hypnotism produces sleep; sleep metabolizes the hypnotism and restores the balance in the organism. **5.** (E. N. Harvey, G. A. Hobart and A. L. Loomis) There are five identifiable electro-encephalic stages in sleep, called stages 0, 1, 2, 3, 4, respectively. Stage 1 EEG is accompanied by rapid eye movements and dreaming. **6.** (N. Kleitman) Sleep is the phylogenetically fundamental passive state. On the lower levels of evolution, in decorticated animals and newborn infants, the environmental or inner stimuli may interrupt the state of sleep and elicit temporary states of "wakefulness necessity." One must also distinguish between primitive sleep and wakefulness controlled by subcortical centers, and the cortical sleep and wakefulness controlled by the cortex. **7.** (W. R. Hess) Sleep is an active inhibitory state controlled by the parasympathetic nervous system; sleep provides for rest and relaxation. **8.** (W. H. Magoun) The synchronized EEG in sleep is caused by the thalamus-cortical system, driven by the pontine mechanisms which produces a reduction in the visceral process. The sleep mechanism is inhibitory in Pavlovian sense and operates opposite the reticular activating system. **9.** (R. Hernandez-Peon) There is no one sleep center. The sleep system is influenced by the neocortex, medulla and the limbic system.

**sleep deprivation, effects of** See *deprivation, sleep.*

**sleep epilepsy** See *epilepsy, sleep.*

**sleep treatment, prolonged** A treatment technique of mental disorders in which extended sleep is induced by chemicals.

**slip, Freudian** See *Freudian slip.*

**slip of the tongue, or lapsus linguae** The inclusion of an incorrect word or phrase in speech which changes the meaning of the sentence. This was interpreted first in psychoanalysis and now quite generally interpreted as expressing a repressed wish or unconscious desire of the individual.

**slope** (mathematics) The inclination of a line as compared to any base line. The slope of a line can be computed by dividing the vertical distance between two points by the horizontal distance. The formula, given two points $(X_1, Y_1)$ $(X_2, Y_2)$ is:

$$SLOPE = \frac{Y_2 - Y_1}{X_2 - X_1}$$

**slope of a curve** (mathematics) The inclination of a line tangent to a curve at any point. The value is constantly changing.

**slow learner** A child who cannot learn at the same rate as his peers because of mental retardation or slower development, but who can profit from academic training at a slower rate.

**small-sample method** A mathematical technique which permits drawing conclusions from a small number of cases.

**Smith, Mahlon Brewster (1919-   )** American social psychologist. Developed (with J. S. Bruner and R.W. White) an early comprehensive account of how social and political attitudes are embedded in the functioning of personality; contributed to the reconceptualization of "mental health" as personal effectiveness and competence; sponsored the application of social psychology to such topical social problems as prejudice, student protest, and population; promoted a view of human agency intended to bridge the gap between polarized humanistic and scientific psychologies.

**smooth curve** A curve with little if any deviations from its direction.

**Snellen chart or test** (H. Snellen) A test of visual acuity consisting of a chart of printed letters ranging from very large to very small which the subject is asked to read at a predetermined distance.

**Snezhnevsky, Andrei V. (1904-   )** Soviet psychiatrist. Main studies in the field of clinical psychiatry. Studied and elaborated a classification of schizophrenia based on the principle of development. Has distinguished three main typical groups of schizophrenia proceeding continuously, without remissions (sluggish, paranoid and malignant forms of schizophrenia), leading to a gradual and gross deterioration; mixed or shift-like forms including a development with attacks and residual psychotic changes between the attacks (and in the form of pseudoneurotic, pseudopsychopathic, hypochondriacal, paranoidal, etc.) and distinct personality changes; recurrent schizophrenia developing in acute affective and affective delusional attacks and with minimal personality changes. Also many works in psychopharmacology.

**sociability** Desire to be with other people; enjoying human company.

**sociability rating** See *rating, sociability.*

**sociable or social type** See *type, sociable or social.*

**social adaptation** The changes necessary to meet the demands made by society and interpersonal situations. See *adaptation.*

**social atom** See *atom, social.*

**social attitude** See *attitude, social.*

**social behavior** 1. Behavior of an individual dependent on the presence of other people. 2. Behavior of a group, social unit or social organization.

**social character** (E. Fromm) By social character it is understood to mean the character matrix shared by members of a social group such as a tribe, nation, or class. It develops in the process of active adaptation to the economic, social and cultural conditions common to the group. The effect of the social character is to make people *desire* doing what they *have* to do in their socially determined role. The social character has a two-fold function: it furnishes society with the specific psychical energies it needs for its proper functioning, and it gives the individual a sufficient degree of satisfaction from behaving according to his character traits, while making him conform with society. The social character is transmitted to the child through the character structure of the parents and through methods of child rearing and education which in themselves are mainly socially determined. The family is the "psychological agency" of society which mediates the social influence in early childhood.

Because social change occurs more rapidly than change in educational methods and ideologies, there is often a "lag" between a traditional form of social character and new social conditions to which it is not properly adapted. This lag often leads to serious maladjustments in the social process.

The concept of social character was first employed by E. Fromm in 1932, using the term "social libidinous structure," and from 1941 onwards the term "social character".

**social character typology** (D. Riesman) The postulation of three character types: tradition-directed, inner-directed, and other-directed whose formation is influenced by society.

**social class** A group of people united because of their fulfillment of certain criteria, e.g., wealth, education, family background, religion, etc.

**social climate** The totality of social factors affecting the behavior of a group and its members.

**social climbing** Vertical social mobility; moving from a lower social class toward a higher one.

**social continuity** See *continuity, social.*

**social control** See *control, social.*

**social conventions** See *conventions, social.*

**social distance scale** See *scale, Bogardus Social Distance.*

**social dynamics** The causes and motives of social behavior.

**social exchange** A profit-centered view in which social interactions are designed to maximize gain for both parties through exchange of rewards; i.e. one rewards the other with something (some statement or behavior) which is more valuable to the receiver than to himself, and in exchange receives a reward which is more valuable to him than to the other individual.

**social facilitation** The energizing effect of a group on the motivation and effort of any given member.

**social factors** Influences stemming from interindividual relations, social organizations, social institutions, norms, or beliefs.

**social influence** The ability of an individual or a group to affect or control some aspect of some other individual or group.

**social instinct** (A. Adler) An innate ability for cooperation, for "seeing with the eyes of another person." The child's innate impulses of affection are directed toward others and, in normal development, the striving for superiority is blended with the social interest.

**social integration** See *integration, social.*

**social learning** See *learning, social.*

**social maturity** An index of the level of social development including the acquisition of social behavior and standards expected at a particular age.

**social medicine** See *medicine, social.*

**social mobility** Flexibility and fluidity of a social organization which permits groups and individuals to change their social affiliation and status.

**social norm** Rule of conduct established by a social organization.

**social perception** See *perception, social.*

**social pressure** Any type of coercion or force applied by an institution or group of individuals.

**social process** 1. A social interaction between individuals. 2. Social change.

**social psychology** See *psychology, social.*

**social status** The position of an individual within his group in relationship to other group members.

**social stratification** The division of a society into strict social classes.

**social structure** The organization of a group in terms of the stratification of persons, interpersonal relationships and any other factors which differentiate the group from other groups.

**social work** The profession which concerns itself with the amelioration of social conditions in a community.

**socialization** 1. The process in and by which the individual learns the ways, ideas, beliefs, values, patterns and norms of his particular culture and adapts them as a part of his own personality. 2. The process of bringing the industry and services of a country under governmental control for the benefit of all people in the country.

**socialized anxiety**  See *anxiety, socialized.*

**sociatry**  (J. L. Moreno) A special approach to the problems of social psychiatry which applies Moreno's rationale of social acceptance and rejection, spontaneity, etc. as the main determinants in psychopathology.

**society**  1. A large number of mutually interdependent individuals. 2. Social organization; a group formed for a fulfillment of a certain task.

**sociocenter**  (J. L. Moreno) The person who is most often chosen in a sociometric test.

**sociocentrism**  An assumption that a particular society is or should be the determinant of the behavior of its members.

**sociocultural determinants**  The social organization, the legal and political system, social norms, religion, economics and other aspects of the ways and manners of a particular society viewed as determinants of individuals' normal or abnormal behavior.

**sociodiagnostic technique**  (B. B. Wolman) A technique of diagnosing behavior disorders using overt interindividual behavior as the main clue. This sociopsychological technique is derived from experimental studies with statogram and uses the power and acceptance dimensions for the assessment of the clinical type of particular sociopsychogenic mental disorder. The sociodiagnostic technique uses Sociopsychological Inventory of Observation and Sociopsychological Diagnostic Interview.

**sociodrama**  (J. L. Moreno) The use of role playing and dramatization to teach socially acceptable behaviors.

**sociogenesis**  The process by which other persons affect the self, either the body or the mind.

**sociogenic mental disorders**  (B. B. Wolman) Mental disorders are either inherited, acquired, or caused by a combination of both. If they are inherited, they are transmitted through the genes. Those mental disorders which are not inherited are acquired through interaction with either the physical or the social environment. Thus mental disorders can be divided into three large categories related to their origins. Those that originate in the organism through heredity or through interaction with the physical environment (injuries, poisons, and so on) are somatogenic (soma means body). The inherited disorders are genosomatogenic, for they are caused by genes; the physically acquired mental disorders are ecosomatogenic, for they are caused by interaction with the environment, the ecos. All other disorders stem from faulty interindividual relations, i.e. they are psychosocial, but since the interaction with the social environment is the cause of morbid conditioning and cathexis, we shall call these disorders sociogenic or sociopsychogenic.

In sociogenic or psychosociogenic disorders the social interaction is the cause, and the psychological or behavioral symptoms are the result.

**sociogram**  (J. L. Moreno) A diagram in which group interactions are analyzed on the basis of mutual attractions or antipathies between group members.

## WOLMAN'S CLASSIFICATION OF SOCIOGENIC MENTAL DISORDERS

|  | Hyperinstrumental Type (I) | Dysmutual Type (M) | Hypervectorial Type (V) |
|---|---|---|---|
| Neurotic Level | HYPERINSTRUMENTAL NEUROSIS (Certain anxiety and depressive neuroses) | DYSMUTUAL NEUROSIS (Dissociative and conversion neuroses) | HYPERVECTORIAL NEUROSIS (Obsessional, phobic, and neurasthenic neuroses) |
| Character Neurotic Level | HYPERINSTRUMENTAL CHARACTER NEUROSIS (Sociopathic or psychopathic character) | DYSMUTUAL CHARACTER NEUROSIS (Cyclothymic and hysteric character) | HYPERVECTORIAL CHARACTER NEUROSIS (Schizoid and compulsive character) |
| Latent Psychotic Level | LATENT HYPERINSTRUMENTAL PSYCHOSIS (Psychopathic reactions bordering on psychosis) | LATENT DYSMUTUAL PSYCHOSIS (Borderline manic-depressive psychosis) | LATENT VECTORIASIS PRAECOX (Borderline and latent schizophrenia) |
| Manifest Psychotic Level | HYPERINSTRUMENTAL PSYCHOSIS (Psychotic psychopathy and moral insanity) | DYSMUTUAL PSYCHOSIS (Manifest manic-depressive psychosis) | VECTORIASIS PRAECOX (Manifest schizophrenia) |
| Dementive Level | COLLAPSE OF PERSONALITY STRUCTURE | | |

**sociology** The science of human societies, groups, organizations and institutions.

**sociometry** (J. L. Moreno) A technique for the measurement of attraction and repulsion among people which uses the method of the sociogram.

**socionomics** The study of nonsocial factors, such as geographical factors, rivers, climate, etc. on social life and social organizations.

**sociopath** See *personality, sociopathic.*

**sociopathic personality** See *personality, sociopathic.*

**sociopharmacology** The study of the effects of drugs upon social systems and upon persons other than the drug taker.

**sociopsychogenic disorders** See *sociogenic mental disorders.*

**socio-psychological-diagnostic interview** (B. B. Wolman) Reflects the subject's perception of himself and his environment in terms of power and acceptance. The interviewer conducts an open-end, focused-type interview. The subject is requested to tell his life history, dwell on his childhood memories, describe his past experiences, etc. The interviewer avoids asking any direct questions, but encourages a free flow of communication and whenever necessary tries to bring out a point by asking a question, such as "And what happened next? What did you do? How did you feel about it? And what was the reaction of others?" etc.

**socio-psychological-diagnostic inventory of observation** (B. B. Wolman) Roughly corresponds to the technique of statogram. In the Inventory of Observations the observer or observers carefully record the overt patterns of behavior of the subject and categorize them in terms of power and acceptance. The observers register empirical data, record them carefully, and tabulate. To increase the objectivity of observations one can employ several observers and correlate their ratings. This observation includes actions (eating, sleeping, working, entertainment) and other interaction and communication with other individuals.

**sociopsychosomatic theory of schizophrenia** (B. B. Wolman) Morbid environmental factors—especially the disturbed intrafamilial setting (social)—cause disbalance in interindividual cathexis of libido and destrudo, which in time affects the intra-individual balance of cathexis and disorganizes the personality structure (psychological). The disorganized personality affects adversely the functions of the glandular and nervous system causing morbid changes in the organism (somatic). Hence the causal sociopsychosomatic chain.

**sociotype** Stereotype applied to a certain social group or clan.

**sodium amytal** See *amytal.*

**sodium pentothal** See *thiopental.*

**sodomy** 1. Sexual intercourse through the anus. 2. Sexual intercourse between a human being and an animal.

**solipsism** An epistemological theory promoted by A. Schopenhauer and others which implies that whatever exists is a product of will and ideas of the perceiving individual.

**solution, comprehensive** (K. Horney) The identification of the self with the idealized self in order to protect oneself from intrapsychic conflict.

**solution learning** (O. H. Mowrer) Acquisition of a tendency to action which is the solution to some problem. Solution learning is problem solving, drive reducing and gives pleasure.

**solution, major** (K. Horney) The neurotic tendency to deny or repress two of the three interpersonel orientations and to recognize only one as a means of reducing basic anxiety.

**soma** The body; the tissues of the body.

**somatic** Pertaining to the tissues of the body.

**somatic disorders** 1. Disorders of the organism. 2. Behavior disorders of organic origin; somatogenic disorders.

**somatogenesis** Having origins in the tissues of the body.

**somatogenic disorders** (B. B. Wolman) All mental or behavior disorders can be divided into somatogenic, which are caused by physiochemical factors and socio- or psychosociogenic ones caused by interaction with the social environment. The somatogenic disorders can be divided into genosomatogenic, i.e. inherited and ecosomatogenic, i.e. acquired in interaction with physiochemical world, such as poisons, infections, etc.

**somatophysic** Refers to a psychological disorder which has a somatic basis.

**somatoplasm** (biology) The protoplasm of the cells of a living organism.

**somatopsychic** Transformation of or transition from an organic to a non-organic process. The influence of alcohol or drugs on behavior is a somatopsychic process.

**somatotonia** (W. H. Sheldon) Temperament component characterized by physical and personal assertiveness, striving for power, desire for risk, and need for adventure and competition, associated with the mesomorphic body-type.

**somatotype** Body type.

**somatotypology** The classification of persons according to body type or physical characteristics, usually with the implication that certain physiological characteristics and body types are correlated differentially with personality characteristics and personality variables.

**somesthesia** The overall bodily sense, including kinesthesis, tactile and other sensations.

**somnambulism** 1. Execution of complex acts, such

as walking or talking, during sleep that normally take place in the waking state. **2.** Refers to hypnotic phase in which subject may appear awake and in control of actions, though his behavior is directed by the hypnotist.

**somnambulism, cataleptic** Cataleptic state taking place during somnambulism.

**somnambulism, complete** (P. Janet) Temporary, hypnotically induced state which is forgotten by the subject sometime after hypnosis is over.

**somnambulism, ecstatic** State of ecstasy occurring during somnambulism.

**somnambulism, monoideic** (P. Janet) Ideational processes centering around a single idea occurring during a somnambulistic state.

**somnambulism, polyideic** (P. Janet) Ideational content containing many ideas occurring during a somnambulistic state.

**somnambulist** One who performs complex acts, such as walking and talking, during sleep.

**somniferous** Sleep-producing.

**somniloquy** Talking in sleep.

**somnolence 1.** Drowsiness, sleepiness. **2.** Unnatural prolonged drowsiness.

**sonant** A vocal speech sound.

**sone** A unit of the ratio scale of loudness which is equal to a loudness at a frequency level of 1000 cycle tone forty decibels above the mean threshold.

**sonometer** An instrument consisting of one or more strings stretched over a resonating box used in auditory experiments and demonstrations.

**sophism** A subtly fallacious argument.

**soporific** A substance which induces sleep.

**sorting test** See *test, sorting.*

**soul 1.** (Aristotle) The vital aspect of life. **2.** (theology) An entity which is believed to exist permanently even after death. **3.** An obsolete term for the mind. **4.** Emotional factors as opposed to the intellectual aspect of personality.

**sound-pattern theory of hearing** See *hearing, theory of: sound-pattern theory.*

**sound pressure level (SPL)** Usual reference level used in specifying decibels or sound intensity. SPL is .0002 dyne per square centimeter. When using decibels the reference pressure level is always indicated, for example, 20 db (SPL).

**sound spectrograph** A device which produces a quantitative representation of a sound. It is a group of sound filters each of which passes energy of only a narrow frequency band. The output voltage of each filter adjusts the brightness of a light which produces a trace on a moving formant belt, thus producing a graphic representation of the components of a sound.

**source** (communication theory) A system that emits a message.

**source trait** (R. B. Cattell) A factor-dimension, stressing the proposition that variations in value along it are determined by a single, unitary influence or source.

**South African Picture Analysis Test** See *test, South African Picture Analysis.*

**space error** A bias in the judgment of the position of stimuli because of its spatial relationship to the observer.

**space perception** Three dimensional perception.

**space response** A type of Rorschach response which includes the use of the white areas of the card rather than the properties of the blot itself. Scored S, it is generally considered a perceptual reversal of figure-ground and interpreted as a form of negativism and/or non-conformity.

**spacial summation** The addition of two or more volleys which results in one motor response. These volleys of nervous impulse can be summated, provided they reach a synapse at approximately the same time.

**span of attention** The number of objects, digits or letters perceived on a brief exposure, usually measured on a tachistoscopic exposure.

**spasm** Involuntary, localized, usually slow, sometimes prolonged muscular contractions which may occur anywhere in the body.

**spasm, nodding** (A. Kanner) Vertical or rotary head movement of infants.

**spastic acathusia** See *acathusia, spastica.*

**spastic colitis** See *colitis, spastic.*

**spasticity** Muscular tension often associated with clonic movements.

**spatial threshold** The smallest distance between two points on the skin surface at which two simultaneous tactile stimuli are perceived as two and not as one.

**spaying** Removing the ovaries of a female animal; sterilization.

**Spearman-Brown formula** A procedure used in the estimation of the reliability of a test which has been changed by the addition or subtraction of similar items:

$$R_n = \frac{n r_m}{1+(n-1)r_m}$$

being the estimated reliability coefficient of a test with $n$ items, $r_m$ being the obtained reliability coefficient of the original test with $m$ items.

**Spearman, Charles E. (1863-1945)** British quantitative psychologist. Invented the rank-difference coefficient of correlation, $\rho$ (Greek letter rho), which has been named after him. Formulated the two-factor theory of human capacity (performance of a task is a function of $G$, general intelligence, and of $S$, the ability specific to the performance of the task), and was a forerunner of later developments in factor analysis.

**Spearman footrule**  See *correlation, Spearman footrule.*

**special education**  Education of children with physical, sensory, intellectual and emotional handicaps, deficiencies or disorders.

**special purpose test**  See *test, special purpose.*

**species**  1. Clan; category. 2. (biology) Biological clan of animals or plants; subdivision of a genus.

**species specific behavior**  See *behavior, species specific.*

**specific energy of nerves**  A belief that each nerve is capable of reacting in a certain way only, irrespective of the nature of the stimuli.

**specific inhibition**  See *inhibition, specific.*

**specification equation**  An equation which predicts performance on a specific behavior or task for an individual, from knowledge of 1) the association of that behavior with a set of factors, and 2) the individual's endowment on each of the factors.

**specificity**  1. Typical or characteristic of a certain class or category of objects or events. 2. Typical of a certain biological species, bodily organ or part of an organism.

**spectrometer**  An apparatus which measures the lengths of the waves of colors on a spectrum.

**spectroscope**  An apparatus which gives a spectrum.

**spectrum**  1. The colors obtained by refraction of a wave of light in a prism. 2. The energy of light obtained by refraction.

**speculation**  Non-empirical reasoning; reasoning without factual evidence.

**speech agnosia**  See *agnosia, speech.*

**speed practice**  Learning process with time intervals between the successive trials.

**speedometer**  (operant conditioning) A stimulus, some dimension of which changes as a function of the rate of responding over some period of time.

**spells, breath-holding**  A condition simulating epilepsy, observed during crying, set off by an event that made the child angry or afraid. The child seems as if in a rage, begins to hold his breath and becomes cyanotic around the lips; there may also be loss of consciousness and/or convulsive movements.

**Spence, Kenneth W. (1907-1966)**  American psychologist and learning theorist. A follower of C. L. Hull, Spence deemphasized the physiological aspects of Hull's theory and rejected the need-reduction concept as the prerequisite for reinforcement. Introduced the response-competition concept based on non-reinforcement and maintained that reinforcement is necessary for the classical aversive conditioning, but not for the instrumental aversive learning. Wrote *Behavior Theory and Conditioning, Behavior Theory and Learning,* and several other studies.

**Spencer, Herbert (1820-1903)**  British evolutionary associationist who wrote major works about the sciences of the mid-nineteenth century. He championed double-aspect monism as a solution to the mind-body problem, and was one of the first to suggest that behavior is a continual adjustment to life circumstances, thus anticipating the later functionalist school.

**Spens syndrome**  (T. Spens) See *Stokes-Adams syndrome.*

**sperm; spermatozoan**  Mature male germ cell.

**spherical aberration**  Failure of rays of light to be refracted by a lens, caused by a curvature of the lens.

**sphincter morality**  (S. Ferenczi) A psychoanalytic term for superego forerunners related to parental prohibitions in toilet training at the anal stage.

**sphingolipids**  A type of lipid; the abnormal metabolism and storage of sphingolipids is associated with metabolic disorders such as Gaucher's Disease and Tay-Sach's Disease.

**sphygmomanometer**  An apparatus which measures the arterial tensions and blood pressure.

**Spielmeyer-Vogt disease**  Juvenile form of amaurotic family idiocy which occurs between the ages of six and twelve and is characterized by mental dysfunction, blindness and death within two years.

**spina bifia (myelomeningocele)**  A birth defect which involves a developmental failure of the bilateral dorsal laminae of the vertebrae to fuse in the midline and develop a single dorsal spinal process. The developmental failure may not be accompanied by spinal-cord or nerve-root abnormality and may be covered by normal skin. When associated with defective formation of the spinal cord, the defective cord and the meninges are visible on the back. This condition is generally accompanied by muscle weakness, skin sensitivity below the defective part of the spinal cord, poor innervation of the bowel and bladder, and various degrees of hydrocephalus, neuromuscular problems, such as difficulties in walking and muscle imbalance leading to curvature in posture.

**spinal cord**  A part of the central nervous system extending from the medulla oblongata to the filum terminale at the level of the first (sometimes second) lumbar vertebra.

**spinal nerve**  See *nerve, spinal.*

**spinal reflex**  See *reflex, spinal.*

**spinal root**  See *root, spinal.*

**spinal tonus**  The tonus retained by the spinal cord following severence of the nerve fibers leading to the brain.

**spindle, muscle**  A receptor found in the equatorial region of muscles which consists of muscle fibers activated by sensory nerve endings, all of which are enclosed in a tissue fluid and a capsule of connective tissue. The spindle has nerve endings of two kinds, depending on their appearance which function as standardization 355

receptors: the annulospiral endings and flower-spray endings.

**spindle tendon** See *Golgi tendon organ.*

**spiritism** 1. Belief in spirits, ghosts, etc. 2. Belief in the possibility of communication with deceased people.

**spiritualism** A monistic philosophical theory which assumes that the world is comprised of one non-material element.

**spirograph** An instrument which measures and records the rate and amount of breathing.

**spirometer** A mechanism used for measuring the amount of air exhaled in one breath independent of the air remaining in the lungs.

**split-half correlation** See *correlation, split-half.*

**split-half method of reliability** See *reliability, split-half, method of.*

**split personality** An obsolete term indicating dissociation and amnesia; also called multiple personality.

**spontaneity test** See *test, spontaneity.*

**spontaneity therapy** See *therapy, spontaneity.*

**spontaneity training** See *training, spontaneity.*

**spontaneous behavior** See *behavior, spontaneous.*

**spontaneous recovery** See *recovery, spontaneous.*

**spontaneous recovery rate** The rate of the disappearance of symptoms without treatment.

**spot, hypnogenic** Point on the body which when touched will induce a hypnotic state.

**Spranger, E. (1882-1963)** German philosopher who developed what is termed the "psychology of structure" emphasizing the whole mental life as a unique structure not to be reduced to more elementary levels. He studied the individual as a whole in relation to his historical environment and identified six ideal cultural types of man based on six human values or goals. These types include the theoretical or knowledge-seeking, the esthetic, the economic or practical, the religious, the social or sympathetic and the practical.

**spread of effect** See *effect, spread of.*

**spurious correlation** See *correlation, spurious.*

**SR** A symbol for stimulus response, or the stimulus response relationship. The symbol is also written *S-R* and *S→R*, stimulus leading to response.

**SRA mechanical aptitude test** See *test, SRA mechanical aptitude.*

**SS interval** See *avoidance, free operant.*

**stabilimeter** A device for measuring the amount of bodily sway a person evinces when he is blindfolded in an erect position attempting not to move.

**stability coefficient** See *coefficient, stability.*

**stage** A naturally occurring level in the developmental process which is separate from other levels.

**stage, postpubertal** Period just after puberty during which much of the growth of the skeleton is completed.

**stages of sensory development** See *sensory development, stages of.*

**staircase illusion** See *illusion, staircase.*

**stammering** See *stuttering.*

**standard** 1. A model or criterion of performance. 2. A fixed unit of measurement used for comparison and in the development of scales.

**standard deviation** (statistics) The index of variability of a distribution. It is derived by the following formula:

$$SD \text{ or } \sigma = \sqrt{\frac{\Sigma(X\text{-}M)^2}{N}}$$

where *SD* or $\sigma$ is the symbol for standard deviation, *X* is any number, *M* is the mean of the distribution, *N* refers to the size of the sample, $\Sigma$ is the summation sign and $\sqrt{}$ is the square root sign.

**standard error of difference** The difference between two means divided by the standard error of that difference. The formula is:

$$\sigma \text{ diff.} = \sqrt{\sigma_{M_1}^2 + \sigma_{M_2}^2} = \sqrt{\frac{\sigma_1^2}{N_1} + \frac{\sigma_2^2}{N_2}}$$

where M = mean and $\sigma$ = the standard error of the mean. It is also known as the critical ratio.

**standard error of estimate** ($\sigma_{est}$ or $\sigma_{xy}$) The standard deviation of the difference between the actual values of the dependent variable and those values which are estimated from a regression equation. The formula is: $\sigma_{est} = \sigma_0\sqrt{1\text{-}r^2}$

where $\sigma_0$ is the standard deviation of the dependent variable and *r* is the correlation coefficient.

**standard error of mean** ($\sigma_{DM}$ or $\sigma_M$)
An estimate of the amount that an obtained mean varies by chance form the true mean. The formula is:

$$\sigma_M = \sqrt{\sigma^2 M} = \frac{\sigma}{\sqrt{N}}$$

where $\sigma_M$ is the standard error of estimate, and *N* is the size of the sample on which the means are based.

**standard measure** See *standard score.*

**standard observer** A hypothetical individual who has normal sensory receptors.

**standard ratio** See *standard difference.*

**standard score** See *score, standard.*

**standard stimulus** One of a group or pair that is used as a basis of comparison with the others in an experiment.

**standardization** The procedure of establishing standards or norms, uniform procedures and acceptable deviations from the norm for a test by administering it to a large group of representative individuals.

**standardization group** See *group, standardization.*

**standardized test** See *test, standardized.*

**Stanford Achievement Test** See *test, Stanford Achievement.*

**Stanford Binet** An English language revision and reconstruction of the Binet-Simon intelligence test by L.M. Terman of Stanford University. First revision in 1916; second (with Maud A. Merrill) in 1937; third in 1959.

**stanine** (statistics) A unit of measure developed by the United States Air Force during World War II which is equal to one-ninth of the range of standard scores of a normal distribution. It has a mean of five and a standard deviation of absolute two.

**stapes** One of the three auditory ossicles in the middle ear resting against the membrane of the vestibular window of the cochlea. Also known as the stirrup.

**staphylococcal meningitis** See *meningitis, staphylococcal.*

**startle reflex** See *Moro response.*

**state** (R. B. Cattell) Dimension describing change-over-time within a single individual or in groups of individuals. Essentially, a factor-dimension in *intra*-individual change as contrasted with a Trait which describes *inter*-individual differences at any one time. State dimensions are discovered by P-Technique or by Incremental Factor Analysis.

**state, hypothetical variable** See *variable, hypothetical state.*

**static convulsion** See *convulsion, static.*

**static reflex** A postular reflex which maintains the balanced posture of the body (stance reflex) or restores it (righting reflex).

**static sense** The sense of equilibrium of posture. The receptors of the static sense organ are located in the semicircular canals in the inner ear.

**stasis** State of rest; static state.

**statistic** Any value that expresses the end result of mathematical operations which represents a population or a sample.

**statistical constant** A value or number that represents or describes the population from which the sample was drawn. The means and standard deviations are examples.

**statistical table** The arrangement of statistical data in horizontal or vertical rows to exhibit any relationships that might occur.

**statistical universe** 1. The basis underlying statistical inferences. 2. The population of cases from which samples can be drawn.

**statistics** 1. The branch of mathematics that gathers and evaluates numerical data, and treats them such that the relation between these facts is clearly shown. 2. A set of values that expresses the end result of mathematical operation which represents a population or sample.

**statistics, descriptive** A branch of statistics which includes the organizing, summarizing and describing of quantitative information or data.

**statistics, nonparametric** The branch of statistics which deals with distributions that are not normal and makes no assumptions with regard to the distribution of the population being sampled.

**statogram** (B. B. Wolman) A research technique in social psychology used for evaluating the status of individuals in small groups. The members of a group rate one another in terms of power and acceptance on quasi-Cartesian coordinates.

**statokinetic reflexes** Postural reflexes which adjust the balance posture while the body is in motion.

**statue of Condillac** The French philosopher-sensualist Condillac maintained that mental life started with simple sensations. He imagined a statue to be endowed first with the olfactory sense, then the other senses until it developed a full scale mental life.

**status** Position; state.

**status epilepticus** Series of grand mal epileptic seizures without interruption which is the most frequent cause of death in epileptics.

**staves** (R. B. Cattell) Units in a scale for converting questionnaire raw scores to units which are standard relative to the population. Exactly like stens, except that staves are only a five-point scale, extending from two and one-half standard deviations below the population average (stave 1) to two and one-half standard deviations above (stave 5). Stave 3 represents the population average.

**Stekel, Wilhelm (1868-1940)** Viennese psychiatrist and sexologist, one of Freud's earliest associates. Developed a modified psychoanalytic technique in which the analyst directly intervenes in the patient's life.

**stens** (R. B. Cattell) Units in a standard ten scale, in which ten score points are used to cover the population range in fixed and equal standard deviation intervals, extending from two and one-half standard deviations below the mean (sten 1) to two and one-half standard deviations above the mean (sten 10). The mean is fixed at 5.5 stens. First proposed by Cattell in 1949, questionnaire raw scores are usually converted to stens, when intending to use them normatively (to compare obtained values with population values).

**step interval** See *class interval.*

**stereoscope** (C. Wheatstone) Device invented in 1833 for simultaneous presenting to each eye of one individual separate two-dimensional pictures of the same event. The resultant two separate retinal images are identical to those that would be produced by the three-dimensional real event and the impression of depth is produced from the binocular view of the two pictures.

**stereoscopic vision** Binocular depth vision resulting from the slightly different retinal projections of the same stimulus. This inevitably occurs since the two eyes are not positioned identically in space.

**stereotaxic atlas** (psychophysiology) A map of the brain which is requisite in experiments or studies of brain stimulation.

**stereotaxis** An orienting response to a solid object stimulus with a direct and immediate reaction to the stimulus.

**stereotype** A rigid or biased perception in which individuals are ascribed certain (usually negative) traits regardless of whether they possess these traits, merely because of their membership in a specific national or social group.

**stereotyped behavior** See *response, stereotyped.*

**stereotyped response** See *response, stereotyped.*

**sterility** The inability to produce offspring due to organic or psychological causes.

**Stern, William (1871-1938)** A German experimental and differential psychologist at Hamburg, who also contributed to child psychology and to applications of psychology to industry and law. He invented the concept of the intelligence quotient, the I.Q., defined as the ratio of mental age to chronological age (times 100).

**steroid disorder** An undesignated metabolic disorder, transmitted by an autosomal recessive gene, which results in a general slight aminoaciduria and an excess of glutamic acid in the blood. Clinical signs include mental and physical retardation, lack of pigmentation in the hair and microencephaly.

**Stevens' power law** (S. S. Stevens) A formulation relating the objective stimulus energy to the subjective sensory experience. It contends that for certain sensory systems equal physical ratios are psychologically equal. In normal tests of the power law the stimulus values are transformed to logarithms so as to mark off equal stimulus ratios and plotted on the x axis of a graph. Since the psychological ratios are also thought to be equal, the response values, plotted on the y axis, are also transformed to logarithms. If the resultant plot of the log of the response as a function of the log of the stimulus is a straight line, the prediction of the power law is fulfilled. This law has been proposed as an alternative to the psychophysical function proposed by Fechner, but neither function is truly satisfactory and both functions cannot be correct at the same time. Consequently the power function has been the center of controversy in psychophysics for the past thirty years.

**stilling test** See *test, stilling.*

**stimulation** 1. The activation of a sense receptor by a form of energy or energy change. 2. The excitation of an organism by a change of energy whether internal or external.

**stimulation, mechanical** Stimulation of a reception by means of pressure.

**stimuli, accidental** Those chance happenings that occur in the environment of a sleeping individual which seem to become part of or to precipitate dreams. For example, a muscle cramp may start a dream of being hurt in that particular area of the body.

**stimulus** 1. An object or an action that elicits action. 2. (physiology) Any inner or outer factor that causes the organism to act. 3. (psychology) Any action or situation that elicits response.

**stimulus, adequate** A stimulus which excites the receptor appropriate to the particular stimulus.

**stimulus attitude** 1. The subject's readiness to respond to a particular stimulus. 2. The subject's set to attend to specific qualities of the stimulus.

**stimulus, aversive** A stimulus that, when applied after a response, decreases the tendency for that response to be activated in similar situations.

**stimulus-bound** 1. Referring to perception which is almost wholly determined by the stimulus aspects. 2. Pertaining to an individual whose reactions are inflexible and almost totally determined by the stimulus situation. 3. Referring to the perception of striking or outstanding aspects of a situation to the exclusion of less central aspects.

**stimulus, comparison** See *comparison stimulus.*

**stimulus, conditioned (CS)** A stimulus which, through classical conditioning, has become an effective stimulus for a response which was originally elicited by another stimulus, the unconditioned stimulus (UCS).

**stimulus, consummatory** A stimulus which triggers off a consummatory response.

**stimulus continuum** A continuous series of stimuli such that between any two, there is always a third.

**stimulus control** (operant conditioning) The extent to which the value of an antecedent stimulus determines the probability of the occurrence of a conditioned response. It is measured as a change in response probability as a function of change in stimulus value. The greater the change in response probability, the greater the amount of stimulus control with respect to the stimulus continuum that is varied. In operant conditioning this term has come to be the favored term over the terms stimulus generalization and discrimination primarily because these latter terms come from attempts to describe processes rather than empirical functions.

**stimulus-controlled P-technique** A P-technique which enters the score values for the intensity of manipulated stimuli as well as for levels of response.

**stimulus differentiation** 1. (Gestalt) The process whereby parts of a homogeneous whole become distinguished in the visual field. 2. The process whereby an organism learns to distinguish two or more stimuli which previously elicited the same response.

**stimulus, discriminative**  In operant conditioning the stimulus which elicits the correct response.

**stimulus, distal**  A stimulus in the environment that acts upon a sense receptor indirectly, through the action of a proximal stimulus, e.g. the chair in the environment is the distal stimulus. The retinal image caused by the chair is the proximal stimulus.

**stimulus equivalence**  See *equivalence, response.*

**stimulus error**  See *error, stimulus.*

**stimulus generalization, primary**  The elicitation of a response learned to a certain stimulus by stimuli that are like or similar to the original stimulus.

**stimulus, inadequate**  A stimulus which excites the receptor for which it is not the appropriate stimulus, resulting in subjective sensation that is inappropriate to the stimulus but in accordance with the receptor. For example, a wool object applied to a receptor for warmth is sensed as warm.

**stimulus, incidental**  A stimulus occurring in a situation for which it is neither essential nor intentional but which nevertheless influences the subject's response.

**stimulus, indifferent**  A stimulus to which a subject has not yet responded in a particular way, as often occurs at the beginning of conditioning experiments to what is to become the conditioned stimulus.

**stimulus, liminal**  A physical stimulus which is just at the threshold or just barely evokes a sensory response on one half of the trials.

**stimulus, neutral**  (I. P. Pavlov)  A stimulus which does not elicit conditioning if applied without the unconditioned stimulus.

**stimulus pattern**  A configuration which consists of a conglomeration of stimuli harmoniously grouped together.

**stimulus population**  A finite number of independent environmental events, only one sample of them being effective at any one time.

**stimulus-produced conflict**  A conflict produced by a stimulus which has been associated with both reward and punishment.

**stimulus, proprioceptive**  Stimulus produced by the act of responding. A response produces sensations which themselves have stimulus qualities.

**stimulus, proximal**  A stimulus that effects a sense receptor directly, e.g. the feel of a pencil, or heat, or an image on the retina.

**stimulus schedule**  The rule whereby an experimentally specified stimulus is intruded into an organism's behavior stream; "reinforcement schedule" is the special case where the intruded stimulus is of the sort historically called a "reinforcement."

**stimulus, sensory**  Any stimulus which affects a sense organ.

**stimulus set**  See *set, stimulus.*

**stimulus, sign**  A part or change in a part of the environment that is correlated with some species specific behavior which is not a reflex response.

**stimulus, standard**  See *standard stimulus.*

**stimulus, structured**  A complex stimulus consisting of distinct interrelated parts.

**stimulus, subliminal**  A stimulus whose magnitude is below the threshold of a receptor.

**stimulus, super-normal sign**  A sign stimulus with one or more of its dimensions amenable to quantification along a continuum. The stimulus occurring in the field is at a point on the continuum; while stimuli below this value occasion responses of less magnitude, stimuli above this value occasion responses of greater magnitude.

**stimulus threshold**  See *threshold, stimulus.*

**stimulus, unconditioned**  A stimulus which evokes an unconditioned response and may serve as a reinforcing agent. Such a stimulus evokes a response without prior learning or conditioning.

**stimulus value**  The qualitative description of the stimulus, usually referring to the intensity of the stimulus.

**stimulus variable**  See *variable, stimulus.*

**St. Louis encephalitis**  See *encephalitis, St. Louis.*

**stochastic**  Relating to events whose probability of occurrence constantly changes.

**stochastic models of behavior**  Theories of learning which view behavior as a stochastic chain.

**stochastic processes**  A branch of probability theory dealing with sequences of events whose probabilities are constantly changing.

**Stokes-Adams syndrome**  (W. Stokes and R. Adams) Heart block due to functional or organic causes.

**stop items**  See *items, stop.*

**story recall test**  See *test, story recall.*

**Stout, George Frederick (1860-1944)**  British systematic psychologist, a forerunner of William McDougall. He emphasized conation (or striving) in his psychology, developing a functional or act psychology that contrasted sharply with the dominant German structuralism. His 1899 *Manual of Psychology* was for decades the most widely accepted systematic psychological statement in Great Britain.

**strabismus**  Failure of eye coordination causing lack of proper fixation in the form of either divergent or convergent squint.

**straight-jacket**  A canvas jacket used to restrain a violent, usually mentally ill patient.

**stratification**  A horizontal layering of a group or society.

**stratified sample**  See *sample, stratified.*

**stratified sampling**  See *sampling, stratified.*

**Stratton's experiment** (G. M. Stratton) An experiment designed to investigate the relationship between vision and tactual-motor coordination. The experiment consists of wearing prisms which turn the visual field through an angle of 180 degrees and studying the effects of this reversed visual experience or tactual-motor experience.

**stream of consciousness** (W. James) The belief that consciousness is a stream of thought, a changing continuum, a unity in diversity rather than a series of discrete separate elements.

**streptococcal meningitis** See *meningitis, streptococcal.*

**stress** 1. A condition of physical or mental strain which produces changes in the autonomic nervous system. 2. Emphasis on particular words in speaking.

**stress interview** See *interview, stress.*

**stretch reflex** Contraction of a muscle as a result of a rapid stretching of the muscle.

**striate or striped muscle** See *muscle, striate or striped.*

**striate body, or striatum** A part of the base of each cerebral hemisphere composed of nerve fibers making up the caudate nucleus, lenticular nucleus and internal capsule.

**strip key** A scoring key which is designed to allow comparison of the key with the subject's responses by aligning the two.

**striped muscle** See *muscle, striate or striped.*

**stroboscopic movement** See *movement, stroboscopic.*

**stroke** A sudden and severe seizure which may be due to a lesion in the brain or spinal cord leading to paralysis.

**Strong vocational interest blank** An inventory designed to assess the extent to which an individual's interests and preferences match those of successful persons in specific occupations in order to predict which career choice would be desirable for the subject. It consists of four hundred items which cover various areas of occupation, amusement, academic subjects and personality traits. The inventory may also be scored for non-occupational interests which can be used in guidance and counseling.

**Stroop Test** See *test, Stroop.*

**structural psychology** See *psychology, structural.*

**structure-function principle** (A. Gesell) In experimental studies with infants, Gesell has proven that development depends both on maturation and learning. When an infant tries to learn a certain behavioral pattern ("function") before he is mature enough (his "structure" is not ready) he will not make much progress in learning. Hence, the structure-function principle which means when the structure is ready, the function may start—that is, maturation must come ahead of learning.

**structure, mental** 1. A hypothetical construct which is believed to account for similarities or recurrence of behavior. 2. A personality viewed as a stable complex organization of interrelated traits.

**structured interview** See *interview, structured.*

**structured learning theory** (R. B. Cattell) That portion of learning theory, complementary to *reflexology,* which explains the emergence of personality and dynamic *structures,* rather than atomic *conditioned reflexes.* It involves description of learning change by the tri-vector analysis: 1) A vector of trait change, 2) of behavioral index (loading) change, and 3) of modulation index change. Under (1) it develops the theory regarding the learning of motivational *sets.* It operates with multivariate, matrix-expressed calculations.

**structured stimulus** See *stimulus, structured.*

**study of values** See *Allport-Vernon-Lindzey Study of Values.*

**Stumpf, Karl** (1848-1936) German psychologist and philosopher. As a law student at Würzburg Stumpf came under the influence of Brentano and, following his advice, went to Göttingen to study with Lotze, under whom in 1868 he received his Ph.D. with a thesis on Plato. From 1870-1873 he was a Privatdozent at Göttingen and then went to Würzburg. In 1879 he was called to Prague where he became an associate of Mach, Hering, and Marty. He was in Halle in 1884 and went to Munich in 1889. Finally, in 1894 he was appointed professor at Berlin, where he remained until his retirement in 1921.

Along with the work of other scientifically-minded philosophers of his time, Stumpf's work is an attempt to supplant Kantian *a priori* schemes with empirical ones. In his first book, which was on the psychological sources of space perception, he defended a nativisitic interpretation which, along with the contributions of Hering, became one of the supports of Gestalt theory.

As a psychological systematist he distinguished four closely related disciplines: Phenomenology, Logology, Psychology, and Eidology. Phenomenology is concerned with the contents of consciousness in the manner of Wundt. Logology is concerned with the relations in these contents that are presumably directly presented, a view shared with Wm. James. Psychology is concerned with mental acts in the Brentano tradition. Eidology is an effort to account for presentations of memory in the absence of external stimulation in sentences like, "I like red." To Gestalters these distinctions seemed too much in the act psychology tradition and thus too imbued with the "old psychology."

Stumpf strongly influenced Wm. James and in turn wrote a book about him (1927). In 1900 he founded the *Verein für Kinderpsychologie* . He studied the language of his son. These interests led him to sponsor Köhler's study of anthropoids in Tenerife. He had as students, Köhler, Koffka, and Lewin, but they later abandoned his work under the influence of Wertheimer.

**stupor, catatonic** See *catatonic stupor.*

**stupor, epileptic** State which frequently follows a

grand mal epileptic seizure in which the individual is almost unconscious.

**stuporous mania**  See *mania, stuporous.*

**stuttering**  A speech nonfluency in which the even and regular flow of words is disrupted by rapid repetition of speech elements, spasms of the breathing and vocalization muscles, and hesitations. There are various forms of this nonfluency, including neurogenic, in which fluency is affected by the periodic and uncontrolled release of electrical potential in areas of the brain which subserve speech formulation or which innervate articulatory musculature; sensorimotor, in which fluency is affected by a physiological delay in the return of various sensory dimensions of the speech signal back to the speaker; evaluational forms, in which fluency is affected by the overmonitoring and criticizing by significant others of the child's developmentally expected nonfluencies, resulting in the disruption of the automaticity of speech due to the child's own criticism of the nonfluencies; and psychogenic, in which fluency is affected by an internal conflict over the content of the speech.

**stuttering Iowa scale**  See *scale, stuttering Iowa.*

**style of life**  See *life style.*

**stylus maze**  See *maze, stylus.*

**subception**  The perception of a stimulus on a preverbal level as evinced by an emotional reaction which is detected by a psychogalvanometer or a longer verbal reaction time to the stimulus.

**sub-coma insulin treatment**  See *insulin treatment, ambulatory.*

**subconscious**  An ambiguous term referring to partial unconscious.

**subconscious personality**  (M. Prince) A condition where complexes of subconscious processes have been constellated into a personal system manifesting a secondary system of self-consciousness endowed with volition, intelligence, etc. This personality is capable of communication and occasionally may become the only personality capable of remembering its own personal subconscious life and can give information about subconscious processes.

**subconscious process**  (M. Prince) A process of which the personality is unaware and thus it is outside personal consciousness but which is a factor in determination of conscious and bodily phenomena, or produces effects analogous to those which might be directly or indirectly induced by consciousness.

**subcortical**  1. Referring to neural structures lying below the cortex which mediate functions that are not controlled by the cortex. 2. Relating to functions which are not controlled by the cortex.

**subculture**  A subgroup of a culture which has its separate mores and customs but which shares some of the basic customs with the general culture.

**subcutaneous sensibility**  See *sensibility, subcutaneous.*

**subject**  1. An individual who participates in an experimental situation. 2. Topic; theme; matter.

**subject complex**  See *complex, subject.*

**subjective**  1. Referring to the subject or person. 2. Referring to experience available only to the subject of the experience. 3. Characterizing systems of psychology which focus on the subject and his personal experiences. 4. Not available to consensual validation. 5. Referring to judgments made without the use of devices or instruments. 6. Referring to sensations originating in internal states. 7. Hallucinatory, illusory. 8. Dependent on the person's own standard prejudices and experiences.

**subjective equality, point of**  1. The subject's choice of a point in a continuous series of stimuli at which two stimuli appear to be equal. 2. (psychophysics) A point in a continuum which is judged to be equal to a standard by one of the following methods: the value which is chosen most frequently as equal to the criterion; the point of intersection between values which are judged greater than the standard and those which are chosen as smaller than the standard' or the point midway between the upper and lower thresholds. 3. (comparative psychology) A point when the experimenter does not perceive any noticeable differences in the organism's responses to two stimuli.

**subjective sensation**  See *sensation, subjective.*

**subjective test**  See *test, subjective.*

**subjectivism**  1. The tendency to evaluate experiences in terms of one's own personal frame of reference. 2. The theoretical viewpoint which stresses personal experience as the sole basis of reality.

**sublimation**  A successful and normal defense against instinctual wishes is called sublimation. Sublimation is a cathexis of instinctual energy into a substitute aim or object or both; it is a channeling of the instinctual demands into a new desire or idea and a desexualized cathexis of libido or destrudo.

**sublimation theory of cultural evolution**  (S. Freud) The theory that aim-inhibited creative activities advance development of cultural civilization.

**subliminal**  1. Below the absolute threshold of perception. 2. Pertaining to stimuli which are not perceived consciously but which are perceived on a preverbal level and influence behavior.

**subliminal learning**  See *learning, subliminal.*

**subliminal perception**  See *perception, subliminal.*

**subliminal stimulus**  See *stimulus, subliminal.*

**subnormal**  Below the normal level, inferior.

**suboccipital puncture**  (Ayer) A procedure developed for the determination of spinal subarachnoid block and other therapeutic purposes.

**subset** ($\subseteq$)  $B$ is a subset of $A$ if every element of $B$ is also in $A$. $B \subseteq A$.

**subset, proper** ($\subset$)  $B$ is a proper subset of $A$ if every element of *B* is also in *A*, and there is at least one element of *A* that is not in *B*. *B⊂A*.

**subshock therapy** See *therapy, subshock.*

**subsidiation** A term referring to the fact that achievement of most or all goals requires prior achievement of a series of sub-goals. For example, before achieving the goal "having one's own home," one may first have to achieve sub-goals as "getting a better-paying job," "gaining the confidence of a banker," etc., the latter two being subsidiated to the former.

**substance** Essence; the essential part; the main part of an issue, problem or communication.

**substantia nigra** A layer of pigmented gray matter which separates the dorsal from the ventral part of the cerebral peduncle.

**substantive sets** (W. James) A part of the stream of consciousness consisting of definite and distinct objects or persons as opposed to transition states which are denoted by prepositional words.

**substitution test** See *test, code.*

**subtest** A part of a test or test battery.

**subtraction method** See *method, subtraction.*

**subvocal speech** Movements of the mouth, larynx and tongue without making audible sounds.

**successive-approximation method** See *conditioning, approximation.*

**successive contrast** See *contrast, color.*

**successive differential reinforcement** See *conditioning, approximation.*

**successive-intervals, method of** A modified version of the method of equal-appearing intervals in which the intervals are differentiated verbally or by the use of samples.

**successive-practice, method of** A method designed to assess the effect of transfer of training by measuring the amount of time saved in learning B as a function of having learned A. A control group is given B to learn without having learned A and the two groups are compared.

**successive reproduction method** See *method, successive reproduction.*

**succorance need** See *need, succorance.*

**sudoriferous glands** See *glands, sudoriferous.*

**sufficient reason, law of** (G. V. Leibniz) The principle which states that the occurrence of an event can always be understood given sufficient information.

**suggestibility** The readiness to accept suggestions.

**suggestion, affective** (E. Jones) The emotional rapport that exists between the subject and the hypnotist in a hypnotic setting. Called hypotaxia by Durand.

**suicide** Killing oneself.

**sulcus** Shallow grooves on the surface of the brain.

**sulfatide lipidosis** A rare lipidosis unusual in that symptoms do not appear until the child is one to one and a half years of age. Weakness progresses to spasticity and severe mental and motor retardation.

**sulfatide variants** Conditions which may represent a bridge between the lipidoses and mucopoly-saccharidoses.

**Sullivan, H. S. (1892-1949)** American psychiatrist and neo-psychoanalyst who developed his own system of psychology deviating from S. Freud farther than any other psychoanalyst. He abandoned the Freudian concepts and terminology, borrowing only some principles in human dynamics such as unconscious motivation, defense mechanisms, and dream interpretation. Sullivan was influenced by A. Meyer's biological method and G. Mead's and K. Lewin's theories of social status, role and interpersonal relation. He distinguished between physical and cultural phenomena. He dealt with bodily needs in a consistently reductionist manner. Sullivan introduced the theory that the release of energy is always controlled by social relations. He specified that the development of personality is the result of interpersonal relations. He theorized that there exists two basic needs, the need for security and the need for satisfaction. A conflict between the two is believed to cause emotional problems. Sullivan introduced a new terminology into his system such as the self-dynamism and re-defined already existing terms such as anxiety. His greatest contribution was in stating that men become themselves in relation to others, that growth, motivation, adjustment and disturbances can be understood only in their social interrelationships.

**summation 1.** The total of a series, or aggregate. The symbol for summation is $\Sigma$ (sigma). **2.** In sensation, the increased intensity effect of the rapid presentation of two stimuli (sensory summation effect). When the stimulation impulses are presented in rapid succession it is known as temporal summation. When the impulses are presented to adjacent areas it is known as spatial summation. **3.** A single effect produced by two or more factors. **4.** The occurrence of a different kind of response when mild stimuli are applied in succession.

**summation curve** The graphic representation of a cumulative frequency distribution.

**summation tone** A combination tone, heard when two tones, separated by 50 cps or more, are sounded simultaneously. The resultant summation tone is the sum of the two frequencies.

**superego** (S. Freud) The intrapsychic, mostly unconscious structure of personality which represents societal and cultural standards. The critical self-attitude of a part of the ego exercising the power of censorship in dreams and serving as the main force in repressing instinctual wishes, and the ideal aspirations of the person which the person may not always rise to. The superego develops as a result of an introjection and identification of the child with the parents. The origin is seen in pregenital stages when the child internalizes the prohibitions and restraints of the parents because of the fear of punishment and the need for their love. The full development of the superego does not occur before the end of the phallic stage, when at the height of the Oedipal phase, fear of castration for the boy, and fear of the loss of love for the girl, forces each to give up their erotic love for the parents of the opposite sex and to regress from object relationship to identification by introjection. The introjected parental figures become the superego with the parental standards and punitive attitudes, and the ego-ideal, the child's admiration for the parents. The hostility of the child for the parents becomes the energy at the disposal of the superego, which once directed at the parents, now becomes aimed at the self. The relation between ego and superego parallels that of the child to the parents. The superego rewards the ego with feelings of self-esteem when it is good and punishes it when the ego is bad with feelings of guilt and low self-esteem. As the person develops, the mature superego becomes more impersonal, incorporating societal and objective standards by which the person lives which are no longer bound to parental demands.

**superego anxiety**    See *anxiety, superego.*

**superego, double**    The presence of two usually antagonistic consciences in a person representing disparate standard of conduct.

**superego, group**    (S. R. Slavson) Term referring to the modification of the superego due to experiences with groups of people exclusive of the parents.

**superego, heteronomous**    A type of superego which demands that the ego behave according to the demands of the moment rather than to a set of internalized standards.

**superego, parasite of the**    Standards and values which take over the functions of the superego for varying lengths of time causing feelings of high and low self-esteem.

**superego, primitive**    A superego which exists earlier and apart from the parental superego. It is believed to be hereditary and to function in organizing the differentiation of the cells in the fetus, according to the principles of development of the particular species.

**superego resistance**    See *resistance, superego.*

**superego sadism**    See *sadism, superego.*

**superego strength**    A source trait governing conscientious, persevering, unselfish behaviors and impelling the individual to duty as conceived by his culture.

**superior adult test**    See *test for superior adults.*

**superiority feelings**    1. An attitude that one is better in some or all ways than most other people which, although it may be true in some cases, is generally disproportionately displayed and thus, is viewed as a defense against intense feelings of inferiority. 2. (M. Klein) The displacement onto an intellectual level of

a boy's feelings of inferiority which he over-compensates for by viewing himself as superior to girls in the area of sex simply because he possesses a penis.

**super-normal sign stimulus**    See *stimulus, super-normal sign.*

**superstition**    1. Explanation of events by a belief usually surviving in a distorted form from an earlier religious system now not accepted in a current religious system nor in the body of established facts. 2. (B. F. Skinner) In an operant conditioning experimental situation, when given periodic reinforcements, hungry animals develop repetitive behavior the precise form of which varies from one experimental subject to another but is constant for a single subject.

**supportive therapy**    See *therapy, supportive.*

**suppression**    1. (physiology) Inhibition of an activity. 2. (psychoanalysis) Conscious repression of a desire or an idea.

**suppression area**    Any area of the cortex which inhibits other cortical activity when stimulated.

**suppression, conditioned**    The presentation of the neutral stimulus with or without the unconditioned aversive stimulus, eventually occasions a decrease of whatever behavior the organism is engaged in at that particular time.

**suppression of insight**    (G. M. Gilbert) A defense mechanism in which the individual resists integrating the cognitive elements of a particular kind of experience that would lead to ego-threatening insights. This mechanism is particularly applicable to attempts to resolve social value and role conflicts of guilt, e.g. hypocritical inconsistency between professed principles and actions in role behavior. The mechanism has some elements in common with cognitive dissonance and denial, but differs from repression in being semi-conscious and merely suppressing the accompanying anxiety.

**suppressor variable**    A variable in a prediction battery which has a zero correlation with the criterion but correlates highly with some other predictor in the battery. Its effect is that it subtracts the variance from the predictor variables not correlated with the criterion, increasing the predictive value of the battery.

**suprapatellar reflex**    A swift reflex in the leg elicited when the index finger, placed above the patella with the leg extended, is struck. The result is a kickback of the patella.

**suprarenal glands**    See *adrenal glands.*

**surface color**    See *color, surface.*

**surgency**    (R. B. Cattell) The high-score (positive) pole of a personality dimension found in questionnaire data, characterized by cheerfulness and alertness.

**surgery, emotional reactions to**    Experiments have shown that the presence of moderate pre-operative fear results in an absence of emotional disturbance during the stressful period following the operation, while the pre-operative presence of extreme fearfulness or the absence of fear, results in post-operative anxiety, anger, and resentment.

**surrogate** 1. A person who functions in an individual's life as a conscious or unconscious substitute for someone else, generally a parent. 2. (psychoanalysis) A person unconsciously substituted for one of the parents. Because the surrogate figure is frequently not consciously recognized as such, unacceptable id-originated feelings toward the person being substituted for, are often expressed in dreams toward the surrogate.

**sursumvergence** A movement of one eye upwards in relation to the other.

**survey research** The assessment of public opinion using questionnaire and sampling methods.

**survey tests** See *tests, survey.*

**survival value** The value of a quality or trait in prolonging the life of an organism or species.

**suture of nerve** Artificial connection of the cut ends of a nerve trunk in order to allow the end which is attached to the cell body to develop along the nerve while the other end degenerates.

**Sydenham's chorea** See *chorea, Sydenham's.*

**syllogism** A kind of reasoning consisting of three statements, two premises and a conclusion. Acceptance of the premises leads to the acceptance of the conclusion which may not always be true.

**Sylvian fissure** The lateral fissure separating the temporal and parietal lobes.

**symbiosis** 1. A relationship consisting of two species which cannot survive without each other. 2. A normal developmental level following birth when the infant is physiologically and psychologically dependent on the mother and when he is not yet separated from the mother as a distinctly separate individual. 3. (E. Fromm) A neurotic dependence of one individual on another. 4. (M. S. Mahler) A pathological involvement between mother and child typical for the symbiotic syndrome in childhood schizophrenia.

**symbiosis, focal** Extremely strong bond between a young child with personality disturbance and one of his parents, revolving around a particular and exclusive set of ego functions, such as intellectual functioning or motor skills.

**symbiosis, normal** (M. S. Mahler) Normal symbiosis is ushered in by cracking of the autistic shell and the lifting of the innate strong stimulus barrier protecting the young infant up to the third or fourth week of life, with the result of inside and outside stimuli impinging from now on upon him. As the instinct for self-preservation has atrophied in the human young, the ego has to take over the role of managing the human being's adaptation to reality, a role that the id is unable to fulfill. The mental apparatus of the young infant is unable to organize his inner and outer stimuli in such a way as to insure his survival,

and the psycho-biological rapport between the nursing mother and the baby complements the infant's undifferentiated ego. Empathy on the part of a mother is, usually, the human substitute for those instincts on which the altricial animal relies for its survival. Normal symbiosis develops concomitantly with the above mentioned lowering of the innate stimulus barrier (J. Benjamin), through the repetitious experience of an outside mothering agency which alleviates the need hunger tension and functions as an auxiliary ego (R. Spitz).

Symbiosis refers to a stage of sociobiological interdependence between the one to five month old infant and his mother, to a stage of preobject or need satisfying relationship, in which the self and the maternal intrapsychic representations have not yet been differentiated: from the second month on the infant behaves and functions as though he and his mother were an omnipotent dual unity within one common boundary (the symbiotic membrane).

The mother's availability and the infant's innate capacity to engage in the symbiotic relationship marks the inception of ego-organization by the establishment of intrapsychic connections on the infant's part between memory traces of gratification and the Gestalt of the human face, and signals a shift of cathexis from inside the body (viscera of the autistic phase) to the periphery, the sensory perceptive organs, from coenesthetic (R. Spitz) to diacritic organization.

**symbiotic child psychosis** (M. S. Mahler) The crucial disturbance in child psychosis consists of the lack or loss of the ability to utilize the mother during the early phases of life as a complement to and organizer of maturation. This causes an absence of a human beacon of orientation, both in the world of reality and in his own inner world, and a gross impairment of the integrating, synthesizing and organizing functions of the ego.

In symbiotic psychosis (Mahler) disturbances in maturation and/or development seriously interfere with the progress of the subsequent separation-individuation process, and results in fixation at or regression to a distorted symbiotic phase, uneven growth, and a striking vulnerability of the ego to minor frustrations.

The symbiotic infantile psychosis is often precipitated by acute panic evoked by such routine separation experiences as enrollment in nursery school, the birth of a sibling, and so on. Basically, however, the symbiotic child psychosis is a reaction of the child to the inherent maturational pressures toward intrapsychic separation from the mother. The paradigm of inherent maturational pressure is behaviorally manifested by the onset of the autonomous locomotor capacities that enable and prompt the toddler to physically separate from the mothering person.

The clinical picture is most often dominated by agitated biphasic fusion and violent isolation attempts, by agitated catatonic-like temper tantrums and panic stricken behavior, followed by bizarrely distorted efforts at restitution.

In many cases of the primarily symbiotic syndrome, the child is compelled to take recourse to a secondary retreat into a quasi-stabilizing (secondary) autism, disrupted by occasional aggressive destructive behavior.

**symbiotic phase** (M. S. Mahler) A stage of development occurring approximately from the age of three months to about two years when the infant relies on his mother for the satisfaction of his physical and emotional needs. During this stage, the infant, having no separate image of himself as an individual, remains emotionally fused with the mother.

**symbiotic psychosis** See *psychosis, symbiotic*.

**symbiotic relatedness** A parasitic style of relating to others in terms of the gratification of one's own neurotic needs.

**symbiotic syndrome in childhood schizophrenia** 1. See *psychosis, symbiotic*. 2. (B. B. Wolman) The second most severe level of childhood schizophrenia, corresponding to catatonia in adulthood. It is characterized by the child's inability to separate from his mother.

**symbol arrangement test** See *test, symbol arrangement*.

**symbol elaboration test** See *test, symbol elaboration*.

**symbol of a construct** (G. A. Kelley) A factor representing the construct which conceptualizes it as well as itself.

**symbol substitution test** See *test, code*.

**symbolic information** See *information, symbolic*.

**symbolic interpretation** Interpretation of the person's thoughts, dreams, and behavior as derivatives of unconscious conflicts.

**symbolism** 1. The use of symbols. 2. (psychoanalysis) The use of symbols to represent repressed material.

**symbolism, abstract** Symbols that signify abstract concepts, for example, the cross and the swastika. Abstract symbolism has had an important role in religious mythology. Although the origin of the symbols may have been forgotten, the ideas which were behind them have remained.

**symbolism, anagogic** An indirect representation of objects of ideas that have an ideal, spiritual or moral significance.

**symbolism, cryptogenic** (E. Silberer) The representation of mental functions in the form of imagery.

**symbolism, dream** See *dream work*.

**symbolism, functional** (E. Jones) A form of symbolism which arises due to the hindering influence of an affective complex.

**symbolism, threshold** (E. Silberer) Symbolism occurring in the transition stage from one state of consciousness to another.

**symbolism, true** Symbolism which represents unconscious material and is unvariable in meaning independent of individual differences. It is believed to evolve from previous generations and have parallels in other races, myths and cultures.

**symbolization** (psychoanalysis) The unconscious process of utilizing symbols so that unconscious material can be allowed into consciousness.

**Symond's Picture-Study Test** See *test, Symond's Picture-Study*.

**sympathectomy** The surgical excision of the sympathetic division of the autonomic nervous system.

**sympathetic ganglion** Any of the nerve clusters of the sympathetic division of the autonomic nervous system which are found on both sides of the spinal cord.

**sympathetic nervous system** See *nervous system, sympathetic*.

**sympathin** A neurohormonal substance. The form E is believed to be produced by a combination of chemical substances discharged in excited effector cells and the endings of sympathetic nerves. The form I is believed to be produced by a combination of chemical substances discharged in inhibited effector cells and the endings of sympathetic nerves.

**symptom** 1. An event indicative of something. 2. Any event or sign indicative of disease or disorder.

**symptom, accessory** (E. Bleuler) A secondary symptom not basic to schizophrenia such as hallucinations, delusions, speech and writing disturbances.

**symptom, fundamental** (E. Bleuler) A symptom which is pathognomonic of schizophrenia, such as disturbances of affect, of thought, autism and schizophrenic dementia.

**symptom, primary defense** (S. Freud) The first defensive measures such as shame taken in the development of obsessional neurosis against memories of pleasurable sexual activities.

**symptom remission** The temporary disappearance of the symptoms of a disorder.

**symptom, secondary defense** (S. Freud) Defensive measure taken in obsessional neurosis when the primary defenses have failed. These include obsessive thought, compulsive activities, doubting, and precautionary and penitential actions.

**symptom-substitution theory** An expression of the contention that simple removal of a symptom through behavior modification, hypnosis or suggestion will result in the appearance of another symptom. The theory rests on the assumption that the personality is a closed-energy system, with the offending behavior or symptom serving as a mechanism for the expression of an internal conflict of drives.

**symptomatology** The study of symptoms.

**symptoms, ego deficiency** (B. B. Wolman) Psychotic symptoms indicative of failure of the ego, e.g. delusions, hallucinations, depersonalization, incontinence, etc.

**symptoms, ego protective** (B. B. Wolman) Neurotic

symptoms indicative of ego's struggle for retaining a behavioral control, e.g. repression, isolation, compulsive acts, phobias, etc.

**Synanon** A residential treatment facility for drug addicts organized by a former alcoholic, C. E. Dederich in 1958. It is a secular treatment center staffed by non-professional former drug addicts. Membership is voluntary and the focus is on personal and social responsibility which is discussed in group therapy sessions.

**synapse** The junction between two nerve cells, neurons. The neural impulse is transmitted across synapses by chemical action of a neurotransmitter.

**synaptic conduction** The transmission of a nerve impulse across the synapse.

**synaptic knob or bouton** The bulblike area in the unmyelinated portion at the ending of the axon which releases substances to transmit the nerve impulse from one neuron to another.

**synaptic resistance** The facilitation or inhibition of the transmission of the nerve impulse occurring at the synapse.

**synchronism** 1. The occurrence of several developmental disturbances at one time. 2. (C. G. Jung) An acausal principle which refers to events which occur together in time but which do not cause one another. This principle is evinced in phenomena such as clairvoyance, telepathy and archetypes.

**syncope** Temporary loss of consciousness due to cerebral anemia. Fainting.

**syncope, vasodepressor** A temporary disturbance of the cardiovascular homeostasis causing fainting due to the sudden drop in blood pressure. It may be of physical or psychogenic origin.

**syncretism** 1. The combination of many elements into one system disregarding the inherent contradictions. 2. (J. Piaget) A level of thinking found in young children characterized by accidental connections made among elements with the absence of any causal or logical types of associations.

**syndromal analysis** See *analysis, syndromal.*

**syndrome** A cluster of symptoms indicative of a clinical entity.

**syndrome, abstinence** Constellation of symptoms seen when medication is withdrawn from a patient physiologically dependent on an addictive.

**syndrome, adaptation** (H. Selye) A cycle of extensive physiological changes in the endocrine and other organ systems due to prolonged and intense stress. The first response to stress, called the alarm reaction, is the release of metabolites in the affected tissues. If this phase is not too severe, the metabolites will stimulate the anterior lobe of the pituitary to release a hormone that influences secretion in the cortex of the adrenal gland which aids the body in its resistance (the countershock phase). Should this intense stimulation continue, however, the adrenal cortex will persist in releasing its hormones. Such prolonged exposure would eventually wear down the adaptive

mechanisms and the individual would enter a stage of exhaustion until the adrenal cortex is unable to secrete any more hormones and the organism dies.

**syndrome, Bassen-Kornzweig** Mental deficiency associated with a genetic metabolic disorder; abetalipoproteinemia.

**syndrome, Brown-Sequard** (C. E. Brown-Sequard) A syndrome following the hemisection of the spinal cord resulting in paralysis of movement on one side and of sensation on the opposite side.

**syndrome, Capgras** A condition described by Jean Marie Joseph Capgras (1873-1950), a French psychiatrist. The patient, upon meeting a familiar person, concludes that this person is an impostor who has assumed the real person's physical identity.

**syndrome, carotid sinus** A syndrome caused by pressure applied over the carotid sinus which results in weakness, slowing of the heart, a decrease in blood pressure and often fainting.

**syndrome, *cri du chat*** See *cri du chat syndrome.*

**syndrome, dependence-independence** Inconsistent interpersonal behavior most commonly seen in latent schizophrenics, comprised of marked shifts in mood from dependent feelings manifested through expectations of strength, unconditional love, and protection from relations, to independent feelings; when dependence needs are frustrated, manifested through aggressive, rebellious, and domineering behavior.

**syndrome, deprivation** In young children, a constellation of symptoms and behaviors, usually associated with maternal loss or absence, characterized by withdrawal, lack of responsiveness to the environment and often depression.

**syndrome, disparagement** A pattern of self-denigration in certain areas of accomplishment as well as a generalized tendency to disparage the abilities of others.

**syndrome, Ganser's** (S. J. M. Ganser) A syndrome consisting of the giving of irrelevant, often absurd answers to questions.

**syndrome, general adaptation** See *general adaptation syndrome.*

**syndrome, Horner's** (J. H. Horner) Ptosis of the eyelid resulting from paralysis of the nerve fibers or from lesions of the cervical sympathetic nerve fibers, usually associated with enopthalmus and absence of sweating on the affected side of the head and the face.

**syndrome, Hunt Ramsay** (J. Ramsay Hunt) Dyssynergia cerebellaris. A geniculate neuralgia associated with severe pain in the middle ear, hyperacusis, facial paralysis and decline in taste and salivation, often associated with herpes zoster infection.

**syndrome, hyperventilation** Respiratory alkalosis resulting from over-breathing and characterized by dizziness, sometimes loss of consciousness, numbness and tonic or clonic motor reactions. The syndrome may be due to anxiety, fear, drugs, or organic brain disease.

syndrome, Klinefelter's (H. F. Klinefelter) A disorder of a defective hormonal balance and underdeveloped testes in males, related to an extra X chromosome. Mental retardation is often present.

syndrome, Klüver-Bucy (H. Klüver and P. C. Bucy) A syndrome, the symptoms of which are loss of the ability to recognize others, loss of fear, and rage reactions, increased sexual activity, memory defects, bulimia, and hypermetamorphosis. It was originally described by Klüver and Bucy in monkeys whose temporal lobes had been removed.

syndrome, mast Presenile dementia inherited through the recessive gene with an onset in the early teens causing intellectual deterioration, spasticity, and dysarthria and by the age of thirty to forty, resulting in complete incapacitation.

syndrome, McArdle's (B. McArdle) A defect of the mitochondrial enzymes which is inherited as a recessive gene. It is characterized by weakness, pain, and stiffness following exercise due to the excessive deposit of glycogen in the muscles resulting from the deficiency of the enzyme, mycophosphorylase.

syndrome, Münchausen (R. Asher) A syndrome characterized by the presentation of false symptoms and false medical and social histories.

syndrome, Pötzl (O. Pötzl) Symbol agnosia for written material with disturbances of color vision found in the presence of lesions in the medullary layer of the lingual gyrus of the dominant hemisphere, including damage of the corpus callosum.

syndrome, Rubinstein-Taybi (J. H. Rubinstein and H. Taybi) A form of mental retardation characterized by congenital malformation including broad thumbs and toes.

syndrome, Sjögren-Larsson (S. Sjögren and T. Larsson) Hereditary syndrome characterized by mental retardation, spastic paralysis and ichthyosis, and occurring through the autosomal recessive type of transmission.

syndrome, striatal Disease of the striatum characterized by rigidity, tremor, hypokinesis, impairment of associated movements and an absence of sensory disturbances or true paralysis.

synergism The principle that responses or ideas result from the combination of coordinated factors working together.

synergism, sexual Sexual excitation resulting from the combined effect of many stimuli occuring simultaneously.

synergy (R. B. Cattell) The energy, representable by an ergic vector by which a group operates, summing the attitude vectors representing the interest strengths of members in the group life.

synonym-antonym test See test, synonym-antonym.

syntactic aphasia See aphasia, syntactic.

syntality (R. B. Cattell) That which determines a group's performance when its situation is given. Analogous to personality in the individual.

syntaxic See syntaxic mode.

syntaxic mode (H. S. Sullivan) The third, logical mode of experiencing the world characterized by consensually validated experiences, judgments and observations and an interpersonal system of communication.

synthesis The combination of elements into a whole.

syntone One who is in affective harmony with the environment.

syntonia A personality trait characterized by a high degree of emotional responsiveness to the environment.

syntonic Possessing the qualities of a syntone.

syntonic ego See ego-syntonic.

syntropic Pertaining to syntropy.

syntropy (A. Meyer) Harmonious association with others.

syphilis A prenatal or acquired venereal disease due to systemic infection with treponema pallidum and almost always acquired in sexual intercourse. Lesions may be produced in any tissue or organ of the body with symptoms characteristic of the site of involvement.

syphilis, cerebral See syphilis, meningovascular.

syphilis, meningovascular Syphilis of the central nervous system involving the leptomeninges and the cerebral arteries. Symptoms do not differ from those caused by other cerebral lesions.

syphilitic insanity Obsolete term for psychosis caused by syphilis.

syphilophobia Fear of syphilis.

system 1. A set of elements which are orderly interrelated to make a functional whole. 2. A set of concepts which provide the framework for arranging the facts and data of a science.

system, action (A. Kardiner) A bodily system which allows an organism to fulfill a need or desire.

system, anabolic The system in constitutional medicine which corresponds to the megalosplanchnic habitus.

system analysis Analysis of the functioning of a system which includes an identification and measurement of errors, and a modification of the system in order to correct the mistakes.

system, dynamic A system which involves a stable exchange of energy among the parts depending on their interrelationships.

system equation See equation, system.

system, kinship (anthropology) The types and degrees of kinship, the terms by which they are defined, and the behavior patterns associated with them in any given culture or society.

system, miniature A set of principles and theoretical laws which are organized to explain a psychological process or group of related psychological facts.

**system, perceptual-conscious** (S. Freud) The surface aspect of the ego which is directed onto the external world, mediates perceptions of it and produces the phenomena of consciousness through its functioning. This system is the receptor of stimulation from without and from the inside of the mind.

**system research** Research involving the investigation of new system designs and the examination of the relationship of man to machine with a view to developing and improving existing systems.

**system, sign** (P. Schilder) The utilization of language as the chief instrument in psychotherapy.

**systematic desensitization** (J. Wolpe) A behavior therapy technique in which deep muscle relaxation is used to inhibit the effects of graded anxiety-evoking stimuli. The patient is trained to relax muscles beyond the point of normal tonus, and anxiety-evoking situations, e.g. those characterizing a phobia are ranked according to their anxiety potency for him. In systematic desensitization, the weakest situation is presented to the imagination of the fully relaxed patient, repeatedly, until it no longer evokes anxiety, and then in progressively stronger situations. There are many variants of this technique, using real stimuli instead of imaginery ones, and various anxiety-inhibiting responses other than relaxation.

**systematic error** See *error, systematic.*

**systemic** 1. Referring to a system. 2. Referring to the body systems.

**systemic-localization** concept The principle that higher mental functions called systems are localized in specific areas of the brain.

**systemic sense** See *sense, systemic.*

**systemogenesis** (P. K. Anokhin) An evolutionary trend based on the original theory of the functional system. This trend reveals new regularities of the brain development in ontogenesis and phylogenesis of animals and man. The main features of systemogenesis are the accelerated and selective development of those structures in ontogenesis which form vitally significant functional systems of a new-born immediately after birth, such as respiration, blood circulation, sucking, feeding, etc. Maturation of structures necessary for these functional systems is rather selective and does not depend upon degree of maturation of the entire organ. For example, the nerve cells of the facial nerve nucleus innervating orbicularis oris, completely mature at a definite time, and their axons innervate the muscle fibers through developed neuromuscular synapses, while other motor neurons of the facial nerve nucleus have not matured yet. Such a type of maturation of the functional system but not of the organ is basic in the evolution of organisms and that is why it was called systemogenesis and not organogenesis.

**systems, informational** (J. P. Guilford) Organized items of information; complexes of interrelated or interacting parts.

**systems theory** An approach to knowledge in which a unit is seen as being a subsystem of a larger and more comprehensive system and also seen as being comprised of various and smaller subsystems. The interactions of the various systems, subsystems, and components of subsystems are focused upon, resting on the assumption that a unit cannot be studied with no understanding of how that unit fits into other larger and smaller systems.

**systole** The period of active contraction of the heart muscle.

**Szondi test** See *test, Szondi.*

# T

**t** **1.** Any particular case in a series. **2.** The amount of time passed since a stipulated event. **3.** (statistics) The ratio of a statistic to its standard error. It is also written with subscripts indicating the value which is observed, ($t_{obs}$), or a critical value ($t_{crit}$).

**T** Transmittance of radiant power.

**T** **1.** (Rorschach) The total time required to respond to all the inkblots. **2.** Temperature given in degrees absolute. **3.** Point of transition. **4.** A total, sometimes written with subscripts indicating which scores are summed.

**T.A.** Toxin-antitoxin.

**$st_R$** (C. Hull) The median reaction time or latency.

**$sT_R$** (C. Hull) The reaction time or latency.

**T data** (R. B. Cattell) Data obtained through the use of tests.

**T distribution** See *test, t.*

**T function** A measure of the reduction of the amount of information needed to locate an element in one category or classification if it has already been located in other categories. The amount of relatedness in the classification of elements.

**T group** A sensitivity training group in which the focus is the learning of human relation skills and personal and interpersonal issues.

**T maze** See *maze, T.*

**T maze, multiple** See *maze, multiple T.*

**T scale** See *scale, T.*

**T technique** (R. B. Cattell) Factor analysis of a correlation matrix from correlating, on a sample of people, the various occasions on which the same test is repeated.

**T-TAT** See *test, Thompson, Thematic Apperception.*

**t test** See *test, t.*

**TAB** (statistics) The estimated frequency of the cell as the intersection of the $A^{th}$ row and the $B^{th}$ column.

**tabes dorsalis** Degeneration of posterior column of spinal cord leading to loss of proprioceptive feedback from muscles and consequent incoordination of walking movements (locomotor ataxia).

**table, correlation** See *correlation table.*

**table, double-entry** A statistical table arranged in rows and columns. Two entering arguments or values are needed to specify a value in the table.

**taboo, incest** The prohibition of sexual intercourse between close relatives.

**taboo; tabu** A social prohibition of objects, persons, dress, words, or actions usually stemming from early cultural conceptions of the object as magical or sacred and thus associated with power, danger, and by extension, the unclean.

**tabula rasa** (J. Locke) The mind of a newborn child is like a clean slate (tabula rasa), and whatever is in the human mind, is derived from the sensory perceptions.

**tachistoscope** An apparatus used in experimental studies of perception, learning, etc., for exposure of small pictures, digits and letters for brief intervals.

**tachycardia** Rapid heart rate which may be due to functional or organic causes.

**tachylogia** Abnormally rapid speech.

**tact** (B. F. Skinner) Verbal response secondarily reinforced.

**tactile agnosia** See *agnosia, tactile.*

**tactile circle** An area of skin whose two tactile stimuli are perceived as one.

**tail** (statistics) The end area of a frequency curve beyond a specified ordinate which is usually less than a third of the distribution. A distribution curves into a tail-like formation toward the base-line at the extremes.

**Talbot-Plateau law** See *law, Talbot-Plateau.*

**talent** High level innate ability in a particular area such as music.

**tally** The recording of a single mark for each occurrence of a certain event or characteristic in order to maintain a cumulative tabulation.

**tand schedule** See *reinforcement, schedule of: tandem.*

**tandem (tand) schedule** See *reinforcement, schedule of: tandem.*

**taphaophilia** Attraction for a cemetery.

**taphophobia** Fear of being buried alive.

**tapping test** See *test, dotting.*

**tarantism** Compulsion to dance.

**taraxein** A chemically unstable protein fraction which is reportedly present in the blood of schizophrenic patients and is believed to be a chemical manifestation of an inborn error of metabolism. Taraxein is said to inhibit the interaction of a brain enzyme and a chemical, diamine, which is produced under situations of psychological stress. This inhibitory action underlies the development of mental disorder. Several experiments have shown that the injection of a protein fraction from the plasma of schizophrenic patients produces psychotic-like behavior in normal subjects.

**Tarchanoff phenomenon** Electrodermal response; production of a mild electric current on the surface of the skin.

**Tartini's tone** Difference in tones.

**taste bud** Nerve ending of the gustatory sense located in the mouth.

**TAT** See *test, thematic apperception.*

**Tau effect** (H. Helson) The interaction of time and space such that if three spots are successively stimulated on the skin, or three lights are flashed successively, if the time between the second and third is less (greater) than that between the first and second, the distance between them is perceived to be smaller (greater) than that between the first two. The converse of this effect, named the Kappa effect, is found when observers are asked to judge the time when the distance between spots is varied; then the shorter (longer) distance is perceived to be stimulated more rapidly (less rapidly) than the longer (shorter) distance between the stimuli.

**tautaphone** (D. Shakow and S. Rosenzweig) A projective device introduced in 1940 consisting of a record of random vocal sounds which the subject is asked to interpret.

**taxis** The involuntary movement of a motile organism or organic bodies involving a change of place toward (positive taxis) or away (negative taxis) from a source of stimulation. Several types of taxes have been distinguished: klinotaxis, tropotaxis, telotaxis, menotaxis, anemotaxis, and geotaxis.

**taxonomic system** A system of classification of data according to their natural relationships.

**Tay-Sachs disease** A type of lipidosis characterized by hypertonicity, listlessness, blindness, spasitic paralysis, convulsions and retardation. Progressive deterioration usually leads to death by age three. About 80 percent of those affected are of Jewish descent.

**Taylor Manifest Anxiety Scale** See *scale, Taylor Manifest Anxiety.*

**taylorism** (industrial psychology) A theory of increased efficiency and productivity in business, management and industry.

**teaching machine** A system of programmed instruction in which the child works independently and at his own pace on academic material presented to him through a console on a mechanical apparatus. The material is presented in either a linear manner or a branching manner.

**technique, critical incident** A method of studying organisms by observing selected samples of their behavior and making inferences about the total organism.

**technique, graphomotor** A projective technique in which the subject is asked to move the pencil freely on a piece of paper. The clinician subsequently interprets the drawing.

**technique, inspection** (R. Monroe) Abbreviated technique for evaluating the Rorschach using only those response patterns which are significant for a given purpose rather than attempting an over-all personality description.

**technique R** See *correlation, R.*

**tele** 1. Purpose. 2. (J. L. Moreno) A unit of attraction or repulsion measured by sociogram.

**telecephalon** The anterior part of the forebrain which includes the olfactory lobes, cerebral cortex and corpora striata.

**teledendrite** Terminal arborization of an axon.

**telegnosis** (parapsychology) Clairvoyance.

**telekinesis** (parapsychology) Movement of objects believed to take place without application of physical force.

**telemetry** A technique for measuring autonomic body changes from the distance using devices such as a miniature radio transmitter which is sensitive to perspiration, changes in heart rate, blood pressure and respiration rate, muscle tension and electrical conductance of the skin.

**teleologic regression** See *regression, teleologic.*

**teleology** 1. The study of behavior as it is related to purposes or as being purposive. 2. The belief that behavior is defined and set off from other phenomena in that it is purposive. **3.** (philosophy) The doctrine that goals have a causal influence on present events, that the future as well as the past affect the present. **4.** (theology) The belief that a universal purpose or design exists which pervades reality, and that all events tend toward its ultimate fulfillment.

**telepathy** Extrasensory perception of thought without the use of any known means of communication.

**telodendron** Teledendrite.

**telotaxis** A taxis in which, as in tropotaxis, the animal makes simultaneous comparisons of stimulus intensity. However telotaxis does not depend on a balance between sources of stimulation; if there are two stimulus sources operating through the same modality the animal orients toward one or the other and not intermediately suggesting that one stimulus source is inhibited.

**temperament** **1.** The predisposition of a person to emotional reactions. **2.** (Hippocrates) A personality type characterized in terms of a humoral theory. There are four types: choleric, melancholic, sanguine and phlegmatic. **3.** (I. P. Pavlov) A personality type which has its basis in the excitation and inhibition processes of the nervous system. There are four types, the excitatory or choleric, the inhibitory or melancholic and the central or equilibrated type which consists of a quiet or phlegmatic and lively or sanguine type.

**temperature spot** Skin surface that is exceptionally sensitive to temperature.

**Temple-Darley Test** See *test, Temple-Darley*.

**temporal lobe** See *lobe, temporal*.

**temporary reflex** See *reflex, conditioned*.

**tender feeling** (W. McDougall) An innate inclination for taking care of children and helpless individuals.

**tenderness** (K. Abraham) The wish to preserve and to take care of. It starts at the anal-retentive phase of psychosexual development.

**tendon** Fibrous tissue connecting a muscle to a bone.

**tendon reflex** A contraction of a muscle.

**tension** **1.** (physiology) Strain which results from muscular contraction and through which muscles, tendons, etc. are stretched and maintained in that position. **2.** Physical sensations which result from muscular strain, tension, and contraction. **3.** Condition of anxiety, tension, and uneasiness which occurs from readiness to alter behavior or readiness to act, especially in situations of threat. **4.** Emotional strain. **5.** (K. Lewin) A state of disequilibrium between an organism and its environment.

**tension system** (K. Lewin) A state of disequilibrium between the individual and his environment. This objective state of disequilibrium is perceived by the individual as a need. Tension and need are two sides of the tension system which entails the psychological field of the individual as well as the objective state of disequilibrium.

**teratology** The study of malformations of the body.

**Terman, Lewis Madison (1877-1956)** American educational psychologist, widely known for test construction. Designed and standardized an American revision of the Binet-Simon intelligence test (Stanford Binet), bringing the IQ concept into widespread usage, and directed construction of the Stanford Achievement Test. Conducted a lifetime longitudinal research on the development of gifted children, and also made naturalistic, test-based studies of masculinity-femininity and marital happiness. See *IQ; Stanford Binet; M-F Test*.

**Terman-McNemmar Test of Mental Ability** See *test, Terman-McNemmar, of Mental Ability*.

**terminal bulb** See *synoptic knob*.

**terminal stimulus** The highest intensity of a stimulus to which the organism is capable of responding.

**terminology** A system of terms, symbols and names used in a particular discipline, profession or occupation.

**test** **1.** A standardized set of questions which are administered to a group or to individuals in order to assess the presence or absence of a particular skill or knowledge. **2.** A measurement which produces quantitative data. **3.** (statistics) A set of operations designed to assess the significance of a stated hypothesis. **4.** (logic) An operation designed to determine the truth or validity of a hypothesis.

**test, ability** Standardized test of maximum performance designed to reveal the level of present ability, either in general or in a specific direction.

**test, absurdities** A task in which the individual must detect and point out the absurdity in a picture, story or writing. An absurdity is an incongruity, something that is obviously the opposite of that which is accepted as fact or truth. The Stanford-Binet tests of intelligence include both picture and verbal absurdities tasks. An example of a verbal absurdity is as follows: "They found a young man locked in his room with his hands tied behind him and his feet bound together. They think he locked himself in." After the presentation of a statement of this type, the subject is asked, "What is foolish about that?"

**test, accuracy** A test that considers only correctness as the criterion and the time taken to perform the tasks is not important.

**test, ACE** The American Council on Education test of intelligence, primarily designed for upper high school students and college freshmen. A language score, a quantitative score and a total score can be obtained for this test.

**test, achievement** A test designed to measure the level of proficiency by testing the individual's performance in a particular area.

**test, adult-child interaction** (J. F. Alexander) Eight card TAT-like test designed to facilitate the categorization of scores in terms of: 1) what kinds of stimuli were employed (symbolization); 2) positive and negative affects and activities (emotional perception); and 3) frequency and degree of organization of a series of defined elements in the story (behavioral continuum).

**test age** The score which is obtained from an age-equivalent scale.

**test, aiming** A task involving quick precise eye-hand coordinations. Aiming is measured by a stylus-and-hole apparatus. The subject's task is to thrust the stylus into progressively smaller holes or into holes momentarily uncovered by a rotating shutter. without touching the sides of the holes. There is also an aiming test that is of paper and pencil design which requires the subject to place dots in small circles as rapidly as he can. This version of the test involves motor speed as well as precision of movement.

**test, alternate-response** A test composed of a number of questions, each having only two possible answers. The subject is required to choose one of the alternatives such as Yes-No or True-False.

**test, altitude** A test specifically designed to obtain a measure of the maximum level of difficulty that an individual can achieve in problem solving.

**test, analogies** Test which requires supplying a fourth term to correctly complete a relationship of four terms in which the relationship between the first and second terms is the same as that between the third and fourth terms, i.e. $M$ is to $N$ as $O$ is to _____.

**test, aptitude** A compilation of tasks which are chosen and standardized so as to yield scores which enable a prediction of a subject's future performance on tasks which are somewhat similar to the tasks on the test.

**test, Army Alpha** Verbal intelligence tests used by the army during World War I, 1917-1918, in combination with the Army Beta test. Also called the Army Alpha Intelligence Test.

**test, Army Alpha Intelligence** See *test, Army Alpha.*

**test, Army Beta** Non-verbal intelligence test used by the army during World War I, 1917-1918, in combination with the Army Alpha test. Also called the army Beta Intelligence Test.

**test, Army General Classification** Also called AGCT. World War I brought with it the necessity of developing a method of measuring the intelligence of the normal adult. The Army Alpha and Army Beta Tests, which were developed at that time, laid an important foundation for the future of mental testing. It was shown that the mental test was much more than a device to help identify the feeble-minded, and that there are degrees of mental ability among those considered normal. The army testing program also brought out the fact that mental testing does not have to be the costly individual procedure previously held to be the only method. Also convincingly shown was the value of the tests for the practical classification of men. The psychologists in World War I had their greatest achievement in the development of the group intelligence test. Following World War I the tests were released for civilian use and group testing continued to be expanded.

There were many tests modeled after the army plan and the psychologists of World War II were faced with the task of sifting the available testing devices in order to find the ones which were or could be made suitable to their needs. In contrast to World War I, military organization had become more complex and individual roles were more highly specialized and therefore, needs were also more specific and varied.

The problem of group intelligence testing had been further clarified during the years between the two wars, and a new Army General Classification Test was prepared and used in World War II. This group intelligence test was used by the army to classify inductees according to their abilities to learn military duties. The technical kind of learning involved in military service forced the emphasis to be on verbal comprehension, quantitative reasoning, and spatial perception. The three subtests designed to measure these processes were a vocabulary test, an arithmetic test, and a block-counting test. Scores were changed to standard units with a mean of 100 and a standard deviation of 20. These final scores were similar to IQ scores but with a greater spread around the mean. Therefore, the very high or very low scores would be of slightly less significance than if computed by the usual method for IQs. The scores obtained from the AGCT are not in part a function of chronological age. See *Army Alpha Test; Army Beta Test.*

**test, association** A technique designed to assess a person's reaction to specific stimuli such as words or colors. The subject may be given a general instruction of saying whatever comes to his mind or may be told to respond in a specified manner.

**test, auditory apperception** (D. R. A. Stone) An auditory projective test introduced in 1953 consisting of five 45-rpm records which have a variety of sounds. There are ten sets of three types of sounds. After hearing a set, the subject is asked to tell a story about the sounds, including what led up to them, what is happening and how it will end. The test is recommended for use with blind subjects or groups.

**test, ball and field** A Stanford-Binet test item which requires the child's demonstrating through drawing how he could search for an object lost in a field.

**test, Bárány** (R. Bárány) The rotation of a subject positioned so that his head lies in each of the three planes bringing the three semicircular canals vertical to the direction of rotation.

**test, Behn-Rorschach** (H. Behn and H. Rorschach) Companion test to the original Rorschach, used for research or with subjects overly familiar with the standard Rorschach.

**test, Bender Visual-Motor Gestalt** (L. Bender) Test

of visual-motor and perceptual functioning requiring the subject to reproduce nine geometric designs characterized by their patterning or configuration, each design presented on a different card. Distortions in the copied designs can be the result of neural injury, variations in level of intellectual performance, or emotional disorder.

**test, Bennett Differential Aptitude** (G. K. Bennett) Aptitude tests used for grades eight to twelve which measure numerical, verbal, mechanical, and abstract reasoning, spatial relations, language usage, and clerical speed and accuracy.

**test, Bennett, of Mechanical Comprehension** (G. K. Bennett) A test of mechanical ability with several levels of difficulty for high school students and adults which uses mechanical problems in printed form.

**test, best answer, or test, best reason** A test in which a number of different answers or solutions to a problem are presented along with a problem; the testee chooses the answer or solution he thinks is the best one.

**test, Binet-Simon** (A. Binet and T. Simon) A series of tests developed in 1905 and 1908 for use in the assessment of school children in France and since adapted for use in many other countries. The test underwent several revisions in France and elsewhere.

**test, Blacky pictures** (G. S. Blum) Cartoons of a dog family with questions derived from a psychoanalytic framework, focusing on castration fears, sexual activity, sibling rivalry and so on.

**test, block design** A kind of performance test which requires the subject to reproduce standard designs with various colored blocks.

**test, Bolgar-Fischer World** (H. Bolgar and L. Fischer) A projective technique developed in 1947 which consists of miniature objects such as houses, animals, vehicles. The subject is asked to do whatever he wants with them. The examiner discusses the subject's work inquiring in order to obtain qualitative data. The test can be used with adults or children.

**test, bone-conduction** A procedure designed to assess how well the subject can hear sounds transmitted to the internal ear via the skull bones. If the subject can hear well, hearing loss can be determined to be due to defective conduction in the middle ear.

**test, Bryngelson-Glaspey** (B. Bryngelson and E. Glaspey) A test which determines proficiency in articulation of speech sounds. The test, introduced in 1941, consists of stimuli pictures designed to elicit verbal responses which assess individual sound in initial, medial and final position and in sound clusters.

**test, cause and effect** A test which requires the testee to state or choose from available options the cause of a specified effect or the effect of a specified cause.

**test, CAVD** (E. L. Thorndike) A battery of four

intelligence tests: completion, arithmetic problems, vocabulary, and following directions.

**test chart** A chart which is employed in the assessment of visual acuity.

**test, children's apperception** (L. Bellak and S. S. Bellak) A projective test modeled after the Thematic Apperception Test and intended for children from three to ten years of age. The test has two forms, one in which the characters are animals and the other in which they are children.

**test, code** A test which requires substitution of one set of symbols by another, e.g. digit-symbol test.

**test, color sorting** See *test, Holmgren.*

**test, completion** A test in which the subject is asked to fill in the missing word, letter or phrase.

**test, comprehension** 1. A form of aptitude test in which the subject is asked to evaluate what he would do in a specific practical situation. 2. A test which assesses a person's comprehension of a written passage by means of questions, following the selection, which the person is asked to answer.

**test, d reaction** In reaction-time experiments, the test in which the subject must withhold his response until he has made an identification of which of the two stimuli has been presented.

**test, developmental, of visual-motor integration** (K. E. Beery and N. A. Buktenica) Form-copying test for the assessment of the degree of integration of visual and motor skills; used with children fourteen years of age.

**test, dexterity** Test to measure the speed and accuracy in performance of manual tasks.

**test, diagnostic** A test for the purpose of identification of the nature and source of the individual's difficulties. For example, a reading test can identify the source of an individual's poor scholastic performance.

**test, diagnostic word** A test which presents auditory verbal stimuli to determine the intensity threshold at which speech can be understood.

**test, differential aptitude** (DAT) A battery of eight aptitude tests including tests of verbal, numerical, abstract, and mechanical reasoning, and spacial relations, clerical speed and accuracy, and two language tests. It is designed for use by high school students.

**test, directions** An intelligence test in which the testee is directed to perform tasks on the assumption that the ability to follow directions is indicative of intelligence.

**test, disarranged sentence** Test item in which the task is to rearrange the given series or words into a meaningful sentence.

**test, dotting** A paper and pencil test of motor ability in which the subject makes as many dots as possible in a unit of time. Also called the tapping test. In a variant of this, the aiming test, the subject is required to aim his dots one in each of a series of randomly placed circles.

**test, Downey's Will-Temperament** (J. Downey) A personality scale introduced in 1924 based on the assumption that various performance tasks, such as writing, express personality characteristics. It consists of twelve such tasks.

**test, draw-a-person** (K. Machover) A projective test developed in 1948 and based on F. Goodenough's test of intellectual ability determined from children's drawings. The subject is asked to draw a person, then a person of the opposite sex. He is then asked specific questions about his drawings. There is one list of questions for children and one for adults which inquire about age, schooling, ambition, marital status of the drawn people. This test is believed to yield information concerning the subject's self-image and body image.

**test, Elizur's, for organicity** Test for brain damage involving figure copying, clock-design constructs, and a digit test. Scores in the organic range on two of the three scales indicate organic damage.

**test for homogeneity** See *test of independence.*

**test for superior adults** Test developed for the assessment of superior adults such as the three grades of tests in the Terman-Merrill tests which are used for adults up to a mental age of over twenty-two.

**test, Forer Structured Sentence Completion** (B. R. Forer) An inventory introduced in 1950 designed to evaluate problematical areas such as interpersonal relations, aggression, and anxieties to plan a course of therapy. It consists of one hundred items. There are separate forms for males and females.

**test, formboard** Any of a group of performance tests which requires fitting geometric forms or blocks into depressions on a board.

**test, four pictures** (D. J. Van Lennep) A projective test introduced in 1948 consisting of four ambiguous pictures showing figures which are alone and in groups. The subject must make up one story integrating the four pictures. Analysis of the results involves the content and formal dimensions such as time and space.

**test, Franck Drawing Completion** (K. Franck) A projective instrument used with children ages six and over in which the child is presented with various stimulus patterns and asked to complete them or make a drawing out of them. The instrument is particularly geared for the assessment of masculinity-femininity.

**test, free association** A test or examination in which the subject is asked to make an association as quickly as possible to each stimulus presented. Any modality of stimulus or of response may be employed but verbal stimuli and responses are the most frequently used. The nature of the response and the time interval between the stimuli and the response are evaluated in terms of the subjects' attitudes, personality or other variables.

**test, free recall** A test in which the subject responds with associations to the test stimuli.

**test, Frostig, of Visual Motor Development** (M. Frostig) A test which is designed to assess the development of perceptual disturbances in which the child is required to perform various perceptual tasks.

**test, gestural interverbal** A subtest of the Parson Language Sample designed to assess skills of the gestural exchange class of language behavior.

**test, good and evil** The precursor of the right and wrong test which is used to determine a person's responsibility in a criminal action. Based on the M'Naghten rule of 1843, English law stipulates that to plead insanity as a defense in a criminal case, it must be shown that the accused was not cognizant of what he was doing or that he did not know that this action was wrong.

**test, Goodenough Draw-A-Man** (F. Goodenough) A test of intelligence for children up to eleven years old in which the child is asked to draw a man. The drawing is scored according to the amount of detail present. It was introduced and standardized in 1926.

**test, Gray Oral Reading** (W. S. Gray) An individually administered test designed for use with children in grades one to twelve in the assessment of speed, accuracy, and comprehension in oral reading which consists of a series of standardized reading paragraphs.

**test, group** A test designed to be given to more than one person at a time.

**test, H** A test of the significance of the differences between two sets of ranked data.

**test, hand** A projective technique in which children six years of age and over are shown a series of nine drawings of hands in various ambiguous poses and are asked what the hand is doing. The last card is blank and requires the child to imagine a hand and describe what it is doing. The scoring, similar to that of the Rorschach and TAT, provides measures of affection, dependence, tension and aggression.

**test, Hanfmann-Kasanin Concept Formation** (E. Hanfmann and J. S. Kasanin) A test originally concerned with the performance of schizophrenics, designed to determine a person's ability to classify twenty-two blocks each being in one of five colors, six shapes, two heights and two widths, into four categories: tall-wide, flat-wide, tall-narrow, and flat-narrow. Performance is analyzed with respect to the person's interpretation of the task, nature of the attempts at solution, and discovery of the correct solution, each of which is classified according to three levels: the primitive, the intermediate and the conceptual which are scored 1, 2, and 3 respectively. These scores are arbitrary values which have not been determined experimentally. This test yields an over-all evaluation of a person's performance and is used to determine deterioration in conceptual thinking.

**test, Healy Picture Completion** (W. Healy) 1. A performance test in which the subject is asked to complete the missing parts of a picture by choosing pieces from a larger number of possibilities. The time limit is ten minutes. This test is a subtest of the Pintner-Paterson Scale of Performance Tests. 2. See *tests, Pintner-Paterson Scale of Performance.*

**test, heel-to-knee** A test for ataxia in which the patient, who is in a reclining position, is asked to raise his foot high, touch the knee with the opposite heel and move the heel along the shin with his eyes open or closed.

**test, Hejna** (R. F. Hejna) A test to assess speech articulation developed in 1959 which consists of pictures designed to elicit verbal responses which will include specific sounds.

**test, Holmgren** (A. F. Holmgren) A test for color blindness in which the subject must classify skeins of wool according to three sample colors.

**test, Horn-Hellersberg Drawing Completion** (C. C. Horn and E. F. Hellersberg) A projective technique used with children in which the child is given a series of stimulus patterns and asked to make a complete drawing out of each. There is a published list of popular responses for grade-school children.

**test, house-tree-person** (J. N. Buck) A projective test introduced in 1948 in which the subject is asked to draw a house, a tree, and a person, each of which is believed to be a self-portrait. The drawings are evaluated in terms of sequence, style and area. The tester conducts an extensive interview following the test. This test is believed to reflect personality characteristics and assess intelligence.

**test, Hunt-Minnesota, for Organic Brain Damage** (H. F. Hunt) A test designed for the detection of organic brain damage, introduced in 1943. It consists of three parts: the vocabulary subtest of the 1937 Stanford-Binet Test, six memory and recall tests, and nine tests which are used to predict validity. In the vocabulary test the number of words the subject defines correctly reflects his basic verbal ability before the deterioration occurred. The validation tests consist of items of information, of counting forward and backward and of following specific instructions; subjects who cannot perform these tests are considered too disturbed, uncooperative or too deteriorated to be tested. The subject receives a score of each of the validation tests to determine whether he scores below the critical score ascertained as necessary for taking the test. This test was developed for use with individuals sixteen years of age and older. It was standardized on a small group of thirty-three patients, aged sixteen to seventy, who had been diagnosed as suffering from organic brain damage.

**test, identification** A test requiring the subject to name an object or part of a picture pointed to by the examiner.

**test, IES** An instrument, based on a psychoanalytic framework, developed and designed to measure impulses, ego and superego in children ten years of age and over.

**test, Illinois, of Psycholinguistic Abilities (ITPA)** A test based on communications theory designed to assess differential language abilities that are considered important in communications and learning disorders. It consists of twelve subtests which attempt to assess the child's communication skills in: 1) three processes of communication (reception, expression and organized process); 2) two levels of language organization (representational and automatic); 3) two channels of language input (auditory and visual); and 4) two channels of language output (verbal and manual expression). The test assesses the degree of the child's ability to, understand spoken words, comprehend visual stimuli, manipulate linguistic symbols meaningfully, express ideas with spoken words, express ideas using movement, produce the correct patterns of standard American language, remember auditory stimuli, remember and reproduce nonmeaningful visual figures, identify a common object from an incomplete visual presentation, fill in the deleted parts from an auditory perception, and synthesize separate parts of a word presented orally to produce an integrated whole word.

**test, incomplete pictures** A test of visual organization in which the subject is required to identify a common object presented in a series of successively completed drawings of that object as early in the sequence as possible. Also used as an indicator of the degree of psychotic impairment.

**test, individual** A test designed to be administered usually by a specially trained individual to only one person at a time.

**test, induction** A test often used as a measure of general intelligence, requiring the subject to derive a principle from several particular instances.

**test, infant** A test measuring infant behavioral development consisting of the performance of various tasks that are expected to be performed at the individual infant's chronological age.

**test, informal** A nonstandardized test designed to give an approximate index of an individual's level of ability.

**test, information** 1. A mental test designed to sample the subject's knowledge of a variety of general facts which theoretically are available to everyone. 2. One of the verbal sub-tests appearing on the Wechsler Intelligence Scales.

**test, intelligence** 1. A standardized test which measures a wide range of abilities, including verbal, numerical and social competence. 2. See *Stanford-Binet.* 3. See *Wechsler-Bellevue Scale.* 4. See *Wechsler Adult Intelligence Scale.* 5. See *Wechsler Intelligence Scale for Children.* 6. See *Wechsler Preschool and Primary Scale of Intelligence.*

**test, inventory** A test covering major areas of pupil achievement for the purpose of yielding a profile of individuals' strengths and weaknesses.

**test, Ishihari** A test used in the detection of color blindness consisting of a number of plates in which figures printed in different hues appear against backgrounds of random dots of varying saturation and brightness. The difference in hue between the figure and ground is not apparent to the color-blind person.

**test item**   A question, an item or a problem which elicits a response which can be measured as a single unit and related to the skill the test is measuring as a whole.

**test, Jung association**   (C. G. Jung) A word association test used in conjunction with physiological measures of emotion yielding strong evidence of emotional reactions to specific words. It is used for the purpose of uncovering complexes and aiding diagnosis.

**test, Kahn, of Symbol Arrangement**   (E. Kahn) A structured play test used in diagnostic evaluation of children and sometimes adults. For use with those six years of age or older, the test involves the arrangement of sixteen small plastic objects, such as dogs, hearts, stars and butterflies.

**test, Kent-Rosanoff**   (G. H. Kent and J. Rosanoff) A free association test consisting of one-hundred words, the associations to which have been standardized so that the frequency of different associations is known and used in determining relative normalcy or eccentricity of thought.

**test, Knox Cube**   (H. A. Knox) A performance in which the subject taps a series of four cubes in various sequences prescribed by the examiner.

**test, Kohs Block Design**   (S. C. Kohs) A performance test of intelligence in which multicolored cubical blocks are arranged by the subject to form designs, the patterns of which are the same as those appearing on presented cards. It is part of the Arthur Performance Scale.

**test, Kuhlmann-Anderson**   (F. Kuhlmann and R. G. Anderson) A series of test batteries designed to measure general intelligence from kindergarten to adulthood.

**test, Kuhlmann-Binet**   (F. Kuhlmann and A. Binet) Binet intelligence tests which have been revised for the purpose of administration for the U.S.A. population.

**test, Kwint Psychomotor**   An inventory of psychomotor activities based on age, and designed for use with brain-damaged children.

**test, Leiter International Performance**   (R. G. Leiter) A series of nonverbal intelligence tests consisting of picture completion tasks, number series, concealed figures and various wooden blocks which are to be matched by the subject according to colors, pictures and forms. The test is designed to be culture-free.

**test, literacy**   A test measuring the ability to read or write.

**test, MacQuarrie, for Mechanical Ability**   (T. W. MacQuarrie) A paper-and-pencil test, which includes such tasks as the tracing of a line through a series of broken lines, an assessment of tapping, block analysis, and counting and pursuit. It is heavily weighted for skills in eye-hand coordination and spatial relations.

**test, Maddox Rod**   (E. E. Maddox) A test of muscular imbalance of the eyes. It uses one or more parallel glass rods fitted in an opaque disk. The rod or rods are held in front of one eye at a time through which the eye perceives a candle flame which is converted by the rod into a line of light. The differential images perceived by the two eyes reflect the degree of heterophogia.

**test, make-a-picture-story**   (E. S. Schneidman) A projective technique designed in 1947 which consists of twenty-two background pictures and sixty-seven separate figures of people of different ages and occupations. The subject is required to choose people for each scene and to make up a story about it. The choice of people, their location, and the story are interpreted to provide information about conflicts, interpersonal relations and self-image.

**test, manikin**   (R. Pintner and D. Paterson) One of the subtests in the Pintner-Paterson Scale of Performance Tests introduced in 1917. It consists of pieces of a man, wooden legs, arms, head and body, which the subject must put together to make a man. The score depends on the quality of the performance.

**test, matching**   A test which requires the subject to choose items from one list and match them with items from a second list according to prescribed criteria.

**test, Meier Art Judgment**   (N. C. Meier) A test of aesthetic judgment introduced in 1940 for use with children in grades seven to twelve. It consists of one hundred pairs of uncolored pictures, one of which is a reproduction of a masterpiece and the other of which is altered in a way to make it inferior. The subject is asked to indicate his preference. His aesthetic judgment is considered to be an index of his artistic capability and talent and to indicate his future success in the field of art.

**test, memory-for-designs**   An instrument designed for use in the assessment of the organic consequences of brain injury. Fifteen geometric figures are presented, each for five seconds, and then removed, the patient then drawing each from memory. Scores from zero to four are assigned on the basis of configuration, Gestalt, reversal and rotation.

**test, mental**   1. The measurement of the presence, absence or degree of particular mental abilities. 2. An intelligence test.

**test, Michigan Picture**   A projective test focusing on school difficulties.

**test, Miller Analogies**   (W. S. Miller) A test designed in 1926 to predict scholastic ability at the graduate school level. It consists of one hundred mostly verbal analogies covering a wide variety of fields of specialization. The subject is asked to determine analogy relationships among words. The time limit is fifty minutes.

**test, Minnesota Clerical Aptitude**   A test of clerical ability introduced in 1946 which consists of two subtests, numbers and names, each of which is made up of identical and nonidentical pairs which the subject has to detect. The tests are designed to measure perception of detail and perceptual speed.

**test, Minnesota, for Aphasia** (H. Schuell and J. J. Jenkins) A test for aphasia developed in 1961. It consists of a variety of linguistic tasks which require the subject to respond orally and in writing.

**test, Minnesota Rate of Manipulation** A test of the rapidity of movement in working at simple tasks with the hands and fingers. It consists of two parts. Part one requires the subject to place sixty blocks into sixty holes in a board. Part two requires the subject to pick up each block, turn it over, and replace it with the opposite hand. The score is the total time required to perform these tasks.

**test, Minnesota Spatial Relations** A test of mechanical aptitude introduced in 1930 which consists of a series of four boards, each of which has fifty-eight cutouts of different shapes. The subject is required to replace them in their correct places. The test is believed to measure speed and accuracy in the perception of details in mechanical and spatial relations.

**test, Monroe Diagnostic Reading** (M. Monroe) A test developed in 1930 to diagnose the factors which interfere with an individual's ability to read, exclusive of intelligence. The test consists of nine parts, some visual and some auditory, which deal with the sensory aspects and the mechanics of reading and writing and attempt to delineate the auditory and visual deficiencies. It is designed for children in grades one to five.

**test, mosaic** A projective instrument used with children two and over in the assessment of global personality traits. The test requires the choice of various ambiguous forms (circles, triangles, etc.) of five colors (red, yellow, blue, green, black and white), and organization of those forms into something the child wishes to make, using as many pieces as he likes. The child's method of procedure and finished product are analyzed in terms of choices of pieces and colors and the finished design.

**test, multiple choice** A type of test which requires the subject to choose the answer he thinks is the best answer or solution to a question or problem.

**test, multiple response** A test in which the testee is required to choose more than one of the given optional answers as correct.

**test, number completion** A test which requires the subject to complete a series of numbers according to an inherent rule, such as 4, 16, 64, _____.

**test, object assembly** 1. A test in which the subject must put together pieces or objects which have been disassembled. 2. Test which uses a jigsaw puzzle.

**test, occupational** A test designed to measure ability for a given occupation.

**test of independence** A test of the degree of agreement between actual and expected frequencies in a plot of two or more variables. Also called test for homogeneity.

**test, omnibus** A type of test in which different kinds of tasks or items are distributed throughout the test rather than being grouped together by kind as in battery tests. There is only one timing and one score for such a test.

**test, one-tailed** (statistics) A test of the null hypothesis which distributes the risk of rejecting the null hypothesis falsely in one tail of the sampling distribution obtained under the null hypothesis. The power is greater than the two-tailed test if the results obtained are in the direction anticipated by the experimenter. If not, the power is decreased.

**test, opposites** Test in which the subject is instructed to respond with the opposite of a stimulus word.

**test, oral** A test in which the testee is required to give his response orally.

**test, Otis Quick Scoring Mental Ability** (A. S. Otis) Three forms of group intelligence tests for different school levels: the Alpha test for grades 1-4, the Beta test for grades 4-9, and the Gamma test for grades 9-16. The tests contain a spiral mixture of verbal, spatial and numerical items and yield a single raw score which can be converted into age norms.

**test, Otis Self-Administering, of Intelligence** (A. S. Otis) Verbal intelligence test consisting of two forms: intermediate examination for grades 4-9 and higher examination for grades 9-16. The test may be used as a group or an individual test, has self-contained items, and is easy to administer and to score.

**test, paired hands, of friendliness** A projective instrument used in the assessment of children's social relatedness. Slides of two hands, one white and one black, are projected in various positions and the child chooses answers from a multiple-choice answer sheet.

**test, paper and pencil** Test in which answers must be written.

**test, Peabody Picture Vocabulary** A decoding or receptive vocabulary test in which the child is required to understand the words spoken by the examiner and to select which of the four pictures is most related to the word. The test is untimed and takes about ten minutes to administer. Norms are available for ages two to eighteen.

**test, performance** A test which requires nonverbal responses rather than verbal. Such tests minimize the role of language and often involve concrete materials, such as blocks, form boards, etc.

**test, Pickford Projective Pictures** (R. W. Pickford) A projective instrument used for children ages five to fifteen consisting of 120 ambiguous line drawings of people in a variety of situations. It is designed to serve as a cathartic experience for the child as well as a means of understanding the child's dynamics. The recurrent themes in the large number of stories reflect the child's worries and preoccupations.

**test, picture arrangement** (S. S. Tomkins) A projective test introduced in 1957 which consists of a set of twenty-five plates, each having three drawings depicting the activities of a person. The subject is required to arrange the drawings in sequence and to tell a story about what is happening. The sequences and the stories are interpreted in terms of quantitative and qualitative criteria respectively. There are norms for the sequences of normal and abnormal subjects.

**test, picture completion** Performance type intelligence test in which the subject is required to find the missing part or parts in a drawing or group of drawings of animals or objects.

**test, picture impressions** A projective instrument used with adolescents and adults, specifically designed to study the patient's expectations regarding the therapist. The four pictures have drawings of a person in a short white laboratory coat.

**test, picture interpretation** Intelligence test in which the subject must interpret what a picture is about. The subject's response is then assessed. Enumeration is considered a lower response than description which is less advanced than an interpretive response.

**test, picture world** A projective instrument, used with children six and over, consisting of unambiguous and reality-oriented scenes about which the child writes his own story, adding additional objects and figures from a list of thirty-six if he wishes so. The child is instructed to make up a world that is as he sees it or as he would like it to be.

**test, placement** Test designed to determine the most appropriate class or course of studies for individual students based on their abilities, achievements and interests.

**test, Porteus Maze** (G. Arthur) A performance test in the Arthur Point Scale of Performance Tests introduced in 1933 and revised in 1943. It consists of a set of mazes of increasing difficulty, each found on a separate sheet. The subject is asked to trace each maze from beginning to end. The test is given to children five to fourteen years old for the assessment of intelligence.

**test, power** A test which is used to measure the level of achievement an individual can reach.

**test, power of** See *power function*.

**test, profile** An instrument which yields several separate measures of different variables resulting in a picture, or profile of the individual's characteristics across several areas.

**test, prognostic** An instrument which is designed so as to enable the prediction of the possible degree of achievement of a certain skill under specified conditions.

**test, progressive matrices** (J. C. Raven) A nonverbal scale of mental ability used in evaluating the individual's ability to apprehend relationships between geometric figures and designs, to perceive the structure of the matrix and of the figure (part) necessary to complete each system of relations (the matrix) presented. The test evaluates the individual's ability to discern and utilize a logical relationship, requiring analytical and integrating operations. There are several sets of the scales: one is for children six and over and adults, and one is for use with the highest quarter of intelligence.

**test, proverb** An instrument which requires the subject to explain the meaning of proverbs.

**test, psychological** See *examination, psychological*.

**test, rate** A test of many items of comparable difficulty which is taken within a certain proscribed time limit, the testee being required to finish as many items as possible with no expectation that all the items will be completed. The score is the total of all the correct responses.

**test, Raven's Controlled Projection** (J. C. Raven) A projective technique used in the assessment of social attitudes, habits and personal relationships in children ages six to twelve. The child is asked to draw whatever occurs to him and simultaneously relate a story about an imaginary child. The examiner provides the framework of the story and the child provides the details in response to eleven questions about preferences, fears, fantasies, feelings and parents.

**test, remote association** A test of creativity developed by S. A. Mednick in 1962 which requires the person to provide a word which links three ostensibly unrelated words. Correct responses are determined according to the criteria of remoteness and usefulness.

**test-retest coefficient** The correlation coefficient between the two administrations of the same test or of comparable forms of the same test.

**test, role construct repertory** (G. Kelly) A test developed in 1955, which determines the dimensions along which people classify other people.

**test, Rorschach Inkblots** (H. Rorschach) A projective test consisting of ten cards on which either black and white, black and white with color, or colored asymmetrical inkblots appear. The subject is presented the cards in a prescribed sequence and requested to tell the examiner what the inkblots could be. Responses are scored according to the various determinants used in a particular response and are indicative of the particular cognitive style and defensive patterns characterizing the individual's personality structure as a whole.

**test, Rosenzweig Picture-Frustration** (S. Rosenzweig) A projective instrument used with children and adults that is useful for sampling reactions to frustration and for determining whether aggression is directed inwardly or externally. The pictures are highly structured scenes of interpersonal frustration events such as the destruction of a treasured object. The scoring system is relatively objective.

**test, Sargent Insight** (H. D. Sargent) A projective instrument which combines sentence completion technique with thematic technique. A series of cartoon-like pictures are presented and a story is begun for the child. The themes covered deal with problem solving in relation to parents, other adults, children, school failure, loss of a loved one, illness, and concepts of time and distance. Scoring focuses on expressions of affect, defenses against affect, and thought processes which are indicative of maladjustment.

**test, scaled** A test in which the questions are arranged in order of increasing difficulty.

**test scaling** See *scaling, test*.

**test, scholastic achievement** Test which measures the testee's knowledge and ability within a certain area of study, such as literature, mathematics, french, chemistry, etc.

**test, scholastic aptitude** A combination of verbal and mathematical tests used to select candidates for college admission.

**test, school and college ability** A group of test batteries consisting of a sentence completion, vocabulary, calculation, and quantitative reasoning subtest, each of which is designed to assess the person's capacity to master educational requirements at the next level.

**test, seashore musical ability** A series of tests consisting of recorded tasks of pitch and loudness discrimination, tonal memory, rhythm, time and timbre, used for the identification of an individual's relative musical ability.

**test, selective answer** A test in which questions are presented along with several alternative answers from which the testee must choose the one that is correct, e.g. a multiple choice test.

**test, self-administering** A test in which the instructions for completion are given directly and clearly in order that the subject can easily follow them without further assistance.

**test, self-marking** A test which is designed in such a way that the subject's answers are recorded as right or wrong automatically.

**test, semantic differential** A paper-and-pencil test which provides the subject with a series of pairs of opposite adjectives, such as "rough-smooth," "active-passive," and requires him to locate himself (or any other person) on the continuum between each of the adjective pairs. The resulting semantic spaces can be defined statistically; adjectives that are associatively similar are identified and their psychological distance from other adjectives is determined.

**test of sensorimotor functions** Instruments and techniques designed to assess the child's developmental status and progress in perceptual and motor behaviors. See *scale, Lincoln-Oseretsky Motor Development; scale, California infant, for Motor Development; Purdue Perceptual-Motor Survey; scale, Movigenic Movement*.

**test, sentence repetition** A test in which the subject is asked to repeat verbatim after the examiner a series of increasingly difficult sentences.

**test, sequential** (statistics) A test used to determine the point at which the addition of further data would not increase the obtained level of significance.

**test, similarities** A test in which the subject is required to state the similarity between two items or to arrange items according to their likeness.

**test, situation** A test which requires the subject to solve an artificial real life problem in order to assess his capability of doing so in a real life situation.

**test sophistication** The gain or change in a test score due to past familiarity with that test or type of test.

**test, sorting** 1. A test used to determine conceptualization by presenting a subject with a series of objects which he must categorize. 2. See *Q-sort*.

**test, South African Picture Analysis** A projective TAT-type instrument designed to measure the subject's relationship to God as well as to man. The stories given to pictures with both human and humanlike animals, are interpreted in an existential framework.

**test, special-purpose** A relatively brief test designed to measure either some single factor-dimension or some special combination of factors in a single score.

**test, spontaneity** (J. L. Moreno) A test in which an individual is placed in a life-like situation with people with whom he is emotionally involved or others who symbolize these people so that he can act out his feelings and practice new behaviors toward them.

**test, SRA mechanical aptitude** A test of mechanical aptitude which involves three subjects designed to assess mechanical information used in the names and uses of tools, form perception and spatial visualization, and the solution of problems using shop arithmetic.

**test, standardized** A test which is compiled empirically, has definite directions for administration and use, has adequate norms, and has data on reliability and validity.

**test, Stanford Achievement** A test designed for use in measuring a pupil's progress in paragraph meaning, word meaning and grammatical usage.

**test, stilling** A test which is composed of a chart of many dots of various hues, saturations, and intensities. The charts are used in the detection of color weakness as the dots are arranged to form numbers which are visible to the naked eye but not to the eye with color weakness.

**test, story recall** A test involving the subject's ability to recall and reproduce details of a story which has been presented to him.

**test, Stroop** (J. R. Stroop) A test developed in 1935 designed to measure an individual's degree of cognitive control. It consists of a series of colored cards on which names of colors other than the color of the cards are printed. The individual is asked to name the color of the card rather than to read the name written. The degree to which individuals are subject to the interference of the printed words is the measure of cognitive control.

**test, subjective** Any test which cannot and does not employ any objective criteria for scoring purposes.

**test, survey** Tests to investigate and study the level and status of a whole group and class.

**test, symbol arrangement** (T. C. Kahn) A projective test developed in 1955 which consists of sixteen plastic geometric shapes, such as hearts, dogs, anchors, crosses. The subject is asked to group the objects into rectangles designated as "love," "hate," "bad," "good," "living," "dead," "small," and "large" on a piece of felt which is divided into fifteen numbered parts. He is asked to free associate to the meaning of each object. A scoring system is available which purports to yield information about the subject's unconscious process of symbolization.

**test, symbol digit** See *test, code.*

**test, symbol elaboration** A projective technique used with children ages six and over in which the child is provided with eleven stimulus patterns and asked to elaborate them by drawing.

**test, symbol substitution** See *test, code.*

**test, Symonds Picture-Study** (P. M. Symonds) A projective technique, designed for use with adolescents, which closely parallels the TAT although the figures in the pictures are more youthful and the pictures more depressive in tone. The subject tells a story to each of the pictures which include a large number of situations and interpersonal relationships. The stories are then analyzed in terms of such themes as family relationships, aggression, economic concern, punishment and separation.

**test, synonym-antonym** A test requiring the subject to indicate whether pairs of words which are presented are the same or opposite in meaning.

**test, Szondi** (L. Szondi) A projective test developed in 1947 in Hungary and introduced in the United States in 1949. It consists of forty-eight cards, which are divided into six sets. The cards have portraits of faces of mental patients on them representing the categories of homosexuality, sadism, epilepsy, hysteria, catatonic schizophrenia, paranoid schizophrenia, depression and mania. Each set of cards has one card representing a category. The subject is asked to choose two cards which he likes best and two which he least likes in each set. The distribution of chosen cards is interpreted in terms of which categories the subject identifies with and which traits he rejects.

**test, t** (statistics) The ratio of a statistic or its standard error used especially when the number of cases in the sample is small. The statistical significance of *t* is dependent on its size and the number of degrees of freedom, or the number of observations minus the number of independent restrictions placed on the sample. A common use of this test is the determination of the significance of the differences between two means.

**test tapping** See *test dotting.*

**test, Temple-Darley** (M. C. Temple and F. L. Darley) A test of articulation developed in 1960 which has standardized stimulus pictures, words and administrative procedures.

**test, Terman-McNemar, of Mental Ability** (L. M. Terman and Q. McNemar) A group administered verbal scale of mental ability which is designed for use with grades seven through twelve, with norms provided for ages ten through nineteen years eleven months. There are seven subjects, including information, synonyms, logical selection, classification, analogies, opposites and best answer.

**test, thematic** Any test in which a person is asked to tell a story.

**test, thematic apperception** (C. D. Morgan and H. A. Murray) A projective test introduced in 1935 consisting of thirty pictures plus one blank card which are used in combinations depending on the sex and age of the subject. The subject is told that the test is one of imagination without right and wrong answers. He is asked to make up a story for each picture which has a beginning describing what has led up to the depicted scene, a middle giving an account of what is occurring in the picture and the feelings of the characters involved, and an end telling what the outcome will be. There is no time limit in this test. The stories should be recorded verbatim. Following the testing procedure, the tester may conduct an interview to obtain more specific information about the given stories for diagnostic purposes.

**test, Thompson Thematic Apperception** (C. E. Thompson) A projective test developed in 1949 based on the Thematic Apperception Test. The test consists of pictures of Negro figures in various combinations and situations. The subject is asked to tell a story about each picture which is interpreted in terms of formal structure and content.

**test, true-false** A form of test in which the subject is presented with certain statements and is required to check whether each statement is true or false. The test may consist of statements concerning a certain area of study or general statements that concern the individual.

**test, Twitchell-Allen Three-Dimensional Personality** (A. Twitchell-Allen) A projective technique used with children consisting of a set of twenty-eight ceramic figures, relatively culture-free and free-form and of neutral color, laid out in a predetermined order in front of the child. The child tells three stories and names each piece, two stories being told to pieces he selects and arranges and one being told to three standard pieces selected and arranged by the examiner. The examiner records verbal associations, stories and expressive motor behavior such as gestures, facial expressions and movements. The several recommended scoring procedures include the naming test in which the child's responses are categorized as to content, determinants, form quality and originality, as in Rorschach scoring; a psychodynamic approach in which stories are analyzed in terms of themes such as sexual, relationship to authority, and struggle between independence and dependence; and an analysis of verbal form and content, taking into account the number of words, parts of speech, and number of different persons in the story. The test is one of the few standardized projective techniques that can be used with visually handicapped children.

**test, two-tailed** (statistics) A nondirectional test of the null hypothesis in which the risk of rejecting the null hypothesis falsely is distributed equally in the two tails of the sampling distribution obtained under the null hypothesis. This test has the greatest power unless it is known that the data implies directionality.

**test, U** (statistics) A nonparametric test used to determine the significance of the differences between means for unmatched groups.

**test value** A temporary value determined by a few observations which is used to limit the variability of an experimental variable.

**test, vector** (statistics) The representation of a test by a vector or straight line.

**test, verbal** 1. Any test which is constructed so as to require verbal ability to perform the tasks. 2. Any test which measures general verbal ability.

**test, Vigotsky** (L. S. Vigotsky) A test of concept formation in which the subject is required to sort blocks of different sizes, shapes and colors.

**test, visual apperception** A projective technique designed for use with subjects twelve years of age and over. The subject is presented with twelve plates consisting of lines randomly drawn under controlled conditions and is asked to color in whatever object or pattern he sees in the doodles and title the finished drawing.

**test, visual-motor Gestalt** See *test, Bender Visual-Motor Gestalt*

**test, vocabulary** A test which is designed so as to assess the skill a person has in using and understanding words.

**test, Weigl-Goldstein-Scheerer** (E. Weigl, K. Goldstein and M. Scheerer) A test of concept formation introduced in 1941 which requires the subject to sort a variety of geometric figures according to color and form and to shift from one category to another. The subject must also verbalize his act to allow for discrimination of concrete from abstract behavior.

**test, Wepman, of Auditory Discrimination** (G. P. Wepman) An individually administered examination that requires five to ten minutes to administer and, attempts to determine whether or not auditory discrimination deficits are present. The subject is required to determine whether two words pronounced by the examiner are alike or different.

**test, whisper** A crude form of hearing test in which the subject, standing with one ear plugged twenty feet from the examiner who pronounces test words in a distinct whisper, tries to hear the words without looking at the examiner's lips.

**test, wiggly block** A test of manual dexterity requiring the subject to reassemble nine blocks cut by wavy lines from a rectangular block.

**test-wise** A term used to describe a person who, having taken a number of tests, will tend to be relatively less naive and have more of an advantage over a person who has not taken a lot of tests.

**test, word association** 1. A projective technique consisting of a list of words which is presented to the subject one at a time. The subject is asked to respond with the first word which comes to his mind. The verbal responses, and non-verbal reactions are recorded. This test is used to assess general adjustment and neuroticism. 2. (C. G. Jung) A test designed for the detection of "complexes" which was developed in 1906. It consists of one hundred words which represent the common emotional "complexes." The verbal content and non-verbal responses are interpreted. 3. (G. H. Kent and A. J. Rosanoff) A test consisting of one hundred words designed in 1910 for the purpose of differentiating between normal and mentally ill people. Standardized norms are available for common and uncommon responses which are believed to differentiate normal from abnormal individuals. This is not always true. 4. (D. Rapaport, et al.) A test developed in 1946 consisting of a list of words designed to provide clinical information concerning the degree of maladjustment and impairment of thought organization. Many of the stimulus words elicit responses involving psychosexual matters.

**test, word-building** A test requiring the subject to construct as many words as possible out of a given number of letters.

**test, work-limit** A kind of test in which each subject performs the same task, the differences between them dependent upon the time required.

**test, X-O** (S. Pressley) A test which pioneered in the area of attitudes and interests. The subject either crosses out or circles certain preferences.

**testability** Characterizing propositions or statements which can be tested for truth.

**testing** The administration of a test or tests.

**testing-of-limits** A special type of structured Rorschach inquiry suggested by B. Klopfer, and usually involving suggestions to a subject concerning certain percepts or characteristics of percepts not mentioned by the subject but ordinarily seen by most subjects. If, after direct suggestion, the subject still maintains no awareness of the percepts in question, the examiner may use a more direct form of suggestion so as to ascertain the extent to which the subject is able to see popular or conventional concepts. Testing-of-limits ordinarily occurs only after the formal inquiry has been completed.

**testis** One of the ball-shaped organs located in the scrotum, and constituting the vertebrate male sex glands.

**testosterone** One of the male sex hormones.

**tests, battery of** 1. A group or series of related tests that are administered at one time. 2. A group or series of tests which, when combined, yield a single score.

**tests, Benton Visual Retention** (A. L. Benton) Ten geometric designs are exposed to a child, each for ten seconds, then removed while the child draws the design. The test measures visual perception, immediate memory and psychomotor reproduction. Used with children eight years of age and over; useful in the detection of severe brain damage in older children.

**tests, California Achievement** (L. P. Thorpe and W. W. Clark) Four batteries of tests, including primary, elementary, intermediate and advanced (running from grade 1 to grade 13), covering the same general areas of reading vocabulary, arithmetic reasoning, reading comprehension, arithmetic fundamentals, spelling, and mechanics of English and grammar, although content and difficulty change with increasing levels. Except for spelling, each test is divided into subtests that are seen as parts of the larger area of school learning; widely different subtest scores are seen as significant for diagnostic purposes.

**tests, California, of Mental Maturity** (L. P. Thorpe and W. W. Clark) Scales arranged on five levels all testing the same factors, such as memory and logical reasoning with the content of each scale adapted to the appropriate level of form and difficulty. At the earliest levels there is an emphasis on nonverbal materials, with increasing use of word knowledge, number concepts and complex nonverbal material at higher levels.

**tests, California, of Personality** (L. P. Thorpe, W. W. Clark and E. W. Tiegs) A set of five scales introduced in 1953, the primary, elementary, intermediate, secondary and adult, which assess the principal sources of an individual's problems. The questions of the test determine the presence of traits in two categories: personal adjustment and social adjustment. Personal adjustment consists of feelings of self-reliance, personal worth, personal freedom, and belonging, withdrawing tendencies and nervous symptoms. Social adjustment refers to social standards, social skills, anti-social tendencies, family relations, school relations, occupation relations and community relations.

**tests, clerical** Usually a battery of tests, which includes tasks such as filing, checking, simple bookkeeping, routine mathematical operations, and sometimes stenography and machine calculation.

**tests, concept formation** 1. Methods of studying how people form concepts and levels of concept formation. 2. See *test, Weigl-Goldstein-Scheerer.* 3. See *test, Vigotsky.*

**tests, cumulative** Tests which measure traits and abilities which increase with age. Scoring is established on a minimally inferential level, usually establishing a criterion and determining a person's score deviation from the criterion.

**tests, Gates-MacGinitie Reading** A series of reading

tests designed to assess vocabulary, comprehension, speed and accuracy in reading at the primary levels.

**tests, Goldstein-Scheerer** (K. Goldstein and M. Scheerer) Five tests designed in 1941 to assess abstracting ability and the capacity to form concepts in abnormal subjects. There is no standardization data or norms available. The tests are used as qualitative measures of the presence of organic disorders. The five tests consist of the following: 1) Goldstein-Scheerer cube test—seeks to determine the subject's ability to copy designs which are constructed with superimposed lines to help the subject who has previously failed to analyze the design. 2) Gelb-Goldstein color sorting test—assesses the subject's ability to sort woolen skeins according to color. 3) and 4) Gelb-Goldstein—Weigl—Scheerer object sorting test and the Weigl-Goldstein-Scheerer color-form sorting test—determine the subject's ability to sort objects according to color, form, and material and to shift from one category to another. 5) Goldstein-Scheerer stick test—requires the subject to reproduce a series of figure designs from memory by means of sticks.

**tests, Iowa, of Basic Skills** A battery of educational achievement tests which provides scores on reading, vocabulary, language, arithmetic and work-study skills. There are norms for each grade at the beginning, middle and end of the year. The measured skills are all assessed in sections that become increasingly more difficult with some overlap between grades.

**tests, Metropolitan Achievement** An instrument used in the assessment of achievement levels for grades 1-2, 3-4, 5-6, 7-8. At the elementary level the test provides in three hours of testing, nine scores assessing vocabulary, reading and arithmetic skills and language usage. Tests of social studies, science and study skills are included at the higher levels.

**tests, nonverbal** Tests which do not utilize verbal material for presentation or solution of the problem. They are also known as performance tests.

**tests, paired-choice** Personality tests which consist of paired items and require the subject to choose which of the statements most applies to him or to a situation.

**tests, personality** Any test or technique used to evaluate personality or to rate personality characteristics or personal traits.

**tests, Pintner-Paterson scale of performance** (R. Pintner and D. Paterson) A group of fifteen performance tests designed for the evaluation of mental ability in persons having serious hearing and speech defects and for non-English speaking individuals, introduced in 1917. The age range of this scale is four to fifteen years although this does not apply to all of the subtests. Three different scoring methods may be used: median mental age, point score, and percentile rank. This scale does not measure the same abilities as verbal tests and should be used to supplement the latter.

**tests, psychomotor** Tests of motor skill in which

the score is dependent upon a certain degree of precise coordination of a sensory process and a motor activity.

**tests, sentence completion** **1.** Projective tests which consist of a series of sentence stems of one or more words which the subject is asked to furnish. They are believed to reflect attitudes, motives and conflicts. The first was developed by A.D.A. Teadler in 1930 which was modified by A. R. Rohde in 1946. **2.** See *Rotter Incomplete Sentence Blank.* **3.** See *test, Forer Structured Sentence Completion.*

**tests, timed** A test which has time limits.

**tests, vocational aptitude** A test which is constructed to measure and evaluate potential achievement in a specific profession through the assessment of ability, personality traits and interests.

**tetanoid epilepsy** See *epilepsy, tetanoid.*

**tetanus** **1.** A state of continuous muscle contraction. **2.** An infectious disease characterized by tetanus.

**tetany** A pathological condition or disease which is characterized by the presence of intermittent tetanus, particularly of the extremities.

**tetartanopia** Partial blindness which affects one fourth of the field of vision.

**tetrachoric correlation** See *correlation, tetrachoric.*

**tetrachromatism** The theory that there are receptors in the eye for four colors.

**tetrad difference equation** See *equation, tetrad difference.*

**texture gradient** Characterizes the perceived increase in density and loss of the separateness of the perceptual field elements with increasing distance from the eye.

**texture response** A type of Rorschach response in which the chiaroscuro (light-dark) features of the blot convey the impression of tactuality to the subject, whose response becomes determined, at least in part, by this impression. Texture responses are generally interpreted as representing deprivation of the more infantile erotic needs.

**thalamic theory of the emotions** (W. B. Cannon and P. Bard) A theory stressing the role of the hypothalamus in the emotions. The theory holds that emotion provoking stimuli give rise to impulses stimulating the hypothalamus in turn activating the cortex and the visceral processes, the cortical activity arousing the emotional experience and the visceral activity preparing the individual for activity.

**thalamotomy** A rarely used procedure in the treatment of depressive states in which there is a bilateral destruction of the medial thalamic nuclei.

**thalamus** Mass of gray matter consisting of numerous nuclei in the diencephalon which relays impulses from various sensory organs to the cortex.

**thalamus, extrinsic** Dorsal thalamic nuclei which funtion to relay incoming impulses from other mechanisms.

**thalamus, intrinsic** Dorsal thalamic nuclei which relay incoming impulses which originate within other thalamic nuclei.

**thalassophobia** A morbid fear of the sea.

**thalidomide** A drug used as a tranquilizer, sedative or hypnotic. When used during pregnancy it causes limb and brain damage to the fetus.

**thanatophobia** Fear of death.

**Thanatos** (S. Freud) A drive toward death. It is present in all organisms arising from the time when organic material developed from inorganic material. With the start of life the death instinct, Thanatos, was born, which aimed at the destruction of life and the re-establishment of inanimate nature. The life force, Eros, and the death force Thanatos, are inseparable. Eros seeks to bring organic material together into larger units whereas the death instinct seeks to disperse organic materials and return life to its original inorganic state. All masochism, sadism, hostility, destruction, violence, etc., are thought to be an expression of the death instinct.

**thanatotic** (K. Eissler) A term describing a person who manifests the death instinct.

**thema** (H. A. Murray) A molar behavioral unit consisting of the interaction between press, the instigating situation, and the operating need.

**thematic apperception test** See *test, thematic apperception.*

**thematic test** See *test, thematic.*

**theme, mythological** (C. G. Jung) The themes revealed in a people's myths are seen as derived from themes that are present in the collective unconscious.

**theomania** The delusion that one is God.

**theophobia** The pathological fear of God.

**theorem** A scientific proposition, statement or premise, expressed in scientific terms, symbols or mathematical equation.

**theorem of intellectual unity and hierarchy of specific intelligences** (C. Spearman) A certain proportion of the variance in any intellectual task can be accounted for by a factor of "general intelligence" (g). However, there are elements to each intellectual task which are common to the specific task and not common to all the tasks.

**theoretical type** See *type, theoretical.*

**theory** Any scientific system is comprised of empirical data derived from observation and/or experimentation, and of their interpretation. The set of statements of propositions explaining factual data is called theory. Some scientists start with empirical data while others pose several theoretical statements and deduce from them the empirical laws. Whichever way scientists proceed, a theory is a system of hypothetical statements concerning a certain area of scientific inquiry.

**theory, crisis** (G. Caplan, et al.) The idea that particular stages of development are crisis periods during which the individual is susceptible to change. During these times the person may progress or regress. Intervention at these times consists of aiding the individual to progress.

**theory, drive-reduction** 1. The proposition that all motivated behavior rises out of drives or needs and the responses which satisfy those drives or needs tend to be strengthened or reinforced. 2. The proposition that all motivation is based on the reduction of a drive, need for drive stimulus and the responses which tend to reduce the drive.

**theory, duplicity** The proposition, now established as fact, that there are separate receptors for color vision (cones) and brightness vision (rods). Cones are primarily sensitive to differences in wave length and rods are primarily sensitive to intensity of light waves.

**theory, interpersonal** (H. S. Sullivan) The belief that personality development is solely the result of interpersonal experiences and situations and can only be observed and studied as it is manifested in such situations. Sullivan postulated that satisfaction and security are the two basic goals of human activity, satisfaction resulting from the fulfillment of bodily needs and security from the feeling of well-being derived from acceptance and love by significant others in the environment. Both needs are present at birth and patterns of comfort and frustration are first established through the infant's and mother's interrelations. The individual's unique patterns of interrelations are called dynamisms, the most important of which is the self-dynamism or self-system, which is formed early by the experience of anxiety. Gradually the infant learns which behaviors, thoughts and actions serve to avoid destruction of the euphoric feeling of satisfaction and security and evoke love and approval from the mother, and which do not. The resulting pattern of protective behaviors and controls form the self-system, which continues to be modified in later life by various threats to one's security. Associated with behavior resulting in satisfaction and security is the individual's perception of himself as "good-me". Associated with forthcoming anxiety is the self perception of "bad-me". When the child's interactions result in intense anxiety his perception of himself as perpetrator is dissociated and becomes "not-me". Sullivan terms these perceptions personifications and states that they also exist in reference to others, for example, the caring, loving mother is "good mother", while the mother in situations associated with the child's anxiety is "bad mother". Sullivan was also concerned with the relation of cognitive processes to personality. He distinguished three modes of cognitive experience: the prototaxic, consisting of sensations, images and feelings found in its purest form in infancy, the parataxic, the next to develop, consisting of the ability to see causal relationships between events occurring close in time but not being logically related, and the syntaxic, the highest and most uncommonly experienced mode of thinking, consisting of consensually validated symbol activity particularly of a verbal nature which produces logical order among experiences. Any of these may be the mode of experience in a given situation depending on the particular interpersonal relationship involved.

**theory, irradiation** 1. The theory, based on the application of irradiation phenomena to learning, that learning consists of the selective reinforcement of one of many occurring responses. 2. (I. P. Pavlov) The spread of excitation or inhibition in nerve centers.

**theory of knowledge** See *epistemology*.

**theory of the ideal observer** See *ideal observer*.

**theory, quantum** See *quantum theory*.

**theory, sampling** See *sampling theory*.

**theory, signal detection** See *signal detection theory*.

**therapeutic community** (M. Jones) A plan for the transformation of the traditional custodian type mental hospitals into centers of incessant therapeutic activity. According to Jones' idea, the entire time a patient spends in a mental hospital must be utilized for therapeutic purposes. Even the architecture of the hospital, its furniture, daily routines, diet, entertainment, etc. must form a part of an overall therapeutic program.

**therapeutic milieu** A therapeutic setting for mental patients in which all personnel are trained in interpersonal and therapeutic techniques and in which the patients take responsibility to help each other. Frequent patient-staff group meetings are held in order to facilitate interpersonal communication.

**therapist** One who is trained in and skilled at the use of techniques for the treatment of various disorders.

**therapy** 1. Activities undertaken to cure diseases and to ameliorate suffering, e.g. psychotherapy, chemotherapy. 2. The curative effects of such activities.

**therapy, active** See *psychotherapy, activity group*.

**therapy, activity group** See *psychotherapy, activity group*.

**therapy, adjuvant or adjunctive** Supplementary or contributory techniques used in psychotherapy such as occupational therapy. Often used synonymously with adjunctive psychotherapy.

**therapy, analytic** See *psychotherapy, psychoanalytic*.

**therapy, art** Participation in the arts such as dance, music, painting and sculpture used as a therapeutic method to offer the patient opportunities for sublimation, outlets to distance himself from his problems and occasions to increase his self-esteem through achievement.

**therapy, aversion** A behavior therapy technique in which an undesired response such as pleasurable emotion to a fetishistic object is inhibited by the evocation of an incompatible response to which the person reacts with avoidance. Stimuli to such responses are either physical, e.g. electrical shock or noxious odors, or conditioned, e.g. the evocation of nausea by suggested images (covert sensitization). See *reciprocal inhibition.*

**therapy, crisis** Therapy provided on a "drop-in" emergency basis.

**therapy, directive group** See *psychotherapy, directive group.*

**therapy, expressive** Therapy which encourages the individual to express feelings without inhibitions and to talk openly about personal problems.

**therapy, insight** Form of psychotherapy which focuses on the uncovering of the deep causes of the patient's conflicts, and the adjustment or removal of the defenses against this insight. This type of therapy aims at helping the patient toward greater self-understanding and utilization of his resources.

**therapy, interpersonal** See *psychotherapy, interpersonal.*

**therapy, interpretive** Psychotherapy focused on the patient's verbal expression of conflicts and their symbolic meaning with the belief that the process will teach the patient to eventually solve his problems alone.

**therapy, occupational** The treatment of mental or physical disorders by giving the patient useful or interesting work to do. The intention is usually to exercise particular muscles and to improve the individual's mental outlook.

**therapy, physical** See *physiotherapy.*

**therapy, physiological** Therapeutic techniques including electroconvulsive shock treatment and drug therapy.

**therapy, placebo** Any treatment or therapy which has an affect on the patient's symptoms, disease or psychological state because it reinforces the patient's expectations though it does not really act on the individual's condition.

**therapy, play** See *psychotherapy, play.*

**therapy, reality** (W. Glasser) A method of treatment in which the therapist plays an active role and the patient is held responsible for his behavior. It is theorized that a person will act the right way if he has fulfilled two basic needs, the need for feelings of self-worth and respect and love for others. Fulfillment of these needs is a sign of responsibility. The therapist focuses on helping the patient do better and be more responsible. It is the patient's responsibility however to change his behavior.

**therapy, recreational** A kind of therapy in which the patient is encouraged to participate in some form of play or recreation in order to enjoy it for its own sake.

**therapy, regressive electroshock** Electroshock treat-

ment in which the patient is given a shock resulting in a short convulsive period and then, through the use of mild electrical current, is maintained in a sleep-like state.

**therapy, relaxation** A kind of therapy in which there is an emphasis on teaching the patient how to relax in the belief that muscular relaxation and lack of tension will promote the decrease of psychological distress and tension.

**therapy, release** (D. Levy) A short-term child therapy concerned with specific symptoms resulting from a traumatic event. It consists of the expression of the traumatic situation which caused the symptoms through play, allowing the child to master his repressed emotions. This type of therapy is believed to be a good prophylactic technique to avert the consolidation of neurotic responses to traumatic situations.

**therapy, religious** Psychotherapeutic help obtained in various aspects of the church such as the confessional which offers a verbal catharsis, pastoral counseling, and participation in church sponsored activities.

**therapy, role** (G. A. Kelly) A form of therapy in which the focus is on helping the client reformulate his constructs or form new ones as a prelude to initiating new modes of action. The relationship of the therapist with the client is a cognitive one. The emphasis is on the present.

**therapy, spontaneity** (J. L. Moreno) Psychodrama and sociodrama techniques designed to allow the person to act out his conflicts and to practice new behaviors which are more adaptable.

**therapy, subshock** Shock therapy in a mild degree.

**therapy, supportive** A type of therapy in which the therapist actively offers reassurance, suggestion, advice, and persuasion to help the person resolve his problems. The therapist attempts to foster a positive relationship and to utilize it to promote improvement. Adjunctive methods may be used, such as physical and/or occupational group, drug or hypnotherapy.

**therapy, three-cornered** See *psychotherapy, role-divided.*

**thermal** 1. Pertaining to heat. 2. Warm; hot.

**thermal sensitivity** The ability to discriminate temperature.

**thermalgia** Sensation of burning pain.

**thermanaesthesia** Loss of ability to discriminate heat or cold by touch.

**thermestosiometer** An instrument which measures the sensitivity to heat of different areas of the skin.

**thermocouple** A thermoelectric device used to measure differences in temperature.

**thermohyperaesthesia** Abnormal sensitivity to temperature stimuli.

**thermohypesthesia** Abnormal insensitivity or indifference to heat or contact with heated objects.

**thermoneurosis** An elevation of body temperature due to neurosis.

**thermophobia** Morbid fear of heat.

**thermoreceptor** Nerve structures (receptors) which are stimulated by temperature fluctuations.

**thermotaxis** 1. The regulation of body temperature. 2. The involuntary movement of an organism toward or away from heat.

**thermotropism** The involuntary movement of an organism or cells involving change or movement or growth toward or away from heat.

**thesis** 1. A proposition which is formally offered for proof or disproof. 2. A systematic treatise, generally dealing with one specific problem. 3. In American universities a treatise written in partial fulfillment for an advanced degree.

**thinking** 1. Cognitive behavior which uses symbols. 2. Representational or symbolic mental process. 3. Manipulation of concepts and precepts. 4. The train of ideas. 5. (J. Dewey) Problem solving activity involving primarily ideational activity. 6. (J. B. Watson) Subvocal or covert speech.

**thinking, abstract** Thinking which is characterized by the use of abstractions and generalizations.

**thinking, associative** A form of thinking based on the use of associative connections.

**thinking, autistic** (E. Bleuler) Thought processes which have meaning to the thinking individual himself; turning away from reality and seeing life in fantastic pictures.

**thinking, conceptual, and brain processes** Thinking on an abstract level which is dependent on the integrative processes of the cortex. Localization of this function in a specific area of the brain does not exist.

**thinking, concrete** (K. Goldstein) A form of thinking found especially in brain-injured individuals when the frontal lobes are impaired. Its characteristics include an inability to detach the ego from the inner or outer sphere of experience; an inability to assume or to shift a specific mental set; a confusion about spatial relationship; an inability to concentrate on two tasks simultaneously, to integrate parts into a whole or to analyze a totality; and an inability to judge, reflect about or plan for the future.

**thinking, magical** A form of developmentally primitive thinking seen in young children, psychotics and normal individuals under conditions of stress and fatigue characterized by primary process, animism, prelogical, and superstitious thought processes.

**thinking, primary process** Form of thought which is characterized by rules of primary process rather than secondary process. Such thinking reflects a tendency towards condensation and displacement. Fantasy or day-dreaming is a form of primary process thinking.

**thinking type** See *type, thinking.*

**thiopental** A barbiturate which is used intravenously as an anaesthetic in surgery and has been used to stimulate the release of repressed feelings.

**thioridazine** Mellaril; a tranquilizer used in the treatment of psychoses.

**thombencephalon** The hind brain.

**Thompson, Clara (1893-1953)** American psychiatrist and neo-psychoanalyst, follower of H. S. Sullivan School; historian of psychoanalysis.

**Thompson Thematic Apperception Test** See *test, Thompson Thematic Apperception.*

**thorazine** Common name for chlorpromazine.

**Thorndike, Edward L. (1874-1949)** Educational psychologist (Columbia Teachers' College), known for his 1) original work on trial-and-error learning in cats, 2) statement of the law of effect, 3) development of educational psychology and experimental education through authoritative textbooks based on the three problems of motivation, capacity, and learning, 4) construction of achievement and higher level intelligence tests, and 5) research on verbal learning.

**Thorndike-Lorge list** A 30,000 word list showing frequencies of English words based on written material such as books and magazines. Words which occur more than 100 times per million are designated AA and those which occur between 50 and 100 times per million as A. The book also includes lists of words occurring four times per 18,000,000 words. These lists are used in verbal and association learning in order to evaluate the results.

**Thorndike's Handwriting Scale** See *scale, Thorndike's Handwriting.*

**Thorndike's trial and error learning** (E. L. Thorndike) The theory that learning proceeds through neural connections between stimulus and response, a stimulus and response being connected when a response to a stimulus leads to a state of satisfaction or pleasure.

**threctia** (R. B. Cattell) The low-score pole of the Parmia-Threctia personality dimension, characterized by timidity, withdrawal, and susceptibility to threat.

**three-component theory** 1. See *trireceptor theory.* 2. See *trichromatic theory.*

**threptic** A conveniently brief term (borrowed by Cattell from Aristotle) for defining "the portion of a trait or a trait variance which is environmentally determined." Thus, *genetic* and *threptic* are complementary terms to be used in behavior genetics in reference to experimentally determinable quantities.

**threshold, or limen** (psychophysics) The minimum stimulus energy or energy change necessary for the experimental subject to indicate an awareness of the stimulus change. Stimulus energy values are usually determined several times for the same subject; the threshold is arrived at by one of several possible statistical treatments of the determined values. Thus the threshold value is statistical, and as such affected by several types of experimental errors as well as the changes within the physiology and nervous system of the subject himself. Thus, a threshold determination does not truly represent one absolute value, but rather a best guess from a range of possible values.

**threshold, absolute (RL)** The minimum intensity or frequency at which a stimulus will be perceived. See *differential threshold.*

**threshold, arousal** The minimum amount of stimulation necessary to produce arousal.

**threshold, brightness** The minimal intensity of a visual stimulus required to differentiate it as brighter than the surrounding or adjacent visual field.

**threshold, difference** The minimum difference between two stimuli that can be responded to as different under the given experimental conditions. Also referred to as the just noticeable difference and JND.

**threshold, response** Minimal value of a state variable that will evoke a response; the state variable is a conceptualization of all internal and external determinants of the response.

**threshold, sensation** See *threshold, absolute.*

**threshold, stimulus** The class of stimuli that occasion at a stated probability a defined response class, e.g. the threshold traditionally is the stimulus that has a 50% probability of occasioning the response.

**thromboangitis obliterans** A disease of the peripheral nerves, arteries, and veins with associated venous and arterial thrombosis, often leading to gangrene. It usually occurs in young and middle-aged males who are heavy smokers. Also called Buerger's disease.

**thumb-sucking** An early manipulation of the body, believed to serve as substitute erotic gratification and calming purposes generally seen only from birth to early childhood.

**Thurstone Attitude Scale** See *scale, Thurstone Attitude.*

**Thurstone, Louis L. (1887-1955)** Quantitative psychologist at Chicago who contributed substantially to the development of the theory of factor analysis, and undertook major factor analyses of human intelligence in a search for primary mental abilities. After he identified seven, he constructed tests to measure them in a more refined manner.

**Thurstone's theory of primary mental abilities** (L. L. Thurstone) The theory is based upon relationships which were found among tests of ability using multiple factor analysis. All of a number of tests correlated, indicating the presence of common factors of which he identified seven: verbal ability (V), the use and understanding of verbal concepts; spatial (S), the dealing with objects in space and the utilization of spatial relationships; reasoning (R), the apprehension and employment of abstract relationships in the solution of problems; word fluency (WF), thinking of words rapidly; number (N), the rapid and correct performance of fundamental mathematical opera-

tions; memory (M), learning and retaining information; perceptual (P), rapid and accurate object identification. Thurstone is in opposition to those which hold that there is a unitary ability involved in intelligence and holds that intelligence can be truly measured only by a measurement and percentile ranking of the seven primary abilities of the theory.

**thwart** Prevention of a consummatory response; one of three is usually used: 1. Withholding the stimulus for the response when the stimulus usually appears as the consequence of previous responses. 2. Mechanically preventing the response, e.g. by making rigid the response key in the Skinner box. 3. By placing the animal in a conflict situation.

**thymergasia** (A. Meyer) Pathological affective and emotional processes.

**thymopathy** General term for abnormal instability of the emotions.

**thymus** An organ located in the anterior superior mediastinum. It develops until the second year of life and atrophies after the age of fourteen.

**thyroid dwarfism** See *cretinism.*

**thyroid gland** One of two endocrine glands at the base of the neck which secretes thyroxin, a hormone which influences growth and development.

**thyrotropic hormone** Also TSH. A hormone secreted by the pituitary gland which stimulates the activity of the thyroid gland.

**tic** 1. An uncontrolled nervous twitch which is of neurogenic or psychological origin. The psychogenic component is a hysterical conversion symptom, whose origin is defensive or reflexive movements. 2. Any compulsive habit.

**tic douloureux** Facial neuralgia characterized by excruciating sharp pain.

**time agnosia** Loss of knowledge about or loss of ability to use time.

**time and motion study** The observation and analysis of movements in a task with an emphasis on the amount of time required to perform the task.

**time-corrected P technique** P technique in which lead-and-lag (staggered) correlations are carried out to maximize the correlations among variables.

**time, d reaction** A form of a choice reaction time experiment; the subject withholds the response until he has identified the stimulus.

**time error** A tendency to incorrectly judge objects dependent on their position in time; e.g. of two identical tones sounded in succession, the first will generally be judged louder.

**time limit method** A procedure in which the test score is arrived at by the totaling of all items done correctly within a certain time limit, the time limit being established so as to preclude all the tasks being completed.

**time out (TO)** (operant conditioning) Time, usually in minutes, during which behavior characteristically does not occur. With pigeons, TO is usually arranged by turning off all lights in the apparatus. With the rat, TO is usually arranged by previously established discriminative stimulus. TO's are used as markers in a series of events, as probes, as a method to eliminate proprioceptive stimulus effects of earlier behaviors, and recently as a form of aversive stimulation.

**time perception**  See *perception, time.*

**time-sampling**  Continuous behavior observations recorded by pre-established categories, made in successive time intervals, each of which is treated as an independent observation unit; interval may be of any appropriate duration; behavior measure is given in terms of number or proportion of intervals containing a given category. See *point-sampling.*

**time score**  See *score, time.*

**timed tests**  See *tests, timed.*

**tinnitus**  A condition characterized by ringing in the ears and other noises in the head caused by disturbances in the receptor mechanisms.

**tissue**  Any organismic structure which is composed of similar elements or cells having a common function.

**Titchener, Edward Bradford (1867-1927)**  British-born psychologist and systematist whose principal contributions were made in the United States. Studied at Oxford, and at Leipzig with Wundt; became professor of experimental psychology at Cornell (1892) where he remained for his entire academic life. Representing the Wundtian tradition with faithful dedication to the pursuit of the pure scientific psychology of the generalized normal adult mind, he became the leading protagonist of structural psychology in opposition to functionalism. Never became part of American psychology. Author of numerous books and articles including *Experimental Psychology: A Manual of Laboratory Practice* (1901-1905); *A Textbook of Psychology* (1909-1910), and *Systematic Psychology: Prolegomena*, a posthumous work (1929).

**TO**  See *time out.*

**toilet training**  Teaching children the socialized manner, time and place of urination and defecation.

**tolerance of incongruity**  The ability to consider incompatible ideas without anxiety and the use of defenses.

**Tolman's purposive behaviorism**  (E. C. Tolman) A system of psychology, rooted in behaviorism, which is a stimulus-response theory interpolated by the interpretation of non-observable factors. Observable factors are the initiating causes of behavior and the behavior itself. The former consists of five independent variables: 1) the environmental stimuli (S); 2) physiological drive (P); 3) heredity (H); 4) previous training (T); and 5) maturity or age (A). Behavior is a function of (f) the five, B=f(S,P,H,T,A). Environmental stimuli and physiological drive are releasing variables; heredity, previous training and age are guiding variables.

The theory holds that the organism actively looks for significant stimuli to plan his "map" and is not the passive receptor of physically present stimuli; behavior is purposive and cognitive. Behavior is not a sequence of causes and effects but a chain of goals and actions leading to the goal object. Behavior is determined by the goal-directed perceptions of the totality of the situation, or the sign-gestalt expectations, a combination of motivating and perceptual elements.

**tonal bell**  (C. E. Ruckmick) A bell-shaped model illustrating the interrelations among the tonal attributes—tonal brightness, volume and tonality.

**tonal gap**  A range of pitches to which an individual is insensitive or partially insensitive although he is sensitive to tones on either side.

**tonal islands**  A region of an individual's normal acuity for pitch or frequency that is surrounded by areas of insensitivity to tones.

**tonal pencil**  A diagrammatic scheme representing the relation of pitch to volume.

**tonal scale**  The range of frequencies audible to the normal human ear—20 to 20,000 cycles per second.

**tonal volume**  A tone's extensity or space-filling attribute.

**tonality**  1. (experimental psychology) The attribute of a pitch by which a tone sounds more closely related to its octave than to the tone adjacent to it in the scale. 2. (music) The relationships among a scale's tones and chords to the keynote or tonic.

**tone**  1. A sound whose physical stimulus or source is a periodic vibration or sound wave in an elastic medium. 2. A unit of measure of the musical interval. 3. An instrument's characteristic timbre. 4. See *tonus.* 5. A quality of the general level of background emotion or feeling.

**tone, interruption**  A tone produced by regular and rapid successive interruptions of a continuous and uniform tone, the pitch of which corresponds to the frequency of the interruptions.

**tone, otogenic**  A perceived tone which is stimulated by activity within the auditory mechanism rather than by external sound waves.

**tone variator**  A device used in the production of pure tones of variable pitch.

**tongue apraxia**  Lack of purposeful tongue movements.

**tonic**  1. Pertaining to tonus. 2. Characterized by a continuous state of muscular tension or contraction.

**tonic contraction**  The contraction of the groups of muscle maintaining muscular tonus.

**tonic convulsion**  See *convulsion, tonic.*

**tonic epilepsy**  See *epilepsy, tonic.*

**tonic fits**  See *cerebellar fits.*

**tonic immobility**  1. Total immobility occurring in some animals as a reaction to certain stimuli; death feigning. 2. Slight contraction of large muscle groups sufficient to cause tautness but not movement.

**tonic reflex** A continuous or immediately renewed tonus which is maintained by some specified stimulus condition.

**tonicity** Normal state of tension of any organ or muscle.

**tonitrophobia** Morbid fear of thunder.

**tonoscope** A mechanism used in converting sound waves to light and, through the stroboscopic effect, measuring changes in pitch.

**tonus** Slight degree of contraction normally occurring in muscles not in active movement. In skeletal muscles due to low frequency efferent impulses; an inherent property of smooth muscles.

**tonus, induced** Muscle tone caused by movement in another part of the body.

**topalgia** Pain localized in a certain spot.

**topectomy** A modification of the lobotomy in which small incisions are made in the frontal lobe and thalamus in an attempt to alleviate psychotic symptoms.

**topographical theory** (S. Freud) Division of the human mind in three layers or strata—conscious, preconscious, and subconscious.

**topography, response** (experimental) Full quantitative specification of all relevant, physically measurable dimensions of a response.

**topological psychology** See *psychology, topological.*

**topology** (mathematics) A part of geometry which investigates properties of a figure which remain unchanged under continuous transformation. These properties are non-quantitative, non-metrical, thus neither magnitudes nor distances count.

**topophobia** Morbid fear of places, especially open spaces such as streets.

**torpor** Total inactivity.

**torticollis** Spasmodic contraction of the muscles of the neck. Also called wryneck.

**total correlation** See *correlation, total.*

**totem** (anthropology) An animal, plant, or inanimate object which is venerated as the group's symbol, the symbol of the group's protective deity or the symbol of the spirit kin of the group.

**totemism** The use of symbolic objects to assure a degree of psychological safety.

**touch spot** An area of skin surface exceedingly sensitive to tactile stimuli.

**touching** (sensitivity training) The use of physical contact among the members of a sensitivity group toward the end of breaking down defenses and barriers to interpersonal communication.

**toxemia** Blood poisoning.

**toxic-infectious psychosis** See *psychosis, toxic-infectious.*

**toxicity, corticosteroid** Large doses of corticosteroids may produce symptoms ranging from mild personality change to psychosis and coma, and in some cases, even death.

**toxicomania** Addiction; craving to be poisoned.

**toxicophobia** Morbid fear of being poisoned.

**toxin** Poisonous product of vegetable or animal cells; organic poison.

**toxoplasmosis, congenital** A disease caused by infection by a parasitic protozoa, called toxoplasma. When contracted by a pregnant woman, it may cause encephalomyelitis and severe mental deficiency.

**t-r systems** Systematic organizations of stimulus schedules; the temporal parameters of these two systems subsume all stimulus schedules within a single descriptive framework, the traditional "contingent schedules of reinforcement" appearing as special or limiting cases of the system's parameters.

**trace conditioned response** A response resulting from the presentation of a conditioned stimulus followed by a blank interval and then by reinforcement.

**trace, perseverative** (C. L. Hull) A neural impulse which continues with diminishing strength for a short period following the cessation of the firing of a neuron.

**tradition directed** (D. Riesman) A term describing a person whose behavior is dictated by rules, rituals and relationships derived from past generations and modified only slightly by later generations.

**train** (experimental) To subject an animal to a series of procedures such that the animal behaves in a desired fashion.

**training, spontaneity** (J. L. Moreno) Training in acting more naturally and spontaneously in real-life situations by practicing these behaviors in a supporting environment.

**trait** 1. An inherited or acquired characteristic which is consistent, persistent and stable. 2. (G. W. Allport) A combination of motives and habits; it is a neuropsychic system that determines to a great extent which stimuli will be perceived (selective perception) and what kind of response will be given (selective action). Each individual's traits determine his behavior in a unique way.

**trait dissection theory of environmental and genetic influence** The model which does not divide a factorial source trait into genetic and threptic variance components but supposes that heredity and environment yield discernibly different factor trait patterns. These may appear as "eidolons," i.e. cooperative factor patterns not far from being mutual images.

**trait organization** The dynamic and cause and effect interrelationships among the various traits which compose the individual's personality.

**trait profile** A chart or diagram which depicts the relative standings of a number of traits as measured by tests or other instruments.

**trait, recessive** A genetically controlled trait which remains latent or subordinate to a dominant trait except in those cases in which both members of the gene pair are recessive.

**trait, unique** 1. A personality trait possessed by an individual, and not found exactly the same in other people. 2. (statistics) A trait which shows a zero correlation when compared to other traits being measured.

**trait variability** The spread, divergence or scatter exhibited by the individual on various trait measures.

**trait view theory** (R. B. Cattell) The theory that the distortion in the estimation of a trait level, either in another (rating) or in oneself (questionnaire response) is a piece of behavior to be predicted like any other from the individual's trait endowment and a behavioral equation specific to the rating or test-taking situation. This model enables one to estimate the true trait levels from the given rating or test levels.

**trance** 1. A sleeplike state which is characterized by a reduced sensitivity to stimuli and a loss or alteration of knowledge of what is happening. 2. The hypnotic state.

**tranquilizer** Any drug which has a sedative effect without inducing sleep.

**tranquilizing treatments** A therapeutic treatment consisting of the administration of drugs to calm or soothe patients.

**transaction** A psychological event or behavior in which all parts of the unit are understood through their interaction with the physical and social environment.

**transactional analysis** See *analysis, transactional.*

**transactional theory of perception** (A. Ames) A complex theory holding that our fundamental perceptions are learned reactions based on our interactions and transactions with the environment. On the basis of past experience, the individual builds up expectancies of what will be perceived and the individual brings them to new experiences and will make perceptions of those experiences conform to the expectancies.

**transcendent function** (C. G. Jung) A unifying mechanism within a person which aims to unite all of the opposing, divergent trends within the personality to form a perfect whole, if not at a conscious level, then at an unconscious one.

**transection** Section or cutting across the long axis of, e.g. a fiber, an axon, or the spinal cord.

**transfer** 1. The effect of either increasing or decreasing the strength of a response complex as a consequence of performing some other response. 2. The effect of a set of responses to one set of stimuli when the same set of responses are made to a different set of stimuli.

**transfer of training** (educational psychology) A theory which maintains that a proficiency acquired in a branch of knowledge or a skill helps in the acquisition of knowledge or skill in another field.

**transfer RNA** Ten to twenty percent of the ribonucleic acid which combined with certain amino acids complements the messenger ribonucleic acid during protein synthesis.

**transferability coefficient** (R. B. Cattell) A correlation showing how much a test measures with one kind of subject the same thing that it measures with other kinds of subjects.

**transference** (psychoanalysis) The patient transfers his past emotional attachments to the psychoanalyst in accordance with the repetition compulsion principle. The analyst is a substitute for the parental figure. Transference may be either negative or positive. In positive transference the patient loves the analyst and wishes to obtain love and emotional satisfaction from him. In negative transference the patient views the analyst as an unfair, unloving, rejecting parental figure and accuses him of all his parents' past injustices. Interpretations of transference make the patient aware of the fact that his infatuation with the analyst is not related to the analyst as a person but is simply a reflection of previous emotional entanglements. Interpretation is necessary for modification of behavior. In the psychoanalytic situation, regression to childhood is necessary for the resolution of conflicts rooted in the past.

**transference, negative** Reliving of hostile feelings toward parents or parental substitute in psychotherapeutic setting and experiencing hostility toward the psychologist or psychoanalyst.

**transference neurosis** Reenacting of the infantile roots of the neurotic conflict in psychoanalytic treatment with the psychoanalyst representing the parental figure.

**transference, positive** See *transference.*

**transference resistance** See *resistance, transference.*

**transformation** 1. (logic) Substitution of a symbol or a proposition by another performed in accordance with the rules of formal logic. 2. (mathematics) A change in mathematical formula without changing the content or the value, performed through operations accepted in a particular branch of mathematics, e.g. $a + b$ can be transformed into $b + a$.

**transformation stage** (C. G. Jung) The fourth stage of analytical psychotherapy in which the patient comes to discover and develop his unique and individual personality pattern.

**transformations, informational** (J. P. Guilford) Changes of various kinds—redefinitions, shifts, revisions, or other modifications—in existing items of information or in their roles.

**transformism** 1. A theory of transformation. 2. (biology) Theory of evolution.

**transitionism** (B. B. Wolman) The proposition that mental phenomena should be explained as a derivative and a continuation of somatic processes.

translocation The transfer of a piece of one chromosome to a non-homologous chromosome, as occurs, for example, in a variant of Down's syndrome of mongolism, where a translocation occurs between a chromosome 21 and one of the D group, such as chromosome number 15. If two non-homologous chromosomes exchange places, the translocation is reciprocal.

transmission 1. Transferring or sending over of objects, symbols and words in communication. 2. (genetics) Carrying of genetic traits from one generation to another. 3. (neurology) Firing of one neuron by another. 4. (medicine) Communicating a disease; contagion. 5. (communication theory) Sending a message. 6. (anthropology and sociology) Carrying over of cultural norms and values.

transmission unit A logarithmic unit of sound intensity, such as decibel.

transmittance Percentage of light energy transmitted through a medium.

transmitter 1. (communication theory) The means by which a message is encoded and begun on its way through a channel. 2. Any device for relaying a message in the form of a signal to a receiver.

transmutation of measures The alteration of a set of measures into an equivalent system.

transmuted score See score, transmuted.

transorbital lobotomy See lobotomy, transorbital.

transposition 1. A change or interchange in position of two or more elements in a system. 2. (music) The change of a musical composition from one key to another. 3. The reaction to the relationships among stimuli rather than to the absolutes of the stimuli, e.g. the organism's learning that to be rewarded he must go to the smaller of two circles and transferring the learning to a situation in which the originally smaller circle is now the larger and reward requires going to the now smaller circle.

transtype variables Variables which can be measured upon members of many different types and species, and thus lead to dimensions on which all types can be placed.

transvaluation of psychic values A significant shift in the value system and the adoption of a new, if not opposite, one.

transverse 1. Lying or going across. 2. Lying at right angles to the body's longitudinal axis of the body.

transvestism See transvestitism.

transvestite 1. One who dresses in clothes of the opposite sex or has strong desire to do so. 2. One who experiences sexual sensation when wearing clothes of the opposite sex.

transvestitism Strong desire to dress in the clothes customarily associated with the opposite sex. 2. Sensation of sexual excitement when wearing clothes of the opposite sex.

tranylcypromine An antidepressant drug of the monoamine oxidase inhibitor group prescribed in the treatment of depressive psychosis.

trapezoid body A strand of fibers located in the pons arising from the cells of the cochlear nucleus.

trauma 1. A physical injury or wound or an experience which inflicts injury on the organism. 2. Psychological damage or an experience inflicting psychological damage.

traumatic neurosis See neurosis, traumatic.

traumatophilia Desire to be hurt; accident proneness.

traumatophilic diathesis See diathesis, traumatophilic.

traumatophobia Morbid fear of being hurt.

treatment, ambulatory Treatment of noninstitutionalized patients; outpatient treatment.

treatment, residential Psychotherapeutic treatment offered in an institutional setting which involves a total program for supporting the child's ego strengths, reinforcing his ego weaknesses, and providing him with adults and peers who will help him to develop more effective modes of interaction.

treatment, variable An experimental or independent variable.

trembling abasia See abasia.

tremograph A device used in the measurement of the amount of involuntary fine movement made by a member of the body or by the whole body.

tremophobia Morbid fear of trembling.

tremor Repeated spastic motions; trembling.

trend analysis (statistics) The analysis of a series of measurements of a variable, taken at different points of time, to discover if there is a direction of change.

trend, neurotic (K. Horney) The group of tendencies in an individual developed during childhood which strive to attain maximum security, thus reducing basic anxiety. Horney distinguished three trends: toward people, away from people, and against people.

trephine 1. A small drill, generally hollow inside, used to cut a hole or plug in the skull. 2. To cut a hole, or plug, in the skull.

treppe The tendency for a muscle tissue contraction to become progressively stronger in response to a stimulus of constant intensity.

trial A single opportunity in which a specific response is elicited or can occur.

trial and error learning See learning, trial and error.

trial and error, vicarious (experimental) Movement of the head of an animal looking at alternative pathways in a maze or at other possible avenues.

tribade A woman with an exceedingly large clitoris who plays the male role in lesbian relations.

**trichlorethylene poisoning** See *poisoning, trichlorethylene.*

**trichotillomania** A compulsion to pull one's own hair.

**trichromatic theory** A theory on color vision which is based upon the facts of color mixture.

**tricyclic compounds** Antidepressant drugs used which appear to act by altering cellular permeability, thereby decreasing the storage or degradation of norepinephrine.

**tridimensional theory of feeling** (W. Wundt) The position that affect or feeling has three dimensions: pleasantness-unpleasantness; excitement-quiescence; tension-relaxation.

**trigeminal nerve** See *nerve, trigeminal.*

**trigeminal nucleus** A bunch of nerve cells located in the pons and medulla giving rise to the trigeminal nerve.

**triorthocresyl phosphate poisoning** See *poisoning, triorthocresyl phosphate.*

**triple-X syndrome** An anomaly of the sex-chromosome in which the patient is anatomically female but has the sex-chromosome complement XXX. The syndrome is often associated with mental retardation.

**trireceptor theory** A theory which holds that there are three types of receptors in the eye, corresponding to the three color primaries of trichromatic theory.

**triskaidekaphobia** A morbid fear of the number 13.

**trisomy** The state of having one extra chromosome per cell, so that there are three representatives per cell of that chromosome instead of the usual diploid number. In Down's syndrome or mongolism there is a trisomy of the twenty-first chromosome. Severe mental retardation, deformities of mouth and eyes, etc. are caused by 13 chromosome trisomy. Physical and mental defects are caused by trisomy of the 18 chromosome.

**tristimulus value** The hue of a sample color stated in the amounts of the three primaries needed to create it.

**tritanopia** A rare type of partial color blindness characterized by the confusion of reddish blue and greenish yellow stimuli.

**troland** A measure of retinal illuminance which corrects for the energy lost in the eye.

**tropism** The involuntary movement of an organism involving change in orientation or growth either toward (positive tropism) or away (negative tropism) from a source of stimulation. See *taxis.*

**tropotaxis** A taxis in which the sense receptors are bilaterally symmetrical enabling simultaneous comparisons of stimulation intensity. Thus the animal can orient to a stimulus source without lateral swings or wavy movements necessary in klinotaxis.

**truancy** Absence from school or home without permission usually due to psychological problems involved in each situation.

**true-false test** See *test, true-false.*

**truism** A statement of the obvious.

**truncated distribution** See *distribution, truncated.*

**truth serum** The use of narcotics such as sodium amythal or sodium pentothal injected intravenously for extracting confessions from subjects.

**TSH** See *thyrotropic hormone.*

**TU** See *transmission unit.*

**tube feeding** Forcefeeding patients who refuse to eat by means of a nasal catheter that terminates in the stomach.

**tubectomy** Excision of the uterine tube.

**tube feeding** Forcefeeding patients who refuse to eat by means of a nasal catheter that terminates in the stomach.

**tuberculomania** A form of hypochondriasis; the morbid belief that one has tuberculosis.

**tuberous sclerosis** See *epiloia.*

**tumescence** Swelling of tissue, especially central tissue.

**tumor, intracranial** A localized intracranial lesion of neoplastic or chronic inflammatory origin, which causes a rise in intracranial pressure. Symptoms may include headache, vomiting, papilledema, aphasia, convulsions, coma, and progressive confusion and disorientation.

**tune** 1. The adjustment of the frequency of mechanical device's sounding body so that it emits a tone of some required pitch. 2. A series of musical notes making a melody.

**tuning fork** A two-toned device made of highly tempered metal which when struck emits a perceptually pure tone of some pitch.

**tunnel vision** Restriction of vision to the central area of the retina with no peripheral vision.

**Turner's syndrome** (H. H. Turner) The affected individuals are anatomically females, but have a deficiency in ovarian tissue and concomitant sexual infantilism. Chromosome complement is XO. Mental retardation is often present.

**twilight vision** The type of vision occurring under conditions of minimal illumination.

**twin** One of two offspring gestated simultaneously and born at the same birth.

**twinned** To be born as a twin.

**twinning** Refers to giving birth to or being a twin.

**twins, enzygotic** See *twins, identical.*

**twins, fraternal** Twins which develop from two separate ova fertilized at the same time; can be of the same or of a different sex since they have different genetic structures.

**twins, identical** Twins which develop from a single fertilized ovum in the same chorionic sac and consequently, of the same sex and the same genetic structure.

**twins, monochorionic** See *twins, identical*.

**twins, monovular** See *twins, identical*.

**twins, monozygotic** See *twins, identical*.

**twins, Siamese** Monozygotic twins joined together at birth over some portion of their bodies due to incomplete splitting of the egg during pre-natal development.

**twitch** A sudden localized convulsive muscle contraction.

**twitch, isometric** A slight muscular contraction occurring as a response to a new stimulus without significant shortening of the muscle.

**Twitchell-Allen Three-Dimensional Personality Test** See *test, Twitchell-Allen Three-Dimensional Personality*.

**two-aspect theory** A theory of the mind-body problem in which mind is body seen from one viewpoint and body is mind seen from another.

**two-factor theory** (O. H. Mowrer) First introduced about 1950 to distinguish between conditioning (Pavlov) and habit formation (Thorndike, Hull). Later (circa 1960) it proved possible to derive the latter from the former; and the two factors which have since been emphasized are positive (rewarding) reinforcement and negative (punishing reinforcement).

**two factor theory of avoidance conditioning** A theory which explains the avoidance of an aversive stimulus. When the organism avoids the stimulus, it is reinforced by the non-occurrence of an event. According to the theory, the situation in which the aversive stimulus initially occurred is classically conditioned to the aversive stimulus. The situation becomes, through classical conditioning, a conditioned aversive stimulus. The escape from this conditioned stimulus is reinforcing. The escape is acquired by instrumental conditioning. Thus avoidance conditioning becomes a special case of escape conditioning and incorporates both classical and instrumental conditioning.

**two point threshold** The minimum distance separating two pointed objects at which, when applied to the skin, they can be perceived as two separate objects.

**two-tailed test** See *test, two-tailed*.

**two-way table** See *scatter diagram*.

**Tyler, Leona E. (1906- )** American psychologist. Author of books on individual differences, tests and measurements, counseling, developmental, and clinical psychology. President of American Psychological Association, 1972-73. Research and theoretical contributions on development of interests and organized choices.

**tympanic membrane** The eardrum.

**type** 1. A category or class of people or things distinguished by the possession of some common characteristic and grouped together on that basis. 2. A person who serves as an ideal example of a group due to possessing fully the characteristics which define that group and distinguish it from others. 3. Pattern of characteristics according to which people are categorized. 4. The end portions of a continuous variable as in an aggressive type or tall type.

**type, aesthetic** (E. Spranger) Personality type characterized by individualism and interest in universal harmony, beauty and gracefulness.

**type, affective reaction** A term used to describe any behavior disorder in which the main symptoms are of an affective or emotional nature. See *affective disorders*.

**type, apoplectic** (Hippocrates) Body type characterized by a thickset, rounded physique.

**type, asthenic** (E. Kretschmer) Body type associated with schizothymic temperament.

**type, athletic** (E. Kretschmer) Body type characterized by well-proportioned body, well-developed muscular-skeletal structure, and physical strength and prowess associated with the schizothymic temperament.

**type, body** Any classificatory scheme of individuals which uses macroscopic anatomical characteristics as guidelines, usually with the assumption that certain psychological characteristics are associated with certain body types.

**type, cerebral** (L. Rostan and C. Sigaud) Constitutional type distinguished by a predominance of brain and nervous system over body.

**type, cerebrotonic** (W. H. Sheldon) Basic temperament component characterized by a rigidity in posture and in movement, inhibition in social situations, self-worry and hypersensitivity, associated with the ectomorphic body type.

**type, choleric** (Hippocrates) Constitutional type characterized by an abundance of yellow bile in the body which was thought to result in an irritable personality type.

**type, cyclothymic** (E. Kretschmer) One of two basic personality types which is primarily associated with the pyknic body-type in Kretschmer's constitutional system. Should a cyclothymic ever become psychotic, his psychosis will be manic-depressive.

**type, dysplastic** (E. Kretschmer) Body type characterized by deviant features, uneven combination of elements, and structure too irregular to be classified in any of the three basic categories of asthenic, athletic or pyknic; most often associated with schizothymic temperament.

**type, economic** (E. Spranger) The economic personality type is characterized by concern about practical matters, self-preservation and economic security. Material values and success are primary goals.

**type, ectomorphic**  1. Somatotype characterized by fragile physique, predominance of linearity, and relatively great surface area as compared to body mass. 2. (W. H. Sheldon) Body type correlated with the cerebrotonic temperament.

**type, endomorphic**  1. Somatotype characterized by a predominance of structures developed from the internal organs on the endodermal embryonic layer and by soft and round body features. 2. (W. H. Sheldon) Body type correlated with the viscerotonic temperament.

**type, erotic**  (S. Freud) The main interest of the erotic type is loving and even more, being loved. Should such a normal type deteriorate, he will become a hysteric.

**type, esthetic**  See *type, aesthetic.*

**type, extraverted**  (C. G. Jung) Personality type characterized by movement of the libido outwards toward the world resulting in all attitudes, values, and interests being directed toward the physical and social environment or an object-directed reference point.

**type, fallacy**  The false assumption that the extremes along a continuum are distinct groups discontinuous from the intermediate range of the continuum rather than an extension of it.

**type, feeling**  (C. G. Jung) Personality type characterized by the dominance in the conscious of the feeling function.

**type, hyperinstrumental**  (B. B. Wolman) A narcissistic type of mental disorder characterized by tendencies to use others, which at the neurosis level is seen as anxiety and depression reactions, and at the psychosis level manifests itself as psychotic psychopathy and so-called "moral insanity."

**type, hypervectorial**  (B. B. Wolman) A type of mental disorder developed in an over-demanding home environment which manifests itself on the neurotic level as obsessive, phobic, or neurasthenic reactions and at the psychotic level becomes schizophrenia called by Wolman *vectoriasis praecox.*

**type, hypoaffective**  (N. Pende) The constitutional type characterized by deficient emotional reactivity.

**type, introverted**  (C. G. Jung) Personality type characterized by a dominance of subjective perception and cognition resulting in a self-centered orientation and involvement with one's own inner world.

**type, intuitive**  (C. G. Jung) Personality type characterized by the dominance in the conscious of the feeling function, which is an irrational process based on the immediate perception of relationships.

**type, irrational**  (C. G. Jung) Personality type characterized by a dominance of either the sensation or intuition functions which are associated with the

intensity of perceptions rather than rational judgments.

**type, learning**  See *learning type.*

**type, melancholic**  (Hippocrates) A constitutional body type characterized by an abundance of black bile in the body which was thought to result in a personality type characterized by sadness.

**type, mesomorphic**  1. Somatotype characterized by a predominance of structures developed from the bone, muscle and connective tissue, the mesodermal embryonic layer. 2. (W. H. Sheldon) Body type correlated with the temperament component of somatotonia. 3. (H. J. Eysenck) A person whose body-build index falls within one standard deviation of the mean.

**type, narcissistic**  (S. Freud) The main interest is self-preservation with little if any concern for other people, and very weak if any superego.

**type, obsessional**  (S. Freud) The main characteristic of the obsessional type is his very strong dictatorial superego, conscience and conservatism. This type may develop the neurotic pattern of obsessive-compulsive neurosis.

**type, oral-aggressive**  (psychoanalysis) Personality type characterized by hostile, critical, negativistic, and overdemanding attitude.

**type, oral passive**  (psychoanalysis) Personality type characterized by passivity, overdependence, inability to accept frustrations and disappointments, day dreaming about personal desires and the feeling that the world owes him protection and concern.

**type, personality**  See *personality types.*

**type, phlegmatic**  (Hippocrates) Constitutional type characterized by an abundance of "phlegm" in the body which was thought to result in an apathetic personality type.

**type, phtisic**  (Hippocrates) Slender, flat-chested body build believed to prove a tendency to develop tuberculosis. Analogous to Kretschmer's asthenic type.

**type, power politics**  (E. Spranger) Personality type characterized by the desire to control people and perception of the world in terms of power, of overcoming obstacles and of domination, and an interest in politics and methods of influencing and ruling.

**type, pyknic**  (E. Kretschmer) Body type characterized by short limbs, thick neck, and rounded or fat body contour, associated with the cyclothymic temperament.

**type R conditioning**  See *conditioning, instrumental.*

**type, rational**  (C. G. Jung) Personality type characterized by a dominance in the conscious of either the thinking or feeling functions which are associated with reasoning and judgments.

**type reaction**  See *reaction, type.*

**type, religious** (E. Spranger) Personality type characterized by a mystical outlook and the pursuit of unity between man and universe. Contemplation and a search for eternal unity are primary goals.

**type S conditioning** See *conditioning, Pavlovian.*

**type, sanguine** (Hippocrates) A personality type characterized by warmth, ardor, and/or optimism and thought to be the result of the influence of blood.

**type, schizothymic** (E. Kretschmer) One of two basic personality temperament's in Kretschmer's constitutional system. This temperamental type is associated primarily with the asthenic and athletic body-type. Should a schizothymic ever be psychotic, he will be a schizophrenic.

**type, sensation** (C. G. Jung) Personality type characterized by the dominance in the conscious of the sensation function, which is an irrational process associated with intensity of perceptions and a concern for the reaction of the individual to the outer world.

**type, sociable, or social** (E. Spranger) Personality type characterized by friendliness, congeniality, and consideration and compassion for others. The desire to help people is a primary goal.

**type T** (E. Jaensch) A personality type prone to eidetic imagery.

**type, theoretical** (E. Spranger) The theoretical personality type is characterized by an inquisitive intellectual approach to life which is systematic and rational and which attempts to see the world as a systematic logically ordered unity.

**type, thinking** (C. G. Jung) Personality type characterized by the dominance in the conscious of the thinking function which is a rational process of reasoning, judgment and interpretation of the perceived objects and relationships.

**type, visual** Person who thinks in visual terms and uses visual imagery predominantly.

**typology** 1. The study of types. 2. A particular system used in the classification of individuals into types.

**tyrosinosis** An overflow aminoaciduria disease with a probable deficiency of p-hydroxyphenylpurivic acid oxidase. In the acute variety the patient experiences in the first few months of life vomiting, diarrhea, enlarging abdomen, and failure to thrive, with death usually occurring within a period of a few months. The chronic type is similar with the onset later in life, with death usually occurring in the first decade of life. The main clinical features are progressive hepatic and renal failure, failure to thrive, and mild mental retardation.

# U

U fibers  Short fibers in the cerebral cortex which interconnect adjacent cortical gyri.

U-hypothesis  (H. Helson) In most organic responses there is a region of optimal functioning wherein errors are minimal and beyond (above and below) which errors rapidly increase. Even classical curves of visual and auditory sensitivity can be regarded as inverted U-functions since they exhibit maximal regions of sensitivity and brightness as a function of wave length, loudness as a function of frequency, etc.

U test  See *test, U*.

ucs  (psychoanalysis) Abbreviation for unconscious.

ulcer, duodenal  See *ulcer, peptic*.

ulcer, peptic  Ulcer due to an inordinate secretion of gastric juices affecting the gastric or duodenal mucosa or the mucosa of the stomach and jejunum of physical or psychological origin. Psychogenic causes involve frustrated wishes for dependency which are transformed regressively into wishes to be fed.

ulcerative colitis  See *colitis, ulcerative*.

ulnar nerve  An afferent sensory nerve found in the hand.

umbilical cord  Cord which connects the navel of a fetus to the placenta of the mother.

unbiased estimate  See *estimate, unbiased*.

uncertainty interval  See *interval of uncertainty*.

unconditioned reflex  See *reflex, unconditioned*.

unconditioned response  See *response, unconditioned*.

unconditioned stimulus  See *stimulus, unconditioned*.

unconscious  1. (philosophy) Several philosophers and scientists, among them Galen, Plotinus, St. Augustine, St. Thomas Aquinas, Montaigne, and Descartes, were aware of unconscious processes.

Paracelsus (1493-1541) implies the influence of ideas people are unaware of. Several authors described their dreams, analyzed the irrational elements in their behavior, and described the surprising motives they were driven by without being aware of them. The idea of unconscious has become a topic of general interest when F. A. Mesmer (1733-1815) claimed to be able to cure people by "magnetic" processes; the hypnotic states, induced by Mesmer, were obviously unconscious. In 1890 G. H. Schubert published a book on "Dream Symbolism." A. Schopenhauer (1788-1860) explained the origins of mental illness by repression of ideas which hurt one's interests and conscious wishes. J. F. Herbart (1716-1841) presented mental life as a struggle of ideas for a place in human consciousness; the repressed ideas continue struggling to attain the conscious surface.

The term unconscious was probably used in print for the first time in 1860 by the French writer H. I. Amiel who wrote about *La Vie Inconsciente* (the unconscious life). This term appeared in 1878 in the dictionary of the French Academy and in 1868 E. von Hartmann published a comprehensive work *The Philosophy of Unconscious*. **2.** (psychoanalysis) In years 1872-1880 there appeared several works dealing with the various aspects of unconscious and the works of Charcot, Bernheim, Liebeault and Janet introduced the concepts of unconscious motivation to psychiatry and psychology. S. Freud developed the concept of unconscious as a part of an overall "topographic" description of "mental layers" or "provinces." The human mind is divided into what one is aware of, i.e. his conscious or consciousness and what he is unaware of, or his unconscious. The unconscious is divided into preconscious and unconscious proper. The preconscious includes all that one has in his mind but not on his mind at a particular moment.

The mind of a newborn child is totally unconscious and only a part of it ever becomes preconscious and conscious. The unconscious processes are "primary processes;" and they are totally irrational, inaccessible to the conscious mind. Their existence can be inferred from dreams, amnesias, slips of the tongue, and symptom formation. Some unconscious wishes are thrown back into the unconscious even before the individual becomes clearly aware of them; such a rejection of the unconscious wishes and impulses is called repression.

**unconscious, collective** (C. Jung) The part of the unconscious composed of acquired traits and cultural patterns transmitted by heredity that is the foundation of the whole personality structure. It is universal, all men being essentially the same, is almost totally divorced from anything personal or individual, and is continuously accumulating memory traces as a result of man's repeated experiences over generations. Archetypes are its structural components.

**unconscious memory** See *memory, unconscious.*

**unconscious, personal** (C. G. Jung) The surface layer of the unconscious, consisting of subliminal perceptions, repressed, suppressed, forgotten and/or ignored experiences, and fantasies and dreams of a personal nature, all of which can be accessible to consciousness.

**unconscious process** See *processes, unconscious.*

**unconscious sadism** See *sadism, unconscious.*

**underachiever** A person who does not perform as well as would be expected from known characteristics or abilities, particularly from measures of intellectual aptitude.

**understanding need** See *need, understanding.*

**undifferentiated areas** (K. Lewin) The life space of an individual which has not been structured and differentiated through learning and perception into inner and outer regions of personality. The life space of a neonate is an undifferentiated field or area.

**undoing** (psychoanalysis) The mechanism of undoing represents a far-reaching loss of contact with reality. Undoing is a fallacious belief that one can undo or nullify previous actions that make one feel guilty. A strong ego admits past blunders and a mature individual assumes responsibility for his behavior. A weak ego fears the superego's reproaches and acts in accordance with a belief that wishing to nullify past deeds can effect such nullification. The mechanism of undoing is a patent distortion of truth; it is a kind of magic. Freud pictured the ego as trying to "blow away" not only the consequences of an event, but the fact that the event itself ever took place.

**unequivocal** Not ambiguous; clear; open to only one interpretation.

**unfinished task** See *Zeigarnik effect.*

**Ungestalt** (Gestalt) Not a Gestalt; that which is not united or an integrated whole.

**ungrouped scores** See *scores, ungrouped.*

**unidextrality** The use of one hand or side of the body rather than the other.

**unidimensional** Possessing only one direction.

**unimodal** A frequency distribution curve having only one mode or peak.

**unintegrated motivation component** (R. B. Cattell) That component in a person's motivation for a given course of action which has poor reality contact and manifests itself mainly through "I wish" expressions.

**uniocular** One-eyed; pertaining to only one eye.

**unipolar** 1. Having only one pole. 2. Referring to variables, tests, or scales which are meaningful at one extreme but not at the other.

**unique factor** See *factor, unique.*

**unique trait** A set of characteristics patterned idiosyncratically in an individual, so that other individuals cannot meaningfully be given scores on this trait. Differences between individuals on unique traits tend to be qualitative.

**unitas multiplex** (W. Stern) A unity composed of elements which contains more than mere empirical unity. The personality is a unitas multiplex because it is a product of the converging influences of hereditary and environmental factors.

**units, informational** (J. P. Guilford) Relatively segregated or circumscribed items of information having "thing" character. May be close to Gestalt psychology's "figure on a ground."

**universal set (S)** A set which includes all objects to be considered in any particular discussion.

**universe, statistical** See *statistical universe.*

**unreality feeling** See *depersonalization.*

**uraniscolalia** Speech defect caused by cleft palate.

**Urban's tables** The tables of the Müller-Urban weights.

**urethra** The organ which conducts urine from the bladder.

**urethral character** See *character, urethral.*

**urethral phase** (S. Freud) The developmental stage between anal and phallic stages. Urethral eroticism is basically autoerotic; it may, however, turn toward others with fantasies about urinating on them or being urinated on. The training in bladder control leads to conflicts with parents, and bedwetting children tend to become over-ambitious, as if trying to re-establish their self-esteem.

**urolagnia** An unusual preoccupation with urine because pleasure is derived from this source.

**US** Unconditioned stimulus.

**use, law of** See *law of use.*

**utilitarianism** An ethical philosophical, social and economic theory which sets practical achievements and well-being of people as the supreme value. The greatest possible happiness of the greatest number of people is believed to be the supreme moral value.

**utility index** (R. B. Cattell) A validity coefficient calculated for a prediction made one year from the time of testing and with known intervening events.

**utricle** An expansion in the vestibule of the inner ear associated with the balance receptors in the semicircular canals.

**uvula** Lump of tissue hanging from the soft palate.

# V

**V** **1.** A verbal comprehension factor. **2.** (Rorschach) Referring directly to the vista response. **3.** Referring to volume. **4.** (C. L. Hull) The magnitude of the intensity of a potential reaction.

**V factor** A verbal comprehension factor.

**V test** (statistics) A modification of the t test used when the samples are large and the variance is unequal.

**vaccinophobia** A morbid fear of receiving vaccinations.

**vacuum activity** (etiology) The occurrence of a fixed action pattern in the apparent absence of its usual releaser. It is hypothesized that this occurs because of a high drive state.

**vaginal plexus** Vaginal nerve network.

**vaginism; vaginismus** A symptom of frigidity; a painful contraction of vaginal muscles which prevents sexual intercourse.

**vagotomy** The cutting of the vagus nerve.

**vagotonia** A condition due to the overactivity of the vagus nerve.

**vagus nerve** See *nerve, vagus.*

**valence** **1.** (E. C. Tolman) Objects that attract an organism have a positive valence, those that repel have a negative valence. Thus valence is a determinant of actions leading toward or away from an object-goal. **2.** (K. Lewin) The concept of valence corresponds to a field force which has the structure of a positive central field; that is all forces in this field are directed toward the attracting-positive valence or away from negative-repulsive valence.

**validation** **1.** The process in which the degree of validity of a measuring instrument is determined. **2.** The process of establishing the objective proof of a proposition, measuring instrument, etc.

**validation, consensual** (H. S. Sullivan) A technique developed in the syntaxic stage of checking one's perceptions against the perceptions of others which correspond to reality. It is similar to S. Freud's reality testing.

**validation, internal** A means of improving the validity of a measuring device by consisting of checking for high correlations between the scores on various subitems of the test and the total score.

**validity** A test's ability to predict performances other than performance on itself, that is, a test's correlation with a factor, life-situation performance, clinical category placement, etc. There are several varieties of validity.

**validity, concurrent** The measure of the extent to which a test measures what it is supposed to measure by correlating the results of the tests with the results of the person's performance or a task which the test presumably assesses. The two correlated measures must be taken at the same time with no time lapse.

**validity, content** A measure of how well items of a test correspond to the behavior which the test attempts to assess or predict.

**validity criterion** An independent external measure of what a test is devised to measure.

**validity, ecological** (E. Brunswik) An established relationship within a set of environmental circumstances between a proximal stimulus and a distal stimulus, such that the presence or occurrence of the proximal stimulus increases the probability that the distal stimulus is also operative and vice versa.

**validity, factorial** (psychometrics) Validity of a test measured by correlation of the test with a factor derived by factor analysis.

**validity, item** The extent to which a test item measures what it is intended to measure.

**validity, predictive** See *predictive validity.*

**validity, sampling** See *sampling, validity.*

**valium** Common name for diazepam, a tranquilizing drug.

**value** **1.** The degree of worth or excellence assigned to or derived from an object. **2.** A quantitative score or measure. **3.** (mathematics) The magnitude of something, or the number or symbol representing the magnitude. **4.** An abstract concept which determines for a person or some social group the relative worth of various goals or ends. **5.** The location of some visual datum on the scale of white to black. **6.** (economics) The determination of what an object will bring in exchange on the market.

**value, absolute** The mathematical value of a number without regard to its positive or negative sign.

**value, difficulty** Measure of the discriminating power of a test item in terms of the percent of a specified group who answer the item correctly.

**value judgment** A reaction to persons, objects, places, events, etc. on the part of an individual in terms implying or employing an assessment of their worth in relation to others rather than in terms of their objective characteristics.

**value system** A set of values adopted by an individual or society, governing the behavior of the individual or the members of the society, often without the conscious awareness of the individual or the members of the society.

**van Bogaert-Nyssen disease** (L. van Bogaert and R. Nyssen) Sclerosis and a degenerative disease of the nervous system. Appears late in life.

**variability** **1.** The degree to which scores in a set differ from each other or from their central tendency. The most common measures are: the range, which is the distance from the highest to the lowest score in a distribution; the average deviation (*AD*), or the average of the differences from the mean of each value in a series,

$$AD = \frac{\Sigma \mid X - \bar{X} \mid}{N}$$

and finally the standard deviation (*S²*) which is an index of the variability of a whole distribution:

$$S^2 = \frac{\Sigma (X - \bar{X})^2}{N-1}$$

**2.** The ability or capacity of an individual or a species to change.

**variability coefficient** See *coefficient, variation.*

**variability, sampling** See *sampling variability.*

**variable** **1.** A factor the quantity of which can be increased or decreased either in discrete steps or along some continuum without any other concomitant change in that factor. **2.** Anything that can change or take on different characteristics appropriate to specified conditions.

**variable, autochthonous** Factors within a system that change relatively independently of forces outside the system. In psychology, common examples are metabolic changes, appetites such as hunger, thirst, and sex, and neural noise from spontaneous neural discharge.

**variable, continuous** A variable, the possible values of which are on a continuum. When between any two values of a variable it is possible to find an intermediate value, the variable is called continuous.

**variable, controlled** See *variable, independent.*

**variable, criterion** A variable the value of which serves as a standard to compare results of other variables.

**variable, dependent** A parameter, usually in an experimental setting, whose values are hypothesized to change as a consequence of changes in the independent variable, i.e. the parameter directly manipulated by the experimenter.

**variable, discontinuous** See *variable, discrete.*

**variable, discrete** A variable, the possible values of which do not form a continuum but a certain scale in which there are no intermediate values between two given values. Thus, there are definite, discrete, and abrupt changes in quantity on this scale.

**variable, distal** (E. Brunswik) A variable which does not directly effect a receptor but is mediated by the action of a proximal variable.

**variable error** See *error, chance.*

**variable, experimental** The independent variable in an experiment which is systematically manipulated in order to observe and investigate its influence on other dependent variables.

**variable, hypothetical process** A class of hypothetical constructs. It is a process hypothesized to occur on the basis of observed effects. The process is also hypothesized to have properties or effects other than those that lead to its postulation.

**variable, hypothetical state** (K. W. Spence) Hypothetical relatively permanent condition or state of an organism which is assumed to result from past interactions with the environment. The state variables are usually specific to fairly circumscribed sets of stimuli and seldom to the total state of the organism.

**variable, independent** **1.** A variable that can be observed and assessed as a determinant of behavior. **2.** The variable that is altered independently of any other variable, usually by the experimenter. **3.** (E. C. Tolman) The initial causes of behavior of which there are six: a) the environmental stimulus, b) physiological drive, c) heredity, d) previous training, e) maturity or age, f) some organismic factors. Experimental independent variables include a) preceding experimental presentations of the stimuli, b) previous occurrences of the behavior, c) the instances of reinforcement of the behavior, d) the drive level or deprivation level of the organism, e) the appropriateness of the goal object, f) the types of stimuli, g) the types of responses required, h) the experimental apparatus. **4.** (B. F. Skinner) The external conditions of which behavior is a function.

**variable interval reinforcement** Partial reinforcement schedule in which reinforcement occurs on the first trial after varying time lapses, but on the average after a certain amount of time.

**variable interval (VI) schedule** See *reinforcement, schedule of: variable interval (VI).*

**variable, intervening** **1.** The unobserved, inferred factors that connect the observed independent variable, the stimuli, with the observed dependent variables, the responses. Thus intervening variables are hypothetical statements about entities, events or processes occurring within the behaving organism. The status of intervening variables in scientific thinking has not been settled. Distinctions have been made between hypothetical constructs, and intervening variables. The former, also called existential constructs, postulate the existence of entities that "fill out" the space between the observables, for example, the theory of genes "fills out" Mendelian genetics. The intervening variable is often defined only in terms of the independent and dependent variables, thus it has a specific and limited operational meaning. **2.** (E. C. Tolman) The intervening variable is a part determinant of behavior, being divided into immanent purposive and cognitive determinants, capacities, and behavior adjustments. These cannot be observed, only inferred. A subsequent revision of this theory postulated (a) need-systems, the drive situation or physiological deprivation at a given time; (b) belief-value, relative value of goal objects to the organism; (c) behavior-spaces, the space, or environment in which the organism operates.

**variable, O** Factors which are present in an organism at any given moment; internal variables which affect an organism's response to a stimulus. These include drive and individual differences such as age. Also called O factors.

**variable, organic or O** An internal state or process of the organism or person which, together with the immediate stimulus, co-determines the response, as for example, an illness or a general attitude.

**variable, polar** (J. Loevinger) A variable which increases as a function of age.

**variable, proximal** See *stimulus, proximal.*

**variable ratio reinforcement** Partial reinforcement schedule in which reinforcement occurs in an irregular pattern every $n^{th}$ trial, on the average.

**variable ratio (VR) schedule** See *reinforcement, schedule of: variable ratio (VR).*

**variable, response** Dependent variable in psychological research that changes with concomitant changes in the stimulus variable.

**variable, stimulus** **1.** The independent variable in psychological research. It is a measurable dimension of a stimulus complex. Changes in the stimulus variable occasion concomitant changes in the response variable. **2.** (psychophysics) Any of the set of stimuli that are compared to standard stimulus.

**variance** The measure of the extent to which individual scores in a set differ from each other. It is the square of the standard deviation computed by the formula:

$$S^2 = {}_i\Sigma(X_i - M)^2 \over N$$

where $S$ and $X$ are the symbols for sample and population variance respectively, $M$ is the mean of the set, $N$ is the size of the set and $\Sigma$ is the summation sign.

**variance analysis** See *analysis of variance.*

**variance, common factor** See *communality.*

**variation** **1.** Change. **2.** Difference. **3.** (biology) The change in an organism or species resulting from hereditary or environmental influences. **4.** (statistics) The extent of deviation of scores from the mean of the distribution.

**variation coefficient** See *coefficient, variation.*

**varicella encephalitis** See *encephalitis, varicella.*

**vasodepressor syncope** See *syncope, vasodepressor.*

**vasopressin** Pituitary hormone mainly used for antidiaretic effect.

**vectorialism** (B. B. Wolman) A sociopsychological attitude based on the desire for helping others without expecting anything in return; it is an unselfish, giving attitude. Originates in the parent-child core.

**vectoriasis praecocissima** (B. B. Wolman) Childhood schizophrenia. See *vectoriasis praecox.*

**vectoriasis praecox** (B. B. Wolman) Schizophrenia. A term introduced in 1957, based on the division of non-organic mental disorders into hypervectorial (schizotype), hyperinstrumental (narcissistic), and dysmutual (cyclic). Vectoriasis praecox indicates a too early and extreme object hypercathexis, called hypervectorialism.

**vegetative nervous system** The autonomic nervous system.

**vegetative neurosis** See *neurosis, vegetative.*

**vehicle** (R. B. Cattell) A mode of expression of interest or motivation which expresses partly the strength of a capacity, e.g. memory, which needs to be discounted in assessing the interest strength itself.

**ventromedial nucleus of the hypothalamus** The portion of the hypothalamus which controls the cessation of eating.

**verbal aphasia** See *aphasia, motor.*

**verbal behavior** See *behavior, verbal.*

**verbal catharsis** See *catharsis, verbal.*

**verbal conditioning in behavior therapy** See *behavior therapy, verbal conditioning.*

**verbal learning** See *learning, verbal.*

**verbal paraphasia** See *paraphasia, verbal.*

**verbal test** See *test, verbal.*

**verbomania** Morbid need for excessive talking; logozzhea.

**verbone** (H. A. Murray) A verbal reaction pattern.

**vergence** A turning movement of the eyes.

**veridical** A term describing that which corresponds to objective reality.

**verification** **1.** The use of empirical data to prove or disprove an hypothesis or the process of proving or disproving an hypothesis using empirical data. **2.** (esthetics) A stage of artistic thought or creation in which the observer or artist reviews an artistic object to ascertain whether the intended effect was achieved.

**vermis** The median lobe of the cerebellum.

**vernier** A closely calibrated scale, ancillary to a larger scale which allows the reading off of fractions from a larger scale.

**Verstehende Psychologie** See *psychology, understanding.*

**vertex** 1. The uppermost point of a geometric figure. 2. Referring to the top of the head. 3. The point where two angular lines meet.

**vertical axis** See *Y axis.*

**vertical group structure** (B. B. Wolman) The distribution of severity of disorder in a psychotherapeutic group.

**vertical mobility** (sociology) Moving upward of a social class system; climbing up the social ladder.

**vertigo** A state of dizziness.

**vesania** (B. de Sauvage) An obsolete term for all mental disorders introduced in 1763.

**vesicle** A sac-like structure which contains liquid.

**vestibule** A bony cavity in the inner ear's labyrinth composed of two sacs—the utricle and saccule—and containing fluid. The hair cells in the utricle and saccule are sensitive to acceleration and deceleration of the body, being the receptor apparatus for that sense.

**VI schedule** See *reinforcement, schedule of: variable interval.*

**vicarious arousal** An emotional response aroused by an empathetic understanding of what another person is experiencing.

**vicarious conditioning** Learning through observation without practice.

**vicarious functioning** Behavioral pattern in which one psychological process is substituted for another.

**vicarious learning** Learning through indirect experience.

**vicarious trial and error** See *trial and error, vicarious.*

**Viennese Circle** See *logical positivism.*

**Vierordt's Law** (K. von Vierordt) The two-point threshold of a mobile part of the body is lower than for a less mobile part of the body.

**Vigotsky Test** See *test, Vigotsky.* Also spelled Vygotsky.

**Vincent learning curve** (L. E. Vincent) A method used in comparing the learning curves of individuals who take different numbers of trials or different lengths of time to achieve the specified criterion of learning. Each subject's data are broken down into equal intervals—either of time or number of trials—allowing the construction of a curve with all subject's having the same beginning and end points

but with different amounts of learning exhibited in any one interval.

**Vineland Social Maturity Scale** See *scale, Vineland Social Maturity.*

**viraginity** A woman being or acting in man-like fashion.

**virilism** The development in a woman of the male secondary sex characteristics.

**virus RNA** See *RNA, virus.*

**viscera** The organs enclosed in the large cavities of the body, especially the abdominal and thoracic cavities.

**visceral drive** A drive which is based upon a physiological need.

**visceral reflex** The response, regulated by the sympathetic and parasympathetic nervous system, of the viscera to conditions of stress.

**visceral sense** A collective term for all those sensations emanating from the viscera.

**visceroceptor; visceroreceptor** A receptor organ in one of the viscera.

**viscerogenic** A term describing that which originates in the viscera.

**viscerotonia** (W. H. Sheldon) Temperament component characterized by love of food, enjoyment of physical relaxation and comfort, sociability and affection, associated with the endomorphic body-type.

**visibility coefficient** A number designating the visibility of a specified sample of radiant energy, usually of a single spectral wave length.

**visibility curve** A graphic representation of the relation of visual intensity, called brilliance, to the wave length.

**vision** 1. The seeing sense with the eye as the receptor whose normal stimulus is light or radiant energy ranging from about 400 to 760 millimicrons. 2. That which is seen. 3. The act of seeing.

**vision, distance** 1. Seeing objects that are more than twenty feet away. 2. Ability to discriminate among stimuli twenty feet or more away.

**vision, indirect** Vision of objects stimulating the marginal area of the retina.

**vision, monocular** Vision with one eye.

**vision, paracentral** Seeing through use of the area immediately surrounding the fovea centralis.

**vision, perimacular** Vision which utilizes the part of the retina which surrounds the macula.

**vision, photopic** Vision under conditions of fairly strong illumination such that full discrimination of colors is possible since the cones are functional; color or daylight vision.

**vision theory** See *color vision theory; duplicity theory.*

**visions, hypnagogic** See *imagery, hypnagogic.*

**vista response** A type of Rorschach response in which the chiaroscuro (light-dark) features of the blot convey the impression of depth or dimensionality. Vista responses are generally interpreted as a form of self-examination and/or attempts to distantiate from the environment.

**visual acuity** The ability of the visual mechanism to discriminate two points in the visual field; the closer together the two points, the greater the acuity.

**visual adaptation** The ability of the eyes to adjust to conditions of continued stimulation or lack of stimulation. See *adaptation, brightness; adaptation, color.*

**visual agnosia** See *agnosia, visual.*

**visual agraphia** See *agraphia, visual.*

**visual alexia** See *alexia, visual.*

**visual aphasia** See *aphasia, visual.*

**visual apperception test** See *test, visual apperception.*

**visual aurae** See *aurae, visual.*

**visual axis** The straight line running from the external fixation point through the nodal point of the eye to the point of clearest vision on the retina.

**visual displacement** The angles describing the eyes' deviations from the primary position when viewing objects.

**visual field** 1. All of the external world that is visible to the unmoving eye of any particular observer at a given moment. 2. The perceived three-dimensional space that forms a frame of reference for perceived objects, forms, distances and movements.

**visual fixation** The movement of the eyes so that the images fall on the central part of the retina.

**visual induction** The effect on the perceptual reaction to one area of the visual field caused by the stimulation from another area of the visual field.

**visual-motor Gestalt test** See *test, Bender Visual-Motor Gestalt.*

**visual organization** The complex relationships existing among the various elements of the visual field, reflecting the fact that the phenomenal visual field always appears patterned and meaningful.

**visual process** 1. Activity of the organism contributing to seeing; operations of the eye, nerve tracts and brain centers involved in seeing. 2. The operation of sight in general.

**visual projection** The process involving the attribution of objective location to a visually perceived object.

**visual purple** A substance found in the rods of the retina which bleaches in white light and which is believed to be involved in the reception of faint visual stimuli.

**visual-righting reflex** An alteration in the position of the head when there is a change from one fixation point to another.

**visual space** The visual field or the three-dimensional subjective field in which objects are perceived and located.

**visual type** See *type, visual.*

**visual yellow** A yellow substance which is sometimes found in the retina when visual purple has been bleached by exposure to light.

**vital statistics** Data concerning birth and death rates concerning human beings.

**vitalism** 1. A philosophical theory of life which maintains that living organisms contain elements not existing in the inanimate nature and these elements account for irreducibility of life to inanimate processes. 2. (Hans Driesch) Presented as a theory of autonomy of the life processes. The life of an organism is entelechy, i.e. realization of a potentiality, sort of a purposeful evolvement. According to Driesch, entelechy is like an artist who uses a material medium within its limitations (easel, paint, etc.) but only he creates the work of art. McDougall, Kantor and other psychologists have been influenced by vitalism.

**vitality** 1. The property or quality of being alive, or being able to maintain life. 2. Vigor, energy or endurance.

**vocabulary test** See *test, vocabulary.*

**vocal cords** The ligaments of the larynx involved in the production of vocal sounds.

**vocal immaturity** Voice disorder due to the inhibition of laryngeal growth, usually caused by dysfunctioning of the sex glands, and characterized by a voice of higher than normal frequency.

**vocal register** The pitch range of an individual voice.

**vocational aptitude** Particular abilities a person possesses which allow the making of a prediction concerning the person's future success in a given field.

**vocational aptitude tests** See *tests, vocational aptitude.*

**vocational counseling** See *counseling, vocational.*

**vocational guidance** Aiding a person in the choice of an occupation.

**vocational interest blank** See *strong vocational interest blank.*

**Vogt-Spielmeyer Disease** (O. Vogt and W. Spielmeyer) A variant of Tay-Sachs Disease. See *Tay-Sachs Disease.*

**voice dysmaturity** Voice disorder resulting from various conditions, such as defects of the larynx, which directly interfere with the development and function of the laryngeal structures.

**volition** 1. The process of deciding upon a course of

action without external pressure. **2.** Voluntary activity. **3.** (content psychology) A complex experience consisting primarily of kinesthetic sensations and images of a goal.

**volley theory of hearing** See *hearing, theory of: volley theory.*

**voluntarism** A philosophical doctrine which assumes the superiority of the will over reason.

**voluntary movement 1.** Movement resulting from conscious intention to move. **2.** Movement of striated muscles under the control of the central nervous system.

**von Bezold assimilation** In the field of color vision von Bezold showed that certain patterns of white lines on chromatic surfaces lightened and black lines darkened the surfaces thus reversing the usual classical lightness contrast effects. Found by H. Helson and colleagues to hold usually for narrow lines on gray as well as chromatic backgrounds.

**voyeurism** Sexual gratification obtained from peeping, especially from watching people engage in sexual intercourse.

**VR schedule** See *reinforcement, schedule of: variable ratio.*

**vulnerability index of a scale to motivational distortion** (R. B. Cattell) An index, obtainable factor analytically, which expresses the distortion in a given questionnaire scale in a given test situation as a function of strength of need to distort. The administration of two scales for the same trait, but of differing vulnerability indices, permits estimation of the true, undistorted score.

**Vvedensky, Nikolay Yevgenyevich (1852-1922)** Russian physiologist, a disciple of I. M. Sechenov. In 1874 he was arrested, being accused of political propaganda and spent three years in prison. After graduation from the University he worked at Sechenov's laboratory. In 1889 he was appointed as Professor of the Petersburg University.

In 1900 he was elected as an Honorable President of Congress of Medicine in Paris. Vvedensky continued Sechenov's trend in the field of physiology of the nervous system. Investigating the problem of the nervous inhibition and of relation of the inhibitory processes to the excitation of the nervous system, he discovered excitation in nerves is a rhythmic one. He elaborated the theory of parabiosis as a state of a "stable unfluctuated excitation" (*Excitation, Inhibition, and Narcosis,* 1901). Vvedensky showed that the inhibitory process can be formed inside the nervous substrate under increase of frequency and power of the coming nervous impulses (Pressimum). Later on, this phenomenon was called the "Vvedensky inhibition."

**Vygotski, Lev Semionovich (1896-1934)** Soviet psychologist, one of the founders of modern scientific psychology in the U.S.S.R. His basic contribution to psychology is the introduction of sociohistoric approach to the psychological sciences and the concept of higher psychological processes which are social by origin, intermediated by tool or sign, and conscious and voluntary. According to his observations, higher psychological processes (as voluntary action, active attention, higher form of memorizing) were started as processes divided between two persons (adult and child) and mainly are inter-psychological processes; only then with the development of child's own speech (first overt, then abbreviated and last, internal) these processes become interiorized and an inter-psychological system of processes is formed. Vygotski studied the development of child's own speech; he proved that not only the contents but the structure of the word meanings undergo development, and the system of psychological processes underlying higher psychological functions basically changes during the child's development. His book *Thought and Language* was published in Russian posthumously (1934) and was translated into several languages and had a profound impact upon the development of psychology in the U.S.S.R.

**w** (Rorschach) A response to a card which utilizes most of the inkblot, although not including some small part of the blot.

**w** 1. (statistics) A weight; also written *W*. 2. A will factor.

**W** 1. (physics) Work measured in joules. 2. (statistics) Referring to a weight; also written w. 3. (statistics) The coefficient of concordance. 4. (psychophysics) The Weber fraction. 5. The word fluency factor. 6. (Rorschach) Referring to the whole response.

**W%** (Rorschach) The percentage of the total number of responses to the cards which are responses to the whole card.

**W response** (Rorschach) A response to a card which utilizes the whole inkblot.

**Wagner von Jauregg, Julius (1857-1940)** An Austrian psychiatrist and neurologist known for the development of a fever treatment for general paresis.

**WAIS** See *Wechsler Adult Intelligence Scale.*

**Wallerian degeneration** (A. V. Waller) (neurology) The breakdown of the myelin sheath of portions of the axon; secondary degeneration.

**wandering mania** See *mania, wandering.*

**wanderlust** See *wandering mania.*

**war neurosis** See *combat neurosis.*

**warm spot** A tiny spot on the surface of the skin particularly sensitive to heat.

**warm-up** Increase in the magnitude of some aspect of the response occasioned by the first few trials independent of any reinforcement contingency.

**Wartegg drawing completion form** A projective technique used with children five and over which consists of a form with eight two-inch boxes, each containing a small stimulus: a line or dots or geometric detail. The child is asked to finish the drawings, title them and tell which he likes best and least.

Formal aspects as well as content of the drawings are considered in the assessment and scoring.

**Washburn, Margaret Floy (1871-1939)** American psychologist and pioneer in struggle for equal educational opportunities for women. Studied with Cattell at Columbia and obtained her doctorate under Titchener at Cornell. Taught philosophy and psychology at Vassar College (1903-37). Widely known for her theory of motor consciousness, for her editorial services on several psychological journals, and for her election (1921) as president of the American Psychological Association, the second woman so honored.

**Wassermann Test** A test or a sample of the blood or cerebrospinal fluid for the presence of syphilitic infection.

**Watson, John Broadus (1878-1958)** American psychologist, founder of behaviorism, whose textbooks on comparative (1914) and general psychology (1918), and popular writings on child rearing (1920's), were highly influential in turning American psychological study away from mental content and toward behavior.

**Watson's behaviorism** (J. B. Watson) A system of psychology holding strictly to the principle that the only valid material for study is that which can be observed from without—the overt and observable behavior of the organism, its muscles, glands and tissues—eliminating states of consciousness as objects of investigation. The goal of his system was to interpret all behavior in physical-chemical terms. The system proposes that all behavior is learned, the instincts being rejected as causative influences. Behavior is viewed as the result of a stimulus-response connection, the connections in existence being those which have been practiced the most recently and frequently. The theory applied the concept of conditioning to the most complex forms of learning and to the emotions. Behavior, even the most complex, was reduced to a sensory-central-motor chain of stimuli and responses. Thus all behavior was divided into explicit and implicit, the

**405**

explicit behavior including observable activities such as talking, walking, etc., and the implicit one including visceral activities, glandular secretion, etc.

**wave amplitude** The height of a wave measured from the crest to the trough.

**wave frequency** The number of times per second a complete wave pattern passes a specific stationary point.

**wave length** The distance, at a specified point in time, between two adjacent crests of a wave. The wave length is in an inverse relation with frequency.

**wave of excitation** 1. An electrochemical change which is propogated in wave form through a living tissue. 2. A neural impulse when seen as an electrochemical change.

**waxy flexibility** See *catalepsy.*

**WAY technique** A projective technique in which the subject is asked to write three short answers to the question "who are you?"

**Weber, Ernst Heinrich (1795-1878)** Pioneer German sensory psychophysiologist, the first to study touch and kinesthesis in elaborate experiments. Discovered a major psychophysical principle which G. T. Fechner later called Weber's law: $\Delta I/I = k$; that is the just noticeable increment ($\Delta I$) in stimulus intensity is a constant fraction ($k$) of the intensity ($I$) already present.

**Wechsler Adult Intelligence Scale** See *scale, Wechsler Adult Intelligence.*

**Wechsler-Bellevue Scale** See *scale, Wechsler-Bellevue.*

**Wechsler, David (1896-  )** American psychologist, author of widely used individual intelligence scales which bear his name: the Wechsler-Bellevue, the Wechsler Adult Intelligence, the Wechsler Intelligence Scale for Children, and the Wechsler Preschool and Primary Scale of Intelligence. First to combine verbal and non-verbal tests into a composite scale, and to introduce the concept of the non-intellective factors of intelligence. Proponent of the view that most intellectual abilities begin to decline at relatively early age (25 or sooner). Principal fields of research: intelligence, diagnostic use of mental test and range of human capacities.

**Wechsler Intelligence Scale for Children** See *scale, Wechsler Intelligence, for Children.*

**Wechsler Preschool and Primary Scale of Intelligence** See *scale, Wechsler Preschool and Primary, of Intelligence.*

**weight coefficient** (statistics) A constant number which is multiplied with a variable so as to alter or modify its relative contribution to a total score or to the variance of the total score.

**weighting** The determination of the relative influence any one element should have in the total by the assignment of a constant by which that element is multiplied.

**Weigl-Goldstein-Scheerer Test** See *test, Weigl-Goldstein-Scheerer.*

**Weigl-Goldstein-Scheerer Color Form Sorting Test,** See *test, Weigl-Goldstein-Scheerer Color Form Sorting.*

**Weissmannism** A theory of genetics which negates the principle that acquired characterictics are inherited and postulates a continuity of germ plasm through generations.

*Weltanschauung* A German word meaning view of the universe, used to describe one's total outlook on life, society and its institutions.

**Wepman Test of Auditory Discrimination** See *test, Wepman, of Auditory Discrimination.*

**Werner, Heinz (1890-1964)** A psychologist who was trained in Germany but later moved to the United States. He is known for his development of the sensory-tonic field theory of perception and an organismic theory of development.

**Werner-Strauss theory** (H. Werner and A. Strauss) An attempt at explaining the difficulties brain-injured children have in learning situations. Brain-injured children tend to be seriously handicapped in the visual, tactual and auditory fields by background interference, leading to a chaotic and disturbing impression of the world around them. Special teaching and training approaches are thought to be needed, aimed at overcoming the excessive distractibility of the brain-injured child by diminishing irrelevant stimuli and at teaching him how to tackle perceptual difficulties by taking him through a carefully designed program of exercises.

**Wernicke, Carl (1848-1905)** A German neurologist known for his work in aphasia. One of the brain areas is named after him.

**Wernicke's agnosia** See *agnosia, Wernicke's.*

**Wernicke's area** An area of the cerebrum in the temporal region that was once thought to be the center for understanding spoken language. The area is involved in language but the relationship is more complex than once thought.

**Wertheimer, Max (1880-1943)** European-born American psychologist. With Wolfgang Köhler and Kurt Koffka, founder of Gestalt psychology. His experiments on apparent movement (phi phenomenon), published in 1912, launched this new psychology. Showed in many contexts that organized wholes cannot be treated as sums of elements "from below," but must be approached "from above," in terms of whole properties and the dynamics of the whole. Demonstrated factors of organization in perception. Undertook major studies and analyses of productive thinking, attempting to describe the processes that occur in it and to show that neither association theory nor the application of traditional logic can account for thinking at its best. Applied Gestalt approach to an understanding of certain problems in ethics. the nature of truth, democracy and freedom.

**Wetzel fibers** (N. E. Wetzel) An instrument used in plotting interrelations of height, weight, and age over a period of years with norms of development being derived from the interrelations.

**Wever-Bray phenomenon** (E. G. Wever and C. W. Bray) Cochleal electrical activity in response to external stimulation combined with the action potential of the auditory nerve.

**Wherry-Doolittle technique** (statistics) A short-cut method used in selecting a small number of tests from a larger number, so the smaller number will yield a correlation with a criterion with only slightly less validity than the multiple correlation of all the tests with the criterion.

**whisper test** See *test, whisper.*

**white matter** The areas of the brain which are light gray in color from the myelin covering of the nerve fibers.

**white-space response** (Rorschach) A response utilizing a portion of the card which is not covered by the inkblot.

**White, William A.** (1870-1937) An American psychiatrist who was instrumental in bridging the gap in America between academic psychiatry and psychoanalysis.

**whole method of learning** See *learning, whole method of.*

**whole response** A Rorschach response which involves the use of the entire blot. Scored *W,* these responses are generally indicative of one's organizational talents.

**wholism** See *holism.*

**Whorf's hypothesis** (B. L. Whorf) Differences in language and linguistic habits lead to differences in behavior in general.

**Wiersma, Enno Dirk** (1858-1940) A Dutch psychiatrist and neurologist who studied genetic origins of mental disorders.

**Wiggly Block Test** See *test, Wiggly Block.*

**Wiktiko psychosis** See *psychosis, Wiktiko.*

**wild boy of Aveyron** (J. Itard) A boy found living in the woods, thought to be a feral child, and brought under the care of Dr. Itard. The boy was unsocialized and spoke no language. The attempt to train him made some inroads but was, for the most part, unsuccessful.

**will** 1. The capacity which is involved in the ability to participate in conscious activity. 2. The total impulses, conscious and unconscious, of the person.

**will therapy** See *psychotherapy, will.*

**will to power** (A. Adler) The guiding force in development which consists of a striving for superiority and dominance.

**Wilson's disease** (S. A. K. Wilson) Hepatolenticular degeneration due to a genetic mechanism consisting of several alleles which results in changes in the level of ceruloplasmin.

**windigo** See *psychosis, Wiktiko.*

**windmill illusion** The illusion that, without real change in direction, the direction of spin of a spoked wheel changes intermittently.

**WISC** See *Wechsler Intelligence Scale for Children.*

**Wisconsin General Test Apparatus** (WGTA) Apparatus used to test discrimination in primates in which the subject chooses between two food cups. The cup that contains the reinforcement is randomly changed from trial to trial.

**wit-work** (S. Freud) The psychological processes, mostly unconscious, which produce wit. They are similar to the processes involved in dream-work.

**witchcraft** The belief and practice of magic and sorcery.

**withdrawal symptoms** Symptoms exhibited by drug addicts when they are removed from the addicting drug, including anxiety, cramps and profuse perspiration.

**Wittkower, Eric David** (1899-    ) Psychoanalyst. Pioneer in psychosomatic medicine. Has published several books (largely on psychosomatic subjects) and over 125 scientific articles. Recent interests include the cultural aspects of and variations in mental disorder.

**wolf child** See *feral child.*

**Wolpe, Joseph** (1915-    ) American, previously South African, psychiatrist, central figure in the development of behavior therapy. Demonstrated that experimental neuroses, whether produced by conflict or noxious stimulation, are learned behavior. Derived from these experiments general theory of neuroses as persistent unadaptive habits acquired by learning in anxiety-generating situations. Evolved reciprocal inhibition theory of psychotherapy on observation that experimental neuroses are progressively diminished through evocation of competing responses, such as feeding in the presence of the stimuli to weak neurotic responses. On this paradigm developed systematic desensitization and other techniques for eliminating human neurotic habits. Major publications: *Psychotherapy by Reciprocal Inhibition,* and *Practice of Behavior Therapy.*

**Woodworth personal data sheet** (R. S. Woodworth) A personality inventory developed in 1920 which consists of one-hundred sixteen items requiring a "yes" or "no" answer. The inventory is a screening device for neurosis where a "yes" answer is a neurotic one. The subject's score of "yes" answers plus his responses on critical items determine his position in the neurotic category.

**Woodworth, Robert Sessions** (1869-1962) American psychologist who served psychology for more than 70 years as experimentalist, teacher, textbook writer and editor. Studied with James at Harvard and Cattell at Columbia. Joined teaching staff at Columbia in 1903 and maintained his association with this university until his death. Revised Ladd's *Physiological Psychology* (1911). During World War I designed *The Personal Data Sheet,* a personality inventory to detect emotional instability for military purposes. (Became prototype for subsequent personality questionnaires). An advocate of dynamic psychology—published *Dynamic Psychology* (1917) —and analysis of dynamic interaction of motivation with perception, learning, and thinking. Wrote an introductory text, *Psychology* (1921) in five editions; *Contemporary Schools of Psychology* (1931, rev. 1948, and a final revision, prepared with Mary Rose Sheehan, published posthumously, 1964); and *Dynamics of Behavior* (1958).

**word association test**  See *test, word association.*

**word-building test**  See *test, word-building.*

**word count**  An assessment and study of the frequency with which certain words or classes of words are used in a representative sample of speech or writing.

**work decrement** (experimental) Decrease in the magnitude of some aspect of the response system as a function of frequency of the response.

**work-limit test**  See *test, work-limit.*

**work sample**  Selected operations or tasks which are taken as representative of some job, often used in the selection of new employees or in the validation of other tests.

**working mean**  See *mean, assumed.*

**working through** (psychoanalysis) The process in which the patient re-experiences and encounters over and over again the troubling conflicts until he is able to master them and face them independently and successfully in everyday life.

**world test**  See *test, Bolgar-Fischer World.*

**WPPSI**  See *Wechsler Preschool and Primary Scale of Intelligence.*

**writer's cramp**  A painful spasm of the muscles of the forearm, hand and fingers of psychogenic origin.

**Wundt, Wilhelm (1832-1920)** German physiologist and psychologist; professor at Leipzig (1875-1917) where he founded the first laboratory for experimental psychology. Developed his scientific psychology of consciousness based directly on experience, from physiology and psychophysics. Trained many early pioneers of psychology from various countries. Author of numerous books and articles on physiology, psychology and philosophy. Probably his most important volume is *Principles of Physiological Psychology* (1873-1874), which presented his system and launched psychology as an independent science.

**Würzburg school**  A school of psychology in Germany, important for its contributions concerning the effect that the preparation of a subject has on an experiment, the fact that responses are not mere products of the stimuli but also depend upon some factors within the mind of the subject, and the influence of what were called determining tendencies (hypnotic or experimental suggestions).

# X

x **1.** The deviation of a class from the mean value of the *x* variable. **2.** Refers to a standardized score which is more commonly referred to as *z*. **3.** The midpoint of an interval. **4.** An uncommon response in the Rorschach test in which the subject reports seeing part of an animal in an inkblot to which the most common response is that of seeing a whole or entire animal.

X **1.** The most commonly used symbol employed to denote the range of possible scores. **2.** Any raw score of the X distribution.

$\overline{X}$ The overlined capital stands for the arithmetic mean of a group of scores.

X´ The capital letter prime stands for a score in the original scale units predicted from another group of scores, Y.

$X_o$ Any variable whose changes are dependent upon the changes in another variable.

$X_1 X_2$ The predicted raw score.

X axis The horizontal axis or abcissa which at a right angle to the Y axis, forms a reference by which any point in space can be located.

x chromosome One of the sex determining chromosomes. Females have xx chromosomes; males have xy chromosomes.

X coordinate See *X axis*.

X-O test See *test, X-O*.

X value The distance from any point to the X axis measured on a line parallel to the Y axis.

xanthocyanopia; xanthocyanopsia Partial color blindness; red and green are not perceived.

xenophobia An extreme fear of strangers.

xi (psychophysics) The point of subjective equality or the point at which the probability of a judgment "greater" is equal to the probability of a judgment "lesser".

# Y

y (statistics) The deviation of a value from the class mean ordinate value. 2. (mathematics) The height or value of an ordinate, the qualitative value representing the distance from the X axis along any line parallel to the Y axis.

Y 1. That which is being predicted by other variables. The dependent variable. 2. Any raw score of the *Y* distribution. 3. (Rorschach) An inkblot response which is determined by a flat gray surface.

Y axis The vertical axis or ordinate which at a right angle to the X axis, forms a reference by which any point in space can be located.

y chromosome One of the sex determining chromosomes. See *x chromosome.*

Y coordinate See *Y axis.*

y intercept (mathematics) The distance from the origin to the point where a line crosses the Y axis.

Y value The distance from any point to the X axis measured on a line parallel to the Y axis.

year scaling See *age-equivalent scale.*

yellow-sighted A heightened color sensitivity for yellow or the tendency to see all objects tinged with yellow.

yellow spot See *macula lutea.*

Yerkes-Bridges point scale An early adaptation of the Binet scale for American conditions which utilized points rather than months of mental age.

Yerkes, Robert Mearns (1876-1956) Yale psychologist and primatologist. Known for 1) invention of numerous laboratory devices for comparative studies of animal behavior, 2) early research on aggressive instincts in cats, 3) formulation of Yerkes-Dodson law, 4) supervision (with L. M. Terman) of army intelligence testing in World War I, and 5) extensive research studies of chimpanzees and gorillas in his Yale Laboratories of Primate Biology (1925-1946).

yoga A method of contemplation used in Indian religious training. Yoga means, literally, yoking or harnessing, controlling one's faculties. The aim of yoga is to separate the eternal element in man from the psychophysical organism by striving for a conscious state in which mental activities, such as perception and imagination, can be suspended. There are physical as well as mental exercises and techniques aimed at attaining this state.

yoked boxes (operant conditioning) Experimental control procedure which separates reinforcement frequency from other variables. In one isolated experimental chamber the organism is reinforced according to the schedule, usually an FR. In another completely isolated experimental chamber, another subject becomes eligible for reinforcement whenever the organism in the first chamber is reinforced. Only when a response in the first experimental chamber is reinforced is a response in the second chamber reinforced. When an FR schedule is operative in the first chamber, usually a VI schedule is operative in the second chamber.

yoked control Experimental control technique in which the experimental subject's reinforcement is dependent upon his responses while for another control subject, the reinforcements are delivered as they were for the experimental subject regardless of the responses of the control subject.

Young-Helmholtz theory See *color vision, theory of: Young-Helmholtz theory.*

Young, Paul Thomas (1892- ) American psychologist, pioneer in the experimental study of motivation and the affective processes. Known for 1) experimental studies of food preferences, palatability, appetite, dietary habits, 2) the role of hedonic processes in behavior and development, 3) experimental studies of sound localization with a right-left reversing pseudophone.

# Z

z (statistics) A standardized score which shows the relative status of that score in a normal distribution. Any raw score may be converted into this score by means of the formula: $z = \dfrac{x\text{-}M}{S}$
where $x$ is the score, $M$ is the mean of scores and $S$ is the standard deviation of the sample of scores.

Z (statistics—R.A. Fisher) A one-to-one function of $r_{xy}$ known as the Fisher r to Z transformation. It is used to test hypotheses about $_{xx}$ as well as confidence intervals on large samples from bivariate normal populations. For each r there is only one Z value. The Z value is used because for almost any value of $_{xy}$, the sampling distribution of Z value is approximately normal. Transformation values are found in appendices of statistical textbooks.

z score A major scoring used in the Beck approach to the Rorschach to evaluate the organizational activity which occurs as certain responses are formulated. Scores are given on a weighted basis depending on the difficulty and complexity of the organization.

Zeigarnik effect (B. Zeigarnik and K. Lewin) An experimental study of uncompleted tests. Settings of a task or a goal creates tension, and the individual tends to act in order to remove the tension by locomotion in the direction of the goal. As long as the task is not completed, a force corresponding to the valence of the goal region motivates the individual, thus the uncompleted tasks are better remembered than the completed ones.

Zeitgeist The spirit of the times; the prevailing cultural climate at a certain epoch.

Zen Buddhism A form of Mahayana Buddhism found chiefly in Japan but recently having an influence in the West, especially the United States. Zen, meaning literally meditation, stresses spiritual discipline through meditation leading to sudden illumination or satori, a stage on the road to full enlightenment. There is a belief in rebirth, the necessity of attaining release, and the possibility of attaining Buddhahood, as well as an emphasis on the spontaneity of illumination and the rapport existing between the individual and nature. Illumination is gained when the unity which transcends the differences between immediate experience and cerebration is recognized and known.

Zen psychology A treatment approach originating in the Orient which concerns itself with existential questions of meaning and strives to attain a state of oneness with the universe which is called "satori". Specific techniques are available to reach this goal, such as training in particular physical posture and meditation, the aim of which is the suppression of worldly desires and conflicts.

Zeno's arrow A logical argument forwarded by the sophistic philosophers in ancient Greece which attempted to prove that motion is impossible.

zero, absolute 1. The temperature at which there is no longer any molecular motion, equivalent to -273 degrees C. or –459 degrees F. 2. The point on a measuring scale where that which is being measured no longer exists, where nothing of the variable remains.

zero correlation See correlation, zero.

zero-order (statistics) Pertaining to a correlation coefficient which has no variables held constant when computed. It is written $r_{12}$, referring to the correlation of variables 1 and 2.

Zoellner illusion See illusion, Zoellner.

zone, hypnogenic See spot, hypnogenic.

zooerasty Sexual intercourse of a human with an animal.

zoology The science of animal life.

zoomorphism An interpretation of human behavior in terms of animal behavior; uncritical application of data obtained from comparative psychology to human behavior.

zoophilia An excessive attraction to animals.

zoophobia A morbid fear of animals.

**Zubin, Joseph (1900-   )** American psychologist and psychopathologist concerned with introducing objective approaches to evaluation of treatment of mental disorders, improvement of classification and diagnosis by use of systematic structured interviews, development of suitable statistical techniques and experimental laboratory and field investigation methods for detection and diagnosis of mental disorders.

**Zürich school**   Carl G. Jung and his followers.

**zygote**   The fertilized ovum.

# APPENDIX A

---

# CLASSIFICATION
## OF
# MENTAL DISORDERS
by
AMERICAN PSYCHIATRIC ASSOCIATION

# THE USE OF THIS MANUAL: SPECIAL INSTRUCTIONS

## Abbreviations and Special Symbols

The following abbreviations and special symbols are used throughout this Manual:

WHO    —The World Health Organization

ICD-8   —The **International Classification of Diseases, Eighth Revision,** World Health Organization, 1968. For use in the United States see: **Eighth Revision International Classification of Diseases Adapted for Use in the United States,** Public Health Service Publication No. 1693, U. S. Government Printing Office, Washington, D. C. 20402.

DSM-I   —**Diagnostic and Statistical Manual, Mental Disorders,** American Psychiatric Association, Washington, D. C., 1952 (out of print).

DSM-II  —This Manual: **Diagnostic and Statistical Manual of Mental Disorders,** Second Edition, American Psychiatric Association, Washington, D. C., 1968.

[ ]      —The brackets indicate ICD-8 categories to be avoided in the United States or used by record librarians only.

\*        —Asterisk indicates categories added to ICD-8 for use in the United States only.

(( ))   —Double parentheses indicate ICD-8 terms equivalent to U. S. terms.

OBS    —Organic Brain Syndrome(s), i.e. mental disorders caused by or associated with impairment of brain tissue function.

## The Organization of the Diagnostic Nomenclature

While this Manual generally uses the same diagnostic code numbers as ICD-8, two groups of disorders are out of sequence: *Mental retardation* and the *Non-psychotic organic brain syndromes. Mental retardation* is placed first to emphasize that it is to be diagnosed whenever present, even if due to some other disorder. The *Non-psychotic or-*

*ganic brain syndromes* are grouped with the other organic brain syndromes in keeping with psychiatric thinking in this country, which views the organic brain syndromes, whether psychotic or not, as one group. Furthermore, the diagnostic nomenclature is divided into ten major subdivisions, indicated with Roman numerals, to emphasize the way mental disorders are often grouped in the United States.

## The Recording of Diagnoses

Every attempt has been made to express the diagnoses in the clearest and simplest terms possible within the framework of modern usage. Clinicians will significantly improve communication and research by recording their diagnoses in the same terms.

## Multiple Psychiatric Diagnoses

Individuals may have more than one mental disorder. For example, a patient with anxiety neurosis may also develop morphine addiction. In DSM-I, drug addiction was classified as a secondary diagnosis, but addiction to alcohol, for example, could not be diagnosed in the presence of a recognizable underlying disorder. This manual, by contrast, encourages the recording of the diagnosis of alcoholism separately even when it begins as a symptomatic expression of another disorder. Likewise mental retardation is a separate diagnosis. For example, there are children whose disorders could be diagnosed as "Schizophrenia, childhood type" and "Mental retardation following major psychiatric disorder."

The diagnostician, however, should not lose sight of the rule of parsimony and diagnose more conditions than are necessary to account for the clinical picture. The opportunity to make multiple diagnoses does not lessen the physician's responsibility to make a careful differential diagnosis.

Which of several diagnoses the physician places first is a matter of his own judgment, but two principles may be helpful in making his decision:

1. The condition which most urgently requires treatment should be listed first. For example, if a patient with simple schizophrenia was presented to the diagnostician because of pathological alcohol intoxication, then the order of diagnoses would be first, *Pathological intoxication,* and second, *Schizophrenia, simple type.*

2. When there is no issue of disposition or treatment priority, the more serious condition should be listed first.

It is recommended that, in addition to recording multiple disorders in conformity with these principles, the diagnostician *underscore* the disorder on the patient's record that he considers the underlying one. Because these principles will not always be applied or used consistently, statistical systems should account for all significant diagnoses recorded in every case.

### Qualifying Phrases and Adjectives

The ICD is based on a classification scheme which allots three digits for the designation of major disease categories and a fourth digit for the specification of additional detail within each category. DSM-II has introduced a fifth digit for coding certain qualifying phrases that may be used to specify additional characteristics of mental disorders. This digit does not disturb the content of either the three- or four-digit categories in the ICD section on mental disorders.

These terms are as follows:

(1.) In the brain syndromes a differentiation of acute and chronic conditions may be provided by .x1 *acute* and .x2 *chronic*. This will help maintain continuity with DSM-I. These qualifying adjectives are recommended only for mental disorders specified as associated with physical conditions and are, of course, unnecessary in disorders seen only in an acute or chronic form.

Those who wish to continue the distinction made in DSM-I between "acute" and "chronic" organic brain syndromes must now add these as qualifying terms. Note also that a recorded diagnosis which merely indicates an organic brain syndrome and does not specify whether or not it is psychotic will now be classified under *Non-psychotic organic brain syndromes.*

(2.) The qualifying phrase, .x5 *in remission,* may also be used to indicate a period of remission in any disorder. This is not synonymous with *No mental disorder.*

(3.) With a few exceptions, all disorders listed in parts IV through IX may be classified as .x6 *mild*, .x7 *moderate*, and .x8 *severe*. But exceptions must be made in coding *Passive-aggressive personality, Inadequate personality,* and the two sub-types of *Hysterical neurosis* because their basic code numbers have five digits. *Antisocial personality* should always be specified as mild, moderate, or severe.

(4.) As explained on page 439, the qualifying phrase *not psychotic* (.x6) may be used for the psychoses listed in pages 430-468 when the patient's degree of disturbance is not psychotic at the time of examination.

## Associated Physical Conditions

Many mental disorders, and particularly mental retardation and the various organic brain syndromes, are reflections of underlying physical conditions. Whenever these physical conditions are known they should be indicated with a separate diagnosis in addition to the one that specifies the mental disorder found.

# THE DIAGNOSTIC NOMENCLATURE:
## List of Mental Disorders and Their Code Numbers

## I. MENTAL RETARDATION

Mental retardation (310-315)

310  Borderline mental retardation

311  Mild mental retardation

312  Moderate mental retardation

313  Severe mental retardation

314  Profound mental retardation

315  Unspecified mental retardation

The fourth-digit sub-divisions cited below should be used with each of the above categories. The associated physical condition should be specified as an additional diagnosis when known.

 .0 Following infection or intoxication

 .1 Following trauma or physical agent

 .2 With disorders of metabolism, growth or nutrition

 .3 Associated with gross brain disease (postnatal)

 .4 Associated with diseases and conditions due to (unknown) prenatal influence

 .5 With chromosomal abnormality

 .6 Associated with prematurity

 .7 Following major psychiatric disorder

 .8 With psycho-social (environmental) deprivation

 .9 With other [and unspecified] condition

## II. ORGANIC BRAIN SYNDROMES

(Disorders Caused by or Associated With Impairment of Brain Tissue Function) In the categories under IIA and IIB the associated physical condition should be specified when known.

## II-A. PSYCHOSES ASSOCIATED WITH ORGANIC BRAIN SYNDROMES (290-294)

290 Senile and pre-senile dementia
.0 Senile dementia
.1 Pre-senile dementia

291 Alcoholic psychosis
.0 Delirium tremens
.1 Korsakov's psychosis (alcoholic)
.2 Other alcoholic hallucinosis
.3 Alcohol paranoid state ((Alcoholic paranoia))
.4* Acute alcohol intoxication*
.5* Alcoholic deterioration*
.6* Pathological intoxication*
.9 Other [and unspecified] alcoholic psychosis

292 Psychosis associated with intracranial infection
.0 Psychosis with general paralysis
.1 Psychosis with other syphilis of central nervous system
.2 Psychosis with epidemic encephalitis
.3 Psychosis with other and unspecified encephalitis
.9 Psychosis with other [and unspecified] intracranial infection

293 Psychosis associated with other cerebral condition
.0 Psychosis with cerebral arteriosclerosis
.1 Psychosis with other cerebrovascular disturbance
.2 Psychosis with epilepsy
.3 Psychosis with intracranial neoplasm
.4 Psychosis with degenerative disease of the central nervous system
.5 Psychosis with brain trauma
.9 Psychosis with other [and unspecified] cerebral condition

294 Psychosis associated with other physical condition
.0 Psychosis with endocrine disorder
.1 Psychosis with metabolic or nutritional disorder
.2 Psychosis with systemic infection

.3 Psychosis with drug or poison intoxication (other than alcohol)

.4 Psychosis with childbirth

.8 Psychosis with other and undiagnosed physical condition

[.9 Psychosis with unspecified physical condition]

## II-B NON-PSYCHOTIC ORGANIC BRAIN SYNDROMES (309)

309 Non-psychotic organic brain syndromes ((Mental disorders not specified as psychotic associated with physical conditions))

.0 Non-psychotic OBS with intracranial infection

[.1 Non-psychotic OBS with drug, poison, or systemic intoxication]

   .13* Non-psychotic OBS with alcohol* (simple drunkenness)

   .14* Non-psychotic OBS with other drug, poison, or systemic intoxication*

.2 Non-psychotic OBS with brain trauma

.3 Non-psychotic OBS with circulatory disturbance

.4 Non-psychotic OBS with epilepsy

.5 Non-psychotic OBS with disturbance of metabolism, growth or nutrition

.6 Non-psychotic OBS with senile or pre-senile brain disease

.7 Non-psychotic OBS with intracranial neoplasm

.8 Non-psychotic OBS with degenerative disease of central nervous system

.9 Non-psychotic OBS with other [and unspecified] physical condition

   [.91* Acute brain syndrome, not otherwise specified*]

   [.92* Chronic brain syndrome, not otherwise specified*]

## III. PSYCHOSES NOT ATTRIBUTED TO PHYSICAL CONDITIONS LISTED PREVIOUSLY (295-298)

295 Schizophrenia

.0 Schizophrenia, simple type

.1 Schizophrenia, hebephrenic type

.2 Schizophrenia, catatonic type

   .23* Schizophrenia, catatonic type, excited*

   .24* Schizophrenia, catatonic type, withdrawn*

.3 Schizophrenia, paranoid type

.4 Acute schizophrenic episode

.5 Schizophrenia, latent type

.6 Schizophrenia, residual type

.7 Schizophrenia, schizo-affective type

    .73* Schizophrenia, schizo-affective type, excited*

    .74* Schizophrenia, schizo-affective type, depressed*

.8*    Schizophrenia, childhood type*

.90* Schizophrenia, chronic undifferentiated type*

.99* Schizophrenia, other [and unspecified] types*


296  Major affective disorders ((Affective psychoses))

.0 Involutional melancholia

.1 Manic-depressive illness, manic type ((Manic-depressive psychosis, manic type))

.2 Manic-depressive illness, depressed type ((Manic-depressive psychosis, depressed type))

.3 Manic-depressive illness, circular type ((Manic-depressive psychosis, circular type))

    .33* Manic-depressive illness, circular type, manic*

    .34* Manic-depressive illness, circular type, depressed*

.8 Other major affective disorder ((Affective psychoses, other))

[.9 Unspecified major affective disorder]

    [Affective disorder not otherwise specified]

    [Manic-depressive illness not otherwise specified]


297  Paranoid states

.0 Paranoia

.1 Involutional paranoid state ((Involutional paraphrenia))

.9 Other paranoid state


298  Other psychoses

.0 Psychotic depressive reaction ((Reactive depressive psychosis))

[.1 Reactive excitation]

[.2 Reactive confusion]
    [Acute or subacute confusional state]
[.3 Acute paranoid reaction]
[.9 Reactive psychosis, unspecified]

[299 Unspecified psychosis]
    [Dementia, insanity or psychosis not otherwise specified]

## IV. NEUROSES (300)

300 Neuroses
  .0 Anxiety neurosis
  .1 Hysterical neurosis
    .13* Hysterical neurosis, conversion type*
    .14* Hysterical neurosis, dissociative type*
  .2 Phobic neurosis
  .3 Obsessive compulsive neurosis
  .4 Depressive neurosis
  .5 Neurasthenic neurosis ((Neurasthenia))
  .6 Depersonalization neurosis ((Depersonalization syndrome))
  .7 Hypochondriacal neurosis
  .8 Other neurosis
  [.9 Unspecified neurosis]

## V. PERSONALITY DISORDERS AND CERTAIN OTHER NON-PSYCHOTIC MENTAL DISORDERS (301—304)

301 Personality disorders
  .0 Paranoid personality
  .1 Cyclothymic personality ((Affective personality))
  .2 Schizoid personality
  .3 Explosive personality
  .4 Obsessive compulsive personality ((Anankastic personality))
  .5 Hysterical personality
  .6 Asthenic personality
  .7 Antisocial personality
  .81* Passive-aggressive personality*
  .82* Inadequate personality*

.89* **Other personality disorders of specified types***

[.9 **Unspecified personality disorder**]

302 **Sexual deviations**

.0 **Homosexuality**

.1 **Fetishism**

.2 **Pedophilia**

.3 **Transvestitism**

.4 **Exhibitionism**

.5* **Voyeurism***

.6* **Sadism***

.7* **Masochism***

.8 **Other sexual deviation**

[.9 **Unspecified sexual deviation**]

303 **Alcoholism**

.0 **Episodic excessive drinking**

.1 **Habitual excessive drinking**

.2 **Alcohol addiction**

.9 **Other [and unspecified] alcoholism**

304 **Drug dependence**

.0 **Drug dependence, opium, opium alkaloids and their derivatives**

.1 **Drug dependence, synthetic analgesics with morphine-like effects**

.2 **Drug dependence, barbiturates**

.3 **Drug dependence, other hypnotics and sedatives or "tranquilizers"**

.4 **Drug dependence, cocaine**

.5 **Drug dependence, Cannabis sativa (hashish, marihuana)**

.6 **Drug dependence, other psycho-stimulants**

.7 **Drug dependence, hallucinogens**

.8 **Other drug dependence**

[.9 **Unspecified drug dependence**]

## VI. PSYCHOPHYSIOLOGIC DISORDERS (305)

305 Psychophysiologic disorders ((Physical disorders of presumably psychogenic origin))

.0 Psychophysiologic skin disorder

.1 Psychophysiologic musculoskeletal disorder

.2 Psychophysiologic respiratory disorder

.3 Psychophysiologic cardiovascular disorder

.4 Psychophysiologic hemic and lymphatic disorder

.5 Psychophysiologic gastro-intestinal disorder

.6 Psychophysiologic genito-urinary disorder

.7 Psychophysiologic endocrine disorder

.8 Psychophysiologic disorder of organ of special sense

.9 Psychophysiologic disorder of other type

## VII. SPECIAL SYMPTOMS (306)

306 Special symptoms not elsewhere classified

.0 Speech disturbance

.1 Specific learning disturbance

.2 Tic

.3 Other psychomotor disorder

.4 Disorders of sleep

.5 Feeding disturbance

.6 Enuresis

.7 Encopresis

.8 Cephalalgia

.9 Other special symptom

## VIII. TRANSIENT SITUATIONAL DISTURBANCES (307)

307* Transient situational disturbances[1]

---

[1] The terms included under DSM-II Category 307*, "Transient situational disturbances," differ from those in Category 307 of the ICD. DSM-II Category 307*, "Transient situational disturbances," contains adjustment reactions of infancy (307.0*), childhood (307.1*), adolescence (307.2*), adult life (307.3*), and late life (307.4*). ICD Category 307, "Transient situational disturbances," includes only the adjustment reactions of adolescence, adult life and late life. ICD 308, "Behavioral disorders of children," contains the reactions of infancy and childhood. These differences must be taken into account in preparing statistical tabulations to conform to ICD categories.

.0* Adjustment reaction of infancy*

.1* Adjustment reaction of childhood*

.2* Adjustment reaction of adolescence*

.3* Adjustment reaction of adult life*

.4* Adjustment reaction of late life*

## IX. BEHAVIOR DISORDERS OF CHILDHOOD AND ADOLESCENCE (308)

308 Behavior disorders of childhood and adolescence[2] ((Behavior disorders of childhood))

.0* Hyperkinetic reaction of childhood (or adolescence)*

.1* Withdrawing reaction of childhood (or adolescence)*

.2* Overanxious reaction of childhood (or adolescence)*

.3* Runaway reaction of childhood (or adolescence)*

.4* Unsocialized aggressive reaction of childhood (or adolescence)*

.5* Group delinquent reaction of childhood (or adolescence)*

.9* Other reaction of childhood (or adolescence)*

## X. CONDITIONS WITHOUT MANIFEST PSYCHIATRIC DISORDER AND NON-SPECIFIC CONDITIONS (316*—318*)[†]

316*[††] Social maladjustments without manifest psychiatric disorder

.0* Marital maladjustment*

.1* Social maladjustment*

.2* Occupational maladjustment*

.3* Dyssocial behavior*

.9* Other social maladjustment*

---

[2] The terms included under DSM-II Category 308*, "Behavioral disorders of childhood and adolescence," differ from those in Category 308 of the ICD. DSM-II Category 308* includes "Behavioral disorders of childhood and adolescence," whereas ICD Category 308 includes only "Behavioral disorders of childhood." DSM-II Category 308* *does not* include "Adjustment reactions of infancy and childhood", whereas ICD Category 308 does. In the DSM-II classification, "Adjustment reactions of infancy and childhood" are allocated to 307* (Transitional situational disturbances). These differences should be taken into account in preparing statistical tabulations to conform to the ICD categories.

**317\*  Non-specific conditions\***

**318\*  No mental disorder\***

## XI. NON-DIAGNOSTIC TERMS FOR ADMINISTRATIVE USE (319\*)†

**319\*  Non-diagnostic terms for administrative use\***

**.0\*  Diagnosis deferred\***

**.1\*  Boarder\***

**.2\*  Experiment only\***

**.9\*  Other\***

---

† The terms included in this category would normally be listed in that section of ICD-8 that deals with "Special conditions and examinations without sickness." They are included here to permit coding of some additional conditions that are encountered in psychiatric clinical settings in the U. S. This has been done by using several unassigned code numbers at the end of Section 5 of the ICD.

†† This diagnosis corresponds to the category \*Y13, **Social maladjustment without manifest psychiatric disorder** in ICDA.

# THE DEFINITIONS OF TERMS

## I: MENTAL RETARDATION[1] (310—315)

Mental retardation refers to subnormal general intellectual functioning which originates during the developmental period and is associated with impairment of either learning and social adjustment or maturation, or both. (These disorders were classified under "Chronic brain syndrome with mental deficiency" and "Mental deficiency" in DSM-I.) The diagnostic classification of mental retardation relates to IQ as follows[2]:

**310 Borderline mental retardation—IQ 68—83**

**311 Mild mental retardation—IQ 52—67**

**312 Moderate mental retardation—IQ 36—51**

**313 Severe mental retardation—IQ 20—35**

**314 Profound mental retardation—IQ under 20**

Classifications 310-314 are based on the statistical distribution of levels of intellectual functioning for the population as a whole. The range of intelligence subsumed under each classification corresponds to one standard deviation, making the heuristic assumption that intelligence is normally distributed. It is recognized that the intelligence quotient should not be the only criterion used in making a diagnosis of mental retardation or in evaluating its severity. It should serve only to help in making a clinical judgment of the patient's adaptive behavioral capacity. This judgment should also be based on an evaluation of the patient's developmental history and present functioning, including academic and vocational achievement, motor skills, and social and emotional maturity.

## 315 Unspecified mental retardation

This classification is reserved for patients whose intellectual functioning

---

[1] For a fuller definition of terms see the "Manual on Terminology and Classification in Mental Retardation," (Supplement to *American Journal of Mental Deficiency*, Second Edition, 1961) from which most of this section has been adapted.

[2] The IQs specified are for the Revised Stanford-Binet Tests of Intelligence, Forms L and M. Equivalent values for other tests are listed in the manual cited in the footnote above.

has not or cannot be evaluated precisely but which is recognized as clearly subnormal.

## Clinical Subcategories of Mental Retardation

These will be coded as fourth digit subdivisions following each of the categories 310-315. When the associated condition is known more specifically, particularly when it affects the entire organism or an organ system other than the central nervous system, it should be coded additionally in the specific field affected.

### .0 Following infection and intoxication

This group is to classify cases in which mental retardation is the result of residual cerebral damage from intracranial infections, serums, drugs, or toxic agents. Examples are:

**Cytomegalic inclusion body disease, congenital.** A maternal viral disease, usually mild or subclinical, which may infect the fetus and is recognized by the presence of inclusion bodies in the cellular elements in the urine, cerebrospinal fluid, and tissues.

**Rubella, congenital.** Affecting the fetus in the first trimester and usually accompanied by a variety of congenital anomalies of the ear, eye and heart.

**Syphilis, congenital.** Two types are described, an early meningo-vascular disease and a diffuse encephalitis leading to juvenile paresis.

**Toxoplasmosis, congenital.** Due to infection by a protozoan-like organism, Toxoplasma, contracted in utero. May be detected by serological tests in both mother and infant.

**Encephalopathy associated with other prenatal infections.** Occasionally fetal damage from maternal epidemic cerebrospinal meningitis, equine encephalomyelitis, influenza, etc. has been reported. The relationships have not as yet been definitely established.

**Encephalopathy due to postnatal cerebral infection.** Both focal and generalized types of cerebral infection are included and are to be given further anatomic and etiologic specification.

**Encephalopathy, congenital, associated with maternal toxemia of pregnancy.** Severe and prolonged toxemia of pregnancy, particularly eclampsia, may be associated with mental retardation.

**Encephalopathy, congenital, associated with other maternal intoxications.** Examples are carbon monoxide, lead, arsenic, quinine, ergot, etc.

**Bilirubin encephalopathy (Kernicterus).** Frequently due to Rh, A, B, O blood group incompatibility between fetus and mother but may also follow prematurity, severe neonatal sepsis or any condition producing high levels of serum bilirubin. Choreoathetosis is frequently associated with this form of mental retardation.

**Post-immunization encephalopathy.** This may follow inoculation with serum, particularly anti-tetanus serum, or vaccines such as small-pox, rabies, and typhoid.

**Encephalopathy, other, due to intoxication.** May result from such toxic agents as lead, carbon monoxide, tetanus and botulism exotoxin.

## .1 Following trauma or physical agent

Further specification within this category follows:

**Encephalopathy due to prenatal injury.** This includes prenatal irradiation and asphyxia, the latter following maternal anoxia, anemia, and hypotension.

**Encephalopathy due to mechanical injury at birth.** These are attributed to difficulties of labor due to malposition, malpresentation, disproportion, or other complications leading to dystocia which may increase the probability of damage to the infant's brain at birth, resulting in tears of the meninges, blood vessels, and brain substance. Other reasons include venous-sinus thrombosis, arterial embolism and thrombosis. These may result in sequelae which are indistinguishable from those of other injuries, damage or organic impairment of the brain.

**Encephalopathy due to asphyxia at birth.** Attributable to the anoxemia  following interference with placental circulation due to premature separation, placenta praevia, cord difficulties, and other interferences with oxygenation of the placental circulation.

**Encephalopathy due to postnatal injury.** The diagnosis calls for evidence of severe trauma such as a fractured skull, prolonged unconsciousness, etc., followed by a marked change in development. Postnatal asphyxia, infarction, thrombosis, laceration, and contusion of the brain would be included and the nature of the injury specified.

## .2 With disorders of metabolism, growth or nutrition

All conditions associated with mental retardation directly due to metabolic, nutritional, or growth dysfunction should be classified here, including disorders of lipid, carbohydrate and protein metabolism, and deficiencies of nutrition.

**Cerebral lipoidosis, infantile (Tay-Sach's disease).** This is caused by a single recessive autosomal gene and has infantile and juvenile forms. In the former there is gradual deterioration, blindness after the pathognomonic "cherry-red spot," with death occurring usually before age three.

**Cerebral lipoidosis, late infantile (Bielschowsky's disease).** This differs from the preceding by presenting retinal optic atrophy instead of the "cherry-red spot."

**Cerebral lipoidosis, juvenile (Spielmeyer-Vogt disease).** This usually appears between the ages of five and ten with involvement of the motor systems, frequent seizures, and pigmentary degeneration of the retina. Death follows in five to ten years.

**Cerebral lipoidosis, late juvenile (Kuf's disease).** This is categorized under mental retardation only when it occurs at an early age.

**Lipid histiocytosis of kerasin type (Gaucher's disease).** As a rule this condition causes retardation only when it affects infants. It is characterized by Gaucher's cells in lymph nodes, spleen or marrow.

**Lipid histiocystosis of phosphatide type (Niemann-Pick's disease).** Distinguished from Tay-Sach's disease by enlargement of liver and spleen. Biopsy of spleen, lymph or marrow show characteristic "foam cells."

**Phenylketonuria.** A metabolic disorder, genetically transmitted as a simple autosomal recessive gene, preventing the conversion of phenylalanine into tyrosine with an accumulation of phenylalanine, which in turn is converted to phenylpyruvic acid detectable in the urine.

**Hepatolenticular degeneration (Wilson's disease).** Genetically transmitted as a simple autosomal recessive. It is due to inability of ceruloplasmin to bind copper, which in turn damages the brain. Rare in children.

**Porphyria.** Genetically transmitted as a dominant and characterized by excretion of porphyrins in the urine. It is rare in children, in whom it may cause irreversible deterioration.

**Galactosemia.** A condition in which galactose is not metabolized, causing its accumulation in the blood. If milk is not removed from the diet, generalized organ deficiencies, mental deterioration and death may result.

**Glucogenosis (Von Gierke's disease).** Due to a deficiency in glycogen-metabolizing enzymes with deposition of glycogen in various organs, including the brain.

**Hypoglycemosis.** Caused by various conditions producing hypoglycemia which, in the infant, may result in epilepsy and mental defect. Diagnosis may be confirmed by glucose tolerance tests.

### .3 Associated with gross brain disease (postnatal)

This group includes all diseases and conditions associated with neoplasms, but not growths that are secondary to trauma or infection. The category also includes a number of postnatal diseases and conditions in which the structural reaction is evident but the etiology is unknown or uncertain, though frequently presumed to be of hereditary or familial nature. Structural reactions may be degenerative, infiltrative, inflammatory, proliferative, sclerotic, or reparative.

**Neurofibromatosis (Neurofibroblastomatosis, von Recklinghausen's disease).** A disease transmitted by a dominant autosomal gene but with reduced penetrance and variable expressivity. It is characterized by cutaneous pigmentation ("café au lait" patches) and neurofibromas of nerve, skin and central nervous system with intellectual capacity varying from normal to severely retarded.

**Trigeminal cerebral angiomatosis (Sturge-Weber-Dimitri's disease).** A condition characterized by a "port wine stain" or cutaneous angioma, usually in the distribution of the trigeminal nerve, accompanied by vascular malformation over the meninges of the parietal and occipital lobes with underlying cerebral maldevelopment.

**Tuberous sclerosis (Epiloia, Bourneville's disease).** Transmitted by a dominant autosomal gene, characterized by multiple gliotic nodules in the central nervous system, and associated with adenoma sebaceum of the face and tumors in other organs. Retarded development and seizures may appear early and increase in severity along with tumor growth.

**Intracranial neoplasm, other.** Other relatively rare neoplastic diseases leading to mental retardation should be included in this category and specified when possible.

**Encephalopathy associated with diffuse sclerosis of the brain.** This category includes a number of similar conditions differing to some extent in their pathological and clinical features but characterized by diffuse demyelination of the white matter with resulting diffuse glial sclerosis and accompanied by intellectual deterioration. These diseases are often familial in character and when possible should be specified under the following:

**Acute infantile diffuse sclerosis (Krabbe's disease).**

**Diffuse chronic infantile sclerosis (Merzbacher-Pelizaeus disease, Aplasia axialis extracorticalis congenita).**

**Infantile metachromatic leukodystrophy (Greenfield's disease).**

**Juvenile metachromatic leukodystrophy (Scholz' disease).**

**Progressive subcortical encephalopathy (Encephalitis periaxialis diffusa, Schilder's disease).**

**Spinal sclerosis (Friedreich's ataxia).** Characterized by cerebellar degeneration, early onset followed by dementia.

**Encephalopathy, other, due to unknown or uncertain cause with the structural reactions manifest.** This category includes cases of mental retardation associated with progressive neuronal degeneration or other structural defects which cannot be classified in a more specific, diagnostic category.

**.4 Associated with diseases and conditions due to unknown prenatal influence**

This category is for classifying conditions known to have existed at the time of or prior to birth but for which no definite etiology can be established. These include the primary cranial anomalies and congenital defects of undetermined origin as follows:

**Anencephaly (including hemianencephaly).**

**Malformations of the gyri.** This includes agyria, macrogyria (pachygyria) and microgyria.

**Porencephaly, congenital.** Characterized by large funnel-shaped cavities occurring anywhere in the cerebral hemispheres. Specify, if possible, whether the porencephaly is a result of asphyxia at birth or postnatal trauma.

**Multiple-congenital anomalies of the brain.**

**Other cerebral defects, congenital.**

**Craniostenosis.** The most common conditions included in this category are acrocephaly (oxycephaly) and scaphocephaly. These may or may not be associated with mental retardation.

**Hydrocephalus, congenital.** Under this heading is included only that type of hydrocephalus present at birth or occurring soon after delivery. All other types of hydrocephalus, secondary to other conditions, should be classified under the specific etiology when known.

**Hypertelorism (Greig's disease).** Characterized by abnormal development of the sphenoid bone increasing the distance between the eyes.

**Macrocephaly (Megalencephaly).** Characterized by an increased size and weight of the brain due partially to proliferation of glia.

**Microcephaly, primary.** True microcephaly is probably transmitted as a single autosomal recessive. When it is caused by other conditions it should be classified according to the primary condition, with secondary microcephaly as a supplementary term.

**Laurence-Moon-Biedl syndrome.** Characterized by mental retardation associated with retinitis pigmentosa, adiposo-genital dystrophy, and polydactyly.

## .5 With chromosomal abnormality

This group includes cases of mental retardation associated with chromosomal abnormalities. These may be divided into two sub-groups, those associated with an abnormal number of chromosomes and those with abnormal chromosomal morphology.

**Autosomal trisomy of group G. (Trisomy 21, Langdon-Down disease, Mongolism).** This is the only common form of mental retardation due to chromosomal abnormality. (The others are relatively rare.) It ranges in degree from moderate to severe with infrequent cases of mild retardation. Other congenital defects are frequently present, and the intellectual development decelerates with time.

**Autosomal trisomy of group E.**

**Autosomal trisomy of group D.**

**Sex chromosome anomalies.** The only condition under the category which has any significant frequency is Klinefelter's syndrome.

**Abnormal number of chromosomes, other.** In this category would be included monosomy G, and possibly others as well as other forms of mosaicism.

**Short arm deletion of chromosome 5—group B (Cri du chat).** A quite rare condition characterized by congenital abnormalities and a cat-like cry during infancy which disappears with time.

**Short arm deletion of chromosome 18—group E.**

**Abnormal morphology of chromosomes, other.** This category includes a variety of translocations, ring chromosomes, fragments, and iso-chromosomes associated with mental retardation.

## .6 Associated with prematurity

This category includes retarded patients who had a birth weight of less than 2500 grams (5.5 pounds) and/or a gestational age of less than 38 weeks at birth, and who do not fall into any of the preceding categories. This diagnosis should be used only if the patient's mental retardation cannot be classified more precisely under categories .0 to .5 above.

## .7 Following major psychiatric disorder

This category is for mental retardation following psychosis or other major psychiatric disorder in early childhood when there is no evidence of cerebral pathology. To make this diagnosis there must be good evidence that the psychiatric disturbance was extremely severe. For example, retarded young adults with residual schizophrenia should not be classified here.

## .8 With psycho-social (environmental) deprivation

This category is for the many cases of mental retardation with no clinical or historical evidence of organic disease or pathology but for which there is some history of psycho-social deprivation. Cases in this group are classified in terms of psycho-social factors which appear to bear some etiological relationship to the condition as follows:

**Cultural-familial mental retardation.** Classification here requires that evidence of retardation be found in at least one of the parents and in one or more siblings, presumably, because some degree of cultural deprivation results from familial retardation. The degree of retardation is usually mild.

**Associated with environmental deprivation.** An individual deprived of normal environmental stimulation in infancy and early childhood may prove unable to acquire the knowledge and skills required to function normally. This kind of deprivation tends to be more severe than that associated with familial mental retardation (q.v.). This type of deprivation may result from severe sensory impairment, even in an environment otherwise rich in stimulation. More rarely it may result from severe environmental limitations or atypical cultural milieus. The degree of retardation is always borderline or mild.

**.9 With other [and unspecified] condition.**

## II. ORGANIC BRAIN SYNDROMES

**(Disorders caused by or associated with impairment of brain tissue function)**

These disorders are manifested by the following symptoms:

(a) Impairment of orientation

(b) Impairment of memory

(c) Impairment of all intellectual functions such as comprehension, calculation, knowledge, learning, etc.

(d) Impairment of judgment

(e) Lability and shallowness of affect

The organic brain syndrome is a basic mental condition characteristically resulting from diffuse impairment of brain tissue function from whatever cause. Most of the basic symptoms are generally present to some degree regardless of whether the syndrome is mild, moderate or severe.

The syndrome may be the only disturbance present. It may also be associated with psychotic symptoms and behavioral disturbances. The severity of the associated symptoms is affected by and related to not only the precipitating organic disorder but also the patient's inherent personality patterns, present emotional conflicts, his environmental situation, and interpersonal relations.

These brain syndromes are grouped into psychotic and non-psychotic disorders according to the severity of functional impairment. The psychotic level of impairment is described on page 439 and the non-psychotic on pages 447-448.

It is important to distinguish "acute" from "chronic" brain disorders because of marked differences in the course of illness, prognosis and treatment. The terms indicate primarily whether the brain pathology and its accompanying organic brain syndrome is reversible. Since the same etiology may produce either temporary or permanent brain damage, a brain disorder which appears reversible (acute) at the beginning may prove later to have left permanent damage and a persistent organic brain syndrome which will then be diagnosed "chronic". Some brain syndromes occur in either form. Some occur only in acute forms (e.g. *Delirium tremens*). Some occur only in chronic form (e.g. *Alcoholic deterioration*). The acute and chronic forms may be indicated for those disorders coded in four digits by the addition of a fifth qualifying digit: *.x1 acute* and *.x2 chronic*.

# THE PSYCHOSES

Psychoses are described in two places in this Manual, here with the organic brain syndromes and later with the functional psychoses. The general discussion of psychosis appears here because organic brain syndromes are listed first in DSM-II.

Patients are described as psychotic when their mental functioning is sufficiently impaired to interfere grossly with their capacity to meet the ordinary demands of life. The impairment may result from a serious distortion in their capacity to recognize reality. Hallucinations and delusions, for example, may distort their perceptions. Alterations of mood may be so profound that the patient's capacity to respond appropriately is grossly impaired. Deficits in perception, language and memory may be so severe that the patient's capacity for mental grasp of his situation is effectively lost.

Some confusion results from the different meanings which have become attached to the word "psychosis." Some non-organic disorders, (295-298), in the well-developed form in which they were first recognized, typically rendered patients psychotic. For historical reasons these disorders are still classified as psychoses, even though it now generally is recognized that many patients for whom these diagnoses are clinically justified are not in fact psychotic. This is true particularly in the incipient or convalescent stages of the illness. To reduce confusion, when one of these disorders listed as a "psychosis" is diagnosed in a patient who is not psychotic, the qualifying phrase *not psychotic* or *not presently psychotic* should be noted and coded .x6 with a fifth digit.

Example: 295.06 *Schizophrenia, simple type, not psychotic.*

It should be noted that this Manual permits an organic condition to be classified as a psychosis only if the patient is psychotic during the episode being diagnosed.

If the specific physical condition underlying one of these disorders is known, indicate it with a separate, additional diagnosis.

## II. A. PSYCHOSES ASSOCIATED WITH ORGANIC BRAIN SYNDROMES (290—294)

### 290 Senile and Pre-senile dementia

#### 290.0 Senile dementia

This syndrome occurs with senile brain disease, whose causes are largely unknown. The category does not include the pre-senile psychoses nor other degenerative diseases of the central nervous system. While senile brain disease derives its name from the age group in which it is most commonly seen, its diagnosis should be based on the brain disorder present and not on the patient's age at times of onset. Even mild cases will manifest some evidence of organic brain syndrome: self-centeredness, difficulty in assimilating new experiences, and childish emotionality. Deterioration may be minimal or progress to vegetative existence. (This condition was called "Chronic Brain Syndrome associated with senile brain disease" in DSM-I.)

#### 290.1 Pre-senile dementia

This category includes a group of cortical brain diseases presenting clinical pictures similar to those of senile dementia but appearing characteristically in younger age groups. Alzheimer's and Pick's diseases are the two best known forms, each of which has a specific brain pathology. (In DSM-I Alzheimer's disease was classified as "Chronic Brain Syndrome with other disturbance of metabolism." Pick's disease was "Chronic Brain Syndrome associated with disease of unknown cause.") When the impairment is not of psychotic proportion the patient should be classified under *Non-psychotic OBS with senile or pre-senile brain disease.*

### 291 Alcoholic psychoses

Alcoholic psychoses are psychoses caused by poisoning with alcohol (see page **439**). When a pre-existing psychotic, psychoneurotic or other disorder is aggravated by modest alcohol intake, the underlying condition, not the alcoholic psychosis, is diagnosed.

Simple drunkenness, when not specified as psychotic, is classified under *Non-psychotic OBS with alcohol.*

In accordance with ICD-8, this Manual subdivides the alcoholic psychoses into *Delirium tremens, Korsakov's psychosis, Other alcoholic hallucinosis* and *Alcoholic paranoia.* DSM-II also adds three further subdivisions: *Acute alcohol intoxication, Alcoholic deterioration* and *Pathological intoxication.* (In DSM-I "Acute Brain Syndrome, alcohol intoxication" included what is now *Delirium tremens, Other alcoholic hallucinosis, Acute alcohol intoxication* and *Pathological intoxication.*)

### 291.0 Delirium tremens

This is a variety of acute brain syndrome characterized by delirium, coarse tremors, and frightening visual hallucinations usually becoming more intense in the dark. Because it was first identified in alcoholics and until recently was thought always to be due to alcohol ingestion, the term is restricted to the syndrome associated with alcohol. It is distinguished from *Other alcoholic hallucinosis* by the tremors and the disordered sensorium. When this clinical picture is due to a nutritional deficiency rather than to alcohol poisoning, it is classified under *Psychosis associated with metabolic or nutritional disorder.*

### 291.1 Korsakov's psychosis (alcoholic) Also "Korsakoff"

This is a variety of chronic brain syndrome associated with longstanding alcohol use and characterized by memory impairment, disorientation, peripheral neuropathy and particularly by confabulation. Like delirium tremens, Korsakov's psychosis is identified with alcohol because of an initial error in identifying its cause, and therefore the term is confined to the syndrome associated with alcohol. The similar syndrome due to nutritional deficiency unassociated with alcohol is classified *Psychosis associated with metabolic or nutritional disorder.*

### 291.2 Other alcoholic hallucinosis

Hallucinoses caused by alcohol which cannot be diagnosed as delirium tremens, Korsakov's psychosis, or alcoholic deterioration fall in this category. A common variety manifests accusatory or threatening auditory hallucinations in a state of relatively clear consciousness. This condition must be distinguished from schizophrenia in combination with alcohol intoxication, which would require two diagnoses.

### 291.3 Alcohol paranoid state ((Alcoholic paranoia))

This term describes a paranoid state which develops in chronic alcoholics, generally male, and is characterized by excessive jealousy and delusions of infidelity by the spouse. Patients diagnosed under primary paranoid states or schizophrenia should not be included here even if they drink to excess.

### 291.4* Acute alcohol intoxication*

All varieties of acute brain syndromes of psychotic proportion caused by alcohol are included here if they do not manifest features of delirium tremens, alcoholic hallucinosis, or pathological intoxication. This diagnosis is used alone when there is no other psychiatric disorder or as an additional diagnosis with other psychiatric conditions including alcoholism. The condition should not be confused with *simple drunkenness*, which does not involve psychosis. (All patients with this disorder would have been diagnosed "Acute Brain Syndrome, alcohol intoxication" in DSM-I.)

### 291.5* Alcoholic deterioration*

All varieties of chronic brain syndromes of psychotic proportion caused by alcohol and not having the characteristic features of Korsakov's psychosis are included here. (This condition and Korsakov's psychosis were both included under "Chronic Brain Syndrome, alcohol intoxication with psychotic reaction" in DSM-I.)

### 291.6* Pathological intoxication*

This is an acute brain syndrome manifested by psychosis after minimal alcohol intake. (In DSM-I this diagnosis fell under "Acute Brain Syndrome, alcohol intoxication.")

### 291.9 Other [and unspecified] alcoholic psychosis

This term refers to all varieties of alcoholic psychosis not classified above.

## 292 Psychosis associated with intracranial infection

### 292.0 General paralysis

This condition is characterized by physical signs and symptoms of parenchymatous syphilis of the nervous system, and usually by positive serology, including the paretic gold curve in the spinal fluid. The condition may simulate any of the other psychoses and brain syndromes. If the impairment is not of psychotic proportion it is classified *Non-psychotic OBS with intracranial infection*. If the specific underlying physical condition is known, indicate it with a separate, additional diagnosis. (This category was included under "Chronic Brain Syndrome associated with central nervous system syphilis (meningoencephalitic)" in DSM-I.)

### 292.1 Psychosis with other syphilis of central nervous system

This includes all other varieties of psychosis attributed to intracranial infection by **Spirochaeta pallida.** The syndrome sometimes has features of organic brain syndrome. The acute infection is usually produced by meningovascular inflammation and responds to systemic antisyphilitic treatment. The chronic condition is generally due to gummata. If not of psychotic proportion, the disorder is classified *Non-psychotic OBS with intracranial infection.* (In DSM-I "Chronic Brain Syndrome associated with other central nervous system syphilis" and "Acute Brain Syndrome associated with intracranial infection" covered this category.)

### 292.2 Psychosis with epidemic encephalitis (von Economo's encephalitis)

This term is confined to the disorder attributed to the viral epidemic encephalitis that followed World War I. Virtually no cases have been reported since 1926. The condition, however, is differentiated from other encephalitis. It may present itself as acute delirium and sometimes its outstanding feature is apparent indifference to persons and events ordinarily of emotional significance, such as the death of a family member. It may appear as a chronic brain syndrome and is sometimes dominated by involuntary, compulsive behavior. If not of psychotic proportions, the disorder is classified under *Non-psychotic OBS with intracranial infection.* (This category was classified under "Chronic Brain Syndrome associated with intracranial infection other than syphilis" in DSM-I.)

### 292.3 Psychosis with other and unspecified encephalitis

This category includes disorders attributed to encephalitic infections other than epidemic encephalitis and also to encephalitis not otherwise specified.[1] When possible the type of infection should be indicated. If not of psychotic proportion, the disorder is classified under *Non-psychotic OBS with intracranial infection.*

### 292.9 Psychosis with other [and unspecified] intracranial infection

This category includes all acute and chronic conditions due to nonsyphilitic and non-encephalitic infections, such as meningitis and

---

[1] A list of important encephalitides may be found in "A Guide to the Control of Mental Disorders," American Public Health Association Inc., New York 1962, pp. 40 ff.

brain abscess. Many of these disorders will have been diagnosed as the acute form early in the course of the illness. If not of psychotic proportion, the disorder should be classified under *Non-psychotic OBS with intracranial infection*. (In DSM-I the acute variety was classified as "Acute Brain Syndrome associated with intracranial infection" and the chronic variety as "Chronic Brain Syndrome associated with intracranial infection other than syphilis.")

### 293 Psychosis associated with other cerebral condition

This major category, as its name indicates, is for all psychoses associated with cerebral conditions *other* than those previously defined. For example, the degenerative diseases following do *not* include the previous senile dementia. If the specific underlying physical condition is known, indicate it with a separate, additional diagnosis.

#### 293.0 Psychosis with cerebral arteriosclerosis

This is a chronic disorder attributed to cerebral arteriosclerosis. It may be impossible to differentiate it from senile dementia and presenile dementia, which may coexist with it. Careful consideration of the patient's age, history, and symptoms may help determine the predominant pathology. Commonly, the organic brain syndrome is the only mental disturbance present, but other reactions, such as depression or anxiety, may be superimposed. If not of psychotic proportion, the condition is classified under *Non-psychotic OBS with circulatory disturbance*. (In DSM-I this was called "Chronic Brain Syndrome associated with cerebral arteriosclerosis.")

#### 293.1 Psychosis with other cerebrovascular disturbance

This category includes such circulatory disturbances as cerebral thrombosis, cerebral embolism, arterial hypertension, cardio-renal disease and cardiac disease, particularly in decompensation. It excludes conditions attributed to arteriosclerosis. The diagnosis is determined by the underlying organ pathology, which should be specified with an additional diagnosis. (In DSM-I this category was divided between "Acute Brain Syndrome associated with circulatory disturbance" and "Chronic Brain Syndrome associated with circulatory disturbance other than cerebral arteriosclerosis.")

#### 293.2 Psychosis with epilepsy

This category is to be used only for the condition associated with "idiopathic" epilepsy. Most of the etiological agents underlying chronic brain syndromes can and do cause convulsions, particularly

syphilis, intoxication, trauma, cerebral arteriosclerosis, and intracranial neoplasms. When the convulsions are symptomatic of such
diseases, the brain syndrome is classified under those disturbances
rather than here. The disturbance most commonly encountered here
is the clouding of consciousness before or after a convulsive attack.
Instead of a convulsion, the patient may show only a dazed reaction
with deep confusion, bewilderment and anxiety. The epileptic attack
may also take the form of an episode of excitement with hallucinations, fears, and violent outbreaks. (In DSM-I this was included in
"Acute Brain Syndrome associated with convulsive disorder" and
"Chronic Brain Syndrome associated with convulsive disorder.")

### 293.3 Psychosis with intracranial neoplasm

Both primary and metastatic neoplasms are classified here. Reactions
to neoplasms other than in the cranium should not receive this
diagnosis. (In DSM-I this category included "Acute Brain Syndrome
associated with intracranial neoplasm" and "Chronic Brain Syndrome
associated with intracranial neoplasm.")

### 293.4 Psychosis with degenerative disease of the central nerv-
ous system

This category includes degenerative brain diseases not listed previously. (In DSM-I this was part of "Acute Brain Syndrome with disease
of unknown or uncertain cause" and "Chronic Brain Syndrome
associated with diseases of unknown or uncertain cause.")

### 293.5 Psychosis with brain trauma

This category includes those disorders which develop immediately
after severe head injury or brain surgery and the post-traumatic
chronic brain disorders. It does not include permanent brain damage which produces only focal neurological changes without significant changes in sensorium and affect. Generally, trauma producing a chronic brain syndrome is diffuse and causes permanent
brain damage. If not of psychotic proportions, a post-traumatic personality disorder associated with an organic brain syndrome is classified as a *Non-psychotic OBS with brain trauma.* If the brain
injury occurs in early life and produces a developmental defect of
intelligence, the condition is also diagnosed *Mental retardation.* A head
injury may precipitate or accelerate the course of a chronic brain
disease, especially cerebral arteriosclerosis. The differential diagnosis
may be extremely difficult. If, before the injury, the patient had
symptoms of circulatory disturbance, particularly arteriosclerosis,

and now shows signs of psychosis, he should be classified *Psychosis with cerebral artiosclerosis.* (In DSM-I this category was divided between "Acute Brain Syndrome associated with trauma" and "Chronic Brain Syndrome associated with brain trauma.")

### 293.9 Psychosis with other [and unspecified] cerebral condition

This category is for cerebral conditions other than those listed above, and conditions for which it is impossible to make a more precise diagnosis. [Medical record librarians will include here *Psychoses with cerebral condition, not otherwise specified.*]

### 294 Psychosis associated with other physical condition

The following psychoses are caused by general systemic disorders and are distinguished from the *cerebral* conditions previously described. If the specific underlying physical condition is known, indicate it with a separate, additional diagnosis.

### 294.0 Psychosis with endocrine disorder

This category includes disorders caused by the complications of diabetes other than cerebral arteriosclerosis and disorders of the thyroid, pituitary, adrenals, and other endocrine glands. (In DSM-I "Chronic Brain Syndrome associated with other disturbances of metabolism, growth or nutrition" included the chronic variety of these disorders. DSM-I defined these conditions as "disorders of metabolism" but they here are considered endocrine disorders.)

### 294.1 Psychosis with metabolic or nutritional disorder

This category includes disorders caused by pellagra, avitaminosis and metabolic disorders. (In DSM-I this was part of "Acute Brain Syndrome associated with metabolic disturbance" and "Chronic Brain Syndrome associated with other disturbance of metabolism, growth or nutrition.")

### 294.2 Psychosis with systemic infection

This category includes disorders caused by severe general systemic infections, such as pneumonia, typhoid fever, malaria and acute rheumatic fever. Care must be taken to distinguish these reactions from other disorders, particularly manic depressive illness and schizophrenia, which may be precipitated by even a mild attack of infectious disease. (In DSM-I this was confined to "Acute Brain Syndrome associated with systemic infection.")

### 294.3 Psychosis with drug or poison intoxication (other than alcohol)

This category includes disorders caused by some drugs (including psychedelic drugs), hormones, heavy metals, gasses, and other intoxicants except alcohol. (In DSM-I these conditions were divided between "Acute Brain Syndrome, drug or poison intoxication" and "Chronic Brain Syndrome, associated with intoxication." The former excluded alcoholic acute brain syndromes, while the latter included alcoholic chronic brain syndromes.)

### 294.4 Psychosis with childbirth

Almost any type of psychosis may occur during pregnancy and the post-partum period and should be specifically diagnosed. This category is not a substitute for a differential diagnosis and excludes other psychoses arising during the puerperium. Therefore, this diagnosis should not be used unless all other possible diagnoses have been excluded.

### 294.8 Psychosis with other and undiagnosed physical condition

This is a residual category for psychoses caused by physical conditions other than those listed earlier. It also includes brain syndromes caused by physical conditions which have not been diagnosed. (In DSM-I this condition was divided between "Acute Brain Syndrome of unknown cause" and "Chronic Brain Syndrome of unknown cause." However, these categories also included the category now called *Psychosis with other [and unspecified] cerebral condition.*)

### [294.9 Psychosis with unspecified physical condition]

This is not a diagnosis but is included for use by medical record librarians only.

## II. B. NON-PSYCHOTIC ORGANIC BRAIN SYNDROMES (309)

### 309    Non-psychotic organic brain syndromes ((Mental disorders not specified as psychotic associated with physical conditions))

This category is for patients who have an organic brain syndrome but are not psychotic. If psychoses are present they should be diagnosed as previously indicated. Refer to pages 438-439 for description of organic brain syndromes in adults.

In children mild brain damage often manifests itself by hyperactivity, short attention span, easy distractability, and impulsiveness. Sometimes the child is withdrawn, listless, perseverative, and unresponsive. In exceptional cases there may be great difficulty in initiating action. These characteristics often contribute to a negative interaction between parent and child. If the organic handicap is the major etiological factor and the child is not psychotic, the case should be classified here. If the interactional factors are of major secondary importance, supply a second diagnosis under *Behavior disorders of childhood and adolescence;* if these interactional factors predominate give only a diagnosis from this latter category.

**309.0 Non-psychotic OBS with intracranial infection**

**309.1 Non-psychotic OBS with drug, poison, or systemic intoxication**

      **309.13\* Non-psychotic OBS with alcohol\* (simple drunkenness)**

      **309.14\* Non-psychotic OBS with other drug, poison, or systemic intoxication\***

**309.2 Non-psychotic OBS with brain trauma**

**309.3 Non-psychotic OBS with circulatory disturbance**

**309.4 Non-psychotic OBS with epilepsy**

**309.5 Non-psychotic OBS with disturbance of metabolism, growth or nutrition**

**309.6 Non-psychotic OBS with senile or pre-senile brain disease**

**309.7 Non-psychotic OBS with intracranial neoplasm**

**309.8 Non-psychotic OBS with degenerative disease of central nervous system**

**309.9 Non-psychotic OBS with other [and unspecified] physical condition**

      **[.91\* Acute brain syndrome, not otherwise specified\*]**

      **[.92\* Chronic brain syndrome, not otherwise specified\*]**

## III. PSYCHOSES NOT ATTRIBUTED TO PHYSICAL CONDITIONS LISTED PREVIOUSLY (295—298)

This major category is for patients whose psychosis is not caused by physical conditions listed previously. Nevertheless, some of these patients may show additional signs of an organic condition. If these organic signs are prominent the patient should receive the appropriate additional diagnosis.

## 295  Schizophrenia

This large category includes a group of disorders manifested by characteristic disturbances of thinking, mood and behavior. Disturbances in thinking are marked by alterations of concept formation which may lead to misinterpretation of reality and sometimes to delusions and hallucinations, which frequently appear psychologically self-protective. Corollary mood changes include ambivalent, constricted and inappropriate emotional responsiveness and loss of empathy with others. Behavior may be withdrawn, regressive and bizarre. The schizophrenias, in which the mental status is attributable primarily to a *thought* disorder, are to be distinguished from the *Major affective illnesses* (q.v.) which are dominated by a *mood* disorder. The *Paranoid states* (q.v.) are distinguished from schizophrenia by the narrowness of their distortions of reality and by the absence of other psychotic symptoms.

### 295.0  Schizophrenia, simple type

This psychosis is characterized chiefly by a slow and insidious reduction of external attachments and interests and by apathy and indifference leading to impoverishment of interpersonal relations, mental deterioration, and adjustment on a lower level of functioning. In general, the condition is less dramatically psychotic than are the hebephrenic, catatonic, and paranoid types of schizophrenia. Also, it contrasts with schizoid personality, in which there is little or no progression of the disorder.

### 295.1  Schizophrenia, hebephrenic type

This psychosis is characterized by disorganized thinking, shallow and inappropriate affect, unpredictable giggling, silly and regressive behavior and mannerisms, and frequent hypochondriacal complaints. Delusions and hallucinations, if present, are transient and not well organized.

### 295.2  Schizophrenia, catatonic type
#### 295.23*  Schizophrenia, catatonic type, excited*
#### 295.24*  Schizophrenia, catatonic type, withdrawn*

It is frequently possible and useful to distinguish two subtypes of catatonic schizophrenia. One is marked by excessive and sometimes violent motor activity and excitement and the other by generalized inhibition manifested by stupor, mutism, negativism, or waxy flexibility. In time, some cases deteriorate to a vegetative state.

### 295.3 Schizophrenia, paranoid type

This type of schizophrenia is characterized primarily by the presence of persecutory or grandiose delusions, often associated with hallucinations. Excessive religiosity is sometimes seen. The patient's attitude is frequently hostile and aggressive, and his behavior tends to be consistent with his delusions. In general the disorder does not manifest the gross personality disorganization of the hebephrenic and catatonic types, perhaps because the patient uses the mechanism of projection, which ascribes to others characteristics he cannot accept in himself. Three subtypes of the disorder may sometimes be differentiated, depending on the predominant symptoms: hostile, grandiose, and hallucinatory.

### 295.4 Acute schizophrenic episode

This diagnosis does not apply to acute episodes of schizophrenic disorders described elsewhere. This condition is distinguished by the acute onset of schizophrenic symptoms, often associated with confusion, perplexity, ideas of reference, emotional turmoil, dreamlike dissociation, and excitement, depression, or fear. The acute onset distinguishes this condition from simple schizophrenia. In time these patients may take on the characteristics of catatonic, hebephrenic or paranoid schizophrenia, in which case their diagnosis should be changed accordingly. In many cases the patient recovers within weeks, but sometimes his disorganization becomes progressive. More frequently remission is followed by recurrence. (In DSM-I this condition was listed as "Schizophrenia, acute undifferentiated type.")

### 295.5 Schizophrenia, latent type

This category is for patients having clear symptoms of schizophrenia but no history of a psychotic schizophrenic episode. Disorders sometimes designated as incipient, pre-psychotic, pseudoneurotic, pseudopsychopathic, or borderline schizophrenia are categorized here. (This category includes some patients who were diagnosed in DSM-I under "Schizophrenic reaction, chronic undifferentiated type." Others formerly included in that DSM-I category are now classified under *Schizophrenia, other [and unspecified] types* (q.v.).)

### 295.6 Schizophrenia, residual type

This category is for patients showing signs of schizophrenia but who, following a psychotic schizophrenic episode, are no longer psychotic.

### 295.7 Schizophrenia, schizo-affective type

This category is for patients showing a mixture of schizophrenic symptoms and pronounced elation or depression. Within this category it may be useful to distinguish excited from depressed types as follows:

#### 295.73* Schizophrenia, schizo-affective type, excited*

#### 295.74* Schizophrenia, schizo-affective type, depressed*

### 295.8* Schizophrenia, childhood type*

This category is for cases in which schizophrenic symptoms appear before puberty. The condition may be manifested by autistic, atypical, and withdrawn behavior; failure to develop identity separate from the mother's; and general unevenness, gross immaturity and inadequacy in development. These developmental defects may result in mental retardation, which should also be diagnosed. (This category is for use in the United States and does not appear in ICD-8. It is equivalent to "Schizophrenic reaction, childhood type" in DSM-I.)

### 295.90* Schizophrenia, chronic undifferentiated type*

This category is for patients who show mixed schizophrenic symptoms and who present definite schizophrenic thought, affect and behavior not classifiable under the other types of schizophrenia. It is distinguished from *Schizoid personality* (q.v.). (This category is equivalent to "Schizophrenic reaction, chronic undifferentiated type" in DSM-I except that it does not include cases now diagnosed as *Schizophrenia, latent type* and *Schizophrenia, other [and unspecified] types.)*

### 295.99* Schizophrenia, other [and unspecified] types*

This category is for any type of schizophrenia not previously described. (In DSM-I "Schizophrenic reaction, chronic undifferentiated type" included this category and also what is now called *Schizophrenia, latent type* and *Schizophrenia, chronic undifferentiated type.*)

### 296 Major affective disorders ((Affective psychoses))

This group of psychoses is characterized by a single disorder of mood, either extreme depression or elation, that dominates the mental life of the patient and is responsible for whatever loss of contact he has with his environment. The onset of the mood does not seem to be related directly to a precipitating life experience and therefore is distinguishable from *Psychotic depressive reaction* and *Depressive neurosis.* (This category is not equivalent to the DSM-I heading "Affective reactions," which included "Psychotic depressive reaction.")

### 296.0 Involutional melancholia

This is a disorder occurring in the involutional period and characterized by worry, anxiety, agitation, and severe insomnia. Feelings of guilt and somatic preoccupations are frequently present and may be of delusional proportions. This disorder is distinguishable from *Manic-depressive illness* (q.v.) by the absence of previous episodes; it is distinguished from *Schizophrenia* (q.v.) in that impaired reality testing is due to a disorder of mood; and it is distinguished from *Psychotic depressive reaction* (q.v.) in that the depression is not due to some life experience. Opinion is divided as to whether this psychosis can be distinguished from the other affective disorders. It is, therefore, recommended that involutional patients not be given this diagnosis unless all other affective disorders have been ruled out. (In DSM-I this disorder was considered one of two subtypes of "Involutional Psychotic Reaction."

### Manic-depressive illnesses (Manic-depressive psychoses)

These disorders are marked by severe mood swings and a tendency to remission and recurrence. Patients may be given this diagnosis in the absence of a previous history of affective psychosis if there is no obvious precipitating event. This disorder is divided into three major subtypes: manic type, depressed type, and circular type.

### 296.1 Manic-depressive illness, manic type ((Manic-depressive psychosis, manic type))

This disorder consists exclusively of manic episodes. These episodes are characterized by excessive elation, irritability, talkativeness, flight of ideas, and accelerated speech and motor activity. Brief periods of depression sometimes occur, but they are never true depressive episodes.

### 296.2 Manic-depressive illness, depressed type ((Manic-depressive psychosis, depressed type))

This disorder consists exclusively of depressive episodes. These episodes are characterized by severely depressed mood and by mental and motor retardation progressing occasionally to stupor. Uneasiness, apprehension, perplexity and agitation may also be present.

When illusions, hallucinations, and delusions (usually of guilt or of hypochondriacal or paranoid ideas) occur, they are attributable to the dominant mood disorder. Because it is a primary mood disorder, this psychosis differs from the *Psychotic depressive reaction,* which is more easily attributable to precipitating stress. Cases incompletely labelled as "psychotic depression" should be classified here rather than under *Psychotic depressive reaction.*

**296.3  Manic-depressive illness, circular type** ((Manic-depressive psychosis, circular type))

This disorder is distinguished by at least one attack of both a depressive episode *and* a manic episode. This phenomenon makes clear why manic and depressed types are combined into a single category. (In DSM-I these cases were diagnosed under "Manic depressive reaction, other.") The current episode should be specified and coded as one of the following:

**296.33\*  Manic-depressive illness, circular type, manic\***

**296.34\*  Manic-depressive illness, circular type, depressed\***

**296.8 Other major affective disorder** ((Affective psychosis, other))

Major affective disorders for which a more specific diagnosis has not been made are included here. It is also for "mixed" manic-depressive illness, in which manic and depressive symptoms appear almost simultaneously. It does not include *Psychotic depressive reaction* (q.v.) or *Depressive neurosis* (q.v.). (In DSM-I this category was included under "Manic depressive reaction, other.")

**[296.9  Unspecified major affective disorder]**

**[Affective disorder not otherwise specified]**

**[Manic-depressive illness not otherwise specified]**

**297  Paranoid states**

These are psychotic disorders in which a delusion, generally persecutory or grandiose, is the essential abnormality. Disturbances in mood, behavior and thinking (including hallucinations) are derived from this delusion. This distinguishes paranoid states from the affective psychoses and schizophrenias, in which mood and thought disorders, respectively, are the central abnormalities. Most authorities, however, question whether disorders in this group are distinct clinical entities and not merely variants of schizophrenia or paranoid personality.

## 297.0 Paranoia

This extremely rare condition is characterized by gradual development of an intricate, complex, and elaborate paranoid system based on and often proceeding logically from misinterpretation of an actual event. Frequently the patient considers himself endowed with unique and superior ability. In spite of a chronic course the condition does not seem to interfere with the rest of the patient's thinking and personality.

### 297.1 Involutional paranoid state ((Involutional paraphrenia))

This paranoid psychosis is characterized by delusion formation with onset in the involutional period. Formerly it was classified as a paranoid variety of involutional psychotic reaction. The absence of conspicuous thought disorders typical of schizophrenia distinguishes it from that group.

### 297.9 Other paranoid state

This is a residual category for paranoid psychotic reactions not classified earlier.

## 298 Other psychoses

### 298.0 Psychotic depressive reaction ((Reactive depressive psychosis))

This psychosis is distinguished by a depressive mood attributable to some experience. Ordinarily the individual has no history of repeated depressions or cyclothymic mood swings. The differentiation between this condition and *Depressive neurosis* (q.v.) depends on whether the reaction impairs reality testing or functional adequacy enough to be considered a psychosis. (In DSM-I this condition was included with the affective psychoses.)

### [298.1 Reactive excitation]

### [298.2 Reactive confusion]
#### [Acute or subacute confusional state]

### [298.3 Acute paranoid reaction]

### [298.9 Reactive psychosis, unspecified]

## [299 Unspecified psychosis]
### [Dementia, insanity or psychosis not otherwise specified]

This is not a diagnosis but is listed here for librarians and statisticians to use in coding incomplete diagnoses. Clinicians are expected to complete a differential diagnosis for patients who manifest features of several psychoses.

## IV. NEUROSES (300)

### 300 Neuroses

Anxiety is the chief characteristic of the neuroses. It may be felt and expressed directly, or it may be controlled unconsciously and automatically by conversion, displacement and various other psychological mechanisms. Generally, these mechanisms produce symptoms experienced as subjective distress from which the patient desires relief.

The neuroses, as contrasted to the psychoses, manifest neither gross distortion or misinterpretation of external reality, nor gross personality disorganization. A possible exception to this is hysterical neurosis, which some believe may occasionally be accompanied by hallucinations and other symptoms encountered in psychoses.

Traditionally, neurotic patients, however severely handicapped by their symptoms, are not classified as psychotic because they are aware that their mental functioning is disturbed.

### 300.0 Anxiety neurosis

This neurosis is characterized by anxious over-concern extending to panic and frequently associated with somatic symptoms. Unlike *Phobic neurosis* (q.v.), anxiety may occur under any circumstances and is not restricted to specific situations or objects. This disorder must be distinguished from normal apprehension or fear, which occurs in realistically dangerous situations.

### 300.1 Hysterical neurosis

This neurosis is characterized by an involuntary psychogenic loss or disorder of function. Symptoms characteristically begin and end suddenly in emotionally charged situations and are symbolic of the underlying conflicts. Often they can be modified by suggestion alone. This is a new diagnosis that encompasses the former diagnoses "Conversion reaction" and "Dissociative reaction" in DSM-I. This distinction between conversion and dissociative reactions should be preserved by using one of the following diagnoses whenever possible.

### 300.13* Hysterical neurosis, conversion type*

In the conversion type, the special senses or voluntary nervous system are affected, causing such symptoms as blindness, deafness, anosmia, anaesthesias, paraesthesias, paralyses, ataxias, akinesias, and dyskinesias. Often the patient shows an inappropriate lack of concern or *belle indifférence* about these symptoms, which may actually provide secondary gains by winning him sympathy or relieving him of unpleasant responsibilities. This type of hysterical neurosis must be distinguished from psychophysiologic disorders, which are mediated by the autonomic nervous system; from malingering, which is done consciously; and from neurological lesions, which cause anatomically circumscribed symptoms.

### 300.14* Hysterical neurosis, dissociative type*

In the dissociative type, alterations may occur in the patient's state of consciousness or in his identity, to produce such symptoms as amnesia, somnambulism, fugue, and multiple personality.

### 300.2 Phobic neurosis

This condition is characterized by intense fear of an object or situation which the patient consciously recognizes as no real danger to him. His apprehension may be experienced as faintness, fatigue, palpitations, perspiration, nausea, tremor, and even panic. Phobias are generally attributed to fears displaced to the phobic object or situation from some other object of which the patient is unaware. A wide range of phobias has been described.

### 300.3 Obsessive compulsive neurosis

This disorder is characterized by the persistent intrusion of unwanted thoughts, urges, or actions that the patient is unable to stop. The thoughts may consist of single words or ideas, ruminations, or trains of thought often perceived by the patient as nonsensical. The actions vary from simple movements to complex rituals such as repeated handwashing. Anxiety and distress are often present either if the patient is prevented from completing his compulsive ritual or if he is concerned about being unable to control it himself.

### 300.4 Depressive neurosis

This disorder is manifested by an excessive reaction of depression due to an internal conflict or to an identifiable event such as the loss of a love object or cherished possession. It is to be distinguished from *Involutional melancholia* (q.v.) and *Manic-depressive illness* (q.v.). *Reactive depressions* or *Depressive reactions* are to be classified here.

### 300.5 Neurasthenic neurosis ((Neurasthenia))

This condition is characterized by complaints of chronic weakness, easy fatigability, and sometimes exhaustion. Unlike hysterical neurosis the patient's complaints are genuinely distressing to him and there is no evidence of secondary gain. It differs from *Anxiety neurosis* (q.v.) and from the *Psychophysiologic disorders* (q.v.) in the nature of the predominant complaint. It differs from *Depressive neurosis* (q.v.) in the moderateness of the depression and in the chronicity of its course. (In DSM-I this condition was called "Psychophysiologic nervous system reaction.")

### 300.6 Depersonalization neurosis ((Depersonalization syndrome))

This syndrome is dominated by a feeling of unreality and of estrangement from the self, body, or surroundings. This diagnosis should not be used if the condition is part of some other mental disorder, such as an acute situational reaction. A brief experience of depersonalization is not necessarily a symptom of illness.

### 300.7 Hypochondriacal neurosis

This condition is dominated by preoccupation with the body and with fear of presumed diseases of various organs. Though the fears are not of delusional quality as in psychotic depressions, they persist despite reassurance. The condition differs from hysterical neurosis in that there are no actual losses or distortions of function.

### 300.8 Other neurosis

This classification includes specific psychoneurotic disorders not classified elsewhere such as "writer's cramp" and other occupational neuroses. Clinicians should not use this category for patients with "mixed" neuroses, which should be diagnosed according to the predominant symptom.

### [300.9 Unspecified neurosis]

This category is not a diagnosis. It is for the use of record librarians and statisticians to code incomplete diagnoses.

## V. PERSONALITY DISORDERS AND CERTAIN OTHER NON-PSYCHOTIC MENTAL DISORDERS (301—304)

### 301 Personality disorders

This group of disorders is characterized by deeply ingrained maladaptive patterns of behavior that are perceptibly different in quality from psychotic and neurotic symptoms. Generally, these are life-long patterns, often recognizable by the time of adolescence or earlier. Sometimes the pattern is determined primarily by malfunctioning of the brain, but such cases should be classified under one of the non-psychotic organic brain syndromes rather than here. (In DSM-I "Personality Disorders" also included disorders now classified under *Sexual deviation, Alcoholism,* and *Drug dependence.*)

### 301.0 Paranoid personality

This behavioral pattern is characterized by hypersensitivity, rigidity, unwarranted suspicion, jealousy, envy, excessive self-importance, and a tendency to blame others and ascribe evil motives to them. These characteristics often interfere with the patient's ability to maintain satisfactory interpersonal relations. Of course, the presence of suspicion of itself does not justify this diagnosis, since the suspicion may be warranted in some instances.

### 301.1 Cyclothymic personality ((Affective personality))

This behavior pattern is manifested by recurring and alternating periods of depression and elation. Periods of elation may be marked by ambition, warmth, enthusiasm, optimism, and high energy. Periods of depression may be marked by worry, pessimism, low energy, and a sense of futility. These mood variations are not readily attributable to external circumstances. If possible, the diagnosis should specify whether the mood is characteristically depressed, hypomanic, or alternating.

### 301.2 Schizoid personality

This behavior pattern manifests shyness, over-sensitivity, seclusiveness, avoidance of close or competitive relationships, and often eccentricity. Autistic thinking without loss of capacity to recognize reality is common, as are daydreaming and the inability to express hostility and ordinary aggressive feelings. These patients react to disturbing experiences and conflicts with apparent detachment.

### 301.3 Explosive personality (Epileptoid personality disorder)

This behavior pattern is characterized by gross outbursts of rage or of verbal or physical aggressiveness. These outbursts are strikingly different from the patient's usual behavior, and he may be regretful and repentant for them. These patients are generally considered excitable, aggressive and over-responsive to environmental pressures. It is the intensity of the outbursts and the individual's inability to control them which distinguishes this group. Cases diagnosed as "aggressive personality" are classified here. If the patient is amnesic for the outbursts, the diagnosis of *Hysterical neurosis, Non-psychotic OBS with epilepsy* or *Psychosis with epilepsy* should be considered.

### 301.4 Obsessive compulsive personality ((Anankastic personality))

This behavior pattern is characterized by excessive concern with conformity and adherence to standards of conscience. Consequently, individuals in this group may be rigid, over-inhibited, over-conscientious, over-dutiful, and unable to relax easily. This disorder may lead to an *Obsessive compulsive neurosis* (q.v.), from which it must be distinguished.

### 301.5 Hysterical personality (Histrionic personality disorder)

These behavior patterns are characterized by excitability, emotional instability, over-reactivity, and self-dramatization. This self-dramatization is always attention-seeking and often seductive, whether or not the patient is aware of its purpose. These personalities are also immature, self-centered, often vain, and usually dependent on others. This disorder must be differentiated from *Hysterical neurosis* (q.v.).

### 301.6 Asthenic personality

This behavior pattern is characterized by easy fatigability, low energy level, lack of enthusiasm, marked incapacity for enjoyment, and oversensitivity to physical and emotional stress. This disorder must be differentiated from *Neurasthenic neurosis* (q.v.).

### 301.7 Antisocial personality

This term is reserved for individuals who are basically unsocialized and whose behavior pattern brings them repeatedly into conflict with society. They are incapable of significant loyalty to individuals, groups, or social values. They are grossly selfish, callous, irresponsible, impulsive, and unable to feel guilt or to learn from experience and punishment. Frustration tolerance is low. They tend to blame others or offer plausible rationalizations for their behavior. A mere history of repeated legal or social offenses is not sufficient to justify this diagnosis. *Group delinquent reaction of childhood (or adolescence)* (q.v.), and *Social maladjustment without manifest psychiatric disorder* (q.v.) should be ruled out before making this diagnosis.

### 301.81* Passive-aggressive personality*

This behavior pattern is characterized by both passivity and aggressiveness. The aggressiveness may be expressed passively, for example by obstructionism, pouting, procrastination, intentional inefficiency, or stubbornness. This behavior commonly reflects hostility which the individual feels he dare not express openly. Often the behavior is one expression of the patient's resentment at failing to find gratification in a relationship with an individual or institution upon which he is over-dependent.

### 301.82* Inadequate personality*

This behavior pattern is characterized by ineffectual responses to emotional, social, intellectual and physical demands. While the patient seems neither physically nor mentally deficient, he does manifest inadaptability, ineptness, poor judgment, social instability, and lack of physical and emotional stamina.

### 301.89* Other personality disorders of specified types (Immature personality, Passive-dependent personality, etc.)*

### 301.9 [Unspecified personality disorder]

## 302 Sexual deviations

This category is for individuals whose sexual interests are directed primarily toward objects other than people of the opposite sex, toward sexual acts not usually associated with coitus, or toward coitus performed under bizarre circumstances as in necrophilia, pedophilia, sexual sadism, and fetishism. Even though many find their practices distasteful, they remain unable to substitute normal sexual behavior for them. This diagnosis is not appropriate for individuals who perform deviant sexual acts because normal sexual objects are not available to them.

### 302.0 Homosexuality

### 302.1 Fetishism

### 302.2 Pedophilia

### 302.3 Transvestitism

### 302.4 Exhibitionism

### 302.5* Voyeurism*

### 302.6* Sadism*

### 302.7* Masochism*

### 302.8 Other sexual deviation

### [302.9 Unspecified sexual deviation]

## 303 Alcoholism

This category is for patients whose alcohol intake is great enough to damage their physical health, or their personal or social functioning, or when it has become a prerequisite to normal functioning. If the alcoholism is due to another mental disorder, both diagnoses should be made. The following types of alcoholism are recognized:

### 303.0 Episodic excessive drinking

If alcoholism is present and the individual becomes intoxicated as frequently as four times a year, the condition should be classified here. Intoxication is defined as a state in which the individual's coordination or speech is definitely impaired or his behavior is clearly altered.

### 303.1 Habitual excessive drinking

This diagnosis is given to persons who are alcoholic and who either become intoxicated more than 12 times a year or are recognizably under the influence of alcohol more than once a week, even though not intoxicated.

### 303.2 Alcohol addiction

This condition should be diagnosed when there is direct or strong presumptive evidence that the patient is dependent on alcohol. If available, the best direct evidence of such dependence is the appearance of withdrawal symptoms. The inability of the patient to go one day without drinking is presumptive evidence. When heavy drinking continues for three months or more it is reasonable to presume addiction to alcohol has been established.

### 303.9 Other [and unspecified] alcoholism

## 304 Drug dependence

This category is for patients who are addicted to or dependent on drugs other than alcohol, tobacco, and ordinary caffeine-containing beverages. Dependence on medically prescribed drugs is also excluded so long as the drug is medically indicated and the intake is proportionate to the medical need. The diagnosis requires evidence of habitual use or a clear sense of need for the drug. Withdrawal symptoms are not the only evidence of dependence; while always present when opium derivatives are withdrawn, they may be entirely absent when cocaine or marihuana are withdrawn. The diagnosis may stand alone or be coupled with any other diagnosis.

**304.0 Drug dependence, opium, opium alkaloids and their derivatives**

**304.1 Drug dependence, synthetic analgesics with morphine-like effects**

**304.2 Drug dependence, barbiturates**

**304.3 Drug dependence, other hypnotics and sedatives or "tranquilizers"**

**304.4 Drug dependence, cocaine**

**304.5 Drug dependence, Cannabis sativa (hashish, marihuana)**

**304.6 Drug dependence, other psycho-stimulants (amphetamines, etc.)**

**304.7 Drug dependence, hallucinogens**

**304.8 Other drug dependence**

**[304.9 Unspecified drug dependence]**

## VI. PSYCHOPHYSIOLOGIC DISORDERS (305)

**305 Psychophysiologic disorders ((Physical disorders of presumably psychogenic origin))**

This group of disorders is characterized by physical symptoms that are caused by emotional factors and involve a single organ system, usually under autonomic nervous system innervation. The physiological changes involved are those that normally accompany certain emotional states, but in these disorders the changes are more intense and sustained. The individual may not be consciously aware of his emotional state. If there is an additional psychiatric disorder, it should be diagnosed separately, whether or not it is presumed to contribute to the physical disorder. The specific physical disorder should be named and classified in one of the following categories.

### 305.0 Psychophysiologic skin disorder

This diagnosis applies to skin reactions such as neurodermatosis, pruritis, atopic dematitis, and hyperhydrosis in which emotional factors play a causative role.

### 305.1 Psychophysiologic musculoskeletal disorder

This diagnosis applies to musculoskeletal disorders such as backache, muscle cramps, and myalgias, and tension headaches in which emotional factors play a causative role. Differentiation from hysterical neurosis is of prime importance and at times extremely difficult.

### 305.2 Psychophysiologic respiratory disorder

This diagnosis applies to respiratory disorders such as bronchial asthma, hyperventilation syndromes, sighing, and hiccoughs in which emotional factors play a causative role.

### 305.3 Psychophysiologic cardiovascular disorder

This diagnosis applies to cardiovascular disorders such as paroxysmal tachycardia, hypertension, vascular spasms, and migraine in which emotional factors play a causative role.

### 305.4 Psychophysiologic hemic and lymphatic disorder

Here may be included any disturbances in the hemic and lymphatic system in which emotional factors are found to play a causative role. ICD-8 has included this category so that all organ systems will be covered.

### 305.5 Psychophysiologic gastrointestinal disorder

This diagnosis applies to specific types of gastrointestinal disorders such as peptic ulcer, chronic gastritis, ulcerative or mucous colitis, constipation, hyperacidity, pylorospasm, "heartburn," and "irritable colon" in which emotional factors play a causative role.

### 305.6 Psychophysiologic genito-urinary disorder

This diagnosis applies to genito-urinary disorders such as disturbances in menstruation and micturition, dyspareunia, and impotence in which emotional factors play a causative role.

### 305.7 Psychophysiologic endocrine disorder

This diagnosis applies to endocrine disorders in which emotional factors play a causative role. The disturbance should be specified.

### 305.8 Psychophysiologic disorder of organ of special sense

This diagnosis applies to any disturbance in the organs of special sense in which emotional factors play a causative role. Conversion reactions are excluded.

### 305.9 Psychophysiologic disorder of other type

## VII. SPECIAL SYMPTOMS (306)

### 306 Special symptoms not elsewhere classified

This category is for the occasional patient whose psychopathology is

manifested by discrete, specific symptoms. An example might be anorexia nervosa under *Feeding disturbance* as listed below. It does not
apply, however, if the symptom is the result of an organic illness or
defect or other mental disorder. For example, anorexia nervosa due to
schizophrenia would not be included here.

**306.0  Speech disturbance**

**306.1  Specific learning disturbance**

**306.2  Tic**

**306.3  Other psychomotor disorder**

**306.4  Disorder of sleep**

**306.5  Feeding disturbance**

**306.6  Enuresis**

**306.7  Encopresis**

**306.8  Cephalalgia**

**306.9  Other special symptom**

## VIII. TRANSIENT SITUATIONAL DISTURBANCES (307)

**307*  Transient situational disturbances[1]**

This major category is reserved for more or less transient disorders
of any severity (including those of psychotic proportions) that occur
in individuals without any apparent underlying mental disorders and
that represent an acute reaction to overwhelming environmental stress.
A diagnosis in this category should specify the cause and manifestations
of the disturbance so far as possible. If the patient has good adaptive
capacity his symptoms usually recede as the stress diminishes. If, however, the symptoms persist after the stress is removed, the diagnosis
of another mental disorder is indicated. Disorders in this category are
classified according to the patient's developmental stage as follows:

---

[1] The terms included under DSM-II Category 307*, "Transient situational disturbances," differ from those in Category 307 of the ICD. DSM-II Category
307*, "Transient situational disturbances," contains adjustment reactions of infancy (307.0*), childhood (307.1*), adolescence (307.2*), adult life (307.3*),
and late life (307.4*). ICD Category 307, "Transient situational disturbances,"
includes only the adjustment reactions of adolescence, adult life and late life.
ICD 308, "Behavioral disorders of children," contains the reactions of infancy
and childhood. These differences must be taken into account in preparing statistical tabulations to conform to ICD categories.

### 307.0* Adjustment reaction of infancy*

Example: A grief reaction associated with separation from patient's mother, manifested by crying spells, loss of appetite and severe social withdrawal.

### 307.1* Adjustment reaction of childhood*

Example: Jealousy associated with birth of patient's younger brother and manifested by nocturnal enuresis, attention-getting behavior, and fear of being abandoned.

### 307.2* Adjustment reaction of adolescence*

Example: Irritability and depression associated with school failure and manifested by temper outbursts, brooding and discouragement.

### 307.3* Adjustment reaction of adult life*

Example: Resentment with depressive tone associated with an unwanted pregnancy and manifested by hostile complaints and suicidal gestures.

Example: Fear associated with military combat and manifested by trembling, running and hiding.

Example: A Ganser syndrome associated with death sentence and manifested by incorrect but approximate answers to questions.

### 307.4* Adjustment reaction of late life*

Example: Feelings of rejection associated with forced retirement and manifested by social withdrawal.

## IX. BEHAVIOR DISORDERS OF CHILDHOOD AND ADOLESCENCE (308)

### 308* Behavior disorders of childhood and adolescence ((Behavior disorders of childhood))[2]

This major category is reserved for disorders occurring in childhood and adolescence that are more stable, internalized, and resistant to

---

[2] The terms included under DSM-II Category 308*, "Behavioral disorders of childhood and adolescence," differ from those in Category 308 of the ICD. DSM-II Category 308* includes "Behavioral disorders of childhood and adolescence," whereas ICD Category 308 includes only "Behavioral disorders of childhood." DSM-II Category 308* *does not* include "Adjustment reactions of infancy and childhood," whereas ICD Category 308 does. In the DSM-II classification, "Adjustment reactions of infancy and childhood" are allocated to 307* (Transitional situational disturbances). These differences should be taken into account in preparing statistical tabulations to conform to the ICD categories.

treatment than *Transient situational disturbances* (q.v.) but less so than *Psychoses, Neuroses,* and *Personality disorders* (q.v.). This intermediate stability is attributed to the greater fluidity of all behavior at this age. Characteristic manifestations include such symptoms as overactivity, inattentiveness, shyness, feeling of rejection, over-aggressiveness, timidity, and delinquency.

### 308.0* Hyperkinetic reaction of childhood (or adolescence)*

This disorder is characterized by overactivity, restlessness, distractibility, and short attention span, especially in young children; the behavior usually diminishes in adolescence.

If this behavior is caused by organic brain damage, it should be diagnosed under the appropriate non-psychotic *organic brain syndrome* (q.v.).

### 308.1* Withdrawing reaction of childhood (or adolescence)*

This disorder is characterized by seclusiveness, detachment, sensitivity, shyness, timidity, and general inability to form close interpersonal relationships. This diagnosis should be reserved for those who cannot be classified as having *Schizophrenia* (q.v.) and whose tendencies toward withdrawal have not yet stabilized enough to justify the diagnosis of *Schizoid personality* (q.v.).

### 308.2* Overanxious reaction of childhood (or adolescence)*

This disorder is characterized by chronic anxiety, excessive and unrealistic fears, sleeplessness, nightmares, and exaggerated autonomic responses. The patient tends to be immature, self-conscious, grossly lacking in self-confidence, conforming, inhibited, dutiful, approval-seeking, and apprehensive in new situations and unfamiliar surroundings. It is to be distinguished from *Neuroses* (q.v.).

### 308.3* Runaway reaction of childhood (or adolescence)*

Individuals with this disorder characteristically escape from threatening situations by running away from home for a day or more without permission. Typically they are immature and timid, and feel rejected at home, inadequate, and friendless. They often steal furtively.

### 308.4* Unsocialized aggressive reaction of childhood (or adolescence)*

This disorder is characterized by overt or covert hostile disobedience, quarrelsomeness, physical and verbal aggressiveness, vengefulness, and destructiveness. Temper tantrums, solitary stealing, lying, and hostile teasing of other children are common. These patients usually have no consistent parental acceptance and discipline. This diagnosis should be distinguished from *Antisocial personality* (q.v.), *Runaway reaction of childhood (or adolescence)* (q.v.), and *Group delinquent reaction of childhood (or adolscence)* (q.v.).

### 308.5* Group delinquent reaction of childhood (or adolescence)*

Individuals with this disorder have acquired the values, behavior, and skills of a delinquent peer group or gang to whom they are loyal and with whom they characteristically steal, skip school, and stay out late at night. The condition is more common in boys than girls. When group delinquency occurs with girls it usually involves sexual delinquency, although shoplifting is also common.

### 308.9* Other reaction of childhood (or adolescence)*

Here are to be classified children and adolescents having disorders not described in this group but which are nevertheless more serious than transient situational disturbances and less serious than psychoses, neuroses, and personality disorders. The particular disorder should be specified.

## X. CONDITIONS WITHOUT MANIFEST PSYCHIATRIC DISORDER AND NON-SPECIFIC CONDITIONS (316*—318*)

### 316* Social maladjustments without manifest psychiatric disorder

This category is for recording the conditions of individuals who are psychiatrically normal but who nevertheless have severe enough problems to warrant examination by a psychiatrist. These conditions may either become or precipitate a diagnosable mental disorder.

### 316.0* Marital maladjustment*

This category is for individuals who are psychiatrically normal but who have significant conflicts or maladjustments in marriage.

### 316.1* Social maladjustment*

This category is for individuals thrown into an unfamiliar culture (culture shock) or into a conflict arising from divided loyalties to two cultures.

### 316.2* Occupational maladjustment*

This category is for psychiatrically normal individuals who are grossly maladjusted in their work.

### 316.3* Dyssocial behavior*

This category is for individuals who are not classifiable as anti-social personalities, but who are predatory and follow more or less criminal pursuits, such as racketeers, dishonest gamblers, prostitutes, and dope peddlers. (DSM-I classified this condition as "Sociopathic personality disorder, dyssocial type.")

### 316.9* Other social maladjustment*

### 317* Non-specific conditions*

This category is for conditions that cannot be classified under any of the previous categories, even after all facts bearing on the case have been investigated. This category is not for "Diagnosis deferred" (q.v.).

### 318* No mental disorder*

This term is used when, following psychiatric examination, none of the previous disorders is found. It is not to be used for patients whose disorders are in remission.

## XI. NON-DIAGNOSTIC TERMS FOR ADMINISTRATIVE USE (319*)

### 319* Non-diagnostic terms for administrative use*

#### 319.0* Diagnosis deferred*

#### 319.1* Boarder*

#### 319.2* Experiment only*

#### 319.9* Other*

# APPENDIX B

## ETHICAL STANDARDS
## OF PSYCHOLOGISTS

by
AMERICAN PSYCHOLOGICAL ASSOCIATION

# ETHICAL STANDARDS OF PSYCHOLOGISTS [1]

*The psychologist believes in the dignity and worth of the individual human being. He is committed to increasing man's understanding of himself and others. While pursuing this endeavor, he protects the welfare of any person who may seek his service or of any subject, human or animal, that may be the object of his study. He does not use his professional position or relationships, nor does he knowingly permit his own services to be used by others, for purposes inconsistent with these values. While demanding for himself freedom of inquiry and communication, he accepts the responsibility this freedom confers: for competence where he claims it, for objectivity in the report of his findings, and for consideration of the best interests of his colleagues and of society.*

## Specific Principles

**Principle 1. Responsibility.** The psychologist,[2] committed to increasing man's understanding of man, places high value on objectivity and integrity, and maintains the highest standards in the services he offers.

  a. As a scientist, the psychologist believes that society will be best served when he investigates where his judgment indicates investigation is needed; he plans his research in such a way as to minimize the possibility that his findings will be misleading; and he publishes full reports of his work, never discarding without explanation data which may modify the interpretation of results.

  b. As a teacher, the psychologist recognizes his primary obligation to help others acquire knowledge and skill, and to maintain high standards of scholarship.

  c. As a practitioner, the psychologist knows that he bears a heavy social responsibility because his work may touch intimately the lives of others.

**Principle 2. Competence.** The maintenance of high standards of professional competence is a responsibility shared by all psychologists, in the interest of the public and of the profession as a whole.

  a. Psychologists discourage the practice of psychology by unqualified persons and assist the public in identifying psychologists competent to give dependable professional service. When a psychologist or a person identifying himself as a psychologist violates ethical standards, psychologists who know firsthand of such activities attempt to rectify the situation. When such a situation cannot be dealt with informally, it is called to the attention of the appropriate local, state, or national committee on professional ethics, standards, and practices.

  b. Psychologists regarded as qualified for independent practice are those who (a) have been awarded a Diploma by the American Board of Examiners in Professional Psychology, or (b) have been licensed or certified by state examining boards, or (c) have been certified by voluntary boards established by state psychological associations. Psychologists who do not yet

---

[1] Copyrighted by the American Psychological Association, Inc., January 1963. Reprinted (and edited) from the *American Psychologist*, January 1963, and as amended by the APA Council of Representatives in September 1965 and December 1972.

[2] A student of psychology who assumes the role of psychologist shall be considered a psychologist for the purpose of this code of ethics.

meet the qualifications recognized for independent practice should gain experience under qualified supervision.

c.   The psychologist recognizes the boundaries of his competence and the limitations of his techniques and does not offer services or use techniques that fail to meet professional standards established in particular fields. The psychologist who engages in practice assists his client in obtaining professional help for all important aspects of his problem that fall outside the boundaries of his own competence. This principle requires, for example, that provision be made for the diagnosis and treatment of relevant medical problems and for referral to or consultation with other specialists.

d.   The psychologist in clinical work recognizes that his effectiveness depends in good part upon his ability to maintain sound interpersonal relations, that temporary or more enduring aberrations in his own personality may interfere with this ability or distort his appraisals of others. There he refrains from undertaking any activity in which his personal problems are likely to result in inferior professional services or harm to a client; or, if he is already engaged in such an activity when he becomes aware of his personal problems, he seeks competent professional assistance to determine whether he should continue or terminate his services to his client.

## Principle 3. Moral and Legal Standards.
The psychologist in the practice of his profession shows sensible regard for the social codes and moral expectations of the community in which he works, recognizing that violations of accepted moral and legal standards on his part may involve his clients, students, or colleagues in damaging personal conflicts, and impugn his own name and the reputation of his profession.

## Principle 4. Misrepresentation.
The psychologist avoids misrepresentation of his own professional qualifications, affiliations, and purposes, and those of the institutions and organizations with which he is associated.

a.   A psychologist does not claim either directly or by implication professional qualifications that differ from his actual qualifications, nor does he misrepresent his affiliation with any institution, organization, or individual, nor lead others to assume he has affiliations that he does not have. The psychologist is responsible for correcting others who misrepresent his professional qualifications or affiliations.

b.   The psychologist does not misrepresent an institution or organization with which he is affiliated by ascribing to it characteristics that it does not have.

c.   A psychologist does not use his affiliation with the American Psychological Association or its Divisions for purposes that are not consonant with the stated purposes of the Association.

d.   A psychologist does not associate himself with or permit his name to be used in connection with any services or products in such a way as to misrepresent them, the degree of his responsibility for them, or the nature of his affiliation.

## Principle 5. Public Statements.
Modesty, scientific caution, and due regard for the limits of present knowledge characterize all statements of psychologists who supply information to the public, either directly or indirectly.

a.   Psychologists who interpret the science of psychology or the services of psychologists to clients or to the general public have an obligation to report fairly and accurately. Exaggeration, sensationalism, superficiality, and other kinds of misrepresentation are avoided.

b.   When information about psychological procedures and techniques is given, care is taken to indicate that they should be used only by persons adequately trained in their use.

c.   A psychologist who engages in radio or television activities does not participate in commercial announcements recommending purchase or use of a product.

## Principle 6. Confidentiality.
Safeguarding information about an individual that has been obtained by the psychologist in the course of his teaching, practice, or investigation is a primary obligation of the

psychologist. Such information is not communicated to others unless certain important conditions are met.

    a.  Information received in confidence is revealed only after most careful deliberation and when there is clear and imminent danger to an individual or to society, and then only to appropriate professional workers or public authorities.

    b.  Information obtained in clinical or consulting relationships, or evaluative data concerning children, students, employees, and others are discussed only for professional purposes and only with persons clearly concerned with the case. Written and oral reports should present only data germane to the purposes of the evaluation, every effort should be made to avoid undue invasion of privacy.

    c.  Clinical and other materials are used in classroom teaching and writing only when the identity of the persons involved is adequately disguised.

    d.  The confidentiality of professional communications about individuals is maintained. Only when the originator and other persons involved give their express permission is a confidential professional communication shown to the individual concerned. The psychologist is responsible for informing the client of the limits of the confidentiality.

    e.  Only after explicit permission has been granted is the identity of research subjects published. When data have been published without permission for identification, the psychologist assumes responsibility for adequately disguising their sources.

    f.  The psychologist makes provisions for the maintenance of confidentiality in the preservation and ultimate disposition of confidential records.

### Principle 7. Client Welfare. The psychologist respects the integrity and protects the welfare of the person or group with whom he is working.

    a.  The psychologist in industry, education, and other situations in which conflicts of interest may arise among various parties, as between management and labor, or between the client and employer of the psychologist, defines for himself the nature and direction of his loyalties and responsibilities and keeps all parties concerned informed of these commitments.

    b.  When there is a conflict among professional workers, the psychologist is concerned primarily with the welfare of any client involved and only secondarily with the interest of his own professional group.

    c.  The psychologist attempts to terminate a clinical or consulting relationship when it is reasonably clear to the psychologist that the client is not benefiting from it.

    d.  The psychologist who asks that an individual reveal personal information in the course of interviewing, testing, or evaluation, or who allows such information to be divulged to him, does so only after making certain that the responsible person is fully aware of the purposes of the interview, testing, or evaluation and of the ways in which the information may be used.

    e.  In cases involving referral, the responsibility of the psychologist for the welfare of the client continues until this responsibility is assumed by the professional person to whom the client is referred or until the relationship with the psychologist making the referral has been terminated by mutual agreement. In situations where referral, consultation, or other changes in the conditions of the treatment are indicated and the client refuses referral, the psychologist carefully weighs the possible harm to the client, to himself, and to his profession that might ensue from continuing the relationship.

    f.  The psychologist who requires the taking of psychological tests for didactic, classification, or research purposes protects the examinees by insuring that the tests and test results are used in a professional manner.

    g.  When potentially disturbing subject matter is presented to students, it is discussed objectively, and efforts are made to handle constructively any difficulties that arise.

    h.  Care must be taken to insure an appropriate setting for clinical work to protect both client and psychologist from actual or imputed harm and the profession from censure.

    i.  In the use of accepted drugs for therapeutic purposes special care needs to be exercised by the psychologist to assure himself that the collaborating physician provides suitable safeguards for the client.

### Principle 8. Client Relationship. The psychologist informs his prospective client of the important aspects of the potential relationship that might affect the client's decision to enter the relationship.

a. Aspects of the relationship likely to affect the client's decision include the recording of an interview, the use of interview material for training purposes, and observation of an interview by other persons.

b. When the client is not competent to evaluate the situation (as in the case of a child), the person responsible for the client is informed of the circumstances which may influence the relationship.

c. The psychologist does not normally enter into a professional relationship with members of his own family, intimate friends, close associates, or others whose welfare might be jeopardized by such a dual relationship.

## Principle 9. Impersonal Services. Psychological services for the purpose of diagnosis, treatment, or personalized advice are provided only in the context of a professional relationship, and are not given by means of public lectures or demonstrations, newspaper or magazine articles, radio or television programs, mail, or similar media.

a. The preparation of personnel reports and recommendations based on test data secured solely by mail is unethical unless such appraisals are an integral part of a continuing client relationship with a company, as a result of which the consulting psychologist has intimate knowledge of the client's personnel situation and can be assured thereby that his written appraisals will be adequate to the purpose and will be properly interpreted by the client. These reports must not be embellished with such detailed analyses of the subject's personality traits as would be appropriate only after intensive interviews with the subject. The reports must not make specific recommendations as to employment or placement of the subject which go beyond the psychologist's knowledge of the job requirements of the company. The reports must not purport to eliminate the company's need to carry on such other regular employment or personnel practices as appraisal of the work history, checking of references, past performance in the company.

## Principle 10. Announcement of Services. A psychologist adheres to professional rather than commercial standards in making known his availability for professional services.

a. A psychologist does not directly solicit clients for individual diagnosis or therapy.

b. Individual listings in telephone directories are limited to name, highest relevant degree, certification status, address, and telephone number. They may also include identification in a few words of the psychologist's major areas of practice; for example, child therapy, personnel selection, industrial psychology. Agency listings are equally modest.

c. Announcements of individual private practice are limited to a simple statement of the name, highest relevant degree, certification or diplomate status, address, telephone number, office hours, and a brief explanation of the types of services rendered. Announcements of agencies may list names of staff members with their qualifications. They conform in other particulars with the same standards as individual announcements, making certain that the true nature of the organization is apparent.

d. A psychologist or agency announcing nonclinical professional services may use brochures that are descriptive of services rendered but not evaluative. They may be sent to professional persons, schools, business firms, government agencies, and other similar organizations.

e. The use in a brochure of "testimonials from satisfied users" is unacceptable. The offer of a free trial of services is unacceptable if it operates to misrepresent in any way the nature or the efficacy of the services rendered by the psychologist. Claims that a psychologist has unique skills or unique devices not available to others in the profession are made only if the special efficacy of these unique skills or devices has been demonstrated by scientifically acceptable evidence.

f. The psychologist must not encourage (nor, within his power, even allow) a client to have exaggerated ideas as to the efficacy of services rendered. Claims made to clients about the efficacy of his services must no go beyond those which the psychologist would be willing to subject to professional scrutiny through publishing his results and his claims in a professional journal.

**Principle 11. Interprofessional Relations.** A psychologists acts with integrity in regard to colleagues in psychology and in other professions.

a.  Each member of the Association cooperates with the duly constituted Committee on Scientific and Professional Ethics and Conduct in the performance of its duties by responding to inquiries with reasonable promptness and completeness. A member taking longer than 30 days to respond to such inquiries shall have the burden of demonstrating that he acted with "reasonable promptness."

b.  A psychologist does not normally offer professional services to a person receiving psychological assistance from another professional worker except by agreement with the other worker or after the termination of the client's relationship with the other professional worker.

c.  The welfare of clients and colleagues requires that psychologists in joint practice or corporate activities make an orderly and explicit arrangement regarding the conditions of their association and its possible termination. Psychologists who serve as employers of other psychologists have an obligation to make similar appropriate arrangements.

**Principle 12. Remuneration.** Financial arrangements in professional practice are in accord with professional standards that safeguard the best interest of the client and the profession.

a.  In establishing rates for professional services, the psychologist considers carefully both the ability of the client to meet the financial burden and the charges made by other professional persons engaged in comparable work. He is willing to contribute a portion of his services to work for which he receives little or no financial return.

b.  No commission or rebate or any other form of remuneration is given or received for referral of clients for professional services.

c.  The psychologist in clinical or counseling practice does not use his relationships with clients to promote, for personal gain or the profit of an agency, commercial enterprises of any kind.

d.  A psychologist does not accept a private fee or any other form of remuneration for professional work with a person who is entitled to his services through an institution or agency. The policies of a particular agency may make explicit provision for private work with its clients by members of its staff, and in such instances the client must be fully apprised of all policies affecting him.

**Principle 13. Test Security.** Psychological tests and other assessment devices, the value of which depends in part on the naivete of the subject, are not reproduced or described in popular publications in ways that might invalidate the techniques. Access to such devices is limited to persons with professional interests who will safeguard their use.

a.  Sample items made up to resemble those of tests being discussed may be reproduced in popular articles and elsewhere, but scorable tests and actual test items are not reproduced except in professional publications.

b.  The psychologist is responsible for the control of psychological tests and other devices and procedures used for instruction when their value might be damaged by revealing to the general public their specific contents or underlying principles.

**Principle 14. Test Interpretation.** Test scores, like test materials, are released only to persons who are qualified to interpret and use them properly.

a.  Materials for reporting test scores to parents, or which are designed for self-appraisal purposes in schools, social agencies, or industry are closely supervised by qualified psychologists or counselors with provisions for referring and counseling individuals when needed.

b.  Test results or other assessment data used for evaluation or classification are communicated to employers, relatives, or other appropriate persons in such a manner as to guard against misinterpretation or misuse. In the usual case, an interpretation of the test result rather than the score is communicated.

c.   When test results are communicated directly to parents and students, they are accompanied by adequate interpretive aids or advice.

**Principle 15. Test Publication.** Psychological tests are offered for commercial publication only to publishers who present their tests in a professional way and distribute them only to qualified users.

a.   A test manual, technical handbook, or other suitable report on the test is provided which describes the method of constructing and standardizing the test, and summarizes the validation research.

b.   The populations for which the test has ben developed and the purposes for which it is recommended are stated in the manual. Limitations upon the test's dependability, and aspects of its validity on which research is lacking or incomplete, are clearly stated. In particular, the manual contains a warning regarding interpretations likely to be made which have not yet been substantiated by research.

c.   The catalog and manual indicate the training or professional qualifications required for sound interpretation of the test.

d.   The test manual and supporting documents take into account the principles enunicated in the *Standards for Educational and Psychological Tests and Manuals.*

e.   Test advertisements are factual and descriptive rather than emotional and persuasive.

**Principle 16. Research Precautions.** The psychologist assumes obligations for the welfare of his research subjects, both animal and human.

The decision to undertake research should rest upon a considered judgment by the individual psychologist about how best to contribute to psychological science and to human welfare. The responsible psychologist weighs alternative directions in which personal energies and resources might be invested. Having made the decision to conduct research, psychologists must carry out their investigations with respect for the people who participate and with concern for their dignity and welfare. The Principles that follow make explicit the investigator's ethical responsibilities toward participants over the course of research, from the initial decision to pursue a study to the steps necessary to protect the confidentiality of research data. These Principles should be interpreted in terms of the contexts provided in the complete document [3] offered as a supplement to these Principles.

a.   In planning a study the investigator has the personal responsibility to make a careful evaluation of its ethical acceptability, taking into account these Principles for research with human beings. To the extent that this appraisal, weighing scientific and humane values, suggests a deviation from any Principle, the investigator incurs an increasingly serious obligation to seek ethical advice and to observe more stringent safeguards to protect the rights of the human research participants.

b.   Responsibility for the establishment and maintenance of acceptable ethical practice in research always remains with the individual investigator. The investigator is also responsible for the ethical treatment of research participants by collaborators, assistants, students, and employees, all of whom, however, incur parallel obligations.

c.   Ethical practice requires the investigator to inform the participant of all features of the research that reasonably might be expected to influence willingness to participate, and to explain all other aspects of the research about which the participant inquires. Failure to make full disclosure gives added emphasis to the investigator's abiding responsibility to protect the welfare and dignity of the research participant.

---

[3] *Ethical Principles in the Conduct of Research with Human Participants,* available upon request from the American Psychological Association.

d. Openness and honesty are essential characteristics of the relationship between investigator and research participant. When the methodological requirements of a study necessitate concealment or deception, the investigator is required to ensure the participant's understanding of the reasons for this action and to restore the quality of the relationship with the investigator.

e. Ethical research practice requires the investigator to respect the individual's freedom to decline to participate in research or to discontinue participation at any time. The obligation to protect this freedom requires special vigilance when the investigator is in a position of power over the participant. The decision to limit this freedom gives added emphasis to the investigator's abiding responsibility to protect the participant's dignity and welfare.

f. Ethically acceptable research begins with the establishment of a clear and fair agreement between the investigator and the research participant that clarifies the responsibilities of each. The investigator has the obligation to honor all promises and commitments included in that agreement.

g. The ethical investigator protects participants from physical and mental discomfort, harm and danger. If the risk of such consequences exists, the investigator is required to inform the participant of that fact, secure consent before proceeding, and take all possible measures to minimize distress. A research procedure may not be used if it is likely to cause serious and lasting harm to participants.

h. After the data are collected, ethical practice requires the investigator to provide the participant with a full clarification of the nature of the study and to remove any misconceptions that may have arisen. Where scientific or humane values justify delaying or withholding information, the investigator acquires a special responsibility to assure that there are no damaging consequences for the participant.

i. Where research procedures may result in undesirable consequences for the participant, the investigator has the responsibility to detect and remove or correct these consequences, including, where relevant, long-term aftereffects.

j. Information obtained about the research participants during the course of an investigation is confidential. When the possibility exists that others may obtain access to such information, ethical research practice requires that this possibility, together with the plans for protecting confidentiality, be explained to the participants as a part of the procedure for obtaining informed consent.

k. A psychologist using animals in research adheres to the provisions of the Rules Regarding Animals, drawn up by the Committee on Precautions and Standards in Animal Experimentation and adopted by the American Psychological Association.

l. Investigations of human subjects using experimental drugs (for example: hallucinogenic, psychotomimetic, psychedelic, or similar substances) should be conducted only in such settings as clinics, hospitals, or research facilities maintaining appropriate safeguards for the subjects.

**Principle 17. Publication Credit.** Credit is assigned to those who have contributed to a publication, in proportion to their contribution, and only to these.

a. Major contributions of a professional character, made by several persons to a common project, are recognized by joint authorship. The experimenter or author who has made the principal contribution to a publication is identified as the first listed.

b. Minor contributions of a professional character, extensive clerical or similar nonprofessional assistance, and other minor contributions are acknowledged in footnotes or in an introductory statement.

c. Acknowledgment through specific citations is made for unpublished as well as published material that has directly influenced the research or writing.

d. A psychologist who compiles and edits for publication the contributions of others publishes the symposium or report under the title of the committee or symposium, with his own name appearing as chairman or editor among those of the other contributors or committee members.

**Principle 18. Responsibility toward Organization.** A psychologist respects the rights and reputation of the institute or organization with which he is associated.

a.   Materials prepared by a psychologist as a part of his regular work under specific direction of his organization are the property of that organization. Such materials are released for use or publication by a psychologist in accordance with policies of authorization, assignment of credit, and related matters which have been established by his organization.

b.   Other material resulting incidentally from activity supported by any agency, and for which the psychologist rightly assumes individual responsibility, is published with disclaimer for any responsibility on the part of the supporting agency.

**Principle 19. Promotional Activities.** The psychologist associated with the development or promotion of psychological devices, books, or other products offered for commercial sale is responsible for ensuring that such devices, books, or products are presented in a professional and factual way.

a.   Claims regarding performance, benefits, or results are supported by scientifically acceptable evidence.

b.   The psychologist does not use professional journals for the commercial exploitation of psychological products, and the psychologist-editor guards against such misuse.

c.   The psychologist with a financial interest in the sale or use of a psychological product is sensitive to possible conflict of interest in his promotion of such products and avoids compromise of his professional responsibilities and objectives.